# Holman
# Concise
# Bible
## Commentary

# Holman
# Concise
# Bible
# Commentary

**Simple, straightforward commentary
on every book of the Bible**

David S. Dockery
**General Editor**

**H**

**HOLMAN
REFERENCE**

Nashville, Tennessee

©1998 Broadman & Holman Publishers
Nashville, Tennessee

ISBN# 0–8054–9337–9

Dewey Decimal Classification: 220.7
Subject Heading: BIBLE. COMMENTARIES
Library of Congress Card Catalog Number: 98–27818

Much of the material in this book previously appeared in the *Holman Bible Handbook,* ©1992 Holman Bible Publishers.

Printed in the United States of America
01 00 99 98    1 2 3 4

**Library of Congress Cataloging–in–Publication Data**

The Holman concise Bible commentary.
    p.  cm.
    Edited by David S. Dockery.
    Includes bibliographical references.
    ISBN 0–8054–9337–9 (hardcover)
    1. Bible—Commentaries.   I. Dockery, David S.
BS491.2.H65  1998
220.7—dc21                                98–27818
                                                  CIP

# GENERAL EDITOR'S FOREWORD

We say it and hear it said so often that it sometimes loses its force: The Bible is God's Word.

Can you imagine what it would be like for God to speak to you? How attentive would you be?

God has spoken and continues to speak through His written Word. John Calvin said that as we read Scripture we do well to hear it as if God were uttering these words to us. When this realization grips us, we listen carefully. If we don't understand at first, we will take actions that will enable us to understand what God is saying—just because of who the speaker is.

God's Word isn't easy. It was originally given in times, places, and cultures very different from our own. God has given to the church in over two millennia men and women dedicated to helping their generation understand God's Word.

*The Holman Concise Bible Commentary* is an excellent first commentary for Bible study. As you use this commentary, you are putting yourself in the company of some of the outstanding evangelical scholars of our time. Each of these writers loves God's Word and has a passion to help you grow in your ability to read, understand, and apply the truths of God's Word in your life.

In addition to the clear commentary, *The Holman Concise Bible Commentary* includes numerous eye-pleasing elements that will make learning a pleasure.

I pray that as you study the Bible your reading and study will be guided by the Holy Spirit's illuminating ministry as in the days of Nehemiah when the people of God celebrated with great joy because they understood the words that had been made known to them (Neh. 8:12).

*Soli Deo Gloria*
David S. Dockery, General Editor

# CONTENTS

# FEATURE ARTICLES

# CHARTS

# MAPS

# CONTRIBUTORS

Daniel L. Akin, Ph.D.
Vice-President for Academic Administration
The Southern Baptist Theological Seminary
Louisville, KY
*Order of the Gospels; Accounts of the Resurrection*

David Allen, Ph.D.
W. A. Criswell Professor of Preaching
Criswell College
Dallas, TX
*New Testament Use of the Old Testament; Old and New Covenant*

James Blevins, Ph.D.
Professor of New Testament
The Southern Baptist Theological Seminary
Louisville, KY
*Hymns and Creeds in the New Testament*

Craig L. Blomberg, Ph.D.
Associate Professor of New Testament
Denver Seminary
Denver, CO
*The Gospel of Matthew*

Darrell L. Bock, Ph.D.
Associate Professor of New Testament
Dallas Theological Seminary
Dallas, TX
*The Gospel of Luke*

C. Stephen Bond, Ph.D.
Editor
Broadman & Holman Publishers
Nashville, TN
*Project Coordinator*

Gerald L. Borchert, Ph.D.
Professor of New Testament
Northern Baptist Theological Seminary
Lombard, IL
*Assurance, Warning, and Perseverance*

Trent C. Butler, Ph.D.
Editor
Broadman & Holman Publishers
Nashville, TN
*Marriage and Family in Israel; Death, Resurrection, and Afterlife in the Old Testament; Messianic Prophecies; Symbolic Actions by the Prophets; Old Testament Apocalyptic*

Robert B. Chisholm, Th.D.
Professor of Old Testament
Dallas Theological Seminary
Dallas, TX
*The Major Prophets*

Christopher L. Church, Ph.D.
Assistant Professor
Baptist Memorial College of Health Sciences
Memphis, TN
*The Gospel of Mark*

E. Ray Clendenen, Ph.D.
Editorial Supervisor
Broadman and Holman Publishers
Nashville, TN
*The Minor Prophets; The Sacrificial System*

George B. Davis, Jr., M.A.
Doctoral Candidate
Cambridge University
Cambridge, England
*New Testament Signs and Miracles*

Raymond Dillard, Ph.D.†
Former Professor of Old Testament
Westminster Theological Seminary
Philadelphia, PA
*The Temple; David as King and Messiah*

David S. Dockery, Ph.D.
President
Union University
Jackson, TN
*General Editor; The Pauline Letters; The Lordōs Supper*

Walter A. Elwell, Ph.D.
Dean of the Graduate School
Wheaton College
Wheaton, IL
*The Kingdom of God in the Gospels; Titles of Christ in the Gospels*

Duane A. Garrett, Ph.D.
Professor of Old Testament
Gordon-Conwell Theological Seminary
South Hamilton, MA
*The Poetic and Wisdom Books*

Ron Glass, Ph.D.
Associate Professor of Bible Exposition
Talbot School of Theology
La Mirada, CA
*Election in the Old Testament*

Stanley J. Grenz, D.Theol.
Professor of Theology
Carey Hall/Regent College
Vancouver, British Columbia, Canada
*Church and State; The Value of Human Life*

Harold W. Hoehner, Ph.D.
Professor of New Testament
Dallas Theological Seminary
Dallas, TX
*Trial of Jesus*

David Howard, Ph.D.
Associate Professor of Old Testament
New Orleans Baptist Theological Seminary
New Orleans, LA
*Egypt; Moses*

F. B. Huey, Jr., Ph.D.
Professor of Old Testament (Retired)
Southwestern Baptist Theological Seminary
Fort Worth, TX
*The Flood; Old Testament Numbers; Patriarchs*

Walter C. Kaiser, Jr., Ph.D.
President
Gordon-Conwell Theological Seminary
South Hamilton, MA
*Covenants, Dates of the Exodus*

Dan G. Kent, Ph.D.
Professor of Old Testament
Southwestern Baptist Theological Seminary
Fort Worth, TX
*Israel's Festivals and Feasts; Tabernacle*

George L. Klein, Ph.D.
Professor of Old Testament
Criswell College
Dallas, TX
*Christ in the Psalms; Vengeance and Vindication*

Thomas D. Lea, Th.D.
Dean, School of Theology
Southwestern Baptist Theological Seminary
Fort Worth, TX
*The General Letters*

A. Boyd Luter, Jr., Th.D.
Professor of Bible
Cedarville College
Cedarville, OH
*Apocalyptic Literature*

D. Michael Martin, Ph.D.
Associate Professor of New Testament
Golden Gate Baptist Theological Seminary
Mill Valley, CA
*The Return of Christ*

Kenneth A. Mathews, Ph.D.
Associate Professor of Divinity
Beeson Divinity School
Birmingham, AL
*The Historical Books*

Eugene H. Merrill, Ph.D.
Professor of Old Testament
Dallas Theological Seminary
Dallas, TX
*The Pentateuch*

Darold H. Morgan, Ph.D.
President Emeritus
Annuity Board of the SBC
Dallas, TX
*The Parables of Jesus*

Robert Stan Norman, Ph.D.
Assistant Professor of Religion
Charleston Southern University
Charleston, SC
*Justification by Faith*

Harry L. Poe, Ph.D.
Vice President for Academic Resources and Information
Union University
Jackson, TN
*Apostolic Preaching; The Holy Spirit and Acts*

John B. Polhill, Ph.D.
Professor of New Testament
The Southern Baptist Theological Seminary
Louisville, KY
*Acts; The Birth of the Church; Greco-Roman Cities; The New Testament and History; Roman Provinces*

Kurt A. Richardson, D.Theol.
Assistant Professor of Historical Theology
Southeastern Baptist Theological Seminary
Wake Forest, NC
*Election in the New Testament*

Richard Rigsby, Ph.D.
Associate Professor of Old Testament
Talbot School of Theology
La Mirada, CA
*Atonement*

J. Julius Scott, Ph.D.
Professor of New Testament
Wheaton College
Wheaton, IL
*Slavery in the First Century*

Mark A. Seifrid, Ph.D.
Associate Professor of New Testament
The Southern Baptist Theological Seminary
Louisville, KY
*Salvation in Paulōs Thought*

Robert B. Sloan, D.Theol.
President
Baylor University
Waco, TX
*Apostasy; Revelation*

Marsha A. Ellis Smith, Ph.D.
Associate Vice President for Academic Administration
The Southern Baptist Theological Seminary
Louisville, KY
*Compiler of charts and maps*

Harold S. Songer, Ph.D. (Retired)
Vice President for Academic Affairs
The Southern Baptist Theological Seminary
Louisville, KY
*Jerusalem in New Testament Times; Pilate*

Klyne Snodgrass, Ph.D.
Dean of the Faculty
North Park Seminary
Chicago, IL
*Gnosticism; Law in the New Testament*

Aida Besancon Spencer, Ph.D.
Associate Professor of New Testament
Gordon-Conwell Theological Seminary
South Hamilton, MA
*Virgin Birth*

Willem VanGemeren, Ph.D.
Professor of Old Testament
Trinity Evangelical Divinity School
Deerfield, IL
*Names of God*

Bruce K. Waltke, Ph.D.
Professor of Old Testament
Regent College
Vancouver, British Columbia
*Themes of Proverbs*

James Emery White, Ph.D.
Senior Pastor
Mecklenburg Church
Charlotte, NC
*The Gospel of John*


[†] deceased

# THE PENTATEUCH

## EUGENE H. MERRILL

The term *Pentateuch* is the title most commonly employed to describe the first five books of the Bible. It derives from the Greek *pente (five)* and *teuchos (scroll)* and thus describes the number of these writings, not their contents.

*Pentateuch* is a satisfactory way of identifying these books. By virtue of nearly two thousand years of usage, it is deeply ingrained in Christian tradition. However, a more accurate and informative term is *Torah* (Hebrew *torah*). This name is based upon the verb *yarah, to teach*. *Torah* is, therefore, *teaching*. Careful attention to this will lead to an appreciation both of the contents of the Pentateuch and of its fundamental purpose: the instruction of God's people concerning Himself, themselves, and His purposes for them.

The enormous amount of legal material in the Pentateuch (half of Exodus, most of Leviticus, much of Numbers, and virtually all of Deuteronomy) has led to the common designation *Law* or *Books of the Law*. This way of viewing the Pentateuch does enjoy the sanction of ancient Jewish and even New Testament usage and is not without justification. However, recent scholarship has shown conclusively that the Pentateuch is essentially an instruction (hence *torah*) manual whose purpose was to guide the covenant people Israel in the way of pilgrimage before their God. For example, Genesis, though containing few laws, still instructs God's people through its narra-tives of primeval history and the patriarchs. The law was the "constitution and bylaws" of the chosen nation. *Torah* is therefore the title best suited to describe the full contents and purpose of this earliest part of the Bible.

Until the Enlightenment in the 1700s, there was a consensus within Jewish and Christian tradition that the witness of the Pentateuch revealed Moses as its author. Both the Old (Deut. 1:5; 4:44; 31:9; 33:4; Josh. 8:31-34; 1 Kgs. 2:3; 2 Kgs. 14:6; 23:25; 2 Chr. 23:18; Ezra 3:2; Neh. 8:1; Mal. 4:4) and New Testaments (Luke 2:22; 24:44; John 1:17; 7:19; Acts 13:39; 28:23; 1 Cor. 9:9; Heb. 10:28) support the tradition of Mosaic authorship. Some pre-Enlightenment interpreters raised incidental questions about chronological discrepancies. For example, they noted reference to kings of Israel in Genesis 36:31, Moses' reference to himself as "a very humble man, more humble than anyone else on the face of the earth" (Num. 12:3), and his authoring the account of his own death (Deut. 34:5-12). These, however, can be explained as either the result of divine revelation of the future or more likely as examples of later additions to the text. Those accepting Moses as a historic person whose life and experience are evidenced by Scripture (Exod. 2:10-11; Heb. 11:23-24) must admit the genuine possibility of his authorship of those writings that traditionally bear his name.

Many scholars affirm Moses' significant contributions to the formation of the Pentateuch but hold that the *final* form of these books evidences some editing after the time of Moses. Such critics in no way deny the divine inspiration of the Pentateuch or the reliability of its history. Rather, they affirm that after the death of Moses, God continued to move people of faith to elaborate those truths Moses taught earlier. Evidence for such retelling of accounts after Moses' death includes the account of his death in Deuteronomy 34, especially 34:10-12, which appears to reflect a long history of experience with prophets who failed to measure up to Moses. Further evidences are historical notes that appear to reflect a time after Israel's conquest of the Canaanites' land (Gen. 12:6; 13:7) and place names that have apparently been updated to those used after Moses' death (see Gen. 14:14 with Josh. 19:47 and Judg. 18:29).

Some radical critics have denied the possibility of God's supernatural involvement in history and questioned the trustworthiness of the history found in the Pentateuch (see "Criticism and the Old Testament"). Yet any adequate view of the Pentateuch must recognize Moses' real contribution and the historical reliability of its traditions (see the discussion of the Pentateuch as history that follows).

Deuteronomy, the last book of the Pentateuch, was composed by Moses in the Plains of Moab (Deut. 1:1-5; 4:44-46; 29:1) just before his death (Deut. 31:2,9,24). The first four books probably share this time and place of origin. Genesis, Exodus, and Leviticus, however, could have been penned as early as the convocation at Mount Sinai, thirty-eight years earlier. This setting in Moab is particularly appropriate because God had already informed Moses that he would not live to cross the Jordan and participate in the conquest and settlement of Canaan (Num. 20:10-13; 27:12-14). It was thus urgent that he bequeath to his people the legacy of divine revelation—the Pentateuch—that the Lord had entrusted to him. The inspired prophet had to address any questions they had about their origins, purpose, and destiny then and there. The date of the final form of the Pentateuch as it came from Moses' hand is about 1400 B.C., forty years after the exodus from Egypt.

The description of the Pentateuch as *torah*, "instruction," immediately reveals its purpose: to educate the people of Israel about their identity, their history, their role among the nations of the earth, and their future. The Pentateuch contains information about such things as creation, the cosmos, and the distribution and dispersion of the peoples and nations. However, this information finds its relevance primarily in relation to Israel, the people to whom Moses addressed himself at Moab.

Biblical literature's true and ultimate purpose cannot be separated from its theological message. The Pentateuch sought to inform God's people of their identity and focus. Though both themes emerge regularly in Exodus and Deuteronomy especially, the focal text where Israel's identity and focus are found is Exodus 19:4-6. Here, on the eve of the Sinai covenant encounter, the Lord spoke to Israel.

> You yourselves have seen what I did to Egypt, and how I carried you on eagles' wings and brought you to myself. Now if you obey me fully and keep my covenant, then out of all nations you will be my treasured possession. Although the whole earth is mine, you will be for me a kingdom of priests and a holy nation.

Here then is what it meant to be Israel and to serve the Lord as Israel. This core text of the Pentateuch presents the central theme to which all the other themes and teachings relate and in light of which they and the whole Pentateuch find their meaning. In this magnificent affirmation the Lord proclaimed that He had brought Israel to Himself. The text immediately presupposes the exodus deliverance, the redemptive act in which God overthrew Egypt ("you yourselves have seen what I did to Egypt") through miraculous intervention ("how I carried you on eagles' wings"). It furthermore declares that the sovereign God of all nations was offering to only one nation—Israel—a covenant that would allow them the privilege of serving all the peoples of earth as "a kingdom of priests and a holy nation."

This pivotal text looks both backward and forward. Reference to the exodus would naturally draw attention to Israel's past. Israel had come out of Egypt, a land of bondage, where it had sojourned for 430 years (Exod. 12:40). The reason for the long stay there had been a famine that forced the patriarchs to flee Canaan for relief. Another reason, however, was that Jacob and his sons had begun to lose their identity as the family of promise by intermingling with and becoming tainted by the Canaanites and their ungodly ways. The sordid affairs of Judah (Gen. 38) illustrate this leaning most clearly.

Moses thus had to reach back into the times of the nation's ancestors to account for the Egyptian sojourn and the exodus event itself. Beyond this he needed to explain who the patriarchs were and why God called them. The answer lay in the ancient patriarchal covenant. One man, Abraham, was called out of Sumerian paganism to found a nation that would be a blessing to all nations who recognized its peculiar nature and calling (Gen. 12:1-3). Israel was that nation, that offspring of Abraham, that now was ready to undertake the role long ago revealed to the founding father.

The purpose for the call of Abraham and the covenant promise entrusted to him are carefully spelled out as well. Humankind, which God had created to be in His image and to rule over all His creation (Gen. 1:26-28), had violated that sacred trust and had plunged the whole universe into chaotic ruin and rebellion. What was required was a people called out of that lostness to exhibit godly obedience before the world, to function as mediators and a redemptive priesthood, and to provide the matrix from which the incarnate God could enter the world and achieve His saving and sovereign purposes of re-creation. That people, again, was Israel. They surely understood their calling, but it likely had never been fully spelled out until Moses did so there on the edge of conquest.

The form this rehearsal of Israel's significance took was, of course, the Book of Genesis. Whether or not the account of these grand events had ever existed in written form cannot be known for sure, though there are strong hints of such in the Book of Genesis itself (2:4; 5:1; 6:9; 10:1; 11:10, 27; 25:12,19; 36:1). Moses, who was about to pass from the scene, shaped the story as we now have it. He wanted to provide Israel with a historical and theological basis for their status as a peculiar people (that is, God's "treasured possession").

The remainder of the Pentateuch is, for the most part, a historical narration of events contemporary with Moses and his generation. Embedded in it are the Sinaitic covenant text (Exod. 20:1–23:33), instructions for the creation of a tabernacle (Exod. 25:1–27:21; 30:1-38; 35:4–39:43; Num. 7:1–8:4), selection and setting apart of a priesthood (Exod. 28:1–29:46), a system of sacrifices and other cultic regulations (most of Leviticus), law and ritual appropriate to the people in the desert (Num. 5:1-4; 9:15-32), and the covenant renewal text (most of Deuteronomy). All of these nonnarrative sections and the narratives themselves relate to the theme of Israel as a community of priests. The Pentateuch then tells where Israel came from and why. It tells how they entered into covenant with the Lord following their redemption from Egypt, what claims this covenant laid upon them, and how they were to conduct themselves as the servant people of a holy and sovereign God.

Interpreters take one of three broad approaches to the Pentateuch as a source for history. (1) Many interpreters read the Pentateuch as a straightforward recounting of events. (2) Radical critics disregard the Pentateuch as a source for history. For example, Julius Wellhausen and his source-critical school saw the narratives—especially those of Genesis—as reflecting the first millennium era in which they were allegedly composed rather than the times of Moses and the patriarchs (second millennium). The form critic Hermann Gunkel coupled this historical skepticism with a dismissal of the supernatural. He viewed the first eleven chapters of Genesis as largely myth and legend and the patriarchal stories as folktale and epic. The most radical critics regarded only the core of the Mosaic traditions, the exodus event itself, as reliable history. Even that event had to be rid of all its miraculous overtones before it could be accepted as history in the strict sense. The rest of the Moses stories were regarded as embellishments of actual events or stories thought up to justify later religious belief and practice. (3) Others see the Pentateuch primarily as a theological interpretation of real persons and events. For these interpreters the narratives were written from the perspective of a later time. Such scholars differ widely over the possibility and value of recovering the "bare facts" behind the biblical *interpretation* of what happened.

Many scholars take the findings of scientific biblical archaeology as confirmation that the Pentateuch is most at home precisely in the second millennium setting in which the Old Testament located it. Thus the discovery of ancient Sumerian and Babylonian creation and flood stories at the library of Ashurbanipal at Nineveh and at other places has lent credence to their antiquity in Israelite tradition. Documents by the thousands from Ebla, Mari, Alalakh, and Nuzi confirm for some interpreters that the lifestyle, customs, and habits of the biblical patriarchs are most at home in the Middle Bronze Age (about 2000–1550 B.C.) where biblical chronology places them. The now well-understood environment of New Kingdom Egypt and Amarna Canaan (about 1570–1300 B.C.) likewise demonstrates that the account of Israel's history assigned to the time of Moses is compatible with that period. In short, the historicity of the Pentateuch is affirmed by much that has been and is being understood about its setting in the ancient world. Though this may not (and indeed cannot) prove the historicity of individual details, especially personal and private episodes and miraculous intervention, evidence suggests the Pentateuch recounts genuine historical events centered around actual historical persons.

The fundamental importance and relevance of the Pentateuch lies in its theology, not in its historicity or even its literary form and content. What truth is God communicating about Himself and His purposes? What meaning *did* that communication have for Old Testament Israel and the New Testament church (biblical theology)? What meaning *does* it have for contemporary Christian theology?

Such questions are obviously related to the matter of the Pentateuch's theme and purpose, matters dealt with previously. The historical, social, and religious setting of the Mosaic writings points to their purpose as that of instructing Israel about its past, its present, and its future. The nation had been redeemed by the great exodus event as a result of Yahweh's free choice of Israel in fulfillment of the promises to the patriarchs. Israel had to understand the context of those promises and their necessary fulfillment in light of the exodus salvation and the subsequent Sinai covenant. Israel now stood as covenant heir and servant people charged with mediating the saving purposes of Yahweh to the whole earth.

The great theme of the Pentateuch, then, is the theme of reconciliation and restoration. God's creation, having been affected by human disobedience, stood in need of restoration. Humanity, having been alienated from God, stood in need of forgiveness. God's saving plan began with a solemn pledge to bless the world through Abraham and his offspring (Israel). The pledge found expression in a covenant granting Abraham descendants and land and designating Abraham as God's instrument of redemption. Centuries later that covenant with Abraham

incorporated within it a covenant of another kind. The Sinai covenant—a sovereign-vassal treaty—offered to Israel the role of redemptive mediation if Israel submitted to God's rule. Israel's acceptance of that servant role produced the whole apparatus of law, religious ritual, and priesthood. These institutions enabled the nation to live out its servant task as a holy people and by that holiness to attract lost humanity to the only true and living God. In brief, that is the theology of the Pentateuch.

The Christian is also part of a "kingdom of priests" (Exod. 19:6; 1 Pet. 2:5,9; Rev. 1:6) with privileges and responsibilities corresponding to those of Old Testament Israel. The church and each and every believer stand within the stream of God's gracious covenant promises. Believers have been made "children of God" (John 1:12), delivered from bondage to sin by an exodus of personal redemption, established on the pilgrim way to the land of promise, and provided with every means through the new covenant of serving as the instruments of God's reconciling grace. The theology of the Pentateuch is important for Christians because it models God's timeless purposes for creation and redemption.

# GENESIS

The Book of Genesis takes its name from the Greek version of the Old Testament (the Septuagint), which called it *Genesis,* meaning *beginning.* This is an accurate translation of *bereshit,* the first word in the Hebrew book. The title is most appropriate to the book's contents, for it concerns the divine origin of all things, whether matter or energy, living or inanimate. It implies that apart from God everything can be traced back to a beginning point when God's purposes and works came into being. *Bereshit* indicates that God brought forth the "heavens and the earth" as the first act of creation (Gen. 1:1).

Jewish and Christian tradition has nearly unanimously attributed the authorship of Genesis to Moses (see "The Pentateuch"). Genesis is the only book of the Pentateuch that does not mention Moses' name or indicate something about its authorship. This omission may well be because the latest events of the book predate Moses by several centuries. Also biblical books seldom designate their authors. Yet the remainder of the Pentateuch builds upon Genesis, without which the constant allusions to the patriarchs and other persons and events would make no sense. The summary of the conclusion of Genesis (Gen. 46:8-27) in Exodus 1:1-7 serves as a bridge between the patriarchs and the exodus deliverance and highlights the continuity of the Pentateuch's story.

***Theme.*** The name *Genesis* describes what is at least a major theme of the book—beginnings. It recounts the beginnings of the heavens and earth, of all created things within them, of God's covenant relationship with humankind, of sin, of redemption, of nations, and of God's chosen people Israel.

Beginnings, however, is not a completely satisfying summary theme because it fails to answer the fundamental historical and theological question —why? To know *what* God did—He created all things "in the beginning"—is important. But to know *why* God acted in creation and for redemption is to grasp the very essence of divine revelation.

The theme of Genesis centers around the first utterance of God to man and woman recorded in the Sacred Text, namely Genesis 1:26-28.

Here God clarifies that He created man and woman to bless them and so that they could exercise dominion on His behalf over all creation. Human disobedience threatened God's purpose for humanity in creation. God responded by calling Abraham, through whom God's blessing would ultimately triumph. Admittedly, this interpretation of the theme derives not only, if at all, from Genesis but from a total biblical theology. Because it is a matter of theology, it will be more productive to consider it later under that heading.

***Literary Forms.*** The three major sections of Genesis are characterized by distinct literary types. The primeval events (Gen. 1–11) are cast in a poetic narrative form to aid in oral transmission. The accounts of the first three patriarchs (Gen. 12–36; 38) are reports about ancestors that were retained in family records. The Joseph narrative (Gen. 37; 39–50) is a short story containing tension and resolution. Within each of these major literary types, however, are other minor types such as genealogies (5:3-32; 11:10-32), narratives in which God appears (17–18; 32:22-30), words from God (25:23), blessings (1:28; 9:1; 27:27-29), and tribal sayings (49:3-27). Genesis presents history in every sense of the term. Genesis, however, presents history in the form of narrative that embraces a host of literary types to communicate its theological message clearly and effectively.

I. God's Creation Goal (1:1–2:25)
II. Sin, Its Consequences/God's Grace (3:1–10:32)
III. Abraham: The Obedience of Faith (12:1–22:19)
IV. Isaac: The Link with God's Promises to Abraham (22:20–25:18)
V. Jacob's Struggle for the Promises (25:19–36:43)
VI. Deliverance through Joseph (37:1–50:26)

**Purpose and Theology.** The purpose of Genesis was to give the nation Israel an explanation of its existence on the threshold of the conquest of Canaan (see Theme). Moses had at hand written and oral traditions about Israel's past and records concerning the other great themes of Genesis. He was, however, the first to organize these, select from them those that were appropriate to the divine redemptive purposes, and compose them as they stand. His task as inspired, prophetic author was to clarify to his people how and why God had brought them into being. He also wanted them to know what their mission was as a covenant, priestly nation and how their present situation fulfilled ancient promises.

Close attention to the themes that link Genesis and the remainder of the Pentateuch clarify these purposes. God had revealed to Abraham that he would be granted the land of Canaan (Gen. 12:1,5,7; 13:15), that his descendants would leave that land for a time (15:13), but that they would be delivered from the land of their oppression to return to the land of promise (15:16). This land would be theirs forever (17:8) as an arena within and from which they would be a means of blessing all nations of the earth (12:2-3; 27:29). Joseph understood this and saw in his own sojourn in Egypt the divine preservation of his people (45:7-8). God had sent him there to save them from physical and spiritual extinction (50:20). The time would come, he said, when God would remember His promise to Abraham, Isaac, and Jacob and would return them to Canaan (50:24).

The link with Exodus is clear in the call of Moses to lead his people from Egypt to the land of promise (Exod. 3:6-10,16-17; 6:2-8). Their charter as a covenant nation—a "kingdom of priests and a holy nation" (Exod. 19:6)—recalls God's promise to bless the nations through Abraham (Gen. 12:3; 22:18). The covenant renewal at the Plains of Moab repeats those same themes. The Lord was about to lead His people into Canaan to possess it as their inheritance (Deut. 4:1; 5:33; 7:1,12-16; 8:1-10; 9:5; 11:8-12,24-25). There they would serve Him as a redemptive agent, a catalyst around which the nations would be reconciled to God (Deut. 4:5-8; 28:10).

The theological message of Genesis, however, goes beyond the narrow concerns of Israel alone. Genesis does indeed provide Israel's reason for being, but it does more. It explains the human condition that called forth a covenant people. That is, it unfolds the great creative and redemptive purposes of God that found focus in Israel as an agency of re-creation and salvation.

God's original and eternal purposes are outlined in Genesis 1:26-28. God created man and woman as His image to bless them and so that they could exercise dominion over all creation on His behalf. The key themes of biblical theology and of Genesis are, therefore, God's blessing and human dominion under God's reign.

The fall of humankind into sin subverted God's goal of blessing and dominion. A process of redemption from that fallenness and of recovery of the original covenant mandate of God had to be effected. That took the form of the choice of Abraham through whose offspring (Israel and ultimately the Messiah) the divine creation purposes might come to pass. That man and nation, joined by eternal covenant to Yahweh, were charged with the task of serving Him as the model of a dominion people and the vehicle through which a saving relationship could be established between Him and the alienated world of nations.

Of course, Israel failed to be the servant people, a failure already anticipated in the Torah (Lev. 26:14-39; Deut. 28:15-68). God's goals cannot, however, be frustrated. So from the nation arose a remnant, a remnant finally compressed to only one descendant of Abraham—Jesus the Christ—who accomplished in His life and death the redemptive and reigning purposes of God. The church now exists as His body to serve as Israel was chosen and redeemed to serve. God's Old Testament people served as the model of the kingdom of the Lord and the agency through which His reconciling work on earth can be achieved through His New Testament people.

The theology of Genesis then is wrapped up in the kingdom purposes of God who, despite human failures, cannot be hindered in His ultimate objective of displaying His glory through His creation and dominion.

### GOD'S CREATION GOAL (1:1–2:25)

*Primeval history* describes the accounts of the creation, the fall, the flood, the tower of Babel, and the distribution of the human race. It embraces all those facets of human experience that led up to and necessitated the call of Abraham to covenant service to the Lord.

The two accounts of creation (1:1–2:3 and 2:4-25) are designed respectively to demonstrate the all-wise and all-powerful sovereignty of God (first account) and His special creation of humanity to rule for Him over all other created things (second account). Though the creation stories are fundamentally theological and not scientific, nothing in them is contradicted by modern scientific understanding. Genesis insists that all the forms of life were created "after their kind" (1:11-12,21,24-25); that is, they did not evolve across species lines. Most importantly, the man and the woman were created as "the image of God" (1:26). In other words, humanity was created to represent God on the earth and to rule over all things in His name (1:26-28). God's desire was to bless humanity and to enjoy relationship with them.

### SIN'S CONSEQUENCES/GOD'S GRACE (3:1–10:32)

The privilege of dominion also carried responsibility and limitation. Being placed in the garden to "work it and watch over it" represented human responsibility (2:15). The tree in the midst of the garden from which humans should not eat represented those areas of dominion reserved to Yahweh alone. The man and woman, however, disobeyed God and ate of the tree. They "died" with respect to their covenant privileges (2:17) and suffered the indictment and judgment of their Sovereign. This entailed suffering and sorrow and eventual physical death. God had created man and woman to enjoy fellowship with Himself and with each other. Their disobedience alienated them from God and each other.

The pattern of sin and its consequences set in the garden is replayed throughout Genesis in the accounts of Cain, the generation of the flood, and the men of Sodom. The fall means that we humans are predisposed to sin. Though God punishes sin, sin does not thwart God's ultimate, gracious purpose for His human creation. Embedded in the curse was the gleam of a promise that the offspring of the woman would someday lead the human race to triumph.

The consequences of sin became clear in the second generation when Cain, the oldest son, killed Abel his brother. Just as his parents had been expelled from the presence of God in the garden, so now Cain was expelled from human society to undertake a nomadic life in the east. Embedded in the curse was the gleam of grace, the "mark on Cain," symbolizing God's protection.

***Blessing and Curse (4:17–5:32).*** Cain's genealogy illustrates the tension between God's blessing and spreading sin. Through the achievements of Cain's descendants, humanity began to experience the blessing of dominion over creation. Progress in the arts and technology was, however, matched by progress in sin as illustrated in Lamech's boastful song of murder. Meanwhile, God's redemptive, creation mandate continued through another son of Adam and Eve—Seth. His genealogy led straight to Noah, to whom the original creation promises were reaffirmed (6:18; 9:1-7).

***Deliverance (6:1–9:29).*** With the passing of time it became increasingly clear that humanity was unwilling and unable to live out the responsibilities of stewardship. Humans again violated their proper place within God's order by overstepping the limits God had placed on them. As a result of the improper inter-

mingling of the "sons of God" (understood as either the angels or the rulers on the earth) and "the daughters of men," God again saw the need to reassert His lordship and make a fresh beginning that could give the human race another chance at obedience.

The consequence of sin was the great flood, a catastrophe so enormous that all life and institutions perished from the earth. God's grace was still active in preserving a remnant on the ark. In response to the worship of His people, God promised never again to destroy the earth so long as history ran its course. God's pledge to Noah reaffirmed the creation promises of blessing and dominion. Though differing in detail from the original statement of Genesis 1:26-28, the central mandate is identical. The new humanity springing from Noah and his sons was called on to exercise dominion over all the earth as the image of God. The sign of the permanence of that arrangement was the rainbow.

Once more, as though to underline the effects of the fall on human faithfulness, Noah fell victim to his environment. Adam had sinned by partaking of a forbidden fruit; Noah sinned by perverting the use of a permitted fruit. Both cases illustrate that unaided humans can never rise to the level of God-ordained responsibility.

When Noah learned of the abuse he had suffered at the hand of his son Ham, he cursed the offspring of Ham—the Canaanites. He blessed those of his other two sons. This set in motion the relationships among the threefold division of the human race that would forever after determine the course of history. God would enlarge Japheth (the Gentiles), but in time Japheth would find refuge in the preserving and protecting tents of Shem (Israel). The Shemites (or Semites) thus would be the channel of redemptive grace.

## THE FLOOD

The cataclysmic deluge described in Genesis 69 as God's judgment on the earth is mentioned elsewhere in the Old Testament (Gen. 10:1,32; 11:10; Pss. 29:10; 104:6-9; Isa. 54:9) and in the New Testament (Matt. 24:38-39; Luke 17:26-27; Heb. 11:7; 1 Pet. 3:20; 2 Pet. 2:5; 3:3-7). That more verses are devoted to the flood than to the creation (Gen. 12) or the fall (Gen. 3) suggests the significance of the account.

### The Old Testament Account

Because of the great wickedness of humanity (Gen. 6:5,11), God resolved to destroy all living beings (6:13) with the exception of righteous Noah and his family (6:9,18). God instructed Noah to make an ark of cypress wood (6:14; "gopher wood," KJV). He told Noah to take his family and seven [pairs] of every clean species and two of every unclean species of animals, birds, and creeping things, along with provisions for the duration of the flood (6:18-21; 7:1-3). The rains lasted forty days and nights, covered "all the high mountains under the whole heaven" (7:19), and destroyed every living creature on land (7:21-23). When Noah and his family emerged from the ark after a year and ten days, he built an altar and offered sacrifices to God (8:14-20). God blessed Noah and his family (9:1) and made a covenant that He would never again destroy the earth by flood (8:21; 9:11). God gave the rainbow as a visible sign of that covenant (9:12-17).

### Date and Extent of the Flood

It is impossible to determine the exact date of the flood, since no archaeological or geological materials have been found that would enable its accurate dating. Estimates have placed it between 13,000 and 3000 B.C.

The extent of the flood has been debated. Arguments for a universal flood include: (1) the wording of Genesis 6–9, which is best interpreted as a universal flood (see 7:19-23); (2) the widespread flood traditions among many, widely scattered peoples that are best explained if all peoples are descended from Noah; (3) the unusual source of water (Gen. 7:11); (4) the length of the flood, whereas a local flood would have subsided in a few days; (5) the false assumption that all life resided in a limited geographical area; and (6) God's limitless ability to act within history.

Arguments against a universal flood have persuaded some scholars to accept a limited flood. Some arguments are: (1) the amount of water needed to cover the highest mountain, which would be eight times as much as there is on earth; (2) the practical problems of housing and feeding so many animals for a year; (3) the destruction of all plant life submerged in salt water for over a year; (4) the view that destruction of the human race required only a flood covering the part of the earth inhabited at that time; and (5) the lack of geological evidence for a worldwide cataclysm. While all of our questions cannot be answered, the biblical data points in the direction of a universal flood.

### Theological Significance

(1) The flood demonstrates God's hatred of sin and the certainty of His judgment on it. (2) God's giving people 120 years to repent before judgment came demonstrates His patience in dealing with sin. (3) The sparing of one family demonstrates God's saving grace. (4) The flood reveals God's rule over nature and over humanity.

**Blessing Reaffirmed (10:1-32).** The "table of nations" demonstrates the fulfillment of God's command to be fruitful and fill the earth. The climactic position of the Shemites focuses attention on Eber for whom the Hebrews (ibri) were named. This ancestor of Abraham anticipates the Jewish patriarchs who are the focus of the second half of Genesis.

**Confusion at Babel (11:1-32).** The story of the tower of Babel separates the genealogy of the descent from Noah to Eber and Peleg and the genealogy that connects Noah to Abraham. In the days

| LIFE OF ABRAHAM | | |
|---|---|---|
| EVENT | OLD TESTAMENT PASSAGE | NEW TESTAMENT REFERENCE |
| The birth of Abram | Gen 11:26 | |
| God's call of Abram | Gen 12:1-3 | Heb 11:8 |
| The entry into Canaan | Gen 12:4-9 | |
| Abram in Egypt | Gen 12:10-20 | |
| Lot separates from Abram | Gen 13:1-18 | |
| Abram rescues Lot | Gen 14:1-17 | |
| Abram pays tithes to Melchizedek | Gen 14:18-24 | Heb 7:1-10 |
| God's covenant with Abraham | Gen 15:1-21 | Rom 4:1-25 Gal 3:6-25 Heb 6:13-20 |
| The birth of Ishmael | Gen 16:1-16 | |
| Abraham promised a son by Sarah | Gen 17:1-27 | Rom 4:18-25 Heb 11:11-12 |
| Abraham intercedes for Sodom | Gen 18:16-33 | |
| Lot saved and Sodom destroyed | Gen 19:1-38 | |
| The birth of Isaac | Gen 21:1-7 | |
| Hagar and Ishmael sent away | Gen 21:8-21 | Gal 4:21-31 |
| Abraham challenged to offer Isaac as sacrifice | Gen 22:1-19 | Heb 11:17-19 Jas 2:20-24 |
| The death of Sarah | Gen 23:1-20 | |
| The death of Abraham | Gen 25:1-11 | |

of Peleg, son of Eber, the earth was "divided" (10:25). Through Abraham and the Abrahamic covenant it someday would be reunited. The Babel narrative thus illustrates the false and defiant sense of humanistic solidarity that sought to evade the creation mandate to fill the earth under God's dominion. The scattering of the nations accomplished that purpose but did not effect compliance to the will of God that made true servanthood a reality. That is why a new covenant, one with redemptive aspects, had to be implemented.

## ABRAHAM (12:1–22:19)

The story of the patriarchs is centered and grounded in the covenant to which the Lord called Abraham. The history of the human race from the fall to Abraham's own day was sufficient to show that the great kingdom purposes of God could not be achieved until humanity could be redeemed and restored to covenant-keeping capacity. The promise had been given that the offspring of the woman would someday prevail over anti-God forces. Now that offspring promise was to find fulfillment in one man and his descendants, chief among whom was to be the Messiah who would effect salvation and dominion.

**God's Promises (12:1-9).** Abraham was called from Sumerian paganism to faith in the living God. God granted him an unconditional set of promises—descendants and blessing. God promised to lead him to Canaan, the earthly scene for the working out of God's promises. On Abraham's arrival in Canaan, he received God's promise of land.

**Promises Threatened (12:10-20).** No sooner were God's promises given than their fulfillment was "threatened." Faced with famine, Abraham deserted

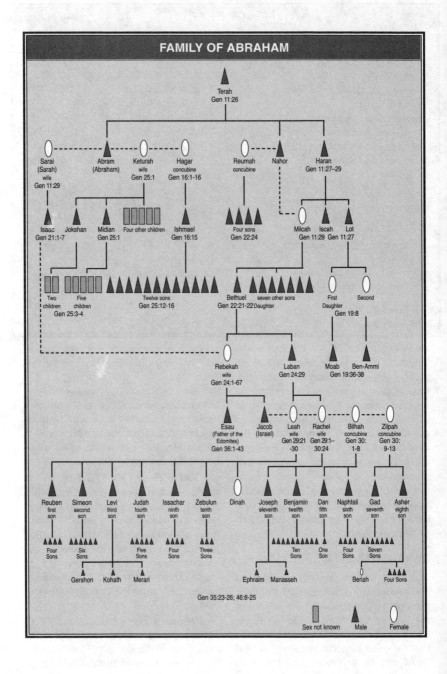

# FAMILY OF ABRAHAM

Terah
Gen 11:26

Sarai (Sarah) wife Gen 11:29

Abram (Abraham)

Keturah wife Gen 25:1

Hagar concubine Gen 16:1-16

Reumah concubine

Nahor

Haran Gen 11:27–29

Isaac Gen 21:1-7

Jokshan

Midian Gen 25:1

Four other children

Ishmael Gen 16:15

Four sons Gen 22:24

Milcah Gen 11:29

Iscah Gen 11:29

Lot Gen 11:27

Two children

Five children Gen 25:3-4

Twelve sons Gen 25:12-16

Bethuel Gen 22:21-22

seven other sons Daughter

First Daughter

Second Daughter Gen 19:8

Rebekah wife Gen 24:1-67

Laban Gen 24:29

Moab Gen 19:36-38

Ben-Ammi

Esau (Father of the Edomites) Gen 36:1-43

Jacob (Israel)

Leah wife Gen 29:21 -30

Rachel wife Gen 29:1– 30:24

Bilhah concubine Gen 30: 1-8

Zilpah concubine Gen 30: 9-13

Reuben first son

Simeon second son

Levi third son

Judah fourth son

Issachar ninth son

Zebulun tenth son

Dinah

Joseph eleventh son

Benjamin twelfth son

Dan fifth son

Naphtali sixth son

Gad seventh son

Asher eighth son

Four Sons

Six Sons

Five Sons

Four Sons

Three Sons

Ten Sons

One Son

Four Sons

Seven Sons

Gershon    Kohath    Merari

Ephraim    Manasseh

Beriah    Four Sons

Gen 35:23-26; 46:8-25

Sex not known          Male          Female

the promised land and placed Sarah—the link with the promise of descendants—in a potentially compromising position as a member of Pharaoh's harem.

***Promises Realized (13:1-18).*** Abraham anticipated the history of his descendants by dwelling briefly in Canaan, sojourning in Egypt (12:10-20), and coming out with riches and honor as Israel did later in the exodus (Exod. 11:1-3; 12:35-36). Then, in his own "conquest" and occupation, Abraham divided the land between himself and Lot. The territories through which he had previously traveled as a nomad now became his in permanent habitation.

***Possessing and Blessing (14:1-24).*** Abraham's dominion over his inheritance was not to be uncontested. The invasion and subjugation of the cities of the plain by the kings of the east represented resistance to Abraham's claim to the land. Abraham, acting on behalf of El Elyon, the Almighty God, overcame this threat. In rescuing Lot's people, Abraham was fulfilling his God-given charge to be a blessing to other nations.

***Descendants and Land (15:1-21).*** Though he had inherited the land by promise, Abraham did not yet have the promised offspring, even after ten years in the land (see Gen. 16:3). The Lord reaffirmed His promise, enlarging it to include innumerable offspring. That host of descendants, Yahweh promised, would go to a land of sojourn, just as Abraham had done. They eventually would return with the riches to fill the land of promise.

***Human Effort (16:1-16).*** Sarah, Abraham's wife, was past the age of childbearing. Thus she and her husband, following the custom of the time, decided that the offspring promise could find fulfillment only if they took matters into their own hands. Sarah presented her slave girl to Abraham as a surrogate mother. In due time a son, Ishmael, was born. This attempt to short-circuit the ways and means of the Lord was to no avail.

***Promise of an Heir (17:1-18:15).*** Once more the Lord affirmed His covenant intentions. Abraham would be the father of nations, but the nations would be born of Sarah, not Hagar. As a token of His steadfast loyalty to His covenant pledge, the Lord established the rite of circumcision.

Soon the Lord appeared as the angel of the Lord, revealing to Abraham and Sarah that she would give birth to the promised offspring within the year.

***Blessing Neighbors (18:16-19:22).*** God reminded Abraham that he was the chosen means of blessing the nations. As an illustration of what that meant, Yahweh revealed to Abraham that He was going to destroy Sodom and Gomorrah, cities whose sinfulness was beyond remedy. Abraham was aware that this implied the death of his own nephew Lot, who lived in Sodom. Abraham exercised his ministry of mediation by pleading with the Lord to spare the righteous and thus the cities in which they lived. Though not even ten righteous ones could be found and the cities therefore were overwhelmed in judgment, Abraham's role as the one in whom the nations could find blessing is clearly seen.

***Promise Threatened (20:1-18).*** Abraham's encounter with Abimelech of Gerar also testifies to Abraham's role as mediator. He had lied to Abimelech concerning Sarah, maintaining that she was only his sister. Abimelech took Sarah into his own harem, putting God's promise of offspring through Sarah in jeopardy. Before matters could proceed further, the Lord revealed to Abimelech that Abraham was a prophet, one whose

## COVENANTS

A covenant is a compact or agreement made between two parties binding them mutually to some agreed upon obligations and benefits. Much of the history of salvation can be traced by noting both the presence and the contents of biblical covenants. Covenants may be either bilateral ("two-sided"), where both parties are obligated, or unilateral ("one-sided"), where only one party is bound by the agreement.

Genesis 15:9-21 offers the best illustration of the unilateral type of covenant. The verb "to make" a covenant is literally "to cut" a covenant. Thus when one made a covenant, several animals were brought, cut in half, and arranged opposite each other. The person or parties making the covenant would then walk through the aisle formed by the carcasses and say in effect, "May it happen to me as it has happened to these slain animals if I do not keep all the provisions of this covenant." (Compare Jer. 34:18-20.)

In a bilateral covenant both parties would take the oath. If one defaulted, the other was released from any further obligations. But in the case of Genesis 15:9-21, the "smoking fire pot with a blazing torch" pictures God as the *only* One who walked between the pieces and thus obligated Himself alone to bring all the blessings and benefits of the Abrahamic covenant. God's blessings were apart from any works of obedience on the part of Abraham or any of the patriarchs who followed him who also enjoyed the benefits of this covenant.

The Sinai covenant offers the best illustration of a bilateral covenant. The people of Israel agreed to accept the terms of relationship God offered (Exod. 19:5-6; 24:3). In their preaching, the later prophets often placed Israel on trial for failure to fulfill their covenant commitments (Jer. 11:10; Ezek. 16:59; Hos. 8:1). In times of spiritual revival, the people of Israel would reaffirm their commitment to the covenant (Deut. 5:2-3; Josh. 24; 2 Kgs. 23:3; 2 Chr.. 15:12).

Scripture presents a fairly large number of covenants. Many were instituted by the one true living God. The primary divine covenants include those made with Noah (Gen. 9:9-17), Abraham (Gen. 15:18; 17:2), Moses (Exod. 19:5-6), David (2 Sam. 23:5; see 7:12-16), and the new covenant of Jeremiah 31:31-34.

The *content* of covenants is more important than their *form*. The content of all these divine covenants exhibits a unity, continuity, and building theme. The form changes since there are different "signs" of the covenant (for example, a rainbow in

---

prayers were effective. Then the plague that Yahweh had brought upon Abimelech because of his dealings with Sarah was removed in response to Abraham's intercession. Once more Abraham's function as dispenser of blessing and cursing is evident.

***Promise Fulfilled (21:1-21).*** At last Isaac, the covenant son, was born. Through Ishmael, God honored His promise that not only the Hebrews but "many nations" would call Abraham "Father" (see 25:12-18).

***Obedience and Blessing (22:1-19).*** Within a few years the Lord tested Abraham by commanding him to offer his covenant son as a burnt offering. The intent was to teach Abraham that covenant blessing requires total covenant commitment and obedience. The narrative also stresses that covenant obedience brings fresh bestowal of covenant blessing. Abraham's willingness to surrender his son guaranteed all the more the fulfillment of God's promises to him.

## ISAAC (22:20–25:18; 26:1-33)

Isaac fulfilled a *passive* linking role quite unlike the other patriarchs, who took an *active* role in the outworkings of God's promises. Already Abraham had waited for Isaac's birth; Abraham stood ready to

Noah's case, circumcision in Abraham's case), types of covenants, and "people" addressed in the covenant. If we keep our eyes on their content, we will note how the everlasting plan of God, both for our redemption and our successful living, was unfolded.

One three-part formula acts as a summation of God's covenant relationship: I shall be your God, you shall be My people, and I shall dwell in the midst of you. The repetition of elements of this formula as part of many of these covenants supplied one of their unifying themes: God would be in the midst of His people and they would be His special possession. (Compare Gen. 17:7; Exod. 6:6-7; 19:4-5.)

In spite of their structural and thematic unity, the major Old Testament covenants exhibit a diversity of focus as history progresses.

God's covenant with Noah focused on preservation. The Abrahamic covenant focused on land and descendants. The Mosaic covenant emphasized obedience to the law of God, and the Davidic covenant focused on preservation of David's dynasty. The new covenant of Jeremiah 31 focused on God's forgiveness of His people, on whose hearts He would write His law. The covenants with Abraham and David and Jeremiah's new covenant anticipated redemption through the promised Messiah.

To clarify the relationship between the old covenant (usually equated with the Mosaic covenant) and the new covenant is difficult. Paul apparently set the promise of the Abrahamic type covenants over against the law of the Mosaic type. But Paul's contrast was in no way absolute or unqualified.

Paul affirmed that the law-covenant did not annul the covenant of promise (Gal. 3:17) and that the promise-covenant did not annul the covenant of law (Rom. 3:31).

At the apex of all the covenants is the new covenant found in Jeremiah 31:31-34. The phrase new covenant is found six times in the New Testament (1 Cor. 11:25; 2 Cor. 3:6; Heb. 8:8; 9:15; 12:24; and possibly in Luke 22:20). The idea is also present in Romans 11:27 and Galatians 4:21-31. Since much of the content of the new covenant repeats the previous covenants' promises, it may be best to represent this covenant as a "renewed covenant." It fulfills the promises of the older covenants, but it is better by virtue of its clearer view of Christ, its richer experience of the Holy Spirit, and the greater liberty it grants to believers.

offer Isaac as a sacrifice. Following the death and burial of Sarah, Abraham made arrangements for Isaac to take a wife from among his own kinfolk of Aramea. Abraham thus worked to ensure that the promise of offspring would continue into the next generation. This done, Abraham died (25:7-8) and was buried with his wife by his sons Ishmael and Isaac. Isaac rarely occupied the center stage. In the following years Isaac, who had been the object of his father's actions, became an object in his son Jacob's struggle for the promises (27:1-40).

A rare scene focusing on Isaac pictures him as the link through whom

God's promises to receive land and to be a source of blessing for the nations were fulfilled. The Lord sent Isaac to live among the Philistines of Gerar as Abraham had done. There Isaac unwillingly blessed the nations by digging wells which the Philistines appropriated to their own use. Isaac and his clan proved to be such a source of nourishment to their neighbors that Abimelech their king made a covenant with Isaac, recognizing his claim in the promised land.

## JACOB (25:19-34; 27:1–36:43)

Isaac served as a passive link with God's promises to Abraham. In contrast, Isaac's

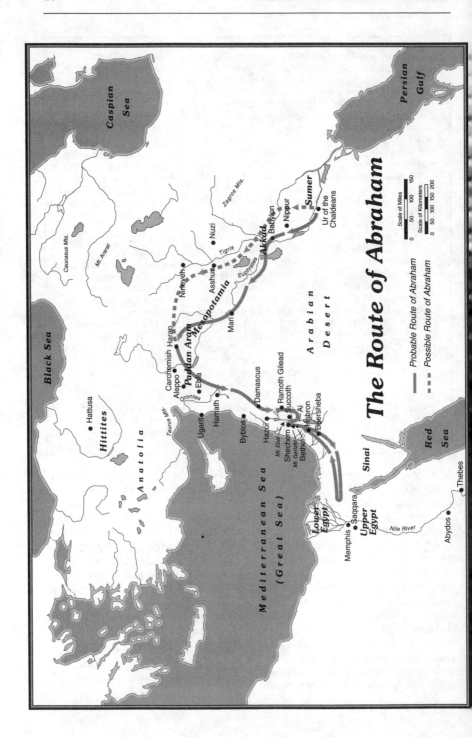

The Route of Abraham

younger son, Jacob, fought throughout his life for the very best that God had promised to give.

### Beginning of Struggle (25:19-26).

Just as the barrenness of Sarah called for Abraham to trust God for offspring, that same deficiency in Rebekah called for earnest prayer from her husband Isaac. Faithful to His promise to Abraham, Yahweh responded and gave not one but two sons, Esau and Jacob. Jacob's grasping Esau's heel in an effort to be the firstborn introduces the major theme of the Jacob stories—Jacob's struggle for the promised blessings.

### Struggle for Birthright (25:27-34).

Contrary to the norms of succession and inheritance, the Lord gave to Jacob the rights of the firstborn, though on the human level Jacob manipulated his brother in order to receive them. Esau, as the older son of Isaac, should have inherited the birthright, the claim to family leadership. He forfeited that, however, in a moment of self-indulgence.

### Struggle for Blessing (26:34-28:9).

Esau still retained his position as heir of the covenant promises in succession to Abraham and Isaac. But when it was apparent through his marriages to Hittite women that he was unworthy of covenant privilege, his mother, Rebekah, set about to replace him with his brother Jacob.

When the day came for Isaac to designate Esau as the recipient of God's promised blessing, Jacob appeared in his place. Blind Isaac, deceived by the substitution, granted his irrevocable blessing. In the ancient world the speaking of a blessing, like the signing of a contract in our day, gave the words binding force. Jacob thus controlled both the birthright and the blessing. Though the means of their acquisition was anything but honorable, the Lord had foretold Jacob's triumph on the occasion of the birth of the twins (25:23).

Enraged by this turn of events, Esau plotted to kill his brother. Rebekah urged Jacob to flee for his life to Paddan-Aram, her homeland, so that he might also acquire a wife from among their kin.

### God's Faithfulness (28:10-22).

God's watchcare became apparent at Bethel, where Jacob encountered Yahweh in a dream. He revealed Himself to Jacob as the God of his fathers, the one who would continue the covenant promises through him.

### Struggle Continues (29:1-31:55).

Thus encouraged, Jacob went on to Haran, where he struggled with his uncle Laban for the right to marry his daughters Leah and Rachel. God's promise of many offspring began to be realized as Jacob fathered eleven sons and a daughter in his wives' struggle for children. In his struggle against scheming Uncle Laban, Jacob became prosperous beyond his wildest expectations. By stealing the household gods, Rachel joined Jacob in the struggle against Laban. With Laban intent on revenge, only God's intervention in a dream brought a peaceful end to the struggle with Jacob.

### Promised Land (32:1-33:17).

Finally, after twenty years Jacob returned to his homeland. On the way he learned that Esau was coming to meet him. Fearing that his own efforts to safeguard himself from Esau's revenge were inadequate, Jacob entreated the Lord to deliver him. The Lord again appeared to Jacob, this time as a human foe, and wrestled with the patriarch through the night. Impressed with his persistent struggle, the "man" blessed Jacob with a change of name (Jacob to Israel, prince of God). The deceiver (ya akob) had become a nobleman, one fit to rule through the authority of the sovereign God. The subsequent encounter with

## PATRIARCHS

The term *patriarch* comes from a Greek word meaning the *head of a tribe* or *family.* The term usually refers to the Israelite forefathers Abraham (Heb. 7:4), Isaac, and Jacob. It is used more loosely of Jacob's twelve sons (Acts 7:8-9) and David (Acts 2:29).

### Date and Historicity

The time of the patriarchs has been estimated between 2200 and 1300 B.C. Available evidence suggests a time early in the second millennium B.C. Some doubt the patriarchs were historical characters, seeing them as legendary figures who explain the names of the tribes of Israel. Yet no evidence has been discovered to refute the existence of the patriarchs.

### Names

Many of the personal names in the patriarchal narratives appear in early second millennium B.C. texts written by other Near Eastern peoples. Texts from Ugarit and Assyria combine the name *Jacob* with the names of local gods (Jacob-el, Jacob-baal). The Old Testament understands Abram to mean *exalted father;* and Abraham, *father of many* (Gen. 17:5). Isaac, from the Hebrew *to laugh,* brought joy to his parents by his birth (Gen. 21:6). Jacob likely comes from the word *grasp the heel.* The patriarchs were Arameans (Deut. 26:5), Semitic peoples of northwestern Mesopotamia.

### History

The patriarchal narratives are found in Genesis 12–50. Genesis 11:31 describes Abraham's migration with his family from Ur of the Chaldeans to Haran in northern Mesopotamia, where God made a covenant with him (12:1-3). The covenant promised innumerable descendants and a land known today as Israel. Abraham lived a typical seminomadic life. He dwelt in tents and moved from place to place, seeking pasture for his flocks. Even before the death of his father, Terah, Abraham journeyed with his family and possessions to Canaan, where he settled at Shechem (12:4-6). He later relocated near Bethel (12:8). During a famine, he lived for a time in Egypt (12:10-20). After returning from Egypt, he and Lot agreed to separate and settle in different areas. Lot chose the Jordan Valley near Sodom, and Abraham settled in Hebron (13:2-18).

God promised Abraham an heir when he was seventy-five and Sarah, his wife, was ten years younger. The child, Isaac, was born twenty-five years later (Gen. 12:2; 17:1,17,21; 21:5). Little information is given about Isaac except the choosing of his wife, Rebekah (Gen. 24), and the blessing Jacob received from him by disguising himself as Esau (Gen. 27). Jacob's twelve sons, the ancestors of the twelve tribes of Israel, were born to Jacob's wives, Leah and Rachel (Gen. 29; 30; 35:16-19). The aged Jacob's blessings on his sons singled out Judah as the one from whom a ruler would emerge (49:8-12).

### Patriarchal Religion

Abraham probably was a worshiper of the Mesopotamian moon god Sin before God made a covenant with him. Joshua 24:2,14 affirms that the patriarchal ancestors worshiped pagan gods in Mesopotamia. Some argue that the patriarchs worshiped one god without denying the existence of other gods. While they became worshipers of the *only* living God, their descendants reverted to polytheism, worshiping the many gods of the Canaanite fertility cults (Exod. 32; Num. 25:1-3; Josh. 24:14; Ezek. 6:13; 20:8). The prophets constantly condemned the people for their worship of their neighbors' gods.

Esau proved to be peaceful. Indeed, Jacob saw in Esau's forgiveness a reflection of God's face.

**Threat of Assimilation (33:18–34:31).** Jacob moved on into Canaan, coming first to Shechem, the first stopping place of his grandfather Abraham (see 12:6). Having secured property there, Jacob built an altar.

The rape of Dinah graphically illustrates the loose morals of the native Canaanites. Shechem's proposal of marriage illustrates the threat of intermarriage. The slaughter of the men of Shechem anticipates Israel's conquest of the land under Joshua.

### Reaffirming the Promises (35:1–36:43).
Jacob traveled on to Bethel, again in the footsteps of Abraham (see 12:8). There, as he had before, Jacob saw the Lord in a vision and received yet another promise of the divine presence and blessing. He would father nations and kings and would inherit the land of his fathers. The list of his immediate descendants attests to the onset of promise fulfillment. Even Esau, who had to settle for a secondary blessing (27:39-40), gave rise to a mighty people.

## JOSEPH (37:1–50:26)
Israel's role as the people of promise was being jeopardized by their acceptance of the loose moral standards of the native Canaanites. The incest between Reuben and his father's servant-wife (35:22) hints at that moral compromise. Judah's marriage to the Canaanite Shua and his later affair with his own daughter-in-law, Tamar, makes the danger clear. To preserve His people, Yahweh removed them from that sinful environment to Egypt, where they could mature into the covenant nation that He was preparing them to be.

This explains the Joseph story. His brothers sold him to Egypt to be rid of their brother the dreamer. God, however, used their act of hate as an opportunity to save Israel from both physical famine and spiritual extinction. The rise of Joseph to a position of authority in Egypt in fulfillment of his God-given dreams illustrates the Lord's blessing

upon His people. Joseph's wisdom in administering the agricultural affairs of Egypt again fulfilled God's promise that "I will bless him who blesses you." What appeared to be a series of blunders and injustices in Joseph's early experiences proved to be God at work in unseen ways to demonstrate His sovereign, kingdom work among the nations.

No one was more aware of this than Joseph, at least in later years. After he had revealed himself to his brothers, he said, "God sent me ahead of you to preserve for you a remnant on earth and to save your lives by a great deliverance." Years later after Jacob's death, when Joseph's brothers feared his revenge, he reminded them that they had intended to harm him, "but God intended it for good to accomplish . . . the saving of many lives." Human tragedy had become the occasion of divine triumph. Joseph's dying wish—to be buried in the land of promise—looks past the future tragedy of Israel's experience of slavery and anticipates God's triumph in the exodus.

### Contemporary Significance.
One obvious contribution of the Book of Genesis to the modern world is its explanation of the origins of things that could be understood in no other way. That is, it has scientific and historical value even if that is not its primary purpose.

More fundamentally, Genesis deals with the essence of what it means to be human beings created as the image of God. Who are we? Why are we? What are we to do? Failure to appreciate God's purpose for humanity has resulted in chaotic, purposeless thought and action. Ultimately, life without true knowledge of human nature as the image of God and human function as stewards of God's creation is life without a sense of meaning. When one lives out life in light of Genesis, life is seen as being in touch and in tune with the God of the universe. God's rule becomes a reality as human beings conform to His goals for His creation. Genesis outlines the Creator's intentions.

As sinners we are unable to realize God's purpose for our lives through our own efforts. Only God's intervention brings promise to our lives. Our salvation is God's work.

***Ethical Value.*** The awful effect of sin is one of the striking themes of Genesis. Sin frustrated the purposes of God for the human race. Sin had to be addressed before those purposes could be realized. Genesis teaches the heinousness and seriousness of sin and its tragic repercussions.

In addition to the story of "the fall," narrative after narrative in Genesis shows people how to live victoriously in the face of anti-God elements at work in this fallen world and describes what happens when they fail to do so. Cain, through lack of faith, dishonored God and then killed his brother. Lamech, in boasting pride, revealed the absurdities of humanistic views of life. The intermingling of angelic and human societies shows the inevitable result of breaking the bonds of God-ordained positions in life. The pride of the Babel tower builders demonstrates the arrogance of people who seek to make a name for themselves rather than to honor the name of the Lord.

The models of faith and obedience—Abel, Enoch, Noah, Abraham, and Joseph—are instructive as well. Their commitment to righteousness and the integrity of lifestyle speak eloquently of what it means to be a kingdom citizen, faithfully at work discharging the high and holy elements of that call.

## Questions for Reflection

1. How does the meaning of the name *Genesis* relate to the contents of the book?

2. Why did God create humankind?

3. What does Genesis teach about the consequences of sin? Does human sin thwart God's ultimate purpose for humanity?

4. What were God's goals in calling Abraham?

5. What events seemed to threaten the fulfillment of God's promises to Abraham? How did God overcome these obstacles?

6. What was Isaac's role in the story of Genesis?

7. Why can the story of Jacob be called "the struggle for God's promises"?

8. How does the story of Joseph inspire hope at times when God seems to have forgotten you?

9. How did Joseph help realize God's promises

    (a) to make Abraham a blessing to the nations?

    (b) to make Abraham the father of a multitude?

10. How do Christians participate in realizing God's promises to Abraham?

## Sources for Additional Study

Butler, Trent C. "Genesis." *Holman Bible Dictionary.* Nashville: Holman, 1991.

Coats, George W. *Genesis,* with an *Introduction to Narrative Literature.* Forms of Old Testament Literature, vol. 1. Ed. R. Knierim and G. Tucker. Grand Rapids: Eerdmans, 1983.

Garrett, Duane. *Rethinking Genesis.* Grand Rapids: Baker, 1991.

Kidner, Derek. *Genesis: An Introduction and Commentary.* London: Tyndale, 1967.

Kikawada, I. M., and Arthur Quinn, *Before Abraham Was.* Nashville: Abingdon, 1985.

Leupold, H. C. *Exposition of Genesis.* 2 vols. Grand Rapids: Baker, 1942.

Mathews, Kenneth A. *Genesis 1–11:26.* The New American Commentary. Nashville: Broadman & Holman, 1996.

Ross, Allen P. *Creation and Blessing.* Grand Rapids: Baker, 1988.

# EXODUS

Exodus, meaning *way out*, was the title the early Greek translation, the Septuagint, gave to the second book of the Torah (see Exod. 19:1).

Some interpreters understand statements within Exodus (17:14; 24:4; 34:27) to mean that Moses is the author of the final form of the book. Other scholars take such statements to mean that Moses wrote only specific portions of Exodus, such as the account of the defeat of the Amalekites (17:8-13), the "Book of the Covenant" (chaps. 21–23), and the instructions in Exodus 34:10-26. Only the most radical critics have denied Moses any link with the materials in Exodus.

Interpreters who accept the traditional authorship of Exodus hold that Moses put it in its present form as early as the sojourn at Sinai (about 1444 B.C.) or as late as the encampment on the plains of Moab just before his death (about 1406 B.C.). Except for Exodus 1:1–2:10, Moses was eyewitness to virtually all the incidents of the book. The early section could certainly have come to him by means of either written or oral sources. The remainder of the book gives every evidence of having been composed as a journal, recorded as the various episodes themselves transpired. *Author* then designates Moses as the final editor of a collection of memoirs. Other interpreters view the Book of Exodus as the product of the inspired reflection of many generations of God's people who worked to discern the meaning of the exodus event for worship and practice.

**Theme.** Deciding on a single theme that unifies all the varied materials of Exodus is difficult. One approach views the Sinai meeting where the redeemed nation encountered Yahweh and agreed to enter into covenant with Him as the theological center. The persecution of Israel in Egypt; the birth of Moses, his exile to Midian, and his return to Egypt as Israel's leader; the plagues upon Egypt; and the mighty exodus event itself—these all lead up to the climax of covenant commitment. Likewise, everything after that—the establishment of methods of worship, priesthood, and tabernacle—flow from the covenant and allow it to be put into practice.

A second approach views the presence of Yahweh with and in the midst of Israel as central. Yahweh's saving presence with Israel results in its deliverance from Egyptian slavery (Exod. 1–15). Yahweh's continuing presence with Israel calls for obedience to covenant commitments and for worship (Exod. 16–40).

A third approach views the lordship of Yahweh as the central theological theme. In Exodus God is revealed as Lord of history (1:1–7:7), Lord of nature (7:8–18:27), Lord of the covenant people Israel (19:1–24:14), and Lord of worship (25:1–40:38).

**Literary Forms.** Exodus includes various literary types and genres including poetry, covenant texts, and legal materials. It is not possible here to examine the entire book and identify the rich variety of literary expression, so a few passages will have to suffice.

One of the great poems of the Old Testament is "The Song of the Sea" (Exod. 15:1-18,21). This piece celebrates Israel's exodus deliverance from Egypt through the Red Sea (15:1a). The poem mixes the traits of a hymn of praise, a coronation song, a litany, and a victory psalm. Its mixed form suggests that it is multipurposed.

The presence in the song of certain themes and terms characteristic of Mesopotamian and Canaanite myths neither suggests that the song is only a myth nor even patterned after a myth. It is merely employing the vivid images and style of

mythical poetry in order to communicate the awesome majesty of Yahweh and His dominion over His foes. On the other hand, the parallels between it and Ugaritic epic poetry of the Late Bronze Age (about 1500–1200) lend credence to its great antiquity and Mosaic composition.

Even greater benefit has come from the discovery that parts of Exodus, specif-

## NAMES OF GOD

| NAME | REFERENCE | MEANING | NIV EQUIVALENT |
|---|---|---|---|
| HEBREW NAMES | | | |
| Adonai | Ps 2:4 | Lord, Master | Lord |
| El -Berith | Judg 9:46 | God of the   Covenant | El -Berith |
| El Elyon | Gen 14:18-20 | Most High God/ Exalted One | God Most High |
| El Olam | Gen 21:33 | The Eternal God | The Eternal God |
| El Shaddai | Gen 17:1-2 | All Powerful God | God Almighty |
| Qedosh Yisra'el | Isa 1:4 | The Holy One of Israel | The Holy One of Israel |
| Shapat | Gen 18:25 | Judge/Ruler | Judge |
| Yahweh-jereh | Gen 22:14 | Yahweh Provides | The LORD Will Provide |
| Yahweh-seba'ot | 1 Sam 1:3 | Yahweh of Armies | LORD Almighty |
| Yahweh-shalom | Judg 6:24 | Yahweh Is Peace | The LORD Is Peace |
| Yahweh-tsidkenu | Jer 23:6 | Yahweh Our Righteousness | The LORD Our Righteousness |
| ARAMAIC NAMES | | | |
| Attiq yomin | Dan 7:9 | Ancient of Days | Ancient of Days |
| Illaya | Dan 7:25 | Most High | Most High |

# MOSES

Moses was the great leader, law-giver, prophet, and judge of Israel. God raised up Moses to lead the nation out of Egyptian bondage into the land promised centuries earlier to Abraham. Moses also was to be the mediator of God's law to his people. His story is told in the Books of Exodus, Numbers, and Deuteronomy; and he is perhaps the most significant human figure in the Old Testament.

Moses was born into slavery in Egypt, where the Pharaoh was persecuting the Israelites. Moses' life was providentially spared as an infant. He spent his first forty years in the courts of the Pharaoh's daughter, where he undoubtedly learned many administrative, literary, and legal skills that would serve him in good stead in his years as Israel's leader and lawgiver.

Moses probably lived early in the New Kingdom era (about 1550–1200 B.C.). This time was the cultural and military peak of Egypt's three-thousand-year history. Moses lived within one hundred years

of King Tutankhamen (about 1347–1338 B.C.), the boy-king whose undisturbed tomb was discovered in 1922. The magnificent objects found in that tomb are typical of the art, wealth, and workmanship amid which the young Moses lived and which was later represented in much of the artistry of the tabernacle.

As an adult, Moses was forced to flee to the Midianite wilderness in the Sinai desert. There he met his wife and spent the next forty years. There he learned practical skills that would help him in leading Israel through the wilderness. During this time, he received God's call at Mount Sinai to lead Israel out of Egypt. He also received the revelation of God's covenant name, *Yahweh*. Moses was a reluctant leader, but he obeyed. He confronted the Pharaoh repeatedly until he let Israel go.

Moses' tenure as Israel's leader lasted another forty years. They were years filled with God's impressive miracles through Moses, such as the parting of the Red ("Reed") Sea, repeated provision of food

and water, and deliverance from enemies. The high point was the year spent at Mount Sinai in the southern Sinai Peninsula during which Moses communed closely with his God and received the Ten Commandments and the rest of the law to deliver to Israel.

Moses was barred from entering the promised land of Canaan because of his sin at Meribah, so he was able only to view it before he died.

Despite this, the universal testimony of the Scriptures is that Moses held an unrivaled place in all of Israel's history. Theologically, the exodus out of Egypt that he helped to effect and the law that he delivered to Israel are twin towers to which the Scriptures refer again and again as key factors in God's dealings with humanity. Personally, we are instructed by Moses' humility and by his life of submission to God's will. His example of obedient faith and his roles as deliverer, lawgiver, author, prophet, and even judge all place him in the first rank of Israel's heroes.

ically 20:1–23:33, resemble in both form and content certain covenant texts and law codes from the ancient Near East. Scholars have observed striking parallels between ancient Hittite texts and covenant and law texts of the Old Testament. One result is that these Exodus passages at least are now thought by many scholars

to be much earlier than some had generally held.

According to some scholars Exodus 20–23 follows the pattern of a sovereign-vassal treaty in which a great king such as the Hittite king initiated a contract with a defeated or less powerful king. Such a treaty made certain demands on the weaker king (now a vassal or agent of the

Hittites) and pledged certain commitments on the part of the Hittite king. Hittite treaty texts invariably contain certain clauses in a generally unalterable order.

The covenant text of Exodus 20–23, like Hittite treaties, contains both basic and specific stipulations. The Ten Commandments (20:1-17) make up the so-called "basic stipulation" section of the covenant text. They lay down fundamental principles of behavior without reference to motive or results.

The second main section, Exodus 21:1–23:19, is otherwise described as the "specific stipulations." Its purpose is to elaborate on the principles established in the Ten Commandments and to address particular concerns faced by the community. The first subdivision of this portion (21:1–22:17) consists of case law. There the statutes read, "If one does thus and so . . . then here is the penalty." The second subdivision (22:18–23:19) is mainly moral absolutes—"Thou shalt not" or "If you do thus and so . . . you shall not do thus and so."

The important theological insight gained by recognizing that Exodus 20–23 is covenant in nature and not just law does not finally depend on comparison with ancient Near Eastern treaties. Exodus "sandwiches" legal material (Exod. 20–23) between narratives that anticipate (Exod. 19) and relate Israel's commitment to the covenant (Exod. 24). This "sandwich" structure suggests the legal portions find their rightful place in the context of the covenant. In other words, Exodus is not an "abstract" legal treatise. Rather, Exodus is law born in the "concrete" situation of Yahweh's covenant commitment to the nation Israel, whom He has freed from Egyptian slavery.

*Literary Structure.* Discovering the literary structure of Exodus is a difficult task. Some interpreters discern a geographic outline.

- Israel in Egypt (1:1–13:16)
- Israel in the Wilderness (13:17–18:27)
- Israel at Sinai (19:1–40:38).

Others focus on content in outlining Exodus:

- Deliverance from Egypt and Journey to Sinai (1:1–18:27)
- Covenant at Sinai (19:1–24:18)
- Instructions for Tabernacle and Worship (25:1–31:18)
- Breach and Renewal of Covenant (32:1–34:35)
- Building the Tabernacle (35:1–40:38)

Still other interpreters focus on a central theological theme. For example, Exodus can be divided into two parts focusing on the *physical* (1:1–15:27) and *spiritual* birth (16:1–40:38) of the nation Israel. The outline that follows takes the presence of Yahweh as the central theme of Exodus.

  I  God's Presence (1:1–13:16)
 II  God's Guidance (13:17–18:27)
III  God's Demands (19:1–24:18)
IV  God's Rules (25:1–31:18)
 V  God's Discipline (32:1–34:35)
VI  God's Abiding Presence (35:1–40:38)

*Purpose and Theology.* The Book of Exodus is the story of two covenant partners—God and Israel. Exodus sets forth in narrative form how Israel became the people of Yahweh and lays out the covenant terms by which the nation was to live as God's people.

Exodus defines the character of the faithful, mighty, saving, holy God who established a covenant with Israel. God's character is revealed both through God's name and God's acts. The most important of God's names is the covenant name Yahweh. Yahweh designates God as the "I AM" who is there for His people and

## NAMES OF GOD

The names the Old Testament uses for God speak of His rule (God, Lord), His perfections (the Holy One of Israel), and His involvement in human affairs (I Am or I Cause to Happen).

### Elohim

Elohim, the usual designation for God, is the Creator, the God of all gods, the transcendent One (Gen. 1:1–2:3).

### El

*El* was known to the Canaanites as the chief of their many gods. The Hebrews freely spoke of their God by the name El.

*El* is generally used in compound names. Examples are *El Elyon* (*God Most High*, Gen. 14:18-22) and *El Shaddai* (*God Almighty*, Gen. 17:1). *El* is frequently compounded with a noun or verb to form personal or place names such as Elimelech *(My God is king)*, Eliezer *(God of help)*, and Elijah *(My God is Yahweh)*.

*El* also occurs in some of Scripture's oldest confessional phrases. Examples are "jealous God" (Exod. 20:5), "God brought them out of Egypt" (Num. 24:8), "great and awesome God" (Deut. 7:21; Neh. 1:5), "great and powerful God" (Jer. 32:18). *El* is common in Job (forty-eight times) and in Psalms (sixty-nine times).

### Adonai

*Adonai* (Lord) is a special form of the common word *adon,* meaning *lord. Adonai* is used only in reference to the one true God, never to refer to humans or other gods. It signifies the exalted being of God, who alone is Lord of lords (Deut. 10:17). He is "the Sovereign" of Israel (Exod. 34:23). *Adonai* also occurs in compounds such as Adonijah (*Yahweh is my Lord,* 1 Kgs. 1:8).

### Yahweh

Yahweh, meaning *I Am,* is a shortened form of God's response to Moses' request for the name of the patriarchs' God (Exod. 3:13-14). The full name identifies God as the Living God *(I Am Who I Am)* or as the God who acts in creation and redemptive history *(I Cause to Be What Is).* Out of extreme reverence for Yahweh's name (Exod. 20:7), the Jews read Adonai (or Elohim) wherever the Hebrew text had YHWH. English Bibles likewise represent the four consonants YHWH by "LORD" or "GOD" in large and small caps.

Yahweh revealed His name in the context of redemption of Israel from Egyptian slavery. With the name came the assurance that Yahweh would fulfill all His promises (Exod. 3:15; 6:2-8). The Lord's name is the concrete confirmation that God who "is" will "make things happen" and fulfill His promises.

Yahweh's name is thus associated with God's faithfulness, by which He binds Himself to His covenant promises. In the familiar words of Psalm 23:1, the Hebrew reads, "Yahweh is my shepherd." A reader of the English Bible can enter more deeply into the spirit of closeness and personal fellowship that existed between Yahweh and His ancient covenant people by substituting the name Yahweh for "the LORD." In Jesus' use of "I am" *(ego eimi),* He claimed to be Yahweh in the flesh (John 8:58).

Shortened forms of Yahweh occur in phrases (Hallelujah, *praise Yahweh*) and in names (Jonathan, *Yahweh gives,* and Adonijah, *Yahweh is Lord*).

### Other Names

In their adversity God's covenant people called on Him by the familial name "our Father" (Isa. 63:16; 64:8). Jesus invites all who come to God through Him to call God "our Father" or "Abba" (Mark 14:36; Rom. 8:15; Gal. 4:6).

Other designations for God include "the Rock" (1 Sam. 2:2; 2 Sam. 22:47), "the Holy One of Israel" (Isa. 1:4; 5:19; 43:3), "the LORD of Hosts" (Sabaoth, "Almighty," Ps. 24:10; Zech. 1:3-4), Shepherd (Isa. 40:11; Jer. 31:10; John 10:11-14), and King (Pss. 5:2; 24:7,10).

acts on their behalf. (See the feature article "Names of God.") Another important name, "the God of Abraham, the God of Isaac and the God of Jacob" (3:6,15-16), pictures God as the One who is true to His promises to the patriarchs.

Exodus also reveals God's character through His acts. God preserved Israel from famine by sending Joseph to Egypt (1:1-7). Pharaohs come and go (1:8); God, however, remains the same and preserves His people through the oppression of slavery (1:8–2:10). Israel's God rescues and saves (6:6; 14:30), guides and provides (15:13,25; 16:4,8), disciplines and forgives (32:1–34:35).

Exodus also defines the character of God's people. Lines of connection to Genesis, especially to the narratives of the patriarchs, demonstrate that the purposes of the Lord for Israel rested on the promises to the fathers. Exodus also looks to the future, to the land of promise, for the land was indispensable to Israel's full nationhood. Exodus stands then at a crossroads between the promises of the past and their culmination in the future.

A theological high point in Exodus appears in 19:4-6, which outlines Israel's true nature and role within God's plan. Yahweh had judged the Egyptians, had delivered His own people "on eagles' wings," and had brought them to Himself at Sinai. There the Lord offered Israel a covenant. If it was accepted and lived out, the covenant would result in Israel's being God's "treasured possession," a chosen "kingdom of priests," and a "holy nation." The people accepted these terms and pledged, "We will do everything the LORD has said" (19:8).

For Israel to be a kingdom of priests implied that God's people functioned as mediators and intercessors, for that is at the heart of the priestly function. Israel was to bridge the gap between a holy God and an alienated world. In other words, Israel was made a servant people, a servant of Yahweh, whose task was to be the channel of reconciliation. This mission was already anticipated in the Abrahamic covenant where Abraham's offspring (Israel) was destined to become the means whereby all the nations of the earth would be blessed (Gen. 12:1-3; 22:18; 26:4).

Israel's call to covenant was founded not on its merit but on God's free choice: "I carried you on eagles' wings and brought you to myself" (Exod. 19:4). The covenant then did not make Israel the people of Yahweh. They were the people of Yahweh by descent from Abraham, Isaac, and Jacob, the recipients of God's promises. Even the exodus, therefore, did not create the people of God. It rescued Yahweh's enslaved people, forged them into a nation, and brought them to the historical and theological

| THE TEN PLAGUES OF EGYPT | |
|---|---|
| PLAGUE | SCRIPTURE |
| 1. WATER TO BLOOD—The waters of the Nile turned to blood. | Exod 7:14-25 |
| 2. FROGS—Frogs infested the land of Egypt. | Exod 8:1-15 |
| 3. GNATS (Mosquitoes)—Small stinging insects infested the land of Egypt. | Exod 8:16-19 |
| 4. FLIES—Swarms of flies, possibly a biting variety, infested the land of Egypt. | Exod 8:20-32 |
| 5. PLAGUE ON THE CATTLE—A serious disease, possibly anthrax, infested the cattle belonging to Egyptians. | Exod 9:1-7 |
| 6. BOILS—A skin disease infected the Egyptians. | Exod 9:8-12 |
| 7. HAIL—A storm that destroyed the grain fields of Egypt but spared the land of Goshen inhabited by the Israelites. | Exod 9:13-35 |
| 8. LOCUSTS—An infestation of locusts stripped the land of Egypt of plant life. | Exod 10:1-20 |
| 9. DARKNESS—A deep darkness covered the land of Egypt for three days. | Exod 10:21-29 |
| 10. DEATH OF THE FIRSTBORN—The firstborn of every Egyptian family died. | Exod 11:1–12:30 |

# EGYPT

Ancient Egyptian history spanned an unbroken period of almost three thousand years, down to the time of the Roman conquest in 31 B.C. It spanned some thirty dynasties, each consisting of several generations of kings. Modern Egyptian people and culture trace direct influences from the ancient periods.

Egypt's history was played out on a long, narrow strip of fertile land following the Nile River, winding more than sixteen hundred miles through Egypt. The Upper Nile (southern part) flows in a narrow valley never more than about twelve miles wide. The Lower Nile (northern part) widens north of Memphis and Cairo into the Nile Delta, emptying into the Mediterranean Sea. The Nile flooded annually, providing irrigation for growing crops in the otherwise arid desert.

The time of the Old Kingdom (the Third through the Sixth Dynasties, about 2700–2200 B.C.) represented an early peak of prosperity and cultural achievement. The Great Pyramids were built during this time.

A second peak was reached during the Middle Kingdom (especially the Eleventh and Twelfth Dynasties, about 2000–1800 B.C.). During this time, Egypt expanded into Syria-Palestine and produced a golden age of classical literature, especially short stories. Following a period of domination by foreign (mostly Semitic) rulers called the "Hyksos" (about 1675–1550 B.C.), the New Kingdom arose. It represented the zenith of Egyptian culture and political power (especially the Eighteenth and Nineteenth Dynasties, about 1550–1200 B.C.).

At this time Egypt controlled territory stretching a thousand miles from the Euphrates River in the north to the fifth set of rapids on the Nile in the south. Egypt's greatest temples and its short-lived but much-celebrated experiment with monotheism under Pharaoh Amenophis IV (Akhenaten) come from this period. Much of its great literature also comes from this cosmopolitan age. Following this, a long period of decline and relative isolation set in. Egypt still ventured forth but was overshadowed by other powers, especially from Mesopotamia.

Israel had scattered contacts with Egypt throughout its history. The most significant contacts were early, the several hundred years between Abraham's and Moses' times (about 2100–1400 B.C.). (Most dates here are approximate, since dating schemes for Egypt vary widely—often by two or more centuries—as do those for early Israel. Synchronizing these for both nations poses even more difficulties.)

In patriarchal times Abraham spent time in Egypt due to a famine in Canaan (Gen. 12:10-20). Joseph was sold into slavery by his brothers, ending up in Egypt. He rose to prominence there, possibly during the late Middle Kingdom, and helped Egypt and surrounding lands prepare for another famine (Gen. 37:50). Many of the customs seen in the Joseph story reflect known Egyptian practices from the period in question.

Following the glory years under Joseph, Israel was subjected to Egyptian slavery for many years until God raised up Moses and delivered Israel (Exod. 1–15). The great event of the exodus (about 1446 B.C.) is not mentioned in Egyptian records. This oversight is not surprising, since ancient Near Eastern chronicles tended to record political successes, not failures.

Egypt's religion was polytheistic. Its major national gods were Ra, the sun god; Osiris, the god of the dead; and Isis, Osiris's wife. Elaborate ritual systems built up around the cults of the dead associated with Osiris. Egyptians also worshiped numerous lesser gods, many of them associated with specific locales and households. In addition, Pharaoh was considered to be divine, in contrast to beliefs about kings in most of the ancient Near East.

## DATES OF THE EXODUS

The Book of Exodus does not give specific data that definitely links the biblical events with specific events or persons in Egypt. We are only told of "a new king" (Exod. 1:8) "who did not know about Joseph," an anonymous "Pharaoh" (Exod. 1:11,19,22; 2:15), and a "king of Egypt" (Exod. 1:15; 2:23).

This much we do know: *Pharaoh,* meaning *great house* and designating the monarch's residence, was used as a title for the king himself for the first time in the Eighteenth Egyptian Dynasty. Also, the Pharaoh of the oppression died (Exod. 2:23) and was not the Pharaoh of the exodus (Exod. 4:19).

The two main views identify the Pharaoh of the exodus as a Pharaoh of (1) the Eighteenth Dynasty (1580–1321 B.C.) or (2) of the Nineteenth Dynasty (1321–1205 B.C.). The first is called the "early date," and the latter is called the "late date."

The early date of the fifteenth century has two main arguments in its favor. (1) The summarizing

statement in 1 Kings 6:1 that there were 480 years from the exodus until the fourth year of Solomon (967 B.C.) yields a date of 1447 B.C. for the exodus (967 + 480 = 1447). (2) The supporting figure from Judges 11:26 comments that three hundred years had elapsed since Israel entered Canaan until the commencement of Judge Jephthah's rule (Jephthah is commonly placed around 1100 B.C. (1100 + 300 = 1400).

Both of these texts would set the exodus at 1446 B.C. and the conquest forty years later at 1410–1400 B.C. They would also make Thutmose III the pharaoh of the oppression (1490–1436 B.C., as dated by Albright, Wright, and Pritchard, or 1504-1450 B.C. as dated by the revised *Cambridge Ancient History).* In this case, Amenhotep II would be the pharaoh of the exodus

Lately, many have pointed to one Greek manuscript that has 440 years instead of 480 or to the fact that 480 is a round number involving twelve generations of forty years each. The first variation is too insignificant to count.

The second argument of round numbers fails because the priestly line in 1 Chronicles 6:33-37 actually yields eighteen generations, not the stylized twelve that many have assumed. Moreover, the numbers recorded in Judges do support the total given in Judges 11:26.

It is important to note that the oppression by the Ammonites (Judg. 10:8–12:14) and the oppression by the Philistines (Judg. 13:1–16:31) occurred simultaneously, one on the east side of the Jordan and the other on the west. Thus the forty-seven years of the Ammonite oppression does not continue the chronology since it fits into the narrative of the Philistine oppression featured in the first Book of Samuel.

Even when the additional fifteen to twenty years for Israel's conquest and settling of land are allowed, we still come up with 480 years from the exodus to Solomon's fourth year.

Over against the early or fifteenth century date for the exodus stands the late or thirteenth century date. Most biblical scholars and archaeologists conclude

position where they could willingly accept (or reject) the responsibility of becoming God's instrument for blessing all nations (see Ps. 114:1-2).

In other words, the offer of covenant entailed function only. It did not make Israel Yahweh's people, for that relationship had long since been established and recognized (see Exod. 3:7; 4:22-23; 5:1). What the Sinai covenant did was to define the task of the people of Yahweh.

In conclusion, the theology of Exodus is rooted in servanthood. It centers in the truth that a chosen people, delivered from bondage to a hostile power by the power of Yahweh, were brought to a point of decision. What would they do with God's offer to make them the servant people long before promised to Abraham? Their willing acceptance of this generous offer then obligated them to its conditions, conditions spelled out in that the Israelites entered Canaan around 1230–1220 B.C., toward the end of the late Bronze Age (generally accepted date is 1550–1200 B.C.).

Four arguments are usually advanced to support this theory.

1. The two store-cities built by the Israelites in Egypt—Pithom and Rameses (Exod. 1:11)—were built just before the exodus. Rameses is equated with Pi-Ramesse built by Pharaoh Ramses II, who ruled from 1240–1224 B.C. This would place the exodus in the thirteenth century.

2. The Transjordan, where Israel was said to have encountered several nations, was thought to be uninhabited from 1800–1300 B.C.

3. Archaeological evidence shows many destruction levels in the cities of Canaan west of the Jordan in the second half of the thirteenth century. Though the Scriptures record that Israel burned the cities of Jericho and Ai (Josh. 6:24; 8:19-21), archaeologists have been unable to confirm that these sites were occupied in the Late Bronze Age, the era of the conquest.

4. The final argument for the late date notes that the capital of Egypt was moved north to Pi-Ramesse in the Nineteenth Dynasty (thirteenth century). The Eighteenth Dynasty of the fifteenth century had its capital in the south at Thebes.

Opponents of the late date have replies for the four previous arguments.

1. Exodus 1:7-14 seems to place the building of these cities as one of the first tasks Israel accomplished during its four centuries of bondage. Rameses is probably to be identified with Qantir. The use of the name Rameses may simply be a case of a modernization of a name much as modern historians might say that Julius Caesar crossed "the English Channel." Note that Genesis 47:11 refers to the area where Jacob's family settled in Egypt as "the district of Rameses." This certainly is a case of updating terms. Exodus 1:11 offers no definitive proof for a late date; archaeology offers no proof for equating Pi-Ramesse with biblical Rameses.

2. The conclusion that the Transjordan was unoccupied at the early date of the exodus was based solely on surface observation of these territories fifty years ago. Since that time excavations at Dibon have demonstrated thirteenth-century occupation. A tomb excavated in Heshbon has yielded a number of artifacts dating from 1600 B.C.

3. The alleged Israelite burning levels in such sites as Lachish, Bethel, and Debir were probably caused by later thirteenth century incursions by the Egyptians, but certainly by the invasion of the Sea Peoples in 1200 B.C.

4. Important inscriptions are now coming to light that indicate that the Eighteenth Dynasty did have a keen building interest in the delta region of Goshen where the Israelites resided. Some texts imply that these Eighteenth Dynasty pharaohs had a secondary or temporary residence in the delta region.

5. The strongest evidence for the early date continues to be 1 Kings 6:1 and Judges 11:26. Many, but not all, conservatives tend to favor the early date. Some archaeological evidence supports this date while other evidence tends to question this conclusion or is itself subject to interpretation and in need of further confirmation.

the Book of the Covenant (Exod. 20:1–23:33) and the remainder of the Book of Exodus.

## GOD'S PRESENCE (1:1–13:16)

### With Oppressed People (1:1-22).

The Exodus story begins by recalling the Genesis account of the descent of Jacob and his sons to Egypt and their sojourn there until after Joseph's death (Gen. 46–50). The Genesis link reminds readers that God sent Israel into Egypt to deliver them from famine. Their prosperity and success in their new land show that Israel was the recipient of God's blessings on creation and to Abraham.

Egyptian hospitality did not long outlive Joseph, however, and within a generation or two before Moses' birth had changed to bitter hostility and oppression. Israel was put under forced labor and eventually subjected to the slaughter of their male newborns. Even in the years of oppression God was with Israel and caused them to prosper. The Lord had revealed to Abraham that his offspring would suffer oppression but that their bondage would be lifted by a great redemptive act. The Egyptians would be judged and the slave people set free to return to their own land (Gen. 15:13-16). Israel's experience of slavery was not a disaster that proved its God to be irrelevant; it was but part of the redemptive plan of the Lord of history. In contrast to the Lord of history stand the pharaohs who came and went (see 2:23) and trembled with fear.

**With Young Moses (2:1-22).** God's saving presence is clear in the early life of Moses, the human agent of God's deliverance. Moses' Levite parents saved him from a cruel death by hiding him in a basket in the Nile. Rescued by Pharaoh's daughter, Moses was reared by his mother, who introduced him to the God of Israel. Though Moses later enjoyed the privileges of the Egyptian royal court, he never forgot his Israelite heritage. When he saw a fellow Hebrew being abused, he came to his rescue, slaying the offending Egyptian official in the process. This rash, though heroic, act forced Moses into exile in Midian. There Moses came to the rescue of the daughters of Reuel (Jethro), a Midianite priest. Moses married Zipporah, one of the shepherd daughters.

**Revelation to Moses (2:23–4:17).** The death of the former king of Egypt paved the way for Moses to return to lead his people to freedom. But first the ever-living God had to reveal Himself to Moses in a convincing display of His power and purposes. God did this at Mount Horeb (Sinai) in the burning bush that was not consumed. In this marvelous appearance the Lord identified Himself as the God of the ancestors of Israel, the One who was

aware of His people's suffering and was coming now to fulfill His pledge of deliverance and land. Though he knew of the God of his fathers and of the ancient covenant promises, Moses needed to know precisely how his God would identify Himself to His people. The answer was as Yahweh, the "I AM," who by that name would redeem them and live among them. (See the feature article "Names of God.")

Moses felt inadequate for the task God gave him. What was crucial was not Moses' "Who am I?" but God's "I will be with you." Moses doubted that the people would accept his leadership or believe his report about the burning bush experience. Therefore Yahweh gave Moses some tangible evidence of His presence and blessing, turning Moses' shepherd's staff into a serpent and causing his hand to become leprous. Still not confident of success, Moses argued that he was not articulate. To still his objections once more, Yahweh promised to make his brother Aaron his spokesman. Indeed, God had already sent Aaron on his way.

**Moses in Egypt (4:18–13:16).** Moses at last yielded to God and made his way back to Egypt with this message for Pharaoh: "Israel is my firstborn son . . . Let my son go, so he may worship me." Along the way Yahweh met Moses and threatened to kill him because he who was about to lead the circumcised people of Israel had failed to circumcise even his own son. Only the quick intervention of Zipporah saved him, for she hastily circumcised her son in obedience to the covenant requirements.

At the edge of the desert Moses met Aaron. Together they entered Egypt to confront the elders of Israel. After Moses had related all that God had said and done, the elders and the people heard with faith and bowed themselves before the Lord.

Pharaoh's question, "Who is the LORD, that I should obey him and let Israel go?" sets the stage for the conflict that dominates the scene through Exodus 15. Before the drama of redemption was over, Pharaoh would "know the LORD" and would yield to His powerful saving presence. But for now Pharaoh intensified the Israelites' sufferings. This led a bitter Moses to accuse Yahweh.

Yahweh renewed His pledge to be with Israel in deliverance, a pledge grounded securely in His very covenant name Yahweh. God commanded Moses to go back to Pharaoh with the promise that the Egyptian monarch would know that there was a higher authority. Moses would seem like God Himself to Pharaoh, and Aaron would be his prophet. By His mighty acts of judgment, God would make Himself known to the Egyptians.

Again and again Moses and Aaron commanded Pharaoh to let God's people leave Egypt to worship. Despite the signs, wonders, and plagues that revealed the mighty presence of the Lord, the king of Egypt would not relent. In round one of the conflict, the rod of Aaron became a serpent that swallowed those of the Egyptian magicians. Three plagues followed. The Nile was turned to blood, the land was filled with frogs, and Egypt was plagued by gnats. Pharaoh's own magicians could duplicate the first two feats, so he was not impressed. Pharaoh did, however, request that Moses and Aaron pray "to the LORD to take the frogs away." Pharaoh was becoming acquainted with Yahweh, the God of Israel. The plague of gnats, the final plague of round one, exceeded the magical powers of the Egyptian magicians and led them to confess, "This is the finger of God."

In round two of the conflict, the plague of flies demonstrated that Yahweh was present in Egypt. In this plague, the grievous disease of the cattle, and the boils, God distinguished between the Egyptians who suffered God's judgment and the Israelites who experienced God's protection.

Round three of the conflict likewise consists of three plagues. Before sending hail, the Lord asserted that He alone is the Lord of history. Yahweh had raised up Pharaoh for the express purpose of demonstrating His mighty power and proclaiming His holy name. Indeed, some of the officials of Pharaoh "feared the word of the LORD," and Pharaoh confessed his sin. Moses' prayer to end the hail demonstrated "that the earth is the LORD'S." Pharaoh, however, again hardened his heart. Plagues of locusts and thick darkness followed to no avail.

The fourth and deciding round of the conflict consisted of but one final plague—the death of the firstborn of every family in Egypt. At last Pharaoh permitted Israel to leave Egypt with their flocks and herds. The structure of Exodus 11–13 underscores the abiding theological significance of this final plague. Here narrative language relating once-for-all saving events alternates with instructional language applicable to the ongoing worship of Israel. The Passover celebration, the consecration of the firstborn, and the feast of unleavened bread serve as continuing reminders of what God did to redeem His people. The firstborn of all the families of Israel belonged to the Lord because He had spared them when He had decimated the families of Egypt.

## GOD'S GUIDANCE (13:17–18:27)

Exodus 1:1–13:16, which focuses on God's powerful, saving presence, builds steadily to its dramatic conclusion—the death of the firstborn of Egypt and Israel's exodus. Exodus 13:17–18:27

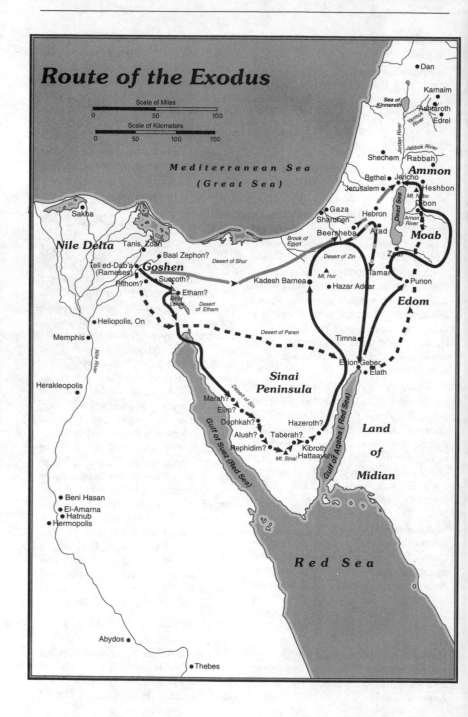

# THE TEN COMMANDMENTS

| COMMANDMENT | PASSAGE | RELATED OLD TESTAMENT PASSAGES | RELATED NEW TESTAMENT PASSAGES | JESUS' TEACHINGS |
|---|---|---|---|---|
| You shall have no other gods before me | Exod 20:3; Deut 5:7 | Exod 34:14; Deut 6:4,13-14; 2 Kgs 17:35; Ps 81:9; Jer 25:6; 35:15 | Acts 5:29 | Matt 4:10; 6:33; 22:37-40 |
| You shall not make for yourself an idol | Exod 20:4-6; Deut 5:8-10 | Exod 20:23; 32:8; 34:17; Lev 19:4; 26:1; Deut 4:15-20; 7:25; 32:21; Ps 115:4-7; Isa 44:12-20 | Acts 17:29; 1 Cor 8:4-6,10-14; 1 John 5:21 | Matt 6:24; Luke 16:13 |
| You shall not misuse the name of the Lord | Exod 20:7; Deut 5:11 | Exod 22:28; Lev 18:21; 19:12; 22:2; 24:16; Ezek 39:7 | Rom 2:23-24; Jas 5:12 | Matt 5:33-37; 6:9; 23:16-22 |
| Remember the Sabbath day by keeping it holy | Exod 20:8-11; Deut 5:12-15 | Gen 2:3; Exod 16:23-30; 31:13-16; 35:2-3; Lev 19:30; Isa 56:2; Jer 17:21-27 | Acts 20:7; Heb 10:25 | Matt 12:1-13; Mark 2:23-27; 3:1-6; Luke 6:1-11 |
| Honor your father and your mother | Exod 20:12; Deut 5:16 | Exod 21:17; Lev 19:3; Deut 21:18-21; 27:16; Prov 6:20 | Eph 6:1-3; Col 3:20 | Matt 15:4-6; 19:19; Mark 7:9-13; Luke 18:20 |
| You shall not murder | Exod 20:13; Deut 5:17 | Gen 9:6; Lev 24:17; Num 35:33; | Rom 13:9-10; I Pet 4:15 | Matt 5:21-24; 19:18; Mark 10:19; Luke 18:20 |
| You shall not commit adultery | Exod 20:14; Deut 5:18 | Lev 18:20; 20:10; Deut 22:22; Num 5:12-31; Prov 6:29,32 | Rom 13:9-10; 1 Cor 6:9; Heb 13:4; Jas 2:11 | Matt 5:27-30; 19:18; Mark 10:19; Luke 18:20 |
| You shall not steal | Exod 20:15; Deut 5:19 | Lev 19:11,13; Ezek 18:7 | Rom 13:9-10; Eph 4:28; Jas 5:4 | Matt 19:18; Mark 10:19; Luke 18:20 |
| You shall not give false testimony | Exod 20:16; Deut 5:20 | Exod 23:1, 7; Lev 19:11; Pss 15:2; 101:5; Prov 10:18; Jer 9:3-5; Zech 8:16 | Eph 4:25,31; Col 3:9; Titus 3:2 | Matt 5:37; 19:18; Mark 10:19; Luke 18:20 |
| You shall not covet | Exod 20:17; Deut 5:21 | Deut 7:25; Job 31:24-28; Ps 62:10 | Rom 7:7; 13:9; Eph 5:3-5; Heb 13:5; Jas 4:1-2 | Luke 12:15-34 |

likewise focuses on God's presence, which here guides, guards, and protects.

By means of the pillars of cloud and fire, the Lord guided Israel from Succoth to the wilderness of Etham, just west of the Red (or Reed) Sea. There they appeared to be boxed in by the sea to the east, the deserts to the north and south, and the advancing Egyptian armies to the west. Once more the Lord hardened the heart of Pharaoh so that through his defeat Egypt would know that Yahweh is God. For a tense night the presence of the Lord guarded Israel from the armies of Egypt. Then Yahweh, in the most marvelous redemptive act of Old Testament times, opened up the sea so His people could go safely through while their enemies perished. For generations thereafter Israel commemorated its salvation by singing the triumphant songs of Moses and Miriam, hymns that praised Yahweh as the Sovereign and Savior.

The journey from the Red Sea to Sinai was filled with miracles of provision of water, quail, manna, and water once more. All this occurred despite Israel's complaining insubordination. Hostile and savage desert tribes likewise fell before God's people as He led them triumphantly onward. When heavy administrative burdens threatened to overwhelm Moses, his father-in-law, Jethro, instructed Moses about how the task could be better distributed.

## GOD'S DEMANDS (19:1–24:18)

Again and again in the account of the plagues, Moses delivered God's message to Pharaoh: "Let my people go, so that they may worship [or serve] me." At last the moment of worship and service arrived, which the exodus deliverance had made possible. At Sinai Israel was to commit itself to God in covenant. Yahweh based His call to covenant commitment on His mighty acts of deliverance. Only

through obedience to God's covenant could Israel fill its role as "a kingdom of priests and a holy nation."

Unanimously they agreed to its terms, so Moses prepared to ascend Mount Sinai to solemnize the arrangement. As Moses was about to go up, Yahweh came down, visiting the mountain with the thunder and lightning of His glorious presence. Moses warned the people to respect the holy (and potentially dangerous) presence of God on the mountain.

As suggested already, the Sinaitic (or Mosaic) covenant is in the form of a sovereign-vassal treaty text well attested from the ancient Near East. The treaty established the relationship between the King (God) and His servants (Israel). Its first section is a preamble introducing the Covenant Maker, the Lord Himself. Next a historical prologue outlines the past relationship of the partners and justifies the present covenant. Then follows the division known as the general stipulations, in this case the Decalogue, or Ten Commandments. After a brief narrative interlude, the Book of the Covenant gives the specific stipulations of the treaty.

Contracting parties often sealed their agreement with oaths and a ceremony that included a fellowship meal. The Sinaitic covenant also had its sacrifice, sealing of the oath by blood, and covenant meal. The covenant or treaty texts also had to be prepared in duplicate and preserved in a safe place for regular, periodic reading. Moses therefore brought down from the mountain the tablets of stone to be stored in the ark of the covenant (24:12-18; 25:16).

## GOD'S RULES (25:1–31:18)

Once Yahweh and His people Israel had concluded the covenant, arrangements had to be undertaken for the Great King to live and reign among them. Therefore elaborate instructions follow for the building of a tabernacle (or worship tent) and its furnishings and for the clothing and consecration of the priests. The priests, of course, functioned as the covenant mediators. They offered sacrifices on the nation's behalf and presented other forms of tribute to the Great God and King.

## GOD'S DISCIPLINE (32:1–34:35)

The covenant fellowship almost immediately fell on hard times, however. Even before Moses could descend from the mountain with the tables of stone and other covenant texts, the people, with Aaron's consent, violated the covenant terms by casting an idol of gold and bowing down to it. This act of apostasy brought God's judgment and even a threat of annihilation. (See the feature article "Apostasy.") Only Moses' intercession prevented the annulment of the covenant with the larger community.

The Lord was attentive to Moses' cry and did not utterly destroy the idolaters immediately. God did renew His promise to bring His people into the land of promise. Yahweh, however, declared that He could not go with Israel lest He destroy the stubborn, rebellious people. Two narratives stressing God's intimacy with Moses only highlight the Holy One's separation from Israel more. God's people would never make it to the land of promise without God's presence. Twice Moses interceded with God on behalf of rebellious Israel. Yahweh twice revealed Himself to Moses as a God of mercy and compassion. God's mercy and compassion—not Israel's faithfulness—formed the basis for renewal of the broken covenant. Descending from the mountain with the tablets of the covenant, Moses appeared before his people, his face aglow with the reflection of the glory of God.

## GOD'S ABIDING PRESENCE (35:1–40:38)

Exodus concludes with Israel's response to God's offer of forgiveness. Without delay the work of tabernacle construction was underway. When it was finally completed, all according to the explicit instruction of the Lord and through the wisdom of His Spirit, the building was filled with the awesome glory of God. By cloud and fire God revealed His presence among the people of Israel whether the tabernacle was at rest or in transit to its final earthly dwelling place in Canaan.

*Contemporary Significance.* The exodus deliverance is to the Old Testament what the death and resurrection of Christ are to the New Testament—the central, definitive act in which God intervenes to save His people. The Old Testament illustrates how God's acts of redemption call for a response from God's people. The proclamation of God's saving acts in the exodus was the central function of Israel's worship (see Pss. 78:11-55; 105:23-45; 106:7-33; 136:10-16). Christian worship focuses on God's saving act in Christ. (Compare the hymns in Phil. 2:6-11 and Rev. 5:12.) God's saving intervention in the exodus formed the basis both for the prophetic call to obedience (Hos. 13:4) and the announcement of judgment on covenant breakers (Jer. 2:5-9; Hos. 11:1-5; 12:9; Amos 2:10; 3:1-2). Today God's saving act in Christ forms the basis for the call to live a Christlike life (Rom. 6:1-14). God's saving acts in the past gave Israel hope that God would intervene to save in the future (Isa. 11:16; Mic. 7:15). Likewise, God's saving act in Christ is the basis for the Christian's hope (Rom. 8:28-39).

The exodus deliverance, the Sinaitic covenant, the wilderness experience, and the promise of a land provide models of the Christian life. The believer, having already and unconditionally been adopted into the family of God, undertakes his or her own "exodus" from bondage to sin and evil to servanthood under the new covenant. Christians live out their kingdom pilgrimage in the wilderness of this world system, as it were, pressing toward and in anticipation of the eternal land of promise to come.

**Ethical Value.** God saved and made covenant with His ancient people Israel and demanded of them a lifestyle in keeping with that holy calling. He demands that same adherence to His unchanging standards of all who call themselves His people. The Ten Commandments are an expression of the very character of a holy, faithful, glorious, saving God. Even the "statutes" and "judgments" designed specifically for Old Testament Israel exemplify standards of holiness and integrity that are part and parcel of God's expectations for His people of all ages.

One can also learn a great deal about practical living and relationships by examining carefully the narrative sections. One must be impressed with the faith of godly parents who, in the face of persecution and peril, placed their son in the hands of Yahweh to wait to see how He would spare him. From his birth, then, Moses enjoyed the benefits of a wholesome spiritual environment in the home.

Clearly Moses himself inspires one to a life of dependence and yet dogged determination. Despite his slowness in responding to the call of the Lord in the wilderness, he went on in faith to challenge the political and military structures of the greatest nation on the earth. By the power of his God he overcame the insurmountable and witnessed miraculous intervention over and over again.

Many other examples could be cited, but these are enough to show that Exodus is timeless in its moral and ethical as well as theological relevance.

## Questions for Reflection

1. What do you think is the central theme of Exodus?

2. What is a covenant? Why is the Sinai covenant important?

3. How is God's presence made known in Exodus? How does God demonstrate His lordship?

4. What does Exodus teach about the character of God? What is the significance of God's name (Yahweh)? What is the significance of God's mighty acts?

5. How is Exodus 20–23 similar to ancient treaties?

6. How does the history of God's dealings with Israel serve as a basis for the demands of the law?

7. What does Exodus teach about the character and responsibilities of God's people Israel? What are the implications for the church?

## Sources for Additional Study

Cates, Robert L. *Exodus.* Layman's Bible Book Commentary, vol. 2. Nashville: Broadman, 1979.

Cole, R. Alan. *Exodus.* Downers Grove: Inter-Varsity, 1973.

Youngblood, Ronald. *Exodus.* Chicago: Moody, 1983.

# LEVITICUS

The name *Leviticus* comes from the ancient Greek translation, the Septuagint, which titled the composition *Leueitikon,* that is, *[The Book of the] Levites.* The Levites are not, however, the major characters of this book. The title rather points to the book as useful to the Levites in their ministry as worship leaders and teachers of morals.

The last verse of Leviticus sets the book in its scriptural context: "These are the commands the LORD gave Moses on Mount Sinai for the Israelites" (27:34). An expanded translation makes that context clearer: "These are the commands [covenant obligations] the LORD [Yahweh, the covenant God] gave Moses [the covenant mediator] on Mount Sinai [the covenant place] for Israel [the covenant people]."

First, Leviticus cannot be understood apart from God's purpose for His covenant people. In the account of Moses' struggle with Pharaoh in Exod. 4–12, God repeatedly called for the freedom of Israel to worship Him (4:23; 7:16; 8:1; 9:1; 10:3; 12:31). In a real sense the exodus deliverance was incomplete until Israel began the worship of God at Sinai (Exod. 3:12), thus fulfilling God's goal for the exodus. Israel was set free from Egyptian slavery and brought into a new, covenant relationship with God precisely so that they might be free to worship.

Second, Leviticus cannot be understood apart from God's desire to be with His covenant people. But because a Holy God cannot condone sin, Israel's experiment in idolatry with the golden calf (Exod. 32) presented God with a dilemma. Twice God warned the Israelites: "You are a stiff-necked people. If I

were to go with you even for a moment, I might destroy you" (Exod. 33:5; also see 33:3). How could a holy God continue to go with a disobedient and rebellious people? Exodus 34–40 and the Book of Leviticus answer that question.

**Theme.** The overall burden of the Book of Leviticus was to communicate the awesome holiness of Israel's God and to outline the means by which the people could have access to Him. This is in line with the great central covenant theme of the Pentateuch, a theme that describes the relationship between the Lord and Israel as one of Great King and vassal (servant) people. Just as a servant had to follow proper protocol to approach the king, so Israel had to recognize its own unworthiness to enter the sacred precincts of God's dwelling place. The gulf between the people and their God could be bridged only by their confession of their unworthiness and their heartfelt adherence to the rites and ceremonies prescribed by Him as a precondition to fellowship.

**Literary Forms.** With the exception of a few narrative passages (Lev. 8–10) and a blessing and curse section (Lev. 26), Leviticus consists of legal material, particularly of a cultic (or ceremonial) nature. Much of this legal material is highly structured in an almost poetic form (Lev. 1–7 and to a lesser extent Lev. 11–15). The final part of Leviticus (chaps. 17–26) is a looser collection of legal material known as the "Holiness Code," an appropriate term given the prevailing notion of holiness there.

The legal form of most of Leviticus (prescriptions and statutes) suggests that it is part of a covenant text. In fact, it deals with the covenant requirements that regulate the means by which the nation and individual Israelites could enter into and maintain a proper relationship with the Lord God. In this sense Leviticus, like much of Exodus, is a body of covenant stipulations designed to help close the gap between God's holiness and humanity's sin.

I. Need for Sacrifice (1:1–7:38)
II. Need for Mediators (8:1–10:20)
III. Need for Separation (11:1–15:33)
IV. Need Atonement (16:1-34)
V. Need for Holy Living (17:1–25:55)
VI. Blessing and Curse (26:1-46)
VII. Dedication Offerings (27:1-34)

***Purpose and Theology.*** Israel was "a holy nation," that is, a nation set apart to be God's special people. As such, Israel was called on to accomplish a special mission for God on the earth by virtue of His saving act. (See Lev. 22:32-33: "I am the LORD, who makes you holy and who brought you out of Egypt to be your God.") Having accepted this covenant role at Sinai, Israel became God's vassal, the mediator of His saving grace to all the nations of the earth. (See "Purpose and Theology" in the Exodus commentary.) Israel's inability to abide by the requirements of God's covenant, however, threatened its status as "a holy nation."

To be a holy nation Israel had to have a means whereby that holiness—or separatedness—could be maintained. Israel needed a set of guidelines stipulating every aspect of that relationship between the nation and its God. God's people had to learn the relationship of holiness as a position and holiness as a condition. As a position holiness means the setting apart of a person, object, or institution for the use of a god. It has no necessary ethical or moral corollary; Israel's pagan neighbors set apart "holy" prostitutes for the service of their gods. Israel set apart a

holy place (the tabernacle), rituals (the sacrifices), persons (the priests), and times (the Sabbath, the feasts, the Sabbatical and Jubilee Years). Whatever has not been designated as holy is common or profane. As a condition holiness comes to embody moral purity and righteousness. God's own personal holiness entails not only His remoteness and uniqueness but also His moral perfection. Persons and things that He sanctifies and declares holy must also exhibit moral uprightness. The Holiness Code of Leviticus 17–25 stresses holiness as a moral condition.

Leviticus outlines how Israel could offer God appropriate homage to cultivate and maintain the relationship brought about by mutual commitment to covenant. Because Israel was unable to live up to its covenant commitments, they could not approach the holy God. Only God could provide a system to purify the sinful people and their worship place so that they could appear before and serve the Holy One. These sacrifices rendered a person righteous who by faith accepted the atoning benefits of the sacrifices. God also provided a system of offerings for a person to express proper understanding of and thanksgiving for the benefits of His grace. The holy people also had to be taught about and continually reminded of the strict lines that separate the holy from the profane by seeing examples of these differences in everyday life.

A thing was holy or unholy only as the sovereign God declared it to be such in line with His own inscrutable criteria and His own inherent holiness. In His sovereignty God listed unclean animals, separating them from the clean ones. He described certain diseases and certain fungi and other phenomena as unclean. Those who came in contact with the unclean became unclean as well. Even bodily secretions were unclean, their appearance being sufficient to mark the individual so affected as unholy.

The apparently arbitrary nature of the categories of clean and unclean makes it clear that holiness is essentially a matter of divine discretion. The sovereign God made these distinctions for educational purposes. Israel as a people separated from all other peoples had to learn from everyday and commonplace examples that God sits in sovereign judgment over all things. They had to learn that He alone reserves judgment about whether or not a person, object, or condition conforms to His definition of holiness. Only in this way could Israel understand what its own holiness was all about and how that holiness was essential if it were to live out the purposes for which it was elected and redeemed.

If Israel was called on to be holy, it was all the more necessary for the priests, who in a sense were the "mediators of the mediators," to be holy before God. The nation with its individuals had access to the Lord but in a limited way. Only through the priests was perfect access achieved. Clearly the priests had to measure up to unusual standards of holiness. Leviticus therefore addresses the matter of the consecration and instruction of the priests as well.

Finally, the sovereign God ordained not only principles of access by which His servant people might approach Him, but He also designated special times and places. Thus Leviticus, like Exodus, instructs the covenant community to meet the Lord as a community at the tabernacle, the central sanctuary that He invested with His glory as a visible sign of His habitation among them. He could not be approached randomly or whimsically. No king holds audience at the discretion of his subjects. Rather, the king establishes regular times of assembly with

his people when he receives their tribute and addresses their concerns. Likewise, the Lord revealed a calendar of ritual, a schedule according to which the community as such could (and should) appear before Him to praise Him and to seek His face on their behalf. Sabbaths, new moons, and festival days were therefore set aside for the regular encounter of the servant nation with its sovereign God. Times and places were not irrelevant, as Leviticus makes clear. In a covenant context they attested to the rule of the Lord among His people and to their need to come where and when He decreed for them to do so.

## NEED FOR SACRIFICE (1–7)

The first major section of Leviticus (chaps. 1–7) deals with the nature, purpose, and ritual of sacrifice. The summary statement that concludes this section sets the entire sacrificial system in the context of God's covenant with Israel at Mount Sinai. God freed Israel from Egyptian slavery so that it would be free to worship. Leviticus 1–7 instructed Israel in how properly to worship God. God desires the fellowship of His people. The Israelites' rebellion, however, made continued relations a problem for a holy God. Leviticus 1–7 introduces those sacrifices that made possible renewed fellowship between God and His people. (See "Purpose and Theology.")

As an expression of tribute and devotion to the Lord, sacrifice had to be offered with a willing heart but also according to clearly articulated and well-understood prescriptions. Different kinds of offerings served a variety of purposes. Therefore an elaborate manual of procedure was necessary to show God's people how to approach the Lord God in an appropriate manner.

***Burnt Offering (1:1-17).*** The burnt offering could consist of an animal of the herd or flock or even of a bird. "Burnt offering" (*olah*) suggests that the victim was totally consumed on the altar; that is, everything was given to the Lord, and nothing remained for either the offerer or the priest. The purpose was to provide atonement for the offerer. By laying a hand on the head of the animal, the offerer was recognizing the substitutionary role of the victim. The animal was, in effect, paying the price of the offerer's sin. Whether bull, sheep, or dove, the animal's death became a "soothing aroma" before God, a means of effecting a harmonious relationship between a person and God.

**Grain Offering (2:1-16).** The grain offering appears always to have followed the burnt offering (Num. 28:1-8) and consisted of flour and oil. Though it too provided a "soothing aroma," it was not totally consumed in fire but was shared with the priests. Thus its purpose was not so much to secure atonement. But as its name (*minhah*, that is, *gift, tribute*) and the use of salt imply, it attested to the covenant relationship (re)established by atonement. That is, the grain offering

## THE SACRIFICIAL SYSTEM

A great deal can be learned about what a society values from what it expresses in rituals. The study of Old Testament ritual, far from being boring and unintelligible, can unlock the fundamentals of biblical theology.

### Meaning

To all who enter a relationship with God through faith, God gives commandments that the faithful follow in evidence of their faith (Deut. 5:29; Rom. 1:5; Heb. 3:18-19; John 14:15). When believers express their faith in obedience, they experience fullness of life (Lev. 18:5; Deut. 30:15-16; Ezek. 20:10-12).

For the Old Testament believer, God's commands were given in the law of Moses. These included instructions on how God was to be approached in rituals of worship and repentance. Ritual that does not arise from hearts committed to God is worthless (Prov. 15:8; Isa. 1:11-17; Hos. 6:6; Amos 5:21-24). Israel tended to neglect justice, mercy, and faithfulness, "the weightier matters of the law" (Matt. 23:23; see Mic. 6:6-8) and to be satisfied with ritual. Yet it is not true that authentic worship is found only in spontaneous acts and that formal, ritual acts necessarily represent sham or hypocrisy.

The sacrifices were a secondary though vital part of Israel's religion. Through them Israel expressed their faith and learned the nature of a holy God, sinful humanity, and the necessity of atonement. They also received forgiveness (Lev. 1:4; 4:20,26,31,35; 5:10,16) based upon Christ's final sacrifice (Rom. 3:25; Heb. 9:9-10; 10:1-4).

### The Offerings

The most common offering in Israel was the burnt offering (Lev. 1). It was presented by the priests every morning and evening and more frequently on holy days. Its main distinction was that the animal was entirely consumed by the altar fire. In response to the faithful offering, God's anger would be turned; and the worshiper would be accepted, freed from punishment by payment of the ransom.

The priest was to eat a portion of the other offerings (joined by the worshiper with the fellowship offering, Lev. 3). The sin or purification offering (Lev. 4:1–5:13) served to purify the sanctuary so that God could continue to dwell with a sinful people. The guilt or reparation offering (5:14–6:7) accompanied compensation that was required in the case of certain sins. The fellowship or peace offerings (Lev. 3) were unique in that these were optional, brought in response to an unexpected blessing (a "thank" offering), a general thankfulness (a "freewill" offering), or a prayed-for deliverance (a "vow" offering).

Finally, the grain offerings (Lev. 2) accompanied the daily burnt offerings or were presented independently in thanks at harvest.

was a harvest tribute paid to the sovereign Lord.

**Peace Offering (3:1-17).** The peace offering could be an animal of the herd, a lamb, or a goat. The purpose was, like the grain offering, not to effect atonement but to celebrate covenant union. It produced a soothing aroma, thereby attesting to God's pleasure with the offerer. So much was this the case that the peace offering actually was viewed as a common meal in which the Lord, the offerer, and the priests "sat down" together to share their respective parts; (see further 7:15-18,28-34).

**Sin Offering (4:1-5:13).** Peace or fellowship between a human being and God could not be achieved as long as sin created a barrier between them, so means had to be found to deal with that problem. Sin could be either unintentional or by choice. The rituals of Leviticus provided atonement only for unintentional sin. The person who sinned by choice ("sin defiantly," NIV; Hebrew "sin with a high hand") was forever cut off from God's people (Num. 15:30; see Ps. 19:13).

The removal of unintentional sin required appropriate sacrifices. These included not only the bull and lamb (here the female, 4:32) but also the goat, dove, or even flour. The nature of the offering depended on the status of the offerer.

| SACRIFICIAL SYSTEM | | | |
|---|---|---|---|
| NAME | REFERENCE | ELEMENTS | SIGNIFICANCE |
| Burnt Offering | Lev 1; 6:8-13 | Bull, ram, male goat, male dove, or young pigeon without blemish. (Always male animals, but species of animal varied according to individual's economic status.) | Voluntary. Signifies propitiation for sin and complete surrender, devotion, and commitment to God. |
| Grain Offering Also called Meal, or Tribute, Offering | Lev 2; 6:14-23 | Flour, bread, or grain made with olive oil and salt (always unleavened); or incense. | Voluntary. Signifies thanksgiving for firstfruits. |
| Fellowship Offering Also called Peace Offering: includes (1) Thank Offering, (2) Vow Offering, and (3) Freewill Offering | Lev 3; 7:11-36 | Any animal without blemish. (Species of animal varied according to individual's economic status.) | Voluntary. Symbolizes fellowship with God. (1) Signifies thankfulness for a specific blessing; (2) offers a ritual expression of a vow; and (3) symbolizes general thankfulness (to be brought to one of three required religious services). |
| Sin Offering | Lev 4:1-5:13; 6:24-30; 12:6-8 | Male or female animal without blemish—as follows: bull for high priest and congregation; male goat for king; female goat or lamb for common person; dove or pigeon for slightly poor; tenth of an ephah of flour for the very poor. | Mandatory. Made by one who had sinned unintentionally or was unclean in order to attain purification. |
| Guilt Offering | Lev 5:14-6:7; 7:1-6; 14:12-18 | Ram or lamb without blemish | Mandatory. Made by a person who had either deprived another of his rights or had desecrated something holy. |

Thus the sin of the priest required the bull, the blood of which was sprinkled within the holy place of the tabernacle. The purification of the congregation as a whole also demanded a bull whose blood was applied by the priest in the way just described. The inadvertent sin of a ruler was atoned by the sacrifice of a male goat, the blood being applied to the great altar. An ordinary person presented a female goat or lamb or even, if poor, two doves or a mere handful of flour. When all of this was done with proper ritual and intent, the sin would be forgiven.

***Trespass Offering (5:14–6:7).*** Atonement for either sins of inadvertence (4:1-35) or sins of omission (5:1-13) had to be followed by appropriate compensation to the one sinned against. The trespass offering was always a ram without blemish. If the offerer had withheld anything from the sanctuary, perhaps a promised offering, a 20 percent penalty had to be added to the offering. If the sin involved the loss or destruction of another's property, the guilty party had to offer a perfect ram and again make restitution of 120 percent. Reparation was expected; for though forgiveness comes by grace, sin always produces damaging consequences, particularly in terms of loss to fellow human beings.

***Priests and Offerings (6:8–7:38).*** Leviticus 6:8–7:36 is a brief "handbook for priests" to instruct these worship leaders in the proper ritual for sacrifices and offerings. Its order of contents conforms largely to that of the sacrifices just outlined.

The law of the burnt offering required that the fire of the altar be kept burning day and night. The continual fire points to the continuing need for sacrifice to atone for the people's sins. The law of the grain offering and sin offerings repeat the earlier instruction (chaps. 2; 4) but from the priests' perspective. The priestly role in the guilt offering and peace offerings specifies in greater detail what portion of the offerings was the priests' share.

Leviticus 7:37-38 summarizes the entire system of sacrifices and sets that system in the context of the Mosaic covenant at Mount Sinai. (See the introduction.)

## NEED FOR MEDIATORS (8–10)

Moses' role as mediator on behalf of rebellious Israel (Exod. 32:30-32; 33:12-17; 34:8-9) points to the need for God-ordained mediators to continue his ministry of intercession throughout Israel's history. Exodus 28–29 specifies that these mediators will be the priests. The second major part of Leviticus—chapters 8–10—describes the establishment of the priesthood in answer to this need.

***Consecration of Priests (8:1-36).*** Moses called for all the congregation to assemble at the front of the tabernacle where they would witness the consecration of Aaron and his sons to the priesthood. Their adornment by the clothing and other trappings gave them identity and symbolically spoke of the meaning and function of their office (9:6-9; see Exod. 28). They were then anointed. And on their behalf Moses offered up a sin offering, a burnt offering, and an offering of consecration that symbolized the total commitment of Aaron and his sons to the priestly ministry. Then, as with all peace offerings, they ate of the ram of consecration during a seven-day period of purification.

***Function of Priests (9:1-24).*** Once Aaron and his sons had been duly set apart, they could and did offer sacrifice, a matter that occupies Leviticus 9. The purpose of these first sacrifices was to effect oneness between God and His people. The great variety of offerings, for both priests and people, attests to the significance of this particular day. The day was to mark the appearance of the Lord among them, an appearance that required their total commitment and purity.

**Failure of Priests (10:1-20).** That the ritual of priestly function and sacrifice must be performed precisely according to divine prescription is highlighted in Leviticus 10. Failure to do so met with most severe judgment. Two of Aaron's sons, Nadab and Abihu, offered "unauthorized fire" before the Lord on the altar of incense. The "unauthorized fire" may have been fire like that used in foreign worship. What is clear is that violation of God's demand to be glorified invited His swift retribution. Aaron and his two surviving sons had to remain in the tabernacle to complete the offerings described in chapter 9. Their failure to eat of these parts of the animals to which they were entitled brought Moses' displeasure. Upon hearing Aaron's explanation—that he was afraid of further offending the Lord—Moses understood and relented.

## NEED FOR SEPARATION (11–15)

God had called Israel to be a people separated for service (Exod. 19:5-6). Israel was, however, constantly tempted to conform to the standards of its neighbors in Egypt and Canaan (Lev. 18:3). The laws of clean and unclean witness the "separateness" of Israel and remind God's people that there can be no compromise of His standards. The Lord had charged Aaron directly to distinguish between the holy and the profane (10:10). Leviticus 11–15 provides examples.

**Clean /Unclean Animals (11:1-47).** The first of these examples was in the area of animal life, for not all were fit for human consumption. Though hygienic principles may be indirectly involved, the major lesson to be learned here was that because God is holy His people must also be holy. Their holiness

or separateness was to be illustrated by their distinctive eating habits.

**Uncleanness after Childbirth (12:1-8).** The second example of the distinction between ritual cleanness and impurity is seen in the uncleanness associated with childbirth. Comparison with the similar legislation in chapter 15 clarifies that impurity stems from bodily discharges associated with birth and not the act or fact of birth itself. Why discharges or emissions are unclean is not so clear. Many scholars have proposed that the loss of bodily fluids, especially blood, may signify the onset of death itself, the ultimate uncleanness.

**Uncleanness of Disease (13:1– 14:57).** Leviticus 13–14 deals with the manifestations of "infectious skin disease" and "mildew" on the body, clothing, or even houses of the afflicted, considering it as a sign of uncleanness. Of all the diseases of the Bible none is deemed more serious or loathsome than those often (though imprecisely) called leprosy. The many symptoms and prescriptions for cure listed indicate a variety of different afflictions. Their cleansing after healing had occurred required the offering of appropriate sacrifices. Similarly, clothing contaminated by such diseases also had to be treated either by washing or, if that failed, by burning. Houses polluted by disease would manifest it by mildew, a condition that had to be remedied by repairing the affected parts of the house or even tearing it down.

**Unclean Emissions (15:1-33).** The final kind of uncleanness dealt with in Leviticus concerns abnormal male emissions by disease, the release of semen, menstrual flow, and other kinds of female discharge of blood. These all were not inherently unclean. But they symbolize impurity and must therefore be cleansed by appropriate ritual and sacrifice in order that the holiness of God's people might be asserted and maintained.

## NEED FOR ATONEMENT (16)

The greatest act of purification—one involving the entire nation—was that achieved on the Day of Atonement. On this day the high priest first offered up sacrifice for himself. He then slaughtered one goat as a sin offering for all the people and expelled another goat (the scapegoat) from the camp as a symbol of the removal of sin from the community. Following a whole burnt offering, the camp was purified of the blood and animal remains by ceremonies of bathing and burning outside the camp. The writer of Hebrews developed images from the Day of Atonement to stress the superiority of Christ's priesthood (Heb. 8:6; 9:7,11-26). Hebrews 13:11-12 uses the picture of the bull and goat burned outside the camp as an illustration of Christ's suffering outside the Jerusalem city walls. According to one interpretation of 2 Corinthians 5:21, Paul alluded to the ritual of the Day of Atonement by speaking of Christ as a sin offering.

## NEED FOR HOLY LIVING (17-25)

The longest section of Leviticus (chaps. 17-25) is sometimes called the "Holiness Code" because it contains an exhaustive list of miscellaneous regulations pertaining to the acquisition and maintenance of holiness in Israel. The previous sections of Leviticus have been concerned primarily with holiness as "position." In chapters 17-25 (especially chap. 19) the focus shifts to holiness as moral condition. These miscellaneous laws may be categorized under eight major headings.

*Sacrifice and Blood (17:1-16).* Because blood was tantamount to life itself and was the God-ordained means of effecting atonement, no animal could be slaughtered outside the tabernacle. In the ancient Near East there was no such thing as ordinary slaughter for meat. For Israel to slaughter meat outside the tabernacle precincts was to shed blood to alien territory and perhaps to alien gods. The Christians of Corinth faced a similar problem regarding meat slaughtered in a pagan context (1 Cor. 8; 10:14-33).

As a metaphor for life, blood was sacrosanct and could not be eaten. This pertained not only to animals offered in sacrifice but to wild game and other edible animals as well.

*Sexual Relationships (18:1-30).* Strict standards of holiness also had to be observed in the area of sexual relationships. Contrary to the practices of the pagan world, the people of the Lord had to marry among their own society but not incestuously. Thus a man could not marry his mother, stepmother, sister or half-sister, granddaughter, stepsister, blood aunt, uncle's wife, daughter-in-law, sister-in-law, stepdaughter, or stepgranddaughter. Likewise, adultery, child sacrifice, homosexuality, and bestiality were strictly prohibited.

*Interpersonal Relationships (19:1-37).* The holiness of God meant that the Israelites had to display holiness in their interpersonal relationships. The frequent echoes of the Ten Commandments (worship the one God, honor parents, keep the Sabbath, 19:3; the prohibitions against stealing, lying, and false swearing, serve as reminders that a lifestyle of holiness was a condition of God's covenant with Israel. Again and again God's people were reminded that moral behavior is not optional for those who call Yahweh Lord. The conduct required of God's people went beyond ritual matters to include providing for the poor, caring for the disadvantaged, practicing justice, loving one's neighbor, respecting the aged, caring for foreigners, and dealing fairly in business and

# ISRAEL'S FESTIVALS AND FEASTS

For the early Hebrews, public worship perhaps centered not in the more familiar sacrificial offerings but in the great annual feasts. These festivals formed an integral part of Old Testament life and are vital to the understanding of much in the New Testament.

All of the annual Jewish religious observances, except the Day of Atonement, were joyous occasions. They were feasts, festivals, and fiestas.

## The Sabbath (Lev. 23:3)

The Sabbath was the most important religious festival for the Hebrews because it came every week. The Sabbath commemorates not only God's rest following creation (Exod. 20:11) but God's freeing Israel from Egyptian slavery (Deut. 5:15).

## Passover (Lev. 23:4-5)

The name "Passover" indicates deliverance from the tenth plague in Egypt, the death of the firstborn. The observance falls in the spring, at the beginning of the barley harvest. It commemorated the exodus from Egypt. Along with Pentecost and Tabernacles, Passover was one of three annual pilgrimage festivals (see Deut. 16:16).

## Unleavened Bread (Lev. 23:6-8)

This seven-day observance immediately following

Passover recalls the Israelites' hasty departure from Egypt. Together the two festivals made up an eight-day celebration something like our Christmas through New Year's Day does.

## Firstfruits (Lev. 23:9-14)

Firstfruits involved the offering of the first sheaf of grain that was harvested. This symbolized that the entire crop belonged to the Lord and that it all was a gift from His hand.

## Weeks (Lev. 23:15-21)

This feast came seven weeks after the Feast of Unleavened Bread. It was a grain (wheat) harvest festival. The people read the Book of Ruth and recited the Psalms. The New Testament calls this festival "Pentecost" from the Greek word for *fifty*.

## Trumpets (Lev. 23:23-25)

The beginning of the civil year was marked by this New Year's Day feast. It was a day of rest, of sacred assembly commemorated with trumpet blasts, and of offerings made to the Lord.

## Day of Atonement (Lev. 23:26-32)

This observance, in many ways the most important annual activity, was a solemn fast. This was the one day of the year the high priest entered the holy of holies in the tabernacle or temple. At this time the scapegoat was sent into the wilderness, signifying the sending away of the people's sins (see Lev. 16).

## Tabernacles or Booths (Lev. 23:33-43)

This fruit harvest festival in the fall was the most joyous occasion of the year. It lasted for seven days. Some say it was a time for the renewal of the covenant.

## Sabbatical Year (Lev. 25:1-7,20-22)

Every seventh year the land was to be given a year of rest. Fields were to lie fallow. Vineyards were not to be pruned.

## Jubilee Year (Lev. 25:8-17,23-55)

Each fiftieth year was also special. Property was to be returned to the family who originally owned it. Hebrew slaves and their families were to be released. Once again the land was to be given rest.

## Purim (Esth. 9:20-28)

This feast, not mentioned in the Mosaic law, is described in the Book of Esther. It was established by Mordecai to commemorate the deliverance from the threats of Haman. It was a time of feasting, gladness, and the giving of gifts to the needy.

## Hanukkah

This feast was established just before New Testament times. It celebrated the recovery and cleansing of the Jerusalem temple by Judas Maccabaeus in December of 164 B.C. John 10:22 calls Hanukkah the "Feast of Dedication." It is also called the Festival of Lights.

# JEWISH FEASTS AND FESTIVALS

| NAME | MONTH: DATE | REFERENCE | SIGNIFICANCE |
|---|---|---|---|
| Passover | Nisan (Mar./Apr.): 14-21 | Exod 12:2-20; Lev 23:5 | Commemorates God's deliverence of Israel out of Egypt. |
| Feast of Unleavened Bread | Nisan (Mar./Apr.): 15-21 | Lev 23:6-8 | Commemorates God's deliverence of Israel out of Egypt. Includes a Day of Firstfruits for the barley harvest. |
| Feast of Weeks, or Harvest (Pentecost) | Sivan (May/June): 6 (seven weeks after Passover) | Exod 23:16; 34:22; Lev 23:15-21 | Commemorates the giving of the law at Mount Sinai. Includes a Day of Firstfruits for the wheat harvest. |
| Feast of Trumpets (Rosh Hashanah) | Tishri (Sept./Oct.): 1 | Lev 23:23-25 Num 29:1-6 | Day of the blowing of the trumpets to signal the beginning of the civil new year. |
| Day of Atonement (Yom Kippur) | Tishri (Sept./Oct.): 10 | Lev 23:26-33; Exod 30:10 | On this day the high priest makes atonement for the nation's sin. Also a day of fasting. |
| Feast of Booths, or Tabernacles (Sukkot) | Tishri (Sept./Oct.): 15-21 | Lev 23:33-43; Num 29:12-39; Deut 16:13 | Commemorates the forty years of wilderness wandering. |
| Feast of Dedication, or Festival of Lights (Hanukkah) | Kislev (Nov./Dec.): 25-30; and Tebeth (Dec./Jan.): 1-2 | John 10:22 | Commemorates the purification of the temple by Judas Maccabaeus in 164 B.C. |
| Feast of Purim, or Esther | Adar (Feb./Mar.): 14 | Esth 9 | Commemorates the deliverance of the Jewish people in the days of Esther. |

trade. The memory of God's mighty acts in delivering Israel from Egyptian slavery was to motivate God's people to lives of compassion and justice. An appreciation of the holiness of God and the memory of what God has done for our deliverance—not from Egyptian slavery but from sin through Christ's death—continue to motivate Christians to holy living. It is thus not surprising that New Testament writers often echo the ethical teaching of Leviticus 19 (for example, Matt. 22:39; Rom. 13:9; Gal. 5:14; Jas. 2:8).

*Capital Offenses (20:1-27).* The laws concerning capital offenses have to be understood against the backdrop of paganism. Capital crimes tended to obliterate the differences between God's holy people and the world at large. Thus the worship of Molech, the god of the Ammonites, was punishable by death. So were other heathen religious practices, cursing of one's parents, and incest and other sexual deviations. Again, Israel was a separated people whose lifestyle was to reflect that separation for service to a holy God.

*Worship and Holiness (21:1– 22:33).* Obviously holiness had to pervade Israel's religious life, so detailed injunctions regulated the priesthood and the eating of sacrificial offerings. The ordinary priests and the high priest had to follow strict guidelines in regard to mourning rites and marriage. They had to adhere to strict criteria of physical perfection to qualify for service. This requirement suggests that inward holiness must have outward, physical expression.

The priests had to be ceremonially clean before partaking of sacrifices. Then they and their families could enjoy their meal together as they took the portions to which they were entitled. All animals devoted in sacrifice had to be perfect specimens, for to offer Yahweh anything but the best would profane His holy name (see Mal. 1:6-8).

*Holy Days (23:1-44).* For the ancient Israelite holy living entailed the proper observance of holy days. These include the Sabbath, Passover and Unleavened Bread, Firstfruits, and the Feast of Weeks (or Pentecost). The fall festivals also were observed, which consisted of the Feast of Trumpets or New Year's Day, the Day of Atonement or Yom Kippur, and the Feast of Tabernacles or Booths, a reminder of Israel's wilderness experience. (See the feature article "Israel's Festivals and Feasts.")

*Consecration and Desecration (24:1-23).* God provided proper protocol in the administering of the affairs of the tabernacle. But He demanded punishment for violation of divine holiness, a point clearly made in the narrative about the blasphemer. This incident gave rise to related cases that directly or indirectly impinged upon the character of God and the requirements mandated to a people who claimed allegiance to Him.

*Sabbatical and Jubilee Years (25:1-55).* The proper observance of Sabbatical and Jubilee years was to testify to Israel's status as a holy people. The land, like the people, had to have rest; so every seventh year was set aside as a year when nothing would be planted. Then after seven such cycles, the fiftieth year too would be set apart for the rejuvenation of the land, the forgiveness of mortgages on it, and the like. The redemption of property was to remind the people that the land was Yahweh's and was actually leased out by Him to them. Likewise, those who had been forced to indenture themselves were to be released on the Year of Jubilee. It was most unfit that Israel, itself a slave people released from bondage by Yahweh, should tolerate bondage within its own borders. A holy people had to be a free people.

## BLESSING AND CURSE (26)

The essentially covenantal nature of Leviticus is made crystal clear in the summary statement of 27:34, which sets the whole book in the context of the Sinai covenant. The lists of blessings and curses that comprise Leviticus 26 reinforce this view of Leviticus as a covenantal text. Such lists are well known from other ancient Near Eastern texts where they impress upon the covenant recipient the seriousness of the covenant commitment. To be obedient resulted in great blessing, but to fail to obey brought judgment.

Thus a general exhortation introduces blessings and curses that follow obedience and disobedience to the covenant terms. The sting of the curses, however, is eased by a declaration of grace. The Lord affirmed that even though His people would sin and suffer exile, repentance was possible. Then God, in line with His ancient covenant promises, would restore them to Himself and to the land.

## OFFERINGS OF DEDICATION (27)

Leviticus closes with regulations concerning offerings of dedication (chap. 27). Placed here, these laws perhaps suggest appropriate ways to respond to the lifestyle choice posed by the blessing and curse. They form a fitting conclusion to Leviticus, for the dedication of oneself and possessions to the service of God is at the heart of holiness. These laws consist of personal vows of service to the Lord, votive gifts of clean and unclean animals, and gifts of one's house or lands. These could all be redeemed or reclaimed for "secular" use by payment of the appropriate redemption price to the priest. The firstborn and tithe could not be dedicated to the Lord because they were already His possession. Whatever was irrevocably devoted to God could not be sold or reclaimed for private use but had to be destroyed as an offering to God.

***Contemporary Significance.*** The Book of Leviticus, without doubt, is one of the most neglected of the Old Testament precisely because modern Christians fail to see what relevance it has to contemporary life. When one realizes, however, that its principal themes or ideals—the holiness of God, His covenant with His people, and the resultant demands for holy living—are timeless and irrevocable, the pertinence of the book becomes immediately evident. God chose Israel to be His servant people and to represent Him and His saving purposes on the earth. This same God in Jesus Christ has redeemed a people in this day to serve a corresponding function. The sacrifices, rituals, ceremonies, and holy days may have lost their legal status for the church. But the principles of holiness they embodied and demonstrated are principles that must characterize the people of the Lord of every generation if they are to serve Him effectively as salt and light.

***Ethical Value.*** The rituals of Leviticus found their fulfillment in Christ's sacrifice and are thus not binding rules for Christian worship. (See the commentary on Heb. 9–10.) In contrast, an appreciation of the holiness of God and the memory of what God has done for our deliverance—not from Egyptian slavery but from sin through Christ's death—continue to motivate Christians to holy living. It is thus not surprising that New Testament writers often echo the ethical teaching of texts such as Leviticus 19 (Matt. 22:39; Rom. 13:9; Gal. 5:14; Jas. 2:8). The detailed and complicated legislation of Leviticus is grounded squarely on the great covenant principles of the Ten Commandments. These laws find their ultimate meaning in the recognition that the God who freed Israel from Egyptian slavery (and freed us) is absolutely holy. True hope and happiness are found only in responding rightly to that God through holy lives of dedicated service. Again and again, Leviticus pleads that these things must be done because "I am Yahweh." That is, human behavior is successful to the extent that it acknowledges the Redeemer's claim to our lives and strives to mirror the holiness of God. No higher motivation for personal and community integrity can be found than in the governing theme of Leviticus: "I am the LORD who brought you up out of Egypt to be your God; therefore be holy, because I am holy" (Lev. 11:45).

## Questions for Reflection

1. Why is the context of Leviticus (27:34) important for understanding its message?

2. How do the instructions for worship relate to God's purpose for the exodus?

3. What was Israel's role as God's people, and why was holiness necessary in fulfilling this role?

4. Why were sacrifices and priests necessary?

5. What were the major types of sacrifices, and what were their purposes?

6. Why is Leviticus 17–25 known as the "Holiness Code"? What does God's demand for holiness teach about His moral character?

7. What do we mean by holiness as "position" and as "condition"?

8. How do the commands to distinguish the ritually clean from the unclean reflect God's lordship?

## Sources for Additional Study

Clements, Ronald E. "Leviticus." *The Broadman Bible Commentary,* vol. 2. Nashville: Broadman, 1970.

Harrison, R. K. *Leviticus: An Introduction and Commentary.* The Tyndale Old Testament Commentaries. Downers Grove: InterVarsity, 1980.

Schultz, Samuel J. *Leviticus.* Chicago: Moody, 1983.

Wenham, Gordon J. *The Book of Leviticus.* The New International Commentary on the Old Testament. Grand Rapids: Eerdmans, 1979.

# NUMBERS

The Hebrew name of this book (bemidbar) means in the desert and is thus a most appropriate way of describing its contents as a treatise whose entire setting is in the Sinai, Negev, and Transjordanian wilderness. The English title "Numbers" translates Arithmoi, the title used by the ancient Greek translation, the Septuagint. The term obviously reflects the census of the tribes of Israel at the beginning of the book and the other lists and totals.

The last verse of Numbers summarizes the whole by saying, "These are the commands and regulations the LORD gave through Moses to the Israelites on the plains of Moab by the Jordan across from Jericho" (36:13). Moses had led the Israelites from Mount Sinai to the borders of the promised land. The concluding verse suggests that Numbers instructs Israel in the preconditions of their possession and enjoyment of the promised land. (See "The Pentateuch" for a discussion of Mosaic authorship and the "Dates of the Exodus" for matters of chronology.)

**Theme.** The Book of Numbers is more than a mere travelogue tracing Israel's journey from Mount Sinai to the plains of Moab. The narratives and laws in Numbers give the conditions of Israel's possession and enjoyment of the promised land. These conditions included an unflinching desire to possess the land God promised, respect for God-ordained leaders, and concern for maintaining the holiness of the covenant community and of the land of promise. Frequent warnings of the danger of rebellion and the certainty of God's judgment on sin likewise prodded Israel ahead to the goal of possession of the land.

Numbers documents that when God's people were faithful to the covenant conditions, their travels and lives went well. When they were disobedient, however, they paid the price in defeat, delay, and death in the wilderness. The book thus teaches subsequent generations that covenant conformity brings blessing but covenant rejection brings tragedy and sorrow.

Numbers also documents the effective organization of the tribes into a discernible religious and political community in preparation for their conquest and occupation of Canaan. This explains the extraordinary interest in the numbering of the tribes, their arrangement for travel and encampment, and the centralizing of the tabernacle and priesthood as the focal point of Israel's life as a covenant people. This also explains the introduction of new legislation, especially of a cultic or ceremonial nature. The commandments and statutes appropriate for the forthcoming settlement in Canaan could not in every case be relevant to the people in a nomadic, transient stage of their lives. Numbers anticipates the possession of the promised land and therefore provides special instruction for those times and conditions.

**Literary Forms.** The great bulk of Numbers describes a nearly forty-year period of Israel's history in a story or almost "diary" form. Moses apparently kept a log book in which he noted significant events that could and did constitute his personal memoirs (see 33:2). Numbers, then, is history but narrative history of an individualistic type.

In addition to narrative materials, Numbers contains census lists (1:5-46;

3:14-39; 4:34-49; 26:5-51), an organization manual for encampment and march (2:1-31), and regulations for the priesthood and Levitical orders (3:40–4:33; 8:5-26; 18:1-32). It also contains laws of sacrifice and ritual (5:1–7:89; 9:1–10:10; 15:1-41; 19:1-22; 28:1–30:16), instructions about the conquest and division of the land (32:33-42; 34:1–35:34), and laws regulating inheritance (36:1-12). Numbers even contains poetry: a portion of "The Book of the Wars of Yahweh" (21:14-15), the "Song of the Well" (21:17-18), the "Song of Heshbon" (21:27-30), and the various prophetic oracles of Balaam (23:7-10,18-24; 24:3-9,15-24).

This rich diversity of forms is one of the major characteristics of biblical history writing. The story of God's redemptive purposes for Israel and all the world is told in narrative punctuated and illuminated by command, exhortation, illustration, proverb, and song. Numbers is thus not mere history but *torah,* instruction in holy living. Though the types of literature in Numbers are diverse, the goal of the possession of God's promised land is a constant unifying factor.

  I. Taking the Promised Land (1:1–10:10)
 II. Rejecting God's Promise (10:11–14:45)
III. Wandering (15:1–22:1)
 IV. Encountering Obstacles (22:2–25:18)
  V. Preparing for Conquest (26:1–36:13)

***Purpose and Theology.*** The diverse materials in Numbers point toward a common goal—the possession of the land God promised the patriarchs. Numbers opens with a census that reveals God had blessed Israel with the strength necessary for the conquest of the promised land (1:1–2:34). Organization for worship (3:1–4:49), instructions

for preserving the purity of God's people (5:1–6:27), and the building of the tabernacle (7:1–8:26) all made possible God's dwelling with this people (9:15)—a necessary condition for reaching the land. Though God equipped His people for conquest (10:11-36), their hearts repeatedly longed for Egypt (11:1-35; 14:2-4; 20:2-5; 21:4-5). They rejected Moses, the leader God had appointed to lead them to the land (12:1-15). Ultimately, Israel rejected God's gift of the land (12:16–14:45). Having spurned God's gift, Israel was condemned to wander in the desert (15:1–22:1). Again and again Israel rebelled against God's chosen leaders and suffered judgment (16:1-50). Even Moses failed to trust in the power of God's word (20:1-29) and was excluded from the land of promise.

God, however, is true to His promises. God overcame obstacles to Israel's possession of the land—the external threat of Balaam's curses (22:2–24:25) and the internal threat of Israel's idolatry and immorality (25:1-18). After the death of the rebellious generation, God again blessed Israel with a force capable of conquering the land (chap. 26). God rewarded the daughters of Zelophehad who, unlike the previous generation, earnestly desired their share in the land (27:1-11; 35:50–36:13). God's provision of Joshua as Moses' successor prepared for the successful conquest of the land.

Even the legal texts in Numbers anticipated life in the promised land. These texts regulated its worship (chap. 15) and maintained its purity (chaps. 19; 35). The Book of Exodus tells how the Israelites placed themselves under God's sovereignty—with all the responsibilities and privileges that entailed—by accepting the terms of the Sinaitic covenant. They became a holy nation (their status) and a kingdom of priests (their function). Num-

# OLD TESTAMENT NUMBERS

In the Hebrew text of the Old Testament numbers are written out as words, never represented by symbols or abbreviations. The numbers most frequently found in the Old Testament are one, two, ten, and seven (in that order).

Hebrew also used separate words for fractions, such as one-tenth (Exod. 16:36), two-tenths (Lev. 23:13), one-third (2 Sam. 18:2), and one-half (Exod. 25:10).

During the Intertestamental Period a system of numerical equivalents for the letters of the Hebrew alphabet was developed. Thus 'alep represented one, bet represented two, and so forth, following the order of the alphabet. Numerals beyond ten were formed by a combination of letters. This system is commonly used to denote chapter and verse divisions in printed texts of the Hebrew Bible today.

Numbers are most frequently found in the Old Testament in the enumeration of age or a census. Much attention has been given to the great ages of certain persons who lived before the flood. Examples are Methuselah, 969 years; Adam, 930 years; Seth, 912 years (Gen. 5:5-27). Bible interpreters understand these large numbers in various ways. (1) Some explain the numbers as based on a different reckoning of time. (2) Others take the numbers as a reference to an entire family rather than one individual. (3) Others see the large numbers as evidence that sin or disease had not yet sufficiently infected the human race to shorten the life span, or due to cosmological conditions that were different, making longevity commonplace. (4) Others believe that these ages had symbolic significance, whose meaning is unknown. (5) Others accept the ages as historical fact without explanation.

The large numbers found in census and enumeration lists (for example, Num. 1:21-46; 1 Kgs. 4:26) have been explained as textual errors or as symbolical numbers. (For example, the large number of people involved in the exodus from Egypt in Exod. 12:37 has been explained as symbolically suggesting power, importance, and victory of the Israelites.) Others insist the numbers should always be taken literally since apparent problems can be explained by careful analysis.

Numbers are sometimes used literally (for example, Asa ruled forty-one years, 1 Kgs. 15:10). Other numbers are approximations (1 Kgs. 20:29; 2 Chr. 17:14-18). Sometimes numbers represent an indefinite number (Judg. 5:30; 2 Kgs. 9:32; Isa. 17:6).

Numbers are sometimes used in the Old Testament for rhetorical or poetic effect. For example, numbers may express a striking contrast between God's limited judgment and great mercy (Exod. 20:5-6) or between military strength and weakness (Lev. 26:8; 1 Sam. 18:7).

A further example is a sequence of two consecutive small numbers, which should be interpreted as an indefinite number or perhaps a large number (Amos 1:3,6,9,11,13; Prov. 30:15,18,21,29).

Much attention has been given to discovering symbolic and mystical significance in biblical numbers. For example, "one" represents unity; "four" is the world; "seven" represents completeness. But the Bible itself neither affirms nor denies hidden meanings, which are often determined by the ingenuity of the one interpreting them.

A system called gematria developed in late Judaism that found hidden meaning in numbers. By giving numerical value to the letters of a word or phrase, hidden meanings were discovered. For example, 603,550 (Num. 1:46) means the sum of all the children of Israel (Num. 1:2). By gematria the enigmatic "Shiloh comes" (Gen. 49:10) has the numerical value of 358, the numerical value of the word messiah. Correct interpretation of a passage will often depend on a proper understanding of how the numerals are being used.

bers tells of Israel's successes and failures in living out the covenant as they made their way to the land of promise. The wilderness became a proving ground, an arena in which Israel had opportunity to display their commitment to the God who had called and commissioned them. It was historically their first opportunity to move beyond the place of covenant reception and enter the sphere of covenant implementation.

Israel's inability or, at least, refusal to exhibit its role as obedient mediator became clear again and again. They rebelled at Taberah and Kibroth Hattaavah (11:3,34). They challenged Moses' authority as covenant representative (chap. 12). They rejected the spies' report that encouraged conquest of the land of Canaan (14:1-10). They rejected the priestly role of Aaron (chap. 16). They committed idolatry and immorality of Baal Peor (chap. 25). Each case of rebellion was met by divine displeasure and punishment. The constancy of the Lord, His faithfulness to His covenant pledge, however, remained unaltered. Indeed, the ancient Abrahamic promise that those who blessed Israel would be blessed and those who cursed Israel would be cursed remained intact (24:9). Even more remarkable, since it came from the lips of the pagan seer Balaam, was the great messianic revelation that "a star will come out of Jacob; a scepter will rise out of Israel" (24:17), a word that confirmed the function of Israel as the source of redemptive and reigning blessing for the whole world (see Gen. 49:10).

## TAKING THE PROMISED LAND (1:1–10:10)

The covenant with Israel had been concluded at Sinai. And its social, political, and religious stipulations had been outlined (Exod. 20–40; Lev.). Then the Lord commanded His people to leave the holy mountain and to make their way to the land of promise.

**Organizing for War (1:1–2:34).** The census of the men of military age revealed a fighting force of 603,550, excluding the Levites. God had fulfilled His promise to Abraham of numerous descendants. With such an army Israel was well equipped to take the promised land. To facilitate moving and encamping such a vast force, explicit instructions as to tribal, clan, and family organization became mandatory.

The Israelite camp was organized with God's dwelling, the tabernacle, at its center. The Levites and priests camped nearest to the tabernacle, the priests guarding the entrance on the east side (3:38). The "lay tribes" camped somewhat farther away, with Judah occupying the position of leadership, again to the east. Such organization lays stress on preserving the purity of the tabernacle. The Levites were responsible for the movement and care of the tabernacle and so remained outside the military census.

**Organizing for Worship (3:1–4:49).** The Levites had been set apart for Yahweh's special service as a substitute for Israel's firstborn sons. Moses organized them according to Levi's three sons—Gershon, Kohath, and Merari. The Gershonites were responsible for the curtains, drapes, and coverings of the tabernacle; the Kohathites, for its furnishings; and the Merarites, for its supporting structure.

**Preserving Purity (5:1–6:27).** The sanctity of the tabernacle—a point made clear by the detailed regulation concerning its handling (chaps. 3–4)—gave rise to a consideration of various ordinances having to do with holiness and separation. Thus Moses addressed ritual uncleanness (5:1-4), sin and restitution, and tests to be administered to a woman

## TABERNACLE

The tabernacle was a portable shrine. It served the Hebrew people as their center of worship during the years of desert wanderings, conquest of Canaan, settlement in the land, and early monarchy. The English word *tabernacle* comes from the Latin Vulgate. It means *tent* or *wooden hut*. The Hebrew term translated "tabernacle" means *to dwell*. Thus the tabernacle represented the Lord's presence with His sojourning people.

### Importance

Exodus 25:31 told the people how to make the tabernacle. Exodus 35:40 reports that they made it just that way. Thirteen chapters out of forty, over a third of the Book of Exodus, concern the making of the tabernacle. (Of course, many details of furnishings, ritual, and priestly activity were included, in addition to the actual construction.)

### Plan

The tabernacle was a rather small prefabricated tent made of a wooden frame and elaborate curtains. It sat in an outer court that measured 150 by 75 feet. The court was formed by a fence of posts and curtains.

The tent faced east and measured forty-five by fifteen feet. The first chamber, the holy place, was thirty by fifteen feet. The holy of holies (the holiest of all) was a cube and measured fifteen feet in every direction.

### Furniture

Six items of furniture were associated with the tabernacle. In front of the tent, nearest the outer fence, sat the huge brazen altar on which the priests offered the sacrifices. Behind it was the large laver or basin for ceremonial washing.

Inside the holy place, at the north wall, stood the table of showbread (bread of the presence). Some think it was an acknowledgment of the Lord's bounty in providing food for His people. On the south side of the holy place stood the seven-branched lampstand (not candlestick).

At the curtain separating the two sections of the tabernacle stood a second, smaller altar, the altar of incense.

Inside the holy of holies the ark of the covenant rested. It was a chest overlaid with gold. Its lid was a slab of solid gold called the mercy seat (RSV; the atonement cover, NIV). Over it the cherubim stood (or knelt, depending on the interpretation). The atonement cover was the X-marks-the-spot where the Lord was enthroned and where He came down to meet His people.

### Meaning

In Exodus 25:8 God instructed Moses, "Then have them make a sanctuary for me, and I will dwell among them." Some commentators find Christian significance in every detail of the tabernacle construction. This approach should not be overdone, lest we miss the main point: the Lord's presence. The New Testament applies this image of God's presence in the tabernacle to Jesus' presence with His first disciples: "The Word became flesh and made his dwelling among us" (John 1:14).

The Book of Hebrews often applies the image of the priest serving in the tabernacle to Christ's saving work (Heb. 6:19-20; 8:2; 9:24; 10:19-20). Because Christ died for us and lives to intercede for us, Christians have access to the presence of God. In the Old Testament only priests could enter the tabernacle building. Lay worshipers had to remain outside the outer fence unless they were allowed to bring their sacrifices as far as the altar just inside. The tabernacle helps us to appreciate the free access Christ provides for us to the Father (Heb. 10:19-20). (See "The Sacrificial System" and "The Temple.")

whose husband accused her of adultery. Since the Nazirite was a classic example of one who set himself apart for divine service, Moses set forth lengthy guidelines concerning the Nazirite vow (6:1-21).

The blessing Moses taught Aaron and the priests captures the very essence of what it means for Israel to be the people of Yahweh—a source of blessing that makes God's gracious presence known.

*A Dwelling for God (7:1–8:26; 9:15).* The tribal leaders of the respective twelve tribes brought their own gifts of tribute to the Lord at the tabernacle, thereby recognizing His sovereignty over all political as well as religious affairs. Day by day the tribes came in succession, bringing silver and gold vessels and a great number of sacrificial animals. More important than even these lavish gifts, however, was Israel's giving of itself to the Lord. They separated and dedicated the Levites to Yahweh as His own special treasure. This had already been commanded (3:5-10), but now it actually took place.

*Celebrating Passover (9:1–10:10).* Appropriately Israel's move from Sinai to Canaan followed celebration of the Passover, the same festival that preceded the exodus from Egypt. Likewise, just as that first exodus was marked by the appearance of the glory of God, who led them by fire and cloud, so the wilderness journey followed His leadership in the same form. The movement and settlement of Israel was determined by the movement and settlement of Yahweh as represented in the symbols of His glorious presence. The signal for that movement and for other occasions in which the Lord would lead His people would be the blowing of silver trumpets, an audible witness to His presence among them.

## REJECTING GOD'S PROMISE (10:11–14:45)

A little more than a year after the exodus and after nearly a year at Sinai (Exod. 19:1), Israel pressed on to the land of promise, mobilized for conquest. Taking their cue from the movement of the cloud of glory, the camp set out in the manner previously commanded. Preceding the whole camp was the ark of God, the symbol of His guiding and protecting presence.

*Longing for Egypt (11:1-35).* No sooner had the journey commenced, however, than the people began to complain and murmur. The result was judgment by fire, a visitation of God halted only by Moses' urgent intercession. The major complaint seems to have been dissatisfaction with the manna God had miraculously provided (Exod. 16:13-20) and a longing for the delicacies of Egypt. So intense was the agitation that Moses seemed crushed under the load of leadership. Graciously, therefore, the Lord provided him with seventy Spirit-filled leaders who could assist him in these matters. He followed this with the provision of low-flying quail, which the people consumed with such gluttonous lust that the Lord once more inflicted them with His judgment.

*Rejecting God's Prophet (12:1-15).* The selection of seventy elders of Israel to assist Moses infuriated his own sister Miriam and brother Aaron. They sensed in this a decrease in their own prestige and leadership. Miriam, a prophetess, had played a leading role in the exodus (see Exod. 15:20-21); whereas Aaron, of course, was the great high priest. Under the pretense of criticizing Moses for having married outside the covenant people, they registered their true feelings by challenging his prophetic authority. The result was Yahweh's severe chastening of them and His reminder that Moses, the covenant mediator, was unique among all of God's servants: God spoke to Moses openly and not in visions and dreams. The sign of that special relationship was in Moses' very ability to restore his stricken sister to ritual cleanliness.

*Rejecting God's Gift (13:1-14:15).* Somewhere in the northern Negev, close to Canaan, the Lord commanded Moses to send out spies who could ascertain the strengths and weaknesses of its inhabitants and prescribe a course of action in regard to conquest (12:16–13:2). The twelve, including Joshua and Caleb, traveled the length of Canaan and returned with a divided report. The land was rich and fertile, they said, but the majority argued it could not be taken because of the superior might of its citizens. Caleb's affirmations of the Lord's presence and power notwithstanding, the people listened to the majority report and refused to press forward. The people rejected God's gift of the promised land.

Once more Moses' leadership was at stake. In fact, the people demanded that he step down in favor of someone who would guide them back to Egypt. His striking response to them—and to the Lord who tested him by threatening to destroy them—is remarkable. If Israel failed to enter Canaan, he said, the whole world would view Yahweh as unreliable. He had to pardon His people for His own name's sake if not for theirs.

Moved by this intercession, the Lord relented but announced to Moses and the people that they would not live to see the land of promise. Instead, they would die in the wilderness, leaving the promises of God to be enjoyed by their children. Only Joshua and Caleb, who had trusted God for victory and conquest, would see for themselves the land of milk and honey.

Having refused the opportunity to enter Canaan with the Lord, the people now perversely determined to do so without Him. Leaving the ark in the camp, they pushed north, only to be confronted and defeated by the Amalekites and Canaanites of the southern hill country. Thus began their forty years of aimless wandering in the wilderness.

## WANDERING (15:1–22:1)

With striking irony the Lord, who had just sentenced the people of Israel to death in the wilderness, outlined immediately the principles of sacrifice and service to be followed by their descendants in the land of Canaan. These generally agree with the procedures of Leviticus 1–7, though there are certain amendments appropriate to a settled rather than nomadic life. Particular attention is focused on the sin offerings, for sin would always be a problem even in the land of promise.

As though to illustrate this fact, the brief narrative of a Sabbath breaker appears after the instruction concerning willful sin. His death by stoning underlined the seriousness of such sin and gave rise to the reemphasis on Israel's need to remember who they were and what the Lord required of them.

***Rejecting God's Priest (16:1-50).*** A second illustration of the continuing problem of sin follows in the story of the rebellion of Korah against Aaron's priestly authority. Korah was a Levite, but not a priest. He resented this exclusion and challenged the claim of Aaron and his sons to hold sole rights as mediators before God. Moses, therefore, arranged for Korah and his followers to appear at the sanctuary, where they and Aaron would offer incense before the Lord. He whose offering was accepted would stand vindicated.

When the moment of truth came, the Lord appeared in His glory, threatening to destroy not only Korah and his collaborators but the entire congregation. Only the intercession of Moses and Aaron prevented this. Korah, with his friends and family, was swallowed up in a great crevice in the earth. Thus the rebellion of competing priests was put down.

God's judgment did not end the murmuring of the people. Again the Lord threatened them with annihilation. Only the faithful mediation of Moses saved them once more, though several thousand of them died of the plague.

**Vindicating God's Priest (17:1-13).** The congregation again challenged God's choice of leaders. When Aaron's rod (the symbol of the tribe of Levi) budded and bloomed, it was clear that the priestly line lay in him and his family and nowhere else.

**Priests, Levites, and Purity (18:1-19:22).** Once this crisis was over, it was necessary once more to spell out the duties and privileges of the priests and Levites. This led naturally to a discussion of other cultic matters, especially purification. This required such things as the slaughter of a red heifer as a sin offering and was applicable to uncleanness incurred by touching a dead body and a tent made unclean by someone's dying therein.

**Failing to Trust God's Word (20:1-13).** The narrative of the journey continues with the account of Israel's arrival at Kadesh Barnea, the center of Israel's desert wanderings for thirty-eight years. In and near Kadesh, Miriam and Aaron died (20:1,28), underscoring the serious consequences of the rebellion of the first wilderness generation. There once again the people rebelled against Moses because of the lack of water. This time, burning with rage, Moses struck the rock rather than speaking as the Lord had instructed him. Numbers later describes Moses' sin as a failure to respect God's holiness (27:14). Moses' rash act resulted in a blessing for Israel—abundant water—but a curse for Moses—rebuke and exclusion from the promised land. According to Psalm 106:32, Moses suffered for the people's sin: "Trouble came to Moses because of them."

**Journeying to Moab (20:14-22:1).** Faithful to his commission, nonetheless, Moses made plans to continue the journey on to Canaan. He first sought permission from the king of Edom to pass through that land on the King's Highway—a petition that was refused. Moses then engaged the Canaanites of Arad in a skirmish that ended in a solid Israelite victory. Encouraged, Israel pressed on. Though persisting in rebellion from time to time, they eventually reached Moab. Their arrival caused great concern to Israel's enemies. Sihon, king of the Amorites, tried to stem the advance of God's people but was unsuccessful. Og of Bashan likewise suffered defeat at Israel's hands. Thus Moses and his followers found themselves at last on the plains of Moab, directly east of the land which the Lord had promised to give them.

### ENCOUNTERING OBSTACLES (22:2-25:18)

The defeat of the Amorites and Bashanites suggested the way was clear for Israel's conquest of the promised land. Before entering the land, Israel would, however, face obstacles to God's promise of land. The first obstacle was external—the threat of curse from Balaam; the second, internal—the threat of compromise to the sexual standards of the Moabites.

**External Threat (22:2-24:25).** Balak, the king of Moab, concluded that his nation would be next to fall to Israel. He therefore engaged the services of Balaam, a famous Mesopotamian seer. The Lord warned him not to collaborate with Balak, for it was fruitless to attempt to curse a people whom God had blessed. Balaam went on to Moab, hoping to satisfy the request of Balak but having learned that he could say only what the God of Israel would permit.

Once at Moab, Balaam commenced a series of curses that were converted by the Lord into magnificent blessings for His people. He first predicted the innumerable host of Israel, then the faithfulness of the Lord to His people, their prosperity and success, and the rise of an Israelite ruler who would subdue Israel's neighbors. Thus Balak's diabolical plan to curse Israel resulted in just the opposite—a magnificent outpouring of God's blessing upon His people and, through them, upon the whole world.

**Internal Threat (25:1-18).** What Balaam could not do, however, Israel's own base inner impulses could and did do. While in the plains of Moab, they came upon the licentious cult of Baal at Peor and soon were attracted to its allurements. Only the zeal of Phinehas, son of the high priest Eleazar, prevented wholesale apostasy. With his spear in hand, he slew the ringleaders of the affair. Thus he brought atonement, but not before thousands of his fellow Israelites perished in a plague sent by God.

## PREPARING FOR CONQUEST (26:1—36:13)

Having now cleared the way for the crossing of the Jordan and the conquest of Canaan, the Lord gave instructions concerning those matters. He first ordered a new census of the tribes and outlined some principles of land inheritance in families where there were no sons. The earnest desire of the daughters of Zelophehad to share in God's gift of land contrasts sharply with the earlier generation's spurning of the gift.

**Moses' Successor (27:1-23).** God revealed His will concerning a successor to Moses, someone who would become covenant mediator in the land of Canaan, which Moses could not enter. This successor was Joshua, the faithful servant of the Lord, upon whom the honor of Moses was bestowed.

**Anticipating Worship (28:1–30:16).** The conditions of settled life dictated adjustment in religious life and practice. Therefore the Lord revealed new regulations regarding sacrifices and holy days and reiterated, with some refinements, laws pertaining to the making and terminating of vows.

**Keeping Israel Pure (31:1-54).** There was also the unfinished matter of the Midianites. They had drawn Israel into the degrading debauchery of Baal Peor (25:16-17) and therefore had to suffer God's awful judgment. Twelve thousand men of Israel were tapped for the assignment. Having slain Balaam and all the kings and men of Midian, they returned in triumph to the camp. Since the rebellion at Baal Peor involved sexual immorality, Moses demanded that those Midianite women who were not virgins also be slain.

**Turning Back Again (32:1-42).** Canaan proper was the land promised to the patriarchs. Yet some of the Israelites, namely, Reuben, Gad, and half the tribe of Manasseh, pleaded with Moses that they be allowed to take their inheritance in the Transjordan, right where they were. These tribes, like the previous generation, seemed ready to reject the land God had promised to give. Moses reluctantly granted their request but only on condition that they help their kindred in the conquest of Canaan and that they forever after be faithful to the Lord.

**Remembering and Anticipating (33:1–36:13).** The recital of Israel's itinerary since Egypt serves as a reminder of God's care through the wilderness years. Moses' final instructions about conquest and the tribal allocations anticipate the fulfillment of God's promise of land recorded in the Book of Joshua. Instructions concerning the Levitical cities and cities of refuge were to safeguard the promised land from pollution caused by shedding innocent blood. The final narrative in Numbers highlights the desire of the daughters of Zelophehad to share in

## PRIESTS IN THE OLD TESTAMENT
### (Listed alphabetically)

| NAME | REFERENCE | IDENTIFICATION |
|---|---|---|
| Aaron | Exod 28–29 | Older brother of Moses; first high priest of Israel |
| Abiathar | 1 Sam 22:20-23; 2 Sam 20:25 | Son of Ahimelech who escaped the slayings at Nob |
| Abihu | See Nadab and Abihu | |
| Ahimelech | 1 Sam 21–22 | Led a priestly community at Nob; killed by Saul for befriending David |
| Amariah | 2 Chr 19:11 | High priest during the reign of Jehoshaphat |
| Amaziah | Amos 7:10-17 | Evil priest of Bethel; confronted Amos the prophet |
| Azariah | 2 Chr 26:16-20 | High priest who stood against Uzziah when the ruler began to act as a prophet |
| Eleazar and Ithamar | Lev 10:6; Num 20:26 | Godly sons of Aaron; Eleazar—Israel's second high priest |
| Eli | 1 Sam 1–4 | Descendant of Ithamar; raised Samuel at Shiloh |
| Eliashib | Neh 3:1; 13:4-5 | High priest during the time of Nehemiah |
| Elishama and Jehoram | 2 Chr 17:7-9 | Teaching priests during the reign of Jehoshaphat |
| Ezra | Ezra 7–10; Neh 8 | Scribe, teacher, and priest during the rebuilding of Jerusalem after the Babylonian captivity |
| Hilkiah | 2 Kgs 22–23 | High priest during the reign of Josiah |
| Hophni and Phinehas | 1 Sam 2:12-36 | Evil sons of Eli |
| Ithamar | See Eleazar and Ithamar | |
| Jahaziel | 2 Chr 20:14-17 | Levite who assured Jehoshaphat of deliverance from an enemy |
| Jehoiada | 2 Kgs 11–12 | High priest who saved Joash from Queen Athaliah's purge |
| Jehoram | See Eliashama and Jehoram | |
| Joshua | Hag 1:1,12; Zech 3 | First high priest after the Babylonian captivity |
| Nadab and Abihu | Lev 10:1-2 | Evil sons of Aaron |
| Pashhur | Jer 20:1-6 | False priest who persecuted the prophet Jeremiah |
| Phinehas | (1) Num 25:7-13 (2) See Hophni and Phinehas | (1) Son of Eleazar; Israel's third high priest whose zeal for pure worship stopped a plague |
| Shelemiah | Neh 13:13 | Priest during the time of Nehemiah; was in charge of administrating storehouses |
| Uriah | 2 Kgs 16:10-16 | Priest who built pagan altar for evil King Ahaz |
| Zadok | 2 Sam 15; 1 Kgs 1 | High priest during the reign of David and Solomon |

the inheritance in the land. God rewarded their desire for His promises by providing laws of inheritance for families that had no male heirs. All was now ready for the final statement of covenant embodied in the Book of Deuteronomy and for the conquest of Canaan related in the Book of Joshua.

***Contemporary Significance.*** God desired the very best for the ancient Israelites—to give them a beautiful land as their home. God likewise desires the best for people today. People, however, are free to choose—either to accept God's gifts of love or else to spurn God's promises. The Israelites who left Egypt rejected God's gift of land and suffered death in the wilderness. Likewise those today who reject God's free gift of salvation in Christ do so at their own peril.

The story of the pilgrimage of Israel from Sinai, the place of initial commitment to God, to the plains of Moab, where Israel stood ready to realize all God's promises, sheds light on the Christian experience. Clearly Israel, like today's believers, experienced times of abysmal failure. Israel's frequent murmuring against Moses (and God) illustrates how God's people then and now are not satisfied with what should be our highest pleasure—to experience God's care and guidance in our lives. Israel's longing for good times in Egypt illustrates that the pleasures of sin remain attractive even to those whom God has redeemed. Then and now rebellion against God has dire consequences. Judgment is not, however, God's final word; those who cling tenaciously to God's promises find themselves rewarded.

***Ethical Value.*** Israel's response to the leadership of Moses and Aaron and to the covenant requirements in general dictated the degree of success or failure that characterized their wilderness sojourn. The principle is crystal clear: whenever there was unqualified obedi-

ence, there was unmitigated success. Whenever there was obstinate rebellion, there was failure. The demand for commitment to God is no less real and necessary today.

The strong ethical message that comes through loud and clear in Numbers is that God has a plan that leads to blessing. But that plan is built around principles and practices of behavior that cannot be compromised or negotiated. God desires to bless His own, but that blessing is predicated upon submission to God's rule. Success in life depends not only on doing the will of God but on doing it in the manner He prescribes.

## Questions for Reflection

1. What were God's conditions for Israel's possession and enjoyment of the promised land?

2. What does Numbers teach
   a. about the dangers of disobedience?
   b. about God's sovereign grace?

3. What is the significance of the location of the tabernacle in the center of the camp?

4. What were the consequences of Israel's rejecting
   a. its God-appointed leaders?
   b. God's gift of the land?

5. What obstacles (external and internal) did Israel face on route to the promised land?

6. Why was Moses not permitted to enter the promised land?

7. How do the daughters of Zelophehad serve as models of faith for Israel?

## Sources for Additional Study

Honeycutt, Roy L. Jr., *Leviticus, Numbers, Deuteronomy.* Nashville: Broadman, 1979.

Jensen, Irving L. *Numbers: Journey to God's Rest-Land.* Chicago: Moody, 1964.

Wenham, Gordon J. *Numbers: An Introduction and Commentary.* Downers Grove: InterVarsity, 1981.

# DEUTERONOMY

The name *Deuteronomy* (from the Greek for *second law*) arose from the Septuagint's translation of the Hebrew phrase meaning *a copy of this law* (Deut. 17:18). Deuteronomy is not a second law but an amplification of the first given at Sinai. The Greek (and hence English) title is thus somewhat misleading. The Hebrew title "these are the words" (from the first two words of the the book) is appropriate for these last words of Moses to Israel. (For discussion of Mosaic authorship and date see "The Pentateuch.")

In recent decades scholars have drawn attention to striking parallels between the Book of Deuteronomy and both Hittite (1400–1200 B.C.) and later Assyrian (850–650 B.C.) treaties. Though many analysts are convinced that Deuteronomy has been influenced by the ancient Near Eastern treaty tradition, it is more than a treaty or covenant text. It is a covenant statement embedded in the farewell address of Moses to Israel (Deut. 1:1-3; 34:1-8).

Israel had completed nearly forty years of wilderness wandering and was about to enter and occupy the land of Canaan. The old, rebellious generation had died. The new generation had to hear and respond to the covenant that God had made with their parents at Sinai. Moses repeated the history of God's faithfulness and exhorted the new generation to be obedient to the covenant mandates. He repeated the covenant terms but with amendments and qualifications appropriate to the new situation of conquest and settlement that lay ahead. In addition, Moses provided for future generations to renew their allegiance to the God of the covenant. Thus Deuteronomy is a "farewell" sermon centered on the covenant, an address that takes its fundamental shape from the pattern of Late Bronze Age covenant documents.

**Theme.** The overarching theme of Deuteronomy is covenant relationships. What would it mean for Israel to be the people of God in the context of conquest and settlement? What privileges and responsibilities did that status as chosen people entail for that generation of Israel and for future generations of God's people?

At the initial revelation of the covenant (Exod. 19:4-6), the Lord stated that He had delivered His people from Egypt "on eagles' wings" and had made them His own special people, "a kingdom of priests and a holy nation." Their calling was to be a servant people who would mediate the saving grace of God to all the nations of the earth. Deuteronomy continues that theme by emphasizing the divine election of Israel (Deut. 7:6-11; 10:12-15). This role of chosen people was to be lived out within the framework of clearly defined guidelines. These covenant stipulations governed every aspect of the political, social, and religious life of God's people.

**Literary Forms.** There is a widespread consensus that Deuteronomy is modeled after well-known ancient Near Eastern (specifically Hittite and/or Assyrian) treaty forms. Though the ancient treaty tradition provides the general structure and outline of the book, Deuteronomy adds exhortations, poetry, and other elaborations appropriate to its larger character as a farewell sermon of Moses.

Study of sovereign-vassal treaties made by the great king of the Hittites with conquered or dependent rulers reveal certain common components, which Deuteronomy embodies in the same general order. Following Peter Craigie (*The Book of Deuteronomy*, 24, 67–68), the following standard elements of Hittite covenant texts and their corresponding place in Deuteronomy may be set forth.

1. The Preamble (1:1-5) provides the setting in which the text is presented to the vassal by the Great King.

2. The Historical Prologue (1:6–4:49) rehearses the past relationships between the contracting parties.

3. The General Stipulations (5:1–11:32) are the basic principles of relationship. These reveal the purposes of the Great King and alert the vassal to the guidelines for implementing those purposes.

4. The Specific Stipulations (12:1–26:15) further define the general stipulations by particular cases. In specific situations the vassal would not always be able to deduce the proper application of the general principle without further guidance. Thus the Great King had not only to lay down generalized expectations but to anticipate peculiar or unique circumstances.

5. The Blessings and Curses (27:1–28:68) outline the consequences of faithfulness and disobedience to the covenant. Faithful obedience to the terms of the covenant, that is, to the stipulations laid down in Deuteronomy, would ensure that the vassal would be appropriately rewarded. Conversely, disobedience would bring swift and sure retribution at the hands of the Great King.

6. The Witnesses to the Treaty (30:19; 31:19; 32:1-43) testify to its worth and

to the commitments made by the contracting parties. Even the Great King acknowledges the need to stand by the promise He has solemnly sworn.

The elements of the ancient Near Eastern treaties can be seen not only in the larger structure of Deuteronomy but also in the organization of smaller units of the book. For example, Deuteronomy 5 contains (1) an introduction of the Great King ("I am the LORD your God," 5:6); (2) a historical prologue ("who brought you out of Egypt, out of the land of slavery," 5:6); (3) covenant stipulations (5:7-21); (4) blessings and curses ("punishing the children . . . of those who hate me, but showing love to a thousand generations of those who love me and keep my commandments," 5:9-10); and (5) the recording of the covenant (5:22).

I. Covenant Setting (1:1-5)

II. Learning from History (1:6–4:40)

III. More Covenant Principles (4:44–6:25)

IV. Auxiliary Covenant Principles (7:1–11:32)

V. Aids/Threats to Worship (12:1–16:17)

VI. God's People (16:18–26:19)

VII. Curses and Blessings (27:1–28:69)

VIII. Commitment Renewal (29:1–30:20)

IX. Future of the Covenant (31:1-29)

X. Moses' Song (31:30–32:43)

XI. End of Moses' Ministry (32:44–34:12)

***Purpose and Theology.*** The Book of Deuteronomy first restates the covenant between Yahweh and Israel for the generation assembled in the plains of Moab prior to the conquest of Canaan under Joshua. Most of the generation who had heard and accepted the covenant at Sinai thirty-eight years earlier had died (Deut. 2:14; see Num. 14:34). Their sons and daughters now needed to hear the covenant for themselves and to affirm their loyalty to it (Deut. 4:1-2; 5:1-5). Provision for future affirmation of the covenant suggests that each generation of God's people has to make the history of God's saving acts its own (26:5-9) and commit itself afresh to the covenant (26:16-19; see 5:3-4).

Second, Deuteronomy's mix of exhortation and covenant prescription suggests that the book was to record for posterity Moses' words of admonition, encouragement, and warning. Those about to enter the land of promise had to learn from the past, he maintained, if they were to fulfill the purposes for which the Lord had created them (Deut. 8:11-20).

The theology of Deuteronomy cannot be separated from its theme and form. As a document influenced by the form of covenant texts, it becomes the vehicle by which the sovereign God expresses His saving and redemptive purposes to His servant nation, His kingdom of priests whom He elected and delivered from bondage in response to the ancient patriarchal promises.

The truth that the God who delivered Israel from Egyptian slavery is the only true God is central to Deuteronomy's presentation of the covenant. Because there is but one God, He demands the total loyalty of His people (6:5; 10:12-13). Because there is but one God, He is to be worshiped in the one place of His choosing (12:5,11; 14:23).

## COVENANT SETTING (1:1-5)

The beginning of Deuteronomy finds Moses addressing the assembly of Israel in Moab, just east of the Jordan River. Forty years had transpired since the exodus, the long trek from Sinai had been completed, the enemies in the Transjordan had been defeated, and everything was in readiness for the conquest of Canaan. Moses therefore delivered a farewell address of covenant instruction and pastoral exhortation.

## LEARNING FROM HISTORY (1:6–4:40)

Hittite treaties included a summation of past relations between the great king and his vassal. Moses likewise recited the highlights of God's dealings with His people since the giving of the covenant at Sinai nearly forty years before. Following this résumé of Israel's failures and successes on route to the promised land, Moses exhorted God's people to treasure God's commands, to avoid idolatry, and to marvel at God's saving acts.

*Failures and Successes (1:6–3:29).* The Lord had commanded Israel to leave Sinai and to press toward the land of promise. The way had been hard, taxing Moses almost to the limit. But eventually they arrived at Kadesh Barnea on the borders of the promised land. There the people rebelled, refusing to enter the land. The Lord thus condemned them to wander in the wilderness until they died. After futile attempts to invade Canaan without God's aid, the tribes pressed north, bypassing Edom and eventually arriving at Moab. From there they sought permission to pass through Amorite territory but were soundly rebuffed by both Sihon, king of the Amorites, and Og, king of Basham. These two the Lord delivered into Israel's hands, thereby allowing Israel to come into possession of the entire Transjordan region. From there Moses had requested that he be allowed to lead his people into Canaan. The Lord, however, denied the request because at Meribah Moses had not trusted God or respected His holiness (33:51; see Num. 20:12).

*Reminders (4:1-40).* Following this sketch of history, Moses reminded his people of their special privileges as recipients of Yahweh's covenant grace. He urged them to remember what God had done in the past in making Himself

## LAW CODES AND COVENANTS
### (2nd Millennium B.C.)

| LAW CODE | | COVENANT * |
|---|---|---|
| Title | Identifies superior partner. | Title |
| Prologue | Shows how the superior partner has cared for the subordinate one in the past, thereby inspiring gratitude and obedience within the subordinate partner. | Prologue |
| Laws | Lists the laws given by the superior partner which are to be obeyed by the subordinate partner. | Stipulations/Laws |
| Blessings and Curses | Provides for the preservation of the text in the temple of the subordinate partner. | Depositions Reading |
| | Witnessed and guaranteed by the gods of both partners. | Witnesses |
| | Pronounces curses on those who disobey and blessings on those who obey. | Blessings and Curses |
| | Ratified by an oath and a ceremony, and sanctions are pronounced against any person who breaks the covenantal relationship. | Oath Ceremony Sanctions |

* Covenants also follow the pattern of an ancient Near Eastern treaty. See the discussion in the introduction to the Book of Deuteronomy.

known to them. The invisible God who acts in history cannot be represented in lifeless stone or wood or in His creation. Idolatry would lead to His punishment of destruction and exile. Israel's motive for serving and worshiping Yahweh exclusively lies in Yahweh's unique intervention on Israel's behalf, freeing them from slavery and making a covenant with them.

**Cities of Refuge (4:41-43).** In a brief narrative interlude Moses set aside three Transjordan cities as places of refuge in the event of manslaughter (see 19:2-13). Such cities were intended to free the promised land from the stain of innocent blood.

## COVENANT PRINCIPLES (4:44–6:25)

A brief introduction sets the covenant in the context of the exodus from Egypt and the successful conquest of the territory across the Jordan.

**The Ten Commandments (5:1-21).** After exhorting the present generation of Israelites to identify with their parents at Sinai, Moses listed the Ten Commandments, the very heart of the Sinai covenant. The Ten Commandments share the basic form of ancient Near Eastern treaties.

The Great King is identified ("I am the LORD your God"), and the history of His dealings with His servant people is outlined. The first command is *the* basic covenant principle. The following commands detail what Israel's exclusive devotion to God entails for Israel's relations with God and interpersonal relations. The form of these commands is virtually identical to that in Exodus 20:2-17. Here, however, remembering the Sabbath commemorates the saving deliverance from Egypt (Deut. 5:15) rather than creation (Exod. 20:11).

**Covenant Mediator (5:22-33).** The following flashback to the Sinai revelation emphasizes Moses' role as covenant mediator to fearful Israel. Moses challenged the new generation "to do what the LORD your God has commanded you" as a condition for prosperous life in the land of promise.

**Love for God (6:1-25).** The fundamental nature of the relationship between Yahweh and Israel consists of the recognition that God is one and that His people, if they are to enjoy the benefits of His promises to the patriarchs, must give Him undivided allegiance and unswerving obedience.

## MORE COVENANT PRINCIPLES (7:1–11:32)

The basic requirement of complete and exclusive love for God (6:5; 10:12) is worked out in various ways in 7:1–11:32.

**Total Destruction (7:1-26).** Because Israel was to serve only God in the land of promise, they were to destroy completely the native inhabitants of Canaan who served other gods. They were also to refuse any entangling alliance with them.

**Yahweh as the Source of Blessing in Canaan (8:1–9:6).** Israel was to acknowledge that Yahweh—not the fertility gods of Canaan—was the source of all blessings in the land. Israel was also to acknowledge that blessing as a product of God's grace, not their righteousness.

**Moses' Role (9:7–10:11).** Moses' role as covenant mediator and intercessor for disobedient Israel is again highlighted. The incidents of the golden calf, the wilderness murmurings, and the rejection of God's gift of land illustrate Israel's persistent rebellion. Moses' appeal to the patriarchal promises and to God's honor resulted in a renewal of the covenant.

**Love (10:12-22).** The oneness and exclusivity of Yahweh demand that He be loved by His people with a love that is synonymous with covenant fidelity. But love for God cannot be divorced from love for others, especially for the disadvantaged. Thus the center and substance of the covenant relationship is not legalism but love.

**Obedience (11:1-32).** Love must be manifest, and in covenant terms that means obedience. Israel had already seen what disobedience could bring. Now they had to understand afresh that the bounties of God's goodness were theirs only as they loved Him and kept His commandments. Now, and when they later entered the land, Israel would have opportunity to pledge its faithfulness to the Lord.

## AIDS/THREATS TO WORSHIP (12:1–16:17)

Having expounded the broad principles of covenant relationship and responsibility (Deut. 5:1–11:32), Moses turned to more specific examples of their application.

**Central Sanctuary (12:1-28).** The native Canaanites worshiped many gods at numerous local shrines. As an aid to the worship of the one true God, there was to be only one sanctuary where Israel's community worship was to be carried out. This could not be at the whim of the people but where Yahweh would cause His name to dwell. Before the building of the Jerusalem temple this central sanctuary was the site of the tabernacle and ark of the covenant.

**Pagan Gods/False Prophets (12:29–13:19).** Israel was to worship not only in the place of God's choice but in the manner of God's choice. God's people were prohibited from adopting the worship practices of the native Canaanites. When animal blood was shed, either for offering or human consumption of meat, the blood could not be eaten because it symbolized life itself and

therefore was sacred. God's people were not to consume blood as the native Canaanites did. God's people were further prohibited from adopting other Canaanite worship practices such as human sacrifice and cultic prostitution.

Canaanite religion depended on soothsayers and enchanters as channels of revelation and power. Since such practices entailed dealing with gods other than Yahweh, it was obviously forbidden for the people of Israel. Any prophet who counseled God's people to defect from Him, even if he came from within Israel itself, was to be put to death.

**Clean and Unclean Animals (14:1-21).** Further differences between Israel and the unbelieving nations around them lay in their perception and use of the animal world. Israel was to demonstrate its calling and character as a holy people by conforming to the Lord's definitions of clean and unclean by eating only those animals that were not forbidden.

**Offerings of Thankful Hearts (14:22-28).** A further expression of reverence of the sovereign God of Israel was the people's generous offer of tribute to Him in the form of tithes of all their increase. This could be in produce or, if the central sanctuary were too far way, in money. Every third year that tithe was to be used to meet the needs of the Levites, God's specially chosen servants, as well as needs of the poor.

**Concern for the Poor and Oppressed (15:1-18).** Israel also acknowledged God as its sole Lord by its distinctive concern for the poor and the oppressed. Every seventh year was a year of release in which poor Israelites were freed of all financial encumbrances that had befallen them as a result of their indenturing themselves to their fellow countrymen.

***Offerings and Festivals (15:19–16:17).*** Deuteronomy 15:19–16:7, like 12:1-28, emphasizes Israel's worship of the one, living God at the central sanctuary. Because the Lord had spared the firstborn of every house of Israel from the tenth plague (Exod. 13:11-16), faithful Israelites were to offer up the firstborn of their herds and flocks annually as an expression of devotion. This was done as part of the Passover celebration and the Feast of Unleavened Bread that followed immediately thereafter. Other occasions for the community of faith to offer tribute to the Great King were the Feast of Weeks (or Pentecost), seven weeks after Passover, and the Feast of Tabernacles in the seventh month of the year.

## GOD'S PEOPLE (16:18–26:19)

***Kingdom Officials (16:18–18:22).*** The implementation of the demands of the covenant on the part of the community required political and religious officials who, under God, could ensure stability and obedience. The first group consisted of "judges and officials." Their task was to apply fair administration of justice without resorting to pagan means. In the interest of justice, Deuteronomy 17:2-7 provides guidelines for admissible evidence. Matters too difficult for resolution at the local level were to be decided by a high court of priests and judges at a central sanctuary, with punishment appropriate to the crime.

Eventually the nation would develop a monarchial government. The king was to be a native Israelite chosen by the Lord Himself. He was to adopt a humble and dependent lifestyle contrary to that of neighboring kings. This would preclude the amassing of horses as a sign of military might and the multiplication of wives as a sign of entangling international political alliances. Finally, he was to trust in the Lord and seek to live by the principles outlined in the very book of the covenant, the Book of Deuteronomy.

The religious officials of Israel included the priests and Levites. Their responsibilities as leaders in Canaan also receive brief attention. Since the Lord was their inheritance, they had no land or properties but were to live off the offerings and gifts of God's people.

The prophets also were important in shaping the course of Israel's life as God's people. All peoples, including the Canaanites, had their prophets. These practitioners of sorcery and incantation were so evil before God, however, that they and their demonic techniques were to be repudiated totally. In their place God would raise up an order of prophets in the tradition of Moses, spokesmen who would speak the true word of the Lord. This is therefore a collective reference to the prophets who would follow. As such, it received its ultimate fulfillment in Jesus (see John 1:21,25,45; 5:46; 6:14; 7:40; Acts 3:22-26; 7:37).

Any among this group of prophets who defected from this high and holy calling by prophesying falsely had to die. The fundamental test of their integrity would be whether or not their predictive word came to pass.

***Civil Law (19:1-21).*** Though Israel was by definition a religious community, it was nevertheless a community composed of individual citizens who were to live together in peace and order. There was, in other words, a social and civil dimension to life as a covenant people. This dictated the need for civil legislation, for rules of behavior in a social setting (Deut. 19:1–22:4).

The first of these dealt with the issue of homicide. The Sixth Commandment had already addressed this in principle (Deut. 5:17), but not all homicide was murder. Killings were to be considered on a case-by-case basis. If the killing was purely accidental, the perpetrator could flee to a designated city of refuge until his case could be judged (see Num. 35:9-34). If, however, the deed was intentional or there was malice aforethought, the killer was to be apprehended and slain by the avenger of the aggrieved party.

The second civil statute concerned the removal of boundary markers. Land was at the very heart of covenant inheritance, so for one to cheat his neighbor by moving property lines was to infringe on God's gift to him. Central to equitable civil law was the innocence of the accused unless proven guilty. One was not to be condemned on the testimony of one witness only; there were to be at least two for corroboration. False witnesses were to suffer the consequences of their perjury to the degree the accused party would have obtained if he had been found guilty and punished, showing that care must be taken to provide justice.

**Holy War (20:1–21:14).** As a nation about to engage the Canaanite nations in wars of conquest, Israel was given guidelines for this undertaking. God's people were to trust that God was with them and that He would achieve the victory (20:1-4). This allowed for many kinds of exemptions from military service. The sheer numbers of troops would not determine the outcome but only faithfulness to the Lord's commands.

In wars against distant nations, terms of peace were to be offered first. If they were accepted, the populace would be spared but would be reduced to the service of Israel and its God. If, however, the cities were devoted to the Lord as part of Israel's inheritance in Canaan, they were to be annihilated lest their peoples draw Israel away into apostasy.

From time to time homicides would occur without witnesses. Israel's sense of corporate solidarity was such that the citizens of the village nearest the corpse were held liable. They were to offer up a heifer as an atonement for the whole community to absolve it of guilt.

As a result of war, prisoners would frequently come under Israelite control. Females in such cases could become the wives of their captors after a period of adjustment. If the arrangement proved unsatisfactory, they were to be freed.

**More Distinctives of Law (21:15–22:4).** Though the Lord nowhere sanctions multiple marriages, He did provide guidelines for making the best of a bad situation. A preferred wife was to have no advantage over a less-loved wife in the allocation of inheritance rights to their respective sons.

Rebellious sons who were unmanageable to their parents could be prosecuted by them and even executed by the civil authorities. In any capital case, however, the corpse was not to lie exposed after sundown but was to be buried that very day (cf. John 19:31).

The final example of civil law has to do with lost property. Any Israelite who found anything belonging to a fellow citizen either had to return it to him or wait for him to come and claim it. If it were an animal that had fallen by the wayside, brotherliness mandated that the beast be lifted up and restored.

**Purity of God's People (22:5–23:18).** As the Mosaic covenant testifies over and over again, Israel was a holy people and was to live a holy life before the world. Like Leviticus (see Lev. 17–25), Deuteronomy also has its "holiness code," its set of guidelines by which Israel was to achieve and maintain its purity. Though the reason for the inclusion of some of these laws may escape the modern reader, in their own time and circumstances they undoubtedly contributed to Israel's understanding of what it meant to be a people peculiar to the Lord and unique among the peoples of the earth.

Transvestism was condemned because it spoke of unnatural mixing of clothing. Rules about the protection of young birds, the building of roof railings, sowing mixed seed, plowing with mixed teams, wearing clothing of mixed material, and wearing garments with tassels either positively or negatively speak of Israel's role as a people distinct from the heathen around them.

Purity or impurity frequently expresses itself in sexual relationships. Thus a man who married a woman who, in his opinion, turned out not to have been a virgin might demand that she prove her purity. If she could, he stood condemned; but if she could not, she was to be stoned to death. Adulterers, both male and female, were to die, as were engaged girls who had undertaken sexual relations willingly. An assailant who raped an engaged woman was to pay with his life. One who raped a maiden who was not betrothed had to marry her, pay her father a generous bride price, and never divorce her. Finally, one was not to engage his father's wife (that is, his stepmother) in sexual relation.

The holiness of God's people also revealed itself in the rejection from its assembly of those who had been emasculated, born out of wedlock, or who were of Ammonite or Moabite descent. This was because these latter refused hospitality to Israel in the wilderness. The Edomites, Israel's kindred people, and the Egyptians, Israel's hosts in times of famine, could, however, eventually enter the covenant privileges.

Both male and female cult prostitutes were strictly forbidden in Israel. Their ungodly gain could not serve as an offering to the Lord. An escaped slave was welcome, however, and in fact was not to be forced to return to his master.

Finally, purification pertained to matters of bodily cleanliness, especially in the context of holy war. Soldiers contaminated by bodily secretions were to purify themselves. They were also to bury their excrement. The reason was that the Lord walked in the midst of the camp. Physical impurity was an affront to a holy God and pointed to spiritual impurity as well.

***Interpersonal Relationships (23:19–25:19).*** Attention to the laws of purity gives rise to an association with precepts governing interpersonal relationships in general. There are areas of societal life which, though not cultic in nature, have moral and ethical implications important to covenant life and faith. Such matters as loans to fellow Israelites and foreigners, vows to the Lord, and the right to help oneself to a neighbor's grapes and grain while passing through his land illustrate the principle that one's fair dealings with both God and others are on the same level.

Similarly, the covenant addresses the problems of divorce and the newlywed; loan security; kidnapping; contagious skin diseases; the charitable care of the poor, weak, and disenfranchised; and the principle of responsibility for one's own sin and of liability to punishment.

Justice demanded that the guilty suffer appropriate punishment, that a brother of a deceased and childless Israelite raise up offspring in his name by marrying his widow, that a woman not dishonor a man sexually, and that weights and measures be according to standard. Justice even extended to the animal world, for the ox was allowed to eat of the grain it was threshing for its owner (see 1 Cor. 9:9). At the other extreme, God's justice demanded that the enemies of His chosen people experience judgment at their hands. Thus Amalek, who had attacked the elderly and defenseless of Israel in the wilderness journey (see Exod. 17:8-16), was one day to be destroyed from the earth.

**Reaffirmation of Covenant (26:1-15).** The specific stipulations section of Deuteronomy concludes with the laws of covenant celebration and confirmation. When Israel finally entered the land of Canaan, they were to acknowledge the Lord's faithful provision. They were to do this by offering their firstfruits to Him while reciting the history of His beneficent covenant dealings with them from the ancient days of the patriarchs to the present. This ceremony appears to have been a part of the celebration of the Feast of Weeks (or Pentecost or Harvest; see Exod. 23:16; Lev. 23:15-21). Following the offering of the first of the grain harvest to the Lord, Israelite farmers were to provide the Levites and other dependent citizens the tithe of their produce. In this manner tribute to God and support of the needy merged into one glorious act of worship.

**Exhortation and Narrative Interlude (26:16-19).** Having outlined the long body of stipulations, Moses commanded the people to obey them, not just perfunctorily but with all their heart and soul. The very essence of the covenant was the pledge they had made to be God's people and the Lord's reciprocal promise to be their God. It was the will of God that Israel continue to be His special people, a holy communion called to be an expression of praise and honor of the Lord.

## CURSES AND BLESSINGS (27:1-28:69)

An element of many ancient treaties was the description of the rewards for faithful compliance to its terms and the punishments befitting disobedience to it. The curses and blessings of Deuteronomy 27-28 show the influence of this treaty form.

**Gathering at Shechem (27:1-10).** The ceremony of blessing and cursing, to take place once Canaan had been occupied, was to occur in the vicinity of Shechem, the site of early patriarchal encounters with God (see Gen. 12:6; 35:4; Deut. 11:26-29). There Israel was to erect great plastered monuments containing the covenant text and an altar of stone upon which appropriate offerings of covenant renewal could be sacrificed.

**Curses for Disobedience (27:11-26).** As God's people, Israel would stand half on Mount Ebal and half on Mount Gerizim to affirm their covenant commitment. As a great responsive chorus, tribal representatives would stand on Mount Gerizim to shout "amen" at the listing of the blessings while others, on Mount Ebal, would do so when the curses were sounded.

The first list of curses deals with representative covenant violations without specifying the form the curses might take.

**Blessings for Obedience (28:1-14).** The blessing section promises prosperity in physical and material ways and reaffirms God's intention to make Israel an exalted and holy people.

**More Curses (28:15-68).** The second list of curses threatens loss of prosperity, disease and pestilence, defeat and deportation with all that would entail, and a reversal of roles between Israel and the nations. Rather than being exalted among them, Israel would become their servant. All of this would result in indescribable misery and hopelessness. In effect, covenant violation would undo the exodus and deliver the nation back into the throes of bondage.

## COMMITMENT RENEWAL (29:1-30:20)

**God's Saving Acts (29:1-9).** Moses rehearsed God's dealings with

Israel in the exodus and wilderness. He exhorted them to pledge themselves to covenant fidelity as the new generation chosen by the Lord to represent Him on the earth. Their commitment was to be personal and genuine. If not, the time of judgment would come in which the nations would question whether or not Israel was in fact the people of the Lord.

**Rebellion, Judgment, Grace (29:10–30:20).** Moses anticipated not only Israel's rebellion and God's judgment but also God's grace toward the repentant. God would visit His people in their day of calamity and exile and would cause them once more to reflect on their covenant privileges.

God then would exercise His grace and restore them to full covenant partnership with its blessings.

**Choices (30:11-20).** Israel's pledge to faithful adherence to the terms of covenant could bring immediate and lasting reward. But disobedience would produce only judgment.

### FUTURE OF THE COVENANT (31:1-29)

**God, the True Leader (31:1-8).** Though the ceremony of covenant renewal is not narrated, it is clear that the new generation of Israelites recommitted themselves to the covenant. (It is implied in 29:10-13.) Moses reaffirmed God's role as the true leader of His people.

**God's Word (31:9-13).** God's provision for the future of the covenant included a leader (Joshua) to succeed Moses as covenant mediator, as well as a law, the covenant text delivered to the priests for safekeeping (31:9-13).

**God's Provision (31:14-29).** God provided Joshua as a successor to Moses. God's provision for the future of the covenant also included a song, whose purpose was to remind the nation of the covenant pledges they had made (see 31:30–32:43). Finally, God provided a record of the law so that future genera-

tions could know God's will (30:24-27). The Lord, true to ancient treaty form, invoked heaven and earth as witnesses to the promises that Israel had sworn.

### MOSES' SONG (31:30–32:43)

This wonderful hymn of covenant commitment extols the God of Israel for His greatness and righteousness despite the wickedness of His people. He had created them and had redeemed and preserved them. They rebelled in turn and followed other gods. This course of action provoked His judgment in the past and would do so in the future. At last, however, God would remember His covenant and bring His people salvation.

### END OF MOSES' MINISTRY (32:44–34:12)

**Narrative Interlude (32:44-52).** Having sung his song, Moses urged his people to subscribe to its demands as a covenant instrument. Then, in response to the command of the Lord, Moses ascended Mount Nebo to await the day of his death. That so great a leader as Moses was not spared judgment when he failed to trust God and respect His holiness served as a stern warning to Israel to avoid his mistakes.

**Moses' Final Act (33:1-29).** Before he left them, Moses offered his fellow Israelites a will and testament similar to that with which Jacob had blessed his sons (see Gen. 49:2-27). After praising the God of deliverance and covenant, he listed the tribes by name, assigning to each a prophetic blessing. He concluded with praise of Israel's Lord and a promise that His chosen ones would ultimately triumph over all their foes.

**Moses' Death (34:1-12).** Having ascended Mount Nebo (or Pisgah), Moses viewed all the land of promise, a land promised to the patriarchs but denied to Moses because of his sin (see 32:51). He then died and was buried by the Lord in an unknown and unmarked grave. With great lament the people of Israel mourned his passing. Though Joshua possessed the spirit and authority of Moses, neither he nor any man to come could compare with this giant on the earth whom God knew "face to face" and who had been the great spokesman for God.

***Contemporary Significance.*** Deuteronomy was addressed specifically to a younger generation of Israelites poised to enter the promised land. However, it conveys timeless principles and theological truths that are appropriate to the modern church and world. That new generation of Israelites serves as a model for God's people in every age. We, like they, are a people with a past in which God has acted for our salvation and has revealed His will for our lives. But it is not enough to have a proud heritage of faith. We, like they, are a people with a present. We too are personally to commit ourselves to God today. Finally, we, like they, are a people with a future dependent on our continuing faithfulness to God.

Deuteronomy's covenant anticipates that new covenant—not written on stone but on human hearts (Jer. 31:33-34)—which is finally fulfilled in Christ (Matt. 26:28; Mark 14:24; Luke 22:20). The God of Israel redeemed them from bondage and chaos and chose to identify with them in an everlasting covenant bond. In and through His Son Jesus Christ, He has graciously offered the same to all people everywhere.

***Ethical Value.*** Deuteronomy's frequent appeal for Israel to love God (6:5; 10:12; 11:1,13,22; 19:9; 30:6,16,20) shows that the aim of Old Testament law was not legalism but love-inspired service. Indeed, when Jesus was questioned about the greatest of the Old Testament laws, He quoted Deuteronomy 6:4-5.

Israel's love—like that of the Christian (1 John 4:19)—is grounded in a prior experience of God's redeeming love. Israel's love for God—again like that of the Christian (1 John 3:18; 4:20-21)—is true love only to the extent it is shared with others (Deut. 10:19). The Ten Commandments underscore that God demands not just respect from people (5:6-15) but respect for other people (6:16-21). While the Ten Commandments have a timeless quality, they are truly significant only to those committed to the God behind them.

## Questions for Reflection

1. What is the meaning of the name *Deuteronomy?* How appropriate is it for the contents of the book?

2. What are the basic elements of the ancient treaty form? How is Deuteronomy like ancient treaties? How is it different?

3. Why is it important for each generation to commit itself afresh to God's lordship?

4. Explain how the command to love God completely and exclusively is the foundation of the whole law. Can one love God and not love others?

5. Why was it important
   a. for the Israelites to destroy the Canaanite population of the promised land?
   b. to worship God at one central sanctuary?

6. What qualities were to distinguish the leaders of God's people? What qualities were to distinguish God's people from the Canaanites?

7. How does the history of Israel from the conquest through the exile to the restoration of Jerusalem illustrate the blessings and curses of the covenant?

8. How does God provide for the future of His covenant people?

## Sources for Additional Study

Craigie, Peter C. *The Book of Deuteronomy.* The New International Commentary on the Old Testament. Grand Rapids: Eerdmans, 1976.

Goldberg, Louis. *Deuteronomy. Bible Study Commentary.* Grand Rapids: Zondervan, 1986.

Kline, Meredith G. *Treaty of the Great King.* Grand Rapids: Eerdmans, 1963.

Merrill, Eugene H. *Deuteronomy.* New American Commentary. Nashville: Broadman & Holman, 1994.

Rad, Gerhard von. *Deuteronomy.* Philadelphia: Westminster, 1966.

Schultz, Samuel J. *Deuteronomy: The Gospel of Love.* Everyman's Bible Commentary. Chicago: Moody, 1971.

Thompson, J. A. *Deuteronomy: An Introduction and Commentary.* Downers Grove: InterVarsity, 1974.

# THE HISTORICAL BOOKS

## KENNETH A. MATHEWS

The Historical Books in the English Bible are Joshua, Judges, Ruth, 1 and 2 Samuel, 1 and 2 Kings, 1 and 2 Chronicles, Ezra, Nehemiah, and Esther. At first the Books of 1 and 2 Samuel were one book, as were Kings, Chronicles, and Ezra-Nehemiah. The Septuagint, the ancient Greek translation, was the first to divide the books. The Latin Vulgate and English versions have continued this practice. (The Hebrew division of these books did not occur until the Middle Ages.) Our English translators, again following the Septuagint, arrange the Historical Books in a loosely chronological order. This continuous narrative traces the history of Israel from the conquest of Canaan by Joshua (about 1400 B.C.) to the restoration of the Jews during the Persian period (about 400 B.C.).

The Hebrew canon arranges the Historical Books differently. The Hebrew canon consists of three divisions (Law, Prophets, and Writings). Joshua, Judges (omitting Ruth), 1 and 2 Samuel, and 1 and 2 Kings are in the second division, the Prophets. Within this division they are designated the Former Prophets (the Latter Prophets are Isaiah, Jeremiah, Ezekiel, and the twelve Minor Prophets). First and Second Chronicles, Ezra, and Nehemiah occur in the Writings as the final four books of the Hebrew canon. They, however, have a reverse order: Ezra, Nehemiah, and 1 and 2 Chronicles. The Books of Ruth and Esther also appear in the Writings. They, with the

Song of Solomon, Lamentations, and Ecclesiastes, constitute the five *Megilloth* (*scrolls*) read by the Jews at various feasts.

The Former Prophets (Joshua, Judges, Samuel, and Kings) continue the narrative of Genesis through Deuteronomy, which tells of Israel's birth and rise as a nation. Deuteronomy concludes with the appointment of Joshua as Moses' successor who eventually led Israel into the land. Joshua through 2 Kings relate the occupation of the land of Canaan, the rise of the Hebrew monarchy, and conclude with the destruction and exile of the nation by the Babylonians.

The heading *Former Prophets* indicates that the rabbis did not read these books as histories (in our modern sense). Although written in narrative form, they were *prophetic*. Like the oracles of the Latter Prophets, these "histories" declared the word of the LORD. They do not give an exhaustive history or a political account (as modern history writing would do). Rather, they interpret Israel's history from the theological perspective of God's covenant with Israel. As prophetic writings, they present God's evaluation and verdict on the history of Israel. They are not merely a history of Israel's religion either. (The Hebrew historians did not differentiate between Israel's political fortunes and its religious life.) The narrative in Joshua through 2 Kings shows that Israel's success or failure as a nation was determined by God's intervention in its history. God's kindness or judgment was in response to the spiritual and moral condition of the people with respect to their fidelity to the Mosaic covenant (Exod. 20–24). In particular, the Former Prophets—especially 1 and 2 Kings—were influenced by Deuteronomy's understanding of the covenant. This understanding emphasizes covenant loyalty and exclusive worship of God and explains how history is affected by a nation's morality.

The authors of Joshua, Judges, Samuel, and Kings are unknown since the works are anonymous. The six books show independence but also have a relationship. Each book can be read as a literary whole, possessing its peculiar literary arrangement and theological emphasis. They also evidence continuity based on their common subject and, in some cases, their common forms of expression. Each contributes to the consecutively told history of Israel. The books overlap in other respects too. David's reign is related primarily in 2 Samuel but continues into 1 Kings 1–2. The death of Joshua is recounted in both Joshua (24:29-33) and Judges (2:8-10). Deuteronomy's style of language and its basic approach to interpreting history significantly influenced all four works.

The traditional view emphasized the discontinuity of the six books, attributing the four works to different authors. Even the early rabbis, however, attributed Judges and 1 and 2 Samuel to the prophet Samuel (with 2 Samuel finished by others). A convincing reconstruction of the history of the writing of these four works has to account both for their differences and distinctives and the apparent continuity of the books.

Some critical scholars believe that Joshua is best understood as the *conclusion* of the Pentateuch rather than the *introduction* to the history of Israel in the land. These scholars use the term *Hexateuch (six-book unit)* to highlight the unity of Genesis through Joshua. The remaining books, Judges through 2 Kings, are regarded as a separate composition. The editor of this history combined extensions of the sources that underlie the Hexateuch.

A competing opinion among scholars treats Deuteronomy through 2 Kings as the work of an unnamed editor deeply influenced by the themes of Deuteronomy. This editor wove sources together during the exile (about 550 B.C.). This history was at first unrelated to and independent of the Tetrateuch (Genesis through Numbers). The composition of this history involved lengthy and complex processes of sewing together written sources, authoring new material, and editing the whole into one narrative. Scholars debate the details of date and authorship, some suggesting one author and others proposing several with two or three editions of the work. Its proponents, however, generally accept that the core of Deuteronomy was authored in the mid-seventh century by an author drawing on ancient traditions from the time of Moses. Later an individual or group supporting Josiah's reforms expanded and reworked this core into the bulk of Deuteronomy through 2 Kings. This expanded history was later issued with minor additions to reflect the fall of Jerusalem in about 550 B.C.

In contrast to the traditional rabbinic opinion, these two critical theories emphasize the continuity of the Former Prophets. But in doing so they create a number of problems of their own. Scholars, for example, are not agreed on the process of compilation or on who the nameless editors were (priests, prophets, or sages?). The criteria used by source critics for discovering the underlying literary strands in the Former Prophets are as suspect as those employed for the Pentateuch. Most troubling to these composition theories is their dependence on a seventh-century date for Deuteronomy. Its literary form has, however, been shown to be much older than proposed. In fact, it corresponds in general to the political treaties among the Hittites (about 1400–1200 B.C.).

The challenge is to give due both to the continuity and disunity evidenced in the Former Prophets. The four books were likely once independent works, largely in their present form. These underwent a brief period of editorial integration after the destruction of Jerusalem. What they share with Deuteronomy is best attributed to the imposing figure of the prophet Moses. His theology of history, reflected in Deuteronomy, became the theological model by which Israel interpreted its history. The Former Prophets play out what in essence Moses had forewarned concerning God's blessing and cursing (Deut. 28).

First and Second Chronicles and Ezra-Nehemiah give a second perspective on Israel's history, complementing the account of Genesis through 2 Kings. First and Second Chronicles parallel this first history from creation to the destruction of Jerusalem. Ezra-Nehemiah continues the account with the return of the exiles from Babylon and the restoration of the religious life of Judah (about 400 B.C.). Since these books were written during and after the exile when there was no monarchy, they focus on the religious life of restored Israel. Temple worship and observance of the law of Moses are particularly emphasized.

Like the Former Prophets, the Books of Chronicles and Ezra-Nehemiah have been ascribed to a single author or compiler. The rabbinic tradition attributed these four books to Ezra the scribe. Some modern scholars who have emphasized the unity of the books in language, content, and perspective follow this position.

## QUEENS OF THE OLD TESTAMENT
### (Listed alphabetically)

| NAME | REFERENCE | IDENTIFICATION |
|---|---|---|
| Abijah | 2 Kgs 18:2 | Mother of King Hezekiah of Judah |
| Athaliah | 2 Kgs 11 | Evil daughter of Ahab and Jezebel; mother of King Ahaziah of Judah (only woman to rule Judah in her own right) |
| Azubah | 1 Kgs 22:42 | Mother of King Jehoshaphat of Judah |
| Bathsheba | 2 Sam 11–12; 1 Kgs 1–2 | Wife of Uriah, then wife of David and mother of Solomon |
| Esther | Esth 2–9 | Jewish wife of King Ahasuerus of Persia |
| Hamutal | 2 Kgs 23:31; 24:18 | Mother of King Jehoahaz and King Zedekiah of Judah |
| Hephzibah | 2 Kgs 21:1 | Mother of King Manasseh of Judah |
| Jecoliah | 2 Kgs 15:2 | Mother of King Azariah of Judah |
| Jedidah | 2 Kgs 22:1 | Mother of King Josiah of Judah |
| Jehoaddin | 2 Kgs 14:2 | Mother of King Amaziah of Judah |
| Jezebel | 1 Kgs 16:31; 18:13,19; 19:1-2; 21:1-25; 2 Kgs 9:30-37 | Evil wife of King Ahab of Israel (who promoted Baal worship, persecuted God's prophets, and planned Naboth's murder) |
| Maacah | 1 Kgs 15:10; 2 Chr 15:16 | Mother of King Abijah and grandmother of King Asa of Judah |
| Meshullemeth | 2 Kgs 21:19 | Mother of King Amon of Judah |
| Michal | 1 Sam 18:20-28; 26:44; 2 Sam 3:13-16; 6:20-23 | Daughter of Saul and first wife of David |
| Naamah | 1 Kgs 14:21,31 | Mother of King Rehoboam of Judah |
| Nehushta | 2 Kgs 24:8 | Mother of King Jehoiachin of Judah |
| Queen of Sheba | 1 Kgs 10:1-13 | Foreign queen who visited Solomon |
| Zebidah | 2 Kgs 23:36 | Mother of King Jehoiakim of Judah |

## RULERS OF ISRAEL AND JUDAH

### RULERS OF THE UNITED KINGDOM

Saul  1 Sam 9:1–31:13
David  1 Sam 16:1–1 Kgs 2:11
Solomon  1 Kgs 1:1–11:43

### RULERS OF THE DIVIDED KINGDOM

| RULERS OF ISRAEL | | RULERS OF JUDAH | |
| --- | --- | --- | --- |
| Jeroboam I | I Kgs 11:26—14:20 | Rehoboam | 1 Kgs 11:42–14:31 |
| | | Abijah (Abijam) | 1 Kgs 14:31–15:8 |
| Nadab | 1 Kgs 15:25-28 | Asa | 1 Kgs 15:8-24 |
| Baasha | 1 Kgs 15:27—16:7 | | |
| Elah | 1 Kgs 16:6-14 | | |
| Zimri | 1 Kgs 16:9-20 | | |
| Omri | 1 Kgs 16:15-28 | | |
| Ahab | 1 Kgs 16:28—22:40 | Jehoshaphat | 1 Kgs 22:41-50 |
| Ahaziah | 1 Kgs 22:40–2 Kgs 1:18 | Jehoram | 2 Kgs 8:16-24 |
| Jehoram (Joram) | 2 Kgs 1:17—9:26 | Ahaziah | 2 Kgs 8:24–9:29 |
| Jehu | 2 Kgs 9:1-10:36 | Athaliah | 2 Kgs 11:1-20 |
| Jehoahaz | 2 Kgs 13:1-9 | Joash | 2 Kgs 11:1–12:21 |
| Jehoash (Joash) | 2 Kgs 13:10—14:16 | Amaziah | 2 Kgs 14:1-20 |
| Jeroboam II | 2 Kgs 14:23-29 | Azariah (Uzziah) | 2 Kgs14:21; 15:1-7 |
| Zechariah | 2 Kgs 14:29—15:12 | | |
| Shallum | 2 Kgs 15:10-15 | Jotham | 2 Kgs 15:32-38 |
| Menahem | 2 Kgs 15:14-22 | | |
| Pekahiah | 2 Kgs 15:22-26 | | |
| Pekah | 2 Kgs 15:25-31 | Ahaz (Jehoahaz) | 2 Kgs 16:1-20 |
| Hoshea | 2 Kgs 15:30—17:6 | Hezekiah | 2 Kgs 18:1–20:21 |
| | | Manasseh | 2 Kgs 21:1-18 |
| | | Amon | 2 Kgs 21:19-26 |
| | | Josiah | 2 Kgs 21:26–23:30 |
| | | Jehoahaz II (Shallum) | 2 Kgs 23:30-33 |
| | | Jehoiakim (Eliakim) | 2 Kgs 23:34–24:5 |
| | | Jehoiachin (Jeconiah) | 2 Kgs 24:6-16; 25:27-30 |
| | | Zedekiah (Mattaniah) | 2 Kgs 24:17–25:7 |

Others, agreeing in principle with the idea of a single author or compiler, have proposed an unnamed author (the "Chronicler"). The Chronicler drew on sources, including the memoirs of Ezra and Nehemiah and the Books of Samuel and Kings. He completed his "Chronicler's History" no earlier than 400 B.C.

In a variation on this view, two different viewpoints are discerned within the history. First and Second Chronicles plus Ezra 1–6 was an early edition by the Chronicler (about 515 B.C.), in conjunction with the prophetic ministries of Haggai and Zechariah. At this time Israel's hope was for a restored Davidic monarchy (1 Chr. 3:17-19; see Ezra 1:8; 3:8; 5:1-2; 6:14; Hag. 2:6-9; 3:23; Zech. 3:1–4:14; 6:9-15). The inclusion of Ezra 7–10 (Ezra's reforms) and Nehemiah's material came later (about 400 B.C.). At this later time the community shifted its emphasis from the monarchy and the religious role of David to the law of Moses. Some prefer, therefore, to speak of a "Chronistic school" rather than one person.

The similar language and content of Chronicles and Ezra-Nehemiah points to a single work. Both works stress, for instance, the role of the temple and worship customs. Further evidence of linkage is 2 Chronicles 36:1-21, which recounts the pilfering of temple articles, and Ezra 1:7-11, which inventories the restored temple treasuries. Most significant is the verbatim agreement of 2 Chronicles' final verses (36:22-23) with the opening paragraph of Ezra (1:1-3a). These verses relate the decree of Cyrus announcing the release of the Jews from captivity. In fact, the last verse of 2 Chronicles ends in the middle of a thought that is completed in the Ezra version (1:3b). This duplication of verses, it is argued, indicates that the books were once bound as a consecutive whole. Evangelical as well as critical scholars hold this view of a single work. Conservative scholarship uniformly holds that the Chronicler used reliable sources and did not materially distort them.

Other scholars, both evangelical and critical, argue that Ezra and Nehemiah were the authors of their own works. Proponents of this position point to significant differences in both language and content between Chronicles and Ezra-Nehemiah. (For instance, Chronicles does not address the subject of mixed marriages.) Finally, the Hebrew arrangement of Ezra-Nehemiah followed by 1 and 2 Chronicles is said to evidence that the two were *not* authored as one piece. The common paragraph shared by the two can best be explained as a much later attempt to bind together what were once separate books.

The arrangement of the Hebrew canon, however, is not a decisive witness for either position. The arrangement is better explained by appeal to the envelope construction created by the repetition of the decree of Cyrus. In this arrangement, like bookends, Ezra begins and 2 Chronicles closes with the decree of Cyrus. This proclamation of freedom embodied the abiding hope that God would yet again gather the Jews dispersed among the nations. By closing the Hebrew canon on this note of freedom, the compiler emphasized this proclamation and therefore encouraged the Jews throughout the Diaspora.

In conclusion, the differences between the books cautions against concluding without more evidence that the works of Chronicles and Ezra-Nehemiah constituted an original Chronicler's history.

Ruth and Esther are included among the five *Megilloth*. These books—Song of Solomon, Ruth, Lamentations, Ecclesiastes, and Esther—are related to the five festivals (and fasts) of the Jewish calendar. Ruth, set at the harvest, is read at the Feast of Weeks (Pentecost), which celebrates the spring gathering (May-June). Esther's story gives the origins of the Feast of Purim and is read on that occasion (14th and 15th of Adar [Feb.–Mar.]). Purim is the only Old Testament feast not legislated by the Mosaic law.

# JOSHUA

The Book of Joshua is named after the book's focal character, who as Moses' successor led Israel into the promised land. The English title is derived from the Greek and Latin translations. The Hebrew name *Joshua (Yehosua)* means *The LORD is salvation*. The shortened form of Joshua (*Yesua*) is *Jesus* in Greek. Traditionally, the Jews assigned the book's authorship to Joshua. However, they recognized the evidence of later contributors too (for example, the report of Joshua's death [24:29]).

The authorship and date are disputed since the book is anonymous. Some interpreters believe the book was completed in the seventh or sixth centuries B.C. after a long process of compilation by unnamed editors as part of a large history influenced by the themes of Deuteronomy. (See "The Historical Books.") Other scholars argue for a view closer to the traditional opinion, dating the book within one generation of the events recorded (fourteenth century B.C.).

The book includes sources that are contemporary with Joshua (for example, 5:1,6; 6:25; 8:32; 18:9; 24:26) and also sources from a later time (for example, "to this day," 4:9; 5:9; 7:26; 10:27; 13:13). The book probably was based on an early core of testimony that was supplemented by an author no later than the tenth century B.C. There are hints that the book came from the early monarchy. (See, for example, the "book of Jashar" quoted in 10:13 and 2 Sam. 1:18.) The Book of Joshua addresses many of the same problems faced by Israel's kings. Leadership, land dispute, the location and role of the tabernacle, and how to deal with Canaanite populations were problems shared by Saul and David.

Although the book is constituted of different sources, this does not mean that they are inconsistent or contradictory. They have been written and gathered under the supervision of God's Spirit to present a unified message to God's people.

**Historical Setting.** Opinions differ on the date of the conquest. The traditional view has set the conquest in the fifth century (1406 B.C.), based on the date of the building of the temple in 966 B.C. This view is derived from the literal computation of 1 Kings 6:1, which places the exodus 480 years before Solomon's fourth year of reign. Other scholars have dated the conquest in the thirteenth century (about 1250 B.C.) because of archaeological evidence from Egypt and Palestine. In the latter view the 480 years of 1 Kings 6:1 is explained as a symbolic number for twelve generations between Solomon and the exodus (see the feature article "Dates of the Exodus").

The dispute cannot be easily resolved since the archaeological record is inconsistent and difficult to interpret. It cannot be decisive by itself, and therefore the question will eventually be decided on the balance of all the evidence.

More important is that varying views exist concerning the nature of the conquest. One school of thought rejects the tradition of a military invasion by Israel. It holds that the "conquest" was a slow infiltration of seminomadic tribes who migrated into Canaan from the desert over hundreds of years. These diverse tribes brought various traditions which together were shaped into a religious heritage adopted as Israel's history. This unsatisfactory opinion does not adequately account for the Bible's testimony of a rapid occupation by Joshua. Also it fails to explain why and how over such a long period of time these diverse tribes became unified.

A second view is that Israel emerged as a result of a social revolution inside Canaan. The people of Canaan rebelled against their kings, rejected Baalism, and adopted the new religion of Yahweh. This view is insufficient by itself since the biblical account does not explain the conquest as a political revolution with religious overtones. Also this interpretation imposes on the biblical traditions a contemporary model of social revolution.

Third, the traditional interpretation of a military invasion has the advantage of the biblical testimony. However, with this invasion the Joshua account also shows that there was some internal conversion to the religion of Yahwism brought by these newcomers. Rahab is an example. Also the four cities of the Hivites (9:17) entered into league with Israel. These examples may reflect a much wider movement within Canaan. Conversion of Canaanite peoples may explain the need for the covenant renewal ceremony in Joshua 24.

**Theme.** Under Joshua's leadership the people of God entered into the land of rest promised to their ancestors, because the people were careful not to depart from the "Book of the Law" of Moses (1:8).

 I. Claiming the Land (1:1–5:15)
 II. Conquering the Land (6:1–12:24)
 III. Distributing the Land (13:1–21:45)
 IV. Living in the Land (22:1–24:28)
 V. Resting in the Land (24:29–33)

**Purpose and Theology.**

1. The Book of Joshua traces the victory of God's people when they possessed the land of Canaan. The book continues the story of Israel's pilgrimage from Egypt to the promised land, demonstrating to all nations that Yahweh is God and He alone is to be worshiped (2:11; 4:24).

2. The Book of Joshua explains that God acts as the sovereign Lord of history who fulfills His promises to His people. The Lord is depicted as Israel's mighty warrior (5:14) who fights for His people and gives them rest from their enemies (11:20; 23:4).

3. The land is an important motif in the book. The promise of land for the patriarchs finds fulfillment in the conquering tribes who received what their fathers failed to enjoy (1:6; 11:23; 21:43-44). The importance of this theme is indicated by the detailed distribution of the land (13:1–21:45).

4. However, God grants His blessing only to a holy and obedient people (3:5; 4:10). Because the Lord is holy (5:15), He punishes the sin of His people (23:15-16) and restores them only upon their repentance (7:11-13).

5. The word of God given through Moses was the standard by which both God's faithfulness and Israel's fidelity were measured. God keeps His promises (21:45; 23:9). The people were to be careful to live according to the law of Moses (1:7,16-17).

6. The Lord accomplishes His purposes for Israel through a chosen leader. Joshua followed in the footsteps of Moses as God's ordained spokesperson (1:5; 4:14).

7. The book also has a message of hope for later generations of the Hebrew people who had lost the land through dispersion or captivity. Future generations of God's people could take hope that since God had achieved this victory for ancient Israel, He could do it again for them.

8. God's people will enter into a final rest through faith in the Lord Jesus Christ (Heb. 4:6-11).

## CLAIMING THE LAND (1:1–5:15)

The opening section shows how God enabled Israel to enter the land. The commander was chosen and the land surveyed (2:1-24). The people crossed the Jordan with the help of the Lord, which was memorialized for future generations. Once in the land, the people renewed their commitment to the Lord and worshiped in celebration.

*Joshua's Commission (1:1-18).* The Lord commissioned Joshua as Moses' successor (see Num. 27:18; Deut. 34:9) to lead Israel into the promised land. God instructed Joshua to be obedient to the law of Moses and to be courageous so that he might succeed.

Joshua commanded the officers of the camp to prepare the people for crossing the Jordan. He reminded the Transjordan tribes of Reuben, Gad, and the half-tribe of Manasseh that they had committed themselves under Moses (see Num. 32) to cross and help their brothers.

The people agreed and echoed the exhortation of God to Joshua, "Only be strong and courageous!"

*Rahab's Conversion (2:1-24).* Joshua dispatched two spies to discover the strength of Jericho. The city was strategically located at the pass leading from the Jordan Valley to the central highlands. The spies entered the house of the prostitute Rahab, who concealed their presence from the king of Jericho.

The story's events confirmed to the spies that Israel's enemies were weak in spite of their towering walls. Jericho's foolish king was easily tricked by the lowly harlot Rahab, whereas the Hebrew spies were clever when they entered into an oath with her. Also the spies learned that the city's population was terrified of Israel. Another assurance of Israel's ulti-

mate victory was Rahab's conversion and admission that the Lord had given the land into their hands.

Rahab showed her faith in God's promises by helping the spies escape. She tied a scarlet thread to her window that signaled her salvation. Rahab's faith in God and her action in behalf of the spies became a model for Christian faith and works (Heb. 11:31; Jas. 2:25).

*Crossing the Jordan (3:1-17).* Joshua ordered the people to prepare for crossing by sanctifying themselves. The priests carrying the ark of the covenant led the procession. The ark symbolized the presence of God. It commonly rested in the tabernacle's holy of holies where the glory of God appeared (see Exod. 25:1-22; see the feature article "Tabernacle").

When the Levites who bore the ark entered the river, the waters stopped flowing at Adam (Tell ed-Damiyeh) near Zarethan. The extraordinary nature of the crossing is emphasized by the author, who explained that the river flooded its banks at that time of year. Yet Israel crossed the river bed on "dry" land.

The miraculous crossing magnified Joshua's leadership because it paralleled Moses' leadership at the Red Sea (4:14). The crossing also proved that the Lord was alive and would drive out Israel's enemies.

*Memorial Stones (4:1-24).* The Israelites erected a monument to commemorate their crossing. It was built of twelve stones, representing the twelve tribes of Israel. The stones were taken from the river where the Levites bearing the ark had stood. When future generations asked, "What do these stones mean?" the monument served to remind them of the miraculous crossing. Because of this miracle Joshua was exalted in the eyes of the people. Another purpose of the miracle was that all nations might recognize the power of God.

***Spiritual Readiness (5:1-15).*** The crossing of the river terrorized the Canaanite populace. Before Israel could proceed, however, the people had to prepare themselves spiritually.

God ordered Joshua to renew their covenant commitment by circumcision, the sign of God's election of Abraham and his descendants (see Gen. 17). Circumcision had been abandoned during Israel's sojourn in the wilderness because of disobedience. This new generation underwent circumcision as a test of their loyalty to the Lord. By following God's directions, Joshua in effect disabled his whole army. Because of their circumcision, God named the place Gilgal, meaning a rolling. God explained that He had rolled away the disgrace of Egyptian bondage.

The people celebrated a new Passover (see Exod. 12; Lev. 23:4-5; Num. 9:1-14). The Passover festival remembered God's deliverance of Israel when the angel of death plagued the firstborn of Egypt. (See the feature article "Israel's Festivals and Feasts.") For God's people today, Jesus is the Passover Lamb who delivers them from sin and death (1 Cor. 5:7).

The people for the first time began to eat food harvested from Canaan. In the wilderness their diet was the manna provided by God. The cessation of manna and their harvest of the land were reminiscent of God's promises that they would possess a land flowing with milk and honey (Exod. 3:8).

Also the Lord prepared Joshua spiritually by appearing to him. Joshua did not recognize the Lord until He identified Himself as the commander of the Lord's armies. Like Moses, Joshua stood on holy ground because of the presence of God (see Exod. 3:1-12). He humbled himself by taking off his sandals.

## CONQUERING THE LAND (6:1–12:24)

Joshua directed three campaigns in Canaan. The central campaign included Jericho, Ai, and Gibeon. The southern campaign was against a five-king coalition, which was led by the king of Jerusalem. The northern campaign was against a coalition of city-states led by Hazor. Through these battles the people learned that Yahweh fought for them and secured their victory.

***Shouting Jericho Down (6:1-27).*** The city of Jericho stood in the way of Israel's possession of the land. The city was one of the oldest in the world, but it was not particularly large. The Bible presents Jericho as a formidable city with imposing walls that could not be scaled.

Joshua and the people marched in silence around the city one time for each of six days. On the seventh day they marched seven times. At the appropriate signal the priests blew their trumpets, and the people gave a mighty shout. The walls collapsed, and the soldiers entered straight into the city.

The organization of the march placed the ark at the center of the parade. The ark indicated that God was in their midst as He was when they crossed the Jordan. No military general could have accepted such a plan, but Joshua was not counting on human ingenuity. The purpose of the strategy was to test their faith and their patience. By faith the walls collapsed (Heb. 11:30).

The spies rescued Rahab and her family, but the rest of the population was killed and the city burned. The city and all that was in it were "devoted to the LORD." The expression "devoted" *(herem)* meant that the city was banned from Israelite possession because it was solely for the Lord (see Deut. 20:16-18). The ban removed any economic motiva-

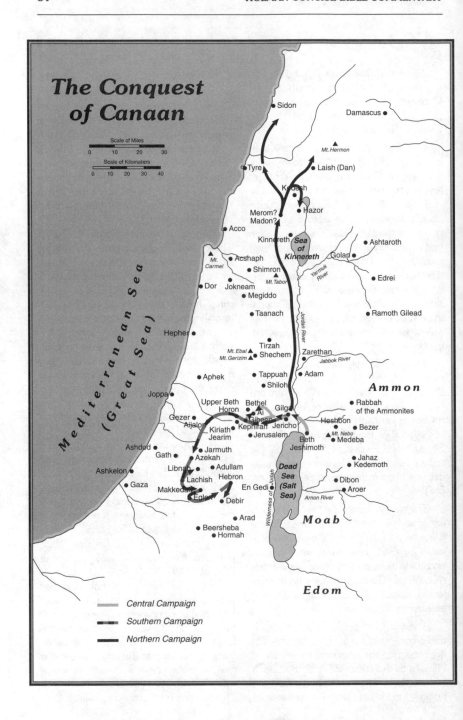

The Conquest of Canaan

Scale of Miles
0    10    20    30

Scale of Kilometers
0    10    20    30    40

Mediterranean Sea (Great Sea)

Sidon
Damascus
Mt. Hermon
Tyre
Laish (Dan)
Kedesh
Merom?
Madon?
Hazor
Acco
Kinnereth
Sea of Kinnereth
Golan
Ashtaroth
Mt. Carmel
Acshaph
Shimron
Mt. Tabor
Edrei
Dor
Jokneam
Megiddo
Yarmuk River
Ramoth Gilead
Taanach
Jordan River
Hepher
Tirzah
Mt. Ebal
Mt. Gerizim
Shechem
Zarethan
Jabbok River
Aphek
Tappuah
Shiloh
Adam
Ammon
Joppa
Upper Beth Horon
Bethel
Ai
Gibeon
Gilgal
Rabbah of the Ammonites
Gezer
Aijalon
Kephirah
Jericho
Heshbon
Bezer
Kiriath Jearim
Jerusalem
Mt. Nebo
Medeba
Ashdod
Beth Jeshimoth
Jahaz
Kedemoth
Gath
Jarmuth
Azekah
Adullam
Wilderness of Judah
Ashkelon
Libnah
Hebron
Dead Sea (Salt Sea)
Dibon
Aroer
Gaza
Makkedah
Lachish
En Gedi
Eglon
Debir
Arnon River
Moab
Arad
Beersheba
Hormah
Edom

Central Campaign
Southern Campaign
Northern Campaign

tion for the Israelites' action. It was a "holy war" because Israel fought at the instructions of the Lord and received no benefits from the city's destruction.

The ban was not always employed by the Israelites, and even when in effect there were exceptions. The exceptions at Jericho were Rahab and some costly metals that were placed in the Lord's treasury. By the grace of God, Rahab was spared from the ban because of her faith (Heb. 11:31).

God placed Canaanite cities under the ban so that Israel would not fall victim to the sinful influence of their enemies (Deut. 20:18). In this case the ban was eternal, and anyone who rebuilt the city was cursed of God. The truth of God's word was demonstrated in the judgment rendered against Hiel, who lost his two sons for rebuilding the city (1 Kgs. 16:34).

**Disobedience and Defeat (7:1-26).** The Israelites stood guilty before God because of the sin of Achan, who took from the devoted things at Jericho. The covenant requirement of community responsibility explains why all Israel suffered as a result of Achan's sin. Since they were bound together as one family, the whole group suffered for one man's sin.

The people acted presumptuously by not consulting the Lord before they launched an offensive against Ai. They met with sudden defeat, and "the hearts of the people melted" with fear (see 2:9).

Joshua interceded for his people and questioned why God had brought Israel to this tragic end. God chided Joshua, explaining that Israel suffered because of sin, not because the Lord had failed Joshua. The sin of Israel meant that God no longer fought for them. Joshua called all the people together, and by the process of casting lots he discovered that Achan was the culprit.

Achan confessed that he "saw . . . coveted . . . and took" the devoted things and hid them in his tent. This incident illustrates James's warning that wicked desires lead to sin, and sin leads to death (Jas. 1:14-15). Achan and his family were stoned, and his possessions were burned (Josh. 7:24-25). Because the entire community was responsible for covenant holiness, all of Israel participated in destroying what pertained to the sin. The site of the stoning was named Achor, meaning *trouble*. The name plays on the name of Achan because he had troubled Israel.

**Obedience and Victory (8:1-35).** God instructed Joshua to attack Ai with all his troops. When Israel had attacked before, they did not have the explicit direction of the Lord; and they were presumptuous and haughty (7:3). Now with their sin behind them, Israel chose to obey the Lord.

Unlike Jericho, where God performed a miracle, Israel accomplished the defeat of Ai through Joshua's God-given military strategy. Although they surprised the city by ambush, the success of the war was dependent upon God's blessing. As long as Joshua stretched forth his javelin in petition to God, the victory was Israel's. This is reminiscent of Moses' uplifted arms when Israel defeated Amalek (Exod. 17:8-13).

Israel destroyed the city but was permitted to take the spoil. Since the place was condemned to be a ruin, its name Ai, meaning *ruin,* was appropriate. Ancient Ai has been identified with the modern site of et-Tell, but this identification is disputed.

Israel had learned through tragedy that their success was solely dependent upon God. Therefore after their victory at Ai they worshiped the Lord with thanksgiving at Shechem. In accordance with Moses' instructions (Deut. 27:2-8), they read the covenant from Mount Gerizim and Mount Ebal. These two mounts form a natural amphitheater. The reading of the law by Joshua reflected the renewed commitment of God's people (see 2 Kgs. 23:2; Neh. 8).

**Gibeonites' Deception (9:1-27).** Moses gave Israel the rules of warfare (Deut. 7:1-2; 20:10-18). He required Israel to destroy the nations nearby in Canaan and spare the nations living afar.

The Gibeonites conspired to trick the Israelites into forming a peace treaty by giving the appearance of traveling from a far country. They wore old clothes, carried mended sacks, and had dry, moldy food. They acted as though they knew only of Israel's early wars under Moses and not their recent victories. They repeatedly flattered Joshua and the elders by referring to themselves as "your servants." Israel failed by not consulting the Lord before entering the covenant. The people grumbled when they learned that the Gibeonites had deceived them. They probably feared God's wrath as at Ai because they were prohibited from falsely swearing an oath in the Lord's name (Lev. 19:12).

When the Gibeonites confessed their trickery, Joshua punished them by conscripting the Gibeonites and their descendants to serve the tabernacle's altar. This oath was observed until the days of Saul, when he ruthlessly broke the treaty (2 Sam. 21:1-2).

Although the Israelites failed God, the fear of the Gibeonites was another assurance that Joshua would succeed among the nations.

**God Fights for Israel (10:1-43).** The Gibeonite deception gave occasion for Israel to fight a coalition of kings in the south. Neighboring Amorite kings led by Jerusalem waged war against Gibeon because of its defection. With the destruction of Jericho, Ai, and now the capitulation of Gibeon and its Hivite cities (9:17; 11:19-20), Jerusalem was threatened on all sides.

The Gibeonites appealed to Joshua for deliverance, and he marched by night from Gilgal to Gibeon. The conflict spread to the countryside as the fleeing Amorites escaped. God intervened miraculously as at Jericho and fought for Israel by hurling hailstones that killed more than even Israel's swords killed.

Since the enemy was in disarray, Joshua wanted to finish the battle before they could regroup the next day. He prayed to the Lord for the sun to delay its descent. Joshua's prayer was also found in another source called the book of Jashar (see 2 Sam. 1:18). The victory was God's more than Israel's: "Surely the LORD was fighting for Israel!" The author declared that there was no day like it.

The kings of the coalition were captured and executed by Joshua, and the southern cities were destroyed according to the Lord's command. Since Jerusalem is not included in the cities captured, it probably survived. Nonetheless the area was incapacitated by Joshua.

**Hamstringing Hazor (11:1-15).** A confederation of kings led by Jabin, the dynastic ruler of Hazor, campaigned against Israel. The military strength of the alliance was its numerous chariots. The battle waged at the Waters of Merom near Hazor.

Unlike the previous accounts, the author did not give as many details of the battle and was satisfied with giving a theological summary. God required Joshua to hamstring the captured horses and burn their chariots. This prevented Israel from relying on military prowess. Like Jericho and Ai, Hazor was burned in accordance with Moses' instructions (Deut. 7:1-2; 20:16-17).

**Counting the Kings (11:16–12:24).** This summary of captured lands and their slain kings is a tribute to God's faithfulness. The passage emphasizes that Joshua took "the entire land." This included the lands of the Anakites, whom the Israelites had initially feared the most (Num. 13:28,33; Deut. 9:2). God incited Israel's enemies to wage war, and then He destroyed them because of their sin (Josh. 11:20). This was the method God used to give the land to Israel as He fulfilled His promise to Moses.

The list of kings begins with Og and Sihon, whom Moses defeated (see Num. 21:21-35). The kings defeated by Joshua were thirty-one. This list of kings includes some kings not specifically mentioned in the narrative. This record of Israel's acquisitions showed future generations what faith could accomplish. It also was a rebuke to those who had refused to take the land.

## DISTRIBUTING THE LAND (13:1–21:45)

The detailed description of Israel's inheritance may be tedious to modern readers. For the author it proved the faithfulness of God's word. The territories given by Moses are listed first and then the land distributed by Joshua.

*Nondistributed Lands (13:1-7).* Joshua was too old to finish driving out Israel's enemies. However, God promised Joshua that the remaining lands would also become an inheritance for Israel. These territories were the Philistine cities, the Phoenician coast, and the mountain area of Lebanon. During the reigns of David and Solomon, Israel conquered these areas (2 Sam. 8:1; 24:6-7; 1 Kgs. 9:19).)

*Transjordan Lands (13:8-33).* Joshua allocated the lands across the Jordan that Moses had promised to Gad, Reuben, and the half-tribe of Manasseh. These tribes had initially questioned Joshua's leadership (1:17), but Joshua proved himself by following the example of Moses.

*West of the Jordan (14:1-5).* The remaining tribes, with the exception of Levi (see 21:1-42), received from Joshua their possessions on the west side of the Jordan. Each allotment was determined by the casting of lots (see Num. 26:55).

*Caleb's Courage (14:6-15).* Caleb was the first of Judah to claim his land. He recalled how forty-five years earlier he had brought a favorable report at Kadesh Barnea when he urged Israel to possess Canaan. Caleb's testimony magnified God's faithfulness. Even in his old age Caleb had the courage and vigor to follow the Lord.

*Judah's Allotment (15:1-63).* Judah was the first tribe to receive its inheritance. It was the largest and most prestigious tribe (see Gen. 49:8-12). Caleb's lot was in Judah. He possessed Hebron by driving out the Anakites. Othniel, in behalf of Caleb, captured Debir and received Caleb's daughter Acsah in marriage. Acsah, like her father, had a zeal for the promises of God. Jerusalem was in Judah's territory, but the Israelites could not dispossess the Jebusites.

*Ephraim and Manasseh (16:1– 17:18).* The lands belonging to the two sons of Joseph, Ephraim and Manasseh, were in the central highlands. Ephraim received its allotment before Manasseh because it had the greater blessing of Jacob (Gen. 48:17-20). Ephraim failed to drive out the Canaanites from Gezer, although Joshua had killed its king (Josh. 12:12). Ephraim chose to use them as forced labor. The city became a royal possession under Solomon (1 Kgs. 9:16).

Joshua distributed land to the families of Manasseh west of the Jordan. He honored all of God's promises, as shown by his giving land to Zelophehad's daughters (Num. 27:1-7). Like Ephraim, Manasseh also chose to coexist with Canaanite cities. Later these areas were subjugated by Israel (see 1 Kgs. 9:15-22). When Ephraim complained that their lot was too small, Joshua challenged them to increase their territory by driving out the Canaanites.

**Shiloh (18:1-10).** The people set up the tabernacle at Shiloh, giving evidence that Israel had gained control of the land. However, seven tribes had not made their claim, and Joshua chided them for their reluctance.

**The Last Tribes (18:11–19:48).** The land was apportioned to Benjamin, Simeon, Zebulun, Issachar, Asher, Naphtali, and Dan. The inheritance of Benjamin was small but strategic; it was a buffer zone between the mighty states of Judah and Ephraim. Its cities of Bethel and Jerusalem were the most influential cities in the worship of Israel. King Saul and the apostle Paul were Benjamites.

The inheritance of Simeon was absorbed by the tribe of Judah according to Jacob's blessing (Gen. 49:7). Simeon may have lost its blessing as a result of Simeon's and Levi's murder of Shechem (Gen. 34:25).

The final lot fell to the Danites. Its territory was very small, and the Amorites were too great for them (see Judg. 1:34). Yet even they succeeded in having a portion with Israel by possessing Leshem, which they renamed Dan (see Judg. 18).

**Joshua the Builder (19:49-51).** The courageous leader Joshua was the last to receive his portion. The people triumphantly gave Joshua his allotment in Ephraim. Joshua was not only a defender of the land but also a builder.

**Cities of Refuge (20:1-9).** The cities of refuge illustrated God's continued grace toward Israel while living in the land. According to Moses' instruction, six cities were set aside as places of safety for manslayers who unintentionally killed

(see Num. 35:9-34; Deut. 4:41-43; 19:1-14).

When the manslayer appealed for refuge at one of the designated cities, the elders protected him from a relative of the deceased who was the avenger. If the elders found the manslayer innocent of murder, he remained in the city until the death of the high priest (see Num. 35:25-28). However, if the slayer was found guilty of homicide, the city executed him (see Exod. 21:12-14; Num. 35:29-34).

**The Levites' Possession (21:1-42).** Rather than receiving a tract of land, the service of the Lord was the Levites' special possession (Deut. 10:8-9). They received forty-eight cities scattered throughout all Israel in accordance with God's promise (Num. 35:1-5). This geographical distribution enabled the Levites to influence all the tribes as they taught them God's precepts (Deut. 33:10).

**God's Promises (21:43-45).** The summary emphasizes the major motif of the book: God fought Israel's battles and fulfilled His promises to their fathers. They rested from their wars and enjoyed the inheritance from the Lord.

## LIVING IN THE LAND (22:1-24:28)

This section shows how Israel preserved itself in the land by carefully observing the word of the Lord. Joshua exhorted them to live in faith, and the people entered into a covenant to serve the Lord. This served as an example of how future generations should live in commitment to one another and to God.

**Unity Preserved (22:1-34).** With the land under the control of Israel, Joshua commended and then released the Transjordan tribes to return to their allotted territories.

The Transjordan tribes erected an altar on the west bank as a testimony to their relationship with their brothers, but Israel misunderstood this as an act of idolatry. Israel gathered for war because they

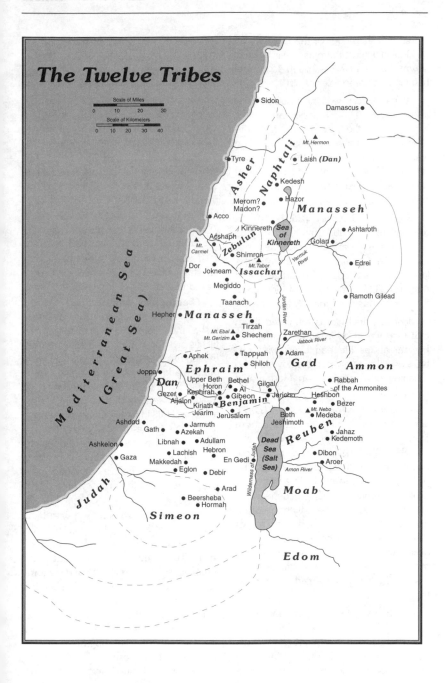

# The Twelve Tribes

Scale of Miles
0    10    20    30

Scale of Kilometers
0    10    20    30    40

Mediterranean Sea (Great Sea)

Sidon •

Damascus •

▲ Mt. Hermon

Tyre •

Laish (Dan) •

*Asher*

*Naphtali*

Kedesh •

Merom? •
Madon? • Hazor

Acco •

*Manasseh*

Ashtaroth •

Kinnereth • Sea of Kinnereth

Golan •

Acshaph •
▲ Mt. Carmel

*Zebulun*

Shimron •

Yarmuk River

Dor •     Joknean •

Mt. Tabor ▲   *Issachar*

Edrei •

Megiddo •

Jordan River

Ramoth Gilead •

Taanach •

Hepher •  *Manasseh*

Tirzah •
Mt. Ebal ▲   • Shechem
Mt. Gerizim ▲

Zarethan •

Jabbok River

Aphek •     • Tappuah    • Adam

Joppa •   *Ephraim*    • Shiloh    *Gad*    *Ammon*

*Dan*   Upper Beth  Bethel   Gilgal •
Horon •   • Ai
Gezer •  Kephirah •  • Gibeon    Jericho •

• Rabbah of the Ammonites

Aijalon •   • Kiriath   *Benjamin*   Heshbon •

Jearim   Jerusalem •                Bezer •

Ashdod •   • Jarmuth              Beth ▲ Mt. Nebo
Gath •    • Azekah              Jeshimoth  • Medeba

Ashkelon •   Libnah •   • Adullam            *Reuben*    Jahaz •
• Lachish  Hebron •                        Kedemoth •

Gaza •   Makkedah •      • En Gedi   Dead Sea (Salt Sea)   Dibon •
• Eglon   • Debir                            • Aroer

*Judah*                     Arnon River

• Arad

Wilderness of Judah    *Moab*

• Beersheba
• Hormah

*Simeon*

*Edom*

feared that the anger of the Lord would be kindled against them as it was at Peor (Num. 25) and at Ai (Josh. 7:6-12). Israel had learned not to tolerate sin.

A delegation led by Phineas was investigated. The Transjordan tribes explained that the altar was built for a witness and not for animal sacrifice. The war was averted, and the altar was named "Witness." This incident showed how Israel should resolve intertribal disputes.

***Farewell Sermon (23:1-16).*** At the end of his public ministry, Joshua summoned Israel and exhorted them not to ally with the nations remaining in the land. God had fought for Israel; but if they turned from their love of God, then they would be abandoned by the Lord.

Joshua's final words reminded them that God would be as sure to carry out His threats as He had been with His blessings. If they violated the covenant by pursuing other gods, then God would expel them.

***Covenant Renewal (24:1-7).*** Joshua convened the tribes at Shechem to renew their oath of covenant loyalty (see 8:30-35). The preamble of the covenant identified God and Israel as the parties of the covenant. The historical prologue rehearsed God's benevolent acts toward Israel. The covenant stipulated the requirements God expected of His vassals. Joshua challenged them to decide whom they would serve: "As for me and my household, we will serve the Lord." The elders consented and ratified the covenant.

Joshua recorded the covenant in the "Book of the Law of God." This implies that Joshua was contributing to Holy Scripture (see 8:31-34; 23:6). Also Joshua placed a memorial stone under a tree as a witness against the people if they failed the Lord.

## RESTING IN THE LAND (24:29-33)

The epilogue ends with three heroes of faith buried in the promised land. Joshua died at at the age of 110 years and received his inheritance as a reward for his courage at Kadesh Barnea (Num. 13-14). Under his leadership Israel served the Lord obediently.

Joseph also believed God would lead His people into the promised land. His bones were buried in Canaan as he requested in faith (Gen. 50:25-26). Unlike Aaron, who died in the wilderness (Num. 20:28), his son Eleazar entered the promised land and was buried there.

These three burials were three seals attesting to God's fulfillment of His promises to the fathers.

***Theological and Ethical Value.*** The Book of Joshua portrays Yahweh first as the God who acts in history to fulfill His promise to the patriarchs by giving the land to Israel. That the land is God's gift is made clear by the stopping of the Jordan River (Josh. 4) and the falling of the walls of Jericho (Josh. 6). God's faithfulness to fulfill His promises in the past (21:43-45) is the ground for confidence that God will continue to be faithful. In time all the promised land would belong to God's people (see 13:1). In time God's people will enjoy the promised rest (Heb. 3–4).

Second, Yahweh is a God with high ethical expectations who punishes sin and rewards faithfulness. Possession of the land of promise was contingent on its inhabitants' conformity to God's moral demands. For their sins the Canaanites suffered a judgment of annihilation and enslavement at the hands of Israel (see Gen. 15:16). When Achan sinned, Israel likewise experienced judgment in the form of defeat (Josh. 7:1-26). Future generations of Israelites would learn the cost of disobedience when the Assyrians and Babylonians would exile them from the land of promise. In contrast, Caleb and Joshua serve as models of those whom God rewards for faithfulness (14:1-15; 19:49-51).

## Questions for Reflection

1. What are the characteristics of godly leadership?

2. What does the Book of Joshua teach about God and His relationship to nature and human history?

3. What are God's expectations of His people?

4. How should God's people live during times of prosperity?

5. How should God's people deal with problems that threaten their unity?

## Sources for Additional Study

Davis, Dale Ralph. *No Falling Words. Expositions of the Book of Joshua.* Grand Rapids: Baker, 1988.

Enns, Paul P. *Joshua.* Grand Rapids: Zondervan, 1981.

Jensen, Irving L. *Joshua: Rest-land Won.* Chicago: Moody, 1986.

# JUDGES

The Book of Judges is entitled after the military and civic leaders who were raised up by God to deliver Israel from its oppressors (2:16-19; Ruth 1:1; Acts 13:20). The Hebrew title *Judges* is followed by the ancient versions and the English tradition.

The judges were not trained arbiters of legal cases as the word *judge* means today. They were Spirit-endowed leaders who were chosen by God for specific tasks (see 3:9-10; 6:34; 11:29; 13:25). As judges they worked to bring about justice for the oppressed people of Israel. To avoid confusion with the modern connotation of *judged,* the NIV has translated "led" in many passages where it is more appropriate in context (4:4; 10:2-3; 12:8-11,13-14; 15:20; 16:31). The verb *led* is used most often by the author to describe the judges' function. The judges also "saved" and "delivered" Israel from their enemies (for example, 3:9,31; 4:14; 10:1; 13:5).

Two of the leaders, Othniel and Ehud, are described as "deliverers" (3:9,15). Only Gideon is not called judge or deliverer, but he is said to have saved Israel (6:14). On one occasion the Lord is described as "Judge" (11:27).

Although the judges were remembered primarily for their military prowess (2:16), they also functioned as civil authorities (see Deborah, 4:4-5). Some judges were not specifically said to have engaged in warfare (see Tola and Jair, 10:1-5).

The Book of Judges is an anonymous writing. The Jewish tradition that Samuel wrote the book cannot be substantiated. Some scholars believe, however, that Samuel best fits the evidence of the book.

Other interpreters believe the traditions of the judges came from times before Israel had a king but that the book was not completed until the seventh or sixth centuries B.C. (see 18:30). These interpreters view Judges as part of a large history influenced by the ideas of Deuteronomy. (See "The Historical Books.")

The book probably was compiled during the early monarchy. The recurring expression "in those days Israel had no king" (17:6; 18:1; 19:1; 21:25) indicates that the book was written from a later period when there was a central authority in Israel.

The book's sources were gradually collected at several stages into a unified whole. The stories of the individual judges (3:7–16:31), with their introduction (2:6–3:6), formed the first part of the book. These episodes were placed by the author in an interpretative framework introducing and concluding each judgeship. (For example, compare the opening and closing of the story of Othniel, 3:7,11.)

The appendix of stories about the Danite migration (Judg. 17–18) and the rape of the Levite's concubine (Judg. 19–21) were added last to illustrate the spiritual depravity of the period. The migration of the Danites actually occurred in the early part of the Judges period. The author, therefore, arranged his book along thematic lines rather than a strictly chronological one (see 18:1-31 with Josh. 19:40-47; also Judg. 1:34; 13:25).

The final step was the addition of 1:1–2:5, which served as an appropriate introduction to the book. It described events during the transition from Joshua to the next generation, while containing some flashbacks to the days of conquest.

Some scholars have questioned the literary and theological integrity of the book. However, the book's composite sources are not conflicting accounts. They rather have a thematic unity and a complementary theological perspective.

The era of the judges included the judgeships of Eli and Samuel, which are recorded in 1 Samuel (see 1 Sam. 4:18; 7:15; 8:1-2). The period of the judges extended from Joshua's death to the reign of Saul (about 1050 B.C.). The beginning of this period is debated since it is dependent on the date of the Exodus. (See "Dates of the Exodus.") If the early date is followed, the period was from about 1400–1050 B.C. The late date places the period from about 1250–1050 B.C.

During this period, the tribes of Israel were loosely bound together around the central sanctuary. The tribes were bound by their common commitment to the covenant made with God at Sinai (Exod. 20; 24). Their unity, however, was weakened by the inroads of Canaanite religion. When the tribes defected from the covenant, God used foreign oppressors to bring Israel to repentance.

**Theme.** Although Israel inherited the land of promise, they repeatedly disregarded their covenant obligations by doing what they "saw fit" (Judg. 21:25). Israel's disobedience resulted in their oppression at the hands of neighboring peoples (3:7-8). Such oppression led Israel to cry to the Lord for help (3:9). God responded to Israel's repentance and cries for mercy by sending judges or deliverers (3:9-10). Israel, however, returned to disobedience following the death of the judge (3:11-12). (See the feature article "The Cycle of the Judges.")

I. Spiritual Disobedience (1:1–3:6)

II. Political Destruction (3:7–16:31)

III. Moral Depravity (17:1–21:25)

***Purpose and Theology.***

1. The Book of Judges continues the unfolding story of Israel's life in the land promised to their fathers. Whereas the Book of Joshua describes Israel's faithfulness and success, Judges depicts Israel's covenant apostasy and the resulting oppression at the hands of their neighbors (2:6-7,10-16). The author tells events in the life of early Israel to warn his own generation about the results of disobedience.

2. The book explains why Israel suffered from their enemies (see 6:13). The fault lay in Israel's sin and not in God's failure to keep His covenant promises. God was longsuffering and merciful as He continued to raise up saviors to deliver His people even though they repeatedly forgot Him and worshiped the gods of Canaan (2:2-3,10-14,20-21). The book further explains that God left the nations among Israel so that He might test Israel's faithfulness (2:22-23; 3:4). Israel was also to learn discipline through warfare (3:1-3).

3. The book also demonstrates that God held Israel to account for its moral and religious behavior. Although they were the elect people of God and the recipients of God's promises, they would not enjoy the blessing of that privileged position if they continued in sin (2:1-15; 9:56-57; 10:11-16).

4. The book shows that the Lord, not the Canaanite deities, is the God of history and salvation. He is the true "Judge" who gave Israel into the hands of their enemies and then by His Spirit empowered deliverers to give them victory over their oppressors. Through miraculous intervention in history and nature, God accomplished His purposes for Israel

(2:16-18; 3:9-10,15; 4:15; 6:34; 7:22; 11:29; 14:6,19; 15:14).

5. An important issue facing the author was the leadership of the nation. The Book of Judges illustrates the kind of moral decay that occurred when there was an absence of godly leadership. There was a decline in the spiritual condition of the judges themselves as each cycle describes the judge and his era. Samson, the last judge of the book, was the embodiment of the immorality of the period.

The book shows what happened to Israel when there was no godly king to lead them. In this way the book advocates the institution of kingship. It must, however, be a kingship characterized by piety. Without godly leadership, the people drifted from the objective standard of God's word, and each "did as he saw fit" (17:6; 18:1; 19:1; 21:25).

6. The Book of Judges also shows the power of faith and prayer. The writer to the Hebrews recognized that the judges accomplished their exploits through faith in God (Heb. 11:32-33).

## SPIRITUAL DISOBEDIENCE (1:1-3:6)

The introductory section explains that Israel failed in the land because of its disobedience, immorality, and intermarriage with the Canaanites.

**Incomplete Obedience (1:1-2:5).** The Book of Judges begins by showing the proper way Israel should have dispossessed the Canaanites. Judah and Simeon joined forces to defeat the Canaanite despot Adoni-Bezek. A second example of success was Caleb's family, whose courage paved the way for the Judahites to control the hill country. Othniel, Caleb's nephew, captured Debir; and Caleb and drove out the Anakites from Hebron (see Othniel, 3:7-11).

However, the Israelites did not follow Caleb's example. All of the tribes, including Judah and Benjamin, failed to drive out the Canaanites completely. Even the nations they did subdue were placed under forced labor rather then destroyed. Israel chose material wealth over obedience to God.

The Lord came to Israel, appearing as an angel, and condemned them for their disobedience. Because Israel had disobeyed, God left their enemies in the land to be as "thorns" and a "snare" to Israel. Israel "wept" before the Lord for its sins, and the place was called Bokim, meaning *weepers*.

**Idolatry (2:6-3:4).** The second reason for Israel's failure was its idolatrous worship. This section previews the seven cycles of the judges who are described in the major section of the book that follows (3:7-16:31). The recurring cycle is Israel's sin, its servitude to foreign enemies, its cries of supplication, and the salvation God provided through a divinely appointed deliverer.

The death of Joshua and his generation explained why Israel began the cycles of sin and apostasy. The new generation did not know the Lord as their covenant God.

The *sin* of Israel was its worship of the Baals and Ashtoreths of the Canaanites. These were the male and female gods of the Canaanite religion. The religion of Canaan was a fertility cult known for its ritual prostitution. Therefore the author spoke of how Israel "prostituted themselves to other gods and worshiped them."

The chastening of the Lord was Israel's *servitude* to foreign nations. God responded to their repentance and *supplication* for deliverance by granting *salvation* through appointed judges. However, when the judge died, Israel repeated its idolatry; and the cycle of sin began again.

The Lord left the nations among Israel to punish them and to test Israel's faith. This testing also meant Israel would learn the discipline of warfare. Because of Israel's sin, the promise of rest and peace in the land was not realized (Josh. 23:1). Ongoing warfare became the pattern for Israel's existence.

***Intermarriage (3:5-6).*** A third reason for Israel's failure was its intermarriage with the Canaanites. The prohibition of marrying the Canaanites was because Israel "served their gods" and not because of racial differences (see Deut. 7:3-4).

## POLITICAL DESTRUCTION (3:7–16:31)

This section describes the seven cycles of Israel's sin and salvation by telling the stories of Israel's judges.

***Othniel (3:7-11).*** Because Israel sought the Baals and Asherahs of Canaan, God used the Mesopotamian King Cushan-Rishathaim to bring Judah to repentance. The name of the king, *Cushan of double-wickedness,* may have been a deliberate epithet given him by his enemies. The Spirit of the Lord came upon Othniel, Caleb's nephew (1:13; Josh. 15:18), and he expelled Cushan from the land. The eight-year reign of Cushan was followed by forty years of peace.

***Ehud and Shamgar (3:12-31).*** Eglon of Moab established a provincial capital at the "City of the Palms" (Jericho) and held Israel under tribute for eighteen years. The Benjamite Ehud brought Israel's annual tribute to the king. Because Ehud was left-handed, his weapon was undetected by the king's bodyguards.

Ehud told the king that he had a secret message from God. The message was the sword of Ehud! He slayed the king and escaped, rallying the people to defeat the Moabites. Israel subjugated Moab and rested from war for eighty years.

While Eglon oppressed Israel in the east, the Philistines troubled Israel in the west. Shamgar kept the Philistines at bay by using an oxgoad (see 5:6). The oxgoad was a farm tool of about eight feet in length that had a metal, chisel-shaped blade at its tip. Shamgar killed six hundred Philistines during his judgeship.

***Deborah and Barak (4:1–5:31).*** Both prose and poetic descriptions are given of Deborah and Barak's victory over the Canaanites. The two accounts, though having differences, are best interpreted as supplementary and not necessarily contradictory. An important theme of this cycle is the role women played in the defeat of the Canaanites.

Israel was oppressed by Jabin, the king of Hazor who ruled over a coalition of cities, one of which was ruled by Sisera. The name Jabin was probably a dynastic title (see Josh. 11:1). Although Joshua destroyed Hazor, the city had been rebuilt because of its strategic location.

Because of Sisera's superior chariots, Israel had been oppressed for twenty years. Deborah, a woman recognized for her civil authority, was a prophetess of God. She called on Barak to lead Israel against Sisera. Barak was reluctant to go without Deborah, and for this reason a woman received the honor of the victory rather than Barak.

With ten thousand soldiers gathered from Naphtali and Zebulun, the Lord routed Sisera's nine hundred chariots at the River Kishon. Sisera fled by foot toward Kadesh. Jael, the wife of Heber who had friendly relations with Jabin, gave him refuge. Sisera fell asleep in the tent of Heber, where Jael killed him by driving a tent peg through his temple. For Sisera to die at the hand of a woman rather than in battle was a grave disgrace for a professional soldier.

## RULERS OF OLD TESTAMENT PAGAN NATIONS
### (Listed Alphabetically)

| NAME | REFERENCE | NATIONALITY |
|---|---|---|
| Abimelech | (1) Gen 20 | Philistine |
|  | (2) Gen 26 | Philistine |
| Achish | 1 Sam 21:10-14; 27–29 | Philistine |
| Adoni-Zedek | Josh 10:1-27 | Canaanite |
| Agag | 1 Sam 15:8-33 | Amalekite |
| Ahasuerus | See Xerxes I |  |
| Ammon, King of (Unnamed) | Judg 11:12-28 | Ammonite |
| Artaxerxes | Ezra 4:7-23; 7; 8:1; Neh 2:1-8 | Persian/Mede |
| Ashurbanipal (also known as Osnapper) | Ezra 4:10 | Assyrian |
| Baalis | Jer 40:14 | Ammonite |
| Balak | Num 22–24 | Moabite |
| Belshazzar | Dan 5; 7:1 | Babylonian |
| Ben-Hadad I | 1 Kgs 20:1-34 | Syrian |
| Ben-Hadad II | 2 Kgs 6:24 | Syrian |
| Bera | Gen 14:2-24 | Canaanite |
| Cyrus the Great | 2 Chron 36:22-23; Ezra 1; Isa 44:28; 45:1; Dan 1:21; 10:1 | Persian/Mede |
| Darius the Great | Ezra 4–6; Neh 12:22; Hag 1:1; Zech 1:1,17 | Persian/Mede |
| Darius the Mede | Dan 11:1 | Persian/Mede |
| Edom, King of (Unnamed) | Num 20:14-21 | Edomite |
| Eglon | Judg 3:12-30 | Moabite |
| Egypt, Pharaoh of (Unnamed) | (1) Gen 12:18-20 | Egyptian |
|  | (2) Gen 41:38-55 | Egyptian |
|  | (3) Exod 1:8 | Egyptian |
|  | (4) Exod 2:15 | Egyptian |
|  | (5) Exod 3:10; 5:1 | Egyptian |
|  | (6) 1 Kgs 3:1 | Egyptian |
| Esarhaddon | Ezra 4:2 | Assyrian |
| Evil-Merodach | 2 Kgs 25:27-30; Jer 52:31-34 | Babylonian |
| Hanun | 2 Sam 10:1-4 | Ammonite |
| Hazael | 1 Kgs 19:15; 2 Kgs 8:7-15 | Syrian |
| Hiram | 1 Kgs 5:1-18 | Tyrian |
| Hophra | Jer 44:30 | Egyptian |
| Jabin | (1) Josh 11:1-11 | Canaanite |
|  | (2) Judg 4:2 | Canaanite |
| Jericho, King of (Unnamed) | Josh 2:2 | Canaanite |
| Merodach-Baladan | 2 Kgs 20:12; Isa 39:1 | Babylonian |
| Mesha | 2 Kgs 3:4-27 | Moabite |
| Nahash | 1 Sam 11:12 | Ammonite |
| Nebuchadnezzar | 2 Kgs 24–25; Dan 1–4 | Babylonian |
| Neco | 2 Kgs 23:29-30 | Egyptian |
| Nergal-Sherezer | Jer 39:3,13 | Babylonian |
| Osnapper | SEE Ashurbanipal |  |
| Pul | SEE Tiglath-Pileser III |  |
| Rezin | 2 Kgs 15:37; 16:5-9 | Syrian |
| Sargon II | Isa 20 | Assyrian |
| Sennacherib | 2 Kgs 18–19; Isa 36–37 | Assyrian |
| Shalmaneser V | 2 Kgs 17:1-6 | Assyrian |
| Shishak | 1 Kgs 14:25-26; 2 Chr 12:2-9 | Egyptian |
| Tiglath-Pileser III | 2 Kgs 15:19,29; 16:7-10 | Assyrian |
| Tyre, Prince of (Unnamed) | Ezek 28:1-10 | Tyrian |
| Xerxes I (also known as Ahasuerus) | Ezra 4:6; Esth | Persian/Mede |

The Song of Deborah is the poetic version of the battle. Deborah praised God for His deliverance of Israel. She described how commerce and village life were disturbed under Canaanite harassment. Israel was disarmed and depended on foreign alliances. The poem honored the tribes who responded to Barak's call and rebuked those who refused.

While the battle began near Harosheth Haggoyim, the decisive moment was at Megiddo near Taanach. Traversing the valley of Jezreel, where these cities are located, is the Kishon River. Evidently the Kishon flooded and swept away the chariots of Sisera. From archaeological findings at Megiddo, scholars have concluded that the battle took place about 1125 B.C.

The final stanzas of her poem repeated the theme of Sisera's shameful death at the feet of Jael. The song concludes with a taunt by depicting Sisera's mother awaiting his return. In fact, Sisera lay dead at the feet of a woman.

**Gideon (6:1–8:32).** The story of Gideon focuses on his struggle to overcome fear. The Midianites, along with other eastern peoples, had oppressed Israel for seven years. The Lord came to Gideon and challenged him to lead Israel like a "mighty warrior."

Gideon passed his first test of faith by tearing down the altar of Baal that belonged to his father. The Spirit of the Lord came upon Gideon, and he prepared for battle against the Midianites. By setting out a fleece of wool, he devised a test to learn that God was with him.

Gideon gathered 32,000 soldiers, but the Lord tested Gideon's courage once again. So that the Lord might receive the credit for the victory, He reduced Gideon's army to ten thousand. He then chose only the three hundred who lapped "the water with their tongue like a dog." These three hundred were selected because they showed that they were more watchful for the enemy.

The Lord reassured fearful Gideon through the dream of a man in the Midianite camp that Gideon would win the battle. The barley loaf in the dream was Israel, and the tent it struck was representative of the nomadic Midianites.

With three companies of one hundred men, Gideon launched a surprise attack; and the Midianite camp fell into panic. In spite of a weak leader, small army, and the foolish weapons of trumpets and torches, Israel won the day because of the power of the Lord.

The Ephraimites complained to Gideon that they were not called to the battle. He satisfied them by praising their part in the war. No longer afraid of battle, Gideon humbled the cities of Succoth and Peniel, which had refused to gave aid to his fatigued army. By executing the Midianite kings, Zebab and Zalmunna, Gideon avenged his brothers.

The grateful Israelites invited Gideon to rule over them. But Gideon refused and declared, "The LORD will rule over you." However, Gideon failed the Lord because he made an ephod that became an object of worship in his hometown, Ophrah. The ephod was the garment of the high priest, which contained the lots used to discern the will of God (Exod. 28:30; 39:1-26). Here the means of discerning God's will became a substitute for God. Gideon succeeded in bringing peace to the land for forty years, but his obsession with knowing the certainty of God's favor became his downfall.

Gideon's career also was marred by his polygamous life. Abimelech, who was born to Gideon by one of his concubines, became a wicked leader in Israel.

**Abimelech, Tola, Jair (8:33–10:5).** The fifth cycle of stories focuses on the treacherous life of Abimelech. It

## JUDGES OF THE OLD TESTAMENT

| NAME | REFERENCE | IDENTIFICATION |
|---|---|---|
| Othniel | Judg 1:12-13; 3:7-11 | Conquered a Canaanite city |
| Ehud | Judg 3:12-30 | Killed Eglon, king of Moab, and defeated Moabites |
| Shamgar | Judg 3:31 | Killed 600 Philistines with an oxgoad |
| Deborah | Judg 4-5 | Convinced Barak to lead an army to victory against Sisera's troops |
| Gideon | Judg 6-8 | Led 300 men to victory against 135,000 Midianites |
| Tola | Judg 10:1-2 | Judged for 23 years |
| Jair | Judg 10:3-5 | Judged for 22 years |
| Jephthah | Judg 11:1-12:7 | Defeated the Ammonites after making a promise to the Lord |
| Ibzan | Judg 12:8-10 | Judged for 7 years |
| Elon | Judg 12:11-12 | Judged for 10 years |
| Abdon | Judg 12:13-15 | Judged for 8 years |
| Samson | Judg 13-16 | Killed 1,000 Philistines with a donkey's jawbone; was deceived by Delilah; destroyed a Philistine temple; judged 20 years |
| Samuel | 1 and 2 Sam | Was the last of the judges and the first of the prophets |

also includes brief comments on the judges Tola and Jair. The people's desire for a king of their own choosing led them to the despot Abimelech, whose career brought continual warfare and insurrection.

Abimelech, born of a Shechemite woman, convinced the citizens of Shechem to make him king and to kill his half-brothers, the seventy sons of Gideon. Only Jotham escaped the slaughter. From Mount Gerizim, which overlooks Shechem, he taunted them by telling the fable of the "Bramble King." He cursed them and predicted that they too would be killed by the treachery of Abimelech.

After three years the Lord caused dissent between the Shechemites and Abimelech. The ensuing bloodshed and cruel deaths of Gaal and the Shechemites was God's vengeance for murdering Gideon's sons.

The rebellion against Abimelech spread to the city of Thebez. Abimelech stormed the city's tower. From the tower a woman dropped a millstone, crushing his skull. To escape the shame of being killed by a woman, he called for his armor bearer to kill him. The careers of Tola and Jair followed Abimelech's debacle. Tola led Israel for twenty-three years.

Jair was probably a contemporary of Tola. He was from Gilead and led Israel for twenty-two years. Since Jair had thirty sons, he probably was a polygamist like Gideon. The prestige of Jair's family is reflected by the donkeys (1 Sam. 25:20) and cities his sons possessed.

***Jephthah, Ibzan, Elon, Abdon (10:6–12:15).*** The sixth cycle concerns the judgeship of Jephthah and includes the minor judges Ibzan, Elon, and Abdon. An important feature of Jephthah's story is Israel's fickleness toward Jephthah. They turned to him for deliverance after they had earlier disowned him. This par-

allels how Israel had treated the Lord. A second theme is Jephthah's hasty judgments.

Because Israel fell into grave idolatry, God raised up the Philistines to trouble Israel in the west and the Ammonites to subdue Israel in the east. The Ammonites had oppressed Israel eighteen years when the Lord heard the cries of the Gileadites.

Jephthah had been exiled by the Gileadites because he was born of a harlot. When the Gileadites were humiliated by the Ammonites, they asked for Jephthah's help and vowed to make him their leader.

Jephthah sent a diplomatic delegation to the Ammonites to argue for Israel's right to their land, but the Ammonites rejected their claims. Then the Spirit of the Lord empowered Jephthah, and he advanced against the Ammonites. To secure the favor of God, he vowed to sacrifice as a burnt offering the first one who came out of his house to greet him upon his return from battle. The Lord gave the victory to Jephthah, but his hasty vow sacrificed his family lineage. His only child, a virgin daughter, was the first to greet him.

Some commentators believe that Jephthah offered her as a human sacrifice. Others believe the sacrifice of Jephthah was her service to the Lord as a perpetual virgin. The text does emphasize her virgin state. The vow, however, refers to "a burnt offering" (see 2 Kgs. 3:27). Both Jephthah and his daughter believed that the Lord expected him to keep the vow. God, however, did not request this "burnt offering." Indeed, the pagan practice of human sacrifice is contrary to God's expressed will (Deut. 12:31; 18:10).

As in the days of Gideon, the Ephraimites were angry that they did not participate in the battle and receive its spoil. Jephthah did not exhibit the patience of Gideon and fought against them. Ephraim fled back across the Jordan, but Jephthah controlled the fords. His armies identified the Ephraimites by a difference in their pronunciation of the word *Sibboleth* instead of *Shibboleth* (*ear of corn*). This intertribal war led to the death of 42,000 Ephraimites. Although the career of Jephthah spanned only six years, his judgeship epitomized the problems of Israel's declining leadership.

Three minor judges—Ibzan of Bethlehem (located in Zebulun, Josh. 19:15), Elon of Zebulun, and Abdon of Ephraim—are mentioned. Ibzan led for seven years and was remembered for his influential family. Elon judged for ten years, but little else is known of him. Abdon was also polygamous and had a prestigious family. He ruled for eight years. These judges may not have engaged in any military missions.

***Samson (13:1–16:31).*** The Philistines oppressed Israel for forty years (13:1), which included the twenty-year career of Samson and the judgeship of Samuel (1 Sam. 1–7). The Philistines were a people from the Aegean region who migrated to Canaan in the mid-thirteenth century and settled in the coastal plain. The Philistines pressured Dan and Judah in the west by infiltrating the tribes through trade and intermarriage.

The story of the Danite hero Samson epitomizes the spiritual and political disarray of the nation. There are many contrasts in the story which the author used to highlight the moral impotence of the people. Samson was strong physically but weak morally. Though he made poor decisions and could not control his emotions, God used his mistakes as occasions to demonstrate His sovereign power. Another startling contrast is the sanctity of his Nazirite vow versus the disregard

he showed for his Hebrew heritage. The victories of Samson were incomplete, and it was not until David that the Philistines were finally subjugated (2 Sam. 5:17-25).

The Lord, who appeared as the angel of the Lord (Exod. 3:1-8; Josh. 5:13-15), announced to Samson's mother that she would bear a son and rear the child as a Nazirite (Judg. 13:2-7). The Nazirite vow included abstinence from any drink derived from the grapevine, abstaining from cutting one's hair, and avoiding contact with a dead body (Num. 6:1-21).

The angel of the Lord confirmed the calling of Samson by revealing Himself to his mother and father, Manoah. As with previous judges, the empowerment of the Spirit began to move Samson. The devotion of his mother, who also took the Nazirite vow, stood in stark contrast to the licentious career that Samson would choose to live.

Against the advice of his parents, Samson wanted to arrange a marriage with a Philistine woman from Timnath. As they journeyed to her home, a lion attacked; the Spirit enabled Samson to kill it. Later, when he returned to marry the woman, he saw that the carcass of the lion had become the home of wild bees. He took honey from the carcass and shared it with his parents. In doing so, he violated his vow by touching the dead lion (see Num. 6:6-12).

Out of this experience Samson made up a riddle at his wedding. He challenged his Philistine guests to solve it for thirty changes of clothing. The riddle was too clever for them, and they forced Samson's new bride to discover the answer for them. The Lord used their treachery, however, to incite Samson against the Philistines. At Ashkelon he killed thirty men to pay his thirty changes of clothing.

When Samson returned to Timnath and learned that his bride had been given to another man, he swore to harm the Philistines more. He burned the wheat harvest of the Philistines by releasing into the fields foxes with lighted torches tied to their tails. The Philistines responded by burning his wife and her father to death, but this only made Samson slay many more.

The Philistines gathered in Judah near Lehi (*jawbone*) to fight Samson, and the Israelites bound Samson to give him over to the Philistines. When he was delivered over, the Spirit came upon Samson again, and with the fresh jawbone of a donkey, he killed one thousand Philistines. God miraculously provided water for Samson, who was dying of thirst from the battle.

Samson's lust for a prostitute at Gaza led him again into trouble. He was surrounded by the people of the city, but he escaped to Hebron by removing the city gates.

The final betrayal of Samson came from yet another woman, named Delilah. The woman enticed Samson to tell her the secret of his strength. After several tests she learned that the cutting of his hair would break his Nazirite vow. During his sleep, a man cut off Samson's braided hair. Samson fell into the hands of the Philistines, who bound and blinded him. Samson was taken to Gaza, where he was forced to grind grain in the prison like a common animal. But his hair began to grow again. The Lord used this last humiliation of Samson to kill the enemies of Israel.

At a Philistine festival to honor their god Dagon, the rulers boasted that Dagon had rendered Samson helpless. The crowd in the temple called for blinded Samson to entertain them. Samson prayed for strength to avenge himself. He pulled down the central pillars of the temple and killed all the Philistines and their rulers. Samson killed more

in this act of death than all those killed during his life. Ironically, his inability to control his lusts meant that the Nazirite's death was more valuable to Israel than his life.

## MORAL DEPRAVITY (17:1–21:25)

The final section of the book gives two parade examples of Israel's moral defection. The first case concerns idolatry by the tribe of Dan. The second case is about intertribal warfare that resulted from the rape and murder of a Levite's concubine by the men of Benjamin.

The author used these two events to show his own generation the need for a righteous king like David. In the tenth century B.C., Dan became a center for the worship of Baal established by the apostate King Jeroboam (1 Kgs. 12:25-33). Also the story of Benjamin cast a poor light on the tribe of Ish-bosheth, Saul's surviving son, who rivaled David for the throne (see 2 Sam. 2:10-11). The opponents of David's dynasty had their roots in the period of the Judges.

Both stories tell of priests who acted corruptly and of tribes who killed for gain. What was needed for an antidote was a righteous ruler like David so that Israel might do what was right in God's eyes (see 17:6; 18:1; 19:1; 21:25).

***Micah's Gods (17:1–18:31).*** The story of Micah shows how Israel adopted the idolatrous religious practices of its neighbors. Micah constructed a private shrine from stolen silver, including an ephod and several idols. He conscripted his son to serve as its priest until he hired a wandering Levite from Bethlehem. Micah foolishly believed he had the favor of God because of his personal shrine and priest.

The Danites, meanwhile, dispatched five spies to search for a new tract of land because they were pressed for space by the Amorites (see 1:34; Josh. 19:47).

On their way to Laish, they discovered Micah's priest and shrine.

Later the Danites returned with six hundred men and stole Micah's valuable idols. His Levite saw the chance to improve his status by serving a whole tribe. The Danites took the Levite with them to Laish, where they dispossessed the people and renamed the city Dan.

Micah's Levite was a direct descendant of Moses. This showed how low the spiritual leadership of the nation had fallen. Whereas Moses had established proper worship at the tabernacle, his descendants were functioning at rival sanctuaries in the land.

*The Levite's Concubine (19:1–30).* The second story tells of a Levite whose concubine left him for her father's house at Bethlehem. The Levite convinced her to return, and together they journeyed toward Ephraim. Along the way they looked for lodging and chose Gibeah (the home of the future king, Saul) rather than the Jebusite city of Jerusalem (the residence of the future king, David) because Gibeah was inhabited by Israelites. There they expected treatment as brothers. Ironically, pagan Jerusalem would have proven a safer refuge.

At Gibeah, however, no one offered them hospitality, except an old man from Ephraim who had migrated to Gibeah. That evening the men of Gibeah came to the old man's house to have sexual relations with the Levite.

The old man was so embarrassed by this breach of hospitality that he offered his virgin daughter and the Levite's concubine. The men refused and pressed against the door, so the Levite pushed his concubine outside. The men ravaged her for their sport and left her for dead. Out of revenge the Levite carved up her body into twelve pieces and sent them to the tribes of Israel. So great an atrocity became a long-remembered symbol of Israel's sin ( see Hos. 9:9; 10:9).

*War with Benjamin (20:1–21:25).* Covenant law required the tribes to punish anyone guilty among them or they would become the object of God's wrath too. Israel learned this in the days of Joshua at Ai (Josh. 7–8). Because Benjamin refused to give up the offenders, all Israel agreed to march against their kindred tribe Benjamin.

The Lord instructed them to attack, but each time the Israelites suffered numerous casualties. This was God's way of punishing Israel for its immorality to bring out repentance and true worship. In the third battle God gave them victory. The whole tribe of Benjamin was destroyed except for six hundred survivors.

The Israelites mourned for their lost tribe Benjamin, and to revitalize the tribe they had to find wives for the six hundred survivors. Jabesh-Gilead had not fought in the war; therefore Israel led a punitive expedition against them and took four hundred virgins for Benjamin. The Benjamites stole two hundred more virgins at the festival of Shiloh.

The final verse captured the spirit of the times: "In those days Israel had no king; everyone did as he saw fit."

*Theological and Ethical Value.* The Book of Judges presents Yahweh as the Lord of history. As such, God used foreign peoples to test the Israelites' loyalty to God and to punish their idolatry. Testing and punishment were not, however, God's ultimate goal for Israel. When God's people repented and appealed to God for aid, God did His heart's desire—He raised up deliverers to save His people. Salvation is the goal toward which God was and is directing history.

As Lord of history, God was free to choose whomever He pleased to act as deliverer. From the human point of view

God's choices are surprising: an assassin (Ehud), a woman (Deborah), a coward from an insignificant family (Gideon), the rash son of a prostitute (Jephthah), and a womanizer (Samson). Many of these chosen deliverers had obvious moral shortcomings. Still, God used them to save His people. True, Christians are called on to make every effort to be holy (Heb. 12:14). But God is sovereign and free to use whomever He chooses to further His saving purposes.

Human sinfulness necessitates governments to enforce morality. In the days of the judges when there was no king, "everyone did as he saw fit" (21:25). Governments have a God-given responsibility to punish wrongdoing (see Rom. 13:3-5). The later history of Israel, however, reveals that just having a king was not the answer to Israel's moral failure. Indeed, Israel's and Judah's kings often led God's people into even greater disobedience. What was most needed was not for God's covenant to be enforced from without but written on the hearts of His people (see Jer. 31:31-34).

## Questions for Reflection

1. What are the effects of immorality on society?

2. In what different ways does God respond to sin among His people?

3. How does God's Spirit work in the world and with God's people?

4. What can be learned from Judges about God's forgiveness and longsuffering?

5. What are some examples of godly leadership in the book?

## Sources for Additional Study

Cundall, Arthur E., and Leon Morris. *Judges and Ruth.* Downers Grove: InterVarsity, 1968.

Goslinga, C. J. *Joshua, Judges, Ruth.* Grand Rapids: Zondervan, 1986.

Lewis, Arthur H. *Judges/Ruth.* Chicago: Moody, 1979.

# RUTH

The Book of Ruth is named for its heroine, whose devotion to God and love for family has endeared her to generations of readers. It tells how God graciously rewarded the faithfulness of the widows Ruth and Naomi by delivering them through their kinsman-redeemer Boaz, who married Ruth and maintained the property of Naomi's family. The story takes place during the time of the judges (about 1150 B.C.). For this reason our English versions and the Greek translation of the Old Testament put the book after the Book of Judges.

In the Hebrew Bible, Ruth appears in the third section of books known as the *Hagiographa* or "Writings." Traditionally, the Jews read Ruth at the Feast of Weeks (Pentecost), which is a harvest celebration.

The authorship of Ruth is unknown. The book is named for its chief character, not necessarily for its author. A late Jewish tradition ascribes the book to the prophet Samuel.

The date of the composition is disputed and has been dated to either the early monarchy (about 950 B.C.) or the postexilic period (about 450 B.C.). Linguistic arguments have not been decisive, since they can be used to date the book either early or late. Also scholars are divided about whether the story fits better with the concerns of the monarchy or the setting of the postexilic period.

The question is complicated by problems concerning the relationship of the story and the genealogy of David, which ends the book (4:18-22). It is unusual for a book to end with a genealogy. Some scholars believe that the story is fictional and originally had no connection with David. In this view an editor during the postexilic period borrowed the genealogy of David from 1 Chronicles 2:4-15 and added it as an appendix to the story.

Recently, however, many biblical scholars have adopted the traditional view of Ruth, accepting it as the historically trustworthy work of one writer from about 950 B.C. They believe that the story presupposes the genealogy. The genealogy in Ruth and Chronicles probably came from a common temple source. These scholars argue that it is unlikely that David would have been linked to a Moabite ancestress unless he was *in fact* her descendant.

**Theme.** Ruth is a story of faithfulness, both human and divine. Naomi demonstrated faithfulness by returning to the land of promise. Ruth demonstrated her faithfulness by accompanying Naomi to Bethlehem and working the fields to provide for her. Ruth further demonstrated faithfulness to her deceased husband by her desire to marry into his family. Boaz demonstrated his faithfulness by fulfilling his covenant role as near kinsman.

Above all, Ruth is a story of God's faithfulness. God was faithful in preserving a family line, which—in God's time—led to King David and ultimately to Jesus. Ruth's story serves as a reminder that our faithfulness plays a part in the fulfillment of God's promises.

 I. Choice of Faith (1:1-22)
 II. Challenge in Faith (2:1-23)
 III. Claim by Faith (3:1-18)
 IV. Child because of Faith (4:1-18)

***Purpose and Theology.***
1. The story provides a transition from the patriarchs to the monarchy. The

genealogy at the end of the book traces the lineage of Boaz from Perez, the son of Judah, down to King David. For many Israelites the most important word of the book was the last—*David*.

2. The story of Ruth shows how God sovereignly, though almost imperceptively, achieves His purposes through the faithfulness of His people. The book speaks about God indirectly through the prayers and blessings of the story's characters. Although the book reflects a strong belief in God's lordship over history, it equally convinces readers that human decisions and actions play a significant role.

3. The book teaches that God's will is sometimes accomplished by common people with uncommon faith. The Book of Ruth does not have miracles or revelations. It does not mention the institutions of Israel's religion, such as tabernacle and prophecy. It has simple people going about everyday affairs.

4. The theological emphasis of Ruth can be summed up by two key words—*kindness (hesed )* and *kinsman-redeemer (goel).* The word *kindness* indicates covenant faithfulness and occurs three times in the prayers and commendations spoken by the characters (1:8; 2:20; 3:10). There is an implied contrast between the story's characters, who are righteous, and those of Judges, who "did as he [they] saw fit" (Judg. 21:25).

The story teaches that God rewards the faithfulness of His people. God accomplished this by using Boaz as the family's "kinsman-redeemer" (2:20; 3:12-13; 4:1-10). *Kinsman-redeemer* refers to a relative who helped a troubled family member so that the family was not dispossessed of land or left without an heir (Lev. 25:25-34; Deut. 25:5-10).

5. The story corrected the Jews when they made the worship of God exclu-

sively the prerogative of Israel. Although Ruth was a Moabitess, she was blessed by God.

## CHOICE OF FAITH (1:1-22)

*Ruth's Dilemma (1:1-5).* Because of famine the family of Elimelech moved from Bethlehem to Moab. "In the days when the judges ruled" describes the hostile and sinful times when the story transpires.

Elimelech was accompanied by Naomi, his wife, and their two sons, Mahlon and Kilion. The story describes them as "Ephrathites." *Ephrath* was another name for Bethlehem (Gen. 35:19; 48:7; Ruth 4:11; Mic. 5:2).

Elimelech died and left Naomi and her sons behind. The sons married Moabite women, Ruth and Orpah. Then they too died, leaving the Moabite widows and Naomi with the dilemma of facing life without the security of a husband or sons. In the ancient world women had security through their husbands and sons.

Nearby Moab was east of the Dead Sea and south of the Arnon River. The Moabites were descendants of Lot (Gen. 19:30-38). They fought the Israelites during the judgeship of Ehud (Judg. 3:12-30). The story of Ruth probably took place during a period of peace.

*Ruth's Decision (1:6-22).* Faced with little hope, the three widows considered the extent of their obligation to the family. Naomi decided to return to her homeland in Bethlehem. She had heard that God "had come to the aid of his people by providing food." This is the first hint that God would save the widows. Ruth 1:6 and 4:13, where Ruth conceived a child with the help of God, are the only passages where the story specifically says that God acted on behalf of His people. Just as God had caused the land to grow, God would bless the house of Elimelech through Ruth's womb.

Ruth and Orpah insisted that they return to Bethlehem, but Naomi urged them to seek "rest," that is, homes, in Moab. She explained that it was impossible for her to marry and have sons who could become their new husbands.

She was referring to the Israelite custom known as levirate marriage. A brother-in-law (Latin *levir*) or other near kinsman married the wife of his deceased brother and had a child in the name of the deceased (Deut. 25:5-10). This practice perpetuated land possession within a family and protected the widow.

Orpah stayed in Moab, but Ruth "clung" to Naomi. The depth of her commitment is poignantly expressed by the Moabitess: "Your people will be my people and your God my God."

***Ruth's Destiny (1:19-22).*** When Naomi and Ruth arrived in Bethlehem, the women of the town asked, "Can this be Naomi?" Naomi answered that her name was no longer *Naomi* but *Mara* because the Lord had afflicted her.

Her reply involves a play on the meaning of her name. *Naomi* means *pleasantness,* and *Mara (mara' )* means *bitterness.* Naomi considered her condition a bitter experience because she left Bethlehem with a full, happy house and had returned empty without children.

They returned to Bethlehem at the time of harvest. This is another hint that their fortunes would change in Bethlehem. Among the plentiful fields, God *would* again restore fullness to Naomi and Ruth.

## CHALLENGE IN FAITH (2:1-23)

***"Chance" Meeting (2:1-3).*** Boaz was a relative of Elimelech. He was a man of importance and wealth who was able to act as Ruth's kinsman-redeemer.

According to Mosaic law, the poor could glean the corners of the fields. Ruth looked for work, and "as it turned out" she came to the field of Boaz.. The Hebrew text says literally "her chance chanced" to work in the fields of Boaz. This expression intentionally exaggerates the way the human eye saw her actions. The author did this to draw attention to the hidden reality of God's providential intervention. This was not accidental but the work of God veiled from Ruth's eyes.

***Ruth's Commendation (2:4-18).*** Boaz invited Ruth to work exclusively in his fields. Ruth was surprised by Boaz's generosity, particularly since she was a Moabitess, a foreigner. Boaz explained that he had already heard a good report about her commitment to Naomi. He commended Ruth for her faithfulness and prayed that God might bless her.

Boaz acted on his prayer. He rewarded Ruth with roasted grain and instructed his laborers to leave stalks behind for her to glean. At the end of her work, Ruth had enough food for Naomi. As God had used Boaz and Ruth to feed Naomi, God would use them to give Naomi a son.

***Ruth's Care (2:19-23).*** Naomi exulted in the Lord when she learned about Boaz because she knew that he was a kinsman-redeemer. She urged Ruth to follow Boaz's instructions because he would care for her safety.

## CLAIM BY FAITH (3:1-18)

***Ruth's Obedience (3:1-6).*** Naomi instructed Ruth to prepare herself properly and approach Boaz during the night at the threshing floor. She obeyed Naomi's instructions carefully. Ironically, Naomi is the one who would find "a home" ("rest," 3:1) for Ruth and not a Moabite husband.

A threshing floor was a stone surface in the fields where the harvest husks were crushed and the grain sifted from the chaff.

***Ruth's Trust (3:7-15).*** Ruth secretly approached Boaz. By lying at his feet, Ruth humbled herself as one of his servants. She trusted God to use Boaz to answer her needs and to protect her. Ruth startled Boaz since women were usually not with the men at night.

She made her request: "Spread the corner of your garment over me, since you are a kinsman-redeemer." By this expression Ruth was asking Boaz for marriage (see Ezek. 16:8). The Hebrew word translated "corner" can also be translated "wings." Boaz had prayed that Ruth might have refuge under the "wings" of God. He was used by God to provide the refuge for which Boaz himself had prayed.

Boaz commended Ruth for her righteous conduct because she chose him instead of a younger man. This was a greater act of loyalty ("kindness," 3:10) than even her initial faithfulness ("kindness") to the family.

Boaz told Ruth that there was another kinsman who had the first right to redeem her. If he declined, then Boaz promised to marry her. He gave Ruth a bounty of grain as an indication of his commitment.

***Ruth's Patience (3:16-18).*** Ruth reported to Naomi about Boaz's promise, and she gave her the grain from Boaz. This was another sign that God was answering their prayers through the hand of Boaz. Naomi told Ruth that she must be patient until the man carried out his pledge that day.

## CHILD BECAUSE OF FAITH (4:1-22)

***Ruth's Redemption (4:1-12).*** Just as the widows had weighed their responsibility, the kinsmen of the Elimelech family discussed their roles. Boaz informed an unnamed kinsman that Naomi's fields were his to redeem. The kinsman agreed to buy the fields, but Boaz added that whoever bought the land ought to marry Ruth to "maintain the name of the dead with his property." The Mosaic law does not tie the role of

purchasing property with the custom of kinsman marriage. Therefore the kinsman could have declined without embarrassment. The kinsman explained that marriage would jeopardize his own inheritance. Boaz happily announced that he would redeem the property and marry Ruth himself.

Both the nearer kinsman and Orpah were not required technically by law to help the family. Ruth and Boaz decided to go beyond the prescription of the law to fulfill the purposes of the covenant. Because of their actions, the redemption of the family could be completed. Through their action, God worked to redeem Israel by making possible the birth of David.

The contract was sealed when the nearer kinsman gave his sandal to Boaz. This symbolized the transfer of his right to redeem.

The elders witnessed it and offered a prayer of blessing. They asked God to give Boaz children as He did the wives of Jacob and the house of Judah through Tamar, who bore Perez. The wives of Jacob bore twelve sons, the progenitors of all Israel; and Tamar bore twin sons to Judah (Gen. 38:27-30).

The blessing implied two comparisons. First, Ruth was a Moabitess, whereas Leah and Rachel were the mothers of Israel. The comparison, however, was not offensive to the elders because Ruth had become integrated into the family of faith.

Second, Tamar and Ruth both were without children. Tamar achieved her ends through trickery, but Ruth received her son through righteous obedience. Judah tried to avoid his responsibility to perpetuate his own son's family line. Ruth and Boaz, the descendant of Judah, went beyond the letter of the levirate law and acted righteously before the Lord. Ironically, the righteousness of a Moabitess, a foreigner to Israel's covenant, brought salvation to Judah's family.

**Ruth's Rest (4:13-22).** God rewarded the couple by giving them the child Obed. The women of the city praised God and recognized that Obed would sustain Naomi and possess Elimelech's property. In this sense Naomi was regarded the mother of the child.

Ruth was more valuable to Naomi than seven sons. Naomi had lost two sons. Through Ruth, who continued the house of her husband and provided Israel with its greatest king, Naomi gained far more. This signals the completed reversal in the life of Naomi. She was no longer empty.

The genealogy linked David with the patriarchs through Perez, the son of Judah. Because of the faithfulness of Ruth and the faithfulness of God, the promises of the patriarchs could be realized through David and his greater Son, Jesus Christ: "A record of the genealogy of Jesus Christ the son of David, the son of Abraham" (Matt. 1:1).

**Theological and Ethical Significance.** The Book of Ruth shows God working behind the scenes in the lives of ordinary people, turning apparent tragedy into joy and peace. The Book of Ruth shows God as concerned not only for the welfare of one family—Naomi and Ruth—but for the welfare of all God's people who would be blessed by David and by David's Son, Jesus Christ. The participation of Ruth, the Moabitess, in the fufillment of God's promises indicates that God's salvation is for people of all nationalities.

By their faithfulness, integrity, and love, the characters of the Book of Ruth mirrored the character of God. They serve as reminders that the lives of godly people are a powerful witness to God's self-sacrificing love.

### Questions for Reflection

1. What does the book teach about the loving care of God?

2. How should the people of God respond to the sorrows of life?

3. How should those who are different in race, color, or economic status be treated?

4. How does the book encourage the people of God to be faithful?

5. Why should the people of God pray?

### Sources for Additional Study

Atkinson, David. *The Message of Ruth.* Downers Grove: InterVarsity, 1983.

Cundall, Arthur E., and Leon Morris. *Judges and Ruth.* Downers Grove: InterVarsity, 1968.

Enns, Paul P. *Ruth.* Grand Rapids: Zondervan, 1982.

# 1 SAMUEL

First and Second Samuel are named for the principle character in the early chapters of the book. Samuel led Israel as its last judge and anointed Israel's first two kings, Saul and David.

First and Second Samuel were originally one book in the Hebrew Bible. The Greek Septuagint and the Latin Vulgate first divided the Hebrew into two books. The Septuagint entitled Samuel and Kings as four consecutive books called "First—Fourth Kingdoms." The Vulgate also had four books but with the title "Kings." In the Hebrew Bible the division into two books was established with the first printing of the Hebrew Bible (A.D. 1488). The English versions followed the Hebrew title "Samuel."

First and Second Samuel are anonymous. According to Jewish tradition, based on 1 Chronicles 29:29, the Books of Samuel were authored by Samuel and completed by the prophets Nathan and Gad. Since 1 Samuel 25:1 records Samuel's death and he seldom appears after the anointing of David (1 Sam. 16:1-13), alternative explanations for the compilation of the Books of Samuel have been sought.

As the Jewish tradition itself indicates, the Books of Samuel are a composite work of more than one hand. Among the materials used were eyewitness accounts, archival materials, independent narratives, and poetry.

Scholars disagree on how and when the Books of Samuel were written. Some believe the work was completed soon after the time of David (1011–971 B.C.). Other scholars have dated the completed work about 650–550 B.C. as part of a larger history influenced by the central ideas of Deuteronomy. (See "The Historical Books.")

Some commentators have charged that 1 Samuel evidences sources of contradictory theological viewpoints (for example, views on kingship). However, this diversity has been explained on other grounds, such as differences in emphasis or supplementation. The book's variety of sources have been integrated into a unified work with a consistent theme.

**Theme.** Through the prophetic ministry of Samuel, God established the monarchy of Israel by choosing David, "a man after his own heart," to rule over His people (13:14). The book helps us see that God is Lord over history. His sovereign plans are accomplished in spite of human failure.

    I. Righteous Leadership (1:1–7:17)
   II. Disobedient Saul (8:1–15:35)
  III. Faithful David (16:1–31:13)

***Purpose and Theology.***

1. The book tells of the transition in leadership from the period of the judges to the rise of the monarchy. The book continues the story of Israel's wars with the Philistines begun in the Book of Judges (see Samson, Judg. 13–16). Samuel was a transition figure who, as the last judge, inaugurated the first king, Saul (10:1), and initiated the dynasty of King David (16:1,13).

During the judges period, the nation was a theocracy. The Lord was its only king and authority. The tribes had no central authority to govern them and were held together because of their common commitment to the covenant with the Lord. With the establishment of the kingdom, God would express His rule in a new way, through His chosen king.

2. The Lord's choice of godly leadership is focal. Samuel is extolled in contrast to Eli and his sons, Phinehas and Hophni. They were rejected by God because of their evil deeds (2:12-36). Under their leadership the Philistines captured the ark of the covenant at the battle of Aphek (4:1b-11); but under Samuel, Israel defeated the Philistines at Mizpah (7:1-17). Yet Samuel's sons were also unfit (8:1-6). So the Lord permitted the people to have a king (8:6-9,19-20; 9:17). King Saul, however, rejected the prophetic word of Samuel for reasons of political expediency (15:26-29). God, who "looks at the heart" (16:7), chose David as His anointed servant to rule over Israel (16:1-13; 28:16-19).

3. For Israel to prevail over its enemies, God required covenant faithfulness and moral responsibility from Israel's leadership. The sin of Israel's leaders resulted in death for them and the people. The Philistine's defeat of Israel under Eli's evil sons (4:1-21) and under wicked Saul (31:1-13) is contrasted with Samuel's and David's victories (7:13; 23:1-5; 30:1-31).

4. God's continued grace is another significant theme in the book. In spite of Israel's repeated failures, the Lord raised up new deliverers in Samuel, Saul, and David. God answered the cry of Hannah (1:9-20), called the boy Samuel (3:1-21), granted the request for a king (8:6-9), and spared David for Israel's golden age to come (18:6-11,24-27; 19:9-10; 21:10-15).

5. The book demonstrates that God is Lord over history. His dominion is exercised over the rise and fall of important figures as well as whole nations. The motif of prophecy and its fulfillment shows that the Lord accomplishes His will in spite of human plans. Also the presence and empowerment of the Holy Spirit in the lives of Saul and David evi-dences God's sovereignty (10:6,10; 11:6; 16:13). When God disapproved Saul, the Spirit departed (16:14).

## RIGHTEOUS LEADERSHIP (1:1–7:17)

In the opening section the godly life of Samuel is distinguished from the failures of the high priest Eli and his sons, Hophni and Phinehas. Although Samuel and the sons of Eli were reared in the same house, their dedication and destinies were very different. The Philistine wars led to the end of Eli's family, but Samuel prevailed over the Philistines and led Israel as judge and prophet.

*Samuel's Dedication (1:1–2:10).* Samuel's unusual birth was an early indication of the special dedication Samuel would have to the Lord throughout his life. Barren Hannah, Samuel's mother, prayed for a son. She vowed to rear the child as a Nazirite (see Num. 6:1-21 and Judg. 13). Because the Lord answered her prayer, she dedicated Samuel to serve at the tabernacle under Eli's care.

Hannah's prayer in song celebrated the righteousness and sovereignty of God. He defeats the proud and exalts the humble. He will protect His saints and strengthen His anointed king.

*Eli's Corruption (2:11-36).* The corruption of the tabernacle at Shiloh by Eli's sons is contrasted with the faithful ministry of young Samuel. Whereas Hannah's son "ministered before the LORD," the sons of Eli "had no regard for the LORD." Eli's servants had contempt for the Lord's offerings, and his sons engaged in temple prostitution. Yet young Samuel, as it would be said of Jesus (Luke 2:52), grew in "favor with the LORD and with men."

A man of God prophesied the death of Hophni and Phinehas and the appointment of a "faithful priest." The immediate context suggests that Samuel is meant (1 Sam. 3), though Samuel did not exhaust this powerful image. This priest has also been identified as the high priest Zadok (1 Kgs. 2:35), or Jesus Christ the priestly Messiah (Heb. 5:1-10; 7:1-28).

**Samuel's Ministry (3:1-4:1a).** Because of the sin at Shiloh's shrine, the "word of the LORD was rare" and "visions" were not seen. However, the word came to Samuel, and the Lord appeared to him at Shiloh. Samuel's ministry reached throughout the land, and the people recognized that he was a prophet of the Lord.

**Judgment of "Ichabod" (4:1b-22).** As in the Book of Judges, God's judgment on sin came in the form of foreign oppression. Here God's judgment fell on the house of Eli through the Philistine's victory over Israel at Ebenezer (see 7:12). The battle had a major impact on the religious life of Israel because the ark of the covenant was captured. Israel's defeat and the deaths of Eli's sons showed that God would not tolerate their sin.

Hophni and Phinehas ordered the ark brought into the battlefield because they believed it would give them victory (see Josh. 6). The Lord rejected their superstitious actions, and they died in the battle. When Eli heard the news of the captured ark, he fell over backward and died. The deaths of his family brought the end to Eli's priesthood, fulfilling the prophecy of the man of God. Eli's daughter-in-law named her newborn son "Ichabod" (*no glory*) to remember this tragic day of the ark's loss.

**Lord of the Ark (5:1-12).** The god of the Philistines was the vegetation deity Dagon. The Philistines believed Dagon had given them victory by defeating the Lord of Israel. The Philistines placed the ark in their temple like a trophy for their victorious deity. The failure of Dagon, however, to stand before the ark showed that the Lord was greater. God brought a plague of tumors upon the Philistines. Perhaps this disease was bubonic plague related to an infestation of rats (see 6:4).

**Ark and God's Holiness (6:1-7:1).** The Philistines feared the Lord and honored Him by returning the ark on a new cart bearing a guilt offering. The Israelites at Beth Shemesh welcomed the ark, but they too suffered death because some men looked unlawfully into the ark (see Num. 4:20). They learned like the Philistines that the Lord was a holy God. They sent the ark to the house of Abinadab at Kiriath Jearim, where it resided until the days of David.

**Samuel's "Ebenezer" (7:2-17).** Unlike the sons of Eli, who sinned, Samuel was faithful. He turned the people away from their worship of the Canaanite fertility deities, Baal and Ashtoreth. As in the Book of Judges, God responded to His people's repentance by raising up a judge or national deliverer. God honored Samuel's faithfulness by giving him victory over the Philistines. Samuel commemorated the victory by erecting a stone at the site. He named it "Ebenezer" *(stone of help),* saying, "Thus far has the LORD helped us." Samuel spent his life serving the Lord as an itinerant judge, priest, and prophet.

## DISOBEDIENT SAUL (8:1-15:35)

Israel's disappointment with the priesthood of Eli and the sin of Samuel's sons led Israel to turn to a new form of leadership. The people, following the example of the nations around them, demanded a king (1 Sam. 8). God granted their desires, and Samuel reluctantly appointed a king. Saul's reign had a promising beginning. King Saul, however, proved unlike Samuel because he did not listen to the word of the Lord. The Lord thus rejected Saul as He had the house of Eli.

**God Permits a King (8:1-22).** The people requested a king because Samuel's judgeship had begun to fail. He was old; and his sons, like Eli's, were wicked men who perverted justice. Also the people wanted the benefits of a central authority like the other nations had. Although Samuel resisted, God graciously permitted Israel to have a king. Samuel warned the people of the troubles of kingship, but they persisted; so God granted their request.

**God Reveals Israel's King (9:1-27).** A Benjamite named Saul searched with his servant for the lost donkeys of his father, Kish. Saul's servant knew of Samuel, the prophet of God. They sought him to inquire of God where they might find the donkeys. On the previous day God had informed Samuel that he would meet a man from Benjamin whom he should anoint king over Israel. God reserved the right to choose Israel's king (Deut. 17:15). Saul remained with Samuel to attend a sacrificial feast. The next day Samuel detained him to receive a message from God.

**Saul Anointed (10:1-27).** The message was that God had chosen Saul to be king over Israel. Samuel anointed him with a flask of oil, indicating the special relationship between God and king (see Deut. 17:15). Because of this custom, the king of Israel became known as the "anointed one" (*Messiah*). Three signs followed the anointing to confirm to Saul that God had indeed chosen him. Saul sought after lost donkeys, but he discovered a kingdom.

Samuel anointed Saul again but this time publicly at Mizpah. The people found Saul hiding among the baggage, and they hailed him king. They longed for a king to rival the nations; ironically, they were elated with a shy keeper of donkeys.

**Saul at Jabesh (11:1-15).** The first test for Saul's reign was the attack of the Ammonites upon Jabesh Gilead across the Jordan. As in the days when the judges ruled, the Spirit came upon Saul, and he became angry. No longer was Saul shy. By exercising his authority as king, he rallied the Israelites. His forces defeated the Ammonites. This confirmed to the people that Saul was an able king.

**Samuel's Final Warning (12:1-25).** With the installation of Saul, Samuel retired as Israel's civic leader. His final sermon defended his leadership and reviewed God's favor in the past. He indicted the people's sinful choice of a king because they had set aside the kingship of the Lord. Samuel proved his charge by calling upon God to send a thunderstorm. It came during the dry season of the year (May-June) when a thunderstorm was unexpected. After the people confessed their sin, Samuel reminded them that they had nothing to fear from God if they continued in the Lord. If they failed to obey the Lord, however, they and their king would be swept away.

**Saul's Foolishness (13:1–14:52).** Saul's son, Jonathan, bravely initiated a war with the Philistines. However, the troops of Israel feared the numerous Philistines gathered at Michmash.

Saul awaited Samuel for seven days at Gilgal to offer a sacrifice to entreat the Lord's blessing. When Samuel did not come at the appointed time (see 10:8), Saul's army began to defect. Saul acted foolishly because of impatience. Out of desperation, he disobeyed the prophet Samuel's instructions and offered burnt offerings. Samuel arrived and rebuked Saul for his disobedience. Because he acted foolishly, Samuel prophesied that Saul would lose his kingdom. God would choose "a man after his own heart." Samuel's rebuke of Saul set the pattern for future relations between the leaders of God's people—prophets and kings. The future history of Israel and Judah illus-

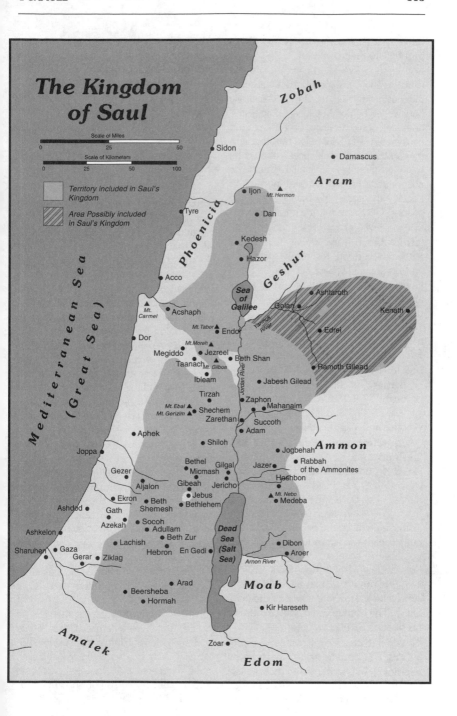

trates that their kings disobeyed God's prophets to their own peril.

Although Israel had no weapons and were greatly outmanned, Jonathan courageously attacked the Philistines while Saul waited behind in Gibeah. The Philistines fell into disarray because of an earthquake, and Saul called for the ark to consult the Lord's guidance. Yet after he saw the Philistines panic all the more, he abandoned the inquiry and hurried to attack. In spite of Saul's impulsive actions, God gave them a great victory.

Saul's pride and hasty decision to restrict Israel from eating during the battle jeopardized his armies' strength and his son's life. Saul built an altar and inquired of the Lord, but the Lord did not answer him because of his unbelief. By casting lots, Saul discovered that Jonathan had unknowingly broken Saul's ban of eating. The men of the camp refused Saul's order to execute Jonathan, saving him from Saul's foolish oath.

Because of his disobedience, Saul never totally defeated the Philistines. In spite of his sin, God graciously gave him victories and a large family.

***Rejection of Saul (15:1-35).*** Saul's pride and desire for economic gain fueled his continued disobedience. Saul went so far as to build a monument for himself. The Lord "grieved" that he had made Saul king over Israel. The Lord instructed Saul by the prophet Samuel to put to death the Amalekites and all their possessions because of their past sins (see the law of holy war, Deut. 20:16-18). Saul, however, permitted Agag, the Amalekite king, and the best of the spoil to live. The Lord rejected Saul because of his sin, and Samuel wept for him.

When Samuel confronted Saul with his sins, Saul tried to justify his actions by explaining that he wanted to make a sacrifice of the spoil to the Lord. Saul had failed to learn that God does not accept ritual without obedience. Samuel refused to support Saul any longer because God had torn away his kingdom. Samuel himself executed Agag in accordance with the Lord's command. Samuel, as the prophet of God, never advised Saul again (see 19:24; 28:11).

## FAITHFUL DAVID (16:1–31:13)

The book's final section focuses on the personalities of Saul and David. Although Saul is king until the end of the book, the story turns to his successor's rise. David's story is told from the viewpoint of Saul's continued failures. Saul's reign was chaotic, marred by personal problems and the threat of Philistine oppression. While it became clearer that Saul was unfit for leadership, David emerged before the nation as God's champion to defeat the Philistines and rule the land. In the end Saul would take his own life.

***God Anoints David (16:1-23).*** The Lord instructed Samuel to go to the house of Jesse in Bethlehem to anoint Israel's new king. Although frightened that he might be found out by Saul, Samuel went to Bethlehem to offer a sacrifice. There he was joined by the family of Jesse. Samuel looked upon Jesse's seven older sons and was impressed by their appearance. But God rejected them and looked instead for one who had a faithful heart. David, the youngest, was called to the house, and the Lord instructed Samuel to anoint him. David was empowered by the Spirit from that day forward.

Since the Lord rejected Saul as king, He withdrew His Spirit; and Saul received an "evil spirit." The identity of this "evil" spirit has been disputed. Some believe that it was a demon. Others argue that it was a troubling spirit causing emotional disturbance (see Judg. 9:23). Some have suggested that the Lord permitted Satan to afflict Saul as punishment for his sin (see 2 Sam. 24:1 with 1 Chr. 21:1).

What is clear is that this spirit was sent by the Lord (see 1 Kgs. 22:20-23) to show that Saul had been rejected. It caused Saul to experience bouts of rage and despondency. Christians do not have to fear that the Lord will remove His Spirit from them, since the Spirit is the believer's permanent possession (Rom. 8:9,12-17; Eph. 1:13; 4:30).

Saul's attendants sought a musician to soothe troubled Saul. David was selected to enter into the service of the king.

### David Defeats Goliath (17:1-58).
The Philistines were at war with Saul. Their greatest champion, Goliath (who stood over nine feet tall) taunted the Israelites for their cowardice. In ancient times it was common for champions of opposing armies to face off in a personal duel. No Hebrew had the courage to face Goliath.

Jesse's older sons were in the battle lines, and Jesse sent David to the field with provisions. David heard the defiant words of Goliath and was zealous to defend the name of the Lord by challenging the giant to combat. With the weapons of a lowly shepherd but armed with the power of God, he killed Goliath, and the Philistines scattered in defeat.

The stunning victory caused Saul to inquire of Abner, the captain of Israel's army, about the lineage of David. Since David was already in the service of Saul, the inquiry of Saul and his address to David seem out of place. Some scholars have suggested that the two accounts of David's introduction to Saul come from separate sources. This conclusion is reasonable, but this does not mean that the stories are two garbled accounts of the same event. Since Saul would reward David with his daughter in marriage, David's lineage became particularly important. Saul, therefore, investigated David's background anew.

### Saul's Fear of David (18:1-30).
David's success in battle and the people's love for him made Saul wildly fearful for his kingdom. Saul's son Jonathan loved David and entered a covenant of loyalty with him. Whenever David returned from battle, the women of the city exclaimed, "Saul has slain his thousands, and David his tens of thousands." Saul, in a fit of rage, attempted to spear David twice. Saul feared him because he realized that God had turned to David.

Saul plotted to kill David by the hands of the Philistines. He offered his daughter Michal in marriage if David would kill one hundred Philistines. When David and his men killed two hundred, Saul feared David all the more. Saul knew that God favored David.

### God's Spirit Saves David (19:1-24).
Saul instructed his men to kill David, but Jonathan intervened. Saul, however, could not control his anger, and again he threw a javelin at David. David fled to his house, where Michal warned him that the king's men planned to kill him in the morning. She helped him escape unseen and then deceived her father about David's whereabouts.

David took refuge with Samuel at Ramah. The Spirit of God protected him from the king by mysteriously causing the king and his men to act "crazy" like the prophets.

### Jonathan's Selfless Love (20:1-42).
David met his friend Jonathan and appealed for his help. Jonathan knew that he would never be king of Israel because the Lord had chosen David to succeed his father. He loved David (18:1; 20:17), and they covenanted together to spare each other's lives. Jonathan agreed to signal David in the field if his father again planned to kill him.

At the Feast of the New Moon, David's absence caused Saul to become enraged, and he charged Jonathan with

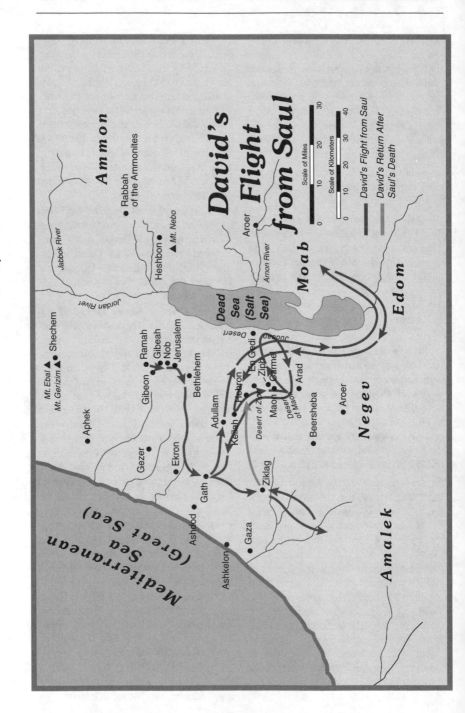

treachery. He tried to kill his own son, but Jonathan escaped to warn his friend David.

### David's Deceptions (21:1–22:5).
For fear of his life, David took matters into his own hands. At Nob he lied to the priest Ahimelech to save himself by receiving food and Goliath's sword. His deception would cost many innocent lives (see 22:18-19).

David mistakenly thought he could find refuge as a mercenary soldier in the Philistine city Gath, but Achish the king discovered his identity. David pretended to be a madman to save himself.

### Saul Murders Priests (22:6-23).
David hid in the wilderness of Adullam where he was joined by social outcasts like himself. He arranged for his family's care in Moab, and he hid in the forest of Hereth at the advice of the prophet Gad. David likely turned to Moab because of his ancestral linkage with Ruth, the Moabitess (Ruth 4:18-22), and because of Moab's hatred for Saul (see 14:47).

Saul learned from Doeg, the Edomite, that David had received comfort from the priest Ahimelech (see 21:1-9). Saul's paranoia led him to think that Ahimelech had conspired with David against him. The deranged Saul ordered the murder of the priests of the Lord! His guards refused to obey, however, because they would not harm the Lord's servants. Doeg, of Edomite descent, had no regard for the Lord and carried out the king's command. Only Abiathar, the son of Ahimelech, escaped to David's camp. There he found safety under David's protection.

### Dependence on the Lord (23:1-29).
David's deception of Ahimelech had led to the death of the Lord's priests. From this tragic episode David learned to depend on the Lord's help to escape Saul. David turned to the priest Abiathar, who possessed the sacred ephod, to inquire of the Lord. He followed God's guidance to save the city Keilah from Philistine invaders. By inquiring of the Lord he also escaped Saul at Keilah and fled successfully from place to place in the wilderness of Ziph. The author presents a striking contrast between Saul, who killed the servants of the Lord, and David, who honored them.

### David Spares Saul (24:1-22).
Saul pursued David into the region of En Gedi. There he went aside into one of the many caves nearby to relieve himself. David and his men were hidden in the back of the same cave. His men urged him to kill the king, but David chose to trust God's providence. However, he quietly cut off the hem of Saul's garment. David later regretted doing it, however, because the hem was symbolic of Saul's position as the Lord's anointed. Once the king left, David called out to him and showed the hem as evidence of his innocent intentions toward the king. Saul openly admitted his sin against David and confessed with his own mouth that the Lord had chosen David to be king.

### David Spares Nabal (25:1-44).
The notice of Samuel's death is not incidental to the author. He shows how the people's love for Samuel's godly leadership continued with David as well.

David kindly protected the flocks of a wealthy herdsman named Nabal (fool). As a result, none of his flocks were stolen or lost to wild animals. It was not unreasonable then for David to ask Nabal to respond kindly to him. But Nabal angrily refused, and David threatened to kill him. The shepherds of Nabal, who had benefited from David's protection, entreated Abigail, Nabal's wife, to intercede. Abigail pleaded with David that the Lord's anointed had no need to avenge himself since the Lord would do so. David gratefully agreed and resisted the evil deed. Later, God struck Nabal dead. This event

exemplifies the Old Testament understanding of God's sovereignty over all
things. Everything happens as part of the
outworking of God's will.

This famous incident involving Abigail
led the author to list David's wives. He
married Abigail from Carmel and Ahi-
noam from Jezreel. His first wife, Saul's
daughter Michal, was given to another
man (see 18:27).

**David Spares Saul Again (26:1-
25).** The Ziphites feared David and
urged the king to pursue him in their territories (see 23:19-24). When David
learned of Saul's arrival, he discovered
the location of the camp. Abishai joined
David in spying out the camp at night.
They discovered Saul asleep with Abner
resting nearby. Although Abishai interpreted the occasion as the Lord's opportunity for him to kill the king, David
rebuked Abishai, pointing out that Saul
was the Lord's anointed. Instead, David
took a spear that was stuck in the ground
at the king's head along with the king's
water jug. David left without detection
because the Lord had caused Saul to fall
into a deep sleep.

David crossed to a distant hill and
called out to awaken Abner. He challenged him to consider his lapse in protecting the king. When the king realized
that David had taken the spear and jug,
he regretted unjustly pursuing David. He
believed that because David had spared
the Lord's anointed that the Lord in turn
would deliver David. Saul confessed a
second time that David would triumph
(see 24:20).

Some scholars hold that this account
is a retelling of how David spared Saul's
life at En Gedi (1 Sam. 24). While there
are a number of similarities, David's different responses show that the two stories are distinct incidents. As a result of
En Gedi and the encounter with Nabal,
David realized that God would care for

him. David left Judah for a life among the
Philistines in order to avoid further contact with Saul.

**David Tricks Philistines (27:1-
12).** David feared that any further
encounters with Saul would lead to
bloodshed. In the service of King Achish
of Gath he would escape Saul's attention.
David's troops were headquartered at
Ziklag, where he raided the enemies of
Judah. He duped the Philistine king into
thinking that he was attacking the towns
of Judah.

The passage does not condone
David's deception of Achish; rather, the
author includes this to show how God
used David even in this situation to aid
the covenant people. Also it continued
the theme of how David outwitted the
foolish Philistines (see 21:10-15).

**The Witch of Endor (28:1-25).**
The Philistines threatened war in the
Jezreel Valley. Out of fear Saul sought a
word from the Lord. Ironically, Saul, who
had once despised the Lord's will (14:18-
19; 15:26), could not discover it now
that he desperately needed it. When God
refused to answer Saul through legitimate
means, Saul sought a spiritual medium.

By deceiving the witch at Endor, Saul
convinced her to bring Samuel from the
dead. Much to her surprise the appearance was a genuine one, and by it she discovered Saul's true identity. God
intervened in an unprecedented way and
actually sent Samuel to prophesy Saul's
judgment (see 15:27-29). Samuel condemned Saul to death because he "did
not obey the LORD." So great was Saul's
despondency that he could not continue.
At the urging of Saul's men and the sor-
ceress, he took food to strengthen himself for his travel.

The passage contrasts the true prophetic word of Samuel with Saul's
attempt to consult the dead (see Saul's
condemnation in 1 Chr. 10:13-14). The

prophetic word would be fulfilled, and Saul could not hope to escape it.

**God Spares David (29:1-11).** This episode precedes the events in chapter 28 since the Philistines were gathered at Aphek (29:1) and then moved to Shunem in the Jezreel Valley (28:4; 29:11). This arrangement serves to heighten without interruption David's success against the Lord's enemies (continued in 1 Sam. 30).

The Philistines refused to include David in their battle against Israel. God used the discontent of the Philistines to spare David from fighting against his own people and jeopardizing, in their eyes, his place as the Lord's anointed. Achish apologetically dismissed David to Ziklag.

**God Strengthens David (30:1-31).** David and his men arrived in Ziklag, where they discovered the city burned and their families captured by raiding Amalekites. So distraught were the men that they threatened to stone David, but the Lord strengthened him. At the instruction of the Lord by the ephod of Abiathar, David pursued the Amalekites.

During the march, two hundred men remained behind because of exhaustion, but four hundred pressed ahead. With the aid of an Egyptian slave who was left behind by the Amalekites, David's men discovered their camp, overtook them, and retrieved all their possessions. David won the hearts of his men and the elders of Judah by sharing with them—even the two hundred who stayed behind—a portion of the booty taken from the Amalekites.

**Saul's Shameful End (31:1-13).** The final chapter resumes the account of the Philistine war (1 Sam. 28–29). The Israelites were defeated and many killed on Mount Gilboa. The proud king died shamefully by ending his own life. His corpse was publicly abused by the Philistines. Three of Saul's sons were also killed in battle, preparing the way for David to be king.

The people of Jabesh Gilead remembered how Saul had delivered them from the Ammonites (see 11:1-11). They journeyed all night to Beth Shan, where Saul's body had been impaled. They stole the body away and honorably buried Saul at Jabesh, where they mourned his death.

**Theological and Ethical Significance.** God desires people "after his own heart" (13:14). Such people mirror God's love and faithfulness. God rejected Eli's sons as worship leaders because of their wickedness. In their place God raised up "a faithful priest" who would do what was in God's heart and mind (2:35). God rejected Saul as king because of his disobedience. God looked at David's heart and chose him to lead God's people (16:7).

God is free to choose leaders for His people (see Deut. 17:15). Samuel was not a Levite, but God chose him to minister as a priest (1 Sam. 1:1). Saul was from the least significant family of "the smallest tribe in Israel," but God chose him to deliver His people (9:16,21). David was the youngest in his family, but God chose him as king (16:11-12).

Christians are to respect those whom God has chosen to lead His people. David showed respect for Saul because he was the Lord's anointed. Christians should also remember that God is the true Leader of His people. No Christian leader can take God's place. God dealt harshly with Eli's sons, who had no respect for God's sacrifices and abused the laypeople who looked to them for religious leadership. God dealt harshly with Saul, who disregarded God's command given through the prophet Samuel. No Christian leader is above God's word.

## Questions for Reflection

1. What influence can godly parents have on the lives of their children?

2. By what different means does the Lord accomplish His purposes for His people?

3. What are the consequences of disobedience to the word of the Lord?

4. What are proper ways the people of God may seek the Lord's will?

5. What kind of person does the Lord choose to lead His people?

## Sources for Additional Study

Baldwin, Joyce G. *1 & 2 Samuel.* Downers Grove: InterVarsity, 1988.

Bergen, Robert D. *1, 2 Samuel.* New American Commentary. Nashville: Broadman & Holman, 1996.

Laney, J. Carl. *First and Second Samuel.* Chicago: Moody, 1982.

Payne, David F. *I & II Samuel.* Philadelphia: Westminster, 1982.

# 2 SAMUEL

First and Second Samuel form an uninterrupted narrative in the Hebrew Bible (compare the introduction to 1 Samuel). Second Samuel continues the story of Israel's monarchy, tracing the history of David's reign from its triumphs to its troubles.

**Theme.** God consolidated the kingdom through the reign of David, who unified the nation, conquered Israel's foes, and received God's covenantal promise of an eternal dynasty and kingdom (7:5-16). Though David sinned, God's grace proved greater than David's sin. Though David suffered consequences of his sin, God continued to watch over him and preserve his rule. Through David, God blessed Israel with its next king (Solomon) and, in time, with Jesus, its Messiah.

I. God Establishes (1:1–10:19)
II. God Chastens (11:1–20:26)
III. God Preserves (21:1–24:25)

**Purpose and Theology.**

1. Second Samuel continues the story of how God established His kingdom through the leadership of Israel's monarchy. In this second portion of Samuel, the anointing of David for rule (1 Sam. 16:12-23) was realized. David secured the borders of Israel, subjugated its enemies, and brought prosperity to the fledgling kingdom.

2. The Davidic covenant is the theological centerpiece of the book (chap. 7). God promised David and his heirs an eternal lineage that would rule over an everlasting kingdom (7:12-16). The Davidic king was God's adopted son who ruled in the name of the Lord and enjoyed God's providential care. This covenant promise became the messianic hope of God's people (see Pss. 2; 110).

The messianic expectation was a source of great comfort in Israel's darkest days (see Isa. 9:1-7; 11; Amos 9:11-15; Zech. 9:9-13). This promise is fulfilled by David's Greater Son, Jesus Christ (Luke 1:31-33).

3. The book also shows how the Davidic covenant affected Israel's national fortunes. The favor of God enabled David to establish Jerusalem as the political and religious center of the nation by bringing the ark into the city and establishing a ruling bureaucracy (2 Sam. 6; 8:15-18). David also experienced victories over the powerful Philistines and Arameans (8:1-14; 10). David's house grew in international prestige, paving the way for a mighty dynastic order. However, while the covenant contained promised blessing, it also included God's chastening for sin. The book details the troubling consequences for the nation because of David's sin (chaps. 12–20).

4. Second Samuel teaches that God is faithful and merciful. God remained loyal to His promise although David at times failed the covenant. David and Bathsheba sinned, and their child died in judgment. God, however, gave Bathsheba the child Solomon, whom the Lord loved (12:24-25). God continued to reveal His will to David through the prophets Nathan and Gad and the priests Zadok and Abiathar (12:1-14; 15:24-29; 24:11-14). Also, He was merciful by safeguarding David during the rebellions of Absalom and Sheba (chaps. 18; 20).

5. The narrative of 2 Samuel indicates that God expects faithfulness and righteousness. The Davidic covenant had the provision of punishing David for sin (7:14-15). Nathan the prophet delivered

a divine oracle of judgment against David for his sin with Bathsheba (12:1-23). God also judged David for his pride in Israel's military strength (chap. 24). Unlike Saul, who tried to excuse his sin, David confessed his sins before the Lord (12:13; 24:10).

6. Second Samuel depicts Israel's God as the covenant Lord of history (5:19b; 6:21-22; 8:14; 12:11; 23:10b; 24:25).

## GOD ESTABLISHES (1:1–10:19)

This section of the book traces the triumphs of David's reign, first over the tribe of Judah and then over all Israel. The high point of David's career was the covenant the Lord made with David and his descendants. Because of God's blessing, David successfully expanded his kingdom by defeating Israel's enemies.

***David's Lament (1:1-27).*** God gave the throne to David; David did not steal the kingdom from Saul. David proved this by dealing swiftly with Saul's alleged killer and publicly lamenting his personal loss of Saul and Jonathan.

An Amalekite came to David at Ziklag and related how he had killed Saul on Mount Gilboa. Most likely the Amalekite was fabricating his story in order to receive a reward (see 1 Sam. 31:3-6; 2 Sam. 18:22). The Amalekite was greeted with David's strongest rebuke. David, who had more cause than anyone to kill the king, had refused to raise his hand against the Lord's anointed (1 Sam. 24:6; 26:23). But this pagan slave did not respect the Lord's anointed. David's men executed the Amalekite for his alleged deed.

David lamented the deaths of Saul and Jonathan. His sorrowful refrain "How the mighty have fallen!" expressed tribute to these great men whom David loved and missed.

***David Anointed at Hebron (2:1-32).*** David showed his dependence on the Lord by inquiring what he should do about Saul's kingdom. The Lord instructed David to go to Hebron. There the elders of Judah anointed him king. His first act as king was the gracious commendation of the men of Jabesh Gilead who had bravely rescued the body of Saul (see 1 Sam. 31:8-13).

David was appointed by God. In contrast, Abner installed the surviving son of Saul, Ish-Bosheth, as David's rival. Ish-Bosheth, meaning *man of shame,* was changed from the original Esh-Baal (*man of Baal;* see 1 Chr. 8:33; 9:39). Ish-Bosheth reigned from Mahanaim in Transjordan during David's rule in Hebron.

With the outbreak of war, Abner confronted Joab, David's general, in battle at Gibeon. Abner was pursued by Joab's brother, Asahel. Abner warned him to stop, but he continued; and Abner was forced to kill him.

***God Strengthens David (3:1-39).*** David's house increased while Ish-Bosheth's foothold weakened. David possessed many sons, a sign in antiquity of strength and blessing.

As a result of his dispute with Ish-Bosheth, Abner defected to David's side. Abner had sexual relations with a concubine in the royal harem. Ish-Bosheth interpreted this as a threat to his throne (see 16:21-22; 1 Kgs. 2:22). Abner was so incensed at this charge that he secretly met with David in Hebron. Abner vowed to bring all Israel under David's rule. David agreed on the condition that Abner return his wife Michal, whom Saul had given to another man (1 Sam. 18:20-27). Abner left under a covenant of peace. When Joab returned to Hebron from battle, he was told of Abner's arrangement with David. Because of his blood feud with Abner (2:23-24), Joab plotted the assassination of Abner without David's knowledge.

David was so distraught at Abner's murder that he took special steps to disassociate himself from the guilt of Joab's wicked deed. He declared a national day of mourning and personally abstained from food. The people concluded from this that David was innocent; his stature increased in their eyes.

***Avenging Saul's House (4:1-12).*** The defection of Abner discouraged Ish-Bosheth's already-dwindling support. Two of his captains, Baanah and Recab, murdered and decapitated the king during his midday's rest. With the death of Ish-Bosheth, David had no serious rival. Mephibosheth, the only surviving son of Jonathan, suffered from a crippling disability and was not a threat (see chap. 9).

Ish-Bosheth's assassins presented the king's head to David as the Lord'S vengeance upon the house of Saul. Although Ish-Bosheth's death advanced David's kingdom, he abhorred their treason and executed the murderers.

***David Reigns (5:1-25).*** After Ish-Bosheth's death the northern tribes joined Judah in making David their king. All Israel anointed him at Hebron "before the LORD." David reigned for forty years (5:4) from 1011–971 B.C.

David marched on Jerusalem to dispossess the Jebusites from their mountain fortress upon Zion. The citadel of Jerusalem became known as the City of David because it became his personal royal possession. The move from Hebron to Jerusalem gave David a military and political advantage. The site was strategically located, easy to defend, and had no strong political association with the northern or southern tribes (see 1 Chr. 12:23-40). The respect Hiram, king of Tyre, showed David's emerging kingdom assured him that the Lord was establishing his throne.

The triumphs of David are no better illustrated than in his victories over Israel's archenemies, the Philistines. Unlike Saul, who failed against the Philistines, David succeeded because he was careful to follow the word of the Lord.

***The Ark of God (6:1-23).*** David wanted to bring the ark of the covenant to Jerusalem from the house of Abinadab, its home base after its capture by the Philistines (1 Sam. 7:1-2). With the ark in Jerusalem, the religious and political life of the nation could be unified around David.

The ark was called the "Name," a reverential reference to the holy name of the Lord. The presence of the ark symbolized the presence of God. Because of its close association with God, the Israelites were instructed that only the Levites (sons of Kohath) should carry it and that it was not to be touched (see Exod. 25:12-15; Num. 4:15; 7:9; Deut. 10:8). The sons of Abinadab, Uzzah and Ahio, set the ark on a new cart, as the Philistines had done (1 Sam. 6:7), and guided it. Uzzah steadied the ark with his hand when it shifted on the cart. God struck him dead at the site of the ark because he showed disrespect for the holy things of God (see 1 Chr. 15:13).

Because of this unusual demonstration of God's holiness and wrath, David learned to fear the Lord. He showed special homage by sacrificing a burnt offering after the ark had been carried six paces. The ark entered the city without incident only when the priests carried it properly. When David brought the ark into Jerusalem, he celebrated with dance and dressed humbly before the Lord.

***The Lord's Covenant (7:1-29).*** God's covenant with David followed his humble display before the Lord and the Jerusalem crowds. After securing his kingdom, David showed his concern for the reputation of the Lord, who dwelt in

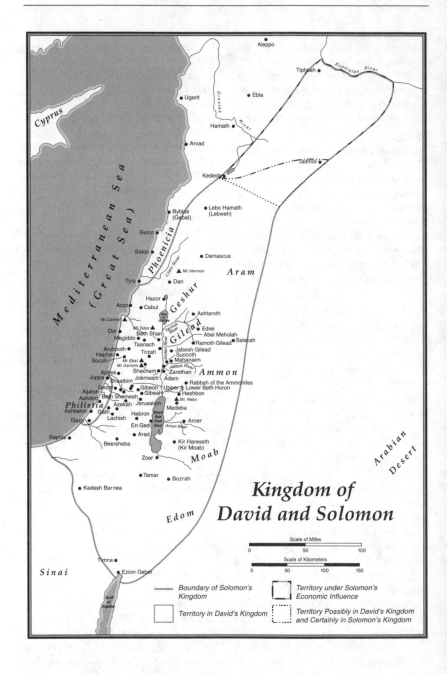

Kingdom of
David and Solomon

Scale of Miles

| 0 | 50 | 100 |

Scale of Kilometers

| 0 | 50 | 100 | 150 |

Boundary of Solomon's Kingdom

Territory under Solomon's Economic Influence

Territory in David's Kingdom

Territory Possibly in David's Kingdom and Certainly in Solomon's Kingdom the wilderness tabernacle and not in an impressive temple structure.

The Lord, however, would build a "house" for David—not a building but a dynasty. The prophet Nathan instructed David in the Lord's covenant. The Davidic covenant consisted of three eternal promises: a dynastic lineage, a kingdom, and a throne. The Lord would be as a father to David's son, the Lord's representative in the earth. If David's descendants sinned, the Lord warned of chastening. But He promised never to annul His covenant.

This covenant gave rise to the messianic hope in the Old Testament. Although David's descendants failed, the people clung to the hope of a Greater David. The angel Gabriel echoed the words of David's covenant when he announced the birth of Israel's King, Jesus the Savior (Luke 1:32-33)

David responded with praise, recognizing God's greatness and the blessedness of His favor. He petitioned the Lord to keep His promise forever so that the Lord might be magnified by all nations.

***David's Victory (8:1-18).*** God's promises for David's kingdom were first realized through the military and administrative successes of his rule. David subjugated the Philistines in the west, the Moabites in the east, Zobah and Damascus in the north, and the Edomites in the south. Indeed, "The LORD gave David victory wherever he went."

The expanding bureaucracy included the mercenary soldiers of the Kerethites (Crete) and Perethites (Philistines?) under the command of Benaiah (see 15:18; 20:7,23). Abiathar was joined by Zadok as priest. Civil advisers included a recorder and a secretary.

***David and Mephibosheth (9:1-13).*** David was not only an effective warrior and administrator, but he also was a beneficent ruler. He desired to honor the pledge he had made to Jonathan and his family (1 Sam. 20:14-15). He inquired and learned from Ziba, a servant in Saul's household, about Mephibosheth, who was Jonathan's only surviving son. Mephibosheth was crippled and lived in obscurity. When he was brought before David, the king calmed his fears and returned Saul's property to him. Mephibosheth lived in Jerusalem and ate at the king's table.

***Ammonites and Arameans (10:1-19).*** David also desired to be generous to the son of his deceased ally King Nahash and sent a delegation to express his sympathies. But David's delegation was charged with espionage and was humiliated by Nahash's son, Hanun. The Ammonites hired Aramean mercenaries and prepared for David's advance. The armies of Joab and Abishai prevailed by outmaneuvering them. But the Arameans under Hadadezer gathered more troops from beyond the Euphrates. David subjugated them, expanding his realm to the east.

The author also recorded this rout of the Arameans in the summary of David's victories in 8:3-8. These two battles, which the author describes in more detail, took place before David's final victory over the Arameans.

## GOD CHASTENS (11:1–20:26)

The sin of David and Bathsheba changes the tenor of the story from David's triumphs to his troubles. The following events tell the consequences of their sin as David's kingdom was rocked by moral and political problems.

***David's Sin (11:1-27).*** Israel's war with Ammon was the background for David's sin against God. The author implied that David should have been at war rather than remaining behind. Perhaps his earlier successes gave him a sense of false security. The author's

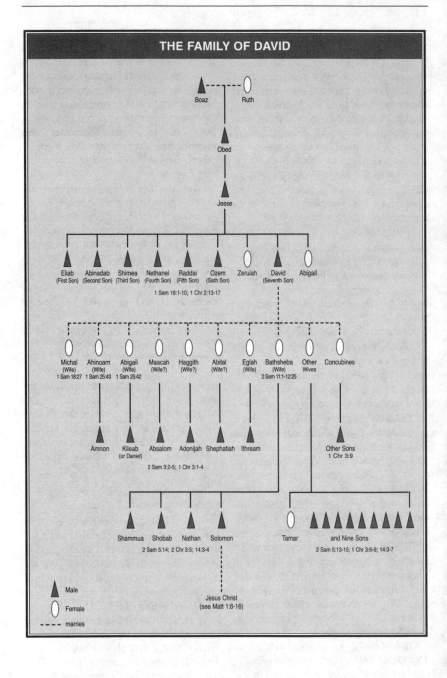

## DAVID AS KING AND MESSIAH

*Messiah* is a Hebrew term meaning *anointed one*. The New Testament term *Christ* represents a translation of this Hebrew word into Greek.

In the Old Testament the king of Israel was often called "the LORD'S anointed." The act of anointing symbolically conferred God's Spirit on the king and designated him as God's representative (1 Sam. 24:6,10).

The ideals for kingship in Israel are perhaps most clearly seen in Psalms. Israel's king was to be a righteous and universal ruler (Pss. 2:8-12; 45:4-7). His rule was to be everlasting (Pss. 21:4; 45:6). He was to befriend the poor and resist their oppressors Ps. 72:2-4, 12-14). He was to be honored as God's Son (Ps. 2:7) and to lead the nation to victory over its foes (21:8-12; 89:22-23). Though no human king could fully measure up to these ideals, they were closely associated with David. David became the standard by which later kings were measured (1 Kgs. 3:3, 14; 2 Kgs. 14:3).

When Israel's prophets spoke of a future ideal King, this Anointed One *(messiah)* was described in terms of the Davidic ideal. David was used as a model, a pointer or type, of what this future King would be like. Like David, the Messiah would be a king of Israel, born in Bethlehem (Mic. 5:2), who would rule in righteousness (Isa. 11:1-16). But the coming King would be more than David. He would have universal rule (Mic. 5:4). He would be "God with us" (Immanuel—Isa. 7:14; Matt. 1:23), the Prince of peace and might God (Isa. 9:6-7). He would be called "Branch" and "The LORD Our Righteousness" (Jer. 23:5; 33:15-16). This Anointed One is the Servant of the Lord (Isa. 42:1-4; 49:1-6; 50:4-9; 52:13–53:12). From his vantage during the exile, when no son of David sat on a throne in Jerusalem, Ezekiel could still hope for a new Shepherd like David (Ezek. 34:23-24; see 1 Sam. 17:34-35).

---

description of David's temptation is reminiscent of Achan's sin (Josh. 7): he saw her, inquired about her, and then he took her.

When Bathsheba learned of her pregnancy, David attempted to cover up his sin. He sent for her husband, Uriah the Hittite, who was in the field of battle. Uriah refused to go home to his wife, even at David's insistence. Uriah did not want to enjoy his wife and home when the ark and armies of God were on the battlefield.

In desperation David plotted with the aid of Joab to murder Uriah by exposing him to the Ammonites in battle. The plot succeeded, and David took Bathsheba as his wife. The sin, however, did not go unnoticed, for "the thing David had done displeased the LORD."

**Nathan's Oracle (12:1-31).** About one year later, God sent Nathan to confront David. Nathan told a parable of a poor man's only ewe lamb taken away by a rich man for his selfish pleasure. David, who as king was responsible for justice in the land, burned with anger against the culprit. Unwittingly, David condemned himself. Nathan accused the king, "You are the man! Nathan declared God's judgment. Because he murdered Uriah by the sword, his household would likewise experience the sword. Since he took the wife of another man, David's wives would be taken. And though David sinned in secret, he would be publicly humiliated before all Israel (see 15:16; 16:21-22). These curses were fulfilled by the deaths of three of David's sons (Amnon, Absalom, and Adonijah) and the strife David's reign experienced toward the end of his life.

To David's credit, however, he did not shirk his guilt as Saul did when Samuel accused him (see 1 Sam. 15). David confessed his guilt openly and lamented his spiritual impurity (see Ps. 51). The judgment of God began with the child of David and Bathsheba. David prayed and fasted earnestly for the child's life. David had felt the heavy hand of God's judgment, but he also knew God's mercies. For that reason he prayed, believing God might deliver the child. Though the child was not spared, David believed that he would see the child again. In the midst of His chastening, God also was merciful to David and Bathsheba. God gave them another child, Solomon, whom the Lord named Jedidiah ("beloved of the LORD"). From their union came the king who would build the Lord's temple and rule Israel during its golden age. Evidence of God's continued forgiveness was Israel's victory over the Ammonites—this time led by David himself.

**Absalom Murders Amnon (13:1-39).** Although God forgave David, the consequences of his sin were immediately seen in his household. Just as David had lusted for Bathsheba, Amnon, the king's eldest son, desired his half-sister Tamar. He lured Tamar into his private quarters and raped her. However, his guilt was too great for his conscience, and he despised her afterward. He dismissed her, and she took refuge in the house of Absalom, her brother.

David, like Eli and Samuel, had no control over his sons. Absalom harbored his hatred for Amnon for two years until an occasion arose to kill him. Absalom held a festival attended by Amnon. At the command, Absalom's servants murdered Amnon. Absalom fled to Geshur where he took refuge with his maternal grandfather, Talmi, the king of Geshur. David wept for his son Amnon, who was special to the king as his eldest and successor to the throne. Yet he longed to see Absalom for the three years they were estranged.

**Absalom Returns (14:1-33).** Perhaps out of concern for the state of the kingdom, Joab wanted David's potential successor returned to the royal house. Similar to Nathan's ruse (chap. 12), Joab sent to the king a woman of Tekoa who pretended to be a woman in mourning. She sought the king's mercy on her only surviving son, who had murdered his brother. When David ruled that the son should be spared, the woman challenged David to reconsider his banishment of his own son Absalom. David agreed and dispatched Joab to retrieve him. David, however, refused to see Absalom's face upon his return to Jerusalem.

**Absalom's Coup (15:1-37).** Four years later the crown prince mounted an insurrection against the king by taking the king's place in the eyes of the people. Ironically, David's kingdom almost collapsed as a result of his own mishandling of his subjects rather than external threats. Absalom began to play the role of king. He had a private standing guard and functioned as final arbiter of judicial cases. Absalom stole away the hearts of the people, and he attempted to steal the kingdom from David. At Hebron, where his father had been declared king, Absalom's coconspirators acclaimed him king. Among their ranks was David's political advisor, Ahithophel.

Joined by a small but loyal contingency of Kerethites and Pelethites, David fled across the Kidron Valley toward the desert. He left behind his royal harem. Ittai the Gittite and his six hundred mercenary soldiers (Philistines from Gath) went with David. David sent Zadok and Abiathar back to Jerusalem with the ark of the Lord. David knew that the ark belonged in the house of God. He believed that if God so desired he would return one day to see the holy place of the Lord. The two priests, as prophetic seers, could aid David by learning of Absalom's plans and inquiring of the Lord in his behalf. Also, David countered the wisdom of Ahithophel by ordering Hushai the Arkite to remain in Absalom's service in order to confound the coup's strategy.

**David's Anguish in Flight (16:1-23).** The dark shadow of Saul again was cast over David as he fled his kingdom. Ziba, Saul's servant and manager of Mephibosheth's estate, maliciously defamed Mephibosheth to better himself (see 19:24-28). David granted the lands of Saul to Ziba. Shimei, a member of Saul's family, cursed David, calling him a "man of blood." This charge probably reflected the enmity many harbored against David. It may refer to David's turning members of Saul's family over to the Gibeonites for execution (chap. 21). Shimei attributed David's pain to the Lord's retribution. David perceived that Shimei's curse, though not altogether just, was part of God's chastening for his sin. David repelled Abishai's ambition to kill Saul's kinsman. David believed that God's vengeance or mercies alone would decide his and Shimei's fates.

Meanwhile, Hushai arrived in Jerusalem to win Absalom's favor. Absalom, not yet ready to trust Hushai, turned to Ahithophel for advice. He counseled Absalom to announce his takeover by the symbolic gesture of publicly sleeping with David's concubines (see 1 Kgs. 2:17-25). Absalom's incestuous act thus fulfilled Nathan's prophecy. The narrator compared the political adeptness of Ahithophel to the word of God revealed to the prophets.

**Ahithophel's Advice (17:1-29).** Hushai's task was a formidable one. Ahithophel advised Absalom to attack David while his troops were in disarray. This time Absalom heard the second opinion of Hushai, who argued that such a tactic would fail because of David's wily experience in warfare. Absalom postponed his attack, which meant that David had the opportunity to withdraw. The Lord "determined to frustrate the good advice of Ahithophel" and thereby doomed Absalom (see 15:34). The outcome of the war was decided before the first blow was struck.

Absalom's strategy was relayed to David's camp at the river fords through Jonathan and Ahimaaz, the sons of Zadok and Abiathar (see 15:35-36). Meanwhile, the wicked Ahithophel took his own life because he knew that Hushai's plan meant the end of Absalom's kingdom (15:15-23).

David in exile set up his provisional base in Mahanaim across the Jordan (see 2:8). Absalom established his military command by giving Amasa, Joab's relative, charge of the army. While Absalom organized for battle, David's friends—Shobi, Makir, and Barzilli—refreshed his fatigued army.

**Absalom's Death (18:1-33).** The story of Absalom's death focuses on David as father rather than as king. David remained behind the battle lines at the advice of his troops. He dispatched his commanders, instructing them to care for Absalom's life. Absalom, on the other hand, entered into the battle as it raged in the forests of Ephraim and beyond. The terrain was so precarious that more died from its pits and thickets than the sword. Absalom himself was its victim. He was caught by the head (see 14:26) in a tree and was suspended in midair. Though reminded of David's instructions to spare Absalom, Joab killed the helpless prince. The tragedy and disgrace of how Absalom died was even sadder because he had no heir. His three sons had apparently also died (see 14:27).

The story's detailed description of the two messengers and David's hopes dashed by their news accentuates the anguish of David the father. David's sin had spelled disaster for his family and crippled his own soul: "O my son Absalom! My son, my son Absalom. If only I had died instead of you—O Absalom, my son!"

**David Returns (19:1-43).** Joab continued to place the state of the nation above the feelings of the king. The aftermath of the war required a stronger show of Davidic leadership. Joab rebuked David for mourning the death of his enemies instead of greeting his triumphant soldiers. David took his place at the gate to receive his troops.

The tribes of Israel urged their leaders to reinstall David as their king. The men of Judah were initially reluctant. David replaced Joab with Amasa in a gesture of reconciliation. No doubt, Joab's demotion was also due to his killing of Absalom. The king also extended his generosity by sparing Shimei's life, hearing out the explanation of Mephibosheth, and sharing Saul's inheritance with Ziba in spite of his treachery. Furthermore, he welcomed to his court the son of his loyal advisor Barzillai.

The undercurrent of strife between Israel and Judah became apparent when the men of Israel were left out of the welcoming party that ushered David home. They interpreted this as exclusion from David's kingdom. The succession of northern tribes from Jerusalem occurred in the reign of David's grandson, Rehoboam (see 1 Kgs. 12:16-20).

**Sheba's Revolt (20:1-26).** The conclusion of this section concerning David's troubles appropriately ends with yet another rebellion. Sheba, a Benjamite, led an insurrection against David. The tribe of Benjamin, the kin of King Saul, had a long-standing feud with David as evidenced already by Shimei (16:7). Now fueled by animosity against Judah, Sheba seized the opportunity to rally the men of Israel to support his coup.

Amasa's slowness to attend to the rebellion forced David to appoint Abishai and Joab to deal with Sheba. When Amasa finally joined Joab's campaign, Joab greeted him with a treacherous kiss and then thrust his sword into Amasa's belly. Meanwhile, Sheba took refuge in Abel Beth Maacah, where the Judahites besieged the city. The people of Israel must have been skeptical of Sheba's chances for success. A woman of the city convinced its citizens to offer the head of Sheba to Joab, thereby averting the city's massacre and ending the schism.

The author concluded this section with a brief report on David's bureaucracy. This final listing of David's officials is similar to 8:15-18 with two important differences. There is no mention of slave labor in David's earlier administration, and also David's sons are absent.

## GOD PRESERVES (21:1–24:25)

The last section of the book is an appendix to David's career as the Lord's anointed. Here the emphasis falls on David's praise for God's sovereign mercies and the mighty warriors the Lord used in the service of the king. The stories of famine, war, and pestilence resulting from Israel's sin were fitting reminders that no king was above the word of the Lord.

**God Avenges (21:1-22).** A three-year famine caused David to inquire how Israel had offended the Lord. It was common in the Old Testament to attribute such catastrophies to the Lord's intervention. King Saul had breached Israel's long-standing covenant with the Gibeonites (see Josh. 9:25-27). Although 1 Samuel does not narrate Saul's murder of these Amorites (who resided in his homeland of Benjamin), such an act was consistent with Saul's policies (see 1 Sam. 22:16-19). David turned over seven descendants of Saul's house (sparing Mephibosheth) to the Gibeonites for execution to avenge their loss. David buried Saul's kin honorably with his and

Jonathan's bones. The execution of Saul's kinsmen may have been the reason Shimei claimed David was guilty of bloodshed (see 16:7-8).

The catalog of wars against the Philistines is a commentary on the continued troubles in the reign of David but also a tribute to God's abiding favor as Israel prevailed over their foes.

**Thanksgiving Hymn (22:1-51).** The core of the appendix is David's tribute to the Lord. This song was also included in the Book of Psalms (Ps. 18). The occasion for David's thanksgiving was his deliverance from King Saul.

David recalled his cry for deliverance. He described the Lord's intervention in words reminiscent of His appearance at Mount Sinai (see Exod. 19; Ps. 68:7-18; Hab. 3). The Lord, awesome in might, came to his personal rescue because David was upright and faithful. God was his Lamp, Rock, and Shield of Salvation, giving David complete victory over all his enemies. The song concludes with a doxology.

**Oracle (23:1-39).** Although other words from David are recorded in the Old Testament books that follow (1 Kgs. 2:1-9; 1 Chr. 23:27), this oracle was David's last formal reflection on the enduring state of his royal house under the covenant care of the Lord. The term "oracle" commonly introduces prophetic address (Num. 23:7; Isa. 14:28; Mal. 1:1). David declared by the Spirit that God had chosen him from all Israel and made an everlasting covenant with his lineage. Those who opposed him would be cast aside as thorns for the fire. This messianic description is fully realized in Jesus Christ, who as David's son establishes the rule of God in the earth.

The catalog of mighty men and their exploits was another tribute to God's enablement of David. Among David's armies were two elite groups of champions who served as the king's bodyguard and special fighting force (see 21:15-22; 1 Chr. 11:10-47). The first group consisted of the "Three" whose exploits against the Philistines were renown (see the cave of Adullam, 1 Sam. 22). Abishai and Benaiah were singled out, although they were not as great as the "Three," because they held high honor in the annals of David's wars. The second group, the "Thirty," is also listed, giving a total count of thirty-seven heroes (including Joab, 22:24-39).

**David's Pride (24:1-25).** The final episode of the appendix concerns the plague the Lord brought against Israel because of David's sin. It parallels the beginning story of the appendix where Israel suffered famine because of Saul's sin (21:1-14). The specific reason for God's anger at Israel is unstated. The Lord, however, used David's census to chasten the people by plague. In the parallel passage (1 Chr. 21:1) the author explained that the immediate cause for David's sin was the work of Satan.

David's taking of the census was an indication of his pride and self-reliance. In the law the taking of a census required an atonement price to avert plague (Exod. 30:11-16). God instructed the prophet Gad to announce His judgment on Israel. God presented David a choice of three punishments—famine, plague, or war. These three sanctions were the curses God threatened to bring upon Israel for breaking the covenant (Deut. 28). David wisely placed himself at the mercy of God and not the temperament of man. The Lord punished Israel by a devastating plague. David confessed that he was guilty for misleading the sheep of Israel.

To make atonement for Israel, the prophet Gad instructed David to build an altar at the threshing floor of Araunah. There David had seen the avenging angel carry out the deadly plague. He would later choose this site for the building of the temple (1 Chr. 22:1).

Araunah offered to give the floor to the king, but David knew that acceptable atonement required a price. He built the altar, offered sacrifices, and prayed in behalf of his people. The Lord acknowledged David's intercession, and the plague ceased.

***Ethical and Theological Significance.*** David's story, like Romans 7:7-25, speaks to the Christian's experience of sin. David was a man after God's own heart (1 Sam. 13:14). Like Paul, he could have said, "In my inner being I delight in God's law" (Rom. 7:22). But like Paul, David saw "another law at work in the members of [his] body, . . . making [him] a prisoner of the law of sin" (7:23). David coveted Uriah's wife, and "sin sprang to life" (7:9). With Uriah's murder, David's sin became "utterly sinful" (7:13).

Nathan's parable roused David's moral outrage at his sin (2 Sam. 12). Today Scripture functions like Nathan's tale to help us see what we are really like. David saw and experienced heartbreak over his sin.

David suffered short- and long-term consequences of his sin. His sin did not, however, thwart God's ultimate, saving purpose for and through him. "In all things God works for the good of those who love him" (Rom. 8:28). God worked through the lives of David and Bathsheba to give Israel its next king (Solomon) and, in time, its Messiah (Matt. 1:6). God continues to work through the lives of repentant sinners. "Thanks be to God—through Jesus Christ our Lord!" (Rom. 7:25).

## Questions for Reflection

1. What does 2 Samuel teach about war and peace?

2. How does personal sin affect family and friends?

3. What responsibilities does a Christian have in civic and business leadership?

4. What character traits made David a great man of God?

## Sources for Additional Study

Baldwin, Joyce G. *1 & 2 Samuel*. Downers Grove: InterVarsity, 1988.

Laney, J. Carl. *First and Second Samuel*. Chicago: Moody, 1982.

# 1 KINGS

The title *Kings* reflects the content of 1 and 2 Kings, which trace the history of God's covenant people under Israel's kings.

Like the Books of Samuel, 1 and 2 Kings were one book in the Hebrew tradition. The division of the book first occurred in the Greek version, which translated Samuel and Kings as four consecutive books entitled *First–Fourth Kingdoms*. Jerome's Vulgate followed the Greek tradition of four books but with the title *Kings*. The English title *Kings* was derived from the Latin Vulgate. The English version followed the Greek and Latin practice of four books but with the Hebrew titles *Samuel and Kings*. The division of Kings was not commonly practiced in Hebrew until the first printed edition in 1488.

The Books of Kings are anonymous. Jewish tradition assigns their authorship to Jeremiah. Rabbinic custom attributed unnamed works to famous religious leaders of the era. Many critical scholars believe 1 and 2 Kings are the last books of a consecutive history from Deuteronomy through Kings. This account is called the "Deuteronomistic History" because many of the major themes of the Book of Deuteronomy recur in the larger history. Other scholars who reject this reconstruction believe that the authorship of Kings is independent of Deuteronomy (see "The Historical Books").

Most commentators agree that much of Kings was written before the destruction of Jerusalem (586 B.C.), although how much is disputed. There is agreement on the date for the completion of the work. The last historical reference in Kings is 562 B.C., the first full year of Babylon's Evil-Merodach's reign (2 Kgs. 25:27). The completion of the book must be after this date but before the return of the exiles to Judah in 539 B.C. since 1 and 2 Kings do not mention this event. The book is dated at about 550 B.C., during the exile.

The author used a variety of sources, many of them early, in the writing of Kings. The sources ranged from royal and temple records to stories about the prophets. Excerpts from three royal annals are specifically cited: "the book of the annals of Solomon" (1 Kgs. 11:41; see also 11:27), "the book of the annals of the kings of Israel" (for example, 1 Kgs. 14:19), and "the book of the kings of Judah" (for example, 1 Kgs. 14:29). The author, however, was not merely an editor but a composer whose work was based on these sources.

The structure of Kings is built upon a fixed framework having introductory and concluding formulas about each king's reign. The structure deviates from this framework with the inclusion of the Elijah and Elisha narrative cycles. The "deviation" points to the force of the prophets as shapers of the history of God's people.

***Chronology of the Kings.*** Interpreters have a problem understanding how the chroniclers calculated the dates for the reigns of the kings. The reigns are dated by comparing the date a ruler began to reign with the number of years his counterpart in the other kingdom had reigned at that time. The length of the reign is provided for each king. However, there are problems reconciling the various dates. Additionally, Judah and Israel may have followed calendars beginning the new year at different times. Finally, there may have been differences in how the rulers counted the beginning of their reigns. Some began counting with their coronation, while others began counting only after their first year of reign. Therefore scholars have attempted reconstructions, including overlapping reigns of a father and son, to help explain the dates.

There is no consensus among scholars on all the dates of the kings. The differences are not so remarkable so as to impede our understanding of the historical background of the period. The dates followed here are those suggested by E. R. Thiele *(The Mysterious Numbers of the Hebrew Kings* [Grand Rapids: Eerdmans, 1965]).

**Theme.** God established Solomon as David's successor over Israel; but Solomon sinned, and God "humbled David's descendants" (11:39) by dividing the nation into two kingdoms. The ten tribes of the Northern Kingdom retained the name *Israel.* The Southern Kingdom took the name of its dominant tribe, *Judah.*

I. Ruthless Succession (1:1–2:46)
II. Riches and Ruin (3:1–11:43)
III. Judah and Israel Divided (12:1–16:34)
IV. Elijah and Micaiah (17:1–22:53)

**Purpose and Theology.**

1. First and Second Kings trace the history of Israel's monarchy during four tumultuous centuries from the reign of Solomon (971 B.C.) to Jehoiachin's imprisonment in Babylon (562 B.C.). They tell of Solomon's reign, including the building of the temple (1 Kgs. 1–11), the era of the Divided Kingdom to the fall of Samaria (1 Kgs. 12–2 Kgs. 17), and the last years of Judah down to the Babylonian exile (2 Kgs. 18–25).

2. This history of 1 and 2 Kings is not merely a political history of the monarchy. It is a prophetic interpretation of how each king affected the spiritual decline of Israel and Judah. The kings who had a greater religious impact receive more attention. For example, Omri was one of the most significant kings in the history of the ancient Near East, but his reign is only mentioned in a few verses (1 Kgs. 16:23-28). Much more is said about his son Ahab. The destruction of Israel and Judah was due to the idolatry advocated by their kings. By reciting this history from a theological perspective, the author both warned against idolatry and encouraged renewed commitment (8:33-34; 11:6,9-13; 13:34; 14:14-16; 18:39; 19:18).

3. First and Second Kings explain how history is governed by God's moral law. The theological perspective of Kings is the same as Deuteronomy's. Faithfulness to God's word is rewarded with blessing, but disobedience reaps God's judgment. This principle is demonstrated in the life of the two kingdoms whose rise and fall were dependent upon their obedience to the covenant of the Lord. The kings were evaluated on the basis of their fidelity to the Lord.

All the kings of the Northern Kingdom were condemned because of their idolatrous worship. In this they followed the ways of Israel's first king, Jeroboam, who introduced calf worship at Dan and Bethel (for example, 15:25-26,33-34). The kings of the Southern Kingdom, Judah, were approved if they followed after their father David (for example, 15:13). Only Hezekiah and Josiah met with full approval because they removed the high places and reformed the defiled worship of the temple (2 Kgs. 18:1-8; 22:1-2; 23:24-25).

4. The people of God are held responsible for their actions. The kings of David's descent experienced the same chastening for their sins as the evil kings of Israel (1 Kgs. 11:9; 14:22). Even a

prophet, the "man of God," suffered death for his unfaithfulness (13:26).

5. God is portrayed as the sovereign Lord of history. The prophets were God's spokespersons who announced the rise and fall of kings and kingdoms because God controls their destinies (1 Kgs. 11:29-32; 13:1-4; 16:1-7; 20:13,28; 22:13-28).

6. God is faithful. Although Judah's kings sinned, the Lord upheld His promise to David (2 Sam. 7:16) by preserving his kingdom and retaining his descendants on the throne (1 Kgs. 11:31-36; 15:3-5; 2 Kgs. 25:27-30). The Lord was faithful to His prophets who heralded His message in the face of danger (1 Kgs. 19:3-4,18; 22:24-28).

## RUTHLESS SUCCESSION (1:1–2:46)

This section completes the succession story of David begun in 2 Samuel 9–20. It depicts the ruthless struggle for power between Adonijah and Solomon as David neared his death. Only God's providential grace preserved the throne intact.

### Solomon Becomes King (1:1-53).

In his old age David needed the warmth and nursing of a servant girl named Abishag. The imminent death of the king explained the struggle that ensued between David's strongest allies. Adonijah, who was David's oldest living son (2 Sam. 3:4), led a conspiracy to make himself king. He was joined by Joab and the priest Abiathar at En Rogel, where they celebrated his impending enthronement. However, Nathan the prophet, Zadok the priest, Benaiah the captain of the king's bodyguard, and Solomon his brother were excluded.

Nathan knew that this meant banishment or death if Adonijah succeeded. Nathan encouraged Bathsheba to ask the king to fulfill his prior commitment to make Solomon king. Perhaps David had interpreted the special naming of Solomon (Jedidiah) by God as indicative of

the Lord's choice (see 2 Sam. 12:24-25 and Deut. 17:15).

David ordered the anointing of Solomon at the spring Gihon. When Adonijah heard the people shout, "Long live King Solomon," he fled for safety in the tabernacle, where he grasped the horns of the altar. The "horns" were the four projectiles at the corners of the altar where the blood of the sacrifice was smeared. Solomon spared Adonijah but placed him under house arrest.

### Solomon's Kingdom (2:1-46).

David's deathbed instructions warned Solomon that only obedience to the Lord would secure his kingdom. He advised Solomon to execute Joab for murdering Abner and Amasa (see 2 Sam. 3:22-27; 20:4-10) and to deal swiftly with Shimei for his treachery (see 2 Sam. 16:5-14). David died after his forty-year rule (1011–971 B.C.), but the kingdom was secure in the hands of his successor.

The enemies of David and Solomon received their retribution. Adonijah was executed because he asked for the hand of Abishag, a member of the royal harem. Solomon interpreted this request as tantamount to staking another claim to the throne. Zadok replaced Abiathar as chief priest because the latter had sided with Adonijah. This banishment of Abiathar fulfilled God's judgment on his ancestor Eli's house (1 Sam. 2:27-36). Benaiah executed Joab and replaced him as captain of Solomon's armies. Shimei also was executed because he disregarded the limitations of his house arrest (1 Kgs. 2:36-46a). The narrator aptly stated the conclusion of this struggle: "The kingdom was now firmly established in Solomon's hands."

## RICHES AND RUIN (3:1–11:43)

The second section of the book concerns Solomon's reign. It focuses on the wisdom he received from the Lord. He was able to assemble an impressive administration and to undertake numerous building projects, in particular the Jerusalem temple. He became an important international figure through wealth, trade, and politics. These accomplishments were God's blessing because of His covenant with David. But the author also tells how Solomon's apostasy caused Israel to lose all he had achieved.

**God's Gift of Wisdom (3:1-28).** Solomon married Pharaoh's daughter, which evidences Solomon's significance in the international community (7:8; 9:24). Solomon loved the Lord and obeyed Him as his father had, but he also practiced sacrifice at local shrines. This custom would become a snare when he turned to idolatrous worship at such high places (see Deut. 12:11-14).

Solomon requested in a dream the wisdom needed to serve the people of God. God granted him wisdom and more (1 Kgs. 3:4-15). An example of his wisdom was his ability to settle a dispute between two prostitutes. The people realized that his wisdom came from God.

**Solomon's Wisdom (4:1-34).** The list of officials, twelve administrative districts, and the necessary provisions for this bureaucracy show how God blessed Solomon in his administrative skills. This change in the tribal boundaries to twelve districts with their heavy taxation angered the northern tribes (see 12:1-17).

God gave Solomon great learning. The extent of his learning exceeded even the famous sages of Egypt and the East. He was gifted in the arts and also possessed unusual knowledge in the life sciences.

**Temple Preparations (5:1-18).** Like his father, Solomon was zealous for the reputation of the Lord. He allied himself with Hiram, king of Tyre in Phoenicia, and acquired from him building materials for the temple. When Hiram witnessed Solomon's wisdom, he praised the God of Israel. Solomon's laborers were drafted from among the Israelites. Samuel had warned Israel of such conscription under a king (1 Sam. 8:11-12,16).

**Temple Construction (6:1-38).** The importance of this event in the life of Israel is indicated by the careful dating of the event and the elaborate description of the temple's architectural plan. The date is the fourth year of Solomon's reign (966 B.C.). (See "Dates of the Exodus.") An architectural parallel to the Jerusalem temple's design is a Phoenician temple from about 850 B.C. recovered at Tell Ta'inat in Northern Syria. The Phoenician craftsmen, who were specialists, were employed for the temple (1 Kgs. 7:13-14; 2 Chr. 2:7,12-13). Between the description of the temple's external features and its luxuriant furnishings the author emphasized the Lord's promise to bless Solomon. The construction required seven and a half years. (See "The Temple.")

**Temple Furnishings (7:1-51).** The palace complex took almost twice as long to build as the temple. The proximity of Solomon's house to the Lord's house reflected the close relationship between God and king (see Ps. 2:7). Included with his own palace and the palace of Pharaoh's daughter was the costly Palace of the Forest of Lebanon with its elaborate halls (1 Kgs. 7:1-12).

The author was more interested in the construction of the temple and returned to describe its furnishings. Huram of Tyre, whose mother was a Hebrew, made the bronze furniture (see Bezalel, Exod. 31:3; 35:31). The bronze work consisted of the two pillars (named Jakin and Boaz) their capitals and designs, ten lavers, and the molten sea. The gold work included the altar, table of bread, lampstands, basins, and door sockets. (See the feature article "The Temple.")

Solomon placed in the temple the gifts and spoils of war dedicated by David (2 Sam. 8:10-12).

**Temple Dedication (8:1-66).** This event was the highlight of Solomon's career just as the bringing of the ark into Jerusalem was David's (2 Sam. 6). Solomon was accomplishing what the Lord promised to David's descendants. After the ark was set under the cherubim

---

## THE TEMPLE

The story of redemption is one of God's overcoming the breach sin caused in His relationship with humanity. The sanctuaries God instructed Israel to build reiterated God's intention to be Immanuel, God in their midst (Isa. 7:14; Matt. 1:23). But contact between a holy God and sinful people was restricted and mediated by priests. Each of Israel's sanctuaries had zones of increasing sanctity. The outer areas were open to all, while the inner court and the temple building were restricted to priests. The most holy place within the temple as restricted to the high priest, who entered there only on the Day of Atonement each year.

In the course of Israel's history God instructed Israel to build three sanctuaries. The first was the tabernacle, a portable shrine that fit Israel's homadic existence during the wilderness period (Exod. 25–40). Once Israel settled the promised land, the tabernacle continued to serve as the central shrine (Deut. 12).

That the tabernacle remained a portable shrine is clear from the sites associated with it: Shiloh (1 Sam. 1–4), Kiriath-Jearim (1 Sam. 7:1), Gibeon (1 Chr. 21:29), and Jerusalem (1 Chr. 23:25-26).

Solomon built the temple in Jerusalem on land David acquired in connection with his disastrous census (1 Chr. 21:1–22:1; 1 Chr. 28:1-19; 2 Chr. 3:1). The architectural details are described in 1 Kings 6–7 and 2 Chronicles 3–4. This temple was destroyed by the Babylonians in 586 B.C.

When Israel returned from the Babylonian captivity, a second temple was constructed in Jerusalem on the site of the first. This work was completed in 516 b.c (2 Chr. 36:22-23; Ezra 1:1–6:18).

The temple of Old Testament times was actually a third structure. By Jesus' ministry, this temple had been under construction for forty-six years (John 2:20). It was completed just before the destruction of Jerusalem by the Romans in A.D. 70.

In addition to these sanctuaries, during the Babylonian captivity God gave Ezekiel an extensive vision of a new Jerusalem, including a temple (Ezek. 40–48). Just as during the wilderness period, the tribes were arrayed around the sanctuary, portraying once again that God was in their midst (Ezek. 48; Num. 2; 9:15–10:36).

God indicated His acceptance of the tabernacle, the first temple, and the temple in Ezekiel's vision by the appearance of the pillar of fire and cloud—the Shekinah glory—to take up residence above the most holy place in those structures (Exod. 40:34-38; 1 Kgs. 8:10-13; 2 Chr. 5:13–6:2; 7:1-3; Ezek. 43:1-12). This pillar was a visible manifestation of God's presence, once again saying to Israel that God was with them, in their midst. Though prophets did say that God's glory would appear there (Hag. 2:1-9; Zech. 2:5,10-13), the Old Testament does not narrate the appearance of the pillar of fire and cloud at the second temple.

The Old Testament views Jesus as the fulfillment of the temple's true meaning: God with us (John 2:19-22; Heb. 10:19-22; Rev. 21:22). God takes residence in the church as His temple; believers enjoy the indwelling presence of God's Spirit (1 Cor. 3:16-17; 2 Cor. 6:16; Eph. 2:21-22; 1 Pet. 2:4-5). The goal of redemption history is in large measure overcoming that breach between God and humanity introduced in the fall. When that relationship is fully restored, in God's new city no temple will be needed (Rev. 21:1-3,22).

in the holy of holies, the whole house was filled with a cloud. The glory of the Lord was so great that it prohibited entry into the temple (see Exod. 40:34-35). This meant that the presence of the Lord was in the temple. The ark was moved in the wilderness from place to place, but the temple provided a permanent dwelling for the ark.

Solomon showed in his prayer that he did not conceive of the Lord as bound to a sacred place like the deities of the Canaanites. The temple could not house the God of heaven. The "Name" of the Lord transcends a mere physical structure.

Solomon anticipated Israel's captivity. He prayed that God would hear the repentant prayers of His people and bring them back to their inheritance (see Deut. 28:15-68). Solomon exhorted the people to walk faithfully before the Lord. The dedicatory service concluded with a fourteen-day feast of worship and celebration.

**The Lord Appears Again (9:1-9).** In response to Solomon's prayer, the Lord appeared as He had at Gibeon (3:4-15). The Lord exhorted Solomon to be obedient and warned that disobedience would result in exile and a rejection of the temple. Second Kings describes how this happened to the two kingdoms of the divided monarchy (chaps. 17; 25).

**Commercial Policies (9:10-28).** Solomon's acquisition of wealth further demonstrated the fulfillment of God's promise to David. He acquired gold from King Hiram in exchange for twenty cities. Solomon's extensive building projects, including fortifying Jerusalem and other royal cities, required him to conscript slave labor and to install Israelites as overseers.

**Queen of Sheba (10:1-29).** Just as Hiram of Phoenicia praised God (5:7), the Queen of Sheba extolled the Lord

because of Solomon's international fame. Sheba has been traditionally associated with South Arabia, which controlled the sea lanes between India and the East. God used Solomon's prestige to bring glory to Himself throughout the world.

Solomon's possession of gold, the extent of his shipping enterprises, and his military armament made him the most powerful king among the nations. He controlled the merchandising of horses from Kue (Cilicia) and of chariots from Egypt. The author attributed all of Solomon's splendor to the divine wisdom God gave him.

**Solomon's Apostasy (11:1-43).** Deuteronomy warned of forgetting God in prosperity (Deut. 6:10-12; 8:7-20). The troubles of Solomon's reign can be traced to the misuse of God's blessing. His success in international trade encouraged him to marry foreign wives for diplomatic reasons. He loved the Lord, but he also "loved many foreign women."

This love for foreign women grew greater than his love for the Lord's commandments. The wives caused him to pursue idolatrous worship. The hills of Jerusalem were dotted with high places sacred to the Phoenician fertility goddess Ashtoreth (see Deut. 16:21; Judg. 3:7; 1 Sam. 7:3-4), the god Molech of the Ammonites (Lev. 18:21), and Chemosh of Moab (Judg. 11:24).

The author concluded that "Solomon did evil in the eyes of the LORD" and did not obey "as David his father had done." Although David sinned against the Lord, his reign was not evil because he never fell into the contemptuous practice of idolatry. This practice brought God's judgment, which entailed Israel's division into two kingdoms. Solomon's wisdom and possessions were not subjected to the Lord. Therefore the Lord raised up three antagonists: Hadad the Edomite,

Rezon of Aram/Syria, and Jeroboam of the tribe Ephraim. Ahijah, the Lord's prophet, incited Jeroboam to lead the ten northern tribes to secede from Jerusalem.

Solomon died after forty years of rule (971–931 B.C.). Rehoboam succeeded his father and reaped the whirlwind of God's judgment.

## JUDAH AND ISRAEL DIVIDED (12:1–16:34)

The book describes the period of antagonism between the two kingdoms of Israel and Judah. Jeroboam's revolt fulfilled God's judgment on Solomon's kingdom. Jeroboam's dynasty was condemned and usurped for its evil idolatry. Israel suffered the bloodshed of war and political coups. In all, nine dynasties ruled Israel in its two hundred years (931–722 B.C.). The kingdom of Judah enjoyed the stability of only one dynastic house since the Lord preserved the throne of David. Yet its kings also committed the idolatrous sins of their northern counterparts. The kings of Judah continually experienced war, and only righteous Asa had a long, prosperous rule.

***Golden Calves (12:1-33).*** This chapter treats the watershed event in 1 Kings. King Rehoboam's refusal to rescind the oppressive forced labor and tax measures of his father, Solomon, split the kingdom. The ten tribes of Israel under Jeroboam seceded from Jerusalem, fulfilling the prophecy of Ahijah (see 11:29-39). Rehoboam attempted to reclaim his kingdom, but the prophetic word from Shemaiah prohibited him. Rehoboam's greatly reduced kingdom became known as Judah. Rehoboam's name means *one who enlarges the people,* but ironically he divided the people.

King Jeroboam built his military command at Shechem, an important religious and political site in Israel's history

(Josh. 24). He knew that his political fortunes were tied to the religious life of the nation. He set up two golden calves at Dan and Bethel (see Hos. 8:4-6; 10:5; Amos 7:8-13). He encouraged local high places and authorized a non-Levitical priesthood. He initiated an annual feast at Bethel in the eighth month to rival the Feast of Tabernacles traditionally celebrated in the seventh month (1 Kgs. 12:25-33; see Leviticus 23:33-43). Jeroboam cried out, "Here are your gods, O Israel, who brought you out of Egypt" (1 Kgs. 12:28). These gods were patterned after the sacred bull of Egypt (see Exod. 32:4) and the calf worshiped by the Canaanites. Yet Jeroboam tied the worship of these calves to the Lord's deliverance of Israel from Egypt. If Jeroboam intended to continue the worship of the Lord, the calves were meant only as pedestals for Israel's invisible God. From the sacred writer's viewpoint these calves were signs of pagan idolatry.

***Man of God (13:1-34).*** An unnamed prophet of the Lord delivered a message of judgment against Jeroboam's royal shrine at Bethel. He predicted that Josiah would destroy the Bethel worship site. This occurred in 621 B.C. when King Josiah of Judah initiated extensive religious reforms (2 Kgs. 23:15-17). When Jeroboam saw that he could not harm the prophet, he enticed him to stay. But the Lord had forbidden the prophet to eat or drink in the Northern Kingdom.

As the man of God left Bethel, an old prophet hoping to fellowship with him met the prophet and, using deceit, persuaded him to stay. The man of God foolishly agreed to dine with him. After the man of God left his host, a lion on the road killed him. When the old prophet discovered the body, he exclaimed, "It is the man of God who defied the word of the LORD." Ironically, the death of the

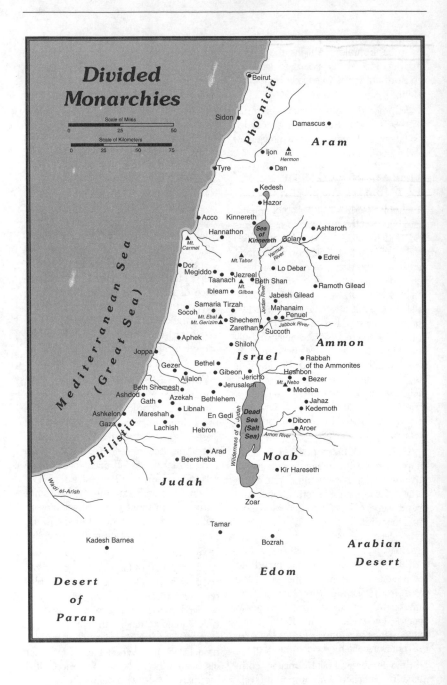

man of God proved that his predictions about Bethel would "certainly come true."

Jeroboam's sinful altar was the reason for his downfall and ultimately the demise of Israel (see 14:16; 15:29; 2 Kgs. 17).

**Denouncing Jeroboam (14:1-20).** Jeroboam's wife, disguised as another woman, visited Ahijah the prophet at Shiloh to learn the fate of her ailing son Abijam. The prophet was not fooled and denounced the house of her husband. He predicted the boy would die and the Lord would raise up another dynasty to cut off the progeny of Jeroboam (see 15:29). The prophet also foretold the exile of Israel. Jeroboam reigned twenty-two years (930–909 B.C.).

**Chastening Rehoboam (14:21-31).** Rehoboam squandered his heritage through spiritual apostasy. His reign was as wicked as Jeroboam's with its high places and male cult prostitutes. Although Judah was preserved because of the promise to David, the Lord in anger punished Rehoboam for his wickedness. He was afflicted by Shishak (Shoshenq), who was the founder of Egypt's Twenty-second Dynasty (945–924). An account of his wars is inscribed on the wall of the temple at Karnak. Rehoboam paid him handsomely from the gold accumulated by Solomon. Rehoboam reigned for seventeen years (930–913 B.C.). *J*

**Abijah and Asa 15:1-24).** Abijah's three-year reign was evil, but God sustained his throne as a "lamp" in Jerusalem for the sake of David.

Asa, however, received a good report from the sacred historian. His reign of forty-one years (910–869 B.C.) included reforms, though he did not remove the high places. During Asa's reign, Baasha of Israel built a fortress near Jerusalem at Ramah. Asa entered a treaty with Ben-Hadad, king of Aram (Syria), who attacked Israel. Baasha left Ramah and dismantled the fortress.

**Nadab of Israel (15:25-32).** Nadab succeeded his father Jeroboam but reigned only two years (909–908 B.C.). He did evil in the sight of the Lord like his father. Baasha assassinated Nadab and killed the whole household of Jeroboam, fulfilling the prediction of Ahijah (see 14:10-11,14). ✻

**Baasha and Elah (15:33–16:14).** The dynasty of Baasha was founded by assassination and ended in the same manner. The prophet Jehu condemned the evil of Baasha and foretold the demise of his house. He reigned for twenty-four years (908–886 B.C.) and was succeeded by his son Elah (886–885 B.C.). In a drunken stupor he was assassinated by Zimri, a court official. Zimri executed the whole family of Baasha just as Jehu had prophesied.

**Zimri's Seven Days (16:15-20).** Zimri's reign, the Third "Dynasty," had the distinction of being the shortest in the history of Israel. He ruled for seven days before he committed suicide in the flames of his palace. His demise was plotted by General Omri, who led an expedition against Zimri for his murder of King Elah.

**The House of Omri (16:21-28).** Omri defeated Tibni, a rival to the throne, and founded the Fourth Dynasty in Israel. His reign was only twelve years (885–874 B.C.). His fame was so great that a hundred years after his death the nation Israel was still called the "house of Omri." Omri had close ties with the Phoenicians, even marrying his son Ahab to the Tyrian princess Jezebel. Omri moved the capital of Israel from Tirzah to Samaria. There the kings of Israel ruled until its destruction by the Assyrians in 722 B.C.

**Ahab and Jezebel (16:29-34).** Ahab and Jezebel reigned for twenty-two

Omri father of Ahab

years (874–853 B.C.). Together they attempted to make Israel a pagan nation devoted to Baal and Asherah, the deities of the Sidonians. Ahab erected an idol of Baal in Samaria and built an image of the Canaanite goddess Asherah. The sacred historian was unimpressed with Ahab's many political accomplishments. Twice he evaluated Ahab's rule as more evil than all his predecessors.

During the reign of Ahab, a man named Hiel, who was from the sinful city of Bethel, rebuilt the city of Jericho. His sons died under the curse Joshua pronounced upon anyone who restored the city (Josh. 6:26). The author included this account to show that the Lord's judgment on sin is certain. Ahab too would suffer for his sins.

## ELIJAH AND MICAIAH (17:1–22:53)

The Elijah cycle of stories departs from the stereotyped reporting of the kings in chapters 12–16. The stories of the prophet Elisha show that the makers of Israel's history were not the kings but the prophets who dramatically shaped the future of each royal house.

Elijah's ministry occurred during Israel's greatest religious crisis under Ahab and Ahaziah (1 Kgs. 22:51–2 Kgs. 1:18). Ahab's reign declined because of wars with Aram and his theft of Naboth's vineyard.

***Trouble for Ahab (17:1-24).*** Elijah the Tishbite is introduced in the book suddenly as an envoy from the Lord. He proclaimed to Ahab a great drought which would end only when Elijah gave the word (see Jas. 5:17-18). The drought was a refutation of Ahab's Baalism because Baal was reputed to be the god of rain and vegetation. This showed that the Lord was the true Lord of nature.

During the three-year drought, Elijah dwelt with a widow and her son in Zarephath of Phoenicia, the native land of Jezebel, where Baal was worshiped. The drought had spread to Phoenicia, and the Lord used the prophet to provide food to this family. When the woman's son became ill and stopped breathing, Elijah prayed three times, and the Lord answered by raising up the boy. Because God did these miracles in Phoenicia, this showed that the Lord was the God of all nations and that Baal did not exist.

***Choosing the Real King (18:1-46).*** For three years Ahab and his servant Obadiah desperately sought the elusive Elijah. Elijah unexpectedly met Obadiah in the road and promised Obadiah that he would see the king. When Ahab met the prophet, he called Elijah the "troubler of Israel." Yet it was Ahab who caused Israel's distress. Elijah proposed a contest with the prophets of Baal and Asherah at Mount Carmel.

The contest was for the benefit of the people to learn who truly ruled Israel—the Baals of Ahab and Jezebel or the Lord God of their fathers. The contest consisted of preparing a sacrifice and praying for the deity to prove his existence by answering with fire from heaven. Baal was reputed to be the god of storm and therefore should at least have been able to bring down fire (lightning).

The prophets of Baal prayed all morning, but there was no answer. Elijah ridiculed their pagan theology. Then in ecstatic frenzy they frantically slashed themselves to draw their god's attention (see Lev. 19:28; Deut. 14:1), but there was no answer. At the evening hour of sacrifice, it was Elijah's turn. He rebuilt the altar of the Lord and called upon God, identifying Him as the "God of Abraham, Isaac and *Israel.*" Fire fell and the people exclaimed, "The LORD—he is God!" The people executed the evil prophets.

God also sent a great rainstorm to end the drought. The storm rained upon Ahab as he hurried to Jezreel. The hand of the Lord empowered Elijah to run ahead of Ahab's chariot to the city.

**Elijah Hides at Horeb (19:1-21).** Elijah's victory, however, turned into fear and depression. Surprisingly, Jezebel was not intimidated by Ahab's report of Elijah's deeds. She vowed to kill the prophet, who ran again but this time away from Jezebel to the desert. In despair the prophet prayed to die (see Num. 11:11-15; Job 6:8-9; Jon. 4:8). The angel of the Lord strengthened him with food, and he journeyed forty days and nights to a cave at Mount Horeb. It was upon the same Mount Horeb, another name for Mount Sinai, that the Lord had revealed Himself to Moses (see Exod. 3; 19).

Elijah complained that the Israelites had abandoned God and that he was the last prophet of the Lord. But Elijah was mistaken. God brought in succession a great wind, an earthquake, and a fire to ravage the mountain. But the prophet did not hear God in these events. Instead, Elijah heard the Lord in a small whisper. By this the prophet learned that sometimes God works in quiet ways.

There were in fact seven thousand who had not worshiped Baal. God sent Elijah to anoint three men who would ultimately destroy Ahab's house—Hazael of Aram, Jehu of Israel, and the prophet Elisha. The call of Elisha was the beginning of a large school of prophets (see 2 Kgs. 6:1-2).

**Ahab's Victory (20:1-43).** The Aramean king, Ben-Hadad, forged a coalition of thirty-two kings who besieged Samaria and held it hostage. Ahab, at the bidding of an unnamed prophet, secretly attacked the drunken Arameans, and the Lord granted Ahab's weaker armies a surprising victory. By this God demonstrated to Ahab that He was the true Lord of Israel. The next year the Arameans, believing that the Lord was a god only of

the hills, attacked the city of Aphek located in a valley. God again granted victory to show that He ruled over hill and valley. In spite of God's grace, evil Ahab violated the rules of holy war and spared the life of Ben-Hadad. The Lord sent another prophet to the king to condemn Ahab for his neglect of the Lord's word. Ahab confirmed the truth of the message by announcing his own judgment.

**Naboth's Vineyard (21:1-29).** The evil plot against Naboth brought God's wrath against Ahab, including the deaths of Jezebel and his son Joram (1 Kgs. 22:37-38; 2 Kgs. 9:24-26,30-37). Because of the law of Moses, Naboth refused the king's request to acquire his vineyard. The law taught that God was the owner of Canaan and that the people, as its tenants, could not dispose of their land (Lev. 25:23; Num. 27:1-11; 36:1-12). Ahab, perhaps respecting the law of God more highly than Jezebel, only sulked about the refusal whereas Jezebel took steps to steal the land. She sent letters to powerful leaders of Jezreel to entrap Naboth with false charges of sedition and blasphemy. He was executed for these crimes, and his land was gobbled up by Jezebel and Ahab.

Yet their murder of Naboth did not go unnoticed. Elijah delivered God's denunciation in the very vineyard Jezebel conspired to get. Although Ahab was the passive player in this evil deed, he was held responsible for failing to stop his wicked wife. The prophet predicted that in the place the dogs licked the blood of Naboth, Ahab's blood also would be the delight of the city's stray dogs. Jezebel also would be a delicacy for the ravenous hounds of Jezreel.

Ahab repented when he heard the word of the Lord. Though he was the most wicked man of Israel, God took mercy on him and prolonged his life. This postponement did not mean, however, that God had changed His opinion on the character of Ahab's reign (see 22:37-38).

**Micaiah's Prophecy and Ahab's Death (22:1-53).** A monument of the Assyrian king Shalmaneser III tells how he fought the united armies of Ahab and Ben-Hadad at Qarqar on the Orontes River in 853 B.C. (see 20:34). The result was probably a stalemate. When the Assyrians retreated, Ben-Hadad renewed his hostilities by capturing Ramoth Gilead near the border of Israel (see 2 Kgs. 10:32-33). Jehoshaphat, the king of Judah, joined Ahab to fight the Arameans. Jehoshaphat was not satisfied with the prophets at Ahab's court and insisted on hearing from the prophet of the Lord. Micaiah, brought from Ahab's prison, predicted that Ahab would be killed in defeat. Ahab ridiculed his prophecy. But Micaiah told him how in a vision he had seen God send a deceiving spirit to mislead Ahab's counselors.

This vision does not mean that Micaiah believed God was a liar. This vision was a pictorial way to explain that God had permitted the false prophets to mislead Ahab to effect His divine judgment. Ahab went into the battle disguised, but God found him through a bowman's arrow! Ahab's bloody chariot was washed in Samaria, and his blood was licked by dogs, just as the word of the Lord had said (see 21:19).

Jehoshaphat's twenty-five-year reign continued the religious reforms of his father Asa. Meanwhile, Ahaziah followed his father Ahab by worshiping Baal. His two-year reign was shortened by the judgment of God (see 2 Kgs. 1:1-18).

**Theological and Ethical Significance.** First Kings, like Deuteronomy, warns against forgetting God in times of economic prosperity. Having known material abundance, many today have left God out of their lives as the ancient Israelites did. Having abandoned faith, many have compromised their values to those of pagan society. The collapse of Israelite society warns of the consequences of sin.

First Kings reveals the power of the word of God in shaping history. The courage of those, like Elijah, whose hearts were captive to the word of God challenges today's Christians to let their presence be felt. After the prophet Micaiah had seen Yahweh's throne room, he was not impressed by King Ahab's threats. Those of us who have experienced the height and depth and breadth of God's love in Christ Jesus should be bold to speak God's word of judgment and grace to our world.

The history of Israel and Judah is the story of a people's failure to fulfill God's purpose for them. God, however, is faithful in spite of human failure. Though we are called to obedience, our hope lies in God's grace. We see this grace most clearly in Jesus Christ, "who as to his human nature was a descendant of David" (Rom. 1:3).

### Questions for Reflection

1. How does prayer affect the lives of God's people? *[handwritten: w/ Δ's things]*

2. How is wisdom more valuable than wealth?

3. How should God's people use their prosperity? *[handwritten: For his Glory]*

4. In what ways does God use wicked instruments to achieve His purposes?

### Sources for Additional Study

House, Paul R. *1, 2 Kings.* New American Commentary. Nashville: Broadman & Holman, 1995.

McNeeley, Richard I. *First and Second Kings.* Chicago: Moody, 1978.

Millard, Alan. *1 Kings - 2 Chronicles.* Ft. Washington, PA: Christian Literature Crusade. London: Scripture Union, 1985.

Vos, Howard F. *1, 2 Kings.* Grand Rapids: Zondervan, 1989.

# 2 KINGS

First and Second Kings form one narrative which recounts the history of Israel's monarchy (compare the introduction to "1 Kings" for a fuller discussion).

**Theme.** God destroyed the kingdoms of Israel and Judah because their kings led the people to do evil by disobeying the covenant of the Lord (22:13).

I. God's Prophet Elisha (1:1–8:29)
II. Decline and Destruction (9:1–17:41)
III. Survival and Final Days (18:1–25:30)

***Purpose and Theology.***

1. Second Kings continues the recital of Israel's demise. One objective of Kings is to show how God was justified in destroying His people. Israel was given over to the Assyrians because it persisted in the idolatrous worship promoted by Jeroboam (17:21-22). Judah suffered the judgment of God because of the sins of Manasseh, whose reign epitomized the evil of Judah's kings. King Josiah's revival of orthodox worship was not sufficient to turn away God's appointed wrath (21:10-15; 23:25-27)

2. The basis of God's judgment was the Mosaic covenant as described in Deuteronomy. The kings fell far short of the divine ideal (Deut. 12). Because Israel broke the law of Moses by worshiping at the pagan high places, God set in motion the curses of the covenant (2 Kgs. 10:21; 17:7-13; see Deut. 28). The recurring theme of divine retribution peaks in the latter half of 2 Kings. (For example, 5:26-27; 9:25-37; 13:2-3; 17:7,25; 19:27-28; 20:16-18; 21:12.)

3. The author showed that the Lord is at work in the history of Israel. God's activity is seen in His warnings delivered by the prophets and His judgment carried out "according to the word of the LORD" (for example, 1:17; 10:17; see 9:25-26,36-37; 10:10; 14:25; 15:12; 17:18-23). His sovereignty is demonstrated by His assigning victory or defeat to nations and by His establishment of kings or deposing of kings. (For example, 5:1; 7:6; 10:32; 13:5; 14:27; 15:37 and 8:13; 9:6.) Through Israel's history, the Lord is proven to be the one true God (5:15; 19:19).

4. Another evidence of God's intervention is Elijah's numerous miracles. Although it was a dark hour in the life of the nation, Elijah's ministry demonstrated that God was still mighty among His people (for example, 2:13-14; 4:34-35; 5:1-18; 13:20-21).

5. Finally, the grace of God is an important theological lesson of the book (13:22-23; 14:26-27). God spared Judah from Assyria and Hezekiah from a fatal illness in response to his prayers for deliverance (19:14-34; 20:1-11). A glimmer of hope concludes this gloomy book of destruction (25:27-30). David's descendant Jehoiachin was alive in Babylon, and there was hope that God would restore Israel and its king. The book was directed to those living in the Babylonian exile. It was their duty to heed the warnings of the book and repent in preparation for the return to their homeland.

## ELISHA (1:1–8:29)

The introductory section continues the story of the prophets, Elijah and Elisha, who delivered the word of the Lord during this decadent period in the life of the nation. Elijah's ministry closed with his ascent to heaven. But his successor,

Elisha, picked up his mantle and performed a double portion of God's wondrous acts. Through the prophetic ministry of Elisha, the Lord guided Israel to victories over their enemies, the Moabites and Arameans. God showed through Elisha that He also is the Lord of all nations who shapes their destinies. While the Lord met the specific needs of His faithful people, He judged the servant Gehazi for his greed.

**Ahaziah Consults Baal-Zebub (1:1-18).** The reign of Ahaziah (853–852 B.C.) was introduced in 1 Kings 22:51-53. When Ahaziah suffered an accident in his palace, he sent messengers to consult the Phoenician god Baal-Zebub to learn if he would recover. But Elijah interrupted the travel of Ahaziah's messengers and announced that the king would die because he sought Baal-Zebub rather than the Lord. Time and again 2 Kings emphasizes that dependence on other gods is a way that leads to death. After three attempts by Ahaziah's delegations, Elijah went personally to the bed of the king to repeat his message. The king died just as the Lord had said through His prophet.

The name Baal-Zebub *(lord of the flies)* was an intentional play on the original name Baal-Zebul, meaning *lord of the lofty abode* or *princely lord.* Beelzebub, the New Testament form of the name Baal-Zebub, became a symbol of Satan by the time of Christ (Matt. 10:25; 12:24-27).

**Elijah's Ride to Heaven (2:1-25).** The final days of Elijah prepared the way for Elisha to follow in his footsteps. Elisha accompanied Elijah from town to town awaiting the arrival of the whirlwind of God that would usher the great prophet into heaven. Elisha swore that he would not leave Elijah's side until he received a "double portion" of Elijah's spirit. As the firstborn, a son received a double portion of a father's inheritance (see Deut. 21:17). When the chariot of fire came for the prophet, Elisha exclaimed: "My father! My father! The chariots and horsemen of Israel!" Elijah had at one time prayed to die under a broom tree (1 Kgs. 19:3-4), but God took him in a whirlwind to heaven. He and Enoch (Gen. 54:24) were the only two men in Scripture to be translated to heaven.

The fallen cloak of Elijah was symbolic of Elisha's spiritual inheritance. With the cloak he duplicated Elijah's miracle of crossing the Jordan River on dry ground. This proved that Elisha had received his ministry.

The company of prophets doubted Elisha's credentials. Elisha demonstrated his authority by healing, that is, purifying, the polluted waters of Jericho. Also he invoked a divine curse upon his detractors, who mocked Elisha by urging him to ascend into heaven like Elijah. Two ravenous bears killed the wicked young men.

**Joram of Israel (3:1-27).** During the reign of Joram (852–841 B.C.), Mesha, king of Moab, rebelled against Israel. Joram recruited King Jehoshaphat of Judah (see 1 Kgs. 22) and the king of Edom to help subjugate Mesha. The absence of water because of dry stream beds hindered their campaign. Elisha, for the sake of David's descendant Jehoshaphat, agreed to consult the Lord in behalf of Joram.

The Lord instructed them to dig trenches, which He flooded with water. When the Moabites saw the water, it appeared red like blood to them, and they mistakenly believed that the three kings had fought among themselves. The reddish appearance has been explained as the water's reflection of a colored red stone known in that area bordering Edom and Moab. The Moabites attacked prematurely and were defeated. When Mesha saw the battle was lost, he offered his firstborn son as a sacrifice to appease the anger of the Moabite deity Chemosh (see 2 Kgs. 16:3; 21:6). Human sacrifice was prohibited by the Lord, who called upon the Israelites to give their firstborn to God as living sacrifices, devoted to His service (Exod. 22:29-30; 34:20; Deut. 18:10). The armies of Israel withdrew out of fear.

The Moabite stone found at Dhiban, Jordan, in 1868 contains an inscription by Mesha, who offered a different interpretation of his wars with Israel. He admitted his subjugation to Ahab but boasted that Chemosh had given him victory over Israel.

**Faithful Servants (4:1-44).** A prophet's widow had no means to pay her creditors except selling her sons into slavery. Elisha multiplied the small amount of oil she possessed, and it was sold to pay her debts.

In Elisha's itinerate ministry, he stayed in the house of a wealthy Shunnamite woman whenever he traveled in Jezreel. Because of her ministry to the prophet, the Lord gave the woman and her aged husband a son. Later, when the boy took ill and died, God answered the prayer of Elisha and restored him to life (see Elijah, 1 Kgs. 17:17-24).

The Lord met the needs of his prophets through Elisha's ministry of miracles. Elisha purified a pot of poisonous stew by throwing flour into it. The Lord fed one hundred of the prophets from only twenty loaves of bread (see Matt. 14:13-21; 15:32-38; John 6:5-13).

**Naaman's Leprosy (5:1-27).** Naaman, the second in command to the king of Aram (Syria), suffered from the dreaded disease of leprosy. A captured Israelite girl told Naaman's wife about Elisha, the Lord's prophet, who could invoke the Lord to heal the general. When Naaman arrived at Elisha's house bearing great sums of money, a messenger instructed Naaman to bathe seven times in the River Jordan. Because of his pride he went away angry, refusing to wash in the muddy waters. His servants convinced him to do so, and the Lord healed him. Naaman declared, "There is no God in all the world except in Israel." Naaman converted to the Lord and regretted that in carrying out his official duties he would have to accompany his king into the temple of their pagan god Rimmon.

Although Elisha had refused a gift from Naaman, the prophet's servant Gehazi secretly detained Naaman to ask for money. But Elisha knew of Gehazi's greed and condemned him to Naaman's leprous disease.

**The Axhead (6:1-33).** Among the miraculous stories about Elisha is his retrieval of a lost axhead. The prophets experienced the blessing of the Lord, and their increasing number required new housing. A prophet's axhead was lost in the Jordan where he was cutting down trees. Elijah threw a stick into the river, whereupon the axhead came to the surface.

The Arameans led two campaigns against the king of Israel. In the first raid the Lord enabled Elisha to tell the king of Israel the precise movements of the Aramean armies so that Israel might escape entrapment. The Aramean armies attempted to kill the prophet, but the Lord's horses and chariots of fire encircled Elisha and his servant. The Lord answered Elisha's prayer and struck them blind. After God restored their sight, Elisha released them for home so that they might warn their king.

Later the Arameans under Ben-Hadad ordered a full-scale invasion of Samaria. The siege caused famine in the city, and the king of Israel blamed the prophet Elisha for their misery. He probably interpreted this as a punishment from the Lord. The king sent a messenger to kill the prophet.

**The Lord Delivers Samaria (7:1-20).** When the king's messenger approached the prophet, Elisha prophesied that within a day they would be delivered. The messenger ridiculed the prophet's words and later paid for it with his life.

That night the Lord created the rumbling noise of an approaching army, and the Arameans left their camp, thinking that mercenary troops had come to Samaria's aid. On the next day lepers discovered the abandoned camp with its provisions. The whole city rushed through the gateway, trampling to death the messenger who had mocked the prophet's message.

**Shunnamite Woman (8:1-15).** The Lord brought a great famine against Israel, and Elisha advised the Shunnamite woman, whose son was brought back to life (4:8-37), to reside in Philistia. After the seven-year famine, her lands were restored to her by the king because he heard of her story from Gehazi, the servant of Elisha.

Elisha went to Damascus to anoint Hazael, Ben-Hadad's military commander, to be king over Aram. Elisha wept because he knew Hazael would oppress the Lord's people. Ben-Hadad was ill, and Hazael, incited by the word of the Lord, assassinated the king.

**Jehoram and Ahaziah (8:16-29).** Jehoram's reign included a coregency with his father Jehoshaphat (853–841 B.C.). Jehoshaphat foolishly married Jehoram to Athaliah, the daughter of Ahab. Jehoram behaved like the wicked kings of Israel, but God spared his reign because he was of the house of David (see 2 Sam. 7:13-16).

Ahaziah's rule (841 B.C.) was wicked like his father's because he was influenced by his in-laws, the family of Ahab.

This ultimately spelled disaster for the house of Judah since his reign was followed by that of his evil queen mother, Athaliah, Ahab's daughter. During Ahaziah's reign, King Joram of Israel was wounded by the Arameans at Ramoth Gilead. Ahaziah visited his uncle Joram at Jezreel, where he was recuperating.

## DECLINE AND DESTRUCTION OF ISRAEL (9:1-17:41)

The second section describes the deterioration and eventual collapse of the northern state of Israel under the weight of its religious paganism and political infighting. Jehu's dynasty rid Israel of its Baalism, postponing God's wrath. But the slide to destruction came quickly afterwards with the rise and fall of four dynasties within the short span of thirty years. The climax of the account is the final chapter of the section, which explains why Israel did not survive (17:7-41). By disregarding the covenant, Israel chose death (Deut. 30:19-20).

Meanwhile, the descendants of David escaped annihilation only by the grace of God. The alliances of Jehoshaphat with Israelite kings (see 1 Kgs. 22; 2 Kgs. 3; 2 Chr. 20:35-37), sealed by intermarriage (2 Kgs. 8:18; 2 Chr. 18:1), threatened the very existence of the Davidic line when Athaliah became queen mother. The salvation of Judah by Joash and the success of Amaziah's reign were the only two periods of stability in the otherwise tottering kingdom to the south.

**House of Ahab (9:1-37).** Jehu, King Joram's commander, defended Ramoth Gilead against the Arameans. Elisha delegated one of the prophets to anoint Jehu king of Israel. The Lord commanded Jehu to avenge the blood of His prophets by killing the ruling descendants of Ahab and Jezebel.

Jehu drove his chariot furiously from Ramoth to Jezreel. When the two kings

Joram and Ahaziah saw him approach, they met him in the field that had belonged to Naboth. When the kings recognized his intentions, they fled for their lives. Jehu killed Joram and tossed his body on Naboth's land, fulfilling God's judgment on Ahab's house (see 1 Kgs. 21:21-22,29). Ahaziah also was fatally wounded.

Jezebel mocked Jehu from her Jezreel residence by likening him to the murderous Zimri (1 Kgs. 16:9-10). Jehu called for the palace guards to toss her from the window. Where her body splattered, horses trampled her and ravenous dogs chewed her body. Her death fulfilled God's vengeance for the murder of Naboth (1 Kgs. 21:23).

*Jehu's Bloody Coup (10:1-36).* Jehu threatened Samaria's officials, and they appeased him by decapitating Ahab's seventy sons. Jehu did this in accordance with the Lord's command (2 Kgs. 9:7-10), but Jehu's coup went beyond the specific directives of the Lord. He slaughtered forty-two relatives of King Ahaziah of Judah, seizing the opportunity to weaken his rival's throne. The bloodbath was remembered for almost one hundred years (see Hos. 4:1-2). He also killed all the relatives and associates of Ahab.

Jehu continued his purge by exterminating the worshipers of Baal and burning their temple. Yet Jehu sinned like his fathers because he did not remove the golden calves at Dan and Bethel. God nevertheless preserved the house of Jehu for four more generations, lasting almost one hundred years.

During his reign (841–814 B.C.), Jehu's kingdom lost the Transjordan to Hazael of Aram. To avert further loss, Jehu made an alliance with the Assyrians. The black stone monument Assyria's King Shalmaneser III erected tells how Jehu became an Assyrian vassal

(841 B.C.). The stone depicts Jehu kneeling before the king and bearing gifts.

*Athaliah and Joash (11:1-21).* With the death of her son Ahaziah, Athaliah seized the throne and killed the royal descendants of David. But God, upholding His promise to David, preserved Joash the son of Ahaziah. Jehosheba, the half-sister of Ahaziah and wife of the high priest Jehoiada (2 Chr. 22:11), hid the boy in the temple for the six years of Athaliah's reign. In conspiracy with the temple guards, army, and mercenary Carites (see the Kerethites of 2 Sam. 20:23), Jehoiada proclaimed Joash king in the temple (11:1-12).

Athaliah was taken and executed by the guards. Jehoiada renewed the covenant of the Lord, and the people removed the idols associated with the Baal worship Athaliah had promoted. Joash was enthroned at the age of seven.

*Joash's Religious Reform (12:1-21).* The forty-year reign of Joash (835–796 B.C.) was righteous in the sight of the Lord because of the religious reforms he introduced in Judah. When the priests failed to raise the funds to repair the neglected temple, Jehoiada collected monies in a chest located in the temple. Joash's rule was marred, however, when he sent the holy articles of God to the Aramean king, Hazael, as payment of tribute. The people God had redeemed from Egyptian slavery were to remain politically free so that they would be free to serve God. Political unrest led governmental officials to assassinate Joash.

*Jehoahaz and Jehoash (13:1-25).* Jehoahaz (814–798 B.C.) succeeded his father, Jehu, but led Israel to worship the Asherah pole, a representation of the Canaanite fertility goddess. The Lord used the Arameans to reduce Israel's army.

Jehoahaz's son Jehoash ruled for sixteen years (798–782 B.C.) and was remembered for his oppression of King Amaziah of Judah (see 14:1-14). During his reign Elisha was dying from an illness, and Jehoash came to his bedside and wept. Elisha instructed him to strike the floor with his arrow. After he struck the floor three times, Elisha predicted that the Lord would give him three victories over the Arameans. The Lord granted those victories over the Aramean king, Ben-Hadad, who succeeded his father Hazael.

God honored both the life and death of the great prophet Elisha. A dead man was brought back to life when his body was placed in the tomb with Elisha's bones.

***Amaziah (14:1-29).*** Amaziah (796–767 B.C.) pleased the Lord during his reign as his father Joash had done. He executed his father's assassins (see 12:20-21) and defeated the rebellious Edomites. His arrogance, however, brought him defeat by Jehoash of Israel. Jehoash broke down the walls of Jerusalem, raided the temple treasuries, and took hostages. Ironically, like his father's, Amaziah's rule ended by a conspiracy of assassins in Lachish.

***Jeroboam II (14:23-29).*** The kingship of Jeroboam gave Israel one of its greatest periods of political stability and territorial growth (793–753 B.C.). The prophet Jonah advocated the expansionistic policies of Jeroboam. The Lord gave Israel a respite from their woes through Jeroboam, but Jeroboam too followed in the wicked ways of his namesake. The prophet Amos condemned the greed and immoral decadence of Israel during Jeroboam's reign. (See "Amos.")

***Azariah (15:1-7).*** Azariah's coregency and reign totaled fifty-two years (792–740 B.C.). Azariah, also named Uzziah, was contemporary with Jeroboam II, giving Israel and Judah their greatest periods of prosperity. The Lord

struck Azariah with leprosy because he offered incense in the temple (see 2 Chr. 26:16-20). He shared his rule with his son Jotham.

***Zechariah to Pekah (15:8-31).*** After Jeroboam's death his kingdom deteriorated rapidly. Zechariah ruled for six months and was killed by Shallum. This ended Jehu's dynasty in the fifth generation as the Lord had foretold (10:30). Shallum ruled only one month before he was assassinated in the ruthless coup of Menahem from Tirzah.

Menahem held his crown for ten years (752–742 B.C.). He paid tribute to the Assyrian monarch, Tiglath-Pileser III (745–727 B.C.), called by his Babylonian throne name "Pul" in the Bible. The annals of Tiglath record the heavy taxation Menahem endured.

Pekahiah inherited his father's policies of appeasement toward Assyria. After a two-year reign (742–740 B.C.), the commander of Israel's armies, Pekah, engineered an anti-Assyrian coup, murdering the king. (The name *Pekah* is a shortened form of the name *Pekahiah*.) His reign was twenty years (752–732 B.C.). Perhaps during this period Pekah ruled from Gilead independently of the Samarian regime until the death of Pekahiah. Eventually the anti-Assyrian policy of Pekah failed when Tiglath annexed portions of Israel and deported its citizens. Hoshea usurped the throne with the backing of Assyria (see 17:1-6).

***Jotham (15:32-38).*** Jotham, who coreigned with his father, Azariah, ruled for sixteen years (750–732 B.C.). His reign pleased the Lord, except that he left the high places for sacrifice. Pekah of Israel and Rezin of Aram collaborated to threaten Jotham at the end of his rule. The prophets Hosea, Isaiah, and Micah were his contemporaries.

***Ahaz (16:1-20).*** Ahaz (735–715 B.C.) was one of the most wicked of kings in Judah's history. He committed the horrible atrocity of human sacrifice and promoted the practice of sacrifice at the high places (see 2 Chr. 28). Ahaz inherited the political problems of his father. The coalition of Rezin and Pekah marched against Jerusalem to force Judah to join in their war against the encroaching armies of Assyria. But Ahaz, against the counsel of the prophet Isaiah (see Isa. 7:1-17), sought the aid of Tiglath-Pileser and bought his intervention with the temple and royal treasuries. Assyria's war resulted in the capture of Damascus (732 B.C.), the humiliation of Samaria (15:29), and the vassalage of Ahaz to Tiglath.

To comply as a dutiful vassal, Ahaz replaced the bronze altar of the Lord in the temple with a replica of the Assyrian altar Tiglath erected in Damascus. He also removed other features of the temple which were offensive to the Assyrian monarch.

***Hoshea (17:1-41).*** Hoshea's (732–722 B.C.) pro-Assyrian policies (15:30) had saved Samaria, but it was at the high cost of vassalage to Tiglath and his son Shalmaneser V (727–722 B.C.). Hoshea tested Shalmaneser's strength and recruited the aid of So, king of Egypt. Hoshea was imprisoned, and Samaria endured a three-year siege led by Shalmaneser and completed by his brother Sargon II (722–705 B.C.). Samaria's destruction in 722 B.C. sounded the end of the northern state of Israel.

While secular history gives political and military causes for a nation's demise, the inspired historian gave religious reasons for the fall of Samaria. The lengthy commentary on Israel's sins exonerated God but also warned Judah not to imitate their northern kin.

Israel sinned against the Lord and disregarded the warnings of the covenant made with their fathers. They made the golden calves of Jeroboam, erected the Asherah pole, committed human sacrifices, worshiped the stars, and practiced sorcery. The Lord removed Israel from the land because they sinned like the Canaanites whom the Lord had removed before them.

Through a policy of resettlement, the Assyrians subjugated the conquered nations of their empire. The nations transplanted in Samaria worshiped the Lord in name but also worshiped their own national deities. Their mixed worship alienated them from the Jews (Ezra 4:1-3; John 4:4-9,39-40).

## SURVIVAL AND FINAL DAYS OF JUDAH (18:1–25:30)

The final section of Kings traces the survival of Judah after Samaria's collapse. From the perspective of the biblical writer, the reigns of Hezekiah and Josiah brought sweeping moral and religious reforms which prolonged Judah's existence for another hundred years. However, this period also saw Judah's most wicked king, Manasseh (chap. 21). Because of Manasseh's heinous sins, Jerusalem fell under God's final judgment of expulsion.

***Hezekiah (18:1-37).*** The account of Hezekiah's career is also recorded in 2 Chronicles 29–32 and Isaiah 36–39. The three sources do not always give a sequential chronology of the events in his reign since the authors gave a thematic presentation of his career.

Hezekiah, unlike his father, Ahaz, trusted the Lord throughout his reign (715–686 B.C.) and introduced radical reforms by removing the high places, destroying idolatrous symbols, and centralizing worship in Jerusalem. Although he inherited vassal status from Ahaz,

Hezekiah rebelled against Sargon (see Isa. 20:1) and his successor Sennacherib. The sacred historian gave Hezekiah the highest commendation (2 Kgs. 18:5). The account of Sennacherib's invasion is also told in Isaiah 36–37. When Sennacherib became king (705–681 B.C.), Hezekiah, with the encouragement of Egypt, rebelled against Assyria. Sennacherib responded (701 B.C.) by surrounding Jerusalem. The Assyrian's annals report that he had Hezekiah caught "like a bird in a cage." Hezekiah paid a handsome tribute, but it did not appease Sennacherib for long.

Sennacherib sent a delegation from his headquarters in Lachish to negotiate a surrender. The Assyrians ridiculed Hezekiah's dependence on Egypt and his hope in the Lord. They addressed Hezekiah's representatives in Hebrew, refusing to speak in the Aramaic language of diplomacy so that the people of Jerusalem would understand their threats.

**God Delivers Jerusalem (19:1-37).** When Hezekiah heard the report of the Assyrians' threats, he consulted Isaiah for a word from the Lord. Through the prophet the Lord promised to deliver Hezekiah by a rumor that would distract the Assyrians. Meanwhile, Sennacherib's attention had turned to the fortress of Libnah and the approach of an Egyptian army led by Tirhakah. Sennacherib sent a letter, threatening Hezekiah a second time not to ally himself with the Egyptians.

Hezekiah took the letter before the Lord and prayed for God's deliverance, knowing that the Lord alone could save him. Isaiah announced the Lord's response, prophesying the salvation of Jerusalem and end of Sennacherib's reign. That night the Lord slaughtered the armies of Assyria, forcing Sennacherib's retreat to Nineveh. Several years

later, as the Lord had foretold, Sennacherib's sons assassinated him in an effort to save their crumbling kingdom.

**God Heals Hezekiah (20:1-21).** Hezekiah became deathly ill, and the Lord sent Isaiah to tell the king to prepare to die. But Hezekiah prayed earnestly, and the Lord through the prophet Isaiah promised to prolong Hezekiah's life for fifteen years. The Lord encouraged the king by a sign, causing the shadow of the king's sundial to move backward ten steps. The thanksgiving hymn of Hezekiah is preserved in Isaiah 38:9-20.

Merodach-Baladan, the king of Babylon (721–710 B.C.), sent a delegation to congratulate Hezekiah for his recovery. Merodach-Baladan is known from ancient annals as Marduk-apla-iddina II, a chieftain of southern Chaldea who led a successful rebellion against Sargon. Although recounted in Kings after Sennacherib's invasion (chap. 19), his visit actually occurred before.

Merodach-Baladan sent envoys to learn of Judah's strength and lure Hezekiah into an alliance. Isaiah condemned Hezekiah for his sinful pride in openly displaying his treasures. The prophet continued with a divine oracle in which he prophesied that Judah's treasures and people would be carried away to Babylon (see 25:21b).

**Manasseh and Amon (21:1-26).** Remarkably, Hezekiah bore a son (Manasseh) who would undo all that he had achieved in turning Judah back to God. During his fifty-five year reign (697–642 B.C.), the longest in Judah's history, Manasseh committed every pagan atrocity. The historian remarked that Judah "did more evil than the nations the LORD had destroyed before the Israelites" and blamed Manasseh for the eventual fall of Jerusalem (21:12-15; 22:16-17; 24:3-4). Although Manasseh experienced a short imprisonment in Assyria (2 Chr. 33:10-13), Assyrian records show that he was loyal for most of his reign.

Such wickedness yielded the fruit of more violence. Amon (642–640 B.C.), the son of Manasseh, was assassinated by palace officials after only two years on the throne.

***Josiah (22:1-20).*** Josiah (640–609 B.C.) began to reign at age eight after the assassination of his father. In his eighteenth year of reign (621 B.C.), Josiah initiated repairs on the temple Manasseh and Amon had neglected. The high priest Hilkiah recovered the book of the law among the rubble of the temple.

When the book was read before the king, he feared the Lord's wrath and sent a delegation to the prophetess Huldah to inquire of the Lord concerning Judah's fate. She prophesied that the Lord would destroy Judah for its idolatry but that Josiah would not witness it because he had repented. Scholars generally agree that this "book" was Deuteronomy or some part of it.

***Josiah's Reforms and Death (23:1-30).*** Josiah renewed the covenant with the Lord and celebrated the Passover in an unprecedented way. He removed all evidence of pagan worship and centralized worship in Jerusalem. As the prophet had predicted (1 Kgs. 13:32), Josiah tore down the shrine at Bethel, which Jeroboam had erected three centuries earlier. The biblical writer gave Josiah the highest commendation of all the kings: "Neither before nor after Josiah was there a king like him who turned to the LORD as he did." Jerusalem enjoyed a national revival under Josiah. However, it came to a crashing halt when the king was killed at Megiddo by Pharaoh Neco. Josiah had attempted to block Neco's efforts to aid the faltering

Assyrians in their last stand against Nebuchadnezzar's Babylonian armies.

***Jehoahaz and Jehoiakim (23:31-37).*** Necho deposed Jehoahaz, Josiah's son, after only three months and imprisoned him in Egypt. He set up in his place another son of Josiah, the puppet king Jehoiakim, also called Eliakim (609–598 B.C.).

***Jehoiachin and Zedekiah (24:1-20).*** The balance of power turned to the Babylonians in 605 B.C. when Nebuchadnezzar defeated the combined armies of Egypt and Assyria at Carchemish in North Syria. After three years of vassalage to Nebuchadnezzar (605–602 B.C.), Jehoiakim attempted an insurrection that failed. Jehoiakim resisted the word of the Lord by burning Jeremiah's scroll that foretold Judah's subjugation to Babylon (Jer. 36:29). The historian attributed Judah's continued subservience to the wickedness of Manasseh, whose reign grieved the Lord.

Jehoiachin, Jehoiakim's son, was eighteen when he ascended the throne at his father's death (598 B.C.). He too rebelled, and Nebuchadnezzar besieged Jerusalem. He deposed the young king after only three months (see Jer. 52:31-34). At that time the temple and palace were stripped (see 2 Kgs. 20:17), and the king's household as well as the city's leading citizens were exiled (see Jer. 22:24-30). Nebuchadnezzar installed Mattaniah, Jehoiachin's uncle, as king and renamed him "Zedekiah."

***Destruction of Jerusalem (25:1-30).*** Zedekiah (597–586 B.C.), in spite of Jeremiah's warnings (see Jer. 37–39; 52), led a final rebellion against the Babylonians in 588 B.C. After a lengthy siege and resulting famine, the city fell in July 586 B.C. Zedekiah fled but was captured and taken to Nebuchadnezzar's headquarters in Riblah. There Zedekiah witnessed the execution of his sons before he was blinded and led to Babylon for imprisonment Nebuzaradan, the Babylonian commander, raided the city, confiscated the temple furniture, and burned Jerusalem to the ground (25:8-21). Gedaliah was appointed governor but was assassinated in an anti-Babylonian coup. For fear of Babylonian reprisals, many of the Jews fled to Egypt.

The final paragraph of the book indicates how the sacred historian responded to the catastrophe. He saw in the improved conditions of King Jehoiachin's imprisonment a message of hope. Babylon's ruler, Evil-Merodach (561–560 B.C.), released Jehoiachin from prison and placed him under house arrest, where he drew a royal stipend from the Babylonian treasury (25:27-30). Although Jerusalem was no more, Israel still had its king. If God so pleased, Judah could be restored to its land.

***Ethical and Theological Significance.*** Again and again 2 Kings warns against the dangers of compromise. Those who compromise their witness for selfish gain risk God's judgment. Gehazi's attempt to profit financially from Elisha's healing ministry is a stern warning to Christians that the gospel is not a "mask to cover up greed" (1 Thess. 2:5).

In 2 Kings dependence on other gods led to death for both individuals and nations. If our security rests on our own wealth or military might, we are trusting in a house built on sand (see Matt. 7:26). The failures of the kings of Israel and Judah remind Christians to fix their trust on God alone.

The kings of Israel and Judah often sought to preserve national security at the expense of their distinctive religious convictions. The people God freed from Egyptian slavery should have avoided political situations that compromised their freedom to worship their God. Baptists have championed a free church in a free state as the best setting for Christians to exercise their discipleship.

The tragic end of the nations of Israel and Judah demonstrates the awful consequences of sin. However, no catastrophe is so great that God cannot work through it to give hope to His people.

## Questions for Reflection

1. What can be learned from 2 Kings about the holiness of God?

2. How should God's people live in a society that is wicked?

3. How can God's people have hope in the midst of social and political unrest?

4. What is spiritual revival? How does God respond to repentance and prayers for revival?

5. In what ways does God use wicked people or nations to achieve His purposes?

## Sources for Additional Study

House, Paul. R. *1, 2 Kings*. New American Commentary. Nashville: Broadman & Holman, 1995.

McNeeley, Richard I. *First and Second Kings*. Chicago: Moody, 1978.

Millard, Alan. *1 Kings–2 Chronicles*. Ft. Washington, PA: Christian Literature Crusade, 1985.

Vos, Howard F. *1, 2 Kings*. Grand Rapids: Zondervan, 1989.

# 1 CHRONICLES

Like the Books of Samuel and Kings, 1 and 2 Chronicles were originally one book. The Hebrew title means *the chronological events of the period.* The Greek version, which divided Chronicles into two books, entitled them "The Things Left Out" or "Omitted." This title reflects the misunderstanding that Chronicles was written to supplement the events left out of Samuel and Kings. The English name is derived from the Latin Vulgate's title, "The Chronicle of the Whole Sacred History."

The Books of Chronicles are not to be confused with the "annals of the kings of Judah" and "annals of the kings of Israel," which were official royal accounts used in writing 1 and 2 Kings (for example, 1 Kgs. 14:19; 15:7).

The Greek and English traditions have the Books of Chronicles in the collection of historical books, with Chronicles followed by Ezra and Nehemiah. In the Hebrew collection, however, Chronicles is the last book in the canon. There it is grouped with the Writings and is preceded by Ezra-Nehemiah.

The author is unknown. Tradition assigned the book to Ezra (see 2 Chr. 36:22-23 with Ezra 1:1-2). The author probably was a Levite or someone closely associated with the temple since Chronicles focuses on worship in Jerusalem. Many scholars believed that an individual or school, called the "Chronicler," produced Chronicles and Ezra-Nehemiah as one continuous history. Others have rejected this idea of a "Chronicler's History," arguing that all ancient traditions separated the books and that they have a different viewpoint (see "The Historical Books" and "Ezra"). For this latter group, the term "Chronicler" is limited to the author of 1 and 2 Chronicles.

The date of Chronicles is about 400 B.C. Chronicles uses sources from an earlier period, particularly the canonical works of Genesis, Samuel, and Kings. Other sources named are "the annotations on the book of the kings" (2 Chr. 24:27); "the book of the kings of Israel and Judah" (27:7; 35:27), which also contained oracles by Isaiah (32:32); "the annals of the kings of Israel" (20:34; 33:18); "the records of the seers" (33:19); and Isaiah's prophetic works (26:22).

**Differences with Samuel and Kings.** While Chronicles shows a dependence on the Books of Samuel and Kings, there are remarkable differences in content and theological perspective.

1. Chronicles was not written to supplement these former works, nor was it simply a rewriting. These books offer a fresh interpretation of Israel's monarchy. Samuel and Kings addressed the exilic community and explained why Israel's monarchy failed. Chronicles addressed the restored community and explained that God still had a purpose for Israel. Chronicles was written from a priestly perspective, whereas Samuel and Kings were written from a prophetic perspective.

2. Chronicles attempts a comprehensive history, beginning with Adam, but Samuel and Kings are limited to the time of the monarchy. In the Book of Kings, Judah still awaits release from captivity, but Chronicles ends with the decree of Cyrus anticipating Judah's return.

3. Chronicles features David and the kings of Judah and avoids commenting on the Northern Kingdom. Even the reign of Saul is treated as a preamble to David's accession. Chronicles tells the positive contributions of David and Solomon and omits unflattering events in their reigns.

4. The palace is center stage in Samuel and Kings, but the temple is central in Chronicles. For the Chronicler the lasting contribution of the kings was religious. Samuel and Kings condemn sin and urge repentance, but Chronicles encourages the faithful to make a new start.

**Theme.** God promised David an eternal throne, choosing David to found the true center of worship in Jerusalem and appointing Solomon to build His temple (28:4-7).

I. God's Redemptive Plan (1:1–9:44)

II. Plan through David (10:1–20:8)

III. Plan of Worship (21:1–29:30)

### Purpose and Theology.

1. First and Second Chronicles give the history of Israel from its ancestral roots in Adam to the period of restoration after the Babylonian exile. An important function of the genealogies that begin Chronicles is to provide continuity in God's plan for Israel. The retelling of Israel's history was to encourage the Jewish community by emphasizing God's selection of Israel and His promises to them. Chronicles shows that the enduring purpose of Israel was the worship of God. Israel could take heart because, although it had no king, the temple remained.

2. The dominant motif is the temple and its service. Chronicles focuses on the institution of worship, especially music, and the role of the Levites. The book gives attention to David's preparations for the building of the temple almost to the exclusion of other accomplishments

(1 Chr. 6:48-49; 22:1–26:32; 28:1–29:9).

3. First Chronicles exhorts Israel to be faithful so that the redemptive plan promised to David might be fulfilled through them (17:7-15; 28:4-7). God's reward for faithfulness is emphasized, particularly in response to prayer (4:9-10; 5:20-22; 16:8-36; 17:16-27; 29:10-19). The Chronicler explained that unfaithfulness was the reason for the failure of Israel's kings and the exile (5:25-26; 9:1b; 10:13-14).

4. Since God is holy, His people were to worship properly as Moses had commanded and as David ordained. As a consequence of God's holiness, anyone who profaned the sanctity of worship or transgressed the law experienced His wrath (13:10-12; 15:11-15; 21:1-8; 27:23-24; 28:7). David sang of God's holiness when he invoked all creation to worship Him (16:10,29,35; 17:20; 29:11,16).

5. The Lord is also sovereign in world affairs, in particular the rise and success of David's kingdom (1:1–9:44; 17:7-15; 28:4-7; 29:25). Three times the Chronicler returned to the giving of the Davidic covenant (17:1-27; 22:6-13; 28:1-10). Chronicles tends to speak of God's direct involvement (14:2,10,15; 18:6,13) whereas Samuel and Kings include intermediate causes. The plans for the Jerusalem temple are attributed to God's direct revelation and not the creation of David (28:12).

6. Leadership is a significant teaching for the author, who sought to encourage Israel in a day when it had no king. The messianic expectation was still alive for the author, who therefore idealized David's role (17:7-15; 28:5; 29:23). The Chronicler emphasized the spiritual leadership of the nation, particularly the Levites and officials (15:2-27; 23:2–26:32; 29:1-9).

## GOD'S REDEMPTIVE PLAN (1:1–9:44)

The genealogies are not a sterile recitation of names. They are a significant statement of Israel's place in the whole sweep of God's plan for the world. The Chronicler found the proper appreciation of universal history in the founding of Israel, the appointment of David, and the building of the temple, where God resided in the world (a foretaste of the true Temple, Jesus Christ, who resided in the world as a man; see John 12).

*From Adam to David (1:1–3:24).* The genealogies from Adam to Abraham, from Jacob (Israel) to David, and from David to his postexilic descendants show the continuity of God's redemptive plan. The divine plan, which began before creation, began to develop in the realm of history in the garden with Adam (Gen. 3:15) and continued through Abraham who would bring blessing to the world (12:1-3). This promise of blessing would be realized in the lineage of David (2 Sam. 7). The genealogy of David is traced by the Chronicler beyond the exile, indicating that the promise had not been abandoned. The purposes of God always outweigh the circumstances of Israel's political misfortunes.

*More Descendants (4:1–5:26).* More descendants of Judah are listed. Among them is Jabez, who is a model of the faith. Simeon's descendants are listed next since this tribe was assimilated into Judah's territory (Josh. 19:1-9). The families beyond the Jordan are listed, with Reuben honored as the firstborn.

*Levi (6:1-81).* The lineage of the high priest is carefully traced and distinguished from the other Levitical families since only Aaron's sons were permitted to offer sacrifice at the temple. The Levites served as temple musicians and carried out other temple duties.

*Remaining Tribes (7:1-40).* The remaining tribes are listed, but Dan and Zebulon are absent since the Chronicler wanted to retain the traditional number of twelve tribes.

*Family of Saul (8:1–9:44).* The narration repeats that Saul was from the Benjamites who lived in Gibeon and not the Benjamites of Jerusalem. The Chronicler reaffirmed that the Lord had chosen David and Jerusalem, not Saul of Gibeon. Those among the tribes who returned from the exile and resided in Jerusalem were cataloged by genealogies.

## PLAN THROUGH DAVID (10:1–20:28)

The episode of Saul's death provides the background for David's kingdom. David's rule was glorious, and the pinnacle of his reign was the bringing of the ark into Jerusalem. God honored David's desire to build a temple by granting him an eternal throne. David prospered all the more because of God's blessing and dedicated to the Lord the spoils of his victories.

*Saul's Unfaithfulness (10:1-14).* Saul's final defeat and suicide are told (see 1 Sam. 31). The Chronicler concluded that Saul's death was God's judgment on unfaithfulness (see 1 Sam. 13; 15; 28).

*God Prospers David (11:1-47).* David became king, according to God's promise (see 2 Sam. 5:1-3). He conquered the stubborn Jebusites in Jerusalem and became increasingly powerful because the Lord was with him (2 Sam. 5:6-12). The evidence of David's strength was the awesome deeds his corp of mighty men accomplished (see 2 Sam. 23:8-39).

*Army of God (12:1-40).* Those who joined David at Ziklag (1 Sam. 27:2-6) were numerous and from many tribes throughout Israel. His army was like the army of God. All the tribes rejoiced at David's coronation as king over all Israel.

*God's Holiness and the Ark (13:1-14).* Saul did not inquire of the

Lord during his reign, but David with all Israel's consent attempted to return the ark of God from Abinadab's house at Kiriath Jearim (2 Sam. 6:2-11).

Although the people were zealous for the Lord, they sinned by transporting the ark improperly on a cart (1 Chr. 15:13). According to Moses' instructions, the Levites were to carry it by poles without touching it. The penalty for disobedience was death (Exod. 25:14; Num. 3:31; 4:15). Uzzah steadied the ark when it slipped from the cart. The Lord struck him dead. When David witnessed this, he feared the Lord as never before. The ark was left in the care of Obed-Edom, and the Lord blessed his household because of the ark.

**God Establishes David (14:1-17).** All the nations began to fear David. Hiram, king of Tyre, sent building materials for David's palace. David knew that the Lord had established his reign and a growing family; (2 Sam. 5:11-16). The Lord led David's armies into battle and delivered up the Philistines (2 Sam. 5:17-25).

**The Ark Rests (15:1-29).** Jerusalem was called the "City of David" because David captured it as a royal possession. He attempted again to return the ark and was successful because he carefully followed the Lord's word (Exod. 25:14; Num. 4:5-6,15). The priests and Levites consecrated themselves in preparation to carry the ark.

David, an accomplished musician himself (see 1 Sam. 16:18,23), prepared the people for worship by establishing a complete orchestra and appointing three Levitical choirs under the direction of Heman, Asaph, and Ethan (Jeduthun; compare the superscriptions of Pss. 50; 73–83; 88–89). When the ark was brought to Jerusalem, David ordered sacrifices offered to God. David's wife,

Michal, Saul's daughter, disdained David's free worship (2 Sam. 6:12-23).

**David's Prayer (16:1-43).** After David worshiped with sacrifice, he called for the Levites to offer thanksgiving, prayer, and praise.

David presented a thanksgiving hymn. The Chronicler compiled excerpts from well-known psalms to convey the meaning of David's hymn for the Chronicler's community (Ps. 96; 105:1-15; 106:1,47-48). David called the righteous to worship, extolled the Lord's grace from the days of Abraham, and concluded by invoking all creation to worship the Creator.

David provided for the daily sacrifice by appointing Asaph to minister at the ark in Jerusalem and Zadok to serve the tabernacle at Gibeon.

**God's Promises to David (17:1-27).** After David had brought the ark to Jerusalem, he decided to build a "house" (temple) for the Lord. By divine oracle the prophet Nathan learned that God would instead build David a dynastic "house." God promised David a kingdom, a throne, and an eternal dynastic house. David's son would build the Lord's house and would rule as God's son over the Lord's kingdom. The Chronicler explained elsewhere that God prohibited David from building the temple because David's career was known for war and bloodshed (22:8; 28:3).

When Nathan reported the oracle, David prayed, admitting his unworthiness and marveling at the magnitude of God's greatness and grace. The ultimate fulfillment of God's pledge is realized in David's Greater Son, Jesus Christ (see Luke 1:32-33).

**David's Conquests (18:1-17).** The sincerity of God's promise to David was evidenced by the immediate victories the Lord granted over the Philistines, Arameans, and Edomites. David

## MUSICAL INSTRUMENTS OF THE OLD TESTAMENT

| TYPE | NAME | SCRIPTURE REFERENCES | LANGUAGE OF ORIGIN | NIV TRANSLATION |
|---|---|---|---|---|
| PERCUSSION | Bagpipe | Dan 3:5,7,10,15 | Aramaic: sumponeyah | pipes |
| | Bells | (1) Exod 28:33-34; 39:25-26 (2) Zech 14:20 | (1) Hebrew: paamon (2) Hebrew: metsilloth | (1) bells (2) bells of the horses |
| | Cymbals | (1) 2 Sam 6:5; Ps 150:5 (2) 1 Chr 13:8;15:16,19; 2 Chr 5:12-13; Ezra 3:10; Neh 12:27 | (1) Hebrew: tseltselim (2) Hebrew: metsiltayim | (1) cymbals (2) cymbals |
| | Sistrum | 2 Sam 6:5 | Hebrew: menaanim | sistrums |
| | Tambourine | Gen 31:27; Exod 15:20; Judg 11:34; 1 Sam 10:5; 18:6; 2 Sam 6:5; 1 Chr 13:8; Job 21:12; Pss 81:2; 149:3; Isa 5:12; Jer 31:4 | Hebrew: toph | tambourine |
| STRING | Harp | (1) 1 Sam 10:5; Neh 12:27; Isa 5:12; 14:11; Amos 5:23; 6:5 (2) Dan 3:5,7,10,15 | (1) Hebrew: nebel (2) Aramaic: pesanterin | (1) lyres, harp(s) (2) harp |
| | Harplike Instrument | Dan 3:5,7,10,15 | Aramaic: sabbeka | lyre |
| | Lyre | (1) Gen 4:21; 1 Sam 10:5; 2 Sam 6:5; Neh 12:27 (2) Dan 3:5,7,10,15 | (1) Hebrew: kinnor (2) Aramaic: qitharos, qathros | (1) harp (2) zither |
| | Zither | Pss 33:2; 92:3; 144:9 | Hebrew: nebel asor | ten-stringed lyre |
| WIND | Double Pipe | 1 Sam 10:5; 1 Kgs 1:40; Isa 5:12; Jer 48:36 | Hebrew: chalil | flutes |
| | Horn, Cornet | Dan 3:5,7,10,15 | Aramaic: qeren | horn |
| | Pipe, Reed | Dan 3:5,7,10,15 | Aramaic: mashroqitha | flute |
| | Ram's Horn | (1) Josh 6:4-20; Judg 7:16-22; 2 Sam 15:10; Pss 47:5; 150:3; Amos 2:2 (2) Exod 19:13 | (1) Hebrew: shophar (2) Aramaic: yobel | (1) rams' horns, trumpets (2) ram's horn |
| | Trumpet | (1) Num 10:2-10; 1 Chr 15:24,28; 2 Chr 15:14; 23:13; Ps 98:6; Hos 5:8 (2) Ezek 7:14 | (1) Hebrew: chatsotsrah (2) Hebrew: taqoa | (1) trumpet (2) trumpet |
| | Vertical Flute | Gen 4:21; Job 21:12; 30:3; Ps 150:4 | Hebrew: uggab | flute |

responded with thanksgiving by giving the spoils of battle to the Lord. The Chronicler concluded: "The Lord gave David victory everywhere he went" (18:6,13). As a result of his new triumphs and expanding kingdom, David increased his governing bureaucracy (2 Sam. 8:15-18).

***Defeat the Ammonites (19:1-19).*** The Lord remained faithful to David by enabling his victory over a coalition of Ammonites and Arameans. David sent a delegation of envoys to befriend Hanun, who succeeded his father, Nahash, as king of the Ammonites. But Hanun spurned David's offer of peace. A major battle ensued, and David's troops outmaneuvered the enemy (2 Sam. 10:1-19).

***Rabbah and Philistia (20:1-8).*** Joab, David's military commander, routed the Ammonites by capturing their capital city Rabbah (1 Chr. 29:1-3; 2 Sam. 12:26-31). David's champions subjugated the Philistine giants (2 Sam. 21:15-22). Typical of the Chronicler, he omitted the embarrassing incident of David's sin with Bathsheba (2 Sam. 11) and left out the account of Absalom's rebellion (2 Sam. 13–19). Chronicles passes over these accounts because they do not serve its purpose. The Chronicler overlooked moral defeats and highlighted David's victories to draw attention to God's sovereignty in David's life. God succeeded in using David to fulfill His purposes for him. David's greatest accomplishments were not political but spiritual—moving the ark to Jerusalem and preparing for the construction of the temple.

## PLAN OF WORSHIP (21:1–29:30)

The final section features the preparations David made for the building of the temple. For the Chronicler this was the most important contribution of the king and predominated his account of David's reign. The temple site was divinely chosen. David organized the Levites and priests for the temple work, organized the army, and held a national convocation. There the people contributed gifts, and David appointed Solomon king and Zadok priest.

***Atonement for Evil (21:1-30).*** While the Chronicler was careful to extol David's virtues, he included the sin of David's census because it explained the choice of the temple site. David took a census of his military troops, presumably because of his pride (see Exod. 30:11-16).

The parallel in 2 Samuel ascribes David's temptation to God (2 Sam. 24:1), but the Chronicler attributed it to Satan. The reason for this difference is the theological purpose of each writing. The Old Testament ascribes all things to the sovereignty of God, indicating His control over all creation (Isa. 45:7). The Chronicler, however, emphasized the holiness of God and therefore featured Satan as the direct cause for David's sin. Elsewhere in the Old Testament, Satan *(the accuser)* acts under God's direction (Job 1:6; Zech. 3:1).

Although David confessed his sin, he suffered the consequences of his evil deed. God sent an angel to chasten Jerusalem by a plague. To atone for his sins, David built an altar of sacrifice at the site of Araunah's threshing floor. David bought the place, though Araunah volunteered it, because David knew that true atonement always requires payment. God consumed the offering with fire from heaven, and the plague ceased.

***Charge to Solomon (22:1-19).*** In Kings David's charge included the elimination of his enemies (1 Kgs. 1–2). The Chronicler, whose interest was in David's role as a spiritual leader, omitted this and told only of Solomon's appointment to build the temple.

David established Araunah's threshing floor as the future temple site. He gathered materials and workmen in preparation for the building because Solomon was inexperienced. He charged Solomon to build the edifice, explaining that he was disqualified because of his reputation as a warrior. Peaceful Solomon would be permitted to build the temple. David illustrated his point by making a word play on the name of Solomon *(shelomoh),* which is similar in sound to "peace" *(shalom).* David finally instructed Solomon to be faithful so that he might have success. David assembled numerous materials and workers to assure Solomon's achievement.

David commanded his officials to help in the task and to serve the Lord with full devotion. He believed that for this purpose God had granted them victory over their enemies.

*Organizing the Levites (23:1-32).* The Chronicler was not concerned with the political details of Solomon's accession (see 1 Kgs. 1–2). He presented the transition as peaceful and orderly.

The appointment and work of the Levites was divinely ordained through Moses (Num. 3:1–4:49). David organized the Levites into three groups by families—Gershonites, Kohathites, and Merarites. The Levites were assigned to assist the priests' work in the service of the temple.

*Organizing the Priests (24:1-31).* Aaron's descendants had the exclusive assignment of ministering before the ark (23:13-14; 24:19; Num. 18:1-7). The descendants of Eleazar and Ithamar were divided into twenty-four orders, which served at the temple in rotation (see Luke 1:5,8-9). The order of service for the remaining Levites was determined by the casting of lots in the same manner for as the priests.

*Music for the Lord (25:1-31).* David established three musical guilds under his supervision. Asaph, Heman, and Jeduthun (Ethan) were Levites David appointed for the musical accompaniment of temple worship (see 15:16-22). The guilds were drawn from all age groups and those with differing musical skills. They were divided into twenty-four courses like the priests.

*Serving the Lord's House (26:1-32).* Levites from the families of Korah and Merari were entrusted with the security of the temple as gatekeepers. They were chosen because of their exceptional ability. The gatekeepers were stationed day and night to protect the temple. The Levites also provided caretakers for the treasuries. The temple's treasuries included gifts dedicated by David, Samuel, and Saul. The Levites collected taxes for the king (25:29-32).

*Army and Administrators (27:1-34).* The twelve army divisions and the officers of Israel's tribes are listed. Population figures were not kept because of God's wrath (see 21:1-7). Administrators over civil matters are named, followed by the members of the royal cabinet.

*Providential Plans (28:1-21).* David assembled Israel to witness his final charge to Solomon. David was precluded from building the temple, but God providentially prepared Solomon to accomplish that task. David repeated the provisions of God's covenant and commissioned Solomon to build the temple (see also 17:1-27; 22:1-19).

David delivered the plans for the temple to Solomon that he had written under the Lord's guidance. Just as the Lord revealed the tabernacle plan to Moses (Exod. 25:1–30:38), the Spirit instructed David's mind.

The plans included the structure of the temple, the treasuries, storehouses, and the holy furniture. The specific document written by David is not preserved in Scripture, but the substance of it probably is found in Chronicles where the temple and its worship are described (1 Chr. 22:1–26:32; 2 Chr. 3:1–4:22). David assured Solomon that the Lord would help him and that the men and materials were prepared.

***Worship through Giving (29:1-30).*** David exhorted the assembly to follow his example of stewardship. The people rejoiced when they saw their leaders give willingly and liberally. David led Israel in worship, praising God for His greatness and acknowledging that the gifts came from the Lord Himself. The congregation recognized Solomon as their king and Zadok as their priest and pledged their allegiance. The Lord exalted Solomon in the eyes of Israel.

David died after forty years of service to the Lord. The Chronicler concluded by referring the reader to the records of Samuel, Nathan, and Gad, which give a comprehensive account of David's reign.

***Theological and Ethical Significance.*** The Persian period, in which Chronicles was compiled, was a time of half-fulfilled hopes. The Jews had been allowed to return from Babylonian exile but without a king. They had been allowed to rebuild the temple, but the "second temple" paled in comparison with the first. The Chronicler reaffirmed for that generation (and ours) that despite the ambiguities of history God is in control and involved in the lives of His people. First Chronicles overlooks the moral defeats and highlights the victories of David to draw attention to God's sovereignty in his life. God succeeded in using David to fulfill His purposes for him. Chronicles challenges today's Christians to trace the high points of God's working in their own lives. Our hope is that the

One who began a good work in us will complete it (Phil. 1:6).

First Chronicles illustrates a responsible use of Scripture. The Chronicler's use of the Pentateuch and Prophets to shed new light on his major sources—the Books of Samuel and Kings—demonstrates that Scripture is the best guide to the interpretation of Scripture. The need to interpret "the old, old story" of Samuel and Kings for a new, postexilic generation led to the writing of 1 and 2 Chronicles. Each generation is faced with the task of confronting their world with the truth of Scripture in a way that speaks to the distinctive needs of its age.

First Chronicles recognizes that the greatest accomplishment of David's dynasty was spiritual—the organization and support of temple worship. Worship continues to be the center of Christian life. Worship empowers believers for lives of Christian service.

## Questions for Reflection

1. How can a person's family roots lead to salvation?

2. What does 1 Chronicles teach about the nature and practice of worship, particularly the use of music?

3. What does God expect of those who lead congregational worship?

4. What can God's people depend on in times of discouragement?

5. What does 1 Chronicles teach about stewardship?

## Sources for Additional Study

McConville, J. G. *I & II Chronicles*. Philadelphia: Westminster, 1984.
Sailhamer, John. *First and Second Chronicles*. Chicago: Moody, 1983.
Wilcock, Michael. *The Message of Chronicles*. Downers Grove: InterVarsity, 1987.

# 2 CHRONICLES

First and Second Chronicles are one continuous narrative (compare the discussion of 1 Chronicles). Second Chronicles describes the construction of the Solomonic temple and the religious life of the nation under Judah's kings.

**Theme.** God dwells in His holy temple and is faithful to His promise to redeem Israel (7:12).

I. God's Temple (1:1–9:31)
II. Spiritual Lessons (10:1–36:13)
III. Cyrus's Decree (36:14-23)

***Purpose and Theology.***

1. Second Chronicles continues the story of God's redemptive plan for Israel presented in 1 Chronicles. The break between the books is a convenient one because the first half ends with David's preparations for the temple and the second describes the building and history of the temple under Judah's kings. Second Chronicles covers four and a half centuries, from Solomon's reign (about 971 B.C.) to Cyrus's edict (539 B.C.).

2. Second Chronicles narrates Israel's past from the standpoint of its religious history. The building of the temple is the central concern (chaps. 2–7). The history of the monarchy is told from the perspective of how temple worship fared under Judah's kings. For example, the reign of Hezekiah is given greater attention because of his special temple reforms (chaps. 29–32). As in 1 Chronicles, the role of temple personnel, music, and festivals is featured (2 Chr. 5:4-14; 11:13-17; 17:8-9; 20:21; 23:2–24:16; 29:4–30:27; 31:2-19; 34:9-30; 35:1-19). The Chronicler explained in his concluding sermon that the temple's destruction occurred because of Judah's sinful leadership and not God's negligence (36:14-19). However, the book ends on a note of promise with Cyrus's edict to rebuild the temple (36:22-23). Although the restored community lived under Persian dominance, the temple's rebuilding indicated God's presence as in Solomon's days.

3. A recurring theme in Chronicles is faithfulness to God's covenant. In 2 Chronicles the kings of Judah are judged on the basis of their fidelity to Moses' commandments (6:16; 7:17-18). Those kings who were faithful prospered in their reigns, such as the reformers Asa (14:4), Jotham (27:6), Hezekiah (31:20-21), and Josiah (34:31-33; 35:26). The kings that were unfaithful to the law of Moses met with disaster. Jehoram experienced disease and defeat (21:12-20), Joash was assassinated (24:24-25), Uzziah suffered leprosy (26:16-21), Ahaz was humiliated (28:19,22), and Manasseh was imprisoned (33:7-11). The presence of a Davidic king by itself did not guarantee God's favor on Israel. Obedience was the Lord's requirement.

4. Second Chronicles emphasizes God's faithfulness, particularly His forgiveness and promises of restoration (6:21,25,38-39; 7:14; 30:9). The Lord accepted the repentant prayers of Rehoboam (12:5-8), Hezekiah (31:25-26), and Manasseh (33:12-13). God also was faithful to His promises to David, although Judah's kings acted wickedly (21:7).

5. An important theme in 2 Chronicles is God's holiness shown by His anger against the wicked. In particular the kings who committed idolatry merited the God's anger (12:5,12; 21:12-19; 25:14-

15; 33:6). Kings Jehoshaphat (19:10), Hezekiah (29:8-10; 30:8), and Josiah (34:21,23-28) understood this principle and implored Israel to obey God's law to avert His anger. Even those kings who won approval, such as Joash (24:17-25) and Hezekiah (32:25), experienced God's anger when they sinned. The Chronicler attributed Jerusalem's fall to God's wrath (36:16).

6. The theme of God's sovereignty in human affairs continues in 2 Chronicles. Cyrus's edict is the parade example of how God intervened to change the course of Israel's fortunes (36:22-23). In its recorded sermons and prayers 2 Chronicles reflects God's intervention (6:5-6; 7:17-22; 9:8; 13:5-12; 20:6-7; 32:6-8; 34:24,28). The Lord established kings (17:5; 20:15; 26:5), aroused enemies (21:16; 28:5; 33:11; 36:17), and afflicted or delivered kings (13:15; 21:18; 32:21-22).

## GOD'S TEMPLE (1:1–9:31)

The introductory section is occupied with the temple and Solomon's role in its construction. The splendor of Solomon's kingdom was evidence for the Chronicler that Solomon as David's son was the recipient of God's covenant promises.

**God Establishes Solomon (1:1-17).** The Chronicler omitted Solomon's early struggle for control (1 Kgs. 1–2). In his view the highlight of Solomon's career was the temple construction. The Lord elevated Solomon in the eyes of the people. Solomon worshiped the Lord at the tabernacle and sacrificial altar at Gibeon. The Lord granted Solomon's request for wisdom but also rewarded him with the promise of riches and power. The Chronicler demonstrated the truth of God's promise by listing Solomon's wealth and military power.

**Letter to Hiram (2:1-18).** Solomon contracted with Hiram, king of Tyre, for building materials and skilled

workmen. In his letter to Hiram, Solomon indicated Israel's God was not a deity who could be housed in a temple. Still the Lord was worthy of the very best talent and materials. Hiram replied by confessing to the greatness of Solomon's God. He agreed to send a craftsman of Hebrew extraction named Huram-Abi and all the materials requested. Solomon conscripted the aliens in his kingdom to form a large labor force.

**Builds the Temple (3:1-17).** The the temple site was Araunah's threshing floor, where David offered atonement for Israel (1 Chr. 21:28–22:1). The Chronicler identified the site as Mount Moriah, where Abraham offered sacrifice (see Gen. 22:2,14). The author emphasized the temple's role as the place of sacrifice where the Lord could be worshiped. More detail is given to the holy of holies than the temple's design because it was the place of meeting with God.

**Temple Furniture (4:1-22).** The bronze altar, molten sea, basins, lampstands, tables, and courtyards are described (see the feature article "The Temple"). The Chronicler listed the bronze work exquisitely made by Huram-Abi and the items of gold Solomon gave.

**Glory of the Ark (5:1-14).** Solomon brought the things David dedicated into the sanctuary. Then he assembled all Israel to accompany the ark into the temple. Typical of the Chronicler's interest, he elaborated on the role of the Levites and the the three musical guilds. The evidence of God's presence was the glorious cloud that filled the house.

**God's Faithfulness (6:1-42).** Solomon extolled God's faithfulness and applied the Davidic covenant to himself, indicating that he had successfully built the promised house of God.

In the presence of all Israel, Solomon humbled himself by kneeling in prayer. His dedicatory prayer centered on God's faithfulness to David and pleaded with God to hear the prayers and supplications that would be offered in the temple. He appealed to God to forgive and restore His people when they offered up prayers of repentance (1 Kgs. 8:12-52). Solomon concluded his prayer with a final hymn of exultation. ***Temple Dedication (7:1-22).*** The Lord answered Solomon's prayer by fire from heaven (see Elijah, 1 Kgs. 18:38-39). The Lord's glory filled the place so as to prohibit the priests from entering. The dedicatory service lasted seven days, followed by the seven-day Feast of Tabernacles. The dedication included sacrifice and Levitical music. Worship gladdened the hearts of the people.

The Lord appeared to Solomon a second time as He had at Gibeon. The Lord's message encouraged the people by expressing God's readiness to hear their prayers of repentance. The Lord exhorted Solomon to walk in the ways of his father David (see 1 Kgs. 9:1-9). This message was a reminder in the author's time that the Lord continued to hear Judah's prayers offered in the temple.

***Kingdom Expansion (8:1-18).*** The Chronicler showed that the Lord blessed Solomon (see 2 Chr. 7:18) by describing his many accomplishments. Solomon had extensive building projects, developed international relations with Egypt and Phoenicia, and created a navy for trade (see 1 Kgs. 9:10-28). Typical of the Chronicler, he highlighted Solomon's religious advances. Solomon was careful not to profane God's holy things, and he followed David's instructions.

***Fame and Wealth (9:1-31).*** The Queen of Sheba (Arabia) visited Solomon and was overwhelmed by his kingdom. She praised the Lord for His love of Israel (1 Kgs. 10:1-13). Solomon's wealth was fulfillment of God's promises to the king (2 Chr. 1:12). The writer included the details of Solomon's wealth and his special throne, indicating that no king possessed as many riches (1 Kgs. 10:14-29).

The Chronicler identified particular prophetic writings as additional sources for Solomon's reign (1 Kgs. 11:41-43). The Book of Kings includes Solomon's foreign marriages and the idolatry that caused Israel to deteriorate (1 Kgs. 11:1-40). Chronicles omits this because the compiler wanted to limit his account to the positive contributions of Solomon to fulfilling God's redemption through David's seed.

## SPIRITUAL LESSONS (10:1–36:13)

The second section of the book reviews the spiritual life of the nation under the kings of Judah during the divided monarchy. After the revolt of the northern tribes is recounted (chap. 10), the narrative alternates between periods of spiritual decay and religious reforms. Special consideration is given to the reformers Asa and Jehoshaphat, Joash, Hezekiah, and Josiah. The final period of degeneracy is the last days of Judah's kings.

***Rehoboam's Selfishness (10:1-19).*** Rehoboam (930–913 B.C.) succeeded his father, Solomon, and was confronted at his coronation by the rebel Jeroboam. Jeroboam appealed to Rehoboam to lighten the burden of taxation his father had levied ( see 1 Kgs. 11:26-40). Rehoboam followed the poor advice of his young counselors by threatening to increase the levy. The northern tribes rebelled, ousting the king and his officials. This fulfilled Ahijah's prophecy of God's judgment against Solomon's house (1 Kgs. 11:29-33). The Chronicler omitted Jeroboam's coronation, because he did not consider Jeroboam or the later kings of the Northern Kingdom legitimate heirs to Israel's throne.

***Rehoboam's Strength (11:1-22).*** Rehoboam wanted to wage war against Jeroboam, but God hindered him (1 Kgs.

12:21-24). Rehoboam then turned his attention to fortifying Judah's cities. Oppressed by Jeroboam, Levites and priests fled to Judah, where they strengthened Rehoboam's kingdom. The strength of Rehoboam's kingdom was also evidenced by the increasing size of his family.

**God's Wrath (12:1-16).** Shishak, king of Egypt, invaded Judah and threatened the city of Jerusalem (1 Kgs. 14:25-28). Shishak, whose Egyptian name was Shoshenq I (945–924 B.C.), ruled from Tanis (biblical Zoan). He was Pharaoh when Jeroboam went to Egypt to escape Solomon (1 Kgs. 11:40). The Egyptian account of his invasion is recorded on the walls in the temple at Karnak (Thebes). There Shishak listed 150 cities captured in Israel and Judah. The prophet Shemaiah interpreted this invasion as God's wrath because of Judah's sin. Rehoboam paid a heavy ransom, including the temple treasuries and Solomon's vast wealth. Because Rehoboam and the people humbled themselves, the Lord saved Jerusalem from total destruction. Rehoboam's reign was remembered for its years of warfare with Jeroboam.

**Abijah's Sermon (13:1–14:1).** The author of Kings condemned the reign of Abijah (Abijam; 913–910 B.C.; 1 Kgs. 15:1-8), but the Chronicler depicted his reign in a more positive light. Using Iddo's account, he included Abijah's sermon delivered before a battle against Jeroboam. Abijah charged Jeroboam with apostasy, arguing that God had made a permanent bond ("covenant of salt," see Num. 18:19) with David's descendants. He defended Jerusalem's worship because it was conducted by priests descended from Aaron as the Lord required. The Lord "routed Jeroboam," giving Judah a great victory because they trusted in the Lord.

**Relying on the Lord (14:2-15).** Asa (910–869 B.C.) enjoyed the blessing of God because he removed the symbols of paganism (1 Kgs. 15:11-12). The Cushite (Ethiopian) Zerah attacked Judah from the south, but Asa appealed to the Lord and won an impressive victory at Mareshah.

**Religious Reform (15:1-19).** The prophet Azariah called for repentance, instigating Asa's religious reforms. Asa removed idols and repaired the Lord's altar. He led Judah to renew its covenant with the Lord not to follow after other gods. Asa also removed the queen mother, Maacah, who had erected an Asherah pole (see 1 Kgs. 15:13). The Lord gave Judah peace and prosperity.

**Wars and Disease (16:1-14).** Baasha, king of Israel (908–886 B.C.) built a fortress at Ramah near Jerusalem. In desperation Asa bribed Ben-Hadad of Aram (Syria) to attack Baasha's territory (1 Kgs. 15:17-22). The prophet Hanani condemned Asa because he relied on Aram rather than the Lord. Asa imprisoned Hanani and oppressed the people. God chastened Judah with continued warfare, and Asa experienced a debilitating foot disease. Asa's funeral was an elaborate spectacle (see 1 Kgs. 15:23-24).

**Righteous Jehoshaphat (17:1-19).** Jehoshaphat's reign (872–869 B.C.) was remembered for his devotion to the Lord. He sent Levites throughout the territory of Judah to instruct the people in the Book of the Law. The Lord rewarded the king with peace and international respect. His fighting forces grew in strength.

**Micaiah Prophecy (18:1-34).** A fuller account of Ahab's reign (874–853 B.C.) is found in Kings. The story of Ahab's death is the only account in the lives of the northern kings the Chronicler used.

Jehoshaphat had allied himself with Ahab through marriage, giving his son Jehoram to Ahab's daughter Athaliah (2 Kgs. 8:18,25-26). He was persuaded to join Israel in a campaign against the Arameans at Ramoth Gilead. In contrast to Ahab, Jehoshaphat insisted on hearing from a prophet of the Lord. Ahab reluctantly called for Micaiah, whom he had imprisoned (1 Kgs. 22:1-9).

The false prophet Zedekiah had predicted a victory for Israel, but Micaiah condemned his prophecy, attributing it to a lying spirit. As Ahab returned him to prison, Micaiah predicted Ahab's death (1 Kgs. 22:10-28). Ahab disguised himself as he entered the battle, and Jehoshaphat alone wore his royal regalia. When the enemy mistook Jehoshaphat for Ahab, they pursued him, but the Lord spared Jehoshaphat. Ahab was "at random" mortally wounded by a bowman (1 Kgs. 22:29-36).

### Jehoshaphat Repents (19:1-11).

The prophet Jehu scolded Jehoshaphat for his alliance with Ahab. He declared God's impending wrath but reminded him that early in his reign he had acted righteously (see 17:3). The king repented and personally led a revival among the people. He appointed judges who feared the Lord. These included Levites and priests, who taught Judah to love the Lord and fear His wrath.

### God Helps Jehoshaphat (20:1-37).

A coalition of Ammonites, Moabites, and others marched against Judah. Jehoshaphat prayed, calling upon God to deliver Judah based on His promises to Abraham. Jahaziel, a Levite, prophesied that the battle was the Lord's, and the Levites worshiped the Lord with a psalm and music. As they worshiped, the Lord responded to their prayers of deliverance by causing the enemy to turn upon one another. The place became known as the Valley of Beracah (bless-

ing). The nations recognized that Israel's God had given them the victory, and they feared Jehoshaphat so that Judah remained at peace.

Although Jehoshaphat acted righteously by removing pagan objects of worship, he failed the Lord later in his reign when he became an ally with Ahaziah, Ahab's son (853–852 B.C.). Together they built a navy, but it never set sail from port. The Lord destroyed it as the prophet Eliezer predicted (1 Kgs. 22:41-50).

### Jehoram the Murderer (21:1-20).

Upon succeeding his father as king, Jehoram murdered his brothers. He was married to Ahab's daughter, Athaliah, and was wicked like his in-laws, the kings of Israel. The Lord used several enemies to trouble his reign (2 Kgs. 8:16-24). The prophet Elijah sent a letter of doom to the king, predicting defeat and disease for the king. The Lord incited the Philistines and Arabs to attack Judah. This is the only account from the life of Elijah that the Chronicler included in his history. Kings does not record this incident.

God inflicted the king with a horrible disease which led to his death. The Chronicler added that no one regretted the king's passing.

### Jehu Kills Ahaziah (22:1-12).

Jehoram's son, Ahaziah (841 B.C.), was wicked like his father. His mother was Athaliah, the daughter of Ahab. Ahaziah visited his uncle, King Joram of Israel at Jezreel, where he was recuperating from a wound received in battle against the Arameans at Ramoth. God used this evil relationship to end Ahaziah's life. Jehu (841–814 B.C.), a commander in Joram's armies, was commissioned by the Lord's prophet to purge Israel of Baalism and take the throne of Ahab and his son Joram (2 Kgs. 9:1–10:36). Jehu executed Ahab's family and also killed

Ahaziah and his relatives (2 Kgs. 9:21-29).

Athaliah (841–835 B.C.) seized her opportunity to rule Judah by executing the legitimate heirs to the throne. However, the Lord preserved young Joash, the true heir to David's throne. Jehosheba, the wife of the priest Jehoiada and sister of King Ahaziah, hid him in the temple for six years (2 Kgs. 11:1-3).

***Joash Becomes King (23:1-21).*** A conspiracy led by the priest Jehoiada plotted to enthrone Joash. The Chronicler emphasized the heroism of the priests and omitted the role of the foreign

| ASSYRIAN RULERS | | |
|---|---|---|
| **RULER** | **DATES OF RULE** | **SCRIPTURE REFERENCE** |
| Ashur-uballit I | 1354–1318 B.C. | |
| Adad-nirari I | 1318–1264 B.C. | |
| Shalmaneser I (Shulman-asharid) | 1264–1234 B.C. | |
| Tukulti-Ninurta I | 1234–1197 B.C. | |
| Ashur-dan I | 1179–1133 B.C. | |
| Tiglath-pileşer I (Tukulti-apil-Eŝarra) | 1115–1076 B.C. | |
| Ashur-rabi II | 1012–972 B.C. | |
| Ashur-resh-ishi II | 972–967 B.C. | |
| Tiglath-pileser II | 967–935 B.C. | |
| Ashur-dan II | 935–912 B.C. | |
| Adad-nirari II | 912–889 B.C. | |
| Tukulti-Ninurta II | 889–884 B.C. | |
| Ashurnasirpal II (Ashur-nasir-apli II) | 884–858 B.C. | |
| Shalmaneser III (Shalman-Ashar-id II) | 858–824 B.C. | |
| Shamsi-Adad V | 824–810 B.C. | |
| Adad-nirari III | 810–782 B.C. | |
| Shalmaneser IV | 782–773 B.C. | |
| Ashur-dan III | 773–754 B.C. | |
| Ashur-nirari V | 754–745 B.C. | |
| Tiglath-pileşer III (Tukulti-apil-Eŝarra III, or Tiglath-pilneser, or Pul(u)) | 745–727 B.C. | 2 Kgs 15:19,29; 16:7-10 |
| Shalmaneser V (Ululai) | 727–722 B.C. | 2 Kgs 17:1-6 |
| Sargon II | 721–705 B.C. | |
| Sennacherib (Sin-abho-eriba) | 704–681 B.C. | 2 Kgs 18–19 |
| Esarhaddon | 681–669 B.C. | |
| Ashurbanipal | 669–633 B.C. | |
| Ashur-etil-ilani | 633–622 B.C. | |
| Sin-shur-ishkun | 621–612 B.C. | |
| Ashur-uballit | 612–608 B.C. | |

Carites (2 Kgs. 11:4). The Levites and priests assembled the people, and they covenanted to make Joash king. Jehoiada ordered the priests to guard the king at all times since they alone were qualified to be in the holy temple precincts. Together they enthroned the king.

The priests captured Athaliah and executed both her and Mattan, the high priest of Baal. The writer was particularly concerned about the holiness of the temple in his telling of the story. The Levites reinstituted the worship of the Lord in the temple as David had provided.

### Restoring the Temple (24:1-27).
Joash (835–796 B.C.) launched a major restoration project of the temple, which had been neglected during Athaliah's rule. He requested the Levites to gather annual monies due the temple from the people (Exod. 30:12-16), but they were slow in fulfilling the charge. So Joash provided a chest in the temple itself where the people brought their tax so that the restoration was carried out (2 Kgs. 12:1-16). The Chronicler mentioned the priest's failure but softened the tone of the account in Kings.

When the priest Jehoiada died, apostasy resurged under Joash's authority. Joash refused to listen to God's prophets. Zechariah, son of Jehoiada, condemned the people for their religious infidelity and was stoned to death in the king's presence. As he died, the priest swore God's vengeance on Joash. The Chronicler explained the tragic end of Joash's rule as God's judgment on Judah's wickedness. Judah was defeated by invading Arameans, and Joash was murdered in his bed (2 Kgs. 12:17-21).

Joash's career illustrated the Chronicler's major theme: God's blessing on David's house but also God's anger when the kings acted wickedly. Zechariah's murder is the last one mentioned in the Hebrew Bible since Chronicles ends the Hebrew arrangement (see Luke 11:51).

### Amaziah's Idolatry (25:1-28).
Amaziah (797–767 B.C.) began his career by avenging his father's assassins. They were placed under trial in accordance with the law (2 Kgs. 14:1-6).

The Edomites rebelled against the young king, and he gathered a vast army of mercenaries, including a thousand hired from Israel. But an unnamed prophet convinced him to release the Israelites and depend on the Lord alone for victory (2 Kgs. 14:7). Judah crushed the Edomites, but the disgruntled Israelites plundered Judah's cities as they marched home. Amaziah angered the Lord because he returned with Edomite gods whom he worshiped. The Lord's prophet condemned the king for his resistance to the Lord's word. Fresh from his victory over Edom, Amaziah challenged the stronger Jehoash of Israel (798–782 B.C.). The result of the conflict was the destruction of Jerusalem's defenses and Amaziah's capture. The Chronicler attributed Amaziah's defeat and his subsequent murder to his sin of idolatry (2 Kgs. 14:8-20).

### Uzziah the Leper (26:1-23).
Uzziah (Azariah) succeeded his father at the age of sixteen. Zechariah tutored Uzziah in the things of God. God blessed Uzziah in all he did; his fifty-two-year reign (792–767 B.C.; coregency, 767–740) was one of the longest and most prosperous among the kings of Judah (2 Kgs. 14:21–15:1-3). The king subjugated many peoples, built a huge army, and pioneered military weaponry. Because of his success he became proud and, though not a priest, attempted to officiate at the altar. God struck the king with leprosy, and his son Jotham carried on in his place (2 Kgs. 15:5-7).

### Jotham's Success (27:1-9).
Jotham (750–732 B.C.) was righteous

like his father, but he did not act presumptuously by entering the temple proper in his reign. His conquest of the Ammonites was attributed to the favor God showed toward him (2 Kgs. 15:32-38).

### Ahab's Wicked Reign (28:1-27).

Chronicles, based on the report of 2 Kings 16:1-20, emphasized the wickedness of King Ahaz's reign (735–715 B.C.). Ahaz was remembered for his practice of human sacrifice and Baal worship. The writer interpreted Judah's war with Israel and Aram (Syro-Ephraimite war) in 732 B.C. as God's judgment upon Ahaz (see Isa. 7). The Chronicler commended the victorious Northern Kingdom for obeying the prophet Oded and releasing the captured Judahites.

The Lord punished Judah further by pressuring it with the raiding armies of the mercenary Edomites and Philistines. Ahaz appealed to the Assyrian king Tiglath-Pileser III (745–727 B.C.), who promptly obliged by marching west, destroying Damascus and conquering Samaria (732 B.C.). Ahaz failed at buying his independence with temple and royal treasuries. He became a vassal of the Assyrian king and bowed to the gods of Assyria. Second Kings 16:10-14 reports that Ahaz reproduced in the Jerusalem temple Tiglath's pagan altar which he had seen at Damascus. Ahaz eventually closed the temple and erected numerous idols in the land. Whereas the Chronicler tried to introduce something positive about each king of Judah, for vicious Ahaz there was nothing good to report.

### Hezekiah's Restoration (29:1-36).

Hezekiah's reign (715–686 B.C.) is given inordinate attention because of the prominence he gave to temple music and worship. Much of the Chronicler's account (chaps. 29–31) is not paralleled in Kings.

The neglect of the temple under Ahaz (28:24) prompted Hezekiah to order the Levites to consecrate themselves and begin repair of the sanctuary. After sixteen days the Levites completed the task and opened the temple once again. After the Levites had cleansed the articles of worship, the king led the congregation in worship through offerings. The musical guilds functioned again as David had intended and performed the psalms of David and Asaph. After the people had atoned for their sins, they offered burnt and thank offerings so numerous that the Levites were requested to assist the overburdened priests. The sight and sounds of the temple brought great joy to the congregation.

### Passover Celebration (30:1-27).

The king planned a great convocation in Jerusalem to celebrate the Passover. He invited their estranged kin in the North who had survived the collapse of Samaria in 722 B.C. under Assyrian might. Because the temple was not yet prepared and many remained ceremonially impure, the Passover was held in the second month rather than the first as the law commanded (see Exod. 12; Num. 9:10-11). Letters were dispatched throughout the land, exhorting the northern remnants to repent of their former ways and join Judah in worship.

The Chronicler, always concerned for the propriety of worship, reported the unusual circumstances attending this celebration which the Lord graciously permitted. Hezekiah's prayer of repentance on behalf of the people was accepted by God. So devoted was the worship of the people that they extended the Feast of Unleavened Bread a second week. The Chronicler compared the joy of Jerusalem on that occasion to the days of King Solomon. The Chronicler extolled Hezekiah's Passover in the same way the author of Kings praised Josiah's (2 Kgs. 23:21-23; see also 2 Chr. 35:18).

**Gifts for the Lord's Work (31:1-21).** The revival spurred the people on to remove the symbols of any illicit worship. Hezekiah reorganized the priests and Levites to serve the temple. At this spiritual outpouring the people happily brought their tithes and offerings as the law commanded. So vast were the offerings that there was an overabundance distributed among the priest. The Lord prospered Hezekiah for his faithfulness (2 Kgs. 18:5-7).

**God Destroys Sennacherib (32:1-33).** The Chronicler, concerned with Hezekiah's religious contributions, shortened the record of Hezekiah's political career in 2 Kings 18:13–19:37 (see Isa. 36:2–37:38).

The Lord delivered Jerusalem in 701 B.C. from the Assyrian armies of Sennacherib (705–681 B.C.) because of Hezekiah's faithfulness. Hezekiah made preparations for war. The king encouraged the people to remain faithful because the Lord was more powerful than the Assyrians or their gods. An Assyrian delegation addressed the people of Jerusalem in their native Hebrew. They threatened the city by ridiculing Hezekiah's dependence on the Lord. The Chronicler was offended by the Assyrian derision of Israel's God when they likened the Lord to an idol, "the work of men's hands." An account of Sennacherib's invasion is recorded on his palace walls in Nineveh in which he boasted that he had Hezekiah caged like a bird.

Yet Hezekiah, supported by Isaiah the prophet, resisted their threats, praying for God's intervention. The Lord honored their prayers and sent an angel of destruction among the Assyrians. Sennecherib retreated to Nineveh, where he was later murdered by his own sons. The people greatly rejoiced at the deliverance and worshiped the Lord anew.

When Hezekiah became ill unto death, the Lord answered the king's prayers for mercy by giving a sign. However, the king became proud, and the Lord convicted him of his sins. His repentance averted the Lord's wrath. The final years of Hezekiah were blessed of God, and he prospered in all that he attempted (2 Kgs. 20:1-21; Isa. 37:21–38:8).

**Manasseh's Repentance (33:1-25).** The Chronicler detailed the despicable acts of this king who indulged in every evil act of idolatry, sorcery, and astrology. The writer of Kings blamed Manasseh's reign for the Lord's destruction of Jerusalem and the deportation to Babylon (2 Kgs. 21:10-15).

The Chronicler's account of Manasseh's reign (697–687 B.C.) departs from the narrative of 2 Kings 21:1-18 by including the unusual story of Manasseh's imprisonment in Assyria. During this exile, he repented and God answered by returning him to Jerusalem (33:10-13). Many scholars have questioned the authenticity of the Chronicler's account. However, its omission in Kings can be attributed to that author's purpose of presenting a case for the apostasy of Judah. Chronicles, on the other hand, demonstrates how God forgives and restores the humble (see 7:14). The Chronicler cited an independent witness to corroborate his story.

Upon his return Manasseh repaired the temple and renewed proper worship. The reference to his repentant prayer gave rise to speculation about its contents in the apocryphal book "The Prayer of Manasseh" (ca. 200–100 B.C.).

His successor was Amon (642–640 B.C.) for whom the Chronicler had no words of commendation (2 Kgs. 21:19-24).

**Book of the Law (34:1-33).** Josiah reigned for thrity-one years (640–609 B.C.) and walked in the way of the Lord as David had done (2 Kgs. 22:1-2). For the author of Kings, Josiah's significance was second only to David's. Therefore more attention is devoted to his reign in Kings than in Chronicles (1 Kgs. 13:2; 2 Kgs. 22:1–23:30).

Chronicles (34:3-7) indicates that religious reform began in Josiah's eighth year (632 B.C.), a full decade before the discovery of the Book of the Law (622 B.C.). The purge of idolatry and high places extended to northern towns as well as Judah, indicating that Josiah's rule was expanding into the old Northern Kingdom without Assyria's interference.

The Levites received money from the rulers and common people to refurbish the temple. As the Levites worked, the high priest Hilkiah found a copy of the Book of the Law (also called "Book of the Covenant"). From Josiah's response most scholars have concluded that it was a portion of Deuteronomy. Upon hearing the book read, Josiah was remorseful and feared the Lord's wrath. The prophetess Huldah declared that the Lord would destroy Judah but preserve Josiah's reign because of his humble contrition. Josiah led the people in a covenant renewal ceremony.

**Josiah's Passover (35:1-27).** Celebration of Passover and the week of Unleavened Bread followed the reforms of Hezekiah (chap. 30) and Josiah. Chro, because of its interest in cultic matters, elaborated on the few verses given to it in 2 Kings 23:21-23.

The celebration occurred in the appropriate month, unlike Hezekiah's Passover renewal. To worship the Lord properly the Levites and priests consecrated themselves and then prepared the sacrifices in behalf of the people. The Levites functioned in their proper order in accordance with the Book of Moses. Typical of the Chronicler, he also included the role of the musical guilds David appointed. The celebration exceeded that of any previous Passover since the days of Samuel. Josiah's reforms culminated with the Passover observed in the same year as the finding of the Book of the Law.

The Chronicler also clarified the events of Josiah's death at the battle of Megiddo, where Pharaoh Neco defeated him (2 Kgs. 23:26-30). Neco was marching through Jezreel to assist the Assyrians, who were pinned down by the Babylonians at Carchemish (North Syria). Ironically, Josiah, whose reign was remembered for its righteousness, died because he failed to adhere to the Lord's command. The prophet Jeremiah (not mentioned in Kings) lamented in song the death of the monarch.

**Judah's Last Days (36:1-13).** The Chronicler gave a brief account of Judah's last kings (see 2 Kgs. 23:30–25:21; Jer. 52:4-27), focused on temple and its ministries.

Jehoahaz (609 B.C.), whom Necho installed, was deposed after only three months and replaced by a second son of Josiah, Jehoiakim. Nebuchadnezzar was victorious at Carchemish and subjugated the petty kingdom of Judah. Jehoiakim's evil reign (609–598 B.C.) ended in deportation by Nebuchadnezzar, who invaded rebellious Jerusalem and plundered the temple. King Jehoiachin (598–597 B.C.) was quickly supplanted with the puppet king Zedekiah (597–586 B.C.), whose rebellion led to Jerusalem's final demise in 586 B.C.

## CYRUS'S DECREE (36:14-23)

The Chronicler's final remarks are a sermon blaming the failure of the priests and leaders to obey the Lord's commands for the temple's and city's destruction. Writing almost two centuries after

Kings, the Chronicler included in his story the return of the exiles, adding that Jeremiah predicted this (Jer. 25:11; 29:10). The Chronicler commented that the land had its Sabbath rest as the law required (see Lev. 26), for the seventy years from the ruin of the temple (586 b.c.) to its rebuilding (516 B.C.).

With the ousting of the Babylonians, the Persian emperor Cyrus inaugurated a new policy toward the exiles. Cyrus's edict, published in the famous Cyrus Cylinder (539 B.C.), was quoted by the Chronicler in its Hebrew version. Cyrus permitted the conquered peoples of Babylon to return to their homelands and revive their religious traditions. For the Jews he ordered the rebuilding of the Jerusalem temple.

Although it appeared that God's promises to David were abandoned, the Chronicler showed through his review of history that God remains faithful and can change history to accomplish His purposes. The story of Israel's fortunes was not finished. These last two verses were

repeated in Ezra 1:1-3a to indicate that the story of God's redemptive work through the temple continued in the accounts of Ezra and Nehemiah.

**Ethical and Theological Significance.** Second Chronicles speaks of the importance of worship and obedience. The Chronicler evaluated the kings of Judah not on their secular accomplishments but on the basis of their faithfulness to God, especially as evidenced in their support of temple worship. The Chronicler's verdict on these kings reminds today's Christians that our lives will someday be judged as well. As we live our lives, we should keep God's goals in mind and strive for His commendation, "Well done, good and faithful servant" (Matt. 25:21).

Sin is serious. The sin of God's people led to the destruction of Jerusalem, the temple, and to the exile. Though God punishes sin, judgment is not God's final word. God "is good; his love for Israel endures forever" (Ezra 3:11). Second Chronicles ends with the exiles'

## BABYLONIAN RULERS

| RULER | DATES OF RULE | SCRIPTURE REFERENCE |
|---|---|---|
| Merodach-Baladan II (Marduk-apal-iddin) | 721–689 B.C. | 2 Kgs 20:12; Isa 39:1 |
| Nabopolassar | 625–605 B.C. | |
| Nebuchadnezzar II (Nebuchadrezzar II) | 605–562 B.C. | 2 Kgs 24–25; Dan 1–4 |
| Evil-Merodach (Amel-Marduk) | 562–560 B.C. | 2 Kgs 25:27-30; Jer 52:31-34 |
| Nergal-Sharezer (Nergal-shar-usur, or Neriglissar) | 560–556 B.C. | Jer 39:3,13 |
| Labashi-Marduk | 556 B.C. | |
| Nabonidus (Nabu-na'id) | 556–539 B.C. | |
| Belshazzar (Bel-shar-usur) | Co-regent with Nabonidus 556–539 B.C. | Dan 5; 7:1 |

being given the freedom to go home and rebuild the temple. Our God is a God of second chances, who through Jesus offers sinners new freedom, a chance to come home to His family, and opportunities for service.

## Questions for Reflection

1. Why are special days of religious celebration important to the spiritual life of a religious community?

2. What does Chronicles teach about spiritual renewal among God's people?

3. In what ways does God chasten His people?

4. How does God reward the faithfulness of His people?

5. What difference does a nation's morality make in its life and destiny?

## Sources for Additional Study

McConville, J. G. *I & II Chronicles.* Philadelphia: Westminster, 1984.

Merrill, Eugene H. *1, 2 Chronicles.* Grand Rapids: Zondervan, 1988.

Sailhamer, John. *First and Second Chronicles.* Chicago: Moody, 1983.

# EZRA

The Book of Ezra is named for the book's principle character. This scribe revived the law of Moses as the basis for Jewish religious and social life during the period of restoration following the Babylonian exile.

In the Hebrew Bible, Ezra-Nehemiah is one book. It occurs in the third and final section (called the "Writings") and precedes Chronicles, which is the last book of the Hebrew Bible. The English Old Testament follows the Latin in separating Ezra-Nehemiah into two books. The English Old Testament with the Greek and Latin places Ezra in its proper chronological sequence, following 1 and 2 Chronicles, as the tenth of the historical books.

There is a continuing debate about the relationship of Chronicles and Ezra-Nehemiah. The last verses of 2 Chronicles (36:22-23) are the same as Ezra 1:1-3a. In fact, Chronicles ends in the middle of a sentence that only occurs in full in Ezra. This overlapping may indicate that the books were intended to be read together.

Many scholars think that Chronicles and Ezra-Nehemiah formed a single historical work, called the "Chronicler's History," authored by an anonymous individual or school of historians. Other scholars, both evangelical and critical, believe that Ezra and Nehemiah have independent authorship from Chronicles. There are significant dissimilarities in language and viewpoint. (See "The Historical Books.")

In Jewish tradition Ezra the scribe is the author of Chronicles and Ezra-Nehemiah. (See the introduction to "1 Chronicles.") While the attribution of all these books to Ezra cannot be demonstrated it is clear that at least he contributed personal memoirs to the book that bears his name and probably had a significant role in the compilation of Ezra-Nehemiah. The Book of Ezra dates in the later half of the fifth century B.C.

Sources for the Book of Ezra included Ezra's firsthand account (probably 7:1–19:15), empirical documents and correspondence written in Aramaic (4:8–6:18; 7:12-26), and registers of Jewish immigrants (2:1-70; 8:1-14).

***Chronology of Ezra and Nehemiah.*** The date of writing is dependent on the chronology of Ezra's return to Jerusalem. The traditional opinion has Ezra's ministry in the seventh year (458 B.C.) and Nehemiah's ministry in the twentieth year (445 B.C.) of Artaxerxes I (Ezra 7:8; Neh. 2:1). Problems exist with the traditional opinion. For example, the high priest in Nehemiah's time was Eliashib (Neh. 3:1,20-21; 13:28), but Ezra ministered during the priesthood of Jehohana, the son of Eliashib (Ezra 10:6).

Because of such problems, alternative opinions have been suggested. Another view dates Ezra's expedition in the seventh year of Artaxerxes II (398 B.C.) after the time of Nehemiah. A third alternative dates Ezra in 428 B.C. by emending Ezra 7:8 to read the "thirty-seventh year" rather than the seventh year of Artaxerxes.

Although the traditional view has difficulties, its arguments are more compelling. For example, scholars have suggested that there was more than one Eliashib and Jehohanan and that Nehemiah and Ezra speak of different ones. Therefore, following the fifth century date for Ezra's ministry, the composition of Ezra-Nehemiah was about 400 B.C. or soon thereafter. If Ezra-Nehemiah were written as part of the Chronicler's History, it was written after 400 B.C. since the genealogies of Chronicles exceed this date (see 1 Chr. 3:19-24; see the "The Historical Books").

The restoration period commenced with the defeat of Babylon by the Persian monarch Cyrus, who ordered the release of the Jews in 538 B.C. The chronology of the period can be summarized by the expeditions that returned from the captivity.

1. Under the Jewish prince Sheshbazzar (538 B.C.) the first group returned. Later the new governor Zerubbabel and high priest Jeshua completed the temple (515 B.C.) with the help of the prophets Zechariah and Haggai (Ezra 16).

2. During the reign of Artaxerses I (464–424 B.C.) Ezra led a second party and initiated religious reforms (Ezra 7–10). This expedition was fifty-eight years after the completion of the temple (458 B.C.).

3. Nehemiah, appointed governor by Artaxerxes I, led the third party and rebuilt Jerusalem's walls. Nehemiah's first term was twelve years (445–433 B.C.; Neh. 1:1–13:6), and the second term was soon thereafter (430 B.C.?; Neh. 13:6-31).

**Theme.** God used pagan kings and godly leaders to restore His people by reinstituting temple worship and reviving the law of Moses.

    I. Rebuilding the Temple (1:1–6:22)
    II. Reform under the Law (7:1–10:44)

**Purpose and Theology.**

1. The Book of Ezra tells the history of the Jews' return from Babylon. It continues the story that Chronicles left unfinished. The first half of the book (chaps. 1–6) concerns the expedition ordered by King Cyrus (538 B.C.) to rebuild the temple under Sheshbazzar of Judah. The book continues the theme of temple and priesthood begun in Chronicles (Ezra 3:1-6,10-11; 6:16-22). The importance of the Levites and priests to the community is evidenced by the careful cataloging of those who returned (2:36-54,61-62). The Levites supervised the rebuilding of the temple and were reorganized in time to officiate at the first Passover celebration (3:8-9; 6:16-20)

Priests and Levites were a major concern of Ezra's administration (chaps. 7–10). Ezra was careful to include them among those returning from exile (7:7,13,24; 8:15-20,24-34). Their sinful intermarriage with Gentiles provoked Ezra's reforms (9:1-2). They were placed under oath (10:5), and the guilty were noted (10:18-24).

2. Ezra's theological focus is how God accomplishes His will through different human agents. God restored His people by moving the pagan ruler Cyrus to release Judah (1:1-2) and by inciting the Jewish people to volunteer (1:5). The Cyrus Cylinder inscription gives the Persian account of Cyprus's decree. It explains that the Babylonian god Marduk called him to release the exiles to return to their homelands. The Hebrew version of this decree applied to the Jews (2 Chr. 36:22-23; Ezra 1:1-4). Biblical writers interpreted the decree as the act of God (Isa. 45:1-3) in fulfillment of Jeremiah's prophecy (Jer. 25:11-12; 29:10). Cyrus and Darius even supplied necessary provisions for the temple (Ezra 1:7-11; 6:8-10). The Gentiles were perceived as coworkers in the building of the Jewish temple (6:22).

The Lord also was responsible for the success of Ezra's expedition. Ezra was called and protected by the Lord's "gracious hand" (7:9; 8:18,22). God used the

Persian government to enable Ezra to accomplish his task (7:27-28).

God accomplished His purposes through special spokesmen as well. The prophets Zechariah and Haggai delivered the message of God, which motivated the people to complete the temple (5:1-2; 6:14). Together pagan kings, godly leaders, common people, and prophets were the Lord's hands and feet to do His bidding.

3. The book reflects the optimism of a restored Davidic throne, keeping the messianic hope alive. Sheshbazzar and Zerubbabel, who returned from exile to lead Judah, were descendants of Judah's king Jehoiachin, who had been taken captive to Babylon. (See 1:8; 1 Chr. 3:18-19 [Sheshbazzar = Shenazzar?]; and 2 Chr. 36:9-10). The prophecies of Zechariah and Haggai during this period depicted the messianic age by idealizing Zerubbabel and Jeshua as the new David and high priest Zadok (Ezra 3:8; 5:1-2; 6:14; Zech. 3:1-4, 14; 6:9-15; Hag. 2:6-9; 3:23).

4. The second half of the book (chaps. 7–10) concerns Ezra's ministry, which began fifty-eight years (458 B.C.) after the completion of the temple (515 B.C.). In the latter half of the book the emphasis shifts to the law of Moses. Ezra was commissioned to teach and establish the customs of Jewish law (7:11,14,25-26). Ezra was a learned scribe devoted to the law (7:6,10-12). He led the people in a spiritual awakening that resulted in a covenant renewal (10:3).

5. The book also expresses the responsibility for human sin. The people of Ezra's day had sinned by intermarrying with the Gentile populace (9:1-2; 10:1-44). Ezra's intercession (9:6-15) and the people's weeping confession (10:1-2) led to a renewal of covenant commitment to the Lord (10:3). The community felt the responsibility of those who had sinned

and collectively dealt with the guilty, including their leaders (10:16-24).

6. Antagonism toward those building the temple was commonplace and official avenues were used to stop the work (4:1-24; 5:3-6:12). However, the author showed that God's help enabled them to finish the work under His watchful eye in spite of opposition (5:5).

7. The people of God as the remnant of Israel is important to the theology of the restoration period. They are the remnant that escaped the wrath of God (9:8,15). Therefore their company, though small in number (chap. 2), was significant because they were "all Israel" (8:25) who were regathered as the "holy race" (9:2).

### REBUILDING THE TEMPLE (1:1–6:22)

The first section centers on the building of the temple. The Lord inspired Cyrus to permit the return of the Jews to worship their God. Those who volunteered for the first expedition are listed. The foundation of the temple was laid, and the people worshiped God. But opposition from their enemies stopped the work. The Lord stirred up the people by the prophets Zechariah and Haggai to complete the work in spite of inquiries from the Persian governor. King Darius authorized and funded the project, which was completed with great celebration.

***Decree of Cyrus (1:1-11).*** In the first year of Cyrus's reign over Babylon (539–530 B.C.), the Persian monarch permitted the Jews to return and rebuild their temple for the purpose of worshiping the Lord. This was attributed to the inspiration of the Lord both by Cyrus and by the biblical writer (see 2 Chr. 29:22-23), who interpreted it as the fulfillment of Jeremiah's prophecy (Jer. 25:11-12; 29:10; see Isa. 44:28–45:3). The prophet Isaiah identified Cyrus as the anointed servant of the Lord. The Cyrus Cylinder reports how the king tolerated the religions of many nations by restoring the images of their deities and rebuilding their sanctuaries. Cyrus's sympathy was politically motivated to encourage the loyalty of his new subjects upon their release.

The Lord also stirred up some of the exiles of Judah to return. Cyrus returned the temple vessels stolen by Nebuchadnezzar (2 Kgs. 25:13-15; 2 Chr. 36:18). Sheshbazzar, identified as the "prince of Judah" (1:8), received the inventory of temple articles and led the exiles to Jerusalem. Sheshbazzar may be the same as Shenazzar, a son of Jehoiachin (1 Chr. 3:18). If this identification is correct, the equation of Sheshbazzar with Zerubbabel on the basis of comparison of Ezra 5:14,16 with Zechariah 4:9 is questionable. Zerubbabel was the son of Shealtiel (3:8) or Pedaiah (1 Chr. 3:19), making him the nephew of Sheshbazzar. Zerubbabel was the grandson of King Jehoiachin (1 Chr. 3:19) and succeeded Sheshbazzar as governor of Judah (Hag. 1:1).

**Register of Remnant (2:1-70).** The author included the register of the remnant to honor those who trusted in the Lord and to show that the prophecy of Israel's return from exile was fulfilled. The registry includes the leaders, general populace, temple personnel, descendants of Solomon's servants, and those of uncertain genealogical claims. The listing is only representative since the total number exceeds those counted. The revised list is repeated with revisions in Nehemiah 7:6-73.

**Worship and Rebuilding (3:1-13).** The first concern of the community was the worship of the Lord. Sacrifice had not been offered for fifty years since Jerusalem's fall (586 B.C.). The seventh month (Tishri) was the most holy month of the calendar when the Feasts of Trumpets, Atonement, and Tabernacles were celebrated (Lev. 23). Zerubbabel and Jeshua, the high priest, supervised the reconstruction of the altar and the offering of sacrifice. The Feast of Tabernacles was the first holy day celebrated.

In the second year of the return (536 B.C.), materials were imported from Lebanon. The temple foundation was laid under the supervision of priests and Levites appointed by Zerubbabel and Jeshua. The Levites led in praise through song and musical accompaniment. The response was a mixture of joy by the young and weeping by the old because they had seen the glory of Solomon's temple. Zechariah reminded the people not to despise a small work done for the Lord (Zech. 4:9-10). Haggai declared that the glory of this temple would exceed that of the former temple (Hag. 2:9).

**Opposition (4:1-24).** The residents of Samaria offered to assist the exiles because they claimed to worship the God of the Jews. Zerubbabel spurned their help because their religion was a mixed cult that included elements of paganism as a result of the Assyrian policies of intermingling foreign populations (see 2 Kgs. 17:24-41). The Assyrian kings from the time of Esarhaddon (681–669 B.C.) had exiled foreigners to the northern provinces of Israel. The Samaritans impeded the work by harassing the builders and hiring counselors. The work stopped for sixteen years (536–520 B.C.) until the reign of Darius.

In a parenthetical summary, illustrations of such ongoing opposition are taken from letters available to the author. The documents come from a later period during the reigns of Xerxes I (486–465 B.C.) and Artaxerxes I (464–424 B.C.). These letters, along with the other materials in Ezra are written in Aramaic, the official language of the court.

A letter from the time of Xerxes ("Ahasuerus"; Esth. 1:1) is only mentioned. But the second, from the period of Artaxerxes, is quoted at length. The authors of the second letter identified themselves as descendants of those deported by Ashurbanipal ("Osnapper"; 668–627 B.C.). They recalled Jerusalem's history of insurrection and charged the Jews with sedition. Artaxerxes ordered the work stopped.

***Authority to Build (5:1-17).*** The prophets Haggai and Zechariah urged and helped the community to renew its labor (Hag. 1:1-4,14; 2:1-4; Zech. 4:9; 6:15). Haggai criticized the people for living in fine homes while the temple lay in ruins (Hag. 1:3-6). Zechariah unveiled the glorious future that awaited the temple in the days of the messiah (the "Branch"; Zech. 3:8; 6:12-15). Tattenai, governor of the provincial areas west of the Euphrates, questioned their authority to build. But their authority came from God, and it was He who watched over them.

Tattenai sent a letter to King Darius (522–486 B.C.) in which he reviewed the history of the Jewish city and the exiles. Tattenai requested a search in the royal archives for Cyrus's authorization for rebuilding, which the Jews claimed.

***Finished Work (6:1-22).*** A search conducted first at Babylon and then Ecbatana (Media) recovered the decree in its official Aramaic version (see 1:1-4).

| PERSIAN RULERS | | |
|---|---|---|
| PERSIAN RULER | DATES OF RULE | SCRIPTURE REFERENCE |
| CYRUS | 539–530 B.C. | 2 Chr 36:22-23; Ezra 1; Isa 44:28; 45:1; Dan 1:21; 10:1 |
| CAMBYSES | 530–522 B.C. | |
| DARIUS I HYSTASPES | 522–486 B.C. | Ezra 4–6; Neh 12:22; Hag 1:1; Zech 1:1,7 |
| XERXES I (AHASUERUS) | 486–465 B.C. | Ezra 4:16 Esth |
| ARTAXERXES I LONGIMANUS | 464–423 B.C. | Ezra 4:7-23; 7; 8:1; Neh 2:1-8 (Probably ruler during the time of the prophet Malachi.) |
| DARIUS II NOTHUS | 423–404 B.C. | |
| ARTAXERXES II MNEMON | 404–359 B.C. | |
| ARTAXERXES III OCHUS | 359–338 B.C. | |
| ARSES | 338–335 B.C. | |
| DARIUS III CODOMANUS | 335–331 B.C. | |

Darius ordered the governor not to stop them but to pay for their expenses out of the royal treasury and to carry out sanctions against anyone who opposed their work. What had jeopardized the work proved under God's care to expedite its completion.

The speedy response of Tattenai enabled the completion of the temple four years later in 515 B.C. (see 6:15 with 4:24). By providential plan, Jewish elders, Hebrew prophets, and pagan kings all contributed to complete the task. The dedicatory service was celebrated with joy and sacrifices. The Levites and priests were organized into their orders as Moses (Num. 3; 18) and David (1 Chr. 24) had ordained. Out of the four surviving orders (2:36-39), twenty-four were formed (see Luke 1:5).

The text reverts to Hebrew at Ezra 6:19 because it describes the reenactment of the Passover. It was the first Passover commemorated in the temple since the fall of Jerusalem. The exiles were careful to worship the Lord in ritual pureness. They rejoiced that the Lord had changed the heart of the Assyrian king for their good. "Assyria" is named rather than Persia because Persia ruled the former region of Assyria and it was Assyria which had begun the captivity of God's people.

## REFORM UNDER THE LAW (7:1–10:44)

This last section concerns Ezra's memoirs, and it warns the restored community not to follow the sins of their fathers. Ezra, a trained scholar in the law, was commissioned by Artaxerxes to return to Jerusalem and teach the statutes of Jewish religious life. Ezra initiated religious reforms that led to repentance and a covenant commitment.

*God's Hand on Ezra (7:1-28).* Ezra's credentials to fulfill God's calling were his priestly genealogy (see 2:62), his knowledge of the law, and his commitment to the law as a practitioner and teacher. God's "gracious hand" of favor was upon Ezra's life. King Artaxerxes recognized Ezra's qualifications and issued a decree written in Aramaic. The decree said Ezra should lead a company of volunteers to supervise proper religious life in Jerusalem and establish a judicial system in accordance with the law of their God. Ezra praised God for the benevolence of the king and took courage from this sign of God's hand on him (7:27-28).

*Spiritual Preparations (8:1-36).* His companions on the journey are listed by family heads. Ezra specially recruited Levites to assist him in teaching the law in Jerusalem. Ezra attributed his success to the Lord. As spiritual leaders the Levites had to meet the qualification of proper genealogical heritage as the law required. Ezra showed his dependence on God by prayer and fasting in preparation for his journey. He recognized that God had answered his petitions.

Ezra's company, bearing an enormous treasure, arrived successfully without incident. Ezra acknowledged that God's protective hand had spared him from the threat of enemies. The treasure was deposited, and the exiles offered sacrifice for all Israel. The provincial governors were notified of Ezra's new administration.

*Ezra's Prayer of Confession (9:1-15).* When Ezra arrived in Jerusalem, the city leaders confronted him with the problem of intermarriage. Echoing the days of Moses, the sins of the people were likened to those of the Gentiles who had ensnared Israel in the past (Exod. 34:11-12; Deut. 7:1-6). The purpose of this segregation was not to create a pure race but to avoid marriages that would lead to spiritual unfaithfulness (see Judg. 3:5-6).

Ezra's distress over the people's sins moved him to pray for God's forgiveness. He recalled the sins of their ancestors who suffered exile for their guilt. He offered thanksgiving that the Lord had spared them as a remnant. Yet he feared that they had repeated their ancestors' sins and neglected their prophets' warnings. He confessed the inadequacy of the people and invoked the continued mercy of God.

***Repentance of the Guilty (10:1-44).*** Ezra's prayer and example of contrition contributed to the people's conviction for their sins. They recommended a covenant renewal and urged Ezra to reform the community. Ezra called for a convocation of all the tribes under threat of confiscation of property and excommunication (see 7:26). Ezra chastened them and ordered them to separate from their pagan wives. Divorce was not God's will for His people (see Mal. 2:16; Matt. 19:4-6), but it was permitted in this situation in order to preserve the spiritual life of the nation (see Deut. 24:1-3). The practice was so widespread that it took three months for a tribunal to hear the cases.

A listing of the guilty ends the book. The religious leaders are listed first. No group escaped the sin nor the punishment. This somber conclusion contrasts with the register of those honored for their faith (Ezra 2). The conclusion indicates that the exiles still had further strides to make in doing God's work.

***Theological and Ethical Significance.*** Before the exile, the national and religious hopes of God's people went hand in hand. After the return from Babylon, temple worship was restored, and the people recommitted themselves to the law of Moses. But a Davidic king no longer ruled over an independant Judah; Judah was a province of the Persian Empire and was ruled by an agent of the Persian king. The Jews survived because they found their identity as God's people not in nationalistic dreams but in renewed commitment to God's Word. Christians should be careful not to limit God to the national interest of any one people.

The Book of Ezra stresses Scripture as the governing principle for the life of God's people. Confronted with the demands of God's Word, we, like those of Ezra's generation, fail to measure up to God's standards. Our repentance, however, must move beyond remorse for moral failure to the reality of changed lives. Ezra's demand for the divorce of foreign wives demonstrates that the demands of true repentance and obedience to God's Word are sometimes painful.

## Questions for Reflection

1. What should be the Christian's attitude toward civil authority?

2. How should the people of God and their leaders labor together to do the Lord's work more effectively?

3. What priority should God's people give to worship and praise?

4. How is Ezra an example for Christians to follow today?

5. What motivates God's people to act courageously in perilous situations?

## Sources for Additional Study

Kidner, Derek. *Ezra and Nehemiah.* Downers Grove: InterVarsity, 1979.

Laney, J. Carl. *Ezra and Nehemiah.* Chicago: Moody, 1982.

McConville, J. G. *Ezra, Nehemiah, and Esther.* Philadelphia: Westminster, 1985.

# NEHEMIAH

The Book of Nehemiah is named for its principal character. In the postexilic period Nehemiah refortified Jerusalem, established civil authority, and began religious reforms.

Ezra and Nehemiah were one book in the Hebrew Bible until the fifteenth century A.D. The English versions follow the tradition of the Greek church fathers and Latin Old Testament by separating them. In the Septuagint, the pre-Christian Greek version of the Old Testament, Ezra and Nehemiah form one book.

The English arrangement of Old Testament books follows the Greek tradition by placing Nehemiah in the proper chronological sequence. Here Nehemiah follows Chronicles and Ezra as the eleventh historical book. In the Hebrew Bible, Nehemiah appears in the third and final section known as the Writings. There Ezra-Nehemiah precedes Chronicles, which ends the Hebrew Bible.

Some scholars believe that Ezra-Nehemiah was formerly the second half of a larger history known as the "Chronicler's History." This history consisted of 1 and 2 Chronicles and Ezra-Nehemiah. This reconstruction has been rejected by many scholars, both evangelical and critical, and continues to be disputed (see introduction to "The Historical Books" and "Ezra"). The Jewish Talmud names Ezra as the author of Chronicles and names Ezra and Nehemiah as joint authors of Ezra-Nehemiah. In any event, the identity of the compiler, who would have used a number of written sources, such as Nehemiah's first-person account, cannot be known. Ezra-Nehemiah dates to the latter half of the fifth century B.C., no earlier than 430 B.C.

The majority of the book is Nehemiah's first-person memoirs (1:1–7:73; 12:27–13:31). Ezra's ministry is reported in the third person (Neh. 8:1–12:30). Among the sources used were genealogical records (Neh. 7:6-73 and Ezra 2; Neh. 12:1-26, especially v. 23), a covenant document (9:38–10:39), and a residency list (11:4-36).

The date of completion for Ezra-Nehemiah is no later than 400 B.C. If considered part of the Chronicler's History, its date may be soon thereafter (see the introduction to "The Historical Books"). Some scholars have dated Nehemiah (and thus the Chronicler's History too) no earlier than the time of Alexander the Great (about 331 B.C.) on the basis of the high priest "Jaddua" named in Nehemiah 12:11,22. The Jewish historian Josephus reported that Jaddua was high priest when Alexander entered Jerusalem. However, the balance of evidence indicates that the Jaddua Josephus named probably is a descendant of the biblical Jaddua.

The chronology of Nehemiah's ministry in Jerusalem includes two periods of administration. His first tenure covered twelve years (445–433 B.C.; Neh. 2:1). He returned for a second term about 430 B.C. (13:6). For a chronology of the period and the relationship of the two reformers Ezra and Nehemiah, see the introduction to "Ezra."

**Theme.** God encircled His people with protection by the walls Nehemiah rebuilt and by the law Ezra reestablished.

I. Rebuilding the Walls (1:1–7:73)
II. Reading the Law (8:1–10:39)
III. Reforming the People (11:1–13:31)

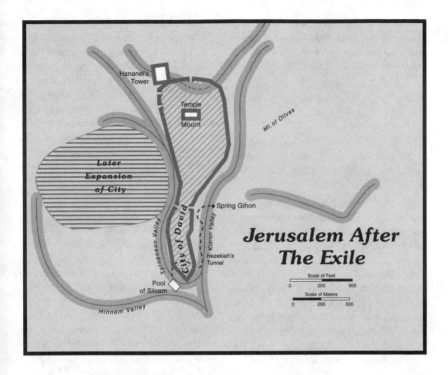

Jerusalem After The Exile

***Purpose and Theology.*** Nehemiah continues the story of the restored community. Whereas the Book of Ezra focuses on the religious restoration of Jerusalem, the Book of Nehemiah describes its political restoration. Nehemiah's rebuilding of Jerusalem's wall restored political integrity and muted the threats of intimidation by neighboring adversaries (chaps. 1–7). However, the book does not neglect the Jews' religious status. The political and religious spheres are inextricably bound together. Therefore another "wall" of protection was the knowledge and observance of God's law. Ezra and Nehemiah together regulated the exiles' social and religious life on the basis of the law of Moses (chaps. 5; 8–13).

1. The book continues the theme of worship, which is pervasive in Chronicles and Ezra. The author drew attention to

the Levites and priests, who were the first to begin work on the wall (3:1,17,22,28) and were prominently listed among those who repopulated the city (11:10-23; 12:1-26,29). They functioned in their expected roles as teachers and temple officials (8:7-8; 9:4; 12:27-36,45-46). The Levites were leaders of Israel's covenant renewal (9:38; 10:9-13,28) and won the community's approval for their service (12:44,47). Yet they did not escape the need for reformation since their sins were exposed (13:4-11,28,30).

2. God is the "God of heaven," who as Creator of the universe is awesome and great (1:5; 2:4,20; 4:14; 9:6,32). The Lord's sovereignty is seen most clearly in His appointment and protection of Nehemiah, accomplished through the mighty kings of Persia (2:8,18). He was the guarantor of Nehemiah's success (2:20), which even his enemies admitted

was divinely accomplished (6:16). God frustrated the plots of the Jews' enemies and was the source for the rallying cry, "Our God will fight for us!" (4:15,20).

But God is not just awesome in might. He is also depicted as a God of covenant steadfastness who dealt faithfully with Israel on the basis of its election (1:5-7; 9:7-37). He is holy and demands a righteous people, a sanctified priesthood, and a hallowed place of worship (12:30; 13:9,23-28,30).

3. Prayer is the fulcrum that engages God to act in Israel's behalf. Nehemiah's prayers sprinkle the narrative with invocations for divine blessing (5:19; 6:9b; 13:14, 22b,31b) or curses upon wicked opposition (4:4-5; 6:14; 13:29). Prayer matched with levelheaded pragmatism marked Nehemiah's ways (2:4-5; 4:9). Confession of Israel's past sin reflected the community's sense of continuity with past guilt and the continuing need for God's merciful intervention (1:4-11; 9:5b-37).

4. Scripture engendered the returned exiles' recommitment to the Lord. The law of Moses, in particular, was the plumb line by which they measured the success of their spiritual rebuilding. The law was read, interpreted, and applied to regulate the community's life (8:1-18; 9:3). The law convicted (8:9; 9:2-3), incited worship (8:11-18), and generated reform (13:1-3,17-22a,23-27).

5. The cooperative work of the remnant was evident in the priests and Levites, rulers, artisans, merchants, and their sons and daughters, who labored side by side to refortify the walls (3:1-32). Their diligence was paralleled by their wits (4:6,16-18). Intimidation was deflected by the community's persistence (4:14; 6:13,19), and their adversaries became fearful of what they said the Jews could not do (4:1-3; 6:16).

6. The book's report on the community's stewardship ties together the themes of community, Scripture, and worship. The Jerusalem walls, even in Nehemiah's day, did not overshadow the temple: "We will not neglect the house of God" (10:39). Thus, the returned exiles swore to fulfill their obligations of service to the house of God through tithes and votive gifts in accordance with the law of Moses (10:32-39; 12:44). The sanctity and perpetuation of temple life were the agenda of Nehemiah's second term as governor (13:4-13,30).

## REBUILDING THE WALLS (1:17:73)

The book opens with Nehemiah's memoirs, which tell the governor's role in refortifying Jerusalem. He reported the opposition he encountered from the Samaritans and showed how God had enabled him to succeed. At God's prompting, Nehemiah took steps to repopulate the city by reviewing those who had first returned.

***Nehemiah's Prayer (1:1-11).*** Nehemiah received a delegation of Jews led by Hanani in modern southwestern Iran, the winter palace of the Persian kings (Esth. 1:2,5; Dan. 8:2). The visit was made in the month of Kislev (Nov.-Dec.) in the twentieth year (445 B.C.) of Artaxerxes I (464–424 B.C.; Neh. 1:1-3). When Nehemiah heard Jerusalem was unprotected, he sought God's help through fasting and prayer. His appeal was based on God's covenant with Israel as given in Deuteronomy. There the Lord threatened the unfaithful but also promised to assist the repentant (see Deut. 9:29; 28:14; 30:1-4). As the king's cupbearer, Nehemiah ended his petition by anticipating an audience with Artaxerxes ("this man," 1:11). Nehemiah's burden for Jerusalem required his personal involvement. The "cupbearer" was a personal butler who functioned as the king's wine taster.

*Nehemiah's Preparations (2:1-20).* After four months of prayer and preparation, Nehemiah was ready to answer the king's inquiries about his sad demeanor. Nehemiah feared the king's response, but with God's help he courageously petitioned the king for the authority to rebuild Jerusalem's defenses. The Lord favored the cupbearer so that the king granted his petition by giving him letters of authority and royal protection. Sanballat's and Tobiah's displeasure was an early omen of trouble (4:1-2; 6:1-7). Sanballat is named in the Elephantine papyri (407 B.C.) as "governor of Samaria." The Elephantine papyri are Aramaic documents of the fifth century B.C. recovered from a Jewish military colony stationed at modern Aswan at the southern border of Egypt.

Upon arriving in Jerusalem, Nehemiah quietly reviewed the condition of the city in preparing to meet with the Jewish leaders. The people accepted the challenge of rebuilding the walls. Sanballat and Tobiah, joined by Geshem the Arab, scoffed at them, accusing them of sedition. The same tactic had been effective against Zerubbabel (Ezra 4:4). Nehemiah answered by asserting that the true authority for his actions came from God.

*Restoring Gates and Walls (3:1-32).* The high priest Eliashib (12:10,22; 13:4) led the work by reconstructing the Sheep Gate. The Fish Gate and wall followed. Workers on the Jeshanah ("Old") Gate and wall included rulers, perfume makers, and women. The Valley Gate and Dung Gate, leading to the city's dumpsite, were next. The restorers of the Fountain Gate and wall included nobility and Levites. Temple servants worked at the Water Gate and wall, and the priests repaired the Horse Gate. The residents near the East Gate and wall repaired it. Among those laboring at and nearby the Inspection Gate were a goldsmith and merchants. People of all occupations participated, including whole families. Despite opposition, they cooperated in their common goal to do the Lord's work.

*Opposition to God's Work (4:1-23).* Sanballat's conspiracy included taunts and threats. Nehemiah prayed for God's intervention, and the people labored "with all their heart" (4:6). The opposition broadened and intensified, but the people responded again with prayer. Rumors weakened their resistance, but Nehemiah organized a civil defense. He exhorted the Jews to remember their "great and awesome" God, who stood able to confound their enemy and fight their battles.

*Economic Oppression (5:1-19).* Internal dissent threatened the building project as much as the threat of war. The absence of food caused the poorer Jews to mortgage their homes and even sell their children into servitude in order to pay indebtedness. They complained that their oppressive creditors were fellow Jews. Nehemiah convened a hearing and charged the creditors with exacting usury (see Deut. 23:19-20). He considered their actions a reproach in the eyes of their Gentile enemies since the community was already struggling to buy back enslaved Jews from the Gentiles. Nehemiah acknowledged he had made loans but not unfairly. The guilty agreed to return the confiscated possessions.

This incident led Nehemiah to defend his conduct during the twelve years of his term as governor. Unlike his predecessors, he did not govern out of greed but placed the building of the wall above his personal interests. By sharing his wealth with many on a daily basis, he set an example for the people.

*Final Intimidation (6:1-19).* With the work near completion, out of desperation Nehemiah's enemies entreated him four times to meet them at Ono, a site located between Judah and Samaria at the southern end of the Plain of Sharon. He refused on the grounds that the Lord's work was more important. Sanballat, frustrated by Nehemiah's refusals, stepped up his intimidation by charging him with sedition. Nehemiah responded with prayer as he had in the past. Sanballat hired Shemaiah and the prophetess Noadiah to give false counsel as though it were from the Lord. Shemaiah advised Nehemiah to take refuge in the temple because he might be assassinated that night. Nehemiah, however, saw the plot for what it was. He did not want such an act of cowardice to discredit him before the people. Again Nehemiah prayed for God's justice.

The wall was completed after only fifty-two days because of the Lord's help. Ironically, the nations became intimidated by the success of the Jews, realizing that they had accomplished an impossible task. Nevertheless, Tobiah convinced some of the Jews to act treacherously by pressuring Nehemiah. Tobiah had close ties with Eliashib the high priest (see 13:4) and also had financial dealings among the Jews.

**Protecting Jerusalem (7:1-73).** Nehemiah charged Hanani with the security of the city because he was able and pious. The city was now secure for new residents (see 11:1-36). God impressed upon Nehemiah the need to keep genealogical records. Therefore Nehemiah began by reciting the first record of the exiles under Zerubbabel's tenure (see Ezra 2:1-70).

## READING THE LAW (8:1–10:39)

The account of Ezra's ministry is told in the third person. Ezra's proclamation of the law began on the first day of the seventh month and continued probably each morning for one week. His reading of the

law encouraged the exiles to rejoice and to celebrate the Feast of Tabernacles in the proper way. By hearing the law, the people came under conviction, and collectively the nation recalled the evil of Israel's past. The result was a covenant renewal in which they pledged themselves to the law.

**Ezra Reads the Law (8:1-18).** The last half of 7:73 introduces chapter 8. The seventh month was the most important month of the ceremonial calendar (see Lev. 23). On the first day of the month (see Num. 29:1), the people assembled and called for Ezra to read the law. The purpose of the reading was so they could understand the law. The people stood in reverence when the law was read; and their response included praise, tears, and joy. The Levites interpreted the law for those who did not understand its meaning.

After hearing the law, the elders urged Ezra to call for a general assembly of all the Jews to observe the Feast of Booths (Tabernacles). Tabernacles was traditionally celebrated for seven days at the time of harvest ingathering (Exod. 34:22). It commemorated God's provision during the wilderness when Israel lived in temporary shelters or booths (see Lev. 23:33-43). For these exiles, this festival was particularly meaningful because they had experienced the second "Exodus" from Babylon. The booths, made of tree branches, were constructed in the city. Not since Joshua's time had the feast been celebrated in this way. The law was carefully followed. The Jews set aside the eighth day (Lev. 23:36) for special assembly.

**Israel Confesses Its Sin (9:1-38).** On the twenty-fourth of the month, two days after the feast, the exiles fasted while dressed in the clothing of contrition. They prepared for confession by sanctification, reading the law of Moses, and worship.

The Levites led a prayer of confession, calling the pilgrims to arise. They praised God as great and gracious. From Abraham's call to Moses' experience at Sinai, God protected and provided for Israel. In contrast to the longsuffering of God, Israel was stiffnecked and rebellious throughout its history. Still, the Lord remained merciful. The prayer concluded with supplications. They admitted that God had justly chastened them by Gentile oppression, but now they prayed that God might see their economic distress and rescue them from oppression. Their prayer of confession concluded with the nation entering an oath of commitment to obey the law of Moses.

***Signing of the Covenant (10:1-39).*** The chapter lists those who signed the oath, beginning with the governor. Also priests, Levites, and rulers are noted. The features of the covenant included (1) submission to the law, (2) separation from foreign marriages, (3) Sabbath observance as the sign of the Mosaic covenant, and (4) service to God through tithes and offerings. They agreed to fulfill what the law required of them. They would pay the temple tax (Exod. 30:11-16) contribute wood for the continual burnt offerings (Lev. 6:12). They would dedicate their firstfruits and firstborn (Exod. 23:19a; Num. 18:17-19) and pay tithes for the Levites and priests (Lev. 27:30-33; Num. 18:21-32; Deut. 12:5-18; 14:22-29).

## REFORMING THE PEOPLE (11:1–13:31)

The concluding section completes the themes already begun in chapters 1–10. The repopulation theme begun in chapter 7 continues with the catalog of new residents in Jerusalem to show a continuity with their ancestral faith and their

hope in a new Israel. The dedication ceremonies of the walls reminds the reader of the opposition the Jews endured yet the success they enjoyed because of God's good favor. Finally, the variety of reforms introduced by Nehemiah enforced the features of the covenant undertaken by the community.

***Settling the Cities (11:1-36).*** The exiles organized their society by lot and by volunteers who migrated to the Holy City. While descendants of all of Israel's tribes returned to Judah, Jerusalem would be comprised particularly of those whose ancestors had populated the city in the days of David's kingdom—Judah, Benjamin, and Levi.

***Dedicating the Walls (12:1-47).*** Nehemiah's memoirs are taken up with the continuing account of the walls. The elaborate festivities planned included Levitical singers and orchestra. The people, aware of their standing before God, cleansed themselves to prepare for the celebration. Ezra and Nehemiah led the two processionals. After marching around the city on its wall, the two parades convened at the temple to offer God thanksgiving. Provisions for the Levites and priests were restored and the choirs David had ordered were reestablished.

***Renewing the People (13:1-31).*** Another line of defense constructed by Nehemiah was the community's spiritual life. The basis for the reforms Nehemiah enforced was the Mosaic law. He attempted to reflect the Mosaic ideal that Ezra's reading of the law had set before the people (chaps. 8–10). The people segregated themselves from foreign influences that would jeopardize their spiritual commitment (see Deut. 23:3-5).

However, Eliashib the high priest (Neh. 3:1,20; 12:22; Ezra 10:6) had already compromised the holiness of God's temple. He cleared the storerooms for the Ammonite Tobiah (Neh. 6:18) to occupy. Nehemiah explained that he was in Persia when Tobiah occupied the temple. Upon his return, he immediately expelled Tobiah and cleansed and restored the storerooms for service. He reinstated the Levitical offerings, which had ceased during his absence, and charged the people with breaking their oath (13:10-14; 10:39; see Mal. 2:8-12). He took further steps against merchants who violated the Sabbath by selling goods to the Jews. He charged the Jews with repeating their fathers' sins and threatened the merchants' lives.

Nehemiah's final action addressed the continued problem of intermarriage (see Ezra 9:1–10:44). To Nehemiah, the different languages he heard spoken by Judah's children indicated that the Jews were losing their distinctive identity as God's people. The problem was the foreigners' religion, not their ethnicity. He argued that the Jews were reviving the sins of Solomon, whose unfaithfulness caused Israel to sin and suffer God's judgment. Nehemiah took drastic action because of the severe threat. He physically chastened those married to foreigners and forced them to abstain from such marriages. So sordid was the situation that even Sanballat's daughter (2:10,19) had married into the priestly line.

Nehemiah concluded his reforms by caring for the needs of the priesthood. Nehemiah was conscious that he was carrying out God's mandates and not his own. With each reform he prayed for God's blessing on his faithful service.

## THE RETURN FROM EXILE

| PHASE | DATE | SCRIPTURE REFERENCE | JEWISH LEADER | PERSIAN RULER | EXTENT OF THE RETURN | EVENTS OF THE RETURN |
|---|---|---|---|---|---|---|
| FIRST | 538 B.C. | Ezra 1–6 | Zerubbabel Jeshua | Cyrus | (1) Anyone who wanted to return could go. (2) The temple in Jerusalem was to be rebuilt. (3) Royal treasury provided funding of the temple rebuilding. (4) Gold and silver worship articles taken from temple by Nebuchadnezzar were returned. | (1) Burnt offerings were made. (2) The Feast of Tabernacles was celebrated. (3) The rebuilding of the temple was begun. (4) Persian ruler ordered rebuilding to be ceased. (5) Darius, King of Persia, ordered rebuilding to be resumed in 520 B.C. (6) Temple was completed and dedicated in 516 B.C. |
| SECOND | 458 B.C. | Ezra 7–10 | Ezra | Artaxerxes Longimanus | (1) Anyone who wanted to return could go. (2) Royal treasury provided funding. (3) Jewish civil magistrates and judges were allowed. | Men of Israel intermarried with foreign women. |
| THIRD | 444 B.C. | Nehemiah 1–13 | Nehemiah | Artaxerxes Longimanus | Rebuilding of Jerusalem was allowed. | (1) Rebuilding of wall of Jerusalem was opposed by Sanballat the Horonite, Tobiah the Ammonite, and Geshem the Arab. (2) Rebuilding of wall was completed in 52 days. (3) Walls were dedicated. (4) Ezra read the Book of the Law to the people. (5) Nehemiah initiated reforms. |

***Theological and Ethical Signifi-cance.*** The Book of Nehemiah illustrates how much a layperson committed to a life of prayer, God's Word, and active obedi-ence can do. Nehemiah serves as a reminder that Christians are needed in leadership positions not only within the church but also in civil government. Those attempting to mold society on the princi-ples of Scripture will doubtless experience opposition like Nehemiah did. Prayer, Nehemiah's most potent weapon, contin-ues to serve Christians in their struggle to do God's will in spite of opposition.

Nehemiah's call for divorce of foreign wives is not an endorsement of divorce or racism but a desperate command for a desperate time. (See Mal. 2:10-16; 2 Cor. 6:14–7:1). The survival of the Jews as a people committed to God demanded *exclusion* of Gentiles *for a time.* The survival of the church demands *inclusion* of *all* who will hear the gospel and commit their lives to Christ.

## Questions for Reflection

1. How should the people of God work together to achieve the Lord's pur-pose?

2. What does the life of Nehemiah teach about the layperson's devotion to God?

3. What is the role of Scripture in the life of the church?

4. How should Christians respond to opposition to God's kingdom?

5. What does the Bible teach about interracial marriage? about marriage to unbelievers?

## Sources for Additional Study

Kidner, Derek. *Ezra and Nehemiah.* Downers Grove: InterVarsity, 1979.

McConville, J. G. *Ezra, Nehemiah, and Es-ther.* Philadelphia: Westminster, 1985.

Vos, Howard F. *Ezra, Nehemiah, and Esther.* Grand Rapids: Eerdmans, 1987.

# ESTHER

The Book of Esther is named after its heroine. Esther used her prominent position as queen of Persia to save the Jewish people from destruction. "Esther" is probably derived from the Persian word *stara,* meaning *star.* Some scholars have related it to "Ishtar," the Akkadian goddess associated with the planet Venus. Esther's Hebrew name was "Haddassah," meaning *myrtle* (Esth. 2:7).

In the Greek and English versions, Esther is the last book in the collection of Historical Books. In the Hebrew arrangement of the Old Testament, the book is one of the five *Megilloth* (*rolls* or *scrolls*) occurring in the third and final section (the *Kethubhim* or *Writings*) of the Hebrew Bible. The book's plot includes the origins of the Jewish festival of Purim. Esther is traditionally read upon that annual celebration (Adar 14 and 15).

The Greek translation has five additions to the Hebrew (and English) text. These additions to Esther supplement the narrative and make the book more religious in tone (see below). Jerome's Latin Vulgate removed the additions and placed them at the end of the book. Luther also separated the additions by placing them with the Apocryphal books.

The author of the book cannot be known. The author probably used sources available from the period. The story mentions the use of royal archives (2:23; 6:1; 10:2). And Mordecai, a key figure in the story, is said to have recorded some events (9:20,23,29-32). Some interpreters have speculated that the author was a Persian Jew.

The date of writing is difficult to determine. The setting of the story is the fifth century B.C. in the reign of the Persian king Ahasuerus (1:1), who is commonly identified with Xerxes I (485–464 B.C.). Scholars have suggested dates of authorship ranging from as early as the fifth century B.C. to as late as the Maccabean period (second to first centuries B.C.). A date of about 400 B.C. coincides well with the linguistic evidence and the author's excellent knowledge of Persian life.

***History and Literary Genre.*** The reliability of the Book of Esther as a historical witness has been challenged. In more recent years many scholars have recognized that it has a historical nucleus. Some of these same scholars believe that the literary genre of Esther is historical novel or historical romance. The Book of Esther, as the argument goes, has the properties of legend and fiction. Internal oddities include Mordecai's age (at least 124 years old if he indeed were deported by Nebuchadnezzar; see 2:6; 3:7) and other questionable exaggerations (for example, 1:4; 2:12; 5:14; 9:16). It is argued that the story's protagonists and the incidents related cannot be corroborated outside the Bible. Furthermore, the Greek historian Herodotus (*History* VII, 114) identified Xerxes' queen as Amestris, not Vashti or Esther.

However, scholars who esteem the book as a reliable historical witness have answered that it shows an accurate and detailed knowledge of Persian life, law, and custom. Archaeological information about the architecture of the palace and about Xerxes' reign harmonizes well with the story's depictions. The occasion of the banquet in the third year (1:3) corresponds to the remarks of the Greek historian Herodotus (*History,* VII.8) that Xerxes convened his leading men in that year to plan a campaign against Greece. Also the name of a court official, *Marduka* (Mordecai?), has been attested in Persian tablets from this time. While it is not possible to identify with certainty this figure as Mordecai, the name gives the story a ring of authenticity.

As for the incongruities, evangelicals answer with alternative explanations. For example, the Hebrew text can be interpreted to mean that Mordecai's ancestor Kish was deported by Nebuchadnezzar (2:6). As for Amestris, some have attempted to equate the names of Esther and Amestris on a linguistic basis, but this has been questioned. Others have accounted for the discrepancy by suggesting that Xerxes had more than one queen or that Amestris was queen during the four years between the removal of Vashti and the wedding of Esther (1:3; 2:16).

If it can be shown that the author intended the book to be read as a literary fiction, it should be interpreted accordingly as one would a parable or allegory without doubting its inspiration. However, if the author intended it as historically verifiable, interpreters should treat it as a reliable account of the Persian Jews. The author indicates that the book should be read as historical when he invites his readers to verify this account by consulting Persian annals where the story's events (and more) can be found (10:2). This is the same kind of invitation found among the histories of Kings and Chronicles. Unless there is compelling evidence otherwise, the trustworthiness of the account should be the interpreter's guide.

**Esther without "God."** Esther is the only book in the Hebrew Bible that does not mention God's name. Also absent is any reference to the law, Jewish sacrifice, prayer, or revelation. It is the

only book of the Old Testament absent from the Dead Sea Scrolls. Opinion about the book's religious value has varied. Luther considered it worthless. The famous Jewish scholar Maimonides (twelfth century A.D.) set it beside the Torah in importance. The book's canonical status has been disputed by Jews and Christians.

One explanation for the book's "secular" nature is that a Jewish author took the story almost verbatim from an official Persian record that omitted God's name. Others have suggested that the author was more concerned about the Jewish people as a nation than their religious practices. However, official records (for example, the Cyrus Cylinder and Moabite Stone) are known to have invoked or referred to deities without reservation. There is no reason the name of Israel's God would have been offensive to Persian religion. Old Testament literature does not make the modern dichotomy between secular concerns and religious ones when describing historical events.

A better explanation is that the absence of religious language best suited the author's theological purposes. The author expressed his theology through the vehicle of story, arranging the events and dialogue to accentuate that theology. He omitted Israel's religious distinctives because he wanted to veil God's presence. The author believed in God's sovereignty but that God's intervention is expressed through human instrumentation.

The author did not directly speak of God's participation; rather, he only hinted at God's presence. He did this through the characters who recognized divine intervention in their lives (4:15-16b). The mention of fasting and the wearing of sackcloth and ashes (4:1-3; 4:16; 9:31) imply that the Jews worshiped since prayer commonly occurred

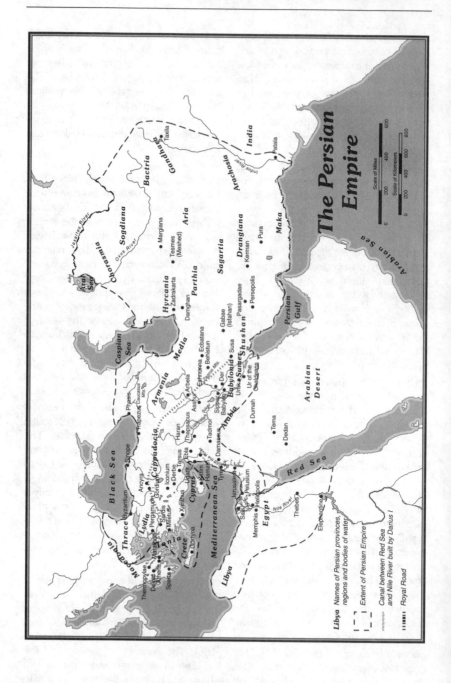

The Persian Empire

with fasting in the Old Testament. The author perceived that God effectively orchestrated the salvation of the Jews, but he did not want God's actions to be obvious.

Another way the story shows God's hand is by reversing the expected outcome of the events. Human intrigue, manipulation, and simple coincidence are the overt explanations for the dramatic changes in the story's conclusion while covertly God is at work. The story's structure further enhances the author's theme of reversals. By omitting reference to religious activities, the author commented on the spiritual status of the Jews living in the Diaspora. These Jews were the ones who did not volunteer to return to Jerusalem as part of the "remnant" through whom God would work again (Ezra 1:4; 9:8-9). Though their faith was fragile, God remained faithful to His covenant by preserving them.

**Theme.** God worked behind the scenes to save the Jews from destruction by exalting Esther as queen of Persia and turning the tables on their enemies (4:14; 9:1).

   I. Vashti's Demotion (1:1-22)

  II. The King's Decree (2:1–3:15)

 III. Haman Threatens Mordecai (4:1–5:14)

 IV. Mordecai Defeats Haman (6:1–7:10)

  V. The King's Decree (8:1–9:32)

 VI. Mordecai's Promotion (10:1-3)

**Purpose and Theology.**

1. The book's primary theological purpose is God's subtle providence in the life of His people. While Ezra-Nehemiah tells how the exiles fared in Jerusalem, the story of Esther answers what happened to those who stayed behind. The author showed through unexpected reversals in his characters' lives how God superintended the deliverance of the Jews. The theme of reversal is best illustrated by the

careers of Haman and Mordecai (7:10–8:2) and the Jews' triumph Jews instead of extermination (9:1).

2. The book also explains the origins of the festival of Purim (*lots*) the Jews celebrated annually on the fourteenth and fifteenth of Adar (3:7; 9:26). While the casting of lots appeared to seal their doom (3:7), the lots became their reason for celebration (9:23-26). The Fast of Esther in Jewish tradition precedes Purim to commemorate the fasting that precip itated their victory.

3. The idea of wealth and power is pervasive in the story with its focus on the Persian court (1:1-9; 3:1-2; 10:1). However, the power of Esther (5:1-3; 7:7) and Mordecai (6:11; 9:4; 10:2), acquired because of their loyalty to the king, triumphed over their Persian enemies. Whereas the Jews were helpless before their Gentile lords, in the end the magistrates feared and honored the Jews (8:17; 9:2).

The moral is that power should be used for righteous purposes and not for self-gratification. Moredecai, for instance, recognized that Esther's power was a gift to be used for her people's deliverance (4:14). Abusive power became Haman's noose (5:11-14; 7:10), whereas Mordecai used authority to help his people (8:7-8; 10:3).

Finally, the book is a parody on Gentile domination. Mighty Xerxes, draped in royal splendor, is depicted as a weak, easily manipulated monarch who was ill-informed about the events of his own kingdom. The prerogative of Gentile authority—the irrevocable law of the Medes and Persians—entraped the king and ultimately brought down Gentile authority (epitomized in Haman). True power is found in the virtues of loyalty, honesty, and fasting in worship of God.

4. God rewards loyalty. Vashti's disloyalty is contrasted with Esther's loyalty to

the king and her people. Another contrast is the bumbling Haman, who was hanged for his conspiracy (7:3-10), while Mordecai was honored for saving the king from assassins (2:21-23). Mordecai, in particular, exemplifies loyalty to the Jewish tradition. He functioned as Esther's Jewish conscience (4:12-14), and as a "Jew" (3:3) he refused to pay homage to Haman the "Agagite" (3:1-2; 5:9). Mordecai attempted to hide their Jewish extraction, but he learned in the end that the revelation of Esther as a Jewess gave them the upper hand (2:10,20). The story shows that those of the Diaspora could be faithful to their heritage while living as honorable citizens of a Gentile state.

5. Another recurring theme is the contrast between festival and fasting. The story begins with Xerxes' elaborate seven-day feast, which ultimately resulted in Esther's appointment as queen. Later, Esther's two feasts resulted in the death of the Jews' archenemy Haman. Finally, Mordecai established the Feast of Purim, enjoyed by Jews and Gentiles for generations to come (8:15,17; 9:17,19,26-28).

The foil for this feasting is Jewish fasting, which was the author's way of expressing this people's commitment to their religious heritage (4:1-3,16). Fasting preceded feasting in the case of Esther's approach to the king (4:16), and thus fasting was also commemorated as part of their Purim (9:31). Their fasting, the outward expression of their trust in God, precipitated their victory and celebration.

6. Finally, the story addresses the problem of social and religious bigotry. Haman's anti-Semitism was frightfully expressed when he swore he would not rest until he rid himself of "that Jew Mordecai" (5:13). The Jews are warned by this story not to escape their heritage. In fact, their spiritual heritage preserved them as a people.

## VASHTI'S DEMOTION (1:1-22)

The Persian King Khshayarsha was known as Ahasuerus in Hebrew and Xerxes in Greek. He is commonly identified with Xerxes I (485–464 B.C.), who is remembered for his devastating naval loss to the Greeks at Salamis in 481. The Greek historian Herodotus described his kingdom as consisting of twenty provinces and extending from India to Ethiopia.

The king convened a royal reception in his third year (483 B.C.) at Susa of Elam (modern SW Iran), which was the winter resort of the Persian kings (Neh. 1:1; Dan. 8:2). Archaeological work has uncovered the elaborate royal palace of the city.

The assembly Xerxes called lasted for 180 days, during which he displayed the splendor of his wealth. It culminated in a seven-day feast of luxurious dining and drunkenness. The opulence of the Persian court is described to indicate the vast resources and power of the king.

In a drunken stupor, the king called for Queen Vashti to "display her beauty" before his guests. Her refusal, probably out of decency, threatened the king's reputation. At Memucan's advice, the king deposed her. Xerxes' action is a parody on Persian might, for the powerful king could not even command his own wife.

## THE KING'S DECREE (2:1–3:15)

The second section of the story concerns the exaltation of Esther and the evil plot by Haman to exterminate the Jews. The role of Mordecai as Esther's cousin and Haman's hated enemy links the two episodes.

*Queen Esther's Rise (2:1-23).* Xerxes, at his attendants' advice, ordered a search for Vashti's successor. The narrator revealed Esther's nationality by first identifying Mordecai's lineage as a Benjamite of the family of Kish. Mordecai was Esther's foster parent and elder cousin. Esther ("Hadassah," her Hebrew name) was among those brought to the king's palace because of her exceptional beauty. At Mordecai's advice she concealed her nationality, a factor that figured in her advantage over the enemy Haman.

One year of purification was required for an audience with the king. Esther was received by the king four years after the deposition of Vashti (479 B.C.; 2:16; 1:3). She won his approval and became queen. The western expedition against the Greeks by Xerxes' Persian ships ended in disaster at Salamis in 481 B.C. His selection of Esther occurred after this debacle.

Mordecai, who may have been in the king's service as a gatekeeper, discovered a plot to kill Xerxes (perhaps because of disaffection over his losses at Salamis). The two culprits were hanged on gallows, and Mordecai's heroism was recorded. From this incident Mordecai learned of Esther's new power at court. The concealment of her identity and the record of Mordecai's deed would lead to Haman's eventual undoing (6:1-2; 7:3-6). The traitors' gallows anticipated Haman's own death for the same crime of treachery (7:10).

**Haman's Plan (3:1-15).** The theme of power is continued by the introduction of Haman as second in position to the king. This incident took place about five years after the installation of Queen Esther (2:16; 3:7). Haman is identified as an "Agagite," perhaps a descendant of the Amalekite king, Agag, who was defeated but spared by King Saul (1 Sam. 15). Israel and Amalek were enemies from Moses' time (Exod. 17:8-16). For the author, the contention

between Haman and Mordecai, a descendant of Kish (as was Saul), typified the enmity between Israel and the Gentiles. This Agagite, however, would not be spared.

While others bowed to Haman, Mordecai refused to worship him because of his Jewish faith—as Daniel had declined to worship Darius (Dan. 6). Haman masterminded a plot to exterminate all the Jews. The divinely appointed day and month was determined by the casting of the *pur,* meaning *lot* (Akkadian). The king was persuaded to permit the mass murder by official decree and sealed by the king's own signet ring (see 8:2,8). Couriers raced throughout the empire to deliver the decree that on the thirteenth day of Adar, some eleven months later, the Jews were to be destroyed. The common people of Susa were shocked by the cold-blooded decree in contrast to the conspirators, who meanwhile confidently celebrated.

### HAMAN'S THREAT (4:1–5:14)

Esther's position enabled her to save the Jews if she were willing to risk her own standing. After recounting Esther's vow of devotion, the author told how Esther took the lead and devised her own scheme to outmaneuver Haman. Ironically, Haman unwittingly devised his own end.

***Mordecai's Plea (4:1-17).*** When Mordecai learned of the murderous plot, he and all the Jews joined in mourning, fasting, and the wearing of sackcloth and ashes. This spontaneous act of grief evidenced the solidarity of the Jews. The custom of sackcloth and ashes included prayers of confession and worship (1 Kgs. 21:27-29; Neh. 9:1-3; Dan. 9:3). Esther learned of the decree from her messenger Hathach, who relayed Mordecai's plea for her help. But Esther explained that she could not approach the king because Persian law meted out death to anyone entering uninvited. Mordecai answered by warning her that as a Jewess her own life was in jeopardy and that God could save His people by another means if she failed. He believed that her exaltation in the palace had a holy purpose. Esther's trust in God was the turning point. She requested a communal fast by all the Jews as they petitioned God (Ezra 8:21-23; see Acts 13:3; 14:23). She replied to Mordecai with courage and confidence in God's will: "If I perish, I perish" (see Dan. 3:16-18).

**Esther's Banquet (5:1-14).** The prayers of God's people were answered because Xerxes received Esther without incident. She invited the king and Haman to a banquet whereupon she would make her request known. Once the guests had enjoyed their fill, Esther wisely delayed her request for another day of feasting—no doubt to heighten the king's interest in the petition.

Haman left in a happy mood, but it was tempered by his fury for "the Jew Mordecai." Haman boasted of his authority, but these boasts would later turn into tears of humiliation (6:12-13a; 7:7-8a). Haman's friends and family would be repaid with their own lives on the very gallows they had recommended for Mordecai (7:10; 9:14).

## MORDECAI DEFEATS HAMAN (6:1–7:10)

This section features the key reversal in Haman's and Mordecai's fates. Mordecai was honored by the king, much to Haman's humiliation. The final indignity of foolish Haman was his pathetic effort to save himself from the gallows.

**Mordecai Honored by Haman (6:1-14).** The unstated reason for the king's insomnia was God's providence. To pass the sleepless night, servants brought the royal annals where Mordecai's deed of saving the king was read (see 2:19-23). Haman was consulted, but ironically his egotism caused him unintentionally to honor Mordecai. The depiction of Mordecai dressed in royalty and being led on horseback by Haman anticipates their inverted roles to come. Even his friends and wife voiced the theological proposition of the book: Mordecai is invincible because he is a Jew.

**Haman's Hanging (7:1-10).** Not only did Mordecai get the best of Haman, but Esther outsmarted him. On the following day, Esther assembled her guests for the second banquet, during which she revealed her entreaty (see 5:7-8). The fivefold repetition of "Queen Esther" in this chapter echoed Mordecai's plea that she had come to power for this moment (4:14). Alluding to Haman's bribe (3:9), she described herself and the Jews as "sold for destruction." She identified Haman as the adversary.

Haman, true to his character as a blundering dunce, begged for the queen's mercy, thus breaking protocol with the king's harem. He magnified his folly by stumbling to her couch, creating the appearance of improprieties and thereby sealing his doom with the irate king. The gallows, whose references tower over much of the narrative (2:23; 5:14; 7:9-10; 8:7; 9:13,25), afforded the Jews their vindication by the hanging of Haman.

## THE KING'S DECREE (8:1–9:32)

This royal decree Mordecai wrote answered Haman's evil decree (see 3:8-11). This parallelism continues the theme of reversal, the decree enabling the Jews to take the offensive against their enemies. The thirteenth of Adar, the day planned for the Jews' destruction, was exchanged for the two-day celebration of Purim because of the Jews' conquest.

**Mordecai's Plan (8:1-17).** Rather than Jewish property falling into Haman's hands (3:13b), Haman's property and authority were given to Esther and Mordecai. But Haman's villainous plot remained, and Esther successfully pleaded for the king's assistance to avert the disaster. The decree Mordecai wrote gave the Jews the right to defend themselves.

Mordecai took Haman's place as second to the king (8:15). Whereas the city of Susa was disturbed at Haman's decree (3:15), Mordecai's edict gladdened their hearts and converted some to the Jewish faith.

***Feast of Victory (9:1-32).*** The dates of the edict and the subsequent victory of the Jews were repeated by the author because they established the traditional calendar for the Feast of Purim. On the thirteenth day of Adar (Feb.–Mar.), the appointed day of Haman's plot, the Jews defeated their enemies. The nations feared the Jews, and local magistrates were favorably influenced by Mordecai's position in Xerxes' court. The king granted a second day of vengeance (the fourteenth of Adar). In Susa eight hundred were killed, and Haman's ten sons were hanged. Among all the provinces, the Jews killed seventy-five thousand.

This explained why Purim was celebrated in the city on the thirteenth and fourteenth and in the provinces on the fourteenth and fifteenth of Adar. The author reiterated that the Jews, however, did not loot their enemies. The motivation for the purging was not economic but an avenging of crimes committed against the Jews. Mordecai gave the official decree establishing Purim. The feast was named Purim because of the *pur* ("lot") cast by Haman. The purpose of the feast was a memorial to Haman's wicked plot, which returned "onto his own head." To promote the feast Esther added her authority to a joint letter distributed with Mordecai.

## MORDECAI'S PROMOTION (10:1-3)

The story concludes in the way it began by describing the power and influence of Xerxes' kingdom. The author refers the reader to the official records of the empire where a full account of the kingdom and the role played by Mordecai could be examined (see 1 Kgs. 14:19; 15:7). Mordecai contributed to the prosperity of the empire and cared for the Jews' welfare. The greatness of Mordecai vindicated the Jews as a people. Their heritage was not a threat to the Gentiles, but rather through Mordecai and the Jews the empire enjoyed peace.

***Theological and Ethical Significance.*** Our modern experience of God is more like that of the Book of Esther than that of many Old Testament books. In Esther, God worked behind the scenes to bring about deliverance for His people. God did not bring deliverance through spectacular plagues or a miracle at the sea as in the exodus. Rather, God worked through a courageous old man who refused to abandon his principles and a courageous woman who valued the lives of her people more than her own life. The Book of Esther calls us to look at the lives of people committed to God if we want to know what God is doing to bring about deliverance in our own world.

The outlook for Mordecai and the Jews looked bleak through much of Esther. Today we may feel that God has abandoned us or that it is not profitable to be on the Lord's side. The last chapters of Esther brought about God's reversal of circumstances. We should live our lives with a view to how our story is going to end. Someday every knee will bow "and every tongue confess that Jesus is Lord" (Phil. 2:10-11). What occassioned fasting and anxious prayer will be forgotten in heaven's feasting (see Rom. 8:18).

As Christians our power and influence should be used for righteous purposes and not for self-gratification. Power is a gift from God to be used for the benefit of His people and His creation. Christian citizenship demands involvement in the affairs of the state. Anti-Semitism and other forms of racial and religious bigotry easily lead to dangerous abuses of power. Today's Christians, like Esther, must be courageous in opposing such abuses.

## Questions for Reflection

1. What is the proper relationship between religion and politics?

2. What does the story of Esther teach about evil and suffering?

3. What godly traits did Mordecai exemplify?

4. What is the purpose of fasting?

5. What does this story teach about the care of God for His people?

## Sources for Additional Study

Baldwin, Joyce G. *Esther*. Downers Grove: InterVarsity, 1984.

McConville, J. G. *Ezra, Nehemiah, and Esther*. Philadelphia: Westminster, 1985.

Vos, Howard F. *Ezra, Nehemiah, and Esther*. Grand Rapids: Eerdmans, 1987.

# THE POETIC AND WISDOM BOOKS

## DUANE A. GARRETT

The Bible is not a manual of religious teachings like the *Baptist Faith and Message* or the *Thirty-Nine Articles* of the Anglican Church. It is the Word of God as it has come to us through the experiences of the people of God. It expresses all the emotions of the life of faith, and it deals with many areas of experience that might seem mundane and unspiritual.

This is nowhere more true than in its poetic and wisdom literature. The Psalms express every emotion the believer encounters in life, be it praise and love for God, anger at those who practice violence and deceit, personal grief and confusion, or appreciation for God's truth. Proverbs not only examines moral issues, but it also helps us deal with the ordinary matters of life, such as indebtedness and work habits. Song of Songs celebrates the joy of love between man and woman. Job and Ecclesiastes make us face our most profound questions and thereby bring us to a more genuine faith in God. In sum, all these books deal with real life.

Traditionally, we speak of Psalms and Song of Songs as being the books of biblical poetry and Job, Proverbs, and Ecclesiastes as biblical wisdom. These books will be the focus of this section. Other Old Testament books, however, share many of the features of poetic and wisdom books. Lamentations is essentially a collection of psalms of lament.

Psalms are also found in the prophets (for example, Jon. 2; Hab. 3). Ruth, Esther, and Daniel have much more in common with wisdom literature than the casual reader might realize. In the Apocrypha, Ecclesiasticus and the Wisdom of Solomon imitate the wisdom features of their biblical counterparts. Even the New Testament has a few psalms and proverbs (Luke 1:46-55,68-79; Acts 20:35; 1 Cor. 15:33).

The five books of Job, Psalms, Proverbs, Ecclesiastes, and Song of Songs still give us the best examples of how biblical hymns, songs, proverbs, and reflections are to be read. This in turn allows us to see how wisdom and poetry have affected the rest of the Bible.

What gave rise to the wide variety of songs, proverbs, and theological reflection we see in this literature? The Old Testament was not written in a cultural or literary vacuum. Many of the motifs and features of Egyptian, Canaanite, and Mesopotamian literature are also found in the Old Testament, especially in the poetic and wisdom passages. Some of the most common are the following:

*Parallelism* is a device in which one line of poetry is followed by a second that in some way reiterates or reinforces the first. Several types of parallelism are found. In *synonymous parallelism* the second line says the same thing in the same word order as the first line. Only the vocabulary differs. For example: "A false witness will not go unpunished / and he who pours out lies will not go free" (Prov. 19:5). See also Psalm 114:8: "Who turned the rock into a pool, / the hard rock into springs of water." In *antithetic parallelism* the second line often reinforces the first by stating the same thought from a negative perspective. For example, "The LORD is king forever and ever; / the nations will perish from his land" (Ps. 10:16). Also: "A gentle answer turns away wrath, / but a harsh word stirs up anger" (Prov. 15:1). With *synthetic parallelism* the second line is not actually parallel to the first, but it reinforces the idea expressed by adding a reason or explanation. For example: "Train a child in the way he should go, / and when he is old he will not turn from it" (Prov. 22:6); "Stay away from the foolish man, / for you will not find knowledge on his lips" (Prov. 14:7).

In *Chiasm* the second line reinforces the first by reversing the sequence of words or phrases. For example, Proverbs 2:4 in the Hebrew order reads:

"If you look for it [A] as for silver [B] and as for hidden treasure [B'] search for it [A']" (author's translation). The word order of the second line [B'-A'] is the reverse of the first [A-B]. Parallelism and chiasm also occur on a much larger scale. Entire chapters or even entire books can be constructed in parallel or chiastic fashion, in which entire blocks of text parallel one another.

Other literary patterns are also found. *Numeric proverbs* enumerate a number of items or occurrences that share a common characteristic. For example: "There are six things the Lord hates, / seven that are detestable to him: /haughty eyes, / a lying tongue" (Prov. 6:16-19).

In an *acrostic poem* each line or section begins with a successive letter of the Hebrew alphabet. The first begins with *aleph,* the second with *beth,* the third with *gimel,* and so on. The twenty-two stanzas of Psalm 119, the Bible's largest acrostic, have eight verses for each consecutive Hebrew letter.

*Rhetorical Devices* are also found. The language of biblical poetry and wisdom is meant to make it entertaining and easy to remember. The Hebrew text contains rhyme, alliteration (repetition of initial sounds), and even puns. Simile, a comparison using *like* or *as,* also occurs frequently (Ps. 131:2; Prov. 25:25). One can also find sarcastic humor (Prov. 11:22; 19:24) as well as paradox, a statement contrary to common sense that is nevertheless true (Prov. 25:15).

Biblical poetry and wisdom are at the same time both great literature and the eternal Word of God. It intrigues and delights us even as it rebukes and instructs. For the reader who gives due attention to these songs and lessons, "They will be a garland to grace your head and a chain to adorn your neck" (Prov. 1:9).

## BIBLICAL PRAYERS

| Type of Prayer | Meaning | Old Testament Example | New Testament Example | Jesus' Teaching |
|---|---|---|---|---|
| Confession | Acknowledging sin and helplessness and seeking God's mercy | Ps 51 | Luke 18:13 | Luke 15:11-24; Luke 18:10-24 |
| Praise | Adoring God for who He is | 1 Chr 29:10-13 | Luke 1:46-55 | Matt 6:9 |
| Thanksgiving | Expressing gratitude to God for what He has done | Ps 105:1-7 | 1 Thess 5:16-18 | Luke 17:11-19 |
| Petition | Making personal request of God | Gen 24:12-14 | Acts 1:24-26 | Matt 7:7-12 |
| Intercession | Making request of God on behalf of another | Exod 32:11-13, 31-32 | Phil 1:9-11 | John 17:9,20-21 |
| Commitment | Expressing loyalty to God and His work | 1 Kgs 8:56-61 | Acts 4:24-30 | Matt 6:10; Mark 14:32-42; Luke 6:46-49 |
| Forgiveness | Seeking mercy for personal sin or the sin of others | Dan 9:4-19 | Acts 7:60 | Matt 6:12,14-15; Luke 6:27-36; Luke 23:33-34 |
| Confidence | Affirming God's all-sufficiency and the believer's security in His love | Ps 23 | Luke 2:29-32 | Matt 6:5-15; 7:11; John 11:41-42 |
| Benediction | A request for God's blessing | Num 6:24-26 | Jude 24 | Luke 11:15-13; Luke 24:50-51 |

# JOB

The Book of Job tells of a righteous man (Job) whom God, at Satan's insistence, afflicted as a test of his fidelity and integrity. Three friends (Eliphaz, Bildad, and Zophar) came to comfort him but were horrified at his anger at God. They tried without success to persuade him to repent of some sin. Job concluded this dialogue with a monologue in which he lamented his fate but continued to protest his innocence.

A fifth speaker, Elihu, tried to make sense of the situation and to point out Job's error. Finally God confronted Job, who could then only prostrate himself and repent. God restored Job's fortunes and declared him to be more righteous than his friends.

What can all this mean? Many say Job answers the question of why the righteous suffer. But in order to understand the meaning of the book, we should first look at its background.

## LITERARY BACKGROUND AND PARALLELS

**Outside the Bible.** The ancient sages wrote a great deal about human suffering. The Mesopotamian myth of Atrahasus tells of human affliction by the apparently blind wrath of the gods. Canaanite literature from Ugarit describes the trials of King Keret who, like Job, lost seven sons. In a Babylonian hymn to Marduk, a sufferer bewails his losses with as much pathos as Job. An even older Sumerian work models the complaints one ought to raise to one's god when calamity strikes. The Egyptian *Protests of the Eloquent Peasant* challenges social injustice and has a structure somewhat like Job's.

The ancient literature of lamentation certainly influenced Job, particularly in the way Job expressed his complaints. But no true parallel to Job exists outside the Bible. The Book of Job does more than grieve over human pain. Job's travail poses questions never considered in any other ancient literature. Its literary structure, moreover, has no true parallel.

**Inside the Bible.** Job is in many ways like other writings in the Bible and yet is in a class by itself. Some of the types of biblical material found in Job follow:

*Laments.* Job repeatedly bewailed what had befallen him, as in 3:1-26; 6:2-7; 10:1-12. See Psalms 22:1-18; 102:1-11; Lamentations 3:1-20.

*Hymns of Praise.* Job often praised God for His power and righteousness, as in 5:9-16 and 26:5-14. See Psalms 94 and 97.

*Proverbs.* Pithy statements of wisdom and metaphor appear in Job 5:2 and 6:5-6. See these respectively to Proverbs 14:30 and Isaiah 1:3. Also note the wisdom sayings in Job 28:28 and Proverbs 1:7.

*Prophetic Speech.* The friends sometimes claimed to have had prophetic experiences, and they preached as the prophets did. See Job 4:12-14; 11:13-20; 32:8.

*Wisdom Poems.* Job has several lengthy poems on the value of wisdom and right behavior. See Job 28 to Proverbs 30:2-4 and Job 8:11-22 to Psalm 1.

*Numeric Sayings.* See Job 5:19 to Proverbs 30:21.

*Reflective Questioning.* Job sometimes bluntly challenges conventional wisdom. See Job 21:17-19 to Ecclesiastes 9:2-3.

*Apocalyptic.* Job has some features in common with books like Daniel and Revelation. The earthly struggle is part of a heavenly conflict between God and Satan (Job 12). Human foes tempt the believer to abandon his perseverance (Job's wife and three friends). But faithful endurance leads to triumph and blessings (Job 42).

The Book of Job draws on many types of literature to set forth its message, but it does not belong to any one of these categories. It must be interpreted as unique both in literary type and message. Job is not a conventional book.

*Date and Authorship.* No one knows when or by whom Job was written. Some have suggested it was written in the Babylonian exile, but the book does not allude to that or any event from Israel's history. It does often allude to other biblical passages, especially Genesis 1–3 and certain psalms of David (see Job 7:17-21 to Ps. 8). This implies it was written after David. A good possibility is that the book appeared in the reign of Solomon or Hezekiah, both of whom encouraged the study of wisdom literature.

   I. Prologue (1:1–2:13)
  II. Dialogue with Three Friends (3:1–31:40)
 III. Elihu's Speeches (32:1–37:24)
  IV. God's Speeches (38:1–42:6)
   V. Epilogue: Job Restored (42:7-17)

*Unity and Integrity.* Some scholars assert that portions of the book are later additions—that is, that they were not written by the original author and are not true to his intentions. The prologue, epilogue, and Elihu speeches are often so regarded. Many allege the writer of the Elihu speeches was a pious Israelite who was offended at much of what Job had to say and felt a need to correct it. But the book makes no sense if the prologue and epilogue are deleted. The Elihu speeches are essential to the plan of the book. We cannot interpret Job by omitting difficult or unusual chapters.

*Central Problem.* The Book of Job confuses modern readers. Often said to be about the problem of why the righteous suffer, it never really solves that problem. To be sure, some readers believe that the prologue resolves the problem: suffering is a test of humanity in a cosmic trial before God and Satan. This concept is present in Job and has validity.

But this hardly explains the whole book. If this is the message of Job, then the dispute between Job and his friends, the very heart of the book, is pointless. Also, although God never said that Satan was the reason for Job's pain, Job was satisfied by God's answer. This implies that the prologue is not the whole answer.

Job actually says remarkably little to explain the problem of pain. Instead, the speakers hurled lengthy and highly poetic speeches at one another in which they alternatively insisted or denied that the wicked suffer retribution for their deeds. Unlike modern Christian theologians, they scarcely considered other explanations for pain and evil. Even God, in His lengthy speeches, said not a word to explain why Job had suffered. The Christian who reads Job for an explanation of the trials and suffering of life may leave more bewildered than comforted.

The fault, however, is not with Job but with us. Although suffering is an important factor in the book, the central question is not why the righteous suffer but why a person should serve God. Or, to put it in the terms of the one who first posed the question, Satan, "Does Job fear God for nothing?" (1:9).

And why should a person fear God? For Job's friends the answer was simple:

because that is the safe thing to do. Wickedness invites the fury of an angry God, but righteousness brings prosperity. This reasoning, moreover, dominates not only the friends but also Job himself at the beginning (1:5). He was one of them. But the undeserved pain of his own life and the condemnation by his friends, like the successive blows of a whip, drove him to face questions he had never faced.

That reality, which he finally proclaimed in chapter 21, was that in his experience the wicked were not often brought to calamity for their sin: "They spend their years in prosperity and go down to the grave in peace" (21:13). In exasperation Job cried out, "Who is the Almighty, that we should serve him?" (21:15) even as he called on his friends to cover their mouths in horror (21:5). Not only his world but theirs had collapsed.

Where is the answer to Satan's challenge and Job's anguished outcry? It is found, of course, in the text of the book itself. In the following comments, we will travel through the book and seek that answer.

## PROLOGUE (1:1–2:13)

The prologue is a tightly woven narrative that blends both chiasm (a pattern repeating ideas in inverted order) and parallelism (a pattern repeating ideas in sequence), as follows:

A   Background of the Story (1:1-5)
B   Dialogue in Heaven (1:6-12)
C   Affliction of Job (1:13-19)
D   Job's Response (1:20-22)
B'  Dialogue in Heaven (2:1-6)
C'  Affliction of Job (2:7-8)
D'  Job's Response (2:9-10)
A'  Background of the Dialogue
      (2:11-13)

In 1:1 Job is declared to have been altogether upright and blameless. At the very outset, therefore, the possibility that his sufferings might be punishment or discipline is thrown out of court. The text does not even allow the possibility that they were preventative disciplines given in order that he would not be tempted to stray. Job was careful about that danger even for his children. This declaration of Job's innocence prevents the reader from escaping the dilemma of the book by the assumption that Job must have been guilty of something. He was not.

Satan (meaning *adversary* or *accuser*) appeared before God in 1:6 and challenged the validity of Job's piety. Some claim that Satan here was merely a loyal angel whose task was that of chief prosecutor, but this misreads the text. His hostility to God was transparent, as was his malice. He was evil. Nevertheless, he posed the central question of the book: "Does Job fear God for nothing?"

Job lost all his wealth and children in the first affliction and his health in the second. Satan's proverb "skin for skin" means that Job valued nothing so much as his own skin, since only skin can equal it. Still, Job did not lose his faith or integrity, even after his wife lost hers. His friends visited him to comfort him, but they sat in horror for a week before anyone could speak.

## DIALOGUE WITH THREE FRIENDS (3:1–31:40)

*Opening Soliloquy (3:1-26).* The day of birth is to the individual what creation is to the whole world. Job cursed the day of his birth and, in doing so, reversed the language of Genesis 1. He called for darkness to overwhelm the day in contrast to the "Let there be light" of Genesis 1:3. He called for the stars and sun to be blotted out (contrast Gen. 1:14-19). Job even invoked the name of Leviathan, a monster symbolic of destruction and chaos (see comments on chap. 41). Job desired creation to revert to chaos (Gen. 1:2). For him the order and structure of the universe had already been turned upside down, and life no longer made sense.

**Eliphaz's First Response (4:1–5:27).** Eliphaz tried to persuade Job that the world's moral order was still stable. God rewards the righteous and punishes the wicked. Eliphaz claimed that both experience and a private revelation supported his case. He asserted that humans are such lowly and foolish creatures that their lives are naturally full of trouble. Still, he urged Job to call upon God, who would hear and help. Ironically, this happened, though not in the way Eliphaz supposed.

**Job Responded and Prayed (6:1–7:21).** Job argued that Eliphaz's doctrine, however orthodox and tidy it might be, failed utterly to answer the hard facts of his experience. Animals only bellow when they are hungry. Likewise Job hungered for some answers. He cried out for wisdom to deal with the calamities and questions that had filled his life. But he would not accept cheap and phony answers, such as Eliphaz had just given. They were as inspired as unsalted egg white. Job lamented his agonies and identified with the sufferings of people everywhere, especially slaves and day-laborers.

Job prayed for mercy. Wondering how he could possibly have been bad enough to merit this treatment from God, he reversed the meaning of Psalm 8. Instead of asking, "What is man?" that God would take notice and exalt him (Ps. 8:4-8), he asked, "What is man?" that he deserves such intense scrutiny and punishment. Job again alluded to Leviathan, here portrayed as a sea monster. Was Job such a threat that he needed to be caged like a wild animal?

**Bildad's First Response (8:1-22).** Eliphaz did not directly accuse Job of having done something to deserve all that had befallen him. Bildad moved closer to doing this first in claiming that Job's children did deserve their fate and second in promising that Job would be restored if he was upright. The "if" naturally implies that he may not be.

Bildad continued Eliphaz's argument that the moral order of the world was not threatened by what had happened to Job. He claimed the accumulated wisdom of generations supported his point. He developed the familiar simile of the two plants in which the one that thrives represents the righteous and the one that withers represents the wicked (see Ps. 1 and Jer. 17:5-8).

**Job Again Responds (9:1–10:22).** In this section Job first responded to his friends and then offered a prayer of complaint to God. But his response was directed more to Eliphaz than Bildad. Job's opening, "How can a mortal be righteous before God?" virtually quoted Eliphaz (4:17).

As Job developed the idea, he turned Eliphaz's meaning upside down. Eliphaz claimed that human folly being what it is, no one has grounds for challenging God's right to punish as He wills. Job replied that God's power and lofty position being what it is, no one, no matter how innocent, has a chance to question God's wrath or make an appeal. Even if he were clean, God would push him into the mud. God's omnipotence and sovereignty, normally objects of praise, had become objects of terror to Job.

Job's despair led him to call for an arbitrator between himself and God. The distance between humanity and God was too great for Job to bridge. He did not develop this idea here but took it up later.

In his prayer Job appealed for mercy on two grounds. First, God had no experience of human mortality and frailty (see Heb. 2:14-18). God ought to understand that it is not easy being human.

Second, Job pointed out that he was God's creature and wondered if God's only purpose in creation was to destroy what He had made. Job's prayer recalled Moses' intercession for Israel (Exod. 32:12). Job again alluded to the creation narrative (see Gen. 2:7). Job had been knit together by God (see Ps. 139:13). But in Genesis 1:31 God saw that all He had made was very good (*tob*). Now Job asked, "Is it good *[tob]* to You that You persecute, that You disdain, the work of Your hands?" (author's translation).

**Zophar's First Response (11:1–20).** Zophar, in an angry retort, was the first to accuse Job of having committed some sin by which he deserved his fate. To be sure, he did not yet make a specific accusation. He was only sure Job must have done *something*.

Zophar's rejoinder turned on the fact that Job, a mere mortal, could not possibly have understood God's ways. He used four dimensions—height, depth, length, and width—to show how far God's ways were beyond Job's (see Eph. 3:18, which uses similar language to encourage Christians to pursue deeper wisdom rather than to prove that it is beyond their reach).

Zophar wished God would rebuke Job. He was sure God could point out Job's sins. Still, like his two friends, Zophar encouraged Job to turn to God, who would hear his prayer and restore what Job had lost.

To the reader, Zophar's speech is laced with irony. God's wisdom is indeed far deeper than Job's, and God would speak to him to that effect. Afterwards God would restore Job's fortunes, as Zophar predicted. But how different it would all be from what Zophar expected. For it was not Job but the three friends whom God would accuse (42:8).

The proverb in 11:12 should probably be translated, "A stupid man will get sense when a wild donkey [perhaps zebra] is born tame." This metaphor of human stubbornness means that some fools are all but beyond hope (see Jer. 13:23). It was a thinly veiled reproach against Job, who had described himself as a braying wild donkey. But in 39:5-8 God said it was He who gave the wild donkey his freedom. What to Zophar was a worthless animal was of far more value to Job and God.

**Second Cycle (12:1–14:22).** The major divisions of this lengthy discourse are as follows: (1) The Shallowness of the Wisdom of the Three Friends (12:2–13:19) and (2) Job's Third Prayer (13:20–14:22).

Job's assault on the advice of his friends is in two parts. First, he proved that he could cite the wisdom of the former generations as well as anyone. Second, he said his argument was really with God and appealed for the friends at least to be quiet if they could not say anything better than what they had already said.

After the initial outburst of anger chapter 12 recites traditional teaching (indeed, much of it could have been said by any one of the friends). The natural world and the teachings of the aged are both guides into wisdom. God's power is irresistible and sovereign: all of life is in His hands, and He brings down the haughty and the proud. Job was in effect saying to his friends: "I know all this. You have told me nothing." But in Job's mouth even orthodoxy appears dark and threatening. God's power appeared almost arbitrary and destabilizing. It negated all human attempts at wisdom.

For Job his friends' hackneyed and conventional arguments were meaningless. They were worthless physicians who always prescribed the wrong medicine. Job even claimed that God could not be satisfied with their hollow defense of divine justice and correctly predicted that God would not be pleased with their refusal to look at the facts of this case objectively. It would have been better by far if they had just let Job take up his case with God, for it was He with whom Job had a complaint. Job knew that God, although He had become like an enemy to him, was still his only hope.

Job's third prayer, like the second, appealed to God to cease tormenting him. In the second prayer, however, Job pleaded on the grounds that he was God's creation (10:8-12). Here he emphasized more his mortality and weakness. This led him to consider the doctrine of resurrection and to wonder if it would be best for him to die and thus rest until the day when the dead rise. Even so, he was tortured by his pain and the brevity of life and concluded this prayer in bleak discouragement.

Some assume that the Book of Job cannot possibly have a true concept of resurrection, but that assumption is groundless. Job 14:14-15 begins with a question, not a confession of faith. Job's sufferings forced him to think about God's ways on a deeper level than ever before. Here the idea of resurrection entered the discussion and gave Job reason to hope (the friends never considered the idea of resurrection).

The term the NIV translates "renewal" may be rendered "transformation." Job here combined the pleas of his two prayers—Job was both mortal and God's creation. The resurrection would both answer his need for immortality and make the creation understandable. God did not make people just to watch them die off. But Job had only begun to deal with this question.

**Eliphaz's Second Response (15:1-35).** Eliphaz now directly accused Job of sin and threw Job's own words back into his face (see 9:20). He was alarmed that Job's attitude might undermine piety and once again claimed that Job needed to recognize his limitations and return to traditional wisdom.

He repeated the argument that since all people are sinful God is justified in punishing whenever He chooses. Another poem on the fate of the wicked was no doubt meant to convict Job and persuade him to repent of whatever sin he had committed.

Does the Book of Job deny the universal sinfulness of humanity? Texts like 15:14-16 give an orthodox if somewhat harsh statement of universal depravity. On the other hand, this text is put in the mouth of Eliphaz, who would be shown to be in the wrong. The characterization of Job as "blameless" (1:1) also seems to contradict universal depravity.

Nevertheless, the book does not claim that some people are sinless. The prologue does not say Job had never committed any sin. It only stresses that he was righteous and that his suffering had nothing to do with any past or potential guilt on his part. Job confessed to having sinned in life (14:16-17) although he was certain he had not deserved what had befallen him.

The book does not imply that everything the three friends said was wrong. Most of what they asserted fully agrees with the rest of the Bible (see Prov. 6:12-15). But they misapplied the biblical teachings. The doctrine of universal sin made them cynical about people (and even about God, although they did not realize it). And the doctrine of retribution made them judgmental. The book does not deny that all have sinned, but it forces the reader to think in terms other than a simple equation of guilt and punishment.

**Job Laments and Prays (16:1– 17:16).** Job vented his frustration over his pain, his confusion about what God had done to him, and his anger at the empty words of his "comforters." But the careful chiasm (a pattern repeating ideas in inverted order) shows that there is more here than an emotional outburst, and a confession of hope stands at the very center of the whole.

That confession returns to the theme of the heavenly Arbitrator or Intercessor. Job was now certain of the reality of the Intercessor. He had previously only wished that such an Intercessor existed (9:33-34). Job had already far surpassed his friends in the understanding of God's ways, and his sufferings would drive him deeper still.

**Bildad's Second Response (18:1-21).** Bildad angrily replied and gave Job another fairly conventional poem on the fate of the wicked (18:5-21). Most significant is the point in 18:20 that men from east and west would be appalled at the fall of the wicked. Surely no one was more famous than Job (1:3), and Bildad here took up Job's own words (17:8). Bildad's slightly concealed meaning was that Job had not only sinned but was one of the proverbial wicked. Job's friends were progressing in bitterness toward him.

**Job Laments and Hopes (19:1-29).** Job again bemoaned his fate and called attention to how those who formerly loved him had abandoned him. He first spoke of God's antagonism to him and then of the contempt he had received from relatives, friends, and subordinates. He pleaded for pity from his friends and warned them that they too might face judgment for their hostility.

In the middle of this cry for love, Job made his most profound confession of hope. The somewhat obscure Hebrew may be translated: "I know that my redeemer lives and that the final One will arise against the dust. After they have done away with my skin, from my flesh I shall have a vision of God. I will have this

vision for myself; my eyes will see that He is no stranger. My heart yearns within me!"

The term "the final One" refers to the divine Redeemer (the Hebrew word is translated "the last" in Isa. 44:6 and 48:12). "Done away with" translates a word elsewhere used of cutting away underbrush (Isa. 10:34). Job assumed his tormented body would soon die and be thrown out like garbage. The phrase "have a vision" ("see") translates a Hebrew word often used of seeing God or a vision (Exod. 24:11; Isa. 1:1).

Job's yearning for an Intercessor and hope for a resurrection came together here, in the middle of deep dejection, in a triumphant assertion of faith. Job's "Redeemer" would arise against the dust. In other words, He would conquer human mortality. Job was therefore sure that he too would rise from the dead and in his body behold God. At the same time, we note that Job's problems were not over. He still did not understand why God treated him as an enemy.

It is pointless to deny that Job looked for a resurrection and a Redeemer. The book, through the sufferings of its hero, points to the two universal human needs: the need for a Deliverer and the need for release from mortality. No one is competent to stand before God, and everyone longs to escape death (in that sense the three friends were correct in their estimate of human sin and divine power). These needs, poignantly portrayed in Job, are dramatically fulfilled in the New Testament.

**Zophar's Second Response (20:1-29).** As Zophar rehashed the fate of the wicked, it is clearer still that Job was the subject. Job had said his Redeemer would arise against the dust (19:25); Zophar said Job's vigor would lie dead in the dust (19:11). He accentuated the unrepentant attitude (19:12-19) and fleeting wealth (19:20-23) of the wicked, which was exactly how the friends regarded Job.

**Job's Response (21:1-34).** All at once Job challenged his friends' tedious sermons on the fate of the wicked. How often, he demanded, had they ever really seen it like this? Far more often the reverse was true: the wicked prospered. Rather than parrot traditional doctrine, the friends should have been dumbfounded. Job's case had undermined the precepts by which they lived. The question remained, Why should we serve God?

**Eliphaz's Third Response (22:1-30).** Eliphaz now hit Job with a frontal assault. He directly accused Job of being a great sinner and particularly charged him with greed and oppression. But the attack began and ended on ironic notes, although Eliphaz did not know it. He sarcastically asked Job if God had rebuked him for his piety, when in fact that was the precise reason for Job's misfortune. He also promised that if Job would repent, he would be able to intercede for sinners. And Job would intercede—for Eliphaz.

The friends had nothing more to say. They repeatedly made their point on the lot of sinners. Their accusations against Job could hardly become any more brutal. Job now began to turn from them.

**Job Looks for Justice (23:1-24:25).** Job mourned here first for himself and then for all the oppressed and suffering. Behind this was a plea for God to vindicate the righteous and punish sinners. The book gives its deepest expressions of struggle in chapter 24. Job voiced the sorrow and bewilderment of believers of every generation. He had not abandoned the faith, however, and returned to traditional expressions of God's justice.

**Bildad's Third Response (25:1-6).** Bildad began a third discourse in which he returned to the idea of God's holiness against human lowliness. His very short speech appears to have been cut off. Job likely interrupted him.

Because Bildad's third speech was so short and Zophar had none at all, many scholars suppose that 26:5-14 concludes Bildad's speech and 27:13-23 is Zophar's missing third speech.

This approach is unnecessary. The friends really had nothing more to say, and Job had no intention of listening to them anymore. Having interrupted Bildad, Job in effect gave Bildad's and Zophar's speeches for them. He did this for two reasons. First, Job somewhat sarcastically showed that he knew their theology better than they. Second, Job suggested that he agreed with them in principle but was dumbfounded by what had happened to him. He knew he was innocent.

**Job's Last Address (26:1-27:23).** Job interrupted Bildad with bitter sarcasm. He described the power of God and the end of the ungodly, but he defiantly maintained that he deserved nothing of what had happened to him. He had nothing more to say to them.

**Hymn to Wisdom (28:1-28).** This poem may be regarded as Job's own words or the author's own transition. It differs from its context and does not begin with the phrase "And Job said." The text does not, however, suggest that these were not Job's words. Either way the interpretation of the chapter is only slightly altered.

The poem contrasts human technical skill in mining out precious metals and gems with the inaccessibility of wisdom. The human condition is indeed pitiful. Although adept at tunneling into the deepest recesses of the earth for treasure, humans are neither willing nor able to penetrate the mysteries of life itself.

The poem concludes with what may be called the heart of biblical wisdom, "The fear of the Lord—that is wisdom." For Job this became far more than a cliche. The former, calm assurance that he understood life had been shattered. The old order of his life was in ruins. He now had to look to God and not to his own wisdom about God.

**Job's Final Discourse (29:1– 31:40).** This discourse is in three parts: (1) Job's former glory, (2) Job's present humiliation, and (3) a negative confession.

Job remembered his former glory especially as a time when he was respected and loved by one and all. He now looked upon his former belief that all was secure as mistaken, although in fact those words would come true (42:12- 16).

Chapter 29 begins and ends with the term "light." In chapter 3 Job cursed the light, but here he remembered when he blessed God's light and others blessed the light of his own face (see Exod. 34:29-35 and Num. 6:25-26).

From a position of highest renown, Job had fallen to complete infamy. He once enjoyed universal respect. Now even the sons of the dregs of society mocked him. His physical pain was more than he could endure, and he awaited death. He voiced another prayer of complaint to God.

Ancient Egyptian literature preserved examples of the "negative confession," a text in which a deceased person's spirit, facing divine judgment, claimed not to have committed sins described in a detailed list. Job 31 is similar to these. Here Job claimed he was not lustful or adulterous, a swindler, or an unjust employer. He was not uncharitable, greedy or idolatrous, or vindictive and cunning. This negative confession, coming as it does at the end of his speeches, implies that Job believed death was near and wanted to end his life with a protest of innocence. He had nothing more to say.

## ELIHU'S SPEECH (32:1–37:24)

Elihu, who is mentioned neither before nor after these six chapters, suddenly appeared and made a particularly wordy speech. Some consider his words to be the high point of the book and claim he resolved the dilemma, but this interpretation is hard to justify.

First, Elihu was overconfident of his own wisdom, especially in 36:4: "Be assured that my words are not false; one perfect in knowledge is with you"). For all his bravado, however, Elihu said nothing that had not already been said: God inflicts pain on people to prevent them from falling into sin; God is the wise and all-powerful Ruler of the world; and the wicked will be destroyed but the repentant will prosper. What Elihu said was not wrong, but everything he proclaimed had already been explored in great detail.

He also wrongly assumed Job was being punished for something. Finally, and most significantly, Elihu was ignored by everyone else in the book. Surely this would not be the case if he were the fount of wisdom he claimed to be.

Some scholars consider the Elihu speeches to be a later insertion by a pious Israelite who was distraught at Job's remarks and sought to correct them. This view also must be rejected. A pious scribe would certainly not put his words into the mouth of such an arrogant young man as Elihu. His speech does provide a transition to God's reply to Job (see 38:1). More importantly, the Elihu speeches perform a special function for the reader.

As we progress through the Book of Job, we feel the same distress Elihu voiced. We are sure there is something wrong with Job's comments but are aware that the three friends failed to answer him. We try to find an alternative answer. Perhaps, we think, God afflicted Job to keep him from falling into sin. We thrash about for a solution much as Elihu did and repeat old arguments without knowing it. And if we are not careful, we fall into the same vain certainty. We think we are wiser than Job and his friends put together.

Job and his friends were each wrong in his own way, but so are we. We need to hear the voice of God.

## GOD'S SPEECHES (38:1–42:6)

The divine speech falls in two parts divided by Job's first response. The first portrays God's dominion over creation, and the second focuses on behemoth and leviathan.

Many interpreters are frankly confused if not disappointed by God's speech. Instead of giving a profound explanation of Job's sufferings, God gave him something of a lesson in natural history. What is the reason for this? Again we must recall that the central question of the book is not why the righteous suffer but whether Job served God for nothing (1:9-11). Both Job and his friends had assumed that life and prosperity were the benefits from service to God.

The meaning of God's reply now begins to appear. Nowhere does He say that Job's affliction was a punishment for sin or even, as Elihu suggested, a way of keeping Job from falling into sin. God did accuse Job of having attributed injustice to God, which Job certainly had. And Job's repentance shows that he came to realize that God had not been unfair. What did God say that so thoroughly convinced Job of his error?

God's words focused entirely on His work in creation (and on the fact that Job was not there). In chapter 3 Job had wanted to bring creation crashing down, but God, in terms that often recall Genesis 1, challenged Job to rethink what he had said.

God repeatedly spoke of the creation of the earth, the morning, and the stars (Gen. 1:1,14-19); the separation of light from darkness and of sea from land (Gen. 1:3,9-10); and the formation of clouds (Gen. 1:6-8). God then called attention to the wild animals such as lions, goats, eagles, and ostriches (Gen. 1:20,24). He emphasized the powerful and wild forces of nature.

In addition, God showed that He has placed all these forces in an order and controls every one. He keeps the sea in its place, separates day and night, feeds the lions, and provides all the animals with what they need to survive. The powers that otherwise would destroy one another and fall into chaos are kept in an ordered balance.

God told Job he had to show he could crush the proud and the wicked if he wanted to be on equal footing with God. Then He turned to the creatures called behemoth and leviathan. The former, behemoth, may have been the elephant or hippopotamus. A powerful creature who dwelt among the lotuses and poplars, he was only the prologue to a much more awesome creature, leviathan.

Leviathan is sometimes interpreted as the crocodile but, even allowing for poetic license, this makes God guilty of considerable exaggeration. For leviathan is invulnerable to human weapons, his eyes and nose flash with light, and fire pours out of his mouth. He is covered with armor and is lord of all creatures. This is more like a terrible dragon than a crocodile.

The Bible and other ancient literature speak of leviathan as a terrible, supernatural creature. Ugaritic texts speak of a serpent with seven heads called "lotan," and Psalm 74:14 says God crushed the heads of leviathan. Isaiah 27:1 calls leviathan a serpent and a sea monster. And in Job, God repeatedly pointed out Job's inability to subdue this monster. What was this beast?

Readers are often confused that although Satan is the prominent adversary of Job 1–2, he seems to disappear after that. Also we note that although the book often speaks of creation and the fall, it has until now said nothing about the agent of the fall, the serpent. A likely solution is that Satan has not been forgotten but has reappeared at the end as the serpent leviathan.

Job had challenged the justice of God, and God had responded that only He, and not Job, is able to control and destroy the chaotic and evil powers. Just as God uses all the natural powers in His creative purpose, even so He allows evil to thrive for a season but always governs it by His providence to bring about the final destruction of the evil one. Therefore it was not for Job to challenge God's moral governance of the world. God knows what He is doing.

*Job Repents (42:1-6).* Against this address from God, Job's complete repentance is not surprising. It is important to see, however, that he repented of having challenged God's justice in his speeches. He did not do as his friends wanted and confess that he had done something to deserve his sufferings.

## JOB RESTORED (JOB 42:7-17)

Job's vindication was complete. God told the friends that they had not spoken what was right, "as my servant Job has." Job's words, however rash, were far better than the hollow defense the friends gave of their religion of rewards and punishments. Job's intercession for them and the restoration of his former glory not only show that his suffering was not punishment but that he was right to refuse to make a meaningless confession of sins he did not commit.

*Theological Significance.* What is the answer to Satan's challenge? Did Job fear God for nothing? The answer, remarkably, is no. Job did not serve God for nothing. Job learned that the real benefit of his piety was not his health and wealth and children; *it was God Himself.* God, the Creator and Judge of all, is bringing about the triumph of righteousness. And Job now knew he could trust God to do all things right, even if it cost Job all he had. For he still had God.

## Questions for Reflection

1. Why do we assume that we are being punished for sin whenever calamity strikes?

2. In what ways did the strict religion of the three friends make them less than human?

3. Do we sometimes wonder why God waits so long and seems to allow sinners to go unpunished? How does Job help us to solve this problem?

4. What is the difference between serving God for God Himself and serving Him in order to be safe from trouble and hardship? How does Job help us to see the difference?

5. How did Job come to see his need for resurrection and for a Mediator? How did God meet those needs for us?

## Sources for Additional Study

Alden, Robert L. *Job*. New American Commentary. Nashville: Broadman & Holman, 1994.

Andersen, Francis I. *Job*. Downers Grove: InterVarsity, 1974.

Janzen, J. Gerald. *Job*. Atlanta: John Knox, 1985.

# PSALMS

The Book of Psalms or Psalter is the hymnal of Israelite worship and the Bible's book of personal devotions. In it we not only find expression of all the emotions of life but also some of the most profound teaching in the entire Scripture.

**Date and Authorship.** The Psalter was not completed until late in Israelite history (in the postexilic era). But it contains hymns written over a period of hundreds of years. Many individual psalms are far older than the whole book.

*Evidence of the Superscripts.* A primary source of information regarding the date and authorship of individual psalms are the superscripts found above many psalms. According to these, some of the authors include David, the sons of Korah, Asaph, Moses, and Solomon. Other psalms, including some of the "Psalms of Ascent" (Pss. 120–134) and "Hallelujah" Psalms (Pss. 146–150) are anonymous. These titles, if taken at face value, would date many of the psalms to the early tenth century (psalms of David) and at least one to the fifteenth century (Ps. 90).

*Meaning and Reliability of the Superscripts.* Some scholars, however, question whether the superscripts are meant to ascribe authorship to the psalms. The phrase *ledawid* used frequently in the psalm superscripts could mean *by David,* but it also could mean *for David.* But most scholars would admit that the word means *by David.* There is no reason to think it is some kind of dedication.

A more serious question is whether the superscripts are reliable. Some scholars believe they were added at a late date and are no more than conjectures that have no real historical value. But there are good reasons to believe the superscripts can be trusted. Many of the psalm superscripts refer to incidents in the life of David about which Samuel and Chronicles say nothing. For example, the superscript of Psalm 60 mentions battles with Aram-Naharaim, Aram-Zobah, and Edom. It would be strange if, in the late postexilic period, rabbis invented this. Another example is the superscript of Psalm 7, which speaks of a certain "Cush the Benjamite" (he is mentioned here only in the OT). If the superscripts were late fabrications, one would expect that they would refer more to incidents from David's life mentioned in Samuel.

Many of the psalm titles contain technical musical terms, the meanings of which were already lost by the time the Old Testament was translated into Greek. For example, *lammenasseah,* "for the choir leader," is wrongly translated "to the end" in the Septuagint, the pre-Christian Greek translation of the Old Testament. A number of these terms are still not understood. Obscure or difficult words in the superscripts include: *song titles* ("Do Not Destroy"; "A Dove on Distant Oaks"; "The Doe of the Morning"; "Lilies"; "The Lily/ies of the Covenant"; and "Mahalath"); *musical instruments or technical terms* ("stringed instruments" and "Sheminith"); *musical guilds or singers* ("Asaph"; "Sons of Korah"; "Heman the Ezrahite"; "Ethan the Ezrahite"); and *types of psalms* ("Songs of Ascent," likely sung by those who were making a pilgrimage to Jerusalem; *maskil,* possibly an instructional or meditative psalm; *miktham; shiggayon).*

Ancient terminology and references to old guilds and bygone events all imply that the titles are very old. This supports confidence in their reliability.

*Davidic Authorship of Psalms.* Many scholars have asserted that David did not write the psalms attributed to him. But there are no historical reasons why David could not have authored those psalms. David had a reputation as a singer and as a devoted servant of the Lord, and nothing in his life is incompatible with his being a psalmist.

One difficulty here is that some of the psalms of David seem to refer to the temple (for example, 27:4), which did not exist in his day. But terms like "House of the Lord," "Holy Place," and "House of God" are regularly used of the tent of meeting and need not be taken as references to Solomon's temple (see Exod. 28:43; 29:30; Josh. 6:24; Judg. 18:31). Certainly David could have written the psalms attributed to him. Other psalms that mention the temple, however, are also ascribed to David (Pss. 5; 11; 18; 27; 29; 65; 68; 138). It is perhaps worth noting that New Testament writers ascribe none of these psalms to David.

*The Date of the Psalms.* Earlier critics dated many of the psalms late in Israel's history, some as late as the Maccabean period. For two reasons, however, this is no longer possible.

First, the Ugaritic songs and hymns show parallels to many of the psalms. The grammar and poetic forms are similar. The Ugaritic tradition of hymn writing is ancient (before twelfth century) and implies that many of the psalms may be ancient too.

Second, a fragmentary, second-century B.C. copy of the biblical collection of psalms was found in the Dead Sea Scrolls. This proves beyond doubt that the psalms were composed well before

the second century B.C., since it must have taken a long time for the written psalms to be recognized as Scripture and for the psalter to be organized.

There is no reason, therefore, to date all the psalms late. Generally speaking, they can be dated to three broad periods: (1) *Preexilic.* This would include those psalms that are very much like the Ugaritic songs, the royal psalms, and those that mention the Northern Kingdom. (2) *Exilic.* This would include the dirge songs that lament the fall of Jerusalem and call for vengeance on the Edomites and others. (3) *Early postexilic.* This would include psalms that emphasize the written law, such as Psalm 119.

*Compilation of the Psalms.* Psalms divides into five sections or "books": (1) Psalms 1–41; (2) Psalms 42–72; (3) Psalms 73–89; (4) Psalms 90–106; (5) Psalms 107–150.

We have no precise information regarding the dates when the five books of the Psalms were compiled or what the criteria of compilation were. Psalm 72:20 implies that a compilation of David's psalms was made shortly after his death. In Hezekiah's time there were collections of the psalms of David and Asaph, which may account for the bulk of the first three books (2 Chr. 29:30). At a later date another scribe may have collected the remaining books of the Psalter. Psalms was put into its final form some time in the postexilic period.

The five books each close with a doxology, and Psalm 150 is a concluding doxology for the entire Psalter. But the numbering of the psalms varies. The Jerusalem Talmud speaks of 147 psalms. The Septuagint divides Psalms 116 and 147 into two psalms each but numbers Psalms 9 and 10 and Psalms 114 and 115 as one psalm each.

***Types of Psalms.*** When studying a psalm, one should ask the following questions: (1) Was it sung by an individual or the congregation? (2) What was the psalm's purpose (praise, cry for help, thanksgiving, admonition)? (3) Does it mention any special themes, such as the king and the royal house, or Zion? By asking these questions, scholars have identified a number of psalm types.

*Hymns.* In this type of psalm, the whole congregation praises God for His works or attributes (Ps. 105). Six subcategories of hymn are: *victory songs,* which praise God for His victories over the nations (Ps. 68); *processional hymns,* sung as the worshipers moved into the temple area (Ps. 24); *Zion songs,* which praise God and specifically refer to His presence in Zion (Ps. 48); *songs of the Lord's reign,* which begin with the words, "The Lord reigns" (Ps. 99); *antiphonal hymns,* chanted by either the priests or choir with the congregation responding antiphonally (Ps. 136); *hallelujah hymns,* which begin or end with "Praise the Lord!" (*hallelu Yah;* Ps. 146).

*Community complaints.* In these psalms the whole nation voiced its complaints over problems it was facing, such as defeat in battle, famine, or drought (Ps. 74). A subcategory of this is the *national imprecation,* in which the people cursed their oppressors (Ps. 83).

*Individual complaints.* These psalms are like the community complaint except that they were prayers given by one person instead of the whole nation. The reason for the prayers might be that the individual was sick, hounded by enemies, or in need of confessing personal sin (Ps. 13). This type of psalm may include substantial imprecation or curses against the psalmist's personal enemies (Ps. 5). A subcategory is the *penitential psalm,* in which the speaker is dominated by the sense of his guilt (Ps. 51).

*Individual songs of thanksgiving.* In these psalms an individual praises God for some saving act. Usually it alludes to a time that the individual was sick or in some other kind of trouble (Ps. 116).

*Royal psalms.* These psalms deal with the king and the royal house. Subcategories include: *wedding songs,* sung at the marriage of the king (Ps. 45); *coronation songs* (Ps. 72); *prayers for victory,* chanted when the king went to war (Ps. 20); *votive psalms,* perhaps sung by the king at his coronation as a vow to be faithful and upright (Ps. 101).

*Torah psalms.* These psalms give moral or religious instruction (Pss. 1; 127). Subcategories include: *testimony songs,* in which the psalmist used his personal experience of God's salvation to encourage the hearer (Ps. 32); *wisdom songs,* in which the psalmist instructed the hearer more in practical wisdom similar to that in Proverbs than in the law (Ps. 49).

*Oracle psalms.* These psalms report a decree of God (Ps. 82). The content of the oracle is often divine judgment, and the psalm concludes with a prayer for God to carry out His decree. But see also Psalm 87, an oracle of salvation for the Gentiles.

*Blessing psalms.* In these psalms a priest pronounced a blessing upon the hearer(s) (Ps. 128).

*Taunt songs.* These psalms reproach the godless for their vile behavior and promise that their doom is near (Ps. 52).

*Songs of trust.* In these psalms the psalmist may face difficulty but remains assured of God's help and proclaims his faith and trust (Ps. 11).

When interpreting a psalm, it is important first to determine what kind of psalm it is. In this way one can see how the psalmist intended it to be read.

## PSALM 1

To avoid walking, standing, and sitting with the wicked is simply to avoid participation in their way of life. "Streams" in 1:3 is best translated as "irrigation canals." The streams of Palestine regularly dried up, but the irrigation canals that came off the great rivers never did.

## PSALM 2

The covenant of David underlies this psalm. The Davidic king is the Lord's anointed (Messiah) and receives the whole world as His domain. All the peoples of the earth are warned to submit to Him. The royal house of Judah obviously never ruled the whole world; the fulfillment is in the greater Son of David, Christ. He is God's Messiah, who was crucified by the rulers of this age (Acts 4:25-26), the Son of God (Ps. 2:7; Matt. 3:17), and the King with an iron scepter (Ps. 2:9; Rev. 2:27). The phrase "Kiss the Son" is unusual in that it is in Aramaic, not Hebrew. The Septuagint reads, "Lay hold of instruction." (See "Christ in the Psalms.")

## PSALM 3

David's prayer for victory over his enemies is more than a plea for himself. It is also a prayer for his people, over whom God made him king.

## PSALM 4

The psalmist called for God to hear him but then turned to address those who doubted or rejected God. He warned them to abandon idols, to be warned that God watches over His own, to meditate in silence and without anger, and to worship and trust the Lord. He then proclaimed his confidence in God.

## PSALM 5

The righteous are outraged by the behavior of the wicked and wait for God to act. This psalm progresses in five stanzas: (1) an opening call for God to hear, (2) an affirmation of God's hatred of evil, (3) a resolution to serve God and a prayer for help, (4) a prayer for the destruction of the wicked, and (5) a prayer for the protection of the righteous.

## PSALM 6

David wrote this psalm when his enemies had him in a desperate situation. He protested that he would be cut off from Israel's worship if he were killed. But he concluded in confidence that God would help him.

## PSALM 7

At a time of conflict, David was driven to see whether or not he was at fault. His protests of innocence did not stem from pride or refusal to acknowledge guilt but from the insight that he could not expect God to help him if he were as guilty as those who opposed him.

## PSALM 8

God is praised as Creator and for having given humanity such a high place in creation. Verse 2 literally reads, "From the mouths of children and babies you have established strength." Matthew 21:16, following the Septuagint, has "praise" instead of "strength." In either case the paradox is that God puts His enemies to shame by infants (see 1 Cor. 1:18-25).

## PSALM 9

In the Septuagint, Psalms 9 and 10 form one psalm. Since the two together form an acrostic, they may well have been originally a single psalm. They were probably separated at an early date to make Psalm 10 an individual complaint psalm. Psalm 9 also has a complaint, but the overall tone is thanksgiving and certainty of victory. David saw in his personal victory a type of God's triumph in the last judgment.

## THE CHARACTERISTICS OF GOD PRESENTED IN THE PSALMS

| CHARACTERISTICS | SELECTED PASSAGES |
|---|---|
| Anger | 5:6; 6:1; 27:9; 30:5; 73:20; 76:7,10; 89:38; 103:8; 106:29,32,40; 108:11; 145:8 |
| Avenger | 9:12; 24:5; 26:1; 53:5; 58:6; 59:4; 68:21-25; 72:4; 86:17; 112:8; 139:19 |
| Creator | 8:3; 24:2; 78:69; 86:9; 93:1; 95:4; 96:5; 119:73; 90–91; 121:2; 124:8; 136:5-9 |
| Deliverer (Savior) | 7:1,10; 9:14; 24:5; 27:9; 37:39; 39:8; 71:2; 80:2; 119:41, 94, 123,146, 173; 132:16 |
| Faithful | 40:10; 54:5; 91:4; 92:2; 94:14; 98:3; 100:5; 115:1; 119:75; 143:1 |
| Forgiving | 25:11; 32:5; 65:3; 78:38; 79:9; 85:2; 86:5; 99:8; 103:3,12; 130:3-4 |
| Glory | 8:1; 24:7; 26:8; 29:1; 63:2; 66:2; 79:9; 89:17; 97:6; 106:20; 113:4; 115:1; 138:5 |
| Good | 13:6; 25:7; 27:13; 31:19; 34:8; 73:1; 86:5,17; 100:5; 106:1; 119:65, 68; 125:4; 145:7,9 |
| Gracious | 67:1; 86:15; 103:8; 111:4; 112:4; 116:5; 119:58; 145:8 |
| Healer | 6:2; 30:2; 103:3; 107:20; 147:3 |
| Holy | 20:6; 22:3; 29:2; 30:4; 68:5,35; 71:22; 77:13; 78:41; 89:18,35; 99:3,5,9 |
| Jealous | 78:58; 79:5 |
| Judge | 7:8,11; 9:4,7-8; 50:4,6; 75:2,7; 98:9; 103:6; 110:6 |
| Justice | 7:6; 9:8,16; 33:5; 36:6; 67:4; 96:10; 99:4; 101:1; 103:6; 140:12 |
| King | 5:2; 9:7; 11:4; 44:4; 47:2-9; 66:7; 68:16,24; 74:12; 89:14; 96:10; 97:1; 145:1,11-13; 145:1,11-13 |
| Living | 18:46; 42:2; 84:2 |

| THE CHARACTERISTICS OF GOD PRESENTED IN THE PSALMS | |
|---|---|
| **CHARACTERISTICS** | **SELECTED PASSAGES** |
| Love | 6:4; 21:7; 25:6; 47:4; 48:9; 52:8; 60:5; 62:12; 66:20; 98:3; 103:4,8,11,17; 106:1,45; 117:2; 119:41,64 |
| Majesty | 8:1; 68:34; 76:4; 93:1; 96:6; 104:1; 111:3; 145:5 |
| Mercy | 4:1; 5:7; 9:13; 26:11; 30:10; 31:9; 41:4,10; 57:1; 78:38; 116:1 |
| Only God | 18:31; 35:10; 73:25; 95:3; 96:4-5; 97:7; 113:5; 135:5 |
| Perfect | 18:30; 92:15 |
| Present | 16:11; 23:4; 35:22; 38:21; 48:3; 73:23; 89:15; 105:4; 110:5; 114:7; 139:7-12 |
| Protector | 3:3; 5:11; 7:10; 33:20; 66:9; 97:10; 115:9; 127:1; 145:20 |
| Provider | 67:6; 68:9; 78:23-29; 81:16; 85:12; 107:9,35-38; 132:15; 136:25; 144:12-15; 145:15 |
| Redeemer | 19:14; 25:22; 107:2; 119:134,154; 130:8 |
| Refuge, Rock | 7:1; 14:6; 19:14; 27:1; 28:1; 42:9; 62:1,8; 73:28; 89:26; 91:2,9; 92:15; 118:8 |
| Repent | 90:13; 106:45 |
| Righteousness | 4:1; 11:7; 36:6; 50:6; 72:1; 89:14; 96:13; 111:3; 119:40; 129:4 |
| Shepherd | 23:1; 28:9; 74:1; 77:20; 78:52; 79:13; 80:1; 95:7; 100:3 |
| Spirit | 51:11; 104:30; 139:7; 143:10 |
| Universal | 24:1; 50:1,12; 59:13; 65:2,5; 66:4; 68:32; 69:34; 86:9; 96:1,7; 99:2-3; 100:1; 138:4; 150:6 |
| Wisdom | 104:24; 136:5; 147:5 |
| Wonder Worker | 40:5; 46:8; 65:5; 66:3,5; 68:7-8; 72:18; 73:28; 74:13; 78:4; 81:10; 86:8,10; 98:1; 107:8,15; 135:8-9; 136:4,10-16; 145:4 |

## HUMAN CHARACTERISTICS PRESENTED IN THE PSALMS

| CHARACTERISTICS | SELECTED PASSAGES |
| --- | --- |
| Afflicted, Poor, Needy | 12:5; 14:6; 22:26; 25:16; 34:2,6; 49:2; 68:5,10; 72:2; 74:19; 76:9; 82:3; 113:7; 136:23; 145:14 |
| Anger | 37:8; 124:3; 138:7; 139:21-22 |
| Blessed | 1:1; 2:12; 3:8; 5:12; 24:5; 34:8; 41:1; 65:4; 84:4,12; 106:3; 119:1; 129:8; 132:15; 134:3 |
| Confident | 3:5; 4:8; 27:1; 30:6; 41:11; 71:5 |
| Covenant/Partners | 25:10; 50:5,16; 74:20; 78:10,37; 89:3,28,34,39; 103:18; 105:8; 106:45; 111:5,9; 132:12 |
| Death/Sheol | 6:5; 16:10; 23:4; 31:17; 44:22; 49:9-20; 55:4,15,23; 68:20; 78:33,50; 82:7; 103:15; 104:29; 115:17 |
| Enemies | 3:1,7; 4:2; 6:10; 8:2; 9:3; 18:37,48; 27:2; 41:2,7; 66:3; 68:1,21; 78:53,61,66; 81:14; 108:12; 129:1; 132:18 |
| Faithful, Godly | 4:3; 18:25; 26:1; 31:23; 37:28; 73:1; 84:11; 85:10-11; 86:2; 97:10; 101:2; 108:1; 125:4; 139:23-24 |
| Fool, Impious | 14:1; 53:1; 74:18,22; 92:6; 94:8; 107:17 |
| Humans, Mortal | 22:6; 33:13; 49:7; 55:13; 56:4; 62:9; 82:5; 89:47; 115:16; 133:1; 139:16; 146:3 |
| Joy | 4:7; 16:9; 20:5; 21:1; 27:6; 28:7; 34:2; 47:1; 48:11; 53:6; 63:11; 68:3; 81:1; 90:14; 98:4; 100:1; 107:22; 145:7 |

## HUMAN CHARACTERISTICS PRESENTED IN THE PSALMS

| CHARACTERISTICS | SELECTED PASSAGES |
| --- | --- |
| King of Israel/ Anointed | 2:2,6-8; 20:6; 28:8; 45:1-9; 61:6; 63:11; 78:70; 84:9; 92:10; 122:5; 144:10 |
| Kings of Earth | 33:16; 48:4; 68:12; 76:12; 94:20; 102:15; 106:41; 110:5; 119:23,46,161; 138:4; 146:3; 149:8 |
| Loving God | 5:11; 18:1; 69:36; 70:4; 91:14; 97:10; 116:1; 119:132; 145:20 |
| Nations/Peoples | 9:5,15,19; 22:27; 44:11; 46:6; 59:5; 67:2; 68:30; 72:17; 78:55; 82:8; 99:1-2; 105:1,13; 110:6 |
| Righteous | 5:12; 11:5; 14:5; 15:2; 17:1,15; 18:20; 23:3; 33:1; 34:15; 37:6,12,16,21,25,30; 55:22; 58:10; 68:3; 72:2; 92:12; 97:11; 106:31; 125:3; 142:7; 146:8 |
| Sacrifice | 4:5; 51:16,19; 107:22 |
| Sin | 5:10; 14:3; 19:13; 25:7; 36:1-2; 51:1,5,13; 52:2; 58:3; 66:18; 68:21; 89:32; 99:8; 103:10,12; 106:6,13-39,43; 107:11,17 |
| Suffering/Afflicted | 22:24; 31:7; 38:3; 41:3; 55:3; 119:50,107,153 |
| Trust | 4:5; 9:10; 13:5; 20:7; 21:7; 22:4,9; 28:7; 37:3; 40:3; 52:8; 62:8; 84:12; 112:7; 115:9; 116:10; 125:1 |
| Wicked | 5:4; 6:8; 7:9,14; 11:2; 23:4; 26:5; 27:2; 32:10; 52:1; 53:1,4; 55:3; 58:3; 59:2; 68:2; 73:3; 82:4; 84:10; 94:3,13,16,23; 104:35; 107:34,42; 119:53,95,119,150,155; 147:6 |
| Wisdom | 90:12; 107:43; 111:10; 119:98 |

## PSALM 10

In every age believers are dismayed at the impunity of the violent, the criminal, the vile, and the ungodly. But God remains the hope of the hopeless. He knows our troubles.

## PSALM 11

The psalmist was aware of the power of evil men but rejected all counsel of despair. He awaited judgment from God. Seated on His throne, God is in control.

## PSALM 12

Truth is trampled underfoot in a corrupt society, and words are only tools of self-interest. But the certain word of God, given in an oraclelike response in 12:5, contrasts with the empty words of people.

## PSALM 13

David's trials were such that he wondered how long he could hold on. But trials produce endurance, and the outcome is joy and singing.

## PSALM 14

God sees the folly and vice of those who live as though He did not exist and declares His anger at those who abuse His people. To treat people as objects of plunder is to be a practical atheist and to invite judgment.

## PSALM 15

Only those who are morally qualified may dwell with God. Anyone who would claim to be God's must be free of slander and greed.

## PSALM 16

Security comes only by trust in the one true God rather than in the many false gods. "Libations of blood" could refer to ceremonies involving human sacrifice or ceremonies in which some blood was poured out and the rest was drunk. Peter cited 16:8-11 and interpreted it as a prophecy of the resurrection in Acts 2:25-31.

## PSALM 17

David asserted his innocence as a prerequisite to his prayer for deliverance from his enemies. He did not claim sinless perfection in 17:3-5, nor did he deny the universal sinfulness of humanity. But he understood that he could not expect God to save him from his enemies if he cherished deceit or violence in his own life.

## PSALM 18

As the superscript says, David gave thanks for the many victories God had given him. In 18:7-15 David described the fury of the Lord in terms reminiscent of the Sinai appearance. Similar language is also found in the ancient Canaanite texts from Ugarit in Syria. David saw his salvation not as personal or private but claimed that God moved heaven and earth—that He set His great power in motion—to save him. God's vindication of David extends to his whole dynasty and thus to the Messiah.

## PSALM 19

God's revelation through nature and through Scripture each have their place. The natural world gives plain evidence of the glory and power of God (see Rom. 1:19-20). The law, however, goes beyond that and instructs and revives the human heart.

Walking in this light, the believer is moved to seek divine forgiveness and approval.

## PSALM 20

The king's victory depended not on his cavalry but on his piety and the power of God. All his people would rejoice to see him return in triumph.

## PSALM 21

Because God had established the Davidic king, the king trusted Him for victory as he went out to meet his foes. The total victory of the king anticipates the messianic judgment.

## PSALM 22

This psalm follows the pattern of many individual complaint psalms in that it begins with a cry for help and concludes in assurance of deliverance with a promise to fulfill vows. The triumphant conclusion is unusually long. David's situation is a type of the sufferings and resurrection of Christ. The psalm anticipates Christ's outcry from the cross (Matt. 27:46), the mockery He received (Luke 23:35), His pain and thirst (John 19:28), the piercing of His hands and feet, and the casting of lots for His clothes (John 19:23-24). But it also looks forward to His victory and the coming of people from all nations to submit to Him. (See "Christ in the Psalms.")

## PSALM 23

The pastoral serenity of the psalm has made it a favorite of generations of readers. Verse 6 contains an implicit promise of eternal life.

## PSALM 24

Worshipers may have chanted this hymn as they entered the temple. Verses 3-6 list the qualifications for entering God's congregation. The hymn may have been antiphonal, with the congregation asking the questions and the priest or choir chanting the body of the psalm.

## PSALM 25

Once again David prayed for deliverance, but here he confessed his sinfulness rather than protested his innocence. He desired his forgiveness to take the concrete form of salvation from personal foes. The overall tone of the psalm is of confident assurance in God's mercy. The psalm is acrostic.

## PSALM 26

Although this psalm is in the form of a "negative confession" (see Job 31), it is not a prideful boast on the psalmist's part (as in Luke 18:11-12). Rather, it teaches the kind of life one must follow to be a part of God's assembly.

## PSALM 27

True righteousness is above all love for God and the joy of worship. The one who so loves God is secure even in the tribulations of life because he or she is accepted in the arms of God.

## PSALM 28

The psalmist prayed for mercy for himself even as he prayed that God would punish evildoers. This came not from selfishness but a profound sense of right and wrong. For those who hate Him to go unpunished would be a perversion of God's justice.

## PSALM 29

A terrible storm displays the power of God. The thunder and rain (29:3), lightning, and wind all speak of His power. It provokes His people to praise.

## PSALM 30

God's anger against His children is for only a moment, but His favor is forever. David confessed, "Thou hast drawn me up" like a bucket from a well. David proclaimed the danger of complacency and the value of prayer.

## PSALM 31

David professed his confidence in God and only then voiced his complaint. He mixed his appeal with trust and concluded in praise and encouragement for others. Compare 31:5 to Luke 23:46; the sufferings of David typify the sufferings of Christ. David prayed that the wicked might lie silent in the grave so that they could no longer slander him. (See

## VENGEANCE AND VINDICATION

Sensitive readers of the Psalms have long been troubled by the harsh expression of vengeance uttered by psalmists, often attributed to David himself. Take for example the statements: "Break the arm of the wicked and evil man: call him to account for his wickedness" (Ps. 10:15); "Let the wicked be put to shame and lie silent in the grave" (Ps. 31:17); "Break the teeth in their mouths. . . . The righteous will be glad when they are avenged, when they bathe their feet in the blood of the wicked" (Ps. 58:6-10). Such unloving statements raise serious ethical questions about the vindictive spirit reflected in these statements. Other prominent curses are found in Psalms 3:7; 5:10; 28:4; 35; 40:14-15; 55; 69; 79; 109; 137; 139:19-22; 140:9-10. Attempts to explain such fierce expressions fall into several categories.

First, some think that these curses only reflect the humanity of the author expressing his deepest desires for vindication when wronged by the wicked. Thus, he was reflecting a lower standard of morality than that found in the New Testament. This explanation does not adequately account for the fact that the verses in which these curses occur are inspired by the very God who taught the virtue of turning the other cheek.

We must also recognize that 1 Samuel portrays David in a very different light. Although provoked almost beyond imagination, David did not respond vengefully but by tolerance and patience. The occasions on which David refused to kill his mortal enemy Saul provide eloquent testimony to this. Furthermore, Leviticus 19:18 forbids any attempt to exact vengeance against personal enemies, arguing against interpreting these curses as personal vendettas.

Second, another explanation sees the curses as only predictions of the enemy's ruin rather than as expressions of the psalmist's desire that the enemy meet an unhappy end. But Psalm 59 is clearly a prayer to God in which the psalmist asks God to wreak havoc on his enemies.

A plausible understanding of these difficult sayings must take account of the significant role enemies play in the Book of Psalms. Their presence goes far beyond the relatively limited number of psalms that curse the psalmist's enemies. The psalmists were often kings or represented the king in some official capacity. God mandated Israel's king to rule over God's covenant people in order to safeguard them and all God had promised to do through them.

Thus, any threat to God's people was also a threat to the very promise of God. In this unique situation, to oppose the God-anointed king was to oppose God Himself. So the king/psalmist prayed that God would judge those evildoers who intended to hinder the work of God, desiring that God and His work on earth would be vindicated.

Because of the unique position held by the king as God's anointed, he represented God's will in a measure unlike that of anyone today. For this reason believers today must not pray curses, for they are not in a position like that of the king/psalmist in ancient Israel.

"Vengeance and Vindication in the Psalms.")

## PSALM 32

The theme and lesson of the psalm is followed by a personal testimony to its truth and further encouragement and exhortation. Paul cited 32:1-2 in Romans 4:7-8. Forgiveness is by God's sovereign mercy, and righteousness comes from faith in Christ rather than by human effort. At the same time, those who genuinely confess live in true obedience rather than mule-headed stubbornness.

## PSALM 33

After an opening exhortation to praise the body of the hymn is taken up with the reasons God should be praised. God's power in creation merges into His sovereign control of human history. National security is in the Lord, not in military power. A communal profession of trust and a prayer conclude the psalm.

## PSALM 34

This psalm is an acrostic. Its primary purpose is to teach the hearer moral lessons about God. The personal testimony is in 34:4-6. The rest of the psalm is made of theological proverbs. The theme is God's continuous care for His own. The psalm does not say that the righteous have no troubles but that God delivers them from their troubles.

## PSALM 35

In this prayer David called down curses on his enemies for their treachery and malice. Above all, David condemned false friendship and ingratitude. The angel of the Lord appears in the psalms only here and in 34:7. (See "Vengeance and Vindication in the Psalms.")

## PSALM 36

This psalm is an "oracle" (a word usually used of prophetic utterances) on the nature of human sin. The wicked continue to love evil even though they too depend on God, the Creator, for life. But their fate is sure.

## PSALM 37

The righteous should not be dismayed over the apparent prosperity of the wicked, for it is fleeting. This psalm, like many passages in Proverbs, reinforces this truth through descriptions of the kindness of the righteous, the fierceness of the wicked, and their respective fates. In addition, it uses personal observation and exhortation.

## PSALM 38

David confessed his sin, described his pain, and complained about his false friends and gloating enemies. The wounds and sickness he mentioned were literal and not symbolic. His isolation and silence were like that of Christ in the passion (see Isa. 53:7 and Mark 14:61). In his pain he saw that his only help was God. (See "Christ in the Psalms.")

## PSALM 39

The meditative silence of a righteous man pondering the brevity of life gives this psalm a quality of distress like that of Job 7. He had been afflicted by God and longed for restoration. He could never again be secure in his possessions and mortal life, for he now saw how transitory they were.

## PSALM 40

This psalm, which begins like an individual song of thanksgiving, becomes a cry for help in 40:9-17. David believed that God would save him again as He had before. Hebrews 10:5-10 cites Psalm 40:6-8 and interprets it as Christ's fulfillment and abolition of the Old Testament sacrificial system. The Hebrew phrase "you have dug ears for me" in 40:6 is difficult. The verb "dug" is often translated "pierced" as in the ritual of Exodus 21:6. But that is unlikely since a different verb is used there and only one ear was pierced. It probably means you opened my ears in the sense you made me obedient (see Isa. 50:5; Jer. 6:10). The Septuagint, followed by Hebrews 10:5, has "a body you have prepared for me."

## PSALM 41

The malice and hypocritical love of his enemies continues to dominate David's psalms of complaint. As in Psalm 38, he spoke here of his own sin and illness. And again David's isolation in suffering, typical of the righteous, was prophetic of the Messiah's affliction (see John 13:18). (See "Christ in the Psalms.")

## PSALM 42

The exact nature of the psalmist's distress is not given, but it brought him to a state of deep depression. Yet he focused not on his trouble but on God and thirsted for God as for water ( Matt. 5:6).

## PSALM 43

Psalms 42 and 43 may have originally been a single psalm. The thought and language of the two are very similar (compare 43:5 to 42:5,11), and the Hebrew meter is the same. Also Psalm 43 has no superscript.

## PSALM 44

God's present abandonment of the nation contrasts with His former mighty presence among them. With remarkable boldness the people call on God to fight for them again.

## PSALM 45

The composition celebrates the wedding of a king of the house of David. Psalm 45:1-9 praises the king, and 45:10-17 instructs and praises the princess-bride. Christians have long seen here an image of Christ and the church (compare 45:6-7 to Heb. 1:8). (See "Christ in the Psalms.")

## PSALM 46

The kingdom of God is like a mighty fortress against which the waters, which here as often in Psalms represent chaos and death, have no power. The psalm looks forward to the eternal reign of God in the new earth but celebrates the present reign of God in this troubled world.

## PSALM 47

Someday, the psalm promises, even the Gentile nations will come and worship the God of Abraham. This has been completely fulfilled in Christ's church.

## PSALM 48

The psalm praises Jerusalem as a type of visible manifestation of the reign of God. The city was glorious and awesome and God made it secure. There God's people think on His love.

## PSALM 49

This psalm draws on themes used extensively in Ecclesiastes. Among these are the transitory nature of life (Eccl. 3:18-21) and the limitations of learning and wealth (Eccl. 2:15-16; 5:8-17). Psalm 49:15 is a clear promise of the resurrection.

## PSALM 50

God here judges the world in a way very similar to the judgment described in Matthew 25:31-46. He accepts the righteous but not because of their sacrificial animals, for which God has no need. He then exhorts them to true piety. The wicked are condemned for theft, adultery, and other sins.

## PSALM 51

This profound plea for forgiveness was written, according to the superscript, after David committed adultery with Bathsheba and murdered her husband. "In sin my mother conceived me" (KJV) may mean that as David's mother and father were sinners, so was he. Or it may mean that he had been sinful from birth. It does not mean that the act of procreation was itself evil.

## PSALM 52

The psalmist taunted a godless and cruel individual for his behavior and asserted that his end was near. He did not ask God to avenge his personal loss but claimed that the godless person would be destroyed for his arrogance and lying.

## PSALM 53

This psalm is almost identical to Psalm 14.

## PSALM 54

The treachery of the Ziphites is described in 1 Samuel 23:19-23; 26:1. As in other psalms, David was so certain of God's help that he vowed a thanksgiving offering.

## PSALM 55

This is the strongest statement in the psalter on the cruelty of false friendship. In Psalm 11:1 the psalmist rejected counsel of flight, but here he was so discouraged by betrayal he longed for it.

## PSALM 56

On the incident at Gath, see 1 Samuel 21:10-15. In structure this psalm is chiastic. (See the introduction to "Psalms.") Between the initial call for help and the concluding vow are two assertions of trust in God. At the center of the psalm is a call for deliverance from the enemy.

## PSALM 57

Praying for help changes the psalmist's attitude from despair to exultant confidence. Surrounded by persons of animal violence, he could sing out joyfully to God.

## PSALM 58

The evil of those who misuse their power for personal gain is here graphically portrayed. They are evil from birth, incorrigible snakes, and ravenous as lions. Their deaths will be as little lamented as that of a slug in the sun. Faith in God is vindicated when they are destroyed.

## PSALM 59

People are instructed when God makes an example of the wicked. This is brought about not by their sudden death but by their gradual and visible demise. In this their true character as wild dogs destined for an ignoble death is clear to all.

## PSALM 60

This psalm is a prayer for victory in battle, but it complains of God's apparent abandonment of His people. God's election of Israel contrasts with His rejection of its neighbors. Shechem and Succoth were on opposite sides of the Jordan and together represent God's (that is, Israel's) ownership of the entire territory.

## PSALM 61

Many seek sanctuary from the weariness and struggles of life. But that asylum is found only in the Rock that is higher and stronger than any human. The prayer for the king to have an eternal reign is fulfilled perfectly in the Son of David, Christ.

## PSALM 62

Trust in God and Him alone. He is like a fortress in that He protects against all who are hostile. People will fail (the Hebrew text reads, "Humans are worthless [as an object of trust]; people are a lie"). Riches are no security. A numeric saying, familiar in wisdom literature, concludes the psalm (see Prov. 30:21-23).

## PSALM 63

So profound was his love for God that even in a desert the psalmist longed for Him rather than water. The worship of God is better than the most delicious food. At night he thought on God rather than sleep (63:6). He stayed close to God in the knowledge that he was safe there.

## PSALM 64

No one is capable of foreseeing and protecting himself or herself from all the plots of evildoers. Only God is a sufficient defense. He turns the schemes of the cruel and the criminal back on their own heads.

## PSALM 65

This song may have been sung in the temple as part of a thanksgiving for a good harvest. The occasion of its singing may have been the Feast of Unleavened Bread at the beginning of the barley harvest or at Pentecost after the general harvest.

## PSALM 66

After a general praise to God and thanks for His deliverance of Israel in the exodus the psalmist testified to his personal

## CHRIST IN THE PSALMS

One of the most controversial questions facing interpreters of the Book of Psalms is how to understand the many references to the "king" or "anointed one" (*Messiah*). Do these references speak of a human king of ancient Israel or point ahead to Jesus as the ideal King and Messiah?

The biblical writers wrote of real-life persons and situations. The king played a most prominent role in ancient Israel's national life. Over sixty references in the Psalms highlight the king's prestige. The original readers of the psalms naturally understood that these references spoke of the human king, whose role was so very important in their day-to-day existence. Because the basic meaning of any text is what the author intended the

original audience to understand, "king" in the Psalms refers primarily to a human king of ancient Israel.

It may be possible for references to the "king" or "anointed one" to both speak of a human king and point ahead to Jesus as the ideal One.

The only clear passage that describes a human king in its Old Testament context who is seen as the ideal messianic King in a subsequent text is Psalm 2. (Hebrews 1:5 treats this psalm as explicitly messianic.) Thus the human king in Psalm 2 functioned as a type, that is, one who had significance in his own historical setting but who also served as a divinely ordained foreshadowing of someone in later biblical revelation.

Generally speaking, references to the king in Psalms speak of the human king in the biblical writer's time. Occasionally, reference to the king was origi-

nally understood as a human king but later applied to the ideal Messiah. In one psalm (Ps. 110) the king can mean none other than the ideal messianic King of kings.

The superscription of Psalm 110 portrays it as Davidic. Surprisingly, the first verse speaks of David's successor as his lord. In ancient Israel this was inconceivable. David was the greatest king, the standard by which his successors were measured. Early in Israel's history this passage was understood as a prophecy of the coming Messiah. Jesus interpreted Psalm 110:1 in this way in a dispute with the Pharisees (Matt. 22:41-45; Mark 12:35-37; Luke 20:41-44). Jesus' riddle—If "David himself calls him 'Lord,' how can he be his son?"—captures the mystery of the incarnation. Jesus is the Son of David but also more than David's son (Rom. 1:3-4).

experience of God's grace. The historical experience of the whole community was repeated in the individual life of the believer.

## PSALM 67

The psalm is built upon the priestly blessing of Numbers 6:24-26.

## PSALM 68

The people praised God for His protection of Israel and for the victories they had received. Israel's triumph over its enemies typified God's final triumph in Christ over all the powers. Paul cited 68:18 to that effect (Eph. 4:8).

## PSALM 69

David typified the suffering of the righteous believer at the hands of the godless,

but this concept finds its fullest expression in the travails of Christ (compare 69:9 to John 2:17 and Ps. 69:21 to Matt. 27:34,48). (See "Christ in the Psalms.")

## PSALM 70

Compare Psalm 40:13-17. The brevity of this psalm matches the urgency of its tone. It is a call to God in a desperate moment.

## PSALM 71

The psalmist, aware that he was aging and his strength was failing, called on God to walk with him as he entered this period of life. Prior experience told him that God would continue to be faithful.

## PSALM 72

The superscript should be translated *For Solomon* since 72:20 implies that the psalm was by David. The song is a prayer for Solomon's coronation. It is based on 2 Samuel 7 and typifies the messianic reign. God's king was to exhibit righteousness, justice, and concern for the poor and oppressed.

## PSALM 73

The psalmist wondered how the wicked could impudently flaunt God's ways and thrive (see Job 21). He wondered if his piety had been for nothing. But he came to understand that God sustained him, not his own will, and that grace would lead him to eternal glory.

## PSALM 74

The psalm was probably written shortly after the Babylonian exile began. The people mourned the destruction of the temple. Remembering God's triumph over chaos at creation (Gen. 1:2), they prayed for God to defeat the enemy that conquered them and to restore the order of the temple.

## PSALM 75

God's determination to judge the earth and punish the wicked is certain. Verse 8 is a familiar prophetic image (see Isa. 51:17; Jer. 25:15-29; 49:12; 51:7).

## PSALM 76

Victory over one of Israel's enemies portrayed here typifies the final victory of God over all earthly powers.

## PSALM 77

Although voiced by an individual, these laments relate to the whole nation and not one person. Compare 77:16-19 to 74:13-17, which alludes to God's victory over the precreation chaos. Here the reference is to the exodus.

## PSALM 78

This psalm recites the events of the exodus, as recorded in the law, and ties the continual rebellion of the Israelites to the secession of the Northern Kingdom (Ephraim) from the house of David.

## PSALM 79

Like Psalm 74, this was apparently written in the Babylonian exile. Unlike the former lament, this psalm emphasizes the plight of the people rather than the destruction of the temple.

## PSALM 80

This psalm again laments the Babylonian captivity and calls on God to remember His former election of Israel. The image of the vine reappears in the prophets (Isa. 5:1-7; Ezek. 15).

## PSALM 81

This psalm begins like a hymn but moves to a long oracle of exhortation from God. It may have been sung at Passover or Tabernacles. Tabernacles was celebrated from the fifteenth of the month, at full moon.

## PSALM 82

God accuses the "gods" of having misgoverned the world. The identity of these "gods" is hard to determine. Some interpret them as spiritual powers that rule the world and others as human judges. But these alternatives are not mutually exclusive. Probably the human powers are treated as the earthly counterparts to spiritual forces (see Col. 1:16). God has determined to judge the powers and rulers who maintain a world system of oppression and injustice.

## PSALM 83

The psalmist listed the nations that he desired to see punished. The psalm likely was written sometime between 900 and 600 B.C., when Assyria was still a threat.

The psalm is not a mere cry for vengeance. Rather, it is a plea for the righteous God to demonstrate His sovereignty by defending His chosen people.

## PSALM 84

The singer celebrates the joy of worship in God's house. The "valley of Baca" was apparently along the path the worshipers took to the temple.

## PSALM 85

The problem the people faced is unclear. They prayed in an optimistic way, sure of God's help; for His love is unfailing.

## PSALM 86

The psalmist based this appeal on the kindness and universal power of God.

## PSALM 87

God has determined to bring even the Gentiles into His kingdom. "This one was born in Zion" means that the Gentile has been adopted into the covenant.

## PSALM 88

The sage Heman "the Ezrahite" is perhaps the same as the son of Zerah in 1 Chronicles 2:6 (see 1 Kgs. 4:31). This psalm shows remarkable parallels to Job, especially in the psalmist's personal affliction and abandonment.

## PSALM 89

Ethan the Ezrahite was possibly the brother of Heman (Ps. 88; see 1 Kgs. 4:31; 1 Chr. 2:6), but the psalm may have been written as late as the exile. It laments that although God made an eternal covenant with the house of David (see 2 Sam. 7), the dynasty now seemed abandoned.

## PSALM 90

In this psalm the community called on God for mercy, but in the tradition of wisdom literature the song strongly emphasizes the shortness of human life.

## PSALM 91

God extends the promise of protection to all who turn to Him. Contrary to Satan's interpretation (Matt. 4:6), Psalm 91:11-12 does not allow reckless behavior.

## PSALM 92

In 92:10 "you have exalted my horn" means that God had given the singer victory. "Fine oils are poured upon me" means that God had lavished favor upon him. The image of the righteous person as a flourishing tree is common in the Bible (see Ps. 1).

## PSALM 93

The permanence of the Lord's reign is the security of all who trust in Him. The pounding of the waves represents the power of death and destruction, but God's eternal regime controls all things. And as God's rule is eternal, so also are His statutes.

## PSALM 94

Distress over the crimes of the wicked gives way to confidence in God's justice. The psalm calls for patience and endurance.

## PSALM 95

Because God is sovereign over all, we must submit to His demand for obedience. Hebrews 3:7–4:11 expounds this psalm in detail. (See "Christ in the Psalms.")

## PSALM 96

The Lord God of Israel rules over all the earth, and all its peoples must bow to Him. This is the great missionary song of the Bible.

## PSALM 97

The power of the Lord is awesome enough to melt even the mountains. Israel can rejoice that its God is greater than all idols and so-called gods. For His people, God's fury promotes not terror but joy.

## PSALM 98

This psalm is a variant of Psalm 96 and follows the same missionary theme. All the world, not Israel alone, must submit to the Lord.

## PSALM 99

The Lord of heaven and earth has chosen Israel as His people and from them has taken His priests and prophets. All the nations, therefore, should acknowledge Him as the sole God and worship at His mountain.

## PSALM 100

The people may have chanted this psalm as they entered the temple or began their worship.

## PSALM 101

In resolving to remain faithful to God, the psalmist especially pledged to keep himself from association with evil men and abide with the righteous. He knew how strong the influence of others could be.

## PSALM 102

This psalm may have been written in the exile. The outcry of the psalmist is individual in perspective but concerns not a private problem but the destruction of Zion.

## PSALM 103

The people praise God for His compassion and forgiveness of sins. Verses 14-18 imply the eternal life of the believer. We are not by nature immortal, but God does not abandon us to death.

## PSALM 104

All creation testifies to the goodness and power of God. This psalm is based on Genesis 1:3-19.

## PSALM 105

This psalm recites the history of the Israelites from the patriarchs to the exodus as a reason for praise. Note the positive tone of the song. Contrary to Psalm 106

(which covers the same history) the sins of Israel are not mentioned. These two psalms form a pair. Psalm 105 ends where Psalm 106 begins: "Praise the Lord!"

## PSALM 106

This psalm praises God by reciting Israel's history from the exodus to the judges' time. God forgave many rebellions. Israel failed to believe at the Red Sea (Exod. 14:10-12). They complained about food in the wilderness (Ps. 106:13-15; Num. 11). Dathan and Abiram rebelled (Num. 16). Israel worshiped the golden calf (Exod. 32). They proved cowards at Kadesh-Barnea (Num. 14). Israel joined Moabite women in sexual sin and idolatry (Num. 25). Israel complained at Meribah (Num. 20:1-13). They accepted Canaanite ways (see Josh. 23) and repeated apostasy in the judges' time (Judg. 1:16).

## PSALM 107

Those who have suffered and then have seen God's salvation all have reason to praise God. This includes homeless aliens; war captives; those punished for their sin with personal illness; and those who have encountered dangers on the sea, famine, and other afflictions.

## PSALM 108

Verses 1-5 are from Psalm 57:7-11, and verses 6-13 are from Psalm 60:5-12.

## PSALM 109

The massive curse on the enemy is founded not on personal vendetta but rather on a sense of justice. (See "Vengeance and Vindication in the Psalms.")

## PSALM 110

This prayer for the Davidic king typologically portrays the glory of the ultimate Davidic King, the Messiah. He is a Lord above even His father David (Matt. 22:41-46) and a priest though not of the

Levitical line (Ps. 110:4; Heb. 7:11-28). He is victor over all His enemies. (See "Christ in the Psalms.")

## PSALM 111

This general song of praise in acrostic form ends with the motto of biblical wisdom (see Prov. 1:7). Here we see the Old Testament proclamation of God's love and grace.

## PSALM 112

This acrostic psalm develops the praise of the Lord entirely along the lines of wisdom literature. (Compare the fates of the righteous and wicked in Prov. 10:3-30).

## PSALM 113

Compare this to the Song of Hannah in 1 Samuel 2:1-10.

## PSALM 114

The congregation praised God for the exodus and conquest. The seas and mountains represent the apparently unconquerable earthly power opposed to Israel.

## PSALM 115

This psalm mocks idols (and those who worship them) in the spirit of Isaiah 40:18-20 and 44:6-20.

## PSALM 116

Compare 116:3 to Jonah 2:5, in another individual song of thanksgiving.

## PSALM 117

Opening and concluding exhortations to praise the Lord envelop the reason He ought to be praised: His enduring love.

## PSALM 118

An individual sang his thanks to God as the congregation responded with praise. Jesus took 118:22 as a prophecy of His rejection by the Jewish leaders (Matt. 21:42). (See "Christ in the Psalms.")

## PSALM 119

This massive psalm is a song in honor of the law. It is in twenty-two eight-verse stanzas, which are organized in acrostic order. Each verse of each unit begins with the same letter. This made the psalm easier to memorize.

## PSALM 120

The peace-loving psalmist was distressed at the slanders spoken against him but was certain that God would save him. Meshech was in Anatolia near the Black Sea, but Kedar was in Arabia. The psalmist did not literally live in these places. The names represent distant barbarian and pagan lands and picture his enemies.

## PSALM 121

Pilgrims going to Jerusalem may have sung this prayer for safety in the journey. The dangers along the way—accidents, wild animals, robbers, heat stroke—are implied in 121:3-6. The "sun" and "moon" represent all the dangers of day and night. A safe trip is promised in 121:7-8.

## PSALM 122

The pilgrims going up to Jerusalem here prayed for the security of the city and the house of David. The city was sacred because God's temple was there.

## PSALM 123

The worshipers in the temple prayed on behalf of their nation. The touching metaphor in 123:2 vividly portrays the people's dependence on God.

## PSALM 124

The people gave thanks for having escaped conquest at the hands of their enemies. The two images of a flood and a bird in a trap portray the helplessness they felt.

## PSALM 125

The psalmist rejoiced in the enduring security of Zion and its people but prayed that God would provide just rulers. God's people were secure in Him but groaned because of the evil powers among whom they dwelt.

## PSALM 126

This touching song may have been sung by the returnees from the Babylonian captivity. It is both a hymn of thanksgiving for restoration to Zion and a prayer for restored prosperity.

## PSALM 127

This psalm acclaims the value of family life under God. Working to the point of fatigue for the sake of one's family is useless; it is better to trust God and be able to rest in His care and protection. When living in God's care, children are not a nuisance or a burden but a gift.

## PSALM 128

This psalm may have been recited as a blessing upon a groom in a wedding ceremony. ("You" and "your" are masculine singular in Hebrew.) The prayer for sons, long life, and prosperity is natural in such a setting. The vine represents not only the wife's fruitfulness but also her cheerfulness (Judg. 9:13) and feminine beauty (Song 7:8).

## PSALM 129

Israel had suffered mightily under the Egyptians, Philistines, Assyrians, Babylonians, and others; but it had survived. Its enemies were cursed with a prayer that they become as insubstantial and insignificant as dried grass on the housetops.

## PSALM 130

The psalmist did not clarify the nature of his troubles or explicitly confess any sin. But he was aware of his sinfulness and need for grace. The closing could suggest this was not a private but a national complaint, but many psalms conclude with a prayer for Israel. The repetition of "more

than watchmen wait for the morning" in 130:6 heightens the sense of longing.

## PSALM 131

The psalmist testified to the tranquility of the one trusting God and exhorted others to trust as well.

## PSALM 132

As the people prayed for the house of David and the temple, they cited God's promises.

## PSALM 133

The image of brotherly unity being like the oil that runs down Aaron's beard is striking. Unity is God's gift and a sacred duty.

## PSALM 134

This psalm exhorts the priests of the temple to praise God and blesses them for their service.

## PSALM 135

This psalm praises the God of Israel for creation and the exodus and conquest. It mocks the foolishness of idol worshipers.

## PSALM 136

Apparently the people responded, "His love endures forever" as the temple priests or choir chanted the body of the psalm. The psalm links the theme of creation to the exodus and conquest. Israel was God's new creation, as miraculous as the first creation.

## PSALM 137

After the beautiful lament of 137:1-6, the reader is jolted by the astonishing ending to the psalm. This brutal blessing shows the Jews' anguish over what had happened to their nation. Other Jews (Daniel, Esther) learned God was with them in the exile.

## PSALM 138

The so-called "gods" of 138:1 may have been supernatural beings who filled

God's heavenly court, or the term may refer to pagan powers and rulers.

## PSALM 139

David praised God for His omniscience and omnipresence. Verses 13-15 draw together the concepts that a person is formed in his or her mother's body and that humans are made from the clay of the earth (Gen. 2:7). Thus we, no less than Adam, are God's creation.

## PSALM 140

David's enemies were out to trap him and especially used slander as their tool.

## PSALM 141

By his willingness to suffer at the hands of the righteous, David showed that he was motivated by integrity and love for God rather than by a selfish desire for personal victory.

## PSALM 142

This psalm follows the normal pattern for the Song of Individual Complaint: introductory affirmation of God's goodness, complaint and appeal, expectation of deliverance, and promise of praise.

## PSALM 143

From beginning to end this psalm is an appeal to God. As part of his plea for help the psalmist also asked for instruction.

## PSALM 144

The martial spirit of this prayer is tempered by the fact that the object of victory is not conquest or military honor but security for the people.

## PSALM 145

Verses 3-7 stress the importance of passing from one generation to the next the tradition of what God has done.

## PSALM 146

It was the duty of the ancient king to be the protector and advocate of the helpless, but many failed in this and instead became oppressors. But God cares for the oppressed, the hurting, and the abandoned. Compare this to Mary's "Magnificat" (Luke 1:46-55).

## PSALM 147

The hymn alternates between praising God as Protector of Israel and as Creator.

## PSALM 148

Heaven and earth and all that is in them are exhorted to praise God.

## PSALM 149

Exuberant, joyful praise of God's people is the weapon by which they conquer all their enemies. Spiritual conflict requires spiritual weapons (see Eph. 6:10-18).

## PSALM 150

The loud, joyful, and exultant tone of this psalm tells us something of the nature of Israel's worship. It could be solemn and grand without tedium or empty pomp. The psalm tells where, for what, how, and by whom the Lord is to be praised.

***Theological Significance.*** The psalms help today's believers to understand God, themselves, and their relationship to God. The psalms picture God as the Creator, who is worthy of praise and is capable of using His creative might to rescue His people from current distress. The psalms picture God as the just Judge of all the world, who rewards the righteous and opposes the wicked. Prayers that God curse the enemies of the psalmist must be understood in part as affirmations of God's justice and the certainty of His judgment. The psalms picture God as the faithful Friend of the oppressed. The psalms offer a refresher course in God's faithfulness throughout Israel's history. The psalms highlight God's promises to David and his descendants, promises that are not finally realized until Christ.

The psalms picture the full range of human emotions: joy, despair, guilt, consolation, love, hate, thankfulness, and dissatisfaction. The psalms thus remind us that all of life is under God's lordship. The psalms likewise illustrate the broad range of human responses to God: praise, confession, pleas for help, thanksgiving. The psalms thus serve as a source book for Christian worship, both public and private.

## Questions for Reflection

1. How can we use the Torah psalms and Wisdom psalms for personal growth?

2. In what ways does the Davidic king in Psalms point forward to Christ?

3. How can the hymns in Psalms be used to enhance our corporate worship?

4. Do the psalms of complaint have any place in our prayer life today? If so, how are they to be used?

## Sources for Additional Study

Alden, Robert L. *Psalms*. 3 Vols. Chicago: Moody, 1975.

Kidner, Derek. *Psalms*. 2 Vols. Downers Grove: InterVarsity, 1975.

Weiser, Artur. *The Psalms*. Philadelphia: Westminster, 1962.

Wiersbe, Warren W. *Meet Yourself in the Psalms*. Wheaton: Victor, 1983.

# PROVERBS

I n spite of its name, the Book of Proverbs is more than a collection of individual proverbs. Chapters 1–9 contain some lengthy discourses, and the book ends with a poem of praise for the virtuous woman (31:10-31). Nevertheless, a great deal of the book is taken up with the individual sayings and proverbs for which it is best known.

**Proverbial Literature.** Every culture has its own proverbs and traditional wisdom. In fact, the study of wisdom and proverbs was a favorite activity of ancient scribes and teachers. Writings that preserve this ancient wisdom have survived from Egypt, Mesopotamia, and Greece.

In ancient times collections of traditional wisdom were the textbooks for educating young men of aristocratic birth. Proverbs often implies that it was written for young men for a similar purpose. For example, the reader is frequently addressed as "my son" (2:1; 3:1,11; 4:1,10; 5:1; 6:1) and is warned to avoid prostitutes (5:3-6; 6:20-35). Although Proverbs can be profitably read by anyone, its interpretation is easier if we keep in mind the original audience for whom it was written.

Proverbs has other features in common with the wisdom writings of the other nations of the ancient Near East. Like them, it is very practical. It deals with ordinary matters of life more than with great philosophical concepts. Also its structure and organization are in many ways like the other wisdom writings, especially those from Egypt.

But Israelite wisdom is distinct from that of the other nations in its assertion that God is the starting point in the search for true wisdom: "The fear of the Lord is the beginning of knowledge" (Prov. 1:7; see 9:10; Ps. 111:10). From beginning to end, Proverbs deals with the practical concerns of an individual who knows God. It teaches the believer how to live. In this sense even when it deals with mundane issues, Proverbs is never "secular."

**Forms of Wisdom Teaching.** Even a casual reading of Proverbs reveals the many creative ways in which the book teaches its lessons. Proverbs is not only interesting to read, but its teachings are also memorable. Some of the major types of expressions follow:

*Proverb.* A proverb is a short, carefully constructed ethical observation (13:7) or teaching (14:1).

*Admonition.* An admonition is a command written either as a short proverb (16:3) or as part of a long discourse (1:10-19).

*Numerical Saying.* The numerical pattern lists items that have something in common after an introduction like, "There are six things, indeed seven" (see 30:24-31).

*Better Saying.* A better saying follows the pattern "A is better than B." See 21:19.

*Rhetorical Question.* A rhetorical question is a question with an obvious answer that still draws the reader into deeper reflection. See Proverbs 30:4.

*Wisdom Poem.* Wisdom poems or songs teach a series of moral lessons, as in 31:10-31. These poems are often acrostic.

*Example Story.* An example story is an anecdote meant to drive home a moral lesson (7:6-27).

***Structure of Proverbs.*** Proverbs is actually a collection of several books:

*The Proverbs of Solomon (Prov. 1–24).* This work includes a title and prologue (1:1-7) and a main text divided into discourses (1:7–9:18), proverbial sayings (10:1–22:16), thirty "sayings of the wise" (22:17–24:22), and additional "sayings of the wise" (24:23-34).

*The Proverbs of Solomon copied by the men of Hezekiah (Prov. 25–29).* This collection has no prologue; it is simply an assortment of individual proverbs.

*The sayings of Agur (Prov. 30).* This collection has seven numerical sayings (30:7-9, 15a, 15b-16, 18-19, 21-23, 24-28,29-31) and several proverbs. Verses 2-9 could be regarded as a prologue.

*The sayings of King Lemuel (Prov. 31).* This two-part book concerns the duties of a king (31:2-9) and the praise of the virtuous woman (31:10-31).

I. Proverbs of Solomon (1:1–24:34)
II. Hezekiah Collection (25:1–29:27)
III. The Sayings of Agur (30:1-33)
IV. The Sayings of Lemuel (31:1-31)

***The Date and Authorship.*** The text says that the above four works are respectively by Solomon, by Solomon as edited by Hezekiah's scribes, by Agur, and by Lemuel as learned from his mother. This means that the bulk of Proverbs (1–29) is essentially from Solomon. Even so, many modern scholars believe that these collections came together long after Solomon. Some believe that Proverbs was not written until over five hundred years after Solomon, although others would date the collections to the late monarchy, some three hundred years after Solomon.

But no hard evidence exists that forces us to abandon the Bible's assertion that Solomon wrote most of the book. Some have argued that passages like Proverbs 8 are too advanced in thought to have come from Solomon. Yet other advanced and complex works of wisdom literature that are far older than Solomon's day appear in ancient Near Eastern texts. In addition, we read in the Bible that Solomon's reign was something of a flowering of wisdom in ancient Israel and that Solomon was at the head of its study (1 Kgs. 10:1-9). That being the case, it is not strange that the greatest Israelite wisdom literature should come from this period.

Agur and Lemuel may be pen names of someone otherwise familiar to us; more likely Agur and Lemuel were simply sages about whom we have no other information.

Since we do not know the identities of the writers, we cannot know the dates of composition. But there is no reason to date these sections very late. Also, although we cannot be sure when something like the present Book of Proverbs first appeared, the reign of Hezekiah (716–687 B.C.) may be a reasonable surmise (25:1).

***Origin of the Individual Proverbs.*** To say that Solomon was the principal author of Proverbs is not to imply that he coined every single proverb in his sections. To the contrary, much of his work was as a collector of the "sayings of the wise" (22:17; 24:23). From whom did these proverbs come?

Certainly a primary source of Israelite wisdom was the family, where traditional teachings were handed down for generations. Proverbs frequently addresses its reader as "my son" and urges him to adhere to the teachings of his father and mother (for example, 1:8).

A second source was in the schools where scribes both compiled and composed wisdom literature. Many such scribes are known from Egyptian literature, and the Bible speaks of scribes and wise men in ancient Israel and Judah (Prov. 25:1; 1 Chr. 27:32; Jer. 18:18).

These men were not only the intellectual class of their day, but they also were the counselors of the kings (Gen. 41:8). Solomon, as king, would have had close contact with such men in order to develop his own studies and writings (1 Kgs. 4:31,34).

It is easy to see, therefore, why Proverbs contains such a variety of types of teachings. The more homey and humorous proverbs may have come from the traditional teachings of the Israelite family (see 11:22 and 26:3). The more literary compositions show the influence of court scribes (1:20-33).

## PROVERBS OF SOLOMON (1:1–24:34)

**Title and Prologue (1:1-7).** The prologue states the purpose for the work in 1:2-7. For the Israelites wisdom not only promoted a life of discipline and prudence, but it also enabled persons to unravel clever and mysterious sayings.

The heart of Israelite wisdom asserts that no one can begin to understand God's ways and life's mysteries apart from God's revelation (1:7). All human attempts at wisdom will ultimately fail.

**Solomon's Discourses (1:8–9:18).** *Discourse 1 (1:8-33).* The teacher warns the young man not to abandon the teachings of father and mother for the sake of lawless companions. Those who accept this kind of peer pressure are on their way to death. Wisdom herself calls on all to learn of her. Those who reject the call have no excuse when disaster strikes.

*Discourse 2 (2:1-22).* The primary benefit of wisdom is the protection she gives. The two main dangers she saves her followers from are the crafty man and the adulterous woman. This again indicates that the book was originally written for young men.

*Discourse 3 (3:1-35).* Wisdom is more than a matter of knowing rules of right and wrong; it is a matter of knowing God. The wise trust in the Lord rather than in their own wisdom. They fear and honor Him and accept His discipline. The Lord, not just their awareness of certain principles, protects them.

*Discourse 4 (4:1-27).* This chapter has all the urgency of a father's appeal to his son. The plea is that the boy learn right from wrong and stay in the right path for all his life. "Wisdom is supreme; therefore get wisdom. Though it cost all you have, get understanding." It is as though father and son were in the marketplace and the father was urging the son to spend his money on wisdom rather than on anything else. The price is the son's whole life.

*Discourse 5 (5:1-23).* Here the father urges his son to avoid every form of promiscuity and be faithful to his own wife. Some may consider the emphasis on the dangers of adultery in these chapters of Proverbs to be excessive. But many go astray and warp their lives precisely here. A primary purpose of wisdom is to teach the reader to avoid self-destruction, and few things are more dangerous and yet so alluring as sexuality. Sexuality itself is not, however, an unhealthy or bad thing. Verses 15-19 eloquently celebrate the beauty and joy of sexual love in its proper place.

*Discourse 6 (6:1-35).* No one can live a peaceful life with financial chaos due to excessive debt. Proverbs urges diligence in labor and caution about entering into contracts and indebtedness. Again the book warns the young man to avoid both the devious man and the wanton woman. The numeric saying in 6:16-19 serves as an easy-to-remember rule of thumb for evaluating character. In the modern day 6:25 applies to pornography as well as to acts of adultery.

*Discourse 7 (7:1-27).* This chapter offends some readers on the grounds that it seems to attack women. The harlot, a woman, is presented as a deadly, wicked

# THEMES OF PROVERBS

The Book of Proverbs begins by challenging the young and simple as well as the wise and discerning to seek wisdom through its study (1:1-7). Ancient wisdom recognized the God-given order underlying creation (3:19-20; 8:22-30) and human society. For ancient wisdom saw God as a just Judge, who observes human conduct and upholds the moral order of His world by rewarding the righteous and punishing the wicked. The bulk of Proverbs takes up the practical application of wisdom. What to do in specific, day-to-day situations was often not directly addressed by the Old Testament laws and the prophets. These problems included how to relate to spouses (12:4; 31:10-31), parents (23:22), and children (19:18). How was one to relate to kings (16:10-15) and subjects (27:23-27), to friends (18:24) and enemies (25:21-22), to rich and poor (14:20-21)? How was one to respond to poverty and riches (18:11; 30:7-9)? Wisdom literature offered the ancient Israelites God-given counsel on such everyday matters.

God inspired Scripture in different ways. God spoke to Moses face to face. God spoke to the boy Samuel as an audible voice. God inspired wisdom teachers through the world they observed. Solomon (1 Kgs. 4:29-32; Prov. 1:1; 10:1; 25:1), Agur (30:1), and Lemuel and his mother (31:1) observed and reflected on the order of creation and society.

For example, seeing the sluggard's untended stone walls lying in ruin and his unworked fields bearing inedible vegetation, the inspired wisdom teacher learned a lesson. He learned that poverty will destroy a lazy individual just as surely as a bandit invades and robs. But through wisdom and discipline, the wise can overcome this evil (see 24:30-34). Although God spoke to the wisdom teachers in a less dramatic fashion than He had to Moses and prophets, those teachers were just as inspired (Prov. 2:6). Their words were just as authoritative as the laws or prophecies. The wisdom teachers referred to their proverbs as "teaching" (torah, also rendered "law"; 1:8; 3:1) and "commands" (2:1; 3:1).

The wisdom teachers viewed life through the lens of Israel's faith, that is, through the law and the prophets (29:18).

They recognized a proper respect for God as the foundation of all wisdom. "The fear of the Lord" (1:7) is the essential spiritual quality for those seeking to learn the inspired teacher's wisdom. What the alphabet is to reading, notes are to music, and numerals are to mathematics is the fear of the Lord is to wisdom.

The wise, motivated by a healthy fear that God will uphold His revealed moral order, accept God's objective standards of wisdom. Those who accept the teachings of the wise and actively pray and search for wisdom come to understand the fear of the Lord (Prov. 2:1-5). With this spiritual attitude God's people find the spiritual strength to master their tongue (21:23) and themselves (16:32; 25:28) and to live in harmony with all creatures and with creation.

The inspired writer was well aware that the righteous may first endure poverty (17:1; 19:1) and even death (1:10-19) before God rewards them. In fact, the righteous person may appear to be knocked out for the full count, but he will rise (24:16). Whereas the Books of Job and Ecclesiastes focus on the morally topsy-turvy world in which the wicked prosper and the righteous suffer, Proverbs looks at the end of the matter. The righteous will ultimately prosper in this life or the next. For the righteous God-fearer, the grave is merely a shadow along the trail (12:28; 14:32). Without this kind of faith it is impossible to please God (3:5; 22:19).

Faith in God's promises and warnings and obedience to His revealed will are contrary to human nature. Folly is bound up in the child's heart (22:15). In fact, sinful humans cannot speak for any extended period without sin (10:19). Like Solomon, persons who stop listening to instruction quickly stray from words of knowledge (19:27). Wisdom is gained through discipline. It is implanted by instruction (22:6; 4:3-4) and pruned with corporal punishment (10:13; 13:24; 23:13-14). Above all, the wise commit themselves in faith to God and pray to Him (15:8,29).

person whom the wise young man will avoid. But no similar warning is issued for the benefit of young girls. Nothing is said about lecherous men. Yet we must remember that the book was written for young men (see "Introduction"). That being the case, we would not expect similar warnings for girls. Verse 6 begins an example story in which the young man is taken in by the harlot and is on his way to destruction. He becomes a bird in a snare or an ox going to slaughter.

*Discourse 8 (8:1-36).* Wisdom calls out for young men to come to her. She both parallels and contrasts with the harlot, who likewise patrols the streets looking for young men. The difference is that wisdom leads young men to life, but the harlot takes them to the grave (compare 7:27 to 8:35). Wisdom is of more value than gold or jewels. More than that, she was present with God at creation. Nevertheless, she should not be interpreted in a mythological sense, as if she were a goddess, or in a Christological sense, as if she were Christ. Lady Wisdom is a personification, not a person (see also 8:12, where wisdom dwells with "prudence"; this too is a personification and not a second person). When the text says wisdom was there when God made heaven and earth, it means that wisdom is not some recent innovation. Principles of right and wrong are not human inventions but are embedded in the very fabric of the created order. Those who reject wisdom, therefore, are going against the very principles God built into the world and are on a path of self-destruction.

*Discourse 9 (9:1-18).* The lady wisdom contrasts with the woman folly. Once again we are dealing only with metaphoric personifications. Like vendors calling for customers to come to their shops, wisdom and folly invite the reader to choose which path to take. It is a decision of life and death

*Proverbs (10:1-22:16). Proverbs on labor, prosperity, and wealth (10:1-32).* Wealth does have value as security from trouble, but riches wrongfully gained will not protect. Diligent workers enrich themselves, but lazy people irritate everyone. Above all, integrity and the Lord's blessing provide the most sure security. Several proverbs on the use of the tongue also appear in this chapter.

*Proverbs contrasting the nature and destiny of the righteous and wicked (11:1-31).* The righteous follow a clear path in life, are delivered from troubles, are generous, and strengthen their communities. The wicked hoard money but are not saved by it, are a curse to their families and communities, and face certain punishment.

*Proverbs urging discernment in dealings with others (12:1-28).* The wise know how to recognize and what to expect of various kinds of people. A good woman will help rather than weaken her husband, and a good man is kind even to his animals. The fool is always sure of himself, speaks without thinking, and is destroyed by his own lies. But the wise both listen and speak well.

*Proverbs on life's realities (13:1-25).* Things are not always as they seem. The wise must learn to look beneath the surface. Verse 23 does not sanction the plundering of the poor by the rich but shows a common tragedy in society.

*Important lessons with touches of humor (14:1-35).* Oxen require feeding, and no one enjoys cleaning up after them. But their strength makes farming much easier and leads to a better harvest. Sometimes we have to give up something for a greater gain. Verse 15 shows that gullibility should not be considered a Christian virtue!

*Proverbs on teaching and instruction (15:1-33).* The wise deal with a problem gently, lead people rightly, and will themselves listen to a rebuke. Fools only do harm when they speak and will not themselves listen to any admonition.

*Proverbs on God's sovereignty over all of life (16:1-33).* All our plans depend on God. Human government is also to be respected. No one is truly independent in life.

*Proverbs on family life and relationships (17:1–19:29).* In any family love is more important than riches. Parents and children are bound to each other by a common identity, although even a servant, if wise and faithful, can take the place of a disgraceful son. Family conflicts can go on forever, and bad relatives can ruin life. Many who would call themselves friends are merely attracted by money and power; they show their real character in dealing with someone who has neither. A faithful friend or relative is a protection from trouble, and a good wife is a gift from God.

*Warnings against wrong choices (20:1–22:16).* The Lord despises fraud, violence, a cold heart, and faithlessness. Drunkenness, laziness, poor investments, and pleasure seeking all lead to destruction. All things are in God's hands, and therefore the fear of God leads to a life worth living.

*Thirty Sayings (22:17–24:22).* Proverbs 22:17–23:14 contains striking parallels to the Egyptian *Teachings of Amenemope.* The Egyptian wisdom book appears to be older, which indicates that Solomon knew and used it. This is not surprising, since an Egyptian influence is seen throughout Solomon's writings. These "sayings of the wise" contain a number of proverbs on proper etiquette in the presence of the rich and powerful, with the warning that it is foolish to try to ingratiate yourself before such men (23:1-8).

Proverbs 23:15–24:22 resembles the discourses in the prologue. It again addresses the reader as "my son,"

encourages the pursuit of wisdom, and warns of the dangers of the immoral woman. This may have been the original conclusion to the Book of Solomon, with 24:23-24 being the equivalent to an addendum or appendix.

*Additional Sayings (24:23-34).* Proverbs 24:23-34 is a further collection of wise sayings. An example story on the danger of laziness appears in 24:30-34.

## HEZEKIAH COLLECTION (25:1–29:27)

*Royal Etiquette (25:1-15).* A proper understanding both of the king's role and of how to behave in his presence was essential for the courtier in ancient Israel. Prudence, discretion, and patience are essential for anyone who would deal with government authorities (see Eccl. 8:2-6).

*Interpersonal Relations (25:16-27).* The one who too frequently visits at a friend's house risks becoming an unwelcome sight. The one who does not know how to read a friend's mood will soon anger him or her. Sometimes the best way to win a conflict is to surprise an adversary with kindness.

*Difficult People (25:28–26:28).* Troublesome and difficult people are recognized by lack of self-control, dogmatic self-assurance, and laziness. They provoke conflict and are deceitful. They should never be honored and cannot be trusted. The apparent self-contradiction in 26:4-5 indicates many proverbs are general statements rather than invariable rules.

*Faithfulness in Love (27:1-27).* Sometimes true love may be hidden in a rebuke just as hatred may be hidden in a kiss. There is no love where there is no fidelity to one's wife and friends. True friends can improve each other's character, but nagging only irritates.

*Need for Law (28:1–29:27).* The powerful and wealthy often exploit the poor. Oppressors govern without benefiting the governed, know nothing of jus-

# MARRIAGE AND FAMILY IN ISRAEL

*Family* is an emotional term that raises strong feelings. Such feelings color our understanding of family. We project our experience onto the written words we read. When *family* describes life far from us in geography and times, we must carefully consider the situation of that place and time. It is easy to think that biblical families were just like our families. In some ways they were quite different.

Israel's family structure resulted from its early experiences of nomadic or seminomadic life and then of agricultural life. Such lifestyles demanded a strong work force either to herd the animals or tend the crops. Often, then, a family consisted of the oldest male, his wife, son(s), daughter(s)-in-law, and grandchildren. Widowed grandmothers, daughters, aunts, uncles, or other relatives might live in the home. If a family had sufficient wealth, slaves would also live with the family. At times a man had multiple wives, but this was not the usual case.

The oldest male served as the family head and as a community elder. He exercised control and gave protection to the family. The Song of Songs shares the love and mutual respect man and woman had for each other. The Ten Commandments show that both father and mother deserved the child's respect. Divorce laws show

God wanted Israel to protect the wife's rights and to offer guidelines in case of divorce (Exod. 21:7-11; Deut. 21:14; 22:13-19,25-30; 24:1-5). The urban woman especially had much freedom to engage in social and business affairs (Prov. 31:10-31).

Birth of children brought great joy to families. Mothers and other women in the family cared for and trained children until puberty. Boys then looked to the father to teach them a trade and adult responsibilities. Fathers taught children the religious tradition of Israel (Exod. 10:2; 12:24-28; 13:8,14; Deut. 4:9; 6:20-25; 32:7; Josh. 4:6-7,21-24; Ps. 44:1; Joel 1:3). The eldest son received special training to become family head.

Marriage was the foundation of Israel's life. A woman left her family to become a part of a man's family geographically. But a man also left his family, giving allegiance to wife above father and mother (Gen. 2:24-25). Marriage forged an emotional, physical, and spiritual unity.

The normal and prescribed practice was one man and one woman sharing mutual love (Prov. 5:15-20; Eccl. 9:9). Marriage—like Israel's relationship to Yahweh, their God—was a covenant relationship not to be broken (Mal. 2:14-15). Only such a union could produce "godly offspring." Marriage occurred at what we would consider a relatively young age, fourteen or a little later. Normally the father

chose a bride for his son, at least in Israel's early days (Gen. 38:6; see also Exod. 2:21; Josh. 15:17; Ruth 3:1-4).

Families apparently negotiated a proper price for the bride called a *mohar* in Hebrew (Gen. 34:12; Exod. 22:16; 1 Sam. 18:25). This apparently repaid the bride's family for the economic loss suffered by losing a valuable family member. At times the future husband could do service for the bride's family rather than pay the *mohar* (Gen. 29:15-30; Josh. 15:16-17; Judg. 1:12-13; 1 Sam. 18:17-27). The practice of families exchanging daughters was also known in the Near East. Payment of the *mohar* signaled the beginning of marriage legally, though the actual ceremony and consummation came later (2 Sam. 3:14; see 1 Sam. 18:25).

Weddings took place at the bride's home. Bride and groom dressed elegantly (Isa. 61:10), the groom having a special head adornment (Song 3:11). The bride wore a veil (Gen. 29:25; Song 4:1). Music and rejoicing marked the event (Jer. 7:34), as did feasting (Gen. 29:22; Judg. 14:10). Festivities lasted for a week (Gen. 29:27; Judg. 14:12). Once begun the marriage continued as a commitment of love and a place for bringing children to know God and His way of life and to learn to become good citizens of Israel, God's people.

tice, amass fortunes by exorbitant interest, and ignore the needs of the poor. Lawlessness brings down societies and families, and people groan under oppressive rule. Governments should establish justice through law. But in the end justice comes only from God.

## SAYINGS OF AGUR (30:1-33)

*Title and Prologue (30:1-9).* We must acknowledge our inability to understand the ways of God before we can accept revelation from God. Compare 30:4 with John 8:23. The prayer of Proverbs 30:7-9 is a clear example of the piety of the wise.

*Various Teachings (30:10-33).* The numerical saying in 30:18-19 is tied to the proverb in 30:20. An eagle in the sky, a snake on a rock, and a ship on the sea all have in common that they move without leaving any tracks. In the same way, those committing adultery assume they can do so without leaving a trace of what they have done.

## SAYINGS OF LEMUEL (31:1-31)

*Title and Prologue (31:1-9).* Although these are the "sayings of King Lemuel," they actually come from his mother. This is one passage of Scripture, therefore, that we may confidently ascribe to a woman (see Exod. 15:21; Judg. 5).

Those in authority should not use their power for self-indulgence and depravity. Instead, they should devote themselves to defending the poor and the powerless.

*The Virtuous Woman (31:10-31).* This poem is an acrostic. Although the object of praise is the virtuous woman, the original audience of the piece was again the young man. The opening question in 31:10 implies that the reader ought to find such a wife for himself. The woman is trustworthy, industrious, intelligent, and kind. She adds dignity to the family and has much foresight and prudence. For all

this she is much loved in her family and is the real center of the home. Above all she fears God. The final verse speaks eloquently against the tendency to regard her role as of inferior significance.

*Theological Significance.* Proverbs challenges believers, especially the young, to learn the lessons of past generations. It gives the practical implications of the confession that God is the Lord of all of life. The truly wise show respect for God and His standards in all life situations. Living faith can never be divorced from lives of faithfulness. Faith must be lived out in the day-to-day world where problems call for practical wisdom. How we relate to others serves as an indicator of our relationship with God.

## Questions for Reflection

1. What does Proverbs mean by the "fool"? Is it simply a stupid person or a buffoon; or does the term have a deeper, moral dimension?

2. Granted that Proverbs 7 was originally addressed to boys, how can its message be redirected in contemporary society for the teaching of girls also?

3. Briefly describe the teaching of Proverbs on wealth.

4. Proverbs has a practical message. How does this supplement the more "spiritual" teachings of the Bible?

## Sources for Additional Study

Alden Robert L. *Proverbs.* Grand Rapids: Baker, 1983.

Bullock, C. Hassell. *An Introduction to the Poetic Books of the Old Testament.* Chicago: Moody, 1979.

Draper, James T., Jr. *Proverbs.* Wheaton: Tyndale, 1971.

Garrett, Duane A. *Proverbs, Ecclesiastes, Song of Songs.* New American Commentary, 1993.

Kidner, Derek. *Proverbs.* Downers Grove: InterVarsity, 1975.

# ECCLESIASTES

M any Christian readers are troubled by Ecclesiastes. From the very beginning, where it declares that everything is meaningless (1:2), it seems unashamedly pessimistic and negative on life. Some wonder why this book is in the Bible. But if we carefully examine its background and message, we discover that Ecclesiastes confronts us and drives us to God in a way that few books do.

**Authorship and Date.** Ecclesiastes tells us it was written by a son of David who was king in Jerusalem over Israel (1:1,12). This points to Solomon since he alone, after David, ruled both Judah and Israel. But many believe that Solomon (who reigned about 961–922 B.C.) could not have written the book and assert an unknown Jewish scribe composed it between 500 and 250 B.C.

*The Language of Ecclesiastes.* The Hebrew of Ecclesiastes is quite unusual and sometimes almost obscure. These peculiarities have led many scholars to believe Ecclesiastes was composed late in Old Testament history. But the Hebrew of Ecclesiastes is not characteristically "late" or "early"; it is simply unusual. The language of Ecclesiastes does have much in common with the language of Song of Songs. Several allegedly late Hebrew words in Ecclesiastes also appear in the Song. For this reason many scholars regard Song of Songs as a late book as well. But it is quite possible they have so much in common because they come from the same hand—Solomon's. (For particulars see the introduction to "Song of Songs.")

*Internal Evidence.* Some argue the text itself hints that Solomon was not the author. For example, in 1:12 the writer states that he "was" king in Jerusalem. The real Solomon, of course, never ceased to be king until the day he died. Some assert that passages like 8:2-3, which exhorts the reader to be tactful in the presence of the king, could not have been written by the king himself.

These arguments are rather weak. If, as it appears, Ecclesiastes was written by an aged man (12:1-7), it is not strange that he would speak of his reign in the past tense. Also it is not clear why a king could not be objective enough to give advice like that found in 8:2-3.

*Literary Evidence.* Certain passages of Ecclesiastes closely resemble other literature from the ancient Near East. For example, the Egyptian *Song of the Harper* exhorts the reader to enjoy life in terms almost identical to those found in Ecclesiastes 3:22 and 9:7-9. The *Gilgamesh Epic,* a Mesopotamian classic, also has parallels to Ecclesiastes 9:7-9 that are far too precise to be accidental.

It is almost impossible to account for the strong similarities between Ecclesiastes and these other ancient texts if we assume Ecclesiastes was written by an obscure Jewish scribe between 500 and 250 B.C. Literary practices changed greatly by that time. A scribe of that late a period would probably not even have known, much less used, the ancient Mesopotamian and Egyptian literature.

Solomon, however, is known to have had wide contacts with the wisdom and learning of the ancient world of his day (1 Kgs. 4:34). He doubtless knew works like the *Song of the Harper* and the *Gilgamesh Epic.* The similarities between Ecclesiastes and those texts are easy to explain if Solomon's authorship is assumed. All in all, therefore, the case for believing Solomon to have written Ecclesiastes is stronger than the case against it.

**Message and Purpose.** Christian readers, after they have shaken off the initial shock of reading Ecclesiastes, have often described it as a defense of the faith or even an evangelistic work. Ecclesiastes shows that many of the pursuits of life, including wealth, education, and power, do not really fulfill. In that way Ecclesiastes shows that life without God is meaningless and drives the reader to faith.

Many readers have pointed out how much stark skepticism is in Ecclesiastes. If Ecclesiastes is an apologetic work, it is surely unlike any other defense of the faith ever written. But the defensive and evangelistic purpose of Ecclesiastes is clearer if one takes into account its original audience. A careful study of the text demonstrates conclusively that its first readers were not "ordinary" people but the wealthy, the powerful, and those who had access to the royal court. Again and again it deals with the study of wisdom (which the average person did not have time to do), the value of wealth, and the problems involved in being in the king's court. These things did not apply as issues in the lives of most people.

Addressed to the intellectual and political elite of Israel, the book's "pessimism" makes sense. It was speaking to the very people who were most likely to build their lives on success, wealth, power, and an intellectual reputation. Ecclesiastes repeatedly points out the futility of such a way of life and urges the readers to face their need for God. In that sense Ecclesiastes is indeed evangelistic and in fact can be read profitably by anyone.

Ecclesiastes should not be called pessimistic or cynical, but it is brutally realistic. In particular Ecclesiastes makes the reader confront the full and dreadful significance of death. Most people, whether or not they are religious, refuse to face what death really is: a calamity that nullifies the achievements of human life. Ecclesiastes strips away the myths we use to shield ourselves from this stark fact.

In pointing out the dreadfulness of death, Ecclesiastes helps us see how profound is our need for resurrection. More simply, Ecclesiastes drives us to Christ. The New Testament shares this perspective; death is not a friend or even a doorway but a terrible enemy. It will be, however, a conquered enemy (1 Cor. 15:26,54-55; Rev. 20:14).

**Structure.** To the modern reader, Ecclesiastes at first appears to have no structure at all. The book does not follow modern standards of setting topics in a hierarchy. But a careful reading shows that Ecclesiastes carefully moves among a group of selected subjects. These include wealth, politics, wisdom, death, and aging. As the book moves to and fro among these and other topics, a complete statement gradually emerges.

I. Introduction (1:1-2)

II. On Time (1:3-11; 3:1-15a; 11:7–12:7)

III. On Wisdom (1:12-18; 2:12-17; 6:10–7:6; 7:11-29)

IV. On Wealth (2:1-11,18-26; 4:4-8; 5:10–6:9; 7:11-14; 10:18-20; 11:1-6)

V. On Politics (3:15b-17; 4:1-3,13-16; 5:8-9; 7:7-10; 8:1–9:6; 9:13–10:20)

VI. On Death (3:18-22; 8:1–9:6)

VII. On Friendship (4:9-12)

VIII. On Religion (5:1-7; 7:15-29)

IX. On Evil (8:1–9:6)

X. On Contentment (9:7-12; 11:7–12:7)

XI. Conclusion (12:8-14)

## INTRODUCTION (1:1-2)

Verse 1 gives the title of the work, and verse 2 gives its theme. The word *vanity* or *meaningless* translates the Hebrew word *hebel,* which originally meant *breath.* From *breath* comes the idea of *that which is insubstantial, transitory, and of fleeting value.* For Ecclesiastes, anything that does not have eternal value has no real value. Everything in this world is fleeting and therefore, in the final analysis, pointless.

## ON TIME AND THE WORLD (1:3-11)

All of nature is in constant motion and yet is going nowhere. This is a parable of human life; it is a long flurry of activity that accomplishes nothing permanent. Not only that, but there is nothing new in this world. "New" does not mean merely *unfamiliar* or *novel* but *something fresh that breaks into the cycle of life and gives meaning and value.* The desperate needs of humanity described here are answered in Christ, in whom we have a new covenant, a new birth, a new commandment, and a new life. Meanwhile, we and this weary creation (Rom. 8:19-22) await the glory of the resurrection: new bodies for ourselves in a new heaven and a new earth.

## ON WISDOM (1:12-18)

Education and intellectual pursuits fail to satisfy our deepest needs. The task of the intellectual, the quest to understand life, is itself a hopeless endeavor. The proverb in 1:15 indicates this: "What is twisted cannot be straightened"; that is, no one can solve an insoluble problem. "What is lacking cannot be counted"; that is, no one can add up unknown sums. We cannot understand life because the problem is too complex, and there is too much we do not know. Only the one who is from above (John 8:23) can answer our deepest needs.

## ON WEALTH (2:1-11)

Ecclesiastes now considers the matter of whether pleasure and luxury can give meaning to life. Solomon experimented in pleasure with his mind still guiding him—in other words, he did not become corrupted but remained in control of himself. Not only illicit pleasures disappointed him but even morally acceptable activities and things done in moderation left him empty. (On Solomon's buildings, gardens, and vineyards see 1 Kgs. 7; 9:1; 10:21; 2 Chr. 8:3-6; Song 1:14; 8:11.)

## ON WISDOM (2:12-17)

In 1:12-18 Solomon had spoken of humanity's inability to solve the riddles of life. The quest for wisdom was hopeless. Now he showed that even what wisdom one gains is of no real value because it does not alter one's destiny. The wise man, no less than the fool, is doomed. Of course, the wise go through life with better understanding of what lies ahead than do fools, but neither can escape death. Attempting to achieve immortality through fame and accomplishments is senseless.

## ON WEALTH (2:18-26)

In 2:1-11 Ecclesiastes points out how the spending of wealth on personal pleasure finally becomes irksome. Now the book exposes the folly of a life devoted to earning money. Many people devote themselves to incessant labor under the justification that they are doing it for their children. But this is no excuse for wasting one's own life. The children may well simply squander all that their parents struggled to accumulate. Going through life with contentment is better than forever trying to increase one's bank account.

## DEATH, RESURRECTION, AND AFTERLIFE IN THE OLD TESTAMENT

Death, resurrection, and afterlife in the Old Testament represent a subject that keeps us in the dark. Death represented a departure after which the individual was "no more" (Ps. 39:13; Job 14:10). Death was pictured as "the place of no return," "the land of gloom and deep shadow," and "the land of deepest night, of deep shadow and disorder, where even the light is like darkness" (Job 10:20-22). Death is also pictured as a place of sleep and rest apart from the world's troubles (3:13).

To die is to join the vast number of ancestors who have already gone that way (Gen. 47:30; 49:29). After death came burial, usually in a family tomb with multiple burials (2 Sam. 17:23). For the aged such death was normal, the person being "old and full of days" (Job 42:17 NASB), having completed the normal accomplishments of life. But not all have that normal experience; some die in punishment before they are full of years (Num. 16:29-30).

Death brought the family and community together to mourn (1 Sam. 25:1). Mourning included tears (Gen. 23:2) and led to recovery (38:12) and consolation (2 Sam. 13:39). Pagan mourning rites such as slashing one's skin were forbidden to Israel (Deut. 14:1). Even touching a corpse was forbidden (Lev. 11:31).

Death is more than a physical event. Sin leads to death (Gen. 2:17; Ezek. 18), but humans can choose life (Deut. 30:15-20). The sin and death relationship is an individual one, but those who understand the relationship have responsibility to warn others (Ezek. 3:17-21).

What happened to the dead? They went through the "gates of death" (Ps. 9:13; Isa. 38:10 ) into the "chambers of death" (Prov. 7:27). They became entangled in the "cords of death" (Ps. 18:4), awash in the "torrents of destruction" (Ps. 18:4), and trapped in the "snares of death" (Ps. 18:5). Unable to partake of the tree of life, the dead returned to dust (Gen. 3:19; see Ps. 90:3). Humans die like animals (Eccl. 3:19).

Nations die as well as individuals. Such a nation can live again (Ezek. 37). Israel can at least say that God gives hope for new life to those sick unto death (Pss. 33:19; 56:13; 116:8). Did Israel have a greater hope for triumph over death than this? The answer rests with the understanding of the

## ON TIME (3:1-15A)

Our existence in this world is a mixture of joy and sorrow, harmony and conflict, and life and death. Each has its own proper moment, and we, as creatures of time, must conform to the temporal limitations that are built into the cycle of life. No permanent state of affairs exists in this world. This is a great source of frustration for people since longing for eternity is planted within us. We can neither be satisfied with what we are nor understand God's purpose in all this. We can only humbly accept what we are in this world and confess our faith that God's way is right. In light of this text, the meaning of the resurrection of Christ as the victory over death is clear.

## ON POLITICS (3:15B-17)

The last line of 3:15, usually translated something like, "God calls back the past," is literally, "God seeks the persecuted." It anticipates the brief discussion of oppression in 3:16-17 and means *God will hold the oppressors accountable.* Ecclesiastes voices dismay at the widespread corruption in places of political power, but it asserts that someday God will judge.

## ON DEATH (3:18-22)

Ecclesiastes states that no one, by comparing the carcass of an animal to a human corpse, can find any evidence that the human, unlike the animal, is immortal. The thought that persons have "no advantage" over the animals

Hebrew concept of Sheol and with our understanding of key verses.

*Sheol* is a Hebrew synonym for death (2 Sam. 22:6). This has led the NIV translators to translate *Sheol* consistently as *death*. Many interpreters, however, see Sheol as the abode of the dead (see Deut. 32:22). All people go to Sheol at death, good or bad (see Gen. 37:35; Num. 16:30). Sheol can be compared to a large animal with an insatiable appetite (Isa. 5:14; see Prov. 30:16). It is excited at the prospect of guests coming (Isa. 14:9). In contrast to heaven, Sheol is the deepest part of the earth and thus the widest distance from the heavens (Amos 9:2). Sheol shuts people off from God and from worship (Isa. 38:18; Ps. 6:5) and shuts people off from God's care (Ps. 88:3-5). Still, Sheol is no place to escape from God (Amos 9:2; see Ps. 139:8).

Two passages are crucial for understanding Sheol. Ezekiel 32:17-32 describes the wicked activities in Sheol. These people speak (v. 21). Isaiah 14:9-17 describes the fate of the Babylonian king in Sheol. There he was greeted by the dead. There former leaders rose from their thrones. They mocked him, saying he was as weak as they. All pomp was gone.

Was this poetic description of death designed to mock and degrade Babylon without picturing life in Sheol literally? Or does it picture Sheol as a place of shadowy existence with earthly rank and power still recognized but in meaningless form?

Death holds no hope for Israel then. It leads only to Sheol, however existence there is pictured. But God does hold hope for Israel (Hos. 13:14). Not only nations can rise. So can individuals. Some Old Testament passages provide language from which the church easily draws hope for resurrection (Job 14:1-22; 19:25-27; Pss. 16:7-11; 17:15; 33:18-22; 71:20).

Three Old Testament passages are mountain peaks from which we can view the clear New Testament hope of resurrection and eternal life. Psalm 49:9-15 promises redemption from Sheol and presence with God. Isaiah 26:19 promises that the earth will give birth to its dead so that the dead will live. Thus the dead can shout for joy. Daniel 12:2 declares resurrection for both the wicked and the faithful, either to eternal contempt or eternal life.

The resurrection of Jesus Christ made totally clear what the Old Testament had begun to point toward. Life after death is a reality, not just a hope. Death in all its ugliness is real. Resurrection through Christ is the beautiful reality that leads from death to everlasting life.

---

astonishes many readers. But it does not mean that we are in all respects like the animals, nor does it contradict the rest of the Bible. It means that humans can no more claim to have the power to beat death than can any other animal. For Christians this should only drive us closer to Christ, who did conquer death in His resurrection. Our confidence is not in some innate power of our own but in the gift from God of eternal life through Jesus Christ (Rom. 6:23). Ecclesiastes forces the reader to see the dreadful terror of death and therefore to cling to God for salvation (see Heb. 2:14-15).

The NIV translation ("Who knows if the spirit of man rises upward and if the spirit of the animal goes down into the earth?") better renders the thought of 3:31 than the KJV's translation.

## ON POLITICS (4:1-3)

The assertion that it is better to be dead (and even better never to have been born) than to have to face all the oppression that exists in the world is hyperbole. But this exaggeration shows how profoundly Ecclesiastes opposes the abuse of political power.

## ON WEALTH (4:4-8)

Ecclesiastes again shows how futile is the life devoted to the acquisition of wealth. The two proverbs in 4:5-6 are set in opposition to each other in order to provide balance in life. Laziness leads to poverty and self-destruction. But it is better to be content with what one has than to

spend life toiling away for more possessions.

## ON FRIENDSHIP (4:9-12)

In all the hardships and disappointments
of life, few things give more real, lasting
satisfaction than true friendship. A friend
is a comfort in need and a help in trouble.
Verse 11 does not refer to sexual relations but to shared warmth between two
traveling companions on a cold desert
night. At the same time, it may imply that
the best friend for life ought to be one's
spouse.

## ON POLITICS (4:13-16)

Political power and the popularity that
accompanies it are short-lived. Those
who have long held power tend to
become inflexible and thus vulnerable.
But the entire struggle, an endless game
of "king of the hill," is pointless.

## ON RELIGION (5:1-7)

Fools assume they know all about God
and are able to please Him. True piety
and wisdom recognize the limitations of
both our understanding of God and our
ability to please Him with our deeds. The
attitude of awe toward God that Ecclesiastes recommends (5:7) is in reality
dependence on God's grace and recognition that the benefits we have from Him
are only by His mercy.

## ON POLITICS (5:8-9)

Corruption of government officials is a
universal occurrence and should not surprise anyone. But anarchy is not the
answer. Verse 9 should be translated: "In
all, this is an advantage to the land: a
king, for the sake of cultivated fields."
Despite all the problems of government,
it is necessary for a well-ordered society
and economy.

## ON WEALTH (5:10–6:9)

Through a series of proverbs and short
reflections, Ecclesiastes warns the reader

not to fall into the trap of the quest for
wealth. Where riches are concerned,
enough is never enough. The laborer has
more peace and better sleep than the
affluent man.

## ON WISDOM (6:10–7:6)

Ecclesiastes here summarizes its position
on wisdom through a series of proverbs
and reflections. We must recognize the
limits of our wisdom. There is much we
will never know. But it is better to go
through life with sobriety and understanding than in inane pleasure seeking.

## ON POLITICS (7:7-10)

Verse 7 is transitional from the previous
passage. Bribery can destroy personal
integrity and lead to injustice in government. Verse 10 counsels readers not to
lose heart or suppose that their generation is the most corrupt that has ever
been. When dealing with injustice, be
patient and careful.

## ON WISDOM AND WEALTH (7:11-14)

Ecclesiastes now compares wisdom to
wealth and considers wisdom better
because it does not disappear in hard
times. The wise understand that both
prosperity and adversity are from the
hand of God and accept both.

## ON WISDOM AND RELIGION (7:15-29)

In this complex section Ecclesiastes discusses the attempt to secure happiness
and divine protection through self-discipline and scrupulous observance of religion and morality. Verses 15-18 at first
appear to say that a little sinning is
acceptable as long as it is not excessive,
but this is not the real meaning. Ecclesiastes here addresses those who follow
the traditional teaching of wisdom that a
disciplined life is prosperous and safe but
a life of indulgence is fraught with disaster. Rigorous self-depravation for the
sake of religion does not really guarantee
a peaceful life. No one can truly please

God by his or her righteousness, since all are sinful. This ought to make us more forgiving of others.

The mystery of human sin and how it impinges on behavior is perplexing, but it does have one clear implication: sin makes domestic life very painful. This text, more than any other, demonstrates our need for God's grace.

On the basis of 7:26-29, some readers think the author was prejudiced against women. In fact, this section reflects on the pain sin has brought upon marriage. It looks back to Genesis 3:16b. There the woman desired to manipulate her husband, but he harshly dominated her. Sin made the home into a battlefield.

Similarly, Ecclesiastes says (again using hyperbole) that a man may find one man in a thousand who can be his true friend, but he will not find a single woman in whom he can have the same confidence. This is not because women are innately worse than men—a woman has the same problem finding a man she can trust but may have one woman friend. Humanity's history of domestic strife and faithlessness fully vindicates this passage.

## GOD'S JUSTICE (8:1–9:6)

The wise know how to behave with discretion and tact toward those in power, but the uncertainty of life makes it difficult to stay on the right path. Many who have power use it ruthlessly for their own gain. That they often seem to go unpunished aggravates the situation. This is, perhaps, the most troubling problem of life. Death levels the differences between the powerful and the powerless, but it aggravates the problem in that the good and bad suffer the same fate. For the reader, however, this should not lead to cynicism. Instead, it should provoke deeper faith that only God knows the end from the beginning and only He can finally set all things right.

## ON CONTENTMENT (9:7-12)

This passage builds upon the certainty of death as described in 9:1-6. Life is short and therefore should not be lived in sorrow. Enjoy the good things of life and do not let ambition for success ruin the time you have. The advice in 9:9, "Enjoy life with your wife," seems to contradict 7:28, but wisdom literature often gives counsel that is paradoxical or apparently contradictory. The reason is that life itself is complicated.

## ON POLITICS (9:13–10:17)

Prudence and political skill are essential for effective governance of a nation, but they are often neglected or lacking. Ecclesiastes presents this concept here first in a short anecdote and then in a series of proverbs and reflections. Whether the wise man saved his city by military strategy or diplomacy is not clear. What is clear is that he was soon forgotten because he was not wealthy or from an influential family. But the worst fate that can befall a nation is that it have ignoble or self-indulgent rulers. Such fools are not even capable of giving a stranger correct directions to the nearest town; they can hardly be trusted in matters of state.

The series of proverbs in 10:8-11 emphasizes the importance of forethought and careful planning. Those who practice cunning often bring about their own demise. They dig a pit for someone else and fall into it themselves. Or they are bitten by a snake while breaking into another's home. But even legitimate activities can be dangerous. Thorough planning must precede any enterprise. In context this means that one must exercise great care in dealing with the intrigues of political life.

## ON POLITICS AND WEALTH (10:18-20)

Three transitional proverbs bridge the gap between the political and economic realms. First, diligence is necessary to maintain an economy, be it the national household or a private home. Second, at least some money is essential in order to enjoy the good things of life; verse 19 is not cynical, as it appears to be in many translations. Third, be careful of those who have power, be it political or economic.

## ON WEALTH (11:1-6)

While Ecclesiastes discourages the pursuit of wealth, it favors wise investment and diligent work. Verses 1-2 speak of long-term investment, not charity. To "give portions to seven or eight" is, in modern terminology, to *diversify investments*. While we do have to look out for dangers on the horizon, we cannot allow ourselves to be so cautious that we do nothing. Better to recognize that all things are in God's hands and proceed with our work with an eye toward all possible contingencies.

## ON CONTENTMENT (11:7–12:7)

This section is in two parts: counsel to youth and a poem on aging and death. To the young, Ecclesiastes advises that their brief time of youthful vigor be spent in joy rather than in anxiety. But they are not free to pursue folly and immoral behavior. Awareness of divine judgment and the fleeting nature of youth should always govern their decisions.

The poem in 12:1-7 is also meant as a warning to the young concerning things to come. Its imagery is in some points obscure, but it is nevertheless poignant and moving. Verse 2 may refer to the day of death or to failing eyesight. Verse 3 describes the loss of strength in the arms ("keepers of the house") and legs ("strong men"), the loss of teeth ("grinders"), and encroaching blindness ("those looking through the windows"). Verse 4 alludes to failing hearing that is yet coupled to the sleeplessness whereby one awakes at the slightest sound. Verse 5 speaks of the general loss of courage, confidence, and sexual drive. Finally, in 12:6-7 death is portrayed as the shattering of a vessel whereby its contents—life—are spilled out.

## CONCLUSION (12:8-14)

The book concludes in four subsections. (1) Verse 8 reaffirms the theme of 1:2. These two verses bracket the beginning and ending of the main body of the work. (2) Verses 9-10 describe Solomon's work. Compare 1 Kings 4:32. (3) Verses 11-12 offer a final word on wisdom. (4) Verses 13-14 conclude with a call to fear God.

True wisdom comes from God, the one Shepherd, and is worthy of acquiring. But one should be wary of endless academic pursuits. Ecclesiastes is not anti-intellectual; still, no one should try to build a meaningful life on the reading and writing of books.

Some readers feel the concluding call to fear God does not follow from all that has gone before, but it is in fact the perfect conclusion. The pursuit of wealth, knowledge, and political power is ultimately unsatisfactory and leads to divine judgment. Life is short and full of mystery. All our attempts to make life meaningful fail. The wise response, therefore, is to cling to God and His grace.

***Theological Significance.*** Ecclesiastes challenges its readers to live in the world as it really is instead of living in a world of false hope. It addresses those who have sought meaning through wealth, education, or political power. For some this search for lasting meaning and value has left them empty. Others have yet to realize the futility of this search.

Ecclesiastes challenges its readers to abandon illusions of self-importance, face death and life squarely, and accept with fear and trembling their dependence on God. Solomon's faith in the justice of God and the goodness of His commands was stronger than his pessimism (8:12 13; 11:9). Even when he did not understand life or God's ways, his response was one of faith. The seeming senselessness of life in the real world drove him to God, the only Giver of permanent worth. Life is God's precious gift. Its fleeting pleasures should be enjoyed, even while pursuing the lasting joy that comes only from God.

## Questions for Reflection

1. How does our mortality render "meaningless" much of what we do in life?

2. What are some ways people try to add meaning to their lives? What does Ecclesiastes say about them?

3. How does Ecclesiastes help us to understand the importance of Christ's resurrection and His victory over death?

4. How would you summarize the teaching of Ecclesiastes on political power?

## Sources for Additional Study

Eaton, Michael A. *Ecclesiastes*. Downers Grove: InterVarsity, 1983.

Garrett, Duane A. *Proverbs, Ecclesiastes, Song of Songs*. New American Commentary, 1993.

Gordis, Robert. Koheleth: *The Man and His World*. New York: Schocken, 1968.

Kaiser, Walter C., Jr. *Ecclesiastes*. Chicago: Moody, 1979.

Wardlaw, Ralph. *Exposition of Ecclesiastes*. 1868; reprint, Minneapolis: Klock and Klock, 1982.

# SONG OF SONGS

The full name of this book is "The Song of Songs, which is Solomon's." Often called Song of Solomon or, after the Latin, Canticles, it is best to call it Song of Songs. But we should note that the Hebrew idiom *Song of Songs* actually means *the best song*.

**Date and Authorship.** The title probably implies that Solomon wrote it, but it could be taken to mean that it was simply part of Solomon's collection and was written perhaps by a court singer. Still, many scholars believe that the Song was written late in Israelite history (500–100 B.C.) and therefore could not possibly have been written by Solomon or his contemporaries (961–922 B.C.). It is important, therefore, to see what evidence there is for dating the book.

Most scholars who regard the Song as a late work do so primarily because some of the vocabulary found in it appears to be incompatible with the earlier date. For example, many argue that the Hebrew word for "orchard" in 4:13, *pardes,* is derived either from the Persian word *pairidesa* or the Greek word *paradeisos* (compare the English *paradise*). It is difficult to see how Hebrew could have borrowed a word from either Persian or Greek as early as Solomon's day.

Some scholars believe that the Song has several Aramaic words. Many Jews spoke this language during the intertestamental and New Testament periods. Finally, the Song frequently uses the Hebrew pronoun *she* (meaning *which, what,* or *who*) instead of the more common *asher* (which has the same meaning). The Hebrew pronoun *she* is relatively rare in the Bible but became common in postbiblical Hebrew. For these reasons, many are convinced that the Song must have been composed very late in Jewish history.

These arguments are not as convincing as they first appear. The word *parades* ("orchard") may come from a Sanskrit root word that is far older than either Persian or Greek. In addition, many words once asserted to be from a late Aramaic background have been found to be more ancient than originally supposed. Also the use of the Hebrew word *she* is not as significant as once was thought. Similar relative pronouns have been found in some ancient Semitic languages, such as Akkadian and Ugaritic. This implies that the use of Hebrew *she* is not an exclusively late phenomenon. In short, the vocabulary of the Song does not prove that it is a late work.

**Geographical Evidence.** The Song of Songs mentions locations from all over ancient Palestine. These include places both in northern Israel (Sharon, Lebanon, Hermon, and Carmel) and in the southern territory of Judah (Jerusalem and Engedi). The Song also mentions the Transjordan territories of Heshbon and Gilead. This geographic outlook reflects a time when all Israel was unified and even territories in the Transjordan were under Israelite dominion. These conditions never prevailed after the death of Solomon.

Song of Songs 6:4 sets the city of Tirzah in parallel with Jerusalem. This implies that at the time of writing, Tirzah was considered the major city of the north and was comparable to Jerusalem in the south. When the kingdom split early in the reign of Rehoboam of Judah (931–913 B.C.), Tirzah immediately became the capital of the Northern Kingdom. But Omri of Israel (reigned 886–874 B.C.) made Samaria the capital of the Northern Kingdom, and from that time forward Tirzah never was prominent again. Song of Songs 6:4, therefore, implies that it was written before Omri's time.

**Cultural Evidence.** The poetic imagery of Song of Songs reflects an age of great prosperity. This also lends support to the belief that it was written in Solomon's day. Only then did Jerusalem possess the spices, perfumes, and luxuries mentioned in the book as well as great quantities of gold, marble, and precious jewels (Song 5:14-15; see 1 Kgs. 10:14-22).

Of course, one can argue that these are only similes and do not prove that the writer actually lived in an age when such things were common. But it is doubtful that a poet would use imagery, described in such detail, that was outside his own frame of reference and experience.

**Literary Evidence.** The poetry we see in Song of Songs is not quite unique in the ancient world. From Egypt, in the period of approximately 1300 to 1100 B.C., come a number of love songs which are remarkably like Song of Songs. Many of the motifs and ideas that appear in the Song are also found in the Egyptian poetry. Outside of this ancient body of literature, however, it is difficult to find any writings comparable to Song of Songs.

What is the reason for this unusual parallel between a book of the Bible and Egyptian poetry? Solomon made an alliance with the Egyptian Pharaoh and married his daughter (1 Kgs. 3:1). The court of Solomon and Egypt doubtless had extensive contacts. Solomon also had contact with wise men—and thus their literature—from all over the world (1 Kgs. 4:29-34).

Solomon likely would have become familiar with the love poetry that had appeared within the previous three hundred years in Egypt. This would explain how the Song has so much in common with its Egyptian counterparts. Solomon, after all, was cosmopolitan in his learning and tastes.

Difficult to explain, however, is why the Song and the Egyptian love poetry have so much in common if the Song were written some 650 years after Solomon. An obscure Jewish songwriter, working a millennium after this kind of love poetry was produced in Egypt, could not have written by accident a work so much like the Egyptian poetry. Nor is it reasonable to argue that he would have known and deliberately imitated an ancient, foreign, and by then probably forgotten art form.

The poetry of Song of Songs reflects Solomon's age better than any other of Israelite history. It is thus best to assume it was written in that period.

**Interpretation.** No other book of the Bible (except perhaps Revelation) suffers under so many radically different interpretations as the Song of Songs. The major approaches are as follows:

*Allegorical Interpretation.* From early times both Christians and Jews have allegorized the Song of Songs. Jews have taken it to picture the love between the Lord and Israel, and Christians have regarded it as a song of the love between Christ and the church. (Traditional Roman Catholic interpreters have often identified the woman with the virgin Mary.) The allegorical approach was standard from the medieval period through the Reformation, but it has few adherents now.

Common allegorical identifications are that the man is Christ and the woman is the church, his kisses (1:2) are the Word of God, the girl's dark skin (1:5) is sin, her breasts (7:7) are the church's nurturing doctrine, her two lips (4:11) are law and gospel, and the "troops with banners" (6:4) is the church as the enemy of Satan. Advocates of this approach claim that the New Testament supports their case, since Ephesians 5:22-33 and other texts describe the church as Christ's bride.

But the New Testament never gives the Song an allegorical interpretation. New Testament passages that do speak of the bride of Christ do not refer to Song of Songs. The material of Song of Songs is grossly inappropriate for worship. It is impossible to imagine a Christian praising Christ in the terms of 1:2,16; or 5:10-16. It is equally bizarre to think of Jesus Christ describing His church in the terms of 7:1-9. This ancient interpretation has rightly been abandoned.

*Dramatic Interpretation.* For the past two hundred years, many interpreters have argued that the Song is a dramatic story. Some say it is a two-character drama in which Solomon and the girl are the main actors. Others take it as a three-character drama in which Solomon, the girl, and a shepherd boy are the main actors.

In the two-character interpretation, the Song tells the story of the romance between Solomon and the one girl he truly loved. The three-character interpretation is altogether different. It says the story tells how Solomon attempted to seduce a beautiful girl but failed because of her faithfulness to her true love, the shepherd boy.

Neither approach is convincing. A romantic drama of this kind was altogether unknown in the ancient Near East. Also both interpretations are at many points forced and unnatural. Considering the size of Solomon's harem and in light of 1 Kings 11:1-6, it is pointless to follow the two-character theory and

assert he had one woman toward whom he was exclusively devoted (see Song 2:2; 7:10).

The three-character theory is equally artificial. According to that approach, for example, chapter 7 describes an attempt by Solomon to seduce the girl and her rebuff of his advances. This would mean that the poetry of 7:1-9a, spoken by the man, was not genuine love but cheap enticement. The girl, moreover, in saying, "Come, my lover, let us go to the countryside" (7:11), was not speaking to the man with her but to an absent lover. This can hardly be the intended meaning.

*Wedding Song Interpretation.* Some have argued that Song of Songs is a wedding song. Some scholars have studied Near Eastern wedding ceremonies and have pointed out similarities between those rituals and the lyrics of the Song. Even so, it is difficult to read Song of Songs as an order of service for a wedding. But even though the Song is not the text of a wedding ceremony, it indicates that the young lovers were marrying each other.

*Love Song Interpretation.* The best interpretation is the most simple and obvious. Song of Songs is a love song in three parts—a man, a woman, and a chorus of women. It has no secret allegories or identifications. It tells no story and has no plot. It is a lyrical expression of romantic love between a couple who are in the process of marrying. Its language and imagery, which go from royal pomp and majesty to the rustic, pastoral setting of the meadow, is meant to convey all the grandeur and glory as well as the simplicity and natural beauty of love.

**Meaning and Message.** One reason for the rise of the allegorical interpretation of the Song is that many felt that a simple love song had no place in the Bible and that, unless it was allegorized, no theological message could be found in it. This concern, however, is misguided. Song of Songs conveys important meaning if left as it is, a love song, and not turned into something it is not.

First, as the Bible is meant to serve as a guide in every aspect of life, so the Song deals with one universal aspect of human life—love, marriage, and sexuality. People need direction and teaching in the matter of how to nurture love for a spouse just as they need guidance in every other matter. The Song teaches that this love relationship is to be both physical and verbal. Again and again the two lovers speak of their desire for and joy in each other. For many couples the inability to express love is a profound problem.

Second, although the Song teaches by example and not by decree, its message is clear. The love the couple shared was exclusive and binding (7:10). By implication this ideal portrait excludes extramarital sex as well as all perversions and abuses of sexuality, such as promiscuity and homosexuality.

Third, Song of Songs celebrates love between man and woman as something that is valid and beautiful even in a fallen and sinful world. In this way Song of Songs testifies in a significant way to the grace of God. Although we are sinners, God tells us that the love relationship is a thing to be cherished and enjoyed. If the Bible said nothing in this area beyond prohibitions and warnings, we might suppose that all sexuality is innately evil and is to be suppressed entirely except for procreation. But because the Song is in the Bible, we understand that it is not sexuality but the misuse and abuse of sex that is wrong. In the Song we see that genuine love between man and woman, and the physical affection that follows, is a good and tender thing.

Fourth, the Song of Songs is unlike its ancient Near Eastern counterparts in one significant respect: it does not turn sexuality into a sacred ritual. In the ancient world fertility cults and religious prostitution abounded. The sexual act was thought to have religious meaning. Not only that, but desperate souls often used incantations and love charms to win the affection of another person. None of this is found in Song of Songs. The romantic love between man and woman is a joy, but it is exclusively a joy of this world.

In this way the Bible avoids the two pitfalls of human religion. It neither condemns sexual love as innately evil and dangerous (as do legalistic cults) nor elevates it to the status of religious act (as do sensual cults and religions).

The Song of Songs, therefore, should be taken as it stands. It is a song of love and an affirmation of the value of the bond between a man and a woman. In this way it adds greatly to our appreciation of God's creation.

## INTRODUCTION (1:1)

This verse is the title; the song actually begins in 1:2. In Song of Songs the groom, the bride, and the chorus each take turns singing their parts, but they do not follow a consistent sequence. At times it is difficult to tell who is singing a given line of lyrics because the Hebrew text does not delineate the parts. But usually the singer is evident.

## BRIDE (1:2-4A)

She calls the groom a king, but this is not to be taken literally. This is the language of love.

## CHORUS (1:4B)

The bride's friends enhance her appreciation for the groom by joining in his praise.

## BRIDE (1:4C-7)

The bride is embarrassed at her dark skin. In contrast to modern standards of beauty, the ancients regarded light skin as most attractive.

## GROOM (1:8-11)

The groom is at the same time a rustic shepherd and yet able to give his beloved gold jewelry. Again, however, this is not to be pressed literally. The pastoral images and the mention of fine jewelry heighten the sense of joy in love.

## BRIDE (1:12-14)

Semitropical vegetation, including henna, grew at the oasis of En Gedi on the western shore of the Dead Sea.

## GROOM (1:15)

"Eyes are doves" means that they are tranquil in appearance. Her eyes convey feelings of peacefulness.

## BRIDE (1:16)

"Our bed is verdant" means it is lush and luxurious, like a tree thick with foliage.

## GROOM (1:17)

It was a luxury to have a house paneled with cedar.

## BRIDE (2:1)

The flower mentioned here is not the modern rose of Sharon but probably a crocus, daffodil, or narcissus.

## GROOM (2:2)

Compared to the groom's beloved, all other women are thorns. True love is exclusive and not distracted by others.

## BRIDE (2:3-13)

He is "like an apple tree," that is, protective ("shade") and pleasurable ("his fruit").

## GROOM (2:14-15)

Despite the endless variety of interpretations that have been heaped upon 2:15, the "little foxes" probably do not represent anything. The man simply invites the woman to join in a chase. This is the kind of childlike play that young lovers often engage in.

## BRIDE (2:16–3:5)

The woman concludes the first section of Song of Songs in 2:16-17 and sings a separate solo in 3:1-5. This section is symbolic of the woman's longing for the groom and is not to be read literally. The proverb that says not to arouse love until it desires (3:5; also 2:7 and 8:4) means that sexual love is to be avoided until the proper time and person arrive.

## CHORUS (3:6-11)

The chorus women call for the Jerusalem girls to come and see Solomon's splendor. This does not mean that Solomon is the singer of the groom's part or a "character" in a story. Instead, the figure of Solomon is more a contrasting poetic symbol here. Every young man in love is a "Solomon in all his glory." The arrival of Solomon stands for the arrival of the groom at the wedding ceremony (see Matt. 25:6). This is a song about a couple just married. But young lovers really do not need the trappings of glory, as Solomon did, since they have each other (see 8:11-12).

## GROOM (4:1-15)

The metaphors seem harsh and unnatural to the modern reader because we take them in too literal a sense. What the poet meant was that aspects of the woman's beauty provoke profound emotional responses. Her neck was like the tower of David in that both were statuesque and caused feelings of admiration and wonder. He did not mean that her neck was unusually long. Similarly, he described the pleasures she gave him in terms of fruits and spices.

## BRIDE (4:16)

This, with 5:1, is the high point of the Song of Songs. Using the metaphor of the garden, she invites her groom to come and enjoy her love.

## GROOM (5:1A)

The man responds. He calls her his bride, which again indicates they are newly married. The poetry is discreet and restrained; it conveys the joy of sexual love without vulgarity.

## CHORUS (5:1B)

The chorus' brief call ("Eat, O friends") breaks the tension of the previous verses and opens the way for a second solo similar to 3:1-5.

## BRIDE (5:2-8)

This section is to be read symbolically and not literally. The main point of the text is to describe that the woman experiences pain and not only pleasure in love. The watchmen who beat her represent this.

## CHORUS (5:9)

This verse introduces the bride's next solo, in which she praises her beloved's beauty. There is no rational transition from the previous segment (5:1-8) because, again, it is not meant to be read as a story.

## BRIDE (5:10-16)

Her beloved is like Lebanon in that he, like it, is majestic. He does not literally look like a forest. Here too the comparisons deal more with emotional response than actual similarity of appearance.

## CHORUS (6:1)

The chorus, following her answer to 5:9, now ask where he has gone.

## BRIDE (6:2-3)

She answers that he has gone to "his garden" (that is, he has come to her).

## GROOM (6:4-9)

He praises his beloved in terms similar to 4:1-15.

## CHORUS (6:10)

The chorus announces the bride's approach and describes her beauty as like that of the moon and sun. See 3:6-11.

## BRIDE (6:11-12)

Verse 12 seems to be saying that her love for the man swept her away. She is about to depart with the groom, as was apparently the custom after a wedding.

## CHORUS (6:13A)

The chorus, representing the bride's friends, long to be with her as they realize they are losing her to her beloved.

## GROOM (6:13B–7:9A)

He answers the chorus in 6:13b and then moves into another song of praise for the bride's beauty.

## BRIDE (7:9B–8:4)

Her wish that her lover was her brother seems strange to the modern reader. The point is that she wishes she were free to display her affection openly. In the ancient world this would have been impossible for a woman with any man except a near relative.

## CHORUS (8:5A)

Once again the song of the chorus contains the idea of movement. See 6:13a.

## BRIDE (8:5B-7)

In saying that her beloved was born under the apple tree, she is alluding to his romantic character. See 2:3.

## CHORUS (8:8-9)

The chorus desires that their young sister remain chaste until the proper time for love arrives. This may answer the proverb in 8:4.

## BRIDE (8:10-12)

The woman says she has reached maturity and found fulfillment (8:10). The thousand shekels Solomon received from his vineyard may be a cryptic reference to Solomon's three hundred concubines and seven hundred wives (1 Kgs. 11:3). The love between the groom and the bride is better than Solomon's sexual extravagance.

## GROOM (8:13)

He calls on everyone to rejoice with him.

## BRIDE (8:14)

She calls the groom away with her.

***Theological Significance.*** The sexual and emotional aspects of love between a man and a woman are worthy of the Bible's attention. Sexuality and love are fundamental to the human experience. As a book meant to teach readers how to live a happy and good life, the Bible naturally has something to say in this area. The Song of Songs celebrates the joy and passion of married love as God's good gifts. The united love of the man and woman in Song of Songs is a reenactment of the love between the first man and woman. As such it witnesses to the triumph of God's gracious purposes for creation in spite of human sin. Likewise, such faithful love beautifully pictures God's love for and commitment to His people.

## Questions for Reflection

1. What are some wrong attitudes toward love and sexuality, and how does Song of Songs correct them?

2. How has God's creation of humanity as male and female made life richer?

3. What can we learn about maintaining a healthy love relationship in courtship and marriage from how the groom and bride express their love for each other?

## Sources for Additional Study

Carr, G. Lloyd. *The Song of Solomon.* Tyndale Old Testament Commentaries. Downers Grove: InterVarsity, 1984.

Garrett, Duane A. *Proverbs, Ecclesiastes, Song of Songs.* New American Commentary, 1993.

Glickman, S. Craig. *A Song for Lovers.* Downers Grove: InterVarsity, 1976.

# THE MAJOR PROPHETS

## ROBERT B. CHISHOLM

The Historical Books showed the dominant role the prophets played in directing and interpreting Israel's history. Not surprisingly, then, the final books of the Old Testament preserve prophetic messages. Traditionally the prophetic books are divided into Major and Minor Prophets, basically on the length of the books.

The Books of the Major Prophets include Isaiah, Jeremiah, Lamentations, Ezekiel, and Daniel. That Isaiah, Jeremiah, and Ezekiel should be classified as major prophets should be self-evident. All three were prominent figures in the history of Israel and have left us with large collections of prophetic messages and biographical materials. Isaiah ministered in Judah from about 742 to 700 B.C. His prophecy addresses issues facing his contemporaries as well as the situation of the future exilic generation in Babylon. Jeremiah lived in Judah during its final days prior to the fall of Jerusalem in 586 B.C. After the fall of the city, he was forced to accompany a group of refugees to Egypt. His prophecy, while focusing on contemporary events, also looks forward to a time of restoration for God's people. Ezekiel was an exile in Babylon whose prophetic ministry took place between 593 and 571 B.C. Like his counterparts Isaiah and Jeremiah, he prophesied both judgment and restoration for God's people.

In the Hebrew Bible, Lamentations and Daniel are included in the Writings, not the Prophets. However, the English Bible, following the earliest Greek translation, places these books with the Major Prophets. Lamentations has traditionally been attributed to Jeremiah and, in lamenting the city's tragic destruction, focuses on an event that occupied a great deal of Jeremiah's attention. The Book of Daniel, of course, contains several prophecies of future events, though they are presented in an apocalyptic literary style that differs significantly from traditional prophetic forms.

## THE PROPHETS IN HISTORY
### (9th—5th century B.C.)

| Prophet | Approximate Dates (B.C.) | Location/ Home | Basic Bible Passage | Central Teaching | Key Verse |
|---|---|---|---|---|---|
| Elijah | 875–850 | Tishbe | 1 Kgs 17:1–2 Kgs 2:18 | Yahweh, not Baal, is God | 1 Kgs 18:21 |
| Micaiah | 856 | Samaria | 1 Kgs 22; 2 Chr 18 | Judgment on Ahab; Proof of prophecy | 1 Kgs 22:28 |
| Elisha | 855–800 | Abel Meholah | 1 Kgs 19:15-21; 2 Kgs 2–9; 13 | God's miraculous power | 2 Kgs 5:15 |
| Jonah | 786-746 | Gath Hepher | 2 Kgs 14:25; Jonah | God's universal concern | Jonah 4:11 |
| Hosea | 786-746 | Israel | Hosea | God's unquenchable love | Hos 11:8-9 |
| Amos | 760-750 | Tekoa | Amos | God's call for justice and righteousness | Amos 5:24 |
| Isaiah | 740–698 | Jerusalem | 2 Kgs 19–20; Isaiah | Hope through repentance and suffering | Isa 1:18; 53:4-6 |
| Micah | 735–710 | Moresheth Gath Jerusalem | Jer 26:18; Micah | Call for humble mercy and justice | Mic 6:8 |
| Oded | 733 | Samaria | 2 Chr 28:9-11 | Do not go beyond God's command | 2 Chr 28:9 |
| Nahum | 686-612 | Elkosh | Nahum | God's jealousy protects His people | Nah 1:2-3 |
| Zephaniah | 640-621 | ? | Zephaniah | Hope for the humble and righteous | Zeph 2:3 |
| Jeremiah | 626–584 | Anathoth/ Jerusalem | 2 Chr 36:12; Jeremiah | Faithful prophet points to new covenant | Jer 31:33-34 |
| Huldah (the prophetess) | 621 | Jerusalem | 2 Kgs 22; 2 Chr 34 | God's Book is accurate | 2 Kgs 22:16 |
| Habakkuk | 608-598 | ? | Habakkuk | God calls for faithfulness | Hab 2:4 |
| Ezekiel | 593–571 | Babylon | Ezekiel | Future hope for new community of worship | Ezek 37:12-13 |
| Obadiah | 580 | Jerusalem | Obadiah | Doom on Edom to bring God's kingdom | Obad 21 |
| Joel | 539-331 | Jerusalem | Joel | Call to repent and experience God's Spirit | Joel 2:28-29 |
| Haggai | 520 | Jerusalem | Ezra 5:1; 6:14; Haggai | The priority of God's house | Hag 2:8-9 |
| Zechariah | 520–514 | Jerusalem | Ezra 5:1; 6:14; Zechariah | Faithfulness will lead to God's universal rule | Zech 14:9 |
| Malachi | 500-450 | Jerusalem | Malachi | Honor God and wait for His righteousness | Mal 4:2 |

# ISAIAH

According to the book's heading, Isaiah prophesied from about 740 until about 700 B.C., during the reigns of the kings Uzziah, Jotham, Ahaz, and Hezekiah of Judah. Several New Testament passages appear to attribute the entire book to the prophet Isaiah (see, for example, John 12:38-41). However, for various reasons modern critical scholars deny much of the book, including chapters 40–66, to eighth-century Isaiah. Appealing to differences in style, as well as to the exilic and even postexilic perspective of many sections, these scholars contend that the prophet's messages have been supplemented by later anonymous writers (two of whom have been labeled Second and Third Isaiah).

Certainly the perspective of chapters 40–66 is much later than Isaiah's time, as the many references to the situations of the exiles, the naming of Cyrus of Persia, the exhortations to leave Babylon, and the description of ruined and uninhabited Jerusalem indicate. However, this need not mean that the author of the chapters lived in this later period. Isaiah could have projected himself into the future and addressed the exilic situation he knew God's people would eventually experience (see 39:5-7). Though such a projection into the future would be unique among the writing prophets, at least on the scale proposed for Isaiah, it would be consistent with one of the major theological themes of the book's later chapters, namely, God's ability to predict events long before He actually brings them to pass.

**Historical Background.** Isaiah lived in momentous times for Israel and Judah. Both nations had experienced prosperity during the first half of the eighth century B.C. But not long after the midpoint of the century, the Assyrians appeared on the horizon like a dark, ominous storm cloud. In an effort to resist the Assyrians, the Northern Kingdom formed a coalition with the Arameans (Syrians). When Judah refused to join the effort, Israel and Aram attacked.

Some of the early chapters of the book reflect this background (see chaps. 7–8). The Assyrians defeated Aram and Israel, reducing the latter to a puppet state. The morally corrupt Northern Kingdom was moving headlong toward final judgment. In 722 B.C. the Assyrians conquered Samaria and made Israel an Assyrian province. Following in the footsteps of the Northern Kingdom, Judah also rebelled against God's commandments.

Isaiah warned his countrymen to change, and the reign of Hezekiah saw a revival of sorts. Hezekiah also resisted the Assyrians. In 701 B.C. the Assyrian ruler Sennacherib marched against Judah and besieged Jerusalem. Isaiah encouraged the king to trust in the Lord, who miraculously delivered the city from the Assyrian hordes. However, Isaiah also foresaw the eventual exile of Judah and addressed the situation of that future generation.

**Theme.** The theme of Isaiah's prophecy may be summarized as follows: God's ideal for His covenant people Israel will indeed be realized but only after His judgment purifies the covenant community of those who rebel against His authority. God is the "Holy One of Israel," who sovereignly controls the destiny of nations but who also demands loyalty from His people.

**Literary Form.** The book contains a multitude of individual literary types, often woven together in a highly artistic and rhetorically effective manner. Among the more common forms are the judgment speech (where the prophet accuses the nation of wrongdoing and announces its coming doom), the exhortation to repentance, the salvation announcement (which promises God's intervention for His suffering people), and the salvation oracle (in which the Lord encourages His people not to fear). Other forms include the disputation speech (where God responds to an accusation or complaint by His people) and the trial speech (where God argues His case with Israel or with the pagan nations). The book contains prophetic messages, mostly in poetic form characterized by parallelism of thought and vivid imagery, and biographical material about Isaiah.

Most of the judgment messages appear in chapters 1–39. The majority of the salvation speeches occur in chapters 40–66. Still it is overly simplistic to say that the theme of chapters 1–39 is judgment and that of chapters 40–66 salvation. In each of the major sections of chapters 1–39, the message moves from judgment to salvation.

I. Judgment and Restoration (1:1–12:6)

II. God's Kingdom (13:1–39:8)

III. Hope and Restoration (40:1–66:24)

**Purpose and Theology.** As a messenger of Israel's and Judah's covenant Lord, Isaiah warned that God's people were about to be judged for breaking their covenant with Him. Though their punishment would be severe, God would ultimately judge the nations as well and reestablish His people in their land.

In the development of this major theme of salvation through purifying judgment, several contributing themes emerge. Isaiah has much to say about Zion (Jerusalem), God's dwelling place. He prophesied and witnessed the city's miraculous deliverance from the Assyrians. The event foreshadowed and became a guarantee of Jerusalem's eventual vindication and glorification before the nations. However, a time would come when Jerusalem would have to endure extreme hardship and its people suffer the humiliation of exile. Nevertheless, God would not abandon the city. He would lead His people out of exile in a grand new exodus and bring them back to the promised land. Once again Zion would be inhabited. This vision was only partially fulfilled about 538 B.C., when the Persian ruler Cyrus allowed exiles to go back to Palestine. The full restoration of Israel awaits a future time when covenant renewal is complete (compare Isa. 55 with Rom. 11:27).

The Servant of the Lord (the focal point of the so-called servant songs of chaps. 42–53) plays a prominent role in the restoration of Israel. Portrayed as a new Moses who mediates a new covenant for the nation, this servant suffers on behalf of God's people and brings them redemption. Subsequent biblical revelation identifies this servant as Jesus Christ. In the earlier chapters of Isaiah we see a more traditional portrayal of the Messiah as a mighty Davidic ruler who conquers the enemies of God and establishes justice in Israel and among the nations.

The book also emphasizes God's sovereignty over the nations. He raised up Assyria and Babylon as instruments to punish His rebellious people but then destroyed them because of their arrogance and cruelty. Time and time again the Lord declared His infinite superiority to the idol-gods of the nations. They were products of human hands and inactive, but He is the sovereign Creator who superintends the universe.

## JUDGMENT AND RESTORATION (1:1–12:6)

**Divine Warning (1:1-31).** See the introduction to "Isaiah" for a discussion of the heading. The Lord summoned the personified heavens and earth, the ancient witnesses to God's covenant with Israel (Deut. 30:19; 31:28), to hear His accusation against His rebellious people. Despite His fatherly concern, they had disobeyed and rejected Him. Though Judah had already experienced the horrors of military invasion and Jerusalem alone had been spared, the nation refused to turn back to God. Comparing His people to the evildoers of Sodom and Gomorrah, the Lord denounced their hypocritical religious acts and demanded that they promote social justice in the land. The Lord delivered an ultimatum. Obedience would bring forgiveness and restored blessings; continued disobedience would result in destruction.

In response to the Lord's denunciation, Isaiah lamented that once-faithful Jerusalem was defiled by social injustice and corruption. The Lord would take up the cause of the oppressed and purify the city of its evildoers. Once again Jerusalem would become a center of justice.

**Restoration (2:1–4:6).** This section begins and ends with a description of purified and restored Jerusalem of the future. In between Isaiah addressed the situation of his own day, warning of impending judgment and condemning the city's proud residents.

*Universal Peace (2:1-5).* Following the Lord's purifying judgment, Jerusalem would become the center of His universal kingdom of peace. Rather than resorting to warfare, the nations would allow the Lord to settle their disputes. In anticipation of this coming age of peace, the prophet exhorted his own generation to seek the Lord's guidance.

*The Lord's Day of Judgment (2:6-22).* Returning to the realities of his own day, Isaiah denounced Judah for its foreign alliances, idolatry, and accumulation of wealth and armaments. He warned that the Lord's Day of judgment was imminent. Like a mighty warrior He would destroy the proud, symbolized here by lofty trees, high mountains, walled cities, and impressive ships. In that day idol worshipers would discard the gods they had formed and flee in terror from God's wrath. Since even the mightiest and most proud could not withstand God's judgment, the prophet urged his contemporaries to no longer place their trust in mortals.

*Jerusalem's Injustice (3:1–4:1).* The focal point of the Lord's judgment would be Jerusalem's arrogant and oppressive leaders. Ironically, in the aftermath of judgment men would refuse positions once coveted for their power and prestige. Those totally incapable of ruling society would be forced to assume leadership.

The pride of Jerusalem's upper classes was epitomized by its wealthy women. Their demeanor and dress were vivid proof that the wealthy profited at the poor's expense. In the day of judgment the signs of wealth and pride would be replaced by those of deprivation and humiliation. The women would wear mourners' sackcloth, not beautiful garments. With their husbands and sons slaughtered in battle, they would beg the few surviving men to marry them.

*Jerusalem's Purification (4:2-6).* Despite its horrors, God's judgment had a positive goal of purification. He would "wash away" the "filth" of Jerusalem's women (an ironic reference to their beautiful garments) and burn away the blood stains left by their violent treatment of the poor. Out of the fire of judgment would emerge a remnant of faithful followers, who would at long last fulfill God's ideal for a holy nation (see Exod. 19:6). He would bless them with agricultural prosperity and protect them from all harmful and destructive forces. The imagery of the "cloud of smoke" and "glow of flaming fire" alludes to the period of the exodus and wilderness wanderings, when a cloud and fire were tangible symbols of God's protective presence and guidance (Exod. 13:21-22; 14:20).

Some see the "Branch of the LORD" as a messianic title (see Jer. 23:5; 33:15; Zech. 3:8; 6:12). But this seems unlikely in this context, where the phrase corresponds to "fruit of the land." Both phrases probably refer to the agricultural abundance the Lord would give to His restored people. The Hebrew word translated "Branch" *(semah)* can refer to vegetation or agricultural growth (see Gen. 19:25, "vegetation"; Ps. 65:10, "crops"; Ezek. 16:7, "plant"). Several prophets, including Isaiah, pictured the age of Israel's restoration as one of renewed agricultural blessing (Isa. 30:23-24; 32:20; Jer. 31:12; Ezek. 34:26; Amos 9:13-14).

**The Lord's Vineyard (5:1-30).** Isaiah marshaled all of his rhetorical skills to emphasize the necessity and inevitability of divine judgment. What begins as a love song quickly hits a sour note. The song tells of a farmer (the Lord) who clears land for a vineyard (God's people). Having made all the necessary preparations, he expected the vineyard to yield good grapes. Instead it produced only bad. Likewise God established Israel to be a model of justice and righteousness. Israel rewarded God's efforts with violent deeds and injustice. (In the Hebrew text wordplay highlights Israel's perversion of

God's ideal. The word translated "bloodshed" in 5:7 [*misah*] sounds like the word for "justice" [*mispat*], while the word rendered "cries of distress" [*seaqa*] sounds like the word for "righteousness" [*sedaqa*].) The farmer's only alternative was to destroy a fruitless vineyard. So the Lord had to judge His sinful people.

A series of judgment speeches follows, each of which begins with the word "woe." Ancient Israelites used this word when mourning the death of a friend or loved one. By employing this word, the prophet was, as it were, acting out the nation's funeral in advance and thereby emphasizing the inevitability of judgment.

In these woe-speeches Isaiah condemned several sins, including socioeconomic injustice, corruption of the legal system, the carousing of the rich, and their spiritual insensitivity. Irony highlights the speeches. Those who accumulated land and houses at the poor's expense would not prosper from their acquisitions. Those who wined and dined would die of hunger and thirst in exile and would themselves be devoured by the grave. Those who challenged the Lord to "hurry" would soon see His instrument of judgment, the Assyrian hordes, advancing "swiftly and speedily." Finally, those who "put darkness for light and light for darkness" in moral and ethical matters would find their sphere of sinful activity darkened by the clouds of judgment.

**Isaiah's Vision (6:1-13).** Isaiah 1–5 describes how God's people rejected their "Holy One" (1:4; 5:24). In Isaiah 6 the prophet tells of his face-to-face encounter with this Holy God. In the year of King Uzziah's death (740 B.C.) Isaiah received a vision of the real King, the Lord, seated on His heavenly throne. Seraphs surrounded Him, chanting "Holy, holy, holy is the LORD Almighty." Overwhelmed by God's splendor, Isaiah

# MESSIANIC PROPHECIES OF THE OLD TESTAMENT

| PROPHECY | OT REFERENCES | NT FULFILLMENT |
|---|---|---|
| Son of Man comes in glory | Ps 102:16 | Luke 21:24,27; Rev 12:5-10 |
| "Thou remainest" | Ps 102:24-27 | Heb 1:10-12 |
| Prays for His enemies | Ps 109:4 | Luke 23:34 |
| Another to succeed Judas | Ps 109:7-8 | Acts 1:16-20 |
| A priest like Melchizedek | Ps 110:1-7 | Matt 22:41-45; 26:64; Mark 12:35-37; 16:19; Acts 7:56; Eph 1:20; Col 1:20; Heb 1:13; 2:8; 5:6; 6:20; 7:21; 8:1; 10:11-13; 12:2 |
| The chief cornerstone | Ps 118:22-23 | Matt 21:42; Mark 12:10-11; Luke 20:17; John 1:11; Acts 4:11; Eph 2:20; 1 Pet 2:4 |
| The King comes in the name of the Lord | Ps 118:26 | Matt 21:9; 23:39; Mark 11:9; Luke 13:35; 19:38; John 12:13 |
| David's seed to reign | Ps 132:11 / 2 Sam 7:12-13,16, 25-26,29 | Matt 1:1 |
| Declared to be the Son of God | Prov 30:4 | Matt 3:17; Mark 14:61-62; Luke 1:35; John 3:13; 9:35-38; 11:21; Rom 1:2-4; 10:6-9; 2 Pet 1:17 |
| Repentance for the nations | Isa 2:2-4 | Luke 24:47 |
| Hearts are hardened | Isa 6:9-10 | Matt 13:14-15; John 12:39-40; Acts 28:25-27 |
| Born of a virgin | Isa 7:14 | Matt 1:22-23 |
| A rock of offense | Isa 8:14,15 | Rom 9:33; 1 Pet 2:8 |
| Light out of darkness | Isa 9:1-2 | Matt 4:14-16; Luke 2:32 |
| God with us | Isa 9:6-7 | Matt 1:21,23; Luke 1:32-33; John 8:58; 10:30; 14:19; 2 Cor 5:19; Col 2:9 |
| Full of wisdom and power | Isa 11:1-10 | Matt 3:16; John 3:34; Rom 15:12; Heb 1:9 |
| Reigning in mercy | Isa 16:4-5 | Luke 1:31-33 |
| Peg in a sure place | Isa 22:21-25 | Rev 3:7 |
| Death swallowed up in victory | Isa 25:6-12 | 1 Cor 15:54 |
| A stone in Zion | Isa 28:16 | Rom 9:33; 1 Pet 2:6 |
| The deaf hear, the blind see | Isa 29:18-19 | Matt 5:3; 11:5; John 9:39 |
| King of kings, Lord of lords | Isa 32:1-4 | Rev 19:16; 20:6 |
| Son of the Highest | Isa 33:22 | Luke 1:32; 1 Tim 1:17; 6:15 |
| Healing for the needy | Isa 35:4-10 | Matt 9:30; 11:5; 12:22; 20:34; 21:14; 7:30; 5:9 |
| Make ready the way of the Lord | Isa 40:3-5 | Matt 3:3; Mark 1:3; Luke 3:4-5; John 1:23 |
| The Shepherd dies for His sheep | Isa 40:10-11 | John 10:11; Heb 13:20; 1 Pet 2:24-25 |
| The meek Servant | Isa 42:1-16 | Matt 12:17-21; Luke 2:32 |
| A light to the Gentiles | Isa 49:6-12 | Acts 13:47; 2 Cor 6:2 |
| Scourged and spat upon | Isa 50:6 | Matt 26:67; 27:26,30; Mark 14:65; 15:15,19; Luke 22:63-65; John 19:1 |
| Rejected by His people | Isa 52:13–53:12 | Matt 8:7; 27:1-2,12-14,38 |
| Suffered vicariously | Isa 53:4-5 | Mark 15:3-4,27-28; Luke 23:1-25,32-34 |
| Silent when accused | Isa 53:7 | John 1:29; 11:49-52 |
| Crucified with transgressors | Isa 53:12 | John 12:37-38; Acts 8:28-35 |
| Buried with the rich | Isa 53:9 | Acts 10:43; 13:38-39; 1 Cor 15:3; Eph 1:7; 1 Pet 2:21-25; 1 John 1:7,9 |
| Calling of those not a people | Isa 55:4-5 | John 18:37; Rom 9:25-26; Rev 1:5 |
| Deliver out of Zion | Isa 59:16-20 | Rom 11:26-27 |
| Nations walk in the light | Isa 60:1-3 | Luke 2:32 |
| Anointed to preach liberty | Isa 61:1-3 | Luke 4:17-19; Acts 10:38 |
| Called by a new name | Isa 62:1-2 | Luke 2:32; Rev 3:12 |
| The King cometh | Isa 62:11 | Matt 21:5 |
| Vesture dipped in blood | Isa 63:1-3 | Rev 19:13 |
| Afflicted with the afflicted | Isa 63:8-9 | Matt 25:34-40 |
| The elect shall inherit | Isa 65:9 | Rom 11:5,7; Heb 7:14; Rev 5:5 |
| New heavens and a new earth | Isa 65:17-25 | 2 Pet 3:13; Rev 21:1 |
| The Lord our righteousness | Jer 23:5-6 | John 2:19-21; Rom 1:3-4; Eph 2:20-21; 1 Pet 2:5 |
| Born a King | Jer 30:9 | John 18:37; Rev 1:5 |
| Massacre of infants | Jer 31:15 | Matt 2:17-18 |
| Conceived by the Holy Spirit | Jer 31:22 | Matt 1:20; Luke 1:35 |
| A New Covenant | Jer 31:31-34 | Matt 26:27-29; Mark 14:22-24; Luke 22:15-20; 1 Cor 11:25; Heb 8:8-12 10:15-17; 12:24; 13:20 |
| A spiritual house | Jer 33:15-17 | John 2:19-21; Eph 2:20-21; 1 Pet 2:5 |
| A tree planted by God | Ezek 17:22-24 | Matt 13:31-32 |
| The humble exalted | Ezek 21:26-27 | Luke 1:52 |
| The good Shepherd | Ezek 34:23-24 | John 10:11 |
| Stone cut without hands | Dan 2:34-35 | Acts 4:10-12 |
| His kingdom triumphant | Dan 2:44-45 | Luke 1:33; 1 Cor 15:24; Rev 11:15 |
| An everlasting dominion | Dan 7:13-14 | Matt 24:30; 25:31; 26:64; Mark 14:61-62; Acts 1:9-11; Rev 1:7 |
| Kingdom for the saints | Dan 7:27 | Luke 1:33; 1 Cor 15:24; Rev 11:15 |
| Time of His birth | Dan 9:24-27 | Matt 24:15-21; Luke 3:1 |
| Israel restored | Hos 3:5 | John 18:37; Rom 11:25-27 |
| Flight into Egypt | Hos 11:1 | Matt 2:15 |

# MESSIANIC PROPHECIES OF THE OLD TESTAMENT

| PROPHECY | OT REFERENCES | NT FULFILLMENT |
| --- | --- | --- |
| Promise of the Spirit | Joel 2:28-32 | Acts 2:17-21; Rom 10:13 |
| The sun darkened | Amos 8:9 | Matt 24:29; Acts 2:20; Rev 6:12 |
| Restoration of tabernacle | Amos 9:11-12 | Acts 15:16-18 |
| Israel regathered | Mic 2:12-13 | John 10:14,26 |
| The kingdom established | Mic 4:1-8 | Luke 1:33 |
| Born in Bethlehem | Mic 5:1-5 | Matt 2:1; Luke 2:4,10-11 |
| Earth filled with knowledge of the glory of the Lord | Hab 2:14 | Rom 11:26; Rev 21:23-26 |
| The Lamb on the throne | Zech 2:10-13 | Rev 5:13; 6:9; 21:24; 22:1-5 |
| A holy priesthood | Zech 3:8 | John 2:19-21; Eph 2:20-21; 1 Pet 2:5 |
| A heavenly High Priest | Zech 6:12-13 | Heb 4:4; 8:1,2 |
| Triumphal entry | Zech 9:9-10 | Matt 21:4-5; Mark 11:9-10; Luke 20:38; John 12:13-15 |
| Sold for thirty pieces of silver | Zech 11:12-13 | Matt 26:14-15 |
| Money buys potter's field | Zech 11:12-13 | Matt 27:9 |
| Piercing of His body | Zech 12:10 | John 19:34,37 |
| Shepherd smitten—sheep scattered | Zech 13:1,6-7 | Matt 26:31; John 16:32 |
| Preceded by Forerunner | Mal 3:1 | Matt 11:10; Mark 1:2; Luke 7:27 |
| Our sins purged | Mal 3:3 | Heb 1:3 |
| The light of the world | Mal 4:2-3 | Luke 1:78; John 1:9; 12:46; 2 Pet 1:19; Rev 2:28; 19:11-16; 22:16 |
| The coming of Elijah | Mal 4:5-6 | Matt 11:14; 17:10-12 |
| Seed of the woman | Gen 3:15 | Gal 4:4; Heb 2:14 |
| Through Noah's sons | Gen 9:27 | Luke 6:36 |
| Seed of Abraham | Gen 12:3 | Matt 1:1; Gal 3:8,16 |
| Seed of Isaac | Gen 17:19 | Rom 9:7; Heb 11:18 |
| Blessing to nations | Gen 18:18 | Gal 3:8 |
| Seed of Isaac | Gen 21:12 | Rom 9:7; Heb 11:18 |
| Blessing to Gentiles | Gen 22:18 | Gal 3:8,16; Heb 6:14 |
| Blessing to Gentiles | Gen 26:4 | Gal 3:8,16; Heb 6:14 |
| Blessing through Abraham | Gen 28:14 | Gal 3:8,16; Heb 6:14 |
| Of the tribe of Judah | Gen 49:10 | Rev 5:5 |
| No bone broken | Exod 12:46 | John 19:36 |
| Blessing to firstborn son | Exod 13:2 | Luke 2:23 |
| No bone broken | Num 9:12 | John 19:36 |
| Serpent in wilderness | Num 21:8-9 | John 3:14-15 |
| A star out of Jacob | Num 24:17-19 | Matt 2:2; Luke 1:33,78; Rev 22:16 |
| As a prophet | Deut 18:15,18-19 | John 6:14; 7:40; Acts 3:22-23 |
| Cursed on the tree | Deut 21:23 | Gal 3:13 |
| The throne of David established forever | 2 Sam 7:12-13,16,25-26 1 Chr 17:11-14, 23-27; 2 Chr 21:7 | Matt 19:28; 21:4; 25:31; Mark 12:37; Luke 1:32; John 7:4; Acts 2:30; 13:23 Rom 1:3; 2 Tim 2:8; Heb 1:5,8; 8:1; 12:2; Rev 22:1 |
| A promised Redeemer | Job 19:25-27 | John 5:28-29; Gal 4:4; Eph 1:7,11,14 |
| Declared to be the Son of God | Ps 2:1-12 | Matt 3:17; Mark 1:11; Acts 4:25-26; 13:33; Heb 1:5; 5:5; Rev 2:26-27; 19:15-16 |
| His resurrection | Ps 16:8-10 | Acts 2:27; 13:35; 26:23 |
| Hands and feet pierced | Ps 22:1-31 | Matt 27:31,35-36 |
| Mocked and insulted | Ps 22:7-8 | Matt 27:39-43,45-49 |
| Soldiers cast lots for coat | Ps 22:18 | Mark 15:20,24-25,34; Luke 19:24; 23:35; John 19:15-18,23-24,34; Acts 2:23-24 |
| Accused by false witnesses | Ps 27:12 | Matt 26:60-61 |
| He commits His spirit | Ps 31:5 | Luke 23:46 |
| No broken bone | Ps 34:20 | John 19:36 |
| Accused by false witnesses | Ps 35:11 | Matt 26:59-61; Mark 14:57-58 |
| Hated without reason | Ps 35:19 | John 15:24-25 |
| Friends stand afar off | Ps 38:11 | Matt 27:55; Mark 15:40; Luke 23:49 |
| "I come to do Thy will" | Ps 40:6-8 | Heb 10:5-9 |
| Betrayed by a friend | Ps 41:9 | Matt 26:14-16,47,50; Mark 14:17-21; Luke 22:19-23; John 13:18-19 |
| Known for righteousness | Ps 45:2,6-7 | Heb 1:8-9 |
| His resurrection | Ps 49:15 | Mark 16:6 |
| Betrayed by a friend | Ps 55:12-14 | John 13:18 |
| His ascension | Ps 68:18 | Eph 4:8 |
| Hated without reason | Ps 69:4 | John 15:25 |
| Stung by reproaches | Ps 69:9 | John 2:17; Rom 15:3 |
| Given gall and vinegar | Ps 69:21 | Matt 27:34,48; Mark 15:23; Luke 23:36; John 19:29 |
| Exalted by God | Ps 72:1-19 | Matt 2:2; Phil 2:9-11; Heb 1:8 |
| He speaks in parables | Ps 78:2 | Matt 13:34-35 |
| Seed of David exalted | Ps 89:3-4,19,27-29 35-37 | Luke 1:32; Acts 2:30; 13:23; Rom 1:3; 2 Tim 2:8 |

acknowledged his and his people's sinful condition. After Isaiah was symbolically purified, the Lord commissioned him as a messenger to His spiritually insensitive people. He was to preach until judgment swept through the land and the people were carried into exile, leaving only a remnant.

**Deliverance through Messiah (7:1–12:6).** The background for these chapters is the Syro-Ephraimitic war (735–733 B.C.), when Aram and the Northern Kingdom invaded Judah and besieged Jerusalem.

*Ahaz's Unbelief, Isaiah's Sign Children (7:1–8:22).* During the Syro-Ephraimitic war, Aram (Syria) and the Northern Kingdom threatened to replace Judah's king, Ahaz, with a nearby ruler. Isaiah urged the king to trust in the Lord's promises to the Davidic dynasty. While Ahaz was inspecting the city's water system in preparation for a siege, Isaiah and his son, Shear-jashub, met the king. The names of the prophet (Isaiah means *the LORD saves*) and his son (Shear-jashub means *a remnant will return*) were symbolic, indicating that God was fully capable of preserving His people through the crisis.

Isaiah challenged Ahaz to ask for a sign of confirmation. When Ahaz refused, Isaiah announced that the Lord would give the king a sign. In the near future a child would be born and named "Immanuel" (meaning *God is with us*). The name would be appropriate because he would be a living proof of God's providential presence with His people. Before the child could distinguish right from wrong, the Lord would deliver Judah from the Aramean-Israelite coalition, demonstrating His sovereignty over Judah's destiny.

However, due to Ahaz's unbelief, this time of deliverance would be shortlived. To punish the king for his lack of faith the Lord would bring upon the land a crisis far worse than the Aramean-Israelite threat. Ironically, the Assyrians, to whom Ahaz looked for help (2 Kgs. 16:7-9), would invade the land and decimate its population. The curds and honey eaten by Immanuel, which at first appeared to be signs of divine blessing, would now attest to the land's desolate condition.

Matthew 1:22-23 states that the birth of Jesus fulfilled the prophecy of Isaiah 7:14. However, one must not conclude from this that the ancient Immanuel prophecy refers *exclusively* to Jesus. The circumstances surrounding the prophecy demand a more immediate fulfillment as well. The context of Isaiah 7:14 indicates that a child would be born in the days of Ahaz who would serve as a sign to that generation of God's providential control of international events and of His people's destiny. This child, who was a sign of God's presence with His people, foreshadowed Jesus, who is "God with us" in the fullest possible sense. Matthew's use of the Immanuel prophecy is consistent with the way he used the Old Testament elsewhere in the early chapters of his Gospel. Matthew 2:14-15 applies Hosea 11:1, which in its context speaks of the historical exodus of Israel out of Egypt, to Jesus' flight to Egypt as an infant. Matthew presented Jesus as a new or ideal Israel, whose experience in early life is patterned after that of the nation Israel. According to Matthew 2:17-18, Herod's slaughter of the innocent children of Bethlehem fulfilled Jeremiah 31:15, which in its context describes the mothers of Ramah (not Bethlehem) weeping as their children were carried off into exile. Herod's action fulfilled Jeremiah 31:15 in that the event described by Jeremiah establishes a pattern to which Herod's oppressive deeds correspond in their character.

The immediate fulfillment of the Immanuel prophecy is described in chapter 8. Isaiah made careful preparations for the birth of a sign-child. He and "the prophetess" (presumably his wife) then had a child, who was named Maher-Shalal-Hash-Baz. Though the child was not named Immanuel, the special significance attached to his name and growth pattern parallels the Immanuel prophecy. Maher-Shalal-Hash-Baz' name, which means *quick to plunder, swift to the spoil,* pointed to the destruction of Judah's enemies. Before he could cry out "daddy" or "mommy," Assyria would plunder both the Arameans and the Northern Kingdom. But the prophecy has its negative side as well. Because of Judah's unbelief, the Assyrians would also invade the Southern Kingdom and, like a flood, bring widespread destruction. This message of judgment concludes with an address to Immanuel, as if he were already living. This is best explained by understanding the preceding verses as describing his birth.

If indeed Maher-Shalal-Hash-Baz and Immanuel are one and the same, some explanation must be given for the different names. Perhaps the names emphasize different aspects of the same prophecy. Immanuel focuses on God's involvement in history, while Maher-Shalal-Hash-Baz, the child's actual name, anticipates the destructive effects of God's involvement. (In the same way Immanuel is applied to Jesus, emphasizing God's personal intervention in history through the incarnation. At the same time, the name Jesus, meaning *the Lord saves,* points to the purpose of God's act.)

Following the message of judgment upon Judah, the prophet, in a sudden burst of emotion, abruptly shifted his perspective. Challenging the nations to attack God's people, he announced that God's presence with His people assured their ultimate deliverance.

Before developing this theme in more detail (see 9:1-7), Isaiah recorded instructions he received from the Lord. The Lord exhorted Isaiah to reject popular opinion and trust in Him. He promised to be a sanctuary for the faithful, but for faithless Israel and Judah He would be like a stumbling block or a snare. In response to the Lord's charge, Isaiah declared his trust in God. He also reminded his listeners that he and his children were God-given signs and encouraged them to look to God's revealed prophetic word, not pagan practices, for guidance.

*The Messiah's Deliverance of God's People (9:1-7).* Dark days were ahead for God's people, especially for the Northern Kingdom. The Assyrians would invade Palestine from the north and humble Israel. Isaiah looked beyond this time of punishment and saw a bright deliverance. Eventually the Lord would save His people from their oppressors, just as He did in the days of Gideon, through whom He annihilated the oppressive Midianites (see Judg. 6–8).

The Lord would accomplish this future deliverance through the Messiah, who would rule on David's throne. The words "For to us a child is born, to us a son is given" link this messianic prophecy with the prediction of Immanuel's birth (see 7:14), suggesting that Immanuel/Maher-Shalal-Hash-Baz foreshadowed the Messiah. Isaiah's son was a reminder of God's sovereign presence; the Messiah would be a much more perfect expression of God's presence.

The Messiah's royal titles attest to his close relationship to God and depict him as a mighty warrior capable of establishing peace in his realm. Four titles are listed, each of which contains two elements. The first, "Wonderful Counselor,"

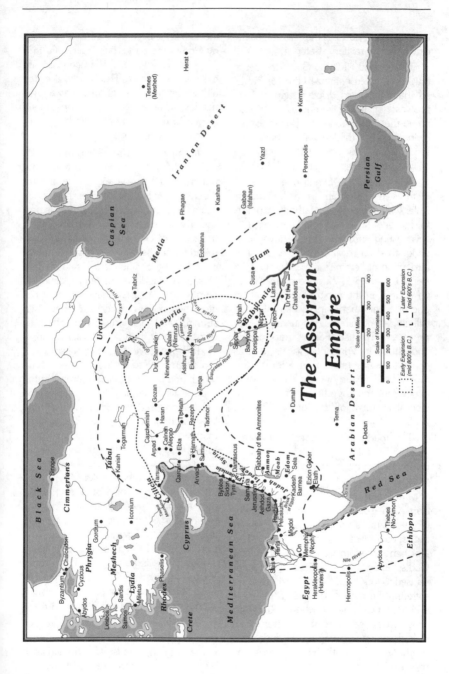

in this context portrays the Messiah as an extraordinary military strategist.

The second, "Mighty God," indicates that God would energize Him for battle so that He would display superhuman prowess against His enemies. (Some argue that this second title points to the divine nature of the Messiah. Others contend that the doctrine of the Messiah's deity is only clearly revealed in the NT.)

The third title, "Everlasting Father," pictures the Messiah as a beneficent Ruler who demonstrates fatherly concern for His people. In the eighth century B.C. "everlasting" probably would have been understood as royal hyperbole (see the attribution of "eternal" life to the king in Pss. 21:4; 61:6-7; 72:5 [compare NIV]). Of course, in the progress of revelation one discovers that Christ's eternal reign will literally fulfill the language of the prophecy. (The title "Father" must not be understood in Trinitarian terms. In this context it is best taken as an idiom, commonly used in the ancient world, for a benevolent and just official or ruler. For a biblical example of the idiom, see Isa. 22:21.)

The fourth title, "Prince of Peace," indicates that the Messiah's kingdom will be characterized by social justice and prosperity.

*Judgment of the Northern Kingdom (9:8–10:4).* Having described the glory of Israel's future, Isaiah addressed the situation of his own times. The Northern Kingdom, despite experiencing God's increasingly severe discipline, refused to turn back to the Lord. Though suffering the ravages of foreign invasion and civil war, the Northern Kingdom proudly claimed to be the master of its own destiny and antagonized Judah, its neighbor to the south. The nation's corrupt leaders continued to enact unjust laws, depriving the poor of their rights. For such a nation divine judgment was inevitable. The punitive measures taken by God in the past would culminate in a "day of reckoning," characterized by exile and slaughter. The words "Yet for all this, his anger is not turned away, his hand is still upraised," which appear as a refrain in this judgment speech, picture the relentless approach of this day.

*Judgment of the Assyrians (10:5–34).* With the appearance of this same refrain in 10:4 one expects a further description of Israel's judgment. But once again the prophet suddenly shifts his perspective by including the Assyrians within the scope of God's Judgment Day. God raised up the Assyrians as His instrument of judgment against Israel and Judah. Obsessed with delusions of grandeur and empire, the Assyrians arrogantly attributed their military success to their own strength and claimed sovereignty over God's chosen city, Jerusalem. From God's perspective this was as absurd as a tool attempting to wield the laborer who uses it or a weapon trying to brandish the warrior who employs it. In anger the Lord announced that He would annihilate Assyria in a single day. Though the mighty Assyrians were comparable to a forest filled with trees, the Lord, like a raging fire, would reduce them to an insignificant number. Like Egypt and Midian, past oppressors of God's people, the Assyrians would experience the harsh judgment of God. When they defiantly marched against Jerusalem, the Lord would cut them down to size, like a woodsman felling a tall tree. This prophecy was fulfilled in 701 B.C. when the Lord decimated Sennacherib's armies outside Jerusalem's walls (see 37:36-37).

In conjunction with Assyria's demise, the Lord promised to restore the once numerous people of Israel, who had been reduced to a mere remnant by the oppressive Assyrians. In that day God's people would place their trust in Him and in the Messiah (compare "Mighty God," 10:21) rather than in foreign alliances.

*The Messiah's Kingdom of Justice (11:1-10).* Assyria's destiny was in direct contrast to that of the Davidic throne. The Lord would chop down the Assyrian empire, but He would cause a new ruler, the Messiah, to spring up from Jesse's family tree. Energized by the Lord's Spirit, this King would possess wisdom, executive ability, and loyalty to the Lord, all of which are necessary to rule in a just and effective manner. His legal decisions would be based on truth, not superficial appearances. He would defend the poor and suppress the wicked. His kingdom would be one of justice, equality, and peace, where the strong no longer prey upon the weak.

*Restoration of God's Exiled People (11:11-12:6).* In the messianic age God's people would also be restored to their former glory. Though exiled throughout the world, God would lead them back to the promised land in a grand new exodus. As in the days of Moses, God would miraculously eliminate all obstacles, prompting His people to once more declare, "The LORD is my strength and my song; he has become my salvation" (see Exod. 15:2). As in the first exodus, God's people would experience His abundant provision and blessing (compare 12:3 with Exod. 15:22-27). Upon returning to the land, the once hostile Northern and Southern Kingdoms would reunite and, as in the days of the Davidic empire, bring their enemies into subjection. In contrast to Isaiah's day, when Israel "spurned the Holy One of Israel" (see 1:4), the Holy One of Israel would be exalted among His people.

## GOD'S KINGDOM (13:1-39:8)

*Judgment Speeches (13:1-23:18).* Before the prophet's vision of universal peace (see 2:2-4; 11:1-10) could become a reality, God had to subdue the rebellious nations of the world. Chapters 13-23 contain a series of judgment speeches against various nations of Isaiah's day and pave the way for the message of universal judgment in chapters 24-27. These judgment speeches serve as a reminder to God's people of His absolute sovereignty over all nations, including both their enemies and allies. God's people need not fear the surrounding nations or rely on their aid.

*Judgment on Babylon and Assyria (13:1-14:27).* Isaiah's first judgment oracle begins and ends with a universal focus. The speech is specifically directed against Babylon, with a brief message against the Assyrians appended in 14:24-25. Some understand the entire speech against the background of the Assyrian period because the Assyrians controlled Babylon during a large portion of Isaiah's ministry and devastated the city in 689 B.C. However, it is more likely that the Babylonian empire, which replaced Assyria as the Near East's leading power, is in view in 13:17-14:23. Isaiah 13:19 specifically associates the city with the Babylonians, and the "king of Babylon," mentioned in 14:4, is most naturally viewed as a Babylonian (see 39:1). Furthermore, the Medes are named as the conqueror of the city.

In Isaiah's day the Babylonians, struggling with the Assyrians for control of Mesopotamia, sought an alliance with Judah. But the prophet knew that the Babylonians would eventually become the enemies of his people and take them away into exile (see 39:1-7). Here he proclaimed judgment against Judah's future oppressor.

The speech opens with a vivid picture of the Lord gathering His armies for war. This coming battle is set against the background of the universal judgment of the Lord's day, which is accompanied by cosmic disturbances and brings widespread terror and slaughter. The Lord would use the cruel Medes as His instrument of judgment and reduce Babylon to an uninhabited heap of ruins.

This prophecy appears to refer to the conquest of Babylon by Medo-Persian forces under Cyrus in 539 B.C. However, Cyrus's takeover of the city, which was relatively peaceful and even welcomed by many Babylonians, fails to satisfy fully the language of 13:17-22. Perhaps the description is a standardized and exaggerated way of emphasizing that the Babylonian empire would be terminated. But the universal and eschatological setting of this speech suggests that a final judgment of Gentile powers, which the downfall of historical Babylon only symbolized and foreshadowed, is also in view (see Rev. 17–18). Since Babylon was a center of Mesopotamian religion and was associated in biblical tradition with rebellion against God (see Gen. 11:1-9), it became an apt symbol of the nations' opposition to God.

The destruction of Babylon would mean deliverance for Israel. In chapter 14 God's people, released from bondage and restored to their land, sang a taunt song against the fallen king of Babylon. They depicted him as descending into the world of the dead, where other deceased kings rose to meet him. These kings ridiculed him, declaring that this once proud world conqueror had been cast down into a bed of worms and maggots. Drawing on their own mythological traditions, these pagan rulers compared the king of Babylon to the petty god "Morning Star, Son of the Dawn," who had had the audacity to think he could ascend the mountain of the gods and rival the high god El's authority. (In 13:13 "God" translates Hebrew *el*, the name of the chief god of the many Canaanite gods. "The sacred mountain" translates Hebrew *sapon*, the name of the Canaanite Olym-

pus, where the gods, here called "stars," assembled.)

It comes as no surprise that words of judgment against Assyria are appended to the oracle against Babylon. Assyria and Babylon were closely associated geographically and in biblical tradition, which attributes the founding of both to Nimrod (see Gen. 10:8-12). As an oppressive Mesopotamian power that ruled Babylon in Isaiah's day, Assyria's decisive judgment foreshadowed that of the coming Babylonian empire and all the hostile nations of the world.

*Judgment on the Philistines (14:28-32).* God's judgment would also fall upon the Philistines. The oracle, which is dated to the year of King Ahaz's death (about 715 B.C.) warns that the Philistines should not rejoice over the apparent relief from Assyrian oppression that they had recently experienced. Though the Assyrians' attention might be diverted to other trouble spots in their empire, they would again invade the west and bring the rebellious Philistines into subjection. In 712 B.C. Sargon captured the Philistine city of Ashdod (see 20:1) and made it an Assyrian province. In 701 B.C. Sennacherib conquered Ashkelon and Ekron. In contrast to these Philistine cities, Jerusalem experienced God's supernatural protection.

*Judgment on Moab (15:1–16:14).* This oracle against Moab is undated, and therefore the time of its fulfillment is uncertain. Like the preceding and following oracles, it probably anticipates one of the Assyrian invasions of the late eighth century B.C. Geographical details and vivid imagery highlight the oracle. In virtually every city the once proud Moabites would lament over their military defeat and its disastrous effects on their land. With dramatic flair Isaiah urged the Moabite fugitives to look to Jerusalem for aid. He then recited Moab's appeal for help, which includes a statement recognizing that only an ideal Davidic ruler could provide relief from the oppressor.

*Judgment on Damascus and Israel (17:1-14).* Though directed against Damascus, the capital of Aram (Syria), this judgment speech deals primarily with its ally, the Northern Kingdom. The oracle was fulfilled between 732 and 721 B.C. when the Assyrians conquered both Aram and Israel and made them provinces. Isaiah warned that Damascus would be reduced to a heap of ruins and lose its power. The prestige of the Northern Kingdom would be diminished, like a man who loses weight during a serious illness. Isaiah compared the coming devastation to a harvest, when the grain is stripped from the fields and the olives are beaten and shaken from the trees. Instead of trusting in God's protection, Israel placed its hope in foreign gods and alliances (compare "imported vines," v. 10), which would prove worthless in the day of calamity. At that time people would recognize the futility of idolatry because God is absolutely sovereign.

Isaiah concluded this oracle with a message of hope for Jerusalem. Though the Assyrian hordes would come sweeping down on Palestine like raging waters, the Lord would only allow them to go so far. When they threatened Jerusalem, He would suddenly sweep them away like chaff or tumbleweed before a powerful wind (see 10:28-43; 14:25; 37:36-37).

*Judgment on Cush (18:1-7).* This oracle pertains to Cush (Ethiopia), located south of Egypt. Possibly it alludes to Cushite efforts to enlist Judah's support in an anti-Assyrian alliance. The Lord would not support the Ethiopian effort, causing it to come to ruin, like unfruitful branches that are pruned. Eventually the Cushites would bring gifts of homage to Jerusalem in recognition of the Lord's sovereignty.

*Judgment on Egypt (19:1-25).* Because the Ethiopians controlled Egypt during Isaiah's time, this oracle is closely related to the preceding one. In the late eighth century B.C. Judah was tempted to ally itself with Ethiopia/Egypt against the Assyrians. Such an alliance was ill-advised, for the Lord was about to bring judgment upon the Egyptians. Following a period of civil strife and turmoil, a foreign ruler would conquer Egypt. This prophecy was fulfilled in the seventh century B.C., when the Assyrian kings Esarhaddon and Ashurbanipal conquered Egypt. Egypt's demise would be accompanied by economic disaster caused by the drying up of the Nile and by a complete breakdown in leadership.

Isaiah foresaw a time when Egypt would recognize the Lord's sovereignty, submit to His rule, look to Him for help, and worship Him. In that day peace would sweep over the war-torn Near East. The rivals, Assyria and Egypt, who oppressed God's people, would join Israel in the worship of the one true God.

*Judgment of Egypt and Cush (20:1-6).* This brief oracle is a fitting conclusion to the judgment message of the two preceding speeches. The oracle is dated to the year of the Assyrian conquest of rebellious Ashdod (712 B.C.). This event demonstrated the helplessness of Egypt, which had encouraged Ashdod's rebellion but then offered it no assistance against the Assyrians. The message spoken in 712 is found in 20:3-6, while 20:2 records the Lord's words to the prophet three years before. During this three-year period the prophet had walked around indecently exposed as an object lesson on Egypt's and Cush's fate. In the near future the Assyrians would conquer Egypt and carry off exiles, who would be taken away stripped and barefoot. The purpose of the prophet's action and the subsequent oracle is obvious. To trust in Egypt/Cush was foolish, for it would lead only to ruin and shame.

*Judgment on Babylon (21:1-10).* Babylon, poetically called "the Desert by the Sea," again takes center stage in Isaiah's vision of judgment (see 13:1–14:23). The prophet's vision of Babylon's defeat at the hands of the Elamites and Medes had an intense physical and emotional effect upon him. In dramatic fashion he urged the unsuspecting Babylonians to get up from their feasts and prepare for battle (see Dan. 5). The drama continues as imaginary messengers are depicted announcing the news of Babylon's defeat to eagerly awaiting watchmen. In conclusion Isaiah assured his audience, a future generation who would experience Babylon's oppression, that his message was authentic. The fulfillment of the prophecy came in 539 B.C. when Cyrus, whose army contained Medes and Elamites, conquered Babylon (see comments on 13:1–14:23).

*Judgment on Dumah (21:11-12).* This very brief, riddlelike oracle concerns Dumah, an oasis in Arabia. Assuming the role of an imaginary watchman, the prophet was asked by an unidentified speaker from Seir (Edom) how long the night would last. Because of its geographical proximity to Dumah, Edom would have taken a keen interest in developments there. The watchman responded that morning was indeed coming, only to be followed again by night. Apparently the night is here a symbol of distress. The prophet was unable to encourage oppressed Dumah. Even though some relief might come, the future remained foreboding.

*Judgment on Arabia (21:13-17).* In a related oracle the prophet foresaw the defeat of other Arabian peoples. He dramatically described the plight of fugitives from battle. He then officially announced that Kedar in the Arabian desert would

fall within one year. This prophecy was probably fulfilled in conjunction with one of Sargon's or Sennacherib's Arabian campaigns.

*Judgment on Jerusalem (22:1-25).* Chapter 22 concerns Judah and Jerusalem. It contains two judgment speeches, an oracle against the "Valley of Vision" and a message addressed to the royal official Shebna. The location of the "Valley of Vision" is unknown, though it is clearly associated with Judah and Jerusalem. The historical background of the oracle is uncertain. It may reflect one of the Assyrian invasions of the late eighth century B.C. (either Sargon's in 712 B.C. or Sennacherib's a decade later).

The Lord denounced the people for their improper response to the crisis. Instead of trusting in the One who founded the City of David, they relied on their own efforts, which included fortifying the city walls and building a new water system. Refusing the Lord's call to repentance, they feasted and fatalistically abandoned any hope of deliverance, implying that the Lord was not in control of the city's destiny. For such people judgment was inevitable. While Hezekiah's repentance (Isa. 37–38; Jer. 26:17-19) and God's decision to demonstrate His sovereignty over the proud Assyrians (10:5-34) postponed Jerusalem's downfall, divine judgment eventually fell upon the city.

The people's lack of devotion to the Lord was epitomized by Shebna, a royal official who displayed inordinate pride by building himself a grand tomb. The Lord announced that Shebna would die in a foreign land and never occupy his specially built tomb. Eliakim would replace him as the royal steward. He would assume responsibility for the nation's care and exercise authority on behalf of the king. For a time his position would be firm and his family honored. However, in due time Eliakim, like all mere human officials, would lose his authority. By the time Sennacherib besieged Jerusalem in 701 B.C., Eliakim had replaced Shebna as steward, and Shebna had apparently been demoted to a scribal office (see 36:3,11,22; 37:2). Beyond this we have no record of the outworking of these prophecies.

*Judgment on Tyre (23:1-18).* Isaiah's oracles against the nations conclude with this judgment speech against Tyre, a prominent commercial center on the Mediterranean coast north of Israel. Tyre's many trading partners were told to mourn, for the Lord was about to bring the proud city low. Tyre should not consider it safe, for even the greatest of cities, such as Babylon, could be conquered (23:13 refers to the Assyrian devastation of Babylon in 689 B.C.). Tyre would experience a seventy-year period of decline. This number may be figurative, suggesting completeness and implying that few, if any, of those who saw its decline would live to view its resurgence. Eventually the city would be restored to its former status, but in that day its wealth would be sent as tribute to the Lord.

The precise details of the prophecy's fulfillment are uncertain. Assyria brought Tyre under its control, leading to an eclipse of the latter's prominence. Later both Nebuchadnezzar (in the sixth century B.C.) and Alexander the Great (in the fourth century B.C.) conquered the city.

***Judgment and Restoration (24:1–27:13).*** Isaiah's message of judgment against individual nations culminates in this section. It describes God's judgment on a universal scale and the establishment of His worldwide rule, using language akin to apocalyptic.

*God Judges the Earth for Its Rebellion (24:1-23).* The Lord would completely destroy the earth for its rebellion against "the everlasting covenant," prob-

ably a reference to God's mandate to Noah (see Gen. 9:1-7). Instead of showing respect for God's image in other human beings, the inhabitants of the earth had shed innocent blood (see 26:21). In the ancient Near Eastern world curses (threatened forms of punishment often involving loss of fertility and death) were attached to formal agreements. Verses 6-13 describe such a curse sweeping over the sinful earth. While the prophet heard the future praise God's just judgment would elicit from His followers, he expressed his chagrin over the present injustice. This prompted him to once more describe the coming worldwide judgment as inescapable and severe as Noah's flood (compare 24:18b with Gen. 7:11). In that day the Lord would defeat all heavenly and earthly opposition and establish His rule from Jerusalem.

*God's People Celebrate His Kingship (25:1–26:6).* Chapter 25 begins with a song of praise spoken by the future generation of God's people who would witness His worldwide judgment and experience His deliverance. They celebrated His conquest of the hostile nations and declared that He had been their faithful protector.

In that day the Lord would host a marvelous feast at Jerusalem in celebration of His kingship. He would eliminate the curse of death from humankind once and for all and remove the disgrace of His covenant people. The imagery of God swallowing up death is powerful irony, in that death was viewed in the Bible (see 5:14) and in pagan mythology as the great swallower of humankind. In contrast to Jerusalem's glorious future, the proud cities and peoples of the Gentile world, epitomized here by Moab, would be humiliated.

This section closes with another song of praise, in which a future generation of

Judeans affirm their trust in the God of Jerusalem, who protects those who place their faith in Him and humiliates the proud oppressor.

*God's People Anticipate His Intervention (26:7-19).* These verses date to a time prior to the announced judgment and deliverance of the preceding chapters. God's faithful people lamented the wickedness around them, expressed their confidence in and devotion to God, and asked for His intervention. In response God assured them that He would restore the nation, using the figure of bodily resurrection to emphasize the miraculous revival His people would experience (see Ezek. 37:1-14).

*The Restoration of God's People (26:20–27:13).* The prophet urged the faithful to hide behind closed doors until the judgment of God passed. The Lord would punish the sinful world for its bloody deeds and subdue those who resist His kingship. These forces are symbolized by the sea monster Leviathan, which in Canaanite myth resisted the kingship of the storm god Baal. Following God's victory over His foes, He would make Israel His "fruitful vineyard" and guard it with unceasing attention (contrast the vineyard image in 5:1-7).

Returning briefly to the present, Isaiah reminded his audience that purifying judgment lay ahead for God's people. Because of their idolatry and lack of spiritual understanding, they would endure warfare and exile and even witness the desolation of Jerusalem. Nevertheless, a day would come when the exiled people would return and worship the Lord in purified Jerusalem.

**Judgment and Hope (28:1–35:10).** Much of this section, which contains several woe-oracles (see 28:1; 29:1,15; 30:1; 31:1; 33:1), is accusatory and threatening, but these chapters also contain words of hope. Though the Northern Kingdom and the Gentile nations were included as objects of divine judgment, the focal point was Judah. Rebellious Judah had to reject the example of the Northern Kingdom and resist the temptation to rely upon foreign alliances. Instead the nations must trust in God alone as the One who is sovereign over the destiny of His people and of the surrounding nations.

*Samaria's Impending Downfall a Warning to Self-confident Judah (28:1-29).* The chapter opens with a woe-oracle against Samaria, the capital city in which the carousing upper classes of the Northern Kingdom took great pride. However, the Lord would send the Assyrians against it like a destructive storm. Samaria would disappear as quickly as a sweet early fig that one grabs with delight and quickly devours (see Hos. 9:10; Mic. 7:1). Eventually judgment would bring God's people to their senses, and they would take pride in Him, not in structures they had made.

Verses 7-13 either continue the description of Samaria's carousers or depict the people of Judah. In either case the religious leaders are portrayed as staggering, vomiting drunkards and the people as sarcastic mockers of the prophet's message. Since they rejected the Lord's offer of true peace, conditioned upon righteous living, He would send against them the Assyrians, whose foreign speech would serve as His mocking response to their jeering mimicry of the prophet.

The remainder of the message is addressed to the leaders of Jerusalem, who boastfully claimed they were safe from harm because they had made a covenant with death (probably an allusion to a foreign alliance in which they were placing their trust). However, the Lord, the only true Protector of the nation and the sovereign Ruler of all things, including death, would bring judgment upon them. He would attack His own people, like He did the Philistines at Mount Pera-zim (see 2 Sam. 5:20-21) and the Amor-ites at Gibeon (see Josh. 10:10-11).

Just as a farmer plows, plants, and harvests at the appropriate times and uses the proper methods for each activ-ity, so the Lord would deal with His people in a wise and appropriate man-ner. While judgment was necessary, the Lord would not allow it to be excessive.

*Warning Spiritually Insensitive Ariel (29:1-24).* The Lord warned that He would bring a military crisis upon complacent Jerusalem, called here Ariel (the meaning and contextual significance of this name are uncertain). The people were characterized by spiritual insensitiv-ity, religious hypocrisy, and an unwilling-ness to trust their destiny to God. The coming crisis would be severe, but God would suddenly rescue the city from the armies outside its walls. This prophecy anticipated the miraculous deliverance of Jerusalem in 701 B.C. Eventually God would restore spiritual awareness, justice, and covenantal loyalty to the land.

*Warnings against Foreign Alliances (30:1-31:9).* The Lord denounced Judah for seeking an alliance with Egypt. Instead of consulting the Lord, the people rejected the prophetic word and sought help from a nation that was inca-pable of following through on its prom-ises. The Lord warned Judah that continued obstinacy would lead to defeat and humiliation. He reminded them that deliverance could only come through repentance and faith. If they cried out to Him, He would graciously and compas-sionately give them renewed spiritual direction and restore agricultural pros-perity to the land. He would appear in glorious splendor and destroy the Assyri-ans, causing His people to rejoice over the demise of their enemies.

Chapter 31 begins with another denunciation of the alliance with Egypt. Though the Egyptians had many horses and chariots, their military might could not prevent their defeat at the hands of the sovereign God. Judah had to repent and trust in the Lord, for He, not Egypt, was the true Protector of Jerusalem. He would miraculously destroy the Assyri-ans, demonstrating again His sovereignty over mere human armies.

*Justice and Peace Reestablished in Judah and Jerusalem (32:1-33:24).* In another of his messianic visions Isaiah anticipated a day when a just king would reign over the land, assisted by compe-tent rulers who would protect, rather than exploit, the people. The spiritual dullness of Isaiah's generation, which resulted in the exaltation of foolish, unjust leaders, would disappear.

Of course, prospects for the immedi-ate future were not as bright. Urging the nation's complacent women to lament, Isaiah warned that the land's agricultural prosperity would soon be swept away and its cities abandoned. Perhaps he pro-claimed this message just prior to Sen-nacherib's invasion of the land in 701 B.C. However, in another of his abrupt shifts in perspective, Isaiah promised that restoration would eventually follow judg-ment. The Lord would again pour His life-giving Spirit upon the land and restore its crops. Justice and genuine security would then return to the land.

Chapter 33 begins with a brief woe-oracle against the "destroyer" and "trai-tor" (probably a reference to Assyria), whose deeds would one day be punished appropriately.

A model prayer follows, in which the people asked for the Lord's gracious intervention and expressed confidence in His ability to defeat the nations. They praised Him as the sovereign King who would reestablish Jerusalem as a center of justice. In support of their request, they lamented the devastating effects of the enemy invasion. In response to their prayer, the Lord announced He would be exalted over His enemies, whose plans would be self-destructive.

Unfortunately, not everyone in Jerusalem was as godly as those who spoke in 33:2-9. The Lord made it clear to the sinners in the city that only those who promoted justice and order would experience His protection and blessing. The righteous could look forward to a grand new era for Jerusalem. The arrogant, terrifying foreign armies would disappear from outside the city's walls. Jerusalem would again be the religious center of the land, experiencing security and prosperity under its divine King's just rule. A forgiving God would eliminate sin and its effects from the city.

*Judgment of the Nations Brings Restoration of God's People (34:1– 35:10).* The theme of God's sovereignty over the hostile nations (see 29:5-8; 30:27-33; 31:4-9; 33:1,18-19) culminates in chapter 34 with a vivid description of universal judgment. The Lord would unleash His anger upon the nations, resulting in widespread carnage and bloodshed. Even the heavens would not escape. The stars, perhaps symbolizing heavenly opposition to God (see 24:21), are pictured as rotting and falling like a leaf or fig to the ground.

The Lord singled out Edom as a representative of the nations (see 63:1-6; Obad.). The prophet compared the bloody slaughter of Edom to a large sacrifice where sheep and cattle are butchered in great numbers. This day of vengeance and retribution on behalf of Jerusalem would reduce Edom to a state of perpetual desolation. By divine decree its weed-covered ruins would be populated only by desert creatures such as owls and hyenas.

In contrast to Edom, God's weakened, discouraged people would be rejuvenated by His mighty deeds on their behalf. This renewal is compared to the miraculous healing of various physical disabilities and to the blossoming of a hot, dry desert. Where once there was only sand and desert creatures, there would now be flowers, green pastures, abundant water, and thick vegetation. Through this garden land would run a highway, upon which no wicked men or dangerous wild beasts would be allowed to go. The Lord's redeemed people would follow this "Way of Holiness" to Jerusalem, entering its gates with joy. The delightful imagery depicts in a striking way the divine blessings and renewed access to God's presence that would follow the future purification and restoration of His people.

*Hezekiah's Reign (36:1–39:8).* These chapters, which repeat 2 Kings 18–20 in many respects, record three significant events of Hezekiah's reign: (1) the Lord's miraculous deliverance of Jerusalem and destruction of the Assyrians, (2) Hezekiah's recovery from a serious illness, and (3) Hezekiah's unwise dealings with the messengers from Babylon. Isaiah played a prominent role in these events, each of which prompted at least one prophetic oracle.

The chapters are not in chronological order. The Assyrian deliverance (chaps. 36–37) followed the events recorded in chapters 38–39. Perhaps chapter 39 comes last because its reference to Babylon provides a frame for chapters 13–39 (see chap. 13, which also focuses on Babylon). Also, by showing that even godly Hezekiah had his faults and ultimately could not prevent Judah's downfall, it paves the way for chapters 40–66, the setting of which is the Babylonian captivity.

# MESSIANIC PROPHECIES

Messianic prophecies are Old Testament passages that refer to a future anointed King who will bring salvation to Israel. Passages may be regarded as messianic prophecies from two different perspectives.

1. From the perspective of the Christian church, many passages qualify as messianic from Genesis 3:15 to Malachi 4:5-6. From this viewpoint one listing numbers 124 passages, each with a specific New Testament fulfillment. This method of identifying messianic prophecies begins with New Testament citations or references connecting the ministry and/or meaning of Jesus' life with the Old Testament.

The method allowed the earliest Christians to witness to Jews by using their Scriptures to prove that Jesus was the goal toward which the Scriptures pointed. It also helped Christians learn more about Jesus and understand His work of salvation. From this point of view the original meaning of the Old Testament passages is not as important as is the contemporary meaning of the passage for the church. The Jews of Jesus' day used a similar method of interpretation to gain the fullest meaning and application of Scripture.

2. From a historical point of view, only a limited number of passages qualify as messianic prophecies. To qualify a passage must represent its original author's reference to a future King of salvation. This method begins with the Old Testament historical setting and selects passages that point to the future, refer to an anointed King, and describe salvation of God's people. This method would speak of incomplete fulfillments in the lives of specific Jewish kings such as Hezekiah, major fulfillment in the earthly ministry of Jesus Christ, and final fulfillment in the second coming. Major passages in view here are 2 Samuel 7; 1 Chronicles 17; Psalms 2; 72; 89; 110; 132; Isaiah 2:2-5; 9:1-7; 11:1-10.

This point of view originates with modern understandings of history and with more recent methods of interpreting ancient literature. It seeks to understand ancient Israel's self-understanding at various points in its history. It asks such questions as: When did Israel begin looking for God to send a new deliverer? What did Israel expect this new kind of deliverer to be and to do? How did various changes in Israel's historical understanding affect the understanding of and expectation of a messianic deliverer?

It asks: In what ways did Jesus of Nazareth fulfill the expectations of Israel? Should the average Israelite in Jesus' day have been able to see that Jesus was the expected Messiah? Did Jesus provide a deeper or different interpretation of Messiah than Israel had known until His day? Whose methods of biblical interpretation did the inspired New Testament writers use as they interpreted Jesus in light of the Old Testament? How can the church today legitimately interpret the Old Testament Scriptures in light of the fulfillment we see in the person of Jesus?

The two points of view thus start with different emphases, different types of questions, and different methods of interpretation. Ultimately they end with the same question: How does the Old Testament help us to understand the life, ministry, and saving work of our Savior, Jesus the Messiah?

Both viewpoints see Jesus as the fulfillment of the religion and hope of the Old Testament. The first viewpoint may find more individual texts pointing to Jesus. The second viewpoint may deem application of some passages to Jesus to be the result of the history of interpretation rather than the meaning of the original author.

Both viewpoints affirm that New Testament writers effectively used the Old Testament to witness to Jesus of Nazareth as Messiah of Israel and Savior of the world. In so doing they see that an original viewpoint was of an earthly king ruling on the throne of his forefather David and restoring political power to the nation Israel. This historical viewpoint developed within Israel's history. This view culminates in the ministry of Jesus the Messiah and Suffering Servant, dying on a cross and being resurrected to ascend to a heavenly throne at the Father's right hand. There He rules not just Israel but the entire universe. This rule will become clear to all nations and people when Jesus returns in the second coming to establish His kingship on earth as well as in heaven.

*The Lord Delivers Jerusalem from the Assyrians (36:1–37:38).* In 701 B.C. the mighty Assyrian army overran the countryside of Judah and, according to Assyrian records, conquered forty-six cities. The Assyrian king Sennacherib sent his field commander to Jerusalem with a message for Hezekiah. With many of the people looking on from the city's walls, the field commander pointed out that Jerusalem's reliance upon its military strategies and its alliance with Egypt was misplaced. He even argued that the Lord would not deliver the city. He erroneously reasoned that Hezekiah's centralization of worship was an affront to the Lord. He claimed that the Assyrians had been commissioned by the Lord to invade Judah.

Troubled by the field commander's use of Hebrew, the language of the people, Hezekiah's officials asked him to use Aramaic, the diplomatic language of the day. He refused, pointing out that the siege would adversely affect all of Jerusalem's citizens. The field commander then urged the people of Jerusalem to reject Hezekiah's appeal to trust in the Lord. He exhorted them to surrender the city, promising them future peace and prosperity (albeit in a new land!). He concluded his speech with an arrogant claim that the Lord could not deliver the city. Jerusalem was no different than other cities, whose gods had been unable to rescue their people from the Assyrians. The people, in obedience to Hezekiah's decree, did not reply to the field commander.

Having torn their clothes in consternation and mourning, Hezekiah's officials reported the message to the king. Hezekiah tore his clothes, went to the temple, and asked Isaiah to pray on behalf of the city. Isaiah sent a salvation oracle back to the king, urging him not to fear, for the Lord was about to punish the Assyrian king for his blasphemy. An alarming report would cause him to return to his own land, where he would be slain by the sword.

Meanwhile the field commander rejoined the Assyrian army, which was now marching to meet an Egyptian army led by Tirhakah. (Though only a prince in 701 B.C., Tirhakah is here called "king of Egypt" in anticipation of his rise to the throne a decade later. Isaiah may have even written or incorporated this account into his prophecy after Tirhakah became king.) Concerned that Hezekiah might derive false hope from this action, Sennacherib sent another message to Hezekiah, assuring him that he still intended to conquer Jerusalem. Once again he emphasized that Hezekiah's God, like the gods of the many lands conquered by the Assyrians, would not be able to deliver the city from his hands.

Upon receiving this letter, Hezekiah went to the temple again, spread the letter out before the Lord, and poured out his heart in prayer. Hezekiah acknowledged that the Lord was the sovereign Ruler of the universe and infinitely superior to the man-made gods of the nations previously defeated by the Assyrians. He asked the Lord to deliver Jerusalem so that the whole earth might recognize His sovereign power.

Through the prophet Isaiah the Lord responded positively to Hezekiah's request. The first part of His response came in the form of a taunt song against Sennacherib. The Lord castigated the Assyrian ruler for his pride, reminded him that his successes were by the Lord's decree, and then announced that He would force the Assyrians back to their own land. In the second part of the message the Lord assured Hezekiah that He would preserve Jerusalem for His own glory and because of His promise to the Davidic dynasty.

The final verses of the chapter record the fulfillment of God's promise. The angel of the Lord struck down the Assyrian hordes in one night, forcing Sennacherib to return home, where two decades later he was assassinated by two of his own sons.

*Hezekiah's Life-Threatening Illness (38:1-22).* The event recorded in chapter 38 probably occurred the year before Sennacherib's invasion. When Hezekiah became seriously ill, Isaiah announced to him that he would die. Reminding the Lord of his faithful deeds, the king pled for his life. The Lord decided to give Hezekiah fifteen more years of life and also promised He would protect Jerusalem from the Assyrians. In response to Hezekiah's request for a confirming sign, the Lord refracted the sun's rays so that the shadow they cast was reversed. (Verses 21-22 are misplaced and belong between 38:6-7. See 2 Kgs. 20:6-9.) Ironically, this sign took place at the "stairway of Ahaz," a structure named for the king who, in contrast to his son, had rejected the Lord's promise of deliverance by refusing to ask for a sign (see 7:10-17).

In response to the Lord's merciful deliverance, Hezekiah offered a song of thanksgiving, in which he recalled his time of need, acknowledged the Lord's intervention, and promised to praise Him all his days.

This account has a twofold purpose. First, Hezekiah serves as an example to God's people of dependence on the Lord in the midst of a crisis. Second, Hezekiah's recovery was representative of the nation's future. Just as the Lord healed Hezekiah and granted him additional years, so He would give Judah and Jerusalem a new lease on life by miraculously removing the Assyrian threat. Nevertheless, like Hezekiah's briefly extended life, so Judah's and Jerusalem's days remained numbered.

*Hezekiah Entertains Babylonian Messengers (39:1-8).* Even godly men have their moments of failure. Hezekiah was no exception. Chapter 39 records an event that occurred shortly after his recovery. The Babylonians, who were seeking to form an anti-Assyrian alliance, sent messengers to Hezekiah. Hezekiah proudly (and foolishly) showed them the riches of his storehouses. It was this kind of self-sufficient attitude that would eventually bring the nation's downfall. The Lord used the occasion to announce through Isaiah that the Babylonians would someday conquer Jerusalem and carry the royal riches and even some of Hezekiah's own descendants into exile. Hezekiah readily submitted to the prophet's words, confident that the rest of his reign would be peaceful. His tone of resignation contrasts sharply with his earlier unwillingness to accept the announcement of his own impending death (see 38:1-3). This may be interpreted negatively (as reflecting self-interest) or positively (as an admission of his own guilt and of God's grace in not bringing immediate punishment).

## HOPE AND RESTORATION (40:1–66:24)

The setting of Isaiah's message shifts to the time of the exile, which earlier passages of the book assumed (11:11-12,15-16; 14:1-2; 27:12-13; 35:10) and prophesied (5:13; 6:12; 27:8; 39:5-7). This final section of the book begins on an extremely positive note, as God affirmed His commitment to His servant nation and promised them deliverance from exile in seemingly unconditional terms. As the section progresses, it becomes apparent that total restoration would not be automatic. Covenantal renewal, mediated through a special servant viewed as an ideal Israel and a second Moses, was necessary. Anticipating that some would reject God's offer of reconciliation, the book's final chapters foresee a final, purifying judgment, out of which a holy community would emerge.

The four so-called servant songs highlight this section (see 42:1-9; 49:1-13; 50:4-11; 52:13–53:12). For years scholars have debated this servant's precise identity. Some conclude that the servant in the four songs is none other than the personified nation Israel. Throughout chapters 40–48 the Lord calls the nation His servant. Isaiah 49:3, located in the second servant song, specifically calls the servant "Israel." However, the solution is not this simple. One of the major tasks of this servant "Israel" is to restore the nation (see 49:5-6,8-9) by suffering innocently on behalf of God's sinful people (see 53:5,8).

These texts require some distinction between the servant "Israel" and the exiled nation. It is best to identify the servant as an individual within the nation who as Israel's representative mediates a new covenant between God and His people (see 49:8). He also fulfills God's original purpose for the nation in that he becomes a channel of divine blessing to the Gentiles (see 42:6; 49:6). Because he embodies God's ideal for the nation, he can be called "Israel." In the progress of biblical revelation Jesus Christ emerges as this ideal Israel who restores God's covenant people and takes His salvation to the nations (see Acts 8:30-35).

## ELECTION IN THE OLD TESTAMENT

Election is the concept representing the Hebrew verb *bachar (select)* or participle *bachir (elect* or *chosen)*, referring to selection by extending preference from among alternatives.

The biblical doctrine of election refers to God's free and sovereign choice of those whom He has appointed to fulfill His purposes. It has particular reference to His decision prior to creation as to whom He would save and how He would bring about their salvation.

Scripture insists that God's saving work is done neither arbitrarily nor outside of His all-inclusive control. Rather, it is accomplished through His sovereign wisdom and power according to His eternal decree.

Election therefore differs from *predestination*. Predestination is the doctrine that God, as omnipotent Ruler over His creation, has planned everything that comes to pass. While the concept of election is included in that of predestination, the latter is broader. Specifically, the Old Testament uses the term *elect* in relation to three subjects:

1. *The nation Israel (Isa. 45:4).* Israel had a unique role as God's elect. God chose them to be His covenant community. He chose them to reveal His sovereignty and holiness to the nations through the prophets and the Scriptures. He chose them to be the vehicle for bringing forth the Messiah.

Israel's election is prominent in Deuteronomy and in Romans 9–11. It was based not on any demonstrated virtue on Israel's part but solely on God's love (Deut. 7:7-8).

2. *A select group of prominent leaders in Israel.* To preserve Israel as the covenant community, God chose certain strategic leaders for their unique positions of authority. Among them Moses, as Israel's intercessor, is called the Lord's "elect one" (Ps. 106:23). David, as the recipient of the Davidic covenant, is described as God's "elect" (Ps. 89:3).

3. *The elect Servant (Isa. 42:1-4).* From before the foundation of the world, God ordained that His chosen "Servant" would someday establish justice upon the earth. The New Testament identifies the Servant as Israel's Messiah, the Lord Jesus Christ. It indicates that not only His reign but His work of redemption was preordained from eternity (Acts 2:23; 1 Pet. 1:20).

## Deliverance of the Exiles (40:1–48:22).

God emphasized that He was both willing and able to deliver His exiled people. Much of the section focuses on God's superiority to the nations and their idols.

*Comfort for Jerusalem and the Exiles (40:1-31).* The chapter begins with a message of encouragement for downtrodden Jerusalem. The city had suffered more than enough; its time of punishment was over. Preparations were to be made for the King's glorious return. The city's restoration was certain, for God's decree is reliable, unlike frail persons and their promises, both of which fade like grass before a hot wind. Jerusalem was to proclaim the good news of God's return to the other cities of Judah. Like a shepherd tenderly holding his sheep to his chest, the Lord would carry the exiles back to the land. The same mighty arm that destroys His enemies (see 51:9-10) would protect His people.

For tired, discouraged exiles this promise of restoration may have seemed like wishful thinking. They felt abandoned by God (see v. 27) and may have wondered if He possessed the ability to deliver them. Perhaps He was a local deity limited to the borders of Judah. To alleviate such doubts, the Lord reminded His people of His sovereignty and might. He is the Creator of the universe, who demonstrated immeasurable power and wisdom in forming the heavens and the earth. He is sovereign over His world, exercising absolute control over the nations and their puny rulers. He is infinitely superior to idols. The stars of the heavens, made gods in pagan thought (see Jer. 19:13), are mere servants who report for duty when God calls. Because His authority, power, and wisdom are unlimited, God is capable of delivering His people from bondage. He gives superhuman strength to those who rely on Him.

*God's Redemptive Program (41:1–42:12).* This section briefly outlines God's program for Israel's redemption. Later chapters then develop this program.

The Lord began by asserting His sovereignty over history and the nations. He was raising up a mighty conqueror (Cyrus the Persian, see 44:28; 45:1) who would subdue the nations and accomplish the Lord's will. Before his relentless march the nations and their idols would be helpless.

Reminding His people of their special position as descendants of Abraham, the Lord assured them that He would protect them and eliminate their enemies. Comparing their distress to the plight of a thirsty man in a desert, the Lord promised to transform their condition. He would, as it were, cause the desert to overflow with abundant waters and blossom into a forest, resulting in universal recognition of His sovereignty.

The Lord challenged the nations' idols to present evidence of their power to predict and fulfill. In response to their silence, He pronounced them to be "less than nothing" and "false." As proof of His own power, He pointed to Cyrus, the "one from the north" whom He was raising up to conquer the nations.

In addition to Cyrus, the Lord would raise up another servant, whose ministry would be characterized by humility and by gentleness toward the downtrodden. Energized by the Lord's Spirit, He would establish justice on the earth, mediate a new covenant for Israel, and release the oppressed. Like Cyrus's conquests, His divinely decreed accomplishments would demonstrate the Lord's sovereignty over history and His superiority to idols. The proper response to this announcement was universal praise.

*Blind and Deaf Israel Summoned as Witnesses (42:13–44:23).* This section is arranged in two parallel panels (42:13–43:13; 43:14–44:20), each of which contains four parts: (1) an announcement of divine intervention in world events, (2) an exhortation to Israel, (3) a message of salvation for God's people, and (4) a declaration of the Lord's sovereignty over the nations and their gods. The following outline reflects the structure of the section:

| Panel A | Panel B |
| --- | --- |
| 1. 42:13-17 | 43:14-21 |
| 2. 42:18-25 | 43:22-28 |
| 3. 43:1-7 | 44:1-5 |
| 4. 43:8-13 | 44:6-20 |

The section concludes with an exhortation to Israel and a call to praise.

Though the Lord had been silent for a lengthy period, He would come like a mighty warrior and lead His people back to their land, demonstrating His superiority to the pagan gods. He made it clear that spiritually unresponsive Israel had experienced His judgment and the hardships of exile because of their refusal to obey His law. Nevertheless, as their Creator He assured them of His continuing presence and supernatural protection. He would raise up the Persians, who would conquer Egypt but allow the Israelites to leave Babylon. Eventually all of God's dispersed people would return to the promised land. Summoning His people as witnesses to His sovereignty over the events of history, the Lord declared His superiority to the gods of the nations.

Speaking as the Redeemer of Israel, who in former times had led His people out of their Egyptian bondage, the Lord announced a new exodus. He would free Israel from their Babylonian captivity and provide for their needs on the journey home. In the past their sinful deeds had invalidated their sacrifices and resulted in severe judgment. (Isa. 43:28 is better understood as a reference to past judgment.) But the Lord reminded them that He is the God who forgives sin. The Lord addressed Israel by its ancient name Jeshurun, which Moses applied to early Israel as the recipient of God's blessings (Deut. 32:15; 33:5,26). Like that earlier generation, exiled Israel would experience an outpouring of divine blessing. Again calling His people as witnesses, the Lord reaffirmed His superiority to all other gods. Certainly the nations' idols could not compare with Him. With great sarcasm the Lord ridiculed idol worshipers. After cutting down a tree, people formed idols from some of the wood and with the rest made fires to cook their meat and warm themselves. They never stopped to think that their god and the wood used for such everyday tasks were made from the same substance.

In conclusion the Lord exhorted Israel to lay hold of His promise of restoration and forgiveness. In anticipation of Israel's redemption, the prophet urged the entire universe to break out in song.

*God Initiates His Redemptive Program through Cyrus (44:24–45:25).* Identifying Himself as the sovereign Creator, who alone controls the events of history, the Lord announced that He would use Cyrus the Persian to restore His people to the land and rebuild the ruined cities. A commissioning account follows, in which the Lord promised Cyrus military success in order that he, and eventually the whole world, might recognize the incomparability of Israel's God. The mention of Cyrus by name is startling, since this ruler did not come on the scene until the sixth century B.C., over a hundred years after Isaiah died. However, such a precise prediction is certainly consistent with the theme of God's ability to predict and fulfill (see 44:26).

Though God had great plans for His exiled people, some grumbled about their condition and questioned God's ways. The Lord reminded such individuals that they had no right to question their Creator's sovereign decisions. To do so would be as absurd as a piece of pottery criticizing the potter who forms it.

The Lord reiterated His plan to use Cyrus as His instrument of redemption. Israel would return from Babylon and rebuild Jerusalem. Foreigners would recognize Israel's privileged position and the incomparability of Israel's God.

Once more declaring His sovereignty and superiority to the pagan gods, the Lord exhorted all nations to turn to Him for salvation. It is wise to submit to God now, for He has issued an unchangeable decree that all will someday bow before Him and acknowledge His sovereignty.

*Exhorting Israel in Light of Babylon's Fall (46:1–48:22).* Here announcements of Babylon's fall are coupled with exhortations to the exiles.

Babylon's idols would be carried away into captivity, unable to rescue themselves, let alone their worshipers. These useless idols were stationary and a burden to the animals that carried them. In contrast, God had always been active in Israel's history and had, as it were, carried His people. He urged those exiles who remained rebellious in spirit to recall His past deeds and to recognize His sovereign hand at work in the career of Cyrus. For those who were willing to trust His promises, a new era was approaching.

In chapter 47 Babylon's fall is described in a taunt song addressed by a vengeful God to the city, which is person-

ified as a proud queen. This once "tender and delicate" queen would now do the work of a commoner or servant and be publicly humiliated. Though God had commissioned her to punish His sinful people, she had shown no mercy, severely oppressing even the very aged. Thinking her position secure, she boasted that she would never experience bereavement. However, the Lord announced that she would suddenly lose both her husband and children. The once self-sufficient queen would be deprived of all means of support. Despite her diviners' and astrologers' attempts to ward off disaster, the judgment of God would overtake the city.

The Lord recognized that many of the exiles only possessed an outward form of religion, while others were outright idolaters and rebels. Throughout Israel's history the Lord had announced His actions beforehand so that His rebellious people would not attribute the events to false gods. Now He was announcing another major event in the nations' history. Though He had punished Israel for its rebellion, He would now bring glory to Himself by delivering it through Cyrus. Because of their disobedience, God's people had forfeited peace and blessing. The Lord was now offering them an opportunity to start over. If they responded in faith and left Babylon, He would care for their needs, as He had done during the wilderness wanderings following the exodus from Egypt. However, the Lord warned that the wicked would not participate in this new era of peace and blessing.

***Restoration of Jerusalem (49:1–55:13).*** Chapters 41–42 introduced Cyrus (see 41:2-3,25) and the Lord's ideal servant (see 42:1-9) as important instruments in God's program for Israel's redemption. Chapters 43–48 focused on Cyrus's role, while chapters 49–55 develop in more detail the ideal servant's part in the drama.

This section is arranged in three panels (49:1–50:3; 50:4–52:12; 52:13–54:17), each of which begins with a servant song followed by an encouraging message for personified Jerusalem. A moving call to covenantal renewal concludes the section.

*The Lord Commissions an Ideal Servant (49:1-13).* Here the Lord's ideal servant, introduced in 42:1-9, recounts his special divine commission. From before his birth the Lord chose him for a special task. The Lord made him an effective spokesman to be used at an opportune time. The servant received the title "Israel" because as an ideal representative of the nation he would restore Israel's relationship to God. In the role of a new Moses the servant would mediate a new covenant for Israel and lead the people out of captivity and back to the promised land. As "Israel" the servant would also fulfill God's original ideal for the nation by being a channel of blessing to the Gentile nations. Though the servant faced rejection and discouragement, he was confident that the Lord would eventually vindicate him. Someday even kings would acknowledge his greatness.

*The Lord Answers Jerusalem's Complaint (49:14–50:3).* The servant's work would have important results for Jerusalem. The city is here personified as a woman who complains of being abandoned by her husband (the Lord) and deprived of her children (the exiled residents of the city). Comparing Himself to a nursing mother, the Lord assured Jerusalem that He could never abandon her. Though she and her children had experienced the harsh consequences of their sin, she would again be inhabited. Her exiled children would return en masse, escorted by the Gentiles. The Lord would

rescue them from captivity and take vengeance on their oppressors.

*The Lord's Ideal Servant Perseveres (50:4-11).* In this third servant song the servant declared his confidence in God. He had not drawn back from the Lord's commission, despite severe opposition and humiliation. He persevered, confident that the Lord would one day vindicate him before his enemies. The song concludes with an appeal for the servant's faithful followers to continue to trust the Lord and with a warning of judgment to those who reject the Lord's guidance.

*A New Exodus (51:1–52:12).* Once more the Lord addressed His people with a message of hope and encouragement. He urged the faithful to consider the example of Abraham and Sarah. From this single individual and his barren wife the Lord formed a nation in fulfillment of His promise. He would do the same for desolate Jerusalem, transforming its ruins into a new Garden of Eden filled with song. God would also extend His blessings to the nations by establishing a just world order.

Overwhelmed by God's reassuring promises, the prophet cried out for and anticipated their fulfillment. He longed for a new exodus, in which God would display the power that destroyed the Egyptians (compared to the mythical sea monster Rahab) and divided the Red Sea.

Speaking as His people's Comforter and as the sovereign Creator of the world, the Lord reiterated His promise to the frightened exiles. He would exert His mighty power on their behalf and release them from their prison.

The Lord would also lift up downtrodden Jerusalem. The city had suffered humiliation at the hands of the nations; now the time of retribution had arrived. The cup of the Lord's wrath would pass from Jerusalem to its oppressors. Never again would the purified city be invaded by foreigners. Though His name had been blasphemed among the nations, the Lord would establish His rule from Jerusalem and reveal His power to the entire earth. The prophet employed vivid imagery, picturing a messenger bringing the good news of God's advent to the watchmen of Jerusalem's walls.

A final exhortation urges the priests to leave the unclean land of exile, implying that the worship system would be reestablished. In contrast to the exodus from Egypt, which was conducted in haste (see Deut. 16:3), there would be no need to hurry because the oppressor would be crushed prior to their departure. As in the first exodus God would accompany His people as their protector.

*Suffering and Vindication of the Lord's Ideal Servant (52:13–53:12).* This fourth servant song describes in greater detail the servant's suffering and vindication, themes introduced in earlier songs (see 49:4,7; 50:6-9). The song begins with the Lord's declaration that His servant would be greatly honored. Just as many had been shocked by the degree of the servant's humiliation, so many nations and even kings would be amazed by his glorious exaltation.

In the central section of the song Israel confessed its former unbelief and acknowledged that the servant's suffering was on their behalf. Responding to the announcement of the servant's future exaltation ("our message" in 53:1 is better translated "the report just heard by us"), Israel confessed that they never had considered such a thing possible for they had not seen God's power revealed through the servant. They regarded him as insignificant and interpreted his intense sufferings as a sign of divine displeasure. Now they were forced to reevaluate their former opinion. They

now realized that the servant's suffering was due to their sins and for their ultimate benefit. Like stray sheep all Israel had wandered from the Lord, and the servant had borne the punishment for their rebellion. He was innocent of wrongdoing, yet he silently endured oppressive treatment and a humiliating death. The Lord had decreed that the servant was to suffer; eventually He would vindicate and bless him.

The song ends as it began, with the Lord Himself declaring His pleasure with the servant. Because the servant submitted to suffering and identified with sinful Israel, he would restore many to the Lord and be richly rewarded for his efforts.

*Jerusalem's Glorious Future (54:1-17).* With Israel's restoration assured by the servant's ministry, Jerusalem's future was bright. Comparing the ruined city to a barren woman, the Lord announced that she would be blessed with an abundance of children (a reference to her returning exiles). Placing her in the role of His divorced wife, He promised a restoration of the marriage. Nothing would ever again separate them. The Lord would adorn the city with beauty and protect it from all assailants.

*A Call to Covenant Renewal (55:1-13).* Using the imagery of an invitation to a banquet, the Lord exhorted His people to receive the blessings He offered. The Lord desired to make an eternal covenant with the nation, which would parallel His covenant with David. Like David, Israel would be living testimony of God's greatness and would rule over nations. If the nation actively sought the Lord and turned from their wicked ways, He would compassionately forgive their sins. They could depend on this merciful response, for God's word of promise, unlike sinful human plans, is always realized. Just as rain does not reverse its course, but falls to the ground and makes the farmer's crops fruitful, so God does not take back His word of promise but rather brings it to fulfillment. The Lord would shower repentant Israel with abundant blessings, which would be an eternal sign of their renewed relationship.

**Purification (56:1–66:24).** Despite God's promise of a new era of blessing and His invitation to reconciliation, the reality of Israel's rebellious spirit remained. Isaiah 56–66 indicates that only the repentant would participate in the new0 era. Those who followed the sinful ways of earlier generations would be excluded. Though many of the promises of chapters 40–55 are reiterated here, the theme of God's purifying, discriminating judgment is also prominent.

*Foreigners and Eunuchs Granted New Status (56:1-8).* In anticipation of God's coming age of salvation, His people should promote justice, one of the chief characteristics of the new era. Without exception, all who demonstrated loyalty to God by keeping His commands would experience His blessings and enjoy access to His presence. Even those who had once been subject to exclusion and strict regulations, such as eunuchs and foreigners (see Deut. 23:1,3,7-8), would freely enter the Lord's temple.

*Sinners Denounced, the Repentant Encouraged (56:9–57:21).* The wicked would have no place in this new community. The Lord warned that judgment was imminent for all the greedy leaders and rebellious idolaters who sought to perpetuate the injustice and spiritual adultery of earlier days. The promised land was reserved for those who trusted in the Lord and displayed a repentant spirit.

*God's Righteous Demands, the Nation's Sinful Deeds (58:1-14).* The Lord denounced the people's hypocritical claims of loyalty and their empty expressions of repentance. Their unjust and violent deeds made their fasts unac-

ceptable. The Lord demanded righteous living, not meaningless ritual. They were to free the oppressed, feed the hungry, give shelter to the homeless, and clothe the naked. In addition to caring for the needs of others, they also were to demonstrate true devotion to God by honoring His Sabbath Day. Then they would experience the Lord's protective presence, enjoy His blessings, and witness the rebuilding of the land.

*Accusation and Confession (59:1-15a).* The Lord was able and willing to restore His people, but their persistence in sin had separated them from God. He could not tolerate their violence, deceit, and injustice. Their evil thoughts produced destructive actions. In contrast to the justice and peace demanded by the Lord, their lifestyle was characterized by bloodshed.

Identifying with and representing the nation, the prophet acknowledged the truth of the preceding accusation. He lamented that justice and truth had disappeared, preventing divine deliverance from becoming a reality. He confessed the nation's many sins and admitted that they had rebelled against and rejected the Lord.

*The Restoration of Jerusalem (59:15b–63:6).* In response to the prophet's confession on behalf of the nation, a message of salvation now appears. The Lord would judge His enemies and return to Jerusalem to rule over His repentant people. He would establish a new covenant with them, enabling them by His Spirit to obey His commandments.

The Lord's glorious return would begin a bright new era for Jerusalem. The city's exiled population would return, and nations would bring their wealth as tribute to the Lord. Signs of the Lord's renewed blessing would be everywhere. Foreigners would rebuild the city's walls.

Its gates would remain open to accommodate the steady stream of visitors bringing tribute. The splendid trees of Lebanon would be used as building materials for the Lord's temple. Those who formerly oppressed the city would acknowledge its special status. God's glorious presence would assure continual peace and justice. In fulfillment of His promise to Abraham, His people would possess the promised land forever and experience extraordinary population growth.

Chapter 61 begins with an unidentified speaker (the prophet? the servant of chaps. 40–55?) relating his commission to proclaim good news to the city's grieving exiles. The Lord had officially decreed a year of release for His captive people. They would rebuild the cities of the land and serve the Lord as a nation of priests (see Exod. 19:6). Foreigners would serve them and bring them their wealth. The Lord would take away His people's shame and give them a double portion of His blessings. The nations would recognize Israel's special relationship to the Lord. The recipient of God's blessings (personified Jerusalem?) rejoiced in His salvation.

The portrayal of Jerusalem's future continues in chapter 62. The restored city's glory would be apparent to all. Though Jerusalem was deserted and desolate, it would someday be named Hephzibah *(My delight is in her)* and Beulah *(Married),* for the Lord would renew His relationship with her. With the threat of foreign invasion forever removed, God's people would enjoy the fruit of their labors.

The chapter concludes with an exhortation to prepare the way for the return of the Lord (see Isa. 40:3-5), who would bring His exiled people with Him (see 40:10) and set them apart as a holy community (see Exod. 19:6).

This section ends as it began, with a description of the Lord as a conquering warrior (Isa. 63:1-6; see 59:15b-19). He comes from Edom (which here represents the hostile nations; compare v. 6 and 34:5-17) with His garments stained with blood. He announces that He has single-handedly crushed His enemies, as if they were grapes in a winepress. One is reminded again that God's kingdom of peace and justice will only come after a powerful and angry display of His judgment against His foes.

*A Prayer for Deliverance (63:7–64:12).* In combination with the confession of 59:9-15a, this prayer forms a frame around the message of salvation in 59:15b–63:6. Once again the prophet represented the nation and provided a model response for God's disobedient, exiled people.

The prophet recalled the Lord's faithful deeds for His people throughout their history. He redeemed them from Egypt and protected them. When they sinned, He was forced to treat them as an enemy, prompting them to recall the days of Moses. The prophet was now doing the same. He longed for a new display of the divine power revealed at the Red Sea.

The remainder of the prayer combines lamentation over the people's current situation, confession of sin, statements of confidence, and petitions for God's deliverance. Confident that God remained their Father and Redeemer, the prophet asked that He might respond compassionately to their plight. He lamented that the Lord had given them over to the hardness of their hearts and that the enemies of God had destroyed His temple. He asked that the Lord might break through the heavens and judge the nations, demonstrating once more His ability to deliver those who trusted Him. He acknowledged their punishment was well-deserved, for they had been totally contaminated by sin. Yet the prophet, confident that their relationship with God was not completely severed, begged Him to relent from His anger. Surely the ruined land and temple were proof that their punishment was sufficient.

*Separation of the Righteous and the Wicked (65:1–66:24).* Chapter 65 contrasts the respective destinies of the righteous and the wicked. Despite the Lord's constant attempts to get Israel's attention, many rejected Him and embraced pagan religious practices. Such stubbornness demanded harsh punishment. However, the Lord would exercise discrimination in judgment. He would preserve the righteous and give them the promised land as a reward. A new world was coming, in which purified Jerusalem would be the focal point. The troubles of the past would be forgotten, and God's blessings would abound. Life spans would dramatically increase; the people would enjoy the fruits of their labor; God would respond immediately to their prayers; all dangers would be eliminated; and peace would prevail.

Chapter 66 begins by contrasting the character of the righteous and the wicked. The righteous were humble, repentant, and showed respect for God's commandments. The wicked were violent, idolatrous, self-willed, spiritually unresponsive, and hostile to the righteous.

A day of retribution was coming, in which the wicked would be purged from the covenant community and the righteous vindicated. The Lord's fiery judgment would destroy the wicked along with their pagan practices. The righteous would take possession of glorified and renewed Jerusalem, where peace and prosperity would abound. The Gentiles would come to Jerusalem on a regular basis to worship the Lord. In the background the smoldering, decaying carcasses of the wicked would serve as a constant reminder of the consequences of rebellion against the Great King.

The Book of Isaiah begins with the Lord accusing His people of rebellion (see 1:2). It ends with a hideous but sobering description of the total and final destruction of the rebellious.

*Theological and Ethical Significance.* For Isaiah God was "the Holy One of Israel" and "the Creator of the ends of the earth." Such a God demanded moral purity and justice from His people and all nations. God's people, like other nations, failed to meet His standards of behavior. The Holy One was thus just in punishing their sin by sending them into exile. God, however, desired to play the part of Savior, Redeemer, and Father to those who would turn to Him in repentance. Isaiah called Israel to hope in God, the Creator who brought order from chaos and the Redeemer who rescued Israel from Egyptian captivity. Such a God would surely again act creatively and redemptively in leading his people home to a restored Jerusalem.

Isaiah challenges Christians to hope in God, who is not through with creation. Old Testament Israel only partially realized God's salvation and peace. God, who acted to save Christians in the past through the Suffering Servant Jesus, will act again to bring history to His desired end of a new heaven and a new earth.

### Questions for Reflection

1. How did Isaiah portray God? What divine names and titles did he employ? What characteristics did he attribute to God? What effect should Isaiah's teachings about God have on our thinking and behavior?

2. Why were God's people so displeasing to Him in Isaiah's day? Is the modern church like ancient Israel in any ways?

3. How does Israel's judgment serve as a lesson to us? What does God's judgment of Israel teach us about His relationship to His people?

4. Why did God remain committed to Israel? In what ways is His devotion to His people portrayed or illustrated in the book?

5. How did Isaiah portray the ministry and future reign of Jesus Christ?

## Sources for Additional Study

Butler, Trent C. *Isaiah. Layman's Bible Book Commentary.* Vol. 10. Nashville: Broadman, 1982.

Martin, Alfred and John. *Isaiah: The Glory of the Messiah.* Chicago: Moody, 1983.

Oswalt, John N. *The Book of Isaiah, Chapters 1–39.* The New International Commentary on the Old Testament. Grand Rapids: Eerdmans, 1986.

Wolf, Herbert M. *Interpreting Isaiah.* Grand Rapids: Zondervan, 1985.

# JEREMIAH

According to the book's heading, Jeremiah was a priest from Anathoth whose prophetic career began in the thirteenth year of Josiah (627–626 B.C.) and continued until the final exile of Judah in 586. Chapters 39–44 indicate that Jeremiah continued to minister after the fall of Jerusalem and was forced to accompany a group of exiles to Egypt.

**Historical Background.** Jeremiah lived during the final days of the Kingdom of Judah. The revival under King Josiah (who ruled from 640–609 B.C.) and the fall of the Assyrian empire (in 612–609) seemingly offered some hope for Judah. The nation's rebellious spirit, however, coupled with the rise of the Babylonians as the new power of the Near East, made calamity inevitable. When Jeremiah denounced Josiah's successors, Jehoahaz (609), Jehoiakim (609–598), Jehoiachin (598–597), and Zedekiah (597–586), he was threatened, imprisoned, and humiliated. Though complaining at times to the Lord, Jeremiah continued to warn of impending judgment.

That judgment came through the Babylonians. In 612 B.C. they conquered Nineveh, the capital of Assyria. In 609 they defeated the last remnant of Assyrian power at Haran. By this time the Egyptians had allied themselves with Assyria in an attempt to stem the Babylonian tide and maintain the balance of power. When they marched northward to help the Assyrians in 609, Josiah tried to stop them and lost his life. His son Jehoahaz took the throne of Judah, but the Egyptians took him into exile three months later and replaced him with his brother Jehoiakim.

In 605 B.C. the Babylonians established themselves as the premier power of the Near East by defeating the Egyptians at Carchemish. Though loyal to Babylon for a time, Jehoiakim eventually rebelled. The Babylonians besieged Jerusalem and in 597 conquered the city. They replaced Jehoiakim's son Jehoiachin, who had only ruled for three months following the death of his father, with his uncle Zedekiah. After remaining loyal to Babylon for a short time, Zedekiah also rebelled.

In 588 B.C. Nebuchadnezzar invaded Judah and began a long siege of Jerusalem that culminated with the fall of the city in August 586. The Babylonians carried many into exile, but some survivors were allowed to remain in the land under the authority of Gedaliah, a governor appointed by the Babylonians. However, in October 586 a small band of dissidents assassinated Gedaliah. Fearing a Babylonian reprisal, many fled to Egypt. Jeremiah, who opposed this course of action and insisted that the Babylonians would not punish the people, was forced to go with the fugitives to Egypt.

**Theme.** Like so many of the other writing prophets of the Old Testament, Jeremiah promised that God would ultimately fulfill His ideal for Israel, but only after a time of purifying judgment and exile. God would not tolerate unfaithfulness among His people. Judgment would sweep away covenant violators and pave the way for the establishment of a new covenant.

**Literary Form.** The book contains a variety of literary types, including prophetic messages given in both poetic and prose style and biographical accounts of

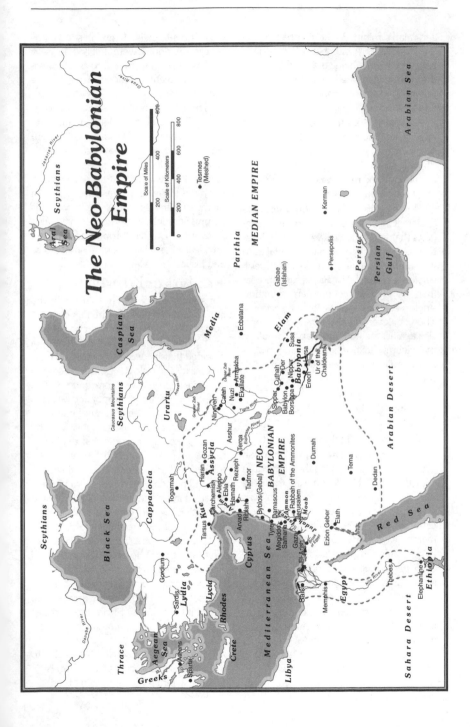

The Neo-Babylonian Empire

Jeremiah's ministry. The first half of the book includes a number of dialogues between Jeremiah and the Lord in which the prophet poured out his heart in prayer. Reports of symbolic acts are also included.

Chapters 1–24 focus on the sin and impending judgment of Judah. The scope of the book broadens in chapters 25–52, where judgment oracles against the nations and messages of Judah's ultimate restoration appear.

A comparison of the Hebrew with the ancient Greek version of Jeremiah suggests that two canonical versions of Jeremiah's prophecies may have circulated in the intertestamental period. The Greek version is about 12 to 13 percent shorter than its Hebrew counterpart, omitting single verses as well as longer sections. The Greek version also arranges the oracles against the nations (chaps. 46–51 in the Hebrew text) differently and places them earlier in the book (as chaps. 25–31).

    I. Jeremiah's Call (1:1-19)
    II. Judah's Downfall (2:1–24:10)
    III. Judah's Alternatives (25:1–51:60)
    IV. A Historical Epilogue (52:1-34)

**Purpose and Theology.** Jeremiah accused Judah of breaking their covenant with the Lord. He denounced the people's unfaithfulness to God, which was seen most clearly in their idolatry and foreign alliances. The leadership of the nation was particularly corrupt. The kings neglected to ensure justice and even persecuted God's prophet. At the same time, false prophets promised deliverance and prosperity.

Jeremiah warned the people not to listen to these lying prophets. The Lord was about to punish Judah for its breach of covenant by bringing upon the nation the curses Moses threatened (see Deut. 27–28). Famine and the sword would destroy multitudes, while many others would go into exile. Jeremiah's warnings of certain doom were fulfilled in 586 B.C., when Jerusalem fell to the Babylonians, an event described in the book's later chapters.

Though much of the book is devoted to the themes of sin and judgment, Jeremiah did see a light at the end of the tunnel. God would someday judge Judah's enemies, including the mighty Babylonians. He would restore His exiled people and make a new covenant with them, enabling them to willingly obey His commandments. The Lord would also restore the Davidic throne and raise up an ideal king who would ensure peace and justice in the land.

## JEREMIAH'S CALL (1:1-19)

For discussion of the heading, see the introduction. Before Jeremiah's conception and birth, the Lord had chosen him to be His prophet. When Jeremiah objected that he was too young and inarticulate for the task, the Lord assured him of His protective presence. The prophet's divinely appointed words would determine the destiny of nations.

Through a pun based on a vision, the Lord assured the prophet that the divine message spoken through him would be fulfilled. When Jeremiah identified an almond branch (saqed), the Lord punned on its name, announcing that He was "watching" (soqed) carefully to assure the realization of the prophetic word.

Through another vision, that of a boiling pot tilting southward, the Lord revealed that Jeremiah's message would be one of impending judgment. The boiling pot symbolized foreign armies that would invade the land from the north as instruments of judgments against God's idolatrous people.

The Lord exhorted Jeremiah to declare His word boldly and fearlessly, promising him protection from his hostile audience.

## JUDAH'S DOWNFALL ( 2:1–24:10)

These chapters contain several judgment oracles against God's people, as well as many of the prophet's emotionally charged prayers to and dialogues with the Lord. The major theme of the section is sinful Judah's coming downfall, yet glimpses of future restoration also appear.

**God Accuses His Unfaithful People (2:1–3:5).** Israel's history was one of apostasy. Early Israel had faithfully followed the Lord and enjoyed His protection. Later generations turned to idols, forgot the Lord's mighty deeds, and defiled the land God had graciously given them. Even the priests, civil leaders, and prophets abandoned the Lord.

Unlike pagans, who maintained loyalty to their worthless gods, Israel exchanged their glorious God and His blessings for useless idols. Consequently they suffered humiliation at the hands of foreigners. Still they sought protective alliances with these same nations.

The Lord compared rebellious and idolatrous Israel to a prostitute and to a good grapevine turned wild. Their guilt was like an irremovable stain in the sight of God. In their frantic pursuit of false gods they were like a skittish female camel dashing about or a lusty female donkey pursuing a mate. Idolatry can only result in shame. The people's idols would prove futile in the coming crisis.

Despite their unfaithfulness, the people claimed to be innocent and accused the Lord of treating them unfairly. In response the Lord pointed to their blatant rebellion and shameless acts of idolatry throughout the land.

**Judah's Alternatives (3:6–6:30).** *A Call for Repentance (3:6–4:4).* Idolatrous Judah was even more corrupt than their sister, the Northern Kingdom, had been. Though the Lord had swept the Northern Kingdom away into exile, Judah had not learned from their northern sister's example. The time for decision had come. Judah's only hope was to repent. The Lord appealed to His faithless people to confess their sins, turn from their idols, and commit themselves to the Lord with renewed devotion. He promised to give them godly leaders and make Jerusalem the focal point of His worldwide rule. Nations would travel to the city to worship the Lord. Judah would be reunited with the exiled Northern Kingdom and would possess the promised land.

*Invasion from the North (4:5-31).* The alternative to repentance was destruction. If Judah persisted in its sin, the Lord would bring a mighty army down from the north to devastate the land. Reference is made to the Babylonians, who would attack with the ferocity of a lion, the power of a whirlwind, and the swiftness of an eagle. The people would flee for their lives; and Jerusalem, abandoned to its doom by its idol-gods, would cry out in panic. Conditions in the ruined and deserted land would resemble those prior to creation, when the earth was formless, empty, and shrouded in darkness.

Throughout the chapter dramatic speeches and vivid imagery are used to emphasize the urgency of the hour. Calls to alarm, lamentations, denunciations, a taunt, and an impassioned appeal for repentance are combined with striking descriptions of the invaders and their effect upon the land.

*A Sinful Society Condemned (5:1-31).* Chapter 5 reiterates why judgment was impending. Without exception the residents of Jerusalem had resisted the Lord's discipline and rebelled against His commandments. Idolatry and sexual immorality were prevalent throughout the land. The people believed the false prophets' message of security. Rich, powerful men exploited others and neglected the cause of the weak and oppressed. Instead of repenting and recognizing God as the source of their blessings, the people stubbornly continued in their sinful ways. Judgment was inevitable for such a nation. The fearsome Babylonians would devour their crops and herds, kill their children, and destroy their cities. Since God's people insisted on acting like pagans, they would serve pagans in a pagan land.

*Jerusalem Attacked (6:1-30).* The invasion threatened in chapters 4 and 5 now takes on even more frightening proportions as the coming siege of Jerusalem is depicted. In succession one hears the Lord's call of alarm to the residents of Benjamin and Judah, the enemy army's call to war, the Lord's summons to this army, a warning to Jerusalem, and the Lord's authorization of foreigners to "glean" His people.

The prophet then interjected a word. Though the people were obstinate and rejected his message of judgment, he was compelled to continue preaching it. God encouraged him to persevere in his proclamation of coming wrath because judgment was inevitable for such a corrupt nation. Even the religious leaders were greedy and deceitful. They glossed over the nation's dire situation and proclaimed a message of false hope. The people refused to obey God's law or to listen to His prophets. Their empty sacrifices would not prevent the coming disaster. The mighty northern army would march relentlessly forward, causing terror and grief among the people. In conclusion the Lord compared Jeremiah's role to that of a metal tester. Having seen the people's moral character revealed in their response to his ministry, Jeremiah observed that they were rebels in need of the hot, purifying fires of divine judgment.

**Hypocrisy and Idolatry (7:1–10:25).** *False Confidence (7:1–8:3).* The people of Judah believed they were safe because the temple, the Lord's dwelling place, was in their midst. The Lord denounced this false confidence, pointing out that only genuine repentance could save such unjust, violent, and idolatrous people. He reminded them of the example of Shiloh, a former dwelling place of the Lord which had not been spared destruction when God judged His wicked people. Though the people brought Him sacrifices, the Lord rejected them as meaningless and hypocritical. He demanded loyalty, not empty ritual. While the people gave the Lord lip service, they also prepared offerings for the "Queen of Heaven" (the Babylonian goddess Ishtar). They sacrificed their children in the Valley of Ben Hinnom south of the city and worshiped the sun, moon, and stars. Apart from repentance, judgment was inevitable. The Valley of Ben Hinnom would be called the Valley of Slaughter, for there the carcasses of the idolaters would be devoured by scavengers. The invaders would desecrate the tombs of the city, leaving the bones exposed to the light of the heavenly bodies the deceased once worshiped.

*Punishment and Lamentation (8:4–9:26).* Though the people claimed to be wise because they possessed God's law, their actions contradicted their words. They disobeyed that same law, refused to repent, and believed the religious leaders who promised peace and safety. The Lord would deprive them of their crops and bring into the land a mighty army, likened to deadly serpents. In that day the doomed and despairing people would lament their fate and acknowledge that their previous hope had been misplaced.

Jeremiah was emotionally shaken by this message of judgment. He described the future cry of the exiles, who in bewilderment would try to reconcile their belief in Jerusalem's inviolability with their situation. He lamented that there was no cure for the nation's sickness and that he did not have enough tears to weep around the clock. He longed to run away, for he recognized that wickedness was everywhere. Even the closest human relationships were polluted by deceit and exploitation.

The time for mourning and lamentation had come, for destruction and exile were on the way. Embodied in the Babylonian army, death would invade the cities and houses of the land, robbing the women of their children and robust young men.

In the coming day of judgment, human wisdom, strength, and riches would be of no avail. Security could only be found in loyalty to the Lord, who as a faithful and just God looks for and rewards these same qualities in His people. Traditional outward signs of a relationship with God, such as circumcision, would also be worthless, if not accompanied by genuine devotion to the Lord (likened in 9:26 to circumcision of the heart; see 4:4). Because God's people lacked this devotion, their physical circumcision would be as useless as that of Gentiles who also observed this practice. Israel would be swept away with the nations mentioned in the coming Babylonian invasion of the west.

*The Incomparable Lord (10:1-16).* The Lord exhorted His people to reject their pagan gods. The man-made wooden and metal idol-gods were inactive and as lifeless as scarecrows. In response Jeremiah praised the Lord, whose greatness infinitely surpasses that of idols. The Lord is the true, living, and eternal God, who created and controls the physical universe and determines the destinies of nations.

*Jeremiah's Lament (10:17-25).* Since God's people had rejected their sovereign King for idols, judgment remained inevitable and lamentation appropriate. Continuing the mood of earlier chapters, the prophet lamented the nation's incurable sickness and impending doom. Appealing to God's justice, he pled that the coming judgment not be unduly harsh and that God would eventually punish the nations for their mistreatment of His people.

**Warnings against Rebellion (11:1-13:27).** *Breach of Covenant (11:1-17).* The Lord reminded His people of the covenant that was to govern their relationship. After the Lord delivered their forefathers from Egypt, He made an agreement with them. If they obeyed His commandments, He promised to be their God and give them the promised land. However, throughout their history the people disobeyed God's law, bringing the punishment (the "curses") threatened in the covenant. Jeremiah's generation had followed in their forefathers' steps by worshiping Baal and other foreign gods. Consequently, they too had to experience the curses of the covenant.

*Opposition to Jeremiah (11:18–12:6).* As the Lord's messenger of judgment, Jeremiah faced opposition, even in his hometown of Anathoth, where some plotted to take his life. Though the prophet had not suspected their hostile intentions, the Lord revealed their schemes. Jeremiah trusted the Lord to vindicate and avenge him. The Lord declared that Jeremiah's enemies would be violently and thoroughly destroyed.

The dialogue between the Lord and His prophet continues in chapter 12. Knowing that God is just, Jeremiah was troubled by the prosperity of the wicked. Confident that God was aware of his loyal character, the prophet asked the

Lord to judge the wicked so that the land might be released from the curse that the sin of the wicked had brought upon it. This time the Lord offered no messages of judgment (see 11:21-23). He warned Jeremiah that the situation would become far worse and that even members of his own family would conspire against him.

*The Lord Abandons and Reclaims His Inheritance (12:7-17).* Though the Lord regarded Judah as His special possession, its hostility forced Him to abandon it. He would allow foreigners to desolate the land. However, He would someday punish these same nations and restore His exiled people to their land. Any nation that then turned to the Lord would be restored, while those that rejected His rule would be annihilated.

*An Object Lesson and a Parable (13:1-27).* The Lord instructed Jeremiah to purchase, wear, and then bury a linen belt. Days later He told the prophet to dig up the now rotten and useless belt. Just as a fine belt brings its owner compliments, so God had intended to glorify Himself through His people. But their pride, stubbornness, and idolatry made them useless. Consequently He would ruin their pride through judgment, just as Jeremiah's belt was ruined by the elements.

The Lord also used a parable to illustrate the coming judgment. Jeremiah was to make the observation that wineskins should be filled with wine. When the people rebuked him for making such an obvious remark, he was to explain the symbolism behind his statement. Just as wineskins were to be used for their designed purpose, so God would deal with His sinful people appropriately. Like wineskins filled with wine, they would be filled with "drunkenness," which is a figurative reference to the staggering effects of God's thorough punishment.

Just as persons cannot change their skin color or a leopard its spots, so the people could not change their propensity for evil. The darkness of judgment would descend on the incorrigible nation, and the people would be swept away into exile like chaff before the wind.

*Jeremiah's Prayers (14:1–15:21). Famine and Sword Are Inevitable (14:1-18).* Jeremiah lamented that a severe drought had swept over the land, confessed the nation's sin, and asked the Lord to restore His favor. In response the Lord pointed to the nation's wickedness, instructed Jeremiah to cease interceding for the people, and announced He would not accept their hypocritical sacrifices. Jeremiah blamed the nation's condition on the false prophets and their promises of peace. These liars would be destroyed with the rest of the nation.

*Prophetic Intercession Is Futile (14:19–15:9).* Once more Jeremiah interceded for the nation, lamenting its condition, confessing its sin, and asking the Lord to intervene. He acknowledged that the Lord was incomparable to the idol-gods and that He alone was the source of the nation's blessings. The Lord declared that not even Moses or Samuel could effectively intercede for such a wicked people. The sins of King Manasseh had angered Him (see 2 Kgs. 21:1-18), and the people had not changed their ways. God decreed that death, famine, and exile would sweep through the land.

*The Lord Vindicates His Prophet (15:10-21).* Jeremiah once again lamented the opposition he experienced (see 12:1-4). Though he was innocent of wrongdoing and had faithfully declared the Lord's word, he suffered reproach. He questioned God's dependability and asked the Lord to take up his cause. The Lord assured him of divine protection and vindication before his enemies. However, the prophet had to confess his lack of faith and persevere in his mission.

**Warnings and Exhortations (16:1–17:27).** *Jeremiah's Restrictions Foreshadow Judgment (16:1–17:4).* The Lord placed several restrictions on Jeremiah that foreshadowed the effects of the coming judgment. Jeremiah was not to take a wife in order to show the devastating effects of judgment upon the nation's families. Many would be left without children and spouses. The prophet was forbidden to attend a funeral, for after the coming disaster people would not even have the opportunity to mourn the dead. Neither was he to attend a feast, for judgment would bring a cessation of joyous celebrations throughout the land.

Once again the Lord pointed out that the people's idolatry had brought this calamity. Though the Lord would someday restore His people to the land through a grand new exodus, the immediate future was only dark. The invaders, like fishermen and hunters, would pursue the people relentlessly. The Lord would repay them double for their idolatry. They would forfeit their place in the promised land and live as slaves in a distant, foreign place.

*Contrasting Fates of the Wicked and Righteous (17:5-11).* The Lord stopped to contrast the wicked and the righteous. Those trusting in human strength and rejecting the Lord were doomed to experience extreme discomfort and eventual death. But those trusting the Lord would flourish, even in times of crisis. Though people can be exceedingly deceptive, God is capable of piercing their minds and motives and dealing with them in a just manner.

*Jeremiah's Prayer (17:12-18).* Appealing to this all-knowing and just God, Jeremiah asserted his faithfulness

to his commission and asked that he be vindicated before his persecutors.

*Sabbath Commands (17:19-27).* Once more the Lord offered the people an opportunity to exhibit a repentant attitude. He exhorted the whole nation, including its king, to demonstrate their loyalty to Him by observing His requirements concerning the Sabbath Day. If they kept it holy by refraining from work, the Lord would bless them and accept their offerings. However, if they rejected this test of obedience, the threatened calamity would come in full force.

**The Potter (18:1–20:18).** *A Marred Pot and an Unpopular Prophet (18:1-23).* The Lord sent Jeremiah to a potter's house, where he illustrated His sovereign control over Judah. As Jeremiah watched the potter shaping a pot, the clay was marred. The potter reshaped the marred clay into a different style pot. The Lord explained that His people were like clay in His hands, which He is free to reshape in accordance with His desires. When He threatens to destroy a sinful nation, He remains willing to reshape that nation's destiny if they are repentant. When He plans to bless a nation, He will alter His purpose if they are disobedient. Though He had once blessed His people, He was now planning disaster against them because of their idolatry and disobedience. Repentance would reshape their destiny, but they refused God's offer.

Jeremiah's proclamation of these truths was not well-received. The residents of Judah and Jerusalem plotted against the prophet, causing him to protest his innocence and again seek vindication from the Lord.

*A Broken Jar and a Disillusioned Prophet (19:1–20:18).* The Lord instructed Jeremiah to buy a jar from a potter and then take some of the civil leaders and priests out to the Valley of

Ben Hinnom (see 7:31). Once there the prophet was to pronounce scathing judgment against Jerusalem because of the idolatry and child sacrifice its residents carried on in the valley. He was then to break the jar, illustrating what God would do to the city. This idolatrous valley would become a burial ground for the slaughtered idolaters.

Having carried out his commission, Jeremiah went to the temple and delivered another announcement of judgment. Pashhur, one of the leading temple officials, had Jeremiah imprisoned and beaten. When released, Jeremiah gave Pashhur the symbolic name Magor-Missabib (meaning *terror all around*) and announced that this official would witness the death of his friends and the exile of the nation. Passhur would die and be buried in a foreign land.

Embarrassed and angry, Jeremiah poured out his heart before the Lord. His words reflect his confused emotions and perspective. He accused the Lord of deception and complained of being caught between a rock and a hard place. When he proclaimed the Lord's word, he was insulted and abused. If he held back from preaching the message, the divine word burned within him until he was forced to declare it. In a sudden burst of confidence Jeremiah affirmed his trust in the Lord. Just as quickly he sank back into depression and cursed the day of his birth.

**Kings and False Prophets (21:1–24:10).** Messages from King Zedekiah's reign begin and end this section. In between are oracles concerning the Davidic throne, Zedekiah's predecessors (Jehoahaz, Jehoiakim, and Jehoiachin), and the false prophets.

*Messages against Judah's Final Kings (21:1–23:8).* Zedekiah sent messengers to Jeremiah in hopes that the Lord might miraculously deliver Jerusalem from the Babylonian armies. The Lord declared that He was fighting with the Babylonians and would not rescue the city. Jerusalem would be ravaged by plague, famine, and sword. Zedekiah and the city's survivors would be handed over to the Babylonians (see 2 Kgs. 23:5-7). Those who wished to escape the slaughter should surrender to Nebuchadnezzar immediately.

Jeremiah 21:11–22:9 contains two exhortations, addressed generally to the royal house. Both focus on the necessity for justice. They come from a time when repentance was still an option and the people were still boasting Jerusalem could never fall. The Lord reminded the king of his obligation to promote justice, warning that a failure in this regard would bring severe consequences. He threatened proud Jerusalem with judgment as well.

The next speech comes after the death of Josiah and the Egyptian exile of his son Shallum (Jehoahaz), both of which occurred in 609 B.C. (see 2 Kgs. 23:29-34). The people were to cease mourning for Josiah and lament Jehoahaz, for the latter's fate (death in exile) was even more foreboding for the nation than Josiah's death had been.

The next oracle (Jer. 23:13-23) concerns Jehoiakim, another of Josiah's sons and Jehoahaz's successor. The Lord denounced the unjust practices used by Jehoiakim in building a beautiful new palace. Jehoiakim's exploitation of the citizenry stood in stark contrast to his father Josiah's righteousness. Josiah's concern for justice in his realm was proof that he truly acknowledged the Lord's authority. Humiliation would overtake proud Jehoiakim and his city.

The future was also dark for Jehoiachin, Jehoiakim's son and successor. The Lord would reject him as king and hand him over to Nebuchadnezzar. He would spend the rest of his d[...] [...]n of (see 2 Kgs. 24:8-17). Non[...] would occupy his throne.

In the final oracle of [...] Lord announced the [...] of ment of the "shepher[...] [...]een nation, who had [...] 26–35 cared for, His [...] [...]ch begin people would b[...] [...]ating from Lord would ev[...] to the land a[...] [...]ent (25:1-38). leaders. In tha[...] [...] Jehoiakim's fourth would reign in [...] [...]rough faithful proph-the land. [...]1, the Lord had repeat-

*Messages against Fals[...]* [...]e nation to repentance. *(23:9-40).* The Lord's judgmer[...] [...]ected the offer and persisted about to fall upon the false prophets wh[...] [...]y. The day of reckoning had failed to denounce evil and promised the [...]Nebuchadnezzar's armies would people peace and security. None of these sweep down from the north and overrun prophets had access to the Lord's heav-Judah and the neighboring states. These enly council or received revelation from nations would serve Babylon for seventy Him, yet they claimed to be His messen-years, after which time the Lord would gers. overthrow their oppressor. This proph-

*Two Baskets of Figs (24:1-10).* Fol-ecy of Babylon's doom was fulfilled in lowing the exile of Jehoiachin in 597 538 when the Persians defeated the B.C., the Lord gave Jeremiah another Chaldean empire and conquered Baby-object lesson. He showed the prophet lon. two baskets, one filled with tasty figs and The coming judgment of the nations the other with inedible ones. The good is likened to an intoxicating cup passed figs represented those already exiled in from mouth to mouth. Judah would take Babylon. The Lord would care for them the first swig, followed by several other and eventually restore the exiles to the nations. Finally Babylon, referred to here land. The bad figs represented Jehoi-by its code-name Sheshach (see 51:41), achin's successor Zedekiah, his officials, would be forced to take a draft from the those who remained in Jerusalem, and Lord's cup. The Lord's judgment is those who had gone to Egypt. They described with other vivid images, includ-would experience humiliation and even-ing a deafening storm, the slaughter of tual destruction. sheep, the shattering of a pot, and a raging lion.

## JUDGMENT AND RESTORATION ( 25:1–51:64)

*Exile and Restoration (26:1– 35:19).* This section begins and ends These chapters outline God's future pro-with events from Jehoiakim's time. gram in detail. The theme of judgment These two chapters contrast Judah's upon Judah, introduced in chapters 1– rejection of God's prophet with the devo-24, is developed. This section also tion of the Recabites. The intervening describes divine judgment on a universal chapters date from the time of Zedekiah. Chapters 27–29 and 34, which condemn the nation's corrupt civil and religious leaders, provide a frame around the messages of hope and restoration in chapters 30–33.

*Jeremiah's Life Threatened (26:1-24).* Early in the reign of Jehoiakim, Jeremiah delivered a message to worshipers at the temple. Disaster was coming if the people refused to repent of their sinful ways. The temple would be destroyed like the shrine at Shiloh, which had once been the Lord's dwelling place (see 7:12-14).

Those who heard his message, including the priests and false prophets, grabbed Jeremiah and threatened to kill him. When royal officials intervened, the priests and prophets accused him of treason. Jeremiah declared that the Lord had sent him, again issued a call to repentance, and protested his innocence. The officials and the people objected to the religious leaders' charge. Several elders reminded the crowd of an event in the nation's history about one hundred years before. The prophet Micah had announced that the city and temple would be destroyed (see 26:18 with Mic. 3:12). On that occasion Hezekiah repented, and God postponed judgment. The elders warned that Jeremiah's opponents were about to bring a terrible disaster upon the city. Ahikam, a high-ranking official in the royal court, also interceded for Jeremiah, and he was spared.

However, a parenthetical note informs us that not all of the Lord's prophets were as fortunate as Jeremiah. One of Jeremiah's contemporaries, Uriah, was forced to flee to Egypt when one of his prophecies of judgment angered King Jehoiakim. Jehoiakim had Uriah extradited and executed.

*Jeremiah Confronts the False Prophets (27:1–29:32).* Early in Zedekiah's reign Jeremiah warned the people not to believe the false prophets' messages of hope and peace. In accordance with the Lord's instructions, Jeremiah made a yoke and placed it on his neck. He then sent messages to the kings of the surrounding nations, informing them that Nebuchadnezzar would subjugate their lands. They were not to believe their lying prophets and diviners who were advocating resistance and predicting deliverance. Resistance would only bring disaster and exile. They should submit to Nebuchadnezzar's authority (symbolized by the yoke) so that they might remain in their lands. The message was the same for Zedekiah. He should reject the messages of hope delivered by the false prophets, who were even promising that the temple articles already carried away to Babylon would be returned. Zedekiah should submit to Nebuchadnezzar's yoke in order to spare the city and the temple further suffering and humiliation.

In that same year Hananiah, one of the false prophets, confronted Jeremiah in the temple (28:1). He declared that within two years the Lord would deliver Judah from the Babylonians, restore the temple articles, and return Jehoiachin and the other exiles. After expressing his personal desire that Judah might experience such blessings, Jeremiah reminded Hananiah that historically the Lord's prophets had been messengers of judgment. Prophets of peace could only be authenticated when their predictions came true. In response Hananiah removed the wooden yoke from Jeremiah's neck, broke it, and once again declared that the Lord would deliver Judah and the surrounding nations from Nebuchadnezzar's yoke. Not to be denied, Jeremiah announced that the Lord would place an unbreakable iron yoke upon Judah and the nations. He then announced that Hananiah would die before the year ended, a prophecy that was fulfilled two months later.

During Zedekiah's reign Jeremiah sent a letter to those who had already been taken to Babylon. He encouraged them to settle down there, marry and have children, and pray for the prosperity of their new home. In seventy years the Lord would restore them to the promised land. They were not to believe the deceiving prophets among them who were giving them false hopes of a quick return. Even greater calamity was about to fall on sinful Judah, and those still living in the promised land would be driven among the nations.

Jeremiah condemned two of these prophets by name. Because of their immoral acts and false prophecies, the Lord would deliver them to the Babylonians for execution, probably on charges of rebellion.

Shemaiah, a false prophet in Babylon, sent several letters back to Jerusalem, informing Zephaniah the priest and others of the contents of Jeremiah's letter to the exiles. Calling Jeremiah a madman, Shemaiah urged Zephaniah to imprison the prophet. When informed by the priest of Shemaiah's words, Jeremiah sent another message to the exiles, denouncing Shemaiah as a false prophet and proclaiming that neither he nor his family would participate in the eventual restoration of the exiles.

*Hope and Restoration (30:1–33:26).* Though dark days were ahead, God would not totally abandon His people. An awful time of frightening judgment would come upon the sin-filled land. Abandoned by its allies and struck down by God, the nation would be like a man with an incurable wound. However, after this time of discipline, God would cure their wound and bring His exiled people back to the land. Exiles from the Northern Kingdom would be reunited with those from Judah, and together they would serve the Lord and His appointed Davidic ruler. The people would increase in numbers and enjoy a renewed relationship with God.

The message of comfort to the exiles continues in chapter 31. Assuring the Northern Kingdom of His everlasting love, the Lord promised to deliver its exiles from their captors. Like a shepherd He would lead them back home and restore their agricultural prosperity and joy. They would come to Jerusalem to worship the Lord and thank Him for His abundant blessings.

Personification highlights 31:15-22. Calling the Northern Kingdom Rachel (the mother of Joseph and grandmother of Ephraim and Manasseh, the two important northern tribes), the Lord exhorted her to cease weeping over her exiled children, for they would someday return to the land. Comparing Ephraim to His son (see v. 9), the Lord declared that He had heard His child's prayer of repentance. Finally, addressing Israel as a young woman (see v. 4), the Lord exhorted her to cease her wandering and carefully observe the road signs guiding her back to the land.

The concluding, riddlelike statement of verse 22 has puzzled interpreters. The woman is undoubtedly Israel, and the man, probably the Lord. Perhaps reference is made to Israel's newfound devotion to the Lord or to its renewed worship around the Lord's throne in Zion (see vv. 4-6,11-13). In that day Judah's devotion to the Lord would also be renewed. The restored exiles would pronounce blessings upon Jerusalem and prosper in their agricultural pursuits.

Chapter 31 culminates with a glorious promise of a new covenant. In days past the Lord had carefully planned and executed the demise of Israel and Judah. In the future He would carefully superintend their restoration. He would forgive their sins and establish a new covenant superior to the Mosaic covenant they had violated. This time God would supernaturally give them the capacity for loyalty that the old covenant had demanded. The Lord took a formal oath that His people would never cease to be a nation or experience His rejection. He promised that Jerusalem would be rebuilt, purified, and never again destroyed.

During the Babylonian siege of Jerusalem in 587 B.C. Zedekiah, who resented Jeremiah's oracles of doom, imprisoned the prophet in the royal palace. When Jeremiah's cousin Hanamel came to visit him, Jeremiah, as commanded by the Lord, redeemed Hanamel's field in accordance with the ancient law of land redemption (Lev. 25:25-28).

Having completed the transaction, Jeremiah prayed to the Lord. He praised God as the almighty Creator and just Ruler over all. He recalled God's mighty deeds in Israel's history and acknowledged that the present crisis was the result of the nation's sin. Aware that the city would fall to the Babylonians, he asked why God had instructed him to purchase a field. What good would a field be once the land was destroyed and the people exiled?

In response the Lord asked, "Is anything too hard for me?" (Jer. 32:27). Yes, He would allow the Babylonians to conquer the city because of its idolatry. The Lord would someday restore the exiles to the land, transform them into loyal worshipers, establish a new covenant with them, and restore their prosperity. In that day people would again buy and sell fields. Jeremiah's purchase of the field foreshadowed this future restoration.

While confined in the palace, Jeremiah received another encouraging message about the future restoration of the land. Though the Babylonians would reduce Judah to a wasteland and fill Jerusalem with carcasses, the Lord would someday forgive His people's sins, bring them back to the land, and cause Jerusalem to prosper. In fulfillment of His eternal promise to David (2 Sam. 7:12-16), the Lord would raise up an ideal Davidic ruler, who would bring justice and peace to the land. Faithful to His irrevocable covenant with the Levites (Num. 25:12-13), He would establish them as His servants.

Zedekiah's Fate (34:1-22). Despite these glowing promises of restoration, the immediate future remained bleak. During the Babylonian siege Jeremiah warned King Zedekiah that the Babylonians would conquer the city and take the king into exile. The prophet assured Zedekiah that he would die a peaceful, not violent, death and would receive an honorable burial.

Jeremiah also denounced the king's unjust treatment of slaves. During the siege Zedekiah and the citizens of Jerusalem pledged on oath to free all Hebrew slaves. Apparently in some cases this was done as an act of repentance for past failures in this regard (Jer. 34:13-15). However, ulterior motives must have been involved; for when the Babylonians lifted the siege, the slave owners reneged on their covenant and revoked the freedom of those just released. Jeremiah sarcastically declared that the Lord had granted these covenant violators "freedom" from their deceitful ways so that they might perish. When the Lord was through with them, they would be like one of the calves cut in two in a covenant-making ceremony. The Babylonians would return to the city and destroy it.

Jeremiah and the Recabites (35:1-19). During the reign of Jehoiakim, the Lord instructed Jeremiah to invite the Recabite family to the temple and to offer them some wine. The Recabites were the descendants of Jonadab, son of Recab (2 Kgs. 10:15-23), a zealous devotee of the Lord and opponent of Baal worship. Jonadab had commanded his descendants to follow a nomadic and ascetic lifestyle, which included total abstinence from wine. Over two hundred years later his descendants were still observing the regulations their forefather established. When Jeremiah set the wine before them, they refused to drink it, faithful to their ancestor's commands.

The Recabites were an object lesson to Judah and Jerusalem. Their unwavering devotion to their ancestor stood in stark contrast to unfaithful Judah's rejection of the Lord's prophets. Judgment would fall on Judah, but the Lord would preserve Jonadab's godly line.

**Judah's Final Days (36:1-45:5).** This section opens and closes with material dating from the fourth and fifth years of Jehoiakim's reign. Baruch, Jeremiah's scribe, plays a prominent role in these chapters that frame the section. The intervening chapters relate in chronological order various experiences of the prophet, beginning with his dealings with King Zedekiah and concluding with his messages to the Egyptian exiles following the fall of Jerusalem.

*Jehoiakim Burns the Scroll (36:1-32).* The Lord instructed Jeremiah to record all of his prophetic messages on a scroll. Jeremiah dictated his messages to the scribe Baruch. Baruch took the scroll to the temple on an official day of fasting and read the prophecies to the people assembled there. When the royal officials heard the reading of the scroll, they told Baruch they must report its contents to the king. After warning Jeremiah and Baruch to go into hiding, they informed the king. As the scroll was read, Jehoiakim cut it up by columns and burned it. He then ordered the arrest of Jeremiah and Baruch, whom by this time

the Lord had hidden. The Lord then instructed Jeremiah to dictate another scroll. He also announced that Jehoiakim would be punished severely for his disrespect.

*Zedekiah Imprisons Jeremiah (37:1-38:28).* During the siege of Jerusalem in 588 B.C. the Babylonians temporarily withdrew from the city to fight an army sent out by Egypt, one of Judah's allies. Jeremiah warned Zedekiah that the city's relief was only temporary. The Babylonians would push back the Egyptians and then destroy Jerusalem. Jeremiah was arrested as a traitor, beaten, and imprisoned for a lengthy period of time in a dungeon. Zedekiah eventually sent for Jeremiah to see if he had any new word from the Lord. Jeremiah repeated his earlier message of judgment, protested his innocence, and asked the king not to send him back to the dungeon. Zedekiah granted his request and sent him to the courtyard of the guard.

While similarities between chapters 37 and 38 might suggest they are parallel accounts of the same events, differences in details make it more likely that chapter 38 records events subsequent to those of chapter 37. While in the courtyard of the guard, Jeremiah continued to proclaim his message of impending judgment. Several royal officials complained to Zedekiah, arguing that Jeremiah should be put to death as a traitor. With the king's approval they lowered the prophet into a muddy cistern, where they intended to let him starve. Ebed-Melech, a palace official, objected to the king, who agreed to let Ebed-Melech rescue Jeremiah from the cistern. Zedekiah again met privately with the prophet. The king expressed his fear that the Babylonians would deliver him over to the hostile pro-Babylonian Jewish party. Jeremiah assured the king that if he surrendered to the Babylonians his life would be preserved. At the same time he warned that resistance would result only in humiliation and ruin. Zedekiah warned Jeremiah to keep their conversation a secret and allowed him to remain in the courtyard of the guard.

*Jerusalem's Fall and Jeremiah's Release (39:1–40:6).* After a long siege Jerusalem fell to the Babylonians in 586 B.C. Zedekiah ran for his life, but the Babylonians captured him near Jericho and brought him to Nebuchadnezzar. Before the king's eyes the Babylonians executed his sons and the nobles of Judah. They then put Zedekiah's eyes out and took him to Babylon. The Babylonians destroyed Jerusalem and carried most of the population away into exile, leaving only the poor behind.

In the midst of this disaster, Jeremiah was not forgotten. By royal order Nebuzaradan, one of Nebuchadnezzar's high-ranking officials, released Jeremiah from the courtyard of the guard and turned him over to Gedaliah.

Details of the prophet's release follow a brief parenthesis indicating that Ebed-Melech was spared (see 38:7-13). After his initial release Jeremiah somehow got mixed in with those being taken into exile. Nebuzaradan freed him and gave him the option to go to Babylon or stay in the land. Jeremiah decided on the latter and returned to Gedaliah, the newly appointed governor.

*Turmoil in the Land (40:7–41:15).* During the Babylonian invasion some of the soldiers and men of Judah had managed to avoid capture. They came to Gedaliah, who promised them safety and encouraged them to return to their agricultural pursuits and serve the king of Babylon. Judean refugees from the surrounding countries returned as well and resumed life in their homeland.

However, all was not well. One of the army officers, Johanon son of Kareah, informed Gedaliah that the king of the Ammonites, who was anti-Babylonian in sentiment (see 27:3; Ezek. 21:18-32), wanted the governor dead and had already sent another of Judah's army officers, Ishmael son of Nethaniah, to do the job. Gedaliah refused to believe this report and declined Johanon's offer to kill Ishmael.

Sometime later (41:1 gives the month, but not the year), Ishmael and ten other men visited Gedaliah in Mizpah. During a meal they suddenly arose and killed Gedaliah, as well as the Judeans and Babylonian soldiers who were present. The next day eighty men passed by on their way to Jerusalem to mourn over the temple and present offerings at its ruins. Ishmael enticed them into the city, where he then slaughtered seventy of the eighty (the ten who were spared promised him provisions) and threw their bodies into a cistern. Taking the residents of Mizpah as hostages, he set out for Ammon. When Johanon heard the news, he and his men pursued Ishmael and overtook him in Gibeon. The hostages were rescued, but Ishmael and eight of his men escaped.

*Jeremiah's Message to the Survivors (41:16–43:7).* Fearing reprisal from the Babylonians for the death of Gedaliah, Johanon and the people of Mizpah started toward Egypt. However, before leaving the land, they asked Jeremiah to seek the Lord's will on their behalf and promised to obey His directions. After inquiring of the Lord, Jeremiah told them to stay in the land and promised that God would cause the Babylonian king to treat them mercifully. He warned that if they disobeyed and fled to Egypt, disaster would overtake them. Jeremiah's warning fell on deaf ears. Johanon and others accused him of collaborating with Baruch in an effort to hand them over to the Babylonians for punishment. With flagrant disregard for the Lord's command, the group fled to Egypt, taking Jeremiah and Baruch with them.

*Jeremiah in Egypt (43:8–44:30).* Jeremiah's exile to Egypt certainly did not bring his prophetic ministry to an end. At Tahpanhes, the site of an Egyptian royal residence in the eastern delta, the Lord instructed Jeremiah to announce the coming fall of Egypt to the Babylonians. The prophet took some large stones and buried them in clay in the brick pavement at the entrance to the palace. He then proclaimed that Nebuchadnezzar would someday erect a throne over the stones. The Babylonian king would devastate Egypt and its temples. The Lord would prove to the Judean refugees that He, not Egypt, was their only source of strength and protection.

Chapter 44 records another of Jeremiah's Egyptian messages. Addressing all of the Judean exiles living in Egypt, the prophet reminded them that God's judgment upon Jerusalem was due to the people's idolatry. Their persistence in worshiping idol-gods would only lead to a further outpouring of God's angry judgment.

The people responded to Jeremiah's warning with hostility. They declared that they would continue to sacrifice to the "Queen of Heaven," the Babylonian goddess Ishtar. They thought disaster had only come upon Judah because Josiah purged the land of foreign gods (2 Kgs. 23).

Jeremiah attempted to correct their faulty reasoning, pointing out that it was idolatry that had brought God's wrath upon the nation. In the face of such obstinacy Jeremiah announced that divine judgment would overtake them in Egypt. As a sign of coming disaster, he prophe-

sied the downfall of Pharaoh Hophra. This prophecy was fulfilled a few years later, in 570 B.C., when Hophra was overthrown by a rival Egyptian party.

*Jeremiah Encourages Baruch (45:1-5).* This brief message, which dates to Jehoiakim's fourth year (605 B.C.) and concerns the scribe Baruch, rounds off chapters 36–45. These words were spoken to Baruch after he recorded Jeremiah's prophecies on a scroll (see 36:1-7). Jeremiah told Baruch not to covet a high position, for judgment would surely come upon the land. Yet Baruch could be assured that the Lord would protect him through the disaster.

**Judgment on Various Nations (46:1–51:51).** These oracles of judgment develop the message of chapter 25. Together with chapter 25 they form a frame around this section of the book.

*Judgment on Egypt (46:1-28).* In 605 B.C. one of the major battles of ancient history took place at Carchemish, located on the Euphrates River in Syria. The Babylonians under Nebuchadnezzar defeated the Egyptians under Necho and thereby established themselves as the major power in the Near East. On the occasion of this battle, Jeremiah proclaimed an oracle against Egypt. In dramatic fashion he imitated the commands of the Egyptian officers as they prepared their troops for battle. He then described the Egyptians' retreat and downfall. Though the Egyptians marched into battle with chariots and weapons, they were doomed to defeat, for the Lord was fighting with the Babylonians.

Chapter 46 also includes a prophecy of the Babylonian invasion of Egypt, which took place in 568–567 B.C. The Egyptian army would scatter before the swarming northern invaders. The Egyptians would be as helpless as trees of a forest before the axes of woodsmen. Pharaoh and the gods of Egypt, including even their chief deity Amon, would be unable to resist the Lord's judgment.

The chapter concludes with an encouraging message for God's people. Once their time of punishment was over, the Lord would deliver them from exile and restore them to their land.

*Judgment on the Philistines (47:1-7).* Divine judgment would also fall on the Philistines. The approach of the Babylonians from the north would cause consternation throughout Philistia. The enemy would sweep through the land, bringing death and destruction. This oracle was fulfilled in 604 B.C. when Nebuchadnezzar overran Philistia and conquered Ashkelon.

*Judgment on Moab (48:1-47).* This lengthy oracle portrays the downfall of Moab, which apparently took place in 582 B.C. at the hands of the Babylonians. This chapter is filled with Moabite place names and vivid imagery. The destruction of their land would cause the Moabites to weep bitterly and flee in panic. In the past Moab had been relatively secure, like wine that had been allowed to settle in one jar. All that was about to change. Moab would be poured out of the jar. Moab's military might would be shattered, causing its pride and joy to be replaced by humiliation and lamentation. Its demise was inescapable. Its people and their chief god Chemosh would be carried into exile. A brief concluding statement promised Moab eventual restoration.

*Judgment on Ammon (49:1-6).* Ammon, another of the Trans-Jordanian states, would also experience judgment. The Ammonites were proud of their agricultural prosperity and wealth, but the Lord would bring disaster upon their land. They and their god Milcom (compare NIV "Molech") would go into exile. As in the case of Moab (see 48:47), Ammon was promised eventual restoration.

*Judgment on Edom (49:7-22).* This oracle, which parallels the Book of Obadiah, threatens Edom with thorough and final destruction. Edom was proud of its wisdom and secure position. Since God's own people were not immune from punishment, then certainly the Edomites would not be spared. Like Sodom and Gomorrah, Edom would become a prime example of devastation and ruin. The Lord would come against them like a lion attacking a helpless flock of sheep.

*Judgment on Damascus (49:23-27).* Damascus, an important city in Syria, would also experience judgment. Arpad and Hamath, two city-states located in northern Syria, are portrayed as being troubled over the news of the fall of Damascus. The strong warriors of Damascus would fall in the streets as the city went up in smoke.

*Judgment on Kedar and Hazor (49:28-33).* Nebuchadnezzar, the Lord's instrument of judgment against nations, would also attack the Arabian tribes located east of Palestine, two of which are specifically named here (the precise location of Hazor is unknown). This prophecy came to pass in 599–598 B.C.

*Judgment on Elam (49:34-39).* The Lord would also judge the distant land of Elam, located east of Babylon. He would shatter Elam's military might and scatter its people among the nations. As in some of the preceding oracles, an encouraging word concludes the oracle (see 46:26; 48:47; 49:6).

*Judgment on Babylon (50:1–51:64).* Though the Lord would use Babylon to punish many nations, He would eventually judge this mighty empire as well. In these two lengthy chapters Babylon's downfall is described in detail.

A mighty nation from the north would capture Babylon. The Medo-Persians conquered the Babylonian empire in 539 B.C. The Babylonians' idol-gods, the chief of which was Marduk, would be unable to rescue the city.

Babylon's demise would be good news for God's people. He had sent them into exile for their sins, but now they would be able to leave Babylon, return to Jerusalem, and enjoy a renewed covenantal relationship with God. Babylon's and Israel's relative positions would be reversed. Like the Assyrians before them, Babylon had mistreated and oppressed God's people. Now the time of reckoning had come. The Lord would overthrow Babylon and regather His scattered people to their land. He would restore Israel's blessings and forgive their sins.

Babylon's fall is vividly portrayed as dramatic calls to battle alternate with descriptions of the city's defeat. The Lord would vindicate His oppressed people before the arrogant Babylonians. Using the invincible northern army as His instrument, the Lord would destroy everything in which Babylon took pride—its civil and religious leaders, warriors, armaments, and wealth. The city would become like Sodom and Gomorrah. (As in Isa. 13–14, the problem of harmonizing this portrayal of Babylon's fall with the Persian conquest of 539 B.C. is difficult. See comments there.) Again employing the imagery of a lion ravaging a flock of sheep (see 50:44-45 with 49:19-20), the Lord declared that the judgment of Babylon would demonstrate He was a God without equal.

The description of Babylon's fall continues in chapter 51. Once more the Lord's vengeance is a major theme. He would vindicate His people before their oppressor, demonstrating His sovereignty over the affairs of individuals and nations. The Lord is the Creator of the universe, who is infinitely superior to the idol gods.

The Babylonians would be unable to stand before the northern army raised up by the Lord. Babylon would be trampled like a threshing floor at harvest time and be reduced to ruins. In response to His people's prayer for revenge, the Lord announced that the Babylonians would reel like drunkards and be slaughtered like sheep. He would humiliate Babylon and its idols, just as the Babylonians had shamed the Lord's people and dwelling place. Before the Lord's retributive judgment all the wisdom, pomp, and might of Babylon would prove futile.

Having recorded his prophecy against Babylon on a scroll, Jeremiah commissioned Seraiah, an officer of King Zedekiah, who was about to travel to Babylon, to proclaim the message when he arrived there. He instructed Seraiah to offer a brief prayer and to drop the scroll into the Euphrates River as an illustration of Babylon's eventual downfall.

## HISTORICAL EPILOGUE (52:1-34)

This chapter is parallel to 2 Kings 24:18–25:30 (see commentary there). The statistical information given in Jeremiah 52:28-30 does not appear in 2 Kings 25, and the account of Gedaliah's death (see 2 Kgs. 25:22-26) is omitted in Jeremiah 52. The chapter gives a detailed account of Jerusalem's fall to the Babylonians. It is probably included to authenticate Jeremiah's message by showing that his prophecies of judgment were fulfilled.

***Theological Significance.*** Jeremiah shows prophecy in full flesh and blood. He wanted to identify with his people and live a normal life. Instead he had to preach against his people and confront other prophets and then ask God, "Why?" Through the prophet's humanity, God spoke to Judah and the nations during Israel's greatest crisis. God showed that obedience, justice, and piety pleased Him and ensured the nation's future. Theological and worship tradition ensured nothing. God could change political sides to discipline His covenant people and then lead them back to Him. Nebuchadnezzar succeeded in conquering Jerusalem because he was God's agent of judgment on His sinful people. In the end, however, the nations in their arrogance would face God's wrath, while Israel would be a people of a new, heartfelt covenant.

Jeremiah affirmed that God's ultimate plan was to bless His people (29:11). God's plans, however, are conditional on human response (18:7-10). Persistent rebellion can bring punishment when God had promised blessing. Repentance can avert disaster when God had promised judgment.

Jeremiah affirms the faithlessness of God's people and their need for God to intervene to save them. Jeremiah anticipates a time when God would write a new covenant on His people's hearts, when God would be known in intimate fellowship, when God would no longer remember their sins (31:31-34). Jeremiah's hopes find fulfillment in the new relationship with God made possible through Christ's death (Heb. 11:12-22).

## Questions for Reflection

1. How did Jeremiah portray God? What roles and characteristics did the prophet attribute to God?

2. Why was God displeased with Judah? Is the modern church like Judah in any ways?

3. In what ways does Jeremiah serve as an example for God's people? What were his strengths? weaknesses?

4. How did Jeremiah characterize the false prophets of his day? How did they differ from Jeremiah? How can modern Christians identify false teachers?

## Sources for Additional Study

Harrison, Roland K. Jeremiah and Lamentations. Tyndale Old Testament Commentaries. Downers Grove: InterVarsity, 1973.

Huey, F. B., Jr. Jeremiah, Lamentations. New American Commentary. Nashville: Broadman & Holman, 1993.

Skinner, John. Prophecy and Religion: Studies in the Life of Jeremiah. Cambridge: University Press, 1922.

Thompson, J. A. The Book of Jeremiah. New International Commentary on the Old Testament. Grand Rapids: Eerdmans, 1980.

# LAMENTATIONS

Though it does not identify its author, tradition has ascribed the Book of Lamentations to Jeremiah. The author of the book, like the prophet, was an eyewitness of Jerusalem's fall and displayed great emotion in his prayers to God. The book was written between the destruction of the city in 586 B.C. and the rebuilding of the temple seventy years later.

**Theme.** The author lamented the fall of Jerusalem. While acknowledging that the calamity was deserved, he longed for God to restore His favor.

**Literary Form.** The book contains five poems, corresponding to the chapter divisions. The central poem is sixty-six verses in length, while the others contain twenty-two verses each. All but the last poem are acrostics, in which the form reflects the successive letters of the Hebrew alphabet. In chapters 1; 2; and 4 the first letters of the first words of the twenty-two verses correspond to the successive letters of the Hebrew alphabet (the order of the letters *ayin* and *pe* varies). In chapter 3 the verses are arranged in blocks of three. Verses 1-3 each begin with the first letter of the alphabet *(aleph),* verses 4-6 with the second letter *(beth),* and so on.

The laments follow the standard pattern seen in the Psalms. (See "Psalms.") They contain typical lament elements such as complaint, petition, and confidence.

I. Jerusalem's Affliction (1:1-22)
II. The Lord's Judgment (2:1-22)
III. Confidence Despite Disaster (3:1-66)
IV. Jerusalem's Downfall (4:1-22)
V. Prayer for Restoration (5:1-22)

**Purpose and Theology.** The author clearly acknowledged the truth of what the preexilic prophets had preached—Judah's sin led to its downfall and to the tragic destruction of Jerusalem and the temple. However, in the midst of this calamity the author acknowledged the Lord's faithfulness and compassion and appealed to these divine attributes. He longed for the day when God would restore His favor and take vengeance on the nations who had tormented them.

## JERUSALEM'S AFFLICTION (1:1-22)

**The Author's Lament (1:1-11).** Jerusalem had once been a queen; now she was a slave. Foreigners had stolen its wealth, polluted its temple, and carried its people into exile. Abandoned by its allies and no longer visited by religious pilgrims, it was like an inconsolable widow, weeping bitterly over her loss. Because of its sin, Jerusalem had been humiliated, like a woman publicly disgraced by sexual sin.

**The City's Lament (1:12-22).** Jerusalem, personified as a woman, lamented that the Lord had poured His anger out upon it. It acknowledged that its sins had brought its downfall and that the Lord had caused its military defeat. It lamented that it had no comforters, for its allies had turned against it and its people had gone into exile or perished. In desperation it confessed its sin and asked the Lord to consider its anguish. Humiliated and abused by its enemies, it pleaded with the Lord to take vengeance upon them.

## THE LORD'S JUDGMENT (2:1-22)

**The Lord's Anger (2:1-10).** The Lord attacked Jerusalem as if it were His enemy. Rather than protecting the city with His powerful right hand, He turned His might against it and poured His angry judgment upon it like fire. Though He once resided in the city, He abandoned His temple and allowed foreigners to pollute it. The city's walls were destroyed and its leaders enslaved, leaving the rest of the population (represented here by the elders and young women) to mourn bitterly over its demise.

**Call to Prayer (2:11-19).** The author lamented the plight of the small children, who were dying from hunger in their mothers' arms. Addressing the personified city, he grieved over its great distress and reminded it that the words of its false prophets had proven to be futile. In accordance with His sovereign decree the Lord had allowed Jerusalem's enemies to humiliate it. In conclusion he urged the people to cry out to the Lord for mercy.

**Lady Jerusalem (2:20-22).** Responding to the author's exhortation, personified Jerusalem pleaded with the Lord to consider its plight. Women were forced to eat their own children to survive, religious leaders had been killed in the Lord's temple, and the streets were littered with the corpses of the city's inhabitants. The Lord had invited its enemies to attack the city, and no one had escaped.

## CONFIDENCE DESPITE DISASTER (3:1-66)

**Judah's Distress (3:1-20).** Speaking as a representative of the suffering people, the author lamented God's hostile treatment of the nation. This hostility and its effects are compared to a variety of unpleasant and life-threatening experiences, including physical sickness, injury, and imprisonment in a dark dungeon. The author compared Judah's distress to traveling a winding path filled with obstacles, being mauled by vicious predators, having an arrow pierce one's heart, being force-fed bitter food, and having one's face rubbed into the ground.

**Confidence in God's Faithfulness (3:21-42).** Despite experiencing the Lord's disfavor, the author retained hope. The Lord's love, compassion, and faithfulness had kept the nation from total destruction. The Lord would eventually deliver those who trust in Him, even though they might have to endure His discipline for a time. The Lord is sovereign and decrees both calamity and blessing. The author urged his compatriots to acknowledge their sins and come before the Lord with a repentant spirit.

**Prayer for Vindication (3:43-66).** After once more describing the horrible effects of the Lord's judgment, the author prayed for divine vengeance upon the nation's gloating enemies. During Judah's abandonment by God, these enemies had taunted and abused God's people. Confessing that God had intervened for him in the past, the author asked that the Lord might pay back these enemies for their misdeeds and cruelty.

## JERUSALEM'S DOWNFALL (4:1-5:22)

**Jerusalem's Glory (4:1-20).** The description of Jerusalem's downfall continues, with emphasis being placed on the contrast between its former condition and present humiliation. The city's children, once considered as precious as gold, were now treated like mere clay pots. As they cried out in hunger and thirst, no one took pity upon them. The once robust princes were shriveled up from lack of food. Starving mothers who used to be filled with compassion even ate their own children. Because of its slow, painful death, Jerusalem's fate was even worse than that of Sodom, which had been destroyed in an instant. Many had thought the city could never fall. But the Lord allowed its enemies to invade it because of the sins of its unjust and corrupt religious leaders. As the people waited in vain for help from Egypt, their enemies scattered them and even captured their king.

**Retribution upon Edom (4:21-22).** Having described the nation's conquest of the city, the author issued a warning to Edom, one of the nations that participated in and profited from Jerusalem's fall. The tables would someday be turned. Jerusalem's time of trouble and exile would come to an end, but Edom would experience humiliation at the Lord's hands.

## PRAYER FOR RESTORATION (5:1-22)

**Heap of Ruin (5:1-18).** After asking the Lord to take note of His people's disgrace, the author described their plight in detail to motivate God to respond in mercy. Foreigners now controlled the promised land, while God's people were as poverty-stricken and helpless as orphans and widows. The people were deprived of life's necessities and suffered horrible atrocities and oppression. Their sin had turned their joy into sorrow and reduced Jerusalem to a heap of ruins.

**Concluding Petition (5:19-22).** In a final burst of energy, the author praised God as the eternal King, asked how long they had to suffer rejection, and prayed that God might restore and renew His relationship with His people.

**Theological and Ethical Significance.** Lamentations says that there is no place like home, especially when it is gone. It shows the honest face of prayer in the midst of tragedy. It frees God's people to question and still experience His presence. It shows that the road to hope is paved with honesty and questioning, mixed with praise. Faith grows in the midst of crisis when God's people take their troubles to Him.

## Questions for Reflection

1. What does this book teach about sin's effects?

2. How should God's people respond when they are disciplined for their sins?

3. What do these laments teach about God's character?

## Sources for Additional Study

Gordis, Robert. *The Song of Songs and Lamentations:* A Study, Modern Translation and Commentary. New York: KTAV, 1974.

Harrison, Roland K. *Jeremiah and Lamentations.* Tyndale Old Testament Commentaries. Downers Grove: InterVarsity, 1973.

Hillers, Delbert S. *Lamentations.* Anchor Bible. New York: Doubleday, 1972.

Huey, F. B., Jr. *Jeremiah, Lamentations.* New American Commentary. Nashville: Broadman & Holman, 1993.

Kasier, Walter. *Lamentations.* Chicago: Moody, 1981.

# EZEKIEL

E zekiel was among the exiles taken to Babylon in 597 B.C. He received his prophetic call in 593 and prophesied between 593 and 571, as the thirteen specific dates given in the book indicate.

**Historical Background.** For events leading up to the fall of Jerusalem in 586 B.C., see the introduction to "Jeremiah."

**Theme.** Ezekiel warned his fellow exiles against any wishful thoughts that Jerusalem might be spared. As portrayed in Ezekiel's visions, the glory of the Lord had departed from the city, leaving it vulnerable to destruction. Judah would pay for its rebellion against the Lord. However, the Lord would eventually restore His people to the land and reestablish pure worship in a new temple.

**Literary Form.** Among the major literary forms appearing in the book are prophetic visions, reports of symbolic acts, parables, and messages of judgment and salvation. Ezekiel used poetic form less than Isaiah and Jeremiah.

Ezekiel 1–24 focuses on the approaching fall of Jerusalem. Chapters 25–32 prophesy judgment upon the surrounding nations, while chapters 33–48 picture the miraculous restoration of the nation and its worship system.

  I. Judgment upon Judah (1:1–24:27)
 II. Judgment upon Nations (25:1–32:32)
III. Restoration of Israel (33:1–48:35)

**Purpose and Theology.** Like the many prophets who preceded him, Ezekiel denounced God's people for their sins and warned that judgment was imminent. As a priest Ezekiel was particularly interested in the temple. In a vision he saw the glory of God leaving the polluted temple and abandoning the defiled city. Through speeches, symbolic acts, and parables Ezekiel prophesied the fall of the city to the Babylonians and the exile of its people.

God's judgment would not be limited to His people. He would also punish the hostile surrounding nations, especially proud Tyre and Egypt.

Though God's people were scattered in exile, He had not abandoned them. He would miraculously restore them to their land, reunite Israel and Judah under an ideal Davidic ruler, establish a new covenant of peace with them, and annihilate once and for all their enemies. Ezekiel's prophecy ends with an idealized vision of a new and purified temple, out of which flows a life-giving river.

## JUDGMENT UPON SINFUL JUDAH (1:1–24:27)

**Ezekiel's Call (1:1–3:27).** *Ezekiel's Vision of God's Glory (1:1-28).* In 593 B.C. the Lord revealed His glory to Ezekiel through an elaborate vision. Ezekiel saw a storm cloud coming from the north. In the midst of the storm four flaming, winged creatures appeared. Each combined human and animal characteristics (much like some of the minor deities depicted in ancient Near Eastern art). Accompanying each creature in all of its movements was a large wheel, the rim of which was filled with eyes. A sparkling platform stood above the creatures' outstretched wings, which made a deafening sound as they moved. Above the platform was a throne made of precious stone. A human figure, glowing like fire and surrounded by radiant splendor, sat on the throne. Realizing that he was seeing a representation of God's glory, Ezekiel fell with his face to the ground.

*Ezekiel's Commission (2:1–3:27).* The Lord lifted Ezekiel up and commissioned him as a messenger to rebellious Israel. He encouraged the prophet not to fear, even in the face of intense hostility and danger. Ezekiel was to proclaim the Lord's word, no matter what the response. To symbolize his commission, the Lord instructed Ezekiel to eat a scroll containing words of lamentation and judgment. He promised to give Ezekiel the determination, perseverance, and boldness he would need to stand up to his obstinate audience.

After this encounter with the Lord, the divine Spirit led Ezekiel to the exilic community at Tel Abib in Babylon, where he sat in stunned silence for a week. The Lord then called him to serve as a watchman who would be responsible for warning his audience of God's impending judgment. Ezekiel was to warn both the wicked and the righteous who were tempted to backslide. If he failed to do so, their blood would be on his head.

No sooner was the commission delivered than heavy restrictions were placed upon it. Ezekiel would not be free to deliver messages of warning wherever and whenever he desired. The Lord instructed him to enter his house, where he would remain confined and incapable of speech. He could only leave his house or speak when specifically directed by the Lord to do so. These restrictions would be an object lesson to God's people that their rebellion was making it increasingly difficult for Him to communicate to them.

*Object Lessons (4:1–5:17).* Ezekiel Acts Out the Siege of Jerusalem *(4:1-17).* The Lord instructed Ezekiel to draw a picture of Jerusalem on a clay tablet (or perhaps a brick) and to stage a miniature siege of the city, complete with siege ramps, enemy camps, and battering rams. The prophet was also to place an iron pan between himself and the city. This action perhaps illustrated the unbreakable nature of the siege or represented the barrier between God and His sinful people.

The Lord also instructed the prophet to symbolically bear the sin (or perhaps punishment) of Israel. He was to lie on his left side for 390 days, corresponding to the years of the Northern Kingdom's sin (or punishment?). He was then to lie on his right side for forty days, corresponding to the years of Judah's sin (or punishment?). (Ezekiel 4:9-17, which describes the prophet conducting various activities, indicates that he did occasionally rise from his symbolic posture.) Whether periods of past sin or future punishment were being symbolized is uncertain. The significance of the figures 390 and forty is also unclear.

At the Lord's command Ezekiel made bread from various grains and stored it in a jar. During the 390-day period (see 4:5) he was to eat a daily portion of eight ounces of bread, supplemented by two-thirds of a quart of water. This restricted diet would symbolize the food rationing that would be necessary during the coming siege of Jerusalem. The Lord also told Ezekiel to cook his bread over a fire fueled by human excrement. Though the Old Testament law does not specifically prohibit this, Deuteronomy 23:12-14 suggests it would be regarded as unclean. Ezekiel's action would foreshadow the plight of the exiles, who would be forced to eat food in an unclean foreign land. When Ezekiel objected that he had always kept himself ceremonially pure, the Lord allowed him to use cow manure as fuel.

*Ezekiel's Hair (5:1-17).* The Lord also told Ezekiel to shave all of the hair off his head and face and to divide the hair into three equal parts. He was to burn one third, cut up another third with a sword, and throw the remaining third into the wind. These actions were to symbolize the coming destruction and exile of Jerusalem's residents. At the same time Ezekiel was to preserve a few strands of hair in the folds of his garment, symbolizing the remnant that would survive the judgment. However, to show the severity and extent of God's judgment, he was to throw some of these strands into the fire.

Jerusalem's sin would be the cause of its downfall. Despite their privileged status, God's people rebelled against the Lord's commandments and polluted the temple with idols. God's judgment would be so severe that the starved people would resort to eating their own family members. Two-thirds of the city's population would perish by famine and the sword, while the other third would go into exile. The surrounding nations would hold Jerusalem up as an object of ridicule.

*Impending Judgment (6:1–7:27).* *Judgment on the High Places (6:1-14).* Throughout the land the people had erected altars to worship pagan gods. The Lord was about to destroy these altars and litter the pagan shrines with the carcasses and bones of those who worshiped there. From north to south the land would be devastated. (The "desert" refers to the southern wilderness. "Diblah" should probably be read as Riblah, a city in Syria.) However, the Lord would preserve a remnant and scatter them among the nations. These survivors would someday acknowledge the Lord's sovereignty and confess their sin of idolatry.

*The Day of the Lord (7:1-27).* Judah's day of judgment had arrived. There would be no delay, for the nation's arrogance and violent, bloody deeds

demanded punishment. The Lord would repay His people for their sins and show them no mercy. His judgment would be thorough and inescapable. Plague and famine would kill those inside Jerusalem, while enemy swords would slay those in the surrounding country. The few survivors would flee to the mountains in terror and mourn their fate. They would discard their silver and gold, realizing that it could not save them. The enemy would plunder their wealth and desecrate the temple. Not even the nation's religious and civil leaders, including the king himself, would be able to ward off this day of judgment.

*The Polluted Temple (8:1–11:25).* *Idolatry in the Temple (8:1-18).* While sitting in his house with some of the exiled elders of Judah, Ezekiel had a startling experience. Transported in a vision to the temple in Jerusalem, Ezekiel saw an idol at the north gate of the inner court. Also present was the glory of the Lord, which he had witnessed two times before (see 1:28; 3:23). Entering the court through a hole in the wall, Ezekiel saw seventy elders of the land offering incense to the images of unclean animals drawn on the walls. Each of these elders also worshiped his own private idol in secret, thinking that his actions were hidden from the Lord. Going back out to the north gate, Ezekiel saw women weeping for Tammuz, a Mesopotamian fertility god who had supposedly been confined to the underworld. Returning to the inner court, he observed twenty-five men worshiping the sun at the temple's very entrance. Such blatant disregard for the Lord demanded punishment.

*God's Glory Leaves (9:1–11:25).* Chapters 9–11 describe the gradual departure of God's glory from the polluted temple. The Lord summoned six executioners and a scribe. The Lord instructed the scribe to place a mark on

# OLD TESTAMENT APOCALYPTIC

Apocalyptic represents the culmination of Israel's existence as a persecuted people. Apocalyptic proved to be one tool God used to transform Israel from a defeated people bemoaning their fate to a people looking to God with hope for deliverance and mission.

Apocalyptic is a term modern interpreters use to describe a type of thought, a body of literature, and a religious/political movement. The term comes from the Greek word *apocalypsis,* meaning *an unveiling* and is used as the title of the New Testament Book of Revelation.

As a type of thought, apocalyptic refers to an understanding of human existence as a battle between the forces of God and those of evil leading to a final confrontation. As a body of literature, apocalyptic includes two biblical books—Daniel and Revelation—as well as parts of other books often described as apocalyptic, especially Isaiah 24–27; Joel; Zechariah 9–14.

Similarly, parts of 2 Thessalonians in the New Testament are apocalyptic. These latter books have apocalyptic subject material but do not exhibit all the literary features of Daniel, Revelation, and other apocalyptic literature outside the biblical canon. Written shortly before, during, and shortly after the ministry of Jesus, the latter include: 4 Ezra, 1 and 2 Enoch, Jubilees, 2 and 3 Baruch, and the Apocalypse of Zephaniah. Christian works, apocalyptic in whole or part, include: Apocalypse of Peter, Shepherd of Hermas, Apocalypse of St. John the Theologian, Book of Elchasar, 5 Ezra, Apocalypse of Paul, Apocalypse of the Virgin Mary, and the Ascension of Isaiah.

As a religious, political movement, apocalyptic encompassed several groups with differing viewpoints concerning the coming kingdom. The perspective on the kingdom determined whether the group became actively involved in seeking to overthrow the foreign rulers and restore Jewish self-rule or whether the group was content to escape to the fringes of civilization to wait for God to act and bring in His kingdom.

The following ideas are common to the apocalyptic thought-world that produced the literature and the religious/political movements:

1. The present world order is so evil that God will act to destroy it.

2. God's people must exercise wisdom in obeying God, following His revealed will, and living ethically and ritually pure lives.

3. God has provided revelations, usually through complex visions filled with symbols, to His chosen leaders.

4. The visions often describe the course of history from a significant moment of the past, through a series of earthly rulers and kingdoms, to the moment of God's intervention to establish His kingdom.

5. A strong contrast is drawn between the stupidity and evil nature of present rulers and the wisdom and intelligence of the heroes of God's oppressed people.

6. Angels and demonic creatures play significant roles.

7. Universal resurrection leading to eternal hope or eternal punishment awaits individuals.

Apocalyptic had roots both in the prophetic and wisdom movements. Israel's prophets pointed beyond the powerful reigns of Assyrian and Babylonian kings to a restoration of a king on David's throne in Jerusalem (Isa. 9; 11; Mic. 2; Jer. 23:5; Zech. 9:9).

Isaiah 53 transformed the hope. The suffering by God's people and by His chosen agent of salvation were the means God would use to save His people.

The prophets likewise transformed the common *Day of the Lord* from a significant event in which God saved His people (Amos 5:18) to a future event when God would judge the evil of the world, particularly the evil of His own people. (See Isa. 2:10-22; 13:6,9; Ezek. 30:3; Joel 2:1-11; Zeph. 1:14-18.) This led to apocalyptic collections featuring the Day of the Lord as a day of victory and salvation (Isa. 24–27; Zec. 9–11).

Wisdom writers showed Israel the normal lifestyle that pleased God, encouraging Israel to seek God's blessings by living according to their wise directions. They also warned Israel of the results of evil living, particularly of following after sexual enticements. On the other hand, Israel's wisdom writers also dealt with the dark side of life (Job, Ecclesiastes). Apocalyptic used such proverbial teaching to characterize its heroes and used them as examples for all of God's people (note Dan. 1–6).

Apocalyptic combines prophetic hope and wise directions for life. It describes the lifestyle of those who can trust God to lead them out of their present, persecuted state. It provides them hope not only for victory but also for eternal life in the resurrection (Isa. 26:19; Dan. 12:2).

the forehead of every faithful person in the city. He then commissioned the executioners to mercilessly slaughter everyone who was not so marked, beginning in the temple precincts. When Ezekiel expressed his concern that the whole nation would be wiped out, the Lord reminded him that judgment was well-deserved. The land was filled with bloodshed and injustice, and the people had lost faith in the Lord.

When the scribe returned from his task of marking the righteous, the Lord told him to gather coals from among the wheels of His flaming chariot and to scatter them over the city in an act of purifying judgment. Once more the vehicle bearing the Lord's throne is described in detail (see 10:9-14 with 1:4-21), with the living creatures of chapter 1 now being specifically called cherubim. As in the earlier vision, a wheel followed each cherub in its movements. The glory of the Lord, which had earlier left the throne above the cherubim and moved to the temple threshold, now mounted the cherubim chariot once more. The cherubim rose up and stopped over the east gate of the temple.

In the gate below were twenty-five men, including Jaazaniah and Pelatiah, two leaders of the people who were giving the city's residents bad advice and assuring them that they would experience no harm (11:1-2). They compared themselves to meat within a pot, which remains untouched by the flames of the fire below. The Lord told Ezekiel to prophesy against them. He would bring the sword against them and drive them out of the city into exile.

As Ezekiel proclaimed the message, Pelatiah died. Again Ezekiel expressed concern that the remnant of the people would be destroyed (compare 11:13 with 9:8). The Lord assured His prophet that He had not totally abandoned His peo-

ple. He was preserving a remnant among the exiles and would one day bring them back to the land. This restored community would reject the idol-gods and worship the Lord with true devotion.

Following this word of assurance, the chariot carrying the glory of the Lord rose up from the city and stopped on the Mount of Olives, east of the city. The Lord had abandoned His chosen dwelling place, leaving it unprotected and vulnerable to invasion. At this point Ezekiel's vision ended, and he reported it to his fellow exiles.

**Object Lessons (12:1-28).** *Ezekiel Packs His Bags (12:1-16).* The Lord instructed Ezekiel to pack his belongings and then, in the sight of his fellow exiles, dig a hole through the wall of his house at evening and pretend he was sneaking away. He was to carry his belongings on his shoulder and cover his face. In so doing he would be acting out the fate of Judah's king, Zedekiah. A few years later, when the Babylonian conquest of Jerusalem became inevitable, Zedekiah would pack his belongings and flee at night from the city. The Babylonians would capture him, put his eyes out, and then take him into exile.

*Ezekiel Trembles as He Eats (12:17-20).* The Lord next instructed Ezekiel to shake violently as he ate and drank. In so doing he was acting out the fate of Judah's and Jerusalem's inhabitants. When the Babylonians swept through the land, anxiety and despair would overtake them to such a degree that they would not even be able to enjoy a meal.

*Faulty Perceptions of Prophecy Corrected (12:21-28).* The Israelites had a saying, "The days go by and every vision comes to nothing" (12:22). The proverb seems to reflect their skepticism concerning the messages of the Lord's prophets. The Lord announced that the saying should be changed to "The days are near when every vision will be fulfilled," for He was about to fulfill His decrees.

Some also erroneously assumed that the prophetic message of Ezekiel pertained to the distant future and was irrelevant to them. The Lord announced that his prophecies would be fulfilled immediately.

**False Prophecy (13:1-23).** There were many false prophets in Israel who claimed to be spokesmen of the Lord and assured the people that all would be well. They were like those who whitewash a flimsy wall to hide its defects. The Lord would purge these deceivers from the covenant community. His judgment would come like a torrential downpour, violent wind, and destructive hailstones and batter the whitewashed wall to the ground.

The Lord also denounced the false prophetesses who misled the people with lying messages gained by divination. (Some interpret the barley and bread of 13:19 as their pay, but the items mentioned were more likely used as part of their rituals.) Their activities had a debilitating effect upon the righteous, and these diviners actually encouraged the wicked to continue in their evil ways. The Lord would expose them as frauds and free His people from their negative influence.

**Idolatrous Leaders (14:1-11).** The Lord denounced several of the elders living in exile because of their hypocrisy. Though they sought a divine oracle from Ezekiel, they harbored an idolatrous spirit within their hearts. The Lord would answer such individuals directly by cutting them off from the covenant community. Any prophet who dared to give an oracle to such hypocrites would be severely punished.

**Jerusalem's Doom (14:12-23).** The presence of a righteous remnant

within Jerusalem would not prevent the city's destruction. Individuals might be delivered, but the city's doom was certain. To emphasize this point, the Lord stated that even if Noah, Daniel, and Job, three individuals famed for their righteousness, were residents of the city, it would not be spared. These men would escape, but they could save no others, not even their children. (The appearance of Daniel in this threesome is problematic. The Hebrew form of the name is spelled differently here than in the Book of Daniel. Furthermore, Daniel was a contemporary of Ezekiel's, while Noah and Job were figures from antiquity. Some have suggested that Danel, a just ruler who appears in a Canaanite tale dating to the second millennium B.C., is in view here. In this case all three examples would be non-Israelites who lived long before Ezekiel's time. However, others object to this identification, arguing that the Old Testament does not mention this legendary figure anywhere else and that the Lord would not use a worshiper of Canaanite gods as a model of righteousness.)

Men and animals would be destroyed by the Lord's judgment, which would come in the form of the sword, famine, wild beasts, and a plague. In addition to preserving any righteous individuals left in the city, the Lord would also allow a few of the wicked to survive and join the exiles in Babylon. When Ezekiel witnessed the degree of their sin, he would then know from firsthand experience that the Lord's judgment of the city had been necessary and perfectly just.

**Sin and Judgment (15:1-17:24).** *Jerusalem the Useless Vine (15:1-8).* The Lord drew a lesson from the wild vine, which is useless for construction purposes. It is typically used for fuel. Once burned, its charred condition makes it even more worthless. One might as well leave it in the fire until it is entirely consumed. Jerusalem was comparable to such a vine. The Lord had already subjected it to His fiery judgment. Like the charred vine it would now be totally consumed.

*Jerusalem the Unfaithful Wife (16:1-63).* The Lord used an allegory to illustrate the ingratitude and unfaithfulness of Jerusalem's citizens. Originally Jerusalem was a Canaanite city, populated by Amorites and Hittites. It was like an unwanted baby, thrown into a field and left to die from exposure. However, the Lord preserved the child's life. Later, after she had grown into a mature, beautiful young lady, the Lord entered into a marriage covenant with her. He clothed her with beautiful garments, provided her with food, and made her a queen. Her fame spread throughout the nations. Intoxicated by her riches and status, Jerusalem turned to other gods and nations. She built pagan sanctuaries, sacrificed her children to idols, and formed alliances with the surrounding nations. She became worse than a prostitute. Rather than receiving payment from her lovers, she paid them.

The Lord would punish her severely for her ingratitude and unfaithfulness. He would publicly expose her and then execute her. The very nations with which it had formed alliances would turn on it and destroy it.

Developing the allegory further, the Lord pointed out that Jerusalem was no different than her mother and her sisters, who were unfaithful to their husbands and children. Like the Canaanites who resided in the city in its early days, Jerusalem's residents sacrificed their sons and daughters to pagan gods. Like the people of Samaria and Sodom, viewed here as Jerusalem's sisters, they neglected justice and did abominable things in God's sight.

Jerusalem's sins even exceeded those of Samaria and Sodom.

Though it would be humiliated for its sins, the Lord would someday restore the city. The Lord would renew His covenant with it and make atonement for its sins.

*A Parable of Two Eagles (17:1-24).* The Lord used another parable to illustrate truths concerning Jerusalem. A powerful eagle came to Lebanon, broke off the top branch of a cedar, transported it to a city of merchants, and planted it there. This eagle also took some seeds from the land of Israel and planted them in fertile soil, where they grew into a vine with leafy branches. However, when another mighty eagle approached, the vine's roots and branches grew toward him. The Lord then announced that the vine would be destroyed by the east wind. According to the interpretation of the parable (see 17:11-18), the first eagle represents Nebuchadnezzar, who carried away to Babylon Jerusalem's king and several nobles. Reference is made to the deportation of Jehoiachin and others in 597 B.C. (see 2 Kgs. 24:8-16). The planting of the vine represents the preservation of a remnant in Judah, headed up by Zedekiah, whom Nebuchadnezzar appointed as his vassal king. The second eagle symbolizes Egypt, to whom Judah looked for assistance when it decided to rebel against the Babylonians. The destruction of the vine points to the demise of Judah, which the Babylonians would severely punish for their rebellion.

However, the future was not entirely bleak. The Lord would break a branch from the top of a cedar and plant it on a high mountain, where it would grow into a large and fruitful tree. Since the cedar branch earlier symbolized the exiled king (compare 17:3-4 with 17:12), the branch mentioned here probably refers to a future king whom the Lord would establish in Jerusalem (represented by the mountain).

**Individual Accountability (18:1-32).** God's people were quoting a proverb that suggested they were suffering unjustly for the sins of earlier generations. The Lord corrected their faulty thinking. He always preserves the righteous and opposes the wicked, regardless of the moral status of their fathers.

To illustrate His point the Lord described a hypothetical righteous man who repudiates idolatry, adultery, and injustice. Such a man can be assured of divine protection. However, if this man has an idolatrous, adulterous, unjust son, this evil child will be destroyed despite his father's righteousness. Again if this wicked man has a son who is righteous, that son will not be held accountable for his father's evil deeds. Instead, like his grandfather, his life will be preserved by the Lord. Each man is judged on the basis of his own deeds, not those of his father.

The lesson for Israel was obvious. If they were experiencing divine judgment, it had to mean that they, like their fathers, were evil. Rather than complaining that God is unjust, they had to repent and turn from their wicked ways, for God desired that they live, not die.

**Israel's Princes (19:1-14).** The prophet offered a lament for Israel's princes which, like the previous messages, contains several parabolic elements. The princes' mother (probably the nation Judah or the city of Jerusalem; see 19:10-14) is compared to a lioness who rears several cubs. One of the cubs grew into a mighty lion who tore people to bits, but he was eventually captured and taken to Egypt. Reference is made to unjust Jehoahaz, whom the Egyptians took captive in 609 B.C. (see 2 Kgs. 23:31-34). Another of the cubs grew strong and brought terror to the land; but he was trapped, put in a cage, and taken

to Babylon. Reference is made here to either Jehoiachin or Zedekiah, both of whom were taken into exile (see 2 Kgs. 24:8–25:7).

Switching the imagery, the Lord compared the princes' mother to a fruitful vine which He destroys in His anger and replants in a desert. The nation's (or city's) downfall and exile is in view.

**Past/Present Rebellion (20:1-44).** When some of the elders in exile came to inquire of the Lord, He refused to answer them. Instead He told Ezekiel to review the nation's rebellious history. From the very beginning, when the Lord confronted His people in Egypt, they resisted His will by clinging to their idols. After He had delivered them from bondage and given them the law, they rebelled in the wilderness. Though the Lord prohibited that generation from entering the promised land, He preserved their children and warned them not to follow in their fathers' footsteps. However, the children, while still in the wilderness, sinned against the Lord. When He finally established them in the land, they worshiped Canaanite gods at pagan sanctuaries. Ezekiel's idolatrous contemporaries were no different. Consequently the Lord would purify them through judgment and exile. Once He had removed the rebellious worshipers of idols, He would restore the nation to the land. The people then would repudiate their former behavior and worship the Lord in purity.

**Fire and Sword (20:45–21:32).** Judgment would sweep through Judah like a raging forest fire. In bringing the Babylonians toward the land, the Lord would draw His sharp and polished sword. Flashing like lightning, this sword would bring destruction throughout the land. On his way to Palestine Nebuchadnezzar would reach a fork in the road, with one branch leading to Jerusalem and the other to Rabbah, a prominent

Ammonite city. To determine his course of action, he would use various methods of divination, including drawing marked arrows from a quiver, consulting his idols, and examining livers. The Lord would cause all indicators to point toward Jerusalem. Nebuchadnezzar would besiege and conquer the city and take its people into exile. Meanwhile the Ammonites, though arrogant and hostile, were not to think that they would be spared. The Lord's sword of judgment would fall upon them as well (see 25:1-7).

***City of Bloodshed (22:1-31).*** The corruption within Jerusalem made its judgment inevitable. Several specific sins are mentioned here, including idolatry, misuse of power, lack of respect for parents, neglect of widows and orphans, desecration of the Sabbath, incest, bribery, and usury. Violence filled the city. Throughout the chapter reference is made to the shed blood of the innocent. The princes and civil officials took the lead in this regard by oppressing the poor and helpless. Even the religious leaders were corrupt. The priests failed to instruct the people in the law and made no distinction between the holy and profane. The false prophets proclaimed lies in the name of the Lord. When the Lord looked for a man to stand "in the gap" and intercede for the nation, no one was found. Consequently He would purify the city by judgment and scatter the people among the nations.

***Two Sisters (23:1-49).*** To illustrate the nation's unfaithfulness, the Lord used an allegory in which He compared Samaria and Jerusalem to two promiscuous sisters named Oholah and Oholibah. (Oholah means *her tent* and Oholibah *my tent is in her.* Perhaps the latter name reflects the fact that God dwelt in the Jerusalem temple.) The sisters had been prostitutes from their youth in Egypt. Though belonging to the Lord (whether as wives or children is not clear), they courted the favor of foreign nations.

Oholah (Samaria) sought alliances with the Assyrians. She is portrayed as lusting after the Assyrian soldiers and prostituting herself among their officers. Ironically, her lovers killed her and carried away her children.

Oholibah (Jerusalem) witnessed the fate of her sister but failed to learn from her example. She also lusted after the Assyrians and later turned her attention toward the Babylonians and others. Vivid language and harsh imagery are employed to depict her nymphomania. The Lord warned that her lovers would turn on her. The Babylonians would come against the land with all their military might and cruelly destroy her population. Oholibah would be publicly humiliated and suffer the fate of her sister Oholah.

***The Cooking Pot (24:1-14).*** On the very day when the Babylonians began their siege of Jerusalem (January 15, 588 B.C.), the Lord gave Ezekiel a parable illustrating the city's downfall. Jerusalem was like a cooking pot, which had been encrusted with deposits (its bloodshed and idolatry). The inhabitants of Jerusalem were like meat and bones cooking inside the pot. The fire burning beneath the pot (the Babylonian siege) would thoroughly cook the meat and char the bones, both of which would eventually be removed piece by piece (a picture of the exile). The empty pot would then be left on the fire until its impurities were burned away.

***Death of Ezekiel's Wife (24:15-27).*** The Lord announced to Ezekiel that his beloved wife was about to die suddenly. However, as an object lesson to Israel, the Lord commanded the prophet not to mourn outwardly over her death, as was the custom. Instead he could only groan to himself. When his wife died shortly thereafter, Ezekiel obeyed the Lord's instructions. When the people observed his silence, they inquired about its significance. He explained that they were not to mourn publicly over the downfall of their beloved city and its temple, just as he refused to lament over his wife's death.

When Jerusalem finally fell, a fugitive would bring Ezekiel the news. At that time the Lord would remove Ezekiel's muteness (see 3:26-27; 33:21-22). He would now speak openly and freely with the survivors of the catastrophe, warning and encouraging them.

## JUDGMENT UPON NATIONS (25:1–32:32)

The nations surrounding Judah would not escape God's judgment. This section contains oracles against seven specific nations. Though all directions of the compass are represented, Tyre (to the north) and Egypt (to the south) receive special attention. The seven oracles against Egypt conclude the section. The wide geographical distribution of the nations mentioned, as well as the use of the symbolic number seven, convey a feeling of completeness.

**Ammon (25:1-7).** The Lord would judge the Ammonites because they rejoiced over Jerusalem's fall. "People of the East," either the Babylonians or marauding tribes from the desert, would plunder Ammon and reduce Rabbah, its most prominent city, to a pasture land.

**Moab (25:8-11).** The Lord would also punish the Moabites, Ammon's neighbors to the south, because they too rejoiced over Jerusalem's fall. The "people of the East" would conquer the fortified cities guarding Moab's northern border, opening the land up to invasion.

**Edom (25:12-14).** Judgment would also fall on Edom (already mentioned in 25:8; compare "Seir"), located south of

Moab. When Judah fell, Edom displayed a vengeful spirit (compare Obad.). The Lord would take vengeance on Edom through His people Israel.

**Philistia (25:15-17).** The Lord would also take vengeance on the Philistines (also referred to here as Kerethites), Judah's neighbors to the west, because they had opposed God's people for centuries.

**Tyre (26:1–28:19).** *The Downfall of Tyre (26:1-21).* Tyre, located on the Mediterranean coast north of Israel, was a prominent commercial center. Despite its wealth and defenses, it would be unable to withstand the Lord's judgment. Many nations would rage against it, like the turbulent waters of the sea. In the immediate future Nebuchadnezzar's armies would besiege and conquer the city. Tyre would be reduced to a heap of rubble which that never again be rebuilt. All along the Mediterranean coast Tyre's trading partners would lament its demise.

Harmonizing this prophecy with history is difficult. Nebuchadnezzar besieged Tyre for thirteen long years (about 586–573 B.C.) and finally made it a vassal state. However, he did not destroy the city to the degree described by Ezekiel (even 29:18 acknowledges this). Many subsequent conquerors (including Alexander the Great in 332) took the city, but it continued to exist into the Christian era.

Several solutions have been offered, none of which is entirely satisfactory. One possibility is that the description of Tyre's downfall is somewhat stereotypical and purposely exaggerated to emphasize that it would be subjected to the Babylonians and experience a significant decline in prestige. Another possibility is that the description of 26:12-14 moves beyond the time of Nebuchadnezzar and encompasses later attacks on the city. Such subsequent attacks ultimately brought the final downfall of the city. Such a blurring of the immediate future with more distant events is typical of prophetic literature.

*The Prophet's Lament over Tyre (27:1-36).* To emphasize the certainty of Tyre's judgment, the Lord told Ezekiel to lament the city's doom in advance. Tyre is compared to a large commercial ship made from the best wood, adorned with beautiful sails, and manned by skilled sailors. Tyre bought and sold every conceivable product, including precious metals and stones, slaves, animals, fabric and clothing, food, and even ivory tusks. Its list of trading partners included virtually every nation and city in the known world. However, a storm (the Lord's judgment) would destroy this great ship. All of its sailors and merchants would sink into the sea, causing its trading partners looking on from the shore to lament over its fate.

*The King of Tyre Denounced (28:1-19).* Singling out the king of Tyre as representative of the city, the Lord announced that this proud ruler and his city would be humiliated. Because of the city's great success and wealth, its king fancied himself a god and took great pride in his wisdom. (Though some see the "Daniel" of 28:3 as the legendary Canaanite King Danel, the reference to his ability to disclose secrets suggests the biblical Daniel, a contemporary of Ezekiel, is in view. Compare comments on 14:14,20.) When the day of judgment arrived, the king would stand humiliated before his executioners, his delusions of grandeur replaced by the painful reality of his mortality.

In anticipation of the king's downfall Ezekiel pronounced a taunting lament against him. He compared the king to a wise, beautiful, and richly adorned cherub who once dwelt in the garden of Eden and enjoyed access to God's holy mountain. This cherub eventually lost his prestigious position because of his arrogance and oppressive economic practices (Tyre's commercial empire is alluded to here). The Lord threw him down from the sacred mountain and destroyed him with fire in the sight of the nations.

The background for the imagery of this lament is uncertain. The mountain of God has parallels in Canaanite mythology. Use of such mythological imagery might be expected in an address to a Phoenician king. (See Isa. 14:4-21, where mythological themes and imagery are used in a taunt directed to the king of Babylon.) Verse 13 appears to refer to the garden of Eden of biblical tradition, but the only cherubim mentioned in the Genesis account are those placed as guardians at the gate of the garden following the expulsion of Adam and Eve (Gen. 3:24). Perhaps Ezekiel drew his imagery from an extrabiblical Eden tradition.

Because of the references to Eden and to the cherub's pride and fall, some have seen a veiled reference to Satan in 28:12-19. However, the allusion to Eden does not support this view. Satan is not specifically mentioned in Genesis 23, let alone portrayed as a cherub. Satan is traditionally associated with the serpent of the Eden account. But even if this interpretation is correct, the serpent is identified as one of the animals created by God (see Gen. 3:1,14), not as a cherub in disguise.

*Sidon (28:20-26).* Sidon, another prominent Phoenician city, would also experience divine judgment. Like Tyre it had treated God's people with hostility. The Lord would destroy the Sidonians with plague and sword.

The Lord would someday restore His people to their land, where they would live in peace, free from the threats of hostile neighbors like Sidon, Tyre, Philistia, Edom, Moab, and Ammon.

**Egypt (29:1–32:32).** *The Lord's Opposition to Pharaoh (29:1-16).* The Lord announced that He was also opposed to Pharaoh, the proud ruler of Egypt. Comparing the king to a crocodile in the Nile, the Lord warned that He would pull him from the river and drag him to the desert, where he would die and be eaten by scavengers. The Lord would turn the entire land (from Migdol in the north to Aswan in the south) into a ruin for forty years and scatter the Egyptians among the nations. Following the forty-year exile, the Lord would return them to their land, but Egypt would never again experience its former glory. God's people, who had once trusted in Egypt, would no longer rely on its help. When and how this prophecy was fulfilled is not certain. Historical records do not indicate that Egypt experienced desolation or exile to the degree described by Ezekiel.

*Booty for Nebuchadnezzar (29:17-21).* In 571 B.C., shortly after Nebuchadnezzar had lifted his long siege of Tyre, Ezekiel received another message pertaining to Egypt. Though Nebuchadnezzar had come away from Tyre with relatively little reward for his efforts, the Lord would give him Egypt, from which he would haul away an abundance of riches. This prophecy was probably fulfilled in 568 B.C., when, according to a Babylonian text, Nebuchadnezzar apparently conducted a campaign against Egypt.

*The Day of the Lord on Egypt (30:1-19).* Egypt's fall is associated with the Day of the Lord, an expression used elsewhere in the Old Testament of those times when the Lord comes as a warrior and swiftly and decisively destroys His enemies. Using Nebuchadnezzar as His "sword," the Lord would destroy both Egypt and its allies. Egypt's great river,

the Nile, would dry up, its idols and princes would prove helpless, and all of its famous cities would be conquered.

*Pharaoh's Power Broken (30:20-26).* Ezekiel received a message concerning Pharaoh in 587 B.C., one year after Nebuchadnezzar had defeated Pharaoh Hophra in battle when the latter had tried to come and aid besieged Jerusalem (see Jer. 37:5-8). By allowing Nebuchadnezzar to defeat Hophra, the Lord had, as it were, broken Pharaoh's arm, a symbol of his military strength. However, the Lord was not finished with Egypt. He would energize the king of Babylon to conquer Egypt. Both of Pharaoh's arms would be broken. When the Egyptians were conquered and scattered among the nations, they would recognize the sovereignty of Israel's God.

*A Fallen Cedar (31:1-18).* The Lord challenged Pharaoh and his armies to learn a lesson from history. Assyria, the mightiest empire in the Near East from 745–626 B.C., had once been like a mighty cedar of Lebanon. It was well nourished and grew tall. Birds lodged in its branches, and animals sought shelter under its shade. Not even the trees of the garden of Eden could rival its majesty and beauty. However, because of its pride, God delivered it over to a ruthless nation (the Babylonians) who chopped it down. No other trees would ever grow so tall. Pharaoh also was like a great tree, but, like Assyria, he and his armies would come crashing to the earth.

*Lamenting Pharaoh's Destruction (32:1-16).* The Lord revealed to Ezekiel a taunting lament the nations would someday sing over fallen Pharaoh. Though he was like a mighty lion or a powerful crocodile, he would be captured, destroyed, and eaten by scavengers. Darkness would settle over his land as a sign of judgment and destruction. Babylon would invade Egypt, destroy its people, and steal its wealth.

*Egypt's Armies Slaughtered (32:17-32).* Pharaoh's armies would be slaughtered and descend into the land of the dead. They would join the armies of other nations who spread terror on the earth but eventually met their demise. These nations included Assyria, Elam (located east of Mesopotamia), Meshech and Tubal (northern nations; see 38:2), Edom, and Sidon.

## RESTORATION OF ISRAEL (33:1–48:35)

*Ezekiel's Commission (33:1-20).* Shortly before the fall of Jerusalem, the Lord renewed Ezekiel's commission as the nation's spiritual watchman (see 3:16-21). One of a watchman's primary responsibilities was to warn his people of approaching danger. As long as the watchman carried out his duty, he was not responsible for those who failed to take his warning seriously and were unprepared when disaster arrived. Ezekiel was in a similar position. He was to warn both the wicked and backsliders of impending doom and call them to repentance. Even though the nation was weighed down with sin, it was God's desire that they turn from their evil ways and live.

*A True Prophet (33:21-33).* In January of 585 B.C., five months after the temple had been destroyed, a fugitive delivered the news to Ezekiel. The evening before, the Lord had opened Ezekiel's mouth, ending his long period of enforced silence (see 3:26; 24:26-27). Now that Ezekiel's prophecies of judgment had been fulfilled, his ministry would be primarily one of encouragement, and his messages would focus on the future restoration of the exiles.

However, he was to deliver one more judgment speech. The survivors who remained in Judah following the destruction of Jerusalem retained delusions of grandeur, thinking that the land was now theirs. Ezekiel corrected their faulty thinking, pointing out that their idolatry and hypocrisy precluded them from enjoying the land. Another wave of judgment would sweep them away. In the past they had not taken Ezekiel's messages seriously, but in the day of judgment they would finally realize that he was a true prophet of the Lord.

*New Covenant (34:1-31).* Israel's leaders, compared to shepherds, had not cared properly for God's flock. These leaders, who were consumed by self-interest, had actually oppressed and exploited the people. The sheep were now scattered and being ravaged by wild beasts (foreign nations such as Babylon). The Lord announced that these incompetent leaders would be eliminated and that He would take over the care of the flock. The Lord would gather His wandering and injured sheep back to Israel, where they would graze peacefully in rich pasturelands. He would reestablish justice among His people and raise up for them a new, ideal Davidic ruler. He would make with them "a covenant of peace," which would assure them of safety from danger and of agricultural prosperity.

*Edom (35:1-15).* God would judge those nations that had traditionally sought the destruction of His people. As a prime example of such a nation, Edom was singled out as an object of God's wrath. The Edomites participated in Jerusalem's downfall, with hopes that they might eventually acquire the land of Israel as their own. They arrogantly taunted God's people in their time of calamity. Edom would taste God's vengeance. He would treat them the same way they had treated His people. The Edomites would be slaughtered by the sword and their land left a desolate heap of ruins.

**Prosperity Returns (36:1-15).** Foreign armies had overrun the mountains of Israel and boasted of their conquests. The Lord swore that He would bring vengeance upon these nations (Edom is again singled out). He would also restore His people to the land. Once again crops would grow in the land, and cities would be populated.

**Restoration (36:16-38).** Israel had polluted the land with their sinful deeds and had brought dishonor to God's name. When Israel went into exile, the nations made wrong assumptions about the character of God. To vindicate Himself and restore His reputation among the nations, the Lord would restore the exiles to the land. He would cleanse their sins, create in them a desire for loyalty, and renew His agricultural blessings. At that time both the nations and Israel would recognize His sovereignty.

**Resurrection (37:1-14).** Ezekiel's vision of the dry bones portrayed in a vivid way Israel's miraculous restoration. In this vision the prophet saw a valley full of dry, disconnected bones, representing the scattered people of Israel. However, suddenly the bones began to come together, and tendons and flesh appeared on them. The breath of life then entered into the corpses, and a multitude of living beings stood in the valley. In the same way the Lord would miraculously revive the nation of Israel. He would deliver them from the grave of exile, place His Spirit among them, and settle them once more in the promised land.

**Reunited (37:15-28).** The day of restoration would also be a day of reunification for Israel and Judah. To illustrate this the Lord told Ezekiel to take two sticks, one representing the Northern Kingdom and the other the Southern Kingdom, and hold them as one in his hand. In the same way the Lord would bring the exiles of both Israel and Judah back to the land and make them one kingdom again. He would raise up a new ideal Davidic ruler to lead them, establish a new covenant with them, and once more dwell in their midst.

**Israel Invaded (38:1-39:29).** These chapters describe an invasion of Israel by distant nations, led by "Gog, of the land of Magog, the chief prince of Meshech and Tubal." Attempts to identify Gog with a historical figure are unconvincing. Magog, Tubal, and Meshech are mentioned in Genesis 10:2 and 1 Chronicles 1:5 as sons of Japheth. In Ezekiel's day their descendants inhabited what is now eastern Turkey. According to 38:5-6 the allies of Gog included Persia, Cush (modern Ethiopia), Put (modern Libya), Gomer (another son of Japheth whose descendants resided to the far north of Israel), and Beth Togarmah (according to Gen. 10:3, Togarmah was a son of Gomer).

Ezekiel envisioned a time when the armies of these nations would attack unsuspecting Israel. The Lord would intervene in power and miraculously deliver His people. A mighty earthquake would shake the land, and the enemy armies would turn in panic on each other. The Lord would rain down hail and sulfur upon them. The slaughter would be comparable to a great sacrifice. Birds and wild animals would devour the flesh and blood of the enemy warriors. Even with this assistance from the animal kingdom, it would take the people of Israel seven months to dispose of all the corpses. The enemy's weapons would provide God's people with a supply of fuel that would last seven years.

Since this prophecy does not correspond to any known historical event, it is best to understand it as still awaiting fulfillment. Gog and his hordes are symbolic of the end time opposition to God's kingdom which will be violently crushed (see Rev. 20:8-9).

**Pure Worship Restored (40:1–48:35).** In this section the Lord gave Ezekiel a vision of restored Israel. He saw a detailed picture of the new temple and received lengthy instructions for the future leaders of the nations. The book concludes with a detailed description of the future geographical divisions of the land.

Scholars differ in their interpretation of this section. Some see its language as symbolic and as being fulfilled in the New Testament church, while others interpret the prophecy as applying to a literal Israel of the future. Some understand these chapters as giving a literal description of conditions in the millennial age. Others understand the vision as an idealized, perhaps exaggerated, portrayal of God's future restoration of His people that is filled with symbolic elements.

*A New Temple (40:1–43:12).* Through the medium of a vision the Lord gave Ezekiel a preview of the new temple. Beginning at the east gate of the outer court, he was given a tour that led into the inner court, its inner rooms, the temple portico, the outer sanctuary, and finally the most holy place. All along the way detailed measurements and descriptions are provided.

Most importantly, God would reside in the new temple. Almost twenty years earlier Ezekiel had a vision of God's glory leaving the Jerusalem temple (see chaps. 8–10). That temple was subsequently destroyed by the Babylonians. Now through another vision the prophet witnessed God's glory returning to the city and taking up residence in the new temple (see 43:1-9).

*Regulations for the New Temple (43:13–46:24).* These chapters contain several instructions and regulations for the priests and rulers who would function in the restored covenant community of the future.

The section begins with instructions for building the temple altar and for its dedicatory sacrifices. Once the appropriate sin offerings were made for seven consecutive days, the altar would be regarded as purified and would be ready for use. From the eighth day on the altar could be used for burnt and fellowship offerings, which expressed the worshiper's devotion to and communion with God.

Because the Lord's glory returned to the temple complex through the east gate of the outer court, this gate would remain shut. Only "the prince" could sit inside this gateway, where he would eat in the presence of the Lord. This prince is identified elsewhere as the ideal Davidic ruler, or Messiah, whom the Lord would raise up to lead His people (34:24; 37:24-25).

In the past rebellious Israelites had violated the Lord's covenant by allowing foreigners to bring their detestable practices into the temple. These foreigners were "uncircumcised in heart and flesh," meaning that they lacked devotion to the Lord as well as the physical sign of being part of the covenant community. Such foreigners were prohibited from entering the new temple.

Because the Levites had been unfaithful to the Lord, they would be demoted. They could tend the temple gates, slaughter sacrificial animals, and assist the people, but they were not allowed to handle the holy objects or offerings of the Lord.

As a reward for their faithfulness the Zadokite line of the Levitical family would function as the Lord's priests. Zadok was a descendant of Aaron through Eleazar and Phinehas (see 1 Chr. 6:3-8,50-53).

In the future allotment of the land a portion must be reserved for the Lord (and His priestly servants) directly in the center of the land. The prince (Davidic ruler) would possess the land bordering the Lord's portion on the east and west.

This mention of the future prince leads to an exhortation to the civil leaders of God's people in Ezekiel's day. They were not to oppress the people but were to promote justice and fairness in the socioeconomic sphere.

The Lord also provided detailed regulations pertaining to offerings and feasts, including the New Year festival, Passover, and Tabernacles. Various regulations pertaining to the prince highlight chapter 46. On Sabbath days and New Moons the prince would lead the people in worshiping the Lord by presenting offerings at the threshold of the east gate of the inner court.

*The River Flowing from the Temple (47:1-12).* Ezekiel envisioned a river flowing from the temple toward the east. The river became increasingly deeper as it flowed through the desert on its way to the Dead Sea. Its fresh water was filled with fish, and fishermen lined its shores with nets. Also lining the river's banks were nourishing fruit trees, the leaves of which possessed healing properties. This life-giving river flowing from God's throne symbolized the restoration of divine blessing which the land would experience.

*Boundaries and Land Allotments (47:13–48:35).* The Book of Ezekiel concludes with a detailed description of the land's future boundaries and allotted portions. The holy city, constructed as a perfect square in the middle of the land, would have twelve gates (three on each of its four walls) named after the tribes of Israel. The city would be named "Yahweh-Shammah," meaning *the Lord is there.*

*Theological and Ethical Significance.* Ezekiel was the priestly prophet of judgment and hope. His message to the exiles in Babylon still speaks to hurting, broken people in need of a God-given second chance. Jerusalem's destruction and its people's deportation to Babylon caused some to question God's ability to save and His commitment to His covenants. Ezekiel interpreted these events in light of God's character.

Ezekiel's strange, opening vision pictures God as without equal, perfect in holiness and power. Such a God would not abide with unrepentant people. Jerusalem fell not because God was unable to save it but because God abandoned His people to their chosen fate.

But judgment was only part of Ezekiel's picture of God. Even in exile, far from home, God was accessible to the prophet. God's faithfulness was Ezekiel's hope. God is the caring Shepherd of His people (Ezek. 34). God is the only hope for new life for the dead bones of the nation Israel (Ezek. 37).

Christians can learn responsibility from Ezekiel. Like Ezekiel, believers are to empathize with the hurt of those around them (3:15). Like Ezekiel, Christians are "watchmen," responsible for warning neighbors of sin's consequences (3:16-21). Ezekiel 34 warns believers not to seek their own interests at others' expense. Rather, Christians are to model God's love and care in their actions. Believers are to share the good news that God is still the Giver of new life and second chances to those who turn to Him in repentance and faith.

## Questions for Reflection

1. In what ways is Ezekiel an example of an obedient, loyal servant of the Lord?

2. How does Ezekiel portray God? What roles and characteristics does Ezekiel attribute to God?

3. Why were Ezekiel's contemporaries displeasing to the Lord? Is the modern church like them in any ways?

4. What do Ezekiel's messages of salvation teach us about God's relationship to His people?

## Sources for Additional Study

Alexander, Ralph H. "Ezekiel." *The Expositor's Bible Commentary.* Vol. 6. Grand Rapids: Zondervan, 1986.

Block, Daniel. *Ezekiel.* 2 Vols. New International Commentary. Grand Rapids: Eerdmans, 1998.

Cooper. Lamar. *Ezekiel.* New American Commentary. Nashville: Broadman & Holman, 1994.

Greenberg, Moshe. *Ezekiel 1–20.* Anchor Bible. New York: Doubleday, 1983.

Taylor, John B. *Ezekiel.* Tyndale Old Testament Commentaries. Downers Grove: InterVarsity, 1969.

# DANIEL

The Book of Daniel has traditionally been attributed to Daniel on the basis of explicit statements made within its pages (9:2; 10:2) and Christ's testimony (Matt. 24:15). Daniel lived in Babylon during the sixth century B.C. and served both Babylonian and Persian rulers.

Modern critics have denied the historical value of the book for several reasons. They regard it as a combination of court legends and apocalyptic visions, the latter being characteristic of intertestamental Jewish literature (see further discussion on "Literary Form").

Only a few observations related to the historical value of the book can be made.

1. The presence of miraculous events, no matter how incredible they may seem (the preservation of Daniel's friends in the fiery furnace and of Daniel in the lions' den), does not necessarily call in question the book's historical value. The sovereign God of the universe does at times intervene in history in supernatural ways, the prime example being the resurrection of Jesus Christ.

2. The book's portrayal of Darius the Mede, while problematic in many respects, does not necessarily prove it is nonhistorical. Some interpreters have used this as proof of the book's fictional nature, pointing out that Cyrus, not this otherwise unknown Darius son of Xerxes, became the king of Babylon following its fall. Others have proposed that Darius may be another name for Cyrus (in this view Dan. 6:28 is translated, "So Daniel prospered during the reign of Darius, that is, the reign of Cyrus the Persian"). Still others suggest Darius was Gubaru, who served as the governor of Babylon under Cyrus.

3. Scholars have debated whether the Aramaic used in the book reflects an early date (the time of Daniel) or late date (about 165 B.C.).

4. Chapter 11 is a watershed in the debate over the nature of the book's prophecies. Many modern interpreters understand it as after-the-fact "prophecy" and use it to pinpoint the book's date to 165 B.C. Verses 2-20 contain a rather detailed and accurate account of Palestinian history from the time of Cyrus (about 538 B.C.) to the time of Antiochus Epiphanes (175–164 B.C.). Verses 21-35 accurately reflect Antiochus's career, but verses 36-45 do not. Thus, it is argued, the author must have written in 165 B.C., after the events accurately recorded in the chapter but before the inaccurate predictions pertaining to Antiochus.

Others regard it as a prime example of supernatural, predictive prophecy. These interpreters argue that 11:36-45 does not contain unfulfilled predictions about Antiochus Epiphanes. Instead it describes the career of a yet future ruler who resembles Antiochus. Such foreshadowing and blending is typical of Old Testament prophecy.

**Historical Background.** Daniel and his friends were taken into exile in 605 B.C. They served mighty Nebuchadnezzar, who ruled the Babylonian empire until 562. Nebuchadnezzar's successors were Evil-Merodach, Neriglissar, Labashi-Marduk, and Nabonidus. Nabonidus spent much of his reign in Tema worshiping the moon god. His son Belshazzar served as his vice-regent. Though the Book of Daniel calls Belshazzar "king," it hints that he was really second in command in the kingdom (5:7,16). Cyrus the Persian conquered Babylon in 539 and made Gubaru governor over the city. Daniel retained a high civil office under the Persians.

**Theme.** Daniel portrays God as the sovereign Ruler of the universe, who controls the destinies of both pagan empires and His exiled people. He revealed His mighty power to the kings of Babylon and Persia, forcing them to acknowledge His supremacy. He revealed to Daniel His future plans to restore His people Israel once the times of the Gentiles had run their course.

**Literary Form.** How we classify the narratives of Daniel depends on our view of their historical value. Those who regard the stories as fictional classify them as court legends. Those who accept their historical value regard them as biographical accounts of Daniel and his friends.

Daniel's visions can be categorized as apocalyptic literature. Because later examples of such literature are falsely attributed to some famous person from the past (pseudepigraphic) and contain after-the-fact prophecy, some assume that Daniel shares these characteristics. Others acknowledge some literary similarities but argue for Daniel as genuine prophecy.

The structure of the book can be viewed in different ways. Chapters 1–6 are largely narratives, while chapters 7–12 contain visions of future events. At the same time, 1:12:4a; 8–12 are written in Hebrew, while 2:4b–7:28 are in Aramaic. The explanation for the bilingual nature of the book is uncertain. Some observe that the Aramaic section focuses on Gentile rulers and nations, while the Hebrew sections are primarily concerned with Israel. Others explain the variation as a structural device. Daniel 2:4b–7:28 is set off from the surrounding

sections because it is a symmetrically arranged unit, displaying a mirror structure (chaps. 2 and 7 correspond thematically, as do chaps. 3 and 6 and chaps. 4 and 5).

    I. Experiences of Daniel and His Friends in Babylon (1:1–6:28)
   II. Visions and Revelations of Future Events (7:1–12:13)

**Purpose and Theology.** The God of Daniel is the sovereign Ruler of the world, who raises up and brings down rulers and determines long beforehand the future of nations. He rewards the faithfulness of His devoted servants and protects them, even when they are far from their homeland. His sovereignty is especially apparent in His dealings with Nebuchadnezzar. To him God revealed future history, demonstrated His power to deliver His own, and gave a vivid lesson on the dangers of pride. Nebuchadnezzar was forced to acknowledge the sovereignty of Daniel's God. The Lord also displayed His sovereignty to subsequent rulers. He announced in dramatic fashion Belshazzar's downfall for his arrogance and lack of respect for the temple vessels. He demonstrated to Darius His power to deliver His faithful servants from even the worst crises.

Through Daniel's visions the Lord demonstrates His sovereignty over history. Human empires rise and fall, but the Lord ultimately shatters Gentile opposition to His program and establishes His kingdom on earth.

## DANIEL AND HIS FRIENDS (1:1–6:28)

**Remaining Faithful (1:1-21).** *Daniel and His Friends Chosen to Be Court Officials (1:1-7).* In 605 B.C. the Babylonians marched against Judah and besieged Jerusalem. They took some temple articles to Babylon, as well as some of Judah's finest young men. Nebuchadnezzar ordered Ashpenaz, his chief court official, to choose the very best of these men and train them for the king's service. Among this group were Daniel, Hananiah, Mishael, and Azariah. They were given Babylonian names, trained in Babylonian language and literature, and placed on a special diet.

*Daniel and His Friends Refuse Unclean Food (1:8-16).* Daniel regarded the food offered by the Babylonians to be defiling. The Mosaic law forbade God's people to eat unclean animals or flesh that had not been drained of blood. Portions of the wine and meat presented by Ashpenaz may have been offered to idols.

Daniel convinced the Babylonians to allow him and his three friends to follow a different diet, consisting only of vegetables and water. After a ten-day trial period they looked even healthier than those who were following the diet prescribed by the king. Consequently they were not forced to eat the king's food or drink his wine.

*God Rewards Daniel and His Friends (1:17-21).* In response to Daniel's and his friends' faithfulness, the Lord gave them superior intellect and gave Daniel the ability to interpret dreams and visions. When the king interviewed the trainees, he found Daniel and his friends to be the cream of the crop and appointed them to his service. Their abilities far surpassed those of the king's wise men and diviners.

**The Dream Interpreted (2:1-49).** *The King Seeks a Dream Interpreter (2:1-16).* During the second year of his reign King Nebuchadnezzar had a troubling dream. He summoned his wise men and diviners and, perhaps to ensure credibility, commanded them to reveal the dream's contents, as well as its interpretation. If they failed, they would be executed; if they succeeded, they would be richly rewarded. The diviners, understandably shaken, objected that the king's request was without precedent and that no one could know what another man dreamed. In anger the king decreed that all the royal diviners be put to death.

*Daniel Interprets the King's Dream (2:17-49).* When Daniel heard what had happened, he and his friends prayed to the Lord for wisdom to know and interpret the dream so that their lives might be spared. When the Lord revealed the dream to Daniel in a night vision, he praised the Lord as the sovereign Ruler of the universe, who is the source of all wisdom.

When Daniel went before the king, he was careful to give God the credit. He told the king that the Lord had revealed to him both the contents and interpretation of the dream. In his dream Nebuchadnezzar had seen a large statue. Its head was made of gold, its chest and arms of silver, its belly and thighs of bronze, its legs of iron, and its feet of iron and clay. A large rock then smashed the feet of the statue, causing it to tumble and shatter. The rock then grew into a large mountain.

Daniel explained to Nebuchadnezzar that the dream pertained to world history. The statue represented successive world kingdoms, which would ultimately be displaced by God's kingdom. Nebuchadnezzar's Babylonian empire was the golden head. The silver chest and arms represented a kingdom that would follow. Just as silver is inferior to gold, so the glory of this kingdom would not match that of Babylon. The bronze portions of the statue symbolized a third world kingdom, while the iron legs represented a fourth empire, which, like iron, would be especially powerful. The mixture of clay and iron indicated that this empire would eventually divide and become vulnerable to attack. God's kingdom (represented by the rock that grew into a mountain) would conquer this empire, bringing human rule to a violent end. Like a mountain His kingdom would be incapable of destruction and would exist forever.

Scholars differ over the identification of the final three kingdoms represented in the vision. Some see the silver portions of the statue as the combined Medo-Persian empire, the bronze parts as Alexander's Greek empire, and the iron legs as Rome. Others see the successive kingdoms as Media, Persia, and Greece.

When Daniel finished, Nebuchadnezzar praised the Lord as the sovereign God who reveals wisdom. He rewarded Daniel and elevated him and his friends to prominent positions in the empire's government.

**Facing Death (3:1-30).** *Daniel's Friends Refuse to Bow to the King's Image (3:1-18).* Nebuchadnezzar made a huge, gold image. The image may have represented his sovereign authority or one of his gods. The king ordered all of his subjects to attend a dedication ceremony for the image. At a designated time they were to bow down to the image. All who refused to worship the image would be thrown into a fiery furnace. When Daniel's friends refused to bow down to the image, the angry king gave them an ultimatum and warned them of the consequences of disobedience. They explained that their loyalty to the Lord prevented them from worshiping images. They also told the king that the Lord was able to deliver them from the furnace if He so desired.

*Daniel's Friends Delivered from the Furnace (3:19-30).* After ordering the furnace to be heated to its maximum temperature, Nebuchadnezzar had Daniel's friends tied up and thrown in. The fire was so hot that its flames killed the soldiers who threw them in. However, when Nebuchadnezzar looked into the furnace, he saw the three men walk-

ing around unbound, accompanied by an angelic being. When the king ordered them out of the furnace, they were completely unharmed. Nebuchadnezzar praised the Lord for delivering His faithful servants, decreed that anyone who slandered the Lord be executed, and promoted the three men.

**Dream of a Large Tree (4:1-37).** This chapter begins and ends with Nebuchadnezzar praising the Lord (4:1-3,34-37). In the intervening verses he related a personal experience through which he came to a greater realization of God's sovereignty and learned the dangers of pride.

*The King Reports His Dream to Daniel (4:1-18).* While lying in his palace, the king had a terrifying dream. When his wise men and diviners were unable to interpret it, he summoned Daniel. In his dream Nebuchadnezzar saw a large fruit tree with beautiful leaves. Animals found shelter in its shade, and birds lodged in its branches. An angelic being then commanded that the tree be cut down and that the stump be bound with iron and bronze. The angel then announced that the man represented by the stump would be overtaken by insanity and would live outdoors like an animal for a specified period of time ("seven times" may refer to seven years; see 7:25).

*Daniel Interprets the Dream (4:19-27).* Daniel informed Nebuchadnezzar that the tree represented none other than the king himself. Though great and mighty, the king would be brought low. For a period of time he would be plagued by an extreme form of insanity (known as boanthropy or lycanthropy) and would actually behave like an animal. Once he was sufficiently humbled, Nebuchadnezzar would be restored to his throne.

*The Dream Comes True (4:28-37).* One year later, Nebuchadnezzar's dream was fulfilled. As he proudly looked about the great city of Babylon, a voice from heaven announced to him that he was about to be humbled. He began acting like an animal, and his hair and nails grew exceedingly long. Finally, God restored his sanity, causing Nebuchadnezzar to praise Him publicly and warn others of the consequences of pride.

**Babylon Falls (5:1-31).** The events of chapter 5 occurred in 539 B.C., twenty-three years after Nebuchadnezzar's death. Belshazzar was now ruling Babylon in the absence of his father, Nabonidus (see introduction).

*A Mysterious Message on a Wall (5:1-12).* Belshazzar held a great banquet for all his nobles and their wives. He ordered that wine be served in the golden and silver goblets Nebuchadnezzar had taken from the Lord's temple in Jerusalem years before. While Belshazzar and his guests drank from the goblets, a hand appeared in thin air and wrote a mysterious message on one of the palace walls. The frightened king sent for his wise men and diviners and decreed that whoever was able to interpret the message would be elevated to third in the kingdom. (Technically speaking Nabonidus was still the king, with Belshazzar being his vice-regent.) When they were unable to decipher the message, the queen (or queen mother) reminded Belshazzar of Daniel, who years before had gained a reputation as a skillful interpreter of dreams and riddles.

*Daniel Interprets the Message (5:13-31).* When summoned by the king, Daniel agreed to interpret the writing, though he declined the king's gifts. Before interpreting the message, however, he reminded Belshazzar of how God had humbled proud Nebuchadnezzar. He also denounced the king for his arrogance and for his disrespect for the temple vessels. Finally, Daniel turned to the cryptic message, which read, "Mene,

Mene, Tekel, Parsin." He interpreted the message as being an ominous warning of impending judgment on Belshazzar's kingdom. "Mene," meaning *mina* (fifty shekels), sounds like a related word meaning *numbered*. Belshazzar's days were numbered and his reign about to come to an end. In similar fashion "tekel," meaning *shekel*, was a play on a related word meaning *weighed*. Belshazzar had been weighed like a shekel on the scales of divine justice and had been found lacking. "Parsin," meaning *half-shekels* (in 5:28 the singular form "peres" is used) was taken as a play on a related word meaning *divided*. Furthermore, it sounds like *Persian*. Belshazzar's kingdom would be divided between the Medes and Persians. This prophecy of Belshazzar's demise was fulfilled that very night.

**Daniel Delivered (6:1-28).** *Daniel Defies the King's Decree (6:1-15).* Daniel continued to prosper under Persian rule. Darius the Mede made him one of three administrators over the 120 districts within his jurisdiction. Daniel was so successful that he aroused the jealousy of other administrators and officials. Knowing that Daniel was loyal to his God, they devised a plot by which they hoped to have him executed for treason. Appealing to Darius's vanity, they convinced the king to issue a decree commanding his subjects to worship him exclusively for one month. Violators would be thrown to the lions. When Daniel defied the decree and openly prayed to the Lord, the conspirators reported him to the king. Realizing he had been tricked, Darius tried to absolve Daniel of guilt; but Daniel's enemies reminded the king that royal decrees could not be altered.

*Daniel in the Lion's Den (6:16-28).* Darius had no other alternative than to throw Daniel to the lions. A stone was placed over the entrance to the den, and the king sealed it with his own ring so that it might not be disturbed. After a long, restless night Darius returned to the den in the morning. To his amazement Daniel was still alive. Daniel explained that the Lord had miraculously preserved him by closing the lions' mouths. The king ordered that Daniel be lifted from the den and his accusers thrown in. Darius then issued an official statement praising Daniel's God as the sovereign Lord of the universe, who miraculously delivers His servants.

## VISIONS AND REVELATIONS (7:1–12:13)

**Four Beasts (7:1-28).** The vision recorded in this chapter occurred in Belshazzar's first year of co-regency (about 556–553 B.C.), prior to the events recorded in chapters 5–6.

*Daniel Reports the Vision (7:1-14).* Daniel saw four beasts emerge in succession from the churning sea. The first resembled a lion but also had the wings of an eagle. As Daniel watched, the creature's wings were torn off, and it stood on two feet like a human. It also was given a heart like that of a person. The second beast resembled a bear with three ribs in its mouth. The third beast looked like a leopard with four wings and four heads. The fourth beast, the most terrifying of all, had iron teeth with which it ripped its victims to bits. It also possessed ten horns, three of which were uprooted before another horn that sprouted up among them. This other horn had human eyes and spoke arrogant words.

In this vision Daniel also saw God, called the "Ancient of Days," seated on His throne with thousands of His servants attending Him. His clothing and hair were white, and His throne, a flame of fire. Books were opened as God prepared to sit in judgment on the fourth beast. The beast, along with its boastful

little horn, were cast into the fire and destroyed. A human figure, called "one like a son of man," then appeared in the clouds and approached the divine throne, where he was granted authority to rule the world.

*The Interpretation of the Vision (7:15-28).* One of the heavenly attendants explained the significance of the vision to Daniel. The four beasts, like the statue seen in Nebuchadnezzar's dream (Dan. 2), represented four successive empires that would rule the earth. The ten horns of the fourth beast, which was of particular interest to Daniel, represented ten kings who would arise from the fourth empire. The little horn symbolized another ruler, who would supplant three of the ten. This little horn would oppose God and persecute His people for a specified period of time (perhaps three and a half years; compare "a time, times and half a time," 7:25). After this the Lord would destroy this ruler and establish His kingdom.

As in chapter 2, interpreters differ about the identification of the four kingdoms. On analogy with chapter 2, the lion probably represents Babylon. The bear is often associated with the Medo-Persian Empire, with the three ribs understood as symbols of its three major victims, Lydia, Babylon, and Egypt. The leopard may very well represent Greece, its four heads reflecting the fourfold division of Alexander's kingdom after his death (8:8,21-22). The final beast may represent Rome, with its ten horns symbolizing a later manifestation of this empire prior to the coming of God's kingdom. In this case the little horn may be equated with the New Testament figure of the Antichrist. However, as with chapter 2, others identify the successive kingdoms as Babylon, Media, Persia, and Greece, with the little horn being associated with Antiochus Epiphanes (see Dan. 8; 11).

The identification of the "one like a son of man" has also occasioned much debate. Many see the title as messianic. Others understand the figure to represent humanity, God's chosen people, or angelic beings (with Michael sometimes being specified as the angel in view).

**A Ram and Goat (8:1-27).** This vision, like that of chapter 7, came during the reign of Belshazzar.

*Daniel Reports the Vision (8:1-14).* Daniel saw a vision of a ram with two horns of unequal length, the longer of which grew up after the other. The ram charged westward, northward, and southward, conquering all who opposed it. However, a goat with a long horn then came from the west, shattered the ram's two horns, and trampled the ram into the ground. None could stand before the goat, but at the height of his power his horn was broken and replaced by four small horns. From one of these horns grew another horn that became increasingly strong and extended its power southward and eastward. It challenged the hosts of heaven, oppressed God's people, and disrupted the sacrifices in the Lord's temple.

*The Interpretation of the Vision (8:15-27).* The angel Gabriel revealed the interpretation of the vision to Daniel. The two-horned ram represented the Medo-Persian empire, and the goat, the Greek empire (of Alexander). The four horns reflected the fourfold division of Alexander's empire following his untimely death. The little horn represented Antiochus Epiphanes, the Syrian ruler (about 175–164 B.C.) who opposed God's people and desecrated the temple.

**Seventy Sevens (9:1-27).** *Daniel's Intercessory Prayer (9:1-19).* In 539–538 B.C., immediately after the Persian conquest of Babylon, Daniel prayed to the Lord on behalf of exiled Israel. Daniel realized that the seventy-year period of Judah's desolation prophesied in Jeremiah 25:11-12 was soon approaching its end. (The prophecy is dated to 605 B.C. [see Jer. 25:1], the year when Nebuchadnezzar besieged Jerusalem for the first time and carried away the first group of exiles to Babylon. If one assumes that the seventy-year period began in that year, then it would be over in 535 B.C.)

Addressing God as Israel's faithful covenant Lord, Daniel confessed the nation's sinful and rebellious condition and acknowledged that they had justly suffered the covenant curses threatened by Moses. He then asked the Lord to forgive the nation's sins and once again look with favor on desolate Jerusalem.

*Gabriel Reveals and Interprets the Vision (9:20-27).* While Daniel prayed, Gabriel appeared to him and announced that "seventy sevens" (490 years according to many) were decreed for Israel and Jerusalem, after which time atonement would be made for their sins. He then explained the chronology of these "seventy sevens." Sixty-nine sevens would separate the time of the decree to rebuild Jerusalem and the coming of the Messiah ("Anointed One"). Sometime after this the Messiah would be "cut off" and the city destroyed by the "people of the ruler who will come." During the seventieth seven this ruler would make a covenant with God's people, which he would then violate halfway through the period.

Understandably this somewhat cryptic vision poses several difficulties and has been interpreted in a variety of ways. Some view the numbers as symbolic, while others take them quite literally and produce elaborate mathematical explanations of their fulfillment. Among the latter, some even contend that this prophecy pinpoints the date of Christ's crucifixion.

*Gabriel's Appearance (10:1–12:13). Daniel's Vision of the Angel (10:1–11:1).* In 536 B.C. Daniel received his final vision. While standing by the Tigris River, he saw a radiant angelic being whose voice thundered. Totally overwhelmed by the vision, Daniel fell into a deep trance. The angel told Daniel to stand up and encouraged him not to fear. He then explained that he had been delayed in coming by the "prince of Persia," apparently a reference to an angel who exercised jurisdiction over the nation Persia. After a three-week struggle, Michael intervened, allowing this angel to come to Daniel. He would soon be off again to fight against the prince of Persia, but before leaving he revealed to Daniel certain future events.

*The Angel Outlines Future Events (11:2–12:4).* Daniel 11:2-35 outlines the course of Palestinian history from Daniel's time to the time of Antiochus Epiphanes. Verse 2 refers to the four Persian rulers who would succeed Cyrus: Cambyses (530–522 B.C.), Pseudo-Smerdis (522), Darius I (522–486), and Xerxes (486–465). It alludes to Xerxes' campaign against Greece. Verses 3-4 then refer to Alexander the Great (336–323) and the division of his kingdom. Verses 5-20 outline the relationship between the Seleucids ("the king of the North"), who ruled Syria, and the Ptolemies ("the king of the South"), who ruled Egypt during the period 321–175. Verses 21-35 focus on the career of Antiochus Epiphanes (175–164), mentioning among other things his Egyptian campaigns and mistreatment of the Jews. Verses 32-35 anticipate the Maccabean revolt against Antiochus.

Most of the details of verses 36-45 do not correspond to Antiochus's career. For example, Antiochus died in Persia, not Palestine (see v. 45). Consequently, some scholars label these verses as unful-filled "prophecy" and understand the preceding verses (vv. 1-35) as "prophecy" after the fact (see introduction). Others understand a switch in perspective beginning in verse 36. The description merges into a portrayal of the Antichrist, whose hostility to God and His people was foreshadowed in the career of Antiochus.

The final verses of this section (12:1-4) anticipate a time of crisis for Israel in which Michael, the nation's guardian angel, would intervene on their behalf. Reference is made to a general resurrection of the righteous and evil.

*Daniel's Final Vision and Instructions (12:4-13).* The angel instructed Daniel to seal up the revelation until the end times. Daniel then saw two other angelic beings standing by the river, both of whom were clothed in linen. One asked how long it would be before the revelation was fulfilled. The other responded that "a time, times, and a half a time" (probably three and a half years) would pass between the breaking of Israel's power and the fulfillment of the vision. Verse 11 apparently gives a more exact measurement of this period (1,290 days). The significance of the figure given in verse 12 (1,335 days) is unclear. In conjunction with verse 11, it implies that there would be an additional forty-five-day period before the complete fulfillment of the vision.

*Theological and Ethical Significance.* Daniel stresses God's sovereignty over world history. History unfolds as part of God's plans and is moving toward God's predetermined goals. Earthly despots wield their cruel power for only a short time. God is in control, and He has set an end to the time His people have to suffer. God's goals for human history include the deliverance of His people from oppression, the resurrection, judgment, and the establishment of His everlasting kingdom. Daniel thus calls God's people of every time to perseverance and hope. Like Daniel and his friends, today's believers are tempted to compromise their values and worship that which is not God. Daniel calls Christians to live out their faith in a hostile world whatever the cost.

## Questions for Reflection

1. What lessons can we learn from Daniel and his friends?

2. In what ways does God demonstrate His sovereignty in this book? What relevance does the doctrine of God's sovereignty have for the modern Christian and for the church?

3. What is the purpose for the book's extensive use of symbolism? How do the

symbolism and vivid imagery contribute to the overall message of the book?

4. In what ways does this book offer comfort and encouragement to Christians?

## Sources for Additional Study

Archer, G. L., Jr. "Daniel." *The Expositor's Bible Commentary.* Vol. 7. Grand Rapids: Zondervan, 1985.

Baldwin, J. G. *Daniel.* Downers Grove: InterVarsity, 1978.

Miller, Stephen. *Daniel.* New American Commentary. Nashville: Broadman & Holman, 1994.

Wood, L. *A Commentary on Daniel.* Grand Rapids: Zondervan, 1973.

Young, E. J. *The Prophecy of Daniel.* Grand Rapids: Eerdmans, 1949.

# THE MINOR PROPHETS

## E. RAY CLENDENEN

The "Minor" Prophets are so named not because of their lesser importance but because of their size. The longest, Hosea, occupies about fourteen pages in an average English Bible, whereas the "Major" Prophets range in size from twenty-four (Daniel) to ninety-seven pages (Jeremiah). Altogether the Minor Prophets are about the size of Ezekiel. In spite of having been written at different times as separate books, sometime in the development of the Hebrew canon these twelve books were all bound together on the same scroll, and in an order that has generally remained unchanged. Consequently, they came to be known in Jewish tradition perhaps more appropriately as "the Twelve." Some have argued that they exhibit an overall plot or structure. Paul House has observed that the first six books, Hosea to Micah, emphasize sin, Nahum to Zephaniah stress punishment, and Haggai to Malachi stress restoration.

As prophetic books they exhibit all the characteristics of the Major Prophets. First, they employ an elevated rhetorical style that often takes the form of poetry (Jonah is the exception, being narrative). Second, they present their messages as received directly from God. Third, they use an inventory of literary forms such as lawsuit, woe, and promise. And fourth, because of the function of the prophets as "enforcers" of God's covenant, these books call for behavioral changes on the part of the disobedient covenant people. As explained in 2 Kings 17:13 (see also Neh. 9:26,30), "The LORD warned Israel and Judah through all his prophets and seers: 'Turn from your evil ways. Observe my commands and decrees, in accordance with the entire Law that I commanded your fathers to obey and that I delivered to you through my servants the prophets.'"

This focus on behavioral change explains the prophets' use of messages of indictment, instruction, judgment, and hope or salvation. Indictment messages identified Israel's sins and God's attitude toward them. Instruction told them what they must do about it; and judgment and hope messages motivated the listeners to obey by explaining the consequences of disobedience (judgment) or of repentance and faith (hope). Messages of judgment involve specific applications of the covenant curses found in Leviticus 26 and Deuteronomy 28 (see, for example, Joel 1:4-20; Amos 4:6-11; Zeph. 1:13; Hag. 1:10-11). They serve, then, as reminders that sin has its consequences.

At least in some cases where judgment is announced with no explicit expression of hope, the possibility of avoiding punishment through repentance may be assumed (e.g., Jonah 3:4; Jer. 18:1-12). But even when judgment is decreed as inevitable due to Israel's continued obstinacy, the function is to motivate repentance on the part of those who survive the judgment (see Jer. 23:20). In these cases the judgment and salvation oracles combine in a special way to motivate right behavior in a "purified" remnant. Our historical perspective allows us to recognize that in some cases announcements of future judgment or salvation concerned the distant future, beyond the lifetime of the prophet's immediate audience (e.g., Joel 3:14-21; Mal. 3:1). But like the assurance of Christ's return for the Christian, this was to have a motivating effect regardless of the time it would occur (e.g., 1 Thess. 4:18; 5:6-11).

The prophets did not always motivate in terms of the future. Incentives to obedience (positive motivation) could be given in terms of (1) past blessings (e.g., Hos. 2:8; 7:15; 11:1-4; 12:10; 13:4-5; Amos 2:9-11), (2) present realities (e.g., Hos. 3:1; 14:8-9; Mal. 1:2; 2:10a), or (3) future blessings (e.g., Hos. 1:7,10-11; 2:14-23; 3:5; 6:1-3,11; 11:10-11; 13:14; 14:4-7; Joel 2:18-3:21; Amos 9:11-15; Zeph. 3:14-20; Hag. 2:6-9). Deterrents to disobedience (negative motivation) likewise could be in terms of (1) past judgment (e.g., Amos 4:6-11; Zech. 1:6), (2) present circumstances (e.g., Hos. 1:9; 4:3; 5:11-12; 6:5; 7:9; 8:7-8; 9:7; Joel 1:2-12; Hag. 1:6,9-11), or (3) future punishment (e.g., Hos. 1:4-6; 2:3-4,6,9-13; 3:4; 4:5-7; 5:2,6-7,9-10,14-15; Amos 2:13-16; 3:11-15; 5:16-23; 6:7-11; 8:7-14).

Recognizing the vital relationship between words of indictment, instruction, judgment, and hope in the prophets is an important step toward understanding their message. For many the word "prophecy" has only one association—"fulfillment." Students of the prophets often concentrate on the "good news" of prophetic fulfillment to the neglect of the rest of the prophet's message. Or in some cases the preference is for social critique. By all means fulfilled and yet-to-be fulfilled prophecy is an important and fruitful subject for study, as is also the divine displeasure with certain social and religious practices. But recognizing the nature of the prophetic books as behavioral exhortation has important implications. In such discourses the most prominent element is the behavioral change being advocated. All the other elements in the discourse must relate to it. Therefore it is a misuse of Scripture to listen to only one of the supplementary elements, such as predictive prophecy, without relating it to the central message of the book.

As written in Sirach 49:10—"May the bones of the Twelve Prophets send forth new life from where they lie, for they comforted the people of Jacob and delivered them with confident hope" (NRSV). Yet the Twelve do more than comfort God's people. Their primary goal is to make us uncomfortable with lives lived outside the will of God.

## Sources for Additional Study

Chisholm, R. B., Jr. *Interpreting the Minor Prophets.* Grand Rapids: Zondervan, 1990.

Craigie, P. *Twelve Prophets.* The Daily Bible Study Series. 2 vols. Philadelphia: Westminster, 1984–85

Feinberg, C. L. *The Minor Prophets.* Chicago: Moody, 1980.

House, P. *The University of the Twelve.* Sheffield: Academic Press, 1990.

Laetsch, T. *The Minor Prophets.* St. Louis: Concordia, 1956.

McComiskey, T. E., ed. *The Minor Prophets: An Exegetical and Expository Commentary.* 3 vols. Grand Rapids: Baker, 1992–98.

Smith, G. V. *The Prophets as Preachers: An Introduction to the Hebrew Prophets.* Nashville: Broadman & Holman, 1994.

Smith, Ralph L. *Micah-Malachi.* Word Biblical Commentary. Waco: Word, 1984.

Stuart, D. *Hosea–Jonah.* Word Biblical Commentary. Waco: Word, 1987.

# HOSEA

Hosea is one of the most autobiographical of the prophetic books in that the opening account of Hosea's own marriage and family formed a vital part of his unique message. God's word of grace and His call to repent are dramatically portrayed and punctuated in the book by Hosea's scorned but constant love for his wife Gomer and by the odd names of his three children. On the other hand, apart from this information about his immediate family, hardly anything is known about Hosea.

According to the first verse, Hosea's prophetic career spanned at least forty years. It began sometime during the reign of Jeroboam II, who ruled Israel, the Northern Kingdom, as co-regent with his father Jehoash from 793 to 782 B.C., then independently to 753 B.C. Hosea's ministry ended sometime during the reign of Hezekiah, who ruled Judah from 716 to 686 B.C. His divinely commissioned marriage to the prostitute Gomer, which brought Hosea such heartache, may have been the beginning of his long career. But rather than ministering in spite of personal sorrow, his troublesome marriage was the foundation stone of his ministry.

Although the Southern Kingdom of Judah is not neglected in Hosea's prophecy (e.g., 1:7,11; 6:11; 12:2), his messages are primarily directed to Israel, often referred to as "Ephraim" (see 5:2,12-14; 6:4; 7:1), or represented by the royal city, Samaria (7:1; 8:5,6; 10:5,7; 13:16). Hosea apparently lived and worked in or around Samaria, probably moving to Jerusalem at least by the time Samaria fell to the Assyrians in 722 B.C.

The reign of Jeroboam II, the Northern Kingdom's greatest ruler by worldly standards, was a time of general affluence, military might, and national stability. There was a bull market, the future looked bright, and the mood of the country was high and optimistic, at least for the upper class (Hos. 12:8; Amos 3:15; 6:4-6). Syria was a constant problem to Israel, but Adad-nirari III of Assyria had brought them relief with an expedition against Damascus in 805 B.C. Then after Adad-nirari's death in 783, Israel and Judah expanded during a time of Assyrian weakness (the time of Jonah). But after Jeroboam's death in 753, Israel sank into near anarchy, going through six kings in about thirty years, four of whom were assassinated (Zechariah, Shallum, Pekahiah, and Pekah). Since Assyria also regained power during this time, Israel was doomed. Of course, the real reason Israel crumbled was God's determination to judge them for their sins, as Hosea and Amos make clear. Most of Hosea's messages probably were delivered during these last thirty years of Israel's nationhood.

***Message and Purpose.*** *Indictment:* According to Hosea, Israel's sins were in four areas. First, they were violating basic covenant requirements of faithfulness, kindness, and the knowledge of God, thereby rejecting God's law. They had become self-satisfied and proud and had forgotten God's grace. They even spoke lies, insolence, and evil against Him. Second, they were engaging in idolatry and harlotry, that is, cult prostitution. Third, they were trusting in human devices (kings, princes, warriors, and foreign covenants) rather than in God.

Finally, they were guilty of injustice and violence, including murder, theft, lying, and oppression of the defenseless.

*Instruction:* Through Hosea the Lord told Israel to stop their promiscuity, idolatry, and all their iniquity and to return to Him in humility and to faithfulness to the law of the covenant.

*Judgment:* Hosea informed Israel that their present distress was because the Lord had abandoned them and that further chastisement would result, including foreign domination, exile, destruction, desolation, and death.

*Hope:* Hosea reminded Israel of the Lord's grace and love in making them a people and in blessing them in the past with His attentive and patient care and His abundant provisions. He was their only hope, and His ways were right. The Lord also assured them that in response to their repentance and faith He would again have compassion on them and redeem them; He would remove unrighteousness, restore the covenant, bringing righteousness and the knowledge of God; and He would rebuild and beautify Israel in the land.

**Structure.** The first three chapters establish a parallel between the Lord and Hosea. Both are loving husbands of unfaithful wives. Hosea's three children, whose names were messages to Israel, serve as an overture to the second main division of the book, which presents its accusations and call to repent in groups of three (see Garrett's commentary). Just as chapter 1, a third-person account of Hosea's family, is balanced by chapter 3, a first-person account, so the final main division of the book alternates between first-person announcements of God's message and third-person reports from the prophet. The messages in this last division deal with falsehood (8:1–10:15), a rebellious son (11:1–13:6), and a final

call to repent (14:1-8); and they end with a final postscript (14:9).

    I. Divine Love (1:1–3:5)
    II. Accusations and Call to Repent (4:1–7:16)
    III. Antiphonal Proclamations (8:1–14:9)

## GOD'S MESSAGE (1:1–2:23)

Hosea's prophetic ministry began with perplexing instructions from God to find a wife among the promiscuous girls of Israel (of which there were apparently many; see 4:14). This is no parable or vision but actual instructions regarding a literal marriage that would give Hosea God's perspective on Israel. Hosea, like the Lord, would have a wayward wife and a broken heart. Gomer bore Hosea three children whose names made them divine judgment oracles. They would bear the shame of their mother's behavior and at the same time represent the shameful behavior and divine condemnation of the children of Israel. Hence they were called "children of unfaithfulness."

Jehu had carried out God's judgment (2 Kgs. 9:7) by putting the last of Omri's dynasty to the sword at Jezreel (2 Kgs. 9:24–10:11), for which God commended him (2 Kgs. 10:30). Hosea's first child, Jezreel, was a message that Jehu's dynasty, which had been just as wicked as Omri's, likewise would suffer annihilation at Jezreel (a better understanding of the Hebrew of 1:4 than the NIV translation). Zechariah, Jehu's last royal descendant, was assassinated by Shallum in 752 B.C., probably at Ibleam in Jezreel (2 Kgs. 15:10).

Hosea's second child, a daughter, would carry the pathetic name meaning "Not Loved" because by her continual unfaithfulness Israel had forfeited God's love. Israel's hope, however, would be in the assurance that "I will certainly forgive them" (1:6; wrongly translated in NIV).

## SYMBOLIC ACTIONS BY THE PROPHETS

The prophetic word became a living word for the prophets. Often God called them to do something beyond preaching. He led them to picture the message in their own lives. They had to live out the meaning and results of God's word to His people. Their actions thus symbolized for the people what God was about to do to and for Israel.

In calling the prophets to symbolic actions, God gave them no easy task. The word had to come alive in their family. For Isaiah the birth and naming of children became acts preaching to the people. He called one son *A Remnant Shall Return* and another *Speedy Is the Spoil, Quick the Plunder* (Isa. 7:3; 8:3).

These strange names made people think as they watched the prophet walk down the street carrying his children. Was *Remnant* a sign of disaster in war or a hope for new growth in

the future? Did *Return* refer to the aftermath of battle or to spiritual return and repentance? Who was fast to spoil and plunder whom? God's people had to listen to the prophet preach to determine the meaning, but the children's names made them curious enough to listen.

Isaiah gave yet another symbolic name to a more mysterious child—*Immanuel, God with Us* (7:14; 8:8,10). This certainly called the audience to attention when Isaiah announced the birth of yet another child of significance (9:6). Jerusalem's citizens knew the prophet was doing more than acting crazy when he wandered the city's streets minus his clothing for three years pointing to God's actions against Israel's enemies to the south (Isa. 20).

Hosea had an even more difficult family task. He had to endure a broken heart and broken marriage along with public indignity and disgrace (Hos. 1:1-9; 2:2-9). God called him to marry a prostitute and then name her children *Jezreel* (the site of a battle), *Not Pitied*

(or *Without a Mother's Love*, indicating the withdrawal of God's love and forgiveness from Israel), and *Not My People* (or *Illegitimate*, indicating Israel no longer had a guarantee of God's election and protection).

Later, God used the names to indicate His renewed covenant with His people (1:10–2:1; 2:14–3:5). Israel had to pay attention to Hosea, if only to hear the latest gossip about his family. As they listened, they learned the nature of God's deep, undying love for His people, a love going beyond all human love, even Hosea's (11:8-11). They also found the ups and downs of their relationship to God described in family terms.

Jeremiah had to abstain from the duties and joys of family life to preach God's word and show the imminent danger God's people faced (Jer. 16:2). In contrast, Ezekiel suffered having to bury his wife without public mourning (Ezek. 24:15-27), symbolizing how Israel would have to react at the news their temple was destroyed.

Hosea's third child, whose name meant "Not-My-People," declared that Israel had utterly broken their covenant with the Lord (see Exod. 6:7; Lev. 26:12). Hope is given here, however, by alluding to the Abrahamic covenant ("like the sand on the seashore"; see Gen. 22:17). Thus eternal promise is placed profoundly beside final judgment, reconcilable only because "the living God" can bring life out of death. This is affirmed by the name "Jezreel," which symbolized

not only judgment but also life, in that the name means "God plants" (see also Ezek. 36:9-11). The theme of 1:11, that the division between Israel and Judah was superficial and temporary, would be repeated later (Ezek. 37:18-25; see also Hos. 3:5).

Hosea 2 is a continuation of the "Lo-Ammi" oracle. The children, representing the common people of Israel, are urged to reject their mother, representing Israel's leadership. The leaders had led the people

Prophetic symbolism thus reached deep into the prophets' personal relationships. It gave them creative ways to show people God's will without saying a word, though often the prophets did explain the meaning of their actions.

The potter shaping and reshaping a pot on his wheel showed Jeremiah and Israel how God could change course and directions with Israel (Jer. 18). Breaking the potter's beautiful jar showed how God could destroy His people (Jer. 19). Jeremiah had to wear an oxen's yoke around Jerusalem and summon foreign ambassadors to call them to submit to Nebuchadnezzar. He even had to command his own king of Judah to wear Nebuchadnezzar's yoke (Jer. 27). Such action brought quick response. An opposing prophet broke Jeremiah's yoke (28:10-11). False prophets used symbolic actions too. Still, the faithful prophet followed God's calling and continued acting out God's word (see Jer. 32; 43:8-9).

Of all prophets, Ezekiel is most known for his symbolic acts. The first chapters of Ezekiel read almost like modern science fiction at its most bizarre extreme. Ezekiel ate a scroll (3:2). He was tied with ropes and became unable to talk (3:24-27). He drew a map of Jerusalem on a tablet and enacted a military siege against his drawing (4:1-4). He lay down on his left side for 390 days and then on his right side for 40 days (4:4-7). He was called to cook food with human excrement for fuel but allowed to use cow dung when he complained (4:12-15). He cut off his hair and beard and then divided the hair into three parts for separate actions (5:1-4). He packed his bags and left the city by digging a hole in the city wall (12:3-8). He trembled and shuddered as he ate food with the people (12:18).

After the exile Zechariah prepared a crown to symbolize God's messiah (Zech. 6:9-15).

The prophets' actions raised many questions for the people. They wondered about the prophets' mental states. They wondered if the prophets were magicians whose power ensured the acts would come true in the real world. They looked to other prophets to cast doubt on the power of the symbolic acts. They even stopped to wonder if God were actually speaking through the prophets and calling them to a faith in a new way of interpreting Yahweh's way with His people.

The prophets themselves knew God had commanded the acts, no matter what suspicions and questions such acts raised for their audiences. The prophets knew they as humans had no power and no magic to give meaning and actual power to the acts. Rather, the prophets depended on God to take the acts, fulfill the message of the acts, and call the people to account for their response to the acts.

Symbolic acts were a vital method for God to speak to His people in warning and hope. In this way He wooed them to return to Him and avoid the judgment their actions had made inevitable.

---

to trust and seek Baal rather than the Lord. After announcing their punishment of depravation (vv. 6-13), Hosea assures them that the Lord would eventually redeem and restore them (vv. 14-23).

## HOSEA'S TESTIMONY (3:1-5)

Even though Gomer, like Israel, had joined herself to another lover and so committed adultery, Hosea was told to take her back. Like Hosea, God would show love to His "wife" even though she had forfeited her right to that love by having relationships with others. Why Hosea had to buy her is unstated. She perhaps had found it necessary to sell herself to someone as a personal slave. As Hosea and Gomer would refrain from conjugal relations for a period after she returned, so there would be a period during which Israel would be without ruler or worship. This probationary period would begin with the fall of Samaria and would be a time when the

Lord would wait for the people of Israel to seek Him (see 5:15). It would end "in the last days" when Israel would seek their messianic king in repentance and faith (Isa. 11:1-10; Jer. 23:5-6; 33:15-16; Matt. 1:1; 21:9; Rom. 11:23). It is apparently the same time that believing Israel will be reunited (2:11).

## THREEFOLD INDICTMENT (4:1-14)

The primary indictment section in 4:1-5:15 begins with a summary of the charges. The Lord accuses Israel in 4:1 of having (1) no faithfulness, truth, or integrity (basing one's life on the principle of truth rather than on expediency), (2) no love, compassion, or kindness, and (3) no knowledge of God. In personal relationships they were characterized by lying, cruelty, and greed. Their understanding of God was perverse, their relationship with Him nonexistent. As a result they were violating the Ten Commandments and suffering the consequences. The common people and women are identified as guilty, but especially are the priests. Those who mislead God's people invite special punishment.

## THREEFOLD WARNING (4:15-5:15)

This section is divided into three bywords of instruction (exhortation) in 4:15; 5:1; and 5:8 mainly directed against Israel. But Judah was also warned that they were in danger of following them in apostasy and punishment. Because of Israel's adulterous idolatry, arrogance, and stubbornness, they were warned that God would blow them away like a whirlwind, eat away at them like a moth or rot, and tear them to pieces like a lion. Hosea refers to the major worship center at Bethel, "house of God," as Beth Aven, "house of wickedness" (4:15; 5:8; 10:5).

## CALL TO REPENT (6:1-7:16)

An exhortation to repent in 6:1-3 is accompanied by the assurance that all God's punishments would be reversed, even death. After a short time in exile, Israel would be resurrected. The New Testament views as messianic fulfillment certain events in Israel's history which Jesus paralleled or completed.

The Lord was to Israel like a father whose heart is broken by a rebellious child. Hosea 6:6, quoted by Jesus in Matthew 9:13 and 12:7, does not reject sacrifice but rather acts of worship not accompanied by faithfulness and love and not based on the knowledge of God (see 4:1). This section describes a nation full of all kinds of violence and immorality. The king and national leadership neglected the nation and devoted themselves to debauchery and striving for power. As a result, the nation was decaying around them and being assimilated and swallowed up by the surrounding nations. A remedy for the crisis was sought everywhere but in the Lord.

## FALSE HOPES (8:1-10:15)

Israel had arrogantly sought success and security through (1) idolatry and (2) military and political power (probably what is intended by the "double sin" mentioned in the summary passage in 10:10). All their efforts would produce the opposite of what they desired. According to 8:7, they were like farmers trying to plant in the wind; the seed is blown away. Whatever seed that grew would be blown away by a storm, which meant that foreigners would come and take it. Israel's idols, temples, and fortresses would be destroyed, and military alliances would drain them dry, enslave them, and carry them away. For their wickedness and rebellion in trusting in the fertility cult of Baal, the Lord would reject them and make the land and people barren.

Rather than a productive vine (Isa. 5; John 15) Israel had become a destructive (not "spreading"; 10:1) vine serving only itself. They had turned the Lord's blessings into gifts for the calf-idols of Baal, while continuing to pay lip service to the Lord's worship. The resultant devastation would be so terrible that many would cry out for the mountains to bury them and the places of their idolatry (10:8; see Deut. 12:2; Luke 23:30). Allusions to Gibeah in 9:9 and 10:9 (see also 5:8) are to the civil war begun by a Levite's concubine being raped, murdered, and cut into pieces (Judg. 19–21). Like Samaria, Gibeah was a hill with a fortress; it served as Saul's capital during his kingship but was later deserted. So it represents both depravity and militarism and may have figuratively referred to Samaria.

Near the end of the section is an exhortation in 10:12 to "sow ... righteousness," "reap ... unfailing love," and "seek the Lord." This verse alludes to the threefold charge against Israel in 4:1 and summarizes a life that pleases God.

### ISRAEL'S REBELLION (11:1–13:16)
Again the Lord grieves as a loving father abandoned by his son ( see 6:4), and again Israel is told they will be delivered over to Assyria, who will oppress them as Egypt did (11:5; see 7:16; 8:13; 9:3,6; 10:6). Yet the Lord refuses to annihilate Israel. He promises a new exodus for a believing remnant. Like Hosea 6:2, 11:1 is understood in the New Testament as a messianic prophecy in that Jesus, God's Son, like Israel, was also brought out of Egypt in the context of hatred (Matt. 2:15; see Exod. 4:22). Whereas Israel was freed from Egypt and became slaves to sin, Jesus practiced perfect righteousness so that He could die as their substitutionary atoning sacrifice.

According to Hosea, dependence on foreign alliances meant trusting in deceit and violence and amounted to playing with fire. Again he exhorts a threefold repentance. He also rebukes Israel by pointing out that although their namesake Jacob (whose name God changed to

Israel) had been a faithless, self-centered conniver, he met God (at Bethel) and was converted. He became a recipient of grace. They, on the other hand, met Baal at Bethel (Beth Aven) and became recipients of spiritual death.

The contemporary idea of an indulgent, tolerant God is contradicted by the remarkable picture given in 13:7-8 of God being like a lion, a leopard, or a bear, tearing, ripping open, and devouring. Yet, as in 6:1-2, although Israel was presently dead in sin, 13:14 declares that the Lord is able to bring life out of death. As Paul in 1 Corinthians 15:55 declares from this verse, God's power extends to personal, bodily resurrection, not just national renewal.

### FINAL CALL TO REPENT (14:1-9)
The book concludes with the prophet's final invitation to repent (even giving a "sinner's prayer"), the Lord's assurance of restoration and blessing for a believing remnant, and Hosea's exhortation to persevere in the study of his prophecy in humble faith.

*Theological and Ethical Significance.* Nothing can quench God's love for His people. Like a marriage partner, God is deeply involved in their lives and is pained by their rebellion and unfaithfulness. God demands love and loyalty from His own. Often God's people then and now have failed to demonstrate wholehearted love for Him. But God stands ready to forgive and restore those who turn to Him in repentance. In buying Gomer's freedom, Hosea pointed ahead to God's love perfectly expressed in Christ, who bought the freedom of His bride, the church, with His own life.

### Questions for Reflection
1. In what ways are today's believers unfaithful to God?

2. How has God demonstrated His persistent love for us?

3. What demands does God's love place upon us?

4. Why is marriage such a good picture of the human relationship to God?

## Sources for Additional Study

Cohen, G. G. and H. R. Vandermey. *Hosea/Amos*. Chicago: Moody, 1981.

Garrett, D. A. *Hosea, Joel*. New American Commentary. Nashville: Broadman & Holman, 1997.

Hubbard, D. A. *Hosea: An Introduction and Commentary*. Tyndale Old Testament Commentaries. Downers Grove: InterVarsity, 1989.

Kidner, D. *The Message of Hosea: Love to the Loveless*. The Bible Speaks Today. Downers Grove: InterVarsity, 1981.

Smith, B. K. *Hosea, Joel, Amos, Obadiah, Jonah*. Layman's Bible Book Commentary. Vol. 13. Nashville: Broadman, 1982.

Wood, L. "Hosea." Vol. 7. *Expositor's Bible Commentary*. Grand Rapids: Zondervan, 1985.

# JOEL

All that is known about the prophet Joel is that he prophesied to Judah (2:1,15,23,32; 3:1,6,8, 16-21) and that his father's name was Pethuel (1:1). Regarding the circumstances under which the book was written, we only know that a particularly devastating locust plague had occurred which Joel took as a symbol of divine judgment. Unlike most of the prophetic books, Joel does not begin with a chronological note synchronizing his messages with a king or any other datable person or event. Scholars have used various arguments to assign dates to the book ranging from the ninth century B.C. to the late postexilic period. The most likely is either the late postexilic after the temple (516 B.C.) and walls (445 B.C.) were rebuilt in Jerusalem or the late pre-exilic period, perhaps the seventh century.

**Message and Purpose.** What is striking about the book of Joel is that there is no indictment section. The only clue to the sins that have called for a prophetic message is in the instruction in 2:12-13 to repent, that is, to "return to me with all your heart" and "rend your heart and not your garments." All the other prophets (except Jonah, which does not use the prophetic genre) have at least some explicit indication of what behavior needed to be changed. Joel is concerned almost wholly with motivation, with messages of judgment and hope.

There are many exhortations in the book, but they are almost all formal rather than ethical/moral exhortations. They are calls to hear (1:2-3), or to war (2:1; 3:9-13) or lamentation (1:5,8,11,13-14;

2:15-16; though some understand these as indirect calls for repentance), or celebration (2:21-23); that is, they are part of the judgment or hope messages. The only true instruction message, in fact, is in 2:12-13.

The main function of prophets in Israel was to call for behavioral changes in God's people (see Introduction to the Minor Prophets). Why, then, would Joel not make clear how Israel's behavior was displeasing God and how He wanted it changed? The answer is that Joel was relying on Israel's knowledge of their tradition (as reflected in Scripture) and on their ability to make connections between what he said and that tradition. This strategy, together with the vividness of his imagery of the locust plague, gave Joel's prophecy its unique power. The tradition which Joel's message calls forth was the biblical teaching on repentance.

Joel's message is strongly dependent on Deuteronomy in language, style, and themes. God had announced to Israel through Moses that failure to obey the Lord and follow His law would mean deprivation, barrenness, failure, ruin, loss, disease, drought, defeat, disappointment, frustration, death, sorrow, exile, shame, and locusts (Deut. 28:38-42; see also 32:22-27). Strong emphasis is placed there on Israel being defeated, devastated, and destroyed by foreign nations and their being "scatter[ed] ... among all nations, from one end of the earth to the other" (28:64). The specific disobedience cited is rejecting the Lord for idols and abandoning His covenant (29:18,25-26; see 32:15-18,21). But compassion, regathering, restoration, and spiritual rebirth are also promised

Israel if from their exile they would "return to the LORD your God and obey him with all your heart" (30:1-10).

Furthermore, these same curses would fall upon Israel's enemies (Deut. 32:39-43). These themes are previewed in Deuteronomy 4:23-40, also with specific references to idolatry (vv. 23,25), including the promise of restoration if they would "seek" the Lord "with all your heart and with all your soul" and "return" and "obey" Him (4:29-30). Immediately following is the call to "ask from one end of the heavens to the other. Has anything so great as this ever happened, or has anything like it ever been heard of?" (4:32; see also 32:7). This is strikingly similar to Joel 1:2-3 (also 2:3).

This same theme (i.e., judgment on Israel's idolatry followed by restoration if they would repent) is found many times elsewhere, such as in Samuel's words to Israel in 1 Samuel 7:3 ("If you are returning to the LORD with all your hearts . . ."), Solomon's prayer before the temple in 1 Kings 8:46-51 (v. 48, "if they turn back to you with all their heart..."), and in praise of king Josiah in 2 Kings 23:25 as one "who turned to the LORD as he did—with all his heart" (see Isa. 6:10; 9:13; 31:6; 55:7; 59:20; Jer. 3:3-4:4; 24:7; Ezek. 18:30-32; Hos. 3:5; 6:1-3; 14:1-9; Amos 4:6-11; Hag. 2:17; Zech. 1:3-6). Joel's message, then, would have triggered this entire script of judgment, repentance, and restoration, making it unnecessary for him to include an explicit citation of Judah's sins. They were guilty of disobeying God's law and abandoning Him for other gods.

Joel's message was concerned primarily with motivating repentance by proclaiming the day of the Lord, which is "at the same time one event and many events" and "refers to a decisive action of Yahweh to bring his plans for Israel to completion" (D. A. Garrett). First, the current locust plague is understood as judgment from God and a harbinger of the day of the Lord (Joel 1:2-20, especially v. 15). Second, Joel announced that a worse judgment was coming through a human army (2:1-11). This is also called the day of the Lord (2:1,11). Joel insisted that their only hope was through repentance (2:12-17). He assured Judah that repentance would be rewarded with physical (2:18-27) and spiritual (2:28-32) restoration associated with the day of the Lord (2:31). Third, he promises an eschatological day of the Lord which would bring judgment against the nations that had opposed the Lord and His people (3:14).

**Structure.** Joel's use of repetition gives the book the appearance of a series of folding doors, in some cases doors within doors. As Garrett has shown, the overall structure balances the section on the locust plague (1:1-20) with a section on the land's physical restoration (2:21-27). The prophecy of an invading army (2:1-11) is balanced by the promise of the destruction of that army (2:20). In the center is the highly prominent call to repent and promise of renewal (2:12-19). But this balanced structure overlaps with another. The prophecy of the destruction of the invading army (2:20) is also balanced with the concluding prophecy of the Lord's vengeance against all the nations (3:1-21). Finally, the assurance of the land's physical restoration through rain (2:21-27) is balanced by the promise of the people's spiritual restoration through the outpouring of God's Spirit (2:28-31).

  I. Locust Plague (1:1-20)
  II. Invading Army (2:1-11)
  III. Repentance and Renewal (2:12-19)
  IV. Army Destroyed (2:20)
  V. Restoration of the Land (2:21-27)
  VI. Spiritual Revival (2:28-31)
  VII. Vengeance on Nations (3:1-21)

## LOCUST PLAGUE (1:1-20)

Joel wrote after a devastating locust plague accompanied by drought and famine. Deprivation extended not only to food and enjoyment but even to temple worship. Israel was to consider this an early warning sign from the Lord and to gather together in fasting and prayer for the Lord's mercy.

## INVADING ARMY (2:1-11)

Whereas chapter 1 considers past and present troubles, the rest of the book looks to the future. As ancient cities had watchmen, Joel was serving as spiritual watchman of Judah. He urgently warned of an approaching enemy, which is likened to an army of locusts. It would be a foreign army (v. 2) that would serve as God's judgment against His people (v. 11). The phrase "like a mighty army" in verse 5 does not mean it was not an army. The Hebrew word for "like" or "as" can express identity (see Joel 1:15; Neh. 7:2, which says literally that Hanani was "like a man of integrity"). The army's unparalleled destruction is described as the day of the Lord.

## REPENTANCE AND RENEWAL (2:12-19)

The destruction of the day of the Lord could be averted only by genuine national repentance and seeking the Lord's mercy with faith. (On the nature and importance of Joel's call for repentance, see the introduction to Joel.)

## ARMY DESTROYED (2:20)

The invading army is identified as "the northern army" (literally, "the northerner"). This term would not be appropriate for a locust plague, which came from the south or southeast. The geography of Palestine is such that enemies had to attack either from the north or the south, but typically an enemy is described as coming from the north (Isa. 14:31;

41:25; Jer. 1:13-15; 4:6; 6:1; 10:22; 25:9; Ezek. 38:15; 39:2; Zeph. 2:13; Zech. 2:6-7). On the stench left by this divinely slain army compare Isaiah 34:2-3, which describes an eschatological destruction of God's enemies.

## RESTORATION OF THE LAND (2:21-27)

These verses describe a reversal of the devastation brought by the locust plague of 1:2-20. Garrett notes that the command not to fear is characteristic of Isaiah's salvation messages (Isa. 40:9-11; 41:10,13,14; 43:1,5; 44:2-3; 54:4; also Jer. 30:10; 46:27-28). In verse 23 the phrase "autumn rains in righteousness" also may be translated "teacher of/for righteousness" (see Job 36:22; Prov. 5:13; Isa. 30:20). It may be a reference or at least an allusion to the messianic seed of Abraham, the prophet promised in Deuteronomy 18:15, who would bring righteousness to the believing remnant (see Jer. 33:14-17).

## SPIRITUAL REVIVAL (2:28-31)

These verses in all their fullness describe events associated with Christ's return to remove evil and to rule in righteousness, when all believers will have the privileges and abilities of prophets (see Jer. 31:33-34). But the Day of Pentecost in Acts 2 inaugurated Christ's rule in an incipient form. For at that time, God gave His Spirit to all believers as a down payment of more to come (Eph. 1:13-14; 2 Cor. 1:22; 5:5).

## VENGEANCE ON NATIONS (3:1-21)

At the final day of the Lord, God will destroy all His enemies and deliver and bless all who trust Him. Converted Israel will be gathered into their land, and the other nations will come against them (see Rev. 16:13-16). God will deliver Israel and judge the nations not only for their unbelief but also for the way they have treated God's people (see Ezek. 38-39;

Zech. 14). After judging the nations, the Lord will bless His people with His presence, with an abundance of good things, and with perpetual security (see Jer. 23:3-8; 30:7-11; 32:37-44; 33:6-18; 46:27-28; Ezek. 28:24-26; 34:22-31; Hos. 2:14-23).

***Theological and Ethical Significance.*** Ruin and destruction lie ahead for all who do not know and trust the Lord. But all who belong to Him through repentance and faith are promised His indwelling presence, as well as eternal abundance, total satisfaction, and security. Believers feeling outnumbered and bullied by the world should be encouraged to know that all the worldly powers someday will be assembled before the Lord to receive His justice. Believers should consider times of crisis as opportunities for reflection on the character of our lives, especially our relationship with the Lord. For unbelievers these are opportunities to recognize our vulnerability and our need for a relationship with the living God.

## Questions for Reflection

1. How do we respond to crises? Do hard times drive us to God?

2. How did Joel's prophecy find fulfillment in the events of Pentecost (Acts 2:16-17)? How did Joel's prophecy find fulfillment in a mixed Jewish-Gentile church (Rom. 10:12-13)?

## Sources for Additional Study

Finley, T. J. *Joel, Amos, Obadiah.* Chicago: Moody, 1990.

Garrett, D. A. *Hosea, Joel.* New American Commentary. Nashville: Broadman & Holman, 1997.

Hubbard, David Allan. *Joel & Amos: An Introduction and Commentary.* TOTC. Leicester: InterVarsity, 1989.

Patterson, R. D. "Joel." *Expositor's Bible Commentary.* Grand Rapids: Zondervan, 1985.

# AMOS

A mos prophesied slightly earlier than Hosea, during the prosperous reigns of Jeroboam II in Israel (see introduction to Hosea) and Uzziah in Judah (792 to 767 B.C. with his father Amaziah, then alone until 740 B.C.). Since Amos mentions no other kings in 1:1, perhaps he prophesied only during their overlapping reigns, from 767 to 753 B.C. Amos was from Tekoa in Judah, five miles southeast of Bethlehem, but God called him to proclaim His word in Israel, the Northern Kingdom. Amos was not a professional prophet but by trade was a "shepherd" and grower of sycamore-figs, a fruit fed to livestock and eaten by the poor (1:1; 7:14). Although the term "shepherd" *(noqed)* is applied to the king of Moab in 2 Kings 3:4, we are not sure whether Amos was a prosperous rancher or just a hired worker (note the expression "tending the flock" in 7:15).

**Message and Purpose.** Indictment: Israel was oppressing the poor, denying them justice out of greed and self-indulgence. It was the kind of society where success owed much to knowing when to keep one's mouth shut. It "encouraged wrongdoing and discouraged standing for principle. When grace transforms a person it brings this aspect of life into focus: a determination to create a society in which righteousness dwells" (Motyer). Israel was at the same time practicing empty religion, mixing idolatry with worship in the Lord's name. A veneer of law and piety covered a core of injustice that the establishment seemed to accept.

*Instruction:* Israel is told to delight in and seek the Lord only and as a corollary to strive for justice, which is "reparation for the defrauded, fairness for the less fortunate, and dignity and compassion for the needy" (Finley).

*Judgment:* Failure to respond would bring destruction, death, and exile.

*Hope:* Israel should respond with gratitude to God's election, redemption, and care of them in the past. God also promised to preserve a remnant and to reestablish the nation in the land with the messianic ruler and to bring them prosperity.

**Structure.** Amos's book comprises three main sections plus an initial introduction (1:1-3a) and a concluding message of restoration (9:11-15). There are eight oracles against the nations in the first main section (1:3b-2:16), each beginning with "This is what the LORD says." The first three of the five sermons in the second main section (3:1–6:14) are introduced by calls to "hear," and the last two by expressions of "woe." The five visions in the third main section (7:1–9:10) each begin with "This is what [the Sovereign LORD/he] showed me," except for the last, which is a theophany (appearance of God). It begins "I saw the LORD." The third vision is followed by a brief narrative (7:10-17) that dramatizes its message.

I. The Prophecy (1:1-3a)
II. Oracles against Nations (1:3b–2:16)
III. Five Sermons (3:1–6:14)
IV. Five Visions (7:1–9:10)
V. Prophecy of Restoration (9:11-15)

## THE PROPHECY (1:1-3A)

This book conveys the words of Amos, which are at the same time the word of the Lord. Although not all vision, it was all "seen," in that it was received from the

Lord, not invented by Amos (see 2 Pet. 1:20-21).

Words of judgment are much more prominent in Amos than words of hope (see 2:13; 4:11; 6:11; 8:8; 9:1,5). Perhaps this explains the ominous reference to the earthquake in 1:1. The thematic synopsis of the book in 1:2 speaks of God "roar[ing]" from Zion like a terrifying beast of prey (see 3:8). Receiving God's word in faith involves believing that the Lord is an awesome and holy God who is prepared to punish wickedness with intense power. He hates sin, especially when it defiles His people. "The people of God had fallen asleep in the comfort of the privileges of salvation and needed to be jolted into the awareness that the only assured certainty of the possession of those privileges was the evidence of a life committed without reserve to being holy as their Saviour God is holy" (J. A. Motyer).

The earthquake mentioned here apparently coincided with the beginning of Amos's ministry and probably provided the initial object lesson for his messages. It must have been especially severe, since it is mentioned with recollections of terror over two hundred years later in Zechariah 14:5. In his excavations at Hazor, Y. Yadin found evidence of an earthquake during that period.

## ORACLES AGAINST NATIONS (1:3b–2:16)

The order of these oracles is significant. The first four form an X with Israel in the center, as if the nation is in God's crosshairs (northeast, southwest, northwest, southeast). The last four were all related to Israel: Edom, Ammon, and Moab as "cousins," then Judah even closer as "brother." Israel would surely have enjoyed hearing of God's displeasure with and plans to judge these other nations. But each time they applauded

they were signing their names to their own judgment decree, tightening the noose imperceptibly around their necks, because they were guilty of the same things.

If these nations (besides Judah) who did not have God's word were guilty before God, far more so were Judah and Israel (see 2:4,11-12). Nothing the nations had done compared with possessing the revelation of God and ignoring it. Rather than presuming on God's favor, they were to have a higher standard of righteousness. In some cases the secret of strength is mobility and flexibility. But the secret of a Christian's life is our connection with God through the immovable foundation of divine truth. When we have left that, we have left our anchor and refuge for castles in the clouds and are destined for destruction.

Like Romans 1:18-32 and 2:14-15, these chapters indicate that "the whole world is under divine observation, subservient to divine assessment and subdued without refuge before divine judgment" (Motyer). The basis for judgment of the foreign nations here is not their erroneous religious beliefs and practices. Rather, they are condemned for such things as barbarity, slave trading, promise-breaking, persistent hatred, and atrocities against the helpless (see Rev. 20:12-13). The refrain, "for three sins of … even for four," implies that God's patience was at an end and their sinfulness was complete (three plus four, seven, symbolizing completeness).

Seven sins of Israel are condemned in 2:6-8. According to 2:9-11, Israel was committing the same sins for which God had removed the Amorites from the land. They had forgotten that all they had was by His grace. So for their faithless rejection of the Lord, the Lord declared a series of seven devastating judgments against them that amounted to their being crushed.

## FIVE SERMONS (3:1–6:14)

The first sermon threatens imminent punishment, then details Israel's sins and punishment. In a striking use of the word "therefore" in verse 2, the Lords grounds His punishment in His relationship with Israel, which demanded gratitude and loyalty. The illustration in verses 3-6 stresses the unbroken connection between sin and punishment. Israel had become so expert in violence and oppression (extortion, robbery, bribery) that they were enslaved to sin and could give lessons to the Egyptians and Philistines. Thus God would so ruin them that only fragments of their luxuriant lifestyle would remain, only enough to "identify the victim."

The second sermon in 4:1-13 comprises a series of seven judgment oracles (each ending with "declares the LORD"; vv. 1-11), a concluding call to "meet your God," and a doxology (v. 13). The first oracle deals with how Israel treated the poor (see Exod. 23:3,6; Lev. 19:15; 25:35; Deut. 15:4-11), the second with apostate, hypocritical worship (4:4-5), and the last five with past judgments God had sent against Israel in vain. The doxology in 4:13 is the first of three in Amos (see 5:8-9; 9:5-6), which some believe were fragments of ancient hymns. As one scholar explains, "The theological contribution these doxologies of Amos make is immense. They affirm that [the Lord] is the all-powerful Creator who is above any might or power from any source, human or other. [He] is the only and unique Protector" (Hasel). Another scholar says of such a God, "Every high and stable thing crumbles beneath him. Men feel secure so long as God remains in heaven, but when He comes to earth in judgment they are gripped by the terrifying realization that they must meet the

holy God in person. If men would tremble before God, instead of before each other, they would have nothing to fear" (Waltke). Amos was one who feared only God (see 7:10-17).

The third sermon (5:1-17), comprised of lament and exhortation, is the structural-thematic center of Amos. Here is Amos's primary message. First, verses 1-2 introduce this lament/funeral dirge. Israel is like a virgin, at one time young, pure, full of life and potential, who was tragically "cut down in her prime" due to her own folly (but see Jer. 31:1-6,21). The remainder of the sermon uses a recurring or concentric structure. A lament of Israel's decimation appears in verse 3 and again in verses 16-17 ("therefore" in v. 16 points back to the accusations). An appeal to repent comes in verses 4-6 ("seek Me/the LORD and live") and again in verses 14-15 ("seek good that you may live"). One who seeks the Lord, that is, who continually endeavors to maintain and deepen his fellowship with the Lord, will strive to see good prevail over evil in the lives of his fellow human beings. Seeking God and seeking good are the two dimensions of biblical religion.

An accusation unfolds in verse 7 (Israel was perverting justice and righteousness) and again in verses 10-13 (they were opposing the truth). At the heart or center of the structure stands the doxology, which praises the Lord's power to create and destroy, to turn blessing into disaster or vice versa (vv. 8-9; see Jer. 10:10-13). The living God will not allow His "worshipers" to continue coming together in His name, singing, and going away unchanged (see James 1:22-27). He despises a religion that leaves life untouched.

The fourth sermon extends the portions lament of the previous one. The day of the Lord will bring calamity to Israel from which no one can escape. Amos corrected the view that God's covenant assured Israel of God's blessing even when they were unfaithful to Him. The Lord despises religious activity in His name that perverts true worship and neglects righteousness. Integrity and compassion were to be just as much a part of true worship as singing and sacrifice.

In the fifth sermon Amos condemned Israel's arrogance, decadence, complacent self-indulgence, and perversion of justice. To combat their false sense of security, he proclaimed the certainty of utter defeat, destruction, and exile.

## FIVE VISIONS (7:1–9:10)

The first two visions (locusts and drought, i.e., "fire") describe events that proclaim God's patience and mercy. The next two visions (the plumb line and the fruit basket) employ wordplay. Their point is that the time for God's patience and mercy is ended; Israel's apostate sanctuaries will be destroyed, and Jeroboam's dynasty would be terminated.

The third vision is dramatized and justified by an explanatory narrative. It recounts an encounter between Amos and Amaziah, the priest at Bethel, and shows that Israel's royal house and religious establishment had rejected God's word. The issue was who had authority at Bethel: Jeroboam, Amaziah, Amos, or God? Amaziah accused Amos of treason, disregarding his claims to be speaking on divine authority. He regarded Amos as a personal and political enemy of the state and of the religious establishment. It is relatively common for the establishment to charge that those confronting them with God's word are "politically" motivated, only interested in power and personal gain. Amaziah might have been surprised to hear Amos praying for Israel in 7:2,5.

The fourth vision of Israel's end is also followed by an explanation that Israel's lack of justice was the reason they were about to meet their end. This day will be a time of terror and great sorrow, for Israel will be abandoned by God.

In the final (and climactic) vision Amos saw the Lord standing beside this counterfeit altar of the counterfeit religion that was propping up the counterfeit kingdom of Jeroboam (see 1 Kgs. 12:25–13:3). He appeared holding a sword as did the "commander of the Lord's army" that Joshua encountered (Josh. 5:13-15). But the enemy against whom He was about to take vengeance was His own people, Israel, who were using a cloak of religion to hide a lifestyle of wickedness.

Concluding this section is a final doxology and judgment oracle. As in the previous doxologies (4:13; 5:8-9), this one defines more exactly and with terror the One just described who is coming in judgment. The point of the final judgment oracle is that Israel was no different from the other nations in one respect—that God would not tolerate their unrighteousness.

## PROPHECY OF RESTORATION (9:11-15)

This final salvation oracle collects and combines earlier trickles and streams of redemptive clues and messages (3:12; 4:6-12; 5:3,4,6,14-15; 7:1-6; 9:8-9) into a great river of celebration. "David's fallen tent" refers to the kingdom promised to David that had suffered years of disobedience and judgment (see 2 Sam. 7:5-16; Isa. 1:8-9; 9:6-7; 16:5; Jer. 23:5; 33:15-17; Ezek. 34:23-24; 37:24-25; Hos. 3:5; Zech. 12:8–13:1; Luke 1:32). A reuniting of Northern and Southern Kingdoms is implied.

"Possess the remnant of Edom" means that the Gentiles (represented by Israel's archenemy, Edom) will be included in God's people. James makes this point from the verse in Acts 15:7-12 (although citing the Septuagint). He applies this eschatological passage to the present, showing that what will ultimately be completely fulfilled in the future has begun to be fulfilled even now (see Acts 15:13-19).

**Theological and Ethical Significance.** The Book of Amos speaks to at least four major issues:

1. *God's relationship to the world.* Not just believers but the entire world is accountable to God. How should a Christian regard the rampant violence, hatred, greed, injustice, and sexual promiscuity in the world? Not with fear and anxiety, because we know of God's sovereign supervision. Not with disdain or arrogance, because we know we stand only by God's grace. Not with callousness or disregard, because we know how God despises all evil.

2. *God's relationship to His people.* If God despises sin among unbelievers, how much more does He hate it in His people? He especially hates acts of worship that are only covers for lives of wickedness.

3. *The nature of God.* Biblical faith may be regarded as "the tension between opposite feelings of fear and longing; at its highest level religion is love accompanied by a humble sense of inferiority, reverent trust in an immensely powerful and fearful deity, who is at the same time just and benevolent" (R. H. Pfeiffer). The God of Amos and of the Bible maintains perfect righteousness with perfect love. He must be approached with fear and humility but also with confidence and devotion.

4. *The future.* God has assured us that not only do believers in Christ, whether Jew or Gentile, have a future, but also the world has a future. Sin will not be allowed to destroy ultimately what God has created, but God's redemptive power will prevail.

### Questions for Reflection

1. What really pleases God? Are our religious priorities God's priorities?

2. What does Amos teach about the responsibilities of nations before God? How is our nation unjust? How can we work to change it?

3. How just are we in our day-to-day dealings with others?

### Sources for Additional Study

Cohen, G. G. and H. R. Vandermey. *Hosea/Joel.* Chicago: Moody, 1981.

Finley, T. J. *Joel, Amos, Obadiah.* Chicago: Moody, 1990.

Hubbard, D. A. *Joel & Amos: An Introduction and Commentary.* Downers Grove: InterVarsity, 1989.

Motyer, J. A. *The Day of the Lion: The Message of Amos. The Bible Speaks Today.* Downers Grove: InterVarsity, 1974.

Smith, B. K. and F. S. Page. *Amos, Obadiah, Jonah.* New American Commentary. Nashville: Broadman & Holman, 1995.

Smith, G. V. *Amos: A Commentary.* Grand Rapids: Zondervan, 1989.

# OBADIAH

Obadiah is the shortest book in the Old Testament. Like Nahum, which is addressed to Assyria, it is addressed not to Israel but to a foreign people, Edom. The land of Edom was a small mountainous area east of the Dead Sea. Its people were descendants of Esau (Gen. 36).

Nothing is known about the author outside this book. No explicit information is given about the time of writing, but most consider that Obadiah 10–14 is best explained against the background of the fall of Jerusalem to the Babylonians in 586 B.C. Since the book prophesies the desolation of Edom, an event which probably occurred late in the sixth century B.C., Obadiah would have been written about the middle of that century.

Edom was noted in the Bible for its pride, treachery, greed, and violence (2 Chr. 20:10,11; 25:14,20; Jer. 49:16; Amos 1:9,11; Obad. 3). Conflict between Israel and Edom was foreshadowed by conflict between the peoples' progenitors, Jacob and Esau (Gen. 25:21-34; 27:34-45). The incident that initiated and fed the conflict occurred on Israel's journey from Egypt to Canaan (Num. 20:14-21). Thus, Edom and Israel fought through most of their history (1 Sam. 14:47; 2 Sam. 8:14; 2 Kgs. 8:20-22; 14:7). But Edom made themselves especially odious to the Jews when Babylon conquered and plundered Jerusalem. When Nebuchadnezzar's forces closed in on Jerusalem and the king of Judah attempted to flee (2 Kgs. 25:3-7), Edom apparently helped capture him. As a reward the Edomites were allowed to participate in the sack of Jerusalem (Ps. 137:7; Ezek. 25:12; 35:15; 36:5; Joel 3:19; Obad. 10–14).

In fulfillment of prophecy (Isa. 34:5-7; Jer. 49:7-22; Lam. 4:21; Ezek. 25:12-14; 35:1-15; Amos 1:11-12; and Obadiah) God devastated Edom in judgment for their hatred and treachery. They were conquered and driven from their homeland by the Nabatean Arabs. By the time of Malachi (probably early fifth century) their cities had become ghost towns populated only by desert creatures (Mal 1:3-4). More than just Israel's archenemy, Edom became a symbol of all the arrogant nations who oppose God and will meet destruction on the day of the Lord (Isa. 34:5-7; 63:1-6; Jer. 49:17-18; Ezek 36:5; Mal. 1:4; Pss. 60:8; 83:6). In postbiblical Jewish writings Edom was used as a symbol for Rome.

***Message and Purpose.*** Interpreting Obadiah is complicated by its form as a prophetic speech to Edom, although all agree that the message was actually intended for and delivered in Israel. The purpose for the book is not stated but must be inferred from the historical and canonical situation. The prophecy was likely delivered to the Jewish survivors of Jerusalem's destruction. It should have been a great encouragement to know that Edom's treachery against them would not go unpunished. In fact, all the enemies of God and His people would receive justice. Also, what seemed to be the end for God's people would not be the end after all.

On the surface Obadiah offers an indictment of Edom's pride (v. 3) and violence against their brother (vv. 10a,11). The only instruction is the series of eight negative commands (prohibitions) in verses 12-14, which are ironic since they involve actions that have already occurred. They are a rhetorical way of citing Edom's actions as specific violations of God's will. Most of the book concerns God's future judgment against Edom and the rebellious nations they represent (vv. 1-2,4-9,15-21). Edom and the nations are offered no hope; there will be "no survivors" (v. 18). Yet one may infer that deliverance could be theirs if they sought refuge on Mount Zion and in the house of Jacob (v. 17).

**Structure.** The first section (vv. 1-9) announces Edom's doom. The heart of the section is verses 2-4, elaborated in verses 5-7, and concluded in verses 8-9. The second section (vv. 10-14) develops the Lord's accusation against Edom, especially in verses 12-14. The final section (vv. 15-21) focuses on universal judgment associated with the day of the Lord.

I. Edom's Judgment (vv. 1-9)

II. Edom's Sin (vv. 10-14)

III. Edom's Judgment (vv. 15-21)

### EDOM'S JUDGMENT (VV. 1-9)

Obadiah reports that the Lord, who supervises the affairs of the world, is summoning the nations to attack Edom and puncture their inflated pride. Of course, the people who answered God's call did not realize they were serving the God of Israel.

Edom's trust in the topography of their land was misplaced. The extent of their devastation will be comparable to the height of their arrogance. Nothing will remain hidden from the invaders. Even Edom's allies and their own kinsmen will betray them and contribute to their downfall; such is the result of Edom's own treachery against Judah (v. 10). But their real enemy was the Lord.

### EDOM'S SIN (VV. 10-14)

Edom is charged here with violence against their brother (the oldest and one of the most heinous crimes; Gen. 4:1-15). The crime was heinous because Judah was being assaulted at the time by foreigners. Human decency, besides Mosaic law, would have demanded that Edom help their kinsmen rather than gloating over and contributing to their pain. In verses 12-14 the charges are rhetorically expressed as warnings not to do what they had done. The principle of retribution stated in verse 15 ("As you have done, it will be done to you") is implied by using the same Hebrew verb in verses 10 ("you will be *destroyed*") and 14 ("[you] *cut down* their fugitives"). "When Edom looked upon Judah's disaster, they were in effect looking into a mirror" (B. K. Smith).

### EDOM'S JUDGMENT (VV. 15-21)

God's judgment against Edom is based on the fact that all the nations who oppose God and His people will be punished on the day of the Lord. Then "the house of Jacob" will take possession of all that belonged to them (see Amos 9:12). This will fulfill and extend God's promise to Israel before the conquest. It will happen not because of Israel's faithfulness but because of the Lord's (Deut. 1:8,21; 2:5; 9:4-6; 30:4-7). Security will be found not in Edom's mountains but in the Lord's Mount Zion (see Mic. 4:7).

**Theological and Ethical Significance.** Obadiah's prophecy declares that God's judgment not just on Edom but on all God's enemies will come on "the day of the Lord" (see Ps. 2). On that day God will also set up the "kingdom that will never be destroyed" (Dan. 2:44). One whose trust is in anything but the Lord is never secure. All who consider themselves great can be sure that the Lord will someday bring them down (see 1 Sam. 2:3-10; Prov. 16:18; Isa. 26:5; Dan. 5:19-23; Jas. 4:6; 1 Pet. 5:5). In particular, the Lord holds accountable those who take advantage of others in their distress.

## Question for Reflection

What is our response when others take advantage of our misfortune? Do we trust God to be just, or do we take matters into our own hands?

## Sources for Further Study

Armerding, C. E. "Obadiah." *Expositor's Bible Commentary*. Grand Rapids: Zondervan, 1985.

Baker, D. W. *Obadiah: An Introduction and Commentary*. Tyndale Old Testament Commentaries. Downers Grove: InterVarsity, 1988.

Finley, T. J. *Joel, Amos, Obadiah*. Chicago: Moody, 1990.

Smith, B. K. and F. S. Page. *Amos, Obadiah, Jonah*. New American Commentary. Nashville: Broadman & Holman, 1995.

Watts, J. D. W. *Obadiah*. Winona Lake, Ind.: Alpha, 1981.

# JONAH

Jonah ben Amittai was a prophet of Israel from Gath Hepher, a village near Nazareth. His book is unique among the Prophets in that it is almost entirely narrative. It recounts how Jonah learned that God was much bigger than he had thought, especially in the extent of His power and His compassion.

The major power in the middle East at that time was Assyria, whose capital was Nineveh. Since the ninth century B.C. the Assyrians had been sending savage military expeditions west into Syria-Palestine (see the feature article in the section on Isaiah). When Jonah prophesied in the early eighth century B.C., Assyria was in a weakened state, making possible the expansion of Jeroboam II in Samaria and Uzziah in Judah (see introductions to Hosea and Amos). God had earlier given Jonah the privilege of delivering the good news that Israel would experience a time of safety and prosperity (2 Kgs. 14:25).

He and all Israel would have been glad if Assyria had continued to disintegrate. But they regained power in the later eighth century, conquered Syria-Palestine again, and in 722 B.C. conquered Samaria and deported its citizens. Jonah was not pleased when God commanded him to go to Nineveh and preach repentance. They worshiped the vicious god Ashur and a multitude of other gods and goddesses. Their brutality and cruelty was legendary. They were known to impale their enemies on stakes in front of their towns and hang their heads from trees in the king's gardens. They also tortured their captives—men, women, or children—by hacking off noses, ears, or fingers, gouging out their eyes, or tearing off their lips and hands. They reportedly covered the city wall with the skins of their victims. Rebellious subjects would be massacred by the hundreds, sometimes burned at the stake. Then their skulls would be placed in great piles by the roadside as a warning to others. Jonah decided that he would rather quit than preach to such people.

Many have regarded Jonah as a parable or didactic fiction, as if factual history were ruled out by literary artistry or the recounting of miraculous events. If this narrative, however, whose form bears at every point the mark of a historical account, were judged unhistorical on either of these bases, then most of the Bible would have to be so categorized. It is pointless to ask whether Jonah really could have been swallowed by a great fish without also asking whether God really could communicate with a prophet. Every aspect of man's encounter with God is miraculous. Jonah is clearly didactic, but it is not presented as fiction or interpreted as such in the New Testament (see Matt. 12:40-41).

***Message and Purpose.*** Jonah is the story of how God taught a lesson to a narrow-minded, sinful prophet. When Jonah refused to go preach in Nineveh and God retrieved him and mercifully delivered him, Jonah was thankful. But when Jonah preached in Nineveh and they repented and were mercifully spared, Jonah was angry, for which God taught him a lesson.

The Book of Jonah ends with an unanswered divine question regarding compassion, suggesting to the reader that Jonah repented and inviting the reader to do the same. Thus, Jonah's overall purpose is to stir up compassion in God's people. God is concerned for all human beings (John 1:7; 1 Tim. 2:1-6; 2 Pet. 3:9) and has the right to show mercy to whomever He wills (Exod. 33:19; Rom. 9:15).

**Structure.** The book has been called "a masterpiece of rhetoric" and a "model of literary artistry, marked by symmetry and balance." Its four chapters divide into two halves by commands from the Lord in 1:1-2 and 3:1-2 to go preach in Nineveh. The first time Jonah fled (1:3), and the second time he obeyed (3:3). Each half begins with an introduction (1:1-3; 3:1-4) and includes two episodes. In the first episode of each half, Jonah encounters a group of pagans, the sailors (1:4-16) and the Ninevites (3:5-10). Each group surpasses Jonah in sensitivity to the Lord's will. The second and climactic episode of each half finds Jonah talking with God (2:1-11; 4:1-11).

I. Jonah's Disobedience (1:1–2:10)

II. Jonah's Obedience (3:1–4:11)

## JONAH FLEES (1:1-16)

To avoid his divine assignment Jonah tried to get as far away from Nineveh as possible. Nineveh was about five hundred miles to the east, so he headed for Tarshish, probably what is now Spain, the farthest western location he knew, about two thousand miles. But God sent a storm and then a great fish to turn Jonah around. The sailors showed more compassion for Jonah than Jonah showed for Nineveh.

## JONAH PRAYS (1:17–2:10)

Jonah, having been thrown overboard, thought his life was over. Suddenly he found himself alive inside a huge fish. The psalm of prayer Jonah uttered was an expression of thanks to God for saving his life. For his own deliverance Jonah was thankful, but Jonah would show a different attitude toward Nineveh's deliv-

erance. In view of his rebellion in chapter 1, his anger in chapter 4, and the pagan sailors' response to God in 1:14-16, Jonah's vow of thanks in 2:8-9 sounds rather self-serving. Also, there is no confession of sin or expression of repentance in Jonah's prayer.

The "three days and three nights" of 1:17 alluded to the notion popular at that time that the journey to the land of the dead *(sheol)* took that long. So Jonah's retrieval from the fish was like a retrieval from death (Matt. 12:39-40). The fish very likely dropped Jonah off at Joppa, where he had started.

## JONAH PREACHES (3:1-10)

Perhaps about a month later, Jonah arrived in the great city of Nineveh ("a very important city" is literally "a city great to God"). After Jonah preached for only a day rather than the expected three days, the people repented. The message God gave Jonah to preach did not explicitly call for their repentance. Rather, it told the Ninevites that they had angered Jonah's God and that punishment was on the way. The Ninevites did not presume that God could be appeased but repented in humility, hoping that "God may yet relent" (3:9; see 1:6), which He did. That God's judgment message was conditional is clear from His sending the prophet, giving them forty days' warning, and postponing Nineveh's destruction (see Jer. 18:7-10).

## JONAH FUMES (4:1-11)

Jonah despised the Ninevites so much that he would rather die than live, knowing he helped them escape destruction. Still hoping God would give Nineveh what they deserved, Jonah waited and watched. Through the incident of the plant and the worm (sent by God like the wind and the fish in chap. 1), the Lord chided Jonah for his double standard. Jonah was concerned for the transitory plant that gave him shade but not for the 120,000 people of Nineveh who despite their limited knowledge had trusted God.

*Theological and Ethical Significance.* God is sovereign over the forces of nature and the affairs of men. God's favor is always by grace; it is never deserved. His mercy is His to give, and without it we are all corrupt and deservedly condemned. Joy is the appropriate response when God lavishes His grace on the vilest of sinners who put their trust in Him (see Acts 10:34-35). God's servants should value the human beings whom He created and seek their salvation. We should also acknowledge God's authority to do what He pleases.

## Questions for Reflection

1. What does God desire for all the peoples of the world?

2. How do we seek to avoid God's command to share our faith with others?

3. How does prejudice compromise our Christian testimony? How do we begrudge God's love for others?

## Sources for Further Study

Alexander, T. D. *Jonah: An Introduction and Commentary.* Tyndale Old Testament Commentaries. Downers Grove: InterVarsity, 1988.

Ellison, H. L. "Jonah." *Expositor's Bible Commentary.* Grand Rapids: Zondervan, 1985.

Gaebelein, F. E. *Four Minor Prophets: Obadiah, Jonah, Habakkuk, and Haggai.* Chicago: Moody, 1977.

Smith, B. K. and F. S. Page. *Amos, Obadiah, Jonah.* New American Commentary. Nashville: Broadman & Holman, 1995.

Walton, J. *Jonah.* Bible Study Commentary. Grand Rapids: Zondervan, 1982.

# MICAH

Bible students often pay too much attention to the supposed meanings of biblical names. Micah's name, however, which means "Who is like the LORD?" foreshadows a crucial question in the climactic final chapter (7:18): "Who is a God like you, who pardons sin and forgives the transgression of the remnant of his inheritance?"

Yet Micah is noted as a preacher of judgment (unlike the false prophets who sought to ingratiate themselves to the rich with words of peace; see 2:6-7,11; 3:5-11). Like Jonah, Micah appears as a prophet outside the book bearing his name. He even has the distinction of being the only prophet quoted by name by another prophet (Jer. 26:18-19, quoting Mic. 1:14). He is cited there as prophesying calamity to King Hezekiah and all Judah; but his words inspired repentance and resulted in God's postponing judgment (see 2 Chr. 29:5-11; 32:24-26).

Micah was from Moresheth Gath in Judah (see 1:14), about twenty-five miles southwest of Jerusalem near the Philistine city of Gath. A contemporary of Isaiah, he prophesied during the reigns of Jotham, Ahaz, and Hezekiah (1:1), who ruled Judah from about 740 (King Uzziah died that year, but Jotham his son had co-reigned with him for about ten years) to 686 B.C. Between 740 and 700 the Assyrians (mentioned in Mic. 5:6 and 7:12) invaded Palestine repeatedly. In 734 northern Israel and Judah lost their independence and became vassals to Assyria. In 722 Samaria was conquered and made an Assyrian province with most of its population being sent into exile. In 716–715 Assyria put down a

Philistine rebellion and laid a punishing fine on Hezekiah's Jerusalem. In 701 B.C. the Assyrians laid siege to Jerusalem, only relenting at the last minute, placing a heavy fine on the city rather than destroying it. This long history of life-threatening conflict with Assyria served as the background for Micah's messages.

***Message and Purpose.*** Although Micah was a prophet of Judah, he preached also to Samaria (1:1) and used the term "Israel" or "Jacob" to refer to both kingdoms as one.

*Indictment:* Israel was guilty of rebellious acts of idolatry. Their leaders—including judges, priests, and false prophets—perverted justice to prey upon the people, by extorting property and depriving women and children of their homes. They were self-serving and used violence when necessary to get what they wanted. Yet they maintained a facade of religion through ritual in the Lord's name.

*Instruction:* Just as Joel contains no explicit indictment message, so Micah contains no explicit instruction message. Nevertheless, instruction may be found in two ways. First, just as the indictment message is furnished from the covenant context of Joel, so Micah's instruction message is furnished: "Return to the LORD your God and obey him with all your heart and with all your soul" (Deut. 30:2,10; 4:29-30; Lev. 26:40-45; 2 Chr. 7:14). Second, Micah's expression of confidence in 7:7 may be intended as a form of exhortation: "But as for me, I watch in hope for the LORD, I wait for God my Savior; my God will hear me." After God's judgment had removed from

Israel every reason for arrogance, the believing remnant should watch prayerfully for the Lord's deliverance, trusting in His promises. Even in the midst of judgment Israel should not simply cry out in pain but should trust His wisdom and power and, like a woman in labor, should look for His purposes to be accomplished (4:9-10).

*Judgment:* As God made Samaria a "heap of rubble" during Micah's ministry, so He would bring destruction on Judah, bringing against them all the curses of the law (failure, frustration, death, destruction, derision) and would eventually carry them into exile to Babylon.

*Hope:* The Lord promises to gather His remnant as a shepherd gathers His sheep and lead them to freedom (2:12-13). He will forgive His people and vindicate them by vanquishing the defiant nations. He will then establish justice, peace, security, and compassion among His people through a Messianic shepherd/ruler. He will rebuild Zion and make His house into a place of worship for all the nations.

**Structure.** Individual messages, though delivered at various times, have been woven into a coherent whole. Micah has three parts, chapters 1-2; 3-5; and 6–7, each moving from judgment to deliverance. All three maintain a balanced message to both the Northern and Southern Kingdoms. The third part is the most prominent. Whereas the first two parts begin with calls to hear the prophet, the third begins with a call to hear the Lord. The third also has the most developed message of hope.

I. From Disaster to Deliverance (1:1–2:13)

II. From Predators to Shepherd (3:1–5:15)

III. From Darkness to Light (6:1–7:20)

## FROM DISASTER TO DELIVERANCE (1:1–2:13)

God's destruction of Israel for their idolatry should have been a sign to Judah, and the destruction of both should be a sign to all nations that a time of retribution is coming. Micah grieves over the terrible calamity coming upon Judah for their rebellion, a punishment which includes the foreign exile of some of their inhabitants. Sennacherib's devastation of Judah in 701 B.C. was extensive, especially at Lachish, where the idolatry of Samaria first obtained a foothold in Judah. Excavations there reveal a pit into which the Assyrians dumped about fifteen hundred bodies together with pig remains and other trash. The devastation reached up to Jerusalem's "gate," but the city was left undamaged (2 Kgs. 18:13-16; 19:31-37).

Micah 2:1-11 condemns those who hatched and carried out unscrupulous plots to steal houses and ancestral lands by perverting justice. The unavoidable penalty would be calamity, involving the loss of all their land, and more importantly exclusion of the guilty from the future assembly of God's redeemed people. Those wanting to hide or justify their wicked behavior tried to silence Micah and other true prophets. But those who evicted the helpless will be evicted by the Lord.

Micah 2:12-13 promises that Israel's divine Shepherd-King will gather and protect His people and then lead them to freedom. This probably refers most immediately to the Lord's deliverance of Jerusalem from Sennacherib (see 2 Kgs. 19:31).

## FROM PREDATORS TO SHEPHERD (3:1–5:15)

This section begins with denunciations of Israel's corrupt leaders, who preyed upon God's people. Pleas for God's aid will be of no help to them. Judges, priests, and prophets abandoned their responsibility to the truth and used their positions for personal gain. Micah, however, strengthened by God's Spirit, declared the truth, which included destruction and the ultimate darkness and silence at God's departure from them.

Juxtaposed to the message of corruption and doom in chapter 3 is the message of glorious exaltation in chapters 4–5. But even there deliverance in the near or distant future alternates with the trials of Israel's present situation. First is the promise that the Lord Himself will someday teach truth and judge righteously on the earth (see Heb. 12:22-24). Here is a picture of the restored temple on Zion to which people from many nations will come to learn of God's ways and to hear His word (see Ps. 86:9; Isa. 2:1-4; 56:6-8; 60; 66:18-21; Zech. 8:20-23; John 12:32; Rev. 21). It heralds a time of peace and security. The promise to assemble the lame, the outcast, and the afflicted uses a common symbol for the return of the exiles (Isa. 35:6; Jer. 31:8; Zeph. 3:19; Matt. 11:5; Luke 14:21). As wonderful as was the restoration led by Zerubbabel, Ezra, and Nehemiah, it fell far short of the glory yet to be accomplished at the Lord's return.

Before this restoration Jerusalem's people will suffer greatly—invasion and even exile to Babylon (4:10). But from defeat and devastation will come victory and liberation. Their divine "king" and "counselor" (4:9) remained in their midst even in exile, working out His plan (see Isa. 9:6; 28:29; Jer. 8:19). He was using empires to tear down and destroy Israel's corruption. God was also using the empires to build His new order for His people. For the new Israel to be created, the old Israel had to die. Israel's judgment was remedial. But just as God used the stubborn pride of the exodus pharaoh to

demonstrate His glory and at the same time bring judgment upon Egypt, so the nations' own pride would bring about their destruction (4:11-13; see Joel 3). Satan, too, out of pride and hatred of God, planned and executed his own downfall by inspiring the rejection and death of God's Son (1 Cor. 2:7-8).

Micah 5:1 returns to Sennacherib's siege of Jerusalem and his humiliation of King Hezekiah. Verse 3 moves further to the Babylonian exile and even until the coming of Messiah. But God was at work to turn humiliation into glorious victory through a Messianic ruler whose human origins (as far as deity is concerned He had no origin), coming not from proud Jerusalem but from insignificant Bethlehem (5:2; see Matt. 2:4-8), represented Israel's humiliation. "Bethlehem, too insignificant to be mentioned by the cartographer of the book of Joshua or in Micah's catalogue of Judah's cities of defense ..., is today incredibly the centre of pilgrimages from around the world and is universally renowned because Jesus Christ fulfilled this verse" (Waltke). It is a biblical principle, in fact, that exaltation by God must always be launched from humiliation (see 1 Cor. 1:18-31; Phil. 2:5-11).

As David's city, however (1 Sam. 17:12; Luke 2:4,11; John 7:42), Bethlehem also represented God's promise of a Davidic descendant whose throne and kingdom would be eternal and who would mediate God's blessings to all mankind (2 Sam. 7:16-19; Isa. 16:5; Jer. 33:17; Matt. 1:1; 21:9; Luke 1:32,69; Rev. 22:16). This may be the sense in which the ruler's "origins are from of old, from ancient times" (see Isa. 11:1). "David" came to be "theological shorthand for Israel's ideal future ruler" (Waltke; see Jer. 30:9; Ezek. 34:23-24; 37:24-25; Hos. 3:5).

According to 5:7-9 the presence of the remnant of God's people among the nations would bring salvation to some ("like dew" in v. 7) and judgment to others ("like a lion" in v. 8), depending upon how their witness would be received (see 2 Cor. 2:14-16). The initial "in that day" in 5:10 echoes similar phrases in 4:1 and 4:6 and refers to God's establishing the messianic kingdom. According to 5:10-15 He will purge and protect His people from reliance on military might, magic, and idolatry, and from fear of the nations.

## FROM DARKNESS TO LIGHT (6:1–7:20)

The final section begins with an indictment against Israel in the form of a lawsuit (6:1-8). Israel is charged with forgetting the Lord's righteous acts and so losing a sense of genuine devotion to Him. Although they tried to buy God's favor with ritual sacrifices, God's primary demand was for justice, mercy, and humble obedience (v. 8; see Isa. 5:7; Hos. 4:1; 6:6; 12:6; Amos 5:24). But Israel was guilty of doing the opposite. They perverted just standards and followed the standard of wicked Omri and Ahab. Their many crimes of commercial fraud and greed are declared to have brought upon Israel the covenant curses of disease, futility, destruction, and shame (see Lev. 26; Deut. 28).

In chapter 7 Micah again turns accusation and sentence into lament (vv. 1-6). One who hunts for integrity in Israel will return empty. The leaders care nothing for God and His covenant as they prey upon His people. A time of judgment would cause panic that would heighten people's selfish character so that even one's closest friend or family member cannot be trusted (see Isa. 3:4-7; Matt. 10:34-36). But in verse 7 Micah testifies to what the righteous remnant should do in the midst of God's judgment. They should resolve to pray and look expectantly for the Lord's deliverance that will be the fruit of His judgment (see Hab. 3:1-2).

The conclusion of Micah in 7:8-20 is a song of victory. It is written from the perspective of God's city, Jerusalem, and its people as they recover from judgment. It celebrates finding the light of the Lord's presence after experiencing the darkness. It also celebrates vindication before the nations who have proudly opposed God and anticipates their submission to Him. It acknowledges the justice of God's dealings with His people and expresses submission to the Lord's will as well as confidence in His faithfulness. Finally, it rejoices in wonder at the Lord's compassionate pardon. Moses' Song of the Sea in Exodus 15 has much in common with Micah's victory song, especially Exodus 15:11— "Who among the gods is like you, O LORD? Who is like you—majestic in holiness, awesome in glory, working wonders?" As God hurled the Egyptians into the depths of the sea (Exod. 15:4-5; Neh. 9:11), so He hurls our sins.

***Theological and Ethical Significance.*** Micah calls attention to God's hatred of unscrupulous self-seeking leaders who use their positions for gain rather than for service. But his main message is that because of God's faithfulness and mercy the darkness of judgment will give way to the light of freedom and joy. Micah's prophecy calls upon God's people to confess their sin, repent, and receive whatever punishment may come from the hands of our gracious God. Whereas His discipline lasts but for a moment, His forgiveness and peace are forever (Ps. 30:5; Isa. 54:7-8).

## Questions for Reflection

1. What does God require of those committed to Him (see Mic. 6:8)? How do we shortchange God?

2. What does Micah teach about the responsible use of power (see Mic. 2:1; 3:1-3,9-12)?

3. What does Micah teach about the qualities of godly leadership (see Mic. 3:8)?

4. What does Micah teach about God's goals for history (see Mic. 4:1-4; 5:2-5)?

## Sources for Further Study

McComiskey, T. E. "Micah." *Expositor's Bible Commentary*. Grand Rapids: Zondervan, 1985.

Waltke, Bruce K. *Micah: An Introduction and Commentary*. Tyndale Old Testament Commentaries. Downers Grove: InterVarsity, 1988.

# NAHUM

The name Nahum means "comforted" (compare Nehemiah, "the Lord comforts"). The theme of his prophecy is the destruction of Nineveh, chief city of the Assyrians, one of Israel's perennial enemies. Nineveh's demise would have brought comfort to Judah and to all victims of Assyria's ruthless imperialism (see introduction to Jonah).

Nahum's association with the village Elkosh (1:1) tells us little about him because its location is uncertain. Although the name Capernaum may come from the Hebrew for "village of Nahum," 1:15 may imply the prophet was from Judah, a likelihood supported by tradition. Some have suggested Nahum was a northern Israelite exile living in Assyria who sent his prophecy to Judah. The prophecy seems to have been delivered in writing rather than orally (the word "book" in 1:1 and the partial acrostic in 1:2-8), perhaps the reason we do not hear of his suffering for his anti-Assyrian ideas. One tradition even locates Elkosh in Assyria (modern Al Qosh, near ancient Nineveh in Iraq).

The prophecy may be dated with assurance before Nineveh fell to the Medes and Babylonians in 612 B.C., since the book is a prophecy of its destruction. Since Nahum assumes an apparently strong Assyrian empire that had Judah firmly in its grip (see 1:12-13), the time of writing was before that empire began to erode, as it did during the last decade of Ashurbanipal's reign (668–626 B.C.) and especially after his death. Perhaps signs could have been seen even earlier, because Ashurbanipal exhausted Assyrian resources quelling a long bloody revolt in Babylon that began in 652.

Nahum's prophecy must also be dated after the almost impregnable city of Thebes (i.e., Luxor, which had stood unviolated for one thousand years) was sacked by the Assyrians in 663 B.C., furnishing Nahum with an object lesson of Nineveh's own vulnerability (3:8-10). The effect of that illustration would have lessened over time, especially as Thebes began to be reestablished as a cultural center in Egypt (see Jer. 46:25; Ezek. 30:15-16). Manasseh, who ruled Judah from 687 to 642 B.C. (see 2 Kgs. 21:1-18), probably submitted to Assyrian sovereignty on the occasion of that Egyptian campaign. After a long career as one of Israel's most wicked and idolatrous rulers, he rebelled against Assyria, probably during the Babylonian revolt, and was taken captive to Babylon (likely just after the revolt was ended about 648 B.C.). There he repented of his rebelliousness, not only against Ashurbanipal but also against God, and was allowed to return to Jerusalem (2 Chr. 33:10-17). His son Amon (642–640) remained a faithful vassal of Assyria but not of the Lord (2 Kgs. 21:19-26). Following Amon's assassination his son Josiah became king at age eight, and at age twenty (about the time Ashurbanipal died) he began an extensive spiritual reformation of the land (2 Kgs. 22:1–23:30; 2 Chr. 34–35). He died in 609 B.C. trying to stop an Egyptian army from reinforcing what was left of the Assyrian army. It is reasonable to presume that Nahum wrote between 663 and 640 B.C., during Judah's fearful subjugation to Assyrian might.

***Message and Purpose.*** Nahum expresses judgment against God's enemies, specifically Nineveh. As such it may be contrasted usefully with Jonah, which also concerned a message to Nineveh. Jonah teaches that God's compassion was not to be limited to His covenant people but was available to all who would humble themselves before Him. Nahum, on the other hand, adds that any who oppose Him, whoever they are, will receive His wrath.

On the surface Nahum is a message to Nineveh of approaching wrath (as Obadiah is to Edom), frequently addressing them rhetorically. But it also speaks at several points to Judah, the actual audience, making it clear that, like Obadiah, the book is in fact a message of hope for Judah (see 1:12-13,15; 2:2). In judging His enemies God will deliver His people. Most Hebrews probably thought of Assyria as a limitless and invincible evil power. Nahum's book, like Daniel's, debunks the idea that any evil kingdom could stand before God or that any human institution is anything but transitory.

Like Micah, Nahum seems to lack a message of instruction. The "So what?" question is not explicitly answered. Yet it may be inferred from 1:12 and 1:15. God had been afflicting Judah for their sins (described in other prophetic books), often using Assyria to deter them from their wicked path (see Isa. 10:5-34). Nahum's message implies that God could remove His affliction if they would repent and that those who fear Him should persist in faithful obedience while awaiting that deliverance. Josiah may have been influenced by Nahum's prophecy. It was during the years of Josiah's reformation that Assyria began to deteriorate and eventually fell. But Nahum's message was even more that when Judah was delivered from Assyrian slavery, they should celebrate with genuine acts of thanksgiving and worship to the Lord (1:15). Although on the surface 1:15 instructs Judah to "celebrate your festivals ... and fulfill your vows," the context leads us to interpret this primarily as a way of stressing Nahum's message of salvation for Judah. But even though the main point is that Judah would again have reason to celebrate, there may be also an implied warning about how they should respond to the deliverance when it came. We know, however, that after Nineveh's fall in 612 and Josiah's death in 609, Judah returned to their wicked ways (2 Kgs. 23:30-37). Then God raised Babylon to afflict and eventually destroy Judah as a nation (2 Kgs. 24:1ff.). Although the Lord "cares for those who trust in him" (1:7), He "will not leave the guilty unpunished" (1:3).

The reason Assyria would receive the Lord's wrath was that they were His enemies (1:2,8), who plotted against Him (1:9,11) in that they opposed and cruelly oppressed the Lord's people (1:13,15; 2:2), just as they preyed on all the nations (2:12-3:1,4,10,19). Like prostitutes and sorceresses they took pride in their beauty and peddled corruption out of lust for money, power, and pleasure (3:4; Ezek. 16:15; 23:1-21; Rev. 17:3-6). Neither was their idolatry overlooked in their judgment (1:14).

***Structure.*** Most agree that the Book of Nahum has a basic twofold structure, the first part concluding either with 1:11, 1:14, 1:15, or 2:2. The first part emphasizes the character of God and the deliverance of His people. The second part, which also has a twofold structure, vividly portrays the fall of Nineveh.

I. God's Vengeance and Refuge (1:1-15)

II. Nineveh's Fall (2:1–3:19)

## GOD'S VENGEANCE AND REFUGE (1:1-15)

Nahum's designation as "vision" prohibits its being dated near the time of Nineveh's fall as if the message were based on Nahum's political savvy and observation of current events. Despite the reference to Nineveh in 1:1, the book uses general references to God's enemies until Nineveh is specified in 2:8 (though NIV supplies it in 1:11,14; 2:1). Neither is God's people specified until Judah is addressed in 1:15 (again NIV adds it in v. 12). This suggests a general and even end-times application for this section. Such application is supported by references to God's sovereign control of nature in the battle song of verses 2-8. The Lord is portrayed as divine Warrior vanquishing the wicked. Emphasis is placed on God's character as His vengeance displays His jealousy and power, and His protection of the faithful displays His goodness and compassion. The Lord is like a husband defending his wife from those who would steal her affections.

Following the battle song, the prophet addresses God's enemies (plural "you" in Hebrew), who plot evil against the Lord (see Ps. 2:1). He addresses Judah in verses 12-13, underlining it by the introductory "This is what the LORD says." Then he addresses the contemptible enemy leader (i.e., the king of Assyria, singular "you") in verse 14. In contrast to the perpetual name promised King David in 2 Samuel 7, Nahum assures the enemy leader of a nameless destiny. This first section concludes in verse 15 with another message addressed to Judah, again emphasized by an initial "Look!" (see Isa. 52:7). It envisions a messenger appearing on the hill bringing news of victory over the enemy and resultant peace. The appropriate response would be jubilant thanksgiving and renewed devotion to the Lord. The assurance given Judah in verse 12 of being afflicted "no more" and in verse 15 of being invaded "no more" either assumed the appropriate response on Judah's part or refers in context only to Assyrian invasion. It also may be interpreted more literally if understood to have end-times implications.

## NINEVEH'S FALL (2:1–3:19)

*First Description (2:1-13).* This section comprises a vision of Nineveh's fall. It is introduced by an ironic call to arms with a parenthetical explanation and concluded by a taunt song. The prophet has been transported in a vision to Nineveh's watchtower, where he witnesses the armies of the Babylonians (who wore red; see v. 3; Ezek. 23:14) and Medes attacking, invading, and sacking the city of Nineveh. In a very real sense, however, the "attacker" (or "scatterer") is the Lord.

Nahum vividly portrays the confusion and panic of a city under attack. According to an ancient Greek historical account, Nineveh fell when the Tigris river overflowed and tore down the city walls, flooding the city, an event that may be reflected in verse 6 (also 1:8).

The concluding taunt compares Assyria to a ravenous lion and Nineveh to its lair, both of which have been destroyed. Assyrian kings often compared themselves to lions and so decorated their palaces. The image of the ravaging lion appears elsewhere in the prophets for the nations whom God used to punish Israel (see Isa. 2:15; 5:26-29; Jer. 4:7; 5:6; 50:17; 51:38; Joel 1:6; Amos 3:12). The section ends with the ultimate condemnation from God: "I am against you" (also 3:5; see Jer. 21:13; 50:31; 51:25).

*Second Description (3:1-19).* Like the previous section, this one includes a description of Nineveh's fall followed by a taunt. It begins as a funerary lament for a much-deserved death. Several wordplays add to the effectiveness of this visionary portrayal of judgment. What was before an "endless" supply of "wealth" (2:9) has been replaced by "piles" of corpses "without number." Because of her "many harlotries" (NIV, "wanton lust" in 3:4) Nineveh has "many casualties."

The Lord promises utter humiliation to a once proud city that trusted in her fortifications. Like Thebes, she is now desolate. Nineveh's fortifications will provide no refuge from the fire of God's wrath. She is as helpless as crops before a locust plague. Also, like a hoard of locusts Assyria will soon disappear. The chapter ends as it began with a lament that turns to celebration because of their "endless cruelty."

***Theological and Ethical Significance.*** The world often displays a disturbing lack of justice. But such lack is largely due to an eroded or illusive standard of morality, which is applauded by many. Regardless of the wishes of the contemporary culture, Nahum teaches that there is an eternal God with an unbending standard of righteousness. He is not only Father and Shepherd; He is also King, Judge, and Warrior, a God of jealousy, vengeance, and wrath (see Ps. 94:1; Isa. 63:1-6; Jer. 50:28-29; Mic. 5:15). He will exercise punitive retribu-tion to vindicate His glorious name and to deliver those who have fled humbly to Him for refuge (Deut. 32:43; Isa. 34:8; 35:4; 59:18; 61:2). Without God's vengeance there will be no justice and no deliverance. His vengeance is in part a result of His jealousy, which is best defined as the zeal with which He maintains His relationship with His people.

### Questions for Reflection

1. How does the expectation of God's wrath add significance to life? What would the alternative mean?

2. What does Nahum teach about God's sovereignty in the world and in history?

### Sources for Further Study

Baker, D. W. *Nahum, Habakkuk, Zephaniah: An Introduction and Commentary.* Tyndale Old Testament Commentaries. Downers Grove: InterVarsity, 1988.

McComiskey, T. E. "Micah." *Expositor's Bible Commentary.* Grand Rapids: Zondervan, 1985.

Maier, W. A. *The Book of Nahum: A Commentary.* Grand Rapids: Baker, 1980.

Patterson, R. D. *Nahum, Habakkuk, Zephaniah.* Chicago: Moody, 1991.

Robertson, O. P. *The Books of Nahum, Habakkuk, and Zephaniah.* The New International Commentary on the Old Testament. Grand Rapids: Eerdmans, 1990.

# HABAKKUK

Most Christians at some time have longed for a chance to dialogue with God, and perhaps even to complain to Him about His behavior. Habakkuk is one of the few who has been given the chance. Like Haggai and Zechariah, he is identified only as "the prophet." Whereas a prophet is usually a spokesman for God, and Habakkuk did that as well, the book starts with the prophet calling a time out to question and complain to the divine Coach on the sidelines. The message or "oracle" of the book largely consists of the answers which he received.

The only clues for the prophecy's date come from (1) Habakkuk's complaint of great wickedness and lawlessness in Judah (1:2-4) and (2) the prophecy of a Babylonian invasion (1:5-11). From 687 until his repentance (perhaps in 648 B.C.), Manasseh led Judah in one of its worst times of wickedness (see the introduction to Nahum). Under his son Amon, from 642 to 640 B.C., Judah again excelled in wickedness. This continued to some extent until Josiah's reform started in about 628 B.C. Following Josiah's death in 609 B.C. Judah quickly abandoned Josiah's significant reforms and continued their disastrous policies of apostasy under kings Jehoahaz (609 B.C.), Jehoiakim (609–597 B.C.), Jehoiachin (598–597), and Zedekiah (597–587). So the time periods for writing that best fit the first clue are 687–648, 642–628, and 609–587 B.C.

Except for periodic times of revolt (especially under the Chaldean Merodach-baladan from 721–689 B.C.), Assyria dominated Babylon from the ninth century until Ashurbanipal's death in 626 B.C. Between 614 and 609 B.C. Nabopolassar and the Babylonians overthrew Assyria and acquired their empire. They defeated Egyptian armies and established their authority over Palestine, including Judah, in 605 B.C. They continued Assyria's policies of oppression under the new Babylonian king Nebuchadnezzar (605–562 B.C.), under whom Babylon reached the height of its power. Judah's rebellion resulted in Babylonian invasion in 601 B.C., at which time the temple was robbed (2 Kgs. 24:1-4; 2 Chr 36:6). A second invasion occurred in 597, when the royal family and 10,000 others were exiled and the temple was robbed again (2 Kgs. 24:10-17). The last invasion was in 588–586 when Judah's cities were ravaged, Jerusalem was devastated, the temple was destroyed, and more citizens were deported (2 Kgs. 24:18–25:21; Jer. 39:1-10). What this tells us about Habakkuk's date depends upon how 1:5-11 is understood. If what is "amaz[ing]" (1:5) is God's orchestrating the Babylonians' rise to power (Baker, Patterson), then the prophecy must have been delivered prior to 626, or at least 614 B.C. On the other hand, if the amazing thing is God's summoning such a "ruthless and impetuous" nation as Babylon, who would exile His people and destroy His city and temple (Armerding), then the prophecy may just have preceded the invasions. The earliest the prophecy could have been delivered, perhaps about 640 B.C., is suggested by the phrase in 1:5, "in your days," indicating the events would occur within the prophet's lifetime.

***Message and Purpose.*** The Book of Habakkuk uses the prophet's perplexities to declare God's instructions to His people who are distressed by a wicked world. The book's primary message is found in the divine speeches. It begins by calling into question God's way of handling wickedness. The first question is, How can He allow it to continue among His people. The second is, How can He use as an instrument of punishment foreign nations more wicked than Israel? The message of the first question and response is that God cannot allow such wickedness to go unpunished without violating His own righteous character. The prophet's initial lament (1:2-4) serves as his *indictment* of Judah. God's first response of *judgment* (1:5-11) should have motivated repentance in his readers. The message of the second question and response is that God also holds the foreign nations responsible for their wickedness and will punish them. A general application is implied in that God will always bring His *judgment* against arrogant plunderers. But the primary message and *instruction* is that those who maintain their faith and hope in Him ("the just") through all this adversity will have life (2:4). To this dual message of vengeance and life the prophet responds with a hymnic confession of faith (3:1-19), thus demonstrating himself to be among the just. The book's purpose is to instruct the faithful in appropriate response to the God of vengeance and life.

**Structure.** Habakkuk is divided into two parts by the two superscriptions in 1:1 ("the oracle that Habakkuk the prophet received") and 3:1 ("a prayer of Habakkuk the prophet"). Section one is built around the prophet's two complaints. The first in 1:2-4 is followed by God's succeeding response in 1:5-11. This leads to Habakkuk's follow-up complaint in 1:12–2:1 and God's response in 2:2-20. Section two contains the

prophet's psalm of confidence in God's grace (3:1-19):

I. Dialogue with God (1:1–2:20)
II. Psalm of Confidence (3:1-19)

## GOD'S SHOCKING SOLUTION (1:1-11)

The book begins with a cry to God: "How long?" This cry is often found in Scripture in complaints against those who persist in sin (e.g., Exod. 10:3; Num. 14:11,27; 1 Kgs. 18:21; Ps. 4:2; Hos. 8:5; Hab. 2:6) and as here in laments calling for God to deliver from distress (Pss. 6:3; 13:1-2; 35:17; 74:10; 79:5; 80:4; 89:46; 90:13; 119:84; Zech. 1:12; Rev. 6:10). The opening speech laments rampant violence and injustice in Judah (1:1-4).

Habakkuk was assured that God was already at work and that he would soon see the results (v. 5). Judah's violence and injustice will be repaid by a people skilled in brutality. If Judah will not fear God, then they will soon fear the enemy He would send against them. Though the Babylonians recognized no law or power outside themselves and would be held guilty, they were tools of discipline in the Lord's hands (1:6-11; see Amos 3:6).

## RETRIBUTION (1:12–2:20)

The prophet knew that because of God's covenant with Israel, His judgment of them would be redemptive rather than destructive ("punish" should be translated "correct" or "reprove"). But the idea that the Holy God would use wickedness to punish wickedness was intolerable. Furthermore, would the cure not be worse than the disease? Before such a "wicked" one, would not all nations be nothing but fish to be hooked and netted to feed the insatiable appetite of this self-indulgent enemy of all that is right?

Prophets often compared themselves to city watchmen, whose responsibility was to report approaching danger or messengers (see 2 Sam. 18:24; Isa.

21:6-9; 52:8; Jer. 6:17; Ezek. 3:17; Hos. 9:8). Their job was to watch for a message from the Lord and deliver it to the people. That role here assumed by Habakkuk suggests that he was not the only one who needed to hear the answers to his questions. "Complaint" in 2:1 is from the same root as "punish/reproof" in 1:12. Habakkuk was not demanding an answer from God but was expecting reproof or correction for his audacious remarks, knowing that God's ways are always right. He knew that a solution to his perplexity could come only from God and that whatever God said would demand and deserve a response from him. He gives this response in 3:1-19.

Habakkuk's answer came in a vision which was to be proclaimed throughout future generations as the Ten Commandments had been (literally, "the tablets"; 2:2; see Deut. 27:8; Isa. 8:1; 30:8; Jer. 30:2). The message (in 2:3-5) was for all God's people distressed by the turmoil of a proud and wicked world. Its essence was "Trust, and you will receive life!" This is the ultimate answer to both of the prophet's complaints. God is going to deal with the wickedness of His people in His own good time, as He is also going to deal with wickedness generally (see Gen. 3:15). His word to the believer continues to be what Abraham learned: watch patiently but expectantly for what God will do. The word for "faith" here means "perseverance in faith." Even when appearances and human reasoning contradict what God has said, trust God. "Man must lay hold of the future that God has revealed, waiting for it with an eager faith and hope that surpass the apparent obstacles to its realization" (Armerding). Such faith, which is the opposite of pride, is both the condition of righteousness (right standing before God) and also its

chief expression (see Gen. 15:6; Rom. 1:17; Gal. 3:11; Heb. 10:38).

Appearances often declare that it is the ones bloated with pride and greed who will live. The Babylonians are used as an example. But God declares in a series of five mocking woes or curses that their self-made glory was a mirage that would be turned to shame. As God would turn the violence of the wicked within Israel back onto their own heads, so He would turn the victimizers into victims and plunder the plunderers. The knowledge of God's glory—not the works of the wicked—is destined to fill the earth (v. 14). This means that the wicked will be removed. All the earth is called to worshipful silence before Him. How many times have believers given such testimony to the living God while under the heel of arrogant, tyrannical rulers! Here the tyrant was Nebuchadnezzar. At other times it has been Antiochus-Epiphanes, or Nero, or Hitler, or Stalin. The statement holds true: Through faithful patience the righteous survive. The tyrant inevitably falls (see Isa. 40).

## PSALM OF CONFIDENCE (3:1-19)

Chapter 3 is Habakkuk's prayer-psalm. The psalmist reverently remembers reports of God's great acts in the past and prays for Him to bring redemption again: "In our time . . . in wrath remember mercy" (v. 2).

Habakkuk 3:3-15 is a poetic portrayal of God's salvation of His people from Egypt (see Exod. 15). Here metaphors of God's actions drawn from many passages of Scripture are mixed together.

Habakkuk 3:16 recounts the psalmist's believing acceptance that God was active in his own moment in time as well as in the past. He would "wait patiently" for God's retribution against the tyrants. He recognized that his was a day for waiting, not for action.

The closing verses announce his joy in the Lord despite the deprivations he had to endure. God was his strength.

**Theological and Ethical Significance.** The Book of Habakkuk represents the kind of faith that became the norm for Judaism and later for Christianity. Israel no longer had the means to try to shape their own destiny. Under the empires they were the passive recipients of whatever good or evil the powerful chose to give them. But in faith they could believe that God would provide what was necessary for His people to serve Him. Believing and waiting became essential elements in their way of life. It should still be so.

## Questions for Reflection

1. What was Habakkuk's solution to the disappointments and frustrations of life?

2. What did Habakkuk say about the value of faithfulness and hope?

3. According to Habakkuk, what did God have in store for the arrogant and the ruthlessly cruel?

4. What did Habakkuk teach about God's faithfulness to His people throughout their history?

## Sources for Further Study

Armerding, C. E. "Habakkuk." *Expositor's Bible Commentary.* Grand Rapids: Zondervan, 1985.

Baker, D. W. *Nahum, Habakkuk, Zephaniah: An Introduction and Commentary.* Tyndale Old Testament Commentaries. Downers Grove: InterVarsity, 1988.

Gaebelein, F. E. *Four Minor Prophets: Obadiah, Jonah, Habakkuk, and Haggai.* Chicago: Moody, 1977.

Patterson, R. D. *Nahum, Habakkuk, Zephaniah.* Chicago: Moody, 1991.

Robertson, O. P. *The Books of Nahum, Habakkuk, and Zephaniah.* The New International Commentary on the Old Testament. Grand Rapids: Eerdmans, 1990.

# ZEPHANIAH

Zephaniah is dated during the reign of king Josiah (1:1), who became king of Judah at age eight in 640 B.C. He began to "seek the God of his father David" eight years later and four years after that began a spiritual reformation of the land, in about 628 B.C. (2 Chr. 34:3). The reformation became more fervent in 621 when the "book of the law" was discovered in the temple (2 Chr. 34:8-33). Zephaniah was probably a major influence on the young king (see 1:4-5; see also the introduction to Nahum) and hence predates the reforms. If the "Hezekiah" who is listed as Zephaniah's ancestor is the king by that name, that would explain the book's tracing Zephaniah's ancestry to four generations. His family connections would have given him access to the king.

**Message and Purpose.** *Indictment:* Zephaniah's focus is on the city of Jerusalem, which is characterized in 3:1 by oppression, rebellion, and defilement. Furthermore, it is said to be devoid of any faith in the Lord (3:2; see 1:12). The corruption of their leaders receives special attention in 3:3-4. Judah was also practicing an apostate religion, attempting to mix pagan elements with worship of the Lord (1:4-6).

*Instruction:* First, Zephaniah calls for his hearers to cease their empty and adulterous affirmations of faith (1:5) and submit to the Lord in silent humility and fear ("be silent" in 1:7). Second, he calls for them to gather in humble and prayerful repentance to "seek the LORD" (2:1-3). Third, God commands those who respond appropriately to the first two exhortations (3:8) to "wait for me." In the midst of human sin believers should not lose heart. They should look confidently for the culmination of God's purifying work, when the remnant will call upon Him and serve Him "shoulder to shoulder" (3:9).

*Judgment:* To motivate its hearers, the book begins in 1:2-6 by announcing an approaching devastation, expressed in terms of universal judgment. Then 1:8-18 announces a specific time approaching (note "on that day" and "at that time" in vv. 9,10,12) when the Lord will punish Judah. That time is then defined as "the great day of the LORD" (1:14) and "the day of the LORD'S wrath" (1:18; 2:2-3). Past judgments that should have motivated God's people to fear the Lord and "accept correction" had not succeeded (3:6-7).

*Hope:* In 2:4-15 "the day of the LORD'S anger/wrath" is said to be against Judah's enemies, which in itself was a message of vindication and deliverance for Judah. It also meant that after Judah's own purifying judgment was complete they would possess their enemies' land (2:6-7,9). God's desire to purify a remnant is expressed in 3:9-13. This motivates God's repentant people to "wait" (3:8). Finally, that future generation is exhorted to celebrate (3:14) because of the Lord's deliverance and the peace provided by His everlasting presence (3:15-20).

**Structure.** The book has a threefold structure governed by the three exhortations to "be silent" (1:7), "gather" and "seek the LORD" (2:1-3), and "wait" (3:8). In the first section the exhortation is sandwiched between two announcements of the Lord's wrath. The exhortations begin the second and third sections and are followed by explanations introduced by "for" (left untranslated in the NIV).

I. Exhortation to Submit (1:1-18)
II. Exhortation to Repent (2:1–3:7)
III. Exhortation to Wait (3:8-20)

## EXHORTATION TO SUBMIT (1:1-18)

Although "the word of the LORD" occurs over two hundred times in the Old Testament and is an appropriate designation for all Scripture (2 Tim. 3:16), only Hosea, Joel, Micah, Zephaniah, and Malachi use it as a title of their prophecy. Since it is God's Word, "it is to be received and believed and in turn is to be mastered and allowed to master the hearts of those who receive it" (Patterson).

The prophecy opens in 1:2-6 with an announcement of total destruction for the whole "earth" (literally "ground" in 1:2-3) that would also include Judah (1:4-6). The order is reversed in the judgment announcement in 1:7b-18, with verses 7b-13 directed against Judah (note the repeated "I will punish") and verses 14-18 again announcing judgment against "man" (NIV, "the people"; v. 17, reflecting v. 3), "the whole world," and "all who live in the earth" (v. 18). The argument is that if a universal judgment day is coming, then God will certainly judge His people. The command to "be silent" (1:7a) was often used in the presence of a person or event of great importance (Num. 13:30; Judg. 3:19; Neh. 8:11; Hab. 2:20; Zech. 2:13). The prospect of such a horrifying outpouring of divine wrath calls for absolute silence.

The language of 1:2-6 describes (hyperbolically) the reversal of creation (note the order) and is reminiscent of the language of the flood (extended to include fish; see Gen. 6:17; 7:4,21-23). The passage shows that man is morally responsible for the condition of the world. The "day of the LORD" is described figuratively in verses 7b-13 as a day of sacrificial worship. The leaders and wealthy citizens of Judah would be the sacrificial animals; the nations apparently are the ones the Lord has "invited" to slay them at His altar. A graphic image is used in verse 12 of the Lord searching Jerusalem with lamps, meaning that no evildoer would go unpunished. Then "the great day of the LORD" is described in verses 14-18 as a time of worldwide devastation that will occur in the last days (see discussion of the day of the Lord in Joel and Obadiah).

## EXHORTATION TO REPENT (2:1–3:7)

This section begins with a summons to "seek the LORD" before the day of judgment arrives. "Seeking" the Lord could refer either to desiring from Him a word of revelation (1:6) or to turning to Him in repentance. It is the opposite, then, of either indifference to the Lord or abandoning Him. Judah was guilty of both, and the Lord had consequently turned His face (or favor) from them (see 1:6; Exod. 33:7; Deut. 4:29; 2 Chr. 7:14; Jer. 29:13; Hos. 3:5; 5:6,15; 7:10). Genuinely seeking the Lord also means seeking righteousness and humility, "the two qualities necessary for spiritual productivity" (Patterson).

Judah should repent not only because of judgment coming against them, but because God was going to judge all their surrounding enemies and give their land to the remnant of Judah. Four representative peoples are specified: Philistia in the west, Moab and Ammon in the east, Ethiopia (Cushites, who ruled Egypt from about 720 to 654 B.C.) in the south, and Assyria in the north (from which direction they came).

Judah's sins are then catalogued in 3:1-5. They had refused to repent despite the Lord's demonstrations of judgment against the Northern Kingdom (3:6-7). Special attention is given to

Judah's leaders. The officials and judges, whose duty was to protect life and property, preyed upon the people. The prophets, who were trusted to bring the people God's word with integrity, were traitors to that responsibility, driven only by self-interest. Priests, responsible to maintain God's favor and presence by nurturing holiness at the temple and by teaching God's law, profaned God's dwelling and violated His law. Although the Lord who always dispenses justice is the opposite of such leaders (see Deut. 32:4), Judah shamelessly committed evil in His very presence.

## EXHORTATION TO WAIT (3:8-20)

In the face of such a dismal picture of human corruption, Zephaniah exhorts believers to "wait" for the Lord to come as witness, to pour out His wrath against all peoples, and to purify a remnant who will seek refuge in Him. To "wait" for the Lord means to "long for" Him (Job 3:21; Isa. 30:18) and to place one's confident hope only in Him (Ps. 33:20; Isa. 8:17; 64:4).

God's purpose is to purify from the nations a people united to worship Him. Their speech will be cleansed of sinful pride and idolatry (Isa. 2:17-18; 6:5; Hos. 2:17). Terms used of the remnant in verse 13 are used of the Lord in verse 5. God's people's character will be like His. It will be a time of right, of truth, and of security (see Jer. 50:19; Ezek. 34:14; Mic. 4:4; 7:14).

The book concludes with a hymn of praise, an exhortation for restored Jerusalem to rejoice in the Lord's redemption. This hymn describes the messianic age when the Lord, their victorious King, will be in their midst, again taking great delight in loving His people (see Deut.

30:9). It ends with the Lord's promise to regather and glorify Israel after their time of punishment is over.

***Theological and Ethical Significance.*** The Book of Zephaniah focuses on the day of the Lord as a time of His wrath upon the nations, including Israel. The purpose of that wrath, however, at least in part, is the ultimate deliverance of Israel from Gentile enemies, the purification of Israel from sin, and the redemption of a people from the nations who will worship and serve the Lord. God has set a time when He will sweep away the proud, the indifferent, and the corrupt. Those who seek the Lord diligently with humble trust, longing for the day of His redemption, will be sheltered in that day. Then they will rejoice in His loving presence.

## Questions for Reflection

1. List God's qualities seen in Zephaniah.

2. What determines how a person fares on the Day of the Lord?

3. Why was it necessary for God to punish Judah? What did God hope to accomplish through those who survived judgment?

## Sources for Further Study

Baker, D. W. *Nahum, Habakkuk, Zephaniah: An Introduction and Commentary.* Tyndale Old Testament Commentaries. Downers Grove: InterVarsity, 1988.

Patterson, R. D. *Nahum, Habakkuk, Zephaniah.* Chicago: Moody, 1991.

Robertson, O. P. *The Books of Nahum, Habakkuk, and Zephaniah.* The New International Commentary on the Old Testament. Grand Rapids: Eerdmans, 1990.

Walker, L. L. "Zephaniah." *Expositor's Bible Commentary.* Grand Rapids: Zondervan, 1985.

# HAGGAI

When the Babylonians destroyed Jerusalem in 587 B.C., Judah was reduced to the status of a province administered from Mizpah, a few miles north of Jerusalem. Judah likely was made part of the province of Samaria until the exiles began to return under Persian authority. Archaeology confirms the severe depopulation of Judah during the exile. Except for the Negev and the northern border, virtually all the fortified cities had been destroyed. The Edomites had begun taking over southern Judah. The exiles must have been exuberant when they saw the Babylonian empire begin to crumble after Nebuchadnezzar's death in 562 B.C. Their exuberance reached its peak when the Persian ruler Cyrus conquered Babylon in October, 539 B.C. and soon after announced that they were free to return to Judah. He even promised to help them rebuild their temple as part of a general policy of restoring foreign cult centers.

The first group of about fifty thousand exiles to return were led by Sheshbazzar, who was appointed governor of the new province of Judah. Sanballot, governor of Samaria, was not pleased at Judah's new status and took every opportunity to oppose them. The other surrounding provinces such as Ammon-Gilead (ruled by Tobiah) and Arabia-Idumea (ruled by Geshem) supported Sanballot in this opposition. The returning Jews also clashed with Jews who had been left in Palestine who thought they were God's remnant and resented the newcomers taking over. Many of them who claimed to worship the Lord but worshiped other gods as well (see 2 Kgs. 17:24-34) may

have joined the opposition. Opposition continued and increased through the reigns of Cyrus (539–530 B.C.), Cambyses (530–522 B.C.), and Darius (522–486 B.C.; Ezra 4:4-5).

The temple foundation was laid fairly quickly under Zerubbabel's leadership, who eventually replaced Sheshbazzar as governor. This initial success was met not only with celebration but also with sadness when this temple was compared with Solomon's (Ezra 1–3; Hag. 2:3; Zech. 4:10). This is the first hint that perhaps this restoration would not satisfy entirely the prophetic announcements of Israel's glorious restoration. This discouragement together with the continuing opposition and concerns over personal affairs caused work on the temple to cease until the preaching of Haggai and Zechariah roused the people once more to work in faith (Ezra 4:24–5:2).

***Message and Purpose.*** *Indictment:* The leaders and people of Judah had allowed external opposition, discouragement, and self-interest to keep them from completing the task of rebuilding the Lord's temple (1:2-4; 2:3). So they and their offerings to the Lord were defiled and displeasing to Him (2:14).

*Instruction:* The Lord's command through Haggai was to "build the house" for the pleasure and glory of God (1:8). Toward that end the Lord exhorted them not to fear but to "be strong ... and work" (2:4-5). Finally, by a parable Haggai instructed them of the need to dedicate themselves and their work to the Lord (2:11-16).

*Judgment:* The Lord called upon them to recognize His chastisement in

## Chronology of Haggai and Zechariah

| | |
|---|---|
| August 29, 520 B.C. | Haggai's first message (Hag. 1:1-11) |
| September 21, 520 | Temple building resumed (Hag. 1:12-15) |
| October 17, 520 | Haggai's second message (Hag. 2:1-9) |
| October–November, 520 | Zechariah's ministry begun (Zech. 1:1-6) |
| December 18, 520 | Haggai's third and fourth messages (Hag. 2:10-23) |
| February 15, 519 | Zechariah's night visions (Zech. 1:7–6:8) |
| December 7, 518 | Delegation from Bethel (Zech. 7) |
| March 12, 515 | Temple completed (Ezra 6:15-18) |

the deprivation they had been experiencing (1:5-6,9-11; 2:16-17).

*Hope:* The Lord informed the people that the completion of the temple would bring Him pleasure and glory (1:8). He further assured them of success through His presence (1:13-14; 2:4-5). He also promised them that He would reward their renewed work and dedication to Him by glorifying the temple and granting them peace (2:6-9) and blessing (2:18-19). Finally, He promised to restore the Davidic throne on the earth through a descendant of Zerubbabel (2:20-23).

**Structure.** Haggai's four sermons (1:1-15; 2:1-9; 2:10-19; 2:20-23) are marked by introductory date formulae. But repetition between messages one and three and between two and four shows that the book has a twofold structure. Both messages one and three refer to "this people" (1:2; 2:14) and include two commands to "give careful thought" (1:5,7; 2:15,18). Messages two and four both have the divine promise, "I will shake the heavens and the earth" (2:6,21) and have a threefold repetition of "declares the LORD" (2:4,23). Furthermore, the first and third messages are introduced by complete date formulae,

which give year, month, and day, with the order in the third message reversed, as in a mirror. The date formulae that introduces the second and fourth messages have only the month and day, again with the second mirrored in the fourth. Finally, at the end of the first and third messages, the date is repeated (1:15; 2:18).

The first two messages both deal with building the temple. The last two messages do not mention the temple explicitly but move beyond it to issues of defilement and restoration.

    I. Rebuilding the Temple (1:1–2:9)
    II. Cleansing the People and Restoring the Kingdom (2:10-23)

### INSTRUCTION TO BUILD (1:1-15)

The quotation in 1:2 shows how the people had been rationalizing their lack of concern for the Lord's affairs. The Lord's oracle and the response to it is given.

The Lord asked a rhetorical question that revealed their selfishness and the emptiness of their rationalization. Although God's house lay desolate, their own houses were finished. In the context of the Mosaic covenant and Israel's restoration according to divine prophecy, they should have been able to discern God's displeasure with them by the trying circumstances they were experiencing. After pointing this out to them, the Lord commanded them to build His house for His pleasure and glory.

Accepting Haggai's authority as God's spokesman and encouraged by the Lord, Judah's leaders led the "remnant" to begin work in the fear of God. The first message ends as it began—with a date, showing that twenty-three days after Haggai's message the rebuilding was underway again (the order in the Hebrew text of 1:15—day, month, year—is the mirror image of 1:1, showing the two dates to be part of the same section and stressing the comparison between the days). If God's earlier prophets had received such positive response, the temple would never have been destroyed!

## GOD'S PRESENCE, GLORY, AND PEACE (2:1-9)

The second message was given during the Feast of Tabernacles (see Lev. 23:33-43), three weeks after the work began. The following day was the anniversary of Solomon's dedicating the newly built temple in 959 B.C. (2 Chr. 7:8-10). The message unfolds in two parts, divided by the announcement of God's word in verse 6. The Lord asked another rhetorical question that recognized the people's discouragement over the apparent disparity between the glory of Solomon's temple and the simplicity of the one under construction (v. 3; see Ezra 3:10-13). Then the Lord exhorted them to work, remembering His faithfulness in the past and His presence with them in the present (vv. 4-5). God's command to "be strong" and not fear probably reminded Judah's leaders of earlier times when God had enabled His servants to complete the tasks He had given them (Deut. 31:6-7,23; Josh. 1:6-9,18; 1 Chr. 22:13; 28:10,20; 2 Chr. 15:7;

32:7; Isa. 35:4; 41:10-14; 51:7-16; Zeph. 3:16; see Dan. 10:19; Zech. 8:9,13; Eph. 6:10).

Having motivated them to work by pointing to past events and present realities, the Lord also encouraged the remnant in verses 6-9 with promises of the future. The terms used are typical of theophanies, where the Lord is described as appearing on the earth, usually in judgment against His enemies (see Judg. 5:4-5; 2 Sam. 22:7-16; Pss. 68:7-8; 77:15-20; Isa. 13:13; Jer. 10:10; Ezek. 38:20; Joel 2:10; 3:16; Nah. 1:5; Hag. 2:21-22; see Heb. 12:26-27). These verses describe the day of the Lord when the wicked will be removed and the nations shall be made subject to Him and will bring tribute to His temple (see Ezra 6:8-12; 7:15-20; Isa. 60:4-14). Thus its glory will exceed that of Solomon's temple, especially because the Lord Himself will be there. It is hard not to see a preliminary fulfillment of these verses in the appearance of Jesus at Herod's temple (see Matt. 2:11; 21:12-15; 27:51; Luke 2:32; John 1:14; 2:19-21; Heb. 1:3).

## CLEANSING AND BLESSING (2:10-19)

In this message the Lord announces His determination to change Judah's deprivation to blessing because they have dedicated themselves to Him. The date is three months after the temple work began, just after the fall planting, which explains why there is no seed left in the barn. After the introduction comes a dialogue with the priests that functions like a parable. The essence of the parable is that although holiness cannot be transmitted by touch, defilement can be. Then the parable is applied in verses 14-19. Israel, originally set apart for the Lord, had become defiled by sin and unbelief so that all they did was unacceptable to God, including offerings and temple building. Only God's grace in response to their humble dedication could cleanse them again. This He had done (see Ps. 51). Thus they are assured that God would turn their curse of deprivation into blessing, and they would have a plentiful harvest.

## GENTILE OVERTHROW AND DAVIDIC RESTORATION (2:20-23)

Here the Lord promises that He will destroy the kingdoms of this world and will establish a new kingdom ruled by a Davidic descendant, the Messiah (see Ezek. 39:19-23; Dan. 2:44). The messianic servant is named David in Ezekiel 34:23-24 and 37:24 because He is the Davidic seed, the fulfillment of the Davidic covenant. The Messiah will also be a descendant of Zerubbabel (see Matt. 1:12-13). The "signet ring" is appropriate as a messianic metaphor because it was jealously guarded as a symbol of one's authority and was used to sign official documents (see Esth. 8:8). As God had cast off king Jehoiachin, so He had placed his grandson Zerubbabel on His finger (Jer. 22:24).

*Theological and Ethical Significance.* Several reasons can be given for the significance of the temple's being rebuilt. First, it was a sign of the people's priorities. Second, it showed that God was with the remnant and that His promises of restoration had begun to be fulfilled. Third, it declared God's glory and thus brought Him pleasure. Fourth, it served to vindicate the Lord since the temple's destruction had disgraced the

Lord's name (Ezek. 11:23; 37:26–27). Fifth, it served as a pledge of the new covenant and the messianic age (Ezek. 37:26; Isa. 2:2-4; 44:28; 52:1-7; Mic. 4:1-4; Mal. 3:1). The restoration of the temple was a sign that God had revoked neither His covenant with Levi nor His covenant with David (see Jer. 33:17-22; Num. 25:11-13; Mal. 2:4). He will provide cleansing and restoration through a glorious temple and a messianic ruler. As one scholar explains, "They are not just building a material edifice; they are participating in the building and establishment of the kingdom of Yahweh in which the promised Messiah is to reign in glory forever."

### Questions for Reflection

1. What work has God called us to do?

2. How can fear, discouragement, and selfishness interfere with the Lord's work?

3. What should motivate us to persevere with the work God has given us?

### Sources for Further Study

Alden, R. L. "Haggai." *Expositor's Bible Commentary.* Grand Rapids: Zondervan, 1986.

Baldwin, J. *Haggai, Zechariah, Malachi.* Downers Grove: InterVarsity, 1972.

Merrill, E. H. *Haggai, Zechariah, Malachi: An Exegetical Commentary.* Chicago: Moody, 1994.

Verhoef, P. A. *The Books of Haggai and Malachi.* Grand Rapids: Eerdmans, 1987.

Wolf, H. *Haggai and Malachi.* Chicago: Moody, 1976.

# ZECHARIAH

Like Jeremiah and Ezekiel, Zechariah was a priest as well as a prophet. This is fitting since the book largely concerns the temple and priesthood and the purification of the people. Zechariah's grandfather Iddo was a priest who returned with Zerubbabel (Neh. 12:4), making it likely that Zechariah was Haggai's younger colleague. Whereas Haggai's focus was on the rebuilding of the temple and the reinstitution of the sacrificial system, Zechariah's was on the people's spiritual transformation.

Many are convinced that chapters 9–14 were written much later than chapters 1–8 and by a different author. The evidence, however, does not require this conclusion, and the thematic unity of the book argues against it.

For the historical situation in which Zechariah wrote, see the introduction to Haggai.

### Message and Purpose.

*Indictment:* Zechariah explained that the Lord's displeasure was on His people because they had abandoned Him in the past. They were also discouraged over opposition and the apparent insignificance of the building project. After Zerubbabel's time, Judah would again have wicked leaders who would mislead the people. This would result in their rejecting the Lord again.

*Instruction:* The Lord called upon Judah to "return" to Him and so remove His displeasure. He exhorted the high priest Joshua and the remnant to faithful obedience in order to retain His blessings. Implied is an exhortation to complete the temple. The Lord also reminded Judah that He required His people to practice justice and mercy.

*Judgment:* The Lord's judgment of the previous generation was intended to teach Israel to repent and maintain their faithfulness to Him. Their future rejection of Him would result in repeated foreign opposition and the scattering of Israel.

*Hope:* The Lord promised to "return" to Israel with blessing as they returned to Him in faithful obedience. He will enable Zerubbabel and Joshua by His Spirit to complete the temple that will prefigure the coming messianic kingdom. Furthermore, He assured them that He would judge the nations that oppressed them, but that even a remnant of the nations would become His worshipers. As He had preserved a remnant of Israel and cleansed them, so the Lord would send the Messiah to provide by his death permanent forgiveness and peace and the total eradication of evil. He will also send His Spirit to bring about national repentance.

### Structure.

Zechariah has two major sections surrounding a central and therefore highly prominent smaller section. The two major sections, each introduced by a date formula, are 1:1–6:8 and 7:1–14:21. The central section (6:9-15) is a narrative describing the commissioning and crowning of Joshua, the high priest. Each of the major sections comprises seven smaller sections plus an introductory section. In each case the seven subsections are arranged in a repetitive structure that revolves around a central and therefore highly prominent subsection. The central subsection in the first major section (3:1-10) describes the commissioning of Joshua, the high priest, with a turban, and the central subsection in the second major section (1:1-17) is a narrative describing the commissioning of Zechariah with two staffs.

I. Zechariah's Night Visions (1:1–6:8)

II. Crowning of Joshua (6:9-15)

III. Two Oracles Concerning the Coming Kingdom (7:1–14:21)

## ZECHARIAH'S NIGHT VISIONS (1:1–6:8)

The book and the visions are introduced in 1:1-6 by an initial call to "return" or repent. It was issued in October/November, 520 B.C., about a month after work on the temple had resumed. The big question facing the generation of the restoration was whether they would return to faith in the Lord or repeat the sins of their fathers.

The night visions apparently were all received February 15, 519 B.C., about six months after the construction had resumed. The main themes of the night visions are (1) God's judgment of the nations, (2) His election and future blessing of Jerusalem, (3) the purification of the land, (4) rebuilding the temple, and (5) the leadership of Zerubbabel and Joshua. The first three visions (the horses and the myrtles, the horns and the craftsmen; the measuring line) assure the people of the Lord's coming judgment against the nations who have scattered Israel, of His renewed love for and promise to bless Jerusalem, and of their success in rebuilding the temple.

The fourth and central vision in 3:1-10 describes the high priest Joshua's appearance before the angel of the Lord, who is also the Lord Himself (vv. 1-2; see Gen. 16:7-13; 21:17; 22:11-12,15-16; 31:11-13). Satan appears in his role as "accuser" of God's people (the meaning of "Satan"; see Job 1:6-7; 1 Chr. 21:1; Rev. 12:10). Joshua, who represents the remnant (Exod. 28:29) that God had

"snatched from the fire" (Amos 4:11), is disqualified from worshiping the Lord by his "filthy" (or "excrement-covered"; Deut. 23:13; Isa. 4:4) attire, representing the defilement caused by Israel's past sins. The change of attire to "rich garments" and "turban" (inscribed "holy to the LORD"; Exod. 28:36-38) shows God's intention not only to cleanse the priesthood and the people but also to bless and honor them by His sovereign grace (see Isa. 61:10).

Joshua's privileged position as head of the temple depended upon his continued faithfulness (vv. 6-7). Joshua and his attendant priests were signs (i.e., models or foreshadowing) of the coming Messiah ("my servant, the Branch"; see 6:12; Isa. 4:2; 11:1; Jer. 23:5; 33:15) and of His heavenly council (see Ps. 110). The temple whose building they were supervising foreshadowed the one the Messiah would build and of which He would be the chief cornerstone (the stone with seven eyes; see 4:10; Ps. 118:22; Isa. 28:16; Rev. 5:6). This vision speaks of a future permanent forgiveness the Messiah would accomplish when He comes to redeem the nation and to establish peace, prosperity, and security on the earth (vv. 8-10; see 1 Kgs. 4:25; Mic. 4:1-8).

The fifth vision of the lampstand and olive trees encourages Zerubbabel and Joshua, represented by the two olive trees, to trust not in financial or military resources but in the power of God's Spirit working through them. As is often the case in the Old Testament, God's Spirit is represented by the oil (see Isa. 61:1-3). The lampstand probably represented the temple that would glorify God in the earth.

The sixth vision of the flying scroll and the measuring basket is a composite like the second vision. It speaks of God's purifying His people. First, He will remove wickedness through a curse of banishment and destruction against covenant violators, specifying the third and eighth commandments. Second, He will exile that wickedness to Babylon which is personified by a woman (see Ezek. 8:1-18, where Ezekiel is carried from Babylon to Jerusalem to behold Judah's wickedness). The fulfillment of God's restoration of Israel demands the complete eradication of wickedness. As the "paradigm of wickedness and of hostility to all the gracious purposes of God" (Merrill), the "mother of prostitutes and of the abominations of the earth" (Rev. 17:5), Babylon is the appropriate dump for such moral waste.

The final vision of the chariots (6:1-8) reflects the first. It describes divine judgment sent throughout the earth (see Jer. 49:36; Rev. 6:1-8; 7:1). Because of the divine program of judgment and redemption outlined in the seven visions, the superficial and false rest and peace established by the nations in the first vision (1:11) is transformed into genuine divine rest in the last vision. The bronze mountains represent the entrance to the divine dwelling (see 14:3-5; 1 Kgs. 7:15-22).

## CROWNING OF JOSHUA (6:9-15)

The oracle in this central and most prominent section of the book forms a hinge between the two larger sections. Like 3:1-10 it describes a messianic prototype receiving the signs of his office. The introduction, "the word of the LORD came to me" (occurring elsewhere only in Jeremiah and Ezekiel), also echoes 4:8, where it introduces an oracle promising Zerubbabel's completion of the temple. Rather than Zerubbabel here, only Joshua and "the Branch" are mentioned. Zechariah is told to make royal crowns (in Hebrew the word is plural) and to crown Joshua. Then the crowns are to be placed in the temple as a reminder of what God was going to do.

But first Joshua receives a divine message that "the Branch" (since the message was for Joshua, "the Branch" designates someone else) would build the temple, be glorified, and rule (see 1 Chr. 29:25). Now the building of the postexilic temple was already assigned to Zerubbabel (4:9), who as a Davidic descendant prefigured the Messiah (Hag. 2:23). But the Messiah would build the temple associated with His earthly kingdom of righteousness, a future temple prefigured by Zerubbabel's (4:8-10). Therefore, this oracle spans both contemporary and future fulfillment of God's purposes. The passage's ambiguity regarding the number of crowns and the number of thrones is due to the need for both Zerubbabel and Joshua to foreshadow the Messiah, who would be both king and priest. In ancient Israel the king's throne as well as the ark in the Holy of holies were both the Lord's throne (see 1 Chr. 29:23). The reference to "harmony between the two" in verse 13 either personifies the Messiah's dual office or perhaps describes the relation between the Lord and His Anointed (see Ps. 45:6-7; 110:1; Dan. 7:9-14; Heb. 1:3,13; Rev. 5:6). Finally, although the future kingdom was assured by God's grace and power, the contemporary "sign" depended upon the diligent obedience of Zerubbabel, Joshua, and the remnant.

## FASTING (7:1–8:23)

These two chapters serve to introduce the two oracles in chapters 9–14, just as 1:1-6 introduces the visions of 1:7–6:8. Themes such as ceremonial days, for example, the holiness of God's dwelling, universal worship of the Lord, regathering the exiles, and the repopulating of Jerusalem are introduced in chapters 7–8 and reappear in chapters 9–14.

Almost two years after the night visions, a little over two years after the rebuilding had begun, a delegation came to Zechariah from Bethel. They came to inquire whether the time for fasting and mourning over Jerusalem had passed. To commemorate various aspects of Jerusalem's fall the Jews had appointed fasting days in months four, five, seven, and ten (v. 5; 8:19).

God's reply unfolds in four parts, each divided by repetition of "the word of the LORD came" (7:4,8; 8:1,18). Additional repetition gives the sections a mirror structure: 7:1-3 is parallel to 8:20-23; 7:4-7 is parallel to 8:18-19; 7:8-12 is parallel to 8:16-17; 7:13-14 is parallel to 8:7-8; and 8:1-6 is parallel to 8:9-15. God's message was that the Jews' fasting had been nothing but hypocritical ritual anyway. It was motivated by self-interest rather than the genuine sorrow for sin and by desire to renew their faithfulness to God.

Then God reminded them of His demand for justice and mercy and that the exile had resulted from Israel's failure to heed His demands. The implication is that such could happen again (which it did in A.D. 70). But the Lord had blessings planned for Israel, a fact that should should motivate them not to be fearful or discouraged but to finish the temple. He had already returned to them (v. 3 should be translated "I have returned") and promised to dwell with them and gather many more from all over the world. This prospect might seem difficult ("marvelous") to them, but not to "the LORD Almighty." Besides completing the temple, the primary response the Lord sought to His gracious acts and promises was not ritual but righteousness, loving one's neighbor as oneself.

The leaders from Bethel had perhaps mainly wanted to call attention to their own "piety." They are informed in 8:18-23 that God was going to do something so wonderful that fasting would be turned to feasting and that their puny worship would be eclipsed by "many peoples and powerful nations" coming to "entreat" and "seek" the Lord (see discussion of Mic. 4–5; also see Mal. 1:11-14).

## FIRST ORACLE (9:1–11:17)

The remainder of the book, probably written after the temple was completed, contains two divine oracles or messages (chaps. 9–11 and 12–14). Both messages deal with God's establishing His kingdom on the earth. Both describe future events, some of which were fulfilled before Jesus' incarnation, some during Jesus earthly ministry, and some when He returns. Each oracle contains three main sections, but the first oracle concludes with a fourth section that acts as a hinge between the two oracles. It is the third of the commissioning ceremonies in Zechariah (see 3:1-10; 6:9-15).

The first and third sections of the first oracle are warrior hymns connected to God's deliverance of Israel from exile. Between them is a denunciation of false shepherds. The first section describes the future victory of God's people through a coming ruler. Judgment of hostile nations is the theme of 9:1-8, a passage that may in part relate to Alexander's conquests in Palestine in the fourth century B.C.

According to 9:9-10, "one of the most Messianically significant passages of all the Bible" (Merrill), God's kingdom will be established through a human ruler (see also Isa. 9:6-7; Pss. 2; 45; 72, especially v. 8 quoted at the end of Zech. 9:10). Although kings sometimes rode donkeys (see 1 Kgs. 1:33), the contrast with the use of a warhorse (see Rev. 19:11-16) seems to suggest humility and peace (the word translated "gentle" is better rendered "humble"). Jesus' fulfillment of verse 9 in His "triumphal entry" in Jerusalem is made clear in Matthew 21 and John 12. In light of Jesus' crucifixion a few days later, the resultant lasting peace and universal divine dominion described in verse 10 suggests either an undisclosed gap between the two verses or that Jesus' fulfillment then amounted to a "historical prototype" of another event yet to come.

Few prophetic passages (see Zech. 13:7-9) that describe messianic glory explain that it would be preceded by suffering and humiliation (Isa. 52:13–53:12 being the most significant exception). In 9:11-17 the Lord promises to return all His people to His land of blessing and to lead them (or rather use them as a weapon) in victory over their enemies. After a denunciation of Judah's leaders as false shepherds, Zechariah 10:36–11:3 promises that the Lord, their Good Shepherd, will deliver His flock from exile.

The last commissioning ceremony in 11:4-17 contrasts with the previous ones in that Zechariah is not just an observer but plays the part of the messianic priest-king. Apparently He is commissioned as the good shepherd (9:16; 10:3) in a vision. He is given two staffs and is sent on a mission to "pasture the flock" (v. 4; see 9:9), which other shepherds are selling for slaughter (v. 5; see 10:1-3). But the Lord announces that He will deliver the flock to foreign oppressors (v. 6) because of the way they treat Him (vv. 7-14). Though He had removed their false shepherds (v. 8) and established peace with the nations and the reunion of Northern and Southern Kingdoms (symbolized by the two staffs), the flock "detested" Him. So He resigned His commission as their shepherd, breaking His staffs. For His services He was paid the insulting price of thirty pieces of silver, the price of a slave, which Zechariah is instructed to throw to the potter in the Lord's house.

The significance of this scenario only becomes apparent as we watch its fulfillment in the Gospels (see Matt. 26:15; 27:3-10). Then at the vision's conclusion Zechariah must play the part of the false shepherd whom the Lord sent to punish the flock for a time before his own judgment. The message is that Israel's deliverance and glory would be preceded by their oppression and suffering, not only by foreigners but their own Jewish leaders, because they would reject the Lord as their Good Shepherd (see 13:7-8).

## SECOND ORACLE (12:1-14:21)

The second oracle focuses on God's deliverance of Jerusalem from her enemies, especially in the first and last sections. Although God will deliver His people over to their enemies for punishment, He will not abandon them (see Jer. 30:11). The first section describes "all the nations of the earth" surrounding Judah and Jerusalem. But they will destroy themselves as they attack Jerusalem, the "immovable rock" (see Isa. 29; Jer. 25; Ezek. 38–39; Joel 3; Obad. 16).

The second section promises a coming national repentance produced by God's Spirit (see Ezek. 36:24-32; Joel 2:28-32). Israel will experience severe and sincere grief over the way they have treated the Lord, that is, His Messiah (see 11:8; 13:7-8; Isa. 53:1-9; John 19:37). The character of the Messiah as both God and man is suggested by referring to Him in verse 10 as both "me" (that is, God) and "him" (see Isa. 9:6-7; a similar phenomenon occurs in passages where the angel of the Lord is referred to both as the Lord and as someone distinct from the Lord; see Gen. 16:7-13; Exod. 3:2-4; Judg. 6:11-27; Zech. 3:1-6). The Lord also promises to cleanse and purify Israel, especially of idolatry and false prophecy, and to preserve and restore the remnant. The "fountain" (or "spring") suggests continual cleansing for those who had "pierced" the Messiah.

The Lord's command in 13:7 that the sword should "strike" (meaning to "kill") His shepherd is shocking. After all, "the man who is close to me" (i.e., God's "neighbor," "associate," or "friend"), is an apparent reference to the Messiah (see Isa. 53:4). The purpose of the Lord's command is, first, that His flock might be scattered and chastised, and, second, that many should perish (see Matt. 26:31). Then after His people are purged and refined they will be revitalized as the Lord's covenant people, cleansed by the blood of the one they had slain. Thus would the Lord fulfill the gospel He proclaimed in Genesis 3:15.

The final section, which elaborates on the first, describes God's deliverance of Jerusalem in the last days and His coronation as King of all the earth. Jerusalem's initial defeat will be turned to victory when the Lord appears (on the splitting of the Mount of Olives, see 6:1). The site of the Lord's deepest agony will witness His greatest glory (see Matt. 26:30-45). The accompanying darkness echoes such passages as Isa. 13:10; 60:19-20; Ezek. 32:7-8; Joel 2:31 (see also Matt. 24:29; Rev. 21:23-24; 22:5). Then the restoration of Jerusalem is described (vv. 8-11) as the destruction of all the Lord's enemies (vv. 12-15). But a remnant of the nations will worship the Lord (vv. 16-19). The culmination of God's work will be the perfect holiness of His people among whom He will dwell, which is expressed figuratively as extending even to the most common items in God's land (vv. 20-21; see Exod. 19:6; Jer. 2:3).

***Theological and Ethical Significance.*** The people of Judah were discouraged because they could not see God

at work. They lacked a sense of gratitude for what God had done and the enthusiasm to persevere faithfully in serving Him. Zechariah's message was that although Judah's immediate future was in their hands, God would see that eventually the small beginning they were witnessing would result in God's worldwide rule from His dwelling in Jerusalem. All His promises concerning Israel and the nations of the world would be fulfilled. Rather than lamenting what we see in the present, God's people should focus on what God has done in the past, what He has promised to do in the future, and what He has instructed us to do in the present. Nothing we do is "small" if it is done in faith and obedience.

Zechariah has been called "the most Messianic, the most truly apocalyptic and eschatological, of all the writings of the OT." Messianic prophecies and detailed descriptions of the dawning of the messianic kingdom give the book an exciting quality. Zerubbabel and Joshua represent the Messiah in His royal and priestly roles. Reflecting on how God's sovereign program of redemption unfolded in the life and ministry of Jesus should lead to eager anticipation of the completion of His plan, expressed in celebratory worship and zealous obedience.

## Questions for Reflection

1. According to Zechariah, what must God's people do to experience His blessings?

2. What does the Book of Zechariah teach about God's plans for His people's future? How does Jesus meet these expectations?

## Sources for Further Study

Baldwin, J. *Haggai, Zechariah, Malachi.* Downers Grove: InterVarsity, 1972.

Baron, D. *The Visions and Prophecies of Zechariah.* Grand Rapids: Kregel, 1972.

Barker, K. L. "Zechariah." *Expositor's Bible Commentary*. Grand Rapids: Zondervan, 1985.

Feinberg, C. L. *God Remembers*. Portland: Multnomah, 1965.

Merrill, E. H. *Haggai, Zechariah, Malachi: An Exegetical Commentary*. Chicago: Moody, 1994.

Unger, M. F. *Zechariah: Prophet of Messiah's Glory*. Grand Rapids: Zondervan, 1963.

# MALACHI

Malachi is the last prophetic message from God before the close of the Old Testament period, providing a fitting conclusion to the Old Testament and a transition for understanding the kingdom proclamation in the New Testament. It is probably no accident that the one prophesied in Malachi 3:1 to "prepare" the way for the Lord's coming to His temple is identified as "My messenger," a word identical in Hebrew to the name of the book's author given in 1:1. It may be that the prophet Malachi and his earliest readers considered that He and this book constituted a preliminary fulfillment of this prophecy.

Nothing is known about the author other than his name. The book emphasizes the message rather than the messenger, since out of a total of fifty-five verses as many as forty-seven are the personal addresses of the Lord.

Although the book is not dated by a reference to a ruler or a specific event, internal evidence, as well as its position in the canon, favors a postexilic date. Reference to a governor in 1:8 favors the Persian period, when Judah was a province or subprovince of the Persian satrapy Abar Nahara, a territory that included Palestine, Syria, Phoenicia, Cyprus, and, until 485 B.C., Babylon. The temple had been rebuilt (515 B.C.) and worship established (1:6-11; 2:1-3; 3:1,10). But the excitement and enthusiasm for which the prophets Haggai and Zechariah were the catalysts had waned. The social and religious problems Malachi addressed reflect the situation portrayed in Ezra 9 and 10 and Nehemiah 5 and 13, suggesting dates either just before Ezra's return (around 460 B.C.) or just before Nehemiah's second term as governor (Neh. 13:6,7; around 435 B.C.).

**Message and Purpose.**

*Indictment:* Malachi presents Judah's sins largely on the people's own lips, quoting their words, thoughts, and attitudes (1:2, 6, 7, 12-13; 2:14, 17; 3:7,8, 13-15). Malachi was faced with the failure of the priests of Judah to fear the Lord and to serve the people conscientiously during difficult times. This neglect had contributed to Judah's indifference toward the will of God. Blaming their economic and social troubles on the Lord's supposed unfaithfulness to them, the people were treating one another faithlessly (especially their wives) and were profaning the temple by marrying pagan women. They were also withholding their tithes from the temple.

*Instruction:* Malachi called the people to turn from their spiritual apathy and correct their wrong attitudes about worship by trusting God with genuine faith as their living Lord. This included honoring the Lord's name with pure offerings, being faithful to covenants made with fellow believers, especially marriage covenants, and signifying their repentance with tithes.

*Judgment:* If the priests will not alter their behavior, the Lord will curse them, shame them, and remove them from service. Malachi also announces a coming day when the Lord of justice will come to purge and refine His people. At that time He will make evident the distinction between the obedient and the wicked and will judge the wicked.

*Hope:* Malachi also bases his instruction on (1) the Lord's demonstration of love for Israel (1:2), (2) their spiritual and covenant unity with God and with one another (2:10), and (3) that coming day when the Lord will also abundantly bless those who fear Him (3:1-6; 3:16-4:3).

**Structure.** Malachi's message is communicated in three interrelated movements or addresses. Each address contains five sections arranged in a mirror-like repetitive structure surrounding a central section *(a b c b a)*. In the first two addresses, the focus is on the center section which contains the Lord's instruction (1:10; 2:15b-16). These addresses begin with positive motivation or hope (1:2-5; 2:10a) and end with negative motivation or judgment (2:1-9; 3:1-6). The second and fourth sections contain the indictment (1:6-9 and 1:11-14 in the first address; 2:10b-14 and 2:17 in the second). The climactic address begins and ends with a general call to repent (3:7-10a; 4:4-6). The indictment is in the center (3:13-15). The second section furnishes positive motivation or hope (3:10b-12), and the fourth section combines positive and negative motivation (3:16–4:3).

I. Honor Yahweh (1:2–2:9)

II. Faithfulness (2:10–3:6)

III. Return and Remember (3:7–4:6)

## THE LORD'S LOVE (1:1-5)

Despite their responsibility under the covenant of Levi (see 2:4,8) to be the Lord's messengers of Torah (2:7), the postexilic priests were dishonoring the Lord, particularly in their careless attitude toward the offerings. They are exhorted to stop the empty worship and to begin honoring the Lord with pure offerings and faithful service. To encourage them the Lord declares His love for them (and for all Israel) in 1:2-5. To challenge them, He threatens them with humiliation and removal from His service (2:1-9).

Judah's disputing God's love shows that they had allowed their difficulties to steal their sense of God's loving pres-

ence. Such an impoverishment resulted in the moral decay denounced in the second address and the spiritual indifference criticized in the third. Following Judah's impertinent question, the Lord asserts that His love for Judah had been abundantly demonstrated in recent history (vv. 3-5). The Lord's love for Israel consists in His having chosen them out of all the nations for an intimate relationship with Himself and His faithfulness to them in that relationship. They should grasp God's love by simply comparing their blessings to Edom's punishments.

## UNWORTHY WORSHIP (1:6-14)

The situation in the first address is that the priests were failing to honor or fear the Lord. The temple altar is compared to a dinner table which the Lord hosted. This table represented hospitality and relationship. One's attitude toward that table revealed one's attitude toward the Lord. Judah's bringing blemished animals to the altar showed how little they valued their relationship with the Lord.

The Lord desired fear and honor manifested in proper sacrifices from pure hearts. But He preferred no ritual to the empty ritual Judah was orchestrating (v. 10; see Isa. 1:10-17; Amos 5:21-23). "Worship" that does not arise from wholehearted devotion to the Lord is sin (Prov. 15:8; Isa. 1:13; Amos 4:4; see Rom. 14:23; Heb. 11:6). The Lord is not dependent upon human offerings or service. They are means of testifying to His greatness and exalting His name. Worship also benefits the worshipers, serving to nourish their relationship with God individually and to encourage one another in the faith. But religious activity performed without genuine love and gratitude to God is not only useless but repulsive to Him because it slanders His character.

The point of 1:11-14 is that although a time is coming when even Gentiles all over the world will fear the Lord, God's own chosen people of Judah, His kingdom of priests who were supposed to mediate His grace to the nations, were profaning Him. Although God's purpose to make himself known and worshiped among the nations would not be thwarted, He would do it more in spite of Israel than by means of them (see Ezek. 36:20-36; 39:7; Rom. 3:1-8; 11:11-12). Still, the Messiah will be an Israelite (Rom. 9:5).

## PRIESTHOOD CURSED (2:1-9)

The "admonition" (better translated "decree") here is that if the priests' attitude and behavior does not change, the Lord will curse them and remove them from service (see Lev. 10:1-3; 1 Sam. 2:29-36; Ezek. 44:6-14; Hos. 4:6-8). God had entrusted them with the spiritual well-being of Israel (see Num. 25:11-13; Deut. 33:8-11). Although Nehemiah "purified the priests and the Levites of everything foreign, and assigned them duties, each to his own task" (Neh. 13:30), according to the gospel writers, by the time of Jesus the Jerusalem priesthood was under God's curse (see Matt. 16:21; 21:23-46). But the promise of a lasting Levitical priesthood was still in effect (Mal. 3:3-4; see also Jer. 33:17-22).

A priest is called here a "messenger of the LORD Almighty." Elsewhere the Lord's "messengers" are either angels or prophets. Whereas those messengers conveyed new words or instructions from God, priests informed His people of the words of His law previously revealed and applied that law to their lives and situations. Malachi's time near the end of Old Testament prophecy and the completion of the Old Testament canon would make the term's use here especially significant. That teachers of God's Word could be described as "messengers" implies the ongoing relevance of God's past instruc-

tions and shows the continuing importance of the role of biblical teacher (and translator) among God's people. Those who proclaim God's written Word are no less important to His redemptive program than those who previously served as "prophets," since both carry God's message (see 2 Pet. 1:19-21).

## MARITAL UNFAITHFULNESS (2:10-16)

The audience of the second address has broadened to all Judah. The indictment is against unfaithfulness to one another, especially against wives, many of whom were being divorced to marry pagan women. Such behavior involved treachery against those to whom one was joined by spiritual kinship (v. 10a; see 1 John 5:1) as well as by a covenant sworn before the Lord (v. 14).

The vertical aspect of Judah's unfaithfulness is in view in verses 11-12. By marrying those who worshiped other gods, the people had committed a "detestable" act which "desecrated" or profaned the Lord's sanctuary. Such unfaithfulness to God also introduced a spiritually destructive element into the covenant community (see Exod. 34:11-16; Deut. 7:3-4; Neh. 13:26; 2 Cor. 6:14-17). Their sin was made more reprehensible by their continuing to sacrifice to the Lord as if all was well (v. 12). Then they complained because He was not honoring the sacrifices (v. 13). The horizontal aspect of Judah's unfaithfulness—the breaking of marriage covenants—is the focus of verses 13-15a. But this had a vertical dimension as well in that God was "witness" to those covenants.

The point of the very difficult verse 15a seems to be that marriage is not only a union of flesh that can be dissolved, but one of God's Spirit. Since the Spirit remains, marriage has an inherent unity that survives human efforts to sever it. The nature or purpose of marital unity is "seeking seed of [i.e., "from"] God." God intended that a man's purpose in departing from his father and mother and in joining himself to a wife by covenant, thus becoming one with her in flesh (Gen. 2:24), should be fruitfulness. By that means God's people were to spread His rule throughout the whole earth, producing and discipling children who would manifest the divine glory in their obedient lives and continue the process until the earth was full of His glory. Although couples can no longer be assured of bearing children (as the Book of Genesis makes clear), they are still to "seek" them, and can reproduce themselves in other ways if necessary, through adoption and/or spiritual discipleship.

The instruction section (vv. 15b-16) begins and ends with the command to "guard yourself" and not "break faith." Between is another difficult passage, whose traditional interpretation as a general condemnation of divorce (reflected in the NIV) is in tension with Moses' apparent permission for divorce in Deuteronomy 24:1-4, Ezra's prescription for it in Ezra 10:5,11, and Jesus' allowance for it in Matthew 19:9. Beginning verse 16 is a particle meaning either "indeed," "for," or "if, when." The syntax favors "if" (see 2:2), producing the literal translation, "'If He hates (and) divorces,' says the LORD God of Israel, 'then He covers his garment with violence,' says the LORD Almighty." The point is that one who divorces his wife simply because He dislikes her (Deut. 24:2) commits "violence" or injustice against her, that is, "cold-blooded and unscrupulous infringement of the personal rights of others, motivated by greed and hate" (see Ps. 73:6). Such a man deprives his wife of the very things a husband is responsible to provide—blessings, good, protection, praise, peace, justice—and He stands condemned by God.

## JUSTICE FROM THE LORD (2:17–3:6)

This paragraph concludes the second address. The sin of unfaithfulness that was widespread in Judah was a case of injustice, failing to give someone their due. Yet Judah, unable to recognize its own corruption, saw its current economic and social troubles (see Hag. 1:6,9-11; 2:16-19; Neh. 9:32-37) as a sign of God's unfairness or unfaithfulness. God's response to their complaints was to announce a coming messianic "messenger of the covenant" who would purge and purify God's people (see John 2:14-17), including the priests.

The divine-human nature of this messenger is indicated by his being both distinct from God, who is speaking, and also identified with Him (see comments on Zech. 12:10–13:9). "My messenger" is not the same but one who will announce the coming of the "messenger of the covenant" (see Heb. 9:15). The New Testament identifies this one as well as "Elijah" in 4:5 and the "voice" of Isaiah 40:3 with John the Baptist (Matt. 3:3; 11:10; Mark 1:2-3; Luke 3:3-6; John 1:23).

God's immutability in the sense of His faithfulness to His relationship with Israel expressed in 3:6 echoes 1:2-5 (see also Hos. 11:9; Ps. 124; Rom. 11:26-29).

## RETURN AND REMEMBER THE LAW (3:7–4:6)

The final address begins and ends with commands. The first section (3:7-10a) contains two commands: first to "return" to the Lord, then to evidence that return by bringing Him the tithes and offerings they had been withholding. Devoting to the Lord a tenth of one's produce as representative of the whole was an expression of faith and a recognition that all one's possessions were a gift of God. The tithe was used to support the temple personnel and the helpless members of society (see Neh. 13:10; Lev. 27:30-33;

Num. 18:21-32; Deut. 12:5-18; 14:22-29; 26:12-15). The "offerings" were the priestly portions of all the sacrifices brought to the temple (Num. 18:8-20).

In 3:10b-12 the Lord promises blessing from heaven, from the land, and from the nations if Judah would be faithful to Him. As in all the Old Testament promises of material blessings, these applied to the nation, not the individual. Applying such promises to individuals is a misinterpretation that the Book of Job and later Jesus (Matt. 19:23-25; John 9:3) speak against.

Judah's complacency toward serving the Lord is exhibited by their speech in 3:13-15. The difficulties they had been encountering, together with their perverse perspective on their own righteousness and their seriously flawed understanding of what it means to have a relationship with God, had led them to a false conclusion. They had decided that there was no advantage in serving God (see Ps. 73:13) and that there was no real difference between righteousness and wickedness (see Isa. 5:20). What perverse thinking our wicked minds can lead us into, when not guided by God's truth!

The final motivation offered to encourage repentance is the coming day when the Lord will separate the righteous and the wicked and will gather together His "treasured possession" (3:16–4:3; see Exod. 19:5; Deut. 7:6; 14:1-2; 26:18; Ps. 135:4). The message alternates between hope (3:16-18; 4:2) and judgment (4:1), combining the two in the last verse. It begins with a figurative anecdote whose point is that the Lord knows those who fear Him. The "scroll of remembrance" may refer to a heavenly book of destiny known from Psalms 40:7; 139:16; Isaiah 34:16; Daniel 7:10; and Revelation 20:12. The fiery element of the coming day in 4:1 echoes similar images in eschatological passages

such as Joel 2:3-5 (see Ps. 21:9; Isa. 31:9). The word for "furnace" here can also mean "oven" and is used as a divine image in Genesis 15:17. The "sun of righteousness" refers to the Messiah whose appearance will be celebrated like the dawn because "in its wings" (i.e., the wings of the dawn; see Ps. 139:9) will be healing for those who fear the Lord (see Deut. 32:39; 2 Chr. 7:14; Isa. 6:10; 53:5; 57:18-19; 58:8; Jer. 33:6; Hos. 14:4).

Because the Lord remembers those who fear Him and honor His name (3:16), He commands Israel in the last section to "remember the law" revealed to Moses (4:4-6). As the people of Israel were to wear tassels as constant reminders of the Lord's instructions (Num. 15:38-40), so Malachi was calling them to a lifestyle guided at all times not by human wisdom, ambition, or societal expectations but by the thoughtful application of God's Word. Only this divine lighthouse can guide God's people to avoid destruction on "that great and dreadful day of the LORD."

Elijah's role as preparatory proclaimer of the time of divine intervention derives from his being viewed as the quintessential prophet of repentance. As he appears with Moses in these final verses of the Old Testament, so he appeared with Moses representing the prophets to testify to Jesus as the Messiah on the mountain of Jesus' transfiguration (Matt. 17:3; Luke 9:29-31). The prophecy here was also fulfilled in part by John the Baptist (Matt. 11:14; 17:10-13; Luke 1:15-17). But Jesus indicated that an additional fulfillment awaits the time of His return (Matt. 11:14; 17:11), perhaps as reflected in the prophecy of the two witnesses in Revelation 11:3 (see Deut. 19:15).

Elijah's coming before the day of the Lord will result in a great revival of faith in Israel, expressed here as fathers and their "children" (or sons) turning (the same verb translated "return" in 3:7) their hearts toward each other. As quoted in Luke 1:17, it describes fathers turning compassionately toward their children and disobedient people accepting the wisdom of the righteous.

***Theological and Ethical Significance.*** Malachi speaks to the hearts of a troubled people whose circumstances of financial insecurity, religious skepticism, and personal disappointments are similar to those God's people often experience or encounter today. The book contains a message that must not be overlooked by those who wish to encounter the Lord and His kingdom and to lead others to a similar encounter. Its message concerns God's loving and holy character and His unchanging and glorious purposes for His people. Our God calls His people to genuine worship, to fidelity both to Himself and to one another, and to expectant faith in what He is doing and says He will do in this world and for His people.

God's love is paramount. It is expressed in Malachi in terms of God's election and protection of Israel above all the nations of the world. Since God has served the interests of Judah out of His unchanging love, He requires Judah to live up to its obligations by obedience and loyalty to Him and not empty ritualism in worship. This love relationship between God and Judah is the model by which the individual is expected to treat his neighbor; we are bound together as a community created by God, we are responsible for one another, and we are required to be faithful in our dealings with one another at every point in life.

As a community devoted to God, God's people enjoy His protection and intercession. But failure to live right before God and our fellow man means not only the natural consequences of a wicked society but also the intervention of God's judgment. Thus, God's people cannot expect the joy of His blessings if we persist to fail in our duties to God and one another; the people must repent because the judgment of God is certain.

But before God would hold Judah in the balance of judgment, He would grant one last call for repentance; a forerunner would precede that terrible day and herald the coming of God's kingdom in the earth.

## Questions for Reflection

1. How can a Christian keep from developing an attitude that displeases God, especially in difficult times?

2. How can we ensure that our worship honors God?

3. How can we ensure that our marriage and family honor God?

## Sources for Further Study

Alden, R. L. "Malachi." *Expositor's Bible Commentary.* Grand Rapids: Zondervan, 1985.

Baldwin, J. *Haggai, Zechariah, Malachi.* Downers Grove: InterVarsity, 1972.

Kaiser, W. C. *Malachi: God's Unchanging Love.* Grand Rapids: Baker, 1984.

Merrill, E. H. *Haggai, Zechariah, Malachi: An Exegetical Commentary.* Chicago: Moody, 1994.

Verhoef, P. A. *The Books of Haggai and Malachi.* Grand Rapids: Eerdmans, 1987.

Wolf, H. *Haggai and Malachi.* Chicago: Moody, 1976.

# THE GOSPELS

## CRAIG L. BLOMBERG    DARRELL L. BOCK
## CHRISTOPHER L. CHURCH    JAMES E. WHITE

The New Testament begins with four books we call Gospels. Whenever we use the term *Gospels,* we must recall that before the Gospels came the gospel, the good news concerning Jesus Christ—His life, death for sins, and resurrection (see 1 Cor. 15:3-4). Jesus preached good news (the gospel) when He began His work (Mark 1:1,15).

All four Gospel books—Matthew, Mark, Luke, and John—tell the story of Jesus. At some points the four books are quite similar. At other points they are quite distinctive. The first three Gospels, called the Synoptics (which comes from a Greek word that means they saw the ministry of Jesus from a similar point of view), have much material in common. For example, over 600 of Mark's 661 verses are in Matthew. About 380 verses in Luke are similar to Mark's material. Some have suggested that all three drew upon a common source. Others have suggested that Matthew was written first and that Mark and Luke were influenced by Matthew. Yet others have maintained that Mark was written first and so in turn influenced Matthew and Luke.

We really do not know how the Gospels came into being. Luke offered a hint that he did thorough research of other accounts about Jesus before he wrote his Gospel (see Luke 1:1-4). We really do not know the historical process in which the Gospels came into being. What we do know is that the four books we have

called Gospels are inspired of God's Spirit and communicate the story of Jesus to us in a powerful way (see the article "The Order of the Gospels").

Each Gospel is ascribed to a person who either witnessed the events described or who obtained eyewitness accounts. Each of the Gospels tells us things that none of the others do. Each Gospel was written by different people at different times in different places with unique situations. All, however, were probably written sometime between A.D. 60–95 (see the introductions to Matthew, Mark, Luke, and John).

Each of the writers shaped the telling of his story to accomplish particular purposes. For example, Matthew focused on Jesus as the Messiah foretold in the Old Testament. Mark presented Jesus as an active Person, a powerful Minister, and a Suffering Servant. Luke portrayed Jesus as the Savior for all people. John specifically explained his purpose in writing his Gospel (see John 20:31). He wanted his readers to understand that Jesus is the Christ, the Son of the living God. We can be thankful that we have four different Gospels. Our knowledge of who Jesus is and what He has done is far richer and deeper because we have more than just one Gospel.

The various purposes of the Gospels can help us understand and appreciate their differences and unique features. The way or time an event or saying of

Jesus is presented is often shaped by the author's overall purpose. This in no way casts doubt on the reliability or trustworthiness of the writing or the historicity of the event. Instead we recognize that while the Gospels can be read together as complementary stories in *harmony* one with another, we also learn that each Gospel must be read and understood on its own. Together these four books present for us the good news about Jesus Christ, the Son of God.

# JEWISH SECTS IN THE NEW TESTAMENT

| NAME | DATES OF EXISTENCE | ORIGIN | SEGMENTS OF SOCIETY | BELIEFS | SELECTED BIBLICAL REFERENCES | ACTIVITIES |
|---|---|---|---|---|---|---|
| **PHARISEES** | | | | | | |
| Pharisees = "the Separated Ones" with three possible meanings: (1) to their separating themselves from people (2) to their separating themselves to the study of the law ("dividing" or "separating" the truth) (3) to their separating themselves from pagan practices | Existed under Jonathan (160–143 B.C.) Declined in power under John Hyrcanus (134–104 B.C.) Began resurgence under Salome Alexandra (76 B.C.) | Probably spiritual descendants of the Hasidim (religious freedom fighters of the time of Judas Maccabeus) | Most numerous of the Jewish parties (or sects) Probably descendants of the Hasidim—scribes and lawyers Members of the middle class—mostly businessmen (merchants and tradesmen) | Monotheistic Viewed entirely of the Old Testament (Torah, Prophets, and Writings) as authoritative Believed that the study of the law was true worship Accepted both the written and oral law More liberal in interpreting the law than were the Sadducees Quite concerned with the proper keeping of the Sabbath, tithing, and purification rituals Believed in life after death and the resurrection of the body (with divine retribution and reward) Believed in the reality of demons and angels Revered humanity and human equality Missionary-minded regarding the conversion of Gentiles Believed that individuals were responsible for how they lived | Matt 3:7–10; 5:20; 9:14; 16:1,6–12; 22:15–22,34–46; 23:2–36 Mark 3:6; 7:3–5; 8:15; 12:13–17 Luke 6:7; 7:36–39; 11:37–44; 18:9–14 John 3:1; 9:13–16; 11:46–47; 12:19 Acts 23:6–10 Phil 3:4b–6 | Developers of oral tradition Taught that the way to God was through obedience to the law Changed Judaism from a religion of sacrifice to a religion of law Progressive thinkers regarding the adaptation of the law to situations Opposed Jesus because He would not accept the teachings of the oral law as binding Established and controlled synagogues Exercised great control over general population Served as religious authorities for most Jews Took several ceremonies from the temple to the home Emphasized ethical as opposed to theological action Legalistic and socially exclusive (shunned non-Pharisees as unclean) Tended to have a self-sufficient and haughty attitude |
| **SADDUCEES** | | | | | | |
| Sadducees = Three possible translations: (1) "the Righteous Ones"—based on the Hebrew consonants for the word righteous (2) "ones who sympathize with Zadok," or "Zadokites"—based on their possible link to Zadok the high priest (3) "syndics," "judges," or "fiscal controllers"—based on the Greek word syndikoi | Probably began about 200 B.C. Demise occured in A.D. 70 (with the destruction of the temple) | Unknown origin Claimed to be descendants of Zadok—high priest under David (see 2 Sam 8:17; 15:24) and Solomon (see 1 Kgs 1:34–35; 1 Chr 12:28) Had a possible link to Aaron Were probably formed into a group about 200 B.C. as the high priest's party | Aristocracy—the rich descendants of the high-priestly line (however, not all priest were Sadducees) Possible descendants of the Hasmonean priesthood Probably not as refined as their economic position in life would suggest | Accepted only the Torah (Genesis through Deuteronomy—the written law of Moses) as authoritative Practiced literal interpretation of the law Rigidly conservative toward the law Stressed strict observance of the law Opposed oral law as obligatory or binding Observed past beliefs and tradition Believed in the absolute freedom of human will—that people could do as they wished without attention to God Denied divine providence Denied the concept of life after death and the resurrection of the body Denied the concept of reward and punishment after death Denied the existence of angels and demons Materialistic | 2 Sam 8:17; 15:24 1 Kgs 1:34 1 Chr 12:26–28 Ezek 40:45–46; 43:19; 44:15–16 Matt 3:7–10; 16:1,6–12; 22:23–34 Mark 12:18–27 Luke 20:27–40 John 11:47 Acts 4:1–2; 5:17–18; 23:6–10 | In charge of the temple and its services Politically active Exercised great political control through the Sanhedrin, of which many were members Supported the ruling power and the status quo Leaned toward Hellenism (the spreading of Greek influence)—and were thus despised by the Jewish populace Opposed both the Pharisees and Jesus because these lived by a larger canon (The Pharisees and Jesus both considered more than only Genesis through Deuteronomy as authoritative.) Opposed Jesus specifically for fear their wealth/position would be threatened if they supported Him |

| DATES OF EXISTENCE | NAME | ORIGIN | SEGMENTS OF SOCIETY | BELIEFS | SELECTED BIBLICAL REFERENCES | ACTIVITIES |
|---|---|---|---|---|---|---|
| **ZEALOTS** | | | | | | |
| Three possibilities for their beginning (1) during the reign of Herod the Great (about 37 B.C.) (2) during the revolt against Rome (A.D. 6) (3) traced back to the Hassidim or the Maccabees (about 168 B.C.). Their certain demise occured around A.D. 70–73 with Rome's conquering of Jerusalem. | Refers to their religious zeal Josephus used the term in referring to those involved in the Jewish revolt against Rome in A.D. 6—led by Judas of Galilee | (According to Josephus) The Zealots began with Judas (the Galilean), son of Ezekias, who led a revolt in A.D. 6 because of a census done for tax purposes | The extreme wing of the Pharisees | Similar to the Pharisees with this exception: believed strongly that only God had the right to rule over the Jews. Patriotism and religion became inseparable. Believed that total obedience (supported by drastic physical measures) must be apparent before God would bring in the Messianic Age Were fanatical in their Jewish faith and in their devotion to the law—to the point of martyrdom | Matt 10:4 Mark 3:18 Luke 6:15 Acts 1:13 | Extremely opposed to Roman rule over Palestine Extremely opposed to peace with Rome Refused to pay taxes Demonstrated against the use of the Greek language in Palestine Engaged in terrorism against Rome and others with whom they disagreed politically (Sicarii [or Assassins] were an extremist Zealot group who carried out acts of terrorism against Rome.) |
| **HERODIANS** | | | | | | |
| Existed during the time of the Herodian dynasty (which began with Herod the Great in 37 B.C.) Uncertain demise | Based on their support of the Herodian rulers (Herod the Great or his dynasty) | Exact origin uncertain | Wealthy, politically influential Jews who supported Herod Antipas (or any descendant of Herod the Great) as ruler over Palestine (Judea and Samaria were under Roman governors at this time.) | Not a religious group—but a political one Membership probably was comprised of representatives of varied theological perspectives | Matt 22:5-22 Mark 3:6; 8:15; 12:13-17 | Supported Herod and the Herodian dynasty Accepted Hellenization Accepted foreign rule |
| **ESSENES** | | | | | | |
| Probably began during Maccabean times (about 168 B.C.)—around the same time as the Pharisees and the Sadducees began to form Uncertain demise—possibly an A.D. 68–70 with the collapse of Jerusalem | Unknown origin | Possibly developed as a reaction to the corrupt Sadducean priesthood Have been identified with various groups: Hasidim, Zealots, Greek influence, or Iranian influence | Scattered throughout the villages of Judea (possibly including the community of Qumran) (According to Philo and Josephus) About 4,000 in Palestinian Syria | Very strict ascetics Monastic; most took vow of celibacy (adopting male children in order to perpetuate the group), but some did marry (for the purpose of procreation) Rigidly adherent to the law (including a strict rendering of the ethical teachings) Considered other literature as authoritative (in addition to the Hebrew Scripture) Rejected temple worship and temple offerings as corrupted Believed and lived as pacifists Believed in the immortality of the soul with no bodily resurrection Apocalyptically oriented | None | Devoted to the copying and studying of the the manuscripts of the law Lived in a community sense with communal property Required a long probationary period and ritual baptisms of those wishing to join Were highly virtuous and righteous Were extremely self-disciplined Were diligent manual laborers Gave great importance to daily worship Upheld rigid Sabbath laws Maintained a non-Levitical priesthood Rejected worldly pleasures as evil Rejected matrimony—but did not forbid others to marry |

# Palestine in New Testament Times

Scale of Miles
0    10    20    30

Scale of Kilometers
0    10    20    30    40

Mediterranean Sea
(Great Sea)

Phoenicia

Litani River

Sidon

Damascus

Mt. Hermon

Tyre

Kefar Dan
Daphne
Caesarea Philippi
(Panias)

Cadasa

Raphana

Ecdippa

Thella

Ptolemais
(Acco)

Mt. Meron

Korazin
Capernaum
Heptapegon (Tabgha)
Gennesaret
Magdala
(Taricheae)
Cana

Bethsaida

Gergesa

Sea of
Galilee

Hippus

Dion

Mt.
Carmel

Sepphoris

Galilee
Tiberias

Emmatha

Abila

Nazareth

Yarmuk River

Gadara

Edrei

Dora

Simonias   Mt. Tabor
Philoteria
Nain

Agrippina

Capercotnei

Ginae

Scythopolis

Pella

Decapolis

Caesarea
Maritima

Samaria

Salim
Aenon

Jordan River

Gerasa

Geba
Sebaste
(Samaria)

Jabbok River

Mt. Ebal   Sychar
Mt. Gerizim   Shechem

Amathus

Apollonia
Antipatris

Anuathu
Borcaeus

Coreae

Lebonah   Acrabeta
Phasaelis

Alexandrium

Perea

Gadora

Joppa

Gophna

Archelais

Philadelphia

Lydda

Bethel   Ephraim
Neara
Jericho
Cypros

Bethennabris

Abila

Jamnia

Emmaus
(Nicopolis)

Jerusalem
Bethlehem   Bethany

Beth-ramatha   Esbus

Qumran   (Essene Community)   Mt. Nebo

Hyrcania
Herodium

Medeba

Azotus
(Ashdod)

Judea

Tekoa

Callirrhoe
Machaerus

Ascalon

Betogabris

Dead
Sea
(Salt
Sea)

Anthedon
Gaza

Hebron
Adora

En Gedi

Arnon River

Raphia

Idumea

Malatha

Masada

Beersheba

Nabateans

Zered River

# MATTHEW

Strictly speaking, the Gospel of Matthew is anonymous. The titles of the Gospels were not added until the second century. But early church tradition unanimously ascribes this Gospel to Matthew. Matthew was also known as Levi, one of Jesus' twelve apostles, and a converted tax-collector (9:9-13; 10:3). Although modern scholarship has called this identification into repeated question, there are no persuasive reasons for rejecting this tradition outright.

**Recipients.** Early church tradition meshes with the style and contents of the Gospel to suggest that Matthew wrote to a Jewish-Christian audience. We have very little way of narrowing down the destination more than that. A few ancient sources favored Palestine, perhaps Jerusalem. Modern scholars often propose Syria, particularly Antioch.

**Date.** The hostility between Jews and Jesus' followers on the pages of the Gospel has suggested to many that Matthew's Jewish-Christian church had decisively broken from the (non-Christian) Jewish synagogue. This often leads to a dating in the mid-80s or later, after the synagogues allegedly introduced a curse on heretics (including Christians) into their liturgy of prayers. Quotations by the Apostolic Fathers suggest an upper limit for the dating of around A.D. 100. References to the destruction of the temple (most notably 22:7) have convinced many that Matthew was writing after that event (which occurred in A.D. 70).

But none of these considerations proves decisive. It is increasingly doubtful whether a formal break between synagogue and church ever occurred at one specific period of time over a wide portion of the Roman Empire. Arguments based on Jesus' prophecies often rule out the possibility that He genuinely could have foretold the future. How one understands the literary relationship between Matthew, Mark, and Luke will also affect the dating. Matthew probably knew and used extensive portions of Mark in his writing. But Mark may be dated from the late 50s to sometime in the early 70s.

Luke apparently also used Mark, and many have dated Luke-Acts to A.D. 62, since that is when the final events of Acts took place. Mark would then have to be earlier, allowing for Matthew to be as early as the late 50s or early 60s. But there are other explanations for the end of Luke. Repeated references in Matthew to Jewish rituals, which could no longer be performed after A.D. 70, may suggest a date in the 60s, which would dovetail with possible Sadducean persecution of Christians between 58 and 65. In light of all the variable factors, we should allow for any date between A.D. 40 and A.D. 100, but perhaps a slight weight of evidence favors a time before the fall of Jerusalem between A.D. 58 and A.D. 69.

**Literary Form.** Despite many counterproposals, Matthew, like the other Gospels, is best described as a theological biography. Little if any detail in the book appears out of sheer historical interest. Matthew was trying to commend his understanding of Christianity to his audience. But theological motive does not exclude historical reliability. Ancient historiography regularly valued both accuracy and ideology even if it did not insist on compartmentalizing the two the way modern historians do. Once Matthew's

# ORDER OF THE GOSPELS

The question of relationship between our Gospels is often discussed, but not easily answered. This is especially so when attention is focused on the Gospels of Matthew, Mark, and Luke, the popularly designated "Synoptic Gospels."

The term *Synoptic* means *to see together* or *to view from a common perspective.* The first three Gospels are so identified because they present the life and ministry of Jesus from a common point of view that is different from that of the Gospel of John.

In general the Synoptics follow the same outline and record similar material. Sometimes their accounts are almost identical. Yet at other times important differences are observed. This phenomena has given rise, especially in the modern era, to what is called "the Synoptic problem."

How are we to understand and explain the literary relationship of these three Gospels? John's Gospel is usually dated later than the Synoptics (A.D. 80–95), and no extensive literary dependence is readily discerned. Therefore we will note the more popular theories as they pertain to the Synoptic Gospels.

## Primitive Gospel Theory

This position suggests that our three biblical or canonical Gospels drew their material from an earlier, more primitive gospel that has not been preserved, probably written in Aramaic. This view has little if any historical support.

## Oral Tradition Theory

This view believes that only an "oral gospel" is behind our Synoptic Gospels. This theory emphasizes that the Gospel material was passed along orally or by word of mouth before being written down. There is some truth in this theory, but it is insufficient to account for (a) the possible existence of early written accounts (see Luke 1:1-3), (b) the different order of events discovered in the Synoptics, and (c) the variations in form, content, vocabulary, grammar, and word order that are evident in our Synoptic Gospels.

## MARKAN PRIORITY

This theory is the most popular theory among contemporary Bible students. It was not advocated until the modern era and the rise of historical criticism. This theory initially began as a two-source theory but is now usually expanded into a four-source theory.

Mark is viewed as the first Gospel written and is the foundation of Matthew and Luke, who incorporated almost all of Mark. Matthew and Luke also utilized another source (usually assumed to have been written) commonly called Q, from the German word *Quelle,* meaning *source.* This second source is said to account for about 250 verses of mostly teaching material of Jesus common to Matthew and Luke but that is not in Mark.

Expanding the two-source theory, an M-source is thought to account for material unique to Matthew, and an L-source is hypothetically set forth to account for material peculiar to Luke. Though the most popular theory, this model faces the difficulties of (a) having no early church support and (b) claiming sources (Q, L, M) with no historical support for their existence.

## Matthean Priority

Matthean priority was the position of the church from the first century until the Enlightenment. This theory sees Matthew as the first Synoptic, Luke, who utilized Matthew, as second, and Mark as third, being an abbreviated combination of Matthew and Luke.

The preaching of Peter is also seen as a significant influence on Mark's Gospel. The strengths of this theory are that (a) it was the unanimous view of the early church, and (b) it can account for the literary relationship that exists between the Synoptic Gospels without assuming hypothetical documents with little or no historical support.

While we do not know for sure how the Gospel writers possibly interacted with one another or what sources may have influenced their work, we are confident that the result of their work has given us three inspired, truthful, and authoritative portraits of our Lord Jesus Christ.

text is interpreted in light of literary conventions of the day, which for the most part do not require modern standards of precision in reporting, we may fairly assume his accounts to be historically trustworthy. But the reason for their inclusion is almost always theological.

  I. Introduction to Jesus' Ministry (1:1–4:16)

  II. Development of Jesus' Ministry (4:17–16:20)

  III. Climax of Jesus' Ministry (16:21–28:20)

*Purpose and Theology.* Matthew most likely wrote his Gospel for several reasons. (1) He wanted to convince non-Christian Jews of the truth of Christianity. (2) He sought to explain to Christians how their religion is the fulfillment of God's promises and patterns of activity in the Old Testament. (3) He wanted to give young believers basic instructions in Christian living. (4) He wanted to encourage his church in the midst of persecution from hostile authorities in both Jewish and Roman circles. (5) He desired to deepen Christian faith by supplying more details about Jesus' words and works.

The Gospel's theological emphases mesh with these purposes. Matthew took pains to demonstrate God's work in Jesus to bring the fulfillment of His promises to His chosen people, the Jews. Through (or even in spite of) their response, Matthew wanted to show how God offers the identical blessings and judgments to all humanity (see 10:5-6 and 15:24 with 2:1-12 and 28:19). He depicted Christ as a teacher (through five main sermons in chaps. 5–7; 10; 13; 18; 23–25). But he portrayed Him as much more than a teacher, the Son of David-Messiah, and Lord of the universe and of human hearts.

Matthew portrays Christian living preeminently as doing the will of God, which is defined as following Jesus in discipleship and obeying all of His commands (7:21-27; 12:46-50; 28:19). Christ does not abolish the Old Testament, but the law can be rightly applied in a believer's life only after one understands how it is fulfilled in Jesus (5:17). Matthew is the only Gospel to use the word "church" (16:18; 18:17). He envisaged his community of followers living on after his death and resurrection and completing his ministry of preaching the kingdom of God so that men and women might enter into a saving relationship with Jesus.

## JESUS' ORIGIN (1:1–2:23)

Matthew began his story by recounting selected events surrounding Jesus' birth (about 4–6 B.C.). The genealogy establishes Jesus' ancestry by which He was a legitimate descendant of David and rightful candidate for the messianic throne. The rest of Matthew's "infancy narrative" is comprised of five quotations from the Old Testament and the stories that illustrate how those texts were fulfilled in Jesus.

In one instance we read of the rather straightforward accomplishment of certain events previously predicted, namely, the Messiah's birthplace in Bethlehem. In two instances texts that were not prophecies at all in the Old Testament are typologically reapplied to events surrounding Christ's birth. Typology is the perception of recurring patterns of action in salvation-history that are too "coincidental" to be attributed to any cause but God. Examples are that the Messiah, like the Israelites of old, was brought out of Egypt and that the mothers in the vicinity of Bethlehem again bewailed the loss of their children. In one instance Matthew quoted a "text" that does not even appear in the Old Testament, but probably he had a more general theme in view. In the most famous case, he cited the prophecy about a child to be born to a virgin. This probably combines direct

| JESUS' MINISTRY AS FULFILLMENT OF SCRIPTURE IN MATTHEW | | |
|---|---|---|
| Aspects of His Ministry | Fulfillment Passage in Matthew | OT Prophecy |
| His virgin birth and role as God with us | Matt 1:18,22-23 | Isa 7:14 |
| His birth in Bethlehem and shepherd role | Matt 2:4-6 | Mic 5:2 |
| His refugee years in Egypt and role as God's Son | Matt 2:14-15 | Hos 11:1 |
| His upbringing in Nazareth and messianic role (the Hebrew term for branch is *nezer*) | Matt 2:23 | Isa 11:1 |
| His preaching ministry in Galilee and role as Light to the Gentiles | Matt 4:12-16 | Isa 9:1-2 |
| His healing ministry and role as God's Servant | Matt 8:16-17 | Isa 53:4 |
| His reluctance to attract attention and His role as God's chosen and loved Servant | Matt 12:16-21 | Isa 42:1-4 |
| His teaching in parables and His role in proclaiming God's sovereign rule | Matt 13:34-35 | Ps 78:2 |
| His humble entry into Jerusalem and role as King | Matt 21:1-5 | Zech 9:9 |
| His betrayal, arrest, and death and role as Suffering Servant | Matt 26:50,56 | The prophetic writings as a whole |

prediction-fulfillment with typology: Isaiah originally had a young woman of his day in view, but the prophecy was not exhaustively fulfilled in her or her child. This left Jews to believe that a great, more complete fulfillment still awaited them.

Two other themes emerge in these opening two chapters. First, Christ would be for all the nations even as He excluded many from His own people who refused to welcome Him. Even before He grew up, the Messiah clearly was not just another Jewish nationalist. His genealogy includes five women, all of whom were shrouded, rightly or wrongly, in the suspicions of having given birth to illegit-imate children. The Gentile magi who came to worship the Christ child are most likely Persian astrologers. They responded properly, however, to God's revelation to them, whereas the political and religious authorities of Jerusalem did not. Second, Herod figures, directly or indirectly, in every passage in chapter 2. Matthew contrasted the one who is truly the King of the Jews by birth with the one who actually rules but turns out to be a temporary intruder.

## PREPARATION FOR MINISTRY (3:1–4:16)

Matthew jumped abruptly to Jesus' adulthood, passing over in silence the intervening years of His life. The events of this section set the stage for and culminate in Jesus' baptism and temptation, both of which would prepare Him for His approximately three-year ministry (about A.D. 27–30). Jesus' cousin John preceded Him in the public eye, fulfilling the prophecies that one like Elijah would come to prepare the way for the Christ (see 11:7-19, esp. v. 14). He became known as "the Baptist" because he called Jews to repent of their sins and demonstrate the rededication of their lives to God by immersion in water, a rite otherwise largely reserved for Gentile proselytes to Judaism. John vividly taught the lesson that one's faith is a matter of personal commitment and not a reliance on ancestral pedigree.

Jesus and John met each other on the banks of the Jordan, where Jesus requested baptism even though He did not need to repent from sin. After initial protests John acceded, recognizing that this formed part of God's will. God used the occasion to testify with a heavenly voice to Jesus' true identity. Jesus is God's Son, the one whom Isaiah called Immanuel ("God with us," 1:23).

Immediately the Spirit orchestrated the circumstances that would permit the devil to test Jesus' understanding of that sonship. Would He use His elevated power and position for self-aggrandizement or for military or political ends? Would He turn out to be another would-be liberator of the Jews from Rome? Or

## PARABLES OF JESUS

Perhaps the most distinctive style of Jesus' teaching was His use of parables. From the outset of His public ministry until the last days in Jerusalem, one comes across His timeless parables. Matthew's word is appropriate at every juncture: "He told them many things in parables" (Matt. 13:3). A parable has been defined as a comparison from nature or daily life designed to teach a spiritual truth.

### Parables and Teaching

Everyone loves a good story. Jesus developed stories from familiar images and ideas that reveal truth about the nature of God, prayer, spiritual values, stewardship, judgment, and the kingdom of God. He

used parables as a teaching device with His disciples, antagonistic religious leaders, and ordinary people.

The Synoptic Gospels contain between fifty and sixty such stories. Add to that number ten brief stories found in John's Gospel. Some of them are very brief, such as the parables of the pearl of great price, the leaven, the hidden treasure. Some are full-length stories like the parables of the good Samaritan, the talents, the sower and the soils, the rich fool, the prodigal son, and others.

### Parables and Daily Life

Jesus was the keenest of observers about daily life. He drew lessons from farmers sowing in the field, from village customs about weddings, from shepherds and sheep, and from banquets. Recall that His audiences were often simple,

uneducated people such as fishermen, farmers, and villagers. They could grasp His lessons easily about an unjust judge or a friend who knocked at the midnight hour. Jesus used good storytelling to project divine truths about redemption, the kingdom of God, and ethical values.

There is a timelessness about these stories as well as a haunting beauty. They always present some powerful lesson about God and His will for life today.

### Parables of the Kingdom

Many of the parables deal with the kingdom of God, a major message Jesus sought to bring to Israel in His day. Matthew 13 is the great chapter on this theme. There Jesus used a series of parables to proclaim the actions of God in His own ministry.

would He follow the way of the Suffering Servant, the way that leads to the cross? The three temptations epitomize all major categories of human temptation, what the apostle John later would call the "lust of the flesh," "the lust of the eyes," and "the pride of life" (1 John 2:16). Where Adam, the nation of Israel, and indeed all humanity had previously failed, Jesus remained faithful. His ministry proceeded according to plan. As it did, He would continue to fulfill Scripture.

## INTRODUCTION (4:17-25)

"From that time on Jesus began to preach" marks the beginning of His major public ministry, mostly spent in Galilee. "Repent, for the kingdom of heaven is near" epitomizes His message

in one sentence. With Jesus' ministry, death, and resurrection, God's saving reign would be inaugurated in the hearts and lives of those who became His disciples. Universal acknowledgment of God's sovereignty in Jesus must await his second coming, but the kingdom has at least been inaugurated. He began to call to Himself those who would be His most intimate associates and trainees. Matthew then previewed the essence of Christ's ministry with the key terms "preaching, teaching and healing," which characterized his activity wherever He went.

## SERMON ON THE MOUNT (5:1-7:29)

Perhaps no portion of Scripture is as well known as Jesus' Great Sermon. It begins

---

### Parables on God's Nature

Some parables illustrate unforgettably the nature of God as Jesus came to reveal this essential truth. Speaking of the love of God to the Pharisees who were grumbling about tax gatherers and sinners around them, Jesus produced some memorable parables in Luke 15.

These parables of Jesus on the nature of God are excellent examples of His understanding of simple truths from daily living. For example, He related the shepherd's concern about a lost sheep, the peasant woman's loss of a dowry coin, the prodigal's lapse so terrible that he was feeding swine when "he came to his senses" (Luke 15:17).

### Themes of the Parables

Though Jesus did not follow a consistent theme in His teachings through par-

ables, He did address some of the major subjects of His ministry through parables. He dealt with the relation of the old covenant with the new covenant in the parables of the barren fig tree and the great feast. His lessons on prayer were highlighted by the parables of the friend who knocked at midnight and the unjust judge. Stewardship was another important theme as portrayed by the stories of the unjust steward and the rich fool.

Jesus' solemn teachings on judgment come through His parables of the wise and foolish virgins and the talents. The parables of Jesus touch movingly on death and resurrection in His parables of the rich man and Lazarus and the wicked husbandman.

### Approaches to the Study of Parables

Contemporary Bible studies strongly insist that Bible

students who seek the message of Jesus through His parables must understand the setting of the story. It is also important to realize that the parable usually has one major lesson to teach. Using an allegorical approach to the study of parables is both inappropriate and inaccurate. Students of Scripture should seek for one primary lesson from each parable.

Jesus' timeless reputation as a Teacher certainly comes from the substance and content of His inspired and authentic lessons. When we add the unique form of these lessons through the parables, we quickly affirm the conclusion of the centuries regarding Jesus' teaching: they "were amazed at his teaching, because he taught as one who had authority" (Matt. 7:28-29).

with the well-loved Beatitudes, which classically exemplify God's inversion of the world's values. In His kingdom or reign, those who are considered fortunate include the poor, sorrowing, humble, righteous, merciful, pure, peacemakers, and persecuted. These are precisely those categories of people too many of us tend to despise and ostracize.

These countercultural values could suggest that Jesus intended His followers to withdraw from the world and form separate communities. Matthew 5:13-16 immediately belies any such notion. Disciples must be salt and light, arresting decay and providing illumination for a lost and dying world.

Such radical ideas understandably would have raised the question of the relationship between Jesus' teaching and the Old Testament. Jesus addressed this topic next. He had not come to abolish the law, yet neither had He come to preserve but rather to "fulfill" it—to bring to completion everything to which it originally pointed. Some believe that Jesus demonstrated just the opposite with His contrasts in verses 21-48. These verses make plain, however, that Jesus was setting up dramatic contrasts between His teaching and the typical interpretations of the law. In some cases He drastically deepened the requirements. He demanded a greater righteousness, as with His discussion of murder, adultery, and divorce. But in other cases He actually set aside certain provisions of the Old Testament in favor of entirely new, internalized regulations, such as with oaths, retaliation, and probably love for enemy.

Throughout these illustrations Jesus used numerous hyperboles. They were not meant to be applied literally, but we nevertheless can understand why portions of this material have been taken as a manifesto for nonviolence in the church and in the world.

Matthew 5:48 closes off this section of the sermon by demonstrating that Jesus was setting forth an ideal. His disciples will never attain to these standards this side of His return, but they are not thereby excused from continuing to strive after those goals.

Matthew 6:1-18 turns to the theme of true versus hypocritical piety. In three closely parallel examples, Jesus treated the practices of almsgiving, prayer, and fasting. In each case the motive for correct religious behavior must be to please God rather than fellow humans. In the middle of the second of these topics, on prayer, Jesus gave the classic disciples' prayer, which has come to be known as the Our Father or the Lord's Prayer. In it He models all the elements of proper prayer in an appropriate sequence. He presented elements such as praise and adoration, leaving room for God's sovereign will to override ours; appeal for kingdom priorities to be manifest on the earth; personal petition and pleas for forgiveness contingent on our practice of forgiving others; and prayer for strength to avoid the tempter and his snares.

Matthew 6:19-34 is united by the themes of wealth and worry. Here Jesus contrasted transient, earthly riches with permanent, heavenly riches. If our priorities correctly reside with the latter, God through His people will take care of the former. The implementation of 6:33 presupposes Christian communities who look after the needy in their own midst as well as throughout the world. Matthew 6:22-24 catches us up short with its bold suggestion that money may be the single biggest competitor with God for ultimate allegiance in our lives, particularly for those who are not in the poorest classes of society. Affluent individuals who call themselves Christians need to read verse 24 again and again and ask themselves who they really are serving.

Matthew 7:1-12 rounds out the body of the sermon by discussing how to treat others. First, Jesus called His followers not to be judgmental in their relationships with others. But His illustrations also underline that once we have properly dealt with our own sins, we have the right and responsibility to evaluate others' behavior and to help them deal with their shortcomings. Second, He reminds us of God's generosity and desire to give us good gifts, though, after the Beatitudes we dare not define "good" in worldly terms like health and wealth. The well-known Golden Rule brings the body of Jesus' message to a climax and epitomizes the ethic underlying it all—treat others as you would want to be treated.

Matthew 7:14-27 forms the concluding warning. There are only two possible responses to Jesus' preaching—obedience or rejection. The narrow versus the wide roads, the good versus the bad fruit, and the wise versus the foolish builders illustrate this warning in three parallel ways. Professions of faith without appropriate changes of lifestyle prove empty. But mere works by themselves do not save; a relationship with Jesus is needed. On Judgment Day many will cry, "Lord, Lord" and appeal to their deeds. Christ will reply, "I never knew you."

## JESUS' HEALING MINISTRY (8:1-9:34)

Chapters 8–9 present nine miracle stories, all but one dealing with Jesus' physically healing the sick. As with His preaching, He astonished people with His authority, this time in working miracles. Matthew interrupted his narrative in two places to present Jesus' teaching on discipleship (8:18-22 and 9:9-17), thus creating three collections of three miracle stories each. The first underlines how Jesus healed the ritually outcast. He deliberately touched the leper, risking defilement, to cure bodily uncleanness.

Then He rewarded the Gentile centurion's unparalleled faith by curing his servant, transcending Jewish boundaries of ethnic uncleanness. Third, He healed Peter's mother-in-law despite conventional taboos based on gender uncleanness. Matthew characteristically inserted an Old Testament fulfillment quotation to demonstrate how Jesus was accomplishing the mission of Isaiah's Suffering Servant by all of this.

The first break in the healings occurs with Jesus' replies to two would-be disciples, both of whom exhibited inadequate responses to His exacting demands. The one man was overeager; the other, undereager. Neither had adequately counted the cost of following Christ. The second group of miracles proves even more dramatic than the first. Jesus stilled a storm, exorcised a Gentile demoniac, and healed a paralytic. In so doing He displayed His power and authority over disaster, demons, and disease. The stilling of the storm is the lone miracle in these two chapters that is not a healing. But Matthew's reference to Jesus' "rebuke" employs language characteristic of exorcisms, so perhaps Matthew saw this miracle as a kind of healing of nature.

After this dramatic series of wonders, Jesus could return again to the question of discipleship. This time He received a more adequate response—from Matthew himself. This in turn triggered Jesus' key pronouncements on the new, radical priorities of His ministry. A correct appreciation for who Christ is, disclosed in the miracles, should lead people to serve Him in discipleship.

The final series of miracle stories includes one passage with two actual healings in it. En route to Jairus's home, Jesus stopped the flow of blood from a chronically hemorrhaging woman. The delay resulted in His not merely curing

## PARABLES OF JESUS

| PARABLE | OCCASION | LESSON TAUGHT | REFERENCES |
|---|---|---|---|
| 1. The speck and the log | Sermon on the Mount (Matt), Sermon on the Plain (Luke) | Do not presume to judge others | Matt 7:1-6; Luke 6:37-42 |
| 2. The two houses | Sermon on the Mount, at the close | Necessity of building life on Jesus' words | Matt 7:24-27; Luke 6:47-49 |
| 3. Children in the marketplace | Rejection of John's baptism and Jesus' ministry | Evil of a fault-finding disposition | Matt 11:16-19; Luke 7:32-34 |
| 4. The two debtors | A Pharisee's self-righteous reflections | Love to Christ proportioned to grace received | Luke 7:41-43 |
| 5. The unclean spirit | The scribes demand a miracle in the heavens | Hardening power of unbelief | Matt 12:43-45; Luke 11:24-26 |
| 6. The rich fool | Dispute of two brothers | Folly of reliance upon wealth | Luke 12:16-21 |
| 7. The barren fig tree | Tidings of the execution of certain Galileans | Still time for repentance | Luke 13:6-9 |
| 8. The sower | Sermon on the seashore | Effects of preaching religious truth | Matt 13:3-8; Mark 4:3-8; Luke 8:5-8 |
| 9. The tares | The same | The severance of good and evil | Matt 13:24-30 |
| 10. The seed | The same | Power of truth | Mark 4:26-29 |
| 11. The grain of mustard seed | The same | Small beginnings and growth of Christ's kingdom | Matt 13:31-32; Mark 4:31-32; Luke 13:19 |
| 12. The leaven | The same | Dissemination of the knowledge of Christ | Matt 13:33; Luke 13:21 |
| 13. The lamp | Sermon on the Mount (Matt), Teaching a large crowd (Mark, Luke) | Effect of good example | Matt 5:15; Mark 4:21; Luke 8:16 11:33 |
| 14. The dragnet | Sermon on the seashore | Mixed character of the church | Matt 13:47-48 |
| 15. The hidden treasure | Sermon on the seashore | Value of God's kingdom | Matt 13:44 |
| 16. The pearl of great value | Sermon on the seashore | The same | Matt 13:45-46 |
| 17. The householder | Sermon on the seashore | Varied methods of teaching truth | Matt 13:52 |
| 18. The marriage | To the critics who censured the disciples | Joy in Christ's companionship | Matt 9:15; Mark 2:19-20; Luke 5:34-35 |
| 19. The patched garment | The same | Newness of God's work in Christ, which cannot be impeded by the old | Matt 9:16; Mark 2:21; Luke 5:36 |
| 20. The wine bottles | The same | The same | Matt 9:17; Mark 2:22; Luke 5:37-38 |
| 21. The harvest | Spiritual wants of the Jewish people | Need of witness and prayer | Matt 9:37; Luke 10:2 |
| 22. The opponent | Slowness of the people to believe | Need of prompt reconciliation | Matt 5:25-26; Luke 12:58-59 |
| 23. Two insolvent debtors | Peter's question | Duty of forgiveness | Matt 18:23-35 |
| 24. The good Samaritan | The lawyer's question | The golden rule for all | Luke 10:30-37 |

## PARABLES OF JESUS (continued)

| PARABLE | OCCASION | LESSON TAUGHT | REFERENCES |
|---|---|---|---|
| 25. The persistent friend | Disciples ask lesson in prayer | Effect of importunity in prayer | Luke 11:5-8 |
| 26. The good shepherd | Pharisees reject testimony of miracle | Christ the only way to God | John 10:1-16 |
| 27. The narrow, or locked door | The question, Are there few who can be saved? | Difficulty of entry into God's Kingdom | Luke 13:24 |
| 28. The two ways | The Sermon on the Mount | Difficulty of discipleship | Matt 7:13-14 |
| 29. The guests | Eagerness to take high places | Chief places not to be usurped | Luke 14:7-11 |
| 30. The marriage supper | Self-righteous remark of a guest | Rejection of unbelievers | Matt 22:2-9; Luke 14:16-24 |
| 31. The wedding clothes | Continuation of the same discourse | Necessity of purity | Matt 22:10-14 |
| 32. The tower | Multitudes surrounding Christ | Need of counting the cost of discipleship | Luke 14:28-30 |
| 33. The king going to war | The same | The same | Luke 14:31-32 |
| 34. The lost sheep | The disciples' question: who is the greatest? (Matt), Pharisees objected to His receiving tax collectors and "sinners" | Christ's love for sinners based on God's love for them | Matt 18:12-13; Luke 15:4-7 |
| 35. The lost coin | The same | The same | Luke 15:8-9 |
| 36. The prodigal son | The same | The same | Luke 15:11-32 |
| 37. The unjust steward | To the disciples | Prudence in using property | Luke 16:1-9 |
| 38. The rich man and Lazarus | Derision of the Pharisees | Salvation not connected with wealth and the adequacy of Scripture | Luke 16:19-31 |
| 39. The importunate widow | Teaching the disciples | Perseverance in prayer | Luke 18:2-5 |
| 40. The Pharisee and tax-gatherer | Teaching the self-righteous | Humility in prayer | Luke 18:10-14 |
| 41. The slave's duty | Teaching the disciples | Humble obedience | Luke 17:7-10 |
| 42. Laborers in the vineyard | The same | God's graciously adequate gift to the unworthy | Matt 20:1-16 |
| 43. The talents | In Jerusalem at the house of Zacchaeus | Doom of unfaithful followers | Matt 25:14-30; Luke 19:11-27 |
| 44. The two sons | The chief priests demand His authority | Obedience better than words | Matt 21:28-30 |
| 45. The wicked vine-growers | The same | Rejection of the Jewish people | Matt 21:33-43; Mark 12:1-9; Luke 20:9-15 |
| 46. The fig tree | In prophesying the destruction of Jerusalem | Duty of watching for Christ's appearance | Matt 24:32; Mark 13:28; Luke 21:29-30 |
| 47. The watching householder | The same | The same | Matt 24:43; Luke 12:39 |
| 48. The watchful slave | The same | The same | Mark 13:34-36 |
| 49. Character of two slaves | The same | Danger of unfaithfulness | Matt 24:45-51; Luke 12:42-46 |
| 50. The ten virgins | The same | Necessity of watchfulness | Matt 25:1-12 |
| 51. The watching slaves | The same | The same | Luke 12:36-38 |
| 52. The vine and branches | At the last supper | The need to abide in Christ | John 15:1-6 |

Jairus's daughter but actually raising her from the dead. Next He gave sight to two blind men. Finally, He restored speech to a mute person.

Throughout these three accounts, the crowds that observed Jesus' miracles began to take sides. In 9:26 Jesus received widespread positive publicity. In 9:31 this continued, but Jesus hinted at possible danger as well. In 9:33-34 the antagonism became explicit. Even as His popularity grew, the Jewish leaders accused Jesus of working His wonders by the devil's power. This charge reflects consistent Jewish hostility over the next several centuries. Interestingly, rabbinic Judaism never tried to deny that Jesus worked miracles but merely challenged the source of His authority.

## OPPOSITION PREDICTED (9:35–10:42)

Jesus' second major "sermon" in Matthew proceeds at once. One might entitle it "The Sermon on Mission: To the Jew First and Also to the Greek." The sermon begins after introductory remarks explaining the need for workers to help Christ proclaim the good news of the kingdom and after a list of the twelve Jesus formally called to this task. It divides sharply into two quite different sections. In 10:5-16 Jesus laid down the stipulations that would apply to the immediate mission He was sending His followers out two-by-two to carry out. They were to travel light and unencumbered, depend on others' hospitality for their daily provisions, and not stay long with any who remain unresponsive to their message. They were to limit their mission to Jewish territories and communities. As God's chosen people, the Jews had the right and the privilege of hearing and responding to this latest and fullest revelation from God before the rest of the world did.

From 10:17-42 Jesus broadened His scope far beyond His earthly life and the immediate mission on which the disciples were embarking. He envisaged the prospect of future hostility from both Jews and Gentiles, both frustrated family members and officials in high places with legal authority to persecute and potentially condemn Christ's followers. He explained the proper reaction to such hostility: Fear God, who can condemn people eternally, more than humans who can merely take away one's physical life.

As at the end of the Sermon on the Mount, Jesus closed His address by reminding His followers that they have only two options—either to give God ultimate allegiance or not. To do so they must acknowledge that they are Jesus' followers, put God above family, and welcome those who are Christ's emissaries. Any other choice will lead to Jesus' disowning them, which results in the loss of eternal life.

## OPPOSITION EXPERIENCED (11:1–12:50)

The hostilities Jesus predicted the disciples would later experience now began to chase His footsteps as well. In chapter 11 the opposition is implicit; in chapter 12 it becomes explicit. John the Baptist had been arrested and understandably began to question whether he had correctly identified the Messiah-Liberator after all. After sending his disciples to interrogate Christ, he was told to consider Jesus' mighty deeds and then to make up his own mind.

But if John was doubting Jesus, some in the audience may have been starting to doubt John. So Jesus discussed the Baptist with the crowds. John too came in some unexpected ways but was nevertheless to be viewed as the forerunner, fulfilling Old Testament prophecy about preparation for the Messiah's advent. In fact, John was the greatest man to live under the old covenant. But he would not live long enough to see Christ's death and resurrection establish the new covenant, so in that sense even the most insignificant Christian was greater than he. The crowds were not to reject the legitimacy of either Jesus or John. Time would vindicate God's wisdom in sending each in unexpected fashion. Turning to still a third audience, Jesus began to upbraid, because of their unbelief, the Jewish cities in which He performed most of His miracles. A proper response should imitate His disciples, who generally represented the powerless and insignificant of the world but who accepted the spiritual rest available in Christ.

In chapter 11 no one opposes Jesus directly. In chapter 12 opposition turns explicit and ugly. First, the Jewish authorities called Jesus on the carpet for breaking their Sabbath laws. Although it cannot be proven that Jesus went beyond the infringement of the "oral law" to violating the Old Testament itself, part of the argument Jesus made on His behalf appeals to Old Testament precedent in which the very provisions of the Mosaic law were violated. Matthew reasoned that in Jesus something greater than both David and the temple (the king and priestly cult) is present. Surely very serious infractions indeed would be needed to have elicited the Pharisees' extreme response. Jesus withdrew from hostilities and in so doing again fulfilled Scripture.

But the antagonism quickly resumed and grew to a fever pitch. Another exorcism led to the identical charge as in 9:34. This time Jesus responded at some length. The Jews dared not accuse Him of being empowered by the devil. They too cast out demons, so their argument could easily turn back on themselves. In fact, it is absurd to imagine Satan warring against himself in this way. More so than any other kind of miracle, the exorcisms should make plain that God's saving rule had arrived.

Verse 28 offers one of the most crucial texts in all of the Gospels, demonstrating that the kingdom had come with Jesus. Having defended Himself, Jesus then unleashed an attack on His accusers. They had better "come clean" and "show their true colors," which would disclose the evil intentions of their hearts. In this context appears the troublesome warning against the one unforgivable sin of which Scripture speaks—blasphemy against the Holy Spirit. Probably we are to understand this sin as the prolonged, hostile, and unrepentant rejection of Jesus as one empowered by the Holy Spirit, which eventually dulls a person's spiritual sensibilities beyond a point of no return (see Rom. 1:18-32). But we dare never play God and pretend we know who such people are; we would invariably err. And all persons fearful of having committed such sin by that very concern demonstrate that they have not.

If the exorcisms prove inconclusive to the Pharisees, what more indisputable sign could Jesus have offered them? "None," Jesus responded, save for His resurrection, which, if the other signs had not proved convincing would not likely seem any more decisive (Luke 16:19-31). As at the end of chapter 11, Jesus concluded with the positive alternative. It is not adequate simply to be exorcised. One must replace the emptiness created by the demons' absence with loyalty to Christ. Those who follow Him and do God's will thus form His true family, even while some literally related to Him must take a back seat.

### KINGDOM PARABLES (13:1-52)

With chapter 13 we reach the midpoint of Matthew's narrative and a turning point in Jesus' ministry. The polarization of response to Jesus made it necessary for Him to concentrate on those who remained open to His message. In His third major discourse, He taught by means of parables. Parables are short, metaphorical narratives designed to teach truths about spiritual realities in ways that reveal insights to those open to Jesus' claims about Himself but that further alienate those who are not so receptive. Even the structure of this sermon reflects the growing polarization. First Jesus addressed the increasingly skeptical crowds, then He turned to His more loyal disciples. The latter do not always catch on any better at first, but they remain faithful and so eventually achieve more profound understanding.

In the more public half of His message, Jesus narrated and interpreted the parable of the sower, told the story of the wheat and the weeds, and recounted the shorter similes of the mustard seed and heaven. The "sower" depicts four kinds of seeds, standing for four ways in which people respond to God's word. The only adequate, saving response is that which perseveres until it bears a bountiful crop of fruit, notwithstanding the obstacles that may first intervene. The "wheat and weeds" warns against premature, human attempts to usurp God's role as Judge and Avenger. Despite the attacks of the enemy in the present age, often in the form of professing Christians superficially indistinguishable from the real kind, disciples are not to usurp God's role. The "mustard seed and leaven" promise great endings for God's kingdom despite inauspicious beginnings.

When Jesus went indoors to finish His discourse with His disciples, He interpreted the "wheat and weeds" for them. Then He told them a series of short parables. Included are parables of the hidden treasure and pearl of great price, the dragnet, and the scribe trained for the

kingdom of heaven. The first two depict the inestimable value of the kingdom and the need to sacrifice whatever it takes to enter it. The dragnet resembles the wheat and weeds but with emphasis on final judgment and the only two destinies humanity faces. Verses 51-52 compare the well-schooled Christian to a homeowner who finds valuable treasures in his storehouse, both old and new. This probably is an allusion to continuities as well as discontinuities between old and new covenants.

## FROM JEW TO GENTILE (13:53–16:20)

Jesus turned in the midst of His teaching from those who refused to respond adequately to His message to those who proved more receptive. In the same way He then turned from those who rejected His miracle-working ministry, in His hometown and homeland, to those outside Israel who would receive Him more gladly. Matthew 13:53–14:12 opens this section by paralleling Jesus' rejection in His hometown of Nazareth with John's rejection and execution by his own governor, Herod. Both reflect an inadequate understanding of who Jesus is. The Nazarenes thought Him merely a prophet. Herod thought Jesus was John resurrected.

The main panel of this section extends from 14:13–16:12. Here Jesus revealed Himself as the Bread of life for Jews and Gentiles alike. First He manifested Himself to Israel. He miraculously fed the five thousand from a few loaves and fishes, reminiscent of manna in the wilderness in the days of Moses and the exodus. Jesus was a new and greater Moses, bringing full, spiritual redemption for His people Israel if they would accept it. Then He walked on the water, showing Himself as equal to Yahweh, Lord of wind and waves. The innocuous greeting

"It is I" exactly echoes God's words to Moses from the burning bush (Exod. 3:14). It more literally reads, "I am"—the very meaning of the name of God. Appropriately Jesus' disciples reached a provisional high point in their understanding of Jesus' identity as they acclaimed Him "Son of God." A flurry of healings on the shores of Galilee rounds out this section.

Despite all these attestations of Jesus' divine origin, the Jewish leaders remained hostile. Matthew 15:1–16:12 thus portrays Jesus' turning from the Jews to the Gentiles, among whom He received a better welcome. In 15:1-20 Jesus had not left Israel geographically, but He certainly had departed ideologically. Here He challenged all of the Jewish "kosher laws." As with the Sabbath, one cannot prove that He went beyond breaking the oral laws to infringing on the written law of Moses, but verse 11 certainly sets the stage for this conclusion. Food, as something that goes into people from the outside, could no longer ritually defile them. In 15:21-28 Jesus left Galilee for Syrophoenicia (the regions of Tyre and Sidon) and met a woman Matthew deliberately referred to as Caananite—an archiving label designed to conjure up horrors of Israel's enemies of old. This woman admitted her secondary place in salvation history (Jesus was sent to the Jews first). But she nevertheless exemplifies "great faith," reminiscent of the Gentile centurion (whose faith Jesus said surpassed that of all He had found in Israel, 8:10). So Jesus granted her request for her daughter's healing. Even more dramatically, He reenacted the miracle of the loaves and fishes, this time for four thousand Gentile men and their families. Whereas many Jews had scoffed, these Gentiles "glorified the God of Israel," particularly as Jesus again performed a host of healing.

Returning to Galilee, His opponents reared their ugly heads at once. Again Jesus met a request for a sign with rebuff. God does not work miracles on demand to satisfy skeptics. Jesus took His disciples and returned immediately to the eastern shores of the lake. En route He warned them against the insidious teaching of the Pharisees and Sadducees. This combination of rival Jewish factions highlights their hostility against Jesus. They willingly set aside their differences in the face of a common enemy.

The concluding portion of 13:53–16:20 contrasts with the introductory section. There inadequate understandings of Jesus led to His rejection. Here, still in Gentile territory, His disciples, and Peter in particular, correctly identified Him as "the Christ, the Son of the living God." Matthew 16:13-20 thus forms the famous "confession" on the road to Caesarea Philippi. In response, and only in Matthew's version of the episode, Jesus praised Peter's insight as heaven sent and called him the rock on which He would build His church, promising Peter the keys to the kingdom. Nothing of the Roman notions of the papacy or apostolic succession appears here. But Jesus did predict the preeminent role Peter would play as the leader of the infant church in integrating new ethnic groups into the Christian community (see Acts 1–12).

The main body of Matthew's Gospel and the culmination of Jesus' public ministry end with a strange warning against spreading the word about Jesus' true identity. The next verse, with which the final main division of the Gospel begins, will dramatically clarify why.

## CORRECTING MISUNDERSTANDINGS (16:21–17:27)

Immediately on the heels of his triumphant confession of Jesus as Son of God, Peter betrayed a serious flaw in his understanding of that sonship. He was not prepared to hear about the road to the cross, to learn of the suffering Jesus must endure. But a Messiah without an atoning death fits in with the goals of Satan, not the plans of God. In fact, disciples too must be prepared to carry their own crosses, experiencing persecution and even death for their Master when need arises. These verses set the stage for the rest of the Gospel, which narrates the unfolding drama of how Christ was in fact crucified but also resurrected. Glory lies ahead, but the cross must precede the crown.

Jesus, nevertheless, gives His three closest disciples a preview of that glory. He provides a glimpse of His majesty no longer incognito, through the miraculous self-disclosure on a high mountain we have come to call the mount of transfiguration. Matthew 16:28 probably predicts this event. Matthew 17:1-9 describes it in more detail. With Jesus appeared Moses and Elijah, key Old Testament prophets and miracle workers, leading the disciples naturally to ask once more about the prophecies of Elijah's return. In striking contrast with the triumph of the transfiguration appears

## TITLES OF CHRIST IN THE GOSPELS

The Gospels contain two classes of titles: those that go back to Jesus Himself and those that are applied to Him by others. There is considerable scholarly discussion about the exact nature of the first group, but the evidence of Scripture must be allowed to speak for itself. Jesus used certain titles for Himself and allowed His followers to refer to Him in certain ways. From these we gain insight into how He understood Himself and His mission.

### Son of Man

This was Jesus' favorite self-designation. It originated in the Old Testament (Dan. 7:13-14), was used during the intertestamental period, and was chosen by Jesus to define His messianic mission. It was serviceable because it had messianic overtones. It also was sufficiently fluid to allow Jesus to inject His own meaning into it. He

needed to do this because the idea of messiahship current in His day was that of a military hero, whereas He came to be the Savior of the world.

Jesus used the title Son of man in four different ways. First, frequently it was a synonym for "I." Jesus was simply referring to Himself (for example, see Matt. 26:24). Second, the Son of man is one who exercises divine authority (for example, see Matt. 9:6). Third, the Son of man fulfills His earthly mission by death and resurrection (for example, see Matt. 12:40; 17:9,12,23). Fourth, the Son of man will return in great glory to establish His kingdom (for example, see Matt. 16:27-28; 19:28). In this way Jesus defined who He, the messianic Son of man, is.

### Son, Son of God, Only Son

The title "Son of God," or "Son" for short, was also a messianic title derived from the Old Testament (2 Sam. 7:11-16). It assumes a

more exalted status, however, when used by or about Jesus. It means in fact that Jesus possesses the qualities of the divine nature. This was quite evident when the heavenly voice cried out to Jesus at His baptism that He was beloved and well pleasing (Matt. 3:16-17), an affirmation reiterated at Jesus' transfiguration (Mark 9:7).

Jesus' own understanding of His unique relation to God as Son is reflected in Matthew 11:25-27 and Luke 10:21-22. Jesus expressed the same idea when confounding the Pharisees (Matt. 22:41-46). In the Gospel of John, Jesus is referred to as God's "one and only Son" (John 3:16), a term that means one of a kind or unique.

### Lord

This was a title of honor used of Jesus, the equivalent of "Master" or "Sir." However, we can see lurking in it something of the failure of the other nine disciples to work a "simple" miracle for which they had long ago been commissioned (recall 10:8). Jesus rebuked their paltry faith and reassured them that even confidence of the size of the proverbially tiny mustard seed would have been sufficient.

Matthew 17:22-27 rounds off this section as it began—with Christ again predicting His suffering, death, and resurrection. A question about whether or not Jesus paid the temple tax leads Him to teach a remarkable lesson about the freedom of God's people from the Old Testament laws coupled with the necessity of avoiding unnecessary offense in transgressing them (a balance Paul would repeat in a quite different context in 1 Cor. 8:10).

## HUMILITY AND FORGIVENESS (18:1-35)

In his fourth major sermon in Matthew, Jesus began to outline regulations for life in Christian community under the sign of the cross. This discourse divides naturally into two sections. The first focuses on humility; the second, on forgiveness (vv. 15-35). In verses 1-9 Jesus called His disciples to a humble demeanor. Positively,

greater significance (Matt. 8:5-13; Mark 2:23-27). In Judaism "Lord" had become the word pronounced when the personal name *Yahweh* appeared in Scripture. "Lord" thus meant *God*. The church later, in light of Jesus' death and resurrection, used it to mean nothing less than that Jesus was God.

### Christ (Messiah)

Jesus was reluctant to acknowledge this title because of the popular misconceptions that abounded about the Messiah, centering on a king to rule on David's throne. Under the proper circumstances, however, He was willing to confess that He was indeed God's Anointed One (Matt. 16:13-20; 26:62-64; John 4:25-26). This title was used so commonly later on in the church that it became virtually a name for Jesus; so "Jesus the Christ" became simply "Christ." (See as an example the shifting use of names and titles in 2 Cor. 12.)

### The Word

In the Gospels this title is found only in John (1:1-14). The expression "word of God" is common in both the Old and New Testaments as defining how God expressed Himself and what the content of that communication was. When referring to Jesus, it makes that self-revelation of God personal. Jesus as the Word of God supremely reveals who God is. If we would know God, we are to look at Jesus, the very expression (Word) of God. "Anyone who has seen me has seen the Father" (John 14:9), said Jesus.

### Savior

It is self-evident in the Old Testament that just as there is only one God, so there is only one Savior (for example, see Isa. 43:3,11; 45:21). This is also true in the New Testament (1 Tim. 2:3; 4:10; Titus 1:3; 2:10). It is all the more significant, then, that Jesus is announced as the Savior of Israel (Luke 2:11) and the world (John 4:42) in the Gospels. Jesus was understood to be divine redemption incarnate and was proclaimed as such by the early church (Acts 5:31; 13:23; 1 John 4:14).

### Holy One of God

This is a term used specifically by supernatural evil beings of Jesus as the one who is pure and holy (Mark 1:24; Luke 4:34; John 6:69). As such He sealed their doom in that He is wholly righteous and they are wholly evil. It identified Jesus with the Holy God (compare Isa. 6).

### Son of David

Son of David is a messianic title frequently used to refer to Jesus in the Gospels (Matt. 1:1; 9:27; 15:22; 20:30-31; 21:9,15). The title expresses hope. The Son of David, who was greater than David (22:41-45), would bring deliverance for those hopelessly in bondage.

this means adopting a childlike dependence on God. Negatively, it means ruthlessly excising from one's life anything that could cause another believer to sin. In verses 10-14 Jesus explained why He can command these things of His followers. God has already demonstrated the ultimate humility in leaving His nearly complete flock of ninety-nine sheep to seek to recover one stray.

Closely linked with humility is forgiveness. When believers offend fellow believers, they should seek reconciliation at almost any cost. Verses 15-20 describe the appropriate process but recognize that at times one party will still refuse to be reconciled. When all other measures fail, the unrepentant sinner must be "excommunicated" from the fellowship. But even then the goal is rehabilitative and not punitive. Treating people like pagans or tax-collectors suggests first of all that they are not considered as members of the community. But it also indicates that, even as Jesus dealt with the literal pagans and tax collectors of His day, they are continually to be wooed to repent so that they might return. Decisions made by the church in keeping with the procedures of verses 15-18 will be ratified in heaven. On the other hand, when believers do repent, forgiveness should be unlimited. For in light of the immense sin God has forgiven each of us, a professing Christian's refusal to forgive a fellow believer who requests it (and demonstrates a change of heart and action) proves so callous that one can only conclude that such a person never truly experienced Christ's forgiveness in the first place.

## TRUE DISCIPLESHIP (19:1–22:46)

In 19:1 Jesus left Galilee for the final time to begin His fateful journey to Jerusalem, where He met His death. En route He worked but one more miracle, focusing rather on teaching those around Him.

He increasingly stressed the nature of discipleship, but as He entered the city, He underlined the theme of impending judgment for Israel.

In 19:1–20:34 Jesus was literally "on the road," journeying to Judea. Matthew 19:1–20:16 describes three encounters with people who accosted Him with various kinds of questions or demands. First, the Pharisees tried to trap Him by asking Him His views on divorce. In His reply Jesus went beyond both competing schools of Pharisaic thought—the Hillelites, who granted divorce "for any good cause," and the Shammaites, who limited it to adultery. Instead, He stressed the permanence of marriage as God's original design. He did agree with Shammai in permitting divorce and remarriage when adultery has already ruptured a union. But unlike Shammai, He did not require it. And very much out of keeping with conventional Jewish sympathies, He pointed out God's call to some to lead a single, celibate lifestyle.

Second, He dealt with His disciples' impatience at certain individuals who asked Him to bless their children. As in 18:1-5, He used this opportunity to teach about childlike dependence on God. Third, He responded to the rich young man's question about how to receive eternal life. His call to this man demanded that he sell his possessions, give to the poor, and follow Him in discipleship. He called other people to deal with their money differently (see Luke 19:1-27); but whenever something becomes an obstacle to doing God's will, it must be jettisoned. This third encounter led Peter, on behalf of the Twelve, to ask what reward they would receive inasmuch as they *had* left families and possessions behind in their itinerant ministries. Jesus' answer points to their eternal reward but also hints at manifold compensation in this life, presupposing

## TITLES FOR JESUS IN SCRIPTURE

| TITLE | SIGNIFICANCE | REFERENCE |
|---|---|---|
| Alpha and Omega | The Beginning and Ending of all things | Rev 21:6 |
| Bread of Life | The one essential food | John 6:35 |
| Chief Cornerstone | A Sure Foundation of life | Eph 2:20 |
| Chief Shepherd | Gives guidance and protection | 1 Pet 5:4 |
| Christ | The Anointed One of God foreseen by Old Testament prophets | Matt 16:16 |
| Firstborn from the Dead | Leads us into resurrection | Col 1:18 |
| Good Shepherd | Gives guidance and protection | John 10:11 |
| High Priest | The Perfect Mediator | Heb 3:1 |
| Holy One of God | Perfect and sinless | Mark 1:24 |
| Immanuel | God with us | Matt 1:23 |
| Jesus | His personal name meaning Yahweh Saves | Matt 1:21 |
| King of Kings, Lord of Lords | The Sovereign Almighty | Rev 19:16 |
| Lamb of God | Offered His life as a sacrifice for sins | John 1:29 |
| Light of the World | One who brings hope and gives guidance | John 9:5 |
| Lord | Sovereign Creator and Redeemer | Rom 10:9 |
| Lord of Glory | The power of the Living God | 1 Cor 2:8 |
| Mediator | Redeemer who brings forgiven sinners into the presence of God | 1 Tim 2:5 |
| Prophet | One who speaks for God | Luke 13:33 |
| Rabbi/Teacher | A title of respect for one who taught the Scriptures | John 3:2 |
| Savior | One who delivers from sin | John 4:42 |
| Son of David | One who brings in the Kingdom | Matt 9:27 |
| Son of God | A title of Deity signifying Jesus' unique and special intimacy with the Father | John 20:31 |
| Son of Man | A divine title of suffering and exaltation | Matt 20:28 |
| Word | Eternal God who ultimately reveals God | John 1:1 |

that fellow disciples share their posses-sions and functions as a large, extended family (see Mark 10:30).

In 20:17-34 Jesus centered further attention on His "passion," eliciting con-trasting responses from His audiences. Verses 17-19 form the third and final passion prediction. Verses 20-28 illus-trate an inappropriate response. James and John, two of the apostles, through a request by their mother, sought status in Jesus' kingdom and were rebuked. Verses 29-34 illustrate an appropriate response. Two blind men recognized Jesus as Son of David, the legitimate Jewish Messiah, and merely begged for mercy. Christ was gracious and healed them of their malady, leading them to follow Him in discipleship.

Chapters 21-22 find Jesus arriving in Jerusalem itself. There He taught about the imminent destruction of the Jewish temple, capital, and nation if its people as a whole and leaders in particular did not repent. Matthew 21:1-22 introduces this topic by a series of object lessons or enacted parables. Jesus began with what has been improperly termed "the trium-phal entry." Six days before the Pass-over, on what we now call Palm Sunday, He rode a donkey into the city. He was acclaimed by the crowds as Messiah and ushered into town in a fashion reminis-cent of conquering warriors and kings of Old Testament and intertestamental times. But the crowds did not recognize what kind of Messiah Christ is. They had no place in their plans for Him to be pre-sented on such a humble animal nor to be arrested and suffer. Hence, the howl-ing mob merely five days later clamored for His crucifixion. As Jesus entered the temple precincts, He did the entirely unexpected. He overturned the benches of the moneychangers, drove out the sac-rificial animals, and accused the Jewish leaders of having corrupted a place of

prayer by turning it into an extortionary marketplace.

This judgment of the temple by "puri-fication" is followed immediately with judgment by threatened destruction. The strange miracle of cursing the fig tree is best interpreted by Jesus' parable that uses identical imagery (Luke 13:6-9). Fig trees often stood for Israel in the Old Tes-tament. Jesus was showing what would happen to the nation if it did not repent.

Matthew 21:23-22:46 presents a series of controversies with the Jewish leaders. Various individuals and groups approached Jesus, each with a question in keeping with their own commitments. But they were not seeking enlighten-ment. Rather, again they were trying to trap Jesus so as to be able to arrest and condemn Him. The temple authorities understandably asked about Jesus' authority. How dare He come in and so disrupt their proceedings? Recognizing the trap, He posed a counterquestion. How do they account for John the Bap-tist's ministry? They could not reply with-out either conceding Jesus' divine authority, since His message parallels John's, or falling out of favor with the crowds who applauded the Baptist. So they refused to answer, and Jesus did likewise. But He recounted a series of three parables that clearly imply His (and John's) God-given authority, even as they successively depict God's indictment, sentence, and execution of Israel.

The parable of the two sons makes the point that performance takes priority over promise. The parable of the wicked tenants predicts that "the kingdom of God will be taken away from [the Jewish leaders] and given to a people who will produce its fruit." The parable of the wedding banquet prophesies the destruc-tion of Jerusalem in response to the Jews' rejection of Jesus but also threat-ens judgment on any would-be Christians who refuse to come to Christ on His terms.

The series of controversies resumed as the Pharisees and Herodians questioned Jesus about paying taxes to the Roman emperor. The former did not support doing so; the latter did. No matter His reply, Jesus would alienate one of the two groups—except that He found a way out! Both God and human governments deserve allegiance, each in its rightful sphere of influence.

The Sadducees took the stage next and ridiculed the resurrection by means of a worst-case scenario. This Jewish sect refused to believe in any doctrine that could not be established from the five books of Moses. So Jesus replied by proving the resurrection from Exodus 3:6 after correcting their mistaken assumption that humans would retain sexuality in heaven.

A lawyer approached Christ to ask about the greatest commandment in the law. Jesus gave not one but two answers, combining Deuteronomy 6:5 and Leviticus 19:18. The lawyer had no dispute with Jesus' reply. The questions ceased as the crowds remained amazed at Jesus' responses. Jesus concluded this round of teaching in the temple by turning the tables on His questioners and baffling them with a question about Psalm 110:1: How can David's son (the Messiah) be merely human if David (king of all Israel) also calls Him his Lord?

## JUDGMENT (23:1–25:46)

Jesus' final discourse takes place in two parts. First, while still in the temple He unleashed a series of warnings against the scribes and Pharisees, in view of God's judgment on Israel. Then with His disciples on the Mount of Olives He predicted the destruction of the temple but also the final judgment of all peoples. The temple invective divides into three sections. In 23:1-12 Jesus warned

against imitating various kinds of undesirable behavior the Jewish leaders too frequently exemplified. In 23:13-36 proceed seven woes decrying their hypocrisy. Matthew 23:37-39 changes the tone as Jesus more compassionately lamented Israel's downfall and hinted at a future restoration.

Chapters 24–25 comprise Jesus' predictions of what will unfold after His death to usher in the end times. Its structure and interpretation are notoriously complex; the following is but one of several viable options. Matthew 24:1-35 describes the signs and times of the temple's destruction and of Christ's return. The disciples asked about both events, probably thinking of them as occurring simultaneously.

Jesus made clear in His reply that they are distinct. First, He reviewed a series of signs that do not herald the end but consistently characterize life in the Christian era. Second, He described the horror of the actual destruction of the temple. Third, He alluded to the subsequent "great tribulation," which for Matthew, at least, seems to embrace the entire period between Christ's two comings (compare "then" in v. 21 and "immediately" in v. 29). Fourth, He described Christ's actual return, an unmistakable, universally visible event. Fifth, and finally, He drew a series of conclusions or implications from this scenario of events.

Of these, two remain crucial in the face of many false prophets, ancient and modern. First, no one, not even Jesus, knows or can predict when He will come back. Second, all of the preliminary signs leading up to but not including Christ's actual return were fulfilled in the generation immediately following Christ's death. This is why Christians ever since have been able to believe Christ could come back in their day. No modern event (such as the restoration of the nation of Israel) can carry any special significance in pointing to the end of the last days; all the things necessary for Christ to come back were completed by A.D. 70. We now must merely remain faithful and expectant.

Verse 36 may also be seen as the first of many implications that form the second half of the Olivet discourse. Here Jesus strung together a series of parables and metaphors to underline one central theme—believers must always be prepared for Christ's return whenever it may occur. Matthew 24:37-44 describes how it will catch many by surprise. Matthew 24:45-51 warns disciples not to assume Christ will stay away longer than He actually does. Matthew 25:1-13 warns them against assuming that He will return more quickly than He actually does. Matthew 25:14-30 teaches proper behavior however long that interval turns out to be—faithful stewardship of every resource with which we have been entrusted.

Whenever Christ does come back, He will judge all humanity, separating people into one of only two categories—sheep and goats, disciples who will be rewarded with eternal life and unbelievers who will be eternally separated from God. The criterion for determining who goes where is how a person has responded to "the least of these brothers of [Jesus]." A popular, modern interpretation is that Jesus was

## TRIAL OF JESUS

With the traitorous kiss of Judas Iscariot at the garden of Gethsemane, Jesus was arrested and brought before Jewish leaders (Matt. 26:49-57; Mark 14:45-33; Luke 22:54; see John 18:2-13). Subsequently, He was tried by the Jewish and Roman leaders.

### Jewish Trial

John recorded a preliminary examination by Annas (high priest A.D. 6–15), the father-in-law of the high priest Caiaphas (A.D. 18–37; see John 18:13-15). Annas questioned Jesus about His disciples and His teaching. Jesus did not answer his question, was then abused, and was sent as a prisoner to Caiaphas (John 18:19-24).

At Caiaphas's house there was the gathering of the chief priests, elders, and scribes, the first of the two phases of Jesus' trial before the Sanhedrin (Matt. 26:57-68; Mark 14:53-65; Luke 22:54,63-65).

The chief priests sought for those who would falsely testify against Jesus in order to put Him to death. Finally, two agreed to testify that Jesus had stated that He would destroy the temple and build it in three days. The high priest questioned Jesus on this, but He made no reply. Next, the high priest asked Jesus if He would make a claim that He was the Christ, Son of God. Jesus replied by stating that He was the Christ and further elaborated by referring to Himself as the "Son of Man" and predicting His future role from Daniel 7:13 and Psalm 110:1 as being seated at the right hand of Power and coming on the clouds of heaven.

Caiaphas, tearing his robe, interpreted Jesus' claim as putting Himself on par with God and thus a blasphemy worthy of death.

The soldiers mocked Jesus and spat on Him. Immediately after this it is recorded that Peter three times denied that he was a disciple of Jesus (Matt. 26:69-75; Mark 14:66-72; Luke 22:55-62).

A second meeting of the Sanhedrin occurred the next morning, Friday, in order to find some semblance of legality to the verdict reached in the previous night's trial and make an official brief for the Roman prefect Pontius Pilate (Matt. 27:1-2; Mark 15:1; Luke 22:66–23:1).

According to Luke's account the morning trial rehearsed the previous night's trial with the exclusion of calling for false witnesses. The only charge they had against Jesus was one of blasphemy. However, the Sanhedrin lacked the power to carry out the death penalty, which was the Roman prefect's prerogative (John 18:31). Hence, they brought Jesus to Pilate.

teaching judgment on the basis of response to the poor and needy of the world, whoever they are. But the more common view throughout the history of the church, which is supported by Matthew's uniform usage of the words "brothers" and "least" or "little ones" elsewhere, is that Jesus' brothers refer to fellow Christians. Those who welcome itinerant Christian missionaries by providing for their physical needs (as in 10:11-14,40-42) demonstrate that they have also accepted the Christian message.

## CRUCIFIXION (26:1–27:66)

From here on events move quickly to the climax of the Gospel—Jesus' death and resurrection. Chapter 26 outlines the events that set the stage for Jesus' condemnation and execution. Chronologically, the items narrated in 26:1-16 precede "Maundy" Thursday night, the night of His arrest. These include a final reminder that Jesus knew exactly what was going to happen to Him. When He submitted, He would do so voluntarily and thoughtfully. The Jewish leaders plotted against Him. Mary of Bethany (see John 12:1-8) anointed Jesus with precious perfume, symbolizing, possibly inadvertently, His coming death and burial. Judas prepared to betray Him.

Matthew 26:17-46 details the final hours Jesus and His disciples shared. They were celebrating the Passover

---

### Roman Trial

Death may have been a valid punishment for blasphemy in terms of the Jewish law, but that would have been of little interest to Rome. New charges had to be formulated for Pilate (Matt. 27:11-14; Mark 15:2-5; Luke 23:2-5; John 18:29-38).

Three accusations against Jesus were presented to Pilate: perverting the nation, forbidding the payment of tribute to Caesar, and proclaiming His kingship (Luke 23:2). Only the last one was of concern to Pilate. He questioned Jesus directly on this point, but Jesus did not answer him.

Being suspicious of the Jewish leaders' motive for their accusations (Matt. 27:13,18; Mark 15:4,10), Pilate found Jesus innocent. The Jewish leaders insisted that Jesus stirred up the people in Judea and Galilee. When Pilate heard that he was a Galilean, he sent Jesus to Herod Antipas, who was in Jerusalem for the Passover (Luke 23:5-7).

Although according to Roman law the accused was to be tried in the province of his misdeeds and not the province of his home, Pilate nevertheless sent Jesus to Herod Antipas, who ruled over Galilee. The reason for this was that Herod Antipas had recently reported to Tiberius that Pilate had caused an unnecessary riot in Jerusalem (Philo, *Legatio ad Gaium,* 299-305). Pilate did not want to make another wrong move that Herod Antipas could relate to the emperor.

On the other hand, Herod Antipas did not want to make a wrong move so that Pilate could tattle on him. In fact, both Pilate and Herod Antipas realized that any reporting done by either could jeopardize either or both of them; thus they made peace and became friends (Luke 23:8-12). It is not difficult to understand why there was no progress in this trial.

Jesus was returned to Pilate (Luke 23:13-16). Since the Jewish leaders were not placated by Pilate's sending Jesus to Herod Antipas, Pilate tried to extricate himself by flogging and releasing Jesus (Luke 23:16,22). Finally he attempted to release Him as an act of clemency at the Passover (Matt. 27:15-23; Mark 15:6-14; Luke 23:17-23; John 18:39-40).

Although Pilate repeatedly confessed Jesus' innocence (Luke 23:14-15,22), the crowd was not satisfied until he released Barabbas, scourged Jesus, and delivered Him to be crucified (Matt. 27:24-26; Mark 15:15; Luke 23:24-25; John 19:16).

Responsibility for the trial, or mistrial, of Jesus rests squarely on both the Jewish and Roman authorities.

meal, the Jewish festival that commemorated the Israelites' liberation from Egypt at the expense of the Egyptian firstborn. Lambs were slaughtered, special meals celebrated, and an elaborate liturgy rehearsed. Extended families ate together on this joyous occasion. Jesus and the eleven (minus Judas) constituted such a "family," and Jesus Himself would soon become the sacrificial Lamb to spiritually liberate all people from their sins. During this "Last Supper" Jesus ate with His followers, He turned the Passover meal into the first celebration of what Christians have come to call the Lord's Supper (or Holy Communion or the Eucharist). As He broke the loaf of bread and drank the cups of wine that formed part of this festive meal, He invested them with new and deeper significance. They symbolized His soon-to-be-broken body and shed blood for the forgiveness of the sins of all humanity, inaugurating God's new covenant, which fulfills the prophecies of Jeremiah 31:31-34. Christians must repeat this ceremony to commemorate Christ's atoning death but also to anticipate His glorious return.

After celebrating this meal in an "upper room" somewhere in Jerusalem, the little troupe adjourned for the Mount of Olives to the east of town across the Kidron Valley. On its western slopes lay the garden of Gethsemane—a wooded olive grove. Here Jesus took His three closest companions aside and asked them to stay awake and pray with Him. Three times they failed Him, even as He had predicted Peter would shortly deny Him three times.

Christ, who alone remained awake, nevertheless teaches profound lessons for us through His praying. As fully human, He no more wanted to endure His coming torture than any of us would. He asked of God if there were any way possible that He might be spared this ordeal. But He left room for God's sovereign will to override His natural human inclinations. It became increasingly clear as He prayed that God required Him to die for the sake of the world, and so He submitted compliantly. Here if ever is proof that all human prayers must include the condition "if it be God's will" (recall 6:10) and that God does not always grant the desires of those who pray even when those prayers are uttered with complete faith and every good motive.

Suddenly Judas arrived with a combination of Jewish and Roman guards. Matthew 26:47-75 narrates the proceedings taken against Jesus by the Jewish authorities. He was arrested, but Jesus made plain that He would countenance no fighting on His behalf. He was bound and led away to the home of the high priest, Caiaphas, where a hastily called nighttime gathering of the Sanhedrin, the Jewish "supreme court," had been convened.

The proceedings that followed broke many later Jewish laws. Perhaps not all of these were yet in effect; perhaps desperate men were willing to set aside legal provisions so as not to let Jesus escape from their hands. Despite the various illegalities, there was a pretense of due process, which itself almost stymied the authorities.

Finally they found some testimony that led the high priest to confront Jesus directly with the question of His self-understanding. Did He claim to be the Christ, the Messiah? He answered with a qualified affirmative, which might be paraphrased, "That's your way of putting it." But since the council was anticipating a merely human liberator, He went on to clarify. He is a heavenly Son of man who will sit at the very right hand of God and return on the clouds of heaven. *Son of man* for Jesus is a heavenly, Christological title based on Daniel 7:13-14. Such claims made Jesus seem too clearly to have been usurping prerogatives reserved for God alone. Caiaphas tore his clothes in grief and cried, "Blasphemy!" Little did he know it was he and not Jesus who was scandalously rejecting God's true revelation.

The council condemned Jesus to be sentenced to death; blasphemy was a capital offense. The Romans had taken the right to execute criminals away from the Jews, however, so they had to appeal to the imperial authorities in town (John 18:31). Before they did, Matthew returned outside to where he had left Peter and narrated the pathetic account of Peter's denial, just as Jesus had prophesied. Peter provided a sad contrast with Jesus, who remained stalwart under life-threatening pressure.

Chapter 27 moves quickly to Jesus' sentence and execution, the events that occurred on the day we now call Good Friday. Verses 1-31 unfold His sentencing. In verses 1-2 the Jews, more legally now that morning had broken, confirmed their verdict. They then sent Jesus to Pilate, the Roman governor. Pilate did not care if Jesus had blasphemed God according to Jewish law, but he would take careful notice if the Jews charged Him with treason against Rome (as, for example, if Jesus claimed to be king, v. 11).

Again Matthew interrupted the chronology to sandwich another event that offers a bitter contrast—Judas' remorse and suicide. Not only did Judas and Jesus dramatically differ, but also Judas and Peter provided instructive contrasts. Both betrayed their master, even if in differing ways. Both were deeply grieved afterwards. But Peter apparently demonstrated true repentance, which would permit him to be reinstated (John 21:15-18), whereas Judas sought absolutely the wrong remedy by taking his own life.

Verses 11-26 proceed with the Roman sentencing of our Lord. Pilate seems to have been convinced that Jesus had committed no crime against the empire but found himself in a delicate position. If the Jews rioted, he could have been in trouble with the emperor for not preserving the peace. What did it matter to him if the price of peace was the life of one Jewish religious fanatic? Despite his own instincts and warnings from his wife, he acceded to the request of the Jewish leaders and the mob they had whipped up into an irrational frenzy.

Verse 25 climaxes this section with a ringing acceptance of the responsibility for Jesus' death on the part of the Jewish crowds present. "His blood be on us and on our children," however, cannot be taken to refer to all Jews of all times. Matthew doubtless envisaged "our children" as the next generation, which was indeed judged by the destruction of Jerusalem in A.D. 70. But Jesus' blood would also be on the heads of Jewish people for good if they turned to Christ for the salvation His shed blood makes available. Meanwhile Pilate handed Jesus over to his soldiers, who mocked Him and then prepared to lead Him to His execution site.

Matthew offered few details about the nature of crucifixion in general or Jesus' experience on the cross in particular. He was more interested in the reactions of other people and of nature itself. The crowds and Jewish leaders mocked and misunderstood. Two who would have alleviated Jesus' suffering were rebuffed. Jesus would endure the agony to the fullest and to the end. An excruciating death that often lasted several days until slow asphyxiation was completed ended abruptly. Jesus sensed alienation from God in a way we can scarcely explain or imagine, yet He seemingly still chose the moment to stop fighting for life.

Even more remarkable was nature's testimony. Darkness accompanied Jesus' final three hours on the cross (from 12:00 to 3:00 P.M.). After His death the temple curtain was ripped open, signifying the new, intimate access with which Jew and Gentile alike may approach God. An earthquake disrupted the cemeteries, and after Jesus' own resurrection other Old Testament saints were raised, apparently demonstrating that Christ's resurrection is indeed the firstfruits of the destiny of all believers (see 1 Cor. 15:20).

The Gentile commanding officer keeping watch at the cross climaxed Matthew's account of the crucifixion by confessing what most of the Jews had failed to accept—Jesus' divine sonship. The burial scene emphasized the reality of Jesus' death, while the guard at the tomb accounted for the standard Jewish explanation of the Christian resurrection claim.

## RESURRECTION! (28:1-20)

Matthew's Gospel fittingly concludes with the most dramatic and glorious miracle in all of Scripture—the resurrection of Jesus Christ. With this event stands or falls Christianity's claim to be the one true way to God (1 Cor. 15:12-19).

Verses 1-10 describe how the women who had watched where Jesus was buried (27:55-56,61) went to the tomb after the Sabbath (Saturday) had passed to give His corpse a more proper anointing. To their astonishment they found an angel instead, beside an open door revealing an empty burial cave. The angel commanded them to go tell Jesus' disciples that He was risen. On the way they met Jesus Himself, who repeated the command. Verses 11-15 comprise the sequel to 27:62-66 and disclose how flimsy alternatives to belief in the resurrection inevitably proved to be.

Verses 16-20 summarize all the major themes of the Gospel—Christ's divine sovereignty and authority, the nature of discipleship, the universal scope of Christian faith, the importance of doing the will of God, and the promise of Christ's presence with His followers in everything they may experience. Verse 19 has understandably come to be known as the Great Commission. Believers' task in life in essence is to duplicate themselves in others, leading men and women in every part of the world to faith, baptism, and obedience to all of Christ's commands. But the final word of the book properly returns our focus to Christ rather than keeping it on ourselves. Even when we are faithless, He remains faithful.

***Theological Significance.*** Matthew's Gospel shows the essential unity between the Old Testament and the New. The prophesied Messiah of the Old Testament has come in the person of Jesus of Nazareth. Matthew presents Jesus Christ as the One who fulfills the Old Testament promises and predictions (1:18–2:23; 5:17-18). While Jesus is presented as the promised King, He is portrayed as a Servant King, whose kingdom is established on His redemptive work.

The kingdom is presented as both present and future. The rule of God over the earth is inaugurated in the person and ministry of Jesus. Its present manifestation is expressed through the moral transformation of its citizens. Followers of Christ reflect an ethical vision of the kingdom as presented in the Sermon on the Mount (5:17:29). They are people who seek first the kingdom of God and His righteousness (6:33). The kingdom awaits its consummation at the return of Christ (24:1-51). In the present time kingdom citizens are to live out their calling as obedient disciples. Disciples express their allegiance to Jesus by obeying His Word (28:19-20).

## Questions for Reflection

1. What are the themes of Matthew's Gospel?

2. What is the significance of the title "Son of Man"?

3. What is the importance of Jesus' statement that He has come to fulfill the law, not to abolish it?

4. What do we learn about the meaning of discipleship from Matthew's Gospel?

5. How can we best understand and apply the Sermon on the Mount for our lives?

## Sources for Additional Study

Blomberg, Craig L. *Matthew.* The New American Commentary. Nashville: Broadman, 1992.

Carson, D. A. "Matthew." *The Expositor's Bible Commentary.* Grand Rapids: Zondervan, 1984.

France, R. T. *Matthew.* Tyndale New Testament Commentaries. Leicester: InterVarsity, 1985.

# MARK

Unlike Paul's letters, the Gospel of Mark does not identify its author or first audience. According to church tradition, John Mark wrote the Second Gospel from Rome, using Peter as his primary source. John Mark's mother hosted a Jerusalem house church (Acts 12:12), and he ministered alongside his cousin Barnabas (Acts 12:25; 15:37,39), Paul (Col. 4:10; 2 Tim. 4:11; Phil. 24), and later Peter (1 Pet. 5:13). Jewish-Christians were likely in Rome in A.D. 45 when Claudius expelled the Jews over the "Christos" disturbance (see Acts 18:2). About A.D. 55 Paul wrote to a Roman church composed of both Gentile and Jewish believers (Rom. 11:17-24). Mark shows signs that it was written to a largely Gentile church; for example, explanations of Aramaic expressions (5:41; 7:34; 14:36; 15:34) and the Pharisees' traditions (7:3-4). If Mark was known and used as a source by both Matthew and Luke, as seems probable, the Gospel was likely written before A.D. 70 and perhaps even a decade earlier.

**Theme.** Discipleship is the central theme of Mark's Gospel. Of all the Gospels, Mark is at once the most frankly realistic in assessing the difficulties of discipleship and the most hopeful. Discipleship is costly (8:34-37; 12:44; 14:3-5), and persecution comes with the territory (10:30; 13:9-13). Mark was not blind to the disciples' misunderstandings (4:40; 6:52; 8:17,33; 9:6; 10:38) and failures (10:13; 14:37,43,50,71). Nevertheless, he expressed hope that beyond failure, those first disciples—and contemporary disciples—experience forgiveness (16:7) and fulfillment of Jesus' promises to be "fishers of people" (1:17, NRSV) and Spirit-inspired witnesses (13:11; see 10:39). Mark's hope was grounded in Jesus, who both trusted in God's goodness and love for Him (1:11; 9:7; 10:18) and submitted to the necessity of His suffering and death as a prelude to His resurrection.

**Literary Form.** Before Mark the early Christians had passed on the story of Jesus orally as isolated stories, short sayings collections, and some longer narrative, such as the passion. Mark was likely the first Christian to write a "Gospel," not a mere biography but an extended treatment of the significance of Jesus' life, death, and resurrection for believers. Most scholars believe that Matthew and Luke, writing some years later, based their Gospels on Mark's. Indeed Matthew parallels about 90 percent of Mark. Mark's distinctives include his fast-paced adventure style ("immediately," thirty-five times); his use of blunt language ("the heavens torn apart," 1:10, NRSV; "the Spirit . . . drove him out into the wilderness," 1:12, NRSV); his appreciation of the humanity of Jesus (1:41; 3:5; 4:38; 6:6; 11:12; 14:33), and his emphasis on the difficulty of discipleship.

I. Introduction (1:1-13)
II. Jesus' Authority Revealed (1:14–3:6)
III. Jesus' Authority Rejected (3:7–6:6a)
IV. Gathering a New Community (6:6b–8:21)
V. Equipping the New Community (8:22–10:52)
VI. Judgment on Jerusalem (11:1–13:37)
VII. Judgment on Jesus: Passion and Resurrection (14:1–16:8)

***Purpose and Theology.*** Though Mark doubtless wrote with the needs of his own church in mind, his Gospel is not an occasional document such as Paul's letters. The concerns Mark addressed were typical of Christians of his generation and are pertinent to ours. Mark wrote to preserve the story of Jesus after the deaths of first-generation Christians such as Peter. Mark, however, was not a mere archivist, for he used the story of Jesus for pastoral purposes.

1. Mark wrote to encourage Christians to persist in faithful discipleship, particularly in the crisis of persecution. Sometimes Mark encouraged perseverance through Jesus' sayings (8:34-38; 13:11). More often he encouraged faithful discipleship through the examples of his characters: *Jesus,* who by His exorcisms and healings triumphed over evil but who committed Himself to a life of humble service, suffering, and death. *John the Baptizer,* who was Jesus' forerunner in proclamation and death. *Those first disciples,* who left all to follow Jesus but who often lacked faith and understanding and who failed Jesus through their rebuke, betrayal, denial, and abandonment. *The women,* who anointed Jesus for His death, who accepted the suffering, dying Christ of the cross and tomb. *Bartimaeus,* who once was blind but then through the mercy of the Son of David saw and followed Jesus in the way of the cross.

2. Mark encouraged Christians to courageous witness. The call of the first disciples included Jesus' promise to make them "fish for people" (1:17, NRSV; see 6:6b-13). Mark encouraged witness in the face of Jewish opposition through the thirteen "conflict stories" illustrating Jesus' authority (2:1-3:6; 3:20-35; 7:1-23; 10:1-12; 11:27-12:37). Mark likewise encouraged witness through the example of his characters: *the friends of the paralytic* who brought him to Jesus; *the former demoniac* who proclaimed how much Jesus had done for him; *the Syrophoenician women* who envisioned a gospel that reached the Gentiles; *the people of Bethsaida* who brought a blind man to Jesus for healing; *those who brought their "little ones"* to Jesus; and ultimately Jesus before the Sanhedrin (14:62; see 13:11). The oldest manuscripts of Mark end with the fear and silence of the women in 16:8. This puzzling ending reminds contemporary disciples that the Jesus story is unfinished until we share the message boldly with our generation.

3. Mark encouraged Christians to hope in the promises of Jesus. Mark might be termed "the Gospel of loose ends." Mark often pointed ahead to promises that were only fulfilled *outside* his story. For example, John promised one who "will baptize with the Holy Spirit" (1:8); Jesus promised that the disciples would "fish for people" (1:17, NRSV), that God's "mustard seed" of a kingdom would become "a great shrub" (4:30-32), and that disciples would be given grace to share Jesus' cup of suffering and baptism of death (10:39). Also John promised that the Spirit would enable disciples to withstand persecution and witness boldly (13:9-13) and that Jesus would meet His disciples in Galilee after the resurrection (14:28; 16:7). Mark doubtless knew traditions such as those Luke incorporated in Acts that related the fulfillment of such promises. That Mark left these "loose ends" suggests that for Mark the "Jesus story" is not finished until it is finished through the bold witness and costly discipleship of His followers.

## INTRODUCTION (1:1-13)

Already in Mark 1:1 the titles applied to Jesus point to His suffering and death. The Greek term "Christ" corresponds to the Hebrew "Messiah," meaning *anointed king.* Jesus would be anointed in preparation for His burial (14:3,8). "Son of God" was used as a title for kings descended from David (2 Sam. 7:14; Ps. 2:6-7). Jesus is, however, a king unlike other kings. By some mystery Mark did not explain, Jesus is both "Son of David" and "David's Lord" (12:35-37). Though the demons discerned Jesus' mysterious identity from the start (1:24,34; 3:11), only the cross opened human eyes to the "Son of God" (15:39).

For Mark the "good news of Jesus Christ" began with John the Baptizer. John's God-authorized ministry (see 11:29-32) fulfilled Scripture (Mal. 3:1; Isa. 40:3). Both John's clothing (2 Kgs. 1:8) and his preaching of repentance and forgiveness (Mal. 4:5-6) recall the prophet Elijah. John's baptism symbolized an inner commitment to lead a changed life. Mark's audience doubtless understood Jesus to be the more powerful Coming One John anticipated. On receiving John's baptism, Jesus was confirmed as the beloved Son who pleased God by His identification with sinners.

The experience of God's affirmation quickly gave way to Satan's temptation. God's Spirit is not just a comfort; here the Spirit thrust Jesus into the situation of testing. Though Mark did not indicate Jesus' triumph over Satan, the exorcisms that follow demonstrate that Jesus had bound the Satanic "strong man" and was plundering his human possessions (3:27).

## JESUS' AUTHORITY REVEALED (1:14-20)

The first major section of Mark highlights Jesus' role as authoritative teacher, healer, and exorcist. Jesus began His ministry following John's arrest (see 6:14-28). The "fulfilled time" was the era the prophets anticipated when God's rule would become a reality. The necessary response to God's work in Jesus was repentance (a change in life direction) and trust in the good news of God's reign.

Jesus' call to the first disciples included both a demand, "Follow me," and a promise, "I will make you fish for people" (NRSV). In the Old Testament fishers caught persons for God's judgment (Jer. 16:16-18). Here persons are caught for salvation. The immediate response of leaving nets and father illustrates the sacrificial commitment of those first disciples.

## RESPONSE TO JESUS (1:21-45)

Jesus, like Paul, frequently taught in the synagogue (1:21,39; 3:1). There Jesus surprised the crowds by teaching "as one having authority," not like the scribes who taught on the basis of legal precedents. Ironically, only the "unclean spirit" knew Jesus' true identity, and His authority exposed it for what it was. This exorcism evidenced the power of Jesus' words, which broke the power of evil and changed lives.

The incident in Simon's home clarifies that discipleship does not necessarily involve severing family ties and abandoning possessions. The grateful service to Jesus by Simon's mother-in-law represents the first of many women modeling proper responses to Jesus.

Jesus' response to His newfound popularity was solitary prayer. Already Simon Peter emerged as the leader of the disciples ("Simon and his companions," NRSV). For the first time Jesus had to clarify His mission for His disciples. "The message" Jesus proclaimed to "the neighboring towns" was the good news sketched in 1:15. By His dual ministry of preaching and exorcism, Jesus established the pattern for the disciples' subsequent mission (6:12-13).

Mark affirmed Jesus' full humanity by portraying the scope of His emotions. According to a few ancient manuscripts, Jesus was moved to anger, not pity, by the leper's request that expressed doubt that Jesus—and the God active in His ministry—willed his healing. Jesus' response and reference to the cleansing laws (Lev. 14) underscored God's willingness to heal. The "free proclamation" of Jesus' authority to heal hindered Jesus' mission to the neighboring towns by forcing Him into the open country.

## BOLD WITNESS (2:1-17)

The healing of the paralytic is the scene of the first of five "conflict" stories in 2:1–3:6. Mark likely included these stories and a later five-part collection (11:27–12:37) as a "guidebook" for bold witness to the Jewish community. The people who brought the paralyzed man to Jesus were fulfilling their role as fishers of people. Earlier the crowds had recognized Jesus as one who taught with authority (1:22,27). Here Jesus demonstrated His authority to proclaim God's forgiveness of sins. The scribes were experts in the Jewish traditions. They objected to Jesus' acting the part of God. In contrast the crowd "glorified God," whose reign was evidenced by Jesus' offer of relationship ("son,"), forgiveness, and healing.

In 2:10 Jesus identified Himself for the first time as "the Son of Man," an ambiguous designation that can mean simply *I* or *human being*. But it also recalls the "supernatural" Son of man to whom God entrusted dominion, glory, and kingship in Daniel 7:13. In Mark, Jesus retained this ambiguity, sometimes using the title in connection with His human experience of suffering and death and sometimes in connection with His future glory.

The toll-collector Levi, like the earlier disciples, abandoned his livelihood—here the customs table—to follow Jesus. "Sin-

ners" included not only immoral persons but those whose occupations prevented their keeping the strict Pharisaic interpretation of the law. Jesus' association with such persons recalls His identification with sinners at His baptism (1:4,9). This table fellowship occasioned the second "conflict" with the scribes, culminating in Jesus' defense of His—and His disciples'—mission: "I have not come to call the righteous, but sinners." Only sinners could respond to Jesus' call to "repent and believe in the good news" (1:15) of God's forgiveness and acceptance.

## CONFLICT (2:18-3:6)

Mark's third "conflict" concerns fasting. Jesus argued that the time of His ministry was a time of joy, like a wedding party, when fasting was inappropriate. The images of new cloth and new wine illustrate the "revolutionary" affect of God's new work in Jesus. What the Jewish leadership feared was true: Jesus was bursting the old categories of Judaism.

Mark's fourth and fifth "conflicts" concern Sabbath observance. The Pharisees interpreted plucking grain as "reaping," an illegal activity on the Sabbath (Exod. 34:21). Jesus' response was twofold. The goal of Sabbath observance was human benefit, and Jesus' "Son of Man" means I had authority over the Sabbath. The Pharisees likewise took the law to prohibit healing unless life was in danger. Mark again recorded Jesus' anger, anger at callousness toward human need and at willful blindness to the deeper goals of the Sabbath—doing good and saving life. The five "conflict" stories conclude with an unlikely coalition of Herodians and Pharisees—political collaborators and orthodox religionists—rejecting Jesus' authority and plotting His destruction.

## JESUS REJECTED (3:7-35)

The Herodians' and Pharisees' rejection of Jesus contrasts with the common people's acceptance. Jesus' popularity exceeded John's (see 1:5), extending into the Gentile areas of Lebanon and Transjordan. Such acclaim occasioned some inconvenience. The silencing of demons suggests that the time was not yet right for the revelation of Jesus' brand of divine sonship (15:39; see 9:9).

Their number points to the Twelve's foundational role in the new people of God. Their responsibility as disciples was twofold: to be with Jesus and to be sent out to preach His message and exercise His authority over demons.

Mark 3:19b-35 is the first of the "sandwiches," texts where Mark inserted one narrative—the "meat" —into another—the "bread"—to highlight their common emphasis. Here both accounts concern the legitimacy of Jesus' ministry: Jesus' family thought Him "out of his mind"; the Jerusalem scribes supposed He was in league with the "ruler of demons." Jesus was the "stronger one" who had entered Satan's world and was "plundering his possessions" through His exorcisms.

Blasphemy against the Holy Spirit involves a stubborn refusal to acknowledge God at work in Jesus and attribution of that work to Satan. Repentance and forgiveness are not possible for those who *consistently* reject God's saving work in Christ. In the "top slice of bread," Jesus redefined His family as the community of those who enter into a student-Teacher relation with Him ("those who sat around him," 3:34; see 4:10) and who obey God's will (see 1:20; 10:29-31).

## PICTURES OF THE KINGDOM (4:1-34)

The parable of the soils provides a framework for interpreting responses to Jesus' message. Jesus' preaching evoked (1) the disciples' obedient following (1:18,20; 2:14); (2) the crowd's amazement; (3) His family's suspicion of insanity (3:21); (4) the Jewish leaders' opposition (2:7,16,24; 3:6,22). As Mark's story unfolds, a rich man has his opportunity to follow Jesus "choked" by love of wealth (10:17-25; see 4:18-19). And the crowds "who received the message with joy" (4:16) join Jesus' opponents in time of persecution (14:43; 15:15). Beyond Mark's conclusion, the disciples—like seed sown on good soil—come to maturity in which they endure persecution (see 13:9-13) and bear much fruit.

Jesus was not a "secret" (He preached and healed in public) but a mystery waiting to be unraveled by the disciples. Jesus' teaching in parables resulted in many not perceiving what He was about and responding with repentance (see 1:15). Strangely, Jesus was simultaneously a riddle and a shining lamp. Disciples who "have" some understanding of Jesus and His mission are "given more." "Outsiders" who refuse to see understand less and less of Jesus and ultimately reject Him completely.

The parable of the growing seed emphasizes that God gives the kingdom growth in ways that are beyond human understanding. Having sown the seed, disciples must trust God to give the growth. The parable of the mustard seed stresses that God's rule, which became real in a small way in Jesus' tiny circle of followers, is destined for a glorious end.

## FAITH IN GOD (4:35-41)

Jesus demonstrated His absolute trust in God by sleeping through the storm on Lake Galilee. The disciples mistook Jesus' trust for apathy: "Don't you care?" Strangely, their fear is not mentioned until Jesus had quieted the storm. Here faith is courage based on trust in God's care no matter what. The disciples' question, "Who is this?" suggests their awe stemmed from the realization that somehow their Teacher did what only God could do.

## LIFE OUT OF CONTROL (5:1-20)

The Gerasene demoniac pictures the horror of a life out of control: isolation, violence, painful cries, self-destructive behavior, and powerlessness of neighbors to intervene or heal. Only Jesus could confront the oppressive forces and leave him "sitting . . . dressed and in his right mind." A Roman legion consisted of between four thousand and six thousand men. Again the crowd's fear comes at the end (see 4:40-41). They feared the power at work in Jesus more than the demonic forces that had worked in their neighbor. They valued swine more than another human being.

Though Jesus denied the man's request to be with Him (see 3:14), Jesus commissioned the Gerasene to fulfill another disciple task: to tell how much the Lord had done for him.

## FAITH AND FEAR (5:21-43)

Mark's account of a girl restored to life and a woman healed is a second example of his "sandwich" technique. He juxtaposed two examples of faith: a synagogue ruler, a highly respected community member, with a now-impoverished woman who lived as an outcast because of her hemorrhage. The woman in the "inner" story "had heard about Jesus" and exemplified faith in daring to touch the fringe of His garment.

Again Mark noted fear at the end of her story. Her fear of illness and death was surpassed by her awe at this one who knew He had healed her. Like the Gerasene she told her story of God's mercy to her. Jesus' address "Daughter" brought her into relationship with Him based on her saving faith. This new relationship makes going in God's peace possible. In the "outer" story Jesus called Jairus to faith that did not fear even death but trusted that God was at work in Jesus to restore life to his daughter. The laughing crowd of mourners viewed as ridiculous a faith that trusted God no matter what. Those who trusted God had the last laugh.

## SCANDAL OF FAMILIARITY (6:1-6A)

At Nazareth Jesus experienced the scandal of familiarity: He's just a carpenter, just Mary's son—who knows who His father really is? We know His brothers and sisters.

But Mark's readers will recall that Jesus' family is now the community of those who do God's will. The Greek term rendered "took offense" (v. 6) is the polar opposite of "believe in" and is often used for the Jewish rejection of Jesus (Matt. 11:6; Rom. 9:33; 1 Cor. 1:23; Gal. 5:11). Jesus "was amazed at their lack of faith" (Mark 6:6) and "could not do any miracles there"except heal a few people. Jesus' miracles were God's response to human need and faith, not magic tricks performed to impress the crowds. John 1:11-12 perhaps provides the best commentary on this account: "He came to what was his own, and his own people did not accept him. But to all who received him, who believed in his name, he gave power to become children of God" (NRSV).

## MISSION OF THE TWELVE (6:6B-44)

Jesus' rejection by "his own" prepares for the gathering of His new people anticipated in 3:35. The mission of the Twelve "sandwiches" the account of John's martyrdom underscoring the danger of preaching repentance. Jesus set the pattern for the mission of the Twelve by His preaching, healing, and exorcisms. Though the authority given the disciples to heal and exorcise demons was a sign of the kingdom, Jesus only commissioned them to preach repentance, not the good news of the kingdom (see 1:15). The mission instructions evidence absolute dependence on God for support and allude to the exodus. The disciples, like Jesus before them, were to experience rejection as well as welcome.

The question of Jesus' identity introduces the account of John's death. John's full significance is seen only later in relation to Jesus, whose fate he foreshadows. Like Jesus, John was arrested, recognized as righteous and holy, nevertheless executed, and laid in a tomb. Jesus' end, however, distinguishes Him as the more powerful Coming One, whose sandals John counted himself unworthy to tie.

"Sheep without a shepherd" serves as an image for God's people without spiritual leadership. Jesus' initial response to the crowd's need was teaching. The details of the crowd seated on "green grass" and fully satisfied recall the shepherd of Psalm 23 who made his sheep lie down in green pasture (Ps. 23:2,5). The miraculous feeding of the five thousand establishes Jesus as the true Shepherd of God, but it also points to the future ministry of the disciples. Jesus' use of the Twelve to feed the crowd of five thousand suggests a pattern for future ministry in which Jesus provides the disciples with resources for ministry.

## HOPE IN LIFE'S STORMS (6:45-56)

Jesus saw the disciples' struggle at the oars and came to them walking on the water. Jesus did not call disciples into the storm to abandon them there. The disciples characteristically failed to "see clearly." They thought He was a ghost. "It is I" suggests the covenant name of God (Exod. 3:14; Isa. 43:10). The reassurance "Do not be afraid" is common in God's Old Testament appearance (for

example, Gen. 15:1; 21:17; 26:24). Mark did not clarify just what the disciples did not understand "about the loaves." Perhaps they thought Jesus was the Shepherd who would care for their needs and lead them through the dangers of death or that He was a new Moses who would lead them across the sea just as He had miraculously fed them. The disciples' failure to recognize Jesus contrasts sharply with the Gennesaret crowd who recognized Jesus "at once" and appealed to Him for aid.

## CONFLICT WITH TRADITION (7:1-23)

The "conflict" with the Jerusalem Pharisees and scribes occasioned by the disciples' eating with unwashed (ritually defiled) hands prepares for the following three narratives in which Jesus and the disciples overcame barriers to ministry to the Gentiles. Verses 3-4 are Mark's explanation for his Gentile readers. This "conflict" was of crucial importance to the later mission of the church: would Jesus' disciples be bound to follow "the tradition of the elders"?

Jesus' response to the Jewish leaders was twofold: the leaders invalidated God's laws in order to keep their human traditions; and sin is a matter of the heart, not the diet. Mark again explained an Aramaic term—corban—for his Gentile readers. Apparently such an offering to God could be retained during the giver's lifetime but could not be used for any other purpose, somewhat like an irrevocable living trust. In calling His disciples to heed the weightier matters of God's law, Jesus affirmed God's Old Testament revelation as the heritage of the church. Verse 19b is Mark's comment, which the disciples did not immediately grasp (Acts 10), on the significance for the Gentile mission of Jesus' teaching on what really defiles.

## JESUS AND THE GENTILES (7:24-37)

Jesus' response to the Syrophoenician woman has a harshness that leaves us uncomfortable: Jews used "dogs" as a derogatory term for Gentiles whom they regarded as unclean as "muts" searching streets for garbage. Interpreting the diminutive as "puppy" does not solve the dilemma either, for a "house pet" does not share the family status of a child. Status in God's household is not a matter of race. Mark 3:35 has already paved the way for a larger family of those who do God's will. The key word in the narrative is "first," which leaves open later ministry to Gentiles. Jesus' role was first Jewish Messiah and then Savior of the world (compare Paul's bringing the gospel to the Jews first and then to the Greeks, Acts 13:46). Jesus commended the persistent faith of this "unclean" woman who knew there must be a place for her in God's grace. In 8:1-10 Jesus would feed a Gentile crowd with bread as He had God's Jewish children (6:30-44).

As a resident of the Decapolis, the league of ten Greek-speaking cities, the deaf-mute probably was a Gentile. As with the Jewish paralytic, friends brought him to Jesus. Experiencing God's grace makes it impossible to keep the good news of Jesus secret. Ironically, the Gentile crowd recognized that Jesus met the expectation of the Jewish Messiah (see Isa. 35:5).

## READING THE SIGNS (8:1-21)

Feeding the four thousand represented Jesus' miraculous provision for the Gentiles much as the feeding of the five thousand represented His care for the Jews (6:30-44). Mark's Roman readers doubtless saw that those who came "a great distance" to be with Jesus foreshadowed the church's mission to the ends of the earth.

The Pharisees' demand for a sign from heaven recalls the Israelites' testing God in the wilderness (Deut. 6:16; 33:8). Jesus perhaps refused to give a sign because ample opportunity had already been given for those with eyes to see what He was about.

The yeast of the Pharisees and of Herod represents their bad influence. The disciples again lacked understanding. Mark did not specify just what the disciples should have "seen" about Jesus—perhaps that they had no need to worry about bread with Jesus there to provide for their needs.

## SUFFERING DISCIPLESHIP (8:22-26)

Mark's central section is "sandwiched" by two accounts of Jesus' giving sight to blind men (8:22-26; 10:46-52). The "meat" in between consists of teaching on the costliness of discipleship and the suffering/glorification of the Son of man.

The healing of the blind man at Bethsaida is distinct from other miracles in the gospel traditions as a two-part healing. The man at first saw distorted images—people who looked like walking trees. Only after a "second touch" from Jesus did he see clearly. Similarly the disciples would soon see that Jesus was the promised Messiah, but their understanding of messiahship would be badly distorted, even Satanic. In this larger section of Mark, Jesus would remind them repeatedly of the necessity of His suffering and death (8:31; 9:31; 10:32,45).

## WHO AM I? (8:27-38)

Jesus' first question at Caesarea Philippi is merely preparatory; the crucial question then, as now, is, "Who do you say I am?" Peter, as usual, spoke for all the disciples in declaring, "You are the Christ." In Mark's account Peter received no "pat on the back" (see Matt. 16:17-19). English translations obscure the harshness of Jesus' response (using the same

# THE KINGDOM
# OF GOD
# IN THE GOSPELS

The kingdom of God is the heart of the New Testament's message. It was announced by John the Baptist (Matt. 3:2). It formed the essence of Jesus' teaching—we are to seek it first and foremost (Matt. 6:33). It constitutes the life of the church— "The kingdom of God is not a matter of eating and drinking, but of righteousness, peace, and joy in the Holy Spirit" (Rom. 14:17). It was the evangelistic message of the early believers (Acts 8:12; 14:22; 19:8; 20:25; 28:23,31). It will someday be all in all when the kingdom of this world is become the kingdom of our Lord and of His Christ, and He shall reign forever and ever (Rev. 11:15; 1 Cor. 15:23-28).

The kingdom of God, also called the kingdom of heaven by Matthew, is not defined geographically by Jesus or the Gospel writers. But along Old Testament prophetic lines, it is seen as the realm where God's will is being done. It is God's sovereign rule and, in principle, embraces all of the created order. In some respects it parallels God's providential control of the world, but this idea does not predominate in the Gospels. The primary focus is on God's redemptive work. The kingdom of God is the realm where God's saving will is known and experienced. It is the realm where God's will is done. Some are attracted to it, some are on the fringe of it, and some are actually in it (Matt. 13:24-30,36-40,47-50). We are not, however, to say who is and who is not—it is God's kingdom, not ours. We must be careful not to drive people away if they are trying to make their way into it. Those who are in God's kingdom are saved, and Jesus is the one who leads them in it.

It is interesting to note that although God's kingdom is the central point of Jesus' teaching and of the Gospels, God is nowhere called a king. This ties in with another prominent element of what Jesus said, namely, that God is our Heavenly Father. Taken together we have a description of God's sovereign, saving rule. He is the Ruler who exercises His sovereignty as a benevolent Heavenly Father, who opens the door of salvation to all who would enter.

The kingdom is both present (Matt. 11:11-12; 12:28; 18:1-5; Luke 17:21) and future (Matt. 6:10; 26:29; Luke 19:11-27; 21:29-31). The saving power of the age to come has broken into this age, and we may be saved now; but the kingdom has not yet fully come. This age grinds on until the end arrives, until God alone is supreme, and we are fully saved.

The Gospels say a great deal about the entrance requirements of the kingdom. To enter into the kingdom and be saved, we must repent and believe the gospel (Mark 1:15). Jesus' preaching of the kingdom was the preaching of the gospel (Matt. 4:23; 9:35). We must do the will of our Heavenly Father to enter (Matt. 7:21), and our righteousness must exceed that of the scribes and Pharisees (Matt. 5:20). We must repent and become as little children to enter (Matt. 18:3; Mark 10:15; Luke 18:17).

Those who have no faith, even if they are children of the kingdom (that is, Jews), will not participate in it (Matt. 8:10-13). We must sell all that we have to purchase the kingdom, which is a treasure beyond comparison (Matt. 13:44-45). If necessary, we must be willing to make extraordinary sacrifices to enter (Matt. 19:12; Mark 9:42-48). Jesus epitomizes all the above by saying that we must be born anew (John 3:3-9).

Because God's kingdom is not of this world (John 18:36), life in the kingdom is a total reversal of this world's values. The Beatitudes define its fundamental principles (Matt. 5:3-12). In addition, we are to be forgiving (Matt. 18:23-35), humble (Matt. 18:4), generous (Matt. 20:1-16), self-effacing (Matt. 20:20-28), and totally committed (Luke 9:57-62).

In sum, those who by faith in the gospel of Christ have become members of the kingdom are God's children, and they are to live their lives accordingly as those redeemed by Him and who will ultimately inherit eternal life.

Greek verb translated "rebuked" in Mark 8:33). Jesus taught plainly that as the Son of man He must suffer rejection and death (contrast 4:11,33-34). About this central truth of the necessity of the Messiah's suffering, death, and resurrection there was to be no misunderstanding. But disciples had a way of calling Jesus "Lord" and then telling Him what kind of Lord to be. Peter's rebuke of Jesus serves as a warning to modern disciples: one can mouth the correct titles and still have a false understanding of who Christ is. To accept Jesus as Lord is to accept not only His glory but also His suffering, rejection, and death. Peter, realizing the deeper implications for his own discipleship said No thank you to Jesus' brand of suffering messiahship. He knew that those who follow this Christ will experience more of the same.

Faithful discipleship in persecution depends on the grace of seeing circumstances from God's perspective rather than in terms of human cost. On the cross Jesus would be tempted to follow the world's way and save Himself (15:30). Though He felt abandoned by God, Jesus did not seek an easy way out. True life is lost by failing to follow Christ in the way of the cross. Just as Christ endured the cross by setting His gaze beyond the pain (see Heb. 12:2), believers are called to endure present sufferings for the gospel in hope of future glory (9:1; see Rom. 8:18).

### GOD'S KINGDOM COMES (9:1-13)

Jesus encouraged the crowds (8:34) and His disciples that some of those listening to His teaching on costly discipleship would not die ("taste death") until they saw that God's kingdom had come in power. The two most probable interpretations of this difficult saying are that (1) God's kingdom came in power at the resurrection and at Pentecost (Rom. 1:4; Acts 1:8), or (2) the transfiguration

served as an anticipation of the powerful coming of God's kingdom at Christ's second coming.

Jesus' altered appearance at the transfiguration offered the disciples a preview of His resurrection glory. Peter again spoke for the disciples who desired to build booths so they could "package" the experience of glory. That God's seal of approval comes on the heels of Jesus' commitment to the way of the cross is no accident. Only after Jesus had risen from the dead would the disciples be able to share God's vindication of the Suffering Servant-Son.

Jesus' reference to the resurrection perhaps sparked the disciples' interest in the coming of Elijah. Jesus shifted their focus to the crucial question: not why Elijah must first come but why the Son of man must suffer. A suffering servant is what the Scriptures demand—other than that Mark did not answer this question any more than he did Jesus' "Why?" (15:34). "Elijah" (John the Baptist) finds his significance as forerunner of the suffering and death of Jesus.

### PRICE FOR NOT PRAYING (9:14-37)

The disciples learned that their inability to exorcise a demon—and fulfill their commission (6:7)—resulted from their failure to pray. The father of the afflicted boy expressed doubts about Jesus' ability to help him. Jesus responded that "everything is possible for him who believes." The father's plea captures the dilemma of many hesitant believers: "I do believe; help me overcome my unbelief!" (9:24). Jesus responded to the man's feeble faith. Healing of the boy who resembled a corpse sets the stage for further teaching concerning Jesus' death and resurrection.

The disciple's discussion of who was the greatest indicates their misunderstanding of the destination of "the way" of the cross they traveled with Jesus. The measure of true greatness is service. In this Jesus set the standard, coming not "to be served, but to serve" (10:45). The child is not a model for discipleship (see 10:15) but an illustration that no insignificant one should be neglected in the disciples' service.

## THE ABSOLUTE VALUE (9:38–10:16)

The Twelve's narrow view of "authorized" disciples prompted Jesus to affirm that all ministering in His name would be rewarded. Intolerance of the work of fellow believers can prove a stumbling block to nonbelievers looking to see our love and unity (John 13:35; 17:23). That the warnings that follow concern common sins is unlikely. This sin prevents one from entering eternal life and results in one suffering in "Gehenna." Earlier Mark noted that *all* sin can be forgiven except rejecting God's saving work in Jesus. Jesus' warning is to avoid causing anyone else to reject Christ and to reject whatever leads one to reject Christ. Hand, foot, and eye—like possessions, family, and physical life—are not absolute values. God's future kingdom is absolute value. To be "salted with fire" is to undergo persecution. The disciples' "saltiness" is their loyalty to Jesus and the gospel that results in their effective witness.

The presence of Christ leads to peace in the community rather than bickering over who is greatest. Jesus noted that Moses permitted divorce because of stubborn hearts that refuse to be reconciled. God's plan for marriage at creation was, however, one man and one woman sharing their lives together for life.

Though Jesus promised to make the disciples "fishers of men" (1:17), when others brought children to Jesus the disciples interfered. Jesus not only permitted the children to come to Him but used them as an example for those needy ones who would receive the kingdom.

## INHERITING ETERNAL LIFE (10:17-45)

The rich man's question follows naturally on 10:15: "What must I do to inherit eternal life?" What is involved in receiving "the kingdom of God like a little child"? Jesus challenged the rich man to trust that God alone was good. Jesus did not dispute the claim to have kept external requirements of the law (see Phil. 3:6): one can keep rules and still miss the heart of the matter. One essential thing was missing in the rich man's life: "Sell what you own . . . then come follow me." The rich man's problem was not wealth per se but the failure to trust that God—not wealth—was the only good and that God's radical call to discipleship was for his own good. Only radical trust in God's goodness makes possible abandoning wealth and following Jesus in the way of the cross. Such absolute trust in God's goodness that is the prerequisite for entering the kingdom is impossible without a work of grace in one's life. And God does the impossible in conversion, radically reordering human values. Jesus promised a reward—and persecution—for those like Peter who left all to follow Him.

At 10:33 Jesus specified the destination of His way—Jerusalem, where He would face condemnation, torture, and death. Jerusalem has already been depicted as the home base of Jesus' opponents (3:22; 7:1). Jesus' acceptance of His role as Suffering Servant stands in sharpest contrast with James and John's demand: "Teacher, . . . do . . . whatever we ask." Our prayer requests say much about us. Later Bartimaeus would ask Jesus for sight so he could follow Jesus in the way of the cross. Here James and John's request for the seats of honor at Jesus' coming in glory confirms that Peter was not the only disciple interested in sharing only the Messiah's glory (8:32) and that the lesson of "greatness through service" (9:35) was not easily grasped. Jesus promised James and John that they would fulfill their calling as disciples by sharing His cup of suffering (see Ps. 75:8; Isa. 51:17,22) and baptism of death. Christian leaders are to be distinguished from secular leaders who "lord it over." Jesus, who came not to be served but to serve, sets the pattern for Christian leaders. His costly "ransom" frees us for service.

## A MODEL FOR DISCIPLES (10:46-52)

Mark's section on discipleship concludes as it began with the healing of a blind man (see 8:22-26). Bartimaeus models true discipleship. His plea for help, "Son of David, mercy me!" is the cry of a dependent, childlike spirit (see 10:15). He asked Jesus not for a "glory seat" (see 10:37) but to see, and all disciples need eyes that see/perceive (see 4:12). By throwing aside his cloak, Bartimaeus evidenced readiness for mission (see 6:9). By following Jesus on the way to Jerusalem, Bartimaeus accepted the way of his suffering Lord. Finally, Jesus had a disciple who saw.

## THE SERVANT MESSIAH (11:1-33)

Jesus entered Jerusalem as one coming in the name, that is, the authority, of the Lord with a God-given mission of salvation ("Hosanna" means *save now*). By riding a colt, Jesus laid claim to His own brand of messiahship—not conquering hero but humble servant (see Zech. 9:9).

The cursing of the fig tree was a prophetic act meant to illustrate God's judgment upon the temple, which had proved unfruitful by not realizing its mission as a place of prayer for all people. What is necessary for experiencing God is not the temple (see 13:1-2) but "faith in God." Indeed, faith makes the temple obsolete. The one who believes can cast the temple mount into the sea (contrast 1 Kgs. 8:29-30). Forgiveness of sins is not

experienced in temple sacrifice but in sharing God's willingness to forgive. The "forgiveness requirement" warns believers not to turn their prayer time into a robbers' retreat.

Understandably, the religious leaders questioned Jesus' authority because cleansing the temple was the responsibility of the Messiah or the end-time prophet (Mal. 3:1-5; Zech. 14:20-21). Leaders had earlier questioned Jesus' authority to announce God's forgiveness (2:1-12), celebrate God's new work (2:18-22), and do good on the Sabbath (3:1-6). Jesus' question suggests that His authority was God given.

## THE VINEYARD? (12:1-17)

The Jewish leadership took the parable of the wicked tenants as a direct attack on them. The parable builds on several common Old Testament images: the vineyard representing God's possession Israel (Isa. 5:1-7); the harvest as judgment time (Jer. 51:33; Hos. 6:11a; Joel 3:13); and the servants as spiritual leaders (Exod. 14:31; Judg. 2:8; 1 Sam. 3:9; 2 Sam. 3:18). Jesus stood in continuity with the ministry of John and the prophets, yet as "beloved Son" He represented more. His special relation to God was deserving of special respect, and through Him God made His ultimate appeal to Israel (see Heb. 1:1-14). This parable—like the passion predictions (Mark 8:31; 9:31; 10:32)—witnesses Jesus' awareness of a special role in God's plan that would end with His death. Mark's Gentile readers likely saw the Gentile mission reflected in the giving of the vineyard to others.

Ironically, the Jewish leadership recognized Jesus' qualifications as a Teacher/Judge of Israel. They saw Him as one who had integrity, who was not swayed by people (11:32; 12:12), and who was truly teaching God's way. By using Roman coinage, Jesus' adversaries

## CONTROVERSY STORIES IN MARK

| Controversy | Reference in Mark |
|---|---|
| Over Jesus' right to forgive sins | 2:1-12 |
| Over Jesus' fellowship with tax collectors and "sinners" | 2:13-17 |
| Over the disciples' freedom from fasting | 2:18-22 |
| Over the disciples' picking grain on the Sabbath | 2:23-27 |
| Over Jesus' right to do good on the Sabbath | 3:1-6 |
| Over the nature of Jesus' family | 3:20-21,31-35 |
| Over the source of Jesus' power to exorcise | 3:22-30 |
| Over the disciples' eating with unwashed hands | 7:1-5,14-23 |
| Over the Pharisees' and teachers of the law's setting aside the commands of God in order to observe their tradition | 7:6-13 |
| Over the legality of divorce and God's intention for marriage | 10:1-12 |
| Over Jesus' authority to cleanse the temple and John's authority to baptize | 11:27-33 |
| Over paying taxes to Caesar and giving God His due | 12:13-17 |
| Over marriage at the resurrection, the power of God, and the witness of Scripture | 12:18-27 |
| Over the most important commandment | 12:28-34 |
| Over the nature of the Messiah—son of David or David's Lord | 12:35-37 |

witnessed their dependence on that government. Christians should fulfill legitimate responsibilities to their government (Rom. 13:6-7). We bear God's image (Gen. 1:27) and must fulfill our responsibilities to God.

### PRIORITY OF LOVE (12:18-44)

The Sadducees illustrate that one can know something of Scripture (the law of brother-in-law marriage, Deut. 25:5-6) and still miss its central message of God's redemptive love. Resurrection relationships are transformed relationships. Indeed Jesus' disciples already experience transformed relationships as God's children (3:34-35; 10:29-30; 13:12-13).

God is the God of the living not because humans are by nature immortal but because God in His love does not abandon us to death.

Not all Jewish leaders opposed Jesus. One authority in Jewish law asked Jesus which commandment takes priority. When Jesus replied that love of God and neighbor were the priorities of the law, the leader concurred that these obligations were more important than all the sacrificial system (see 11:15-17). Jesus answered that this scribe was near allowing God to rule in his life; all he lacked was to follow Jesus as a disciple (10:21).

In Mark 12:35-37 Jesus took the offensive in asking the religious leaders a question (see 8:27). The riddle of David's son who is David's Lord expresses the mystery of the incarnate Lord, "who as to his human nature was a descendant of David, . . . and who through the Spirit of holiness was declared with power to be the Son of God by his resurrection" (Rom. 1:3-4).

Jesus warned the scribes who used religion to get ahead and to take advantage of others. A widow evidenced characteristics of true discipleship. She showed devotion to God first, freedom from materialism (10:21), and total trust in the good God who would care for her (10:18).

## DESTRUCTION COMING (13:1-13)

Jesus' teaching on the destruction of the temple/Jerusalem and the coming of the Son of man in Mark 13 are difficult to untangle. Despite this difficulty, two primary pastoral emphases are clear in the warnings to beware of deception and to be prepared for Christ's return. The disciples' amazement at the temple complex demonstrated they did not appreciate the prophetic acts of 11:12-21 and prepared for Jesus' prediction of the utter destruction of Jerusalem's temple. Notable among events preceding the destruction of the temple is the appearance of messianic pretenders. Believers are warned not to be taken in by such pretenders or to mistake "the beginning of the birth pains" for God's judgment on Jerusalem.

Acts and Paul's letters witness that the events related to the early Christian community in 13:9-13 were fulfilled before the destruction of the temple in A.D. 70. Paul, for example, was beaten in synagogues five times (2 Cor. 11:24), testified before governors (Acts 18:12-13; 24:1-2; 25:7-8) and kings (Acts 9:15; 26:1-2). And he was accused of spreading the gospel throughout the known world (Acts 17:6; see Rom. 15:19). Peter and others bore Spirit inspired witness (Acts 4:8-22).

## AN EVENT WITHOUT EQUAL (13:14-37)

The events of 13:14-23 concern the Roman campaign against Judea. "Never to be equaled again" in verse 19 suggests an event within human history rather than its conclusion. The "abomination that causes desolation" refers to the defiling of the temple. As before, Jesus cautioned believers about false messiahs and false prophets. In the midst of judgment, God "has shortened" the days of war for the sake of believers ("the elect").

The events surrounding the coming of Christ belong to a time after the destruction of Jerusalem. The coming of Christ in power and glory (see 9:1) is an event whose cosmic repercussions echo Old Testament descriptions of the coming of God for judgment (for example, Isa. 13:10; 34:4). Jesus here emphasized His coming to save the elect.

The fig tree lesson is likely a warning to be prepared for Christ's coming, though "this generation" suggests that the destruction of Jerusalem was in view. "That day," which was unknown even to the Son, is the time of Christ's return. Christians' duty in the interim is to perform assigned tasks rather than speculate about God's timetable. The church must not repeat Israel's failure to be found fruitless when visited by Christ (see 11:12-21).

## APPROACHING DEATH (14:1-11)

Mark's final section concerns events surrounding the human judgment against Jesus (14:1–15:47) and God's judgment for Jesus (16:1-8). The plotting of the Jewish leadership to secure Jesus' death sets the somber tone. A woman was again a model of discipleship. Anointing Jesus with expensive perfume was a "beautiful" act demonstrating freedom

from wealth (see 10:21-25) and acceptance of Jesus' suffering and death (see
8:31-33). Ironically, Mark preserved the
names of those who sought seats of
honor for themselves (10:37) and not
this woman, who sought only to pour
love on Jesus. The section concludes by
telling the readers that Judas agreed to
betray Jesus to the chief priests for
money.

### THE LORD'S SUPPER (14:12-31)

Mark's account of the Lord's Supper
repeatedly emphasizes its Passover setting. As "Son of Man" Jesus would go to
His death in accordance with Scripture
just as the Passover lambs were sacrificed. As in the account of the entry into
Jerusalem (11:1-6), the instructions
regarding preparations underscore the
significance of the event. What Jesus
meant by giving His body is clarified by
His comments on the cup. His blood
would establish a new covenant (see Jer.
31:31) by being "poured out for many."
The Lord's Supper also looked beyond
the cross. Jesus would experience the
blessedness of God's kingdom and would
be reunited with His disciples in Galilee
after the resurrection.

Jesus' acceptance of His God-
ordained fate is contrasted with the disciples' denial of theirs. Distressed at the
thought of a traitor in their midst, first
one then another dismissed the possibility of his own betrayal. Later Peter spoke
for the group: "Even if all fall away, I will
not." The prediction of his denial points
to the difference in the lives of faithful
witnesses under pressure after Easter (see
13:9-13).

### PRAYER IN CRISIS (14:32-53)

At Gethsemane Jesus responded to crisis
with prayer. Gethsemane called into
question Jesus' foundational beliefs.
Jesus addressed God as "Abba," His
"Papa," who loved Him (1:11; see 9:7).

Gethsemane threatened faith in such a
Father. Jesus taught that everything was
possible for one who believed and prayed
(9:23; 11:23-24). Gethsemane raised
the awful possibility that something was
not possible for God—the passing of
Jesus' hour of suffering and death. Mark
shows a frankly human Jesus, "deeply
distressed and troubled," repeatedly falling on the ground in anguished prayer.
Despite the test of faith, Jesus emerged
reaffirming faith in God's possibilities and
recommitting Himself to God's will. The
disciples' repeated failure warns contemporary believers to be alert and pray in
time of temptation.

Judas, one of the Twelve, betrayed
Jesus. His betrayal cautions that it is not
enough to be near Jesus, to have been
called to discipleship, to have received
Jesus' love. Discipleship entails commitment of life to this suffering Christ.
Another disciple responded to the arresting mob with violent resistance. The
response is inappropriate: Jesus had
already accepted the necessity of His suffering and death (8:31; 9:31; 10:32,45).
In a real sense the betrayer and arresting
mob were unnecessary; Jesus did not run
from His fate. He would die to satisfy
Scripture rather than human plans.
Though the disciples were called to be
with Jesus (3:14) and had promised to
die with Him, they all abandoned Him.

### WITNESS UNTO DEATH (14:54-72)

The picture of Peter following "at a distance" and warming himself at the fire
contrasts sharply with that of Jesus on
trial for His life. The shadow of the cross
was heavy when Jesus revealed the mystery of His identity to the high priest. Yes,
He was the Son of God ("the Blessed
One,") and the Son of man, to whom
God had entrusted judgment (Dan. 7:13).
Jesus' faithful witness under pain of
death contrasts with Peter's denial of discipleship. The servant girl's charge, "You

also were with . . . Jesus" echoes Jesus' commission that the disciples "might be with him" (3:14). Peter's concern for comfort and safety led him in the end to brokenness and weeping.

### THE KING OF THE JEWS (15:1–16:8)

Jesus was doubtless brought before Pilate on charges of being a revolutionary. Jesus' response to Pilate's question, "Are you the King of the Jews?" was guarded, "So you say" ( NRSV). Jesus was a king, but not the kind to which Pilate was accustomed (see 10:42-45). Ironically, Pilate released Barabbas, a real terrorist, and sentenced the innocent Jesus to death.

The soldiers mocked Jesus with a purple robe and crown of thorns. The symbols are both awful and beautiful. Jesus embraced His role as suffering, dying Messiah with royal dignity. The inscription above the cross defined the charge: "THE KING OF THE JEWS." The cross redefined the meaning of Messiah. Jesus taught His disciples that "those who want to save their life will lose it" (8:35). At the cross the crowds jeered for Jesus to do just that—save His own life. But Jesus believed what He taught His disciples: Those who lose their life for the sake of what God is doing in the world will save it (8:35). Jesus could face the cross because He trusted God with His life. Ironically, the Jewish leaders confessed that Jesus had saved others. Their insult, "He can't save himself," was a great half truth. Jesus could not save Himself and still trust God and submit to the necessity of His death. Jesus' cry, "My God, my God, why have you forsaken me?" points to the sense of abandonment Jesus experienced when He bore our sins. It would be a mistake to think God aloof from the cross event. The tearing of the temple veil "from top to bottom" demonstrates that "God was reconciling the world to himself in Christ"

(2 Cor. 5:19). Strangely, when Jesus felt God was farthest from Him, a centurion saw clearly that Jesus was God's Son. God doubtless was pleased with Him (1:11; 9:7).

The women who had followed Jesus from Galilee accepted His suffering and death but "from a distance." Joseph of Arimathea exhibited boldness when the most a disciple could do was see to Jesus' proper burial.

The women's desire to anoint Jesus' body though appropriate at another time (14:3-9) was not the proper response for Easter morning disciples. The "young man" seated at the empty tomb said it all: "You're looking for Jesus in the wrong place; God has raised him from the dead; he's not here!" (author's translation). God had vindicated Jesus. The message for the disciples points to restoration after they had denied and abandoned Jesus.

The oldest manuscripts of Mark end at 16:8 with the women silent and fearful. As noted in the introduction, Mark might be termed "the Gospel of loose ends," for Mark often pointed ahead to promises that are only fulfilled outside his story. That God would raise Jesus from the dead following His suffering and death and that Jesus would then meet His disciples in Galilee are but two such promises. Mark doubtless knew traditions relating the fulfillment of such promises; he would have had no reason to write a Gospel had he doubted these promises. That he left these "loose ends" suggests that for Mark the "Jesus story" is not finished until it is finished in you and me through our bold witness to the resurrection.

***Theological and Ethical Significance.*** The Jesus who confronts us in Mark makes us uncomfortable. He is hard to understand and even harder to follow. This is the Jesus most clearly seen to be God's Son only when He has suffered and died on the cross. What those first disciples were so slow to understand, what the centurion and Mark grasped, and what Paul preached is this: "Christ crucified . . . the power of God and the wisdom of God" (1 Cor. 1:23-24).

Mark challenges us, his readers, to open our eyes and see Jesus for who He really is. Mark dares us to follow the example of this suffering, dying Servant of the Lord. Our discipleship will be costly. It may call for leaving families, giving up horded resources, even giving up life itself. All too often we, like those first disciples, will fail Jesus. We too misunderstand; we too lack faith; we too retreat under pressure; we too remain silent and comfortable while others wait to hear that we have been with Jesus. Our stories of discipleship, like Mark's story, are incomplete. But Jesus' promises stand sure. Like those first disciples, Jesus will forgive our failures and make us into what He desires—bold witnesses and followers in His way of costly discipleship.

## Questions for Reflection

1. What does Mark teach us about suffering and discipleship?

2. What does Mark teach about the full humanity of Jesus?

3. What can we learn from Mark's positive and negative examples of discipleship?

4. What role do suffering and death play in Jesus' messiahship?

5. Why do we sometimes live as though we are ashamed of Jesus' example and clear teaching on suffering?

## Sources for Additional Study

Brooks, James A. *Mark*. The New American Commentary. Nashville: Broadman, 1991.

Garland, David E. *Mark*. NIV Application Commentary. Grand Rapids: Zondervan, 1996.

Lane, William L. *The Gospel of Mark*. The New International Commentary on the New Testament. Grand Rapids: Eerdmans, 1974.

Marshall, I. Howard. *Mark: A Bible Study Book. Understanding the New Testament*. Philadelphia: A. J. Holman, 1970.

# LUKE

T he Gospel of Luke according to church tradition was written by the sometime companion of Paul, Luke. (This is indicated by the "we" passages in Acts 16:10-17; 20:5-15; 21:1-18; 27:1–28:16.) He likely was a medical doctor, possibly from Antioch of Syria. Though he was not Jewish, it is not known whether he was a native Syrian or a Greek.

No one knows the locale from which Luke wrote his Gospel.

The date when the book was written is disputed. Two possibilities exist: a date about a decade or so after A.D. 70 and a date in the sixties of the first century. Those who favor a date in the seventies or eighties suggest that Luke knew about the destruction of Jerusalem in A.D. 70, but

| THEMES IN LUKE | | |
|---|---|---|
| **THEME** | **EXAMPLES FROM LUKE** | **REFERENCE** |
| **Theology** | Word of God<br>Jesus as Savior<br>The present kingdom of God<br>The Holy Spirit | 5:1; 6:47; 8:11,13-15,21; 11:28<br>1:69; 2:11; 19:9<br>11:20; 19:9<br>1:35,41,67; 2:25-27; 3:22; 4:1,14; 11:13; 24:49 |
| **Concern for women** | Elizabeth<br>Mary<br>Anna<br>The widow of Nain<br>The "sinner" who anoints Jesus' feet<br>Women disciples<br>The woman searching for her lost coin<br>The persistent widow petitioning the unjust judge<br>The sorrowful women along the way to the cross | 1:5-25,39-45,57-66<br>1:26-56; 2:1-20,41-52<br>2:36-38<br>7:11,12<br>7:36-50<br>8:1-3<br>15:8-10<br>18:1-8<br><br>23:27 |
| **Concern for the poor/warnings to the rich** | Blessings on the poor<br>Woes on the rich<br>The rich fool<br>The rich man and the beggar Lazarus | 6:20-23<br>6:24-26<br>12:16-20<br>16:19-31 |
| **Concern for social outcasts** | Shepherds<br>Samaritans<br>Tax agents and "sinners"<br>Gentiles/all people | 2:8-20<br>10:25-37; 17:11-19<br>15:1<br>2:32; 24:47 |
| **The Christian life** | Gratitude and joy<br><br>Prayer<br>Proper use of material possessions<br>Changed social behavior in imitation of God<br>Repentance/faith | 1:46-55,68-79; 2:14; 15:7,10,24,32; 17:16,18; 24:53<br>3:21; 6:12; 9:18; 11:1-13; 18:1-14<br>6:32-36; 10:27-37; 12:32-34;16:1-13<br>9:3-5,16; 10:2-16,38-42; 12:41-48; 22:24-27<br>3:7-14; 5:32; 10:13; 11:32; 13:3-5 15:7-10; 24:47 |

this is not certain since there is no specific reference to this event in any text. The best one can do is see possible allusions to it in 19:41-44 and 21:5-24. The decision is linked to the date of Acts, which ends with events in A.D. 62. If these books were written later, it is curious why later events are not explicitly narrated in Acts. It is also curious why Jewish and Gentile relations form such a central portion of dispute in Acts. This was a problem for the early church and was less a problem in the eighties. These factors slightly favor a date for the Gospel in the sixties.

**Recipients.** Luke was explicitly written to Theophilus (1:1-4). Theophilus appears to have had some exposure to the faith, as Luke's introduction makes clear. In fact, it is quite likely that he was a Gentile believer struggling with his association in a movement that had Jewish origins. Indications that Theophilus was Gentile are reflected in Luke's explaining certain Jewish customs or names (Acts 1:19).

Did God really plan to include Gentiles among His people? Why do the Jews, for whom the promise of God was originally intended, reject the gospel so strongly? Theophilus may have been wondering if he was in the wrong place. So Luke wrote to reassure Theophilus about God's plan. Luke may also have been writing with an eye on those who were raising doubt for Theophilus. Luke showed how God legitimized Jesus and attested to Him as the one sent to bring God's promise.

**Sources.** Luke said that he had predecessors, but he did not name them for us (Luke 1:1-4). Three views of sources exist.

1. Many scholars regard it as likely that Luke used Mark, some special source material only Luke had, and tradition (or, better, a collection of traditions) which he shared with Matthew.

2. Others prefer to suggest that Luke used Matthew and had his own special source material. This means that in terms of order Mark is last of the Synoptic Gospels and that Luke did not know or use Mark. In this view Mark is seen as a summarizing Gospel of the other Synoptics.

3. A few see Luke as the last of the Synoptic writers, with Matthew and Mark preceding him.

Any of the options is possible, but it is hard to explain Luke 1-2 if Luke knew Matthew's infancy account. Lukan rearrangements of parables and accounts from Matthew are also hard to account for if the second or third hypothesis is taken. Against the second option is explaining how Mark is a summary Gospel and yet omits so much of Jesus' teaching and parables. So it is slightly more likely that the first option holds.

**Themes.** Luke highlights God's plan. It explains how Jesus was not only Messiah but also the Prophet like Moses (see Deut. 18:15), the Suffering Servant, and the one who is Lord. Luke gradually reveals this view of Jesus, bringing the reader from a messianic, prophetic understanding of Jesus in Luke 1-2 to a view that reveals the total authority Jesus bears (Luke 22:69). It is often said that Luke presents Jesus as the "Son of Man," but this emphasis is not, strictly speaking, unique to Luke's Gospel and should be avoided in summarizing Luke. Luke is interested in Jesus as Messiah-Servant-Prophet-Lord. A full portrait of Jesus is a major concern of Luke's work.

Luke details how many in Israel became hostile to Jesus and His teaching. The bulk of this discussion comes in chapters 9-13. Many of the parables unique to Luke touch this question. The nation holds a large degree of blame in slaying Jesus as Luke 23 makes clear. But there is always hope for the nation. Luke never gave up on Israel as even in

## VIRGIN BIRTH

The angel Gabriel declared that "no promise is impossible with God" (Luke 1:37). To cause the elderly Zechariah and Elizabeth to conceive was as easy for God as to cause Mary of Nazareth to conceive a child without a human father. The "virgin birth" is the theological term for Mary, a virgin, becoming pregnant with the child Jesus through the power of the Holy Spirit. Luke, the careful and accurate compiler of eyewitness events (1:1-4), included several details that describe Mary's pregnancy as being without a human father.

1. Mary is described as a virgin (parthenos) betrothed to a man called Joseph (1:27).

2. Mary said she could not bear a child because "I do not know a man" (1:34).

3. The angel said the pregnancy would come about when the Holy Spir-it came over Mary and "the power of the Most High" overshadowed her (1:35).

4. Jesus is described as "the son, so it was thought, of Joseph" (3:23).

Matthew in addition recounts:

5. Joseph, when he discovered that his betrothed Mary was pregnant, intended to terminate their engagement (1:18-19).

6. The virgin birth was a fulfillment of Isaiah 7:14 (Matt. 1:22-23).

7. Joseph did not have any sexual relations with Mary until after Jesus' birth (1:25).

8. The rest of the New Testament has several possible allusions to the virgin birth. Jesus' enemies questioned His father (John 8:19,41). Some of Jesus' neighbors in Nazareth described Him as "the son of Mary" (Mark 6:3). Paul described Jesus as "born of woman" (Gal. 4:4) and as the human "from heaven" (1 Cor. 15:45-48).

Usually parthenos refers to a young woman who is unmarried and therefore who has had no sexual relations with a man. For instance, Philip's four daughters are called parthenos (Acts 21:9). Parthenos was also used to describe young unmarried men who had had no sexual relations with a woman. Paul contrasted a virgin with a married person (1 Cor. 7:25-28), and the 144,000 in Revelation 14:4 are virgin men.

Matthew cited the pregnancy of Mary and the birth of Jesus as a fulfillment of Isaiah 7:14. When King Ahaz of Judah refused to ask a sign of God, God gave him a sign: "A virgin in the womb shall conceive and bear a son, and you shall call his name Immanuel." Before this child was of the age of accountability (twelve?), the land of the two kings who threatened Ahaz would be deserted (Isa. 7:17).

Acts 28 Paul was speaking to Jews about the promise.

Luke also spent much time explaining the proper response to Jesus. His favorite description is "repent." This picture comes in the mission statement of 5:31-32, the picture of the prodigal in 15:11-32, the picture of the tax collector in 18:9-14, and in the picture of Zacchaeus in 19:1-10. Repentance reflects a humble reception of what God offers on God's terms. It means "agreeing with God" about sin and Jesus and thus involves a genuine turning from sin toward God. This is something Paul called faith. But the opportunity Jesus brings requires that believers be commit-ted to pursuing the lost, even the tax collector and sinner.

Luke highlighted the walk of the believer. He noted the danger of excessive attachment to wealth (12:13-21). He warned about the cost of following Jesus (14:25-35). He called for believers to love God and other people, even those who persecute (6:20-49; 18:18-30). In fact, the disciple's love is to stand out as something distinct from the love the world gives by its love for enemies and its care for every type of person. Disciples are to persist in suffering (9:23; 18:8; 21:19), watch for God's return (12:35-48; 17:22-37; 21:5-38), rejoice (1:14; 2:10; 10:17; 24:41,52), and pray (11:1-13; 18:1-8).

Isaiah and his wife, the prophetess, shortly had a child whom they named Mahershalalhashbaz *(The spoil speeds, the prey hastes)* as a sign that soon Damascus and Samaria would be conquered by the Assyrians (Isa. 8:4,18). Both Damascus and Samaria fell within thirteen years of the original prophecy (732–722 B.C.). Thus the prophecy in Isaiah has at least two fulfillments, one in Mahershalalhashbaz and one in Jesus. Isaiah may have expected a more perfect future fulfillment because he and his wife did not call their child "Immanuel," even though "God" had been "with them" to protect Judah from its adversaries.

The virgin birth of Mary's child early became an important aspect of Christian doctrine because it insured that Jesus was indeed "holy, Son of God" (Luke 1:35). Having had a human mother, Jesus was fully human. Having had the Holy Spirit cause conception, Jesus was fully God. Therefore Jesus could truly be the perfect intermediary between, and representative for, God and humanity (Heb. 2:17; 4:15; 7:26-28).

The bishop of Antioch, Ignatius, who lived during the first century A.D., mentioned the virgin birth at least five times in his eight letters that have been preserved for us. For example, to the Smyrneans he wrote: The Lord Jesus Christ "is in truth of the family of David according to the flesh, God's Son by the will and power of God, truly born of a virgin" (1.1; see also *Ephesians* 7.2; 18.2; 19.1; *Trallians* 9.1).

Justin Martyr, who lived in the second century A.D., explained in his *First Apology* that Jesus "was begotten by God as the Word of God in a unique manner beyond ordinary birth" (22). "For 'behold, the Virgin shall conceive' means that the Virgin would conceive without intercourse . . . God's power . . . caused her to conceive while still remaining a virgin" (33).

The New Testament does not present the virgin birth of Jesus as some outlandish event but as simply the fulfillment of a promise by Almighty God made to a poor but devout Hebrew woman. Even as the *shekinah* glory filled the tabernacle and as an eagle shelters its young under its wings (Exod. 40:35; 19:4; Ps. 91:4), God's Spirit "overshadowed" *(episkiadzo)* and filled Mary (Luke 1:35). Although a Jew would consider for God to "change into a human" or "a human into God the "most grievous impiety" (Philo, *Embassy to Gaius* XVI), Mary believed (even if she may not have fully understood) because she agreed that "no promise is impossible with God."

***Literary Form.*** Luke is a Gospel, a form unique to the Bible. The account operates like a narrative. It is more than a biography because it is selective and has a theological message to convey. It is history but only a selective history. We are told nothing about the details of Jesus' childhood. Rather, we move from Jesus' birth directly to His ministry with only one incident at the age of twelve and the ministry of John the Baptist intervening briefly. A Gospel is a theological, pastoral explanation of the significance and impact of Jesus' life, death, and resurrection. So characters, setting, movements of time and location, mood, and the arrangement of events are all a part of telling the account of Jesus' ministry.

All the Gospels tell the events surrounding Jesus in their own way, sometimes presenting events not in their historical, chronological order but according to topical concerns. A *synopsis* easily reveals these rearrangements (compare Mark 6:1-6 and Luke 4:16-30 or the order of the temptations in Matt. 4:1-11 versus Luke 4:1-13). Luke's narrative is dominated by two features: the gathering of disciples in Galilee (4:14–9:50) and the journey to Jerusalem. During the journey, rejection heightens, and Jesus prepares His disciples for His departure (9:51–19:44). Here one can find the central elements in Luke's Gospel.

Luke also has many miracle accounts and parables. These emphasize the power and teaching of Jesus. Luke has more parables than any of the other Gospels. Most parables deal either with God's plan or the walk of the disciple. The explanation of His miracles and their significance comes in Luke 7:18-35 and 11:14-23.

**Theology.** When we look at Luke's portrait of God, the major feature is that He is the God of design and concern. Many texts allude to God's plan or to what must be (1:14-17,31-35; 2:9-14; 4:16-30; 24:44-49). The major scheme Luke applies to make this point is promise and fulfillment. Luke's use of the Old Testament often involves descriptions of Jesus (1:46-55,68-79; 3:21-22; 4:17-19; 7:22; 9:35; 13:31-35; 19:27; 20:41-44; 21:27; 22:69; 24:43-47). Other texts emphasize the immediacy of the realization of the plan "today" (2:11; 4:21; 5:26; 13:32-33; 19:5,9,42; 23:42-43). John the Baptist is the bridge in the plan (3:1-19; 7:18-35). So God's work is central to Luke. Nothing that happens to Jesus takes God by surprise.

The emphasis on Jesus has already been noted. He had many roles: teacher, prophet, prophet like Moses, Messiah, Servant, Son of man, and Lord. Luke wanted to stress the person of Jesus. He said little about how Jesus saved on the cross. In fact, only one text tackles the issue of the cross directly (22:18-20), though allusions to Jesus as the Servant occur as Jesus' baptism shows (3:21-22). Luke wanted his reader to appreciate who does the saving.

Also important to Luke is the arrival of the kingdom. In fact, the kingdom in Luke has two stages. It has already come in the authority Jesus shows over the forces of evil and in the hope of the coming of the Spirit or in the arrival of new covenant promise (10:9,18; 11:9; 17:20-21; 22:18-20; 24:49). Yet there comes a time when the kingdom will come in even more splendor (17:22-37). This combination is known as the kingdom already and not yet. Jesus will manifest His rule in stages. What comes now is but a foretaste of what will come. Part of what Jesus brings now is the Spirit (3:15-18). Though this is more emphasized in Acts, the promise is stated in Luke (24:49).

When one looks at who benefits from Jesus' coming, the simple answer is to say all people. But Luke drew attention to the poor, tax collectors, sinners, and women, since these neglected groups indicate the comprehensive nature of God's salvation. The makeup of God's new community includes all who come in faith and repentance to Christ.

When Luke discussed the blessings of salvation, he used terms like forgiveness, life, peace, the kingdom, and the Spirit. These are various ways to state that God blesses the one He saves, not with material wealth, but with spiritual riches. When Luke sought to assure Theophilus, he made sure that Theophilus was aware of how much he had received from God. The promise of God is rich in benefits.

The outline of Luke breaks down largely into geographical divisions to show the progress of Jesus' ministry.

I. John the Baptist and Jesus (1:1–2:52)

II. Preparation for Ministry (3:1–4:13)

III. Galilean Ministry (4:14–9:50)

IV. Jerusalem Journey (9:51–19:44)

V. Jerusalem (19:45–24:53)

**Purpose.** Luke wrote his Gospel for a wide variety of reasons.

1. Luke wanted to confirm the message of God's promise and salvation through Jesus.

2. He wished to portray God's faithfulness both to Israel and to all persons while explaining why so many in Israel tragically rejected Jesus.

3. He wanted to lay the foundation in Luke for his defense in Acts of the full membership of Gentiles as a part of God's people and promise.

4. He wished to offer a word of conciliation and explanation to Jews by showing how responding to Jesus is the natural extension of Judaism.

5. He wished to show that God's promise extends to all men and women by showing the variety of social classes and people who responded to Jesus.

Luke is an extremely personal Gospel, showing how people can be related to God and share in the full blessing of His promise. It is also a cosmic Gospel, since it reveals and explains God's plan. The question of fulfillment is tackled both at the racial (Jew, Gentile) and individual level. God's plan is shown as wise, thought out, and on course. The death of Messiah was always expected, and so was His resurrection. Now the call of God's people involves the commission to take the message of repentance for the forgiveness of sins to all the nations in the power of the Spirit (24:43-49).

## ELIZABETH AND MARY (1:1-80)

After a crucial preface in which Luke explained his task, the author launched into a unique comparison of John and Jesus by showing how both represent the fulfillment of promises made by God. John was like Elijah, but Jesus had Davidic roles to fulfill and possessed a unique supernatural origin. John was forerunner, but Jesus was fulfillment. Everything in Luke 12 points to the superiority of Jesus over John, who obediently prepared the way.

Mary's hymn praises the faithfulness of God to His promise and His blessing of those who are humble before Him, setting up a major Lukan theme. Her praise is personal in tone. Zechariah reiterated the hope in national, Davidic terms and set forth the superior relationship of

Jesus to John. In doing so, Zechariah links spiritual promises and national promises to Davidic hope, another theme Luke would develop in the Gospel. The goal of salvation is to free God's people to serve Him without fear and to enable them to walk in God's path of peace. In these accounts Mary pictures the one who trusts God, Elizabeth is the one who rejoices in God, while Zechariah learns to trust God.

## JESUS' BIRTH (2:1-52)

Jesus' birth took place in humble circumstances, but all the figures surrounding His birth were pious and responsive to the hope of God. Jesus was praised by a priest, by a humble virgin, by shepherds, and by a prophet and prophetess at the temple. All reflect high expectation from people who are portrayed as walking with God. Only the word of Simeon to Mary gives an ominous ring. The old man noted that Jesus would be a "light for revelation to the Gentiles and for glory to . . . Israel." In fact, Jesus would be a cause of grief for Mary and division in Israel. Jesus is the "salvation" of God, but in the midst of hope is the reality that fulfillment comes mixed with pain and suffering.

Jesus' own self-awareness concludes the introductory overture in the Gospel. Here the young boy declares that He must be about the work of His father in the temple. Jesus notes His unique relationship to God and His association with God's presence and teaching.

This section, dominated by Old Testament allusions, opens the Gospel with notes of fulfillment and indications of God's direction. These emphases continue through the entire Gospel. John and Jesus are placed side by side in the stories of Luke 1, and then Jesus has the stage in Luke 2. The structure imitates the theology of forerunner-fulfillment.

# THE NEW TESTAMENT AND HISTORY

There are at least three ways to approach the question of the New Testament and history. The first is to examine the historical perspectives in the New Testament writings themselves. Jesus, for instance, lived and died in the specific historical context of first-century Palestine.

The Gospels, however, show little concern with the events of the time, except as they bear directly on Jesus. It is in the story of Jesus' death and resurrection that historical references are most apparent with Jesus' appearance before the Roman procurator Pilate. For the most part, the Gospel writers were most concerned with Jesus Himself, His teachings, and His ministry rather than the larger social and political movements of the time, which are the characteristic concerns of historians.

Among the Gospel writers, Luke was the exception. He showed a definite historian's perspective. He was careful to set Jesus within the framework of world history, listing the Roman Emperor and the Syrian governor at Jesus' birth (Luke 2:1-2). He gave all the relevant rulers when John the Baptist began his ministry: the emperor, the Judean governor, the minor Jewish kings, and the Jewish high priests (Luke 3:1-2).

This historian's viewpoint is perhaps even more pronounced in Luke's second volume, Acts. He related the death of the Jewish King Herod Agrippa I (Acts 12:20-23). He showed Paul encountering the political leaders of his day: the Roman proconsul of Cyprus (Acts 13:4-12), the proconsul of Achaia (Acts 18:12-17), the governors of Syria, Felix and Festus (Acts 24:24-25:5), and the Jewish King Agrippa II (Acts 25:13-26:32). Luke wanted to make clear that the events involving the young Christian movement were of worldwide significance. They were "not done in a corner" (Acts 26:26).

An equally strong concern with history is found in Revelation. The theme of the book in a real sense is that God holds the keys to all history. All the affairs of nations and their leaders stand before God's ultimate judgment. He is the Alpha and the Omega. All time, all history, begins with His creation, and in His own time He will draw the final curtain on it.

A second approach asks, What do the non-Christian historians of the first century have to say about Christianity? Actually, there are not many such references, but the few that exist are significant. The Roman historian Suetonius, in his biography of the emperor Claudius, related that Claudius in A.D. 49 expelled all the Jews from Rome because of a riot instigated by a certain "Chrestus." In addition to explaining a reference in Acts to this event (Acts 18:2), Suetonius's remark probably also is good evidence that Christianity had reached Rome by A.D. 49, for "Chrestus" most likely refers to Christ (Latin Christus). In his writings the Jewish historian Josephus referred to three New Testament figures—Jesus, John the Baptist, and James the brother of Jesus. Although the present form of Josephus's reference to Jesus has been somewhat reworked by later Christian scribes, the latter two accounts are considered reliable and confirm the impact early Christianity had on the larger Jewish community.

A final approach deals with the historical setting in which the New Testament came into being. Jesus was a historical figure whose birth, ministry, and death occurred in first-century Palestine under Roman occupation. Paul wrote to actual congregations in Asia Minor, Greece, and Rome. Revelation was written during a period when Christians were being persecuted for their refusal to participate in Roman emperor worship. In short, God sent His Son to redeem the world at a definite time in human history. All the New Testament writings are in a sense "historical documents," for they reflect the faith and mission of the early Christian movement. To understand the New Testament in light of the larger backdrop of its own contemporary world enhances our understanding of its message and our ability to communicate that message effectively in our own day.

## DIVINE SON (3:1-38)

John and Jesus remain side by side in this initial section on Jesus' ministry. John was the "one who goes before" (Isa. 40:3-5), while Jesus is the "One who comes." Only Luke among the Gospel writers lengthens his citation of Isaiah 40 to make the point that salvation is seen by all persons. In addition, only Luke contains the section where the ethical dimensions of John's call to repentance in terms of compassionate response to others is made clear. John also warns about judgment, calls for repentance, and promises the coming of One who brings God's Spirit. John baptized Jesus, but the main feature of the baptism is one of two heavenly testimonies to Jesus (9:35 has the other).

John had promised that Jesus would bring the Spirit, but in 3:22 Jesus was anointed with the Spirit. The first hints of fulfillment occur here. The heavenly testimony calls Jesus "my son, whom I love; with whom I am well pleased." This fusion of Isaiah 42:1 ("one in whom I delight") and Psalm 2:7 ("my Son") marks out Jesus as a regal, prophetic figure who as a chosen Servant of God brings God's revelation and salvation. The universal character of Jesus' relationship to humankind is highlighted in the list of His ancestors. He is "son of Adam, . . . son of God." Jesus not only has connections to heaven but also connections with those created from the dust of the earth.

## FAITHFUL IN TEMPTATION (4:1-13)

Jesus' first actions were to overcome temptations from Satan, something Adam had failed to do. So the section shows Jesus as anointed by God, representative of humanity and faithful to God. God's promise comes in through a man who is able to deliver what God offers and who can deal with sin by being faithful to God.

## WHO IS JESUS? (4:14-30)

Jesus' teaching and miracles dominate this section. Major teaching blocks include His declaration of the fulfillment of God's promise in the synagogue and the Sermon on the Plain (6:17-49). Both passages are unique to Luke in that the synagogue speech represents Jesus' self-description of His mission, while the sermon represents His fundamental ethic presented without concerns about Jewish tradition that Matthew's Sermon on the Mount possesses.

The section's fundamental question is, Who is Jesus? The unit pictures the growth of faith that comes to those whom Jesus gathered around Himself. Their discovery is the vehicle Luke used to answer the question of Jesus' identity. The reader is to identify with the disciples and the crowds who witness and discuss Jesus. The reader is to share in the reflection their discussions and reactions raise. Jesus followed up the disciples' response in faith with the first discussions of the hard road of discipleship. The section shows that following Jesus is full of blessing, but it is not easy.

In the synagogue speech, Jesus raised the note of fulfillment through the appeal to Isaiah 61:1 and 58:6. He said that the anointing of God promised in this passage is fulfilled today. In the context of Luke, the anointing looks back to the anointing with the Spirit in Luke 3:20-22. As such the appeal to Isaiah was not just to the picture of a prophet, as allusions to Elijah and Elisha in verses 24-28 suggest but also asserts Jesus' regal role. Jesus would bring salvation to all those in need: poor, blind, and captive. His presence means release from bondage, particularly bondage rooted in the activity of Satan, as His subsequent miracles in 4:31-44 show. Rejection, like that in

Nazareth, will not be met with failure but with the taking of the message to others, an indirect allusion to the inclusion of Gentiles. The mission's scope is summarized here.

## JESUS' AUTHORITY AND MISSION (4:31–6:11)

Jesus' ability to bring salvation is pictured in a series of miracles. These miracles show the authority of Jesus, even over evil spirits that oppress people and cause them suffering. The healings are a metaphor for the spiritual obstacles Jesus can overcome. Jesus healed, but His healings picture much more than physical resuscitation.

Beyond deliverance there also is mission. Disciples are called to be fishers of men. Unlike the fisherman, who catches fish to devour them, disciples fish to snatch people from the grip of death and damnation. But the offer of hope will yield negative reaction. The first hints of official opposition came with the miracles of divinelike authority, when the Son of man claimed to be able to forgive sins and healed on the Sabbath. This healing of the paralytic is significant because it shows the "picture" quality of miracles. Jesus healed the paralytic, but more importantly it "pictured" His absolute authority to forgive sin.

In contrast to the negative reaction came the positive responses. Levi, a hated tax gatherer, was called. And four controversies emerged, one of which involved the type of company Jesus kept, while the others centered on the Sabbath. In the midst of this debate, Jesus gave some mission statements: His task was to call the sick to repentance. His authority was such that to do good on the Sabbath is the requirement.

## LOVE LIKE CHRIST (6:12–49)

So Jesus organized the disciples who were responding and issued a call. The Twelve were chosen. Then Jesus offered blessing to the humble and poor while warning the rich and oppressive. His Sermon on the Plain is a call to love others in the context of accountability of God. Such love is to be greater than the love a sinner shows. It is not conditional love. It is love shown to the one who persecutes. Jesus' death for sinners will be the prime example of such love. If the world is to recognize God's disciples, their love will have to be different. Such love recognizes sin in the self before it hastens to deal with sin in others. Real wisdom is to respect the authority of Jesus' teaching and respond with obedience. The mission and message of Jesus are introduced here, as well as the fundamental elements of a disciple's ethic.

## MESSIAH FOR ALL PEOPLE (7:1–8:3)

Luke 7:1–8:3 concentrates on who Jesus is and the appropriate response to Him. A Gentile centurion understood faith better than those in the nation, as the contrast between Israel and the nations surfaced. The crowd believed that Jesus was a prophet when He raised the widow of Nain's son much like Elijah and Elisha had done. John the Baptist wondered whether Jesus was the Coming One, probably because Jesus' style of ministry did not reflect the ruling, judging Messiah John had anticipated. Jesus replied that His eschatological works of healing and preaching give the affirmative answer (Isa. 29:18; 35:5-6; 61:1). He is the One who brings the time of fulfillment. The difference in the two ages is so great that John, as the best of men born up to the day of Jesus, is less than the least of those who share in the age to come.

An exemplary faith is displayed by the woman who anoints Jesus and by those women who contribute to His ministry. Here the breadth of Jesus' ministry is emphasized as women, who were held in low esteem in the first century, are raised

## DISCOURSES OF JESUS

| Where Delivered | Nature or Style | To Whom Addressed | The Lesson to Be Learned | References |
|---|---|---|---|---|
| 1. Jerusalem | Conversation | Nicodemus | We must be "born of water and the Spirit" to enter the kingdom | John 3:1-21 |
| 2. At Jacob's Well | Conversation | Samaritan Woman | "God is spirit" to be worshiped in spirit and truth | John 4:1-30 |
| 3. At Jacob's Well | Conversation | The Disciples | Our food is to do His will | John 4:31-38 |
| 4. Nazareth | Sermon | Worshipers | No prophet is welcomed in his own hometown | Luke 4:16-30 |
| 5. Mountain of Galilee | Sermon | The Disciples and the People | The Beatitudes; to let our light shine before men; Christians the light of the world; how to pray; benevolence and humility; heavenly and earthly treasures contrasted; golden rule | Matt 5–7; Luke 6:17-49 |
| 6. Bethesda—A Pool | Conversation | The Jews | To hear Him and believe on Him is to have everlasting life | John 5:1-47 |
| 7. Galilee | Conversation | The Pharisees | Works of necessity not wrong on the Sabbath | Matt 12:1-14 Luke 6:1-11 |
| 8. Galilee | Eulogy and Denunciation | The People | Greatness of the least in heaven; judged according to the light we have | Matt 11:2-29; Luke 7:18-35 |
| 9. Galilee | Conversation | The Pharisees | The unforgivable sin is to sin against the Holy Spirit | Mark 3:19-30; Matt 12:22-45 |
| 10. Galilee | Conversation | The Disciples | The providence of God; nearness of Christ to those who serve Him | Mark 6:6-13; Matt 10:1-42 |
| 11. Galilee | Conversation | A Messenger | Relationship of those doing His will | Matt 12:46-50; Mark 3:31-35 |
| 12. Capernaum | Sermon | The Multitude | Christ as the Bread of life | John 6:22-71 |
| 13. Genessaret | Criticism and Reproof | The Scribes and Pharisees | Not outward conditions, but that which proceeds from the heart defiles | Matt 15:1-20; Mark 7:1-23 |
| 14. Capernaum | Example | The Disciples | Humility the mark of greatness; be not a stumbling block | Matt 18:1-14; Mark 9:33-50 |
| 15. Temple–Jerusalem | Instruction | The Jews | Judge not according to outward appearance | John 7:11-40 |
| 16. Temple–Jerusalem | Instruction | The Jews | To follow Christ is to walk in the light | John 8:12-59 |
| 17. Jerusalem | Instruction | The Jews | Christ the door; He knows His sheep; He gives His life for them | John 10:1-21 |
| 18. Capernaum | Charge | The Seventy | Need for Christian service; not to despise Christ's ministers | Luke 10:1-24 |
| 19. Unknown | Instruction | The Disciples | The efficacy of earnest prayer | Luke 11:1-13 |
| 20. Unknown | Conversation | The People | Hear and keep God's will; the state of the backslider | Luke 11:14-36 |
| 21. House of Pharisee | Reproof | The Pharisees | The meaning of inward purity | Luke 11:37-54 |
| 22. Unknown | Exhortation | The Multitude | Beware of hypocrisy; covetousness; blasphemy; be watchful | Luke 12:1-21 |
| 23. Unknown | Object Lesson | The Disciples | Watchfulness; the kingdom of God is of first importance | Luke 12:22-34 |
| 24. Jerusalem | Exhortation | The People | Death for life; way of eternal life | John 12:20-50 |
| 25. Jerusalem | Denunciation | The Pharisees | Avoid hypocrisy and pretense | Matt 23:1-39 |
| 26. Mount of Olives | Prophecy | The Disciples | Signs of the coming of the Son of man; beware of false prophets | Matt 24:1-51; Mark 13:1-37 |
| 27. Jerusalem | Exhortation | The Disciples | The lesson of humility and service | John 13:1-20 |
| 28. Jerusalem | Exhortation | The Disciples | The proof of discipleship; that He will come again | John 14–16 |

up as examples of faith. Here also in two scenes poor women, wealthy women, and women oppressed by Satan are all brought to equal honor by Jesus.

## JESUS CAN BE TRUSTED (8:4-56)

Jesus can be trusted. With the parable of the seed and the image of the word as light, a call is made to trust God and His word, as revealed by Jesus. Those who yield fruit cling to the word patiently and with a good heart, while the obstacles to fruitfulness include wealth, persecution, and the worries of life. Jesus then showed His total authority by exhibiting sovereignty over nature, over demons, and over disease and death. All the forces of life bow at His feet.

## THE CENTER OF PROMISE (9:1-17)

In the context of such authority, He sends out the message of promise. He sends out a mission of proclamation of the kingdom, as word about Him reaches as far as Herod. The picture of Jesus' ability to provide comes in the multiplication of loaves. Jesus is the source of life and resides at the center of promise.

## LISTEN AND FOLLOW JESUS (9:18-50)

At this point the story moves from teaching and demonstration of authority to confession and call to discipleship. Peter confessed Jesus to be the Christ. Then Jesus explained what kind of Messiah He would be; He would suffer. Those who follow Him must have total and daily commitment in order to survive the path of rejection that comes with following Jesus. The second heavenly testimony to Jesus comes at the transfiguration. The divine voice repeats the endorsement made at the baptism with one key addition, the call to "listen to him" (see Deut. 18:15). Jesus was a second Moses, who marked out a "New Way."

The section closes with the disciples' failing, thus showing their need for Jesus

to instruct them. Jesus issued calls to trust and be humble, two basic characteristics of discipleship. If one is to learn and grow, one must listen to Him.

## TRUSTING ON THE WAY (9:51-12:48)

Over 40 percent of this section contains material unique to Luke. There is a high concentration of teaching and parable. In fact, seventeen parables are in this unit, fifteen of which are unique to Luke. The "journey" is not a chronological, straight-line journey, since Jesus in 10:38-42 was near Jerusalem, while later in the section He was back in the north. Rather, it is a journey in time, in the context of the necessity of God's plan.

Jerusalem and the fate that met Jesus there drew near. The section explains how Jerusalem and the cross happened. Journey notes dot the section (9:51; 13:22; 17:11; 18:31; 19:28,44). Jesus traveled to meet His appointed fate in Jerusalem (13:31-35). The section's thrust is that Jesus gives a new way to follow God, which was not the way of the Jewish leadership. Its theme was "listen to him." So this section discusses how Jesus' teaching related to current Judaism. Jesus fulfilled the promise and is the Way, but His way is distinct from that of Israel's leadership. The difference surfaces great opposition, a theme dominating Luke 9–13. All are invited, but some refuse. As the new way is revealed, the seeds of discontent leading to Jesus' death are also made manifest.

The journey starts with the disciples learning the basics of discipleship: mission, commitment, love for God, love for one's neighbor, devotion to Jesus and His teaching, and prayer. Here we see the call to be a neighbor in the example of the good Samaritan. The choice of the Samaritan is a surprise, since Samaritans were not respected in Israel. Here again Jesus showed His racial breadth. Here is the example of Mary's choosing the "better" thing, which was to sit and listen to Jesus. Here Jesus revealed devotion and submission to God as He taught the disciples the Lord's Prayer, which is really to be the Community's Prayer. Also raised are notes of challenge to Judaism's leadership and a scathing indictment of them by Jesus. Their way is not God's way. Discipleship is fundamentally trusting God, not people or riches, for everything while remaining faithful to Him. If God is sovereign and cares for creation, fear Him and trust Him.

## THE NARROW WAY (12:49–14:24)

Jesus called on the crowd to know the nature of the times of His ministry. Israel was turning away; and the time for them to respond, without facing judgment, was short. The only sign Jesus would give was the sign of Jonah, the message of repentance.

The Lukan focus on repentance here is unique to his Gospel, for in Matthew the "sign" was resurrection. For Luke the comparison was with the preaching of Jonah and the message of Jesus. Israel was like a fruitless tree that the owner of the garden was ready to remove. But tragedy is the end of all people unless they repent. Israel's house would be desolate until they recognized Jesus as sent by God. Nevertheless, blessing would still come to the earth regardless of how the nation responded. Jesus wanted His people, the Jews, to repent but knew their refusal.

Renewed Jewish condemnation of Jesus' Sabbath healings shows that the warnings and divine authentication were unheeded. Jesus said the door was closing, so be sure to enter the narrow way. He also warned that those at the table would not be those who were expected to be there. Israel ran the risk of missing out on blessing, but the table would still be full with the blessed from the corners of the earth.

## SEEK THE LOST (14:25–15:32)

With Israel duly warned, most of the journey section concerns discipleship. Disciples in the face of rejection need absolute commitment. Their mission, even though others grumble at it, is to seek the lost, just as God does. God rejoices in finding lost sinners, so Jesus' call is to pursue them as one would a lost sheep, a lost coin, or a wayward son. When the lost come, open arms are to await them. Celebration and joy greet them in heaven.

## SERVE AND WAIT (16:1–18:30)

Beyond mission is discipleship. Discipleship expresses itself in service to others, so the disciple is generous with resources. He is not like the rich man, who ignored Lazarus. Though false teaching is a threat, it is overcome with forgiveness of the brother, deep faith, and service. Disciples are to see themselves as slaves who do their duty, something Paul also knew (Rom. 1:1).

Disciples are to live, looking for the hope of the King's return, when the promise of the currently inaugurated kingdom is consummated with judgment and the expression of Jesus' total authority. That coming will be sudden, so be ready. It will be visible, so no one will have to hunt for it. The return will be a time of severe judgment but also a time of vindication for the saints. So in the meantime, disciples should live lives of humility, should devote themselves completely to God because disciples trust all to the Father.

## MESSIANIC AUTHORITY (18:31–19:44)

Now Jesus turned to Jerusalem. He again displayed His authority when He predicted His suffering and healed as the "Son of David." The last miracle before Jerusalem returns to Jesus' Davidic, regal association, returning to the theme of Luke 12 and the issue of His trials.

Zacchaeus pictures the transformed sinner and rich man. He is a picture of the mission of Jesus, the lost who can be sought and saved. The parable of the pounds shows the need for faithfulness and the reality that the disciple, as well as the nation of Israel, is accountable to the king. Jesus entered Jerusalem as a king, but the leadership rejected the claim. Jesus warned the nation that they had failed to respond to God's promise and faced judgment. Their tragic fall drew near. Though opposition resulted in death for Jesus, opposition resulted in something much worse for the nation. Jesus predicted the nation's terrible defeat by Rome in A.D. 70. Thus the nation was the loser, while God's plan advanced in triumph.

## THE FINAL CONFLICTS (19:45–21:4)

In this concluding section, Luke explained how Jesus died and why apparent defeat became victory. Luke showed how God revealed who Jesus was. In addition, the task of disciples in light of God's acts becomes clear. Luke mixed fresh material with that present in the other Gospels.

The final battles in Jesus' earthly ministry occur here, recalling earlier confrontations in Luke 11–13. Jesus cleansed the temple, signaling His displeasure with official Judaism. The leaders failed to embarrass Jesus in various controversies concerning His authority to act as He had, concerning an individual's political-economic responsibilities, and concerning resurrection. Jesus' source of authority is like that of John the Baptist; it comes from God. That which is to be rendered to God is to be given to God and is to be separated from the rights God has granted to government to operate. Resurrection changes people, so that

life in the next world is different from and transcends life in this world.

In the midst of these controversies and at their end, Jesus told a parable and asked a question, which give an overview of God's plan. They revealed God's commitment to His Son despite Jewish rejection. The nation's rejection would cost them. The kingdom would go to new tenants. The question about Psalm 110 gives the reason. The Messiah is not just David's Son; He is David's Lord, who is to be seated at God's right hand. When we see Jesus, we see more than a king; we see the person God has chosen to share His authority and His rule. Jesus' death is a transition, not an end to God's plan. Jesus reveals how things stand when He condemns the scribes' hypocrisy, while praising a poor widow's simple, generous, and sacrificial faith. Blessing is not a matter of position but of the heart. The widow may have been poor, but in terms of life she was wealthier than the wealthy because her priorities were right.

## LOOKING TO THE END (21:5-38)

In light of the nation's refusal, Jesus predicted the fall of the temple and of Jerusalem, events that themselves are a foretaste of the end. The fall of Jerusalem will be a terrible time for the nation, but it was not yet the end, when the Son of man returns on the clouds with authority to redeem His people (Dan. 7:13-14). This discourse on the end is hard to understand because it describes events that lead up to the fall in A.D. 70 and the events of the end together. In Luke the events of the fall of Jerusalem are largely in view from verses 5-24. But these events are like those of the end. Disciples are to watch and be faithful. The events of A.D. 70 are a guarantee that the end also comes, since the one set of events does picture the other.

## CHRIST'S EXALTATION (22:1–23:25)

Luke 22–23 describes the moments before Jesus' death. Jesus directed where the Last Supper was held and told the disciples to prepare it. Jesus, though betrayed, was innocent, but His death would bring the new covenant and was a sacrifice on behalf of others. In His last discourse Jesus announced the betrayal, pointed out that greatness is in service, appointed eleven to authority, predicted Peter's denials, and warned of rejection. Jesus was in control, even as His death approached.

As Jesus prayed, He exemplified trust in the face of rejection, something He had exhorted the disciples to possess. The trails centered on who Jesus is. The crucial answer comes in 22:69. Jesus "from now on" would be manifest as the exalted Lord, who is seated with authority at the side of God. The allusion to being seated at the right hand repeats the allusion to Psalm 110, a passage to which Luke would return in Acts 2:30-36. Messiahship means lordship, that is, authority over God's plan and salvation. No judgment the leadership makes can prevent that from happening. In fact, ironically and unwittingly they help bring this authority to pass. Jesus was on trial, it seems; but, in fact, He was the Judge.

But it was not only the leadership that was guilty. As Pilate and Herod debated what to do about Jesus, the people were given the final choice. Despite Pilate's repeated protestations of innocence and Herod's similar reaction, the people asked for Jesus to be slain and Barabbas to be freed. Justice was absent, both in the request and in the failure of the leaders to carry out their impression. Passively and actively, the responsibility for Jesus' death widens. Everyone, whether actively or passively, shares in the responsibility of Jesus' death (Acts 4:24-28).

## GOD TRIUMPHS (23:26-56)

So the innocent died, while a criminal was freed. Here is the first cameo of the significance of Jesus' death as He prepares to face His departure. Next a second image of the significance of Jesus' death follows. Jesus was crucified between two thieves. One derides, but the other believes and receives the promise of life in paradise. Here is a picture of division of opinion and of eternal fate, which Jesus brings. A centurion confesses the righteousness of Jesus, the final word at the scene of the cross. Luke made clear that Jesus died unjustly, yet in the face of injustice God still works. Luke describes Jesus' death with Old Testament allusions that picture Jesus as an innocent sufferer who relied on God (Pss. 19; 22:8-9; 31:6; 69:22). The injustice is transcended in God's plan through the coming resurrection.

## RESURRECTION (24:1-12)

Luke closes with three scenes of resurrection and vindication. First, 24:1-12 announces the empty tomb, but the news of the excited women is greeted with skepticism. The angelic announcement told the women to recall the predictions of suffering proclaimed during the journey to Jerusalem. Luke 24 often notes that such events *must take place*. God's plan emerges at the end of the Gospel, just as refrains of its presence began the Gospel in the various hymns and announcements declaring its presence.

## OVERCOMING DESPAIR (24:13-35)

Second, the experience of the Emmaus disciples pictures the reversal the resurrection brought to the disciples' despair. These two disciples mourned the departure of the Prophet of Israel who might have redeemed the nation. But instruction in Scripture and the revelation of Jesus Himself shows that God had a plan, which included Jesus' death. God has indeed raised Jesus, vindicating both Jesus and the plan. Despair turns to joy upon understanding the nature of God's plan and Jesus' role in it, a major note in Luke. Events that on the surface appeared devastating to Jesus' claims, in fact, were foundational to what God was doing. Jesus' death should not cause despair because it allowed heaven to open its gates to humankind.

### GOD'S PLAN FULFILLED (24:36-53)

Third, Luke reported Jesus' final commission, instruction, and ascension. Just as Luke 12 opened with the hope of Old Testament promise fulfilled, so Luke 24:43-47 returns to the central theme of Jesus the Messiah as the fulfillment of God's plan and promise. Jesus' final Gospel appearance yields a commission, a plan, and a promise. The disciples were reminded again that Scripture taught the suffering and exaltation of Messiah. Jesus also told them that they were called as witnesses to preach repentance. The plan was to go to all the nations, starting from Jerusalem. The promise was the gift of the Father, the Holy Spirit (24:49; 3:15-17). As the Baptist promised, so it had come to pass. Enabling power from heaven, from on high, would come in the distribution of the Spirit upon those who had responded to the message of Jesus (Acts 2:16-39).

## The Temple

The temple was located in the northeastern corner of the city directly west of the Mount of Olives. The temple area, which was approximately three hundred yards wide and five hundred yards long, was entirely walled with the main gates being in the south wall.

Immediately inside the temple walls a portico existed with three rows of massive marble columns on the north, east, and west and four in the south. The eastern portico was known as "Solomon's Colonnade" (John 10:23; Acts 3:11; 5:12). All of the colonnades were fully open to the large, open area paved with variously colored stones and known as the court of the Gentiles. There animals were sold, and money was exchanged (Mark 11:12-19).

Making one's way through the area of the Gentiles toward the temple building itself, one passed through a low stone fence (Eph. 2:14). This fence marked the limit for the Gentiles, and through its openings only Jews could pass (Acts 21:27-29).

The temple building was within a walled enclosure with one large entrance opening to the east, called the Beautiful Gate (Acts 3:2). Inside the gate was the area called the court of the women, where the temple offerings were received (Mark 12:41).

Only male Israelites could proceed to the next area closer to the building itself. The area immediately adjacent to the front of the building where the great altar was set was open only to the priests. The facade of the building was approximately 150 feet wide and 180 feet high.

The temple itself contained two main rooms. First was the holy place, where the seven-branched lampstand and the altar of incense (Heb. 9:2; Exod. 30:6) were and where only priests chosen by lot could enter (Luke 1:9). The inmost room, called the holy of holies, was entered only once each year and only by the high priest in the ceremony of atonement (Heb. 9:25).

## Christian Symbol

The author of Hebrews used imagery drawn from the temple and its ritual to explain what Jesus accomplished: He entered into the holy of holies to win our redemption (9:11-14) and gives to all Christians the spiritual privilege limited to the high priest (10:19-22) in Jewish ritual.

Jesus' ascension pictures the exaltation He predicted at His trial (22:69). God's plan does not involve a dead Messiah but one who sits at God's side. In exaltation Jesus is vindicated, and the plan to reach all nations of people goes on. Jesus, the Messiah, is Lord of all, so the message can go to all (Acts 2:14-40; 10:34-43).

The Gospel of Luke closes with the disciples rejoicing that out of the ashes of apparent defeat, victory and promise arose. The new way was still alive, and the risen Lord showed the way. Theophilus could be reassured (1:1-4), while the history continues in Acts.

***Theological and Ethical Significance.*** How does God want people to receive the message? The centrality of repentance as a summary term for responding adequately to God's message is prominent throughout Luke's message. The fundamental dynamic of responding to God is agreeing with Him about the seriousness of sin, turning to Him to forgive it, and trusting Him to forgive sin and deal with it. In short, we know that God has dealt with the sin problem so we can walk with God (1:77-79; 5:31-32).

As disciples follow Christ, they can count on rejection. They are to hold to the word and endure (8:1-14) and watch for the Lord's return, being faithful until He comes again (12:35-48; 18:1-80; 17:22-37; 21:5-38). The fact of Jesus'

# ACCOUNTS OF THE RESURRECTION

The resurrection of Jesus Christ is the central event of the Christian faith. Its importance is well stated by the apostle Paul in 1 Corinthians 15:17: "If Christ has not been raised, your faith is futile; you are still in your sins."

The reality and nature of the resurrection has been debated from the time of Jesus until the present. A number of different theories have been set forth to explain exactly what happened. These can be summarized as follows:

1. *Swoon theory.*—Jesus did not actually die. He passed out on the cross and was later revived and appeared to His followers.

2. *Spirit theory.*—Jesus appeared only in a spirit form to His disciples. His body remained in the tomb.

3. *Hallucination theory.*—The disciples experienced mass and personal hallucinations. They thought they saw the risen Jesus, but they were mistaken.

4. *Legend/Myth theory.*—This is the most popular view among people with antisupernatural biases. In it the idea of "resurrection" is considered simply a first-century prescientific metaphor that expresses that in Jesus something significant was present. "Resurrection" is not to be understood as a literal bodily event of rising from the dead.

5. *Stolen body theory.*—The body of Jesus was illegally removed from the tomb by the (a) Jews, (b) Romans, or (c) disciples of Jesus (see Matt. 28:11-15).

6. *Wrong tomb theory.*—The followers of Jesus went to another tomb by mistake, found it was empty, and erroneously assumed Jesus had risen.

7. *Hoax theory.*—The early church deliberately and knowingly fabricated the resurrection for personal profit.

8. *Mistaken identity theory.*—The disciples mistakenly identified someone else as Jesus after His crucifixion and burial.

9. *Literal/Bodily resurrection theory.*—Jesus of Nazareth was supernaturally resurrected from the dead bodily. The tomb was actually empty, and Jesus on numerous occasions appeared to His followers up until His ascension (see Luke 24:50-53; Acts 1:6-11).

No one actually saw the resurrection event within the tomb. The evidence is overwhelming, however, in pointing to theory 9, a literal bodily resurrection, as the best explanation of the biblical and historical data. The following evidences are noted:

1. Naturalistic theories are weak and forced to manipulate the evidence due to their antisupernaturalism.

2. The birth of the church during this time period.

3. The transformation of the disciples into bold witnesses who were willing to die for their faith.

4. The change in the day of worship by people raised as devout Jews from the Sabbath to Sunday.

5. The testimony of women as the first to see the risen Lord. (A woman's testimony carried little if any official or legal value in the first century. That they actually saw Christ first is the best explanation for Scripture's testimony to the historicity of the event.)

6. The empty tomb and the articles of clothing left.

7. The unlikely nature of mass hallucinations.

8. The fact that the reported appearances lasted forty days and then suddenly and completely stopped.

9. The fifty-day interval between the resurrection and the proclamation of it at Pentecost in Jerusalem (see Acts 12).

10. The unexpected nature of the resurrection.

11. The character of Jesus and His claims that He would indeed rise.

12. The fact that neither the Romans nor the Jewish leaders could disprove the resurrection event by producing the body of Jesus.

13. The conversion of a skeptic like James (the half brother of Jesus) and the subsequent conversion of an antagonist like Saul of Tarsus (see Acts 9:1-31).

It is extremely difficult in all of these cases, and impossible in some, to explain these thirteen events, and others that could be listed, apart from the resurrection of Jesus Christ. When all the information is gathered and evaluated, the bodily resurrection of Jesus can be concluded to be both a historical reality and the foundation of the Christian faith.

return and the reality that He returns bringing judgment should bring perspective to the temporary suffering endured by His disciples. Though some rejection exists now, reception in heaven awaits in the future (23:42-43; Acts 7:55-56). This truth has been called Luke's individual eschatology, where Luke described how heaven receives the individual faithful to Jesus.

Luke's Gospel is pastoral, theological, and historical. The reality of God's plan affects how individuals see themselves and the community to which they belong. Old barriers of race are removed. New hope abounds. The message of Jesus is one of hope and transformation. Anyone, Jew or Gentile, can belong. At the center is Jesus, the promised Messiah-Lord, who sits at God's right hand exercising authority from above. He will return one day, and all are accountable to Him. His life, ministry, and resurrection/ascension show that He can be trusted. He can bring God's promises to completion, just as He has inaugurated them. In the meantime being a disciple is not easy, but it is full of rich blessing that transcends anything else this life can offer. This is the reassurance about salvation Luke offered to Theophilus and others like him.

## Questions for Reflection

1. What are the themes of Luke, and what additional ones did you find in your own reading of the Gospel?

2. What various roles does Jesus Christ have according to Luke?

3. What elements are part of the disciple's walk?

4. What attitudes should a disciple have about money, suffering, the poor, the rejected, and the lost?

5. What role does hope and looking for Jesus' return play in the disciple's walk?

## Sources for Additional Study

Bock, Darrell. *Luke*. NIV Application Commentary. Grand Rapids: Zondervan, 1995.

Evans, Craig. *Luke*. New International Bible Commentary. Peabody, Mass.: Hendricksen, 1990.

Stein, Robert. *Luke. The* New American Commentary. Nashville: Broadman, 1992.

Tiede, David L. *Luke*. Augsburg Commentary on the New Testament. Minneapolis: Augsburg, 1988.

# JOHN

The Gospel of John is perhaps the most intriguing of the four accounts of the life and teaching of Jesus found in Scripture. More of a theological treatise than a historical narrative, John put the challenge of the incarnation before his readers—God in human flesh.

**Authorship and Date.** The authorship of the Gospel of John has been traditionally ascribed to the apostle John, the son of Zebedee and the brother of James. The Gospel itself, however, does not put forth the author's name (which has made the authorship of John a much-debated issue among interpreters). The only reference to the author is the "disciple whom Jesus loved" (21:20,24). The apostle John is usually seen as the author because the Gospel exhibits many marks that intimate it was written by one who was an eyewitness to the life and ministry of Jesus, such as the aroma of the broken perfume jar in the house at Bethany (12:3).

Even individuals who were anonymous in the Synoptics are given names in John's Gospel (6:7-8; 12:3; 18:10). Many other aspects of the Gospel point toward the apostle John. Examples are the author's knowledge of Palestinian geography, Jewish customs, and the author's inclusion within the inner circle of disciples (listed by the Synoptic Gospels as Peter, James, and John). Writers in the earliest periods of Christian history, such as Irenaeus and Tertullian, also attribute the Gospel to the apostle John.

Who was John the apostle? John was "the disciple whom Jesus loved" (13:23; 19:26; 20:2; 21:7,20,24). John's brother was James, and together they were called the "sons of thunder" by Jesus (Mark 3:17). John's mother was Salome, who served Jesus in Galilee and later witnessed His crucifixion (Mark 15:40-41). Formerly a follower of John the Baptist, the apostle John was perhaps only twenty-five years of age when called to be a follower of Christ.

Beyond this Gospel, John has been traditionally understood to have written the three epistles bearing his name as well as the Book of Revelation. After Christ ascended to heaven, John became one of the principal figures of the church at Jerusalem, along with Peter and James (Acts 3:1; 8:14; Gal. 2:9). Second only to the apostle Paul in the number of books written that are included in the New Testament canon, John served as the pastor of the church at Ephesus. The emperor Domitian later exiled him to Patmos, where he wrote the Book of Revelation (Rev. 1:9). Most interpreters have concluded that John's was the last of the four Gospels to be written, most likely between A.D. 60 and 95.

**Literary Form.** The literary form of the Gospel of John is just that—a gospel. What is a gospel? The word itself comes from the Anglo-Saxon word "godspell," which literally means good news. In reference to the four Gospels in the New Testament, what we have is a narrative of the good news of Jesus Christ.

John made use of many features of Hebrew poetry, most notably parallelism. The Gospel of John does not contain parables, as do Matthew, Mark, and Luke, but rather brings forth the many allegories present in the teaching ministry of Jesus.

| COMPARISON OF THE GOSPELS | | | |
|---|---|---|---|
| Event or Point of Comparison | In Synoptic Gospels? | In Gospel of John? | Scripture Reference |
| Wedding at Cana | No | Yes | John 2:1-11 |
| Encounter with Nicodemus | No | Yes | John 3:1-14 |
| Encounter with Woman at the Well | No | Yes | John 4:1-45 |
| Washing of the Disciples' Feet | No | Yes | John 13:1-17 |
| Last Supper | Yes | No | Luke 22:7-23 |
| Jesus' Final Priestly Prayer | No | Yes | John 17:1-26 |
| Extensive Prologue to the Gospel | No | Yes | John 1:1-18 |
| Concluding Epilogue to the Gospel | No | Yes | John 21:1-25 |
| Birth Narratives | Yes | No | Luke 2:1-20 |
| Jesus' Use of Parables | Yes | No | Matt 13:1-52 |
| Casting Out Demons | Yes | No | Mark 1:21-28 |
| Jesus with Tax Collectors | Yes | No | Luke 6:27-32 |
| Jesus Heals Lepers | Yes | No | Luke 17:11-17 |
| Jesus with Children | Yes | No | Mark 10:13-16 |
| Sermon on the Mount | Yes | No | Matt 5:1–7:27 |
| Discourses on the End Times | Yes | No | Matt 24:1-51 |
| Emphasis on Miracles | Yes | No | Matt 8:1–9:8 |
| Emphasis on Interpretation of Miracles/Signs | No | Yes | John 5:1-47 |
| Jesus' Teaching on Hell | Yes | No | Matt 23:1-39 |
| Temptations of Jesus | Yes | No | Matt 4:1-11 |
| "I AM" Sayings | No | Yes | John 14:6 |

***Purpose and Theology.*** The theme of John's Gospel is that God had taken human form in the person of Jesus Christ. For this reason John's Gospel is often seen as the most evangelistic of the four Gospels. John's emphasis on the nature of Christ—as opposed to the more chronological, historical accounts of Jesus' life in Matthew, Mark, and Luke—has fostered the popular classification of Matthew, Mark, and Luke as "Synoptic" Gospels. This means they put forth a similar view and emphasis, while the Gospel of John falls into a class all to itself.

Virtually every reader of the four Gospels finds the Gospel of John unique in its approach and treatment of the life of Jesus. For example, note the omissions from the Synoptic accounts of the life of Jesus: the genealogy of Jesus, His birth, His boyhood, His temptation, His transfiguration, His appointing of the disciples, His ascension, and the Great Commission. Yet we find uniquely in John Christ called the Word, the Creator, the Lamb of God, and the great "I AM." The contrasts between John and the Synoptics have been framed in many different angles by a host of interpreters. Perhaps the most succinct statement of their distinctions is to say that the Synoptics present theology from a historical point of view, while John presents history from a theological point of view.

The purpose of John's Gospel is not a question for speculation. It contains the most clearly stated purpose statement in all of Scripture: "That you may believe that Jesus is the Christ, the Son of God, and that by believing you may have life in his name" (20:31). The key word here is "believe," found in John close to one hundred times. This gives the Gospel two primary purposes. First, John's Gospel sought to confront individuals with the life and claims of Christ in order that they

might surrender their lives to Christ's rule. Therefore the first purpose of John's Gospel is evangelistic. Second, it is possible to translate "may believe" in John's purpose statement as "may continue to believe," which would intimate the purpose of not only winning individuals to faith in Christ but also that of strengthening the family of faith that is already walking with Christ.

The central theological theme of John is the nature of Jesus Christ. This Gospel teaches us that the Word was God, and that Word became flesh (1:1,14). John's Gospel presents Jesus as God Himself in human form. This is perhaps presented most clearly in the seven "I am" statements found in chapters 6–15, which portray Christ as the "bread of life" (6:35,48), "the light of the world" (8:12; 9:5), "the door" (10:7,9), "the good shepherd" (10:11,14), "the resurrection, and the life" (11:25), "the way, the truth, and the life" (14:6), and "the true vine" (15:1-5). There are even moments in John's Gospel where Jesus equated Himself directly with the Old Testament name for God Himself, "I AM" (Yahweh, see Exod. 3:14), such as in 8:58. When one has seen Jesus, one has seen the Father (chaps. 12; 14).

The ancient heresy of Docetism, however, is not to be found in this account of the life of Jesus. The Docetic view emphasized Christ's divinity to the exclusion of His humanity. John's Gospel balances the proclamation that Jesus was God in human form with the equal proclamation that Jesus was fully human (2:24; 4:6-7; 6:51; 11:35; 19:5,28,34-35). Other unique features in the Gospel of John in relation to the purpose of showing that Jesus was God in human form include the "seven witnesses" (John the Baptist, Nathanael, Peter, Martha, Thomas, John, and Christ Himself) who proclaim the divinity of

Jesus and the "seven miracles" (turning water into wine, healing the nobleman's son, healing the man at Bethesda, feeding the five thousand, walking on the water, healing the blind man, and the raising of Lazarus), which demonstrate the unique person of Jesus Christ as the Son of God.

Many other theological themes present themselves in this Gospel, such as the clear choice to accept or reject Christ. This decision, placed before every individual, permeates the Gospel (1:11-13; 3:36; 5:24-29; 10:27-29). Sin is treated primarily as unbelief, the rejection of Christ, which leads to judgment and death (chap. 8). The Gospel of John contains more teaching about the Spirit than any other Gospel. The unity and witness of the church is also a theme that is given careful attention.

  I. Introduction (1:1–2:11)
 II. Public Ministry of Christ (2:12–4:54)
III. Opposition to Christ (5:1–12:50)
IV. Final Words and Deeds of Christ (13:1–21:25)

### THE WORD BECAME FLESH (1:1-18)

No other book in the Bible has a prologue as overtly theological as does the Gospel of John. First, John made a clear and decisive statement regarding the nature of Jesus: "the Word was God" and that "Word became flesh." John wanted it known that Jesus Christ was fully God in human form. That is the meaning of "incarnation," from the Latin *incarnatus,* which means *made flesh.* God has made Himself known through Christ. Christ was both "Word" and "flesh," not one to the exclusion of the other, and thus was the perfect and only God-man. Christ made His "dwelling" with us, a word associated with "tent" or "tabernacle," intimating the literalness of God's coming to humanity. This word usage should not be lost on the reader, for the tabernacle of the Old Testament was an earthly building filled with the glory of God (Exod. 40:34-35).

In using the term "Word" *(logos),* John was using a term familiar to both Jews and Greeks, though each attributed a different meaning to the term. For the Greek mind the "Word" referred to the rational principle that supervised or governed the universe. To the Jew, "Word" was a reference to God. Thus John wanted to equate the "Word" with God while noting that the Word was distinct from the Father. John stated that Jesus was with God "in the beginning" and that through Christ "all things were made." Jesus is therefore seen as co-eternal with God and as the Creator.

John then discussed the purpose of the Word becoming flesh, namely that Christ brought life, a life that serves as the "light" for all people. The life Christ offers is beyond that of mere human life; it is life eternal with God. Therefore Jesus brought the light of truth and the life of salvation. The questions and concerns of this world that find no ultimate answers are met by the Light that pierces all darkness with the brilliance of truth, yet this truth has been rejected.

The bitter irony of this should not be lost on the reader. John emphasized this irony, stating that though He created the world, the world did not recognize Him. Though He came to His own, His own did not receive Him. God has come to the world for acceptance and relationship. Those who accept the Light, who believe in the message Christ proclaimed about Himself, are given the "right to become the children of God." To be born into the kingdom of God is not something achieved on human energy (see Eph. 2:8-9) but by the grace of the living God through Christ Jesus. This is to be balanced by the emphasis on the need to "receive" Christ. Though we bring nothing to God and contribute nothing to our salvation, the gift itself is dependent on our willingness to receive it from the one who offers it.

## JOHN'S ROLE (1:19-28)

The role of John the Baptist is explained with clarity in relation to Christ. John the Baptist was sent from God (1:6). John was not himself the Light (1:8). He came as a witness to Christ (1:7,15).

John the Baptist offered the words of the prophet Isaiah about the nature of his identity: "I am the voice of one calling in the desert, 'Make straight the way for the Lord' " (see Isa. 40:3). Some had thought he might be Isaiah, the great prophet who had never died but had been taken to be with God (2 Kgs. 2:11). Many believed that Elijah would return to the earth in order to announce the coming end of the world. John denied being Elijah. A word should be mentioned, however, regarding Jesus' reference to John as Elijah in the Synoptics (Matt. 11:14; 17:10-13). What was at hand in Jesus' mind was how John was a fulfillment of the prophecy recorded in Malachi 4:5 (see Luke 1:17).

What was the purpose of John's testimony? First, to fulfill prophecy (Isa. 40:3). Second, to call people to repentance. Third, to draw people's attention toward the coming of the Messiah, Jesus Christ. What was the purpose of John's baptism? Clearly it was not Christian baptism, for that is the mark of one's acceptance of Christ as personal Lord and Savior. John's baptism was "a baptism of repentance for the forgiveness of sins" (Luke 3:3). It looked forward to the coming of the Messiah and served to prepare the people for the coming of the kingdom of God.

## LAMB OF GOD (1:29-34)

John the Baptist's confession upon seeing Christ, that here was "the Lamb of God, who takes away the sin of the world!" is of great significance. The Jews used a lamb as a sacrifice for the Passover Feast, which celebrated Israel's deliverance from bondage in Egypt (Exod. 13:1-10; see John 13:1). Isaiah offered the idea of the Suffering Servant in terms of a sacrificial lamb (Isa. 53). John was declaring that Jesus was the true sacrificial lamb for the passover; His death would now serve as the deliverance of God's people from their sins. As Paul wrote in his letter to the church at Corinth, "Christ, our Passover lamb, has been sacrificed" (1 Cor. 5:7).

John the Baptist then gave testimony that he saw "the Spirit come down from heaven and rest" on Jesus. This confirmed to John that Jesus was the Messiah. For he then declared: "I have seen and I testify that this is the Son of God."

## WITNESSING ABOUT JESUS (1:35-42)

The calling of Andrew, Simon Peter's brother, was the direct result of John the Baptist's testimony concerning Jesus as the Lamb of God. The second person mentioned in this account is not named, but many surmise that it was the author of this Gospel, the apostle John. Andrew immediately sought his brother, Simon Peter, and proclaimed that the Messiah had been found. Upon encountering Simon, Jesus declared that he would "'be called Cephas' (which, when translated, is Peter)," Both "Cephas," which is Aramaic, and Peter, which is Greek, mean *rock*.

That Peter would be given this name is interesting in light of the fact that he was anything but "rocklike." Peter was impulsive and undisciplined in spirit, a rough-hewn man of raw emotion. Yet Christ was calling those whom He would develop, and Peter would indeed become the pillar of the church, the "rock" upon which the early church would depend (Matt. 19:18; Acts 2).

## SON OF MAN (1:43-51)

Jesus used the term "Son of Man" as His favored description for Himself. It has been suggested that the title "Son of God" is Jesus' divine name (Matt. 8:29); "Son of David," His Jewish name (Matt. 9:27); and "Son of Man," the name that ties Jesus to His earthly mission. The term itself is based on Daniel 7:13-14, where it served as a reference to God.

## PROVIDING PURE WINE (2:1-11)

Jesus' first miracle was at a wedding at Cana of Galilee where He turned water into wine. A wedding feast during this period of history might last as long as a week, with poor hospitality treated as a serious offense; and this celebration had run out of wine. The symbolism of this event should not be lost on the reader, for the water used for purification was replaced by wine, that which would come to symbolize the blood of Christ. The blood of Christ did indeed supplant the Jewish ceremonial system in regard to the predicament of sin in light of a holy God.

That Jesus was aware of His "time" and the progress of His mission is evident throughout this Gospel (7:6,8,30; 8:20). The cross was ever before Jesus, and His movement toward that inevitable moment was to remain on God's timetable (12:23,27; 13:1; 16:32; 17:1). As is the pattern of this Gospel, miracles are referred to as "signs" (semeion), intimating that they served as authentication for Jesus' nature and mission. In the Synoptics the most commonly used word for miracles is dunameis, which refers to mighty works that demonstrate the power of God.

## GOD'S STANDARD (2:12-25)

In the clearing of the temple, Jesus brought forth God's standards of what is right and what is wrong. Present for the Passover, a time of remembrance for Israel's deliverance from Egypt, Jesus encountered individuals who were profiteering from the religious festival. Jews who had traveled great distances needed to purchase animals for sacrifice, as well as exchange their money into local currency. They encountered entrepreneurial individuals who offered both services. While legalism was denounced by Jesus, holiness was maintained. The issue at hand was not business or profit making as such but the mockery of the entire sacrificial system of the temple and the exploitation of devout men and women by greedy individuals who were capitalizing on religious sentiment.

This spectacle aroused the indignation of the Jews. Their concern was not the moral issue of whether the sellers and money exchangers should have been there in the first place but on what grounds Jesus took it upon Himself to expel them. The Jews called for a "sign," and Jesus responded, "Destroy this temple, and I will raise it again in three days." Jesus was referring to the temple of His body, but his Jewish antagonists associated His comments with the temple building, providing the groundwork for some of the mockery and ridicule Jesus was subjected to while hanging on the cross (Matt. 27:40; Mark 15:29).

## GOD'S SAVING LOVE (3:1-21)

There can be little doubt that this section in John's Gospel is the most renowned in all of Scripture, with verse 16 serving as the most familiar single verse in all of the Bible. There is good reason for this, for John 3:16 presents the clearest, simplest statement of the good news Christ came to bring to the world. What is that good news? First, that God loves you. Second, that God's love was so great that He sent His only Son to tell the world about God's love. Third, that anyone who will believe in God's Son will never die but will live forever with God. Belief, of course, means far more than mere intellectual assent. Rather, it means placing one's life and trust in complete surrender to the one in whom you believe.

The heart of Jesus' message to Nicodemus is that men and women, in order to come to God in faith, must be "born again." This is not optional, according to Jesus, but a necessity. By this Jesus meant being "born of the Spirit." The reference to "water and the Spirit" has many possible interpretations, such as (1) water referring to purification; (2) synonymous with "born of the Spirit"; (3) baptism, either John's or Christ's. The latter of these three interpretations, that baptism is necessary for salvation, is the least desired understanding (Eph. 2:8-9). To be considered as well is that the Greek

manuscript does not have an article ("the") with the word "Spirit"; therefore it would be grammatically incorrect to separate Spirit from water. What is to be maintained is that to be "born again" is a gift from God through the Holy Spirit as a result of the death, burial, and resurrection of Christ. To be born again is to become a member of God's family through faith in Jesus Christ, initiated by repentance and the desire to lead a new life to the honor and glory of Christ (1 Pet. 1:23; 2 Cor. 5:17). Jesus' purpose was never to condemn the world, for that is something we do to ourselves through our own willful choice to reject Christ, but rather Jesus' purpose was to save the world.

| THE SEVEN SIGNS IN JOHN | | |
|---|---|---|
| **SIGN** | **REFERENCE** | **CENTRAL TRUTH** |
| 1. Changing water to wine | 2:1-11 | Points to Jesus as the Source of all the blessings of God's future (see Isa 25:6-8; Jer 31:11-12; Amos 9:13-14) |
| 2. Healing the official's son | 4:43-54 | Points to Jesus as the Giver of life |
| 3. Healing the invalid at Bethesda | 5:1-15 | Points to Jesus as the Father's Coworker |
| 4. Feeding the five thousand | 6:1-15,25-69 | Points to Jesus as the life-giving Bread from heaven |
| 5. Walking on water | 6:16-21 | Points to Jesus as the divine I AM |
| 6. Healing the man born blind | 9:1-41 | Points to Jesus as the Giver of spiritual sight |
| 7. Raising Lazarus | 11:1-44 | Points to Jesus as the Resurrection and the Life |

## JESUS THE DISCIPLER (3:22-36)

When students of the life of Christ list the priorities of His ministry, many items come to mind: the miracles, the crucifix-

ion, and of course, the resurrection. But one of the most significant items on Jesus' agenda is found in this: "Jesus and his disciples went out into the Judean countryside, where he spent some time with them." Jesus took twelve men and poured His life into theirs, discipling them in thought and deed in order that they might become the foundation of the church following His death, burial, and resurrection.

During this time an argument developed between some of John's disciples and a certain Jew over ceremonial cleansing. The appropriate means of achieving ceremonial purification was of great interest to many in the Jewish community. In coming to John over the matter, the question of Jesus' ministry in relation to John's ministry was surfaced. The loyalty of these disciples to their master, John, is evident as they allowed envy to enter their thinking regarding Jesus. John's reply affirmed his previous testimony about Jesus, as well as providing an important insight into John's character.

Knowing a teachable moment had presented itself, John informed his students that one "can receive only what is given him from heaven." The point of this affirmation is clear. Knowing God has given everything, one who loves God will not envy another person's gifts, abilities, or accomplishments. John understood his role in relation to Jesus to be that of the "best man" to the groom at a wedding. John instructed those that had supported and followed his ministry that Jesus must become greater, while he "must become less."

John knew that he was "from the earth," while Jesus, as God's Son, was "from heaven." John taught his disciples that their relation to Jesus determines life itself, for rejection of Jesus brings about God's wrath. Therefore the one who accepts Jesus and the truth of His message avoids God's wrath, participates in the life of the Spirit, and has life eternal. That life is not as a gift in the future but life eternal as a present reality that begins at the moment Jesus is accepted in faith and engaged in relationship.

## SOURCE OF LIFE (4:1-26)

Not wanting to be seen in competition with John's ministry, Jesus returned to Galilee. In that journey "he had to go through Samaria." It should be noted that Samaria was not a geographic necessity for Jesus' trip but a necessity for His mission. The division between Jews and Samaritans was legendary, a division Jesus did not and would not recognize. Samaritans were rejected because of their mixed Gentile blood and their differing style of worship, which found its center on Mount Gerizim. On this mountain Samaritans had built a temple that rivaled the Jewish temple in Jerusalem.

Jesus' excursion into Samaria resulted in one of the most fascinating dialogues recorded in Scripture. Resting by a well, Jesus encountered a Samaritan woman who had been living a life of habitual immorality. Their conversation proceeded upon two levels, the spiritual and the temporal, with the woman constantly finding excuses for Jesus' probing of her inner world. Her first shock was that Jesus would even speak to her, an act unheard of for that day between a Jewish man and a Samaritan woman. Jesus continually responded not to her questions but to her needs, offering her the opportunity of receiving "living water."

Here we see much regarding the intent of Jesus' ministry, to bring persons to a realization of the state of their life in order to lead them to repentance and a new life in Him. This new life is a life that honors and worships God in spirit and truth in daily life. The location of worship is not important, but the Object is! The English word "worship" is from the Anglo-Saxon *weorthscipe*, literally read-

## MIRACLES OF JESUS

| MIRACLE | BIBLE PASSAGES | | | |
|---|---|---|---|---|
| Water Turned to Wine | | | | John 2:1 |
| Many Healings | Matt 4:23 | Mark 1:32 | | |
| Healing of a Leper | Matt 8:1 | Mark 1:40 | Luke 5:12 | |
| Healing of a Roman Centurion's Servant | Matt 8:5 | | Luke 7:1 | |
| Healing of Peter's Mother-in-law | Matt 8:14 | Mark 1:29 | Luke 4:38 | |
| Calming of the Storm at Sea | Matt 8:23 | Mark 4:35 | Luke 8:22 | |
| Healing of the Wild Men of Gadara | Matt 8:28 | Mark 5:1 | Luke 8:26 | |
| Healing of the Lame Man | Matt 9:1 | Mark 2:1 | Luke 5:18 | |
| Healing of a Woman with a Hemorrhage | Matt 9:20 | Mark 5:25 | Luke 8:43 | |
| Raising of Jairus's Daughter | Matt 9:23 | Mark 5:22 | Luke 8:41 | |
| Healing of Two Blind Men | Matt 9:27 | | | |
| Healing of a Demon-possessed Man | Matt 9:32 | | | |
| Healing of Man with a Withered Hand | Matt 12:10 | Mark 3:1 | Luke 6:6 | |
| Feeding of 5,000 People | Matt 14:15 | Mark 6:35 | Luke 9:12 | John 6:1 |
| Walking on the Sea | Matt 14:22 | Mark 6:47 | | John 6:16 |
| Healing of the Syrophoenician's Daughter | Matt 15:21 | Mark 7:24 | | |
| Feeding of 4,000 People | Matt 15:32 | Mark 8:1 | | |
| Healing of an Epileptic Boy | Matt 17:14 | Mark 9:14 | Luke 9:37 | |
| Healing of Two Blind Men at Jericho | Matt 20:30 | | | |
| Healing of a Man with an Unclean Spirit | | Mark 1:23 | Luke 4:33 | |
| Healing of a Deaf, Speechless Man | | Mark 7:31 | | |
| Healing of a Blind Man at Bethesda | | Mark 8:22 | | |
| Healing of Blind Bartimaeus | | Mark 10:46 | Luke 18:35 | |
| A Miraculous Catch of Fish | | | Luke 5:4 | John 21:1 |
| Raising of a Widow's Son | | | Luke 7:11 | |
| Healing of a Stooped Woman | | | Luke 13:11 | |
| Healing of a Man with the Dropsy | | | Luke 14:1 | |
| Healing of Ten Lepers | | | Luke 17:11 | |
| Healing of Malchus's Ear | | | Luke 22:50 | |
| Healing of a Royal Official's Son | | | | John 4:46 |
| Healing of a Lame Man at Bethesda | | | | John 5:1 |
| Healing of a Blind Man | | | | John 9:1 |
| Raising of Lazarus | | | | John 11:38 |

ing "worthship." Worship is attributing worth and honor to the living God.

## CHRIST'S MISSION (4:27-38)

When the disciples rejoined Jesus, they did not dare ask Him about His conversation with the Samaritan woman but rather inquired about His physical well-being. Perhaps they thought hunger had deprived Him of the sense necessary to know better than to talk with such a woman. Jesus then continued the education of the disciples, instructing them that His "food" was to "do the will of him who sent me and to finish his work."

Jesus was clearly on a mission, a mission that was God-informed and God-directed (5:30; 6:38; 8:26; 9:4; 10:37-38; 12:49-50; 14:31; 15:10; 17:4). What was that mission? To confront people—all people, as the Samaritan woman demonstrated—with the truth of Himself. Jesus told them that the "fields are ripe for harvest" and that in entering that field for work, it makes no different whether one plants the seed or brings in the crop. This is an important truth, for there should never be competition among Christians regarding differing fields of service. All should share in the joy of seeing the kingdom of God extend.

## SAVIOR OF THE WORLD (4:39-42)

Jesus' encounter with the woman at the well, and her subsequent sharing of that conversation, resulted in many Samaritans believing in Jesus. After they met Jesus themselves, they believed not because of what the woman said but because they had come to believe themselves "that this man really is the Savior of the world." This confession of the Samaritan believers, that Jesus was the "Savior of the world," is only found in the New Testament here and in 1 John 4:14. Only through Jesus is the world able to be saved, and that salvation is indeed for everyone in the world.

## TRUE BELIEF (4:43-54)

After his time in Samaria, Jesus returned to Galilee. There he met a royal official whose child was near death. Jesus commented how the belief of the Galileans was tied to His production of miraculous signs and wonders. This provides an interesting contrast, for the Samaritans believed "because of his words," while the Jews believed because of "miraculous signs and wonders." As Jesus would later say to Thomas following His resurrection, "Blessed are those who have not seen and yet have believed" (20:29).

## SEEKING GOOD HEALTH (5:1-15)

After an unspecified period of time, Jesus traveled to Jerusalem for a "feast of the Jews." The name of this feast is not mentioned, but it was probably one of the three pilgrimage feasts that Jewish males were expected to attend: Passover, Pentecost, or Tabernacles.

There Jesus passed by the Bethesda pool, where a number of invalids had placed themselves. The waters, when stirred, supposedly had miraculous powers of healing. A man who had been there for thirty-eight years was asked an interesting question by Jesus: "Do you want to get well?" Many depended on their condition for financial support given by healthy individuals out of pity. Another possible reason for this question relates to the man's spirit; many who have experienced prolonged pain or misfortune have surrendered even the will to attempt to overcome their situation in life. When the invalid shared with Jesus his difficulty of getting into the pool for healing, Jesus proclaimed: "Get up! Pick up your mat and walk." The man was instantly healed.

This healing took place on a Sabbath. The Jews' response was not joy over his healing but concern that he was violating the Sabbath by carrying his mat! The law of Moses did not forbid such a practice, only the Jewish interpretation of the law of Moses forbade it. Jesus found the healed man, and as with the Samaritan woman at the well, addressed the deeper condition of the man's relationship with God. Jesus' words are interesting: "Stop sinning or something worse may happen to you." This injunction could be easily misinterpreted, either into a perspective that equates health with spiritual obedience or an idea that God bestows calamity upon the disobedient. For Jesus the consequences of sin are far more serious than any form of physical illness. He did not say that one can actually stop sinning but, in accord with the entire biblical witness, that believers should not purposefully live a life of sin.

## SON OF GOD (5:16-30)

John then informs his readers that because of this healing on the Sabbath, the Jews began to persecute Jesus. Legalism is a dreadful distortion of God's will for those whom He created to live in fellowship with Him. Not outer deeds but inward postures matter to God. When the inner world is ordered around God's dictates, then the outer world will exhibit utter holiness, a holiness defined by the life and ministry of Jesus. At this rebuke the Jews were outraged, not because Jesus was wrong (they didn't answer His reply regarding healing on the Sabbath) but because "he was even calling God his own Father, making himself equal with God." The Jews did not object to the idea of God as Father but that Jesus somehow was in a special relationship to God as His Father, thus intimating that Jesus was equal with God.

Jesus then gave a clearly defined response about the relationship between the Father (God) and the Son (Himself). First, the Son can do nothing without the Father. Second, the Father loves the Son and reveals everything to Him. Third, the power to bestow life itself is shared by the Father and the Son. Fourth, God has given all judgment over to the Son. Fifth, the Father and the Son share equal honor. Sixth, belief in the words of the Son result in eternal life. Finally, the very consummation of the age will be by and through the Son.

The Jews' objection was in light of their staunch monotheism (the belief in one God). Christians are monotheists as well yet maintain that the nature of the One True God is that He is Triune —three Persons, one God. To the Jewish mind Jesus' claim to be God was blasphemous in view of the fact that it intimated two Gods. Of course, nothing of the sort was in mind in Jesus' self-declaration as the Son of God. Rather, Jesus was proclaiming that He was God in human form, the second Person of the Trinity.

## TESTIMONY TO JESUS (5:31-47)

Testimony regarding Jesus includes John the Baptist, the works of Jesus, God Himself, the Scriptures, and Moses. In this Jesus clearly distinguished the worth of human testimony from God's testimony concerning that which is of worth and the worth of human praise compared to the praise that flows from God.

## NO EARTHLY KING (6:1-15)

The feeding of the five thousand is the one miracle, apart from the resurrection, that occurs in all four of the Gospels. The number was far greater than five thousand, for this figure refers only to men, since woman and children were not counted (Matt. 14:21). This miracle led the people to try to make Jesus king by force. God's design was not that Jesus manifest Himself as an earthly king but as the Suffering Servant who would give His life as a ransom for many (Mark 10:45).

## JESUS' DIVINE ACTS (6:16-24)

This "sign" pointed to the divine nature of Jesus, demonstrated by His power and authority over the natural, created world. The crowds seemed more interested in Jesus' "signs" than in Jesus' truth.

## BREAD OF LIFE (6:25-59)

After the feeding of the many thousands, it is not surprising that these same numbers sought Jesus out again. When they found Him, Jesus read their hearts and confronted them with their motive: "You are looking for me, not because you saw miraculous signs, but because you ate the loaves and had your fill." Jesus then encouraged them not to devote themselves to such pursuits but rather to "food that endures to eternal life."

This eternal food is the teaching of Jesus. When asked about what works were necessary to appease God, Jesus replied in a decidedly different fashion than they anticipated. Rather than outlining a list of do's and don'ts, Jesus replied, "The work of God is this: to believe in the one he has sent." Salvation is not something that is attained through human effort, but instead it is a freely given gift. The only "work" necessary is

to receive the gift of God for eternal life through His Son, Jesus Christ.

The crowd then asked for a sign, as Moses gave with the manna, that Jesus was indeed the One sent from God. This revealed that their primary interest was food, attempting to goad Jesus into giving them bread in exchange for their faith.

This interchange resulted in the first of the seven "I am" statements found within the Gospel of John. Jesus replied, "I am the bread of life." The Greek language at this point is strongly emphatic, reminiscent of God's own "I AM" recorded in Exodus 3:14. Jesus stated that all who come to Him in saving faith will never be driven away and that it is God's will that all should so come. Such statements did not please the Jews. Jesus was claiming to have come from heaven, and this was unacceptable for them to bestow upon one "whose father and mother we know."

In reply Jesus maintained the following: first, that no one can come to the Father through Christ except as the Father wills. Second, to be in relationship with God is to be in a relationship with Jesus. Third, only the Son, Jesus, has seen the Father; Fourth, the bread of life

| "I AM" SAYINGS IN THE GOSPEL OF JOHN | |
|---|---|
| SAYING | REFERENCE IN JOHN |
| I am the Bread of Life. | 6:35 |
| I am the Light of the World. | 8:12 |
| I am the Gate for the Sheep. | 10:7 |
| I am the Good Shepherd. | 10:11,14 |
| I am the Resurrection and the Life. | 11:25 |
| I am the Way, the Truth, and the Life. | 14:6 |
| I am the True Vine. | 15:1,5 |
| I am a King. | 18:37 |

(Jesus) is that which comes from heaven, and only by eating of that bread, given for the world, can life eternal be gained. The Jews understood this to mean that Jesus was going to give of His actual flesh for them to eat. Jesus added to their confusion by stating that "unless you eat the flesh of the Son of Man and drink his blood, you have no life in you."

This verse is subject to many misinterpretations, such as thinking that it refers to the Lord's Supper, or Eucharist. Nowhere, however, is it taught in Scripture that the taking of the Lord's Supper is the single requirement for salvation. The sole requirement for salvation is not partaking of the elements of the Lord's Supper but faith in Christ. So what is the flesh and blood of which Christ spoke? Clearly it is the flesh and blood He offered to the world at the moment of His death, an offering made to the world for acceptance, resulting in eternal life for those who accept His death on their behalf as an atonement for their sin.

## HOLY ONE OF GOD (6:60-71)

Jesus knew from the beginning which disciple would eventually betray Him. At this point many who had followed Jesus ceased to do so. When Jesus asked the Twelve if they too wished to depart, Peter responded for them all: "Lord, to whom shall we go? We believe and know that you are the Holy One of God."

## GOD'S TIME (7:1-13)

Some might wonder why Jesus would purposefully stay away from Judea because the Jews there were waiting to take His life, especially in light of the fact that Jesus willingly went to His death at the time of the crucifixion. Simply put, it was not time. The time for surrendering of His life would come, but not now; there was more God desired to be accomplished through His life. All would transpire at the moment God intended.

## AUTHORITATIVE TEACHER (7:14-24)

At the appropriate time, halfway through the Feast of the Tabernacles, Jesus revealed Himself and began to teach. The crowds were surprised that Jesus had not studied under any of the noted Jewish scholars. Jesus responded to their amazement. His teaching was not his "own" but "comes from him who sent me." This interchange should not be taken as a disparagement of education or learning. Jesus was uniquely empowered and gifted by God for His mission, and His words were God's words.

## SPIRIT PROMISED (7:25-44)

Many falsely understood that no one would know the origin or birthplace of the Messiah, and since they knew of Jesus' origins, He could not be the Messiah. This is to be understood in light of the Jewish tradition, though not a biblical idea, that the Messiah would be a man of mystery. As a result they tried to seize Jesus, but apparently they were unable to lay even a single hand upon Him because "his time had not yet come." On the last day of the feast, Jesus promised to all who would believe in Him "streams of living water," which the author of the Gospel interpreted for us as the Spirit given later at Pentecost.

## PROPHET FROM GALILEE? (7:45-52)

The temple guards sent to arrest him exclaimed, "No one ever spoke the way this man does." The Pharisees simply dismissed them as deceived, arguing that since none of the Pharisees had expressed belief in Jesus, then He was not to be accepted. The Pharisees elevated their own sense of learning and understanding. In so doing, they exaggerated the ignorance of the average person. This produced a spiritual pride that led them to believe that true understanding rested solely with their own musings. Then Nicodemus, who had spoken with

Jesus earlier, reminded them all that no one was to be judged without a hearing. The response was the adamant stance that no prophet could come from Galilee, which was patently false, since Jonah the prophet was from Galilee.

## SINLESS JUDGE (7:53–8:11)

This story is certainly in line with Jesus' character and teaching, but it does not appear in the earliest and most reliable manuscripts. This does not deny the story's authenticity, only that it may have been added at a later date. (See NIV note.)

The teachers of the law and the Pharisees had brought a woman who had been caught in adultery to the feet of Jesus in order that He might pronounce the proper judgment upon her. The purpose was to trap Jesus, for if He neglected to suggest stoning, as the law required, He could be charged with being a lawbreaker. (The actual law prescribed stoning only if she was a betrothed virgin; the man was to be stoned as well, see Lev. 20:10; Deut. 22:22-24.) If however, Jesus did advocate stoning, then He would bring the wrath of the Roman government to bear upon Himself. How did Jesus handle the dilemma? "If any of you is without sin, let him be the first to throw a stone at her." Brilliantly, He did not break the law; yet He ensured the woman would not be stoned. When all had left, Jesus addressed the woman's two greatest needs, self-esteem and a new life. For her self-esteem, He assured her that He, who was without sin, did not condemn her. For her deepest need, that of a new life, Jesus said, "Go now and leave your life of sin."

## LIGHT OF THE WORLD (8:12-30)

The second of Jesus' seven "I am" statements occurs here: "I am the light of the world." The relationship between Jesus and His Father is of such a nature that

Jesus could say that if "you knew me, you would know my father also."

Teaching about His identity and nature, Jesus revealed that He is from above and not of this world. Further, "if you do not believe that I am the one I claim to be, you will indeed die in your sins." Such a statement could only elicit a shocked, "Who are you?" Jesus answered that He was who He had always claimed to be, the One sent from the Father, the Son of man.

Many have wondered how a loving God can condemn persons to hell. Our response should be that He does nothing of the sort. Individual persons condemn themselves by choosing to reject Jesus Christ and the truth He came to share with the world.

## TRUTH THAT SETS FREE (8:31-41)

Jesus made clear that holding to His teachings is essential in order to claim to be one of His disciples. Further, His teachings should be accepted as absolute truth. This truth, and no other, has the power to set a person free. Many philosophies and ideologies make the claim for truth, but all truth is God's truth, and therefore all claims for truth must be judged in light of God's revealed truth and knowledge. To adhere to a false view of reality is to be held captive to ignorance. To live a life apart from God's rule is to be held captive to sin. The truth of Jesus sets individuals free from all such bondage. The Jews refused to listen to the truth of Jesus, instead insisting on clinging to their own understandings. Perhaps the most telling verse is when Jesus stated that they had "no room" for His word.

## WHO IS YOUR FATHER? (8:42-47)

If God was truly their Father, then they would love Him. Jesus' made clear that His origin was divine, His mission God planned, and His purpose God willed.

People cannot hear what God has to say if they do not belong to God. If people choose to listen to the evil one in terms of what is considered truth, then they close out the voice of God. The basic disposition of Satan is that of a liar, a perverter of truth, one who deceives all who will allow him to direct their lives and thoughts.

### THE ETERNAL I AM (8:48-59)

Desperate to discredit Jesus, the Jews accused Him of being a Samaritan as well as demon possessed. Jesus denied the charge and immediately resumed His charge that they were living apart from God. He added that if anyone kept His word, "he will never see death." At this the Jews were outraged. Jesus was placing Himself above even Abraham. With one voice they asked in indignation, "Who do you think you are?" Jesus responded that God glorified Him, that He knew God, and that He kept God's word. Further, Abraham "rejoiced at the thought of seeing my day; he saw it and was glad." This brought utter incredulity to the crowd. They challenged Him, for here Jesus—far from even the fifty-year-old mark—was claiming to have seen Abraham.

Jesus gave one of the most important answers to any question posed to Him in the entire Gospel of John. "'I tell you the truth,' Jesus answered, 'before Abraham was born, I am!'" "What was Jesus saying? That He was God Himself! The only other time the phrase "I am" was used to describe someone was in Exodus 3:14, where God used that very phrase as His name. Here Jesus claimed that name for Himself. No identity statement could be clearer. Jesus claimed to be God Himself in human form. The Jews did not respond with words but picked up stones to kill Him for blasphemy (see Lev. 24:16). Jesus hid Himself and slipped away from the temple grounds.

### SIN AND SICKNESS (9:1-12)

Jesus performed more miracles related to giving sight to the blind than any other miracle. Such an activity was forecast in prophecy as a messianic act (Isa. 29:18; 35:5; 42:7). Jesus came to clear the sight of human beings who had become blinded to the things of God.

The disciples of Jesus, espousing a common perspective of the day, desired to know who sinned in regard to this man's affliction. They understood that such things occurred either as a result of an individual's personal sin or because of sin in the life of one's parents. The rabbis taught that no one died unless there had been sin, and no one suffered unless there had been sin. Even a child could sin in the womb, they suggested, or even in the preexistent state prior to conception. Refuting this entire system of thought, Jesus proclaimed that neither "this man nor his parents sinned." Instead, this man was there at that moment for God to work in His life in order to glorify Jesus.

Jesus suggested that there would come a time when the work of the kingdom of God will not be able to continue. That time is not the end of His life, as the "we" in verse 4 suggests, but when the consummation of the age takes place. Until that day God's people must do all they can to combat evil and do good in the name of Christ.

### POWER OF TESTIMONY (9:13-34)

The man who had been healed testified that his own perspective was that Jesus was a Prophet. This was not the answer the Pharisees wanted to hear. Questioning the formerly blind man again, he said "One thing I do know. I was blind but now I see!" This simple testimony has been the incontrovertible evidence for the Christian faith for centuries. His final words carried the greatest sting: "If this man were not from God, he could do nothing." The Pharisees became enraged, accused the man of being a sinner, and excommunicated him from the synagogue.

## SIGHT MEANS GUILT (9:35-41)

The healing of this blind man took place on two levels: at the physical level his sight was restored. On the spiritual level he had come to faith in Christ. This man serves as a paradigm for Jesus' entire ministry. The Pharisees who witnessed this event responded only in indignation that Jesus would intimate that they were blind. Masterfully, Jesus responded that if they were truly blind, they would be guiltless, but since they claimed sight, their guilt remained.

## THE GOOD SHEPHERD (10:1-21)

One of the great images of Jesus is as the "good Shepherd." First, He is the gate to the sheep pen, meaning that no one can enter the fold through any other means than Jesus Himself. Only through Jesus Christ can anyone be made right with God leading to eternal life. Second, Jesus leads His sheep. No other voice is the true voice of leadership. Third, as the good Shepherd, Jesus protects His flock—even to the point of death. Unlike someone who watches sheep for employment, Jesus is a Shepherd motivated by love for His sheep.

As the good Shepherd, Jesus mentioned that there are other sheep that will listen to His voice and will one day be brought into the fold. More than likely what is in view are the Gentiles who would come to believe in Christ. The idea is not many shepherds with many flocks but one Shepherd joined together as one flock (see Eph. 2:16). Jesus was not forced into being the good Shepherd; He willingly took the role upon Himself, and for this He is loved by God.

## ONE WITH THE FATHER (10:22-42)

The Feast of Dedication was the celebration of the dedication and subsequent reopening of the temple by Judas Maccabeus in December of 165 B.C., after it had been desecrated by the Syrian ruler Antiochus Epiphanes in 168 B.C. (see Dan. 11:31). This event is commonly referred to as "Hanukkah" or "The Feast of Lights."

Jesus stated that His sheep are given eternal life and that no one can "snatch them out of my hand." When a person comes to Christ as Savior and Lord, nothing can remove that person from the state of salvation against their will. If one is truly saved, then that person can rest assured that they are held in the hand of God, protected from any assault to their state of redemption.

Jesus also declared that "I and the Father are one." Jesus and God are not, according the Christian doctrine of the Trinity, identical persons but separate persons who are of identical nature.

At this the Jews picked up stones to kill Him, for it was blasphemy for a man to claim to be God (10:33). Jesus responded to their anger by pointing back to the Old Testament where, in accord with the worldview of the ancient Near East, rulers and judges, as emissaries of the heavenly King, could be granted the honorary title "god" (Ps. 82). If they could be culturally comfortable with that title for those to whom the Word of God came, why did they rebel against the idea that the Messiah would be God's Son ? And if this does not make sense, Jesus argued, then simply look at my life and the miracles performed. This did not persuade the Jews, and again they tried to seize Jesus for execution.

## DYING WITH JESUS (11:1-16)

Lazarus was the brother of the sisters Mary and Martha. Mary had poured per-

## NEW TESTAMENT SIGNS AND MIRACLES

From a biblical perspective, a miracle is an extraordinary work of God that may transcend the ordinary powers of nature. Throughout Scripture miracles are most prevalent at crisis points in salvation history. They authenticate God's presence in historical acts. The basic New Testament terminology used to describe these events includes "signs" (John 2:11; 10:41), "wonders" (Matt. 24:24; Mark 13:22), "power" (Matt. 7:22; Luke 10:13), and "work" (Luke 24:19; John 5:20).

Jesus underscored the relationship between His miraculous ministry and the arrival of the kingdom of God (Matt. 12:28). His supernatural activity signified the coming of a new age in God's program (Luke 4:18-21). Despite the revelatory nature of Christ's miracles, their testimony was not always recognized; they had to be interpreted by faith.

The miracle accounts in the Gospels reveal different theological themes. Mark placed more emphasis on Christ's deeds than the other Gospel writers. Consequently, of the four Gospels, Mark contains the highest proportion of miracles. In Mark the focus of miracles involves tension and confrontation as Christ interacted with His opponents and His own disciples. While Matthew stressed healing miracles, Mark centered on exorcisms; Christ is the one who "binds" Satan (3:27).

However, despite the power evident in Christ's activity, miracles can only be comprehended by faith; they do not produce faith. The disciples misunderstood the miraculous elements of Christ's ministry (4:40; 6:52). They needed Jesus' teaching and His person to comprehend these events properly (4:40; 5:34).

While Mark stressed Jesus' deeds, Matthew highlighted Christ's teaching. Thus miracles are organized around instructive sections for theological purposes. In Matthew miracles reveal Jesus' sovereign power and His ability to forgive sins (chaps. 89). They also show His authority over the law and over Satan (chap. 12).

Furthermore, Matthew used miracles to show transition in Christ's ministry. The disciples were involved in Christ's activity (chaps. 14–15). As they learned from His actions, they became a means by which Jesus' ministry was extended.

Miracles do not play as great a role in Luke as they do in Mark. Primarily they express Jesus' authority over natural forces and the demonic realm. In Luke miracles have more of a validating force than they do in the other Gospels. They authenticate faith in Jesus (7:16; 9:43). As people witnessed the power of God operative in Jesus, they both "saw" (10:23-24; 19:37) and "feared" (5:26; 8:35) the divine truth in Him.

The Gospel of John records only seven miracles or "signs" from Christ's ministry. (See chart "Seven Signs in John.") As signs these miracles serve as symbols of the true significance of Jesus. However, while many marveled at Christ's supernatural exploits, only true believers saw the spiritual implications of the signs. The signs confronted Jesus' audience with the necessity of decision. While some rejected the actual meaning of the signs (2:23-25; 4:45), others grew in understanding because of these events (2:11; 11:42).

---

fume on the feet of Jesus and wiped them dry with her hair (12:3). Jesus loved all three of them. His two-day delay was probably to ensure that the miracle He was about to bestow would be clearly understood to be a resurrection from the dead, not a resuscitation from a severe illness. His disciples urged Him not to go, for there were individuals there who desired to seize and kill Him. Thomas, often known as the doubter, here revealed the depth of his personal commitment to Jesus when he said to his fellow disciples: "Let us also go, that we may die with him."

### EMOTIONS OF JESUS (11:17-37)

One of the most moving scenes in the life of Jesus is the death of Lazarus. Here we see not only the power of Jesus to raise the dead, but the emotions of Jesus moved by the grief of those around Him. Martha's faith is evident as she approached Jesus, four days after the death of Lazarus, and professed belief that He could save her dead brother. When Mary came as well and Jesus saw her grief and the grief of those with her, he was "deeply moved in spirit and troubled." Scripture then tells us that Jesus wept.

## RESURRECTION AND LIFE (11:38-44)

What could testify more to the divine nature of Jesus than to exhibit the power needed to raise someone from the dead? Wishing to teach an important truth about how God hears and answers the prayer of belief, Jesus prayed aloud. Note that the raising of Lazarus serves as something of a foreshadowing of the power to resurrect all believers one day to fellowship and eternal life in Christ. Unlike Lazarus, who was raised only to die again, Christians will be raised to eternal life.

## ONE MAN FOR THE WORLD (11:45-57)

The resurrection of Lazarus caused many to place their faith in Jesus. It also led to a meeting of the Sanhedrin. The Sanhedrin was the high court of the Jews. In the New Testament period, it was composed of three groups: the chief priests, the elders, and the teachers of the law. Its membership reached seventy-one, including the high priest, who served as the presiding officer. Under Roman jurisdiction the Sanhedrin was given great power, but it could not impose capital punishment (18:31).

Their concern was self-preservation. If Jesus continued as He had, then people would continue to place their faith in Him as the Messiah. If the Romans then heard that a Messiah was being her-

alded by the Jews, they would come and destroy the threat, including the Sanhedrin. Therefore much of the opposition to Jesus was sociopolitical in nature.

The remark by Caiaphas about their ignorance was one of rudeness. He understood the political dimension more fully than the others, who were actually thinking in terms of guilt or innocence. For Caiaphas it did not matter whether Jesus was guilty or innocent of wrongdoing. What was important was that the death of one man was worth the viability of the Jewish nation under Roman rule. Historically, Caiaphas was in error; for despite the death of Jesus, the Jewish nation perished in A.D. 70.

The prophecy of Caiaphas was truer than he could have imagined. He prophesied the death of Jesus for the Jewish nation in order to alleviate political tensions, not knowing that Jesus' death would be for the spiritual salvation of the Jewish nation and for the world.

## DEVOTION OR DEATH (12:1-11)

This portion of John's Gospel contains a host of important elements. First, there is the devotion of Mary. The perfume used was expensive, a luxury item for herself, selflessly given in devotion to Jesus. That she poured it on the feet of Jesus was an act of humility, for attending to the feet of another person was the work of a servant. Wiping the oil with her hair was also unusual, for respectable women did not unbraid their hair in public. Mary exhibited unrestrained love and devotion to Jesus that went against personal cost and concern for perception.

Second, is the deceit and corruption of Judas. This is the sole passage that reveals the wicked character of Judas prior to his betrayal of Jesus. While the author of this Gospel relates Judas's dishonesty in hindsight, at the time Judas must have been highly esteemed, for he was trusted with caring for the money bag. All too often individuals have been able to deceive people regarding their relationship with God, but never is God Himself deceived, for He sees into the very heart of every person.

Third, is the judgment of Jesus on both Mary and the poor. Jesus affirmed Mary's act of devotion and linked it to His own burial. Mary did not intend for this to be the significance of her act, but it was perceived by Jesus in this manner, knowing of the growing shadow of the cross. In discussing the use of the expensive perfume on Himself rather than selling it to assist the poor, Jesus said, "You will always have the poor among you." Unfortunately, many throughout the centuries of Christian history have misinterpreted this statement by Jesus as an excuse to neglect the poor. This was far from the intent of Jesus, who exhibited care and concern for the poor throughout His ministry. The point Jesus was making was that Mary's act of devotion at that particular time and place was worthy of the cost.

## PRAISING THE KING (12:12-19)

The triumphal entry into Jerusalem coincided with the Passover Feast. The palm branches were symbolic and used in celebration of victory. The response of the crowds to Jesus was spectacular. The shout of "Hosanna!" is a Hebrew term meaning save which had become an expression of praise.

The Gospel of John emphasizes the royalty of Jesus. Here is the only Gospel that records that the people also shouted, "Blessed is the King of Israel!" The crowd's exultation, as well as Jesus' riding a colt, was not seen by the disciples until after His death, burial, and resurrection as the fulfillment of prophecy. This moment, perhaps more than any other, was the high mark of Jesus' popularity and influence. In only a matter of days, however, the "Hosanna!" would turn to "Crucify him!" (19:15).

## THE HOUR IS COME (12:20-36)

The request of some Greeks to interview Jesus occasioned a lengthy response from Jesus regarding the road that lay before Him. Throughout the Gospel, Jesus had avoided situations that would hasten His death. But now the "hour" had come for "the Son of Man to be glorified." Jesus' death and subsequent resurrection is what is in mind by the term "glorified." Jesus presented Himself as a role model for our perspective on life. Life should not be loved from a temporal perspective but hated as that which represents our sinful separation from God our Creator. This is not, as the life of Jesus demonstrated, a rabid asceticism but an attitude that puts more importance on the world to come.

Jesus understood that His death would bring life to many. Nonetheless, Jesus' heart was "troubled," which is all John wrote in relation to the Gethsemane passages of Jesus' final hours recorded in the Synoptics. Jesus' troubled heart surely came more from the idea of bearing the weight of the sin of the world as a sinless Being than the mere physical and emotional agony that awaited Him. While Jesus contemplated praying to God for deliverance from that which awaited Him, He remained on the course God had willed for His life.

Not only would Jesus' death offer liberation to men and women from the bounds of sin, but it would bring judgment upon the world and drive the prince of the world from its midst. The cross achieved salvation for those who would believe, brought judgment upon the world for the refusal to believe, and defeated Satan's rebellion once and for all. The lifting up of Jesus on the cross would be the beacon that would draw all persons—meaning without regard to sex, race, social status, or nationality—to Himself for deliverance from sin.

## GOD OR THE WORLD (12:37-50)

How could the Jews have witnessed so many miraculous deeds and remain in unbelief? The answer is found in prophecy. Jews both would not and could not believe. They would not believe when they should have according to what they had witnessed. They could not believe, not because they had freedom of choice removed from them, but because they had purposely rejected God and chosen evil. Thus God turned them over decisively to their choice. Those who had chosen to believe were afraid to make their decision public for fear of excommunication. Even these believers were indicted for caring more for the approval of others than for the approval of God.

What is Jesus' relation to those who reject Him? John made clear that it is not judgment (12:47). It is not that judgment for unbelief will not take place (12:48), only that the primary mission and role of Jesus was not judge but Savior (12:47b). Again, the close relationship between God and Jesus is clearly exhibited in regard to thought and deed (12:44-45,49-50).

A word should be given regarding the difference between "last day" and "last days." The latter refers to the current period of time, begun when Christ entered the world (Acts 2:17; Heb. 1:2; 1 Pet. 1:20; Jude 18). The "last day" (singular), however, refers to the consummation of time and history when the great resurrection and judgment will occur of all persons (1 John 2:18).

## HUMBLE SERVANT (13:1-17)

The love of Jesus for His disciples, and those who would come to be His disciples, is shown in the washing of the disciples' feet. The servant motif, so prevalent in the Gospel of Mark (Mark 10:45), is

here revealed as well in the Gospel of John. Servanthood is a direct extension and representation of love (13:1). What enabled Jesus to perform this act of utter humility was a keen understanding of who He was, where He had come from, and where He was going (13:3). This is a key to humility in all persons—a healthy and balanced understanding of who they are.

If Jesus, Lord and Teacher, washes our feet, how much more should we wash one another's feet (13:14). What is at hand is not the institution of an ordinance of foot-washing, as this passage has sometimes been interpreted, but the lifestyle of humble servanthood.

## SATAN AND THE BETRAYER (13:18-30)

At the moment that Jesus identified Judas as His betrayer, Scripture tells us that "Satan entered into him"; and Jesus said, "What you are about to do, do quickly" (13:27). This is the only use of the name "Satan" in the Gospel of John, and it is unclear whether here is actual possession or simply the motivation from Satan to evil. The fellow disciples, however, did not realize what Jesus was referring to, thinking that it had something to do with Judas's responsibilities as keeper of the money bag (13:28). Jesus had to be betrayed, but Judas did not have to be that betrayer. It has often been commented that the difference between Judas and Peter, both of whom betrayed Christ, is that Peter sought forgiveness, but Judas did not.

## MARK OF DISCIPLESHIP (13:31-38)

After Judas's departure, Jesus made clear that His time with the disciples was short (13:33). The heart of this passage is found in verses 34-35: "A new command I give you: Love one another. As I have loved you, so you must love one another. By this all men will know that you are my disciples, if you love one another." "Here Jesus was saying that love among Christians must be in the vanguard of all that we are about. Further, if we fail in this endeavor, then the world will be given the right to deny that we are disciples of Christ. Our love for one another will be the distinguishing mark of authenticity that we truly follow Christ.

## REMEDY FOR ANXIETY (14:1-4)

Such words from Jesus regarding His upcoming departure, not to mention the forecast of Peter's betrayal, cast a net of depression upon the meal. Now come words of comfort from Jesus: "Do not let your hearts be troubled. Trust in God; trust also in me" (14:1). Trust in God is the one true remedy for anxiety. Jesus completed the remedy for their concern by painting a beautiful portrait of the life that awaits them upon their reunion (14:2-4).

## WAY, TRUTH, LIFE (14:5-14)

Jesus responded that a life given in belief and faith in Him will pave the way to eternal fellowship with Him (14:6). Jesus' claim to be the way, the truth, and the life is of great importance. Jesus is not one among many ways to God but the only way to God. The early church was even called "The Way" because of its insistence upon this point (Acts 9:2; 19:9,23). That Jesus embodies and proclaims the truth is a theme throughout the Gospel of John. Jesus also offers life itself, life through God the Father, the Creator and Giver of all life.

The last verse in this section has been fuel for much debate regarding proper interpretation and application. Was Jesus saying that we have unlimited power over God in determining what He will or will not do for us if we simply pray in Jesus' name? Clearly not, for this would be out of accord with the rest of the scriptural

witness. God is sovereign over all and subject to none. We are to pray in accordance with the will of God as exhibited in the life and teaching of Jesus. When we pray in that manner, surely it will be answered. To pray in Jesus' name is to pray in accord with Jesus' will and mission. Such a prayer request is far different from an idea of prayer as some type of shopping list handed to God that He is then bound to perform. Yet the enormous spiritual power that courses through the spiritual veins of the believer should not be underestimated in light of our involvement with the growing kingdom of God. The Holy Spirit empowers believers to do and to be all that Christ would have us to do and to be.

## THE COUNSELOR (14:15-31)

John's Gospel pays much attention to the Holy Spirit. This is the first of several passages that teach about the nature and role of the Holy Spirit in the life of the church and the individual believer (15:26; 16:7-15).

Here the Holy Spirit is referred to as the "Counselor" who will be with the disciples forever (14:16). Note that Jesus called the Holy Spirit "another" Counselor, suggesting that the work of the Holy Spirit would take the place of His role in their lives. The word "Counselor" is a legal term that goes beyond legal assistance to that of any aid given in time of need (1 John 2:1). The Greek word is Paraclete, which suggests adviser, encourager, exhorter, comforter, and intercessor. The idea is that the Spirit will always stand alongside the people of God. The Holy Spirit is also referred to as the "Spirit of truth" (14:17). This means that truth is that which characterizes the nature and mission of the Spirit. The Spirit testifies to the truth of God in Christ and brings people toward that truth through conviction leading to repentance and faith. The Spirit will continue to bring the presence of Christ into the lives of the disciples (14:16-18,20).

To love Jesus is to obey Jesus (14:15,23). If one does not obey Jesus, it is an act of lovelessness (14:24). Obedience and love cannot be separated for the believer. The Holy Spirit will also serve as a reminder to the disciples of all that Jesus has taught (14:25), sent forth by both God and the Son (14:26). The role of the Holy Spirit as the One who "reminds" the disciples of what Jesus said and taught should not be overlooked in regard to its importance in relation to the writing of the New Testament and for the ongoing life of the church. Jesus' effort is one of comfort as He prepares to leave His disciples for the agony of the cross. Here Satan would be allowed to stir people's hearts toward great evil, but never is that to be understood as Satan having power over Jesus (14:30). Jesus willingly submitted to the cross in order to fulfill God's will (14:31).

## THE TRUE VINE (15:1-17)

Here Jesus put forth another declarative "I am" statement, this time asserting that He is the "true vine" and that God is the gardener (15:1). In the Old Testament the "vine" is frequently used as a symbol of Israel (Ps. 80:8-16; Isa. 5:1-7; Jer. 2:21). This symbol was often used when Israel was lacking in some way. Jesus, however, is the true Vine.

Two scenarios are presented that should be seen as representative for the Christian life: first, the one who is on the vine and producing fruit (Matt. 3:8; 7:16-20) and second, the one who is on the vine who is not producing fruit. The productive vine is pruned for greater production, while the nonproductive vine is cut off for destruction. The key to producing fruit is one's relationship to the vine, to "remain in the vine" (15:4-5,7). Apart from Christ nothing can be accomplished (15:5). The verse "Ask whatever you

wish, and it will be given you," as with 14:13, needs to be seen in the context of one who is firmly part of the vine (15:16). When one is in such a close and dynamic relationship with Christ, requests coincide with His will. In other words, asking whatever you wish and having it granted is dependent upon the first clause of the verse: "If you remain in me and my words remain in you" (15:7).

## PLANTED IN CHRIST (15:18–16:4)

What is the result of a life that remains firmly planted in Christ? Here the suggestion is that you will be hated by the world (15:19). Christ was hated and rejected because of the conviction that pierced the heart of every person He encountered. Because of the life and teaching of Christ, individual persons know the truth and therefore have no excuse for those choices which deny God's rule (15:24).

This conviction will not end with the life and ministry of Jesus, for the Counselor, or Holy Spirit, will continue to testify to the hearts and minds of persons through truth of Christ and the claims of Christ (15:26), as will the disciples (15:27). Why did Jesus share this with His disciples? "So that you will not go astray" (16:1). Jesus prepared His followers for the reality of the cross they too would bear because of His name.

## WORK OF THE SPIRIT (16:5-16)

Jesus chided His disciples for their concern over their own situation upon His departure rather than concern over where Jesus was going to be (16:5). Again turning to His discussion of the Holy Spirit, Jesus made clear that His departure was worthwhile if only to allow for the coming of the Counselor whom Jesus Himself would send (16:7).

In a carefully detailed statement, Jesus outlined the convicting work of the Holy Spirit, all related to the work and person of Christ. First, the Holy Spirit will convict the world in the area of sin that results from disbelief in Jesus (16:9). Second, the Holy Spirit will convict the world in the area of righteousness in light of the life of Jesus (16:10). Third, the Holy Spirit will convict the world in the area of judgment because Jesus defeated the prince of the world who now stands condemned (16:11). Only through the Holy Spirit can an individual be brought to repentance leading to faith. It is not good works that elevate our status before God but the cross-work of Christ. The Holy Spirit enables the follower of Christ to live out the Christ life.

The Spirit of Truth will guide the disciples into all truth (16:13). His purpose will be to reveal Christ (16:14). The mark of the work of the Holy Spirit, then, is whether Christ is made central and glorified.

## I HAVE OVERCOME (16:17-33)

The disciples were experiencing understandable anxiety and confusion regarding all that Jesus had shared with them. Jesus comforted them by proclaiming that no matter how dark the hour may prove to be, the dawn will follow! Two "dawns" seem to be at hand, the first being the resurrection and the second being the day they will be with Jesus forever in heaven.

Prior to Jesus' death, the disciples had no need to pray in His name, for Jesus was there to be asked personally! This dynamic element of conversation was not to be lost, only now it would be through the Counselor that Jesus would send. The death, burial, and resurrection of Jesus serves as the intercession on our behalf before God, thereby eliminating the need for Jesus' direct intercession (thus not a contradiction of Rom. 8:34; Heb. 7:25; 1 John 2:1). Persecution will surely come, including trials from living in a fallen world, difficulties in life, and even discipline from God. But Jesus' words of

comfort are paramount with His passionate plea to "take heart! I have overcome the world" (16:33).

## HIGH-PRIESTLY PRAYER (17:1-5)

Here we have the beginning of the longest recorded prayer of Jesus (17:1-26). Many interpreters have called it Jesus' "high-priestly" prayer. In the first section of the prayer, Jesus noted that the cross would bring glory to Himself, for it was the will of God and the means of salvation for all who would believe.

## PRAYING FOR DISCIPLES (17:6-19)

Most of this portion of Jesus' prayer is devoted to the welfare of the disciples. Jesus prayed specifically for their protection in the area of unity (17:11), emphasizing again the importance of the unity of the body of Christ, the church. This is not organizational unity but interpersonal, relational unity. Jesus also prayed that they would be protected from the evil one, or Satan (17:15), who is more than active in the world and bitterly opposed to the things of God (1 John 5:19). Finally, Jesus prayed that God would sanctify them through the word of truth (17:17). Sanctification is the divine process whereby God molds us according to His holiness. It is the bringing to bear upon our lives the moral absolutes of the living God in such a way that they affect how we live and think. Sanctification and revelation are inextricably intertwined, for without God's revelatory word to our life the process of sanctification cannot begin.

## CHURCH'S UNITY (17:20-26)

Here Jesus' prayer turns specifically to those who would come to believe through the disciples' message and testimony (17:20). Again the theme is unity (17:21-23). Christians form the body of Christ (1 Cor. 12:13) and the household of faith (Eph. 2:19).

Some divisions and controversies are necessary and unavoidable. The purification of the church is as insistent a theme as the unity of the church. Jesus Himself said that He came not bearing peace but a sword. What He meant was that the truth of God can never be neutral, but it divides truth from that which is false by its very nature. Jesus' plea for unity has to do more with the petty controversies and bitter divisions that often plague relationships. The love that binds Christians together should overcome all such grievances, demonstrating to the world that the people of God are unique and unprecedented in their fellowship, drawing the nonbelieving world to faith in Christ.

## EMBRACING THE CUP (18:1-11)

John is the only Gospel that records that the attack on the servant of the chief priest was carried out by Simon Peter on a man named Malchus (18:10). Luke recorded Jesus' healing of the man's wound (Luke 22:51).

His concern for the disciples at the moment of His own arrest is evident (18:8). Peter's effort at defending Jesus was rebuked by Jesus Himself, for despite Peter's good intentions, the "cup" that was before Jesus had to be embraced. It should be noted that "cup" was often used as a reference to suffering (Ps. 75:8; Ezek. 23:31-34), as well as the wrath of God (Isa. 51:17,22; Jer. 25:15; Rev. 14:10; 16:19).

## PETER'S DENIAL (18:12-18)

The two interrogations may have been enacted to give the semblance of a fair trial for Jesus, though it was far from just by any stretch of the imagination. Peter's first denial, all four Gospels report, came as the result of the challenge of a slave girl. She asked Peter if he was one of the disciples of Jesus, which Peter promptly denied (18:17).

## THE JEWISH TRIAL (18:19-24)

The interrogation of Jesus by the high priest brought out Jesus' response that what He had taught had been taught publicly and that nothing had been taught in private that was not openly said to the crowds. This brought a blow to the face as if such a reply was improper when answering the high priest (18:22). This blow was illegal for such questionings. Jesus' reply was that what He had said was simply the truth and should not be rejected or reacted to with such violence. Note that John treated the Jewish trial with great brevity, devoting the majority of his narrative to the Roman trial.

## DRAMA OF BETRAYAL (18:25-27)

Peter's second and third denials, followed by the prophesied crow of the rooster, are recorded just before John recorded Jesus' interaction with Pilate (13:38). Two plots are being simultaneously revealed by John, (1) Peter's denials and (2) Jesus' interrogations and mock trial. Both constitute a drama of betrayal, one by the people who should have received Christ as King and one by a person who should have remained loyal to Christ as King.

## JESUS THE KING (18:28-40)

One of the most ironic observations in all of Scripture is made by the apostle John. In order to avoid ceremonial uncleanness, the Jews who had plotted to kill an innocent man and were now executing that plan did not enter the palace of the Roman governor (18:28). The decision to take Jesus to Pilate was to ensure that He would be killed.

This Gospel records three major conversations held between Jesus and an individual person who was being confronted with the truth and the claims of the gospel. In John 3 Nicodemus was a religious man who sought Jesus in order to pursue his spiritual questions. The

## PILATE

Pontius Pilate was the Roman procurator in Judea from A.D. 26–36. Procurator was the title for a governor of a Roman province under direct imperial rather than senatorial control. Pilate was thus responsible to the emperor, Tiberias Caesar, for the military, financial, and judicial operations in Judea.

The emperor personally supervised some provinces, such as Judea and Egypt, because of their instability or crucial importance to Rome. Judea qualified on both counts as the land bridge to Egypt, Rome's breadbasket, and as a rebellious population longing for independent Jewish rule (see John 8:31-33 and Mark 15:7).

A procurator held an authority by delegation from the emperor, called the *imperium*. The *imperium* was the power of life or death over persons in a subject population. Pilate reflected this with accuracy when he said to Jesus, "Don't you realize I have power to free you or to crucify you?" (John 19:10).

Pilate's responsibility for maintaining peace and order was the reason for his being in Jerusalem at the time Jesus was arrested. Passover season commemorated the deliverance of the Jews from Egypt (Exod. 12:1-36) and was the time of year when Jewish patriotism was at its height.

Pilate, whose residence was at Caesarea on the Mediterranean coast, was in Jerusalem to take personal command of the resident Roman forces in the event of any uprising or act of rebellion in Judea's largest Jewish city. He personally interrogated Jesus rather than delegating it to a regular judge (for example, see Matt. 5:25 and Luke 18:2-6) because Jesus was accused of claiming to be a king—a charge that assumed He was trying to recruit revolutionary forces to launch a rebellion against Roman authority (see Matt. 27:11-14; Mark 15:2-5; Luke 23:2-5; and John 18:33-38). Pilate sentenced Jesus to death even though he knew the charge was fallacious (Matt. 27:18), but the soldiers clearly believed they had a revolutionary leader in custody and mocked Jesus (Matt. 27:27-31; Mark 15:16-20; Luke 23:11; John 19:2-3).

Pilate was certainly less than noble in dealing with Jesus as he did, revealing both an indifference to human life and an ugly willingness to cooperate with the Jewish leaders in an execution on the basis of a false charge (Matt. 27:18). See the article "Trial of Jesus."

Additional information about Pilate from non-Christian sources supports the picture of Pilate's character revealed in the New Testament. Philo reported that Tiberius was infuriated with Pilate for his insensitivity in governing and accused him of taking bribes as well as performing numerous executions without any trials (*Embassy to Gaius*, 302-4).

Josephus recounted two incidents in which Pilate himself sparked Jewish demonstrations in Jerusalem—one by flaunting Roman images of the emperor on military equipment and the other by attempting to confiscate temple funds for works he wanted done related to the water supply for Jerusalem (*Antiquities*, 18.55-62).

The incident that resulted in Pilate's being returned to Rome in A.D. 36 by Tiberias was his ordering the unwarranted execution of a number of Samaritan villagers for a religious march to Mount Gerizim (*Antiquities*, 18.85-87). Nothing is known of Pilate after his recall in A.D. 36, but several fictional accounts of his later years appeared during the ensuing centuries. Some of these accounts have Pilate becoming a Christian while others stress his despondency over the way he treated Jesus.

Samaritan woman in John 4 was neither religious nor a skeptic but rather one who represented worldliness in its most common form. She was indifferent to the spiritual, living a life of moral self-indulgence. Pilate, however, is indicative of the modern secularist. Hardened to that which would speak to his soul, he was neither open nor inquisitive about the gospel.

Pilate's first question was perfunctory, almost a leading question in order to investigate the nature of the Jewish complaint. Jesus' answer was disarming and brought about a transparent reply from Pilate regarding the political tensions that had led Jesus to his feet. Speaking in terms Pilate would understand, Jesus admitted being a King but a King of far more than an earthly, temporal realm. Many individuals throughout Christian history have misinterpreted the kingdom of God in earthly terms.

As was His custom, Jesus then turned the discussion toward His mission. He informed Pilate that His kingly role was identified with testifying "to the truth. Everyone on the side of the truth listens to me" (18:37). Pilate's response has become legendary: "What is truth?" (18:29). Was it a serious question? sarcastic? We simply do not know. What is clear is that upon voicing the question, Pilate went out to the Jews and dismissed their charges against Jesus and offered to release Him in celebration of the Passover. The Jews, however, demanded Barabbas, a man who was both an insurrectionist and a murderer (Luke 23:19).

## SOURCE OF POWER (19:1-16A)

The physical and emotional torment that Jesus suffered is beyond description. He was not only physically beaten but ridiculed and mocked. Perhaps as one last effort to have Jesus released, Pilate presented Him before the crowd after His beating in order to see if now they could accept His liberation (19:4). The Jews, however, insisted on His death because Christ claimed to be the Son of God (19:7).

Pilate's claim that he had the power to free or crucify Jesus brought the following response: "You would have no power over me if it were not given to you from above. Therefore the one who handed me over to you is guilty of a greater sin" (19:11). What should perhaps be noted here is Jesus' intimation that Pilate, though not the initiator of the death of Jesus, was not without sin.

## THE HOUR (19:16B-27)

Every word of John's Gospel leads to this moment, for the "hour" had finally come. As if one last effort to cleanse Himself from guilt, Pilate had the title "Jesus of Nazareth, the King of the Jews" fastened onto the cross where Jesus was crucified in Latin, Aramaic, and Greek (19:19). Every prophecy regarding the Messiah, even to the gambling for His clothing, was fulfilled (19:24; see Ps. 22:18).

Crucifixion was the Roman means of execution for slaves and criminals. The victim was nailed to a cross shaped either in the traditional form, or in the shape of a *T, X, Y,* or *I.* The nails were driven through the wrists and heel bones. Present at the cross were Jesus' mother, His mother's sister, Mary the wife of Clopas, and Mary Magdalene (19:25). Also present was the author of this Gospel, the apostle John, whom Jesus instructed to care for His mother (19:27).

## IT IS FINISHED (19:28-37)

The actual death of Jesus was preceded with words fitting the narrative John had written: "It is finished" (19:30). What was finished? The mission of Jesus, the Son of God, to die a substitutionary death for sinful persons. As a result of His death on our behalf, our sin was atoned for, and eternal life through Jesus became attainable through trusting faith.

With these final words Jesus "bowed his head and gave up his spirit" (19:30). This rather unusual way of describing someone's death intimates that Jesus died voluntarily as an act of the will. After the death of Jesus, a soldier pierced His side, "bringing a sudden flow of blood and water" (19:34). From a medical standpoint the mix of blood and water from the spear's thrust was the result of piercing of the sac that surrounds the heart (the pericardium) as well as the heart itself. The author of the Gospel, the apostle John, then offered his testimony that he was a witness to this event and that even to the final moment every detail fulfilled the prophecies concerning the Messiah (19:35-37; see Exod. 12:46; Num. 9:12; Ps. 34:20; Zech. 12:10).

## THE BURIAL (19:38-42)

After the death of Jesus, most of the disciples were nowhere to be found, yet at that moment two individuals who had previously been afraid to make their allegiance known came boldly forward to care for the body of Christ. These two were Nicodemus (John 3) and Joseph of Arimathea, a rich member of the Sanhedrin who had agreed to the condemnation of Jesus (Matt. 27:57; Luke 23:51). Jesus was laid in a tomb following a traditional Jewish preparation.

## THE RESURRECTION (20:1-9)

The first person to the tomb of Jesus was Mary Magdalene. Upon seeing the stone removed from the tomb, she ran to Peter and John, exclaiming that they had taken Jesus from the tomb. Mary did not understand that Jesus' body had not been stolen but that He had been raised from the dead. Peter and John ran to the tomb, finding only the strips of Jesus' burial clothes. Peter and John, as did Mary, failed to understand that the resurrection had taken place (20:9).

## FIRST APPEARANCE (20:10-18)

Commentators often have suggested that Mary Magdalene was the first to see Jesus following His resurrection because she was the person who needed to see Him the most. After all the others had left the empty tomb, she stood alone by its side weeping. Two angels appeared to her, asking her why she was expressing such grief. After answering that someone had taken her Lord away and she didn't know where He was, she turned and saw Jesus.

The tenderness of the moment when he said "Mary" and her recognition of Him and cry of "Rabboni!" (teacher) is one of the emotional highlights of the entire Gospel. Jesus' warning not to "hold on" to Him for He had "not yet returned to the Father" is at first confusing (20:17). When Jesus spoke of not having returned to the Father, clearly the ascension is in view. Also to be considered here is the idea that Jesus was not to be held to in the same sense as before the resurrection, for now Mary's relationship with Him would be through the Holy Spirit (16:5-16).

## FORGIVENESS OF SINS (20:19-23)

Jesus encountered a group of frightened disciples behind locked doors and gave them what they needed most—Himself. He showed them His hands and His side in order to dispel any doubt that they were seeing anything but their crucified Lord (20:20). As with the "Great Commission" recorded in Matthew 28, Jesus decisively gave His followers the command to go into all the world and continue His ministry. To enable them to respond to this task, they received a precursor of the full coming of the Holy Spirit at Pentecost—almost as a deposit for that which was to come fully fifty days later—breathed to them now from the very mouth of Jesus (20:22).

Jesus stated that if the disciples forgave anyone, they were forgiven, and if they did not forgive them their sins, they were not forgiven. At first glance this is a remarkable statement that seems out of step with the role and authority of the disciples. It was not the disciples who could forgive sins but Jesus. The literal reading from the Greek is more clear, stating: "Those whose sins you forgive have already been forgiven; those whose sins you do not forgive have not been forgiven." God's forgiveness is not dependent upon human forgiveness, but rather forgiveness is extended by God as a result of individual responses to the proclamation of the gospel by fellow human beings.

## DO YOU BELIEVE? (20:24-31)

Thomas's doubt was that of many in the modern world. Unless he could see, taste, touch, and hear what was being presented as reality, he would not accept it as the truth. As Jesus noted, however, "blessed are those who have not seen and yet have believed" (20:29).

John's purpose statement is included here, following the resurrection, in order that the reader may know the reason for this carefully detailed narrative of the life and teaching of Jesus. This Gospel was "written that you may believe that Jesus is the Christ, the Son of God, and that by believing you may have life in his name" (20:31). The purpose of the Gospel of John is to present Jesus as God in human form and that through faith in Jesus, individuals would embrace salvation to eternal life.

## MIRACLES CONTINUE (21:1-14)

The miraculous catch of fish, an almost casual appearance and fellowship of the risen Christ with the disciples, constitutes the third recorded appearance of Jesus following His resurrection. Here Jesus demonstrated again His power over the natural world.

## DO YOU LOVE ME? (21:15-25)

Following their breakfast meal on the shores of the Sea of Tiberias, Jesus turned to Peter and asked a series of questions related to Peter's devotion. The first word for love, used in Jesus' first two questions, refers to a love that involves the will and personality. The second kind of love, indicated by the word for love used in the third question of Jesus, refers more to the emotions than to the will.

Regardless of whether or not much is to be made of these word distinctions, the key issue is that of love for Christ, and this Peter surely expressed. His earlier three denials are here answered in three affirmations of love and service. Jesus clearly wanted love for Him to include both will and emotions, demonstrated in a life of discipleship and devotion to the church.

Then Jesus forecast the kind of death Peter would die in order to glorify God. The early church understood the "stretching out of hands" mentioned here to mean crucifixion. Tradition understands the death of Peter to have been by upside-down crucifixion.

The final words of the Gospel of John change from firsthand narrative to that of a plural perspective. It would seem that the Gospel of the apostle John was preserved and then another author, equally inspired by the living God, added his own testimony on behalf of a community of faith as witness to the truth of all that the apostle had written. Not everything from the life of Christ was recorded but only those things the author felt supported the goal of leading individuals to belief in Jesus as the Son of God who came to take away the sins of the world.

*Theological and Ethical Significance.* From this Gospel we learn much about God as Father. Contemporary believers are indebted to John for their habit of referring to God simply as "the Father." The Father is active (5:17), bringing blessing on those He has created. He is love (3:16; see 1 John 4:8-10). We know love because we see it in the cross; it is sacrificial giving, not for deserving people but for undeserving sinners. He is a great God whose will is done in bringing about our salvation (6:44).

The Gospel throughout focuses on Jesus Christ. It is clear that God in Christ has revealed Himself (1:1-18). God is active in Christ, the Savior of the world, bringing about the salvation He has planned (4:42).

John's Gospel tells us more about the Holy Spirit than do the other Evangelists. The Spirit was active from the start of Jesus' ministry (1:32), but the Spirit's full work was to begin at the consummation of Jesus' own ministry (7:37-39). The Spirit brings life (3:1-8), a life of the highest quality (10:10), and leads believers in the way of truth (16:13). The Spirit thus universalizes Jesus' ministry for Christians of all ages.

In response to the work of God in their lives, Christians are to be characterized by love (13:34-35). They owe all they have to the love of God, and it is proper that they respond to that love by loving God and other people.

## Questions for Reflection

1. John presented a portrait of Jesus as fully God and fully man. What are the dangers in emphasizing either Christ's humanity or divinity to the exclusion of the other?

2. John presented a challenging call to believe in Christ as Savior and Lord. What did John mean when he said to believe in Christ and you will be saved? Is it mere intellectual assent or something that involves one's entire life?

3. Essentially Jesus' final recorded prayer was for believers to be unified. What does it mean for believers to be unified? What did Jesus say happens to our witness to the world regarding His truth and claims if we are not unified?

4. What is the relationship between the risen Jesus and the Holy Spirit? How does the Holy Spirit make Jesus present in our lives?

## Sources for Additional Study

Barrett, C. K. *The Gospel According to St. John*. Second Edition. Philadelphia: Westminster, 1978.

Bruce, F. F. *The Gospel of John: Introduction, Exposition and Notes*. Grand Rapids: Eerdmans, 1983.

Carson, D. A. *The Gospel of John*. Grand Rapids: Eerdmans, 1991.

Morris, Leon. *The Gospel According to John*. New International Commentary. Grand Rapids: Eerdmans, 1971.

# THE ACTS OF THE APOSTLES

T he Book of Acts is an exciting and powerful portrait of the history of the early Christian church. From the upper room to the Roman capital, this narrative chronicles the spread of the gospel. Without it we would know little about the apostles and their mission to the Jewish and Gentile world.

Acts follows the activities of two apostles in particular: Peter and Paul. For this reason it has been called "the Acts of the Apostles." The book might better be named "The Acts of the Holy Spirit," however, for the Spirit is the one who provides the power and motivation for the missionary activity of the apostles. Through Acts we follow the unhindered movement of the gospel around the shores of the Mediterranean Sea. We move from Jerusalem to Samaria, from Palestine to Asia, from Greece to Rome. By the time Acts ends, the gospel has been proclaimed throughout the Roman world with miraculous success.

# ACTS

## JOHN B. POLHILL

Acts is unique among the books of the New Testament. It is the only book which relates the story of the earliest church which was created soon after the resurrection of Christ. It is part of a two-volume work by the same writer, Luke, who related the story of Christ in his Gospel and the story of the apostles' witness to Christ in Acts. Luke is the most prolific writer in the New Testament. The Gospel of Luke and Acts comprise nearly a third of its entire contents.

**Luke the Author.** Both Luke and Acts are anonymous. Luke nowhere identified himself in either work, but from an early period, tradition has designated him as author of both writings. One of the earliest witnesses to the tradition was Irenaeus, bishop of Lyons in Gaul (modern France). Writing in the last quarter of the second century, Irenaeus pointed to the passages in Acts which are written in the first person plural. These occur in the portions of Acts which deal with the ministry of the apostle Paul. They include 16:10-17 (Paul's Macedonian call and early ministry in Philippi); 20:5–21:18 (Paul's journey from Philippi to Jerusalem); and 27:1–28:16 (Paul's trip from Caesarea to Rome). Irenaeus concluded from these "we" passages that the author of Acts was a companion of Paul who accompanied him on these occasions. He identified Paul's traveling companion as Luke.

Luke is mentioned three times in the New Testament, all three in the "greet-ings" sections of Paul's epistles. Paul identified him as a "fellow worker" in Philemon 24 and as "the beloved physician" in Colossians 4:14. In 2 Timothy 4:11 Paul lamented that "only Luke" was with him. He probably was facing martyrdom and may have had special need of his physician friend.

Although we have little direct information on Luke, we can learn a lot about his person from his writings. For instance, he wrote in a very natural and literate style of Greek. The name *Luke* is a Greek name, and he was almost certainly a Gentile. (His concern for Gentiles in both Luke and Acts indicate as much.) Luke was cultured. He knew Greek literary conventions. For instance, he began both his volumes with formal prefaces which included dedications to a certain Theophilus (Luke 1:1-4; Acts 1:1-2). He had a concern for linking Christianity with world history. Of all the Gospel writers, he alone was careful to date events by the reigns of kings, governors, and high priests (Luke 2:1-2; 3:1-2); and in Acts he referred to the Roman emperors on several occasions (11:28; 25:10ff.).

Luke liked to travel. He often mentioned places of lodging in his Gospel: There was no room for Mary and Joseph in the inn (Luke 2:7), but the Samaritan provided for the wounded Jew in an inn (Luke 10:34-35). In Acts, Luke took great delight in detailing Paul's travels, right down to the last little island. He must also have liked to eat. He included in his Gospel more instances of Jesus dining and more parables with a meal setting than any of the other Gospel writers. This interest is also apparent in Acts, where so much of the life of the early church is set around the "breaking of bread," and where table fellowship was a major issue for the Jewish and Gentile Christian congregations.

Luke had a great concern for people, particularly the oppressed of his day—the poor, targets of prejudice like Samaritans and eunuchs, and those with limited privileges like women. He was hard on the rich. His culture and profession may indicate that he came from some means himself. He had little toleration for those who had the resources to help the needy but failed to do so. As for women, he showed in his Gospel how much the Christian faith owes to women like Mary and Elizabeth, and in the Acts he highlighted leaders like Lydia and Priscilla.

**Luke's "Episodic" Style.** Luke liked to tell a good story. He wrote with skill and dramatic flare. Acts is no dull history. Rather than giving a bare chronicle of events, Luke chose to illustrate the story of the early church with selected key incidents or "episodes." An example of this is the account of Paul's work in Ephesus in chapter 19. The chapter covers a three-year ministry of Paul in the city. We know from Paul's letters and subsequent Christian history that during this period Paul wrote a number of epistles and established many churches, not only in Ephesus but also in the surrounding cities. Acts 19 does not mention these things. Instead, it gives four incidents out of Paul's three year ministry there—his witness to some disciples of John the Baptist, his preaching each day in a lecture hall, his leading the Ephesian converts to burn their magic books, and his encounter with the local guild of idol makers. This is certainly no formal "his-

tory of the greater Ephesian mission." It is a very effective way to give a person a sense of what really counted in that mission—Paul's faithful witness to Jesus, the opposition that his witness aroused, and the ultimate triumph of the gospel over all its opponents.

There are exceptions to Luke's anecdotal style. Sometimes he chose to give a summary of what went on during a given period in the life of the church rather than highlight specific incidents. Known as the "summaries," there are four in all, clustered in the first five chapters. First, there is the summary dealing with the church at prayer as it awaited Jesus' promise of the Spirit's coming (1:12-14), then the summary of the early church's fellowship (2:42-47), the summary of its sharing in material blessings (4:32-35), and finally, the summary of its witness in the power of the Spirit (5:12-16). These summaries give us a vivid picture of the life of the earliest church and of the forces which drove it.

Another "non-episodic" type of Acts passage is the "speech," in which Christians witness to Christ. Speeches occur in various settings—before crowds in the Jewish temple or in the streets of Gentile cities, before Jewish and Gentile courts. Some are only a few verses in length, while some are nearly a chapter (e.g., 7:2-53). Almost a third of the entire text of Acts contains speeches. There are ten lengthy ones.

Three are Peter's—at Pentecost (chap. 2), in the temple square (chap. 3), and at the home of the Gentile Cornelius (chap. 10). The longest speech of all is that of the martyr Stephen in chapter 7. Six speeches are Paul's. Three occur on his missionary journeys—one on each journey and each to a different kind of audience. Paul addressed *Jews* at Pisidian Antioch on his first mission (13:16-41), *Gentiles* at Mars Hill on his second journey (17:22-31), and

# ASCENSION OF CHRIST

The ascension of Christ is that occasion when at the close of His earthly ministry the risen Christ Jesus was take up into heaven. It was a moment of joy for the disciples, for He said they were to be His witnesses among all the people of the earth. It was a moment of worship, for He blessed them with His outstretched hands and promised His power for the mission He had assigned to their care (Luke 24:47-51; Acts 1:2-3,8-9).

Some have a problem thinking of Jesus "going up" into heaven. But for Luke to note that from the disciple's perspective Jesus was taken up from them is completely natural. Jesus was taken up, much as a father picks up his child and carries him away. Luke described the event this way, "After he said this, he was taken up before their very eyes, and a cloud hid him from their sight" (Acts 1:9). The cloud symbolized the mysterious, majestic presence of God with His people (compare Luke 9:34-35 and Exod. 13:21-22).

A careful reading of Luke and Acts raises the question about when the ascension occurred. Luke 24 seems to imply that Jesus was taken up into heaven in the late evening of the day He arose. But Luke's account in Acts clearly says the ascension happened forty days after the resurrection (Acts 1:3). Though several suggestions have been made to harmonize these accounts, two explanations provide the most plausible solution.

1. Jesus did in fact ascend to to heaven on Sunday evening as Luke 24 indicates. However, He returned to the earth for special appearances throughout the forty days until a second public ascension happened as described in Acts 1:3. John's account of the resurrection appearance lends weight to this line of reasoning. On Easter morning Jesus said to Mary Magdalene, "Do not hold on to me for I have not yet returned to the Father" (John 20:17). One week later He invited Thomas: "Put your finger here; see my hands. Reach out your hand and put it into my side" (John 20:27). Apparently He had ascended on Sunday night and returned to be with the disciples a week later (John 20:26).

2. Others suggest that Jesus was raised up and glorified in one great exaltation early on Sunday morning. He returned for each of the appearances throughout the day and through the forty days as the risen and glorified Son of God. Peter Toon calls this the "secret and invisible" ascension that was followed for the benefit of the disciples forty days later by the "visible symbolic demonstration" of that earlier ascension.

The ascension means that the humanity of God's creation into which He emptied Himself at the incarnation (Phil. 2:7) has been taken into glory. All things human can be redeemed from the effects of sin, so that what God intended from the beginning (see Gen. 1:31, "It was very good") can now be fully achieved. The ascension means that Christians are never without a voice before the Father. Jesus, the Great High Priest, lives now in glory to intercede for His brothers and sisters (Rom. 8:34; Heb. 7:25).

The ascension means that the heavenly reign of our Lord has begun, and one day what is now dimly seen will be fully realized as He becomes all in all (see Eph. 1:20-23; Rev. 3:21). It means that God the Father is fully satisfied with the Son and has seated Him at the Father's right hand, where He reigns as our Great High Priest (Heb. 1:3; 1 Pet. 3:22).

The ascension is a visible reminder that Jesus has left the task of world missions to His disciples, empowered by the Holy Spirit whose work would not start until Jesus went away (John 16:7; Acts 1:8). The ascension is the sign that Jesus will come again to receive His people unto Himself (Acts 1:11). The description of the ascension is the dramatic assertion that Jesus was taken up into heaven to be with the Father with whom He reigns then, now, and forever.

# THE HOLY SPIRIT AND ACTS

The Acts of the Apostles might as accurately have been named the Acts of the Holy Spirit. While the Gospels describe the ministry of God the Son, Acts describes the ministry through the church of God the Holy Spirit. Rather than a strict contrast between the work of Son and Spirit, however, Acts shows the continuity of the work of the incarnate God through His Holy Spirit. Christ Himself is present in His church through His Spirit.

The Holy Spirit is not an "it" but the very presence of God in the life of a Christian. Peter made the understanding clear in the episode of Ananias and Sapphira. Peter charged them with lying to the Holy Spirit (5:3), with lying to God (5:4), and with tempting the Spirit of God (5:9). He did not refer to three things they had done. He spoke of the Spirit in three ways, but he meant the one Spirit who proceeds from the Father and the Son. Likewise, the "Spirit of Jesus" is used to refer to the Holy Spirit when Paul and Timothy were not allowed to go into Bithynia (16:6-7).

The Book of Acts begins with the resurrected Lord promising the gift of the Spirit to His disciples. With the Spirit would come the power to carry out the mission of taking the gospel to the world (1:8). Jesus declared the mission in a geographic progression beginning in Jerusalem, spreading to the region of Judea, crossing the cultural barrier to Samaria, and on to the rest of the world. As the book unfolds, the Holy Spirit bore testimony to the advance of the church at each of these crucial stages.

On the day of Pentecost, the Holy Spirit fell on the church in power (2:1-4). As a result of that day's preaching and witnessing by all the church (2:4,6,14), about three thousand people were added to the church (2:41). The early church understood the baptism of the Holy Spirit (1:5) as the fulfillment of the promise of God through the prophets. Peter preached the first gospel sermon based on the prophecy concerning the coming of the Holy Spirit in Joel 2:28-32 (2:16-21). Furthermore, Peter stressed the gift of the Holy Spirit as a central element of salvation (2:38).

When Philip carried the gospel to Samaria, the church in Jerusalem sent Peter and John to pray for the converts to receive the Holy Spirit (8:14-17). Likewise, the conversion of Paul reached its climax when Ananias came to him that he might regain his sight and be filled with the Holy Spirit (9:17). The gift of the Holy Spirit to Cornelius and other Gentiles as they heard the gospel convinced Peter and the other apostles that God had granted salvation to the Gentiles (10:44–11:18; 15:8).

When he met a group of disciples of John the Baptist in Ephesus, Paul asked them about the Holy Spirit as a diagnostic question. The fact that they had never heard of the Holy Spirit demonstrated to Paul the need to preach the gospel of Jesus to them. Paul baptized those who believed, and when he laid hands on them, they received the Holy Spirit (19:1-6).

Acts contains no fixed order of sequence related to baptism, laying on of hands, and the reception of the Spirit. Some conversion accounts make no reference at all to laying on of hands. The governing principle seems to be that those who have faith in Jesus receive His Holy Spirit to apply the benefits of salvation.

*Christian leaders* on his third missionary journey (20:17-35).

Luke recorded three more major addresses of Paul after his arrest in Jerusalem: before a Jewish mob in the temple court (22:1-21), before the Roman governor Felix (24:10-21), and before the Jewish King Agrippa (26:1-29). When reading Acts, we often give the least attention to these speeches. They are not

Thus baptism and laying on of hands have no sacramental significance for salvation. Instead, they symbolically declare faith in what God has done.

The latter seems more likely because Luke gave a long catalog of the many nationalities present in Jerusalem who witnessed this event (2:5-13). He stressed that each of these heard the Christians speaking "in their own language" (vv. 6,8). Some would appeal to a "miracle of hearing" in which the Christians would have spoken in ecstatic language that would have been miraculously transformed into the native language of the foreigners as they listened. But this would require almost a greater activity of the Spirit on the nonbelievers than the Christians, and that seems most unlikely.

In a real sense Pentecost witnessed the birth of the church. Its mission began then. The three thousand converted on that day (v. 41) drew from the whole crowd of Pentecost pilgrims and in a real sense anticipated the worldwide mission the remainder of Acts details. At Pentecost all the converts were Jews (v. 5), but they came from all parts of the civilized world, and many doubtless returned to their homeland

witnessing to Christ.

The key factor at Pentecost was the gift of the Spirit. In Old Testament times the Spirit of God had often been active in the lives of inspired individuals like the prophets. The new phenomenon, however, was the universal nature of the gift of the Spirit. The Spirit was poured out on all the Christian band gathered in the upper room. The gift was to the whole church. See the article "The Holy Spirit and Acts."

Peter saw this clearly. So he began his Pentecost sermon by citing Joel's prophecy of the final times in God's saving activity. At that time the Spirit would be poured out on all flesh, and all who called on the Lord's name would receive the Spirit and be saved (2:17-21). Hereafter in the Acts narrative the Holy Spirit is a vital part of the conversion experience and a permanent gift to those who are saved (Acts 2:38; 8:17; 9:17; 10:44).

If Pentecost relates the foundation of the church, then the remainder of Acts spells out the implications. In Acts the role of the Spirit is above all that of empowering the church for its witness.

The Spirit gave Peter the courage to address the Jewish Sanhedrin (4:8) and

Stephen courage to debate in the Diaspora Jewish synagogues of Jerusalem (6:10). In fact, the Spirit led in every major breakthrough in the expanding Christian mission—with Philip as he witnessed to an Ethiopian eunuch (8:29,39), with Peter's conversion of the Gentile Cornelius (11:12), and with the Antioch church as it commissioned Paul and Barnabas for their missionary journey (13:2).

The Spirit prevented Paul from working in Asia and Bithynia and provided the vision of the Macedonian call that led him to Philippi and his first work on European soil (16:6-10). Paul's courage to undertake the risky trip to Jerusalem and his resolve to witness in the capital city of Rome—these too are the work of the Spirit (19:21; 20:22). Indeed, some would call Acts "the Acts of the Holy Spirit." Luke probably would not reject such a title as inappropriate to his book. Were one to ask him what gave birth to the church, he would undoubtedly point to Pentecost and the gift of the Spirit there and quickly add that the same Spirit constitutes not only the birth but the continuing vitality of the church.

as engaging as the episodes. A careful study of them will prove rewarding, however. The speeches give the most direct presentation of the gospel of all the material in Acts.

**Themes of Acts.** Many themes run throughout Acts. One is the relationship between the Jewish and Gentile churches. Luke was concerned to show how the church began in Jerusalem, in the heart of

## THE BIRTH OF THE CHURCH

When was the church born? In a sense we could trace it back to God's call of Abraham and the history of Israel as the people of God.

In the more restricted sense of the church as the new people of God, the body of Christ, its roots are certainly to be found in the mind and ministry of Jesus Himself. His intention to establish a community of faith is clearly reflected in His response to Peter's confession (Matt. 16:13-19) and in His words about a new covenant at the last supper (Luke 22:20).

Jesus' intention also is reflected in His choosing an inner circle of twelve disciples in continuity with the twelve tribes of Israel, the original covenant people of God. The twelve did not constitute a church, however, for the basis of His new covenant was Jesus' own death and resurrection. The people of the new covenant were to be redeemed and forgiven of sin, a people with God's law written on their hearts (see Jer. 31:31-34).

That act of forgiveness and deliverance took place on the cross. Only through God's decisive atoning work in Jesus' death could

a new covenant people come into being. Ultimately, Calvary gave birth to the church.

A community needs organization and direction, and this was no less true for that original band of disciples who witnessed the appearances of their risen Lord. More than anything else, it was the Holy Spirit who gave them this sense of direction. The coming of the Spirit is anticipated by Jesus in His words to the disciples at the last supper (John 13:31–17:26). There He promised not to leave them desolate after His departure from this world (14:18). He promised instead to come to them in the person of the Spirit (Paraclete), who would teach them, guide them, and be His own abiding presence in their lives (14:6; 15:26; 16:7-15).

In the Pentecost narrative of Acts 2, this coming of the Spirit is vividly depicted as the foundational event in the constitution of the new community of Christian believers. The risen Christ strictly charges the eleven apostles to wait in Jerusalem for the coming of the Spirit (Acts 1:5). At His ascension He commissioned them as witnesses to the world, but this was to take place only

through the power of the Spirit (1:8).

So the apostles and larger band of disciples gathered together in an upper room, some 120 in all, awaiting this promised event (1:12-14). Their minds were certainly on the community, for their main undertaking during this waiting period was to choose a twelfth apostle, filling the vacancy left by Judas and completing the apostolic leadership necessary for the young Christian community (1:15-26).

Then at Pentecost, some fifty days after Jesus' resurrection, the Spirit came, apparently on the whole band who had gathered in the upper room (2:1). The Spirit's coming was both audible, like the sound of the wind, and visible, as a flame with tongues of fire lapping on the head of each one present (2:2-3).

The result was that all were "filled with the Spirit" and began "to speak in tongues" through the Spirit's leading (2:4). Scholars are sharply divided as to whether the phenomenon was that of glossolalia (unintelligible ecstatic speech) such as Paul described in 1 Corinthians 14 or whether it was a miracle unique to Pentecost of speaking in foreign languages.

Judaism, and how it expanded with an even greater impact on the Gentiles. Luke showed how Jewish and Gentile Christians with their major differences learned how to have fellowship together, a lesson still very relevant to the life of the church.

Perhaps the dominant theme in Acts is that of the Christian witness to Jesus

and its triumph over all opposition. There are many sub-themes related to this major emphasis. One is the spread of the Christian witness both geographically and to various ethnic groups. At the very beginning of Acts, Jesus commissioned His disciples to be His witnesses—in Jerusalem, in all Judea and

The latter seems more likely because Luke gave a long catalog of the many nationalities present in Jerusalem who witnessed this event (2:5-13). He stressed that each of these heard the Christians speaking "in their own language" (vv. 6,8). Some would appeal to a "miracle of hearing" in which the Christians would have spoken in ecstatic language that would have been miraculously transformed into the native language of the foreigners as they listened. But this would require almost a greater activity of the Spirit on the nonbelievers than the Christians, and that seems most unlikely.

In a real sense Pentecost witnessed the birth of the church. Its mission began then. The three thousand converted on that day (v. 41) drew from the whole crowd of Pentecost pilgrims and in a real sense anticipated the worldwide mission the remainder of Acts details. At Pentecost all the converts were Jews (v. 5), but they came from all parts of the civilized world, and many doubtless returned to their homeland witnessing to Christ.

The key factor at Pentecost was the gift of the Spirit. In OT times the Spirit of God had often been active in the lives of inspired individuals like the prophets. The new phenomenon, however, was the universal nature of the gift of the Spirit. The Spirit was poured out on all the Christian band gathered in the upper room. The gift was to the whole church. See the article "The Holy Spirit and Acts."

Peter saw this clearly. So he began his Pentecost sermon by citing Joel's prophecy of the final times in God's saving activity. At that time the Spirit would be poured out on all flesh, and all who called on the Lord's name would receive the Spirit and be saved (2:17-21). Hereafter in the Acts narrative the Holy Spirit is a vital part of the conversion experience and a permanent gift to those who are saved (Acts 2:38; 8:17; 9:17; 10:44).

If Pentecost relates the foundation of the church, then the remainder of Acts spells out the implications. In Acts the role of the Spirit is above all that of empowering the church for its witness.

The Spirit gave Peter the courage to address the Jewish Sanhedrin (4:8) and Stephen courage to debate in the Diaspora Jewish synagogues of Jerusalem (6:10). In fact, the Spirit led in every major breakthrough in the expanding Christian mission—with Philip as he witnessed to an Ethiopian eunuch (8:29,39), with Peter's conversion of the Gentile Cornelius (11:12), and with the Antioch church as it commissioned Paul and Barnabas for their missionary journey (13:2).

The Spirit prevented Paul from working in Asia and Bithynia and provided the vision of the Macedonian call that led him to Philippi and his first work on European soil (16:6-10). Paul's courage to undertake the risky trip to Jerusalem and his resolve to witness in the capital city of Rome—these too are the work of the Spirit (19:21; 20:22). Indeed, some would call Acts "the Acts of the Holy Spirit." Luke probably would not reject such a title as inappropriate to his book. Were one to ask him what gave birth to the church, he would undoubtedly point to Pentecost and the gift of the Spirit there and quickly add that the same Spirit constitutes not only the birth but the continuing vitality of the church.

Samaria, and finally to the end of the earth. Acts can be outlined as roughly corresponding geographically to Jesus' commission—Jerusalem (chaps. 1–7), Judea and Samaria (chaps. 8–12), to the end of the earth (chaps. 13–28). Many would see Acts 1:8 as the "thematic verse" for all of Acts.

There is another part of Jesus' commission in Acts 1:8 that is perhaps even more central to Acts than the geographical emphasis—Jesus' insistence that His commission is to be undertaken only *after* the Holy Spirit has come upon the disciples. The Holy Spirit is central in Acts. Luke made it clear that there would be no Christian mission without the guidance of the Spirit. The young movement never undertook any new endeavor without the express guidance of the Spirit. Sometimes this was with considerable resistance from the would-be witnesses, such as Peter with the Gentile Cornelius (chap. 10). The Spirit is not mentioned by name in eleven of Acts' twenty-eight chapters. The Spirit's presence, however, is implicit in all of Acts. He is the driving force behind the Christian mission.

A closely related theme is that of the providence of God. God is always looking out for the Christian witnesses in the story of Acts. This is sometimes evident in visions and dreams that assure the Christians in threatening times that His purposes in them will be fulfilled and that they have nothing to fear. God is indeed behind the church's witness. His word triumphs. His witnesses often suffer for bearing that word, but when they are faithful in their witness, the gospel triumphs.

Acts presents an inclusive gospel. It is for Jew and for Greek, for Judean and Samaritan, for Lystran peasants and Athenian philosophers, for the Dorcases and the Agrippas, for Paul the proud Pharisee and for the humble, seeking eunuch of Ethiopia. The gospel is for all people. We are called to witness to all.

*Structure of Acts.* The title *Acts of the Apostles* is something of a misnomer. The book deals primarily with only two apostles—Peter and Paul. Of the 28 chapters of Acts, Peter is central in nine chapters, Paul in sixteen, Stephen in two, and Philip in one. Many accordingly outline the book under two main headings: Peter and the Jerusalem church (chaps. 1–12) and Paul and the Gentile mission (chaps. 13–28). Others outline the book according to the geographical scheme of 1:8 as outlined above. In what follows, Acts is presented under the rubric of the Christian witness as it progressed from Jerusalem to Rome in an ever-widening circle of outreach.

## SPIRIT-EMPOWERED CHURCH (1:1–2:47)

The first two chapters of Acts in many ways correspond to the first two chapters of the Gospel of Luke, Luke 1–2 dealing with the birth of the Savior, Acts 1–2 with the birth of the church. Just as Jesus was born of the Holy Spirit (Luke 1:35), the same Spirit is the vital force in the life of the church. Acts 1 and 2 relate the coming of the Spirit to the church. Acts 1 deals with the events leading up to the Spirit's coming, and chapter 2 relates that coming at Pentecost.

*Literary Prologue (1:1-2).* The first two verses of Acts link the book with the Gospel, Luke's "first book," and give a brief summary of the Gospel's contents—Jesus' deeds and His teaching, up to the time of His ascension. Like the Gospel (Luke 1:3), the book is dedicated to "Theophilus," who may have been a real person (perhaps a new Christian) or may have been a symbolic name. (The Greek means "lover of God.")

*Preparations for Pentecost (1:3-5).* After Jesus' death and resurrection, He appeared to His disciples over a forty day period. During this time He gave them "convincing proofs" that He was alive. These became important as they bore witness to His resurrection. He also instructed them about the kingdom of God. Most likely He opened up to them the Old Testament Scriptures about the Messiah. His scriptural interpretation would become important for the Christian preaching to the Jews. Finally, Jesus instructed the disciples to wait for the Spirit in Jerusalem.

*Call to Witness (1:6-8).* The disciples wondered if Jesus' resurrection heralded the immediate coming of God's kingdom. They asked Him in rather narrow nationalistic terms if God was getting ready to "restore the kingdom to Israel?" Jesus rejected both their concern for determining the date and their Jewish exclusivism. He replaced both concerns with a worldwide mission. When the kingdom comes is not our concern. What we do until it comes is: we are to be His witnesses. The witness is to be worldwide. Acts ends with Paul's ministry in the city of Rome, the capital of the Empire. Some would see "ends of the earth" as referring to Rome. Its meaning in the Old Testament prophets is "far distant lands," and that is probably what Jesus intended. The disciples were not to begin the witness yet—only after they had been empowered by the Holy Spirit.

***Ascension of Christ (1:9-11).*** Only Luke relates Jesus' ascension, here and in his Gospel (Luke 24:51). Jesus was caught up in a cloud and taken from the disciples' view. In the Bible, clouds are often associated with appearances of God, as at Mount Sinai and at Jesus' transfiguration (Luke 9:28-36). The two men in white were angels, divine messengers. They assured the disciples that Jesus would one day return on the clouds just as they had seen Him depart. For the disciples, the ascension meant their forty-day communion with the risen Christ was now at an end. He would not join them in the upper room again. For us, the ascension is a reminder that Christ has risen to the right hand of God and rules as Lord of our lives. It also assures us of the certainty of His return—on the clouds of heaven, just as He departed this earth..

***The Upper Room (1:12-14).*** The ascension took place on the Mount of Olives, a "Sabbath day's journey" from Jerusalem (about three-fourths of a mile). The disciples gathered in an upper room,

complying with Jesus' instruction to await the coming of the Spirit. It was a large group, numbering 120 (v. 15). In Palestinian homes, the top floors were often without partitions. Only the upper floor of a large house would accommodate such a crowd. Their main concern was prayer. Indeed, prayer was a hallmark of the earliest church (1:24; 2:42; 3:1; 4:24; 6:6). Among the women whom Luke mentions were those who had accompanied Jesus from Galilee and witnessed His crucifixion (Luke 8:2; 23:55; 24:10).

***Apostolic Circle Restored (1:15-26).*** There was one item of business which needed the apostles' consideration—the replacement of Judas. This section deals with that. First, verses 16-20 relate the gory details of Judas's suicide. He purchased a field with his ill-gotten gain. Then, he fell down in it and ruptured himself so that all his entrails spilled out. Matthew 27:3-10 gives a somewhat fuller account of Judas's death, which speaks of his hanging himself. The two accounts are not difficult to harmonize.

Verses 21-26 relate how Matthias was chosen to replace Judas. The choice was made by prayer and the casting of lots. It was felt that God would make the choice, designating His choice by controlling the lots. Why did they feel it necessary to replace Judas? Later, when James was beheaded, there is no indication he was replaced (12:2). Perhaps it was felt that at this important "birthtime" for the church, the "new Israel," it was important to have the full contingent of twelve apostles, corresponding to the twelve tribes of Israel. It is important to note the qualifications of an apostle. It had to be someone who witnessed *all* of Jesus' ministry, from the time of His baptism by John to His ascension.

**Miracle at Pentecost (2:1-13).** The second chapter of Acts deals with the miracle of Pentecost. It falls into three parts: 2:1-13 relates the miraculous manifestation of the Spirit, 2:14-41 summarizes Peter's speech at Pentecost, and 2:42-47 depicts the life of the greatly increased Christian community after Pentecost. The first part can be further divided into two segments: the descent of the Spirit on the believers, and their witness in the temple area.

1. *The Gift of the Spirit (2:1-4).* Pentecost was the spring harvest festival, referred to in the Old Testament as the Festival of Weeks, coming seven weeks (50 days) after Passover. "All" the Christians were gathered together when the Spirit descended, all 120 of them. They were probably still assembled in the upper room, which must have been near the temple grounds. Luke describes the experience as being both audible and visible. The sound was like a violent wind. The sight was like a giant flame with lapping tongues that rested on each of them. All were filled with the Spirit, and each began to "speak in other tongues." The phrase is ambiguous. It could refer to ecstatic speech, the phenomenon of *glossalalia* or "tongue-speaking" which Paul dealt with at Corinth (1 Cor. 14:1-25). It could also refer to speaking in other languages. In Greek, the word *glossa* can mean either "tongue" or "language." Since the next section speaks of the temple crowd hearing them in their own native tongues ("dialect"), it seems more likely that it was a miracle of speaking in other languages rather than in the ecstatic, non-rational *glossalalia.*

2. *The Witness to the Spirit (2:5-13).* Evidently the Christians rushed forth from the upper room into the temple courtyard. Crowds would be gathered there to celebrate the festival. It was a natural place to witness. The Spirit-filled Christians met there "Jews from every nation under heaven." They are described as "staying" in Jerusalem. Evidently, these were Jews from outside Palestine who had taken up residence in Jerusalem. They represented most of the civilized Roman world, including the Near East, Asia, north Africa, Rome, the islands (Crete), and the desert (Arabia). They heard the witness of the Christians, all in their own languages. The Christians are described as declaring the wonders of God. They were *praising* God. The crowd was divided. Some acknowledged the miracle and wanted to know more. Others were skeptical and accused the inspired Christians of drunkenness. Throughout Acts, the gospel creates division. Even the clearest miracle brings no response apart from faith.

What was the significance of Pentecost? Everything! Without Pentecost there would have been no further story in Acts. The coming of the Spirit furnished the power for the Christian mission. That is the significance of the "roll call of nations" in verses 9-11. Already at the very beginning the worldwide mission was symbolized in the witness in all these languages, representing all the areas of the civilized world. At this point they were all Jews. Most were probably Jerusalem residents and wouldn't return home. But, symbolically anyway, the mission had begun.

Another significance of Pentecost was the *universal* outpouring of the Spirit. In the Old Testament, God's Spirit resided only with selected individuals like the prophets. Here in the church, the new people of God, the Spirit rested on everyone, young and old, male and female alike. As Joel had prophesied long before, this was a sign of the final times. Peter made Joel's prophecy the starting point for his sermon.

**Peter's Sermon (2:14-41).** Peter's Pentecost sermon is the first of the major Acts "speeches." It is built around a number of Old Testament texts, through which Peter interpreted the significance of the Pentecost miracle to the Jewish crowd. He probably spoke in western Aramaic, the language of Palestine in that day. Peter's sermon falls into three parts.

1. *Scriptural Proof Concerning the Pentecost Experience (2:14-21).* Peter began his sermon by quoting Joel 2:28-32, a prophecy which spoke of God's outpouring of the Spirit on all His people. Joel depicted this as a sign of the last days, when God would visit His people in a special way. Peter declared that Joel's prophecy was fulfilled in the Spirit's descent at Pentecost. The days of the Messiah had arrived.

2. *Scriptural Proof Concerning Christ's Messiahship (2:22-36).* Peter now needed to convince the Jewish crowd that *Jesus* was God's promised Messiah. This he sought to do by proving and that the Messiah must die and rise again, that the resurrection was a sign of the Messiah. He began by introducing them to Jesus, with emphasis on His death and resurrection. Then he quoted Psalm 16:8-11 to prove that the Messiah, a descendant of David, would conquer death, just as Jesus had done in His resurrection. Finally, he quoted Psalm 110:1 as an Old Testament text that also points to the resurrection and exaltation of the Messiah.

3. *Invitation and Response (2:37-41).* Having set forth Jesus as their Messiah, Peter now called on his Jewish audience to repent and be baptized, and they would receive the same Spirit that they had just witnessed so powerfully. The response was also miraculous. Three thousand were added to the Christian community that day.

**Life of the Community (2:42-47).** The concluding verses of chapter 2 comprise a summary of the community life in the early Jerusalem church. They emphasize the remarkable unity of the early Christians. Note the qualities that marked their common life. They gave their attention to the *apostles' teaching:* They were eager to learn all they could about their Lord. They gave themselves to one another in their *fellowship* together. They shared at the table: *Breaking bread* probably included both a common meal and the Lord's Supper. They *prayed* together. Their witness was marked by *signs and wonders:* They continued to experience the power of the Spirit. They *shared,* not only of themselves but of their *possessions:* They held everything in common and gave freely to the needy. They met regularly with fellow Christians in *household fellowships* and continued to worship and witness in the Jewish *temple.* It was an ideal time. God blessed their faithfulness. They grew steadily in numbers day by day.

## APOSTLES WITNESS (3:1–5:42)

Chapters 3–5 are all set in Jerusalem. At this point in the life of the church, their witness was solely to the Jews of Jerusalem. These chapters are closely intertwined. The story begins with a healing in the temple square. This attracted a crowd to whom Peter preached. The crowd made the Jewish authorities uneasy, and they arrested Peter and John. Peter and John were interrogated by the Sanhedrin regarding the healing of the man and were dismissed with a warning to desist from preaching Christ. The Christians did not heed the warning of the Sanhedrin and continued their witness of Jesus. Now *all* the apostles were arrested and hauled before the Sanhedrin for their failure to observe its prohibition.

**Peter Heals (3:1-11).** This section relates one of the "signs and wonders" mentioned in 2:43. It also illustrates the Christian witness in the temple. Peter and John went to the temple in the afternoon at the time of the afternoon prayers and sacrifices, the time when there were crowds to witness to. Handicapped persons were often found there because they depended wholly on the alms for which they begged. A lame man was seated at the "Beautiful Gate." This probably was the Nicanor Gate, a gate within the sanctuary which separated the outer Court of the Women from the Court of the Men, where one could observe the sacrifices. When the man was healed he probably leapt into this Court of the Men, the sanctuary proper which had formerly been excluded to him because of his physical handicap. In a sense this symbolized his full acceptance by Jesus.

Of all the healing stories of Acts, this one is the most like the healings of Jesus in the Gospels. There is a major difference. Jesus healed by His own authority. The apostles healed "in the name of Jesus."

**Peter's Sermon (3:12-26).** The healing of the lame man attracted a crowd. Peter seized the opportunity to preach. It is Peter's second major sermon in Acts. Much like the Pentecost sermon, it draws from Old Testament texts and concepts which point to Jesus as Messiah. Preaching to a Jewish audience, Peter began by pointing to their rejection of Jesus as Messiah and their responsibility in His death. Then he pointed to the evidences that Jesus is the Messiah, the "author of life"—His resurrection and His power which healed the lame man. He stated that their rejection of Jesus need not be final. Jesus is coming again, and they could repent and be ready for His second coming. Finally, he appealed to the Old Testament for confirmation from "Moses and all the prophets" that Jesus has ushered in the final times.

**Peter and John (4:1-22).**

*1. Arrested and Interrogated (4:1-12).* The Sadducees and the temple guard halted Peter's speech, but not before he had evoked a considerable response. It is not altogether clear why Peter and John were arrested. The Sadducees represented the aristocracy who had made peace with the Romans. Perhaps they were worried that Peter's messianic message might lead to a popular movement against the Romans that would bring reprisals. The two were held overnight and brought next morning before the Jewish high court, the Sanhedrin.

The Sanhedrin consisted of seventy members. The majority of these were Sadducees, mostly from high priestly families. The high priest himself was presiding officer. A minority of the members were Pharisees. They were popular with the people, and their opinion carried considerable weight. The inquiry centered on the question of credentials. By what authority ("in what name") had Peter healed the lame man? Peter responded with a sermon on the concept of "name," which witnessed to the name of Jesus, the Messiah, the "stone rejected by its builders." Inspired by the Spirit, Peter even had the courage to accuse the Sanhedrin's members for their role in Jesus' death. He ended with an implicit appeal for the high court to commit to Jesus, the only "name" in whom salvation is to be found.

*2. Warned and Released (4:13-22).* The members of the Sanhedrin were in a quandary. The apostles were popular with the people for healing the man, and the Sanhedrin could not deny the clear evidence of the healing. On the other hand, they wanted the messianic preaching to stop. Their solution was to issue a formal ban on the Christian message. This would establish legal responsibility should the apostles continue preaching Christ. Peter told them what to expect: How could he not continue to testify to the power of God he had seen at work in Christ?

***Prayer of the Community (4:23-31).*** The rest of the Christian community undoubtedly had been in prayer for the two apostles during their trial. With their release and return, they now offered a prayer of thanksgiving. They thanked God for delivering His own in times of trial. When the rulers gathered against Christ, God delivered Him. Just now the two apostles had been delivered from the same authorities. They did more than express their thanks, however. They prayed that God would fill them with power to continue their witness even more boldly despite the rulers' threats. God immediately answered their prayer. They received a renewed sense of the Spirit's power, a new boldness for witness.

***Common Life (4:32-37).*** This third of the summaries focuses on the early church's practice of sharing material goods. There were two dimensions to this. First, they "shared everything they had." They did not claim owner's rights; their attitude was "what's mine is yours." Second, those with the means voluntarily sold some of their own property and brought the proceeds to the apostles for distribution to the needy. The church did not practice common ownership but charity on a voluntary basis. Barnabas is held up as an example of one who gave a particularly generous gift. Barnabas was a major figure in the ministry of Paul. He appears frequently throughout Acts 9–15. His nickname "Son of Encouragement" is borne out amply by the role he plays in the subsequent narrative.

***Serious Threat (5:1-11).*** The church's community of sharing was not without abuse. One couple in particular

sought to get more credit for a gift than they merited. They sold a piece of property and brought *part* of the proceeds to the apostles. They lied about their gift, claiming to give all, but keeping part for themselves. Peter dealt with them separately. He first confronted the husband Ananias. When exposed, Ananias fell dead at Peter's feet. Later his wife Sapphira was confronted. She likewise lied about the gift. Once exposed, she too fell dead at Peter's feet. Husband and wife bore equal responsibility for their sin in lying to God's Spirit. They also bore an equal judgment.

This judgment seems particularly harsh to us, but we must remember that this was a time of great unity in the church, of remarkable growth and experience of the Spirit's power. Ananias and Sapphira introduced an element of distrust which threatened the unity and witness of the church. It was almost as if God removed this "root of bitterness" from the fellowship lest it hinder its progress. Their experience is also a reminder that the same Spirit that brings God's blessing can also express His judgment.

***Apostles' Miracles (5:12-16).*** The final summary on the life of the early church focuses on the power of its witness. The apostles were known for their miracles and their testimony to Christ. They witnessed regularly in Solomon's Portico, a colonnaded area along the wall of the temple. The people's response was mixed. Some kept an awestruck distance from the Christian manifestation of the Spirit's power. Others joined them, and the Christian community continued to grow.

***Apostles before the Council (5:17-42).*** The apostles' bold witness in the temple area was bound to catch the notice of the authorities, who had strictly forbidden them to witness to Christ

## APOSTOLIC PREACHING

While the many letters in the New Testament give a full account of the teaching of the apostles, only the Book of Acts actually gives a record of apostolic preaching. In their public preaching, the apostles directed their message to the unconverted. They stressed the gospel of Jesus Christ and preached for conversions. The apostles reserved their doctrinal and ethical instruction for the church (Acts 2:42).

Though only lengthy accounts of preaching by Peter, Paul, and Stephen appear in Acts, their preaching represents the commonly held concept of the gospel. The same basic message of the gospel occurs in the full accounts of preaching. Where only a commentary on preaching occurs, the comment tends to highlight one of the essential elements of the gospel common to full messages.

Peter preached five major sermons in Acts: outside the house where the Holy Spirit fell upon the church (2:14-40), at Solomon's Colonnade (3:11-26), before the rulers and elders (4:8-12), before the Sanhedrin (5:29-32), and before Cornelius and his guests (10:34-43).

Paul preached numerous sermons in Acts, but only three appear in substantial form: at Antioch of Pisidia (13:16-41), at Athens (17:22-31), and before Agrippa (26:2-23). In addition to these, however, a brief commentary on other of his preaching appears: in Damascus (9:20), in Lystra (14:15-17), in Thessalonica (17:2-3), in Corinth (18:5), and in Ephesus (19:14; 20:21).

Acts also makes reference to the content of the preaching of Stephen (7:1-56), Philip (8:5,12,35), and Apollos (18:28). Other places in Acts mention only that the apostles preached the word. Because of the consistency of the message in the other passages, we may assume that when they preached the word, they proclaimed the gospel of Jesus Christ.

The message preached by the apostles had several essential elements in common.

1. They proclaimed that Scripture had been fulfilled. They consistently proved Jesus was the Christ in accordance with, rather than in contradiction to, Scripture. Their message of salvation had continuity with all God had been doing from creation on to save people. They did not bring a new religion but the climax of all God had promised.

2. The fulfillment came in the person of Jesus, whom they proclaimed as Messiah or Christ: Son of David and Son of God.

3. Salvation comes through the death, burial, and resurrection of Jesus, who has ascended to the right hand of God from whence He will come again to judge the world.

4. Salvation consists in the forgiveness of sins and the gift of the Holy Spirit. When sin is taken away and the Holy Spirit comes in, a person has received eternal life.

5. The appropriate response to this gospel is repentance toward God and faith in the Lord Jesus. Believers made this response public through baptism.

When the apostles took the message beyond the Jews, they had to lay a foundation that was unnecessary where people shared the same theological presuppositions. At Lystra and Athens, Paul had to begin by declaring the Creator God (14:15-17; 17:22-31).

Peter could speak to Jews in Jerusalem of Jesus as Lord, a holy title among the Jews. The Gentiles used the term "lord" very loosely.

To express the same divine title, Paul spoke of Christ as the Son of God. Peter did not explain the relationship between the death of Christ and the forgiveness of sins. The Jewish law made clear that atonement came through blood sacrifice. Peter did not need to explain it. For the Gentiles, however, Paul explained the relationship, especially in his letters, that Christ died for our sins (1 Cor. 15:3).

(4:18). This time *all* the apostles were arrested and held in jail overnight awaiting a hearing before the Sanhedrin.

*1. Arrest, Escape, and Rearrest (5:17-26).* God was very much with His messengers, and His angel released them miraculously in the night. The apostles did not flee. They remained in the area and witnessed to the people who gathered at the temple at daybreak. Ironically, the Sanhedrin had no one to try at its morning session. The apostles were finally located, back at the very witnessing for which they were supposed to be on trial. Their miraculous release was undeniable, and so they were led "without force" to the Sanhedrin.

*2. Appearance before the Sanhedrin (5:27-40).* The majority of the Sanhedrin were ready to order the death of the apostles for continuing their witness. But one of the Pharisaic minority urged moderation. He was Gamaliel, a leading rabbi, the teacher of Paul (22:3). He cited two former movements which claimed God's guidance but came to ruin and Gamaliel assured the Sanhedrin that the Christian movement would also fail if it lacked God's blessing. On the other hand, they could not stop it if God were behind it. The Sanhedrin heeded Gamaliel's advice and released the apostles, but not before giving them the flogging prescribed by Jewish law (thirty-nine lashes on the bare flesh with a leather whip).

*3. Release and Witness (5:41-42).* Though once again forbidden by the Sanhedrin to witness, the apostles continued their bold testimony to Christ. They were assured by now that although they might suffer disgrace and bodily punishment, God's word would prosper.

## WIDER WITNESS (6:1–8:40)

With chapter six, the gospel begins to move beyond Jerusalem in fulfillment of Jesus' commission (1:8). The key figures in this widening mission were the "Hellenists," non-Palestinian Jewish Christians who had settled in Jerusalem and whose language and ways were Greek. They are introduced in 6:1-7. Then the witness of two of them is related: Stephen's in 6:8–8:3, and Philip's in 8:4-40.

*The Seven (6:1-7).* A problem developed in the church's program of providing for its needy—in particular, for

its widows. It was a problem of communication. There were the native Palestinians who spoke Aramaic. There were also the Hellenists ("Grecian Jews"), Greek-speaking Jews who originated outside Palestine but now had come to reside in Jerusalem. All were Christian Jews. The problem arose because the Aramaic-speaking apostles were responsible for the food distribution to *all* the Christian widows. The Greek-speaking widows were being neglected because of the language barrier.

As a solution, the apostles requested that the Greek-speaking Christians select seven of their own to provide for the Greek-speaking widows. This was done, and the seven were duly installed. This is often viewed as the establishment of the diaconate, but the word *deacon* never occurs in this passage. The seven seem to have been selected to meet a specific need, not to fill an official church position. In any event, the primary ministry of the most prominent two of the seven was evangelism.

*Stephen's Arrest and Trial (6:8–7:1).* One of the seven was Stephen. Filled with "God's grace and power," he performed miracles and bore a powerful witness to Christ. In particular he preached in the Greek-speaking Jewish synagogues comprised of Jews from various parts of the Roman empire who had come to live in Jerusalem. Stephen encountered considerable resistance in these synagogues, but no one could refute his persuasive arguments. So his opponents resorted to treachery. They "hatched a frame-up" and brought false accusations against him before the Sanhedrin. Two false charges were made: he spoke against the Jewish law (=Moses), and he spoke against God. Specifically, the charge of speaking against God maintained that he had threatened to destroy God's house, the temple. In verse

15 Luke prepares us for Stephen's martyrdom that is to follow. Stephen's face shone with the radiance of divine inspiration for his testimony, a testimony which would lead to his death.

**Stephen's Speech (7:2-53).** On the surface Stephen's speech, the longest in Acts, seems like a bare recital of selected events from Israel's history. It does not appear to answer the charges against him. In actuality, it is a carefully chosen summary of Israel's history which serves to turn the charges back on Stephen's accusers. They, not he, were the resisters of God. They, not he, had blasphemed God's temple. His speech can be divided into five main parts.

*1. The Promises to Abraham (7:2-8).* Stephen began with God's covenant with Abraham. His main point was that Abraham never owned so much as a "foot of ground" in the holy land. The promises to Abraham all came outside the Holy Land. Stephen was beginning a critique of the narrow Jewish nationalism that confined God to the land of Israel and particularly to the temple.

*2. The Deliverance through Joseph (7:9-16).* Stephen continued his implicit critique of the "Holy Land" theology by pointing out how God had delivered Israel through Joseph, again *outside* the Holy Land. He also began a second theme. The sons of Jacob *rejected* Joseph, whom God had chosen. Israel *always* rejected its leaders. This is a major theme throughout the speech.

*3. The Deliverance through Moses (7:17-34).* The treatment of Moses is the longest of the speech. It falls into three sections, each covering forty years of Moses' life. Verses 17-22 cover Moses' early years, his birth and education in Pharaoh's house. Verses 23-29 cover the forty years between Moses's flight from Egypt and his vision of the burning bush. Verses 30-34 begin the final section of Moses's life—the Exodus and wilderness wandering. Again, the same two themes are prominent: God was with Israel in a special way *outside* the Promised Land, and Israel continued to reject its leader whom God had sent.

*4. The Apostasy of Israel (7:35-50).* In this section Stephen's polemic became more direct. Israel rejected Moses' leadership. They turned from God to idolatry. In verses 44-47 he began a critique of the temple. He implied that Israel did a better job of worshipping God in the wilderness, when they had a tent of worship that could be moved from place to place. With Solomon God was tied down to a single holy place, the temple. Yet God cannot be confined to buildings made by human hands. Their charge against Stephen was not altogether erroneous. He *did* criticize the temple *worship* of his day. The temple was supposed to be a house of prayer, but it had become a place where Israel confined God, where it tied Him down exclusively to its own land and people.

*5. The Rejection of the Messiah (7:51-53).* Stephen launched into a frontal assault. Israel had always rejected its leaders—Joseph, Moses, and now Jesus, the "Righteous One." Stephen's accusers had heard enough. They abruptly ended his speech.

Stephen's speech is highly significant to the early Christian mission. He criticized the Jewish nationalism with its exclusive theology of temple and land. This critique provided the rationale for an inclusive worldwide mission. His martyrdom *launched* that mission.

**Stephen's Martyrdom (7:54-8:1a).** Scholars are divided as to whether Stephen was formally sentenced to stoning, the customary Jewish method of execution, or whether he died by mob violence. The latter seems more likely. Under the Romans, the Jews could not carry out executions. What began as a formal trial deteriorated into a lynch mob, so furious were the Jewish leaders at Stephen's words. Saul is introduced to the story of Acts as the onlooker holding the stoners's garments. As the dying Jesus had committed His spirit to God, so did Stephen to Jesus (Luke 23:46). Also like Jesus, he asked forgiveness for his killers (Luke 23:34). We call Stephen the first Christian "martyr." The word *martyr* comes from the Greek word *martus,* which means "witness." Like all martyrs, Stephen was a witness to his Lord, even to the death.

**Persecution and Dispersal (8:1b-3).** Two things directly resulted from Stephen's martyrdom. First, the Christians in Jerusalem were persecuted and scattered. The apostles and the rest of the Aramaic-speaking church seem to have remained in the city. It was the Hellenists, Stephen's fellow Greek-speaking Christians, who had to flee. Among them was Philip, who proceeded to Samaria. Second, Saul came forth as the prime persecutor of the Christians. He too was a Greek-speaking Jew. His life was soon to change radically (9:1-31).

**Witness of Philip (8:4-40).** Like Stephen, Philip was one of the seven chosen to care for the Greek-speaking widows. Like Stephen, his primary role became the proclamation of the gospel, first to the Samaritans, then to an Ethiopian eunuch.

*1. The Mission in Samaria (8:4-25).* Like Jesus before him (John 4), Philip reached out to the Samaritan people. This was the first group beyond Judaism to hear the gospel. Nestled between Judea and Galilee, the Samaritans were the remnants of the ten northern tribes of Israel. They held a form of the Jewish religion, which included the books of the law for scripture, a messianic expectation, and a holy mountain. They were wholly rejected by the Jews. Philip had considerable success among the Samaritans and drew the attention of a charlatan named Simon, who had for some time astounded the Samaritans with his tricks. Philip's Samaritan witness also attracted the attention of the mother church in Jerusalem, which sent Peter and John to check it out. The two apostles quickly determined the legitimacy of Philip's word and joined in it by laying their hands on the Samaritans, who thereupon received the Spirit.

This was too much for the old magician Simon. He wanted the power to grant the Spirit too and offered to pay Peter for the secret of Spirit-conferral. Peter replied that God could not be bought and warned him that he was looking at full exclusion from God's people if he failed to repent. The Samaritan mission as a whole was a great success. Peter and John evangelized other villages there.

*2. The Witness to the Ethiopian Treasurer (8:26-40).* Philip had been the first to reach beyond Judaism, preaching to the "half-Jewish" Samaritans. Now he witnessed to a Gentile, an Ethiopian who was either a Jewish proselyte (convert) or "God-fearer" (worshipper of God who had not formally converted to Judaism). He is identified as a eunuch, the treasurer of the Ethiopian queen. It was a strange place to witness, at Gaza in the desert on the road to Egypt. Philip had not gone there on his own. The Spirit led him there. In fact, the Spirit directed every step in Philip's witness to the Ethiopian. The story is marked by uncanny "coincidences" that make the Lord's leading unmistakable.

The eunuch was reading from the servant portions of Isaiah, which point to Jesus' atoning death perhaps more clearly than any other Old Testament passage—the perfect preparation for

Philip's witness. When the treasurer professed his faith and requested baptism, they immediately arrived at a rare desert oasis. The Spirit had clearly been in everything that happened. As soon as the eunuch was baptized, the Spirit snatched Philip up and transported him to the cities of the coast.

In the first century, the word *eunuch* often was used of treasurers and could refer to one who either was or was not emasculated. In former times, eunuchs were always castrated to make them trustworthy keepers of the monarch's treasury and harem. One is inclined to see the Ethiopian treasurer as a eunuch in the ancient sense. He had been to Jerusalem to worship. Like the lame man at the Beautiful Gate (3:1-10), he would not have been allowed into the sanctuary because of his physical condition. In Christ, however, he found full acceptance. There are no second-class Christians.

## PETER JOINS WITNESS (9:1–12:25)

Acts 9–12 completes the narrative of the church's witness in Jerusalem and all Judea. The conversion of Paul and the witness of the Antioch church link with the work of the Hellenists and prepare for the Gentile mission of Paul. Peter's ministry to Cornelius results in the leading apostle endorsing the witness to the Gentiles. The twelfth chapter gives a final glimpse into the Jerusalem church before the narrative focuses altogether on Paul and his mission to the Gentiles.

### Paul's New Witness (9:1-31).

1. *Paul the Converted (9:1-22).* Paul's conversion is related three times in Acts, here and in two speeches of Paul; before a Jewish crowd in the temple yard (22:3-21), and in his address to King Agrippa (26:2-23). There are minor differences between the three accounts, mainly due to the different audiences to whom they were addressed. The present

account is the primary account. It falls into three divisions.

*Verses 9:1-9* relate the vision of Christ which came to Paul the persecutor on the Damascus Road. It was an objective experience. Paul's companions saw a light and heard a noise but only Paul experienced the vision itself. In persecuting the church Paul was persecuting Christ Himself ("Why do you persecute *me*"). Paul now understood that Christ truly lived, that He was indeed the risen Messiah. In his letters Paul referred to his experience as an actual appearance of the risen Lord (e.g. 1 Cor. 15:8).

*Verses 10-19a* relate the interlocking visions of the blinded Paul and the Christian Ananias in Damascus. Ananias was understandably reluctant to approach this notorious persecutor, who had come to Damascus expressly to arrest Christians like himself. Ananias was instructed to come to Paul, restore his sight, baptize him, and reveal his commission to him. The commission is given in verses 15-16. Paul would now be a witness for Christ; the former persecutor of Christ would himself be persecuted for his own witness to Christ.

*Verses 19b-22* complete the account of Paul's conversion. Paul lost no time in witnessing in the Damascus synagogues. His zeal as a persecutor was surpassed in his zeal for Christ.

There have been attempts to "explain" Paul's conversion—everything from a disillusioned Pharisee to an epileptic. The simplest and yet most profound explanation is that Christ took hold of him and turned him about-face—from a zealot controlled by his own will to an equally zealous disciple directed by Christ.

2. *Paul the Persecuted (9:23-31).* After some time of witness in Damascus and the surrounding Arabian region (Gal. 1:17), Paul was so pursued by the Jews

and the authorities of Damascus that he had to escape the city in a most unusual way. Paul related the incident in his own words in 2 Cor. 11:32-33. He also told of his first post-conversion visit to Jerusalem in Galatians 1:18-24. The apostles were at first reluctant to receive their former arch-enemy, but Barnabas—ever the encourager—intervened for Paul. Like Stephen, however, Paul aroused the opposition of the non-Christian Greek-speaking synagogues of Jerusalem. He fled to his native Tarsus. There he spent some ten or more years before Barnabas sought him out and brought him to Antioch (11:25-26). They are Paul's "silent years." We have no record of his ministry in Tarsus.

**Coastal Towns (9:32-43).** With Paul in Tarsus, the scene shifts back to Judea and the ministry of Peter. Two healing stories are related, both with close resemblances to Jesus' healings. The story of Aeneas reminds one of Jesus telling the paralytic to rise, take up his bed, and walk (Mark 2:9). The story of Tabitha brings to mind Jesus' raising of Jairus's daughter. Even the words are similar: *Talitha* ("little girl," Mark 5:41), and *Tabitha*. Tabitha lived in Joppa. Peter settled there for a while in the home of Simon the tanner.

**A Gentile God-fearer (10:1–11:18).** It would be hard to overestimate the importance of Peter's encounter with Cornelius. Peter was the leading apostle. This incident convinced him that God was including the Gentiles in His kingdom. As a result, Peter later became the defender of Paul's Gentile mission (Acts 15:7-11). Luke emphasized the importance of this event. He emphasized the significance of Peter's and Cornelius's visions by repeating them no fewer than three times in this passage. He presents the incident in his characteristic dramatic

fashion. It can be outlined in seven scenes.

*1. The Vision of Cornelius (10:1-8).* Cornelius is identified as a Roman soldier, residing at Caesarea, and a particularly pious "God-fearer." God-fearers were Gentiles who devoutly believed in God and attended the synagogue but who had not become full converts ("proselytes") to Judaism. Cornelius had a vision of an angel who directed him to send to Joppa for Peter.

*2. The Vision of Peter (10:9-16).* Peter's vision was more graphic—of a sheet descending to earth filled with all sorts of animals, both clean and unclean. Three times he was instructed to "kill and eat" of these animals. To do so was to break the Jewish food laws. It went against everything Peter had been taught from his childhood. How could a heavenly voice direct him to break the food laws?

*3. Peter's Visit to Cornelius (10:17-23).* Peter's vision coincided with the arrival of the messengers from Cornelius. Directions from the Spirit to accompany them served to convince Peter that God had something special in store at Cornelius's house. Next day Peter went with the messengers on the thirty-mile journey to Caesarea.

*4. Shared Visions (10:24-33).* When Peter arrived at Cornelius's house, both he and the centurion shared their visions with one another in some detail. The narrative is quite repetitious, but this serves to underline the importance of the events.

*5. Peter's Witness (10:34-43).* Convinced by his vision that God considered no one "impure or unclean" Peter now proceeded to share the gospel with Cornelius and his fellow Gentiles. It is Peter's third and final major sermon in Acts. The sermon basically was a summary of Jesus' ministry, emphasizing the significance of His death and resurrection. What was really striking about it was Peter's opening statement which recognized that God accepts people of all races and nations.

6. *The Impartiality of the Spirit (10:44-48)*. Peter didn't finish his sermon. The Spirit descended on the gathering of Gentiles, who outwardly demonstrated the Spirit's presence by their ecstatic speech. Recognizing their possession of the Spirit, Peter arranged for their baptism. Now he fully understood his vision. He had no trouble accepting the hospitality of his Gentile brothers and sisters in Christ, although it surely involved some relaxation of the kosher food laws.

7. *Endorsement of the Witness to the Gentiles (11:1-18)*. The final scene takes place in Jerusalem, where Peter was questioned by some of the more conservative Jewish Christians about his having dined with Gentiles. Peter related the whole incident to them. Both visions are given in detail for the third time. The reader cannot miss the importance of the event. Peter's critics could not deny the Spirit's work, so they had to agree with Peter that God was including the Gentiles in Christ. Not all the details had been settled. The issue would arise again in the Jerusalem Conference of Acts 15. But the general principle of the Gentile mission had been agreed upon. The door was now open for the mission of the Antioch church.

***Antioch's Witness (11:19-30).*** The church of Antioch in Syria was established by some of Stephen's fellow Hellenists who had fled the persecution in Jerusalem. Antioch was a city of Greek culture and language. The Christian Hellenists witnessed to the Jews of the city first but eventually turned to the Gentiles. They were the first Christian congregation to undertake a Gentile mission. That

is probably why the name *Christian* was first used there. "Christian" is a Latinized formation and was undoubtedly used first by the Gentiles whose attention had been drawn by the Christian outreach.

Antioch's Gentile mission came to the attention of the Jerusalem church, which sent Barnabas to check it out. Barnabas quickly determined its authenticity and joined in the outreach himself. He remembered Paul, who was himself a Greek-speaking Jew of the Dispersion, one who would be particularly suited for a ministry to Gentiles. Barnabas went to Tarsus, found Paul, and brought him to Antioch. There the two witnessed for a whole year. The Antioch outreach prepared the two for their own mission to the Gentiles, which they would soon undertake.

*Verses 27-30* relate a special project undertaken by the Antioch church. Agabus, a Christian prophet from Jerusalem, predicted that a severe famine would soon occur throughout the Roman Empire. A major famine did indeed occur at that time, during the reign of Claudius. The Antioch Christians saved up and assisted the Judean churches when the famine struck. Paul and Barnabas administered the offering. It served as a pattern for Paul, who would later undertake a major collection from his Gentile congregations for the Judean Christians.

***Persecution Jerusalem (12:1-25).*** Chapter 12 is the last chapter in Acts that deals with the Jewish-Christian congregation in Jerusalem apart from Paul. It is a model of Luke's dramatic style. It falls into four segments.

1. *Herod Agrippa's Persecution of the Apostles (12:1-5)*. Herod Agrippa I was the grandson of Herod the Great. He ruled over Judea between A.D. 41 and 44. Reared in Rome, one of the major concerns of his reign was to win the favor of the Jews. He must have

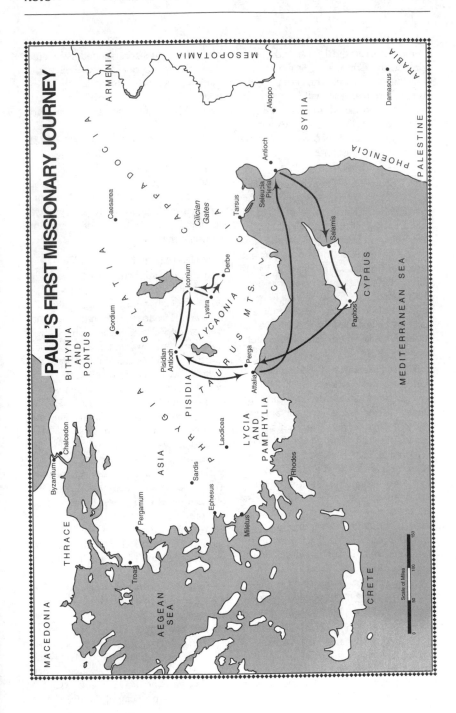

PAUL'S FIRST MISSIONARY JOURNEY

ordered the execution of James in an attempt to please the Jewish leaders who opposed the Christians. He would have done the same to Peter had not the Passover season intervened when executions were not considered proper. He held Peter in jail until the feast days were past. Herod had clearly become the archenemy of the Christians.

*2. Peter's Miraculous Deliverance from Prison (12:6-19a).* Herod's plans for Peter were not to be. Peter was delivered from prison by an angel of the Lord. Luke tells the story in a delightful way. Peter was to come to trial on the next day, but he was sound asleep, as if he had not a worry in the world. His trust was in God. Peter's escape was certainly none of his own doing. The angel had to rouse him, direct him how to dress himself, and lead him each step of the way until safely outside. Only then did Peter fully awaken.

The scene shifts to the house of John Mark's mother, where the Christians were gathered together to pray for Peter. Rhoda ("Rosie"), the little servant girl, was so excited to see Peter that she left him at the gate. The Christians inside could not believe her good news. They found it easier to believe that Peter had been executed and his ghost returned to earth than that their prayer for his release had been answered. Peter gave them a message for James, Jesus' brother, who from then on became the leader of the Jerusalem church, as Peter hastened off to a safer place.

*3. Herod's Self-destructive Arrogance (12:19b-23).* The soldiers paid for Peter's escape with their lives, but Herod got his as well. On a formal occasion in the theater at Caesarea, Herod appeared in especially fine regalia. The Jewish historian Josephus also records the event and says that Herod wore a garment of silver plates which glistened brilliantly in

the rays of the sun. The people hailed him as a god. Josephus stated that Herod neither affirmed nor denied their acclamation. He was immediately struck down, "eaten by worms" in Luke's words. He died for his blasphemous arrogance.

*4. Peace for the Church (12:24-25).* Chapter 12 has come full circle. The murderer of James now lay in his own grave. The church was at peace. Its witness could continue. Paul and Barnabas returned to Antioch, and the stage was set for the next step in the advancing Christian mission.

## THE GENTILES (13:1–15:35)

The church at Antioch was ready to expand its outreach. The Spirit led it to do so through a mission undertaken by Paul and Barnabas. They had great success among the Gentiles. This stirred quite a debate over the extent to which Gentiles should be made to embrace the Jewish law. A formal meeting was convened in Jerusalem to discuss the issue.

**Paul and Barnabas (13:1-3).** The Antioch church had already reached out to Gentiles in its own city. While some of its leaders were fasting and praying for further leading, the Spirit directed them to send Paul and Barnabas on a mission. The others then "commissioned" Paul and Barnabas to the new ministry, fasting, praying, and laying their hands upon them as an expression of solidarity and support. The Antioch church would be Paul's sponsor on all three of his missionary journeys.

**Sergius Paulus Converted (13:4-12).** Barnabas and Paul began their mission on Cyprus, an island in the Mediterranean Sea about sixty miles west of Antioch's port city (Seleucia). Barnabas was a native of Cyprus (4:36). They took John Mark along as their helper. They traveled westward across the width of the island to its capital city of Paphos. There they met Sergius Paulus, the Roman governor of the island. Paulus wanted to know more of Paul's message, but Paul was hindered by a charlatan named Elymas, who had been profiting from his association with the governor. Paul confronted the magician, who was immediately struck with blindness. His blindness was only temporary, but it served to demonstrate the power of the Lord whom Paul represented. The governor became a believer, the first in a long list of Roman officials to whom Paul would witness.

Verse 9 noted that "Saul" was also called "Paul." Before this, Luke had always referred to him by his Hebrew name Saul. From now on, he is called by his Roman name Paul. He would be working among Gentiles and had just witnessed to one who happened to share the Paulus name with him.

### Paul's Address (13:13-52).

*1. The Setting (13:13-16a).* From Cyprus the two missionaries sailed to the coast of Pamphylia (southern Turkey today). John Mark left them, returning to Jerusalem. It is unclear why he did so. It was a sore spot with Paul (15:38). Paul and Barnabas continued on their journey, traveling the difficult trail that led from the coast to Antioch, which was located 3,600 feet up in the mountains on the border of Phrygia and Pisidia. There was a Jewish synagogue in Pisidian Antioch, which the two visited on the Sabbath. Paul was invited to speak. He preached a lengthy sermon, his first major address in Acts.

*2. The Sermon (13:16b-41).* Since he was preaching to Jews, Paul's sermon had much in common with Peter's sermons of Acts 2 and 3. It was mainly constructed around Old Testament texts. It can be outlined in three sections. *Verses 16b-25* remind one of Stephen's sermon. They summarize Israel's history from the Exodus to David. Paul high-

lighted events which emphasized God's promises and His mercy to His people. In *verses 26-37* he introduced the Jews of Pisidian Antioch to Jesus, the promised Messiah. He told them of the death and resurrection of Jesus and quoted Old Testament texts which pointed to these events. Finally, he concluded his sermon with an appeal for them to repent and believe in Jesus. He emphasized that salvation is through faith in Jesus, not by works of the law. This became a favorite theme in Paul's epistles, which he would write later.

*3. The Sermon's Aftermath (13:42-52).* The response to Paul's sermon was largely favorable, and he was invited to preach again on the next Sabbath. Especially impressed were a number of proselytes (Gentile converts to Judaism). This proved to be Paul's undoing. Next Sabbath "almost the whole city" had gathered at the synagogue to hear Paul. The proselytes had invited their Gentile neighbors. The members of the synagogue became jealous at this great Gentile response (v. 45). They turned against Paul, but he responded by turning to the Gentiles, pointing out how it was necessary for him first to witness to the Jews. Now, in accordance with Isaiah's prophecy, he would be a "light" to *all* the peoples of the earth. To this there was an overwhelming response of faith from the Gentiles, but a violent rejection by the Jews. Paul was forced to leave the region.

With this incident, Paul established a pattern which he continued to follow. Whenever he arrived in a new town, he always began his witness in the synagogue. Only when the synagogue rejected him did he turn to an exclusively Gentile witness.

### Acceptance and Rejection (14:1-7).
Paul and Barnabas continued their witness in the mountainous regions of

the Roman province of Galatia (southern Turkey), traveling from Antioch some ninety miles southeast to Iconium. Luke summarized the time spent there. It was a typical pattern for Paul's witness—beginning in the synagogue, having a divided response from both Jews and Gentiles. Some believed; others passionately opposed Paul. When the opponents hatched a plot to kill the two missionaries, they traveled to Lystra, some twenty miles south of Iconium.

**Preaching to Pagans (14:8-21a).** Lystra evidently had no Jewish community. For the first time, Paul and Barnabas witnessed exclusively to Gentiles. It was not easy. There were major communication problems. The account of their ministry there begins with Paul's healing a lame man at the gates of the temple of Zeus just outside the city. At Paul's word, the man leapt up and walked, much like the lame man healed by Peter at the Beautiful Gate (3:1-10).

This, however, led to much confusion on the part of the pagan crowd. They concluded that the gods were visiting them, calling Barnabas Zeus and Paul, the chief speaker, Hermes (the "mouthpiece" of the gods). Since they spoke in their provincial dialect, Paul and Barnabas at first did not realize what was happening. The Lystrans had a local tradition that Zeus and Hermes had once come to their region in human form and been entertained unawares by an elderly couple. The Lystrans were convinced that it was happening again. The priest of Zeus didn't want to miss the opportunity to pay personal homage to his god and prepared sacrifices for the pair (vv. 11-13).

Only then did Paul and Barnabas realize what was happening. They tried to stop the sacrifices, insisting that they were only human. Paul tried to straighten them out by sharing a word about God. He spoke of God's mercy and provi-

dence. These were pagans who believed in many gods. Paul had to convince them that there was only one true God before he could begin to share the gospel of God's Son. The Lystrans did not understand. Paul's eloquence only convinced them all the more that this was a god speaking (v. 18). But crowds are fickle. Quickly they turned from sacrifice to stoning when the Jews of Antioch and Iconium arrived. The hostile crowd stoned Paul, but God delivered him from the ordeal. Paul and Barnabas went to Derbe for a brief but successful ministry there.

**Return to Antioch (14:21b-28).** Paul and Barnabas could have kept traveling southeast from Derbe the 150 miles through the mountain passes to Paul's home town of Tarsus. Instead they chose the more arduous alternative of retracing their route. They wanted to revisit the churches they had established, making sure of their spiritual health and that they had good leadership. The only place not revisited was Cyprus. They sailed directly from Attalia (coast of southern Turkey) to Antioch, their sponsoring church. There they gave their missionary report, particularly highlighting the great response of the Gentiles.

**Debate in Jerusalem (15:1-35).**
*1. The Criticism from the Circumcision Party (15:1-5).* Paul's Gentile mission evoked considerable discussion. Paul had not required his Gentile converts to be circumcised or to live by the Jewish law in matters such as the food regulations. He had not required Gentiles to become Jews in order to be Christians. But there were some Jewish Christians who differed with him on this. They felt that Gentiles converts should be circumcised and live by the letter of the Jewish law—in short, convert to Judaism in order to be followers of Christ. Those who felt this way were mainly Judean.

# ROMAN PROVINCES

Rome's primary administrative division for its overseas territories was that of the province. Although the use of the term *province* is rare in the New Testament (only in Acts 23:34; 25:1), there are many references to the provinces by name.

The Roman provincial system was set up over subject territories as a means of maintaining peace and collecting tribute. In the New Testament period (mid-first century A.D.) there were thirty-two such provinces in all. Eleven were designated as senatorial provinces under the jurisdiction of a proconsul, who usually served a one-year term of office.

Senatorial provinces were those territories where the peace was secure, and the proconsul usually had only a small military detachment under his command. In contrast were the twenty-one imperial provinces. These were under the jurisdiction of an imperial legate (or governor) who was appointed by the Roman emperor and served an open-ended term of office.

Full Roman legions (six thousand soldiers) were maintained in imperial provinces, since these were territories along the frontiers of the empire or places where revolt against Roman rule might arise.

In addition to the provinces were territories under the rule of a client-king, who was loyal to Rome and paid tribute to the empire. Many of the first-century provinces originated as such client-states, which were eventually ceded to Rome by the rulers. Thus Bithynia became a province in 74 B.C. when its king turned it over to direct Roman rule.

In the same manner Pamphylia became a province in 189 B.C.; Galatia, in 25 B.C.; and Cappadocia, in A.D. 17. Other territories were organized into provinces after Rome conquered them in war, such as Macedonia and Achaia in 148 B.C.

The official status of Judea is somewhat unclear. It was a client-state under Herod and his sons but later came under Roman procurators during the ministries of Jesus and Paul. During this period it still may have maintained its client-state status, with the procurator sharing jurisdiction with the Jewish high priest and being subject to the governor of Syria. (See the article "Pilate.")

After the Roman suppression of the Jewish revolt in A.D. 70, Judea was definitely organized as a Roman imperial province.

One often encounters provincial names in Paul's Letters and in the Pauline portion of Acts. Paul himself was born in Tarsus, a city of Cilicia, which in his day was a part of the province of Syria. Likewise in Syria were Damascus, where Paul was converted, and Antioch, where the church was located that sponsored him on his missionary journeys.

On his first mission Paul worked in the senatorial province of Crete and converted the Roman proconsul there (Acts 13:12). From Crete, Paul went to Perga in the imperial province of Pamphylia and from there to Lystra, Antioch, and Iconium, all cities in his day belonging to the imperial province of Galatia.

On his second missionary journey Paul worked in the Greek-speaking senatorial provinces of Macedonia and Achaia. Philippi and Thessalonica are located in Macedonia; Athens and Corinth are located in Achaia. The primary focus of his journey was Ephesus, capital of the senatorial province of Asia. Other provinces mentioned briefly in the Acts narrative of Paul's journeys are Bithynia, along the Black Sea, and Lycia, just west of Pamphylia and under joint provincial administration with it.

Paul preferred to use provincial names when referring to these churches rather than the cities where the churches were located. "Achaia" was his word for Corinth, and "Asia" was his word for Ephesus. When he spoke of "Macedonia," it was not always clear whether he had Philippi or Thessalonica in mind.

Other New Testament writers referred to the Roman provinces. First Peter is addressed to the Christians in the provinces of Asia Minor—former Bithynia, Galatia, Asia, and Cappadocia (1:1). Revelation is addressed to seven churches in the province of Asia (1:4). The geographical term "Italy" also appears in the New Testament (Acts 27:6; Heb. 13:24). Italy is the term used for the territory under direct Roman jurisdiction as distinct from its foreign territories. In the first century all Italians from just north of Florence to the boot of Italy were considered citizens of the city of Rome.

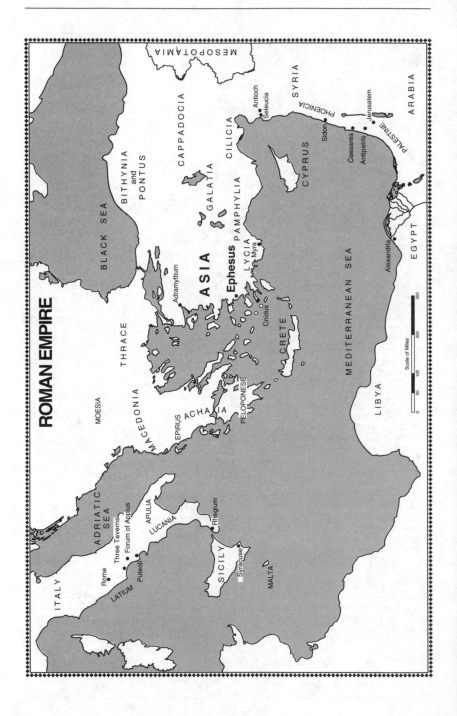

They came to Antioch and created a sharp debate with Paul and Barnabas over the issue. It was decided to have a formal meeting in Jerusalem to resolve the issue. Paul and Barnabas headed up the Antioch delegation.

*2. The Debate in Jerusalem (15:6-21).* The lines were clearly drawn. The one position, represented primarily by Jewish Christians of a Pharisaic background, insisted that Jews had always had a means of accepting Gentiles—by their undergoing circumcision and embracing the letter of the Mosaic law. Paul represented the other viewpoint. He too had been a Pharisee, but he had come to see that everything had changed with Christ. Christians were the new people of God, and to be a Christian one did not have to first become a Jew.

Paul, however, did not defend his position in the meeting. Instead he bore testimony of how God blessed him and Barnabas in their mission to the Gentiles. Paul's position was defended by two influential figures—Peter, the leading apostle, and James, the brother of Jesus and ruling elder of the Jerusalem congregation. Peter pointed out how God had shown him through Cornelius that He accepted the Gentiles. Gentiles should not have to live by Jewish ways. In Christ, salvation is by grace alone, for Jew and Gentiles alike. James basically reinforced Peter's arguments, giving scriptural proof for God's inclusion of the Gentiles.

Like Peter and Paul, James did not feel that the Gentiles should be circumcised or have to live by the Jewish law. He realized, however, that there remained a problem of fellowship. Jewish Christians lived by the Jewish food laws and Gentile Christians did not. How could they sit together at the same table? James therefore proposed a solution which asked the Gentile Christians to abstain from certain food and to main-tain sexual purity. ("Blood" refers to meat from which the blood had not been drained, which was forbidden to Jews.)

*3. The Decision in Jerusalem and Its Report to Antioch (15:22-35).* James's solution was accepted by the whole council. A letter was drawn up which set forth the four regulations. It was addressed to the church of Antioch and its mission field. Judas Barsabbas and Silas were appointed as official delegates to deliver the letter.

## THE GREEK WORLD (15:36–18:22)

This portion of Acts covers Paul's second mission. Accompanied by Silas and Timothy, Paul for the first time left the east and witnessed in the cities of Greece in the western world.

*Parting Company with Barnabas (15:36-41).* Paul asked Barnabas to accompany him as he revisited the churches established on their first mission. Barnabas wanted to take Mark, to give him another chance, but Paul strongly opposed taking such a "quitter" with them. So Barnabas went with Mark on a mission to Cyprus, and Paul took Silas (Silvanus in Paul's letters). Barnabas "rescued" Mark. Later Mark would be one of Paul's coworkers (Col. 4:10). Paul went on foot this time—through Syria north to his native Cilicia and eventually through the mountain passes to the churches established on his first journey.

*Derbe, Lystra, and Iconium (16:1-5).* Revisiting his former mission field, Paul met Timothy at Lystra. He is described as a "disciple," which indicates that he was probably a convert from Paul's earlier work there. Paul wanted to take him on the mission. Timothy had a Jewish mother, which made him legally a Jew, but he had not been circumcised. Paul had him circumcised so as to give no offense in the synagogues where he witnessed. He shared the Jerusalem letter with all the churches of his first missionary journey.

**Called to Macedonia (16:6-10).** Paul's group left the area of Paul's first mission and started north (through central Turkey). Paul would have turned west into the province of Asia over to the coast where the populous city of Ephesus was located. The Spirit prevented this. So Paul continued north, this time headed for the province of Bithynia with its towns along the coast of the Black Sea. Again, Paul was prevented by the Spirit (v. 7). He finally ended up on the Aegean coast at Troas, and there he discovered where he was being led.

In a vision at Troas, a Macedonian man begged him to come minister in Macedonia. Macedonia was not far geographically, a couple of days by sea. Ethnically, it was a different world—the land of Alexander the Great, the Greek world. Here for the first time Luke used the first person plural. His "we" perhaps indicates that he first joined Paul at Troas.

**Witnessing in Philippi (16:11-40).** Paul preached first in the city of Philippi, in the northeastern section of Macedonia. It was a Roman colony city, with a nucleus of Roman citizens, Roman government, and a major Roman highway running through it. We first learn of Paul's Roman citizenship in the course of his Philippian ministry. Luke's account falls into four main parts.

*1. Founding a Church with Lydia (16:11-15).* Philippi evidently did not have a Jewish community large enough to support a synagogue. But, there was a Jewish place of prayer outside the city, mainly attended by women. On the Sabbath, Paul joined them there for worship. One of them, Lydia, was a Gentile Godfearer, like Cornelius. She was a woman of some means. Having believed and been baptized, she invited Paul and his entourage to her home. Subsequently,

the Christians of Philippi held their house church at Lydia's.

*2. Healing a Possessed Servant Girl (16:16-24).* As Paul witnessed in Philippi, he was pestered by a servant girl who was possessed by a spirit with predictive powers. The spirit incessantly proclaimed Paul's relationship to God and the saving power of his message. Annoyed by the demon and feeling compassion for the girl, who was being exploited by her owners, Paul exorcised the spirit. Having lost a source of income, the owners hauled Paul before the town magistrates. Their charges against him were false but carried enough conviction with the authorities to have Paul and Silas flogged and thrown into jail.

*3. Converting a Jailer's Household (16:25-34).* Like the apostles before them (5:17-21), Paul and Silas were miraculously delivered from their confinement, by an earthquake in the night. Also, like the apostles, they did not flee, but remained at the scene to bear witness. The jailer expected to lose his life for loss of the prisoners. Instead, he gained life, true life in Christ through the witness of Paul and Silas. They witnessed to all his household. All were baptized. Joy filled their home.

*4. Humbling the City Magistrates (16:35-40).* The next day, Realizing that Paul and Silas had committed no real offense, the town magistrates sent orders to the jailer to release them. Paul would not go. He divulged his Roman citizenship and noted that he and Silas had been scourged without a hearing, which was strictly forbidden for Roman citizens. He demanded that the magistrates come with a personal apology and escort them out. Paul realized this was an important precedent. Preaching the gospel was not an offense. He had broken no laws. He wanted the record set straight—not just in Philippi but wherever he witnessed.

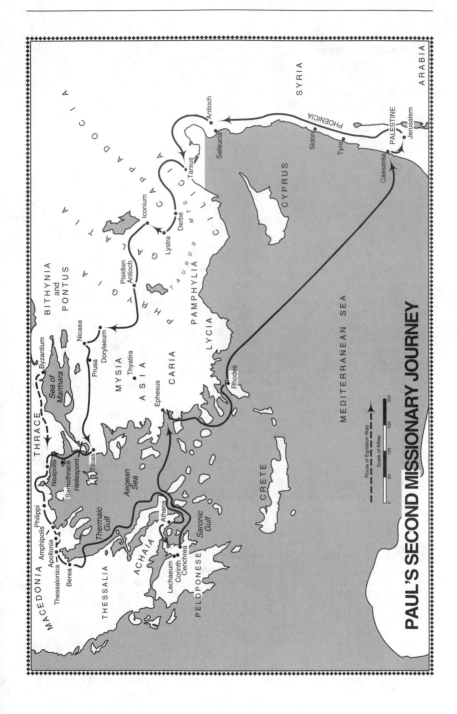

PAUL'S SECOND MISSIONARY JOURNEY

## GRECO-ROMAN CITIES

Paul's ministry was primarily conducted in the great cities of the Roman Mediterranean. Paul came from an urban background, having been born in Tarsus, the major city of Cilicia.

Tarsus had been under Roman rule since 67 B.C. and had the status of a free city, which afforded it considerable local autonomy. The leading citizens of free cities held Roman citizenship, and Paul's family enjoyed this status (Acts 22:28).

Growing up in Tarsus, Paul would have encountered all the characteristic marks of a Greco-Roman city—its temple, its theater, its bustling agora (marketplace), and its noted school of philosophy. Through the latter, Paul may well have been first exposed to the Stoic philosophical language and argumentative methods he employed extensively in his epistles.

Paul was converted in another great city of the Roman Empire: Damascus. Damascus was an ancient city dating well back into the second millennium before Christ. In the fourth century B.C. it came under Greek rule by Alexander and his successors and under Roman rule in 64 B.C. During this period the city was completely rebuilt on the Greek grid-system city plan, which consisted of streets criss-crossing at right angles.

Like all Greco-Roman cities, Damascus was surrounded by a defensive wall, had a prominent temple (to the Roman Jupiter), and extensive marketplace. The Jewish king Herod the Great built a Greek-style gymnasium there. The main street, "Straight Street," was where Paul lodged when Ananias was sent to him (Acts 9:11) and is still in use in modern Damascus. The city wall proved instrumental in Paul's bizarre escape in a basket (Acts 9:25; 2 Cor. 11:32).

Paul's sponsoring church for his mission work was located in Antioch in Syria. The church had been established by Greek-speaking ("Hellenist") Jewish Christians who had already begun to witness to the Gentiles of the city (Acts 11:19-26; 13:1-3).

Antioch was a Greco-Roman city from the very beginning, having been established in 300 B.C. by the Syrian king Seleucus I as his capital city. In Paul's day it was a bustling commercial center, the third largest city of the Roman Empire. Like many of the major cities of the day, it was a harbor city, located sixteen miles upstream on the Orontes River with the Port of Seleucia at the mouth where the river flowed into the Mediterranean.

The city had been under Roman rule since 64 B.C. Fortified by both inner and outer walls, it had a palace, a colonnaded forum (civic center), a theater, a splendid main street with polished stones and colonnades on both sides built by Herod the Great. It had an aqueduct that brought water from springs in the south of the city, a gymnasium, Roman-style public baths, an amphitheater, a theater, and an impressive temple. Though the latter was dedicated to the Greek Artemis, the ancient fertility cult of Daphne still flourished in Antioch whose sacred prostitution probably contributed to the city's reputation for immorality.

Paul's first missionary journey was primarily conducted in the Roman province of Galatia, where he preached in many Greco-Roman cities (Acts 13:13–14:28). Among these was Antioch in Pisidia, where the ruins of its Roman-style temple, aqueduct and theater are still visible today.

To the south-east of Antioch, the city of Iconium lay on the main east-west highway. Along with Derbe, Lystra is as yet unexcavated, but official inscriptions in Greek found in the vicinity of both testify to the dominant Greco-Roman culture pervasive in that area in Paul's day.

On Paul's second missionary journey he worked in the major cities of the Greek world. His first stopping place on Greek soil was Philippi (Acts 16:11-40). Since Philippi was located some thirteen miles inland from the Aegean Sea, its port city was Neapolis, where Paul landed.

Philippi had been settled in ancient times because of the extensive copper and gold mines in the region. Originally named Krenides, it was rebuilt in the fourth century B.C. by the father of Alexander the Great, Philip of Macedonia, for whom it was named. It was again reorganized and rebuilt by the Romans beginning in 42 B.C. after the successful defeat of Caesar's assassins by Antony and Octavian on the plains just outside the city.

At this time Philippi was given the status of a Roman colony, which meant that it had a nucleus of Roman citizens for its population, many of these "colonists" having come from the ranks of the soldiers who shared the victory there. A colony enjoyed many privileges, such as being under Roman law, election of their own officials, and exemption from provincial taxes.

This explains why Paul so enjoyed demanding the personal apology of the Philippian magistrates for beating and imprisoning him without a hearing (Acts 16:37-39). It was illegal to treat a Roman citizen in such a fashion, and loss of their colony status could result from such an infraction. Prominent among Paul's first converts was Lydia, a "seller of purple" (Acts 16:14). A Latin inscription excavated at Philippi refers to merchants of purple goods, thus giving further testimony to the prominence of that trade in Philippi.

Thessalonica was the second major city of Macedonia in which Paul worked (Acts 17:1-9). Some ninety miles southwest of Philippi,

Thessalonica was capital of one of the four major political divisions of Macedonia. Like Tarsus, it had the status of a free city. Like Philippi, the via Egnatia, the main east-west Roman highway, ran through it. Located on an inlet of the Aegean, it was a major port city. Because of opposition from the Jews of Thessalonica, Paul had to flee to the smaller town of Berea some fifty miles to the southwest.

Paul next went to Athens, the city that epitomized Greek culture. Like many Greek cities, Athens was dominated by a hill known as the acropolis. This hill overlooked the city. (There were similar acropolises at Philippi and Corinth.)

On the acropolis stood several temples, the most notable being the Parthenon, dedicated to Athene, the patron goddess of the city. Northwest of the acropolis was the agora (marketplace) where Paul may have observed the idol dedicated "TO AN UNKNOWN GOD" (Acts 17:23). It was here in the agora that he debated with the curious Athenian philosophers (Acts 17:16-21).

On the west side of the acropolis was the Areopagus (Latin "Mars Hill") where from ancient times a court was held that governed matters of religion and morals. The court itself eventually took on the name of its original meeting place. So there is some question about whether Paul's appearance before the Areopagus was on the actual hill itself or some other location where the court met.

Paul evidently did not

start a major Christian community in Athens at this time but departed for Corinth, where he worked for some eighteen months (Acts 18:1-18).

Corinth probably was the most important commercial center of Greece in Paul's day, located on the Peloponnesus, the southern portion of Greece connected to the northern mainland by a narrow isthmus just to the north of Corinth. Corinth thus had two ports, one on each side of the isthmus. Lechaion to the west gave access to the Adriatic Sea; and Cenchreae on the east, to the Aegean.

Although this region was settled as early as 3000 B.C., the city of Paul's day was less than a hundred years old. The ancient city had been leveled in 146 B.C. as the result of a war with Rome. It was reestablished as a Roman colony in 44 B.C. by Julius Caesar. Corinth was excavated in the nineteenth century and is an excellent example of a Roman city.

At the main entrance to the city stands the temple to Apollo, the patron god of the city. On the acropolis overlooking the city stands a temple to Aphrodite, goddess of love. Along the wall of the city is a temple to Asklepius, god of healing. A Jewish synagogue has been excavated, and this may be the same site where Paul preached. A large theater that seated eighteen thousand people has a plaza outside dedicated to Erastus, the treasurer of the city. Erastus may have been the same person Paul sent greetings from to the Romans (Rom. 16:23).➜

Corinth had a large agora. A large bema, or judgment seat, of blue and white marble was discovered on its southern side. This may be the same bema from which the proconsul Gallio heard the Jews' case against Paul (Acts 18:12-17). As a major port city, Corinth was particularly cosmopolitan, and it is easy to see why Paul had to deal so extensively with both religious and moral problems when writing the Corinthian Christians.

Paul's third missionary period was mainly conducted in Ephesus, where he spent two and a half to three years. Ephesus was capital of the province of Asia, having been under Roman dominion since 133 B.C. The site was extensively excavated in the nineteenth century. Among the ruins uncovered are a stadium that Nero built in Paul's day, a theater with a capacity of twenty-four thousand, and a main street thirty-five feet wide with colonnades fifteen feet deep on either side. Its most impressive edifice was the temple to Artemis (Latin Diana), with dimensions of 180 feet by 360 feet. It had sixty-foot columns and was extensively overlaid with gold leaf.

Artemis worship had its roots in the ancient Asian fertility cults of the Mother Goddess. The temple in

Ephesus was considered one of the wonders of the ancient world and attracted many visitors to its spring festival. Small wonder Paul attracted the ire of the local merchants when he criticized the cult's idolatry (Acts 19:23-41).

Ephesus was an important commercial center, located on a natural harbor and the main Roman highway. By now it should be apparent that Paul carried on his main work in the metropolitan centers, the major Greco-Roman cities.

Two further Greco-Roman cities held prominence in Paul's career, Caesarea and Rome. He was imprisoned in Caesarea for more than two years (Acts 23:31; 26:32). In Paul's day the Roman governors kept their residence in that city. Although there had been some settlement in the vicinity at least as early as the fourth century B.C., the city of Caesarea was primarily the contribution of Herod the Great, who desired a major harbor in that area. It was built entirely in the Greco-Roman style, complete with a theater, a hippodrome for chariot races, and an amphitheater for athletic events and gladiatorial combat.

Most impressive was Herod's harbor, with its two massive stone breakwaters. He also built himself a palace or praetorium

there, and this subsequently became the governor's residence and the place of Paul's imprisonment (Acts 23:35).

The most impressive city of all was the last Paul visited—Rome, the largest city of the empire, the city that ruled the world. Paul, of course, was a prisoner, waiting to appear before Caesar. He was under house arrest (Acts 28:30-31) but definitely with freedom to preach and perhaps to move some about the city.

The ancient world was comprised largely of city-states. The more powerful of these often carved out for themselves empires—Nineveh, Babylon, Carthage. No matter how extensive the empire, the city always remained the central governing power.

In Paul's day, Rome's power embraced the entire Mediterranean world. Knowing the importance of cities, Paul especially wanted to witness to the city of his world. He wrote a letter to the Christians who preceded him there to prepare the way (Rom. 15:14-29). He reached his goal, even if it was as a prisoner. Paul's missionary work may thus be characterized as urban evangelism, for he worked almost exclusively in the metropolitan centers of his day.

**Establishing Churches (17:1-15).**
*1. Acceptance and Rejection in Thessalonica (17:1-9).* Leaving Philippi, Paul's group traveled to Thessalonica,

the capital of Macedonia, which like Philippi was located on the main east-west Roman highway. For the first three weeks there Paul preached in the synagogue. He had to leave the synagogue but evidently spent more time in the city, supporting himself with his tent-making trade (1 Thess. 2:9). Eventually his Jewish opponents stirred up a mob from the marketplace rabble who stormed the house where he had been staying. They falsely accused Paul of sedition against Caesar. Jason, the owner of the house, was evidently a Christian. He was made to pay security to guarantee that Paul would no longer remain in Thessalonica.

2. *Witness in Berea (17:10-15)*. Paul and Silas went on to Berea, a sizable Macedonian town about fifty miles southwest of Thessalonica. Luke described the Berean Jews as "more noble" than those of Thessalonica. They studied their Old Testament with Paul to see if it pointed to Christ. Unfortunately, once again Paul's visit was cut short when the Thessalonian Jews came to Berea and turned the crowds against him.

**Witnessing to Athenian (17:16-34).** Paul was escorted by some of the Berean brothers to the coast and eventually to Athens. Silas and Timothy remained behind. Paul did not stay long in Athens. It was primarily a stopping place where he waited for Timothy and Silas to join him. It became the setting for one of Paul's most significant addresses, the speech to the Athenian intellectuals on the Areopagus (Mars Hill).

1. *The Athenians' Curiosity (17:16-21)*. By Paul's day, Athens had lost its political and economic power. It was still the intellectual and cultural center for all of Greece. The remnants of its former grandeur were everywhere, particularly its many statues. Paul was offended by the idols of the Greek gods which were to be seen on all sides. They would soon become the subject matter for his sermon. He witnessed to the Jews on the Sabbath in the synagogue, but every day he engaged the Greek philosophers in the marketplace, particularly the Epicureans and the Stoics, the two leading Athenian schools of thought.

Paul's message was strange to them. They thought he was proclaiming new gods—Jesus and the "goddess Resurrection." They called him a "babbler" (literally, a "seed-picker," someone pecking after any new idea). In reality, Luke said, *they* were the seed-pickers, always looking for the latest. They led Paul to the Areopagus. This could either refer to the venerable Athenian court of that name or to the hill at the foot of the Acropolis where the court had formerly met. The hill had become the Athenian equivalent of Hyde Park. It probably is there that they led Paul.

2. *Paul's Testimony before the Areopagus (17:22-31)*. Paul's speech on the Areopagus is a masterpiece of missionary preaching. Paul sought to establish as much rapport with the Greek philosophers as possible without compromising the gospel. He began with an attention getter, pointing to an idol he had seen in the marketplace as "the unknown god." The Greeks had perhaps erected it in case they might have left a god out whom they would not want to offend. In any event, the God they did not know was the only real God, and Paul now proceeded to present Him. He pictured Him as the God who made all things, the providential God who sets all boundaries of time and space. The philosophers could easily follow this, particularly the Stoics. They would especially agree that "we are his offspring," where Paul actually quoted a Stoic poet.

But in verse 29 Paul began to attack the Greek culture more directly. If we are born in God's image, he said, then we are wrong when we make idols. Idolatry gets things backward; it makes God into man's image. God will no longer tolerate such ignorance, Paul continued. He is coming to judge us for our ignorance and idolatry, to judge us by a person whom He raised from the dead (vv. 31-32). Paul lost most of his Athenian intellectuals right there. The idea of a man rising from the dead was sheer folly to their thinking.

3. *The Mixed Response (17:32-34).* There were three responses to Paul's address. Many mocked him. Others wanted to hear him further. A few believed: the sermon was not a failure. Paul knew that one could go only so far in accommodating the gospel. One cannot avoid the very center of the gospel, the folly of the cross.

**A Church in Corinth (18:1-17).** In Paul's day Corinth was a more influential city than Athens—more populous, more powerful politically and economically. It was a new city. Having been virtually destroyed by the Romans in 146 B.C., it was refounded by Julius Caesar as a Roman colony in 44 B.C. It was cosmopolitan, a port city with harbors to the Adriatic on the west and the Aegean on the east. Paul's stay in Corinth can be dated with some precision. Gallio was proconsul of the Roman province of Achaia for one year between A.D. 51–53. (Achaia covered southern Greece, including Corinth, Delphi, and Athens.) Paul spent eighteen months or more in Corinth (vv. 11,18) during this time frame.

1. *The Mission in Corinth (18:1-11).* Paul's arrival in Corinth is related in verses 1-4. He found there some fellow Jewish tentmakers who may already have been Christians, Priscilla and Aquila. They had recently come from Rome because Claudius had expelled the Jews from the city. (The expulsion is recorded by Roman historians. It took place in A.D. 49 and seems to have been provoked by riots in the Jewish population of Rome involving the message about Christ.) Paul began his Corinthian witness in the synagogue, as usual.

Again, Jewish opposition became so strong that he eventually had to abandon the synagogue and concentrate on the Gentiles (vv. 5-6). Paul moved next door, to the house of Titius Justus, who had been attached to the synagogue as a Gentile God-fearer. Others came over from the synagogue, including Crispus, one of the ruling elders. (Paul mentioned Crispus's baptism in 1 Cor. 1:14.) Paul remained in Corinth for at least eighteen months because he had been assured by God that his work there would be blessed.

2. *Before the Proconsul (18:12-17).* Toward the end of his stay he was hauled by the Jews before the tribunal of Gallio. The Jews accused Paul of teaching in a fashion contrary to the law. Gallio quickly ascertained that it was a matter of Jewish rather than Roman law and refused to hear the case. It is uncertain why the Jews beat Sosthenes in front of the proconsul, It is possible that this synagogue ruler may have become a Christian: Paul mentioned his "brother" Sosthenes in 1 Corinthians 1:1.

**Returning to Antioch (18:18-22).** This section rounds out Paul's second missionary journey, giving his itinerary from Corinth to Antioch. He sailed from Corinth to Ephesus, accompanied by Priscilla and Aquila. The couple remained in Ephesus to establish the witness there. Paul did not stay but promised to return later. He sailed on to Caesarea, then "went up and greeted the church." This was the Jerusalem church. Jerusalem was on a hill. In biblical language, one always "goes up" to Jerusalem. Paul's haircut at Cenchrea may have marked the beginning of a vow. The vow would have been a Nazarite vow. When taking such a vow, one would not cut his hair until the end of the vow's period, usually in a ceremony in the temple (see 21:21–23,26). His visit to Jerusalem complete, Paul went "down" to his sponsoring church of Antioch.

## OVERCOMING OPPOSITION (18:23–21:16)

Paul's "third missionary journey" was a journey only at the beginning and end. For the most part it was an extensive three-year ministry in Ephesus. Luke devoted only one chapter to that ministry, but we know from Paul's letters that it was a time when many churches were established and many of his letters written.

### Apollos in Ephesus (18:23-28).
Paul began his third mission by visiting for the third time the churches established on his first missionary journey. His ultimate destination was Ephesus, where he had left Priscilla and Aquila. Before Paul's return, the two encountered Apollos, who came to Ephesus from Alexandria. Luke described him as a Jew who knew of Jesus and taught accurately about Him. He was deficient in this Christian knowledge, knowing only of John's baptism (v. 25). Priscilla and Aquila soon instructed him more accurately. He eventually went to Corinth. Paul in 1 Corinthians referred to Apollos's ministry in Corinth a number of times.

### The Disciples of John (19:1-7).
When Paul first arrived in Ephesus he encountered twelve men who had been disciples of John the Baptist. They had been baptized by John and knew John's message of the coming Messiah but did not know that Jesus was the Messiah. Neither did they know of the gift of the Spirit. Paul convinced them that Jesus was the fulfillment of John's preaching. They were thereupon baptized. With the laying on of Paul's hands, they received an outward demonstration of the gift of the Spirit which confirmed that God had accepted them.

### Preaching in Ephesus (19:8-12).
As always, Paul began his witness in the synagogue. He witnessed there for three months until opposition forced him to move to a secular lecture hall. For two years he continued testifying there to both Jews and Greeks. He worked many miracles, so much so that people would bring items of cloth for him to touch in the hope that they could heal their sick with them.

### False Religion in Ephesus (19:13-20).
Paul encountered two types of false religion in the city. The first was embodied in seven self-styled Jewish exorcists who claimed to be sons of a high priest. (There never was a high priest name Sceva.) They observed Paul's exorcisms in Jesus' name and decided to exorcise a demoniac in Jesus' name. The demon would not acknowledge their power, fell upon them, and sent them away naked and humiliated. They learned that there is no magic in the name of Jesus as such. Jesus works only through those who are committed to Him. A second sort of false religion was the magical scrolls for which Ephesus was famous. These contained all sorts of strange words and spells. Paul convinced the Ephesian Christians of the worthlessness of such things. They brought their magic books and had a massive public burning.

### Determination (19:21-22).
We know from Paul's letters that he planned to take a collection from his Gentile churches to the Christians in Jerusalem. After that he intended to go to Rome (Rom. 15:22).

### Craftsmen of Ephesus (19:23-41).
The temple of Artemis (Diana) at Ephesus was one of the architectural wonders of the ancient world. People came from all over the world to worship Artemis. The goddess and her temple were the source of much pride and profit

for the Ephesians. Paul's preaching against idolatry and superstition brought him into conflict with the economic interests who profited from the worship of Artemis.

1. *Instigation of a Riot by Demetrius (19:23-27).* A silversmith named Demetrius profited greatly from replicas of the temple he made. Realizing that Paul's preaching against idolatry had ramifications for his business, he called together his fellow smiths. He set before them the real reason for his concern: Paul's threat to their business. He quickly moved to issues of public pride: Paul was endangering Ephesus's reputation (v. 27b).

2. *Uproar in the Theater (19:28-34).* The artisans carried their concerns into the streets, crying "Great is Artemis of the Ephesians." A mob quickly gathered, seized two of Paul's companions, and rushed to the open-air theater. This was the largest structure in town, seating some twenty-five thousand persons. Paul was prevented from going into the theater by the Christians and some friendly officials who were concerned for his safety. Alexander must have been a spokesperson for the Jews. The Gentile crowd may have identified the entire Jewish community with Paul, and Alexander's role may have been to dissociate them.

3. *Pacification by the City Clerk (19:35-41).* The theater was the gathering place for the *demos,* the assembly of all the voting citizens of Ephesus. The town clerk was the convener of the *demos* and the liaison between it and the Roman provincial officers. He realized that the mob in the theater could be viewed as an unscheduled, illegal assembling of the *demos*, which could create real problems with the Roman officials. He quieted the crowd with three observations. First, Ephesus's reputation was secure; they had no need to worry. Sec-

ond, the Christians were innocent of any direct crime against Artemis or the temple. Third, they should resort to the regular courts. An illegal assembly could only lead to trouble.

**Journey to Jerusalem (20:1–21:16).** At the end of his three-year ministry in Ephesus, Paul revisited the congregations of Greece. He was gathering his collection for Jerusalem. He also wanted to say a final farewell. He would not be returning, for he planned to begin a new mission in the west, with Rome as his sponsoring church (Rom. 15:28).

1. *Final Ministry in Macedonia and Achaia (20:1-6).* Leaving Ephesus, Paul went to Macedonia (Philippi and Thessalonica) and then south to Greece (Corinth). He spent three months in Corinth. Acts does not mention Paul's collection, but his epistles of this period do (2 Cor. 8; 9; Rom. 15:25-29). The Jewish plot may have involved sabotaging this large relief fund. The men mentioned in verses 4 and 5 were the official delegates of the churches, who accompanied Paul with the collection. The "we" reappears. Luke may have joined Paul at Philippi and traveled on with him to Troas (v. 6).

2. *Restoration of Eutychus (20:7-12).* This story is one of those delightful Lukan anecdotes, full of colorful detail—a full meal, a lamp-filled room consuming all the oxygen, a long-winded apostle, a young man seated in the window. It is often debated whether Eutychus was actually dead or just had the wind knocked out of him. The text seems to indicate he was dead. It was Easter season, and Eutychus's raising would have been a vivid reminder of the resurrection.

3. *Voyage to Miletus (20:13-16).* Paul could not sail on to Palestine without saying farewell to the Ephesians. He chose, however, not to stop there. Perhaps it was still not safe for him there. Also, he

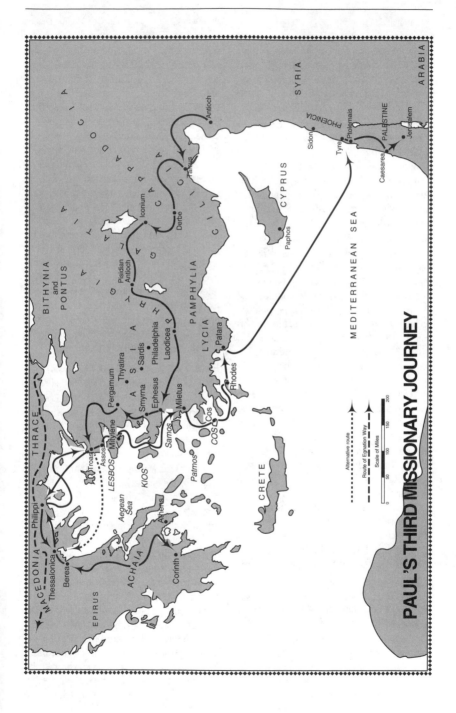

**PAUL'S THIRD MISSIONARY JOURNEY**

worried that the Ephesian Christians might prevail on him to stay longer than his plans allowed. So Paul stopped instead at Miletus and summoned the leaders of the Ephesian church (thirty miles to the north) to meet him there.

4. *Farewell Address to the Ephesian Elders (20:17-35).* Paul's Miletus address is the only major speech of Paul which Luke recorded for his third missionary period. It is the only speech in Acts addressed to a Christian audience and as such is the most like Paul's epistles, which were also addressed to Christians. It can be outlined in four parts.

First, Paul pointed to his *past* example during his three-year ministry in Ephesus. He emphasized his witness to both Jews and Gentiles in the face of constant opposition. Second, he pointed to his own *present* prospects. He was on his way to Jerusalem, led by the Spirit, aware that he was facing real danger. He was saying his farewell to Ephesus; he would not be returning there. Third, Paul looked toward the more distant *future* of the Ephesian church. He warned the church that "fierce wolves" would come and ravage the flock. (His prediction did indeed come true, as false teachings constantly besieged Ephesus in later years [e.g., Rev. 2:6]). Finally, Paul offered a benediction for the church and a reminder of how he had always avoided greed in his ministry to them, urging them to follow his example. He concluded with Jesus' saying that it is more blessed to give than to receive. This saying is only found here.

5. *Final Leave-taking (20:36-38).* Paul said farewell. The reminder that he would not return set an ominous tone for Paul's journey to Jerusalem.

6. *Voyage to Jerusalem (21:1-16).* The same Spirit that was driving Paul to Jerusalem was preparing him for the ordeals he would experience there by issuing warnings of the danger through the Christians at each stopping point along the way (20:22-23). When Paul reached Tyre, the Christians there shared with Paul how the Spirit had revealed to them the dangers which would meet Paul in Jerusalem. The next warning came at Caesarea, where Paul stayed in the home of Philip (see 8:40). Paul had encountered the Judean prophet Agabus once before, when he predicted the famine (11:28). Now Agabus shared a prophetic act, binding himself with Paul's belt to symbolize that Paul would be bound in Jerusalem. Paul assured everyone that he understood the dangers at Jerusalem but was prepared in the Spirit to take whatever fell his lot there, even to death if need be. Paul and his entourage set out from Caesarea to Jerusalem, a journey of about sixty-five miles. Luke was with Paul (note the "we"), as were the delegates who accompanied his collection.

## PAUL WITNESSES (21:17–26:32)

The warnings came true. Paul was arrested in Jerusalem and remained a prisoner to the very end of his story in Acts. His imprisonment subjected him to many trials. The trials were an opportunity for witness, which he did not allow to slip by. This long section of Acts is filled with Paul's speeches: before a Jewish crowd in the temple yard, before a Roman governor, and before the Jewish king. God's words to Ananias had come true which predicted that Paul would bear Jesus' name before Gentiles, kings, and the people of Israel (9:15).

*Witness before the Jews (21:17–23:35).* The setting of this section is Jerusalem. Paul was received with some apprehension there by the Jewish Christian leaders and became the target of an unruly mob in the temple courtyard. Taken into protective custody by the Roman soldiers, Paul remained a prisoner in Jerusalem until a plot by some

## TEN MAJOR SERMONS IN ACTS

| | Reference in Acts | Audience | Central Truths |
|---|---|---|---|
| Peter's mission sermons | 1. Acts 2:14-41 | An international group of God-fearing Jews in Jerusalem for Pentecost | The gift of the Holy Spirit proves now is the age of salvation. Jesus' resurrection validates His role as Messiah. |
| | 2. Acts 3:11-26 | A Jewish crowd in the Jerusalem temple | The healing power of Jesus' name proves that He is alive and at work. Those who rejected the Messiah in ignorance can still repent. |
| | 3. Acts 10:27-48 | The Gentile Cornelius and his household | God accepts persons of all races who respond in faith to the gospel message. |
| Stephen's sermon | 4. Acts 7:1-60 | The Sanhedrin | God revealed Himself outside the Holy Land. God's people capped a history of rejecting the leaders He had sent them by killing the Messiah. |
| Paul's mission sermons | 5. Acts 13 | Jews in the synagogue in Pisidian Antioch | Paul's mission sermons illustrate the changing focuses of early Christian mission work: first Jewish evangelism, second Gentile evangelism, third development of Christian leaders. |
| | 6. Acts 17 | Pagan Greeks at the Areopagus in Athens | |
| | 7. Acts 20 | Christian leaders of the Ephesian church | |
| Paul's defense sermons | 8. Acts 22:1-21 | Temple crowd in Jerusalem | Paul's defense sermons stressed that he was innocent of any breach of Roman law. Paul was on trial for his conviction that Jesus had been raised from the dead and had commissioned Paul as a missionary to the Gentiles. |
| | 9. Acts 24:10-21 | The Roman Governor Felix | |
| | 10. Acts 26 | The Jewish King Agrippa II | |

zealous Jews forced the Roman tribune to remand him to the governor at Caesarea. Central to this section is Paul's defense before the Jews: first before the mob at the temple, then before the Sanhedrin.

*1. The Concern of the Jerusalem Elders (21:17–26).* The Jerusalem Christians received Paul "warmly," especially in light of the large collection he had brought them. James, however, expressed their concern about rumors to the effect that Paul was teaching his Jewish converts to abandon circumcision and Jewish customs. This was not true. Paul did not require Gentile Christians to become Jews; he also did not ask Jewish Christians to abandon their Jewish heritage (see 1 Cor. 9:19-23). James was concerned that the rumors might damage the church's witness to Jews. He suggested that Paul prove his faithfulness to Jewish customs by participating in a vow taken by four Jewish Christian brothers. The time was nearing for their vow to end in a ceremony at the temple where they would cut their hair. Paul agreed to participate in the ceremony and to underwrite the expenses.

*2. The Riot in the Temple Area (21:27-36).* Paul's presence in the temple area was noticed by some Asian Jews, who likely knew him from his Ephesian ministry. They falsely accused Paul of a breach of Jewish law, claiming that he had taken Trophimus, an Ephesian Gentile, into the temple. (Gentiles were forbidden to enter the sanctuary.) They soon attracted a mob, which would have killed Paul had the Roman soldiers not intervened.

The troops were quartered in the Tower of Antonia on the corner of the temple wall. Stairs led from the tower into the temple courtyard. The soldiers took Paul into custody, binding him with chains until they could ascertain the reasons for the riot. The press of the mob was so intense they had to lift Paul up the stairs to their barracks.

*3. Paul's Request to Address the Crowd (21:37-40).* Paul turned the riot into an occasion for witness. Requesting permission to speak, Paul surprised the commander with his native Greek language. He was a citizen of a respectable city (Tarsus), not a wild insurrectionist.

*4. Paul's Speech before the Temple Mob (22:1-21).* Paul's address can be divided into four parts. First, Paul informed the Jewish crowd of his Jewish heritage. He was reared a strict Jew and educated in the Jewish law under one of its greatest teachers, Gamaliel. He was zealous for God. Seeing Christians as dangerous heretics, he persecuted them, even to death. *Verses 6-11* give Paul's own account of his conversion. It is similar to that of 9:1-9. *Verses 12-16* elaborate Ananias's role in Paul's conversion. Paul was addressing a Jewish crowd; so he emphasized that Ananias was a devout Jew. Finally, Paul told of his vision in Jerusalem on the occasion of his first visit there after his conversion. At that time the Lord directed him to witness no longer to the Jews of Jerusalem but to go to the Gentiles.

*5. The Attempted Examination by the Tribune (22:22-29).* The mention of Paul's Gentile witness infuriated the Jewish crowd. The soldiers quickly hauled Paul into their quarters, where they were ordered to examine Paul by scourging. At this point Paul divulged his Roman citizenship. It was forbidden to scourge a citizen without a trial. When informed of Paul's Roman citizenship, the commander (a tribune in rank) came and questioned Paul about it. Paul impressed him that he was a native-born citizen, not one who had purchased a citizen's rights like the tribune. Realizing that he could not examine Paul by scourging, the tribune resorted to other means in his attempt to determine the case against Paul.

6. *Paul before the Sanhedrin (22:30–23:11).* Since the mob's accusations against Paul seemed to involve primarily the Jewish religion, the tribune decided to take Paul before the main Jewish judicial body, the Sanhedrin—for a hearing, not a trial. The session began with Paul declaring that his conscience was clear before God. The high priest responded by ordering him to be struck on the mouth for blasphemy. If Paul had a clear conscience, it meant that his message about Jesus was right and that the high priest's denial of that message was wrong. In the priest's mind, Paul *had* to be blaspheming. Paul answered the action by calling the high priest a "whitewashed wall," a hypocrite. He retracted his statement when reminded that the Jewish law forbade one to speak ill of a high priest. He may, however, have felt that one who doesn't behave like God's priest didn't deserve to be treated like one.

Paul then addressed the charges against him, stating that he was a Pharisee and was on trial for proclaiming the resurrection. This divided the house. The majority of the Sanhedrin were Sadducees. They did not believe in a resurrection. The Pharisees did. They began to violently debate the issue. Things became so intense that the tribune had to remove Paul from the scene. The hearing yielded no substantive information about the charges against Paul. It must, however, have been unsettling for Paul. God reassured him in a night vision that He would be with him. God had a purpose for Paul: to witness in Rome as boldly as he had witnessed in Jerusalem (v. 11). From this point on in Acts, the story of Paul moves rapidly toward Rome.

7. *The Plot to Ambush Paul (23:12-22).* Paul was not safe in Jerusalem; there were many there who wanted him dead. Forty men took a solemn vow to neither eat nor drink until they had killed him. They secured the collusion of the Sanhedrin in their plot. The plot was overheard by Paul's nephew, who informed Paul. Paul in turn sent his nephew to the tribune with this news.

8. *Paul Sent to Caesarea (23:23-35).* Realizing the extreme danger to Paul in Jerusalem, the tribune Lysias decided to send him to the provincial governor, Felix, who resided in Caesarea. Lysias wrote a formal letter to Felix detailing the situation. He took no chances with the zealots, sending Paul to Caesarea by night with a huge contingent of soldiers.

***Witness before Gentiles and the Jewish King (24:1-26:32).*** Paul remained in prison in Caesarea for at least two years. His case was heard by two Roman governors and by the Jewish king. When it appeared that he might be sent back to Jerusalem for trial, Paul invoked his citizen rights and appealed for a trial before the emperor. Not only would this rescue him from the Jerusalem zealots; it would provide an opportunity to witness in Rome, where God was leading him (23:11)

1. *The Trial in Caesarea (24:1-23).* Paul first appeared before the Roman governor Felix. Felix was a freed slave of the imperial family. The Roman historian Tacitus stated that he never fully overcame his background, ruling like a king but with the mind of a slave. Within a week of Paul's arrival, he set a trial in Caesarea. Three people spoke.

First came the charges of the Jewish prosecution against Paul in the person of a lawyer named *Tertullus.* Tertullus's charges were either vague or unsubstantiated: (1) Paul stirred up riots against the Jews throughout the world, (2) he was a leader of the Nazarenes, and (3) he had desecrated the Jewish temple.

Second to speak was *Paul (24:10-21)*. He denied the first and third charges: he came to the temple to worship, not to desecrate it, and he stirred up no crowds there. He admitted being a Nazarene, but preferred to call himself a follower of "the Way." He was a loyal Jew, living by the law and sharing the resurrection hope (v. 15). (Paul shared a belief in the resurrection with many Jews, like Pharisees. Where he differed with them was his belief that the resurrection had already occurred in Jesus.) Paul now turned to the riot itself, pointing out that the Asian Jews who started it had not come to Caesarea to accuse Paul. This was a breach of Roman law: accusers *had* to be present.

*Felix* was the third speaker. Speaking briefly, he dismissed the hearing, stating that he would continue no further until Lysias came from Jerusalem to clarify matters. Felix was well-disposed toward Paul, giving him some freedom to move about and to be visited by his friends.

*2. Paul and Felix in Private (24:24-27)*. Felix kept Paul in prison for two years, not wanting to offend the Jews by releasing him. He conversed with Paul often, hoping to receive a bribe. Luke mentioned his wife Drusilla. She was a Jewish princess, whom Felix is said to have tricked into marrying him through the help of a sorcerer. Perhaps this had something to do with his becoming nervous when Paul preached about self-control, righteousness, and the coming judgment.

*3. Festus Pressured by the Jews (25:1-5)*. Felix was removed from office for mismanaging an incident of conflict between the Jews and Gentiles of Caesarea. He was succeeded by Porcius Festus. On his first visit to Jerusalem, the new governor was approached by the Jewish leaders concerning Paul. Planning another ambush, they urged Festus to bring him to Jerusalem for a trial.

*4. Paul's Appeal to Caesar (25:6-12)*. Paul's accusers came to Caesarea and brought unsubstantiated charges against him. Paul denied them all, but Festus wished to pacify the Jews. Unaware of the danger to Paul in Jerusalem, he suggested that they hold a trial there. All too aware of the danger in Jerusalem, Paul resorted to the one legal recourse he had that would insure against his being taken there for trial. He took the matter out of Festus's hands by exercising his rights as a Roman citizen to a trial before Caesar. Festus consulted with his advisers and agreed to process the appeal.

*5. Festus's Conversation with Agrippa (25:13-22)*. Agrippa II ruled over only several small territories, but he had the title "King of the Jews," which gave him several prerogatives, the most significant of which was the appointment of the high priest. He lived with his half-sister Bernice, the source of much scandal. Festus used the opportunity of a visit from Agrippa to see if the Jewish king might cast some light on the charges against Paul. Festus would need to draw up formal charges against Paul in connection with the appeal to the Roman emperor.

*6. Paul's Address before Agrippa: the Setting (25:23-27)*. The hearing before Agrippa occurred with great ceremony because of the presence of the king. Festus opened with a brief reference to the Jewish accusations against Paul. He expressed his hope that Agrippa could help him draw up formal charges. He also stated his own opinion about Paul's innocence of any capital offenses.

*7. Paul's Address before Agrippa: The Speech (26:1-23)*. Agrippa requested Paul to respond. Paul moved quickly to the main issue—the Jewish messianic hope, which was fulfilled in Christ and confirmed by His resurrection. Paul followed with his personal testimony. He pointed to his former zeal as a persecutor of Christians. He told of his conversion in an account very similar to that before the Jewish crowd (22:6-16) and Luke's initial narration (9:1-l9). Since his hearers now were primarily Gentile, he dwelt at some length on his call to witness to the Gentiles. Paul concluded with a summary of the gospel for which he was on trial: in accordance with the Scriptures, Christ died and rose to bring light and life to Jew and Gentile alike.

8. *Paul's Appeal to Agrippa (26:24-29)*. At the mention of the resurrection, Festus interrupted, accusing Paul of madness. Like the Athenian intellectuals, the idea of the resurrection was foolishness to him. Paul did not back off. He turned to Agrippa and asked the king if he were not aware of the Christians. He pointed out that what had happened in Christ was not hidden but occurred fully in the open for all to see. Did Agrippa not believe the prophets? If he did, he too would believe in Christ, for they all pointed to Christ. The king responded tragically, asking Paul if he intended to convert him to Christ with so brief a witness (v. 28). Bold and persistent, Paul insisted that he would wish for *all* those present to become followers of Christ.

9. *Paul's Innocence Declared by Governor and King (26:30-32)*. Festus had already declared Paul's innocence of anything deserving death (25:25). Agrippa went further: Paul did not even merit imprisonment. He added that Paul could have been freed if he had not made the appeal. But there had been an appeal, and it could not easily be undone. More than that, all that had transpired was in God's purposes. Paul was on his way to Rome: this was God's design for him (23:11).

## JEWS AND GENTILES (27:1–28:31)

Paul was on his way to Rome. Acts 27:1–28:16 relates the difficult journey, and particularly the shipwreck which Paul experienced. Much of the narrative merely relates in detail the whole life-threatening experience. Through it all, the providence of God shone through. God was with Paul and *all* his traveling companions so that Paul could bear his witness in the capital city of Rome.

*Journey to Rome (27:1-28:16).* Paul's voyage to Rome is one of the most exciting stories in Acts. It is considered by naval historians to be one of the finest sources for ancient navigational technique. Luke was an avid traveler, which is amply reflected in this section of Acts.

1. *The Journey to Fair Havens (27:1-8)*. A centurion named Julius was responsible for Paul. Aristarchus the Macedonian and Luke were allowed to accompany them. The centurion was kind to Paul, allowing him to visit the Christians of Sidon when the ship put in there. At Myra (southern Turkey) they transferred to a vessel headed for Italy. It was probably a grain ship. Myra was a common stopping point for grain ships headed from Egypt to Rome. It was already well into the fall, and sea travel was not easy. The usual and most direct route to Italy went to the north of Crete, but the wind prevented this. They sailed around Crete to a small port on the southern coast named Fair Havens.

2. *The Decision to Sail On (27:9-12)*. Because Fair Havens was not well-suited for wintering, the centurion and the ship's officers decided to sail on. Undoubtedly under God's influence, Paul warned them that the voyage was destined to end up disastrously.

3. *The Northeaster (27:13-20)*. They were headed for another Cretan port

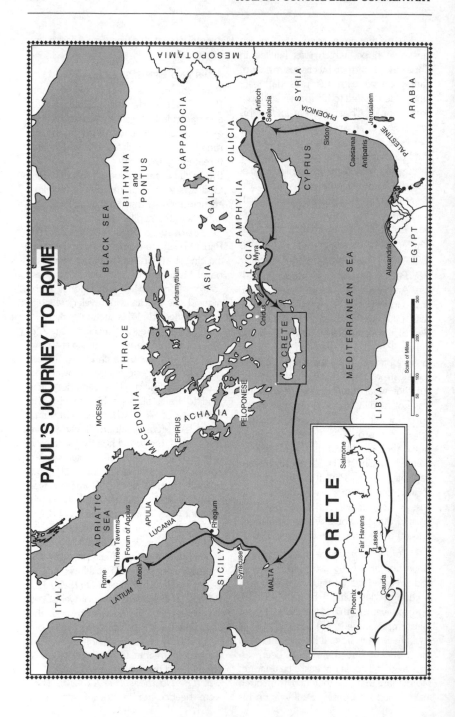

PAUL'S JOURNEY TO ROME

named Phoenix. They never made it. A violent Mediterranean storm overcame them. They took all possible measures, undergirding the ship with cables, throwing the ship's tackle and much of its cargo overboard.

4. *Paul's Words of Assurance (27:21-26).* While the storm raged unabated, Paul had a vision in which an angel assured him that God would deliver him and all those aboard the ship. God had a purpose for Paul—to witness in Rome before Caesar. Paul's presence guaranteed the safety of everyone. Paul urged them to take courage. Their ordeal was not over, however. The angel had also informed Paul that the ship would run aground on an island.

5. *The Prospect of Landing (27:27-32).* After two weeks of the storm, the sailors sensed they were near land, but the shores were rocky. Fearing they would break up, the sailors lowered the lifeboat in an attempt to save their own necks. Realizing what they were up to, Paul warned the centurion, and the boat was cut free. The crew would be needed in the rescue operation when the ship ran aground.

6. *Paul's Further Encouragement (27:33-38).* Paul continued to assure all 276 people aboard the ship that everyone would survive. He urged them to take some nourishment. Most of them were pagans. Paul witnessed to them through blessing the food with his prayer of thanksgiving to the God who was rescuing them.

7. *The Deliverance of All (27:39-44).* In the morning they saw a small bay where they planned to run the ship aground. They never made it. Striking a sandbar, the stern was broken up in the surf. Aware that they would forfeit their own lives if they lost any of their charges, the soldiers on board were ready to kill their prisoners. The centurion prevented

them, wishing to save Paul. Everyone was eventually rescued, just as the angel had assured Paul.

8. *Paul's Deliverance from the Viper (28:1-6).* They had landed on the island of Malta. The friendly Maltese helped them build a fire to warm themselves and dry out. In assisting with the fire, Paul was bitten by a poisonous snake. Roman folklore told a story of a fugitive who escaped shipwreck only to be killed soon after by a viper. The Maltese probably had in mind some such story when they expected Paul to die (v. 4). When he didn't, they tried to worship him as a god.

9. *The Hospitality of Publius (28:7-10).* The voyagers wintered on Malta. The islanders provided amply for their needs. Paul healed many sick persons on Malta, including the father of the chief administrator of the island.

10 . *The Final Leg to Rome (28:11-16).* Luke continued his travel narrative in some detail. The shipwrecked voyagers were able to continue on a ship from Alexandria that had wintered on Malta. The ship took them to the port of Puteoli, 130 miles south of Rome. Paul continued to Rome by foot. He was met about 40 miles south of the city by some brothers from the Roman church. When they reached Rome, Paul was placed under house arrest with a Roman soldier guarding him but also with some freedom of movement.

**Witness in Rome (28:17-31).** In Rome Paul continued his usual pattern of witness, beginning with the Jews.

1. *First Meeting with the Jews (28:17-22).* Paul was not free to go to the synagogues, so he invited the Jewish leaders to come to his house. He told them of his arrest in Jerusalem and of the events leading up to his appeal to Caesar. He assured them that he had no intention of making any counter charges against his fellow Jews. His only desire

was to share the message of Christ. Palestinian Judaism did not have direct jurisdiction over the synagogues of the Jewish Dispersion. That seems to be reflected in their response to Paul that they had received no word about him from Judea. They were, however, aware of the Christians.

2. *Separation from the Jews (28:23-28).* The Jewish leaders arranged a day to hear Paul at length. They brought many other Jews with them. Paul witnessed to them all day long. There was a divided response. Some believed, others rejected Paul's message. Paul then replied that he was turning to the Gentiles, quoting Isaiah 6:9-10 as a prophecy of the Jews' refusal to believe. His words seemed final, but they had seemed so on many occasions before. In town after town, Jewish rejection caused Paul to leave the synagogues and witness to the Gentiles. But, he would return to the synagogue in the next town. Paul never gave up on his people.

3. *Bold Witness to All (28:30-31).* Acts ends with Paul under house arrest for a period of two years, witnessing to all who came to see him. He had the freedom to carry on his witness to God's kingdom and to the Lord Jesus. Why does Acts end so abruptly? What happened to Paul? Did Luke intend to write a third volume which would begin with Paul's trial? We do not know. Luke almost surely did know the outcome of Paul's appeal. Later tradition has it that Paul was released, that he carried on a ministry in the west, and that later, during Nero's persecution of the Christians, he was martyred in Rome by beheading. Perhaps Luke deliberately stopped short in Paul's story in order to leave it open, as if to say "the Christian witness is a continuing story." The witness must still go on, "boldly and without hindrance."

## Questions for Reflection

1. Discuss the themes of Acts. Why were these themes important to Luke's readers? Why are they important to you?

2. How does Acts connect the Gospels and the Epistles? What does this teach us about the unity of the New Testament?

3. What are the distinguishing characteristics of the church in Acts? Are these emphases present in your church?

4. What can we learn about communicating the gospel message to our modern world from the preaching of the apostles, particularly in Acts 17?

## Sources for Additional Study

Longenecker, Richard. "The Acts of the Apostles." *The Expositor's Bible Commentary.* Grand Rapids: Zondervan.

Polhill, John B. *Acts.* New American Commentary. Nashville: Broadman & Holman, 1992.

Stott, John R. W. *The Spirit, the Church, and the World: The Message of Acts.* Downers Grove: InterVarsity, 1990.

# THE PAULINE LETTERS

## DAVID S. DOCKERY

Thirteen letters in the New Testament bear the name of Paul. They inform us about Paul, his beliefs, his ministry, and his activity. The letters generally focus on issues within the life of the church. As various issues and problems developed, help from the apostles was often sought. Sometimes messengers brought word to Paul of problems in the churches. His letters responded to these concerns. As a result the writings contain instruction; advice; rebuke; and exhortation in theological, ethical, social, personal, and liturgical matters.

Paul's Letters were written over a span of less than twenty years. His place among the writing apostles came by virtue of his intimate relationship and personal encounter with the risen Christ and the instruction he received from the Lord. These special experiences qualified him to be classified as one of the apostles, equal in authority to the twelve appointed by Jesus.

The Acts of the Apostles traces the key events in the life of Saul of Tarsus, the persecutor, who became Paul the apostle to the Gentiles. That story starts with his approving presence at the martyrdom of Stephen (Acts 7:58–8:3). He had studied the Jewish law with the great rabbi Gamaliel in Jerusalem (Acts 22:3). He surpassed his peers with a tremendous zeal to uphold the traditions of his people (Acts 26:5; see Gal. 1:13-14; Phil. 3:5). As he traveled to Damascus to persecute the believers there, he encountered the exalted Christ, and his life was radically changed (Acts 9:1-31).

Later he spent time alone with God in Arabia (Gal. 1:17). Here he came to realize that the crucified Jesus was raised from the dead, and He is Lord of all (Acts 9:5). The good news of salvation accomplished by Jesus' death and resurrection was the message to be proclaimed to all (Gal. 2:15-21). Surprisingly, Paul learned that this good news applied equally to both Jews and Gentiles (see Gal. 3:28). Paul's mission was specifically focused on the Gentiles, whom Paul had previously rejected (see Acts 9:15; Gal. 1:15-17). Paul ministered in Antioch from where his mission work (with Barnabas) began (Acts 11:25-26; 13:1-3). Three mission journeys took him across the four Roman provinces of Galatia, Asia, Achaia, and Macedonia. From these various locations he wrote his Letters (see the chart showing the relationship between his writings and his mission work, p. 540).

| PAUL'S MISSION TRAVELS AND LETTERS | | | |
|---|---|---|---|
| **Book of Acts** | **Activity** | **Approximate Date** | **Writing** |
| 9:1-19 | Paul's Conversion | 34–35 | |
| 9:26-29 | Visit to Jerusalem | 37–38 | |
| 11:27-30 | Second Visit to Jerusalem | 48 | |
| 13-14 | First Mission (Cyprus and Galatia) | 48–50 | Galatians |
| 15 | Jerusalem Council | 50 | |
| 16:1–18:22 | Second Mission (Galatia, Macedonia, Greece) | 51–53 | 1, 2 Thessalonians |
| 18:23–21:14 | Third Mission (Ephesus Macedonia, Greece) | 54–57 | 1, 2 Corinthians Romans |
| 21:15–26:32 | Arrest in Jerusalem, Trials and Imprisonment in Caesarea | 58–60 | |
| 27–28 | Voyage to Rome, Roman Imprisonment | 60–63 | Philemon Colossians Ephesians Philippians |
| | Release, Further Work, Final Imprisonment, and Death | | 1 Timothy Titus 2 Timothy |

# ROMANS

Romans has been called the most important letter ever written. Paul wrote his letter to the Romans from Corinth during his third missionary journey around A.D. 56–57 (see Acts 20:2-3).

**Setting.** Paul had never been to Rome, but Christians had been there for several years. We do not know how the church began in Rome. Most likely it started sometime shortly after Pentecost when new believers returned home and started to spread the gospel (see Acts 2:10-11).

Paul understood the importance and influence of a strong church in Rome. He wanted to strengthen the existing work in that place initially through the letter and secondly by visiting them (1:8-15; 15:14-33). For this reason Paul methodically and systematically outlined the foundational meaning of salvation in Jesus Christ, the foundation of Christianity. He described the human condition, the meaning of the gospel, God's plan for men and women, God's purpose for Israel, and the responsibilities of the Christian life and ministry.

Phoebe carried the letter to Rome. She was a "servant," or minister, of the church at Cenchrea (16:1), a marine suburb of Corinth.

**Literary Feature.** Romans is both a systematic theological treatise on central themes and a missionary document that applies those themes to practical issues in the Roman church.

The authenticity and integrity of this letter has rarely been doubted. Some have questioned whether chapters 15–16 were a part of the original letter. Four reasons have been suggested for this division.

1. Some manuscripts ending at chapter 14 circulated in the late second and early third centuries.

2. The letter has three doxologies that could possibly serve as endings (15:33; 16:24; 16:27).

3. Chapter 14 includes 16:25-27 in some manuscripts.

4. The so-called inappropriateness of the personal greetings in chapter 16.

The shorter version ending at chapter 14 indicates an influence from Marcion whose bias against Judaism and the Old Testament would have led him to find the discussion of the preparatory work of Judaism (15:1-29) to be offensive. As for the so-called misplaced endings, it was not uncommon for Paul to interject a doxological emphasis at any point in his writings (for example see 11:33-36). Finally, the people mentioned in chapter 16 probably were people with whom he had worked before and now were located in Rome.

All sixteen chapters of this grand epistle should be viewed as a literary whole. The letter is not only a summary of the apostle's thought on salvation in Jesus Christ, but also an expression of his desire to fellowship with the Roman Christians and recruit their support for his mission work to Spain.

**Purpose and Theology.** It is clear from the last two chapters of the letter that Paul planned to take the contribution from the Gentile churches to the Christians in Jerusalem (see 1 Cor. 16:1; 2 Cor. 8–9; Rom. 15:25-29). From Jerusalem he planned to sail for Rome (15:23-24). One important purpose for the letter was to alert the Romans of his coming so they could help him with his journey to Spain (15:24,28). Paul wanted to inform them of his plans and have them pray for their fulfillment (15:30-32).

In addition to this missionary purpose Paul stated the means by which the righteousness of God had been revealed (1:17). The thematic statement of chapters 1–8 is found in 1:16-17 (see Hab. 2:4). The theme of God's righteousness is paramount throughout the book. The first three chapters show that both Jews and Gentiles are under sin and that the atonement of Christ is applicable to both (3:21-31). Chapter 4 shows how the Old Testament promises to Abraham and David are significant for both since Abraham is the spiritual father of believing Gentiles and Jews.

In chapters 5–8 Paul expounds the meaning of this gift of righteousness. Whether Jew or Gentile, those who trust in the redemptive work of God in Jesus Christ will have "peace with God" (5:1) and will live free from the wrath of God. They will be freed from the penalty and power of sin (chap. 6) but will still struggle experientially with reality of sin and the power of the law (chap. 7). Chapter 8 gloriously describes the believers' freedom from death.

A third emphasis is related to the possible conflict between the Jewish and Gentile segments in the church at Rome. Whether the Judaizers, who had hounded Paul's ministry elsewhere (see Galatians), had reached Rome we do not know. Paul emphasized the historical and chronological priority of the Jews (see 1:16; 2:9-10). He stated the "advantage" in being a Jew (see 3:1-2; 9:4-5) and pointed out that "since there is only one God," He is the God of the Gentiles and Jews (3:29-30). "Jews and Gentiles alike all are under sin" (3:9) and are redeemed by the sacrifice of Christ (3:21-31).

In chapters 9-11 Paul explained Israel's place in the future purposes of God. Believing Gentiles had been brought into God's program of salvation, but God did not cast off Israel (11:1,2). God will graft them back into the tree from which they have been temporarily separated because of their unbelief. This God will do if they trust in Jesus as the true Messiah and Savior (11:23). God continues to have a believing "remnant" (11:5) "until the full number of the Gentiles has come in" (11:25).

The final theological theme runs throughout the letter. It is a defense and vindication of God's nature. Paul refuted those implied undertones that questioned God's goodness, justice, and wisdom as seen in His plan of salvation. God is "just and the justifier" of those who believe in Jesus (3:26). Paul exulted in "the depth of the riches of the wisdom and knowledge of God" (11:33). He challenged the questioners, "Let God be true, and every man a liar" (3:4).

I. Introduction and Theme (1:1-17)
II. The Human Condition and God's Wrath (1:18–3:20)
III. Righteousness by Faith (3:21–4:25)
IV. God's Righteousness Explained (5:1–8:39)
V. God's Faithful Purposes (9:1–11:36)
VI. Righteousness in Christian Living and Service (12:1–15:13)
VII. Conclusion (15:14–16:27)

### INTRODUCTION (1:1-15)

Paul identified himself as a "servant" of God, an "apostle" who was "set apart for the gospel of God." He offered greetings to the Christians at Rome. Paul told them of his prayers for them and his eagerness to proclaim the gospel there.

## DOCTRINAL EMPHASES IN THE LETTERS OF PAUL

| Paul's Letters | Purpose | Major Doctrine(s) | Key Passage | Other Key Doctrines | Influence of the Letter |
|---|---|---|---|---|---|
| Romans | To express the nature of the gospel, its relation to the OT and Jewish law, and its transforming power | Salvation | Rom 3:21-26 | God Humanity The Church | Martin Luther (1515), through preparing lectures on Romans, felt himself "to be reborn." |
| 1 Corinthians | To respond to questions about marriage, idol food, public worship; to discourage factions; to instruct on resurrection | The Church The Resurrection | 1 Cor 12:12-31 1 Cor 15:1-11 | God Humanity | The hymn on love in Chapter 13 is among the most familiar and loved chapters in Paul's writings. |
| 2 Corinthians | To prepare readers for Paul's third visit and to defend Paul and the gospel he taught against false teachers | The Church Jesus Christ Salvation | 2 Cor 5:11-6:2 | God | Called by C.K. Barrett "the fullest and most passionate account of what Paul meant by apostleship." |
| Galatians | To stress freedom in Christ against Jewish legalism while avoiding moral license | Salvation | Gal 2:15-21 | Christian Ethics The Church Election | A sermon on the Book of Galatians brought peace of heart to John Wesley. "I felt I did trust Christ alone for salvation." |
| Ephesians | To explain God's eternal purpose and grace and the goals God has for the church | Salvation The Church | Eph 2:1-22 Eph 3:14-21 | God Jesus Christ | Called by Samuel Taylor Coleridge "one of the divinest of compositions." |
| Philippians | To commend Epaphroditus; to affirm generosity; to encourage unity, humility, and faithfulness even to death | Christian Unity Joy in Salvation | Phil 1:3-11 | Christian Ethics The Church Prayer | Bengel (1850) described as "Summa epistlae, gaudes, gaudete," which means "The sum of the epistles is 'I rejoice; rejoice ye.'" |
| Colossians | To oppose false teachings related to a matter and spirit dualism and to stress the complete adequacy of Christ | Jesus Christ | Col 1:15-23 | The Church Prayer God | Arius of Alex. (318) used Col 1:15, from a hymn on the supremacy of Christ, to undermine Christ's deity. Arianism pronounced heretical at Councils of Nicea (325) and Constantinople (381). |

## DOCTRINAL EMPHASES IN THE LETTERS OF PAUL (continued)

| Paul's Letters | Purpose | Major Doctrine(s) | Key Passage | Other Key Doctrines | Influence of the Letter |
|---|---|---|---|---|---|
| 1 Thessalonians | To encourage new converts during persecution; to instruct them in Christian living; and to assure them concerning the second coming | Last Things | 1 Thess 4:13-18 | Evangelism<br>Prayer<br>God | Every chapter of 1 Thessalonians ends with a reference to the second coming. |
| 2 Thessalonians | To encourage new converts in persecution and to correct misunderstandings about the Lord's return | Last Things | 2 Thess 1:3-12 | Prayer<br>The Church<br>Evil & Suffering | With only three chapters, the letter is one of Paul's shortest yet because of 2:3-10 one of the most extensively studied. |
| 1 Timothy | To encourage Timothy as minister, to refute false doctrine, and to instruct about church organization and leadership | Church Leaders | 1 Tim 3:1-15 | God<br>Christian Ethics<br>Salvation | Known as a "pastoral epistle" since the early part of the eighteenth century, Thomas Aquinas (d.1274) described 1 Timothy as a "pastoral textbook." |
| 2 Timothy | To encourage Christians in the face of persecution and false doctrine | Education | 2 Tim 2:14-19 | Evil & Suffering<br>Jesus Christ<br>Prayer | Used by Augustine (d.430) in book four on *Christian Doctrine* to support the importance of Christian teachers. |
| Titus | To instruct church leaders, to advise about groups in the church, and to teach Christian ethics | Salvation | Titus 2:11-14 | God<br>Christian Ethics<br>The Church<br>Sin | Called the "Magna Charta" of Christian liberty. |
| Philemon | To effect reconciliation between a runaway slave and his Christian master | Christian Ethics | Phlm 8-16 | Prayer<br>The Church<br>Discipleship | Called by Emil Brunner (d.1965) a classic testimony to what is meant by Christian justice. |

## THEME (1:16-17)

The theme is summarized in these two verses as the revelation of a righteousness of God. "The righteous will live by faith" is as some have suggested a summary of Pauline theology as a whole.

The negative manner is a sober reflection of the reality that the gospel is something of which Christians will, while still in the world, continually be tempted to be ashamed (see Mark 8:38; Luke 9:26; 2 Tim. 1:8).

The gospel is the almighty power of God directed toward the salvation of men and women. Paul's understanding of the gospel made him not yield to the temptation to be ashamed of the gospel but live to proclaim it.

For Paul, eternal issues were at stake. Those whose minds were blinded and failed to believe and obey the gospel were perishing (2 Cor. 4:3). They would ultimately fall under the divine wrath (2 Thess. 1:9). Everyone who believes, whether Jew or Gentile, the gospel effectively becomes the power of God for salvation.

This gospel reveals "a righteousness of God." Righteousness denotes the right standing God gives to believers. Believers are righteous (justified) through faith and by faith but never on account of faith. Faith is not itself our righteousness, rather it is the outstretched empty hand that receives righteousness by receiving Christ. Paul's concept of righteousness or justification is a complete and total work of God, and we can do nothing to earn it. (See article on "Justification by Faith", p. 549.)

## GOD'S WRATH (1:18-32)

Before Paul set forth his message of righteousness by faith (3:21–8:31), he showed the need for it. The human race stands condemned, helpless, and hopeless apart from God.

Even though God had given sufficient revelation of his existence and power in the world through creation, men and women had nevertheless become idolatrous and polytheistic with resulting moral degradations. Paul claimed that God gave them up to their dishonorable lusts, passions, conduct, and all kinds of evil. The refusal to acknowledge and glorify God results in a downward path: worthless thinking, moral insensitivity, and religious stupidity.

## ALL FACE JUDGMENT (2:1-16)

The focus of this section is on the fact that God will judge all people. Obviously some Gentiles had high ethical standards and moral lifestyles. They were not characterized by the blanket judgment expressed in 1:18-32. They condemned the widespread idolatry and corruption among those around them. But Paul insisted that God's judgment applied to them as well. They were responsible because they too were guilty of the same kinds of things. The judgment is based on God's revelation in creation (1:18-32) and in their consciences. Paul's emphasis is on God's just judgment.

## JEWS ARE GUILTY (2:17-29)

The Jews had no better standing even though they had received God's special revelation through the law of Moses. Though they knew the will of God expressed in the law, they had not kept the law. One's heritage does not make one a true Jew with right standing before God. Rather, true Jews are only those who have received the regenerating work of the Spirit in their hearts.

## JUDGMENT IS JUST (3:1-20)

Paul described the advantages of the Jews: primarily they have been "entrusted with the very words of God." To suggest that God is unfair (as the questions of 3:5,7 appear to do) is to blaspheme God. Those who question God's judgment are therefore themselves condemned. Paul brings together a series of Old Testament quotations to show that Jews and Gentiles have all sinned, and therefore all are held accountable to God.

## JUSTIFIED BY FAITH (3:21-31)

The gravity of the situation is summarized in 3:23: "All have sinned and fall short of the glory of God." God thus has provided a righteousness for unrighteous people through the atonement of Jesus Christ. The way of forgiveness and freedom has been offered to all, Jews and Gentiles, through the sacrificial death of Christ.

Four words need special explanation. In verse 24 he said that all who believe "are justified." *Justified* is a legal term meaning to *declare righteous*. On the basis of what Christ has accomplished for sinners on the cross, God now views those who believe in Christ from an eschatological perspective. That is, He sees them not as they are but as they will be in Christ. He sees them as He sees Christ: perfect, holy, and without sin (see 2 Cor. 5:21).

God's justification of those who believe is provided "freely by his grace." Grace points to God's free and unmerited favor by which God has without charge to believers declared them to have a right standing in His sight.

God could declare persons righteous only by dealing with their sin. This He did in the "redemption that came by Jesus Christ." The term *redemption* means *a price was paid*. The death of Christ on the cross was the payment price for human sin that secured release from the bondage to sin, self, and Satan.

In verse 25 Paul stated that Christ Jesus was presented as "a sacrifice of atonement" (sometimes translated "propitiation" or "expiation"). Perhaps the idea of satisfaction best illuminates this

Pauline concept for us. In Jesus Christ His Son, God has graciously satisfied His own holy demands and directed against Himself His own righteous wrath that the sinner deserves. By Christ's sacrifice God has satisfied, or propitiated, His own wrath.

As a result God is both "just and the one who justifies" those who have faith in Jesus. Therefore Jew and Gentile alike stand justified not by their works but by their faith in the finished work of Christ.

## FAITH (4:1-25)

The apostle had shown that God declares Jews and Gentiles righteous by their faith in Jesus. How was this different from God's dealings with His people in former times? Paul demonstrated the unity and continuity of God's plan by illustrations from Abraham and David. Paul showed that God declared Abraham righteous by faith, not by works or ritual or the law. Neither Abraham nor any other person had anything to boast about before God because of what he had done but by his faith in God's promise (see Gen. 15:6).

## GRACE ABOUNDS (5:1-21)

Paul argued that by the impact of this righteous gift believers are given salvation from the wrath of God. God has reconciled godless and unrighteous enemies to Himself. Thus they "have peace with God through our Lord Jesus Christ." Paul, by way of a typology, demonstrated that sin and death came to men and women through Adam; righteousness and life, through Jesus Christ. Sin had been intensified by the transgression of the law. Thus greater grace was needed. But where sin abounded, grace abounded all the more.

## NEW LIFE IN CHRIST (6:1-14)

God's provided righteousness involves more than declaring believers righteous on the basis of faith. He declared the duty

# JUSTIFICATION BY FAITH

Justification is the act of God whereby He declares that a sinful person is righteous, based on a belief and trust in Jesus Christ rather than in the person's own good works. It is a change of state from guilt to righteousness.

*Biblical Overview.* The concept of justification has its background in the Old Testament. The Hebrew term for *to justify* or *to be righteous* indicated that one was declared free from guilt. The idea carried legal connotations. This can be seen in usages where justification is contrasted with condemnation (see Deut. 25:1; Prov. 17:15; Isa. 5:23). It can also be found in settings that imply a process of judgment (see Gen. 18:25; Ps. 143:2).

Justification was not merely an ethical quality of character. Rather, it emphasized being righteous; that is, having a right relationship to a certain standard. This standard was God's very own nature and person. As such only He could could perfectly judge whether a person had lived up to the criterion for the relationship. Therefore justification in the Old Testament involved declaring that a person had been faithful to the requirements of the relationship in accordance to the standard given by God.

The New Testament further advances this idea, mainly in Paul's writings. His understanding of justification is the starting place for developing the implications of the central truth of the gospel, namely, that God forgives believing sinners.

From justification flows the understanding that God gives grace and faith equally to all people (Rom. 1:16; Gal. 3:8-14). The concept of grace is defined in accordance with justification (Rom. 3:24). Paul's explanation for the saving significance of Christ's life, death, and resurrection arises from justification (Rom. 3:24; 5:16).

The revelation of God's love at the cross of Jesus (Rom. 5:5-9), human liberation from sin's bondage (Gal. 3:13; Eph. 1:7), a reconciled relationship with God (2 Cor. 5:18; Gal. 2:17), adoption into God's family (Gal. 4:6-8), and assurance in the Christian life (Rom. 5:1-11) are also examined in light of justification.

*Theological Considerations.* Imputation is an act of God whereby He credits Christ's righteousness to sinners who believe and accept His gift. They are then pronounced by God as righteous.

This is not to say God considers believers merely as if they had never sinned. This would only indicate they were innocent. Justification goes beyond this understanding. Christ has paid the penalty for sin and guilt and has fulfilled the just requirements of the law. God the Father applied Christ's perfect work to the believer's life in such a way that he or she is restored to a right standing with God. In this way God declares a person *righteous*.

The basis for a believer's justification is the death of Jesus Christ. People are not able to justify themselves by performing good works (Rom. 3:28; Gal. 2:16). Christ was "made sin" (2 Cor. 5:21) in the place of sinners, dying as their substitute. God's justice was demonstrated by punishing sin through the death of Christ (Rom. 3:21-26). In Christ's death God justified Himself (by punishing sin), as well as justifying believing sinners (by crediting Christ's righteousness to them).

The way a person receives God's justification is through faith. Faith is an absolute reliance in Jesus Christ and His work for salvation. Faith should not be considered a good work (Rom. 3:28), for it rests on grace (Rom. 4:16) and excludes works (Eph. 2:8-9). Faith is a condition that has no merit in itself; rather, it rests upon the merit oferson and work of Jesus Christ. Justification is something that is completely undeserved. It is not an attainment but the gracious gift of God. Not every sinner is justified, only those who believe in Jesus Christ.

Good works do not procure justification. Works, however, are the way people demonstrate that they are justified by faith (Jas. 2:18).

Paul is the only New Testament writer to use "justify" as a term for God's act of accepting people when they believe. When James spoke of being justified, he used the word in a general sense of proving a genuine and right relationship before God and people. James wanted to deny the character of a superficial faith that does not produce works for God's kingdom.

to reject sin and do what is right because of the new life received in Christ.

Paul argued that it would be a perversion of grace to argue that since grace results in freedom and [grace] increases where sin increases, people should continue in sin so that grace can abound. Paul contended that those who have been justified by Christ have died to the power of sin, which no longer has enslaving power. Believers have been identified ("baptized") with the death and resurrection of Christ, the source of their spiritual life. Since believers are dead to sin and its power, they must realize they have new life in Christ and not yield themselves to unrighteousness.

## SLAVES OF RIGHTEOUSNESS (6:15-23)

Paul stated that sin results in death. Believers have been set free from sin and no longer are in bondage to it. Now believers are slaves of righteousness and alive to God. They are now to reject sin and do what is right by serving God.

Chapter 6, like chapters 3–5, asserts the importance of Christ's death. Again the death of Christ is reasserted, but not in isolation as the death of the righteous for the unrighteous. Here the believer has been joined to Christ. Death to sin calls for resolute separation from sin, and resurrection means a new type of life in response to God.

## THE HUMAN CONTRADICTION (7:1-13)

In chapter 7 Paul pictured himself in a representative way as one wanting to live righteously and fulfill the demands of the law but frustrated by sin that still indwelt him. Nowhere else in Paul's letters, and nowhere else in ancient literature, is there such a penetrating description of the human plight and contradiction as in 7:1-25. There is a remarkable parallelism

between what chapter 6 says about sin and what chapter 7 says about the law.

Paul addressed the issue of the believer and the law by a somewhat imperfect analogy with the husband and wife. These verses demonstrate the character of the law. It is "holy, righteous, and good." Paul described the role of the law in his transitional experience before his conversion.

## THE CHRISTIAN STRUGGLE (7:14-25)

The interpretation of these verses is as difficult as any in the New Testament. The text is gripped with tension. Paul painted for the readers a picture of the Christian life with all its anguish and its simultaneous hopefulness. This is the ongoing struggle with which believers are involved throughout their lives. Deliverance is promised. Victory is sure, but it is an eschatological hope.

Paul described one who hates sin and judges it in his or her life. In this struggle the believer constantly continues to strive for the good. Both the struggle of chapter 7 and the deliverance of chapter 8 are true and real in the believer's journey. Though Paul spoke autobiographically of the tensions of life as he experienced them, it remains apparent that he spoke by implication for all who have the struggle and need for God's enablement and blessing.

## NO CONDEMNATION (8:1-17)

Paul's exposition shifted to a focus on the role of the Holy Spirit, who brings pardon and power for the children of God. Those who have been justified have been freed from death. "Therefore, there is now no condemnation for those who are in Christ Jesus." God will give life to their mortal bodies through His spirit, who indwells believers. If believers live according to the sinful nature, they will die; but if by the Spirit believers put to death the misdeeds of the body, they will live.

In contrast to the control of sin, which enslaves to the point of fear, believers have received the Spirit of adoption. So instead of retreating in fear, Christians can approach God in an intimate way, calling Him "Abba, Father." "Abba" is a transliteration of the Aramaic term for father, implying great familiarity and intimacy (see Mark 14:36; Gal. 4:6). The portrait is one of solidarity and relatedness through the Spirit.

Verse 17 concludes and climaxes a list of conditional "ifs" (see 8:9-11,13). He lifts the issue of suffering beyond their own inner moral struggles to suffering together with Christ as a prelude to being glorified together with Him.

### REDEMPTIVE SUFFERING (8:18-27)

Hope transforms suffering. Paul pointed to creation's longing for its redemption and believers' eagerly awaiting their ultimate adoption and redemption. Here we see God's plan of redemptive suffering moving to its fulfillment at the end of the age.

The Spirit Himself groans for believers as they pray and anticipate their glorification. Even though the Spirit groans with words that cannot be expressed, the Father knows what the Spirit is thinking. Though believers during this in-between time are often unsure and unaware of what to pray, the Holy Spirit communicates their concerns for them.

### MORE THAN CONQUERORS (8:28-39)

Paul's conclusion to the first half of the book emphasized the majesty and glory of God and pointed to the certainty of God's redemptive plan. All that happens to them rests in the sovereign hand of God, who in all things "works for the good of those who love him." Believers gain assurance knowing that God is for them (8:31). In all the testings and suffer-ings that confront believers, they can be confident that they are more than con-querors through Christ who loved them. Believers can expect difficulties in this age; yet they can be certain that nothing will be able to separate them from the love of God that is in Christ Jesus."

### ISRAEL'S PLACE (9:1-5)

The apostle could not deal with the issue of men and women, whether Jew or Gentile, being given a right standing before God without addressing the place of Israel in God's plan. Paul stated with great emotion his concern for the Jews, his own people. They had a special place in God's purposes in the past. They were the recipients of adoption, glory, cove-nants, the law, the promises, temple worship, and the patriarchs.

### GOD IS FAITHFUL (9:6-13)

Paul here described God's sovereign choice of His people. Everything that has taken place in redemptive history has been due to God's faithfulness to the promise He gave to Abraham and his descendants. With Jesus, Paul could affirm that "salvation is from the Jews" (John 4:22). The problem for Paul was, How could Israel, as the recipient of all these blessings, fail to receive and recog-nize the promised Messiah?

Paul answered that God elected Abra-ham, but not all the descendants of Abra-ham receive his promises. The choice of God had nothing to do with their charac-ter or worth; it was a matter of God's pur-pose.

### GOD CHOSE ISRAEL (9:14-33)

Paul contended that there is no injustice with God. His choices show forth his power so that His name might be pro-claimed in all the earth. He had chosen Israel to serve His purposes as Lord over all. Only by faith are people declared righteous before God. Those who attempted to establish their righteousness on any other basis stumbled over the Messiah.

## BELIEVE AND CONFESS (10:1-21)

Paul argued that only a remnant of Israel ever believed (9:27-29). In rejecting Christ Israel was following a precedent already at work in earlier days. The Jews' zeal was commendable but nevertheless misguided. The only way of acceptance before God was faith in Christ and was (and is) within the reach of all. Those who believe in their heart and confess with their mouth "Jesus is Lord" will be saved. People cannot believe unless they can hear, and they cannot hear without a preacher. Though Israel heard, they still rejected God's message.

## CALL TO HUMILITY (11:1-24)

Next, Paul claimed that since a remnant of Israel had believed the gospel, it was a clear indication that Israel as a whole will yet believe. Though God may have temporarily rejected Israel, He has not finally or irrevocably rejected them. When Israel rejected God's message, the opportunity was given to the Gentiles, who were grafted into the tree. Gentiles, however, were warned not to be proud of their acceptance but humbly to rely on God's grace.

## ISRAEL IN HIS PURPOSE (11:25-36)

Israel's alienation is not necessarily final. God still has a future and purpose for Israel. The Gentiles are saved by a temporary hardening of Israel, which will continue until the "full number of the Gentiles has come in." Still, within God's purposes "all Israel will be saved." Paul coded this section by praising the marvelous wisdom of God demonstrated in His purposes for both Jews and Gentiles.

## BE TRANSFORMED (12:1-2)

Paul appealed for the dedication of the whole of life to God. The basis of the appeal rested in the mercy of God. As believers are transformed in their minds and conformed to the image of Christ, they will be able to discern, desire, and approve the will of God. God's will is good and holy; it is sufficient for every need. Only through spiritual renewal can believers do the will of God.

## SPIRITUAL GIFTS (12:3-21)

Believers' dedication to God and the accompanying transformed lifestyle is lived out through the exercise of spiritual gifts (see 1 Cor. 12–14). Christians are to live together in love as members of Christ's body, the church. With their various gifts they are to serve one another. The rest of the chapter consists of a series of short exhortations that focus on the outworking of love in all relationships and under all circumstances.

## CHRISTIANS AND RULERS (13:1-14)

Christians should recognize that civil government is ordained of God. Government is God's servant to discipline the disobedient and carry out His righteous will. Love is the sum of the Christian's duty. Christian conduct is vitally related to the hope of Christ's return and the believer's ultimate transformation.

## RELATIONSHIPS (14:1-23)

Harmonious relationships are important. Believers should live without judging others and without influencing others to violate their consciences. Not only should the mature not hinder the weak with their freedom, but the weak must avoid restricting those who have discovered Christian freedom. Mutual love and respect are the marks of true disciples of Christ.

## PLEASE OTHERS (15:1-13)

The apostle described how Christian living involves the desire to please others and not oneself. A need exists to welcome others as Christ Himself has received Gentiles as well as Jews to be His people.

## CONCLUSION (15:14–16:27)

This concluding section contains Paul's travel plans and his role as a minister to the Gentiles. He stated his aim to proclaim the gospel where it had not been preached. He wanted to go to Rome in order to extend the Christian mission westward to Spain. He requested prayer from the church for his mission.

Chapter 16 closes typically with greetings and commendations from various individuals. Greetings are offered to twenty-seven people, including a significant number of women. Paul appealed for the church to avoid divisions and disunity. He offered greetings from his colleagues and closed with an appropriate doxology: "To the only wise God be glory forever through Jesus Christ. Amen."

***Theological Significance.*** Paul's message to the Romans means that the church must proclaim that God is the giver of salvation, the gift of righteousness, and this gift is for all who will receive it by faith. The church must not call for a faith that can be separated from faithfulness. Assurance must be grounded not in human decision but in the atoning and justifying work of Jesus Christ.

The thematic emphasis of the believer's righteousness in Christ means that our acceptance and worth before God cannot be earned but only received. When we feel depressed, discouraged, or defeated, we must remind ourselves that God has reconciled us, accepted us, and given us value and significance in His sight because of the work of Jesus Christ for us.

When troubled from all sides, we are reminded that God is for us, and nothing can separate us from the love of Christ (8:31-39). When divisions occur in the church, we must turn to Paul's exhortation for mutual love, concern, and service for one another. No one has a superior place in Christ's body because of inherent worth, heritage, accomplishments, or background. There is, therefore, no place for human boasting or claim of special privilege. All nations are invited to come to Christ, in whom there is no condemnation for those in Christ Jesus.

### Questions for Reflection

1. How did Paul express the idea of right standing before God?

2. How are believers to understand their relationship to the law?

3. How are believers to live with the tensions of struggle, suffering, and victory as described in chapters 7–8?

4. How does Israel's unbelief relate to God's redemptive purpose?

5. What did Paul say about the responsibilities of Christians in their service in the church and relationships with one another (12:1–14:23)?

### Sources for Additional Study

Cranfield, C. E. B., *Romans: A Shorter Commentary.* Grand Rapids: Eerdmans, 1985.

Hendriksen, William. *Exposition of Paul's Epistle to the Romans.* New Testament Commentary. Grand Rapids: Baker, 1980.

Moo, Douglas J. *Romans 1–8.* Chicago: Moody, 1990.

Mounce, Robert H. *Romans.* New American Commentary. Nashville: Broadman & Holman, 1995.

Vaughan, Curtis and Bruce Corley. *Romans: A Study Guide Commentary.* Grand Rapids: Zondervan, 1976.

# 1 CORINTHIANS

The letter (1:1-2; 16:21) as well as church tradition acknowledges Paul as the author of 1 Corinthians. This affirmation generally has gone unchallenged. The letter was written around A.D. 55 near the end of Paul's three-year ministry in Ephesus (see 1 Cor. 16:5-9; Acts 20:31).

**The City of Corinth.** Corinth was one of the chief commercial cities of the Roman Empire. Its location made it a natural center of commerce and transportation. It had two ports: Cenchrea, six miles to the east of Corinth on the Aegean Sea (see Rom. 16:1), and Lechaeum, a port on the Corinthian Gulf that opened westward to the Adriatic Sea. Sailing in those days was very hazardous, and rounding the southern tip of Greece was a troublesome voyage. To avoid this detour, eastbound shipping between Rome and Asia used the isthmus at Corinth as a portage, unloading their cargoes and carrying them overland to be reloaded at the opposite port. Corinth was thus called the bridge of the seas. It was also a gateway for north-south routes between the Peloponnesus and mainland Greece. As a commercial center it was famous for arts and crafts.

Ancient Corinth was completely destroyed in 146 B.C. by the Roman general Mummius because it had taken the lead in an attempted revolt by the Greeks against the rising power of the Roman Empire. At that time its art treasures and wealth were said to have equaled those from Athens. For nearly one hundred years the city lay in ruins. In 44 B.C. Julius Caesar sent a colony of soldiers to rebuild it, making it the seat of the Roman province of Achaia. Almost immediately it assumed the former prominence it had as the richest and most powerful city of Greece.

Corinth had two patron deities. Poseidon, god of the sea, was appropriately reflected in the naval power and devotion to the sea. The other deity, Aphrodite, goddess of sexual love, was reflected in the city's reputation for immorality. The temple was central to the worship of Aphrodite. It boasted one thousand female prostitutes available to the people of the city and to all the visitors. Most of these women were famous for their great beauty. The income of the temple prostitutes provided a major source of the city's income. This practice, coupled with the looseness often characteristic of a port city of a mixed and transient population, gave Corinth a reputation far beyond the cities of its day.

To demonstrate this fact, the Greeks invented a term, *to Corinthianize,* which meant *to live an immoral life.* To call a young woman "a Corinthian" meant she was an immoral person. Paul wrote what perhaps was a descriptive account of Corinth in his letter to the Romans (see Rom. 1:18-32).

**The Church at Corinth.** The church was a picture of converts who had come out of this background (see 1 Cor. 6:11). The church had several problems, among them a leadership problem producing divisions in the church (1:10-17). Immoral practices were not being dealt with (5:1–6:20). An enthusiastic group in the church flaunted their spiritual gifts (12:1–14:40). A legalistic group was concerned about dietary laws (8:1–10:32). Some were abusing the Lord's Supper (11:17-34), and others were offering false teachings regarding the resurrection (15:1-58). These matters—in addition to its multiethnic makeup of Greeks, Romans, and Jews and a mixture of social classes including rich, poor, and slave—made for a unique and troubled congregation.

**Occasion.** Paul had been to Corinth and stayed for eighteen months (see Acts 18). During this time he had established the church. He possibly visited again for a short time between the letters to the Corinthians and the time he was in Corinth when he wrote Romans. Some have conjectured four visits and have rearranged the order quite a bit.

The apostle had received information from different sources concerning the conditions in the Corinthian church. Members of Chloe's household had informed him of the various factions in the church (1:11). Stephanus, Fortunatus, and Achaicus came to Paul in Ephesus to bring a contribution to his ministry (16:17).

**Purpose and Theology.** Paul dealt with several problems in this letter. He learned of these matters through the report from Chloe's people (1:11), common rumors (5:1), and from information received from the church (7:1; 8:1; 12:1; 16:1). Paul wrote to answer the questions the Corinthians had put to him, but he had other concerns as well. Although the church was quite gifted (1:4-7), it was equally immature and unspiritual (3:1-4). Paul wanted to restore the church in its areas of weakness. Through the inspiration of the Holy Spirit, he expounded the Bible's clearest exposition on the Lord's Supper (11:17-34), the resurrection (15:1-58), and spiritual gifts (12:1–14:40).

Yet the focus of 1 Corinthians is not on doctrinal theology but pastoral theology. This letter deals with the problem of those who bring division to the body of Christ (1:11–3:4), with the treatment of fellow Christians who sin (5:1-13), with matters of sexuality in marriage and divorce (7:1-40), with propriety in church worship (11:2-34), and with disputes about food (8:1–11:1).

## INTRODUCTION (1:1-9)

Paul began this letter in customary fashion, identifying himself (with Sosthenes) as the writer. The recipients were primarily "the church of God in Corinth" (see Acts 20:28; 2 Cor. 1:1). Generally, however, the letter was addressed to "all those everywhere who call on the name of the Lord Jesus Christ." The greeting is followed by a typical Pauline salutation (see Gal. 1:3; Eph. 1:2) and a lengthy expression of thanksgiving. Here he offered thanks for their reception of the gospel, their giftedness, and particularly for God's faithfulness.

## CONCERNING DIVISIONS (1:10-17)

Paul's first major topic was the problem of divisions in the church. Some were claiming to follow Paul, some Apollos, others Cephas (Peter), and yet others Christ. The leaders themselves were not the cause of division. Most likely the superspiritualists claiming to follow Christ were the major source of the problem.

Paul disclaimed responsibility for the situation and showed its sinfulness and folly. God does not act in the way human wisdom might expect. God redeemed men and women by the foolishness of the cross, not by anything that would enhance human pride. The gospel message did not originate in profound human thought but in the Holy Spirit Himself.

### INFANTS IN CHRIST (1:18–3:4)

The Corinthian church showed a great misunderstanding of the essential truth of the gospel. The Corinthians evidenced a wrong concept of wisdom, a wrong concept of the gospel, and a wrong concept of spirituality. It must be remembered that God's wisdom is something that those "without the Spirit" cannot accept. The Corinthians had an improper attitude regarding church leaders. They demonstrated they were "mere infants in Christ."

### PARTNERS IN GOD'S WORK (3:5-9)

Paul and Apollos were not in competition with each other. They were partners in the work of God. One "planted" while another "watered." Each one did his part, but God brought about the growth.

### CHRIST THE FOUNDATION (3:10-23)

The foundation of the church was not the church leaders but Jesus Christ. Each person builds on this foundation. What is built may be something valuable or something worthless. Final evaluation of the value of one's work will be revealed at the day of judgment. Paul explained the condition for rewards with appropriate warnings for leaders and followers.

### CHRISTIAN LEADERS (4:1-21)

Paul's warnings do not mean human leaders are unimportant. People are saved only by Christ, and there is no other basis for salvation. Church leaders build on the foundation. From this thought Paul appealed to the Corinthians to act on what he had written. The apostle emphasized both the responsibility of leaders and the importance of their example. They were "entrusted with the secret things of God." These secret things granted to these leaders are things that human wisdom cannot discover but can only be revealed by God to His people.

### CONCERNING IMMORALITY (5:1-13)

The apostle had heard reports of sexual immorality among them. He reminded the church that incest was considered a reprobate act even by pagans. The Corinthians, however, had apparently done nothing to deal with the detestable evil. Worse than that they were proud of this situation. Paul urged them to discipline the man involved by handing him "over to Satan so that the sinful nature may be destroyed and his spirit saved on the day of the Lord." This abandonment to Satan was to be accomplished not by some magical incantation but by expelling the man from the church (see 5:2,7,11,13). To expel him meant to turn him over to the devil's territory, severed from any connection with God's people.

Paul ordered the church not ever to eat with such a man. This means that intimate association with an immoral person, especially together at the Lord's table, would cause the unbelieving world to think that the church approves such ungodly living. The church must exercise spiritual discipline over the members of the church (see Matt. 18:15-18).

### THE SPIRIT'S TEMPLE (6:1-20)

Paul then chastised them for their factious spirit. Their active part in lawsuits before heathen judges evidenced their carnality. Sexual relations outside the marriage bond are a perversion of the divinely established marriage union. Believers have been bought by Christ.

# THE LORD'S SUPPER

The Lord's Supper was instituted by the command of Christ and by His example as well. On the night before His death, Christ gathered with His disciples to eat the Passover meal (see Matt. 26:26-29; Mark 14:22-25; Luke 22:17-20).

Since the Supper was celebrated in connection with the Passover, we may assume the bread was unleavened. Jesus gave thanks (*eucharisteo*, from which the idea of Eucharist comes) for the meal. That the institution of the Lord's Supper was connected with the Passover meal is clear in the phrase "after the Supper" (1 Cor. 11:25), meaning after the Passover meal. It is practically certain that 1 Corinthians was written before the completion of the Gospels, which means that Paul's account is the earliest record we have of the institution of the Lord's Supper.

*The Names of the Supper.* The Supper is identified six different ways in the New Testament: (1) Lord's Supper (1 Cor. 11:20); (2) Lord's Table (1 Cor. 10:21); (3) Breaking of Bread (Acts 2:42; 20:7); (4) Communion (1 Cor. 10:16); (5) Eucharist (1 Cor. 11:24); and (6) Love Feast (some manuscript readings of 2 Pet. 2:13; Jude 12).

*The Meaning of the Supper.* The Supper's initial focus was table fellowship around a common meal. As the bread and wine were taken, the Lord's presence was to be recalled in the words "in remembrance of me" (1 Cor. 11:24). To recall means to transport an action that is buried in the past in such a way that its original potency and vitality are not lost but are carried over into the present. It is a remembrance of the life and death of the Lord.

Just as the Passover was the means that dynamically allowed Jews to relive the past experience of their forebears in the land of Egypt, the Lord's Supper takes believers back to the scenes of the Lord's redemption, leading them again to receive the blessings of the Lord's passion.

The bread symbolizes His sinless life that qualified Him to be a perfect sacrifice for sin. It represents His body in which He actually bore our sin on the cross (1 Pet. 2:24). His shed blood is represented by the wine. Believers are to look upon these elements as taking them back to the scenes of the Lord's death.

The believers' participation in the Supper represents their response to the Lord's love that bore the cross.

The Supper is a basic announcing of the gospel (1 Cor. 11:26), a sermon by the entire church in silence. The Supper tends to quicken the anticipation for the second coming (see Matt. 26:29). It thus points beyond itself to a future hope in the kingdom of God.

As believers participate in the Supper, they are reminded of the oneness within the body of Christ and of the fellowship that is shared among fellow believers. The observance is one that is so simple a believing child can partake with a sense of understanding. Yet it also contains so many doctrinal ramifications that even the most mature believer will not fully comprehend its meaning.

*The Practice of the Supper.* The church is commanded to continue the ordinance of the Lord's Supper (1 Cor. 11:24). The Supper provides a needed emphasis on the death and resurrection of the Lord that established the new covenant (1 Cor. 11:25; see Jer. 31:31-34).

There are no specific guidelines about how and when the Supper should be observed. Yet the implications from the New Testament teach us that the Supper should be regular, frequent (1 Cor. 11:20), and normally on the first day of the week (see Acts 20:7).

*Conclusion.* Past, present, and future are thus gathered up in one sacred and joyful festival of the Lord's Supper in apostolic practice and teaching. Indeed, in this ordinance the whole of what Christianity means is expressed. One Lord, incarnate, atoning, and triumphant is the sum and substance of the observance.

Here is seen a dramatic interrelationship between human relationships and relationship with God. The essence of the experience is fellowship and worship, eating together, while at the same time remembering the death of the Lord Jesus Christ in our behalf.

The body is a temple of the Holy Spirit. Christians must glorify God in their bodies.

## CONCERNING MARRIAGE (7:1-40)

The Corinthians had raised a series of questions for Paul. He responded to their concerns by addressing the issue and then offering principles for them to deal with the issue. Paul maintained marriage as the normal rule of life (see Eph. 5:21-33). He offered general principles for marriage. He then gave advice to the unmarried and then to the married. People should lead the kind of life God assigns them. He did note a definite value in celibacy because celibates are free to serve the Lord without the cares that are inseparable from marriage. In verse 10 Paul had appealed to Jesus' teaching regarding the permanence of marriage. If a believer is separated from her spouse, Paul argued that in light of Christ's command she is not to marry again. Rather, the separated couple should be reconciled. Verses 12-16 offer advice concerning separation/divorce when an unbeliever abandons a believer. In this case the abandoned believer is under no obligation to remain married to the unbeliever.

Paul offered further advice concerning contentment. He concluded this topic with counsel for virgins and widows.

## CONCERNING FOOD OFFERED TO IDOLS (8:1-13)

Most meat that was available in the marketplace came from animals sacrificed in the temple. To the more scrupulous in the community all of this meat would be suspect. Some Corinthians felt more mature because they were convinced that idols had no reality—"for there is but one God." Therefore any food offered to idols was still fit to eat. Love, not knowledge, is the key to Christian conduct. It would be better not to eat meat, even if one's conscience allows, than to lead a fellow believer into sin.

## CHRISTIAN DISCIPLINE (9:1-27)

Paul practiced the principles he described. As an apostle he had certain rights and privileges. One of these rights was to be maintained by those to whom he preached. But Paul stressed that one should subordinate one's own interests to those of others, especially those of Christ and His gospel.

It is not necessarily who begins but who completes the Christian life that counts. Thus it is a life of discipline, not license, that is important.

## A WAY OF ESCAPE (10:1-13)

The apostle showed how the Israelites, despite their rights and privileges, suffered in the wilderness. Through the use of typological interpretation of the Old Testament events, Paul warned the Corinthians not to grumble or dabble with idolatry. Christians, however, need not be fearful in the face of temptation, for God has provided help and a way of escape for those who will take it.

## CHRISTIAN FREEDOM (10:14–11:1)

Spiritual fellowship at the Lord's table served as a stern reminder that the Corinthians should have nothing to do with idols. One cannot share simultaneously in the Lord's table and in the table of demons.

A summary of the discussion brings chapters 8–10 to a conclusion. The food had not been affected even if it previously was offered to idols, since all food belongs ultimately to God. It is not that the meat had been contaminated. The problem remained with the weak Christian whose conscience was tainted. The strong believers should have passed the meat by out of concern for the good of the congregation and other believers. Believers must always act in a spirit of

| PAUL'S LISTS OF SPIRITUAL GIFTS | | | | | |
|---|---|---|---|---|---|
| Spiritual Gift | Rom 12:6-8 | 1 Cor 12:8-10 | 1 Cor 12:28 | 1 Cor 12:29-30 | Eph 4:11 |
| Apostle | | | 1 | 1 | 1 |
| Prophet | 1 | 5 | 2 | 2 | 2 |
| Teacher | 3 | | 3 | 3 | 5 |
| Pastor | | | | | 4 |
| Miracles | | 4 | 4 | 4 | |
| Discernment of Spirits | | 6 | | | |
| Word of Wisdom Knowledge | | 1 | | | |
| Evangelists | | | | | 3 |
| Encouragers | | 4 | | | |
| Faith | | 2 | | | |
| Healings | | 3 | 5 | 5 | |
| Tongues | | 7 | 8 | 6 | |
| Interpretation | | 8 | | 7 | |
| Ministry/Serving | 2 | | | | |
| Administration | | | 7 | | |
| Leaders | 6 | | | | |
| Helpers | | | 6 | | |
| Mercy | 7 | | | | |
| Giving | 5 | | | | |

love, in a spirit of self-discipline, with the good of the community in mind, and with God's glory uppermost in mind.

## ORDERLY WORSHIP (11:2-34)

The next issue Paul addressed concerned the different head coverings that appropriately distinguish women and men as they pray or prophesy in worship. Paul praised the church at this point because they had not departed significantly from the substance of what he had previously taught. He had no praise for what he heard about their behavior at the Lord's Supper. Their action did more harm than good. The Lord's Supper should be a celebration of unity; instead divisions among the church were magnified.

Paul repeated the words of institution to point out they are participating in Christ's body and blood (see 10:16-17). To participate in an unworthy manner, with divisions among them, profanes the supper and invites God's judgment. Paul exhorted them to examine their motives, their methods, and their manners as they gathered to worship the Lord at His supper (see the article "The Lord's Supper").

## JESUS IS LORD (12:1-3)

The exercise of spiritual gifts in the church was a subject on which the Corinthians had asked for advice. Many of them were attracted by the more spectacular gifts. All spiritual gifts are given by the Spirit. No one speaking by the Spirit's power will use derogatory words about Jesus. The confession "Jesus is Lord" is the touchstone of the Spirit's genuine work in the community.

## GIFTS OF THE SPIRIT (12:4-31A)

Paul named nine gifts of the Spirit. Their use is compared to the functioning of the various parts of the human body for the good of the whole. All believers have been "baptized by one Spirit into one body." The same Spirit brings refreshment and unity to the whole body. Paul emphasized the unity of the church expressed in variety. As chaos would take over in the human body if each part tried to do the work of other parts, so problems will break out in the church unless each member makes his or her proper contribution for the good of the whole.

## GRACE OF HEAVENLY LOVE (12:31B-13:13)

Paul now explained the right way to exercise all spiritual gifts. Higher than all the gifts of the Spirit is the grace of heavenly love. Paul declared that even the most spectacular manifestations of the gifts, even tongues or prophecy, mean nothing unless motivated by love. Christians may be talented, gifted, devoted, generous in their giving, or endowed with mountain-moving faith; but it is of no value if love is not present.

Spiritual gifts have their place for a time, but love endures forever. Above all else love is the one thing needful. Faith, hope, and love form a heavenly triad of spiritual graces that endure forever, but "the greatest of these is love."

## THE WAY OF LOVE (14:1-25)

Paul applied this grand truth to the Corinthian church by exhorting them to "follow the way of love." While all gifts should be desired, Paul maintained that prophecy should be the gift of choice in the church meetings. The Corinthians desired tongues more than other gifts. Paul claimed that tongues without interpretation is of little value to anyone except to the speaker. The goal of the practice of any spiritual gift is the edification of others. When tongues speakers speak only to themselves, they edify no one. The confusion seems like madness to those outside the church.

Outside there is perhaps a role for tongues, either for private devotion or as a sign of judgment. Inside the church tongues should not be used unless an interpreter is present. Prophecy, however, should be exercised inside the church or outside the church because it both builds up and convicts.

## STRENGTHEN THE CHURCH (14:26-40)

All gifts are allowed to function with the goal of mutual edification in mind, not selfish demonstration. Both tongues speakers and prophets must speak in turn. Each utterance should be properly evaluated. Women should refrain from interrupting with their questions.

Two principles remain valid for the church of any place or time period: (1) all "must be done for the strengthening of the church," and (2) "everything should be done in a fitting and orderly way."

## THE RESURRECTION (15:1-19)

Paul knew that at Corinth there were doubts about the resurrection. He affirmed that the resurrection of Jesus is essential for the gospel message. The consistent testimony of the church was that Jesus died for our sins, rose again, and appeared to numerous witnesses. Paul pointed out that if the Corinthians consistently maintained their antiresurrection argument, Christ could not have been raised. If Christ has not been raised, there is no hope, and all gospel proclamation is in vain.

## RESURRECTION FOR BELIEVERS (15:20-34)

The resurrection of Christ carries with it the promise of resurrection from the dead for all believers. Just as the firstfruits presented to God on the first day of the week following Passover guaranteed the coming harvest (Lev. 23:9-11), so Christ's resurrection guarantees the resurrection of believers.

The hope of the resurrection encourages men and women to become Christians. The same hope provided Paul with boldness to proclaim the gospel and endure the suffering that accompanied his calling.

## RESURRECTION BODY (15:35-58)

The resurrection body will be one adapted to its new spiritual environment. The physical body is weak, dishonorable, and perishable. It will be raised in Christ as spiritual, glorious, powerful, and imperishable. The resurrection will take place when the last trumpet sounds. With genuine excitement the apostle shared his real hope: the transformation of the dead who will be raised. Those alive at Christ's coming will also be transformed "in the twinkling of an eye." Thanks to the victory of Christ, death will be finally abolished. This is great encouragement for all believers to persevere faithfully in the Lord's service, knowing that "labor in the Lord is not in vain."

## CLOSING REMARKS (16:1-24)

Paul told them to set aside some money week by week so that it would be ready to be taken to Jerusalem for the needs there (see 2 Cor. 8–9).

Paul planned to remain at Ephesus to make use of ministry opportunities there. In the meantime the Ephesians could expect a visit from Timothy. A closing formal exhortation to firm faith and love led Paul to conclude with his customary greetings and benediction.

*Theological Significance.* If Paul were to write a letter to the average church today, he probably would rewrite much of 1 Corinthians. The Corinthians' world was much like our modern world. The people had the same thirst for intellectualism, the same permissiveness toward moral standards, and certainly the same fascination for the spectacular. The church resembled our churches—extremely proud, affluent, and fiercely eager for acceptance by the world.

In doctrine there existed a mixture of orthodoxy and error. In ethics the church manifested widespread immorality and worldliness. Two valuable contributions come from this letter. First, we have the doctrinal and pastoral expositions of the topics discussed. Second, we have Paul's approach to the problems. Paul carefully defined each issue and then offered helpful principles to deal with them. What we learn from the apostle's method is as important for the contemporary church as the solutions he articulated.

## Questions for Reflection

1. What are the problems Paul addressed in this letter?

2. What are the principles Paul developed to deal with the problem of food sacrificed to idols?

3. What is the significance of the resurrection for believers?

4. What is the goal of spiritual gifts?

5. How does God's wisdom compare and contrast to human wisdom?

## Sources for Additional Study

Blomberg, Craig. L. 1 Corinthians. NIV Application Commentary. Grand Rapids: Zondervan, 1994.

Fee, Gordon D. The First Epistle to the Corinthians. The New International Commentary. Grand Rapids: Eerdmans, 1987.

Gromacki, Robert G. Called to Be Saints: An Exposition of 1 Corinthians. Grand Rapids: Baker, 1977.

Lea, Thomas D. and Curtis Vaughan. First Corinthians. Grand Rapids: Zondervan, 1983.

Morris, Leon. The First Epistle of Paul to the Corinthians. Tyndale New Testament Commentaries. Grand Rapids: Eerdmans, 1958.

# 2 CORINTHIANS

Paul is the author of this letter (1:1; 10:1). It is the apostle's most personal and pastoral letter. While it is a different kind of letter than Romans or even 1 Corinthians, it is characterized by his style. It contains more autobiographical material than any of his other writings.

The letter is difficult to date, for we do not know the amount of time that separated 1 and 2 Corinthians. It has been variously dated between A.D. 55 and 57.

**Destination and Situation.** See 1 Corinthians.

**Purpose and Theology.** The primary purpose of 2 Corinthians was to prepare the church at Corinth for another visit from Paul. The letter was penned at a difficult time between Paul and the Corinthians. Paul communicated his thankful relief that the crisis at Corinth had somewhat subsided. Moreover, Paul wrote to them concerning the collection that he wanted to gather for the church at Jerusalem.

Paul exercised extraordinary vigor in declaring his role and authority as an apostle. His opponents, the so-called "super apostles" (see 2 Cor. 10–13), had challenged Paul's apostolic status and leadership. In return Paul authenticated his apostolic calling and ministry.

The self-portrait of Paul is one of the most fascinating features of this letter. Second Corinthians gives invaluable autobiographical information. Dominant motifs include Paul's gratitude to God and Christ (1:3; 5:14) and his ministry as a continuing triumph in Christ (2:14). Paul shared the risen life of Christ (4:10-11). Simultaneously he gloried in infirmities and was content with weaknesses, persecutions, and calamities for the sake of Christ (12:9). His ministry was characterized by integrity and suffering (1:8-12; 6:3-10; 11:23-29), marks of a true apostle. His message as an ambassador of Christ focused on the message of reconciliation (5:11-21) and Jesus Christ as Lord (4:5).

Paul's collection for the church at Jerusalem had an important role in his missionary efforts. He devoted two chapters to this matter (chaps. 8–9). They provide some of the most helpful teaching on Christian stewardship found in the New Testament.

**Events between 1 and 2 Corinthians.** The reconstruction of these events is helpful for understanding the issues addressed in the letter. However, there is no universal agreement on these matters.

1. The Corinthians probably rectified most of the practical abuses Paul addressed in 1 Corinthians.

2. However, because of the arrival of the intruders (Paul's opponents), conditions at the church had deteriorated, thus calling for Paul's painful visit (see 2:1; 12:14; 13:1-2).

3. Titus was sent from Ephesus to Corinth with the severe letter in which Paul called for the discipline of the wrongdoer (2:3-9; 7:8-12). Paul instructed Titus to organize the collection for Jerusalem (8:6). Titus was to meet Paul in Troas or in Macedonia (2:12-13; 7:5-6).

4. Paul left Ephesus, then suffered his affliction in Asia (1:8-11), and then crossed to Macedonia to organize the collection in the churches there (2:13; 8:1-4).

5. Titus arrived in Macedonia with the report of the Corinthians' response to the severe letter (7:5-16).

6. On returning to Macedonia and hearing of new problems at Corinth, the apostle wrote 2 Corinthians.

7. Paul spent several months at Corinth (Acts 20:2-3), at which time he authored Romans.

*Unity of the Letter.* Some have suggested that chapters 10–13 were the severe letter, written prior to chapters 1–9; but strong evidence for this hypothesis is lacking. Most likely the severe letter has not survived. The letter, as we now have it, forms a coherent whole as the structure and outline indicate. The history of the church has been nearly unanimous in affirming the letter's unity. No existing Greek manuscripts present the letter in any other form.

## INTRODUCTION (1:1-2)

The letter begins with a standard greeting. The identification of Paul as an apostle, one specially commissioned by Christ, is significant for Paul's defense of his calling and ministry.

## APOSTOLIC EXPERIENCE (1:3-11)

Paul knew what it meant to suffer, but it was in suffering that Paul experienced God's comfort. Paul uniquely described the value of an experience of suffering before relating the experience from which the value came. Paul praised God as the source of all comfort, the comfort he wished to pass along to the Corinthians. The apostle thought he might not survive the difficult experience. God's intervention seemed like a resurrection in his life. This reinforced Paul's conviction that God's resources alone, not human effort, can provide comfort and refuge.

## APOSTOLIC EXPLANATION (1:12–2:11)

Paul's opponents suggested that Paul really had no desire to visit them. Paul's first explanation was an appeal to his clear conscience before God. He claimed he was not ambivalent about his intentions; he truly wanted to visit them. Paul's purpose was for vindication, not accusation. This meant he desired their joy, not their pain. Thus the apostle called for redemption, not retaliation.

## APOSTOLIC MINISTRY (2:12–7:16)

*Triumph of Ministry (2:12-17).* At this key transitional point in the letter, Paul began to explain the nature of apostolic ministry. He began to recount his journey from Ephesus to Philippi, when he sought news of the Corinthians' response to the severe letter. At this key transitional point in the letter, Paul explained the nature of apostolic ministry. This was followed by further explanation of his ministry and motives.

The apostolic ministry follows the ministry of Jesus, in that it includes both suffering and glory. Even in suffering there is triumph in Christ. Paul borrowed a picture from the Roman army. The perfumes of a Roman triumph were joy to the triumphant victors and death for the defeated prisoners. Similarly, Jesus' triumph is a sweet aroma of triumph for believers, but it is a symbol of death for unbelievers.

*Authentic Ministry (3:1-18).* Paul noted that the true minister does not need human endorsement because changed lives are the authentic endorsement of genuine ministry. Paul could not validate his own ministry. The certainty of a valid ministry is only from Christ.

Paul's boast was not in himself but in the new covenant in the Spirit, which unlike the old covenant is not fading away. Paul followed the Jewish interpretation of Exodus 34:29-35, which taught that Moses put a veil over his face so the people would not see the glory fade. The new covenant does not veil the presence of God; it is permanent, and through the Spirit of God it reveals God. The old covenant of the letter was a ministry of death. The new covenant gives life. The old covenant was external, engraved on stones. The new covenant was internal, engraved on human hearts.

*Transparent Ministry (4:1–5:10).* There was no deceit in Paul's ministry, for the ministry was received, not achieved. Paul's message was not about himself but about Jesus, who is the Light. The apostolic ministry is a manifestation of light. Paul himself was only a weak container that held the priceless pot: the message that "Jesus Christ is Lord." The only power in the gospel is God's power. The contrast between weakness and power was typified by the apostle's ministry, modeled on the sufferings of Jesus that flowed to others.

Yet the ministry was a continuation of renewal. Even in the midst of suffering, Paul exemplified courage. This was possible because he looked beyond the decay of the outer person to the renewal of the new person. Paul's life was one of faith, focusing on unseen realities. Because the future includes Christ's judgment, Paul exerted great effort to please Christ in all things.

*Service of the Ministry (5:11–6:13).* Now the apostle claimed that the motivation for service is the love of Christ. No one should live for himself or herself but for Christ. Paul's job, like ours, was to proclaim the reconciliation accomplished by Christ. We who are the recipients of divine reconciliation have

the privilege, like Paul, to be heralds to minister God's message throughout the world. Reconciliation is the removal of human enmity toward God. This was accomplished by Christ, who "had no sin" but was made to "be sin for us, so that in him we might become the righteousness of God."

Following this train of thought, Paul stated that from his side he was reconciled to the Corinthians. Paul had nothing against the Corinthians. If there was any blockage in the relationship with him, it must have been on their side.

*Separation of the Minister (6:14–7:1).* Paul seemed to suspect the block in the relationship was brought about by the Corinthians' love of the world. Paul pointed out that the light cannot be a part of the darkness. Christians must not be bound to unbelievers in a way that will affect their moral purity.

*Concluding Explanation (7:2-16).* This section of the letter concludes with one more appeal to the Corinthians and another explanation of his ministry and motives. Paul was not criticizing them but appealing to them in love. Thus he asked them to "make room for us in your hearts."

## APOSTOLIC FELLOWSHIP (8:1–9:15)

In the context of restored relationships Paul turned to the topic of the collection for the church in Jerusalem. These two chapters deal exclusively with the subject of the church's need for renewed stewardship. In 1 Corinthians 16:1-4 Paul had appealed for help in the Jerusalem relief fund. Jerusalem had been impoverished through the famines in Judea in the 40s. The collection was both an act of charity as well as a symbol of unity between the Gentiles and Jews in the church (see Acts 11:27-30; Gal. 2:10). The Corinthians had promised to give and had failed to participate. Paul now appealed for the Corinthians to complete what they said they would do.

Paul taught that believers should give sacrificially and spontaneously, with spiritual motives. Paul taught that they should give freely, for God values the eagerness to give, not necessarily the amount of the gift.

Paul explained that Titus and two men from the Macedonian churches would handle the money. Paul would have nothing to do with money himself. The handling and administration of the money is as important as the giving of the money. It is important for the church and the world to see the honesty with which the church handles its finances.

Paul then reminded them of the extent of God's giving for them. Out of appreciation for God's gift, believers should give joyfully.

## APOSTLESHIP DEFENDED (10:1–13:14)

*Accusations against Paul (10:1-11.* There is not only a subject change at this point but an abrupt change in tone. Paul's apostleship had been attacked. Here he vigorously defended it.

Paul was accused of being two-faced and worldly. Paul's opponents claimed to have a closer relationship with Christ than Paul had. These accusers said Paul's presence was contemptible.

*God's Commendation (10:12-18).* Paul would not enter the game of comparing himself with these other ministers. He noted that God had used him, not the interlopers, to plant the Corinthian church. Whatever ministry his opponents might have had was dependent on his work. Paul's concern was not with the commendation of others. In the end only God's commendation counts.

*Credentials (11:1-33).* The Corinthian rebellion was serious enough to force Paul into the corner of self-defense.

The apostle was shocked at how quickly they had turned away from apostolic teaching. Paul's pastoral concern was evidenced by his godly jealousy for the church.

Paul proclaimed the gospel in Corinth without payment, although he had the right to receive their support. He refused payment to avoid suspicion concerning his motives. The critics judged Paul for refusing payment, for they quickly received it. Paul was surprised that the Corinthians could not see through the hypocrisy of the opponents.

The irony is that his tenderness and pastoral concern was used against him as a supposed weakness. They claimed Paul was a false apostle and knew it; thus he did not receive their money. Paul turned the argument around and suggested the true sign of an apostle was a form of weakness, for true apostles suffer. Paul then chronicled his experiences of suffering. This was repulsive to Paul, so he related one particular experience of weakness. Yet that weakness was indeed his glory.

*Ecstasy and Agony (12:1-10).* The opponents' criticisms forced Paul to say what he did in this chapter. They claimed true apostles had special revelations. Paul knew this boasting was senseless, but he related a time around A.D. 42 when he experienced the inside of heaven. Paul disliked sharing this account, for he knew that God's strength is more easily seen in the apostle's weakness. In fact, God allowed Satan to afflict Paul to keep him humble and to demonstrate the power of God in his life. If vulnerability revealed God's power, Paul gladly accepted the weakness.

*Concern (12:11-21).* Paul found this all distasteful. His ministry was not validated by special experiences but by his concern for the church. Paul planned to come to them again. He would again refuse their money. Paul's ministry was characterized by constant concern for people and a consistency in actions and motives.

***Conclusion (13:1-14).*** Paul claimed he would without fail make another trip to visit them. He warned them at this time that he would have to deal with their sin. He would do so firmly with the power of God. He admonished them to examine their faith and to restore fellowship with him and with one another. The letter concludes without the usual greetings but with a beautiful benediction. The benediction is Trinitarian in form and has played an important role in the worship of God's people through the centuries.

***Theological Significance.*** In this letter we learn of the importance of restoring relationships in ministry. An important lesson on dealing with opponents and appealing to God for confirmation of one's ministry is contained herein. The most important aspect of this letter is Paul's inspired insights regarding the nature of ministry. Ministry involves suffering, joy, comfort, and hard work. Primarily ministry is the power of God working in and through us to accomplish God's purposes.

We learn of the importance of sacrificial and spontaneous giving. These important principles regarding Christian stewardship need to be expounded in every congregation. Believers are to follow Christ in giving freely with joy and love.

Finally, we learn of the significance of Christ's reconciling work in restoring our broken relationship with God. Because of what He has done for us, we are a new creation, participants in the new covenant, and His ambassadors to proclaim the message of reconciliation. Because we have been reconciled to God, we should be reconciled to other believers. The importance of the unity of the church cannot be neglected.

## Questions for Reflection

1. What is the spiritual value of times of suffering in our lives?

2. What are the primary characteristics of an authentic ministry?

3. What does it mean to be reconciled to God?

4. What principles concerning Christian stewardship can be applied to our own situations?

5. How is God's power revealed in our weakness?

## Sources for Additional Study

Bruce, F. F. *1 and 2 Corinthians.* New Century Bible. London: Oliphants, 1971.

Harris, Murray J. "2 Corinthians." *Expositor's Bible Commentary.* Vol. 10. Grand Rapids: Zondervan, 1976.

Hughes, Philip E. *Paul's Second Epistle to the Corinthians.* New International Commentary. Grand Rapids: Eerdmans, 1962.

Robertson, A. T. *The Glory of the Ministry.* New York: Revell, 1911.

# GALATIANS

There can be little doubt that the apostle Paul wrote the letter to the Galatians. This conclusion has seldom been called into question because the circumstances portrayed in the epistle, the details concerning Paul's life found in Galatians, and the theology of the book all coincide closely with information found in Acts and Paul's other letters. Galatians may have been written from Syrian Antioch in A.D. 48–49 or from Antioch, Corinth, Ephesus, or Macedonia in the early to mid-50s.

**Recipients and Location.** The ethnic Galatians of Paul's day were descendants of the cults who had migrated from Gaul to north-central Asia Minor several centuries before. By the New Testament era, however, the Roman province of Galatia included territory well to the south of the original Galatian kingdom. It is difficult to determine in which of these areas "the churches of Galatia" (1:2) were located.

If Paul was writing to churches in North Galatia, the only possible occasions when he could have been that far north are found in Acts 16:6 and 18:23. Both of those passages make passing mention that Paul had traveled through the region comprising Phrygia and Galatia, providing no additional information about ministry. It is quite possible that this was when Paul planted and revisited churches in North Galatia, near what is today Ankara, the modern capital of Turkey. It is also unusual, however, that Acts would give virtually no background.

On the other hand, if Paul wrote to churches in South Galatia, the beginning of those congregations is prominently displayed in Acts 13–14. Much of the

apostle's first missionary journey is focused in the southern Galatian cities of Pisidian Antioch, Lystra, Derbe, and Iconium. Even details about the evangelism, disciple making, teaching, and appointing of leadership in the new congregations are available (Acts 14:21-23).

One other consideration must be weighed in attempting to determine who were the recipients of the Book of Galatians. The primary subject developed in Galatians is "the truth of the gospel" (Gal. 2:5,14), which was also the focus of the Jerusalem Council in Acts 15. Therefore we must ask whether the letter was written before or after the Council met. That question becomes even more necessary to address because Paul made mention in Galatians 1–2 of two trips he had earlier taken to Jerusalem.

If Paul wrote sometime after the Jerusalem Council, the visit in Galatians 2 is referring to the Council, though that is not readily apparent from a comparison of the passages. Also no mention of the pertinent findings of the Council in Galatians casts doubt on the later dating and North Galatian recipients.

Placing Galatians before the Jerusalem Council does not answer all possible questions. But it is quite plausible to parallel Galatians 2 with Paul's earlier visit to Jerusalem in Acts 11–12. Also the apostle's subject and purpose in writing Galatians fit well in the situation prior to the Jerusalem Council's addressing the issues surrounding the gospel. If that conclusion is correct, Galatians is the earliest of Paul's epistles.

**Theme.** The hub that holds Galatians together is its treatment of the gospel. Much like a scientist approaching data from every conceivable angle, so the apostle Paul considered "the truth of the gospel" (2:5,14): its origin, content, reception through justification by faith in Christ, scriptural support, and practical outworking. Considering its shorter length, Galatians actually is proportionately more saturated with "gospel truth" than even Romans. Perhaps the key verse of this power-packed letter is Galatians 2:16: "Know that a man is not justified by observing the law, but by faith in Jesus Christ."

*Literary Form.* In most respects the letter to the Galatians is quite similar to Paul's other letters, as well as the standardized epistles of the day. It has a well-defined introduction (1:1-5), body (1:6–6:10), and conclusion (6:11-18). There is not, however, the characteristic thanksgiving section, as in most of Paul's other letters (see Phil. 1:3-11). Paul probably could find nothing to be thankful for in connection with the Galatians' rapid defection from the true gospel (Gal. 1:6-9).

From a literary standpoint there is one more issue of a longstanding nature, plus a quite recent one, that are worthy of note. Paul's use of the allegory about Abraham's sons in Galatians 4:22-31 has been debated throughout church history. The meaning of the allegory is not in question but whether Paul was sanctioning the use of allegorical interpretation of Scripture. By and large the conclusion has been that the apostle was turning the false teachers' own brand of allegorizing back on them to make his point and was not other otherwise recommending the allegorical approach.

The recent issue has to do with whether Galatians is purposefully structured like a formal "apologetic letter" of that day. Certainly there are interesting parallels, especially related to 1:6-9 and 2:15-21. But there is not enough evidence presently to draw the firm conclu-

sion that Paul crafted Galatians as an apologetic letter. Besides, the hurry in which Paul composed the epistle argues against such a highly stylistic framework for composition.

*Purpose and Theology.* Paul had three closely related purposes in mind in writing Galatians.

1. He was defending his authority as an apostle against those who claimed otherwise.

2. He was stating, explaining, and proving the gospel message.

3. He was applying the gospel message to daily Christian living by the power of the Holy Spirit.

The basic theology of Galatians is related to the truth of the gospel and its implications. Its ultimate ramifications are as clear-cut as that turning from this gospel equates with deserting God and deserving "accursed" status (1:6-9), while faith in Christ is the only grounds for justification in God's eyes and for eternal hope (2:16; 5:5).

The false "gospel" (1:6-7) the Jewish teachers in Galatia were proclaiming relied upon "the works of the law" (2:16; 3:2), apparently emphasizing distinctives like circumcision (5:2-3). Paul made it clear that the motivation behind such "works" is "the flesh" (3:3; 5:19-21), that aspect of humankind that struggles against the Lord (5:17). Tragically, there is no saving power in the pursuit of fleshly works (2:16; 5:21).

Much of the emphasis on the gospel in Galatians has to do with its proper reception and application (2:16–6:10). But Paul also presented a strong historical foundation for his message. At the very beginning (1:1), the apostle stated his basic assumption concerning the resurrection of Jesus Christ (1:1), which validated Christ's redemptive work and deliverance of believers (1:4). This "good news" of justification of faith in Christ's death alone (3:1-2) is the only means of salvation. Also faith in God's promises has always been God's means of pardon and blessing (3:6–4:31). Thus the only aspect of the gospel that is new since Abraham (3:6-9) was Christ coming to live and die in "the fullness of the time," God's perfect timing (4:4).

An amazing transformation takes place when a person trusts Christ and is justified eternally (2:16; 5:5). Paul called this change "a new creation" (6:15; see 2 Cor. 5:17) and deliverance from the present evil age (1:4). This incredible new status of salvation came about because Christians have been crucified with Christ (2:20), freed from bondage to sin (3:22-25), adopted as children and heirs of God (3:26–4:7), and given the Holy Spirit to dwell within (3:2; 4:6).

After becoming a Christian, the need for faith in Christ does not diminish. In living daily by faith, the power of Christ (2:20) and His Spirit (4:6) allows believers to have God's guidance (5:18) and to avoid the sinful behavior promoted by the flesh (5:13,16,19-21). Living by faith harnesses the Holy Spirit's power (5:5) for a loving, radiant life (5:6) that produces a spiritual "bumper crop," both short-term (5:22-23) and over a lifetime (6:8-9).

   I. Salutation and Preview of Themes (1:1-5)
   II. Error (1:6-9)
   III. Apostolic Authority(1:10–2:14)
   IV. The Gospel Message (2:15-21)
   V. Meaning and Scriptural Basis (3:1–4:31)
   VI. Implications for Christian Living (5:1–6:10)
   VII. Signature, Summaries, Salutation (6:11-18)

## SALUTATION AND PREVIEW (1:1-5)

Like the introduction of most letters in the New Testament era, the name of the writer ("Paul") and readers ("The churches of Galatia") are given, as well as Paul's standard greeting ("Grace to you and peace"). There are also several distinctive elements that are linked to the development of thought in the rest of the epistle. For example, the resurrection of Christ is mentioned only here, then assumed throughout the letter. Also the capsule summary of the gospel in terms of redemption and deliverance from "this present evil age" is uniquely worded, though similar thought patterns emerge later in Galatians. Paul's divinely granted apostleship will become the first theme developed at length in the body of the letter (1:10-2:14).

## ERROR (1:6-9)

Paul was astounded that so soon after his ministry among the Galatians they had defected from the gospel of grace in Christ. To turn away from Paul's message was, in effect, to turn away from God and to turn to a perversion of the true gospel. It was being passed off by the false teachers as an alternate gospel but was, in reality, merely a confusing counterfeit. Paul was so concerned by this development that he twice pronounced a curse ("anathema") on any being, including an angel, distorting the gospel among his readers.

## APOSTOLIC AUTHORITY (1:10-2:14)

The apostle was well aware that his strong criticism would be unpopular with his readers. It was not his intention to be a people pleaser but to please God and to serve Christ, from whom he received his gospel message by direct revelation on the Damascus Road (Acts 26:12-18).

To back his authority as an apostle (1:1) and to show that he had wrestled with the issue of the gospel of grace repeatedly before, Paul presented a selective overview of his own experience. First, he recalled his own misguided zeal for the Jewish law and traditions and his

# LAW IN THE NEW TESTAMENT

How the Old Testament law should be applied was one of the most debated issues during the ministry of Jesus and in the early church. The Jewish authorities constantly were offended by Jesus' actions and teachings on the law (for example, see Matt. 12:1-8).

The early church had a major disagreement over whether circumcision should be required of Gentile Christians (Acts 15). Paul even had to warn against useless quarrels about the law (Titus 3:9).

*Law in the Teaching of Jesus.* The popular notion that Jesus set aside the Old Testament law is wrong. In Matthew 5:17 Jesus stated explicitly that He did not come to destroy the law but to fulfill it.

The discussions of the law in Matthew 5:20-48 show that obeying the law is not accomplished by some external act. Rather, obedience to the law of God includes the "heart," what people think and feel at the core of their being.

Jewish teachers understood the focus of the law to be on proper religious observances and on separation from unclean foods and unclean people. Jesus had little concern for such ritual purity. He focused instead on mercy and love for all people (Matt. 9:9-13). Jesus summarized the law with the two greatest commandments, the commands to love God and neighbor (Matt. 22:34-40).

*The Law in the Early Church.* For the early church the law was still the word of God and a guide for life, but it was no longer the center of attention. Jesus was now the focus of Christian thinking. In light of Jesus' coming, early Christians concluded that certain parts of the law were no longer in effect. Still, all of the Ten Commandments are reaffirmed in the New Testament except the command to keep the Sabbath holy.

Such decisions about how to apply the law took time and often caused disagreement, as the Book of Acts shows. Stephen deemphasized the role of the Jerusalem temple (Acts 7:47-50). Peter had a vision about unclean foods from which he concluded that neither food nor people should be called unclean (Acts 10:9-16,28; see Mark 7:19).

The Jerusalem Council decided that Gentiles did not have to keep the Jewish law to be Christians (Acts 15). Gentiles did not have to be circumcised. This was a crucial decision that made mission activity easier and kept Christianity from being a sect of Judaism.

The epistle to the Hebrews set aside the ineffective priesthood of the Old Testament with its animal sacrifices (7:11-18). Jesus is viewed as the eternal Priest whose death and resurrection were once and for all effective. The sacrifices mentioned in the law are only shadows of what is now a reality in Christ (9:11-14).

*The Law in the Writings of Paul.* Paul wrote most of the explicitly negative statements about the law in the Bible. He viewed the law as in some sense temporary (Gal. 3:19-25). He argued it did not lead to salvation or a righteous life. In fact, Paul thought the law was powerless to bring life (Rom. 8:3). That is the work of God through Jesus and the Holy Spirit.

Rather, the law created an opportunity for sin and led to death (Rom. 7:7-13; also see 5:20).

However, Paul still valued the law as holy, good, and spiritual and as an indication of the will of God to be lived (Rom. 7:12,14; 8:4,7). Even while saying that Christians are not under the law, Paul also expected Christians to fulfill the law by loving their neighbors as themselves (Gal. 5:14-18; Rom. 13:8-10).

Paul's conflicting statements have created frequent debate about how he viewed the law. For example, does Paul's statement "Christ is the end of the Law" (Rom. 10:4) mean "Christ is the goal of the Law" or "Christ is the setting aside of the Law"? Probably his intention is "Christ is the goal of the Law." (Compare the use of the same word translated "end" in the KJV in Rom. 6:22.)

For Paul the important point was not law itself but whether God's Spirit is at work in a person's life. Without God's Spirit the law is an occasion for sin and rebellion and leads to death (Rom. 7:5-13). With God's Spirit the law is an occasion for obedience and showing love to one's neighbor.

*Relevance for Modern Christians.* The Old Testament law cannot be ignored by modern Christians. The focus can never be on its ritual and ceremonial practices or on legalistic observance. Christians should study the law in light of Jesus' life, death, and resurrection to learn about God's relation to humans and His desire for them to live in love. They can then understand why James 1:25 refers to the law as "the perfect Law that gives freedom."

intense persecution of the church. Certainly no one among the Galatian churches, or even the Jewish false teachers, could rival the unsaved Paul's works, if that were the true issue of the gospel (Phil. 3:4-6).

In his great care to demonstrate that his apostleship, and specific role as apostle to the Gentiles, came from God, Paul next recounted his conversion and what happened in regard to the gospel over the following years. He noted that his call to salvation was independent of human agency and that he did not immediately consult the other apostles in Jerusalem to verify, or even clarify, his calling or message. After three years Paul did travel to Jerusalem for a brief conference with Peter. But he remained largely unknown among Jewish Christians, except for reports of his ministry in Tarsus and Syrian Antioch (Acts 11:25-26), which were joyfully received by the churches in Palestine.

Next Paul described what would have been the decisive opportunity for the leadership of the Jewish church in Jerusalem to correct his gospel of grace if it needed to be corrected. Well over a decade later Paul revisited Jerusalem, accompanied by Barnabas and Titus, a ministry associate who was a Gentile. If circumcision were really part of the "truth of the gospel," the inner circle of leaders—Peter, John, and James, the half-brother of Jesus—would necessarily have required Titus to be circumcised, especially given the pressure exerted by some Paul called "false brethren." The outcome of this important meeting was apparently full recognition of Paul's gospel message and primary mission field among the Gentiles and a request for Paul and the churches he worked with to continue support of the poor.

A final incident is presented in this section to clear up apparent confusion among Paul's readers. Sometime after the cordial agreement reached in Jerusalem, Peter visited the church in Syrian Antioch, then under the leadership of Paul and Barnabas (Acts 11:26–13:1). While there, criticism from other Jews who had arrived from the church in Jerusalem pressured Peter into hypocritical behavior. Peter's actions strongly implied that it was necessary for Gentiles to observe Jewish distinctives, although God had decisively taught him at a much earlier point that was not true (Acts 11:1-18). As a result, Paul found it necessary to confront Peter because of his dangerous hypocrisy.

## GOSPEL MESSAGE (2:15-21)

This section not only crystallizes the essence of the gospel of grace versus the counterclaims of the Jewish false teachers, but it also serves as a major hinge in the letter. The argument appears to either continue or emerge directly out of Paul's face-off with Peter at the end of the long preceding autobiographical portion. It also prepares for the following exposition of justification by faith alone by stating the central thesis to be proven.

Paul's logic was tight, so as to make his conclusions virtually undeniable. He answered key objections: Jews do not have to sin in the same gross ways as Gentiles to be sinners (Rom. 1–3). Nor does a message of grace provoke more and more sin (Rom. 6:1-14). Having corrected such common misperceptions, the apostle proclaimed that no one can be justified by God by "the works of the Law," although the law of Moses does play an important role in convincing of "deadness" in sin (Gal. 3:10-25; Rom. 7:7-12). Rather, the only channel of justification is faith in Jesus Christ, and the road of growth in the Christian is also full identification with the death and resurrection of Christ by faith (5:5).

## OLD TESTAMENT BASIS (3:1–4:31)

Because the distorted "gospel" being propagated by the Jewish false teachers was based on an understanding of the law of Moses and other Jewish distinctives, Paul now wisely expanded and backed his gospel of justification by faith in Christ from the Old Testament. Paul moved back and forth from personal appeal to more formal argument throughout this lengthy section.

Initially, the apostle pointedly inquired whether the Galatians received the Holy Spirit at salvation by doing the works of the law or by believing the gospel message they had heard from Paul. He then posed an important follow-up question: Is your progress in the Christian life by such works or by faith? Since they had heard the message of the cross so clearly portrayed by Paul, their "foolish" attraction to the false gospel of the Jewish teachers was without any real excuse.

In order to counter any possibility of different answers to those questions, Paul referred to the example of Abraham, father of the Jewish nation, and the relationship of that example to the law. Abraham's faith was credited to his account as righteousness, and all who follow that classic example are Abraham's spiritual children and are similarly blessed.

On the other hand, those who try to attain righteousness through observing the law are cursed (1:8-9), according to the law itself. Fortunately, Christ's death on the cross, in which he was cursed for us, according to the law, provided the payment by which anyone might receive the blessing of Abraham and the Holy Spirit by faith. This is seen to be true because the fulfillment of the promises to Abraham are in Christ, his ultimate descendant, not in the law, which did not invalidate the earlier covenant God made with Abraham.

That does not mean the law was without divine purpose. The law convicts all people of sin, holding them in captivity until the message of faith in Christ was revealed. The law played the role of both a jailer and a guardian of underage children in preparing for believers to be full-fledged children of God, on equal footing spiritually and joint heirs of God's promise no matter their ethnic, social, or sexual gender backgrounds.

Paul then developed a cultural illustration to underline how amazing it is that because Christ became a man at just the right point in history, now any person can, by faith, become an adopted adult child of God. Each believer has full rights and privileges, including the indwelling Holy Spirit. In being freed from the virtual slavery of spiritual "childhood" outside of Christ, the apostle then ironically asks how the Galatians could return to slavery to such weak principles, which cannot provide spiritual strength, such as the law.

He wanted them to know he was concerned for them in their time of spiritual weakness just as they had shown great concern for Paul in his earlier time of physical infirmity. The apostle reminded them how, in initially receiving the gospel from him, the Galatians had honored him and nursed him back to health. He wanted them to know he was risking a fellowship he valued greatly by telling them the hard truth, unlike the false teachers, who were courting their favor for an improper purpose. He related to his beloved spiritual children his deep agony and confusion over their misguided spiritual status.

As the capstone of his argument concerning justification by faith from the Old Testament, Paul created an allegory from the two sons of Abraham: Ishmael and Isaac. In this twist on the method of the false teachers, Paul paralleled Ishmael, the child of a slave, to the covenant of the law made at Mount Sinai and the current spiritual slavery of Jewish legalism. He presented Isaac, the child of free Sarah, in line with the promise to Abraham and the New Jerusalem, the Jewish future hope. He concluded by implying that persecution of those in line with the promise by those in spiritual slavery is to be expected. But that will not last because those in spiritual slavery will be banished by the "father." Paul intended to leave little doubt that the doom of the false teachers and their message is certain before the Lord.

## CHRISTIAN LIVING (5:1–6:10)

Having secured the argument for freedom in Christ through justifying faith alone, Paul examined the nature of that liberty. While again rebuking the tendency to turn back to legalism, he also deplored the opposite extreme of license. Paul expertly showed that freedom in Christ is a Spirit-guided lifestyle within the limits of a new "law" given by Christ: the law of love.

Paul quickly warned against circumcision, which has no spiritual value in Christ. He reminded them that they could not keep part of the law and ignore the rest. And to attempt to be justified by keeping the law of Moses is to turn completely away from God's grace. The route of spiritual freedom in Christ is faith, faith that shows love in the short run and that waits eagerly but patiently for the Christian's eternal hope.

The apostle next laments how the false teachers had confused the Galatians, halting their forward progress in Christ. He longed for an end to the leaven of false teaching spreading among them, wishing that the agitators would do away with themselves. Still, he displayed confidence that the Galatian churches would return to a proper viewpoint.

The danger of misunderstanding freedom in Christ is a tendency toward self-indulgence, which can express itself in destructive words and actions toward other believers. True spiritual freedom manifests itself in love, both for God and for one another. Such loving behavior is against the grain of the flesh. Thus it is necessary to live in the power of the Holy Spirit and thus be guided by the Spirit in our attitudes, decisions, and actions. To fail to follow the lead of the Spirit as a Christian is to manifest a sinful lifestyle that is unworthy of the kingdom of God. On the other hand, the believer who is controlled by the Spirit shows forth qualities that reflect supernatural godliness beyond the requirements of the law.

Such a life of Spirit-prompted love does not go on automatically however. It is necessary to remain consciously in step with the Holy Spirit, and it is easy to do otherwise. Even though the flesh was, in a very real sense, crucified with Christ, the tendency to pride, and even to gross sin, still exists. Mature Christians must, in the power of the Spirit, restore such errant believers. Also they must be available to support Christians overloaded with cares or responsibilities. It is right for every person to work up to their capacity, but not go beyond it. Nor is it proper for a person to boast because someone else has fallen under a load within that person's capacity.

The life of love even includes support of biblical teachers who have financial needs. These are the kinds of good works that bring about a long-term harvest of eternal worth. The opposite route of sowing to the flesh only eventuates in corrupt fruit. The difference in the two final outcomes is whether we choose to do what is right in all situations, especially toward fellow believers, here and now.

## CONCLUSION (6:11-18)

At this point Paul began the conclusion to Galatians by taking the manuscript from his unnamed scribe and writing with large, bold script. He then effectively summarized the issues of the entire letter by setting the pridefulness of those pushing circumcision on the Galatians over against the cross of Christ and the new creation that begins when a person becomes a believer. The apostle then pronounced a benediction of peace and mercy upon all Gentile and Jewish believers with proper perspective. He requested peace for himself in regard to the persecution he had suffered for the sake of the message of the cross and new creation. He ended as he began, and proceeded throughout, with a note of grace (1:3; 2:21).

## Questions for Reflection

1. Why did Paul say that to turn away from the gospel of salvation through faith in Jesus Christ is "desertion" from God and pronounce a curse upon each behavior?

2. How did Paul's own personal background serve as important evidence supporting his message of justification by faith in Christ without works?

3. How does the Old Testament, especially the foundational example of Abraham, back the truth of the gospel, as proclaimed by Paul?

4. How should Christians relate to such precious unseen realities as being crucified with Christ, being adopted children of God and rightful heirs, and having the indwelling Holy Spirit?

5. How can the believer draw upon the resources of the Holy Spirit for guidance and victory over the flesh, as well as a loving, fruitful life in both the short term and over the long haul?

6. How can you discern the difference between someone shouldering their proper responsibility and one who is overburdened? How can you support the person crushed by the overload?

## Sources for Additional Study

Fung, Ronald Y. K. *The Epistles to the Galatians*. New International Commentary. Grand Rapids: Eerdmans, 1988.

George, Timothy. *Galatians*. New American Commentary. Nashville: Broadman & Holman, 1994.

Guthrie, Donald. *Galatians*. New Century Bible. Grand Rapids: Eerdmans, 1973.

Stott, John R. W. *The Message of Galatians*. The Bible Speaks Today. Downers Grove: InterVarsity, 1968.

# EPHESIANS

Paul referred to himself by name as the author of the Book of Ephesians in two places (1:1; 3:1). Today some scholars think the book contains a writing style, vocabulary, and even some teachings that are not typical of the apostle. Yet others regard the book as the crown of all of Paul's writings. If that is the case, then it would mean a disciple of Paul had surpassed him in theological insight and spiritual perception. Of such an erudite disciple the early church has no record. Furthermore, pseudonymity (a writer writing with someone else's name) probably was not practiced by early Christians. We can conclude, in line with the undisputable acceptance of Pauline authorship in the early church, that there is no reason to dispute the Pauline authorship of Ephesians.

Paul penned the letter while in prison (3:1; 4:1; 6:20). Disagreement exists concerning whether Paul was imprisoned in Caesarea (Acts 24:22) around 57–59 or in Rome (Acts 28:30) about 60–62 when he wrote this letter. Paul most likely wrote Colossians, Philemon, and Philippians during the same imprisonment. The evidence for a Roman imprisonment seems more likely. Tradition confirms this conclusion. This being the case, it is plausible to suggest that Paul wrote the letter from Rome around 60–61. This would have transpired while Paul was housed in guarded rental quarters (Acts 28:30).

**Destination.** In spite of the traditional heading (1:1), relatively little is known about the recipients of the letter called Ephesians. (Several important and early manuscripts do not contain the words in Ephesus [1:1].) The letter was carried to its destination by Tychicus, who in Ephesians 6:21 and Colossians 4:7 is identified as Paul's emissary. The Ephesian and Colossian letters probably were delivered at the same time since in both letters the apostle noted that Tychicus would inform the churches concerning Paul's situation.

We can suggest the following possible scenario. While Paul was imprisoned in Rome, the need arose to respond to new religious philosophies influencing the Asia Minor area. The impetus to write the letters came to Paul from Epaphras, who informed him of the threats to Christianity in the Lycus Valley. In a response Paul wrote a letter to the church at Colosse. About the same time, either shortly before or shortly thereafter, he penned a more expansive and general letter intended for churches in Asia Minor, including Laodicea (see Col. 4:16) and Ephesus.

What we call Ephesians was probably a circular letter, with Ephesus being the primary church addressed. Paul stayed at Ephesus, the capital city of the province of Asia, for almost three years (see Acts 20:31). These factors help explain the absence of personal names of Ephesian believers. After the Ephesians read it, the letter would have been routed to Colosse, Laodicea, and other churches in the area.

**Literary Features.** The salutation and structure of Ephesians is quite similar to Colossians. Many topics are commonly treated in both letters. The message is strikingly similar. Of the 155 verses in Ephesians over half contain identical expressions with those in Colossians. Colossians, however, is abrupt,

# ELECTION IN THE NEW TESTAMENT

Election is the operative principle of God's covenant with Israel. The background for the doctrine of election in the New Testament is the Old Testament.

*Old Testament Background.* In the Old Testament "election" relates directly to Israel's understanding of its own origins. Election signifies the meaning and expression of Israel's destiny: God's giving of Himself to be their God and His selection of them to be His people. With this election they will know the blessing of His abiding presence.

In nonreligious biblical usage, election indicates the "choice" of an individual person, place, or thing out of a wide selection. When pertaining to persons, election points to their selection for or appointment to an office (see Gen. 13:11; Exod. 18:25; 1 Sam. 8:18). Thus there can also be a passive use of the word *elected,* which often indicates the great worth and usefulness of something or someone.

Theologically, election signifies God's selecting His people from the nations to be holy and wholly for Himself. They have been chosen to be His inheritance (see Deut. 7:6; 10:5). Outside of Deuteronomy, "election" is used frequently by Isaiah: "You are My Servant, I have chosen you and have not rejected you; fear not!" (Isa. 41:9). The object of God's choice, the Servant of God, names him "Chosen." But the idea here is much more one of office rather than personal condition to which God's servant is called.

Within the elected community God chose individuals for specific duties (for example, see Deut. 18:5, the Levites; Ps. 105:26, Aaron) and in an extended sense Judah (Ps. 78:68) and Abraham (Neh. 9:7).

The election of the king is special in this regard (Deut. 17:15). Above all, David was elected by the Lord (1 Sam. 10:24). Also according to Deuteronomy and other related Old Testament literature, God elects the place for the holy of holies (Deut. 12:18)—particularly Jerusalem (1 Chron 6:6; Zeph. 1:17).

*New Testament Teaching.* In the New Testament election has several different usages that correspond to the usages of the Old Testament. Jesus chose the twelve from the group of His disciples (Luke 6:13) and told them that He had chosen them "out of the world" (John 15:19).

Election is entirely a work of God. He claims persons for Himself and His own purpose: this is His glory. Indeed, our knowledge of election always comes as an already accomplished fact. "He chose us in Christ before the foundation of the world" (Eph. 1:4) and "the elect whom he chose" (Matt. 13:20) indicate that election is an action of God prior to and independent of any human action or condition. Through the means of God's gracious election, He actually bestows all spiritual blessings that accompany salvation (see Eph. 1:4-14).

Characteristically, however, the New Testament teaching of election is always descriptive and never discloses God's reasoning behind this action.

One fact is unmistakable: the mystery of God surrounds this gracious expression of His almighty will.

Where the New Testament indicates a basis for election, grace and love are mentioned to the exclusion of any righteous works or superior value of an individual. Faith is the means by which God's work of election is made known. A most serious and holy consequence is connected with the knowledge of election: the renunciation of all pride and the pursuit of a righteous and holy life before the Lord.

Faith matures in the knowledge of election, and every Christian virtue flourishes (Col. 3:12). This understanding certainly supplies believers with confidence in the promise of the sanctifying power of the Holy Spirit (1 Pet. 1:2). Obedience to all of Christ's commands serves to confirm election (2 Pet. 1:10). This knowledge builds within the believer an understanding of a shared faith within a large community of spiritual people of God.

Personal security in salvation is also an outcome. But this is based upon the fact, first of all, of God's securing a people for Himself who will be living witnesses of His electing grace to the whole world. Election then is that will and action of God to call undeserving persons to share in His glory.

We should note finally the most special case of election, that of Jesus, the Son of God (Luke 9:35). This designation of Christ seems to relate to the fact that believers are elect through Him; and remaining "in Christ," they enjoy every spiritual blessing (Eph. 1:3).

argumentative, and seemingly compressed. Ephesians presents a bigger, finished picture that is meditative, instructive, and expansive.

Though Colossians and Ephesians contain many similarities, it is important to observe the distinctives of Ephesians. When the content of Ephesians that is common to Colossians is removed, there remain units of material unique to Ephesians.

| 1:3-14 | an expanded benediction |
|---|---|
| 2:1-10 | a confessional statement on the new life |
| 3:14-21 | a prayer to understand the mystery of Christ |
| 4:1-16 | an extended exhortation to Christian unity |
| 5:8-14 | a section on walking in the light |
| 5:23-32 | a theological expansion on the household roles |
| 6:10-17 | a unique picture of the Christian's spiritual warfare |

***Purpose and Theology.*** The book hints at several purposes. The apostle taught that Jewish and Gentile believers are one in Christ. This oneness was to be demonstrated by their love one for another. Paul used the noun or verb form of love *(agape)* nineteen times (about one-sixth of the total uses in all the Pauline letters). Ephesians begins with love (1:4-6) and ends with love (6:23-24).

Paul implicitly addressed matters raised by the mystery religions in the Lycus Valley. The letter has much to say about the mystery of redemption (1:7) and the divine intention for the human race (1:3-14). Additional themes treated include grace (1:2), predestination (1:4-

5), reconciliation, union with Christ (2:1-21), among others.

Central to the message of Ephesians is the re-creation of the human family according to God's original intention for it. The new creation destroys the misguided view that God accepts the Jew and rejects the Gentile. Paul claimed that this distinction was abolished at Christ's sacrificial death. Thus no more hindrance remains to reuniting all humanity as the people of God, with Christ as the head (1:22-23). The new body, the church, has been endowed by the power of the Holy Spirit to enable them to live out their new lives (1:3–2:10) and put into practice the new standards (4:1–6:9).

In sum we can say that the overall emphasis of Ephesians is on the unity of the church in Christ through the power of the Spirit.

I. Introduction (1:1-2)

II. God's Purposes in Christ (1:3–3:21)

III. God's Purposes in the Church (4:1–6:20)

IV. Conclusion (6:21-24)

## INTRODUCTION (1:1-2)

Paul identified himself by name and calling. He offered greetings in the manner common to the Pauline letters. Absent is the usual mention of Paul's companions.

## GOD'S PURPOSE (1:3-14)

Paul offered praise to God for his glorious blessings in Christ. This section is one long sentence in the original text made up of carefully balanced clauses. This extended benediction surveys the redemptive activity of the Triune God. Some have seen here a hymn of three stanzas of uneven length. Each stanza concludes with a reference to the praise of God's glorious grace. The theme of this section is God's eternal purpose in history.

Paul theologized about God's purposes. In Christ, God "chose us . . . before the creation of the world to be holy and blameless in his sight." The spiritual blessings granted to believers are the work of the Trinity: the Father's electing, the Son's redemptive work, and the Spirit's sealing. God now has made known His purposes, has forgiven our sins, and granted hope to His own.

God the Father loves His Son, and believers who have been redeemed by the Son are also the object of God's love.

## GOD'S POWER (1:15-23)

The entire letter was written within a framework of prayer. This section is an extended prayer. Paul prayed that his readers would have the spiritual insight to perceive the truth that is hidden in God. It can be unlocked only in the experience of life and fellowship with Him. The prayer issues from his opening section, constituting a request that believers may appropriate all that is contained in that beautifully rich sentence.

Paul's prayer began with thanksgiving for their faith and love. In 1:17-23 he made four requests for them: (1) to know and experience God; (2) to know the hope of His calling; (3) to know of His glorious inheritance; and (4) to know of His great power. Paul expounded on this great power available to believers exhibited in Christ's resurrection, ascension, rule, and headship.

## REDEEMED BY GRACE (2:1-10)

Chapter 2 continues Paul's thoughts about God's eternal purposes in Christ. In 2:1-10 Paul discussed how sinful people who deserve nothing but God's wrath can be redeemed by His grace.

Paul described the human condition in 2:1-3. He explained how people were "dead in transgressions and sins," cut off from the life of God and controlled by their own selfish desires. Beyond this

they were ensnared by the power of Satan. As a result men and women apart from Christ are without life, without freedom, and without hope.

By His grace He has granted new life to believers. The basis for the new life is God's great love and mercy. Believers have been united with Christ in His resurrected life. Formerly people apart from Christ were dead, enslaved, and objects of wrath. In Christ believers are now alive, enthroned, and objects of grace.

God's purpose for believers is spelled out in 2:7-10. He has restored us, "expressed in his kindness to us in Christ Jesus." The memorable words in verses 8-9 express a central idea in Paul's theology. He declared that the nature of God is to give freely because of His own love. God does not deal with people on the level of human achievement but on the level of their deepest needs.

He provides salvation as His gift to men and women. He then creates a disposition of faith within them so that they may receive His gracious gift. Salvation is completely God's achievement, a pure gift of God. Salvation is His workmanship. We are saved to live a totally different life "to do good works, which God prepared in advance for us to do."

## RECONCILIATION (2:11-18)

Paul explained Christ's peace mission in this section. Those who were separated from the covenant have been united, those who were alienated have been reconciled, and those who were far off have been brought near.

The first ten verses of chapter 2 dealt with personal reconciliation. The remainder of the chapter turns to corporate reconciliation, particularly the reconciliation of Gentiles. For centuries the Jews (the "circumcision") looked with contempt on the Gentiles (the "uncircumcision"). The Jews thought they were participants in God's covenant by their heritage. They believed the Gentiles were distant from this covenant. Thus Paul described the Gentiles with the term "without."

They were without Christ, without citizenship, without covenants, without hope, and without God. Their condition was not due to their heritage or even to God but to their own sinfulness and spiritual bankruptcy.

Paul exclaimed the good news in verses 13-18. Apart from Christ the Gentiles were hopeless. "But now in Christ Jesus" Gentiles and Jews are reconciled to God and to one another. The enmity, the barrier, has been broken down. This is the meaning of reconciliation—to bring together again. In Jesus Christ, Jew and Gentile became one because of His crosswork. The law and its accompanying barriers created the barriers. Now those barriers have been nullified. Not only has Christ made peace, "He himself is our peace." Jews and Gentiles are no longer strangers; they are called in one hope as one people of God.

## THE NEW SOCIETY (2:19-22)

Some modern theologians assert that God has acted in Christ to reconcile all the world to Himself. Consequently, the church's primary concern is not to seek to effect the reconciliation of all people to Christ but merely to proclaim that all have already been reconciled. This type of universalism is not what Paul taught in this chapter. In fact, the apostle opposed that kind of thinking.

It is only in response to the cross of Christ (called faith in 2:8) that peace exists vertically between humans and God and horizontally between humans. This new society, called the church, is depicted at the end of chapter 2.

The church is pictured as a nation ("fellow citizens,"), a family ("a household"), and a "building." This new building is "built on the foundation of the apostles and prophets, with Christ Jesus himself as the chief cornerstone." The purpose of the church is for believers to be "built together to become a dwelling in which God lives by his Spirit."

## THE DIVINE MYSTERY (3:1-13)

After discussing the union of Jewish and Gentile believers in the church (2:11-22), Paul began to offer a prayer on their behalf. However, he stopped unexpectedly in the middle of the sentence and digressed on the subject of the divine mystery. He explained the meaning of the mystery and returned to his prayer in 3:14.

Paul was assured that his readers understood something about his unique ministry. He indicated this saying, "Surely you have heard about the administration of God's grace that was given to me." Paul described the details of his unique and privileged ministry in. The word "administration" that he used to refer to this ministry has the sense of a stewardship or trust to be shared (translated "trust" in 1 Cor. 9:17 and "commission" in Col. 1:25). Paul was to administer God's grace, which had been granted to him, particularly to the Gentiles.

The apostle identified the unique aspect of his ministry as a "mystery" in 3:6. A mystery is something previously concealed but now made known in the gospel. In 1:9 "mystery" spoke of God's purpose of gathering together all things under the headship of Christ. In chapter 3 it refers to one aspect of that ultimate goal, the inclusion of Gentiles in the blessings of the gospel and the terms on which this is done.

Paul then moved another step in verses 7-12 to declare his unique role as a minister of the good news of salvation to the Gentiles. His service was carried out in the church in the service of the gospel. The church is the agency of the divine mission. Thus the church is central to history, to the gospel, and to Christian living.

## UNITED IN HIS LOVE (3:14-21)

Paul now continued the prayer he started in 3:1. What he described in 2:11-22 is now the subject of his prayer. He desired for the church to be united experientially. He wanted them to know and experience Christ's love and share it with one another.

Paul addressed his prayer to the Father. He expressed his aspiration for the saints to be strengthened, grounded, and filled. He asked that they comprehend Christ's love and be filled unto God's fullness. His confidence in prayer was grounded not in his abilities or his readers' but completely in God's abundant power. Astoundingly he claimed that God can do abundantly more than we can ask or even imagine. Following these majestic words the apostle concluded with a beautiful doxology.

## THE CHURCH (4:1-6)

Ephesians is the perfect balance between doctrine and duty. The first three chapters deal with doctrine, the believers' spiritual blessings in Christ. The last three chapters focus on the church's responsibility to live in unity, variety, maturity, purity, and victory. We learn from Paul's balanced perspective the need for both orthodoxy (right belief) and orthopraxy (right living).

Commentators have suggested that the pivotal verse of the entire letter—indeed, the key that unlocks its structure—is 4:1. It brings together the themes of chapters 1–3 and in a stirring appeal announces Paul's emphasis of chapters 4–6. The church's privileged position and calling carries with it weighty responsibilities. Paul exhorted the church to worthy living. He emphasized the character and effort required for

such exemplary living. Then with characteristic Trinitarian emphasis the apostle claimed the church could so live because it is energized by the Spirit, established by the Lord, and empowered by the Father.

## THE CHURCH'S GIFTS (4:7-16)

Borrowing an illustration from Psalm 68:18, Paul described the gifts given to the church. God is both sovereign and generous in His distribution of the various gifts.

The gifts in fact are gifted persons: apostles, prophets, evangelists, pastors, and teachers (or pastor-teachers). Apostles and prophets were already mentioned in 2:20 and 3:5 as the foundational gifts to the church. In a strict sense apostles were witnesses of Christ's resurrection and were commissioned by Him to preach. It broadly included those associated with such men, who also were commissioned for ministry (for example, see Acts 14:4,14; 1 Thess. 2:6). Prophets, under the direct inspiration of God, carried out a preaching ministry that included both foretelling and forthtelling.

Evangelists ministered in a manner itinerant and external from the church. They were missionaries to the unconverted empowered with special insight into the gospel's meaning. Pastors and teachers most likely constituted two sides of one ministry. This ministry was indigenous and internal to the church. Persons with this gift shepherd the flock and instruct them in divine truth.

All of these gifted people carry out equipping ministries so that service ministries can be actualized. Or as Paul put it, "to prepare God's people for works of service, so that the body of Christ may be built up until we all reach unity in the faith."

Paul stated the goal of the church in 4:13-16. The church is to grow up in Christ so it will avoid spiritual immaturity, instability, and gullibility. The atmosphere of spiritual maturity is described in terms of truth and love. Maturity is defined totally in relationship to the corporate Christian body. Maturity is an ongoing process of being "joined and held together" in relationship with the body of Christ.

## HOLY LIVING (4:17–5:21)

In this very practical and challenging section Paul focused on holy living. Believers are to walk in purity as well as unity. The apostle first showed negatively how believers should not walk. Then he provided positive aspects of Christian conduct.

Paul distinguished between those characterized by rebellion, obstinacy, and darkened understanding and those who respond to Jesus Christ as both subject and teacher. The first group is called the "old self" or unregenerate self. The second group is called the "new self." Paul exhorted believers to live out the reality of their new position with an inward renunciation and restoration.

The conclusion of chapter 4 includes ethical exhortations grounded in theological truth. Believers are to rid themselves of vices like "bitterness," "anger," and "slander" and instead imitate the compassionate kindness of Christ.

Believers are to walk in love, please God by avoiding evildoers, and walk in wisdom. The church is enabled to do this by the empowering (filling) of the Holy Spirit. When this happens, believers can together praise God, constantly offer thanksgiving in all things, and mutually submit one to another.

## NEW RELATIONSHIPS (5:22–6:9)

Paul now applied his teaching to particular life relationships. Wise believers filled with the Spirit who mutually submit one to another are to live out these truths in household relationships. Three relationships are addressed: wives and husbands, children and parents, servants and masters. In each of these relationships the first partner is exhorted to be submissive or obedient. The second person in the relationship shows submissiveness by Christlike love and concerned care. All relate to one another as service to the Lord. All concerned experience personal worth, value, security, and significance when these reciprocal relationships are exercised under the lordship of Christ.

## WARFARE OF THE NEW PEOPLE (6:10-20)

Paul made sure believers recognized that as new people who have been granted new life in a new family with new relationships they still would endure spiritual warfare. The closing portion of Paul's letter explained his account of the Christian's conflict with evil forces.

Believers must adorn themselves with the armor of God in order to stand against the devil's schemes. Five defensive weapons are identified: (1) the enabling nature of truth that resists lying and false doctrine; (2) the covering quality of righteousness that resists accusations of conscience and despondency; (3) the stabilizing quality of peace that resists slander and selfishness; (4) the protective ability of faith that resists prayerlessness and doubt; and (5) the encouraging nature of salvation that resists fear and disappointment.

Two offensive weapons are included in the armor of God: (1) the sword of the Spirit, which is the word of God, and (2) prayer. It is fitting that this prayerful and meditative letter concludes with an exhortation to prayer and a request for prayer.

## CONCLUSION (6:21-24)

We learn that Tychicus was the bearer of the letter. Paul concluded the letter with words of grace and peace. The unusual benediction provides a fitting benediction to Paul's majestic letter.

***Theological Significance.*** This letter lifts us to a new vantage point from which we are united with the risen and ascended Christ. Believers are not to have a limited or merely earthly perspective. When we view life from the heavenly realms (1:3), we can understand that the church's strength is not in human resources but in the grace and strength of God alone. The church's warfare is not with people but with spiritual powers (6:10-17). The church, the people of God, does not function merely to carry out routine activities. It is to reveal the wisdom of God and to proclaim the rich redemption provided by Jesus Christ (1:3-11; 3:2-13). This grand book gives us a purpose for living in line with God's purposes in history (1:10). This is accomplished as we live in submission to Christ, the head of the church, indeed the head over all things (1:22).

## Questions for Reflection

1. What is important for Paul's concept of the new life?

2. What did Paul identify as his special ministry? How does the church today carry out this ministry?

3. How do spiritual gifts (gifted people) contribute to the unity and maturity of the church?

4. Why do contemporary Christians often ignore the evil forces at war against the church? How can the church apply Paul's teaching on spiritual warfare?

## Sources for Additional Study

Bruce, F. F. *The Epistle to the Ephesians.* The New International Commentary. Grand Rapids: Eerdmans, 1984.

Dockery, David S. *Ephesians: One Body in Christ.* Nashville: Convention, 1996.

Stott, John, R. W. *God's New Society: The Message of Ephesians.* The Bible Speaks Today. Downers Grove: InterVarsity, 1979.

Vaughan, Curtis. *Ephesians: A Study Guide Commentary.* Grand Rapids: Zondervan, 1977.

# PHILIPPIANS

The letter to the Philippians was written while the apostle Paul was in prison probably from Rome about A.D. 62, though we cannot know for sure. Other possible locations for the writing of the letter could have been Ephesus or Caesarea (sometime between A.D. 54 and 62).

**The Recipients.** The Philippian church was founded about A.D. 50–51, approximately a decade before the writing of the letter, during Paul's second missionary journey (Acts 16:12-40). Paul and Silas arrived in Philippi and apparently found no Jewish synagogue. There was, however, a place of prayer by the riverside where some women met on the Sabbath to pray. One of these women, Lydia, believed the gospel message Paul preached. As a result of her gratitude to God and to the missionaries, she opened her home to them.

After the missionaries had settled in Philippi, they were arrested when Paul exorcised a demon from a slave girl because her masters aroused opposition against the preachers. They were beaten, thrown into prison, and fastened in stocks. Yet Paul and Silas were still able to praise God and sing hymns. While they were in prison, there was an earthquake, and all the doors were immediately opened. The events of the evening set the stage for the conversion of the jailor and his household. Through the ministry of Paul and Silas, many in Philippi became Christians, and a church was established (see Acts 16).

When Paul and Silas, along with Timothy, left Philippi, Luke, the doctor, remained. Luke apparently did much to help stabilize the young congregation and enhance its outreach ministry.

Philippi was a Roman colony located on the great northern east-west highway, called the Egnatian Way. Philippi took its name from Philip II, Alexander the Great's father. Just west of town near the Gangitis River, Antony and Octavian defeated Cassius and Brutus in 42 B.C. In 30 B.C. Octavian made the town a Roman colony for retired soldiers and bestowed upon Philippi the full privileges of Roman citizenship. The Philippians took great pride in their privileges as Roman citizens and lived as faithful citizens of Rome, a point to which Paul appealed for illustration purposes in 3:20.

Women in this colony, as in most of the province of Macedonia, were treated with respect. As reflected in the church (Phil. 4:2-3), the women in this area were active in public life.

**Theme.** A continuous note of joy in Christ is sounded throughout the letter. Despite Paul's testings and the difficulties encountered by the church (Phil. 1:27-30), the theme of joy in Christ is echoed eighteen times in the four chapters of this letter. An exemplary text of this theme is Philippians 4:4: "Rejoice in the Lord always. I will say it again: Rejoice!"

**Literary Form.** As the letter now stands, there is some question concerning its unity and sequence. This has led some scholars to hypothesize that Philippians contains two or three letters joined together by the collector of Paul's letters. The questions involve the placement of the matter concerning Timothy and Epaphroditus (2:19-30), which might be expected to come at the end of the letter rather than the middle. Also the farewell and benediction (4:4-9) seem appropriate for the letter's closing. The conclusion, however, does not occur until after the section concerning the Philippians' generous gifts (4:10-20), which some might expect to begin the letter. In addition there is an emotional outburst (3:2) that is surprising.

While some expect Paul to have been more logical and orderly, the literary structure of the book reveals the hypothesis, however interesting, to be unprovable. The fact that Philippians is an informal letter, probably produced over a period of time, helps explain the roughness of style and the questionable sequence of the letter.

Much discussion has also centered around the origin and interpretation of 2:5-11. It is widely held that this section exemplifies an early Christian hymn or confession that Paul used in support of his appeal for humility. Whether or not this is the case, there is no reason to doubt that Philippians 2:5-11 formed a part of the epistle as originally composed by Paul.

***Purpose and Theology.*** Paul wrote this letter for several reasons:

1. He wanted to explain why he was sending Epaphroditus back to them (2:25-30).

2. He wanted to let them know of his plan to send Timothy to them (2:19-24).

3. He wanted to thank the Philippian church for their concern for him and their generous gifts to him (4:10-20).

4. He desired to inform them of his own circumstances and the advancement of the gospel (1:12-26).

5. He wanted to exhort the church to live in humility, fellowship, and unity (1:27–2:11; 4:2-3).

6. He also needed to warn them concerning the false teachings of legalism, perfectionism, and careless living (3:1 4:1).

The letter is extremely practical, but the guidance and warnings are theologically based: Paul's joy was grounded in Christ, as is all of life. In this sense the letter is thoroughly Christ-centered. The preexistence, incarnation, and exaltation of Christ is set forth in 2:5-11. Christ's incarnation is offered as an example for Paul's appeal to humble living and Christian unity (2:1-4).

Paul explained his doctrine of justification by faith in contrast to a false legalism (3:1-9). He contended for a sanctified life by identification with Christ through faith, sharing in His sufferings, death, and the power of His resurrection (3:10-11). Paul exhorted the church to set its mind on heavenly, rather than earthly, realities because Christians are destined for life in the age to come (3:17–4:1).

I. Greetings (1:1-2)
II. Paul's Joy (1:3-11)
III. Paul's Response (1:12-26)
IV. Paul's Plea (1:27–2:18)
V. Paul's Commendation (2:19-30)
VI. Paul's Warning (3:1-11)
VII. Paul's Exhortation (3:12–4:1)
VIII. Paul's Advice (4:2-9)
IX. Paul's Thanksgiving (4:10-20)
X. Conclusion (4:21-23)

## GREETINGS (1:1-2)

The letter addressed the church in Philippi. Paul and Timothy, who were servants of Christ Jesus, wrote to the saints. "Saints" refers to all believers set apart for God's service. The mention of overseers and deacons indicates a developing maturity in the organization of ung church.

## PAUL'S JOY (1:3-11)

Paul's concern and love for the church was evidenced by his thanksgiving and prayer for them. His prayer is full of joy because of their fellowship in the gospel, the confidence of God's continued work in their lives, and because they also shared in God's grace along with Paul. Paul desired for them to abound in richer and deeper spiritual understanding so that they will be blameless until the day of Christ. The day of Christ will be a time of judgment of the believers' works at the Lord's appearing when their faithfulness will be rewarded.

### DIFFICULT CIRCUMSTANCES (1:12-26)

Paul demonstrated a confident joy in the midst of his situation. If Paul was writing from Rome, his tribulations included mob violence, imprisonment, shipwreck, personal stress, and long detention under the palace guards (2 Cor. 11:23-33). Paul rejoiced that in spite of his circumstances the gospel was being preached, even by those opposing him.

Paul informed them of his past and present situation and consciously weighed the alternatives for his future. The joy of Paul's life was grounded in his Christ-centered life. He stated, "For me, to live is Christ and to die is gain." Dying was gain because it meant to be with Christ, the better by far. Yet it was the Lord's will for Paul to remain in this life because it was more helpful for the Philippians' progress and joy in the faith.

### CHRISTIAN UNITY (1:27-2:18)

In this very significant section of the letter, Paul urged the church members to dismiss their pride and to live and serve together in unity. Anything less falls short of the gospel's standards. True unity will be realized by authentic meekness and selflessness, ultimately exemplified in the earthly life of Jesus. The attitude the church should exhibit was the one Jesus maintained.

Jesus' self-emptying served as the basis for the apostle's exhortation. Philippians 2:5-11, possibly a quotation from an early hymn in praise of Christ, taught that Jesus' self-emptying led to His exaltation by the Father. Jesus existed in the very nature of God and made Himself nothing, not giving up His deity but His heavenly glory and privileges. He lived a life of humble obedience and humbled Himself even to the point of dying for sinners on the cross. He was then gloriously exalted in His resurrection and ascension.

Paul's exhortation to unity involved Christians' working out their salvation with fear and trembling. This action brings about a spiritual community void of complaining and friction. They are encouraged to live as lights in the world, thus holding out the word of life to others and providing joy for the apostle on the day of Christ.

### HUMILITY (2:19-30)

Paul was willing to sacrifice himself in service for the church at Philippi and warmly commended his coworkers, Timothy and Epaphroditus, for their humble and sacrificial service as well. He told of his plan to send Timothy to them when there was further news for him to give. Also he offered an explanation for Epaphroditus's return to them. Paul wanted to be sure the Philippians did not think that Epaphroditus failed in his task to serve Paul.

### SELF-RIGHTEOUSNESS (3:1-11)

Paul warned of the dangers of turning aside to depend on legalistic standards rather than on the grace of God in Christ. Paul labeled these false teachers "dogs, those who do evil, mutilators of the flesh." The church must have been aware of these false teachers, Judaizers, who followed Paul everywhere, insisting that Gentile believers should be circumcised and keep the ceremonial law in order to be saved. Instead, Paul taught that true circumcision involved faith in Christ. He offered himself as an example of one who in his past trusted in human achievement instead of the justifying grace of

God and the all-sufficiency of Christ. (See the article "Justification by Faith.")

The object of joy, of concentration, indeed of all of life is Christ. Paul's purpose in life was to know Christ experientially, becoming like Him in His death and attaining to the resurrection from the dead.

## CHRISTIAN MATURITY (3:12–4:1)

Like an athlete who does not waste time looking around or looking back, Paul exerted his all-out effort to reach the finish line of Christian maturity. He did not presume to have attained perfection and therefore fully pursued the goal of God's upward call in Christ Jesus. He likewise called for the Philippians to move forward in their Christian lives.

Simultaneously in this exhortation he strongly denounced the false teachings of careless living, on the one hand, and spiritual perfectionism on the other. He appealed for unity and maturity by reminding them that they were citizens of heaven. Because the Philippians were intensely proud of their Roman citizenship, they would have quickly grasped all that Paul meant. Finally, he reminded them that they would be transformed at the coming again of the Lord Jesus Christ.

## JOY AND PEACE (4:2-9)

There was some hint of division in the church. Paul appealed to Euodia and Syntyche to agree with each other and for the entire church to stand firm in the Lord. Paul offered them a prescription for receiving God's peace, to rejoice in the Lord, and to let their thoughts be filled with that which is good, lovely, and true.

## THANKSGIVING (4:10-20)

Paul rejoiced and offered thanksgiving for the Philippians' generous care for him. He had learned to be satisfied in whatever situation he found himself in the Lord's service. This word of contentment and thanksgiving came from a man in prison facing death, a man who had been beaten, stoned, and hounded by his enemies. The basis for such contentment was found in his confidence that he could do everything through Christ who gave him strength (4:13). Paul commended them for their generosity. From the first, even at great cost to themselves, they had shared with the apostle. In all of this Paul displayed his attitude toward material things and urged them to realize that God would meet all their needs according to His glorious riches in Christ Jesus.

## CONCLUSION (4:21-23)

Paul concluded his letter with a benediction and personal greetings. He also sent greetings from Caesar's household, which included Christian members of the emperor's staff.

**Theological Significance.** In this letter we learn the importance of church unity (1:27-30) and Christian humility (2:1-4). Christ's humility serves as the basis of Christian humility, which is the key for genuine Christian unity. Paul's suffering during his imprisonment also serves as a foundation for teaching abasement and humility (1:12-18; 4:10-13). Alongside abasement and suffering is joy, the great theme of the letter. In all of life's circumstances believers can experience joy. For it is in suffering and sacrifice that true joy is found. Paul's exhortation to rejoice is a much-needed and practical word for believers at all times in all situations.

### Questions for Reflection

1. What does this letter teach us about hardship and suffering?

2. What should be our attitude concerning material things?

3. What can we learn about what Jesus has done for us in providing our salvation and offering us an example of selfless living?

4. How can we demonstrate unity in our churches so as to avoid conflict and bickering?

5. What can we learn through the examples of Timothy and Epaphroditus?

## Sources for Additional Study

Bruce, F. F. Philippians, *A Good News Commentary*. San Francisco: Harper and Row, 1983.

Martin, Ralph P. *The Epistle of Paul to the Philippians.* Tyndale New Testament Commentaries. Grand Rapids: Eerdmans, 1959.

Melick, Richard R., Jr. *Philippians, Colossians, Philemon.* The New American Commentary. Nashville: Broadman, 1991.

Motyer, J. A. *The Message of Philippians.* Downers Grove: InterVarsity, 1984.

# COLOSSIANS

Tradition supports the letter's claim that Paul was the author (Col. 1:1). Paul had never been to Colosse, but he wrote to them to address matters raised by Epaphras (1:7). The letter would have been written about the same time as Ephesians and Philemon (around 60–61). (See the discussion of dates in Philippians and Ephesians.)

Some people today doubt Pauline authorship on the grounds of the book's theology and style. But some obvious differences in the theological perspective do not force one to conclude that someone other than Paul wrote Colossians.

**Destination.** Colosse was an important city in Phrygia on the upper Lycus River in what is today South Central Turkey. It served as a trading center at a crossroads on the main highway from Ephesus to the east. In Roman times relocation of the road leading north to Pergamum brought about both the growth of Laodicea, a city ten miles away, and Colosse's gradual decline.

In New Testament times Colosse was a small city with a mixed population of Phrygians, Greeks, and Jews. Paul may have instructed some from Colosse during his stay in Ephesus (see Acts 19:10). Epaphras, a leader in the church at Colosse, visited Paul in prison in Rome and told him about the church's situation (Col. 1:7; 4:12). Epaphras was later imprisoned with Paul (Phlm. 23). Paul wrote to the Colossians to address the concerns raised by Epaphras at the same time he wrote to the church about Onesimus (Phlm. 16).

**Purpose.** Paul's purpose was to address the false teaching in the church.

To identify the false teaching has been a puzzling problem for students of Paul's letters. Some think the problem was basically a form of Gnosticism. Others think it was a Jewish mystical asceticism. Still others suggest a type of legalistic separatism. Some think it was a syncretistic (combined forms) movement with aspects of each of these ideologies. What we do know is that the false teaching

- attacked the centrality of Christ (1:15-19; 2:9-10);
- focused on speculative philosophical traditions (2:8);
- observed dietary prescriptions and prohibitions (2:16,21);
- observed certain religious rites of a Jewish nature (2:16);
- venerated angels (2:18);
- tended toward asceticism (2:20).

The readers were admonished to "see to it that no one takes you captive through hollow and deceptive philosophy, which depends on human tradition and the basic principles of this world rather than on Christ" (2:8). Paul countered this false teaching with correct teaching, focusing on the supremacy of Christ (1:15-23), ministry and the church (1:24–2:7), and other exhortations (3:1–4:6).

**Theology.** Paul's major teaching centered around the question Who is Jesus Christ? The apostle insisted that no chasm existed between the transcendent God and His material creation. Christ is both the Creator and Reconciler (1:15-23). He is the exact expression of God and brings together heaven and earth. A need for a hierarchy of angelic powers is nonexistent since Christ is fully divine and fully human. Indeed "in Christ all the full-

## GNOSTICISM

Gnosticism is difficult to define because it is used of a collection of divergent movements. The term is derived from the Greek word for knowledge (gnosis). Usually Gnosticism is used of a second-century Christian heresy that was a major threat to the church. The main ideas in Gnostic systems include the following:

1. A dualism in the universe between God and a lesser, evil being usually called the Demiurge.

2. God is unknowable and is neither concerned about the world nor has anything to do with it.

3. Various beings emerge from God and join in male and female pairs to form concentric barriers around God.

4. The female being in the last barrier, without her male partner, gave birth to the Demiurge.

5. The Demiurge created the world, and therefore anything material (including the body) is evil.

6. But a spark of the divine was also placed in humans (or at least some of them) that needs to be awakened and called back to the divine.

7. A revealer calls humans and shows the way through the barriers. Christ was viewed as the revealer, but He was not truly human. He only took over the body of Jesus at the baptism and left before His death.

8. Knowledge of one's true self and of the character of the universe is the way to salvation. Salvation is achieved when at death or the end of the world a person passes through the barriers and is reintegrated into God.

With these core ideas a variety of Gnostic systems developed with different emphases. Some of them had very strict rules, while some had no rules.

*Origins of Gnosticism.* Little is known about the origins of Gnosticism. It had no one founder, even though the name Simon Magus (see Acts 8) was often associated in church traditions with the rise of Gnosticism. Gnosticism had no founding text, nor can a specific time of beginning for the movement be identified. Some of the ideas in Gnosticism were already current in New Testament times. But although debated, there is no evidence that Gnosticism existed before Christianity.

Some facts about the origin of Gnosticism are clear. This religion arose because of a deeply felt spiritual need. One of the main concerns was the problem of evil. The Gnostic understanding of the universe was a way to protect God from any responsibility for the evil in this world. Ideas were gathered from various religions, especially Judaism. The focus on knowledge and light is present in nearly every religion.

Until recently most of what was known about Gnosticism was obtained from quotations of church fathers. In 1945 the discovery of a Gnostic library at Nag Hammadi, Egypt, provided firsthand evidence of Gnostic beliefs.

*Relevance of Gnosticism.* Gnosticism is obviously important for an understanding of church history. It is also important theologically. We too must deal with the problem of evil. Many of the errors of Gnosticism are still dangers. Often there is a tendency to reject God's created world and to view the body as evil or to view Christ as not fully human. Or, like the famous Gnostic Marcion, many people are tempted to reject the authority of the Old Testament.

Gnosticism is also important for reading the New Testament.

Already the ideas of Gnosticism were emerging. First John 4:2 stresses the necessity of acknowledging that Jesus Christ has come *in the flesh.* Timothy was warned against a "falsely called knowledge" (1 Tim 6:20). Gnostic tendencies are sometimes identified as the problems in 1 Corinthians and Colossians, but other explanations of the difficulties in these churches are more likely.

Also an awareness of Gnosticism reminds us that in Christianity knowledge does not save; a faith relationship with Christ does.

---

ness of the Deity lives in bodily form, and you have this fullness in Christ, who is the head over every power and authority" (2:9-10).

Second, he dealt with the issue of genuine spirituality. Paul developed the basis for genuine worship and spirituality by refuting the false spirituality that encouraged an unspiritual pride (2:6-23). He exhorted them to abandon sins of the old life and cultivate the virtues of the new life (3:5–4:6).

I. Introduction (1:1-14)
II. Christ's Supremacy (1:15-23)
III. Ministry for the Church (1:24–2:5)
IV. Warnings against False Spirituality (2:6–3:4)
V. Exhortations for Ethical Living (3:5–4:6)
VI. Conclusion (4:7-18)

**Theme.** The theme of this letter centers on the supremacy of Christ in all things.

### INTRODUCTION (1:1-14)

Paul followed a standard form of salutation, thanksgiving, and prayer in the first part of the letter. It is perhaps longer than some of his other letters because Paul was not personally acquainted with the people of Colosse. The salutation carried greetings from both Paul and Timothy. Words of high commendation and thanksgiving follow for the well-being and spiritual health of the Christian community at Colosse.

These opening words are followed by Paul's prayer for their knowledge and godly conduct. The prayer centered on spiritual blessings, not on physical or material things. He prayed for spiritual insight, genuine obedience, and moral excellence. The prayer went right to the heart of the false teaching invading the church.

The false teachers promised a special insight and a superior spirituality. Terms like knowledge, wisdom, and spiritual understanding were a part of the false teachers' vocabulary. So Paul employed these types of words in his prayer. The prayer requested that God "fill" them "with the knowledge of his will." The term "filled" is a key word in Colossians. It was likewise an important term for the false teachers. Paul used it here and in 1:19,25; 2:2,9-10; 4:12,17. It carries the idea *of being fully equipped or controlled.* Paul's prayer then was for the Colossians to be controlled by the full knowledge of God's will, which would lead to obedience and moral excellence.

### CHRIST'S SUPREMACY (1:15-23)

The false teachers challenged the true nature and deity of Jesus Christ. Their teaching possibly involved the worship of angels or some other beings (2:15,18,20) who negated or minimized the supremacy of Christ. The false teachers declared that salvation was achieved by knowledge rather than faith. Paul's answer to these matters begins in this important section.

Many think that 1:15-20 was a pre-Pauline hymn that Paul used and applied for the Colossian situation. Regardless, whether reworked or original, Paul presented Christ as preeminent in relation to the entire creation and in relation to humanity and the church because of His resurrection. This hymn or early creed celebrated Christ as the sovereign Creator and Redeemer of all things.

Paul described Jesus as Lord of creation, the "firstborn." The term "firstborn" stresses uniqueness and sovereignty rather than priority in time. Jesus is the "firstborn" because He is the agent of creation and the heir of creation.

Paul developed a physiological metaphor to establish the relationship of head over the body. As the head Christ sends life into the whole body. The church responds in humble adoration, acknowledging that Christ is head over all. God was pleased for His fullness to dwell in Christ and through Him to reconcile all things to Himself. The reconciliation spoken of in verses 19-20 is discussed with reference to humankind. Through Christ's physical death they have been reconciled to God. The purpose of Christ's reconciliation is to achieve a new

## SALVATION IN PAUL'S THOUGHT

The message of salvation was central in Paul's thought. He addressed the issue from the perspective of Christ's work on the cross for us. Common themes include justification by faith, new life in Christ, freedom, grace, and assurance. We will examine Paul's thought with a focus on the doctrine of justification by faith.

Justification (or righteousness) by faith summarizes Paul's teaching tat faith in Christ now secures the vindication of the believer in the final judgment. It represents Paul's understanding of the gospel. Paul emphasized that Christ's giving of Himself on the cross on behalf of us and our sins was necessary and sufficient for the salvation of all, both Jew and Gentile.

Paul's pronouncements on this matter always appear in contexts in which relations between believing Jews and Gentiles are at issue. In Galatians the question at hand was whether Gentile believers must be circumcised and adhere to the law of Moses in order to be assured of salvation. Paul vigorously attacked this suggestion and those who would press it upon the Galatian churches (Gal. 5:1-12; see Phil. 3:1-11).

In Romans Paul addressed a predominantly Gentile church with a Jewish minority, who were in danger of rejecting one another. Here Paul's aim in unfolding his understanding of justification by faith was to secure allegiance to his gospel. This would provide the basis for mutual acceptance by the opposing groups (Rom. 15:7-13). In all these instances Paul's claim that righteousness was given through faith opposed the idea that it was given through the law (Rom. 3:21; Gal. 3:11), works (Rom. 4:2,6), or works of the law (Rom. 3:20,28; Gal. 3:2).

Variations on the theme of justification appear in the Corinthian correspondence. In these letters Paul stressed that it is Christ and the shame and suffering of His crucifixion that effects our righteousness (see 1 Cor. 1:22-25,30).

In Ephesians Paul developed the topic further. The apostle taught that grace was the ultimate and faith the mediate means to salvation (Eph. 2:8-9). Similarly in the Pastoral letters we find the formulation "justification [or salvation] by grace" (2 Tim. 1:9; Titus 3:7). All of these statements elaborate the theme of justification by faith for Gentile readers. Paul did this also in Romans, where in speaking to Gentile readers he explained that being justified by faith means possessing peace with God and the assurance of salvation (Rom. 5:1-11).

It is important to bear in mind that justification by faith was only one aspect of Paul's gospel. For Paul participation in Christ involved more. It also meant being made new in Christ, indwelt and empowered by the Spirit for obedience to God (Rom. 6; 8:1-17).

According to Paul it is impossible to share in one aspect of salvation without sharing in all of them. Those justified by faith manifest the fruit of the Spirit in their lives (Gal. 5:16-26). The freedom that the gospel brings is not a freedom for oneself or one's sinful desires but a freedom for service to God and love for one's neighbor (Gal. 5:13-14). Paul did not expect believers to be sinless, but he did expect to see progress and evidence of the presence of Christ in the believer's life (see 2 Cor. 13:5).

The basis for Paul's exhortation to believers lies in what God has done for them in Christ, including justification. They obey not in order to become new persons but because Christ has made them new persons already (see Gal. 5:25; 1 Cor. 5:7).

Christians must again and again by faith appropriate God's saving promises made in the gospel (Gal. 3:3; 5:5-6). Our appropriation of this teaching must always be guided by the purposes for which Paul's arguments were formed. They were not intended to provide an excuse for sinful behavior or a lax spiritual life. They were given instead to shatter all human pretense at righteousness before God, to expose the ultimate sickness and depravity of human nature, and to apply the saving cure of Christ and His cross.

creation in which estranged people may know and approach God.

## MINISTRY FOR THE CHURCH (1:24–2:5)

The second major part of the letter described Paul's apostolic ministry for the church. Paul's ministry task involved making known the mystery of God concerning Christ to the Gentiles in general and to the churches of Colosse in particular. Paul's service was to make known to Gentiles the "mystery" that God had kept hidden from the world but has now revealed to people like Paul. Paul worked to bring about the inclusion of the Gentiles into the church so he could "present everyone perfect in Christ."

Paul's efforts on behalf of the Gentiles were intended to help them know the meaning of God's "mystery" about Christ. By mystery Paul meant that God has now revealed something formerly concealed. The mystery is the fact that Gentiles are now made fellow members with Jewish Christians.

## CHRIST IS DIVINE (2:6-15)

Paul wanted to make sure the Colossians did not follow those who set forth Christ as merely an important visionary or religious leader. Christ is uniquely divine and preeminent. This is the foundation for true spirituality. The exhortation to live in him [Christ] is surrounded by themes that are clearly a response to the false teaching that threatened them. The context emphasizes "as you received Christ Jesus" and "as you were taught." Paul obviously considered the false teachers a real threat to the church. He warned, "See to it that no one takes you captive through hollow and deceptive philosophy."

The right antidote for false teaching is right teaching about Christ, in whom "all the fullness of Deity lives in bodily form." In Christ believers have received all they have and all they need. Christians are not subject to any forms of legalism, nor does legalism do them any good spiritually. Jesus Christ alone is sufficient for our every spiritual need, for all of God's fullness is in Him. The believers' covenant relation, their lives, their freedom, and their victory are all in Him.

## CAPTIVE TO CHRIST (2:16–3:4)

The spiritual life has its dangers and its warnings. Paul warned the church against those who would make the Christian life just a set of rules. The basis for resisting legalism involves focusing on the believer's relationship with Christ. Believers no longer are captive to religious tradition or human bondage. Instead, they are captive to Christ. In view of this privileged identification with Christ, the church must realize its great responsibility: "Set your minds on things above."

The life in Christ is a profound reality (see Gal. 2:20). It is a life that draws its existence from the very center of all reality, Jesus Christ Himself. The admonitions that follow are controlled by the thought of the full life that belongs to all who are in Christ (see Rom. 6:4-5).

## PUT SIN TO DEATH (3:5-11)

Paul exhorted the Colossians to put to death whatever belonged to their "earthly nature" (3:5). This suggests that they had not been living consistently with the principle of a spiritual death and resurrection in their conversion. Some think it is only coincidental that Paul listed five vices in 3:5 and five more in 3:8 and then five virtues in 3:12. More likely Paul was responding to the heretics' list of vices and virtues. The list initially focused on sexual sins. Those who commit such sins bring the wrath of God on themselves. In their former way of life the Colossians practiced this kind of sin. Now they were commanded to differentiate themselves from such conduct.

## PUT ON LOVE (3:12-17)

This section completes Paul's exhortation to the Colossians to maintain a holy lifestyle. Paul admonished them "to clothe yourselves with compassion, kindness, humility, gentleness and patience." Over all these they should "put on love, which binds them all together in perfect unity."

The heretics were obviously causing divisions in the church. The way to unity included letting the peace of Christ and the word of Christ rule in their hearts. This required obedient application. So Paul said, "Whatever you do, whether in word or deed, do it all in the name of the Lord Jesus, giving thanks to God the Father through him."

## FAMILY LIFE (3:18–4:1)

Paul turned to the issue of household relationships. He addressed husbands and wives, parents and children, and slaves and masters. As in Ephesians 5:21–6:9, Paul arranged his discussion to treat the subordinate person first (wife, child, or slave). Paul immediately followed each statement with a reminder of the responsibility of the second member of each pair. The distinctly Christian contribution to the ordering of family life was the stress on reciprocal responsibilities. Even in culture where family relationships were given an importance and significance not widespread in antiquity, it was generally assumed that husbands and fathers had rights to be exercised but few duties. Wives and children assumed they had duties but no or few rights. Paul stressed that all household members had rights and duties. Paul here taught a picture of family life implicit in Jesus' teaching concerning marriage (see Mark 10:2-16).

## CONDUCT AND SPEECH (4:2-6)

This section concludes with further instructions to continue in prayer and to conduct themselves in a worthy manner toward others. Believers' conduct and speech should be carefully controlled and used with great wisdom and love.

## CONCLUSION (4:7-18)

Paul's lengthy conclusion included personal news, greetings, and final instructions. The conclusion gives the letter, which is strategically polemical in places, a real personal touch. The apostles referred to Tychicus, who carried this letter plus Ephesians and Philemon, and to Onesimus, the runaway slave who accompanied him. They were to give a report to the church concerning Paul and Epaphras as well as pertinent information regarding Onesimus's situation.

Paul often sent greetings from those with him. He mentioned Aristarchus, Mark, Jesus (Justus), Epaphras, Luke, and Demas. Mark was the cousin of Barnabas and companion with Paul and Barnabas on the first journey (see Acts 12:12,25; 13:4). But Mark had turned back before the journey was finished, and Paul did not want to take him on future journeys (see Acts 13:4,13; 15:37). Evidently Mark had reconciled himself with Paul.

The reference to a Laodicean letter in 4:16 has called forth numerous suggestions. Some have identified Paul's letter to the Ephesians as this letter. Others have suggested that Philemon was the letter to which Paul referred. Still others have identified the reference to a lost letter to the Laodiceans. We cannot know for sure. Archippus was encouraged to fulfill the temporary ministry he had received. He fittingly asked to be remembered in prayer. Paul concluded with a brief benediction written in his own hand. This probably implies that Paul dictated the letter to a secretary and then signed it himself (see Rom. 16:22).

***Theological Significance.*** In Colosse a religious philosophy appeared that challenged the essence of Christian teaching. It contained Jewish elements (2:16), had an aspect of angel worship (2:18), and had a strong ascetic emphasis (2:20-23). This philosophy brought divisions to the church. It had some parallels with Christianity, but its teaching about Christ was wrongheaded. Today similar movements exist that confront the church's theology about Christ as well as its spirituality. The proper response needed in the church then is the same today. These contemporary New Age teachings must be recognized for what they are. The church must readily affirm that "in Christ all the fullness of the Deity lives in bodily form" (2:9). Any effort to approach God through angelic or human intermediaries is not only misguided, but it is a denial of Christ and authentic Christian teaching.

## Questions for Reflection

1. How is the gospel threatened by combining portions of truth and portions of error from various theological traditions?

2. How does the church deal with false ascetic movements? legalistic movements?

3. What is involved in a distinctively Christian understanding of Jesus Christ?

4. What are the implications of Paul's teaching in Colossians for the church's contemporary response to New Age movements?

### Sources for Additional Study

Bruce, F. F., *The Epistles to the Colossians to Philemon, and to the Ephesians.* The New International Commentary. Grand Rapids: Eerdmans, 1984.

Martin. R. P. Colossians and Philemon. *New Century Bible.* Grand Rapids: Eerdmans, 1981.

Melick, Richard R., Jr. *Philippians, Colossians, Philemon.* The New American Commentary. Nashville: Broadman, 1991.

# 1 THESSALONIANS

Galatians probably was the first of Paul's letters to be written, and 1 Thessalonians was the second. Paul traveled to Thessalonica, the capital city of Macedonia, on his second missionary journey around A.D. 51. Luke reported the brief visit, Paul's preaching ministry there with Silas, and the subsequent persecution that drove them out of the city (see Acts 17:1-9). Many people believed in Jesus Christ before they were compelled to leave. From Thessalonica, Paul went to Berea, Athens, and then Corinth. Timothy and Silas, who had been with Paul at Thessalonica, rejoined Paul in Corinth (see Acts 18:5; 1 Thess. 3:6). Paul wrote 1 Thessalonians in response to Timothy's report shortly after his arrival.

***Purpose of the Letter.*** Paul received the report that the Thessalonians were strong in faith and were making favorable progress. He wrote this letter to defend himself against enemies who spread false rumors and to answer the Thessalonians' questions. Paul's experience with the opposition of the Jews in Corinth, terminating in his expulsion from the synagogue, may well have been the reason for his strong condemnation in 1 Thessalonians 2:14-16. The controversy over the law had plagued the churches of Macedonia. Paul's Jewish adversaries had accused him of being a heretic, a deceiver, and a religious adventurer who made a living by victimizing an ignorant public. The letter to the Thessalonians was Paul's answer to these issues.

***Theology of the Letter.*** Paul's basic theology about salvation, Christ, and His return make up the essence of the letter. Here we learn there is one living and true God (1 Thess. 1:9) who has loved men and women (1 Thess. 1:4) and has revealed Himself to them (1 Thess. 2:13). This revelation concerned His Son, the Lord Jesus Christ (1 Thess. 1:3,8,10) who died and rose again (1 Thess. 4:14) for our salvation (1 Thess. 5:9). The Holy Spirit imparts joy, authoritative truth, and prophetic wisdom (1 Thess. 1:6; 4:8; 5:19). The apostle taught that holiness of life is required of all Christians (1 Thess. 4:3; 5:23).

Paul often mentioned the gospel (1 Thess. 1:5; 2:2-4,8; 3:2), though not in the framework of justification by faith. He affirmed that Jesus' death and resurrection are the core of the gospel, but the greatest single doctrinal emphasis of this letter concerned the return of Christ (1 Thess. 1:10; 2:19; 3:13; 4:13-18; 5:23). This teaching indicates that the expectation regarding the return of Christ was the hope of the earliest church. The motivation for Christian living was based on this anticipation. The hopelessness of death was reversed and abandoned because of this confident hope.

I. Salutation (1:1)
II. Personal Relations (1:2–3:13)
III. Church Problems (4:1–5:11)
IV. Concluding Exhortations (5:12-28)

## SALUTATION (1:1)

The salutation included the identification of the writer, the recipients, and a Christian greeting. Paul, Silas, and Timothy were the authors, though obviously Paul was the primary writer. The letter is addressed "to the church of the Thessalonians, who are in God the Father and the Lord Jesus Christ." This opening word describes the church's union with the Godhead, which meant a new sphere of life on an infinitely higher plane.

## FAITH, HOPE, AND LOVE (1:2-10)

The first part of the letter deals primarily with the response of the church and the nature of Paul's ministry.

Paul offered thanksgiving for the Thessalonians' faith. This letter started Paul's practice of beginning his letters by thanking God for his readers (all of his letters except the first letter to the Galatians contain such a statement). Paul's words were not mere rhetorical flattery. He was giving credit to One who brought about their spiritual progress.

The apostle's trilogy of faith, hope, and love is introduced at this early part of the letter. Paul described the church service as "work produced by faith, labor prompted by love, and endurance inspired by hope in our Lord Jesus Christ." He commended their courageous service that excluded self-pity. The early church associated faith with work (see Gal. 5:6; Jas. 2:18), love with labor (see Rev. 2:2,4), and hope with endurance (see Rom. 5:2-4; 8:24).

Paul found in the fruitfulness of their lives an adequate proof that God loved them. The knowledge of God's prior choice of these believers was the root of Paul's thanksgiving. The heart of divine election is God's sovereign decision to choose a people for Himself, making them peculiarly His own.

The power of the gospel to bring about conviction and transform lives encouraged the apostle. He knew the Holy Spirit was the source of that power. The Thessalonians welcomed the message and were converted. In spite of difficult circumstances and severe suffering, they had a joy that could only be supplied by the Spirit. They rapidly became imitators of Paul and the Lord and thus became a model to all believers throughout Macedonia and Achaia.

The apostle affirmed that these converts played a substantial part in the ever-widening scope of Christian witness. Their testimony echoed the preaching that had undergirded the mission to Thessalonica. They had turned (been converted) from idol worship to the worship of God. They turned to serve the living God and to wait for His Son from heaven. Early Christianity universally maintained that the resurrected and ascended Christ would return. Their expectancy of this event implied its imminency. Ultimately the faith, hope, and commitment of all believers should be focused on the person of Jesus, in whom God's gracious favor found its most pointed expression.

## GOD-APPROVED MINISTRY (2:1-9)

Chapter 2 is new material, but it is closely related to chapter 1 as the following chart shows:

| 2:1-6 | expands | 1:4-10 |
|---|---|---|
| 2:7-12 | restates | 1:5,9 |
| 2:13-16 | echoes | 1:6-8,10 |

Chapter 2 is a defense against insinuations about his alleged ulterior motives. The apostle was subjected to a constant barrage of accusations. The Thessalonians themselves may have begun to question Paul's sincerity. No evidence of organized opposition on a wide scale exists. Estrangement could have developed unless treated immediately. So Paul addressed his readers most affectionately.

Paul claimed their ministry (Paul as well as Timothy and Silas) was above suspicion. It was bold and powerful because God had approved their ministry to preach the gospel. The success of their mission, in spite of sustained opposition, was due largely to their courage inspired by God. The approval of God was more significant for Paul and his team than the success of the mission. Yet the success of the work offered important validation of his motives and message. Verses 7-8 picture Paul as one who had found sufficient reason to endure suffering and the questions surrounding his character. He denied that flattery was the means of his ministry. Also greed and human praise were not the motivations for his ministry.

### WORTHY OF GOD (2:10-16)

Paul appealed to the sensitive nature of their ministry in order to silence those who attacked him. To the hesitant he offered exhortation; to the weary he offered encouragement; to the weak he offered strength and direction. His motivation was to help each convert see what it meant "to live lives worthy of God, who calls you into his kingdom and glory."

Christian ministers are expected to offer practical guidance to fellow Christians, but not as dictators. Christian leaders cannot rule by decree. If they are to be true to the Spirit of Christ, they must lead by example. The example must be modeled after the Lord Jesus Christ (see 2 Cor. 1:12; Phil. 2:7).

Paul returned to the theme of thanksgiving in verse 13. His thanksgiving for them was an aspect of his vindication and served as a demonstration of his guileless interest in them. They had listened to him and welcomed his message as "the word of God, which is at work in [those] who believe." The manner of speech was Paul's. At the same time God was uttering His own powerful, creative word through him. The word had evidenced its power in their daily experience.

The words of verses 15-16 have been the source of careful scrutiny. Some think Paul spoke mistakenly about the Jews.

Others reject Pauline authorship of these verses. These options are hardly worthy of Holy Scripture. Certainly the words here reveal Paul's heartfelt concern and exasperation with his countrymen. Yet to read this as personal vindication is to misunderstand Paul's point. It is the rejection of the gospel that moved Paul to bitter denunciation reminiscent of the prophets of God.

### MY GLORY AND JOY (2:17–3:5)

Paul again expressed deep feeling for the Thessalonians. He described himself in sharp contrast to the persecutors just mentioned in 2:14-16. He declared that the Thessalonians were his glory and joy—not only at Christ's return but even at that very time.

We are allowed to see into Paul's heart in 3:1-5. Paul's deepest concerns for the church are here expressed. He needed to know how the Thessalonians were doing in the midst of persecution. Paul's mission was to strengthen and encourage them in their faith (see Rom. 1:11; 16:25; 1 Thess. 3:13). He knew dependence on God in faith was their only recourse in adversity.

### FAITH THAT LACKS (3:6-13)

Timothy's report of the favorable feelings of the Thessalonians toward him assured Paul that the church had not cast him off as one who exploited them. The encouraging report rejuvenated Paul (as it did elsewhere; see Rom. 1:12; 2 Cor. 7:4; Phlm. 7). Along with rejoicing, Paul prayed continually for the believers in Thessalonica that God would supply what was lacking in their faith.

The prayer reflects the transition in Paul's life from anguish to exhilaration. The prayer served to conclude what he had said in this section (2:13:13) and prepared the readers for what Paul had to say in the second half of the letter. He prayed that God would enable him to visit his friends. Then he asked the Lord to perfect and enlarge the love the Thessalonians had already displayed toward one another.

Love toward God and toward others turns us away from selfish concerns and opens the way to moral perfection that is the condition of holiness. This radical transformation of character Paul desired for the church then and God desires for believers today so that they may face Christ's return without fear or shame. Daringly Paul set himself as a standard of love to be emulated, a step he could take only because of his imitation of Jesus (see 1 Thess. 1:5-7).

## SEXUAL MORALITY (4:1-12)

The second section of the letter shifts to ethical or doctrinal issues. Up to this point the letter has been intensely personal. Now it shifts to instruction and exhortation.

Paul encouraged his readers to purity of life, love, and faithful work. The word "finally" was used to indicate the transition in Paul's thought. He addressed matters of moral irregularities and brotherly love.

Pagan culture looked upon sexual immorality either indifferently or favorably. Had church members slipped into immorality they probably would not have thought it strange. Paul gave general guidelines concerning pleasing God and then specific ones focused on sexual morality. To please God is to do His will, and His will is the sanctification of the believer.

Verses 6-8 provide theological reasons for his ethical exhortations. These include the judgment of God and God's calling on their lives; the words themselves are God's words. To reject these words is to reject God.

Paul turned from negative commands in verses 1-8 to positive concerns in verses 9-12. The manner of the believer's lifestyle should be characterized by mutual edification. God's will includes the necessity of moral purity and love relationship with people, which demands openness and self-sacrifice on the part of believers.

## HOPE IN GRIEF (4:13-18)

This important paragraph holds out hope for believers during times of sorrow. The believing community should not grieve over those who have died in Jesus because God will bring them with Jesus at the return of the Lord. Paul desired that these believers not grieve as those who are without hope.

The "Lord's own word" further confirmed the fact that the Christian dead will experience no disadvantage at the Lord's return. Paul said the living believer will not have an advantage at the Lord's appearing. In fact, the Christian dead will rise first. After that those "who are still alive" will be "caught up with them in the clouds to meet the Lord in the air." These encouraging words provided great comfort to those whose family members had already died. Also it served as the basis for an evangelistic appeal to those who have no hope. Paul exhorted the believers to comfort one another with these words.

## DAY OF THE LORD (5:1-11)

In this section Paul continued his discussion about the Lord's return with particular emphasis on the meaning of the Day of the Lord. Since the Day of the Lord will come suddenly and unexpectedly, bringing destruction on those who are spiritually insensitive, believers should maintain spiritual alertness. The good news for the Thessalonians and for all believers is that their destiny is not wrath but eschatological deliverance through Jesus Christ. Again Paul exhorted believers to comfort one another.

Believers should encourage and build up one another in the faith because one day we will live with Christ. The simultaneous truths concerning the return of Christ and the resurrection of believers offer hope and meaning for living. The flip side is that at the Day of the Lord, God's wrath will be revealed. There is no universalism in this text. People need to be saved from the wrath to come by placing their faith and hope in the Lord.

## CONCLUDING EXHORTATIONS (5:12-28)

The concluding section stresses the responsibilities to the different people in the Christian community. Paul told them they were responsible to church leaders. Leaders were to guard against abusing their authority.

Verses 14-15 focused on their responsibilities to others. They were to warn when necessary, encourage the timid, and show kindness to one another. Responsibilities to oneself and to one's spiritual relationship with God can be seen in 1 Thessalonians 5:16-18. Compliance with other commands and exhortations in the book is impossible apart from personal communion with God. To "be joyful always; pray continually; give thanks in all circumstances" is possible even in the midst of persecution when one recognizes God's superintendence over all things (see Rom. 8:28).

Paul shifted the focus from the personal to the community in 1 Thessalonians 5:19-22. Here Paul reflected on the believers' responsibilities in Christian worship. They were not to underestimate the importance of prophecy while holding "on to the good." Finally they were to be free from every kind of evil that attempts to parade itself as a genuine representation of the Spirit.

Paul offered edifying words of blessing for the church. These comments underscore the importance of prayer in carrying out the purposes of God. Paul's signature theme—"the grace of our Lord Jesus Christ"—concludes this pastoral and encouraging letter.

**Theological Significance.** The letter is more practical than theological. It is God-centered throughout. God chose them unto salvation (1 Thess. 1:4). His will is the guide for all believers (1 Thess. 4:3). He calls His people to holy living (1 Thess. 4:7) and imparts sanctification to them so they can live obediently. He raised Jesus from the dead (1 Thess. 4:14) and will raise believers to be with Him at the Lord's return (1 Thess. 4:13–5:11).

The letter was written specifically to reassure those who were concerned about believers who had already died. Words of comfort and hope from Paul about the resurrection of believers provide equally good news for the church of all times in all places. This good news serves as a basis for practical and godly living.

### Questions for Reflection

1. How does what Paul says about the nature of ministry speak to church leaders and church members today?

2. What is the relationship between the promise of the Lord's return and holy living?

3. How can the true character of Christian love be communicated in a secular world that has degraded the idea of love?

4. In what way is Paul's teaching about the Christian life in 1 Thessalonians 4:1-12 binding on Christians today?

### Sources for Additional Study

Bruce, F. F. 1 and 2 Thessalonians. Word Biblical Commentary. Waco: Word, 1982.

Hiebert, D. E. The Thessalonian Epistles. Chicago: Moody, 1971.

Marshall, I. Howard. 1 and 2 Thessalonians. Grand Rapids: Eerdmans, 1983.

Stott, John R. W. The Gospel and the End of Time. Downers Grove: InterVarsity, 1991.

# 2 THESSALONIANS

Paul's authorship of 2 Thessalonians has been questioned frequently in recent years in spite of the fact that it has extremely strong support throughout church history. The objections to Pauline authorship are threefold: (1) The style of 2 Thessalonians is said to be more formal than 1 Thessalonians. (2) The vocabulary is supposedly too different from the rest of Paul's writings (ten words in 2 Thessalonians are not used elsewhere in Paul). (3) The unique approach to eschatology in 2 Thessalonians (the "man of lawlessness" is not mentioned elsewhere). However, these arguments are not convincing in light of the similarity of content between 1 and 2 Thessalonians.

The interval between 1 and 2 Thessalonians must have been rather short, for the second epistle does not presuppose major changes in the inner constitution of the Thessalonian church or in the conditions under which Paul was writing (see introduction to 1 Thessalonians).

**Occasion of the Letter.** The second letter was apparently evoked by alarm on the part of the Thessalonians who had been informed that the Day of the Lord had arrived.

The agitators who had confused the Thessalonians apparently appealed for authority either to the utterances of inspired prophets within the church, or to some phrases from Paul's writings, or possibly to a forged epistle (2 Thess. 2:1). Some who anticipated the Lord's soon return had ceased working and depended on others to supply them with life's necessities (3:11).

The church members were uncertain of their position because of inexperience.

They needed reassurance in order to cope with opposition of pagan culture and their own doubts raised by their own misunderstandings (2:15). Discipline was needed to keep the lazy ones from disrupting the community life (3:13-15).

**Purpose and Theology.** Paul's purpose in writing 2 Thessalonians paralleled his first letter to them.

1. He wrote to encourage the persecuted church (1:4-10).

2. He attempted to correct the misunderstanding about the Lord's return. (Much of the letter, 18 out of 47 verses, deals with this issue.)

3. He exhorted the church to be steadfast in all things (2:13-3:15).

4. Paul's emphasis was on the return of Christ when the church will be gathered to Him (2:1) and the wicked will be judged (1:6-9; 2:8).

5. Paul instructed the church concerning the man of lawlessness (2:1-12).

The man of lawlessness has no exact parallel in history. The mystery of lawlessness was already at work but was restrained by some "secret power" (2:7) so that it might burst forth at any time in uncontrollable fury. The man of lawlessness is a human being possessed by demonic power who claims for himself the prerogatives of deity. The end times will be accompanied by a rise of organized evil. A blasphemous attempt to supplant the worship of God by the worship of a man who will be the final manifestation of Satanic power will culminate the final apostasy. The force that holds back (2:6) the completion of the mystery of lawlessness has been variously interpreted as (1) the Roman imperial rule, (2) the Jewish nation, (3) the church, or (4) the Holy Spirit.

I. Salvation (1:1-2)

II. Encouragement for the Church (1:3-12)

III. Instructions to Correct Misunderstandings (2:1-12)

IV. Injunctions to Steadfastness (2:13–3:18)

## SALVATION (1:1-2)

The letter started by identifying Paul, Silas, and Timothy as its senders. No doubt Paul was the primary author. The letter's beginning followed the pattern of most Pauline letters (see 1 Thessalonians).

## ENCOURAGEMENT (1:3-12)

The Thessalonians were commended for their growing faith and their maturing love and patience. Paul offered praise and thanksgiving to God for their lifestyles.

Paul offered hope to his readers by noting the forthcoming reversal in God's judgment of the present roles of the persecuted and the persecutors. While the Thessalonians were at that time facing persecution, the persecutors had to face judgment at the coming of the Lord Jesus Christ. Those who reject the good news of the gospel "will be punished with everlasting destruction and shut out from the presence of the Lord." God's people can be encouraged by knowing they will be vindicated at the Lord's coming and will realize they have neither believed nor suffered in vain.

The first chapter concludes with Paul's prayer that God's purposes for the church will be fulfilled in them. Paul expressed his desire that glory will be ascribed to Christ for all He will do in the lives of the believers.

## MISUNDERSTANDINGS (2:1-12)

Some were wrongly teaching that the Day of the Lord had already occurred. Paul countered these false teachers by noting things that must precede the second coming of Christ. Before the Lord's coming the "man of lawlessness" must be revealed. Paul spoke of one who would hold back the mystery of lawlessness. The identification of this person or power remains unclear. Since the second century many have understood the restraining force as the Roman Empire. Others have suggested a supernatural power such as an angel; others have identified this power with the gospel message, the church, or the Holy Spirit. We cannot be sure about such an identification, but we can know that the coming of Christ will mean the overthrow of evil and those who oppose the gospel and take pleasure in unrighteousness.

Because of their deliberate rejection of the truth, God will send them "a powerful delusion so that they will believe the lie." The "lie" is not just any lie but the great lie that the man of lawlessness is God.

## REMAIN FAITHFUL (2:13-17)

Before taking up the discussion of the power of evil in people's lives, Paul offered thanksgiving for the Holy Spirit's work in the life of the church. He also encouraged them to remain faithful to all they had been taught. In typical Pauline style the apostle prayed that God would encourage their hearts and strengthen them in every good word and deed.

## PRAY FOR ME (3:1-5)

Paul in turn requested that they pray for him. He wanted God to bless and prosper the proclaimed word. He also expressed his concern to be delivered from wicked and evil men.

Paul noted that these evil men did not have faith. In sharp contrast to their faithlessness God is faithful (3:2-3; see 1 Cor. 1:9; 2 Cor. 2:18). The apostle expressed confidence that God would continue to direct their paths. Before Paul's rebuke of the idle, he prayed that God would direct their hearts into God's love. There should be no hard feelings among those who are completely indebted to the love of God.

## WHY QUIT WORKING? (3:6-15)

Some in Thessalonica had ceased working in light of the imminent return of the Lord. While Paul maintained his confidence in the Lord's return, he rebuked the idleness of those who passively waited. Paul instead urged them to be examples in the community, to earn their own living, and not to grow weary in well doing.

The problem was mentioned in the first letter (1 Thess. 4:11-12; 5:14) and had apparently grown worse. Paul responded in a most serious fashion, giving more attention to this matter than any in the book except for Christ's return per se. Christians must not be loafers or busybodies. Worse than being idle, they were interfering in other people's lives. Paul strongly urged the faithful believers not to associate with those who rejected his teaching. They, however, should not be treated as enemies but admonished as brothers.

## CONCLUSION (3:16-18)

Paul concluded the letter with words of grace and peace and with his personal signature. Paul normally dictated his letters (see Rom. 16:22). Probably Silas penned the letter, but Paul added something in his own handwriting (see 1 Cor. 16:21; Gal. 6:11; Col. 4:18). The book included encouragement, instruction, rebuke, and admonishment. But it is a word of grace from beginning to end, concluding with "the grace of our Lord Jesus Christ be with you all."

*Theological Significance.* The emphasis on the second coming of Christ reminds us to be ready for Christ's coming at any time. We must be prepared, for He will come as suddenly as a thief in the night. Those who have died and those who are still alive will be united with Christ at His return. These words provide hope and encouragement for the church at all times.

Likewise, we must be alert to the evil schemes of the man of lawlessness. The church gains strength from the instruction about the wicked activity of Satan with all power and pretended signs and wonders. Believers are empowered with the truth that the man of lawlessness will be finally destroyed by the Lord Jesus at His coming (2:12). In the meantime the church must remain faithful and steadfast to the goodwill and providential purposes of God.

### Questions for Reflection

1. What should our attitude be concerning the return of the Lord?

2. Compare and contrast the different features in Paul's teaching regarding the second coming in 1 and 2 Thessalonians.

3. Why must believers avoid idleness in their expectancy of the Lord's coming?

4. How is Paul's teaching about the return of Christ relevant for pastoral and evangelistic ministry today?

# THE RETURN OF CHRIST

The Lord Jesus, who was raised from the dead and ascended to the Father, will return. This conviction is expressed repeatedly in the New Testament.

The church used several terms to refer to the return of Christ. *Parousia*, meaning either *coming* or *presence*, often described the Lord's return (see Matt. 24:3; 1 Cor. 15:23; 1 Thess. 2:19). *Epiphaneia* in religious usage described the *appearing* of an unseen god (see Titus 2:13). The revelation *(apocalypsis)* of the power and glory of the Lord was eagerly anticipated by the church (for example, see Luke 17:30; Rom. 8:18).

The phrase "the day of the Lord" (an Old Testament theme) is also common in the New Testament. "That day," "the day of Christ," and similar phrases were used as synonyms.

Often the writer implied that he was living in the last days (Acts 2:17; 1 John 2:18). The reference to time in many passages listed above, however, is ambiguous (see 1 Cor. 1:8; 5:5; Phil. 1:6,10; 1 Thess. 5:2; 2 Thess. 1:10). The character of that "day" is clearer than its timing. It is a day of judgment.

*The Gospels.* Jesus taught His disciples to expect a catastrophic conclusion to history. At that time God would effect a general resurrection and a final judgment with appropriate rewards for the just and the unjust (Matt. 7:21-27; 24:1-51; Mark 12:24-27; 13:1-37; Luke 11:31-32; 21:5-36).

Although the signs of the end receive considerable attention in the Gospels (Matt. 24; Mark 13; Luke 21), the time of the end remains obscure. Some sayings imply the end is near (Matt. 10:23; Mark 9:1; 13:30). Others imply a delay (Matt. 25:5; Mark 13:7,10). The clearest statements indicate that the time cannot be known (Matt. 24:36,42,44; Mark 13:32-37; Luke 12:35-40).

Acts 1:6-8 expresses the same conviction: the time cannot be known. According to Jesus, the disciples' task was to bear witness to the gospel. The time was left in the Father's hands.

*The Epistles.* As the church aged, questions arose. What happens to those who die before Jesus' return (1 Thess. 4:13-18)? What will His return be like, and when will it occur (1 Thess. 5:1-11; 2 Thess. 2:1-12)? What will happen to us and our world (1 Cor. 15:12-13,23-28)? Does His delay make His promised return a lie (2 Pet. 3:3-10)?

The New Testament answers these questions with a strong affirmation concerning Christ's return. The New Testament is not as clear regarding the time of His appearing. Yet the epistles clearly reveal a persistent faith in the return of Christ (Rom. 8:19-39; 2 Tim. 4:1). His lordship is real. His victory is assured. His people will share His glory at His return (Rev. 19:6;22:17). Thus the responsibility of the church is patience, faithfulness, and witness (see Acts 1:7-8; 1 Cor. 15:58; 1 Thess. 4:18).

# 1 TIMOTHY

Paul's three letters to Timothy and Titus are called the *Pastoral letters*. These letters were written near the end of Paul's life to guide his two younger associates.

Some have suggested that Paul did not write these letters. Arguments against Pauline authorship are basically threefold. (1) These letters cannot be placed within the framework of the chronology of Acts and are thus assumed to have been written after Paul's death. (2) The content of the letters is said to be different from Paul's teaching elsewhere. (3) Differences in vocabulary are said to be so great that the same author could not have written these three letters and Paul's earlier works.

In response it should be noted that Acts 28 and Philippians 1:25-26 imply that Paul was released from his first Roman imprisonment. Several writers in the early church indicate a release, a further period of activity (during which 1 Timothy and Titus were written), and reimprisonment (when 2 Timothy). Also, the different subjects addressed and the needs of the recipients account for the differences in style, vocabulary, and doctrine. The characteristics discussed are not those of the second century and the contents of the letters are appropriate continuations of Paul's earlier concerns. If Luke was the one who wrote down Paul's thoughts, as was certainly possible, then Luke's input may explain some of the unique vocabulary. There is no compelling reason to deny the claim of Paul's authorship of these letters written sometime between A.D. 64 and 67.

**Occasion.** The letters were written to deal with the false teaching which was negatively impacting the young churches. The churches were apparently in more danger from internal threats than from external persecution. Paul urged his apostolic associates to counter the internal danger with sound teaching, by providing an example of godly living, and by organizing and training leaders for the congregations.

First Timothy suggests Timothy was at Ephesus while Paul wrote from Macedonia (1 Tim. 1:3). Timothy probably was still located in Ephesus when he received 2 Timothy (2 Tim. 1:18). The second letter was written from a Roman prison. Titus received his letter in Crete (1:5,12). Paul's whereabouts between Macedonia (1 Tim.) and Rome (2 Tim.) cannot be known for certain. The order of the letters then was 1 Timothy, Titus, and 2 Timothy.

**Purpose and Theology.** The letters to Timothy and Titus share many similar characteristics. Unlike Paul's other letters the letters to Timothy and Titus are personal words to his apostolic helpers. These letters address the need for pastoral oversight in the churches (thus the name Pastoral letters, a name given to these three letters in the eighteenth century). They focus on church organization, the importance of apostolic doctrine, and the refutation of false doctrine. First Timothy and Titus carefully describe the qualifications of Christian leaders.

Not only is there emphasis on orthodox doctrine (1 Tim. 1:8-11; 2 Tim. 1:13-14; Titus 2:1) and church leadership (1 Tim. 3:1-15; 2 Tim. 2:22-26; Titus 1:5-9), but other important matters are addressed as well. Paul wrote to give Timothy and Titus guidance in their ministries (1 Tim. 1:18-2:7; 2 Tim. 2:1-7; Titus 2:7-8,15; 3:9). An emphasis on godly living also characterizes the letters (1 Tim. 1:3-7; 2:8-10; 2 Tim. 1:3-12; 2:14-19; Titus 3:1-11).

I. Introduction (1:1-2)
II. Warning against False Teachers (1:3-20)
III. Guidelines for Church Worship (2:1-15)
IV. Instructions for Church Leadership (3:1-13)
V. Maintaining the Truth (3:14–4:16)
VI. Miscellaneous Instructions for the Church (5:1–6:10)
VII. Personal Charge to Timothy (6:11-21)

## INTRODUCTION (1:1-2)

The letter begins like other Pauline letters. Paul the apostle is named as the author, Timothy is named as recipient, and then follows a greeting. Timothy is affectionately called "my true son in the faith" (1:2). The phrase indicates the spiritual relationship between Paul and Timothy. We cannot be sure whether Timothy was a convert of Paul, but certainly Timothy had a special role on the Pauline mission team (see 1 Tim. 1:18; compare 1 Cor. 4:17; Phil. 2:19-24; 2 Tim. 1:2; 2:1).

## FALSE TEACHERS (1:3-20)

**1:3-11.** Paul emotionally warned Timothy about the danger of false doctrine. Timothy was urged to stay in Ephesus, indicating perhaps some inclination on Timothy's part to leave Ephesus to rejoin Paul. Timothy's assignment was to restrain those in the congregation who were teaching false doctrine.

These false teachers were probably forerunners of second-century Gnostics. In this letter Paul characterizes these false teachers as: (1) teachers of Jewish myths and fictitious stories based on obscure genealogies; (2) conceited; (3) argumen-

tative; (4) desiring to teach Old Testament law, yet they knew not what they teach; (5) full of meaningless talk; (6) teaching false ascetic practices; and (7) using their positions of religious leadership for personal financial gain.

**1:12-20.** Paul's measuring rod for evaluating what is and is not sound teaching was the message of God's grace in Christ with which he had been entrusted. At this point Paul's inventory of sinners, of which he knew he was the chief, initiated a powerful sense of gratitude. Paul's thanksgiving developed from the fact that God in His grace had provided Paul a privileged place of service. Paul expounded the doctrine of God's grace as experienced in his life and as seen in Timothy's ministry.

## CHURCH WORSHIP (2:1-15)

From his concerns about false teachers Paul turned to issues relating to the worship of the church. Paul began with instructions concerning prayer and then moved to matters regarding the roles of men and women.

**2:1-7.** Paul urged that "requests, prayers, intercession and thanksgiving be made for everyone." Prayer is an exceedingly important part of the church's worship. The apostle stresses the importance of special prayer for persons in high places of authority in the state.

Prayer is addressed to God "who wants all men to be saved." Paul here cited three basic truths of the gospel. (1) There is only one God. (2) God can only be approached through the Man who was God in the flesh, the man Christ Jesus. (3) This man gave himself as a ransom for the human race. Paul was not teaching universalism for salvation is possible only for those who know the truth through a relationship with Jesus Christ.

**2:8-15.** Christian men and women should pray to God. Women should adorn themselves modestly and sensibly.

Some maintain that Paul's teaching about women here is historically conditioned. Others see these verses as normative teaching for every age. Some type of prohibition remains. Some believe that Paul prohibited teaching only by women who had not been properly taught themselves. Such women tended to domineer over men. Others suggest that Paul did not allow women to be official teachers in the Christian community, meaning they could not function as overseers (see 3:1). Christian churches differ about the role of women in the church, but the abiding authority of Scripture must not be jettisoned in the ongoing discussion.

## CHURCH LEADERSHIP (3:1-13)

**3:1-7.** Continuing his instructions on how the church should conduct itself, Paul turned to the matter of leadership. Paul said that church leadership is a noble task. Here Paul described the qualifications for those who aspire such leadership.

The term "overseer," one of several terms used for church leaders, was used to refer to the presiding officials in civic or religious organizations. Here it refers to those who provided leadership for local congregations, rather than leaders over a group of churches, such as the office of episcopal bishop developed in the second century. The term "elder" and "overseer" are used interchangeably in Acts 20:17,28; Titus 1:5-7; and 1 Peter 5:1-5. These leaders are to teach the Scriptures (1 Tim. 3:2; 5:17), and to provide direction and administration for the church (3:5; 5:17), to shepherd the flock of God (Acts 20:28), and to guard the church from error (Acts 20:28-31).

An overseer must be a person of noble character. These leaders should be respected by other members of the church and by those outside the church. The overseer must be above reproach, should conform to a high view of sexual morality, should be able to discipline the family, should not be a new Christian, and should not be under the domination of strong drink. Only a person of excellent character should serve as an overseer (1 Tim. 3:1-7).

**3:8-13.** Then Paul moves to discuss the qualification of deacons. The qualifications for deacons are virtually the same as those for elders. Generally the service of deacons (the word means one who serves) was meant to free the overseers to give full attention to prayer and the ministry of the Word (see Acts 6:2-4). The two church offices mentioned in the New Testament are overseer and deacon (see Phil. 1:1). Before being elected as deacons they should have experience in church work (1 Tim. 3:8-10,12-13)

First Timothy 3:11 applies the same qualifications for women. The Greek for the phrase "wives" simply means "the women" and therefore could refer to deacons' wives or less likely to female deacons (see Rom. 16:1).

## MAINTAINING THE TRUTH (3:14–4:16)

**3:14-16.** Paul informed Timothy of his hopes to come to see him and the church at Ephesus. He majestically described Christ in words many scholars believe were adopted from an early hymn of adoration to Christ.

**4:1-10.** As the repository and guardian of the truth, the church continually must be aware of the strategies of the enemies of the truth. Paul stressed that Timothy's pastoral duties involved guarding the truth and refuting the heretics. The church was instructed to confront the false teaching by teaching correct doctrine and by godly living.

The false teachers taught a false asceticism, forbidding marriage and the eating of various foods. But Paul maintained that God has given these things to be appreciated and used for God's glory.

**4:11-16.** The apostle moved from the general concerns of the church to personal exhortations specifically for Timothy. Paul recognized that Timothy was a young man and that some of the older believers might be tempted to look down on his youth. Timothy was to be an example for the church "in speech, in life, in love, in faith and in purity." He was to give himself to the public proclamation of the Scriptures through the use of gift given to him. Since God had called Timothy and the church had sanctioned his ministry through the laying on of hands, Timothy was to strive to live up to these high responsibilities.

## MISCELLANEOUS INSTRUCTIONS (5:1–6:10)

**5:1-16.** From the instructions about how Timothy was to live out his call to pastoral ministry, Paul turned his attention to the various groups that make up the church. The general principle passed on by Paul was to treat different people as one would treat the members of one's own family.

First, Paul addressed the care of widows. Specifically he offered guidelines for helping widows in need, for enabling widows as workers in the church, and suggestions for the younger widows. Younger widows were to be encouraged to marry again and get new husbands to support them. The church, then, would have the responsibility to care for the older widows who have no families to take care of them.

**5:17-25.** The overseers/elders were not only to teach but to provide oversight for the church. These leaders who do double duty are worthy of "double honor." That such honor involves financial support is indicated by the two illustrations in v. 18.

Early church leaders, like modern ones, were not perfect. Their imperfec-

tions need to be dealt with. Criticisms of leaders should be rejected unless they can be proven to be conclusively true. Formal discipline should be exercised with care and caution when needed. These leaders must be examined thoroughly. They should not be chosen or ordained too quickly.

This section gives advice for slaves and masters and the rich and poor in the congregation. Paul recognized that money could be made into a false god and bring all kinds of evil to those with misplaced affections. However, money rightly used can advance the work of God and be changed into a heavenly treasure.

## CHARGE TO TIMOTHY (6:11-21)

Finally, Paul urged Timothy to do his very best to a man of God. Timothy had been a partaker of eternal life since he had first believed the gospel, but Paul encouraged Timothy to claim the gospel's benefits in greater fullness. Timothy should fight a good fight as a soldier of God in his pursuit of holiness, his persistence in service, and in the protection of the gospel. In order to do this Timothy, like all believers, must focus his adoration on the glorious Christ.

The letter concludes with a brief benediction, "Grace be with you."

***Theological Significance.*** The letter to Timothy develops a theology of the church. The church needs organization to do its work effectively. Church leaders give guidance and enablement for the Christian community to carry out its service. The church is to be a pillar and bulwark, a custodian of the truth. The church must strive always to avoid heresy and to teach the truths of the gospel to succeeding generations.

### Questions for Further Reflection

1. What are practical ways for the church to guard the gospel?

2. What are the responsibilities of church overseers?

3. How can false doctrine be recognized? How should it be refuted?

4. What is the church's responsibility for the care of widows?

**Sources for Additional Study**

See Titus.

# 2 TIMOTHY

## INTRODUCTION (1:1-7)

Paul began this letter in a similar way to 1 Timothy. In the first letter Paul greeted Timothy as "my true son in the faith." Here it is "my dear son."

Paul offered thanks for Timothy's heritage and for God's gift to Timothy. Paul appealed to helpful reminiscences and urged Timothy to stir up his gift. Gifts are not given fully developed; they need to be strengthened and matured through use.

## KEEP THE FAITH (1:8-18)

In light of the gift that had been divinely given to Timothy, Paul urged him not to be ashamed "to testify about our Lord." Paul also urged Timothy not to be ashamed of "me his prisoner." The aged apostle wanted to strengthen the courage of his young colleague.

Paul offered a strong admonition to Timothy to keep the faith in the midst of suffering. The apostle's appeal was based on his testimony of God's grace in his own experience. Timothy was to guard the gospel that Paul had entrusted to him. This was possible only through the enabling "help of the Holy Spirit who lives in us."

During this time the apostle had been deserted by Phygelus and Hermogenes. Perhaps this took place when Paul was arrested and taken to Rome for his final imprisonment. In contrast to the actions of the majority, some, such as Onesipho-rus, helpfully befriended Paul. Those must have been difficult days for Paul, forsaken by friends and facing imminent death. It is hard to understand why God's servants suffer like this, but for Paul it was a privilege not only to believe in Christ "but also to suffer for him" (Phil. 1:29).

## BE STRONG (2:1-13)

In this section Paul provided special advice to Timothy. After exhorting Timothy to "be strong in the grace that is in Christ Jesus, Paul declared his frequent message about preserving and passing on the truth.

Paul gave three examples for Timothy to follow: (1) a soldier who wants to please his commander, (2) an athlete who follows the rules of the game, and (3) a farmer who toils faithfully. The three figures of speech used here are found in 1 Corinthians 9:6,24-27. Paul encouraged Timothy to faithful devotion and self-discipline in his service for the Lord. Again the apostle's exhortations were grounded in his own experience of suffering.

## FALSE TEACHERS (2:14-26)

Paul then offered advice regarding false teachers in the church. Positively, he urged Timothy to be an unashamed workman. Negatively, Timothy was to avoid godless chatter. Paul contrasted true and false teachers, noble and ignoble vessels, and the kind and the quarrelsome.

Not only was Timothy to refute the heretical teachers, but he also was to practice and encourage godly behavior and attitudes. Paul concluded this section by saying that a good minister must gently instruct "those who oppose him" so that God might grant them a "change of heart."

## LAST DAYS (3:1-9)

Like his remarks in the first letter (see 1 Tim. 4:1), Paul predicted the moral decline that would come in the last days. This does not at all deny that these conditions have been and will be present throughout the church age. It does say that the characteristics enumerated here will be more intensive and extensive as the end approaches.

In verses 2-4 Paul listed almost twenty different vices that will characterize people in the last days. Generally they all describe those who place self in the place of God as the center of their affections. These people are to be avoided, even though they have "a form of godliness."

Paul began the chapter by pointing out the characteristics of those who love money and pleasure. Then he focused on their depraved living and thinking. These false teachers preyed on "weak-willed women." Such women were apparently easy prey because they wanted to pose as learned people. They were "always learning but never able to acknowledge the truth. Paul compared the false teachers to "Jannes and Jambres." Neither of these men is mentioned in the Old Testament, but according to Jewish tradition they were the Egyptian court magicians who opposed Moses (see Exod. 7:11).

## SCRIPTURE (3:10-17)

Paul again appealed to his own experience and exhorted Timothy to continue the work. Paul urged Timothy not to be led astray by these imposters. Instead, Timothy should continue in what he had learned and had "become convinced of." Timothy could be convinced of the truth taught in the Scriptures because (1) it had made him "wise for salvation through faith in Christ Jesus," and (2) the Scripture is "God-breathed." Paul affirmed God's active involvement in the writing of Scripture. The Lord's superintending work is so powerful and complete that what is written is God's truthful and authoritative word.

## PREACH THE WORD (4:1-18)

Paul's concluding charge stressed the need to preach the word (4:1-5). Like Timothy, all believers are to be prepared in any situation to speak a needed word, whether of correction, rebuke, or encouragement. Christian workers must be ready to endure hardship as Paul had done.

Paul viewed his approaching death as the pouring out of a "drink offering." A drink offering referred to the offering of wine poured around the base of the altar during the Old Testament sacrifices (see Num. 15:1-12; 28:7; Phil. 2:17).

Paul's plea to Timothy closed with personal requests and reference to his "first defense." An important lesson can be learned here about divine support in the midst of human opposition.

## FINAL GREETINGS (4:19-22)

The letter concludes with greetings to Priscilla and Aquilla and the household of Onesiphorus. The household of Onesiphorus was mentioned with great appreciation in 1:16-18. But we know little about this devoted believer.

Paul then sent greetings from four members of the church at Rome and all the brothers. Paul pronounced a personal benediction on Timothy ("your spirit" in 4:22a is singular) before concluding with a corporate blessing "God be with you all" ("you" in 4:22 is plural).

***Theological Significance.*** Second Timothy teaches us about the importance of our theological heritage (1:14). Paul had much to say about what God has done in Christ, our Savior. Jesus Christ has been revealed, destroyed death, and given us life and immortality (1:8-10). The foundation of the Christian life is what God has already done for us in Christ. We should live boldly, for we have received "a spirit of power, of love and of self-discipline" (1:7). These truths about the gospel and Christian living are available to us in God's inspired Scripture (3:15-17). Now we, like Timothy, should pass on these truths to faithful men and women who can teach others also (2:2).

## Questions for Reflection

1. What does it mean to guard the faith?

2. What is the significance of the three examples of Christian living listed in chapter 2?

3. What advice did Paul offer regarding false teachers?

4. What can we learn about the nature of Scripture from this letter?

5. Why is it important to preach the word?

## Sources for Additional Study

See Titus.

# TITUS

## INTRODUCTION (1:1-4)

Paul had been released from Rome. He probably then went to the island of Crete, as well as to Ephesus and Macedonia. Titus, Paul's colleague in ministry, was left behind to work. The letter to Titus was written later to offer him advice and encouragement.

Paul began the letter by identifying himself as "a servant of God." Only here did Paul use this phrase. Elsewhere he used "servant of Christ" (see Rom. 1:1; Gal. 1:1; Phil. 1:1). Paul's salutation is quite long for such a short letter. In the salutation Paul emphasized the purpose of his letter.

Titus is identified as "my true son in our common faith." This designation points to the endearing and intimate relationship between writer and reader. This special relationship assured that in Crete, Titus rightly represented the aged apostle.

## ELDERS (1:5-9)

The first subject of this letter provided Titus with instructions concerning church leaders. Verse 5 states Titus's task, and the following verses in the paragraph dentify the character qualities needed in the new leaders.

Titus was to appoint leaders in every place where there was a group of believers. Probably the entire congregation selected these leaders with the encouragement of Titus. He had the official responsibility, as a representative of Paul, to appoint them to office.

The character qualities identified here corresponds closely to 1 Timothy 3:1-7. Yet differences should be noted. These differences help us see how Paul applied general truths to particular situations. Unlike 1 Timothy, no deacons were mentioned here, suggesting that the organizational structure was not as advanced in Crete. The leaders' character should be blameless, and their doctrinal commitments must be faithful to the biblical message.

## FALSE TEACHERS (1:10-13)

The elders were needed to defend the truth being attacked by the false teachers. Paul described the false teachers in 1:10-13. They were (1) "rebellious" because they rejected the demands of the gospel message; (2) "mere talkers" because they tried to use impressive speech, even though it accomplished nothing; and (3) "deceivers" because they were leading astray the church members. These false teachers could not and should not be trusted because they were "liars." Paul's own observations about these people confirmed the negative assessment of one of Crete's own prophets. Just as Paul gave principles with which to appoint church leaders, so he also provided Titus with guidelines to deal with the false teachers.

The error is described in terms of "Jewish myths" or "the commands of those who reject the truth." These false teachers should be rebuked from the perspectives listed in 1:15-16.

Believers who have been purified by the work of Christ can perceive all things as pure. Unbelievers, especially legalistic ascetics, do not enjoy true freedom in Christ. These false teachers were attempting to set up human standards against which matters of purity and impurity could be judged. But Paul identified these standards as corrupt.

## SOUND DOCTRINE (2:1-15)

Paul turned his attention to the various groups in the congregation. He gave instructions for the older men, the older women and younger women, young men, including Titus, and slaves. To all of these Paul stressed the importance of building up the spiritual life of believers as the best defense against error.

Verse one serves as the basis for Paul's instructions. Paul told Titus to "teach what is in accord with sound doctrine." Sound doctrine must lead to ethical conduct in the lives of all the people in the church.

God's grace provides the foundation for Paul's instructions and exhortations. God's grace has saved us, and it teaches us both by teaching us what to do and by providing enablement to live appropriately. God's grace flows from the work of Jesus Christ who "gave himself for us" in order "to redeem us from all wickedness and to purify for himself a people that are his very own, eager to do what is good." God's grace enables us to live rightly in the present while giving us a future perspective as well. We eagerly await for the appearing of Jesus Christ, who is our Savior and our great God. These are the truths Titus should teach to encourage the church and rebuke the heretics.

## CHRISTIAN LIVING (3:1-11)

Paul moved his thoughts to the duties of all believers, especially in relation to the government and the non-Christian world. Verses 1-2 remind Christians of their duty to government leaders and authorities. It is important to note that early Christian teaching was not limited to the way of salvation, but included exhortations concerning the practical implications for daily life (see Rom. 13:1-7; 1 Pet. 2:13-17).

Some might suggest that such a response to ungodly leaders was inappropriate. Paul met this objection by reminding them of their own pre-Christian condition. It is only by God's "mercy" that we are saved. God brought about our salvation by changing our lives through the work of the Holy Spirit who was "poured out on us" By God's gracious gift of Christ's righteousness to us God now declares us justified in His sight and heirs of eternal life. (See the article "Salvation in Paul's Thought.")

Paul concluded his letter with further instructions about false teachers. Their stubborn refusal to listen to correction revealed their inner corruption.

## CONCLUDING REQUESTS (3:12-15)

Paul announced his plans for the future. Another worker, Artemas or Tychicus, would be sent to replace Titus in Crete. Titus did not need to carry the burden alone. This transition situation offered Paul one more chance to stress the idea that believers need to be characterized by noble deeds. All the workers with Paul joined in sending greetings. Paul's typical closing blessings are addressed to all to whom Titus was to share Paul's greetings.

***Theological Significance.*** Like the other pastoral letters, Paul's letter to Titus focuses on keeping the faith and refuting heresy. Especially significant, considering the nature of the Cretan heresy, are the repeated emphases on doctrinal fidelity (2:11-14; 3:4-7) and faithful living (1:16; 2:7,14; 3:1,8,14). The letter makes it plain that the Christian life is grounded in the grace of God (2:11-14). Believers must recognize this truth and rebuke heresy and avoid legalism (1:10-16). This can be done only by grace; grace that saves, grace that teaches, grace that strengthens, and grace that enables. In so doing we can see the relationship between doctrine and practice.

## Questions for Reflection

1. What are the primary qualifications for a church leader?

2. How can we avoid the trap of legalistic Christianity?

3. What is the relationship between Christian doctrine and Christian living?

4. What duties do believers have as citizens? Why should believers be subject to rulers and authorities?

5. How does a focus on Christ's glorious appearing affect Christian living?

## Sources for Additional Study

Fee, Gordon D. *1 and 2 Timothy, Titus.* San Francisco: Harper and Row, 1984.

Guthrie, Donald. *The Pastoral Epistles.* Grand Rapids: Eerdmans, 1957.

Kent, Homer A., Jr. *The Pastoral Epistles.* Chicago: Moody, 1982.

Lea, Thomas D. and Hayne P. Griffin, Jr. *1, 2 Timothy, Titus.* The New American Commentary. Nashville: Broadman, 1992.

Stott, John R. W. *Guard the Gospel.* Rev. ed. Downers Grove: InterVarsity, 1997.

# PHILEMON

Paul's authorship of the letter has strong support in all spheres of the church. It is closely linked with the epistle to the Colossians. The letter was carried by Onesimus to Philemon with Tychicus (Col. 4:7-9; Eph. 6:21-22). The letter was written near the end of Paul's first Roman imprisonment at the same time as Ephesians and Colossians, about 60–61.

**Destination.** The recipient of the letter was Philemon, a wealthy resident of Colosse. The church members of Colosse who met at Philemon's house were among the first readers (Phlm. 2). Archippus possibly had some official capacity at the church (see Col. 4:17).

**Purpose.** Philemon had a slave, Onesimus, who had run away from his master and who perhaps had stolen money from him as he went (Phlm. 18). Somehow Paul met Onesimus in prison. Onesimus became a believer in Christ and repented of his past deeds. Onesimus was responsible to return to Philemon. Paul wrote to Philemon to intercede for Onesimus, asking Philemon to allow him to return. Paul asked Philemon not only to receive him but to receive him as a brother.

**Theology.** This short letter teaches much about the sense of brotherhood that existed in early Christianity. We see the tension between the sense of equality in Christ (see Gal. 3:28) and the societal differences. Paul did not endorse slavery, nor did he want slaves to rebel against their masters. The teaching of this letter has served as an impetus for the abolition of slavery.

I. Introduction (vv. 1-3)
II. Philemon (vv. 4-7)
III. Onesimus (vv. 8-22)
IV. Conclusion (vv. 23-25)

## INTRODUCTION (VV. 1-3)

Paul identified himself as a "prisoner of Christ Jesus." This introduction also identified Paul with Onesimus. Although the letter is obviously directed to one person, Apphia, Archippus, and the church in Colosse are also mentioned. Apphia was most likely a relative of Philemon, perhaps his wife. Archippus may have been the pastor of the church. Verse 3 follows the pattern of Paul's usual benedictions (see Col. 1:2).

## PHILEMON (VV. 4-7)

The situation that had developed between Philemon and Onesimus required the mediation of an advocate. Paul needed to speak effectively for Onesimus and with respect to Philemon. Paul offered good words of commendation and appreciation about Philemon. Whether or not this was intended to help Paul win a hearing through the psychology of commendation we cannot know. Verses 6-7 include a prayer for Philemon.

## ONESIMUS (VV. 8-22)

A transition occurs at verse 8. Paul offered five appeals for Onesimus. He started with Philemon's reputation as a person who brought blessing to others. Paul could have appealed to Philemon, but instead he appealed in love. The third basis of his argument focused on the conversion of Onesimus. Paul then explained how valuable Onesimus had been to him. The final appeal related to God's providence over the entire situation.

## SLAVERY IN THE FIRST CENTURY

Slavery, the legal possession of an individual by another, was the primary "energy source" for the Greco-Roman world. Slaves were employed in agricultural and manufacturing enterprises, construction, mining, governmental positions, education of children, cultural and entertainment activities, as well as many routine household duties.

In the Roman Empire slavery was unrelated to race. It probably began as generals chose to enslave conquered enemies rather than liquidate them. It was also a form of punishment for crimes or a means of dealing with debtors unable to repay loans.

Unwanted, exposed children were frequently rescued, raised, and sold as slaves. Children of slaves were themselves slaves. Some kidnap victims were sold into slavery. Some voluntarily became slaves for religious reasons or chose security in benevolent bondage over insecurity in freedom and poverty.

By the first century there were thousands of slaves in all parts of the Empire. Their status and treatment differed greatly. Slaves were not completely without legal rights. They were free from taxation and military service, had the right to common-law marriage, and could join social groups or associations.

Yet their lot was determined by the will of their masters. Essentially they were nonpersons, property, "human tools" (Aristotle). Abuse, harshness, and brutality were frequent. Runaway slaves could be subject to torture and death. Kind and considerate treatment was extended if not on humanitarian grounds, then because it was prudent to care for one's "property." Slaves were valuable property. In New Testament times the price of a slave was about nine times the wages paid a laborer for a year. A slave could be sold privately or at public auction at the will of the owner.

Slaves had the hope of freedom. Some bought their freedom. More often it was given, either formally in the will of the owner, by pronouncement of an official, or informally. In the latter case former slaves had no legal proof of their new status. Slaves might gain freedom by being sold to a god; the walls of some ancient temples contain hundreds of names of such individuals. As a "freedman" the former slave had basic civil rights, the possibility of achieving citizenship, but retained some obligations to the former owner.

The New Testament attests that slaves were members of the early church. Both Christian slaves and masters are told their relationship must be controlled by their common relationship in Christ. Philemon was enjoined to receive the runaway slave Onesimus "as a beloved brother" (v. 16), thus elevating the nonperson to the status of an equal. Slavery furnishes New Testament imagery for the status of the sinner under sin and of the Christian to God. In his incarnation Christ accepted the role of slave (Phil. 2:7). Terms such as "ransom" and "redeem" reminded New Testament readers of the parallels between the purchase of their spiritual freedom and that of the physical freedom of the slave.

---

Legally Philemon could have punished Onesimus. Some slave owners were cruel; others, more merciful in these situations. Paul carefully convinced Philemon that he should receive his disobedient slave and forgive him. This situation was quite difficult for Philemon. How should he respond? If he were too easy on Onesimus, his other slaves might rebel or try to "become Christians" to receive special treatment. If he were too hard, it might disrupt the church. Paul recognized this dilemma and offered a helpful suggestion.

Paul volunteered to become a business partner with Philemon and help him deal with the Onesimus situation. Two suggestions followed: (1) "Welcome him as you would welcome me." (2) "If he has done you any wrong or owes you anything, charge it to me." Philemon was then able to receive Onesimus as though he were receiving Paul. Paul did not suggest that Philemon ignore the slave's crimes and forget about the debt Onesimus owed. Instead Paul offered to handle the debt himself. The apostle assured Philemon his debts would be paid.

Obviously we see here many things that remind us of our relationship with Jesus Christ. God's people are so identified with Jesus Christ that God receives them as He received His Son (see Eph. 1:6).

Paul hinted that Onesimus should be treated as a free person. He asked Philemon to receive Onesimus "as a dear brother." Philemon was implored to do "even more" than Paul asked.

## CONCLUSION (VV. 22-25)

Paul concluded the letter with his usual greetings from those with him, including Epaphras, a leader in the Colossian church. One final request and a benediction bring the letter to a close.

*Theological Significance.* Early Christians did not mount an open crusade against slavery. They focused on the message of the gospel but did not ignore its social implications. In other places Paul seemed to accept slavery as a reality in the Roman Empire (see 1 Cor. 7:20-24; Eph. 6:5-9; Col. 3:224:1), but he did not endorse it. There are no indications that Paul had any thoughts of abolishing it. We cannot impose issues from the nineteenth or twentieth centuries back into the New Testament, but the importance of Philemon as a social document cannot be neglected. The expression of Christian love melted the fetters of slavery and counted master and slave alike as *brothers* and *sisters* in the family of God. More importantly the gospel message is beautifully illustrated in Philemon.

### Questions for Reflection

1. What is the relation between the church's evangelistic and social ministry?

2. What can we learn from Paul about dealing with conflict situations?

### Sources for Additional Study

See Colossians.

# THE GENERAL LETTERS

## THOMAS D. LEA

The "General letters" are those writings in which the author designated the recipients in general terms rather than with a specific location. Exceptions to this are 2 and 3 John, addressed to specific individuals. Some New Testament scholars do not regard Hebrews as a General letter, pointing out that the author spoke to a specific group of believers (Heb. 5:1–16:12). Most of the General letters take the name of the writer as the title. By contrast most of the Pauline letters take the name of the recipients as the title. We can clearly observe the difference between the specific address of the Pauline letters ("To all the saints in Christ Jesus at Philippi," Phil. 1:1) and the broad address of the General letters ("To the twelve tribes scattered among the nations," Jas. 1:1).

The letter to the Hebrews addresses a warning to Jewish-Christian believers who were considering abandoning the riches of Christ and returning to the empty rituals of Judaism (5:1–16:6). James penned a warning to Jewish Christians who were neglecting obedience to the practical commands of the Bible (2:1-13). The apostle wrote 1 Peter to steady both Jews and Gentiles against painful persecution that threatened to consume them (4:12-19). The readers of both 2 Peter and Jude faced challenges from heretical teaching that threatened to sap their spiritual vitality (2 Pet. 2:1-3; Jude 3-4).

John wrote his first letter to urge his readers to right action (2:6), a right attitude (4:11), and right belief (4:1). In his second letter he warned against false teachers (vv. 7-11), and in his third letter he dealt with a church dispute (vv. 9-10).

In the ancient Greek manuscripts of the New Testament, the General letters usually appear before the Pauline writings. In modern listings of New Testament books that order is reversed. The dates of the General letters, which are later than most Pauline letters, make this arrangement best.

With the possible exception of James, all the General letters appeared near the end of Paul's life or after his death. They discussed problems the church faced in its later growth and expansion. Such writings as 2 Peter, Jude, and 1 and 2 John touch on the subject of false teaching. This was a normal problem in a growing church encountering alien ideas and viewpoints. Hebrews, James, 1 Peter, and 3 John provide encouragement for Christians who faced harassment and persecution.

All the writers presented a picture of a Savior whose strength could sustain them (Heb. 4:14-16). They called for a demonstration of new stamina and steadfastness (Jas. 1:2-4; 1 Pet. 4:19). Some of the writers called on the readers to show compassion for one another (1 John 3:16-20) and basic practices of honesty and integrity (Jas. 5:1-6). Because modern Christians also face these problems, the words of the General letters can provide us strength and help in our spiritual battles today.

# HEBREWS

The Book of Hebrews is anonymous in that the name of the author is not mentioned in the book. The original readers knew who the writer was, but he remains unknown to us. Despite the difficulties in determining the author of Hebrews, its majestic picture of Christ commended its contents to the early church.

The writer of Hebrews presented Christ as superior to the Old Testament prophets, angels, Moses, Joshua, and Aaron. He laced magnificent discussions of Christ's person and work into frighten-

## NEW TESTAMENT USE OF THE OLD TESTAMENT

A study of the New Testament's use of the Old Testament must include not only an assessment of Old Testament quotations as they are found in the New Testament. It also must include matters of a broader scope, such as the relationship of the two Testaments, the nature and meaning of prophecy and fulfillment, methods of interpreting the Old Testament used by New Testament writers, and their development of biblical themes. These aspects of such an important study can only be touched upon in a survey article of this nature.

The relationship of the two Testaments is foundational to our understanding of the New Testament's use of the Old Testament. Without question, the New Testament authors attributed full authority to the Old Testament Scriptures. The New Testament is never viewed as being in conflict with the Old Testament but rather as the ful-

fillment of what God had begun to reveal in the Old Testament (see Heb. 1:1-2). The New Testament writers viewed the Old Testament as invested with divine authority, and in their use of it by way of quotations they treated it as the very Word of God.

We are surprised to discover that 250 quotations of the Old Testament are in the New Testament. In addition, there are a number of allusions to the Old Testament that are not specific quotations but where it is obvious that an author was employing Old Testament phraseology. Eliminating all allusions that are not of a direct nature, there are at least 278 different Old Testament verses cited in the New Testament: ninety-four from the Pentateuch, ninety-nine from the Prophets, and eighty-five from the Writings.

Something of the authority with which the New Testament authors quoted the Old Testament can be seen in their use of citation formulas. Sometimes the New Testament authors used citation formulas such as "it is written" or "Scrip-

ture says." The former emphasizes the permanent nature as well as the binding character of that which has been written. Jesus withstood the temptation of Satan in the wilderness by three times introducing Old Testament quotations with the phrase "it is written." The latter emphasizes the fact that Scripture "speaks" (present tense) to us today. The desire of the author of Hebrews to emphasize the continuity of the old and new covenants is seen in the fact that eighteen of our twenty-five Old Testament citation formulas appear in the present tense.

Many times God is referred to as the Author of Scripture, emphasizing its divine origin. The joint nature of the origin of Scripture is attested in the use of the names of the human authors as well as the divine Author. For example, Matthew 1:22 reads, "What the Lord had spoken through the prophet." In Acts 1:16 we read, "The Holy Spirit spoke long ago through the mouth of David."

ing passages warning against apostasy (1:1–2:4). The superiority of Christ led the writer to appeal for faith (chap. 11), stamina (12:3-11), and good works (13:16).

**Authorship.** The early church historian Eusebius quoted the biblical scholar Origen as saying, "Who it was that really wrote the Epistle [Hebrews], God only knows" (*Ecclesiastical History* 6.25). Despite this verdict many varied opinions about the authorship have arisen.

Christians in the Eastern Roman Empire regarded Paul as the author. Hebrews contains statements similar to Paul's view of the preexistence and creatorship of Christ (compare Heb. 1:1-4 with Col. 1:15-17). Both Hebrews 8:6 and 2 Corinthians 3:4-11 discuss the new covenant. These factors inclined some observers to consider Paul as the author.

Christians in the Western Roman Empire originally questioned Pauline authorship of Hebrews. They observed that the statement of 2:3 suggested that the author was not an apostle. Also the

---

In the Gospels there are approximately thirty-nine Old Testament quotations attributed to Jesus. Many times Jesus' use of the Old Testament reflects a literalist interpretation. At other times He used the Old Testament in a "this is that" or fulfillment type of interpretation. For example, in Luke 4:16-21 the fulfillment theme is prominent in our Lord's use of the Old Testament. Jesus treated the Old Testament as the very Word of God, giving it the highest authority when He said of it that "not the smallest letter, not the least stroke of a pen, will by any means disappear from the law until everything is accomplished" (Matt. 5:18).

In Acts there are twenty-seven Old Testament quotations attributed to various Christian leaders. Their use of the Old Testament reveals that they understood it from a Christocentric perspective. In the Pauline epistles there are no less than eighty-three quotations (excluding allusions).

As in Acts, Paul's under-standing and use of the Old Testament was couched in a Christological setting as well. Oftentimes Paul's Old Testament quotations can be found in clusters as he would seek to bolster an argument with quotations from many parts of the Old Testament (see for example, Rom. 3:10-18 and 9:12-29).

The New Testament writers interpreted many of the events concerning Christ and the church as having been prophesied in the Old Testament. In addition, the New Testament writers, under the inspiration of the Holy Spirit, have taken many Old Testament passages and interpreted and applied them in a greater perspective beyond their original context. For example, Habakkuk 2:14, "The righteous will live by faith," is quoted three times in the New Testament: Romans 1:17; Galatians 3:11; and Hebrews 10:38.

Sometimes a question arises when one compares the New Testament citation with the Old Testament original in that it would appear the New Testament writers used some freedom in their quotations both in respect to form and meaning. Several factors should be kept in mind. First, modern-day rules of precision in quotation did not apply to the biblical writers. Second, as a result, Old Testament quotations were oftentimes paraphrased by the New Testament writers. Third, quotations had to be translated from Hebrew to Greek. Fourth, New Testament writers often simply alluded to an Old Testament passage without intending to quote it verbatim. These and other reasons account for the fact that some quotations are not "exact."

In conclusion, the New Testament writers believed the Old Testament to be directly relevant to them, and they used it accordingly. Their statements indicate that the Old Testament in its entirety is meaningful and relevant for the first-century church as well as for us today.

Old Testament quotations in Hebrews come from the Greek Septuagint, but Paul used both the Hebrew text and the Septuagint. Further, none of Paul's other writings are anonymous; and the polished Greek style of Hebrews does not resemble the explosive, dynamic style of most of Paul's writings. Shortly before A.D. 400, Christian leaders in the West extended acceptance to the Book of Hebrews. They absorbed it into the Pauline collection of writings without distinguishing it from the rest.

Tertullian advocated Barnabas as the author of Hebrews. Barnabas's background as a Levite would qualify him to write the book, but support for his authorship is lacking in the early church. Martin Luther suggested Apollos as the author. In Apollos's favor is his reputation for eloquence (Acts 18:24), but against him is the absence of early church tradition accepting him as author. Some have suggested Luke as the author. His knowledge of Greek would favor him, but Luke was a Gentile. The outlook of Hebrews is definitely Jewish. The nineteenth-century church historian Adolph Harnack mentioned Priscilla, the wife of Aquila, as the author. She and her husband would have known Pauline theology and Jewish practice, but the early church was silent about nominating her as author.

Modern Greek texts of Hebrews bear the title "To the Hebrews." It is best to accept this title and recognize that we cannot know for sure who wrote Hebrews. Despite our ignorance of the author, we can use and understand what he wrote.

**Date.** The date of writing Hebrews is difficult to determine. We must date the book before A.D. 95, when Clement referred to it. The writer used present tense verbs in 10:11 ("performs" and "offers") to describe the ministry of the priests in the Jerusalem temple. This indicates that sacrifices were still being offered in the days of the writer.

The Roman army destroyed the temple in A.D. 70. Persecution intensified as that day drew near (see 10:32-34). Timothy was still alive (13:23). The best option for the date is the mid to late 60s before the Romans destroyed the temple.

**Recipients.** The above title for Hebrews reflects the conviction that Jewish Christians were the original readers of the writing. Frequent appeal to the Old Testament, extensive knowledge of Jewish ritual, and the warning not to return to Jewish ritual support this conviction.

One might feel that the Jewish Christians who read Hebrews lived in Palestine. According to 2:3, however, the readers may not have seen nor heard Jesus during His earthly ministry. The verse suggests that the readers had been dependent on the first hearers of the Christian message to share it with them. Doubtless, most Palestinian Christians had heard Jesus' preaching and teaching. According to 6:10 the readers of Hebrews had resources enough to assist other believers. Palestinian Christians were poor and needed aid (Acts 11:27-30; Rom. 15:26). These facts indicate that the readers were not from Palestine.

The statement in 13:24, "Those from Italy send you their greetings," sounds as if Italians away from their home were returning greetings to friends in Rome. If this is true, Rome is the probable destination of the writing. A second fact favoring this view is that a knowledge of Hebrews first appears in Clement's First Epistle, which was written in Rome.

**Purpose.** Wherever the recipients lived, they were well-known to the writer. He described them as generous (6:10) but immature (5:11-14). He was aware of their persecution (10:32-24; 12:4), and he planned to visit them soon (13:19,23).

The writer rebuked the readers for not meeting together often enough (10:24-25). They were in danger of lapsing into sin (3:12-14). Perhaps the readers were a Jewish-Christian group who had broken away from the chief body of Christians in the area. They were considering returning to Judaism to avoid persecution. The author wrote to warn them against such apostasy (6:4-9; 10:26-31) and to help them return to the mainstream of Christian fellowship.

**Theme.** The writer of Hebrews presented Jesus Christ as the High Priest who offered Himself as the perfect sacrifice for sins (8:1-2; 10:11-18). Christ had superiority over every aspect of Old Testament religion. Understanding this principle could prevent the readers from abandoning Christ and returning to Judaism (10:26-29).

**Literary Form.** The language of Hebrews is elegant and carefully constructed. Its excellent Greek does not clearly show up in English translations that strive for readability.

Was the writer penning a letter to a specific group of Christians, or was the letter a summary of a sermon made available to several Christian congregations? The reference to "I do not have time to tell" in 11:32 seems to indicate a sermon; however, the writer knew specific details about the congregation (5:11-12; 6:9-10; 10:32-34; 12:4; 13:7). This suggests a letter written to a specific location. The statement in 13:22 also requires that we view the writing as a letter penned in the style of an earnest warning to a specific congregation.

**Theology.** The letter to the Hebrews emphasizes the person of Christ. It presents a Jesus who is truly human (2:18), realistically tempted (4:15), and obedient to death (3:2; 13:12). The suffering of Jesus taught Him the value of obedience (5:8).

Hebrews also emphasizes the finality of Christ's work. The sacrifices offered by Jewish priests in the temple reminded the worshipers of sin, but the sacrifice of Christ removed sin (10:1-4). The priests of Judaism repeatedly offered sacrifices that did not take away sin (10:11). Christ's single offering of Himself forever removed the sin that hindered fellowship with God (10:12-14).

I. God Has Spoken (1:1-3)
II. Angels (1:4–2:18)
III. Moses (3:1-19)
IV. Joshua (4:1-13)
V. Aaron (4:14–10:18)
VI. Spiritual Endurance (10:19–12:29)
VII. Final Exhortations (13:1-25)

## GOD HAS SPOKEN (1:1-3)

The author emphasized that God had spoken in the past through the prophets at many different times and in varied ways. He stated that the revelation God had given through Jesus was superior to that through the prophets. This was true because Jesus was the Heir, Creator, divine Reflection, Image of God, and Sustainer of the world. Jesus had cleansed our sins and then taken His seat at God's right hand as a token of His finished work.

## ANGELS (1:4–2:18)

Our writer presented angels as servants God created to minister to believers. He portrayed Christ as God's Son, who received the worship of angels and had an eternal existence. The superiority of Christ made the failure to believe on Him a fearsome experience. The author concluded that Christ's incarnation and crucifixion enhanced His superiority and qualified Him to become a spiritual trailblazer for believers. This was true because the sufferings of Christ better equipped Him to help us as we suffer.

## MOSES (3:1-19)

Christ was God's Son who reigned over the household of God's people. He was superior to Moses, who was merely a servant within God's household. Jesus' superiority to Moses made it a more serious matter to reject Jesus than to reject Moses. Our writer referred to the experience of Israel in Numbers 14:1-35 as an illustration of the seriousness of unbelief.

## JOSHUA (4:1-13)

The writer showed that Joshua failed to lead the people of God to rest because of their unbelief. Jesus promised rest to His people if they believe and follow the promises of the gospel. This rest is not fully available in this life, but by faith we may experience a portion of its blessings now (see chap. 11).

## AARON (4:14-10:18)

*Our High Priest (4:4-5:10).* Our writer began with a summary of Christ's work as our High Priest. Christ is our great High Priest who represents us in God's very presence. God appointed Aaron as a high priest to represent people before God. Because Aaron was surrounded with weakness, he was able to have compassion on other weak, sinful people. Christ also faced hardship, and He learned the value of obedience by His commitment to God's will. God called Christ to serve as a high priest after the order of Melchizedek. Our author explained this idea more fully in chapter 7.

*Warning against Apostasy (5:11-6:20).* The immaturity of the readers prevented their usefulness and skillful performance for God. The writer warned his readers that no one could ever repeat the experience of repentance and conversion if he committed apostasy.

Some see this warning as a teaching that a true Christian can lose his salvation. That position would contradict the teaching of such New Testament passages as John 10:27-29; Romans 11:29; and Philippians 1:6. Others see the warning as hypothetical and not a realistic possibility. The repetition of the warning here and also in 10:26-31 makes this interpretation less likely. Others see the warning as directed at those who are almost Christians but not genuine Christians. In opposition to this view is the fact that a passage such as "shared in the Holy Spirit" could not be used of one who was not a Christian. The preferred interpretation is to view this passage as addressed toward professing Christians. The writer urged them to show the reality of their faith by enduring in their commitment to Christ without falling away. The writer spoke to his readers in accordance with their profession, but he urged them to show their true faith by producing real works.

The work and love the readers showed convinced the writer that none of them were apostates. However, he wanted all of them to press on to achieve full maturity by obeying the promises of God.

*Melchizedek (7:1-28).* The writer reached back to the story of Melchizedek (Gen. 14:17-20) to explain the nature of Jesus' priesthood. Melchizedek's name and hometown suggest that he was the "king of righteousness" and the "king of peace." The Bible did not record any beginning or ending for his life. His eternal priesthood of righteousness was like that of Christ. Abraham's action of giving tithes to Melchizedek showed that the priest was a great man.

Because the priesthood of Aaron did not bring people into obedience to God, He changed the priesthood. He installed Christ as the Priest after a new order, that of Melchizedek. Our writer felt that the priesthood of Christ was superior to that of Aaron for three reasons. First, God initiated this priesthood with an oath, not merely by some worldly rules.

## APOSTASY

*Apostasy:* Defection; rebellion. The classical Greek term *apostasia* brought to mind a military or political context and referred to rebellion against established authority. In the major English translations the actual word apostasy occurs seldom (NASB 6; RSV 3; NEB 2; NIV 0; KJV 0), but as a reference to rebellion against the Lord, the idea is widespread. In the Old Testament it is Israel's greatest national sin, that is idolatry, or forsaking the worship of the Lord (Exod. 20:3; Deut. 6:5,14; 29:14-28).

The Greek term *apostasia* occurs twice in the New Testament. In Acts 21:21 it refers to an accusation against Paul that he had encouraged Jews to "forsake" Moses. In 2 Thessalonians 2:3 it refers to the great defection or falling away from the faith that will precede the return of Christ.

Various other New Testament contexts point to religious defection, the causes of which vary: affliction or persecution (Matt. 13:21; 24:9-13), false teachers (Matt. 24:11; 2 Tim. 4:30), erroneous views of Christ (1 John 2:18-23; 2 John 7-9), and unbelief (Heb. 3:12-14).

The theological issue raised by the question of apostasy is of paramount importance. The historic doctrines of Christian assurance and the security of the believer are not, however, nullified by the fact that there are those who make Christian professions and/or attend Christian worship who later forsake, either by woreed, their earlier confession.

The Pauline doctrine of the Spirit is an unequivocal scriptural affirmation of the security of the believer. Paul's references to the Spirit as "firstfruits" (Rom. 8:23) and "pledge" (2 Cor. 1:22; Eph. 1:14) indicate that Christians have already begun to experience the gift of eternal life.

For Paul all who hear and believe the gospel receive the gift of the Spirit, which is God's pledge (promise, guarantee, earnest) of the resurrection (Eph. 1:13-14; Rom. 8:11,23,38-39). In this connection the Pauline verb "to predestine" (Rom. 8:28-30; Eph. 1:5,11) is not so much a reference to what God decided before the world began (though Paul certainly affirmed Christ's death and the mystery of the gospel as part of God's eternally predestined purpose; see 1 Cor. 2:7-8; Acts 4:27-28). Rather it is a reference to God's unalterable promise to resurrect unto glory the one who believes in Jesus. Christians are predestined to be raised like Christ. Thus, "having been justified by faith" (Rom. 5:1), having received the Spirit as God's pledge of love (Rom. 5:5; 8:35,39), we may know that "we shall be saved from the wrath of God through him" (Rom. 5:9; compare 5:10).

Hebrews 6:1-8 (esp. v. 6) is interpreted by some to refer to the realistic possibility of losing one's salvation, but the argument is hypothetical. Just as it is impossible for Christ to be crucified twice (see 9:2510:18), so also is faith a once-for-all experience (see 6:4). Furthermore, Hebrews 6:13-20 is one of the strongest affirmations in the New Testament of the certainty of our future hope, which is grounded in the faithfulness of God.

Certainly the fact of sin is a Christian tragedy, but even extremes of sin cannot nullify the promise of God (note that even the incestuous man of 1 Cor. 5:1-5, who is to be "handed over to Satan," will "be saved in the day of the Lord Jesus"). As for those who make Christian confessions only later to renounce them and defect from the faith, we may perhaps say with John, "They went out from us, but they were not really of us" (1 John 2:19).

Second, Christ's priesthood was permanent. Christ would never deliver His office to someone unqualified to handle it. Third, the character of Christ was superior to that of the Aaronic priests. Christ was exactly the type of high priest weak believers needed.

*A New Covenant (8:1–9:28).* Our author indicated that in addition to beginning a new order of priesthood, Christ inaugurated a new covenant. Jeremiah 31:31-34 foretold this new covenant. It provided three benefits for those who lived under it. First, it pro-

## ASSURANCE, WARNING AND PERSEVERANCE

For many Christians who struggle to understand their faith and the meaning of salvation, the question of security looms very large. Texts like John 10:27-29 affirm that no one will pluck them out of the hand of the Lord. They seem to provide assurance concerning security.

Texts like Hebrews 6:4-6 and 10:26-27, however, with the warnings of the impossibility of being renewed, seem to offer insecurity. Because this issue of security touches Christians at a deep level, a few would like to reword the texts of Hebrews or dismiss the entire book from their authoritative canon.

This way of dealing with the New Testament will not work because such disturbing texts can be found throughout other parts of the Bible (see 1 Cor. 10:6-22). Instead, we must realize that there is a built-in tension written into the biblical texts. Remember that God knows what people are like and that Jesus was not confused by their "believing" (John 2:23-25). Remember also that in Hebrews 6 there is not just one "impossible" but two (6:4,18): the one a warning and the other an assurance.

This built-in tension in the Bible reminds us that when God sent Jesus, He was not playing a game. The cross was the most serious moment in the history of the world. God expects us to treat it with utmost seriousness. Believing is not just a matter of words; it involves the way we live (see Jas. 2:14-26). Therefore the entire Bible is laced with warnings about the way we live.

Nevertheless, we must also understand that we do not save ourselves, whether it is at the beginning point of justification (Rom. 3:21-31) or throughout our lives to the point of death and our glorification (Rom. 6:22-23). It is by the gracious working of God that we are renewed daily (2 Cor. 4:16). Our security then is not rooted in our ability to save or uphold ourselves. Our security is in the power of God to save and to forgive us repeatedly since we all continue to sin (1 John 1:8-10).

This life therefore is a pilgrimage with God. It is a pilgrimage that takes seriously both assurance and warning. In this pilgrimage we have a sense of security outlined in the classical definition of the "perseverance of the saints." This means that those who continue to believe in Christ *will* attain their heavenly rest (Heb. 4:9-13; 2 Thess. 2:13-15).

The contemporary popularized statement "once saved, always saved," however, can create a problem because it is an unfortunate oversimplification of this classical doctrine. It makes God's gracious working with us a static momentary action that loses the emphasis of pilgrimage and the great struggle of Christian life reflected throughout the New Testament, to say nothing of the similar Old Testament messages about God and His people.

The purpose of the Bible is twofold. (1) Everything possible is done in the midst of a hostile world to call Christians to a faithful life. (2) Everything possible is done to remind Christians of the assurance of God, who calls them to draw near to the throne of grace (Heb. 4:16).

This tension between assurance and warning is the context for Christian living. Tension is present throughout the Bible because the Bible deals with the intersection of human weakness and divine strength. Genuine Christians take seriously the warnings of the Bible and rely firmly upon its gracious assurances.

---

vided a new awareness of God's laws and a new nature by which to obey God. Second, it gave a personal knowledge of God that inspired a loyalty and commitment to Him. Third, it provided a complete forgiveness of sins. Christians today have inherited the benefits of this new covenant in their relationship with God.

The old covenant made provision for removing external pollution by the use of animal sacrifices and familiar rituals. Under the new covenant Jesus surrendered His life to God in sacrifice for sin.

The sacrifice of Christ is more effective for us today in three ways. First, it did not limit itself to the mere removal of ceremonial pollution. It cleansed the conscience from guilt and thus inspired holy living. Second, it resulted in the removal of sin by the shedding of Christ's blood. Third, by entering God's presence, Christ showed that He has offered a perfect sacrifice. Because Christ has fully removed all sins, Christians have the hope that He will one day return to complete their salvation by taking them to be with the Father.

*Once for All (10:1-18).* The author explained the permanence of Christ's sacrifice. The repetition of the sacrifices offered by the Jews on their Day of Atonement (Lev. 16) could never make the worshipers perfect. Their sacrifices served as an annual reminder of the sins of the people. What God truly wanted was not merely the offering of an unthinking animal but a conscious, volitional choice to follow Him. That is what Jesus gave when He came to do God's will. Jesus' choice to offer Himself as a sacrifice for our sin earned for Christians acceptance in God's sight. The constant offering of Levitical sacrifices testified that sins still remained. The once-for-all death of Christ forever took away all sins. When these sins are removed, no further need for sacrifice remains.

## THE PRACTICE OF SPIRITUAL ENDURANCE (10:19-12:29)

*Stamina in Obedience (10:19-39).* The writer of Hebrews found the readers tempted to pull away from Christ. Hebrews attempted to call them to God and to fellowship with one another by describing a veil by which all believers could enter God's presence. This veil symbolized the life of Jesus presented to God when He suffered for our sins (1 Pet. 3:18). Because Christians had complete access to God, they could draw near to Him with an inward and outward cleansing. They also needed to consider how to stimulate one another to good works by meeting together.

In no instance should Christians fall into a pattern of neglecting fellowship with one another. The author warned his readers that turning away from Christ would expose them to divine judgment. He insisted that his readers show genuine faith by continued commitment to Christ. They had already suffered for their faith, but they needed to demonstrate stamina in obeying God.

*Heroes of Faith (11:1-40).* As an incentive to endurance before God, the writer presented a gallery of Old Testament heroes of faith. Faith gives reality to things that cannot be seen. By this faith the Old Testament believers received a positive witness from God. In the generations before the flood, Abel, Enoch, and Noah all responded by faith to demonstrate obedience to God. Their faith pleased Him. Abraham demonstrated his faith by forsaking the comforts of Ur and Haran to follow God to the promised land. By faith Abraham and Sarah bore Isaac as a child of their old age. Moses showed his faith by leaving the wealth of the Egyptian palace to suffer hardship with the Hebrew people. The writer presented Gideon, Samson, David, Samuel, and many other heroes as examples whose faith Christians should follow. The promises the Old Testament believers had expected were coming true in the events New Testament Christians were experiencing.

*Endure (12:1-29).* The writer also found encouragement for endurance from Jesus' example. Jesus had already run the race of faith, and God had placed Him on the throne. When Christians consider the hardship He faced, they can find strength and fresh courage. God allows all Christians to experience hardship so that they might develop holiness. Even though God's chastisement seems hard for the time, it will eventually produce righteousness in those who follow Him.

The character of God provided another incentive for endurance. God desires that all persons seek after holiness. God will not tolerate a disobedient, self-serving lifestyle. The presence of God at Sinai caused thunder, lightning, and fright among the people who saw Him. If God's speaking on earth at Sinai produced fear, how much more would

His words from heaven through Jesus produce fear! The writer showed that God's kingdom was unmovable. This gives Christians the grace to serve Him with stamina and reverence.

## FINAL EXHORTATIONS (13:1-25)

Christians have practical duties with one another. They must show sympathy to those in prison, and they must avoid all immorality. God has promised never to leave Christians, and that promise helps to banish greed.

---

## OLD AND NEW COVENANT

Definitionally, a covenant is an agreement between two parties, whether equals or not, that signified a relationship whereby the two bound themselves to each other, either conditionally or unconditionally.

Theologically, the term was used to describe the relationship God initiated by His grace between Himself and humankind to those who were willing to bind themselves through a personal commitment of faith. This is reflected in the oft-occurring phrase in the Old Testament "I will be their God and they shall be my people."

A covenant was made by a sacrifice. Hence the Hebrew idiom for its establishment was "to cut a covenant" (Gen. 15:7-21). From God's perspective His covenant is unconditional and unilateral in establishment, but from humankind's perspective it is conditional and two-sided. God commands His people to keep His covenant through obedience and alternatively judges

and blesses them according to their response.

The word covenant in the New Testament is diatheke, and it functions as the equivalent for the Old Testament berit. It occurs thirty-three times, nearly half of which are either Old Testament quotations or references to the Old Testament covenants. But the concept of the "new covenant" did not originate in the New Testament, for Jeremiah 31:31-34 speaks of God's intention to establish a new covenant.

The phrase "new covenant" is found six times in the New Testament: 1 Corinthians 11:25; 2 Corinthians 3:6; Hebrews 8:8; 9:15; 12:24. The new covenant is the fulfillment of the old in that it is identified with the death of Jesus and the Christian age. It is superior to the old covenant according to Hebrews 7:20-22; 8:6 and displaces the old according to Hebrews 8:13; 10:9.

The new covenant was established by the shed blood of Jesus on the cross. In the Gospel accounts of the last supper, it was Jesus Himself who related His

coming death to the establishment of the new covenant. He is, by virtue of His death, the Mediator of a new covenant (Heb. 9:15; 12:24). The sacrificial offering by Jesus on the cross constituted the beginning of the new covenant and is complete and unrepeatable. Entrance into the covenant relationship is by faith in Christ.

The Book of Hebrews is the New Testament epistle most concerned with the relationship between the old and new covenants. The writer's intent was to show both continuity and discontinuity between the two covenants.

Continuity can be seen in that God is the initiator of both covenants, and both are based on sacrifice. Discontinuity can be seen in that the new covenant supersedes the old due to the final nature of the death of Christ.

The old covenant was enacted upon inferior promises, lacked finality, and lacked efficacy in that it provided no power to keep its conditions. In contrast, the new covenant is unconditional, final, and spiritually efficacious.

Christians must follow the faith of their leaders. When Christians submit to those who care for their spiritual needs, this allows the leaders to do their jobs with joy and not with hardship or frustration.

God is pleased with spiritual sacrifices that Christians offer. These sacrifices are commitment, praise, and unselfish sharing of goods.

In the last section of Hebrews the author urged prayer for himself and reported on Timothy's release from prison. He shared a doxology in 13:20-21 and an expression of greeting in 13:24-25.

**Theological Significance.** The author of Hebrews points us to the superiority of Jesus Christ. He is superior to the prophets (1:1-3), superior to the angels (1:42:18), and to Moses (3:14:13). He provides a superior priesthood on the basis of a superior covenant (4:14–10:31). Not only is Jesus superior to the foundational aspects of Judaism, but He also is superior to any aspect of contemporary religion. This means that Jesus is not just one good option among many ways of drawing near to God; He is the only way. Because of the superiority of Jesus we must not neglect such a great salvation that He has provided with His sacrificial death (2:3; 10:1-18).

Jesus, the superior Savior, is also the superior Priest. We can come to Him in times of trouble, suffering, and struggle. In Him we will find a sympathetic Priest (4:14-16) who offers grace in time of need. Thus we can and should draw near to Him in worship (10:19-25), live by faith (11:1-40), persevere to the end (12:1-29), and live a life of love (13:1-25).

## Questions for Reflection

1. In what way is Christ superior to the angels (1:5-14)?

2. What is the significance of suggesting that Christ is a priest after the order of Melchizedek (7:1-10)?

3. Why was the sacrifice of Christ more effective than that of the Old Testament priests (10:1-18)?

4. What were some of the specific deeds of faith the Old Testament heroes in Hebrews 11 performed?

5. How does the writer of Hebrews explain God's purpose in chastisement (12:4-11)?

6. What are some of the sacrifices that please God (13:9-16)?

## Sources for Additional Study

Brown, Raymond. *The Message of Hebrews.* Downers Grove: InterVarsity, 1982.

Bruce, F. F. *The Epistle to the Hebrews.* The New International Commentary on the New Testament. Grand Rapids: Eerdmans, 1964.

Guthrie, Donald. *Hebrews.* Tyndale New Testament Commentaries. Grand Rapids: Eerdmans, 1983.

Guthrie, George. *Hebrews.* NIV Application Commentary. Grand Rapids: Zondervan, 1998.

# JAMES

Martin Luther, whose vigorous voice led to the birth of Protestantism during the Reformation, described the Book of James as a strawy writing. The epistle's emphasis that a believer was justified by works (2:24) clashed with Luther's conviction that the believer becomes just by faith.

Most Christians would feel that Luther erred in his evaluation. The firm demands of the Book of James call wandering Christians back to obedience to God's Word. It is especially useful in pointing out ethical application of the gospel of grace. With the concern of a pastor, James spoke to his readers in urging them to face trial with stamina (1:2-18). He also spoke with the firmness of a prophet in urging them to show evidence of their genuine faith (2:14-26).

**Authorship.** The Book of James came slowly into widespread circulation in the early church. Many factors contributed to this. Its brevity and practical nature made it seem of small significance in comparison to a book like Romans. Christians in the early church also disagreed concerning the identity of James, the author of the epistle. Those who identified the name with the Lord's brother tended to view the book as genuine Scripture. Those who rejected the link between James and Jesus tended to ignore the Book of James. Church councils meeting at Rome (A.D. 382) and Carthage (A.D. 397) accepted James as Scripture. This acceptance gave support to the view that James, the Lord's brother, was the author.

The text of James provides little information about the author other than his name, but the mention of the name provides an important clue to his identity. Few persons with the name of James could succeed in identifying themselves merely by their first name. The writer must have been an important James.

Four persons in the New Testament have the name of James. James, the father of Judas (not Iscariot), is mentioned in Luke 6:16 and Acts 1:13. James, the son of Alphaeus, appears in Matthew 10:3 and Acts 1:13. Both are obscure figures who lacked the importance to have been recognized by the mere designation "James." James the apostle was martyred under Herod Agrippa I in A.D. 44 (see Acts 12:2). He died before the time in which most people feel the Book of James appeared. The Lord's brother was an unbeliever during Jesus' earthly ministry (John 7:2-5), but an appearance of the risen Christ to him apparently led him to become a believer (1 Cor. 15:7; Acts 1:14). He rapidly became a leader in the early church (Gal. 2:6-9). The New Testament pictures him as a committed Jew who recognized Jesus as Messiah and Lord and showed spiritual sensitivity to the working of God. James the Lord's brother would be important enough in the early church clearly to identify himself by the designation "James."

Other features of the epistle of James also confirm the likelihood of identifying the author with Jesus' brother. James 1:22 and 5:12 contain echoes of Jesus' teaching in Matthew 7:20-24 and 5:34-37, respectively. The brother of the Lord could have heard this teaching. James 5:14-18 portrays our author as a man of prayer, and this agrees with the extrabiblical portrait of James, the Lord's brother. The tradition is that the Lord's brother spent such time in prayer that his knees became as hard as those of a camel (Eusebius, *Ecclesiastical History* 2.23). It is not possible clearly to prove that the Lord's brother is the author of this epistle, but he is the most likely candidate from among the Jameses in the New Testament.

**Date of Writing.** Many scholars feel the Book of James is one of the earlier New Testament writings. Three features suggest an early date. First, James described a large gap between the rich and the poor (5:1-6). When the war against Rome broke out in A.D. 66, the rich suffered great losses, and conflict between rich and poor ceased. The impact of this observation pushes the writing to an earlier time rather than later. Second, the church organization mentioned in James seems undeveloped as seen in the mention only of elders as church leaders (5:14). Third, Christians were fervently expecting the return of Christ (5:7-9). It is felt that such fervor would be more true of the initial generations of Christians. All of these features support the acceptance of an earlier date.

**Recipients.** The address of the epistle of James to "the twelve tribes scattered among the nations" (Jas. 1:10) suggests that the readers were Jewish Christians who lived outside of Palestine. Several features confirm the truth of the suggestion. First, the term for "meeting" (2:2) is the Greek word for "synagogue." The word does not suggest that the readers met in a Jewish synagogue, but it indicates that Jewish Christians used this name to describe their place of meeting. Second, the statements of 5:1-6 present the picture of poor believers being intimidated by the wealthy. These rich people may have attended church meetings (2:1-3), but their presence did not indicate conversion. Third, the term "scattered among the

nations" (1:1) reflects a single Greek word that referred to Jews who lived out of their homeland. All of these facts suggest that the Lord's brother directed a message to Jewish believers who had left their native country of Palestine.

**Theme.** The epistle of James makes a unique contribution in the New Testament with its strong ethical emphasis. Its ethical teaching is scattered throughout the writing. James clearly taught that a faith that lacked works was empty, vain, and useless. James's frequent use of the imperative mood indicates his passionate feeling about the issues he faced. His fiery words resemble those of an Old Testament prophet. He shared ethical commands that touched upon both personal morality and social justice.

**Literary Form.** James's writing is similar to the Old Testament wisdom literature in Proverbs and Psalms. Both sources treat such subjects as the use of the tongue, the dangers of wealth, and the need for self-control. Some students of James have also pointed out a similarity with synagogue homilies or sermons.

James's writing reflected a vivid imagination. We can see his use of vigorous figures of speech in his comparison of the wavering man to "a wave of the sea, blown and tossed by the wind" (1:6). He also was a close observer of nature. We can see this from his description of the effects of the sun's heat (1:11), horticulture (3:12), and rainfall (5:7,18).

I. Greeting (1:1)
II. Trials (1:2-18)
III. Hear and Do (1:19-27)
IV. Don't Be Partial (2:1-13)
V. Show Mercy (2:14-26)
VI. Control the Tongue (3:1-18)
VII. Avoid Worldliness (4:1-17)
VII. Be Just (5:1-6)
IX. Endure (5:7-12)
X. Pray (5:13-18)
XI. Lift the Fallen (5:19-20)

***Purpose and Theology.*** James wrote to Jewish Christians facing trials and persecution. Under the threat of persecution the readers considered compromising their Christian commitment and accommodating themselves to worldliness. James spoke as a pastor to urge his friends to develop spiritual stamina in facing persecution. He also spoke as a prophet to urge those who considered compromise to give evidence of their faith.

Some students of James suggest that the book lacks doctrinal emphases. It is true that James assumed some doctrinal similarity between himself and his readers and did not elaborate on all his beliefs. He did affirm the unity of God (2:19; 4:12) together with an emphasis on divine goodness (1:17), graciousness (4:6-8), and judgment (2:13). He emphasized strongly the return of Christ (5:7-11). In 1:12-15 he presented an analysis of temptation and sin, suggesting that human desire was the source of sin. Much of the content of James represented an effort to call individuals and the church back to full commitment to God and to complete concern for one another.

## GREETINGS (1:1)

It is significant that James chose not to mention his relationship to Jesus. His statement that he was a servant of Jesus indicated his humility. The expression "twelve tribes" represented the children of Israel (Acts 26:7). The fact that they were "scattered" suggested they were Jews living outside their Palestinian homeland. James spoke to his readers as Christians, for only believers would see Jesus as the "Lord Jesus Christ."

## TRIALS (1:2-18)

James urged his readers to look at trial from God's attitude. The trial itself was not an occasion of joy, but it could pro-mote joy by becoming an occasion for producing stamina in the life of a committed believer.

In trial the believer must ask for an understanding of the purpose behind the divine permission of the difficulty. An incentive to do this is that God will give generously to those who ask and will not humiliate them for asking. Those who face trial with perseverance receive a crown of life from God as a reward for their stamina.

James moved from a discussion of trial to a discussion of inward enticement to sin in 1:13-18. First, he warned believers not to blame God for temptation in their lives. God does not dangle evil before people to entice them to sin. Second, he stated that the desires of his readers were responsible for luring them to disobedience. Third, he taught that God gave only "good and perfect" gifts to believers and would not vary from that principle.

## HEAR AND DO (1:19-27)

Because his readers might compromise under trial, James warned them of the urgency for demonstrating their faith with works. His appeals can be summarized under the command, "Be doers of God's Word and not mere listeners."

In 1:19-25 James presented three figures of speech that explained how God's Word could help believers. First, he compared God's Word to a seed that could be planted within each Christian to grow into salvation. Second, he pictured God's Word as a mirror that clearly reflected the condition of the one who looked into it. Third, he described God's Word as a law that provided freedom. Listening to God's Word could provide the strength to produce obedient living.

In 1:26-27 James indicated that a true response to God's Word involved both outward activity and inward control. Ministry to orphans and widows was the outward activity. Separation from the world was evidence of inner control.

## DON'T BE PARTIAL (2:1-13)

In 2:1-4 James rebuked his readers for demonstrating favoritism to the rich who attended their services while ignoring the poor. The display of partiality for the rich was contrary to their own interests, for the rich were actually their oppressors. Such partiality was also contrary to God's law. James reminded his audience that they would be judged for their inconsistency.

## SHOW MERCY (2:14-26)

James warned that a faith that merely spoke kind words to the poor without offering them help was not a saving faith. Just as Abraham and Rahab demonstrated their obedience to God by works, James urged his friends to show their faith by works. James explained that a faith that merely affirmed correct belief without producing a changed life was lifeless.

## CONTROL THE TONGE (3:1-18)

James insisted that Christians show their obedience to God by controlling their tongues and all of their desires. He explained that the tongue had great power for both good and evil. He also pointed out the stubbornness and inconsistency of the tongue. He urged his readers to demonstrate heavenly wisdom rather than earthly wisdom. Earthly wisdom produced envy and selfish ambition. Heavenly wisdom produced peacemakers who were merciful and considerate of one another.

## AVOID WORLDLINESS (4:1-17)

James saw an epidemic of worldly living among his readers. In 4:1-10 he warned against worldliness and showed its effects on the prayer life of his recipients. In 4:11-12 and in verses 13-18 he showed,

respectively, that worldliness produced a critical spirit and a godless self-confidence.

In describing the effect of worldliness on the prayer life, James showed that his friends resorted to scheming, quarreling, and striving in order to obtain their wishes. They failed to receive what they truly needed because they did not ask. Whenever they did ask, they failed to receive because their request was tinged with self-will. James's description of God in 4:5 demonstrated that God tolerated no rivals and wanted complete commitment from His followers. God could make heavy demands on His followers, but He could also provide the grace to meet those demands. In 4:7-10 James uttered in rapid-fire fashion ten imperative appeals to submit to God and avoid worldliness.

One evidence of worldliness James cited was the presence of a critical spirit. He saw that Christians were defaming one another in the same way that the ungodly defamed Christians. James warned that those who belittled fellow Christians had set themselves up as judges and had assumed a position that rightly belonged only to God.

Probably the arrogance James denounced in 4:13-17 came from self-confident Jewish businessmen who planned their lives without reference to God's will. James warned his readers that life resembled a transitory vapor and that all of life must be planned with reference to God's will. The sin James described in this paragraph is an example of a sin of omission.

## BE JUST (5:1-6)

James leveled harsh warnings against wealthy landowners who valued the dishonest accumulation of material goods above the demonstration of justice. He accused the rich of the sins of dishonesty, wanton living, and injustice. He implied that God had heard the cries of the oppressed and would punish the unjust treatment meted out by the rich.

## ENDURE (5:7-12)

James used three illustrations to encourage a lifestyle of persistent devotion in serving the Lord. First, he spotlighted the farmer who planted and then waited for rains in order to produce a crop. Second, he mentioned the Old Testament prophets who spoke boldly for God despite suffering. Third, he commended Job, who faced tragedy, family misunderstanding, and physical suffering in obeying the Lord.

In times of distress Christians could easily use God's name in a careless, irreverent way. James warned against invoking God's name to guarantee truth and instead called for truthfulness so consistent that no oath was needed.

## PRAY (5:13-18)

James urged believers to use prayer in all the seasons of life. In times of affliction Christians are to pray to God for help and strength. In times of blessing believers are to praise God instead of congratulating themselves (5:13b). In instances of critical sickness the sick person was to summon the leaders of the church for prayer. Prayer for the sick could result in either physical healing or spiritual blessing. In times of sin and struggle mutual intercession could promote spiritual victory. Elijah prayed with such force that God withheld rain from the earth for three and a half years and gave it again at his request.

## LIFT THE FALLEN (5:19-20)

James operated with a realism about the spiritual life. He insisted that those who continue in sin show their lostness despite their profession of faith. He promised that the believer who won back a wanderer would save the sinner from eternal death and win blessings for himself.

***Theological Significance.*** James reminds us in a forthright way that faith involves doing. It is not enough to be hearers of the word; we must be doers as well. We cannot just say we are believers; we must show it in our lives. This must be evident in the way we control our tongues and the way we relate to others. The rich must share with the poor. The Christian community must live out its faith by demonstrating love and a working faith to those inside and outside the body of Christ.

## Questions for Reflection

1. What does James 1:2-8 teach about a correct response to trials and afflictions?

2. Refer to James 2:14-26 for a discussion of the question, Can a faith without works produce salvation?

3. Explain James's ideas concerning the power, stubbornness, and inconsistency of the tongue.

4. Explain how worldly living affects the prayer life of the Christian.

5. How does the certainty of the return of Christ provide stamina for facing suffering?

6. Does James promise that prayer for the recovery of the sick should always produce healing? Use such passages as 2 Corinthians 12:7-10 and 2 Timothy 4:20 in arriving at an answer.

## Sources for Additional Study

Davids, Peter. *Commentary on James.* Good News Commentary. San Francisco: Harper and Row, 1985.

Moo, Douglas J. *James.* Tyndale New Testament Commentaries. Grand Rapids: Eerdmans, 1985.

Motyer, Alec. *The Message of James.* The Bible Speaks Today. Downers Grove: InterVarsity, 1985.

Vaughan, Curtis. *James: A Study Guide.* Grand Rapids: Zondervan, 1969.

# 1 PETER

The epistle of 1 Peter was written to Jewish and Christian believers living in the northern part of Asia Minor. They faced persecution because of their commitment to Christ. Peter wrote to urge them to show stamina and commitment. Peter also wanted his readers to show a Christian lifestyle that would convert pagan sneers and accusations into appreciation and respect. To accomplish this, he urged all Christians to obey their leaders, servants to be subject to their masters, and husbands and wives to demonstrate honor and submission to one another. The vivid descriptions of Christ's suffering and death (2:21-25; 3:18) could serve as an encouragement for Christians to conquer evil and endure to the end.

**Authorship.** Leaders of the early church made frequent reference to 1 Peter, and there is no evidence of any dispute about authorship at this time. In the twentieth century some students of 1 Peter have questioned whether the apostle wrote the book.

Some have pointed out that the polished Greek of 1 Peter could hardly come from a man viewed as "unschooled" and "ordinary" (Acts 4:13). However, it is certainly possible that Peter could have developed ability in Greek in the years after Jesus' death. Also, Silas (5:12) may have served as a secretary, or amanuensis, to assist Peter in the expression of some of his ideas. Other students of 1 Peter have felt that the type of persecution mentioned in 4:14 refers to a time when it was a crime merely to be a Christian. They generally locate this time in the 90s or in the second century A.D. Peter would have been dead by this date.

However, the expression "insulted because of the name of Christ" may mean only that believers were insulted because of their loyalty to Christ, not that it was a crime to be a Christian.

It is best to accept Peter's claims for authorship in 1:1. Added support for this acceptance comes from recognizing the similarity between statements in 1 Peter and the Petrine speeches of Acts (see Acts 10:42 and 1 Pet. 4:5). Such statements as those of 1 Peter 2:13-17 sound as if Peter could have learned them by listening to Jesus' words in Matthew 17:24-27. The similarity to Jesus' teaching provides added support for Petrine authorship.

**Date.** Each chapter of 1 Peter contains a reference to suffering by someone (1:6-7; 2:21-25; 3:13-17; 4:12-19; 5:10). It is known that Nero brought persecution on Christians in Rome in the early 60s. Many feel that the Neronian persecutions caused a ripple effect in outlying provinces such as those in Northern Asia Minor.

The Neronian persecutions probably did not reach such an intensity that Christians were forced to choose between obedience to God and obedience to the state. Peter had articulated the Christian position concerning this choice in Acts 5:29. The teaching of the Christian attitude toward the state in 2:13-17 more resembles the response to the government we would expect during Nero's time. When persecution intensified in the late 90s and the early second century A.D., the Christian response would be to call for commitment to God rather than the state.

***Recipients.*** The area in which Peter's readers lived, mentioned in 1:1, was far off the beaten path of travel and commerce. The Bible contains no record of how the gospel reached this area. Although the area contained colonies of Jews, Gentiles were numerically predominant. The order in which the provinces are mentioned might suggest the route followed by the letter carrier. He could have landed in Pontus, followed a circuit through the provinces, and left the area at Bithynia.

Peter's references to preconversion sins of idolatry (4:3) and evil desires they had when they lived in ignorance (1:14) suggest a way of life more true of Gentiles than Jews. The statement in 2:10 that they "were not a people" could not be made of Jews. Although the term "strangers" is the Jewish term for those dispersed from the homeland of Palestine (1:1), it is likely that Peter used it to refer to the church. Peter saw believers as a pilgrim people on earth who had been set apart by God to do His will.

***Theme.*** Peter elaborated upon the subject of suffering throughout the entire epistle. He offered words of hope to his readers as they faced suffering (1:4-5; 5:4). He pictured suffering as purposeful (3:14; 4:14). Christians were to endure it patiently (2:21; 3:9), and they were to demonstrate joy despite hardship (4:13). They could draw encouragement from following the example of Christ in suffering (2:21-25). God's will often demanded that believers endure suffering (4:19).

***Literary Form.*** Students of 1 Peter have discussed widely the literary forms within the book. Many find extensive evidence of the presence of hymns, creeds, or fragments of sermons in such passages as 2:4-8 and 2:21-25. Some view the entire writing as a sermon preached at the baptism of a group of Christians. They view the opening section through 4:11 as a message spoken to candidates for baptism. They locate the performance of baptism at 1:21-22 and feel that the "Amen" at 4:11 concludes the address to the candidates.

The concluding section beginning with 4:12 is viewed as an address to the entire church gathered for the rite of baptism. Although these discussions are enlightening and enriching, they are often inconclusive and unconvincing. Peter may have used material from different sources in writing this book, but it is best to see that he made it his own material under the leadership of the Holy Spirit.

Peter made frequent reference to the Old Testament, sometimes by quotation (2:6-8) and sometimes by allusion (3:6,20). This frequent use suggests that Jewish readers were at least among the recipients of the letter. Some of Peter's emphases resemble those of Paul. For example, there is a similarity between Peter's words about relationships between wives and husbands in 3:1-7 and Paul's discussion in Ephesians 5:22-33.

I. Greetings (1:1-2)

II. Salvation (1:3-12)

III. A Demand for Holiness (1:12–2:3)

IV. God's People (2:4-10)

V. Christian Witness (2:11–3:12)

VI. Suffering as Christ (3:13–4:19)

VII. Assurances (5:1-9)

VIII. Praises to God (5:10-14)

***Purpose and Theology.*** Peter urged his readers to live in accordance with the hope that they had received in Christ (1:3). He gave guidance for them to use in their relationships with one another (3:1-12), and he urged them to endure suffering joyfully for Jesus' sake (4:19). His chief aim in writing was to provide them encouragement in Christian living.

Peter often used theological ideas to drive home his ethical demands. He presented the death of Christ as a stimulus for Christians to endure suffering (2:21-25). He also affirmed the resurrection as a chief source of Christian hope and confidence (1:3). He presented the return of Christ as an incentive for holy living (1:13). He portrayed the nature of the Christian call (2:9-10) as a basis for individual Christians to obey Christ at home (3:1-7), to obey Him as servants (2:18-20), and to follow Him as citizens (2:13-17).

## GREETINGS (1:1-2)

Peter addressed his readers as "God's elect" and "strangers" who were "scattered." Although such terms as "chosen" were sometimes used in reference to the Jews (Isa. 43:20), Peter designated the church as a special people temporarily away from their heavenly home. Election began with the foreknowledge of God the Father, included the sanctifying work of the Holy Spirit, and was sealed by the redemptive work of Jesus Christ.

## SALVATION (1:3-12)

Peter's first epistle alternated between teaching and preaching, between proclamation and application. In this initial section Peter pictured salvation as based on the hope inspired by Jesus' resurrection. This salvation produced an unfading and imperishable inheritance given to them by God. The believers are promised protection with God's power through faith.

The faith of Peter's readers was deepened by their trial. These trials came because of their commitment to Jesus, they were a necessary part of their experience, and they could deepen their faith. The faith of the believers filled them with joy and brought them into living contact with Jesus.

In 1:10-12 Peter indicated that the prophets had reported the grace and glory of salvation. Peter stated that the prophets understood that Messiah must suffer, but they tried to learn the time and circumstances when this would occur.

## A DEMAND FOR HOLINESS (1:13-2:3)

Peter explained that the character of God and the high cost of redemption were incentives to produce holiness in his readers. He also demanded that holiness show itself in earnest love for other believers and in a forsaking of all malicious attitudes.

Peter's words in 1:13 are equivalent to saying, "Roll up your sleeves and go to work." He mentioned that the return of Jesus Christ was to give them hope and stability in the face of persecution. Christians would show their response to God's holiness by leaving the "evil desires" of their past ignorance and by adopting God's own behavior as their pattern.

In 1:17-21 Peter indicated that a proper reverence for God and an appreciation of the high cost of redemption demanded holy living. The readers would understand redemption as the freeing of a slave by paying a price. The payment that released Christians from an "empty way of life" was the "blood of Christ." Peter noted that God had determined the performance of this work of Christ before the beginning of time. He had only recently made His plan evident in the incarnation, passion, and resurrection of Jesus.

Peter urged his readers to express their holiness by genuine love for one another. The quotation of Isaiah 40:6-8 (vv. 24-25) showed that the experience of this love came from the creative activity of God. Peter directed his readers to put aside malice and hypocrisy in their response to God's holiness. He also encouraged them to grow as believers by appropriating the nurture inherent in the gospel message.

## CHURCH AND STATE

Throughout church history the Christian community has sensed a somewhat ambiguous relationship to civil government. This relationship tends to follow a variant of three basic models. The first is characterized by a close link between the two realms almost to the point of fusion, sometimes with the state co-opting the church for its own purposes.

In the second model this situation is reversed, as the church seeks to utilize the civil power to its own benefit. The third model maintains that church and state are to exist side by side, each exercising authority in its own sphere and not interfering with the other. Advocates of each model claim the support of the Bible and the Christian heritage.

Similar to other ancient nations, the Hebrew commonwealth saw no division between the civil and religious spheres. Israel was in some sense a theocracy, for Yahweh was to be the sole sovereign over the nation. Yahweh exercised rulership through various representatives, including judges, prophets, and kings, who for this reason exercised both political and religious authority. Nevertheless, these two aspects of national life were not completely fused, as was

the case among Israel's neighbors. This is evidenced, for example, by the prophetic movement, which provided a religious critique of the monarchy.

The New Testament was written in a quite different context. For the Christian church, in contrast to Israel, was an entity quite separate from the Empire. As a response to this situation, the New Testament writers offered two basic principles, one positive and one negative, for the proper Christian relationship to the state.

The Pauline epistles and 1 Peter enjoin believers to be good citizens. This includes submitting to and honoring those in authority (1 Pet. 2:13-17), paying taxes (Rom. 13:7), and praying for leaders (1 Tim. 2:2). For this they appeal to the function of government in acting as God's agent in punishing persons who do wrong. Yet the underlying motivation appears to be the authors' interest in the good reputation of the Christian community, and this for the sake of the gospel proclamation.

At the same time, believers must always follow a higher allegiance—to God. Peter and John articulated this during their conflict with the Jerusalem authorities (Acts 4:19-20). This principle likewise lies behind the conflict presented in Revelation, as the martyrs defied the injunc-

tions of the satanically influenced civil order (see Acts 6:9; 13:7-8).

Both principles build from Jesus' response to the Pharisees' tricky question concerning paying taxes (Matt. 22:15-21). In external matters—taxes and perhaps social conventions—disciples are to honor civil laws because these matters fall under the jurisdiction of civil authority (the coin carries Caesar's imprint). But the emphasis of Jesus' response rests with the matter of personal allegiance. Here God alone has claim to lordship, as indicated by the implied but unstated parallel: the human person carries the imprint of the Creator.

In keeping with these principles and as a result of historical experience, certain Protestant groups (such as the Baptists) have generally advocated the third model, the separation of church and state. This outlook places restrictions on both spheres. It denies the civil government the prerogative of seeking to shape the religious beliefs of its citizens, of meddling in the church's internal affairs, or of determining the nature of the church's message. The separation model, however, is not intended to eliminate religion from national life or to silence the voice of the church in matters of civil concern.

## GOD'S PEOPLE (2:4-10)

Peter used three images to describe the church in this section. First, he portrayed

the church as a living body that gave sacrificial service to God. Christ was a life-giving Stone who enabled His followers to produce such spiritual sacrifices as obedience (Rom. 12:1), praise, and practical ministry (Heb. 13:15-16). Second, he described the church as a building or structure founded on Christ as the cornerstone. He quoted Old Testament passages from Isaiah 8:14; 28:16 and Psalm 118:22 to show that Christ was a foundation stone for believers and a rock which caused tripping for unbelievers. Third, he used the language of Exodus 19:5-6 and Hosea 2:23 to portray believers as a select nation reflecting the glories of God. God had fashioned special recipients of His mercy from those who previously never belonged to anyone.

## CHRISTIAN WITNESS (2:11–3:12)

Peter was eager for God's people to demonstrate distinctive, obedient behavior in order to convince critics of their faith. He urged them to apply this behavior in relation to their rulers, their earthly masters, in their families, and to one another.

In 2:11-12 Peter suggested three reasons Christians must discipline their lives. First, Christians were foreigners to their pagan environment and were not adjusted to it. Second, if Christians yielded to the flesh, they would wage battle against their best selves. Third, self-discipline and obedience had a wholesome influence on unbelievers.

In relation to the government Peter urged voluntary submission for the purpose of commending Jesus' lordship. In relation to their owners slaves were to be subject. An incentive for showing this subjection even in the presence of provocation was the moving example of Christ's obedience. In the home women were to win their unsaved husbands to Christianity by serving them and showing them respect. Husbands in return were to live in an understanding way with their wives and treat them as full heirs of God's

grace. Peter concluded this section by urging all Christians to practice compassion and forgiveness. They were to treat others not as they had been treated by their accusers but as God had graciously treated them.

## SUFFERING AS CHRIST (3:13–4:19)

In this section Peter directly faced some of the difficult suffering of his readers. He encouraged them to respond righteously to those who had caused their suffering by reflecting on Christ's vindication despite His suffering. He urged a full commitment to God's will, and he presented Christ's return as an incentive for watchful action. He demonstrated that a knowledge of future glory provided an additional encouragement to obedience.

Peter instructed his recipients that even if they suffered for righteous living God would bless them (Matt. 5:10). He urged them to serve the Lord even in the face of unjust treatment, for that unjust treatment might be a part of a divine plan to glorify Himself.

In 3:18 Peter presented Christ's suffering as mediatorial because through it He brought believers to God. The death of Christ took place in the realm of the flesh, but the resurrection of Christ occurred in the realm of the Spirit.

Christ's experience in 3:19-20 took place at a time after Christ was made alive in the realm of the Spirit. The "spirits in prison" refer to supernatural beings or wicked angels who opposed the work of God (see Gen. 6:1-4; 2 Pet. 2:4-5; Jude 6). Preaching to them was not an offer of an additional chance for repentance but an announcement of doom.

The exact location of these disobedient spirits is not specified. Some interpreters have seen this as a description of Jesus' descent into hell. Peter stated that Jesus went to the place where these spirits were confined, an unnamed location. If we equate the spirits in prison with the angels who sinned in 2 Peter 2:4, then their location is Tartarus ("cast them down to Tartarus," 2 Pet. 2:4). In Greek thought this place of punishment was lower than Hades. Peter's readers would understand that evil spirits lay behind their persecution. The coming defeat and doom of these spirits would be a source of encouragement to the readers. The knowledge of their ultimate vindication would give believers an additional incentive to obey. The judgment of the flood served as a warning of God's coming judgment on the world (3:20). The ark that saved a few through water illustrates the salvation available in Christ.

In verse 21 Peter presented baptism as a copy of the Old Testament deliverance from judgment. The conviction of sin calls for a faith response to Christ. The act of baptism portrays this response. Salvation comes to believers because Christ has arisen from the dead. Not only has He arisen from the dead, but He has also been installed in a place of power and authority over all His enemies.

In 4:1-6 Peter issued a further call to holy living. He called on his readers to arm themselves by a cocrucifixion with Christ so that sin would no longer be an option for them. Some who had received the gospel message earlier had since died. Their death showed that they experienced the common judgment that sin brings on all people. Despite their death they had entered into life eternal.

In 4:7-11 Peter presented the return of Christ as an incentive for disciplined, watchful behavior. The fact of Christ's return should promote love, hospitality, and a proper use of spiritual gifts.

Peter urged his friends to prepare themselves for a coming trial by commitment and stamina. Instead of offering complaint, they should rejoice that their suffering allowed them to share in Christ's glory. Peter warned his readers against disgracing Christianity by evil deeds or indiscreet action. Peter argued in 4:17-18 that even if believers must face difficulty, the fate of unbelievers would be absolutely terrifying.

## ASSURANCES (5:1-9)

In 5:1-4 Peter outlined the duties of elders and assured them of divine rewards for faithful service. Peter urged the elders to assume their tasks for the right reasons, not because they felt obligated but because they freely chose to do it. At Christ's return the faithful leaders were promised an unfading crown of glory.

In 5:5-9 Peter urged Christians to practice humility and endurance. Christians were to show this humility to one another. They were also to demonstrate a lowliness in the face of circumstances that God allowed. Christians needed to avoid carelessness because their adversary Satan could overpower them.

## PRAISES TO GOD (5:10-14)

Peter expressed praise for God's grace, which allowed Christians growth even after suffering. Silas is probably the same as Paul's helper in Acts 15:40. "She who is in Babylon" is a reference to the church at Rome.

***Theological Significance.*** First Peter calls the contemporary church to faithfulness in Christian living and Christian duty. Peter provided guidance for the church in times of persecution and suffering and offered hope for difficult situations. This hope is grounded in the death and resurrection of Christ. The sufferings and sacrifice of Christ on the cross were central for Peter's theology and ethics. He called for the church to be holy since Christ has redeemed us from an empty way of life (1:18). The church must respond to persecution and oppression with patience and perseverance "because

Christ suffered for you, leaving you an example, that you should follow in his steps" (2:21). The church must do good and live for God in all situations since "it is better if it is God's will, to suffer for doing good than for doing evil. For Christ died for sins once for all, the righteous for the unrighteous, to bring you to God" (3:17-18). The church can take heart and gain courage from this stirring letter that encourages us by testifying about "the true grace of God" (5:12).

## Questions for Reflection

1. Explain how trials develop genuineness in faith. Does genuineness automatically develop through trial? What response on our part promotes the development of faith through trial?

2. Read 1:17–2:3 and then list some of the results a commitment toward holiness should produce in the life of a Christian.

3. Write a definition for the various terms used in reference to Christians in 1 Peter 2:9. How should an understanding of these terms contribute to growth in our Christian life?

4. Harmonize the behavior mentioned in 1 Peter 2:13-17 with the principle spoken in Acts 5:29.

5. Using Peter's words in 1 Peter 3:1-7, explain responses of a husband and a wife within a home. Does Peter's description suggest that the wives and husbands are Christians or non-Christians?

6. What instruction about spiritual gifts does Peter provide in 1 Peter 4:10-11?

7. List the motives and incentives for effective ministry Peter gave in 1 Peter 5:2-3.

## Sources for Additional Study

Davids, Peter. *1 Peter*. New International Commentary. Grand Rapids: Eerdmans, 1990.

Grudem, Wayne. *1 Peter*. Tyndale New Testament Commentaries. Grand Rapids: Eerdmans, 1988.

Kelly, J. N. D. *A Commentary on the Epistles of Peter and Jude*. Grand Rapids: Baker, 1981.

Vaughan, Curtis and Lea, Thomas D. *1, 2 Peter, Jude. Bible Study Commentary*. Grand Rapids: Zondervan, 1988.

# 2 PETER

Peter wrote his second epistle to counter the influence of heresy within the church (2 Pet. 2:1). He appealed for spiritual growth as an antidote to defeat heresy, and he urged his readers to live holy lives in anticipation of Jesus' return (2 Pet. 3:11-12).

The brevity of the letter resulted in its being ignored for centuries by the church. Few Christians made use of it until the time of Origen (A.D. 250), and today many feel that the name Peter is a pseudonym.

**Authorship.** The author claimed to be Peter in 1:1 and asserted that he was an eyewitness of Jesus' transfiguration (1:16-18). His claim to be an apostle and the admission of friendship with Paul (3:15) clearly indicate that the writer intended to be seen as Peter.

Several features have contributed to the questioning of the genuineness of Petrine authorship. The epistle was little used in the early church. No clear second-century usage of the book appears. There are few usages in the third century, and only in the fourth century did it gain general acceptance. Origen's use of the book indicated that he knew of it, but he classified it among the disputed books of the New Testament. Despite these difficulties the church eventually accepted it as genuine and as worthy of inclusion in the canon.

Some have questioned the relationship of 2 Peter to Jude. Second Peter 2 and Jude have sections that are almost identical. Did one copy the other, or did both copy a common source? Many feel that Peter copied Jude, and this would lead to dating the book far beyond Peter's lifetime. Some evidence exists

that the false teachers are seen as future in 2 Peter (2:1) but already present in Jude 4. This feature would point to an earlier date for 2 Peter.

Still others have found that the cumbersome language of 2 Peter is unlike that of 1 Peter. Some of the words used in 2 Peter are difficult, unfamiliar words which a Galilean fisherman might not know. It is possible that a helper assisted Peter with the writing and that this fisherman had learned better Greek with the passing of time.

Peter's reference to Paul in 3:15-16 is interpreted by some as a suggestion that Paul's epistles had been written, collected, and distributed. This would obviously have been at a time long after Peter's death. A reading of Peter's statements in 3:15-16 demands only that Peter had read those writings of Paul available up to the time of Peter's own writing. Peter could have found these writings through his widespread travels.

Those who deny Petrine authorship of 2 Peter have not succeeded in showing how a pseudepigraphical author could avoid being called dishonest. Despite some difficulties it is better to accept the claim of the epistle for Petrine authorship.

**Date.** Peter anticipated that his death would be soon (1:14-15). Assuming Peter wrote both 1 and 2 Peter, we can observe that Peter called this his second writing to the same readers (3:1). There is little specific information by which to arrive at an exact date, but it seems likely that 2 Peter was written shortly after 1 Peter. A time in the mid to late 60s shortly before Peter's demise seems acceptable.

**Recipients.** This letter lacks a specific address as 1 Peter contains. If we assume that Peter wrote the letter, "my second letter" (2 Pet. 3:1) would indicate that he was writing to the same group that received the first letter. The statement of 1:16 suggests that Peter had spoken or preached to this group, but we have no knowledge of when or how this occurred. It seems best to suggest that Peter wrote to churches located in the northern part of Asia Minor.

The letter contains little indication of Peter's location as he wrote. We may leave this as an open question, for a decision on this issue does not affect our interpretation of the book.

**Theme.** Peter centered his emphasis on an exposure of the work of malicious false teachers (2 Pet. 2). Whereas the first letter of Peter dealt with external opposition to the readers, this letter focuses on internal opposition within the church.

In chapter 1 Peter urged that his readers grow in the virtues of faith, goodness, knowledge, self-control, perseverance, godliness, kindness, and love (2 Pet. 1:5-9). Growing Christians would not be susceptible to heretical influence.

In 2 Peter 2 he described the moral errors of the heretics, and in 2 Peter 3 he exposed their doctrinal error in the denial of Jesus' return. He concluded with an appeal for growth as an antidote to pernicious heresy.

**Literary Form.** Several passages in 2 Peter indicate that Peter wrote to a specific congregation (2 Pet. 1:16; 2:1; 3:1). The entire letter is an earnest warning against false teachers and an appeal for growth in maturity. Peter made little use of the Old Testament in quotations (but see 2 Pet. 2:22), but there is frequent allusion to Old Testament characters and events (2 Pet. 2:4-8).

I. Greetings (1:1-2)
II. God's Provisions (1:3-21)

III. Danger (2:1-22)
IV. Hope (3:1-13)
V. Closing Commands (3:14-18)

**Purpose and Theology.** Peter felt strongly that his death was near (2 Pet. 1:14-15). He wanted to leave a spiritual testament that would provide helpful instruction after his departure. He provided warning against the character and false teaching of heretics who would infiltrate the church (2:1-19; 3:1-4). To provide protection against their errors, he urged a development of proper Christian virtues (1:3-11) and a constant growth in God's grace (3:17-18).

Peter held to a high view of Scripture (1:19-21), and he viewed Paul's writings as "Scripture" (3:16). He designated Jesus Christ as "Savior" and "Lord" (1:1-2), and he outlined his observation of Jesus' transfiguration (1:16-18). He affirmed the return of Christ (3:1-4) and asserted God's sovereign control of the events of history (3:13). He used the certainty of Christ's return as an incentive to appeal for godly living (3:14).

## GREETINGS (1:1-2)

Peter identified himself as a servant and an apostle of Jesus Christ. He addressed his words to those who had received faith in Christ. His references in 1:16; 2:1; and 3:1 suggest that he had a specific congregation in mind. Peter wanted his readers to experience God's loving favor and spiritual wholeness because of their clear, personal knowledge of Jesus.

## GOD'S PROVISIONS (1:3-21)

Peter presented four sources of power for spiritual development in his readers. He wanted the commitment of his readers to be a throbbing, pulsating experience that was maturing in its understanding.

First, he assumed the calling and election of his readers. Their special position in God's plan had provided a union with

Christ which allowed them to overcome the moral corruption of the world. The new birth of these readers and their receipt of God's blessings provided an incentive to nurture eight qualities of Christian character in their lives. If Peter's readers developed these Christian graces, they would not fall into spiritual ruin, and they would have a glorious entrance into God's presence.

Second, Peter mentioned his own witness as an incentive for spiritual growth. Peter's use of the future tense may suggest that he was considering writing a document in the future that would remind his readers of his teaching. Peter felt that his coming death made the writing of this testament imperative. He intended, as long as he was alive, to stimulate his friends to devoted commitment by repeated reminders.

As a third source of power Peter mentioned the majestic glory of Christ. The recipients of 2 Peter had likely encountered those who mocked the idea of a powerful, heavenly Christ who could strengthen them for godly living. Peter had been an eyewitness of Christ's majesty in the transfiguration. He could testify that the glory of Jesus was a reality they could experience.

A final source of power for the readers was the prophetic message of Scripture. Peter felt that the transfiguration and other events in Jesus' life made the scriptural picture of Jesus more sure and certain. Christians are able to find guidance from this word until Christ returns in person. Peter stated that the Scripture was reliable because it had a divine rather than human origin.

## DANGER (2:1-22)

Peter used pictorial words to warn his readers of the danger they faced from the false teachers. In 2:1-3 he pictured the immorality and greed of the false teachers. In 2:4-9 he used Old Testament

examples of judgment on sin in order to show the certainty of punishment for followers of the false teachers. He described God's condemnation of the angels who sinned (v. 4), the judgment of the world of Noah (v. 5), and the destruction of the cities of Sodom and Gomorrah. He promised deliverance for the godly by referring to the preservation of Noah and Lot. He denounced the pride, lust, and greed of the heretics. He indicated that those who followed the empty teachings of the heretics were deluded by empty promises.

In 2:20-22 Peter warned that those who had made a superficial commitment to Christ and had turned back to sin were in a more culpable state than before their response. The false teachers had experienced some knowledge of Christian truth which had given them short victory over worldly corruption. A true knowledge of Jesus would have affected them permanently. They were in a worse condition because they had turned from the truth about Christ which they had once received. Their condition of willful rejection made their disobedience a more blameworthy experience. The two proverbs in verse 22 show the folly of returning to a lifestyle of disobedience after an initial response toward Christ. Peter would scarcely use the terms "dog" and "sow" of believers. The passing of time had demonstrated that the false teachers had made a pretense of faith in Christ, but their faith was not genuine.

## HOPE (3:1-13)

Peter discussed a doctrinal failure of the false teachers, their denial of Jesus' return. In 3:1-4 he reminded his readers of the incentive to obedience provided by the promise of Jesus' return. False teachers were looking skeptically at such promises because the stability of the universe did not indicate that God was about to break again into history.

Peter responded to the denials of the heretics by suggesting that the present regularity of the world was not an argument for permanent continuance in the same form. The God who held the universe together by His word could alter it with the same word. In favor of a belief in Jesus' return, Peter also argued that God viewed time differently from human beings. The true explanation for the delay in Christ's return was to allow an opportunity for sinners to respond in faith to Jesus. Peter believed that Christ's promise to return would be fulfilled with destructive power at a time when sinners would least expect it.

The fact of Jesus' promised return could provide strength for a new attitude of holiness and commitment. Peter hinted that Christians could "speed" Jesus' return by renewed vigor in evangelism and devout living.

### CLOSING COMMANDS (3:14-18)

Peter reminded his readers that an anticipation of Christ's future return carried with it the incentive to produce a holy life. He referred to Paul's writings as a support for Peter's belief that divine patience was a factor in the delay of Jesus' return. Many see a reference by Peter to Romans, but Peter left his Pauline source unstated. Peter acknowledged the difficulty of some of Paul's teachings, but he suggested their authority by naming them as "Scripture." Peter boldly stated that his recipients could protect themselves spiritually by mature Christian growth. The "knowledge" they needed was a development in personal acquaintance with Christ.

***Theological Significance.*** The abiding emphases in 2 Peter, with its call for spiritual growth (chap. 1), its warning of false teaching (chap. 2), and its call for holy living in view of the Lord's certain return (chap. 3) are just as relevant for our generation as they were for Peter's. Such features as these have commended it to the consciousness of the church as an inspired writing. Peter's two letters help the church focus its response to external opposition (1 Peter) as well as to evildoers who have come into the church (2 Peter).

### Questions for Reflection

1. Was Peter suggesting that works earn salvation from God, or was he suggesting that they prove the possession of salvation? What is the difference between these options (1:5-11)?

2. What did God do in order to deliver Noah and Lot from a compromise with temptation? Has God helped you in a similar way?

3. Do the proverbs of 2:22 teach that actions demonstrate the nature of an individual or that actions change the nature of an individual?

4. In 3:1-7 Peter argued that both he and the false teachers saw that there was regularity in nature. What opposite conclusions did both draw from that regularity?

5. According to 3:10-13, what should the hope of Christ's return produce in the life of a Christian?

### Sources for Additional Study

Green, Michael. *The Second Epistle of Peter and the Epistle of Jude.* Tyndale New Testament Commentaries. Grand Rapids: Eerdmans, 1968.

Vaughan, Curtis and Lea, Thomas D. *1, 2 Peter, Jude. Bible Study Commentary.* Grand Rapids: Zondervan, 1988.

# 1 JOHN

Leaders in the early church assumed that John the apostle wrote this letter although the author never identified himself by name. Polycarp, Irenaeus, and Tertullian all argued for apostolic authorship of this epistle.

Evidence supporting apostolic authorship is the similar vocabulary between the Gospel and the epistle. Such terms as "light" and "eternal life" appear in both writings. The author claimed that he was a companion of Christ during His earthly ministry (1:1-4). His description of his readers as "dear children" (2:1) indicates a person of sufficient authority to address his audience in this manner. All of these features point toward apostolic authorship. Some who question apostolic authorship favor an authorship by "John the elder" mentioned in Eusebius (*Ecclesiastical History* 3.39). Some feel that the term "John the elder" is merely an alternate way of referring to John the apostle.

**Date.** Little specific material is available for a precise dating of 1 John. Tradition indicates that John later spent a significant ministry in Ephesus. The epistle is usually dated during that ministry. The close link with the Fourth Gospel demands a date during the same period as the writing of that Gospel. Most who assume a common authorship for Gospel and epistle will date the epistle in the mid-90s.

**Recipients.** The letter has no named recipients mentioned within it. Identification of the readers as "dear children" (2:1) and "Dear friends" (2:7) suggests they were a group well known by John. It is best to view the letter as addressed to a group of people perhaps in more than one Asian community. John personally knew them and wrote to warn them of the infiltration of false teaching (4:1-2).

**Theme.** The epistle of John presents three criteria for testing the Christian profession of teachers and individual Christians. First, professing Christians needed to present righteousness as the right behavior (2:3-4). Second they must demonstrate love as the correct attitude of Christian living (4:8). Third, they needed to hold to the correct view of Christ as the proper teaching of Christians (4:3). Those who demonstrate these three traits have eternal life. John would repeat these three themes several times in the epistle as tests to determine the presence of eternal life.

**Literary Form.** The letter lacks an introduction and greeting from the author. It expresses no thanksgiving and lacks a concluding salutation. The author never mentioned the name of another Christian in the writing. He never quoted the Old Testament. The epistle reads like a sermon, but there are sections in which there are clear indications that John wrote to specific people with specific problems (2:1,26).

The style of writing involves much repetition, often with deceptively simply phrasing of words. John alternated emphases on the necessity of right attitude, right action, and right belief. John believed that the practice of these patterns demonstrated the possession of eternal life and distinguished believers from unbelievers.

I. Fellowship with God (1:12:6)
II. New Commandment (2:7-17)
III. False Teaching (2:18-28)

**Purpose and Theology.** John wrote to strengthen the joy (1:4) of his readers and to give them assurance of their relationship with Jesus Christ (5:13). He also wanted to prepare them for dealing with false teachers (4:1-3).

John advocated the genuineness of Christ's humanity (1:1-2), and he called those who questioned the reality of Jesus' incarnation "antichrists" (4:1-3). He presented the death of Christ as an atoning sacrifice for sins (2:2), and he taught the return of Christ (2:28). He denied the idea that Christians could make a practice of sinning (3:8-9), and he called for a demonstration of the reality of faith by ministry (3:16-18).

He opposed both moral laxity and theological errors centering around the person and work of Christ. He opposed Docetism, the denial of the reality of Christ's body, by teaching that he had heard, seen, and touched Christ (1:1). He also emphasized that the same Jesus Christ appeared at both the baptism and the crucifixion (5:6).

## FELLOWSHIP WITH GOD (1:1–2:6)

John began the epistle with a proclamation of the apostolic message. He proclaimed the preexistence and genuine humanity of Christ. He expressed that he was a reliable witness of Jesus' message. In verse 4 he expressed that producing joy in his readers was one of the purposes of this letter. John emphasized that a full experience of joy depended on genuine fellowship with Christ.

In 1:5–2:6 John emphasized the importance of right action in the Christian life. He began with a declaration of the divine character in 1:5-7. John stated

that God had revealed Himself as a God of perfect purity. Anyone who desired fellowship with Him must walk in obedience to His revealed will. John explained that those who denied the practice of sin were deceived, but those who admitted their sin experienced forgiveness and cleansing.

John wrote these words in order to prevent his readers from committing sin. He felt that whenever we commit sin, Christ functions as our advocate in the Father's presence and assures our standing before Him (2:1). Christ functions for believers both as a defender and as an atoning sacrifice. The sinlessness of Jesus qualifies Him to be our defender or advocate.

Christ volunteered to serve as our atoning sacrifice for sin. The term translated "atoning sacrifice"is sometimes rendered "propitiation." The term suggests that our sin against God demands that some form of sacrifice be given to satisfy God's offended holiness. Something in God's nature demanded this propitiation, but something in that same nature was moved with love to provide it. The love of the Father led Him to provide the sacrifice of His Son.

The revelation of God's purity and holiness led John to emphasize that obedience to God's commands provides fellowship with God. Those who would enjoy fellowship with God must follow in the love, holiness, and service that characterized Christ.

## NEW COMMANDMENT (2:7-17)

John emphasized the importance of right attitude as an evidence of genuine Christianity. A believer will love Christian brothers and not the world.

John indicated that the command to love others was a new command. It is new in that Christ's own example of love filled the command with new meaning and application. The response to the

## ATONEMENT

The English word *atone* means *to make reconciliation*. It is based on the English phrase at one. Generally the word atone refers to the condition "at-one-ness" or "reconciliation." Specifically the word is used to refer to the process by which obstacles to such reconciliation are removed. The entire Bible demonstrates that outside of some atoning action, humankind is estranged from God. This alienation, brought on by sin, must be remedied.

In the Old Testament *atone* and *atonement* are based on the Hebrew *kpr*, which means *to cover* or, as some have suggested, *to wipe clean*. Words based on *kpr* are found primarily in the Pentateuch with a few references elsewhere. The Septuagint translated *kpr* and its derivatives primarily by the word family containing *exilaskomai*, *exilasmos*, and *hilasterion*.

The word *atonement* is not found in most translations of the New Testament. (However, the NIV has "atone," "sacrifice of atonement," "place of atonement," and "atoning sacrifice." Also note that Romans 5:11 in the KJV has "atonement," but it renders *katallage* and is properly translated "reconciliation," as seen in all modern translations.)

The *concept* of atonement pervades the fabric of New Testament thought. In the New Testament atonement is centered in Christ's incarnation and especially His work on the cross. The New Testament presents human beings in their natural condition as totally estranged from God. They are "alienated and hostile in mind, engaged in evil deeds" (Col. 1:21). This alienation and hostility outside of Christ is the basic presupposition of New Testament anthropology. It graphically presents humanity's need for atonement. The cause for human estrangement is persistent rebellion to the will of God. God's holiness and righteousness make clear that sin cannot be ignored; sin has its retribution. "The wages of sin is death" (Rom. 6:23). Outside of God's intervention and provision, humanity is absolutely helpless to remedy the situation (Rom. 5:6,8). The sinner is "dead in . . . trespasses and sins" (Eph. 2:1).

God provides deliverance from that which held humankind away from Him. In His infinite compassion and love, He provides atonement in the person of Jesus Christ. The stated purpose of the incarnation was that Jesus came "to seek and to save that which was lost" (Luke 19:10). Christ's atoning work is particularly connected with His death on the cross. "We are reconciled to God through the death of His Son" (Rom. 5:10). This death provided "propitiation in His blood," which must be accompanied "by faith" (Rom. 3:25).

command of love clearly indicates character. One who habitually fails to love others shows that he lives in the darkness of sin and not in the light of God's presence.

In 2:12-14 John assured his readers that they were recipients of strength and help from the Word of God to assist in their spiritual struggles. In 2:15-17 John urged his readers not to love the pagan, self-centered lifestyle that surrounded them. Such a worldly love excluded love for God and also led the Christian to focus on a style of living that was slowly dying.

## FALSE TEACHING (2:18-28)

John emphasized the importance of right belief as an indication of genuine Christianity. The term "antichrist" described those who disrupted fellowship in the churches by holding the wrong doctrine about Christ. The distinctive beliefs of these false teachers are in verses 22-23.

Believers stood secure against the false teaching of the antichrists because of three sources of strength. First, they had the anointing of the Holy Spirit. This provided the capacity to understand spiritual things. Second, they had made a

God is the source of atonement. In the Old Testament God had provided the sacrificial system to effect reconciliation, but in the New Testament God not only initiates atonement but He also brings it to completion. In no sense is the merciful Son championing the rights of humankind against the severe Father who gives forgiveness only grudgingly. "God was in Christ reconciling the world to himself" (2 Cor. 5:19).

The result of the atonement is that the breach between God and humanity is bridged. Fellowship with God is restored because that which has disrupted that relationship has been removed. Through Christ's sacrifice not only is humanity's sin removed, but we also are delivered from our former "futile way of life" (1 Pet. 1:18). Another consequence of the atonement is that the individual in Christ is delivered from selfishness and enabled to live with Christ as Lord (Rom. 14:9;

2 Cor. 5:15).

The New Testament presents a rich and varied treasury of expression concerning the atonement. The words *hilasterion, hilaskomai,* and *hilasmos* are from a root word meaning *appease* or *propitiate.* In Romans 3:25 the word *hilasterion* is rendered "propitiation" in the KJV and NASB. It is translated "sacrifice of atonement" in the NIV and "expiation" in the RSV. In Hebrews 9:5 the same word is translated "mercy seat" in the KJV, NASB, and RSV and "place of atonement" by the NIV. In Hebrews 2:17 the word *hilaskomai* is translated "reconciliation" by the KJV, "propitiation" by the NASB, "atonement" by the NIV, "expiation" by the RSV. The same word in Luke 18:13 is rendered "be merciful" in the KJV, NASB, and RSV and "have mercy" in the NIV.

In both 1 John 2:2 and 4:10 the word *hilasmos* is translated "propitiation" by the NASB, "atoning sacri-

fice" by the NIV, and "expiation" by the RSV.

A second word family containing *lytron, lytroo, apolytrosis,* and *antilytron* should be explored. The first of these words is fairly consistently understood as "ransom" by the KJV; the second is given as "redeem" or "redeemed"; the third and fourth are "ransom." The Bible student should also consider the sacrificial terminology applied to Christ.

Sin effectively keeps people from God. In His atoning work God has secured reconciliation through the work of Jesus Christ. "For he himself is our peace, who . . . broke down the barrier of the dividing wall, by abolishing in his flesh the enmity . . . establishing peace, and might reconcile them both in one body to God through the cross, by it having put to death the enmity" (Eph. 2:14-16). In Christ atonement for the believer has been made complete.

personal commitment to the Christian message. Third, they were living in union with Jesus Christ.

## RIGHT LIVING (2:29–3:10)

John again emphasized the importance of right action as a demonstration of Christian commitment. Christians who had been divinely begotten of God had the privilege of experiencing God's love and living as members of His family. They were to demonstrate their family membership by righteous living. John indicated that Christ had come to take away our sins (3:5). Jesus had died for the purpose of causing us to stop sinning.

John pointed out that the person who made a practice of sinning had never known Christ. In verse 9 he indicated that the experience of a believer in conversion rendered the practice of sin a moral impossibility. John was not suggesting that a Christian will never commit an act of sin. He did indicate that a believer could not live in the practice of sin.

The conclusion in verse 10 pointed out the importance of righteous behavior and also underscored the significance of loving other believers. It makes a good transition from discussion of right action to another presentation of the proper attitude, an attitude of love.

## THE VALUE OF HUMAN LIFE

What does it mean to be human? What is personhood? Is it ever morally justifiable to take human life? These and other emotionally charged questions, all of which revolve around the perennial issue of the value of human life, are being raised anew in the current debates concerning a host of complex ethical issues.

The Bible clearly puts forth what may be termed a high view of the value of human life. In contrast to many contemporary outlooks, however, the Scriptures do not ground this evaluation in society or even in the human person, as important as that is, but squarely in the creative activity of God. This activity gives a special place in creation to human beings as those who bear the image of God.

These themes are sounded in the opening chapters of the Bible. The first creation account reports God's intent as expressed on the sixth day of the creative week: "Let us make man in our image" (Gen. 1:26). God's purpose comes to fruition in the creation of human beings—male and female—each of whom, as

a result, is to share in the divine image. Genesis 1 and 2 indicate that the image of God is a multi-sided concept. It refers to the responsibility of acting as stewards over creation. It includes as well the relational nature of human beings: we are created to live together in community with one another and with God. As a result, human life is of value because God has entered into a covenant with humans, entrusting them with a special purpose, a specific role in the divine plan for creation.

Creation in God's image subsequently became an integral part of the Hebrew mind-set. It forms a basis for biblical injunctions concerning fair treatment of others. God's covenant with Noah after the flood, for example, includes a serious penalty for murder, based on an appeal to the creation of each person in the divine image (Gen. 9:6). So ingrained was this idea that James could matter-of-factly state to his original Hebrew-Christian readership, "With the tongue we praise our Lord and Father, and with it we curse men, who have been made in God's likeness" (3:9). He appealed to human creation in the divine image as a basis for respecting other humans

even in our speaking to and about each other.

Creation in God's image and the resulting value of human life is incomplete, however, without the future orientation given to it by the New Testament. For Paul, Jesus Christ is preeminently the image of God (2 Cor. 4:4; Col. 1:15).

Believers truly participate in the image in that they are being transformed into Christ's likeness (2 Cor. 3:18), a process directed toward the coming of God's kingdom at Christ's return (1 John 3:2). As a result, the value of human life is ultimately based on God's salvation purpose, which is directed toward the future completion of all God's activities. At that point God's purposes in the creation of humans will find its full realization.

On the basis of these considerations, the value of life can and should be seen as bestowed on all humans by God as God's gift. Because all persons are the objects of God's love in Christ and are all potential participants in God's kingdom, all human life is valuable. God calls all humans and human society to acknowledge the value God and God alone has placed in each human being.

## PRIORITY OF LOVE (3:11-24)

John mentioned the importance of the demonstration of a proper attitude, love, as evidence of genuine faith. John presented love as the proof that we have passed from death into life. He located the chief revelation of love in the sacrificial death of Jesus Christ. The chief

manner in which we as believers demonstrate our love is by our kindness and mercy in ministry to others.

In verses 19-24 John indicated that our love brought with it an assurance of our standing with God. If we demonstrate this love, we are able to set our hearts at rest in God's presence. The assurance that love brings will carry with it an experience of boldness before God and also an assurance of effectiveness in the practice of prayer.

## FALSE TEACHING (4:1-6)

John expressed the importance of right belief as an evidence of genuine Christianity. John was speaking of people who claimed to be Christians but who spoke as deadly opponents of Christianity. He was also referring to church services much more informal than our own. In these early services visitors could stand and claim to speak by the Spirit of God. John wanted to provide direction to distinguish between the true and the false.

John directed his readers to test the words of those who claimed to speak for God because of the possibility of the presence of false prophets (v. 1). The test by which the utterances were to be judged was the acceptance of Jesus Christ as God's incarnate Son. As his readers struggled with the presence of false teaching, John assured them that the victory ultimately belonged to them. He also indicated that the worldly message of the false prophets would attract an audience that was gullible in their acceptance of falsehood.

## GOD'S LOVE (4:7-21)

In this section John again underscored the importance of a demonstration of love. He presented love as a disposition that originated in the divine nature.

John appealed for believers to love for two reasons. First, such love has its source and dynamic in God. Second, God is characterized by love. Both reasons blend together so that one runs into the other. The greatness of the divine love for us leaves us with an incentive to love one another. Our practice of love for one another provides evidence that God's love for us has attained its goal.

In verses 13-16 the apostle discussed the relationship between love and the indwelling of God. He suggested that it is not enough merely to know that God is love. Believers must live daily in the sphere of divine love. In so doing they genuinely live in God's presence and have God living in them.

In verses 17-21 John mentioned two evidences of the presence of a ripened fruit of love in a Christian's life. First, such love provides confidence on the day of the coming judgment. Second, this love leads to a genuine concern for fellow Christians.

## VICTORY OF FAITH (5:1-12)

John began this section by stating the chief confession of faith that should characterize Christians. Christians are those who believe that Jesus is the Messiah, the Son of God. Those who are genuine believers demonstrate it by their love for God and obedience to His commandments. The faith that provides strength for spiritual victory is the faith that Jesus is God's incarnate Son.

In verse 6 John outlined more specifically who Jesus is as the Son of God. John's opponents held that Jesus was a mere man to whom the divine Christ spirit came at baptism and from whom this spirit departed before crucifixion. John taught that Jesus was the divine Son of God at both baptism and crucifixion, throughout the entire course of His life.

In verses 7-12 John showed that our faith in Jesus Christ has a good foundation. The KJV text makes a reference to the Trinity in verse 7 that most modern translations omit. The best texts of verses 7-8 suggest that the Spirit, the water, and the blood all unite in their witness to Christ. The Spirit presented His witness at Jesus' baptism and throughout the totality of Jesus' ministry. The terms "water" and "blood" are a reference, respectively, to Christ's baptism and death. John also referred to the witness of the Father and to the witness of personal experience. The truth to which all of the preceding witnesses testified was that eternal life is available only through God's Son, Jesus.

## ETERNAL LIFE (5:13-21)

In 5:13 John indicated that he had written this epistle to lead believers to an assurance that they possessed eternal life. John suggested that assurance that we have been accepted with God provides an assurance toward receiving answers in prayer. He urged that Christians practice intercessory prayer, particularly for fellow believers caught in the trickery of sin. He concluded with the statement that Jesus' death had made possible holiness in the life of each Christian, the new birth, and a genuine knowledge of God.

*Theological Significance.* This letter speaks to contemporary Christians in a significant way. Today there are many people who profess to know God and have fellowship with Him but do not demonstrate such faith at all. John's tests concerning obedience, love, and belief provide warnings for the unfaithful as well assurance for genuine believers. To be sure that we know God, we must keep His commandment. If we lack love for others, it indicates we do not know the love of God in our hearts. Foundationally we must believe rightly about Jesus Christ. He is the Christ, the Son of God, who has come in the flesh. This important triad calls the contemporary church to a strong, balanced faith. We must grow stronger and stronger in all areas of our Christian life.

## Questions for Reflection

1. List the three evidences of eternal life John focused on in this epistle.

2. Who were the "antichrists"? What special doctrinal truth did they deny?

3. List the purposes for the writing of 1 John according to the statements of 1:3-4 and 5:13.

4. When John urged his readers to show love for a Christian brother (3:17-18), what type of demonstration of love was he seeking?

## Sources for Additional Study

Marshall, I. Howard. *The Epistles of John.* The New International Commentary on the New Testament. Grand Rapids: Eerdmans, 1978.

Stott, J. R. W. *The Epistles of John.* Tyndale New Testament Commentaries. Grand Rapids: Eerdmans, 1964.

Vaughan, Curtis. *1, 2, 3 John.* Bible Study Guide. Grand Rapids: Zondervan, 1970.

# 2 JOHN

The brevity and lack of a specific address for 2 John led to its neglect in the early church. Few early Christian leaders made reference to it, but some knew of the epistle. Eusebius placed it and 3 John among the disputed books of the New Testament, but after his time both writings were generally received with little dispute.

The writer described himself as "the elder," and many have seen this as an affectionate title for the aged apostle John. This epistle has a similarity of style and vocabulary with 1 John and with John's Gospel. The false teaching of 2 John 7 is similar to that of 1 John 4:1-3. Some have felt that an unknown "John the Elder" penned this writing, but this elder is a shadowy figure whose existence is uncertain. It is best to see John the apostle as the elder who wrote these words.

**Date.** The interval between the writing of 1 John and 2 John was not great. The false teaching John had mentioned in 1 John 4:1-3 was still a problem for the readers of 2 John. A date in the mid-90s seems most likely.

**Recipients.** John wrote to "the chosen lady and her children." This may be a reference to a personal friend of John. Some have pointed to the use of "lady" in verses 1,5 and the description of her children in verses 1,4 as evidence to take the term in reference to a person. Some have even named the woman as "Kyria" (the Greek word for "lady") or "Electa" (the Greek word for "chosen").

Another more likely interpretation is to see "lady" as a personification for a local church and its members. The Greek word for "church" is feminine in gender.

This gender is normally used in speaking of the church. Also a church would more likely have a reputation for truth than a single family (2 John 4).

**Theme.** John mentioned twin themes in writing 2 John. First, he urged his readers to practice love with one another (2 John 5). Second, he called them to practice truth in affirming the correct doctrine about Jesus (2 John 7-11).

**Literary Form.** This writing is more clearly in letter form than 1 John. John mentioned specific recipients and also included a final greeting. He wrote to a specific community with a doctrinal problem. The epistle contains no reference or allusion to the Old Testament.

I. Greetings (vv. 1-3)
II. Encouragement (vv. 4-6)
III. Warning (vv. 7-11)
IV. Conclusion (vv. 12-13)

**Purpose and Theology.** The false teachers whom John denounced denied the true humanity of Jesus Christ. Their specific error was likely Docetism, a denial of the reality of Jesus' human body. The false teachers traveled among the churches and took advantage of Christian hospitality. John expected his readers to offer hospitality to traveling Christians, but he urged his readers to refuse such hospitality to itinerant heretics (vv. 10-11).

John also urged his readers to practice love with one another. This love would lead them to walk in obedience to God's commands (vv. 5-6).

## GREETING (VV. 1-3)

John described himself as an "elder." The term may refer either to an official title (see 1 Pet. 5:1), or it may describe John affectionately as an old man.

John designated his recipients as "the chosen lady and her children." Some have felt that her name was "Kyria" and others have chosen "Electa." If her name were "Electa," we would have to say that she also had a sister of the same name. If the recipient were an individual, she would likely be anonymous. The phrase is more likely a reference to some local church over which the elder had authority. The "children" were members of that church. John's statement of love and the command to love would be more suitable for a church than for a person. The command not to host false teachers is also more suitable for a local church than for a single home.

The feature that united John with his readers was their common love for the truth (vv. 1b-2). Grace indicated God's provision of salvation, and God's gift of mercy demonstrated the depth of human need of it. Peace is a description of the character of salvation.

### ENCOURAGEMENT (VV. 4-6)

John had met some of the children of the lady, perhaps members of the church, in his travel. Their conduct had impressed him. The meeting led to a single request: Love one another. That request led John to consider the link between love and obedience. If we love God, we will obey Him. Our love for Him expresses itself in our obedience.

### WARNING (VV. 7-11)

John warned against deceivers who led others astray. The doctrine they stressed involved a denial of the incarnation. Christians affirmed the genuine humanity of Jesus when they said, "Christ has come in the flesh." Jesus did not become Christ at the baptism or cease to be Christ before His death. He was Christ come in the flesh.

John warned his readers against losing their reward for faithful service by falling into doctrinal error (v. 8). He affirmed that one who erred at this important point did not have God.

John included an additional warning in verses 10-11. He warned against providing any sort of official welcome for those who erred in their doctrine of Christ. John was not promoting intolerance, nor was he violating his earlier appeal to "love one another." He was warning against extending any form of support for those who erred at the point of the genuine humanity of Christ. We should not apply John's words to cause us to separate from those whose opinions we happen to dislike.

### CONCLUSION (VV. 12-13)

Although John had much he desired to communicate to his readers, he did not want to use another sheet of papyrus for writing. He preferred to speak face to face so that he could not be misunderstood. He anticipated a time of future visitation so that they might experience a future completion of joy.

John's concluding word in verse 13 sounds more like a message of greeting from members of one church to the recipients to whom he wrote.

### Questions for Reflection

1. What is the relationship between our love for God and our disobedience to Him (see John 14:15)?

2. Many Christians today use the term "antichrist" to refer to a powerful leader at the end time. How does John's use of the term contrast to this?

3. Did John suggest that we should be rude to those with whom we disagree doctrinally?

### Sources for Additional Study

See the list at the conclusion of 1 John.

# 3 JOHN

There is little evidence for the use of 3 John before the third century. The brevity and lack of a specific address for the letter would have contributed to its neglect. Eusebius classified the letter among the disputed writings of the New Testament, but the church came to accept it as a product of the apostle John.

The use of the term "elder" in common with 2 John makes it likely that both writings came from the same writer. Both letters also make reference to the practice of walking in the truth (2 John 4; 3 John 3). These similar practices plus the opinion of early Christian leaders make the acceptance of apostolic authorship the wisest choice.

**Date.** The similarities just mentioned make it likely that both 2 John and 3 John were written near the same time. It is possible that the writer referred to 2 John in his description of writing to the church in 3 John 9. No clear scriptural evidence exists, however, of the order of writing the two letters. A date in the mid-90's seems most likely.

**Recipients.** John named the recipient of 3 John (v. 1), but we have no idea of the specific location to which he wrote. Church tradition has placed John at Ephesus during the latter years of his life. It seems reasonable that this is a letter to some churches in Asia for which John had pastoral responsibilities. It is not certain from 3 John that both Gaius and Diotrephes belonged to the same church, but both men probably lived close together.

**Theme.** This letter presents a contrast between the truth and service demonstrated by Gaius and the arrogance shown by Diotrephes. John emphasized that "truth" was a type of behavior that agreed with the doctrine Christians professed (3 John 8). The autocratic behavior of Diotrephes violated this behavior. John wanted to bring his domineering practices to an end.

**Literary Form.** This writing has the form of a typical letter. Both the author and recipient are identified. A conclusion with a collection of Christian greetings appears at the end. The misbehavior of Diotrephes provided a specific occasion for the writing of the letter.

I. Greeting (v. 1)
II. Gaius's Hospitality (vv. 2-8)
III. Diotrephes (vv. 9-11)
IV. A Future Visit (vv. 12-14)

**Purpose and Theology.** John wrote both to commend and rebuke. He commended Gaius for his unselfish behavior and Christian hospitality. He rebuked the domineering Diotrephes for his dictatorial practices. He also praised Demetrius (v. 12), who probably carried the letter. The length of the letter allows little opportunity for theological expression.

## GREETING (V. 1)

John's use of the term "elder" duplicates that of 2 John. It is impossible to determine whether Gaius was the same as others mentioned by that name in the New Testament (see Acts 19:29; 20:4). It was one of the most common names in the Roman Empire.

## GAIUS'S HOSPITALITY (VV. 2-8)

John acknowledged that the spiritual growth of Gaius was progressing well and wished that his physical health might be in the same condition. Some traveling missionaries ("brothers"), probably sent out by John, had commended Gaius for his loyalty to the truth of the gospel and his demonstration of love. John regarded Gaius as his spiritual child and indicated that a report of his spiritual growth filled him with joy.

John was fearful that the aggressive opposition of Diotrephes might lead Gaius to refrain from showing hospitality to traveling believers. He urged Gaius to continue what he had been doing.

Since we cannot know whether Gaius and Diotrephes attended the same church, we are uncertain of the nature of John's warning about Diotrephes. If both men were in the same church, John may have commended Gaius for not buckling under to Diotrephes. If they were in nearby churches, John could have warned Gaius about the high-handed actions of Diotrephes.

## DIOTREPHES (VV. 9-11)

John denounced Diotrephes for his pride, his wicked words, and his inhospitable treatment of traveling Christian missionaries. The motives for Diotrephes' actions do not seem to have been theological but personal and moral.

Diotrephes was dominated by personal ambition.

John may have feared that Gaius would follow carelessly the bad example of Diotrephes. This led him to warn Gaius to choose his examples carefully. Gaius was to follow those who practiced good, not evil.

## A FUTURE VISIT (VV. 12-14)

John commended Demetrius to the care of Gaius. He complimented Demetrius with the statement that "everyone" spoke well of him.

John's heart was full of thoughts and ideas to convey to his readers, but he withheld them in anticipation of a future visit. He had much more to say than he could include on a single sheet of the writing material known as papyrus.

### Questions for Reflection

1. For what actions did John commend Gaius? How can we duplicate his actions today?

2. For what actions did John rebuke Diotrephes? What forms would his disobedient actions take today?

### Sources for Additional Study

See books listed for 1 John.

# JUDE

The author identified himself as "a servant of Jesus Christ and a brother of James." In presenting himself as a brother of the Lord's half-brother (Jas. 1:1), he modestly neglected to mention his own relationship to Jesus (Matt. 13:55; Mark 6:3). Some have identified Jude as "Judas son of James" (Luke 6:16), but the author did not claim apostleship. He was initially an unbeliever (John 7:3-5), but he here displayed a vigorous faith.

The frequent use of the book in the early church, especially references by Tertullian and Origen, made it less controversial than 2 Peter. Some found its reference to apocryphal books a cause for questioning its genuineness.

**Date.** Suggestions for dating this letter vary widely. Little evidence is available for making a conclusive decision.

Some claim that the reference to "the salvation we share" (v. 3) implied a time in which Christians had agreed upon a body of widely accepted doctrine. This would be later than the likely lifetime of Jude. The reference to this common faith need mean no more than the common beliefs held by all Christians.

Others have suggested that the wickedness of the false teachers described in verses 5-13 represented a Gnostic viewpoint that appeared only during the second century. Jude's description would fit any heresy in which immorality was prominent. It is possible to link Jude's references clearly with a specific sect.

**Recipients.** No address for the readers appears in Jude. The readers might have been Jews or Gentiles who lived anywhere. Jude had a concrete situation in mind, but it is impossible to locate it precisely. The statements of verses 17-18 have led some to suggest that the readers knew apostles within the region of Palestine. This is a possible but unproven hypothesis.

**Theme.** Jude began with the intention of discussing the theme of "salvation." Awareness of the infiltration of false teachers led Jude to emphasize two features. First, he warned against and condemned false teachers who were heavily influencing his area. Second, he urged his readers to greater firmness and commitment.

**Literary Form.** Despite the lack of a specific address, Jude's letter is directed to a specific situation. It is more impersonal than John's epistles. Jude was fond of mentioning items in triads (v. 2: "mercy, peace, and love"; v. 11: Cain, Balaam, and Korah). The majestic doxology provides a moving conclusion to Jude's words (vv. 24-25).

I. Greetings (vv. 1-2)

II. Occasion for Writing (vv. 3-4)

III. Be Alert (vv. 5-16)

IV. Resist (vv. 17-23)

V. Doxology (vv. 24-25)

**Purpose and Theology.** Jude intended to produce a message about the common salvation he shared with his readers (v. 3). His awareness of the appearance of heresy led him to change his emphasis to a denunciation of the heresy surrounding him. Jude gave direction for halting the advance of heresy among his readers in verses 17-23.

The epistle contains little theological content because the purpose was largely practical. One controversial feature of the book is the references to the apocryphal books of 1 Enoch (v. 14) and the

Assumption of Moses (v. 9). Some have seen these references as a liability to accepting the authority of Jude, but Paul quoted a heathen poet in Acts 17:28. He also referred to a noncanonical writing in 2 Timothy 3:8. Jude appears to have viewed his references to the Apocrypha as authoritative, and he apparently accepted the historicity of the incident in the Assumption of Moses. He used his references more as an illustration to substantiate his points.

### GREETINGS (VV. 1-2)

Jude identified himself as a follower of Jesus Christ and "a brother of James." Jude was listed among the brothers of Jesus (Mark 6:3). His brother James is the probable author of the epistle of James. Jude gave no geographical designation to his readers, but he presented them as those who were "called," "loved by God," and "kept by Jesus Christ." Jude wished his readers an experience of mercy that would allow them to know the benefits of peace and love.

### OCCASION FOR WRITING (VV. 3-4)

Jude had prepared to write a letter on the theme of "salvation" when he learned of the entrance of false teachers. He urged his readers to contend for the faith by living godly, obedient lives. He described the false teachers as "godless men," who stood condemned before God because of their denial of Jesus' lordship.

### BE ALERT (VV. 5-16)

Jude pictured the heretics as deserving to receive God's judgments just as the unbelieving Jews, the sinning angels, and the cities of Sodom and Gomorrah had merited judgment.

He showed that the false teachers were arrogantly defying God by their perverse moral behavior. They disdained angelic creatures whom they failed to understand. Jude commended the exam-

ple of the angel Michael, who did not deal with the devil's protests on his own authority. Jude used this story from the apocryphal Assumption of Moses to demonstrate a proper attitude toward the supernatural.

In verses 10-13 he used historical examples from the Old Testament to characterize the false teachers as materialistic and immoral. They were as greedy as Balaam and as rebellious as Korah.

In verses 14-15 Jude cited a statement from 1 Enoch to prove the reality of divine judgment upon the ungodly. Jude was not necessarily viewing 1 Enoch as inspired, but he was referring to a book his readers would know and respect.

### RESIST (VV. 17-23)

Jude reminded his readers that the apostles had warned against the divisiveness and spiritual emptiness of the coming false teachers. The recipients were to build themselves up with prayer and obedience. They also were to offer help to wandering believers who need both an experience of divine mercy and the wisdom to avoid corruption.

### DOXOLOGY (VV. 24-25)

Jude's mind focused on the power of almighty God who alone could provide the strength needed for full obedience. In verse 24 he praised God for His sustaining power toward believers. In verse 25 he ascribed "glory, majesty, power and authority" to God because of the work of Jesus Christ.

***Theological Significance.*** Jude's warnings regarding false teachers need to be sounded again in today's churches. The people of God must contend for the faith that has been entrusted to them. Jude reminds us of the seriousness of the Christian faith and Christian teaching. False teachers who oppose the truth must be prepared to face the judgment of

God. True believers must faithfully maintain the truth and keep themselves in the
love of God. The exhortations to watch,
pray, convince the doubters, and lead
others into the way of salvation must be
heard and obeyed.

## Questions for Reflection

1. What is the best way to "contend"
for the Christian faith? See Jesus' words
in John 13:34-35; 14:21.

2. List some of the characteristics of
the false teachers Jude mentioned in
verses 5-16. How common are these
traits today?

3. List some of the truths about God
Jude mentioned in verses 24-25.

## Sources for Additional Study

See books listed for 2 Peter.

# THE REVELATION

## ROBERT B. SLOAN

The Book of Revelation is a work of intensity. Forged in the flames of the author's personal tribulation, it employs the language of biblical allusion and apocalyptic symbolism to express the heights and depths of the author's visionary experience. The result is a work of scriptural and prophetic magnitude.

To encourage Christian faithfulness, Revelation points to the glorious world to come (a world of "no more mourning, no more crying, no more pain," 21:4; compare 7:16) at the reappearing of the crucified and risen Jesus. This now-enthroned Lord will return to conclude world history (and the tribulations of the readers) with the destruction of God's enemies, the final salvation of His own people, and the creation of a new heaven and a new earth.

The intensity of the prophet's experience is matched only by the richness of the apocalyptic symbolism he employs to warn his readers of the impending disasters and temptations that will require their steadfast allegiance to the risen Lord. To be sure, the Lord will come in power and majesty, but not before His enemies have exercised a terrible (albeit limited by the divine mercy) attack upon those who "hold to the testimony of Jesus" (6:9; 12:17; 20:4).

The author's situation was one of suffering. He was a "fellow-partaker in the tribulation" that is "in Jesus," who because of his testimony to Jesus was now exiled to the island of Patmos (1:9). The situation of the recipients, that is, "the seven churches that are in Asia" (1:4), seems not yet so dire. To be sure, a faithful Christian in Pergamum had suffered death (2:13), and the church in Smyrna was warned of a time of impending persecution (2: 10). But the persecutions described in Revelation, though a very real and threatening prospect for the churches of the Roman province of Asia, are still largely anticipated at the time of John's writing.

John's readers might have felt secure, but John knew such security would be short-lived. He called them to faith in the coming Christ and loyal obedience to Him during the time of persecution and tribulation to come. "To him who overcomes I will give the right to sit with me on my throne. . . . He who has an ear, let him hear what the Spirit says to the churches" (3:21-22).

# APOCALYPTIC LITERATURE

The Greek word *apokalypsis* ("apocalypse"), found in Revelation 1:1, provides the title for the final and climactic book of the Bible. In modern literary study Revelation, Daniel, several other biblical books (to a lesser degree), and a wide range of extrabiblical Jewish writings have been characterized as examples of biblically related apocalyptic literature. Similarities in thought and form have also been noted with certain Persian apocalyptic writings and elsewhere.

*The Age of Apocalyptic Literature.* It is almost universally agreed that the first full-blown example of biblical apocalyptic is the Book of Daniel. Other limited Old Testament inclusions of apocalyptic may be seen in Ezekiel and Zechariah. Certain scholars place Daniel during the Maccabean period of Jewish history, specifically about 165 B.C. But there is no compelling evidence against dating it in its stated sixth-century B.C. setting along with Ezekiel or viewing Zechariah as having a fifth-century B.C. point of origin.

Differences in the literary characteristics and thought patterns between earlier biblical apocalyptic and that of the intertestamental period must be viewed as a further, and only partly related literary, development. That conclusion becomes even clearer when we realize that Daniel, Ezekiel, and Zechariah all contain numerous characteristics of biblical prophecy as well as apocalyptic. They could be categorized as "prophetic-apocalyptic," perhaps more as a hybrid of the two types of literature than as a transitional form, especially considering that the New Testament Apocalypse (Revelation) also describes itself as prophecy (see Rev. 1:3; 22:18-19).

There is a sense in which the period between the early second century B.C. and the later second century A.D. represented the "flowering" of apocalyptic in Jewish circles. That is true even if only because so many apocalyptic books or portions, mostly extrabiblical, were written during that time. A number of such works have been traced to separatist groups like the Qumran community, famous for most of the Dead Sea Scrolls.

It is also accurate to refer to the latter part of that period as the high point and climax of biblical apocalyptic. The emergence of the Book of Revelation as well as Christ's Olivet discourse, often referred to as a "little apocalypse," represent the end of canonical apocalyptic literature. Jewish apocalyptic of a somewhat different style continued on in earnest for another century or so before beginning to give way to more formal mainstream Judaism.

Overall it seems fair to say that apocalyptic flourished during periods of foreign domination, starting with the Babylonian exile. The Maccabean era and the persecution of the church under the Roman Empire during the latter first century A.D. were similar historical contexts. After the second Jewish revolt against Rome in A.D. 135, apocalyptic began to decline and eventually ceased after the fourth century A.D.

*Characteristics and Theology of Apocalyptic.* There are several literary characteristics common to apocalyptic, as well as a relatively consistent pattern of theological thought. That does not mean that there may not be significant differences between various apocalyptic books. But the strikingly similar characteristics and theology marks them as legitimate examples of the apocalyptic form.

One agreed-upon characteristic is that all apocalyptic works claim to have been written by significant biblical characters. Books like Daniel and Revelation almost certainly were written by historical figures, as supported by strong internal and external evidence. However, most other apocalypses only assert that they were authored by important Old Testament (and some New Testament) figures (for example, Enoch, Ezra, Solomon) to gain a hearing, a feature called pseudonymity. Thus the actual writers of the bulk of apocalyptic works are unknown. Apocalyptic writing is also known by its use of visions and symbolism. The revelations, dreams, and visions were often narrated or interpreted by an angelic figure. Sometimes the writer is even caught up into the heavenly realm. The striking symbolism of Daniel's visions is found to accurately portray the sweep of history in advance by its interpretive sections and later fulfillments. →

But such symbolism was taken to bizarre extremes by much of later apocalyptic. Also many of the pseudononymous apocalypses are little more than history that has been recast to appear to be futuristic prophecy, with the actual uncertainty about what was still future masked by vague symbolism.

In addition, apocalyptic focused side by side on the movement of world history, especially as it related to the Jewish people and coming of the Messiah. Apocalyptic writers were not just predicting the future but fitting its development into a theological framework, frequently with a climax of messianic intervention on behalf of God's people. For example, Daniel 7 builds upon the earlier vision in Daniel 2. But it clarifies the wider progression of beastlike world empires (7:3-8) by showing that the messianic figure, "The Son of Man," will gain everlasting victory through God's power (7:9-14), delivering and vindicating "the saints," God's people (7:21,25-29).

The above consistent literary characteristics are paralleled by a broader theological pattern. Several interlocking theological emphases show up again and again in these writings, making vivid use of the literary style of apocalyptic. Again biblical and extrabiblical apocalypses are comparable at a number of points but also quite different at others.

Studies of apocalyptic often note that it is "dualistic" (God versus Satan) and "deterministic" (history is determined in advance in moving toward God's ultimate victory). These outlooks have been used to compare biblically related apocalyptic to other types, such as the Persian form. However, the much more specific emphasis on what could be called spiritual warfare at its highest level and the loving but just sovereignty of God over history marks Jewish and Christian apocalyptic as truly distinctive. For example, the unseen angelic conflict in Daniel 10 leads into the movement that climaxes in the resurrection and divine judgment in Daniel 1112. Also the climactic stratagems of the devil, his ongoing war against God, are ended by the appearing of Christ in Revelation 19:1120:3.

Two other related theo-logical perspectives can be called "eschatological realism" and an "imminent expectation" (possible near occurrence) of the final events. Some scholars describe the conclusion that the end times will be a time of "great tribulation" (Dan. 12:1; Matt. 24:21; Rev. 7:14), suffering, and catastrophic events as pessimism. However, because that is the straightforward conclusion of what the apocalyptic works set forth, and because there is an inarguable, optimistic conclusion (God's victory), it is better to view this overall pattern in terms of biblical realism.

With many of the extrabiblical apocalypses, this combination of anticipated suffering and possible near-term divine intervention combined to produce an ethically passive attitude. It apparently seemed to such apocalypticists that there was nothing that could be done except to hang on until the Lord intervened. However, biblical apocalyptic is marked by numerous challenges to godly living in light of the possible soon arrival of the climactic events of history (Dan. 13:2-3; Rev. 1:3; 21:7-8).

# REVELATION

According to early Christian traditions, the Gospel of John, the three epistles of John, and Revelation were all written by the apostle John. Revelation is the only one of these books that actually claims to be written by someone named John.

The author does not claim to be the *apostle* John. Given the authority and prestige of the Twelve, no other first-century Christian leader was associated closely enough with the churches of Asia Minor to have spoken so authoritatively and to have referred to himself simply as John unless he were, in fact, the apostle. There are certainly differences of style and language between the Fourth Gospel and Revelation—as well as some remarkable similarities of thought and terminology. Regardless of the problems related to the authorship of the Fourth Gospel, however, it is not implausible to assume that the John of Revelation was, in fact, John the apostle, the son of Zebedee.

**Date.** Scholars have traditionally suggested two possible dates for the writing of Revelation. Suggested dates are based upon the repeated references to persecution (1:9; 2:2-2,10,13; 3:9-10; 6:10-11; 7:14-17; 11:7; 12:13–13:17; 14:12-13; 19:2; 21:4). It is well-known that the Roman emperor Nero (A.D. 54–68 ) persecuted Christians, and many think that a persecution took place under Domitian ( A.D. 81–96) as well.

From the middle of the second century A.D., Christian authors usually referred to Domitian's reign as the time of John's writing, but there is no historical consensus supporting a persecution of Christians under Domitian, while hard evidence does exist for a persecution under Nero. In this century most New Testament scholars have opted for the later date under Domitian (about A.D. 95), though there has been a resurgence of opinion arguing for a setting just following the reign of Nero (about A.D. 68). The reference in 17:10 to "seven kings," of whom "five have fallen, one is, and the other has not yet come," fits well with this later dating. Nero was fifth in the line of Roman emperors beginning with Augustus (then Tiberius, Caligula, Claudius, and Nero). The evil Nero, who persecuted Christians, died of a mortal wound (13:3,14; 17:11). His name yields the number 666 when put into Hebrew from Greek (13:18), thus for John it would stand as the ultimate exemplar and prototype of the coming antichrist.

Whichever date is chosen, however, the setting must be clearly related to a time of persecution for the author and an anticipated expansion of persecution for the original audience.

**Literary Forms.** Revelation has traditionally been called an "apocalypse." Although the kind of literature was not known in the first century, what modern scholars now call "apocalyptic literature" certainly existed. In any case, John called himself a "prophet" and his work a "prophecy" (1:3; 22:10,19). But he also gave it some of the features of a letter, or epistle, including an epistolary "greeting," an epistolary "conclusion" (22:21), and the overall tone of a Christian letter of "instruction," designed to be read aloud in worship (1:3,11; 2:7,11,17,29; 3:6,13,22).

Within Revelation we find other forms of literature as well, especially hymns.

Perhaps more so than any other book in the New Testament, the Book of Revelation may be called a book of Christian worship. Vision, symbol, prophecy, sermonic exhortation, Scripture citation, narrative, prayer, and dialogue are all frequently interspersed with heavenly (and sometimes earthly) choruses of praise and adoration. The Father is worshiped in hymnic praise for His creative power and sovereign purposes (4:8-11). The Lamb (Christ) is worshiped at His enthronement for His faithfulness unto death, a sacrifice of great redeeming power for the redemption of His people (5:8-14). Or, again, the Lord God, the Almighty, is worshiped for His triumph over evil through Christ (11:15-18). Heaven rejoices at both the expulsion of Satan upon the enthronement of Christ (12:10-12) and at the judgment of the great harlot upon the coming of Christ (19:1-7). The saints also rejoice with a "new song" of salvation (14:1-5) and at their redemption from the beast (15:2-4). Then, as now, God is worthy of all worship and devotion, for He has mercifully accomplished salvation for all who approach Him through Christ.

**Theology.** The Book of Revelation is often treated as if it constituted a world of its own within the canon of the New Testament. Certainly its status as apocalyptic literature, with its exceedingly strange symbolic images, its angelic guides, visionary experience, and cosmic as well as earthly catastrophes, justifies the commonly held perception of it as "strange" and "unusual." But the extraordinary images, symbols, and experiences reflected in Revelation should not mislead us into isolating the book from the world of New Testament theology.

The Book of Revelation, in spite of its unusual language and symbolic traditions, has the basic apostolic theology at its core. The rest of the New Testament speaks profoundly about the same crucified, risen, and exalted Jesus who is variously portrayed in the Book of Revelation. Some of these portraits include: the strangely dressed, apocalyptic Son of man of chapter 1; the Lord of the churches of chapters 2–3; the Lamb/Lion of Judah of chapter 5; the Lord of judgment who pours out woes upon the earth by way of the seals, trumpets, and cups of chapters 6–19; the Child who is to rule the nations and who is exalted to the right hand of God of chapter 12; the Lamb and Son of man of chapter 14; the Word of God, who is the King of kings and Lord of lords who comes to do battle riding a white horse and having a robe dipped in blood of chapter 19; and the One who reigns upon the throne of God and is likewise the heavenly temple of chapters 20–22.

The focus of Revelation clearly falls upon the future coming of Christ. His coming will defeat the powers of Satan, those evil forces that oppress the people of God. The One who will come is none other than the same crucified and risen Jesus. The churches and those within them who have devoted themselves to the lordship of Jesus Christ are exhorted to remain faithful in the hour of affliction to Christ the crucified and risen Lord. Such exhortations to perseverance are widespread in the New Testament. (See Matt. 10:22; John 15; Acts 14:22.) They represent still a central need and obligation of authentic Christian living.

The Book of Revelation thus reflects the basic, apostolic theology that may be attested throughout the New Testament. This "apostolic theology" may be summarized as follows:

1. The events accomplished by God, particularly as they pertain to the person of Jesus Christ, have all been done in fulfillment of Scripture (Matt. 1:22-23).

2. God has powerfully acted for our salvation, especially through the death and resurrection of Jesus (Acts 2:23-32).

3. This same Jesus is now the exalted Lord. Having ascended to the right hand of God and taken His place on God's throne, He now executes the purposes of God as the Living Lord of the cosmos (Acts 2:32-36).

4. All who believe and confess the person of Jesus Christ will experience the salvation of God (Acts 2:38).

5. God's Spirit has been poured out on all those who name the name of Christ (Acts 2:38; Rom. 5:5; 8:9).

6. Commitment to God through Christ means participation in a fellowship of worship and instruction (Acts 2:41-42; Rom. 9:24-26).

7. This same Jesus will come again to rescue those who have confessed Him in faithfulness (see Mark 13:24-27).

## INTRODUCTION (1:1-8)

Written to "the seven churches" of the Roman province of Asia, John's work is a "revelation" of "what must soon take place." Given to John by Jesus Christ, it is a message committed by God to the Lord to show to His "servants." John wrote his prophecy in the form of a letter, beginning with a greeting of grace and peace from each person of the triune God. The theme of John's work is clear: the Lord God, the Almighty One Him-self, has guaranteed the final vindication of the crucified Jesus before all the earth. The victory of Christ is assured. His people will rejoice in their final deliverance, but those who have rejected Him will mourn His coming, for it will mean judgment for them.

## JOHN'S VISION (1:9-20)

While in exile on the island of Patmos, John saw the risen Lord. It happened as he was in the Spirit on the Lord's Day. Suddenly he heard behind him a loud voice like the sound of a trumpet. The voice declared that John should write down what he would see and send it to the seven churches: to Ephesus, Smyrna, Pergamum, Thyatira, Sardis, Philadelphia, and Laodicea. John turned to see the source of the great voice. Interestingly enough, before mentioning Christ, he said he saw first of all "seven golden lampstands." We read later on that the seven golden lampstands are "the seven churches."

Thus the significance of John's visions, a message to the seven churches, should not be overlooked. Indeed, not merely in chapters 23 do we find the seven letters in which the churches are addressed but in the entire Book of Revelation (1:3; 22:10,16-19). There is certainly no textual evidence that the letters, either individually or as a collection, circulated apart from the rest of John's literary work. It is a serious mistake to think that certain portions of Revelation were not important for, or relevant to, the original audiences. The whole of the Revelation is relevant to the churches (then and now), for they are fellow partakers with John in "suffering and kingdom and patient endurance that are ours in Jesus." Each church must heed not only its own letter, but all of the letters, and indeed the entire Revelation (22:18-19), since it warns of coming judgment and pronounces a blessing on all those who persevere in the

## HYMNS AND CREEDS IN THE NEW TESTAMENT

The New Testament is a virtual hymnbook setting forth the praise songs and creeds of the early church. The major problem A.D. for modern scholars has to do with the criteria one might use in pinpointing a hymn in the biblical text. Contemporary scholars have set forth certain stylistic and contextual criteria.

*Criteria for Hymns.* Under stylistic characteristics we find a definite use of the verb *to be* in the second and third persons: *you are* and *he is.* The verses are carefully constructed with numerous parallelisms and relative clauses affirming praise to God. The vocabulary of the hymns also includes words not found elsewhere in the New Testament. The hymns also tend to make use of the term "all."

Certain contextual criteria include the use of introductory formulas such as verbs of saying *(lego).* The content of the hymns involves Christological elements and assertions of God's saving deeds or pleas for God to render help. Many of these hymns end with the phrase "forever and ever."

*The Philippian Hymn.* One of the best known of the New Testament hymns is found in Philippians 2:6-11. This hymn is written in the third-person style, and the praise of the believing community remains in the background. No Christological title is used except that of Lord Jesus Christ in verse 11.

One encounters a brief outline of the basic Christological facts: He humbles Himself, takes on the form of a servant, becomes a human being, humbles Himself, dies, is elevated and given a name above every other name. In the Greek text one can sing this hymn to the modern church tune "Man of Sorrows."

Some scholars divide this hymn into six stanzas with three lines in each. Others in contrast see three stanzas. The first speaks of the preexistence (vv. 6-7a), the second the incarnation (vv. 7b-8), and the third the exaltation (vv. 9-11). Many scholars conclude that Paul took over a hymn as a unit from the early church and made use of it in his Philippian letter.

*Revelation Hymns.* The Book of Revelation is also filled with hymns. The twenty-four elders serve as a choir that sings many hymns of praise to God. In chapters 45 alone we find five hymns. The four living creatures begin the music by singing softly, "Holy, holy, holy" in 4:8. There follows three hymns that all start with the phrase "worthy."

In 4:11 the twenty-four elders join the living creatures in praising God as the creating God. In 5:9-10 they sing a hymn of praise to Christ as a lamb appears on stage. The choir grows to thousands of angels, and they join in singing 5:12, another worthy hymn. Finally everyone in the universe comes together to sing 5:12, a hymn of praise to God and the Lamb.

*1 Timothy Hymn.* The early church often used these hymns for teaching and training new members. In 1 Timothy 3:16 we find a hymn that contains the early Christological teaching of the church. From such hymns the church developed its early creeds:

Who was made manifest in the flesh;
who was made righteous in the Spirit;
who was seen by the angels;
who was preached in the world;
who was taken into glory;
(this can be sung in Greek to the tune of "Rock of Ages").

Thus in a simple hymn the church could teach some of the most important aspects of its faith in Christ. The passages reflect hymns of the faith that were used for training and teaching.

*Singing Greek Hymns.* The music dimension of the New Testament needs to be rediscovered. The tunes used two thousand years ago remain unknown. Yet one can set them to modern church tunes and rediscover some of the thrill of singing words used by the early Christians.

hour of affliction and die in faithfulness to the Lord (14:13). John's authoritative book is not a literary mystery for those struggling to live in a difficult time of persecution and suffering. John's book is an exhortation to the churches to remain faithful to Jesus Christ, to persevere in the hour of trouble knowing that Christ, who is the Lord of the churches, the One who walks among the seven golden lampstands (1:13; 2:1), will return to rescue and vindicate His people.

Having seen the seven golden lampstands, John then saw in the middle of the lampstands a glorious human figure. He saw none other than the heavenly Son of man Himself, clothed in a robe reaching to His feet, having a golden girdle worn high around His breast (in contrast to the workman who wore his belt in a lower position around the waist, so he could tuck his robe about it while at work). Like the Ancient of Days in Daniel 7:9-10, this glorious figure had hair "like white wool, as white as snow" (Rev. 1:14). His eyes, which were penetratingly powerful to judge and discern, were like a flame of fire. His feet, alluding probably to Daniel 10:6, were like burnished bronze. His voice, which John had already likened to the sound of a trumpet, was also like the sound of a mighty waterfall, similar to the description in Ezekiel 43:2 of the voice of God.

In His right hand He held seven stars, which are the angels of the seven churches. Proceeding from the mouth of the Glorious One was a sharp two-edged sword with which He would smite the nations (19:15), but which also stood as a reminder even to the churches that He is the Lord of judgment (2:12). Overwhelmed with this vision of the glorious Son of man, John fell down as a dead man. But the Glorious One laid His right hand upon John and said: "Do not be afraid. I am the First and the Last. I am

the Living One." This description is virtually synonymous with the title of Alpha and Omega given to the Lord God in 1:8. It combines the sacred name revealed at the burning bush of Exodus 3:14 with the description of the Lord, the King of Israel, beside whom there is no other God, given in Isaiah 44:6.

This Living One, this One who possesses the absolute life of God, was Himself once dead but now is alive forever more (Rev. 1:18). This is, of course, none other than the crucified and risen Lord Jesus Christ. Though "born of a woman, born under law" (Gal. 4:4) and Himself thus susceptible and vulnerable to death, this Jesus, having endured the pangs of death, has now been raised to absolute life and can never die again (Rom. 6:9; Heb. 7:16-25).

Every feature in John's description of the Risen One suggests the presence of power and majesty. The Living One then instructed John to write an account of the things he both had seen and would see, that is, an account of "what will take place later."

## THE SEVEN CHURCHES (2:1–3:22)

The letters to the churches of Ephesus, Smyrna, Pergamum, Thyatira, Sardis, Philadelphia, and Laodicea have a fairly consistent format. First, after designating the recipients, the risen Lord as Sender introduces and describes Himself using a portion of the visionary description of the glorious Son of man found in 1:9-20. There follows an "I know" section of either commendation or criticism. Next appears typically some form of exhortation. To those who received criticism, the usual exhortation was to repent. However, to the churches of Smyrna and Philadelphia, for whom the Lord had only praise, the exhortation was one of assurance (2:10; 3:10-11). Each letter concludes, though the order may vary, with both an exhortation to "hear what the

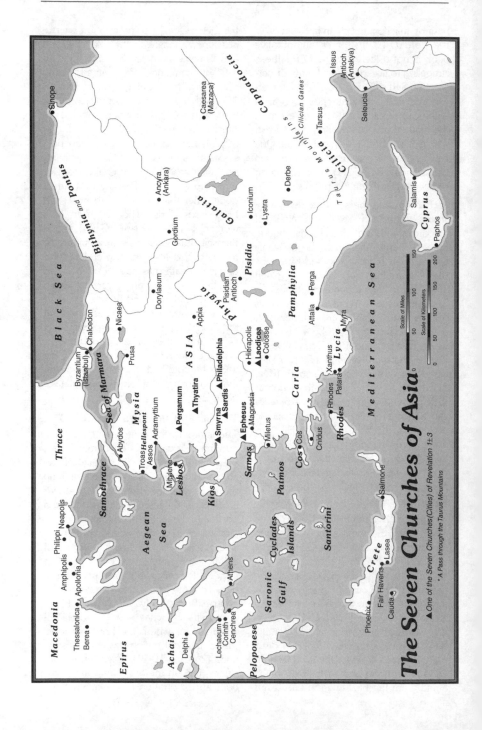

The Seven Churches of Asia

▲ One of the Seven Churches (Cities) of Revelation 1:3

* A Pass through the Taurus Mountains

Spirit says to the churches" and a promise of reward to the "overcomer," that is, the one who conquers by persevering in the cause of Christ.

The church at Ephesus (2:1-7) was told to return to its first love or else its lampstand would be removed out of its place, a judgment implying the death of the church, though not the individual loss of final salvation. The church at Smyrna was tenderly encouraged to be faithful unto death, while the churches of Pergamum and Thyatira were sternly warned to beware of false teaching and the immoral deeds that so often accompany erroneous theology.

The church at Sardis was told to wake up and complete its works of obedience. The church at Philadelphia was promised, in the face of persecution by the local synagogue, that faith in Jesus would assure access into the eternal kingdom. Christ alone has the key of David and has opened the heavenly door that no one else can shut. And the church at Laodicea was told to turn from its self-deception and repent of its lukewarmness.

These warnings and encouragements were sent to seven real churches. No doubt the fact that "seven" are referred to has some symbolic significance and may well mean that the seven churches represented many Christian communities in Asia Minor. However representative the seven churches may have been, they were nonetheless seven very real churches to whom John was known and for whom he was instructed by the Risen Lord to write these words of warning and hope.

Some commentators refer to the seven churches as seven epochs of world history, but there is not the slightest hint in the text that the seven churches are to be understood in such a way. In fact, it is only a very forced and erroneous reading of church history that can make the letters to the seven churches appear as prophecies regarding seven epochs of world history.

Again, there is absolutely no hint in the text that John intended for us to understand these seven letters in that way. Instead, it is abundantly clear that the letters were written to real congregations, engaged in the very real struggles of faith and perseverance in the midst of impending, and sometimes actual, persecution. God's word to one situation clearly had relevance for other situations in the first century. It is therefore not surprising that we, too, may read these letters, and indeed the entirety of the Revelation, and hear the voice of God in them. Thus, we read Revelation in the same general way that we would read Paul's letters to the Corinthians. That is, after doing our best to understand the historical situation of and the inspired message to the intended, first-century audience, we then seek, as a people who continue to stand under the authority of God's Word, to apply the ancient message to our lives and situations today.

## GOD'S SOVEREIGNTY (4:1–5:14)

Chapters 45 represent the pivot point of the book. They tie the risen Lord's opening exhortations to the churches (chaps. 2–3) to the judgments and final triumph of the Lamb (chaps. 6–22). Seen in this way the exhortations to the churches are in fact warnings of both the coming afflictions and God's ultimate triumph, the latter of which may serve as a spur of hope to enable the recipients of the prophecy to endure the former. These chapters also provide the historical and theological basis of the risen Lord's authority over both the church and the world by depicting His enthronement and empowering to carry out the judging and saving purposes of God.

## MILLENNIAL PERSPECTIVES ON REVELATION

| POINT OF INTERPRETATION | AMILLENNIAL | HISTORICAL PREMILLENNIAL | DISPENSATIONAL PREMILLENNIAL | POSTMILLENNIAL |
|---|---|---|---|---|
| Description of View | Viewpoint that the present age of Christ's rule in the church is the millennium; holds to one resurrection and judgment marking the end of history as we know it and the beginning of life eternal | Viewpoint that Christ will reign on earth for a thousand years following His second coming; saints will be resurrected at the beginning of the millennium, nonbelievers at the end, followed by judgment | Viewpoint that after the battle of Armageddon, Christ will rule through the Jews for a literal thousand years accompanied by two resurrections and at least three judgments | Viewpoint that Christ will return after a long period of expansion and spiritual prosperity for the church, brought about by the preaching of the gospel; the Spirit's blessing; and the church's work toward righteousness, justice, and peace. The period is not a literal thousand years but extended time of spiritual prosperity. |
| Book of Revelation | Current history written in code to confound enemies and encourage Asian Christians; message applies to all Christians | Immediate application to Asian Christians; applies to all Christians throughout the ages, but the visions also apply to a great future event | "Unveiling" of theme of Christ among churches in present dispensation, also as Judge and King in dispensations to come | Written to encourage Christians of all ages, but the visions also apply to a great future event. |
| Seven candlesticks (1:13) | Churches | | Churches, plus end-time application | Churches |
| Churches addressed (chaps. 2–3) | Specific historical situations, truths apply to churches throughout the ages; do not represent periods of church history | | Specific historical situations and to all churches throughout the ages; shows progress of churches' spiritual state until end of church age | Specific historical situations, truths apply to churches throughout the ages; do not necessarily represent periods of church history |
| Twenty-four elders (4:4,10; 5:8,14) | Twelve patriarchs and twelve apostles; together symbolize all the redeemed | Company of angels who help execute God's rule (or elders represent twenty-four priestly and Levitical orders) | The rewarded church; also represents twelve patriarchs and twelve apostles | Symbolizes all the redeemed |
| Sealed book (5:1-9) | Scroll of history; shows God carrying out His redemptive purpose in history | Contains prophecy of end events of chapters 7–22 | Title deed to the world | Portrays God carrying out His redemptive purpose in history |
| 144,000 (7:4-8) | Redeemed on earth who will be protected against God's wrath | Church on threshold of great tribulation | Jewish converts of tribulation period who witness to Gentiles (same as 14:1) | Redeemed people of God |
| Great tribulation (first reference in 7:14) | Persecution faced by Asian Christians of John's time; symbolic of tribulation that occurs throughout history | Period at end time of unexplained trouble, before Christ's return; church will go through it; begins with seventh seal (18:1), which includes trumpets 1-6 (8:2–14:20) | Period at end time of unexplained trouble referred to in 7:14 and described in chapters 11–18; lasts three and a half years, the latter half of seven-year period between rapture and millennium | Symbolic of tribulation that occurs throughout history |
| Forty-two months (11:2); 1,260 days (11:3) | Indefinite duration of pagan desolation | A symbolic number representing period of evil with reference to last days of age | Half of seven-year tribulation period | A symbolic number representing an indefinite time and evil influence |
| Woman (12:1-6) | True people of God under old and new covenants (true Israel) | | Indicates Israel, not church; key is comparison with Gen 37:9 | True people of God under old and new covenants |
| Great red dragon (12:3) | All views identify as Satan | | | |

## MILLENNIAL PERSPECTIVES ON REVELATION

| POINT OF INTERPRETATION | AMILLENNIAL | HISTORICAL PREMILLENNIAL | DISPENSATIONAL PREMILLENNIAL | POSTMILLENNIAL |
|---|---|---|---|---|
| Manchild (12:4-5) | Christ at His birth, life events, and crucifixion, whom Satan sought to kill | Christ, whose work Satan seeks to destroy | Christ but also the church (head and body); caught up on throne indicates rapture of church | Christ at His birth, life events, and crucifixion, whom Satan sought to destroy |
| 1,260 days (12:6) | Indefinite time | Symbolic number representing period of evil with special reference to last days of age | First half of great tribula- after church is raptured | Indefinite time |
| Sea beast (13:1) | Emperor Domitian, personification of Roman Empire (same as in chap. 17) | Antichrist, here shown as embodiment of the four beasts in Dan 7 | A new Rome, satanic federation of nations that come out of old Roman Empire | Roman Empire |
| Seven heads (13:1) | Roman emperors | Great power, shows kinship with dragon | Seven stages of Roman Empire; sixth was imperial Rome (John's day); last will be federa-tion of nations | Roman Emperors |
| Ten horns (13:1) | Symbolize power | Kings, represent limited crowns (ten) against Christ's many | Ten powers that will combine to make the federation of nations of new Rome | Symbol of power |
| 666 (13:18) | Imperfection, evil; personified as Domitian | Symbolic of evil, short of 777; if a personage meant, he is unknown but will be known at the proper time | Not known but will be known when time comes | Symbol of evil |
| 144,00 on Mount Zion (14:1) | Total body of redeemed in heaven | | Redeemed Jews gathered in earthly Jerusalem during millennial kingdom | Redeemed people of God |
| River of blood (14:20) | Symbol of infinite punishment for the wicked | Means God's radical judgment crushes evil thoroughly | Scene of wrath and carnage that will occur in Palestine | Symbol of judgment on the wicked |
| Babylon (woman—17:5) | Historical Rome | Capital city of future Antichrist | Apostate church of the future | Symbol of evil |
| Seven mountains (17:9) | Pagan Rome, which was built on seven hills | Indicate power, so here means a succession of empires, last of which is end-time Babylon | Rome, revived at end time | Pagan Rome |
| Seven heads (17:7) and seven kings (17:10) | Roman emperors from Augustus to Titus, ex-cluding three brief rules | Five past godless kingdoms; sixth was Rome; seventh would arise in end time | Five distinct forms of Roman government prior to John; sixth was imperial Rome; seventh will be revived Roman Empire | Roman emperors |
| Ten horns (17:7) and ten kings (17:12) | Vassal kings who ruled with Rome's permission | Symbolic of earthly powers that will be subservient to Antichrist | Ten kingdoms arising in future out of revived Roman Empire | Symbolic of earthly powers |
| Bride, wife (19:7) | Total of all the redeemed | | The church; does not include Old Testament saints or tribulation saints | Total of all the redeemed |

## MILLENNIAL PERSPECTIVES ON REVELATION

| POINT OF INTERPRETATION | AMILLENNIAL | HISTORICAL PREMILLENNIAL | DISPENSATIONAL PREMILLENNIAL | POSTMILLENNIAL |
|---|---|---|---|---|
| **Marriage supper** (19:9) | Climax of the age; symbolizes complete union of Christ with His people | Union of Christ with His people at His Coming | Union of Christ with His church accompanied by by Old Testament saints and tribulation saints | Union of Christ with His people |
| **One on white horse** (19:11-16) | Vision of Christ's victory over pagan Rome; return of Christ occurs in connection with events of 20:7-10 | Second coming of Christ | | Vision of Christ's victory |
| **Battle of Armageddon** (19:19-21; see 16:16) | Not literally at end of time but symbolizes power of God's word overcoming evil; principle applies to all ages | Literal event of some kind at end time but not literal battle with military weapons; occurs at Christ's return at beginning of millennium | Literal bloody battle at Armageddon (valley of Megiddo) at end of great tribulation between kings of the East and federation of nations of new Rome; they are all defeated by blast from Christ's mouth and then millennium begins | Symbolizes power of God's Word overcoming evil forces |
| **Great supper** (19:17) | Stands in contrast to marriage supper | | Concludes series of judgments and opens way for kingdom to be established | Stands in contrast to marriage supper |
| **Binding of Satan** (20:2) | Symbolic of Christ's resurrection victory over Satan | Curbing of Satan's power during the millennium | | Symbolic of Christ's victory over Satan |
| **Millennium** (20:2-6) | Symbolic reference to period from Christ's first coming to His second | A historical event, though length of one thousand years may be symbolic, after Armageddon during which Christ rules with His people | A literal thousand-year period after the church age during which Christ rules with His people but especially through the Jews | A lengthy period of expansion and spiritual prosperity brought about by the preaching of the gospel |
| **Those on thrones** (20:4) | Martyrs in heaven; their presence with God is a judgment on those who killed them | Saints and martyrs who rule with Christ in the the millennium | The redeemed ruling with Christ, appearing and disappearing on earth at will to oversee life on earth | Saints and martyrs who rule with Christ |
| **First resurrection** (20:5-6) | The spiritual presence with Christ of the redeemed that occurs after physical death | Resurrection of saints at beginning of millennium when Christ returns | Includes three groups: (1) those raptured with church (4:1); (2) Jewish tribulation saints during tribulation (11:11); (3) other Jewish believers at beginning of millennium (20:5-6) | The spiritual presence of the redeemed with Christ |
| **Second death** (20:6) | Spiritual death, eternal separation from God | | | |
| **New heavens and earth** (21:1) | A new order; redeemed earth | | | |
| **New Jerusalem** (21:2-5) | God dwelling with His saints in the new age after all other end-time events | | | |

Chapter 4 asserts the sovereign authority of the Creator God. Surrounded by the adoring and powerful four creatures and twenty-four elders, the Lord God the Almighty is holy, sovereign, and worthy of all worship. For He has created all things, and all things exist because of His gracious, sovereign will. John's vision of God upon His throne is reminiscent of Daniel 7 and Ezekiel 1, each of which is calculated to impress the reader with the God of might and glory.

Chapter 5 depicts the delegation of the divine authority to the risen Lord by introducing a sequence of events again reminiscent of Daniel 7. In Daniel 7 the people of God were oppressed by four terrible beasts, symbolic of evil empires and kings. Similarly, Revelation is written to people who either were, or soon would be, experiencing persecution from powers of evil. In Daniel 7 the heavenly thrones of judgment are established, the books of judgment are opened, and authority to carry out God's judgment, and thus to rescue the people of God from the evil nations, is committed to a human figure. This human figure, a glorious "son of man," mysteriously appears before the throne of God in the clouds of heaven.

Similarly, in Revelation 5 we see both a book of judgment (in this instance one with seven seals held in the right hand of God) and a glorious, redemptive agent of God. But now, instead of an unidentified human figure, we learn that the exalted agent of God is none other than the crucified Jesus, the Lamb and Lion of God. This Jesus, because of His conquering obedience to the will of God, is now (being) enthroned and therefore is worthy to take the book and break the seals.

The events portrayed here are highly symbolic but are not for that reason to be regarded as sheer myth. For the scene readily suggests an otherwise well-known and important historical and theological moment within biblical history, namely, the ascension and enthronement of Jesus. Besides explaining the visible absence of Jesus and/or the end of the resurrection appearances, the ascension of Jesus is His enthronement as heavenly Lord (see Acts 2:33-36; Eph. 1:20–2:31; Col. 1:18), His empowering now to execute the judgments of God. He is worthy to take the book, *for He was slain*. His redemptive death, that is, His obedience to the will of God, has revealed Him as qualified for the role of heavenly Lord. He has "triumphed," a word which for John referred to Jesus' triumphal suffering and subsequent enthronement (see 3:21) and may therefore now as the heavenly Lord assume the role of divine Agent and Executor. All power in heaven and on earth has been given to Him (Matt. 28:18). He may take the book and break the seven seals of judgment and thereby execute the purposes of the sovereign, Creator God. At His enthronement the heavens rejoice (5:8-14; 12:5-12), for He truly is worthy, and the people of God now have their reigning Savior.

## THE SEVEN SEALS (6:1–8:5)

The breaking of the first four seals brings forth four horsemen of different colors. These riders, paralleling the chaos predicted in Mark 13, represent God's judgments through the upheavals of war and its devastating social consequences: violence, famine, pestilence, and death. The fifth seal is the plea of martyred saints for divine justice upon their oppressors. For now they are told, they must wait, for the number of the martyred of God's people is not yet complete.

A careful look at the sixth seal is important for understanding the literary structure and episodic sequence of Revelation. When broken, the sixth seal brings forth the typical signs of the end: a great earthquake, the blackening of the sun, the reddening ("blood red") of the moon, and the falling of the stars of heaven (Matt. 24:29-31; Mark 13:24-27). Though Revelation is but a few chapters old, we are brought to the end of world history. The sky is split apart like a scroll; mountains and islands are moved. And the mighty as well as the lowly of the earth realize that the great day of God's (and the Lamb's) wrath has come, and nothing can save them.

The earthquake is a consistent sign in Revelation for the destruction that immediately precedes the end (see 8:5; 11:13,19; 16:18-19) of history and the appearance of the Lord. The repeated references to the earthquake at strategic spots in Revelation do not mean that history itself repeatedly comes to an end but that John employed the well-known literary technique of "recapitulation" (see Gen. 12), that is, the retelling of the same story from a different "angle" so as to focus upon other dimensions of and characters in the same story.

Thus, in Revelation we are repeatedly brought to the end of history and the time of Christ's return. But John withheld his final (and fullest) description of this world's end until the end of his document (19:1–22:5). In the meantime he used the literary technique (among others) of retelling to prepare his readers for both the traumas and hopes of human history. He wanted to prepare his readers for the fact of judgment coming at the hands of the enthroned Lamb of God (6:1-17), for both His protection of His people (7:1-17; 11:1) and their responsibility to bear witness to the earth regarding Him (10:1–11:13), for the redemptive purposes of judgment (8:6–9:21), for the coming persecution (11:7; 12:1–13:18), and for the finality of God's judgments (15:1–18:24). There was much for John to explain regarding the suffering of the

saints and the apparent triumph of evil, facts that seem to deny the Christian confession that Christ has been raised and enthroned as Lord. Does He protect His people? Will He truly come again? Why must we suffer, and "how long, Sovereign Lord," must we wait? The merciful but mysterious ways of God with humankind require, for the sake of completeness, the retelling of the story of human history from several points of reference, replete with the certainties of both judgment and salvation through Christ.

The description of the judgments initiated by the breaking of the first six seals would no doubt tend to overwhelm John's audience, but final wrath is not the lot of the people of God (see Rom. 8:35,39; 1 Thess. 5:9). Therefore, John interrupted the sequence of judgments leading to the seventh seal to remind us that the people of God need not despair, for "the servants of our God" (7:3) have the promise of heaven.

Chapter 7 is actually two visions, with the second both interpreting and concluding the first. The sealing of the 144,000 employs starkly Jewish symbols to describe those who know God through Jesus Christ. Clearly John was referring to Christians as the 144,000. For 7:3 refers to the "servants" of God, a term consistently used throughout Revelation to refer either to Christians in general or the Christian prophet, but never to the non-Christian Jew (or Gentile). Language employed in the Old Testament to refer to the Jews is characteristically used in the New Testament to refer to those who know God through Jesus Christ (for example, 2 Cor. 6:16-18; Gal. 3:29). Those who are in Christ are the beneficiaries of the promises made to Israel (Rom. 4:13-17; Gal. 3:8-9,15-29).

The number 144,000 is an intensification (12 x 12 x 10 x 10 x 10) of the original number twelve (itself an obvious allusion to the twelve tribes). This indicates that the 144,000 comprise the full number of God's people, God's people now being all (Jew or Gentile) who are followers of Jesus. (Note 12:1-17; the woman who has a crown of *twelve* stars and brings forth Christ is *Israel*. Her true offspring is first Jesus—the fulfillment of Israel's history—and His followers, that is, Jews and Gentiles "who obey God's commandments and hold to the testimony of Jesus," v. 17.)

In the second vision the 144,000 have become "a great multitude, which no one could count." Who are they? Using his favorite descriptions of heaven (see 21:3-4,23; 22:1-5), John said that they are those who have "come out of the great tribulation," now to experience the joys of heaven and relief from the tribulations they have endured. Compare 7:14-17 with 21:1-6; 22:1-5. The numberless multitude of 7:9 is not a reference to non-Christian Jews (or Gentiles); it refers rather to all who have trusted Christ. It is the Lamb's bride, the holy city, the new Jerusalem (20:2). To have "come out of the great tribulation" does *not* mean that they exited the earth *before* the hour of tribulation. To the contrary, they did indeed experience the tribulations of this evil age; but now in heaven they enjoy the presence of God, where they will hunger *no more* nor thirst *any more*. No longer subject to death (21:4), they will drink of the water of life, will no more experience the oppressive heat of the sun, and will have every tear wiped from their eyes. As the true Israel of God, Christians ("the servants of our God") have the seal of God. Having refused the mark of the beast (13:16-17), they hold to the testimony of Jesus in spite of persecution and therefore have the promise of final heavenly deliverance from this evil age of great tribulation.

Revelation 8:1-5 describes the seventh seal and again the traditional signs of the end, including "peals of thunder, rumblings, flashes of lightning and an earthquake." These signs represent the very end of human history and the coming of the Lord, but the prophet was not yet ready to describe the Lord's return. He still had too much to say (based on what he saw) about the nature of judgment, the mission of the church, and the persecutions of the beast to bring his prophecy to an end. Therefore, before describing fully the end, John had to start over. Using the symbolic vehicle of the seven trumpets, he declared that the judgments of God also have a redemptive purpose because they are signs, partial expressions, of the coming final judgment.

## THE SEVEN TRUMPETS (8:6–11:19)

The seven seals were divided between the four horsemen and the remaining three seals, with a narrative break between the sixth and seventh seals to remind the people of God of the Lord's promise of final protection and their hope of eternal glory. A similar pattern occurs with the seven trumpets.

The first four trumpets describe partial judgments ("a third") upon the earth's vegetation, the oceans, fresh waters, and the heavenly lights. The last three trumpets are grouped together and are also described as three "woes" upon the earth, emphasizing God's judgment upon humankind. The fifth trumpet (and first woe) releases hellish locusts who will sting those not having the seal of God. The sixth trumpet (and second woe) brings forth a mighty army of infernal horsemen who kill a third of humankind. But all these judgments have no redemptive effect, for the rest of humankind who are not killed by these plagues refuse to repent of their immoralities. The warnings have fallen on deaf ears.

Just as the interlude between the sixth and seventh seals assured the recipients of Revelation that the people of God are safe from the eternally destructive effects of God's wrath, so also between the sixth and seventh trumpets we are reminded of God's protective hand on His people. But in the trumpet interlude we also learn that God's protection during these days of tribulation does not mean isolation, for the people of God must bear a prophetic witness to the world.

In 10:1-18 John's call (after the pattern of Ezek. 2:13:11) is reaffirmed. He is told to eat a bittersweet book and "prophesy again about many peoples, nations, languages and kings." The note of protection and witness is again struck in 11:1-13, where the measuring of the temple of God alludes to God's protective hand upon His people during the hour of turmoil. These persecutions will last for forty-two months, but His people, the "holy city," will be neither destroyed nor silenced. For the "two witnesses" will bear witness during this time, also called "1,260 days," to the mercy and judgment of God. Note well: the "42 months" and the "1,260 days" refer to the same time period seen from different perspectives, for the days of witness are also days of opposition (11:2-7; 12:6,13-17). Negative references to persecution and the activity of Satan and the beasts are consistently called "42 months" (11:2; 13:5), whereas positive references to the sustaining hand of God or the prophetic testimony of His two witnesses are called "time, times and half a time" (12:14), or "1,260 days" (11:3; 12:6).

It seems unlikely that the "two witnesses" ("two" suggests a confirmed, legal testimony) are two individual persons, for they are also called "two lampstands," terminology already interpreted in 1:20 to mean the church. Also we must note that the "1,260 days" of the woman's flight and protection from Satan in 12:6 is as well a reference to the protection of God's people, though under a different image or symbol. Note, too, that in 13:5-7 the same beast from the abyss, who here in 11:7 attacks the two witnesses and overcomes them, is said in 13:7 to "make war against the saints" and "to conquer them."

Though engaged in great spiritual warfare, the church, like Moses and Elijah of old, must faithfully maintain a courageous and prophetic witness to the world, a witness even unto death. Although the earth rejoices that the testimony of the church is in the end apparently snuffed out, the temporary triumph of evil ("three and a half days") will turn to heavenly vindication as the two witnesses (the people of God) are raised from the dead. Though John was not yet ready to describe more fully the resurrection of Christ's followers and the bliss of heaven, we have in the resurrection of the two witnesses the depiction of the church's great hope: the resurrection of all those who hold to the testimony of Jesus (compare 11:7-11 with 13:15; 20:4-6).

The seventh trumpet (and third woe) again introduces the earthquake, lightning, and thunder. The end of history has come, the time for the dead to be judged and the saints to be rewarded. Clearly the very end has come, for the heavenly chorus now treats the coming of the reign of God (and Christ), as well as the day of judgment, as *past events*. The chorus sings, "The kingdom of the world *has become* the kingdom of our God and of his Christ, and he will reign for ever and ever."

John has again brought us to the point of our Lord's return and, indeed, has begun to describe the rejoicing that will accompany His return (19:1-10). But he is not yet ready to describe the actual coming of the King of kings and Lord of lords. There is (sadly) more to relate regarding "the beast that comes up from the Abyss" to make war with the two witnesses, the people of God. It is that awful forty-two months, the period of persecution (and protection/witness), that John must now unfold.

## THE DRAGON'S PERSECUTION (12:1–13:18)

Chapter 12 is crucial for understanding John's view of the sequence of history. The number three and a half was associated by Christians and Jews with times of evil and judgment (see Luke 4:25). John variously referred to the three and a half years as either "42 months" (11:2; 13:5) or "1,260 days" (11:3; 12:6) or "a time, times and half a time." For John it was the period of time when the powers of evil will do their oppressive works. But during this time, God will protect His people while they both bear witness to their faith (11:3) and simultaneously suffer at the hands of these evil powers (11:2,7; 12:13-17; 13:5-7).

All commentators agree that this terrible period of tribulation will be brought to an end with the coming of the Lord. The critical question, however, is when the three-and-a-half-year period of persecution and witness *begins*. Though some scholars have relegated the three and a half years to some as-yet-unbegun moment in the future, chapter 12 unmistakably pinpoints its beginning with the ascension and enthronement of Christ. When the woman's (Israel's) offspring is "caught up to God *and to His throne,"* there is war in heaven, and the dragon is cast down to the earth.

Heaven rejoices because it has been rescued from Satan, but the earth must now mourn because the devil has been cast down to earth, and his anger is great.

He knows that he has been defeated by the enthronement of Christ and that he has but a short time. The woman, who (as Israel) brought forth the Christ and also other offspring (those who hold to the testimony of Jesus), now receives the brunt of the frustrated dragon's wrath. As the enraged dragon now seeks to vent his wrath upon the woman, she is nonetheless nourished and protected for "1,260 days," that is, for a "time, times and half a time."

John's altogether brief description of the life of Christ (only His birth and enthronement are here specifically referred to) should not mislead the reader into thinking that it is the *infant* child who is "caught up to God and to His throne." This passage does not have for its main purpose the telling of the life of Christ, for John knew his readers to be familiar with the decisive events in Christ's history. Rather, the passage seeks to show the *continuity of persecution* as inaugurated by Satan against the woman (Israel) and her child (Christ) and continued against the woman and the rest of her offspring (Christians).

It is, of course, the crucified and risen Lord who is enthroned and whose accession to the throne brings the defeat of the powers of darkness (see Eph. 1:19-23; 1 Pet. 3:22; see Rom. 1:4; Col. 4:15-20; 1 Tim. 3:16). The account of the dragon's defeat in, and expulsion from, heaven clearly commences with, and is caused by, the *enthronement* of the woman's offspring. Likewise, *note well* that the story of 12:6, where the woman flees to the wilderness and is protected by God for "1,260 days," has two unmistakable plot "links" in the developing story line of chapter 12. First, the woman's flight and the "1,260 days" of protection in 12:6 clearly commence with the enthronement of 12:5. But in 12:14-17 it is the *persecution of the dragon,* who has now been cast down from heaven to earth, that motivates the woman's flight to the wilderness. Thus what we have in 12:14-17 is the resumption and amplification of the woman's story which was begun in 12:6.

Note the parallel references in 12:6 and 12:14 to the "desert," nourishment, and "time, times and half a time," or it's equivalent, "1,260 days." This dual plot connection—where two events are seen in connection with the woman's flight—between the *enthronement* of the woman's offspring (Christ) and the *dragon's pursuit* of the woman is neither odd nor surprising. It is the enthronement that (virtually simultaneously) produces the war in heaven, which results in the dragon's expulsion and which then immediately causes the now-enraged dragon to persecute the woman and "the rest of her offspring." It is not only clear that the "1,260 days" of 12:6 is the equivalent of the "time, times and half a time" of 12:14 but that the one particular period of persecution/protection in question commences both with the enthronement of Christ and the subsequent—and, for all practical purposes, simultaneous—expulsion of the dragon from heaven.

The dragon then brings forth two henchmen (chap. 13) to help him in his pursuit of those who believe in Jesus. Satan is thus embodied in a political ruler, the beast from the sea (13:1), who will speak blasphemies for "forty-two months" and "make war against the saints," while the second beast (or "false prophet," 19:20), who comes up from the earth, seeks to deceive the earth so that its inhabitants worship the first beast.

Thus, in chapters 12–13 each of the various ways of referring to the three and a half years is a reference to a single period of time that began with the enthronement of Christ and will conclude

with His return. The time period is not a literal three and a half years but the *entire time between the ascension and the return of Christ,* which will permit the dragon to execute his evil work upon the earth (see Gal. 1:4; Eph. 2:2). Almost two thousand years have elapsed since our Lord ascended to the right hand of God, but the evil period known as the three and a half years continues. Satan still rages, but his time is short, and his evil will cease at the return of Christ.

## A SUMMARY (14:1-20)

After the depressing news of the ongoing persecutions of God's people by the unholy trinity, John's readers need another word of encouragement and warning. Chapter 14 therefore employs seven "voices" to relate again the warnings and promises of heaven. First is another vision of the 144,000. The 144,000, as before, are the full number of the people of God. It is certainly a reference to Christians, for they "were purchased from among men and offered as firstfruits to God and the Lamb."

Using the common biblical imagery of sexual immorality as a reference to idolatry, John called these followers of the Lamb "blameless." That is, they did not "defile themselves" with the beast. They are the men and women who have been faithful in their worship of the one true God through Jesus Christ and have not been seduced by the Satanic deceptions of the first beast and his ally, the false prophet. They will be rescued and taken to heaven's throne, where with one voice they will sing a new song of salvation.

Another voice is heard, that of an angel announcing the eternal gospel and warning the earth of coming judgment. The remaining "voices" (or oracles) follow in rapid succession. The fall of "Babylon the Great" an Old Testament symbol for a nation opposed to the people of God, is announced. Then the people of God are warned not to follow the beast, and those who follow him are warned of the coming torments of their separation from God. After that a blessing is pronounced on those who remain faithful. Finally, two voices call for harvest. One calls upon the Son of man to reap the earth as a giant wheat harvest, while the last voice likens the reaping of the earth to a grape harvest, for the coming of the Lord will mean the treading of the winepress of the fierce wrath of God the Almighty.

## THE SEVEN CUPS (15:1–16:21)

Just as the seven seals and the seven trumpets depict different aspects of God's judgments through Christ, so now another dimension of His judgment must be revealed. The seven cups of wrath are similar to the seven trumpets and the seven seals, but they also are different; for there comes a time when the wrath of God is no longer partial or temporary but complete and everlasting. The outpouring of the seven cups of wrath means that God's judgment is also final and irrevocable. The partial judgment ("one-third") of the trumpets suggests that God uses the sufferings and evils of this life as a warning to draw humankind toward repentance and faith. But such tribulations also foreshadow the final hour of judgment, when God's wrath is finished and there is delay no longer.

The seven cups of wrath represent the judgments of the Lamb on the earth, especially on those who have received the mark of the beast. Between the sixth and seventh seals and the sixth and seventh trumpets we were told of God's protection of, and mission for, the people of God. But with the seven cups there is no break between the sixth and seventh outpourings of judgment. Now only wrath is left; there is no more delay. Babylon the Great, the symbol for all who have vaunted themselves against the Most High God, will fall. With the pouring out of the seventh cup of wrath, there is again the great earthquake accompanied by "flashes of lightning, rumblings, peals of thunder," for the end has come.

The notion of God's wrath is not always a welcome subject to the Bible reader, but its reality as a clear-cut teaching of both Old and New Testaments is inescapable. The reality of evil, the reality of human freedom, the righteousness of God, and the longing of God to have creatures, who though distinct from Him as real creatures nonetheless freely relate to Him in trust and love, make inevitable the notion and reality of God's wrath. A righteous God responds to those who persist in their evil refusal to acknowledge their rightful Lord.

God longs to see His rebellious children lay down their arms and come home to Him. God has mercifully acted by all possible means—even to the extent of taking to Himself, through His Only Begotten Son, the very penalty that He has prescribed for sin—to bring His wayward children home. Wrath brings grief even to the heart of God, but God will not coerce our love of Him. He has given His children their freedom, and He will not destroy their humanity by removing that freedom, even when His children stubbornly persist in using that freedom in rebellion against Him. Incredibly enough, in spite of the overwhelming mercies of God revealed through Jesus Christ, there will be those who refuse His mercies. In such cases the faithful God of creation and redemption will faithfully respond in keeping with His own nature and word by giving His rebellious sons and daughters what they have stubbornly insisted upon, namely, everlasting separation from Him. Surely, as God's wrath, this is the height of torment and misery—to be separated from the One who is the true source of life, to be cut off from one's merciful Creator and thus to experience everlastingly the eternal death that comes from the rejection of Him who is the source of everlasting life. But we must neither deny nor even lament the wisdom of God for His past or future assertions of wrath. Our God evidently loves righteousness, justice, and mercy to such an extent that He will not brook our cowardly tolerance of evil. We may not lightly dismiss the fact that heaven is neither silent nor embarrassed when evil is punished. Heaven rejoices at the justice and judgment of God (19:1-6).

## THE FALL OF BABYLON (17:1–18:24)

Chapter 17 retells the sixth cup, the fall of Babylon the Great, and chapter 18 gives a moving lament for the great city. She has not fulfilled God's purposes for her. All of her mighty works, industry, craftsmanship, political power, and artistic skill are brought to nothing, for she has played the harlot and worshiped the beast rather than devoting her skills and energies to God and to the Lamb.

## REVELATION OF THE LAMB (19:1–22:5)

Heaven now begins to rejoice because Babylon the Great has fallen and it is time for the appearing of the Lamb's bride. The great marriage supper of salvation is ready to commence. Although he has withheld a description of the coming of the Lord on at least three earlier occasions, John is now prepared to describe the glories of the Lord's appearance.

All of heaven rejoices over the righteous judgment of God upon evil. The Lamb's bride, the people of God, has made herself ready by her faithfulness to her Lord through the hour of suffering. Therefore "it was given her" (salvation is always a gift of God) to clothe herself in fine linen, for "the wedding of the Lamb" has come.

Heaven is opened, and the One whose coming has been faithfully petitioned from ages past, the Word of God, the King of kings and Lord of lords, appears to battle the enemies of God in a conflict whose outcome is not in doubt. When the Lamb comes with His heavenly armies, the first beast and the second beast are thrown into the lake of fire from which there is no return. The dragon, who is the serpent of old, the devil and Satan, is cast into a hellish abyss that is shut and sealed for a thousand years. Since the powers of evil reigned for "three and a half years" (the period of time between the ascension and return of our Lord), Christ will reign for a "thousand years." The dead in Christ are raised to govern with Him, and God's rightful rule over the earth is vindicated.

This thousand-year reign is called the millennium. The term *millennium* is derived from the Latin (*mille,* one thousand, *annum,* year) and means *a period of one thousand years.* The biblical words for *thousand* are *eleph* in Hebrew and *chilioi* in Greek. In multiple Old Testament instances the term is used in counting, even as it is in the New Testament (see Gen. 24:60; Luke 14:31). Occasionally the term is used to mean a large number without specific units being intended (see Mic. 5:2; 6:7; Rev. 5:11). The particular references used to establish a doctrine of a thousand years associated with Christ's final coming are found in Revelation 20:2-7.

The biblical materials do not present a systematic eschatology in which all of the diverse references about the end times are brought into one teaching. Therefore in Christian history differing strands of interpretation have emerged. Christian interpreters seeking a coherent systematic doctrine of the last things relate the apocalyptic elements of Old Testament prophecy (especially the Book of Daniel);

the apocalyptic elements in the New Testament (especially Matt. 24–25; Mark 13; 2 Peter; Jude; and the Book of Revelation); Paul's writings about the final coming (especially 1 Thess. 4:13-18 and 2 Thess. 2:1-11—the man of lawlessness); Paul's views about the relationship of Jews and Gentiles (Rom. 9–11); and the references to antichrist(s) in 1 John.

Our concern with millennial issues, that is, whether the return of Christ is before the millennium (premillennialism) or after the millennium (as in either postmillennialism or amillennialism), is a concern whose significance is greatly exaggerated with respect to the interpretation of the Book of Revelation. What ultimately mattered for John is that the followers of Christ, those who have suffered the afflictions and persecutions of this present evil age, will one day be rescued and vindicated by the appearance of Christ, whose coming will destroy the powers of evil. It is abundantly clear in the New Testament that the shape and promise of the future hope should exert an influence upon our present behavior and moral devotion to Christ (see Rom. 8:18-25). Indeed, the very point of Revelation is to encourage Christian perseverance in the present in light of the coming triumph of God through Jesus Christ.

The interpretation of the relationship of the thousand-year kingdom to the return of Christ given in the commentary above could be called a form of premillennialism. Each of the views has something to commend it. Postmillennialism is wrong in its placement of the return of Christ at the conclusion of the thousand-year kingdom. Yet postmillennialism has accurately captured a significant motif in biblical prophecy in both the Old and New Testament. That is, we must live and preach in hope. We must preach the gospel not in the expectation that no one will believe, but we must proclaim the gospel to the ends of the earth, believing that God will somehow use our witness to His glorious salvation through the person of Jesus Christ to bring about a mighty triumph for the kingdom of God. Though we certainly cannot bring the kingdom of God on earth through human means, the preaching of the gospel does indeed offer hope for the transformation of life.

Amillennialism is to be commended for its emphasis upon the current reign of Jesus Christ. Indeed, the Book of Revelation makes abundantly clear (see the exposition above of chaps. 5 and 12) that Christ indeed has overcome and as such has been raised and exalted to the right hand of God. He is currently Lord of the churches. He is indeed currently Lord of the cosmos. He is the one into whose hands all power in heaven and on earth has been given. He has been raised far above all rule and authority and power and every name that is named (Eph. 1:19-21).

Still, only premillennialism can properly explain the episodic sequence of Revelation 19–20.

At the conclusion of the "thousand years," the dragon is to be released. He is permitted another brief time of deception, but his time is short-lived. Following this final episode of deception at the conclusion of the thousand years, the dragon is recaptured and this time cast into the lake of fire and brimstone, "where the beast and the false prophet are also." The fate given to the beast and the false prophet at the return of Christ is also finally meted out to the dragon at the close of the reign of Christ. Then the final judgment takes place, at which all not included in the Book of Life are thrown into the lake of fire.

Chapter 21 is often thought to refer to the period following the thousand-year reign, but it is more probably a retelling of the return of Christ from the viewpoint of the bride. Here we have clear-cut clues about the fact of a literary "retelling." Just as chapter 17 was a recapitulation of the seventh cup and the fall of the harlot, Babylon the Great (compare the language of 17:1-3, which clearly introduces a "retelling" with the language of 21:9-10), so chapter 21 recapitulates the glorification of the bride of the Lamb. Now the story is told with the focus upon the bride. To be the bride is to be the holy city, the New Jerusalem, to live in the presence of God and the Lamb, and to experience protection, joy, and the everlasting, life-giving light of God. The tree of life grows there, and there the river of the water of life flows. There will no longer be any night; there will no longer be any curse, for the throne of God and of the Lamb is there. And there His bond-servants will serve Him and reign with Him forever and ever.

## CONCLUSION (22:6-21)

John concluded his prophecy by declaring the utter faithfulness of his words. Those who heed his prophecy will receive the blessings of God. Those who ignore the warnings will be left outside the gates of God's presence. Solemnly and hopefully praying for the Lord to come, John closed his book. The churches must have ears to hear what the Spirit has said. Under the threat of an everlasting curse, the hearers are warned to protect John's sacred text: neither to add to nor to take away from the words of his prophecy. The people of God must, by His grace, persevere in the hour of tribulation, knowing that their enthroned Lord will soon return in triumph.

***Theological Significance.*** It is extremely helpful to remember what the very first verse of the book says about this book. It is a revelation that God gives to His church, a revelation of Jesus Christ.

The greatest purpose of the book is to show us Jesus Christ. A suffering church does not need a detailed forecast of future events. It needs a vision of the exalted Christ to encourage the weary and persecuted believers. We see Jesus Christ standing in the midst of the churches. We see Him portrayed as the Lamb of God who died for the sins of the world. We see Him as one who rules and reigns. He is the one who takes His church to be with Him in the new heavens and the new earth, where we will worship Him forever and ever. Amen.

## Questions for Reflection

1. How does Revelation differ from other New Testament books?

2. How is Revelation like other New Testament books in terms of basic Christian doctrine?

3. What is the central theme of Revelation?

4. What is the central exhortation of Revelation for Christians?

5. What events in the experience of Jesus are referred to in Revelation 12, and how do the "1,260 days" and "42 months" relate to those events?

6. How does the message of Revelation relate to our current situation?

7. How do the "42 months" or "1,260 days" and the "1,000 years" relate to the return of Christ?

## Sources for Additional Study

Beasley-Murray, George R. *The Book of Revelation.* New Century Bible. Grand Rapids: Eerdmans, 1981.

Dockery, David S. *Our Christian Hope: Bible Answers to Questions about the Future.* Nashville: LifeWay, 1998.

Ladd, George E. *A Commentary on the Revelation of John.* Grand Rapids: Eerdmans, 1972

Mounce, Robert H. *The Book of Revelation.* New International Commentary on the New Testament. Grand Rapids: Eerdmans, 1977.

Newport, John P. *The Lion and the Lamb: A Commentary on the Book of Revelation for Today.* Nashville: Broadman, 1986.

Walvoord, John. *The Revelation of Jesus Christ.* Chicago: Moody, 1976.